RIA's Complete Analysis of the Tax and Benefits Provisions of the American Recovery and Reinvestment Act of 2009

With Code and ERISA Sections as Amended and Committee Reports

Here's your copy of RIA's industry-leading
"Complete Analysis of the Tax and Benefits Provisions of
the American Recovery and Reinvestment Act of 2009".
We appreciate your patronage.

Here's a list of handy reference numbers:

1-800-950-1216—To place an order for this or other publications
1-800-431-9025—If you have questions about a previously placed
order or a customer service issue
1-800-742-3348—If you have a question about product content

THOMSON REUTERS

RIA's Complete Analysis of the Tax and Benefits Provisions of the American Recovery and Reinvestment Act of 2009

RIA

Sue Ellen Sobel,
Supervisor

Alexis Brown
Adel Faltas
Amelia Massiah
Jennifer Stryshak

Data Analyst

Lisa Alcock
Denise Dockery

Citator Data Managers

Janie Davis
Ivette Terry

Paralegals

Joann Casanova
Catherine Daleo
Monica Grier
Danny Wang

Indexing

David Thompson,
Manager

Janet Mazefsky,
Assistant Manager

Tom Adewolu
Oslin Busby
Michael Chernicoff
George Flynn
Linda Lao
Andrea Leal
Irene Richards
Arlene Verderber

Legal Resource Center

Peter Durham,
Manager

Pierre Calixte
Sandra Crowder
Patricia Link
Edward Mack
Theresa Scherne
Bernadette Stanton
Michael Stanton
Holly Yue

Velma Goodwine-McDermon,
Supervisor

Charyn Johnson
William Lesesne

Product Development

Ruth F. Raftery
(J.D., C.P.A., NY, NJ, PA Bar)
Director, New Product Development, Tax Products

Nicole Gagnon
Director, Customer Insight

Todd Gordon,
Director, New Product Development

Kim Chirls,
Lead Project Manager

End-User Technical Services

Jose Fiol,
Team Lead

Steven McGill,
Design Lead

Eric Bauer
Jay Loyola
Tanya McDonald
Joseph Oliveri

Product Technology

Perry Townes,
Vice President

Jay Liu,
Director

Nicole Severson,
Senior Checkpoint Product Manager

Tim Bills,
Manager

Garrett McAlister,
Manager

John Melazzo,
Manager

Laurie Mitchell,
Manager

Dennis Wendell,
Manager

Gene Wojna,
Manager

Jason Shen,
Architect

Eileen Wood,
Information Manager

Daryl Alexander
Ron Bergeron
Mohan Bhairavabhatia
Geoff Braine
Isabel Cimitile
Resa Cirrincione
Tracey Cruz
Chris DiGanci
Andy Dreistadt
Tatyana Fersht
Janine Francesca
Peggy Frank
Terri Ganssley
Anthony Guglielmo
Michelle Harmon
Lori Jones
Jay Kwon
Terry LaGoy
Cynthia Lewis
Jackie Lynott
Chris Macano
Dave Mark
Alex Maskovyak
Ejelonu Onukogu
Pamela J. Otruba
Amish Parikh
Michelle Paulin
Michael Perrone

Dan Pirro
Steve Pitamber
Jason Rapaccuiolo
Patricia Reilly
Marguerite Rice
Ruth Russell
Becky Sears
Alfred Sehayek
Esme Smartt
Young Sone
Margaret Taylor Volpe
Torrod Taylor
Alana Trafford
Vivian Turner
Rhonda Waller
Jieping Wang
Karen Wharton
Steve Wisniewski
Hongtu Zhang
Teresa Zhang

Content Technology

Brian McNamara,
Senior Director

Gale Metz,
Director

Alanna Dixon,
Manager

David Levine,
Manager

Christopher Grillo,
Project Manager

David Bantel
Bob Bridier
Mary Jo Catlett
Karen de Luna
Louie Diaz
Nadine Graham
Steven Haber
Chris Jungheim
Stephen Karg
Julie Lu
Darren McNelis
Scott Murphy
William Peake

Tasso Quidera
Irina Resnikoff
Derek Sanders
Ayca Tank
Linda Wiseman

Manufacturing & Fulfillment Services

Rick Bivona,
Director

Anthony Scribano,
Scheduling and Fulfillment Manager

Gail Gneiding,
Manufacturing and Outside Composition Manager

Rachel Hassenbein,
Associate Fulfillment Manager

John Disposti,
Senior Manufacturing Coordinator

Greg Miller,
Associate Production Manager

Enid Skolnik,
Associate Fulfillment Manager

Bryan Gardner,
Senior Manufacturing Coordinator

Lourdes Barba
Linda Gottlieb
Chris Harrington
Jennifer Kalison

Table of Contents

¶ 1. Organization of the Book

RIA's Complete Analysis of the Tax and Benefits Provisions of the American Recovery and Reinvestment Act of 2009

This book contains RIA's Complete Analysis of the Tax and Benefits Provisions of H.R. 1, the American Recovery and Reinvestment Act of 2009 (generally referred to in the Analysis as the "2009 Recovery Act") as signed into law by the President on Feb. 17, 2009 (PL 111-5, 2/17/2009), and H.R. 2, the Children's Health Insurance Program Reauthorization Act of 2009 (generally referred to in the Analysis as the "2009 Children's Health Insurance Act") as signed into law by the President on Feb. 4, 2009 (PL 111-3, 2/4/2009).

The tax and benefits provisions of the 2009 Recovery Act appear in Titles I, II, III, and VII of Division B of H.R. 1, i.e., (PL 111-5, 2/17/2009).

The tax and benefits provisions of the Children's Health Insurance Act appear in Act Secs. 704 and 311 of PL 111-3, 2/4/2009.

Key provisions in the 2009 Recovery Act. The 2009 Recovery Act includes tax breaks for businesses and many tax breaks for individuals as well as energy incentives and important bond changes. Highlights include—

• *Tax breaks for business.* These include extended bonus depreciation and increased expensing for 2009, longer NOL carrybacks for some, deferral on debt discharge income from reacquisitions of debt, reduced capital gains tax for holders of qualified small business stock, and a shortened S corporation built-in gain holding period.

• *Tax breaks for individuals.* These include a refundable tax credit of up to $400 per worker ($800 per couple filing jointly), phasing out completely at $190,000 for couples filing jointly and $95,000 for single filers, eased child tax credit and earned income tax credit rules, a beefed-up tax credit for higher education, an enhanced credit for first-time home purchases with the removal of the repayment requirement, a tax deduction for state sales and excise taxes paid on the purchase of new cars, including light trucks and SUVs, motorcycles and motor homes, and a 65% subsidy for COBRA premiums for up to nine months.

• *AMT relief.* The 2009 Recovery Act boosts AMT exemption amounts for individuals for 2009, and also provides that for 2009, personal nonrefundable credits may offset AMT and regular tax. Additionally, interest on qualifying private activity bonds issued in 2009 or 2010 isn't treated as an AMT preference (nor is there an ACE adjustment for interest on tax-exempts issued in 2009 or 2010).

- *Energy incentives.* These include a three-year extension of the production tax credit (PTC) for electricity derived from wind (through 2012) and for electricity derived from biomass, geothermal, hydropower, landfill gas, waste-to-energy, and marine facilities (through 2013), extension through 2010 and expansion of tax credits for home energy efficiency for purchases such as new furnaces, energy-efficient windows and doors, or insulation, a tax credit of up to $5,000 for families that purchase plug-in hybrid vehicles and a new manufacturing investment tax credit for investment in advanced energy facilities, such as facilities that manufacture components for the production of renewable energy, advanced battery technology, and other innovative next-generation green technologies.

viewpoint: David E. Hardesty, a CPA specializing in tax planning, especially for Internet, software, and other entrepreneurial enterprises, a vice president of the CPA firm of Wilson Markle Stuckey Hardesty & Bott in Lakespur, CA, an adjunct professor at Golden Gate University's Graduate School of Taxation, and the author of WG&L's Electronic Commerce: Taxation and Planning, comments on the tax provisions of the 2009 Recovery Act as follows:

Here is something we have not seen for a long time—a demand-side stimulus package. There is not much in this bill to make the average business owner happy. Among other things, there are the one-year extensions of 50% bonus depreciation, higher Code Sec. 179 deductions, and first-year auto depreciation limits; and an expansion of carryback years for some net operating losses. However, most of the stimulus package is aimed squarely at individual taxpayers. This is a far cry from the tax bills of the Bush years. In addition, it seems the package is not aimed at all individuals. The package is targeted mostly to the middle class and lower middle class.

Things not in this tax package, which could have been, are measures aimed at the upcoming sunset of the Bush tax cuts. Recall that many major changes in the Internal Revenue Code have long been scheduled to take place after 2009. The estate tax is scheduled to disappear in 2010, only to reappear in 2011 in pre-2002 form; preferential dividend and long-term capital gain rates are scheduled to expire after 2010; and the top individual tax rates are scheduled to jump back up to pre-2002 levels. The implosions of the stock and debt markets have inflicted serious damage on investors. These upcoming tax law changes will be another blow to this group. It is therefore surprising that Congress did not include something in the bill to encourage the investor class, which must be feeling quite fragile right now.

Key provisions in the 2009 Children's Health Insurance Act. The 2009 Children's Health Insurance Act provides that group health plans must permit special enrollment arrangements for employees related to eligibility under either Medicaid or the Children's Health Insurance Program, and increases the corporate estimated tax payments for July, August, and September 2013 by 0.5 percent, to 120 percent of the payment otherwise due, and reduces the next payment accordingly.

Contents. A complete list of items discussed, arranged by paragraph title and number begins at ¶ 2 . . . . p. xiii.

Analysis of the Tax and Benefits Provisions of the American Recovery and Reinvestment Act of 2009. This section includes the Analysis of the tax and benefits provisions of the 2009 Recovery Act and the 2009 Children's Health Insurance Act arranged in topical order. Each analysis paragraph starts with a boldface title. That is followed by a list of the Code or ERISA sections amended, added, affected, repealed by or related to the change, the Act section that caused the change, and the generally effective date for the change. Each analysis paragraph discusses the background for the change, the new law change, and the effective date for that change. Analysis paragraphs may include (1) illustrations and observations providing practical insight into the effects of the change, (2) recommendations explaining how to take advantage of opportunities presented by the law change, (3) cautions explaining how to avoid pitfalls created by the law change, and (4) client letters and interoffice memos highlighting important law changes. The Analysis is reproduced at ¶ 100 *et seq.* . . .
. . . . p. 1.

Client Letters and Interoffice Memos. Client letters and interoffice memos are included on the following topics:

- Tax changes affecting individuals and families in the American Recovery and Reinvestment Act of 2009;

- "Making Work Pay" tax credit in the American Recovery and Reinvestment Act of 2009;

- Enhanced first-time homebuyer credit in the American Recovery and Reinvestment Act of 2009;

- Tax break for new car buyers in the American Recovery and Reinvestment Act of 2009;

- Expanded tax credit for college in the American Recovery and Reinvestment Act of 2009;

- Business tax changes in the American Recovery and Reinvestment Act of 2009; and

- Energy tax incentives in the American Recovery and Reinvestment Act of 2009.

- AMT relief in the American Recovery and Reinvestment Act of 2009.

- Expanded work opportunity credit in the American Recovery and Reinvestment Act of 2009.

- Up to five-year carryback of 2008 net operating losses for small businesses in the American Recovery and Reinvestment Act of 2009.
- Expanded nonbusiness energy property credit in the American Recovery and Reinvestment Act of 2009.
- Qualified tuition programs—"529 plans"—enhanced in the American Recovery and Recovery and Reinvestment Act of 2009.
- Expanded child tax credit in the American Recovery and Recovery and Reinvestment Act of 2009.
- Changes to plug-in electric vehicle credit in the American Recovery and Recovery and Reinvestment Act of 2009.

The Client Letters begin at ¶ 1401 *et seq.* . . . . p. 295.

The Interoffice Memos begin at ¶ 1415 *et seq.* . . . . p. 329.

Code as Amended. All Code sections that were amended, added, repealed, or redesignated by the tax and benefits provisions of the 2009 Recovery Act and the 2009 Children's Health Insurance Act, appear in Code section order as amended, added, repealed, or redesignated. New matter is shown in italics. Deleted material and effective dates are shown in footnotes. The Code as Amended is reproduced at ¶ 3000 *et seq.* . . . . p. 401.

ERISA as Amended. All ERISA sections that were amended, added, repealed, or redesignated by the tax and benefits provisions of the 2009 Recovery Act and the 2009 Children's Health Insurance Act, appear in ERISA section order as amended, added, repealed, or redesignated. New matter is shown in italics. Deleted material and effective dates are shown in footnotes. ERISA as Amended is reproduced at ¶ 3500 *et seq.* . . . . p. 701.

Act Sections Not Amending Code. This section reproduces in Act section order, all tax and benefits provisions of the 2009 Recovery Act and the 2009 Children's Health Insurance Act sections, or portions thereof that are tax or ERISA related but do not amend specific Code or ERISA sections. The Act Sections Not Amending Code are reproduced at ¶ 4000 *et seq.* . . . . p. 751.

Committee Reports. For the tax and benefits provisions of the American Recovery and Reinvestment Act of 2009, this section reproduces all relevant parts of (1) H Rept No. 111-8 Part 2 for HR 598, a predecessor bill to H.R. 1, (2) JCX-10-09 and JCX-12-09 related to the Senate Finance Committee version of H.R. 1, and (3) Conf Rept No. 111-16 for Division B of H.R. 1. The relevant Committee Reports for the tax and benefits provisions of the American Recovery and Reinvestment Act of 2009 are reproduced at ¶ 5000 *et seq.* . . . . p. 801.

For the tax and benefits provisions of the Children's Health Insurance Program Reauthorization Act of 2009, this section also reproduces all relevant parts of JCX-3-09. The relevant Committee Reports for the tax and benefits provi-

Act Sections Amending ERISA. Arranged in Act section order, this table shows all changes to ERISA made by the 2009 Recovery Act and the 2009 Children's Health Insurance Act, including conforming amendments. The table is reproduced at ¶ 6007 .... p. 1,073.

Federal Tax Coordinator 2d ¶ s Affected by Act. Arranged in FTC 2d ¶ order, this table shows the FTC 2d paragraphs that have been affected by the 2009 Recovery Act and the 2009 Children's Health Insurance Act. The table is reproduced at ¶ 6008 .... p. 1,075.

United States Tax Reporter ¶ s Affected by Act. Arranged in USTR ¶ order, this table shows the USTR paragraphs that have been affected by the 2009 Recovery Act and the 2009 Children's Health Insurance Act. The table is reproduced at ¶ 6009 .... p. 1,077.

Tax Desk ¶ s Affected by Act. Arranged in Tax Desk ¶ order, this table shows the Tax Desk paragraphs that have been affected by the 2009 Recovery Act and the 2009 Children's Health Insurance Act. The table is reproduced at ¶ 6010 .... p. 1,079.

Pension Explanations ¶ s Affected by Act. Arranged in Pension and Profit Sharing 2d ¶ order, this table shows the Pension and Profit Sharing 2d paragraphs that have been affected by the 2009 Recovery Act and the 2009 Children's Health Insurance Act. The table is reproduced at ¶ 6011 .... p. 1,081.

Current and Prospective Effective Dates. Arranged in Code section order, this table shows the topic related to a change to each specified Code section made by a Tax Act passed by the 108th, 109th, 110th or the 111th Congress, the current and/or prospective effective date of that change, and the Complete Analysis ¶ in which the topic is or has been analyzed. The table is reproduced at ¶ 6012 .... p. 1,083.

Index. A detailed index, which directs the reader to the appropriate Analysis paragraph, is reproduced immediately after the aforementioned Tables for the Complete Analysis. .... p. 1,301.

¶ 2. Contents

¶ 100. Individual Provisions

¶ 101. Refundable "making work pay credit" of up to $400 ($800 on joint return) is allowed for 2009 and 2010

Code Sec. 36A, as added by 2009 Recovery Act § 1001(a)
Code Sec. 36A, 2009 Recovery Act § 1001(b)
Code Sec. 36A, 2009 Recovery Act § 1001(c)
Code Sec. 6213(g)(2)(N), as amended by 2009 Recovery Act § 1001(d)
Code Sec. 6211(b)(4)(A), as amended by 2009 Recovery Act § 1001(e)(1)
Generally effective: Tax years beginning after Dec. 31, 2008, and before Jan. 1, 2011
Committee Reports, see ¶ 5001

Earned income credit. Eligible individuals are allowed an earned income credit (EIC) equal to the credit percentage times the amount of the individual's earned income for the tax year that doesn't exceed the statutory earned income amount. (FTC 2d/FIN ¶ A-4201; USTR ¶ 324; TaxDesk ¶ 569,001)

"Earned income" for EIC purposes includes: (a) wages, salaries, tips, and other employee compensation, if those amounts are includible in gross income, plus (b) net earnings from self-employment, less one-half of self-employment tax. (FTC 2d/FIN ¶ A-4222; USTR ¶ 324.05; TaxDesk ¶ 569,023) Taxpayers may elect to treat excludable combat pay as earned income for EIC purposes. (FTC 2d/FIN ¶ A-4224.1; USTR ¶ 324.05; TaxDesk ¶ 569,025.1)

Recovery rebate credit for 2008. The 2008 Economic Stimulus Act provided a refundable credit (the recovery rebate credit) for 2008. The credit was available to "eligible individuals," i.e., any individual other than a nonresident alien, a dependent, or an estate or trust. Most taxpayers received the credit during 2008 in the form of an advance rebate. The rebates were intended to deliver a fiscal stimulus to the economy. (FTC 2d/FIN ¶ A-4014; USTR ¶ 64,284; TaxDesk ¶ 568,513)

FICA tax. A 7.65% Federal Insurance Contributions Act (FICA) tax is imposed on employers and employees, consisting of the 6.2% social security tax plus the 1.45% Medicare tax. For 2009, the social security tax is computed on the first $106,800 of the employee's wages. The 1.45% Medicare tax is computed on the employee's total wages. (FTC 2d/FIN ¶ H-4687; USTR ¶ 31,114; TaxDesk ¶ 541,002)

FTC 2d References are to Federal Tax Coordinator 2d
FIN References are to RIA's Analysis of Federal Taxes: Income
USTR References are to United States Tax Reporter: Income
PE References are to Pension Explanations

New Law. The 2009 Recovery Act provides eligible individuals a refundable income tax credit (the "making work pay credit") for the two tax years beginning in 2009 and 2010. (Com Rept, see ¶ 5001)

Allowance and amount of credit. Eligible individuals (defined below) are allowed an income tax credit for the tax year equal to the lesser of (Code Sec. 36A(a) as added by 2009 Recovery Act §1001(a)):

(1) 6.2% of the taxpayer's earned income (defined below) (Code Sec. 36A(a)(1)), or

(2) $400 ($800 for a joint return). (Code Sec. 36A(a)(2))

> *observation:* Thus, a taxpayer with $6,451.61 of earned income ($12,903.22 on a joint return) would get the maximum credit. Because the credit rate (6.2%) is the same as the social security tax rate, the credit can be thought of as offsetting social security tax on those amounts of earned income.

> *illustration (1):* Taxpayer A, a single individual, had $5,400 of earned income in 2009. A's credit is $334.80 ($5,400 × 6.2%).

> *illustration (2):* Taxpayers B and C, joint filers, had $10,800 of earned income in 2009. Their credit is $669.60 ($10,800 × 6.2%).

> *illustration (3):* Taxpayer D, a single individual, had $12,000 of earned income in 2009. D gets the maximum $400 credit, which is less than $744 ($12,000 × 6.2%).

> *illustration (4):* Taxpayers E and F, joint filers, had $24,000 of earned income in 2009. They get the maximum $800 credit, which is less than $1,488 ($24,000 × 6.2%).

The term "earned income" has the meaning given that term by Code Sec. 32(c)(2) for the EIC, with the following modifications:

. . . earned income doesn't include net earnings from self-employment that aren't taken into account in computing taxable income, and

. . . earned income does include combat pay excluded from gross income by reason of Code Sec. 112, see FTC 2d/FIN ¶ H-3106; USTR ¶ 1124; TaxDesk ¶ 138,005. (Code Sec. 36A(d)(2))

Reduction for economic recovery payments or credits to government retirees. The otherwise allowable credit for any tax year is reduced by the amount of:

. . . any payments that the taxpayer received during that tax year under 2009 Recovery Act §2201, which provides for $250 economic recovery payments to recipients of social security, supplemental security income (SSI), railroad retirement, or veterans disability or pension benefits (see ¶ 102), or

... any credit allowed to the taxpayer under 2009 Recovery Act §2202, which provides a $250 refundable credit to certain government retirees (see ¶ 103). (Code Sec. 36A(c))

> *illustration (5):* Taxpayer G is a social security recipient and also has income from part-time work that entitles her to a $400 making work pay credit. G must reduce the $400 credit amount by her $250 economic recovery payment, which leaves her with a making work pay credit of $150.

> *observation:* The making work pay credit is allowed for both 2009 and 2010, while the economic recovery payment is a one-time payment that most eligible individuals will receive in 2009. The credit must be reduced only for the tax year in which the economic recovery payment is received.

An individual's failure to make this reduction is treated as a mathematical or clerical error. (Code Sec. 6213(g)(2)(N) as amended by 2009 Recovery Act §1001(d)) This allows IRS to assess any tax resulting from that failure without having to send the taxpayer a notice of deficiency that allows the taxpayer to file a petition with the Tax Court. (Com Rept, see ¶ 5001) See FTC 2d/FIN ¶ T-3622; T-3902.1; USTR ¶ 62,134.02; TaxDesk ¶ 821,002; 836,019.

Who is eligible for credit. An "eligible individual" for purposes of the making work pay credit is any individual, except for (Code Sec. 36A(d)(1)(A)):

... a nonresident alien (Code Sec. 36A(d)(1)(A)(i));

... an individual who can be claimed as a dependent by another taxpayer for a tax year beginning in the calendar year in which the individual's tax year begins (Code Sec. 36A(d)(1)(A)(ii)); and

... an estate or trust. (Code Sec. 36A(d)(1)(A)(iii))

> *observation:* Students who are (or can be) claimed as dependents by their parents aren't eligible individuals, even if they have enough income to be required to file a return. It makes no difference if the parent chooses not to claim the child as a dependent, because the dependency deduction is still "allowable" to the parent.

FTC 2d References are to Federal Tax Coordinator 2d
FIN References are to RIA's Analysis of Federal Taxes: Income
USTR References are to United States Tax Reporter: Income
PE References are to Pension Explanations

Social security number requirement. The term "eligible individual" doesn't include any individual who doesn't include on the tax return for the tax year (Code Sec. 36A(d)(1)(B)):

... the individual's social security account number (Code Sec. 36A(d)(1)(B)(i)), and

... for a joint return, the social security account number of one of the taxpayers on the return. (Code Sec. 36A(d)(1)(B)(ii))

Thus, each tax return on which the making work pay credit is claimed must include the social security number of the taxpayer. A joint return must include the social security number of at least one spouse. (Com Rept, see ¶ 5001)

For this purpose, a social security account number doesn't include a taxpayer identification number (TIN) issued by IRS. (Code Sec. 36A(d)(1)(B))

> **🅡🅘🅐observation:** IRS will issue an individual taxpayer identification number (ITIN), on application, to an alien individual who isn't eligible for a social security number. See FTC 2d/FIN ¶ S-1508.1; USTR ¶ 61,094; TaxDesk ¶ 570,109. Although ITINs are valid for filing tax returns, they aren't valid for the making work pay credit.

> **🅡🅘🅐observation:** The social security number requirement means that an individual must be authorized to work legally in the U.S. in order to claim the making work pay credit. On a joint return, at least one of the taxpayers must be authorized to work legally in the U.S.

> **🅡🅘🅐observation:** The joint return rule will be helpful where a U.S. Armed Forces member is married to a foreign spouse who is ineligible for a social security number. However, the rule isn't limited to military families.

An individual's omission of a required social security account number is treated as a mathematical or clerical error. (Code Sec. 6213(g)(2)(N)) This allows IRS to assess any tax resulting from that omission without the having to send the taxpayer a notice of deficiency that allows the taxpayer to file a petition with the Tax Court. (Com Rept, see ¶ 5001) See FTC 2d/FIN ¶ T-3622; T-3902.1; USTR ¶ 62,134.02; TaxDesk ¶ 821,002; 836,019.

Phaseout of credit. The credit is phased out at a rate of 2% of the eligible individual's modified adjusted gross income (AGI) above $75,000 ($150,000 for joint returns). (Com Rept, see ¶ 5001) Thus, the amount allowable as a credit for the tax year is reduced (but not below zero) by 2% of so much of the taxpayer's modified AGI as exceeds $75,000 ($150,000 for joint returns). (Code Sec. 36A(b)(1))

observation: The maximum credit of $400 is completely phased out at modified AGI of $95,000. For joint filers, the maximum credit of $800 is completely phased out at modified AGI of $190,000.

illustration (6): Taxpayer H, a single individual, was eligible for the maximum credit of $400 but had modified AGI of $90,000. H's credit is $100: $400 − [2% × ($90,000 − $75,000)].

illustration (7): Taxpayers I and J, joint filers, were eligible for the maximum credit of $800 but had modified AGI of $180,000. Their credit is $200: $800 − [2% × ($180,000 − $150,000)].

illustration (8): Taxpayer K, a single individual, was eligible for the maximum credit of $400 but had modified AGI of $100,000. K gets no credit, because 2% of $25,000 ($100,000 − $75,000) equals $500, which wipes out the $400 credit.

illustration (9): Taxpayers L and M, joint filers, were eligible for the maximum credit of $800 but had modified AGI of $200,000. They get no credit, because 2% of $50,000 ($200,000 − $150,000) equals $1,000, which wipes out the $800 credit.

For this purpose, the term "modified AGI" means the taxpayer's AGI for the tax year increased by any amount excluded from gross income under:

. . . the foreign earned income exclusion under Code Sec. 911, see FTC 2d/FIN ¶ O-1100 ; USTR ¶ 9114; TaxDesk ¶ 191,000,

. . . the exclusion of income from American Samoa under Code Sec. 931, see FTC 2d/FIN ¶ O-1432; USTR ¶ 9314, or

. . . the exclusion of income from Puerto Rico under Code Sec. 933, see FTC 2d/FIN ¶ O-1451; USTR ¶ 9334. (Code Sec. 36A(b)(2))

Credit is refundable. The making work pay credit is refundable. (Com Rept, see ¶ 5001) The credit is allowed by new Code Sec. 36A, which is part of Subpart C of Part IV of Subchapter A of Chapter 1 (2009 Recovery Act §1001(a)) of Subtitle A of the Code.

observation: The credits in that subpart are refundable, i.e., the excess of those credits over the tax is considered an overpayment (see FTC 2d/FIN ¶ A-4001; USTR ¶ 64,014; TaxDesk ¶ 568,501).

FTC 2d References are to Federal Tax Coordinator 2d
FIN References are to RIA's Analysis of Federal Taxes: Income
USTR References are to United States Tax Reporter: Income
PE References are to Pension Explanations

observation: IRS points out that, because the credit is refundable, most low-income workers will qualify for the full credit. (IR 2009-13, Feb. 21, 2009)

illustration (10): Taxpayer N, a single individual, has tax liability of $300, after considering all tax credits other than the making work pay credit. N is entitled to the maximum making work pay credit of $400. The $400 credit will wipe out N's tax liability and, in addition, N will receive a $100 refund or credit against future taxes.

Withholding to be reduced. IRS is to provide an accelerated delivery of the credit in 2009 by revising its income tax withholding schedules. The revised schedules will be designed to reduce taxpayers' income tax withheld for the remainder of 2009 so that the full annual benefit of the credit is reflected in income tax withheld during the remainder of 2009. (Com Rept, see ¶ 5001)

observation: IRS says that, for employees who are subject to wage withholding, the making work pay credit will typically be handled by automated withholding changes in early spring. Those changes may result in an increase in take-home pay.

Although the credit must be claimed on 2009 income tax returns, its benefit will generally be spread out over the paychecks that employees receive from this spring until the end of the year. Taxpayers won't get a check mailed to them by IRS as they did for the economic stimulus payment in 2008.

New withholding tables that incorporate the credit were released on Feb. 21 and will be incorporated in new IRS Pub. No 15-T, which will be mailed to employers in mid-March. IRS asks employers to start using the new tables as soon as possible but no later than April 1.

Employees don't have to take any action, such as filling out a new Form W-4, to have the credit reflected in their take-home pay. However, employees with multiple jobs or married couples whose combined incomes place them in a higher tax bracket may choose to submit a revised W-4 to make sure enough tax is withheld.

Many higher-income taxpayers will see little or no change in their take-home pay because they are subject to the phaseout discussed above.

Taxpayers who don't have taxes withheld by an employer during the year can claim the credit on their 2009 tax return. (IR 2009-13, Feb. 21, 2009; IRS website, "The Making Work Pay Tax Credit")

observation: Self-employed individuals, who aren't subject to wage withholding, can receive the credit in advance by reducing the amount of their estimated tax payments. But they should take care not to overshoot the mark and become liable for the estimated tax penalty, see FTC 2d/FIN ¶ S-5260; USTR ¶ 66,544.02; TaxDesk ¶ 571,353.

Termination after 2010. The making work pay credit won't be available for tax years beginning after Dec. 31, 2010. (Code Sec. 36A(e))

Treatment of U.S. possessions. Special credit rules are provided for residents of U.S. possessions. The Commonwealth of Puerto Rico and the Commonwealth of the Northern Mariana Islands are treated as U.S. possessions for this purpose. (2009 Recovery Act §1001(b)(3)(A))

The treatment of each possession depends on whether it has a "mirror code tax system." A U.S. possession has a mirror code tax system if the income tax liability of the possession's residents under the possession's income tax system is determined by reference to the U.S. income tax laws as if the possession were the U.S. (2009 Recovery Act §1001(b)(3)(B))

Mirror code possessions. For U.S. possessions that have mirror code tax systems (2009 Recovery Act §1001(b)(1)(A)), i.e., the U.S. Virgin Islands, Guam, and the Northern Mariana Islands (Com Rept, see ¶ 5001), the U.S. Treasury will make payments to that possession equal to that possession's loss for tax years 2009 and 2010 by reason of the making work pay credit. (2009 Recovery Act §1001(b)(1)(A))

The amount of the payments will equal the aggregate amount of making work pay credits allowable to that possession's residents against its income tax. (Com Rept, see ¶ 5001) Treasury will determine these amounts based on information provided by the possession's government. (2009 Recovery Act §1001(b)(1)(A))

Non-mirror code possessions. For U.S. possessions that don't have mirror code tax systems (2009 Recovery Act §1001(b)(1)(B)), i.e., Puerto Rico and American Samoa (Com Rept, see ¶ 5001), the U.S. Treasury will make payments to the possession in an amount that it estimates to be equal to the aggregate credits that would have been allowed to that possession's residents for tax years 2009 and 2010 if a mirror code tax system had been in effect in the possession (2009 Recovery Act §1001(b)(1)(B)), i.e., if the making work pay credit provided to U.S. residents were provided by the possession to its residents. There will be two payments, one for 2009 and one for 2010. (Com Rept, see ¶ 5001) A possession won't receive the payments unless it has a plan, approved by the U.S. Treasury, under which it will promptly distribute the payment to its residents. (2009 Recovery Act §1001(b)(1)(B))

FTC 2d References are to Federal Tax Coordinator 2d
FIN References are to RIA's Analysis of Federal Taxes: Income
USTR References are to United States Tax Reporter: Income
PE References are to Pension Explanations

No double credit. No making work pay credit against U.S. income taxes will be allowed to any person (2009 Recovery Act §1001(c)(2)):

... to whom a making work pay credit is allowed against possession income taxes (2009 Recovery Act §1001(b)(2)(A)), e.g., under that possession's mirror income tax (Com Rept, see ¶ 5001), or

... who is eligible for a payment under a non-mirror code possession's plan for distributing to its residents the payment described above from the U.S. Treasury. (2009 Recovery Act §1001(b)(2)(B))

Credit disregarded for federal programs. Any credit or refund of the making work pay credit allowed or made to any individual, including a credit or refund to a resident of a U.S. possession, isn't taken into account as income and isn't taken into account as resources for the month of receipt and the following two months for purposes of determining the eligibility of the recipient or any other individual for benefits or assistance, or the amount or extent of benefits or assistance, under any federal program or any state or local program financed in whole or in part with federal funds. (2009 Recovery Act §1001(c))

Credit treated as negative tax in deficiency computation. Any excess of the making work pay credit over the income tax is taken into account as a negative amount of tax in computing a taxpayer's tax deficiency. (Code Sec. 6211(b)(4)(A) as amended by 2009 Recovery Act §1001(e)(1)) For how deficiencies are computed, see FTC 2d/FIN ¶ T-1501; USTR ¶ 62,114; TaxDesk ¶ 822,501.

☐ **Effective:** Tax years beginning after Dec. 31, 2008 (2009 Recovery Act §1001(f)), and before Jan. 1, 2011. (Code Sec. 36A(e))

¶ 102. One-time $250 payment to be made to recipients of social security, SSI, railroad retirement, and veterans disability or pension benefits

Code Sec. None, 2009 Recovery Act § 2201
Generally effective: Feb. 17, 2009
Committee Reports, see ¶ 5079

Cash benefits provided under federal law include the following:

... Title II of the Social Security Act authorizes cash benefits for retired and disabled workers and their dependents and survivors under the Old Age and Survivors Insurance (OASI) and Disability Insurance (DI) programs.

... Title XVI of the Social Security Act authorizes monthly cash benefits for blind and disabled persons and persons age 65 or over who have limited income and resources under the Supplemental Security Income (SSI) program.

... The Railroad Retirement Act of 1974 authorizes cash benefits for retired and disabled railroad workers and their dependents and survivors.

... Title 38 of the U.S. Code authorizes cash benefits for certain veterans and their dependents and survivors. (Com Rept, see ¶ 5079)

The 2009 Recovery Act provides eligible individuals with a refundable income tax credit (the "making work pay credit") for 2009 and 2010, see ¶ 101. The amount of the credit is based on the individual's "earned income," as defined for earned income credit (EIC) purposes. Under this definition, earned income doesn't include social security, SSI, railroad retirement, and veterans benefits. See FTC 2d/FIN ¶ A-4222; USTR ¶ 324.05; TaxDesk ¶ 569,023.

> *observation:* An individual with only those benefits and no earned income isn't entitled to the making work pay credit.

New Law. The 2009 Recovery Act provides for one-time $250 economic recovery payments to:

... adults eligible for social security benefits;

... adults eligible for railroad retirement benefits;

... adults eligible for veterans compensation or pension benefits; and

... individuals of any age eligible for SSI benefits, other than individuals who receive SSI while in a Medicaid institution. (Com Rept, see ¶ 5079)

To receive an economic recovery payment, the individual must have been eligible for one of the above four benefit programs for any of the three months before the month of enactment. (Com Rept, see ¶ 5079)

Specifically, the U.S. Treasury is directed to make a $250 payment to each individual who, for any month during the three-month period ending with the month which ends before the month that includes Feb. 17, 2009, is entitled to a social security Title II benefit, railroad retirement benefit, or veterans benefit, or is eligible for an SSI cash benefit, as specified below under "Qualifying benefit payments." (2009 Recovery Act §2201(a)(1)(A))

> *observation:* Thus, to be entitled to the $250 payment, an individual must have been eligible for one of the four benefit programs for any of the following three months: Nov. 2008, Dec. 2008, or Jan. 2009.

> *observation:* IRS won't be making these $250 payments. IRS advises individuals who may qualify for a payment to contact their re-

FTC 2d References are to Federal Tax Coordinator 2d
FIN References are to RIA's Analysis of Federal Taxes: Income
USTR References are to United States Tax Reporter: Income
PE References are to Pension Explanations

spective agencies for more information. (IRS website, "The Economic Recovery Payment")

observation: The Social Security Administration (SSA) says that nearly 55 million social security and SSI beneficiaries will receive a $250 payment. That payment will be separate from the beneficiary's regular monthly payment. (SocialSecurityOnline, FAQs)

Certification of recipients. The Commissioner of Social Security, the Railroad Retirement Board, and the Secretary of Veterans Affairs are directed to certify the individuals entitled to receive economic recovery payments and provide Treasury with the information needed to disburse the payments. A certification won't be affected by any later determination or redetermination of the individual's entitlement to, or eligibility for, one of the four benefit programs. (2009 Recovery Act §2201(b))

Individuals ineligible for payment. An economic recovery payment will be made only to individuals whose current address of record under a benefits program listed below under "Qualifying benefit payments" is in:

. . . one of the 50 states;

. . . the District of Columbia;

. . . Puerto Rico;

. . . Guam;

. . . the U.S. Virgin Islands;

. . . American Samoa, or

. . . the Northern Mariana Islands. (2009 Recovery Act §2201(a)(2))

observation: Under this rule, a social security recipient who lives in a foreign country won't get an economic recovery payment.

Prisoners, fugitives, etc. An otherwise eligible individual won't receive an economic recovery payment if the individual's federal program benefits have been suspended because the individual is in prison, is a fugitive, is a probation or parole violator, has committed fraud, or is no longer lawfully present in the U.S. (Com Rept, see ¶ 5079) This rule applies to individuals who, for the most recent month of the individual's entitlement in the three months before the month of enactment (i.e., Nov. 2008, Dec. 2008, or Jan. 2009), have been suspended from receiving:

. . . social security or railroad retirement benefits (2009 Recovery Act §2201(a)(4)(A));

. . . veterans benefits (2009 Recovery Act §2201(a)(4)(B)); or

. . . SSI cash benefits. (2009 Recovery Act §2201(a)(4)(C))

Decedents. No economic recovery payment will be made in the case of an individual who died before being certified to receive the payment. (2009 Recovery Act §2201(a)(4)(D))

No double payments. An individual will receive only one $250 economic recovery payment, even if the individual is entitled to or eligible for more than one benefit or cash payment specified below under "Qualifying benefit payments." (2009 Recovery Act §2201(a)(3))

> 🄡*observation:* For example, an individual who receives both social security and SSI will be entitled to only one payment. An individual who receives social security and who also receives veterans or railroad retirement benefits will likewise be entitled to only one payment. (Social-SecurityOnline, FAQs)

If the individual is also eligible for the making work pay credit, that credit must be reduced by the economic recovery payment (see ¶ 101).

Qualifying benefit payments. Individuals who are entitled to or eligible for the payment of the following benefits are eligible to receive an economic recovery payment (2009 Recovery Act §2201(a)(1)(A)):

Title II social security benefits. Monthly insurance benefits payable, without regard to Sec. 202(j)(1) and Sec. 223(b) of the Social Security Act (42 USC §402(j)(1) and 42 USC §423(b)), under the following Social Security Act sections (2009 Recovery Act §2201(a)(1)(B)(i)):

... Sec. 202(a) (42 USC §402(a)) (2009 Recovery Act §2201(a)(1)(B)(i)(I));

... Sec. 202(b) (42 USC §402(b)) (2009 Recovery Act §2201(a)(1)(B)(i)(II));

... Sec. 202(c) (42 USC §402(c)) (2009 Recovery Act §2201(a)(1)(B)(i)(III));

... Sec. 202(d)(1)(B)(ii) (42 USC §402(d)(1)(B)(ii)) (2009 Recovery Act §2201(a)(1)(B)(i)(IV));

... Sec. 202(e) (42 USC §402(e)) (2009 Recovery Act §2201(a)(1)(B)(i)(V));

... Sec. 202(f) (42 USC §402(f)) (2009 Recovery Act §2201(a)(1)(B)(i)(VI));

... Sec. 202(g) (42 USC §402(g)) (2009 Recovery Act §2201(a)(1)(B)(i)(VII));

... Sec. 202(h) (42 USC §402(h)) (2009 Recovery Act §2201(a)(1)(B)(i)(VIII));

... Sec. 223(a) (42 USC §423(a)) (2009 Recovery Act §2201(a)(1)(B)(i)(IX));

... Sec. 227 (42 USC §427) (2009 Recovery Act §2201(a)(1)(B)(i)(X)); or

... Sec. 228 (42 USC §428). (2009 Recovery Act §2201(a)(1)(B)(i)(XI))

FTC 2d References are to Federal Tax Coordinator 2d
FIN References are to RIA's Analysis of Federal Taxes: Income
USTR References are to United States Tax Reporter: Income
PE References are to Pension Explanations

Railroad retirement benefits. Monthly annuity or pension payments payable, without regard to Sec. 5(a)(ii) of the Railroad Retirement Act of 1974 (45 USC §231d(a)(ii)), under the following sections of the Railroad Retirement Act of 1974 (2009 Recovery Act §2201(a)(1)(B)(ii)):

... Sec. 2(a)(1) (45 USC §231a(a)(1)) (2009 Recovery Act §2201(a)(1)(B)(ii)(I));

... Sec. 2(c) (45 USC §231a(c)) (2009 Recovery Act §2201(a)(1)(B)(ii)(II));

... Sec. 2(d)(1)(i) (45 USC §231a(d)(1)(i)) (2009 Recovery Act §2201(a)(1)(B)(ii)(III));

... Sec. 2(d)(1)(ii) (45 USC §231a(d)(1)(ii)) (2009 Recovery Act §2201(a)(1)(B)(ii)(IV));

... Sec. 2(d)(1)(iii)(C) to an adult disabled child (45 USC §231a(d)(1)(iii)(C)) (2009 Recovery Act §2201(a)(1)(B)(ii)(V));

... Sec. 2(d)(1)(iv) (45 USC §231a(d)(1)(iv)) (2009 Recovery Act §2201(a)(1)(B)(ii)(VI));

... Sec. 2(d)(1)(v) (45 USC §231a(d)(1)(v)) (2009 Recovery Act §2201(a)(1)(B)(ii)(VII)); or

... Sec. 7(b)(2) (45 USC §231f(b)(2)) with respect to any of the Title II social security benefit payments described above. (2009 Recovery Act §2201(a)(1)(B)(ii)(VIII))

Veterans benefits. Compensation or pension payments payable under (2009 Recovery Act §2201(a)(1)(B)(iii)):

... Sec. 1110, 1117, 1121, 1131, 1141, or 1151 of title 38, United States Code (2009 Recovery Act §2201(a)(1)(B)(iii)(I));

... Sec. 1310, 1312, 1313, 1315, 1316, or 1318 of title 38, United States Code (2009 Recovery Act §2201(a)(1)(B)(iii)(II));

... Sec. 1513, 1521, 1533, 1536, 1537, 1541, 1542, or 1562 of title 38, United States Code (2009 Recovery Act §2201(a)(1)(B)(iii)(III)); or

... Sec. 1805, 1815, or 1821 of title 38, United States Code. (2009 Recovery Act §2201(a)(1)(B)(iii)(IV))

The payment must be made to a veteran, surviving spouse, child, or parent, as described in paragraph (2), (3), (4)(A)(ii), or (5) of Sec. 101, title 38, United States Code, who received that benefit during any month within the three-month period ending with the month which ends before the month that includes Feb. 17, 2009, i.e., during any of the following months: Nov. 2008, Dec. 2008, or Jan. 2009. (2009 Recovery Act §2201(a)(1)(B)(iii))

SSI cash benefits. Cash benefits payable under Sec. 1611 of the Social Security Act (42 USC §1382), other than under subsection (e)(1)(B) of that section, or 1619(a) of the Social Security Act (42 USC §1382h). (2009 Recovery Act §2201(a)(1)(C))

Time and manner of payments. Treasury must begin disbursing economic recovery payments as soon as practicable, but no later than 120 days after Feb. 17, 2009, i.e., no later than June 17, 2009. (2009 Recovery Act §2201(a)(5)(A))

> *observation:* The SSA plans to pay all eligible social security and SSI beneficiaries by late May 2009. Payments should be received no later than the first week of June 2009. (SocialSecurityOnline, FAQs)

Termination. No economic recovery payments will be disbursed after Dec. 31, 2010, even if a determination of entitlement to, or eligibility for, a payment is made after that date. (2009 Recovery Act §2201(a)(5)(B))

Electronic payments. Economic recovery payments may be disbursed electronically in the same manner as a benefit payment or cash benefit under the applicable program listed above under "Qualifying benefit payments." (2009 Recovery Act §2201(a)(5)(A))

> *observation:* The SSA will deliver the $250 payments in the same way the social security or SSI benefit is delivered. If an individual's monthly benefit is delivered by check, the SSA will deliver the $250 payment by check. If the individual receives a monthly direct deposit or Direct Express debit card payment, the $250 payment will be received in that way. (SocialSecurityOnline, FAQs)

Payments to representatives and fiduciaries. If an individual has a representative payee or fiduciary for benefit program purposes, the individual's economic recovery payment will be made to that payee or fiduciary. The payee or fiduciary must use the entire payment only for the benefit of the individual who is entitled to it. (2009 Recovery Act §2201(d)(1))

This rule applies to payments to recipients of:

... social security Title II or SSI benefits (2009 Recovery Act §2201(d)(2)(A));

... railroad retirement benefits (2009 Recovery Act §2201(d)(2)(B)); and

... veterans benefits. (2009 Recovery Act §2201(d)(2)(C))

Payments not included in gross income. An economic recovery payment isn't considered gross income for purposes of the Internal Revenue Code of 1986 (2009 Recovery Act §2201(c)(2)), i.e., for income tax purposes. (Com Rept, see ¶ 5079)

FTC 2d References are to Federal Tax Coordinator 2d
FIN References are to RIA's Analysis of Federal Taxes: Income
USTR References are to United States Tax Reporter: Income
PE References are to Pension Explanations

Payments disregarded for federal programs. An economic recovery payment isn't regarded as income or regarded as a resource for the month of receipt and the following nine months, for purposes of determining the eligibility of the recipient or the recipient's spouse or family for benefits or assistance, or the amount or extent of benefits or assistance, under any federal program or under any state or local program financed in whole or in part with federal funds. (2009 Recovery Act §2201(c)(1))

Payments protected from assignment. Economic recovery payments are protected by the assignment and garnishment provisions of the four benefit programs (Com Rept, see ¶ 5079), as if the economic recovery payment were a benefit payment or cash benefit to the individual under the applicable program listed above under "Qualifying benefit payments." (2009 Recovery Act §2201(c)(3))

The following assignment and garnishment provisions apply:

. . . Sec. 207 and Sec. 1631(d)(1) of the Social Security Act (42 USC §407 and 42 USC §1383(d)(1)),

. . . Sec. 14(a) of the Railroad Retirement Act of 1974 (45 USC §231m(a)), and

. . . 38 USC §5301. (2009 Recovery Act §2201(c)(3))

Administrative offset allowed. The payments will be subject to the Treasury Offset Program. (Com Rept, see ¶ 5079) For purposes of 31 USC §3716, which allows an administrative offset of claims by federal agencies, an economic recovery payment isn't considered a benefit payment or cash benefit made under the applicable program. Thus, all amounts paid will be subject to offset to collect delinquent debts. (2009 Recovery Act §2201(c)(4))

> **(RIA)** *observation:* The Treasury Offset Program is a centralized debt collection program developed by the Financial Management Service to assist federal agencies in collecting delinquent debts. When a delinquent debtor is to receive a payment from a federal agency, the payment is intercepted and the debt plus assessed administrative fees are offset against it.

☐ **Effective:** Payments are to begin as soon as practicable, but no later than 120 days after Feb. 17, 2009, i.e., no later than June 17, 2009. (2009 Recovery Act §2201(a)(5)(A)) No payments are to be made after Dec. 31, 2010. (2009 Recovery Act §2201(a)(5)(A))

¶ 103. Refundable $250 credit is allowed to certain government retirees ($500 for joint return where both spouses are eligible)

Code Sec. None, 2009 Recovery Act § 2202
Code Sec. 36A(c), 2009 Recovery Act § 2202
Code Sec. 6211(b)(4)(A), 2009 Recovery Act § 2202(c)(2)
Code Sec. 6213(g)(2), 2009 Recovery Act § 2202(b)(2)
Generally effective: Feb. 17, 2009
Committee Reports, see ¶ 5080

Under Title II of the Social Security Act, a person is eligible for social security benefits only if he or she has insured status as the result of sufficient employment that was covered by the social security system and for which social security payroll taxes were paid. (Com Rept, see ¶ 5080)

Federal employees hired before 1983 were covered by the Civil Service Retirement System (CSRS) and, unless they were eligible for the CSRS-Offset or elected to enroll in the Federal Employees Retirement System (FERS), they aren't eligible for social security benefits on the basis of their federal service. (Com Rept, see ¶ 5080)

In addition, some state and local government employees aren't covered by the social security system and thus aren't eligible for social security benefits on the basis of their public service. (Com Rept, see ¶ 5080)

The 2009 Recovery Act allows a refundable "making work pay credit" for 2009 and 2010 for individuals with earned income (see ¶ 101).

The 2009 Recovery Act also provides a one-time $250 economic recovery payment for recipients of social security, supplemental security income (SSI), railroad retirement, and veterans disability or pension benefits (see ¶ 102).

> **observation:** Certain government retirees who have no earned income and who don't receive social security, SSI, railroad retirement, and veterans disability or pension benefits aren't eligible for the making work pay credit or for the economic recovery payment.

New Law. Under the 2009 Recovery Act, eligible individuals are allowed a $250 credit against income tax (the "credit for government retirees") for the first tax year beginning in 2009. The credit is $500 for a joint return where both spouses are eligible individuals. (2009 Recovery Act §2202(a))

FTC 2d References are to Federal Tax Coordinator 2d
FIN References are to RIA's Analysis of Federal Taxes: Income
USTR References are to United States Tax Reporter: Income
PE References are to Pension Explanations

"Eligible individual" defined. The term "eligible individual" means any individual (2009 Recovery Act §2202(b)(1)):

... who receives during the first tax year beginning in 2009 any amount as a pension or annuity for service performed in the employ of the U.S. or any state, or any instrumentality thereof, that isn't considered employment for purposes of the Federal Insurance Contributions Act (FICA), and (2009 Recovery Act §2202(b)(1)(A))

... who doesn't receive an economic recovery payment (see ¶ 102) during that tax year. (2009 Recovery Act §2202(b)(1)(B))

Thus, the credit is allowed for individuals who receive a government pension or annuity from work not covered by social security and who aren't eligible to receive an economic recovery payment. (Com Rept, see ¶ 5080)

If an individual is also eligible for the making work pay credit, the amount of that credit is reduced by the credit for government retirees. (Com Rept, see ¶ 5080) See ¶ 101.

Social security number required. The term "eligible individual" doesn't include any individual who doesn't include on the tax return for the tax year (2009 Recovery Act §2202(b)(2)):

... the individual's social security account number (2009 Recovery Act §2202(b)(2)(A)), and

... for a joint return, the social security account number of one of the taxpayers on the return. (2009 Recovery Act §2202(b)(2)(B))

For this purpose, a social security account number doesn't include a taxpayer identification number (TIN) issued by IRS. The term "TIN" is defined in Code Sec. 7701(a)(41), see FTC 2d/FIN ¶ J-9001. (2009 Recovery Act §2202(b)(2))

> *observation:* IRS will issue an individual taxpayer identification number (ITIN), on application, to an alien individual who isn't eligible for a social security number. See FTC 2d/FIN ¶ S-1508.1; USTR ¶ 61,094; TaxDesk ¶ 570,109. Although ITINs are valid for filing tax returns, they aren't valid for the credit for government retirees.

Any omission of a correct social security account number that is required on a return under the above rule is treated as a mathematical or clerical error under Code Sec. 6213(g)(2) (see FTC 2d/FIN ¶ T-3628; USTR ¶ 62,134.02; TaxDesk ¶ 836,017). (2009 Recovery Act §2202(b)(2))

> *observation:* Thus, IRS may summarily assess the additional tax due because of the omission (and resulting ineligibility for the credit) without sending the taxpayer a deficiency notice and giving the taxpayer an opportunity to petition the Tax Court. The taxpayer must be given an

explanation of the asserted error and has 60 days to request that IRS abate its assessment. See FTC 2d/FIN ¶ T-3622; T-3902.1; USTR ¶ 62,134.02; TaxDesk ¶ 821,002; 836,019.

Credit is refundable. The credit for government retirees is a refundable credit. (Com Rept, see ¶ 5080) It is treated as allowed by Subpart C of Part IV of Subchapter A of Chapter 1 (2009 Recovery Act §2202(c)(1)(A)) of Subtitle A of the Code.

> *observation:* The credits in that subpart are refundable, i.e., the excess of those credits over the tax is considered an overpayment (see FTC 2d/FIN ¶ A-4001; USTR ¶ 64,014; TaxDesk ¶ 568,501).

> *illustration:* Taxpayer has tax liability of $150, after considering all tax credits other than the credit for government retirees. Taxpayer is also entitled to a $250 credit for government retirees.

> The $250 credit will wipe out taxpayer's tax liability. In addition, taxpayer will receive a $100 refund or credit against future taxes.

Credit disregarded for federal programs. Any credit or refund of the credit for government retirees isn't taken into account as income and isn't taken into account as resources for the month of receipt and the following two months for purposes of determining the eligibility of the recipient or any other individual for benefits or assistance, or the amount or extent of benefits or assistance, under any federal program or any state or local program financed in whole or in part with federal funds. (2009 Recovery Act §2202(d))

Credit treated as negative tax in deficiency computation. For purposes of the Code Sec. 6211(b)(4)(A) deficiency rules, the credit for government retirees is treated in the same manner as the making work pay credit (see ¶ 101). (2009 Recovery Act §2202(c)(2))

> *observation:* Any excess of the making work pay credit over the income tax is taken into account as a negative amount of tax in computing a taxpayer's tax deficiency, see ¶ 101. The same rule applies for the credit for government retirees. For how deficiencies are computed, see FTC 2d/FIN ¶ T-1501; USTR ¶ 62,114; TaxDesk ¶ 822,501.

☐ **Effective:** Feb. 17, 2009. (Com Rept, see ¶ 5080) The credit is allowed for the first tax year beginning in 2009. (2009 Recovery Act §2202(a))

FTC 2d References are to Federal Tax Coordinator 2d
FIN References are to RIA's Analysis of Federal Taxes: Income
USTR References are to United States Tax Reporter: Income
PE References are to Pension Explanations

¶ 104. First-time homebuyer credit is extended to purchases before Dec. 1, 2009 and increased to $8,000 ($4,000 for marrieds filing separately); recapture is waived unless residence is sold or ceases to be a principal residence within 36 months of purchase

Code Sec. 36(h), as amended by 2009 Recovery Act § 1006(a)(1)
Code Sec. 36(g), as amended by 2009 Recovery Act § 1006(a)(2)
Code Sec. 36(b), as amended by 2009 Recovery Act § 1006(b)(1)
Code Sec. 36(b)(1)(B), as amended by 2009 Recovery Act § 1006(b)(2)
Code Sec. 36(f)(4)(D), as amended by 2009 Recovery Act § 1006(c)(1)
Code Sec. 36(g), as amended by 2009 Recovery Act § 1006(c)(2)
Code Sec. 1400C(e)(4), as amended by 2009 Recovery Act § 1006(d)(1)
Code Sec. 36(d), as amended by 2009 Recovery Act § 1006(e)
Generally effective: Residences purchased after Dec. 31, 2008 and before Dec. 1, 2009
Committee Reports, see ¶ 5006

An individual who is a first-time homebuyer of a principal residence in the U.S. after Apr. 8, 2008 and, under pre-2009 Recovery Act law, before July 1, 2009 is allowed, subject to an income phase-out, a refundable tax credit for 10% of the purchase price, up to a maximum of $7,500 ($3,750 on a separate return). The credit is allowed for the tax year in which the taxpayer purchases the home unless the taxpayer makes an election as described below. (FTC 2d/FIN ¶ A-4270, ¶ A-4271; USTR ¶ 364; TaxDesk ¶ 568,851)

Two credit recapture rules generally apply. Under a "regular recapture rule," the credit is recaptured ratably over 15 years with no interest charge, beginning in the second tax year after the tax year in which the home is purchased. For each tax year of the 15-year recapture period, the credit is recaptured as an additional income tax equal to 6-⅔% of the amount of the credit. (FTC 2d/FIN ¶ A-4280; USTR ¶ 364.01; TaxDesk ¶ 568,860)

Under an "accelerated recapture rule," if the taxpayer sells the home, or the home ceases to be used as the principal residence of the taxpayer or the taxpayer's spouse, before the complete repayment of the credit, any remaining credit repayment amount is due on the tax return for the year in which the home is sold or ceases to be used as the principal residence. The credit repayment amount can't exceed the amount of gain from the sale of the residence to an unrelated person. (FTC 2d/FIN ¶ A-4281; USTR ¶ 364.01; TaxDesk ¶ 568,861)

However, neither the regular nor accelerated recapture rule applies in any tax year ending after the taxpayer's death. (FTC 2d/FIN ¶ A-4282; USTR ¶ 364.01; TaxDesk ¶ 568,862) In the case of an involuntary conversion of the home, recapture isn't accelerated if a new principal residence is acquired within a two-year period. (FTC 2d/FIN ¶ A-4283; USTR ¶ 364.01; TaxDesk ¶ 568,863) And in the case of a transfer of the residence to a spouse or to a former spouse incident to a divorce, the transferee spouse—and not the transferor spouse—will be responsible for any future recapture. (FTC 2d ¶ A-4284; USTR ¶ 364.01; TaxDesk ¶ 568,864). Under pre-2009 Recovery Act law, there were no other exceptions to the credit recapture rules. (FTC 2d/FIN ¶ A-4270, ¶ A-4280, ¶ A-4281; USTR ¶ 364.01; TaxDesk ¶ 568,860, ¶ 568,861)

A taxpayer can elect to treat a home purchased during the eligible period in 2009 as if purchased on Dec. 31, 2008 for purposes of claiming the credit on the 2008 tax return and for establishing the beginning of the recapture period. Under pre-2009 Recovery Act law, this election applied for all first-time homebuyer credit purposes except the Code Sec. 36(c) definitions (i.e., the definitions for first-time homebuyer, principal residence, purchase, purchase price, and related persons, and the eligible period ended on June 30, 2009. (FTC 2d/FIN ¶ A-4272; USTR ¶ 364; TaxDesk ¶ 568,852)

Under pre-2009 Recovery Act law, the credit couldn't be claimed if the purchase of the residence was financed by tax-exempt mortgage revenue bonds. (FTC 2d/FIN ¶ A-4279; USTR ¶ 364; TaxDesk ¶ 568,859)

New Law. Under the 2009 Recovery Act, the first-time homebuyer credit is extended to apply to principal residences purchased before Dec. 1, 2009. (Code Sec. 36(h) as amended by 2009 Recovery Act §1006(a)(1)) Correspondingly, for purposes of the election to treat the purchase of a principal residence as having been made on Dec. 31, 2008, the last date of purchase has also been extended until Nov. 30, 2009. (Code Sec. 36(g) as amended by 2009 Recovery Act §1006(a)(2))

The maximum amount of the credit is increased from $7,500 to $8,000. (Code Sec. 36(b) as amended by 2009 Recovery Act §1006(b)(1)) For married individuals filing separately, the maximum credit is increased from $3,750 to $4,000. (Code Sec. 36(b)(1)(B) as amended by 2009 Recovery Act §1006(b)(2))

> ✒ *observation:* The $8,000 maximum credit applies to taxpayers other than married individuals filing separately. That is, it applies to single filers and married couples filing joint returns.

Recapture rules. The 2009 Recovery Act provides that for a principal residence purchased after Dec. 31, 2008 and before Dec. 1, 2009 for which a first-time homebuyer credit is allowed, the "regular recapture rule" won't apply. (Code Sec. 36(f)(4)(D)(i) as amended by 2009 Recovery Act §1006(c)(1))

FTC 2d References are to Federal Tax Coordinator 2d
FIN References are to RIA's Analysis of Federal Taxes: Income
USTR References are to United States Tax Reporter: Income
PE References are to Pension Explanations

observation: That is, recapture of the credit is waived for qualifying home purchases occurring during the period Jan. 1, 2009 through Nov. 30, 2009. This change transforms the credit from the equivalent of an interest-free loan (under pre-2009 Recovery Act law) into direct financial support for qualifying home purchases.

Also for a principal residence purchased after Dec. 31, 2008 and before Dec. 1, 2009 for which a first-time homebuyer credit is allowed, the "accelerated recapture rule" will apply only if the taxpayer disposes of the residence, or the residence ceases to be the principal residence of the taxpayer or the taxpayer's spouse, during the 36-month period beginning on the date of purchase of that residence by the taxpayer. (Code Sec. 36(f)(4)(D)(ii))

observation: Thus, if the taxpayer sells the home, or the home ceases to be used as the taxpayer's (or the taxpayer's spouse's) principal residence within 36 months of purchase, the taxpayer will have to repay the credit. The repayment will be due on the tax return for the year in which the home is sold or ceases to be used as the principal residence. It's not clear how the waiver of the "regular recapture rule" affects the "accelerated recapture rule" in this case. Presumably, because the taxpayer will not have made any ratable repayments during this up-to-36-month period, the entire amount of the credit (not to exceed the amount of gain from sale to an unrelated person) will have to be repaid at this time.

Election to treat purchase as made Dec. 31, 2008. The election to treat pre-Dec. 1, 2009 purchases as made in 2008 applies for all first-time homebuyer credit purposes, except the Code Sec. 36(c) definitions *and* the above new rules on waiver of recapture. (Code Sec. 36(g) as amended by 2009 Recovery Act §1006(c)(2)) In other words, the waiver of recapture applies without regard to whether the taxpayer makes an election to treat the pre-Dec. 1, 2009 purchase as occurring on Dec. 31, 2008. (Com Rept, see ¶ 5006)

No D.C. homebuyer credit. No D.C. homebuyer credit (see FTC 2d/FIN ¶ A-4251; USTR ¶ 14,00C4; TaxDesk ¶ 568,801) is allowed to any taxpayer with respect to a purchase of a residence after Dec. 31, 2008 and before Dec. 1, 2009, if the first-time homebuyer credit can be taken by a taxpayer (or the taxpayer's spouse) with respect to the purchase. (Code Sec. 1400C(e)(4) as amended by 2009 Recovery Act §1006(d)(1)) Thus, taxpayers qualify for the more generous first-time homebuyer credit rather than the D.C. homebuyer credit for qualifying purchases in 2009. (Com Rept, see ¶ 5006)

Qualified mortgage revenue bond financing permitted. The rule which prohibited the taking of the credit if the purchase of the residence was financed with the proceeds of qualified mortgage revenue bonds has been eliminated.

(Code Sec. 36(d) as amended by 2009 Recovery Act §1006(e)) So, the purchase of a home may be financed with the proceeds of a mortgage revenue bond, i.e., a qualified mortgage issue the interest on which is tax-exempt under Code Sec. 103 (relating to interest on state and local bonds, see FTC 2d/FIN ¶ J-3001; USTR ¶ 1034; TaxDesk ¶ 158,001). (Com Rept, see ¶ 5006)

☐ **Effective:** Residences purchased after Dec. 31, 2008 (2009 Recovery Act §1006(f)) and before Dec. 1, 2009. (Code Sec. 36(h))

¶ 105. Standard or itemized deduction is allowed for sales and excise taxes imposed on most new vehicles purchased on or after Feb. 17, 2009 and before 2010

Code Sec. 63(c)(1)(E), as amended by 2009 Recovery Act § 1008(c)(1)
Code Sec. 63(c)(9), as amended by 2009 Recovery Act § 1008(c)(2)
Code Sec. 164(a)(6), as amended by 2009 Recovery Act § 1008(a)
Code Sec. 164(b)(6), as amended by 2009 Recovery Act § 1008(b)
Code Sec. 56(b)(1)(E), as amended by 2009 Recovery Act § 1008(d)
Generally effective: Purchases on or after Feb. 17, 2009 and before 2010
Committee Reports, see ¶ 5008

Individuals who don't elect to itemize their deductions are allowed, instead, to deduct a standard deduction in determining taxable income. The standard deduction includes the basic standard deduction, the additional standard deduction for aged and blind, the disaster loss deduction, and for 2008 and 2009, the real property tax standard deduction. The standard deduction isn't allowed for alternative minimum tax (AMT) purposes, except for the disaster loss deduction component, which is allowed. (FTC 2d/FIN ¶ A-2800, ¶ A-2801, ¶ A-8300, ¶ A-8305; USTR ¶ 634; TaxDesk ¶ 562,001)

An itemized deduction is also allowed for various state and local taxes, including state, local, and foreign income, war profits, and excess profit taxes. Further, a taxpayer can elect to take an itemized deduction for state and local general sales taxes, in lieu of state and local income taxes. Taxpayers can use either actual expenses, or IRS-provided state and local sales tax tables, to figure their itemized state and local general sales tax deduction. However, no deduction is allowed for any general sales tax imposed at a rate other than the general rate of tax, except that sales tax on food, clothing, medical supplies, and motor vehicles is deductible even if imposed at a lower tax rate than the general rate. Also, for motor vehicles, if the taxpayer paid sales tax at a higher rate than the general rate, he or she can deduct only the amount of tax he or she would have

---

FTC 2d References are to Federal Tax Coordinator 2d
FIN References are to RIA's Analysis of Federal Taxes: Income
USTR References are to United States Tax Reporter: Income
PE References are to Pension Explanations

paid at the general tax rate. Taxpayers who use the IRS tables (instead of actual expenses) in addition to IRS table amount can deduct an additional amount for state and local sales taxes paid on specified items, including the purchase (or lease) of a motor vehicle (but not as to amounts paid in excess of the general tax rate). (FTC 2d/FIN ¶ K-4000, ¶ K-4001, ¶ K-4500, ¶ K-4510 *et seq.*; USTR ¶ 1644, ¶ 1644.01, ¶ 1644.03; TaxDesk ¶ 326,006, ¶ 326,019.1 *et seq.*)

Under pre-2009 Recovery Act law, state and local sales tax paid on the purchase of a motor vehicle weren't allowed as a standard deduction, or as an itemized deduction unless a taxpayer elected to deduct state and local general sales taxes in lieu of state and local income taxes.

New Law. The 2009 Recovery Act provides that qualified motor vehicle taxes are deductible either:

(1) as an itemized deduction for "qualified motor vehicle taxes" (Code Sec. 164(a)(6) as amended by 2009 Recovery Act §1008(a)) ; or

(2) as a new (additional) component of the standard deduction (the "motor vehicle sales tax deduction"). (Code Sec. 63(c)(1)(E) as amended by 2009 Recovery Act §1008(c)(1))

For purposes of the Code Sec. 164(a)(6) itemized deduction (see (1), above), "qualified motor vehicle taxes" are defined as any state or local sales or excise tax imposed on the purchase of a qualified motor vehicle (defined below). (Code Sec. 164(b)(6)(A) as amended by 2009 Recovery Act §1008(b)) For purposes of the standard deduction (see (2), above), the "motor vehicle sales tax deduction" is the amount allowable as a deduction under Code Sec. 164(b)(6). But the term doesn't include any amount taken into account as adjusted gross income (AGI) under Code Sec. 62(a). (Code Sec. 63(c)(9) as amended by 2009 Recovery Act §1008(c)(2))

observation: Because the Code Sec. 63(c)(1)(E) motor vehicle sales tax (standard) deduction is defined as the amount allowable under the Code Sec. 164(b)(6) itemized deduction, the definitions (of qualified motor vehicle taxes, above, and qualified motor vehicle, below) and limitations (the purchase price and modified AGI limitations, below) provided under Code Sec. 164(b)(6) also apply for purposes of the standard deduction.

viewpoint: Attorney-CPA Michael A. Spielman, author of WG&L's *U.S. International Estate Planning* treatise, and a Senior Manager in the Transaction Advisory Services Practice of Ernst & Young LLP, where he advises public and private companies and private equity firms on the tax aspects of mergers and acquisitions, notes that because the above-described deduction is available for only state and local sales or excise taxes imposed on new vehicle purchases, it won't apply to similar taxes that may be incurred by U.S. citizens or residents on new vehicle purchases made abroad. However, U.S. citizens or residents living abroad who incur state or local sales taxes on a new vehicle purchase in the U.S. may still use the deduction, subject to the purchase price limitation and income phaseouts (described below).

The deduction is limited to the amount of qualified motor vehicle taxes attributable to the first $49,500 of the purchase price (the "purchase price limitation"). (Code Sec. 164(b)(6)(B)) That is, the deduction is limited to the tax on up to $49,500 of the purchase price of a qualified motor vehicle. (Com Rept, see ¶ 5008)

> **observation:** Code Sec. 164(b)(6)(A), Code Sec. 164(b)(6)(B), and the Committee Report above, don't make clear whether the deduction for state and local sales and excise taxes can be claimed for more than one vehicle. Use of the singular "a" in the Code provisions and the committee reports suggests that the deduction is allowed for only *one* "qualified motor vehicle" purchased in 2009 (after Feb. 16, 2009, as described below). However, the Code isn't absolutely clear as to whether the deduction can be claimed for the purchase of more than one qualified motor vehicle during the applicable period. IRS will likely issue guidance clarifying this point.

> **observation:** Another point on which the new Code provisions are unclear is whether, in the case of married taxpayers, each spouse can deduct qualified motor vehicle taxes on up to $49,500 of the purchase price of his or her own vehicle, whether they file jointly or separately. Here, too, guidance is needed from IRS.

The amount of taxes treated as qualified motor vehicle taxes that can be taken as a deduction is phased out ratably for a taxpayer with modified adjusted gross income (modified AGI) between $125,000 and $135,000 ($250,000 and $260,000 on a joint return) (Com Rept, see ¶ 5008) (the "modified AGI limitation"). Specifically, the amount otherwise deductible (after application of the purchase price limitation) is reduced (but not below zero) by the amount that bears the same ratio to allowable qualified motor vehicle taxes as the excess (if any) of the taxpayer's modified AGI for the tax year over $125,000 ($250,000 for a joint return), bears to $10,000. (Code Sec. 164(b)(6)(C))

For this purpose, modified AGI means the taxpayer's AGI determined without regard to Code Sec. 911 (foreign earned income and foreign housing costs exclusions for U.S. citizens or residents living abroad, see FTC 2d/FIN ¶s O-1101 *et seq.*, O-1161 *et seq.*; USTR ¶ 9114; TaxDesk ¶ 191,001 *et seq.*),

---

FTC 2d References are to Federal Tax Coordinator 2d
FIN References are to RIA's Analysis of Federal Taxes: Income
USTR References are to United States Tax Reporter: Income
PE References are to Pension Explanations

Code Sec. 931 (exclusion of income from sources within American Samoa, see FTC 2d/FIN ¶ O-1432; USTR ¶s 9314, 9314.02), and Code Sec. 933 (exclusion of income from sources within Puerto Rico, see FTC 2d/FIN ¶ O-1450 et seq.; USTR ¶ 9314.04). (Code Sec. 164(b)(6)(C))

> **(RIA) observation:** Thus, income that would otherwise be excluded from gross income under Code Sec. 911, Code Sec. 931, or Code Sec. 933 is included in determining modified AGI for purposes of the above limitation.

> **(RIA) illustration (1):** Taxpayer purchases a car for $25,000 in a locality that imposes a 6% sales tax. The taxpayer's modified AGI is $130,000. The qualified motor vehicle taxes are $1,500. The purchase price limitation doesn't apply. However, because the taxpayer's modified AGI exceeds $125,000 by $5,000, the taxpayer's deduction for qualified motor vehicle taxes is reduced by $750 ($1,500 × $5,000/$10,000). Thus, a $750 qualified motor vehicle tax deduction is permitted.

> **(RIA) illustration (2):** Taxpayer purchases a car for $25,000 in a locality that imposes a 6% sales tax. The taxpayer's modified AGI is $135,000. The qualified motor vehicle tax is $1,500. The purchase price limitation doesn't apply. However, because the taxpayer's modified AGI exceeds $125,000 by $10,000, the taxpayer's qualified motor vehicle tax deduction is reduced by $1,500 ($1,500 × $10,000/$10,000). Thus, no deduction is permitted here.

A qualified motor vehicle is:

• a passenger automobile or light truck (as defined in title II of the Clean Air Act), the gross vehicle weight rating of which isn't more than 8,500 pounds and the original use of which begins with the taxpayer,

• a motorcycle (within the meaning of 49 CFR §571.3, see below), the gross vehicle weight rating of which isn't more than 8,500 pounds and the original use of which begins with the taxpayer, and

• a motor home (within the meaning of 49 CFR §571.3), the original use of which begins with the taxpayer. (Code Sec. 164(b)(6)(D))

> **(RIA) observation:** For definitions under title II of the Clean Air Act (42 USC §7521 et seq.), see FTC 2d/FIN ¶ L-18024.1; TaxDesk ¶ 397,106. 49 CFR §571.3 relates to the Federal Motor Vehicle Safety Standards definitions.

Qualified motor vehicle taxes aren't treated as part of the cost of the acquired property or, for a disposition, as a reduction in the amount realized on the disposition. (Code Sec. 164(b)(6)(E))

A deduction of qualified motor vehicle taxes isn't allowed for taxpayers who make an election under Code Sec. 164(b)(5) to deduct state and local general sales taxes in lieu of state and local income taxes. (Code Sec. 164(b)(6)(F))

> **observation:** Code Sec. 164(b)(6)(F) prevents a taxpayer from getting a double deduction for state and local sales taxes paid on a qualified motor vehicle, because a taxpayer who elects (under Code Sec. 164(b)(5)) to take an itemized deduction for state and local general sales tax in lieu of state and local income tax computes the amount of that deduction by including the state and local sales taxes paid on the purchase (or lease) of a motor vehicle.

> **observation:** The above 2009 Recovery Act rules provide an increased deduction for 2009 for taxpayers who are taking either the standard deduction or an itemized deduction for state and local income taxes—i.e., for those who aren't electing to take an itemized deduction for state and local sales taxes in lieu of state and local income taxes.

> **observation:** Taxpayers who have qualified motor vehicle taxes for 2009 will have to determine which deduction maximizes their tax benefit for 2009: (i) a standard deduction that includes qualified motor vehicle taxes, (ii) an itemized deduction for state and local income taxes, plus an itemized deduction for qualified motor vehicle taxes, or (iii) an itemized deduction for state and local general sales taxes claimed in lieu of the itemized deduction for state and local income taxes.

> **illustration (3):** For 2009, assume X will itemize rather than take a standard deduction, and that X has state and local income taxes of $4,000, qualified motor vehicle taxes of $2,500, and a total of $5,000 of state and local general sales taxes (including the taxes paid on the applicable qualified motor vehicle). Assuming the modified AGI limitation doesn't apply, to maximize his deduction, X would claim the itemized deduction for state and local income taxes, plus the qualified motor vehicle taxes under Code Sec. 164(b)(6), for a total of $6,500 in taxes. If, instead, X elected to claim an itemized deduction for state and local general sales taxes under Code Sec. 164(b)(5), X's deduction would be only $5,000. Note that under pre-2009 Recovery Act law, X would have elected to take the $5,000 itemized deduction for state and local general sales taxes because it would have been greater than his $4,000 itemized deduction for state and local income taxes.

FTC 2d References are to Federal Tax Coordinator 2d
FIN References are to RIA's Analysis of Federal Taxes: Income
USTR References are to United States Tax Reporter: Income
PE References are to Pension Explanations

observation: If a taxpayer isn't subject to a state income tax and generally takes the Code Sec. 164(b)(5) itemized deduction for state and local general sales taxes, the taxpayer isn't likely to benefit from instead claiming the 2009 Recovery Act Code Sec. 164(b)(6) itemized deduction for qualified motor vehicle taxes. That's because Code Sec. 164(b)(5) provides a broader deduction (i.e., for state and local general sales tax paid for the year, not just state and local sales taxes paid on a qualified motor vehicle) and thus should produce a larger deduction than under new Code Sec. 164(b)(6).

Another factor generally favoring taking an itemized deduction under Code Sec. 164(b)(5), rather than under Code Sec. 164(b)(6), is that a claim under Code Sec. 164(b)(5) won't be restricted by the purchase price limitation, or modified AGI limitation discussed above, as it would be under Code Sec. 164(b)(6). (But a claim for state and local sales taxes on a motor vehicle made under Code Sec. 164(b)(5), as described above, will be limited to the extent that tax doesn't exceed the general tax rate. Also see the discussion below of issues raised with respect to AMT liability and deduction of qualified motor vehicle taxes.)

Qualified motor vehicle taxes and the AMT. The 2009 Recovery Act specifically provides that the qualified motor vehicle component of the standard deduction is allowed as a deduction for AMT purposes. (Code Sec. 56(b)(1)(E) as amended by 2009 Recovery Act §1008(d))

observation: Taxpayers who claim the Code Sec. 164(b)(6) itemized deduction for qualified motor vehicle taxes can also deduct these taxes in computing AMT liability because they aren't one of the taxes specifically listed as not deductible for AMT purposes.

Specifically, for purposes of determining a taxpayer's AMT liability, Code Sec. 56(b)(1) provides that the taxes described in the following Code sections *can't* be deducted from the taxpayer's alternative minimum taxable income (AMTI, the amount [after subtraction of an "exemption amount"] on which the taxpayer's AMT liability is computed):

. . . Code Sec. 164(a)(1) (i.e., state, local, and foreign property taxes);

. . . Code Sec. 164(a)(2) (i.e., state and local personal property taxes);

. . . Code Sec. 164(a)(3) (i.e., state, local, and foreign income, war profits, and excess profits taxes); and

. . . Code Sec. 164(a)(5)(A)(ii) (i.e., state and local general sales taxes, taken as an itemized deduction in lieu of state and local income taxes), see FTC 2d/FIN ¶ A-8308; USTR ¶ 564.02; TaxDesk ¶ 697,008.

Because the 2009 Recovery Act doesn't add the taxes described in Code Sec. 164(a)(6) (i.e., the new itemized deduction for qualified motor vehicle taxes) to the above Code Sec. 56(b)(1) list, those taxes *can* be deducted from AMTI in computing a taxpayer's AMT liability. Thus, whether taken as a standard deduction or as an itemized deduction under Code Sec. 164(a)(6), qualified motor vehicles taxes may reduce a taxpayer's AMT liability.

Note, however, that if state and local sales taxes on a qualified motor vehicle are instead claimed as part of the Code Sec. 164(a)(5) itemized deduction for state and local general sales taxes, by operation of Code Sec. 56(b)(1), the taxes can't be deducted from AMTI in computing AMT liability.

observation: A taxpayer is subject to the AMT if his tentative minimum tax liability is greater than his regular tax liability, for the tax year. The tentative minimum tax is computed on the "taxable excess," which is the taxpayer's AMTI reduced by the AMT exemption amount. (See FTC 2d/FIN ¶ A-8101; USTR ¶ 554.01; TaxDesk ¶ 691,002) Note that the 2009 Recovery Act increases the AMT exemption amounts for 2009 to $46,700 for unmarried individuals, to $70,950 for joint filers, and to $35,475 for married individuals filing separately (see ¶ 201).

observation: If a taxpayer would be subject to the AMT before taking any deduction for state or local income taxes or state or local sales and use taxes under Code Sec. 164(b)(5) into account, the taxpayer would never benefit by electing to deduct the state or local sales or use taxes in lieu of state and local income taxes, because this deduction wouldn't be allowed in computing the AMT, and so the taxpayer would lose the benefit of any deduction for sales or excise taxes paid on a qualified motor vehicle. While making the Code Sec. 164(b)(5) election would reduce his regular tax, the AMT would be increased by the same amount that the regular tax was reduced.

In the following *RIA Illustrations,* assume, solely for purposes of simplification, that allowing the deduction for sales or use taxes on a qualified motor vehicle in computing AMT won't affect the amount of the AMT exemption used in determining the taxable excess (AMTI less exemption amount) on which the tentative minimum tax is computed.

illustration (4): A married couple who file a joint return live in a state that has no state or local income tax. They itemize their deductions and are in a 28% tax bracket for regular income tax purposes and a 26% tax bracket for AMT purposes. In 2009, they pay state sales

FTC 2d References are to Federal Tax Coordinator 2d
FIN References are to RIA's Analysis of Federal Taxes: Income
USTR References are to United States Tax Reporter: Income
PE References are to Pension Explanations

taxes of $5,000, including taxes of $2,500 on the purchase of a qualified motor vehicle. Before taking into account any deduction for the
payment of those taxes, their tentative minimum tax is $26,000 (26% of
taxable excess of $100,000) and their regular income tax is $25,500.
Thus, they owe an AMT of $500 ($26,000 less $25,500). The total tax
payable will be $26,000 (i.e., regular income tax of $25,500 plus AMT
of $500). In effect, the total tax is the tentative minimum tax.

If they elect to deduct their sales taxes under Code Sec. 164(b)(5),
their taxable income will be reduced by $5,000 and their regular in-
come tax will be reduced by $1,400 (28% of $5,000) to $24,100. How-
ever, their taxable excess will remain at $100,000 because, as described
above, sales taxes under Code Sec. 164(b)(5) aren't deductible in computing AMTI. Thus, the tentative minimum tax will remain at $26,000,
and the AMT will increase to $1,900 ($26,000 less $24,100). The total
taxes payable will remain at $26,000 (i.e., regular income tax of
$24,100 plus AMT of $1,900).

On the other hand, if the taxpayers don't make the election to deduct
sales taxes under Code Sec. 164(b)(5), they will be able to deduct the
$2,500 in sales taxes they paid for the purchase of a qualified motor ve-
hicle under Code Sec. 164(b)(6) against both regular income tax and
the tentative minimum tax. Thus, their regular income tax will be reduced by $700 (28% of $2,500) to $24,800, and their tentative mini-
mum tax will be reduced by $650 (26% of $2,500) to $25,350. While
their AMT will increase by $50 to $550, the total taxes payable will be
reduced by $650 from $26,000 to $25,350 (i.e., regular income tax of
$24,800 plus AMT of $550).

🅡 *observation:* If a taxpayer wouldn't be subject to the AMT before
taking any deduction for state or local income taxes or state or local
sales and use taxes into account, then whether the taxpayer would be
better off electing to deduct sales and use taxes under Code
Sec. 164(b)(5) instead of taking the deduction for state or local sales or
excise taxes paid on a qualified motor vehicle under Code
Sec. 164(b)(6) would depend mainly on how much the regular income
tax exceeds the tentative minimum tax. The larger the excess, the more
likely it is that the taxpayer will benefit by making the election to deduct sales and use taxes under Code Sec. 164(b)(5).

🅡 *illustration (5):* Assume the same facts as in *RIA illustration (4)* except that the taxpayers' regular income tax is $27,000, i.e., $1,000 more
than their tentative minimum tax of $26,000. If they don't make the
election to deduct sales and use taxes under Code Sec. 164(b)(5), their
regular income tax will be reduced by $700 (28% of $2,500 sales tax
paid on purchase of qualified motor vehicle) to $26,300. This still will

be $950 more than the tentative minimum tax of $25,350 ($26,000 reduced by $650), so no AMT will be owed.

On the other hand, if they do make the election, their regular income tax will be reduced by $1,400 (28% of $5,000) to $25,600. Their tentative minimum tax will remain at $26,000, and they will owe an AMT of $400. Their total tax including the AMT will be $26,000, but this still will be $300 less than the $26,300 of regular income tax they would owe if they don't make the election to deduct sales and use taxes.

illustration (6): Assume the same facts as in *RIA illustration (5),* except that the taxpayers' regular income tax is $26,300, i.e., $300 more than their tentative minimum tax of $26,000. If they don't make the election to deduct sales and use taxes under Code Sec. 164(b)(5), their regular income tax will be reduced by $700 (28% of $2,500 sales tax paid on purchase of qualified motor vehicle) to $25,600. Their tentative minimum tax will be reduced by $650 (26% of $2,500) to $25,350, so no AMT will be owed. Their total tax will be the regular income tax of $25,600.

On the other hand, if they do make the election, their regular income tax will be reduced by $1,400 (28% of $5,000) to $24,900. Their tentative minimum tax will remain at $26,000, and they will owe an AMT of $1,100. Their total tax including the AMT will be $26,000, or $400 more than they would owe if they don't make the election to deduct sales and use taxes.

Termination of deduction. The above provisions don't apply to purchases after Dec. 31, 2009. (Code Sec. 164(b)(6)(G))

☐ **Effective:** For purchases of qualified motor vehicles on or after Feb. 17, 2009 in tax years ending after that date (2009 Recovery Act §1008(e)) and before Jan. 1, 2010. (Code Sec. 164(b)(6)(G))

FTC 2d References are to Federal Tax Coordinator 2d
FIN References are to RIA's Analysis of Federal Taxes: Income
USTR References are to United States Tax Reporter: Income
PE References are to Pension Explanations

¶ 106. Up to $2,400 of unemployment compensation is excludible from recipient's gross income for 2009

Code Sec. 85(c), as amended by 2009 Recovery Act § 1007(a)
Generally effective: Tax years beginning in 2009
Committee Reports, see ¶ 5007

Under pre-2009 Recovery Act law, an individual had to include in gross income any unemployment compensation benefits received under the laws of the U.S. or any state. (FTC 2d/FIN ¶ H-3000, ¶ H-3007; USTR ¶ 854; TaxDesk ¶ 132,506)

New Law. For any tax year beginning in 2009, gross income doesn't include so much of the unemployment compensation received by an individual as doesn't exceed $2,400. (Code Sec. 85(c) as amended by 2009 Recovery Act §1007(a)) That is, up to $2,400 of unemployment compensation benefits received in 2009 are excluded from gross income by the recipient. (Com Rept, see ¶ 5007)

☐ **Effective:** For tax years beginning after Dec. 31, 2008 (2009 Recovery Act §1007(b)) but only for tax years beginning in 2009. (Code Sec. 85(c))

¶ 107. Hope credit is increased and expanded (and re-named the "American Opportunity Tax Credit") for 2009 and 2010

Code Sec. 24(b)(3)(B), as amended by 2009 Recovery Act § 1004(b)(1)
Code Sec. 25(e)(1)(C)(ii), as amended by 2009 Recovery Act § 1004(b)(2)
Code Sec. 25A, 2009 Recovery Act § 1004(b)(8)
Code Sec. 25A, 2009 Recovery Act § 1004(c)
Code Sec. 25A(i), as amended by 2009 Recovery Act § 1004(a)
Code Sec. 25B(g)(2), as amended by 2009 Recovery Act § 1004(b)(4)
Code Sec. 26(a)(1), as amended by 2009 Recovery Act § 1004(b)(3)
Code Sec. 904(i), as amended by 2009 Recovery Act § 1004(b)(5)
Code Sec. 1400C(d)(2), as amended by 2009 Recovery Act § 1004(b)(6)
Code Sec. 6211(b)(4)(A), as amended by 2009 Recovery Act § 1004(b)(7)
Generally effective: Tax years beginning in 2009 and 2010
Committee Reports, see ¶ 5004

Individual taxpayers are allowed a personal nonrefundable income tax credit (i.e., a credit that can reduce the taxpayer's regular tax liability to zero, but that can't result in a refund)—collectively called the "higher education credit" — equal to the sum of the Hope credit and the Lifetime Learning credit which apply for higher education expenses at accredited post-secondary educational institutions.

Under pre-2009 Recovery Act law, the Hope credit was equal to a credit of up to $1,800 (for 2009) per eligible student for qualified tuition and related (QT&R, see below) expenses paid for the first two years of the student's post-secondary education in a degree or certificate program. To claim the Hope credit, the student couldn't have completed the first two years of that post-secondary education before the beginning of the tax year for which the credit was claimed. (FTC 2d/FIN ¶ A-4500, ¶ A-4501; USTR ¶ 25A4; TaxDesk ¶ 568,901)

Specifically, for 2009, under pre-2009 Recovery Act law, the Hope credit equalled: (1) 100% of the first $1,200 (an inflation adjusted amount) of QT&R expenses, plus (2) 50% of the next $1,200 (an inflation-adjusted amount) of QT&R expenses, paid for education furnished to an eligible student in an academic period, i.e., for a total maximum Hope credit for 2009 of $1,800. (FTC 2d/FIN ¶ A-4523, ¶ A-4524; USTR ¶ 25A4.03, ¶ 25A4.04; TaxDesk ¶ 568,923, ¶ 568,924)

And, under pre-2009 Recovery Act law, for each eligible student, the Hope credit couldn't be claimed if the credit had been claimed for that student for any two earlier tax years. (FTC 2d/FIN ¶ A-4530; USTR ¶ 25A4.03; TaxDesk ¶ 568,930)

Generally, under pre-2009 Recovery Act law, QT&R expenses for the Hope credit included, with specific exceptions, tuition and fees (excluding nonacademic fees) required for the enrollment or attendance of the taxpayer, his spouse, or tax dependent, at a post-secondary educational institution eligible to participate in the federal student loan program. (FTC 2d/FIN ¶ A-4537; USTR ¶ 25A4.07; TaxDesk ¶ 568,937)

The otherwise allowable Hope credit is phased out ratably for taxpayers with specified (inflation adjusted) modified adjusted gross income (modified AGI) amounts. Under pre-2009 Recovery Act law, for 2009, the Hope credit was phased out at modified AGI of between $50,000 and $60,000 ($100,000 and $120,000 for joint filers). (FTC 2d/FIN ¶ A-4517; USTR ¶ 25A4.02; TaxDesk ¶ 568,917)

And, under pre-2009 Recovery Act law, for tax years beginning after Dec. 31, 2008, the Hope credit couldn't be claimed against a taxpayer's alternative minimum tax (AMT) liability. (FTC 2d/FIN ¶ A-4901, ¶ A-4902; USTR ¶ 264; TaxDesk ¶ 569,601, ¶ 569,602)

New Law. The 2009 Recovery Act modifies the Hope credit and renames the modified credit the "American Opportunity tax credit" (Com Rept, see ¶ 5004), hereinafter referred to as the "modified Hope credit." Specifically, for

FTC 2d References are to Federal Tax Coordinator 2d
FIN References are to RIA's Analysis of Federal Taxes: Income
USTR References are to United States Tax Reporter: Income
PE References are to Pension Explanations

tax years beginning in 2009 and 2010 (Code Sec. 25A(i) as amended by 2009 Recovery Act §1004(a)), the Act:

. . . increases the maximum credit amount to $2,500 per eligible student per year for qualified QT&R expenses;

. . . expands the definition of QT&R expenses to include course materials;

. . . allows the credit for the first four years of the student's post-secondary education in a degree or certificate program;

. . . increases the modified AGI range at which the credit is phased-out;

. . . permits the credit to be claimed against AMT liability; and

. . . allows 40% of the credit to be refundable. (Com Rept, see ¶ 5004)

> *observation:* Because most individuals are calendar year taxpayers, the fact that the modified rules apply for tax years beginning in 2009 and 2010 means that for most individuals, the modified rules apply for 2009 and 2010.

> *observation:* The 2009 Recovery Act doesn't modify the rules applicable to the Lifetime Learning credit, which, as noted above, a taxpayer may claim in addition to a Hope credit (collectively, as a higher education credit) for a particular tax year. Thus, existing requirements for eligibility for the Lifetime Learning credit continue to control a taxpayer's eligibility to claim that credit for 2009 and 2010.

> The Lifetime Learning credit (an up to $2,000 per year credit) is calculated on a per family (i.e., per return) basis—in contrast to the modified Hope credit which is calculated on a per student basis. However, expenses paid with respect to a student for whom a modified Hope credit is claimed aren't eligible for the Lifetime Learning credit—i.e., both credits can't be claimed for the same student in the same tax year.

Maximum credit increased. For 2009 and 2010, the modified Hope credit equals the sum of (Code Sec. 25A(i)(1)):

(a) 100% of so much of the QT&R expenses paid by the taxpayer during the tax year (for education furnished to the eligible student during any academic period beginning in the tax year) as doesn't exceed $2,000, plus (Code Sec. 25A(i)(1)(A))

(b) 25% of the QT&R expenses so paid as exceeds $2,000 but doesn't exceed $4,000. (Code Sec. 25A(i)(1)(B))

> *observation:* That is, the maximum modified Hope credit a taxpayer may claim for 2009 or 2010 is $2,500—100% (1.0) × the first $2,000 of QT&R expenses + 25% (.25) × the next $2,000 of QT&R expenses.

Thus, the 2009 Recovery Act increases the maximum credit for 2009 by $700 (from $1,800 to $2,500).

Note that under the 2009 Recovery Act, the amount of QT&R expenses eligible for the credit aren't adjusted for inflation for either the 2009 or 2010 tax year.

observation: As described in (a) band (b) above, the increased credit amount is only available for QT&R expenses paid in 2009 or 2010 for education furnished to the eligible student during any academic period beginning in 2009 or 2010. However, many educational institutions require payment in advance of a semester. For example, some educational institutions may have required payment for the semester that began in Jan. 2009 in the last quarter of 2008. In these cases, QT&R expenses paid in 2008, even though they're for a 2009 academic period, wouldn't qualify for the modified Hope credit for 2009.

Credit allowed for first four years of post-secondary education. For 2009 and 2010, the modified Hope credit is allowed with respect to QT&R expenses paid for the first four years of the student's post-secondary education in a degree or certificate program, if the student has not completed the first four years of post-secondary education before the beginning of the fourth tax year. And, for each eligible student, the modified Hope credit may be claimed for four tax years. (Code Sec. 25A(i)(2)) That is, the modified credit extends the application of the credit to two more years of post-secondary education. (Com Rept, see ¶ 5004)

observation: Thus, a taxpayer who had maximized the benefit of the Hope credit under pre-2009 Recovery Act law for an eligible student— i.e., by having already claimed a Hope credit for the first two years of the eligible student's post-secondary education before the 2009 tax year—may, under the 2009 Recovery Act, be able to claim the modified Hope credits for two additional years of post-secondary education for that same student.

Definition of QT&R expenses expanded. For 2009 and 2010, the definition of QT&R expenses for purposes of the modified Hope credit is expanded to include course materials (Com Rept, see ¶ 5004)—i.e., the definition is modified so that it includes tuition, fees, *and* course materials. (Code Sec. 25A(i)(3))

Modified AGI range for phase out of credit increased. For 2009 and 2010, instead of applying Code Sec. 25A(d) (the phase out rules generally applicable

FTC 2d References are to Federal Tax Coordinator 2d
FIN References are to RIA's Analysis of Federal Taxes: Income
USTR References are to United States Tax Reporter: Income
PE References are to Pension Explanations

for both the Hope and Lifetime Learning credits), the modified Hope credit (determined without regard to the following phase out rule) is reduced (but not below zero) by the amount that bears the same ratio to the credit (as so determined) as (Code Sec. 25A(i)(4)):

. . . the excess of (Code Sec. 25A(i)(4)(A))—(i) the taxpayer's modified AGI (as defined in Code Sec. 25A(d)(3), i.e., as defined under pre-2009 Recovery Act law, see FTC 2d/FIN ¶ A-4524; USTR ¶ 25A4.04; TaxDesk ¶ 568,924) for that tax year (Code Sec. 25A(i)(4)(A)(i)), over (ii) $80,000 ($160,000 for a joint return) (Code Sec. 25A(i)(4)(A)(ii)), bears to

. . . $10,000 ($20,000 for a joint return). (Code Sec. 25A(i)(4)(B))

That is, the modified Hope credit that may otherwise be claimed in 2009 and 2010 is phased out ratably for taxpayers with modified AGI between $80,000 and $90,000 ($160,000 and $180,000 for joint filers). (Com Rept, see ¶ 5004)

> **✔ observation:** Thus, under the 2009 Recovery Act, for 2009, the amount of modified AGI at which a taxpayer must start to reduce his or her credit is increased by $30,000 (from $50,000 to $80,000) (and by $60,000 for joint filers, from $100,000 to $160,000). This will allow more taxpayers to claim the full benefit of the credit in 2009 (and 2010).
>
> Note that the 2009 Recovery Act does not provide for an inflation adjustment of these modified AGI threshold phase out amounts for either the 2009 or 2010 tax year.

> **✔ illustration (1):** Thus, for 2009 and 2010, a taxpayer's modified Hope credit must be reduced (but not below zero) by a fraction, the numerator of which is the amount of the taxpayer's modified AGI that is over $80,000 ($160,000 for joint filers) and the denominator of which is $10,000 ($20,000 for joint filers).
>
> For example, if a single taxpayer's modified AGI for 2009 is $85,000, the taxpayer's otherwise allowable modified Hope credit would be reduced by 50% (i.e., $5,000 [$85,000 − $80,000]/$10,000).

> **✔ observation:** Thus, different phase out rules apply for 2009 and 2010 for the modified Hope credit and the Lifetime Learning credit. For 2009, the Lifetime Learning credit continues to be phased out at modified AGI between $50,000 and $60,000 ($100,000 and $120,000 for joint filers).

Credit allowed against alternative minimum tax (AMT). The 2009 Recovery Act provides that the modified Hope credit allowed under Code Sec. 25A(i) isn't subject to the limitation under Code Sec. 26(a)(1) (which provides that Subpart A personal credits can't exceed the excess, if any, of the taxpayer's regular tax liability for the tax year over the tentative minimum tax for the tax year, determined without regard to the AMT foreign tax credit, see FTC 2d/FIN ¶s A-4901, A-4902; USTR ¶ 264; TaxDesk ¶s 569,601, 569,602). (Code Sec. 26(a)(1) as amended by 2009 Recovery Act §1004(b)(3))

Instead, for tax years to which the Code Sec. 26(a)(2) limitation (under which nonrefundable personal tax credits generally may offset both regular and AMT liability) doesn't apply (i.e., any tax year beginning after 2009, as modified by the 2009 Recovery Act, see ¶ 204), so much of the credit allowed under Code Sec. 25A(a) (i.e., the higher education credit) as is attributable to the modified Hope credit can't exceed the excess of (Code Sec. 25A(i)(5)):

... the sum of the taxpayer's "regular tax liability" as defined in Code Sec. 26(b) (i.e., a taxpayer's income tax, not including the AMT and other special taxes, see FTC 2d/FIN ¶ A-4905; USTR ¶ 264.01; TaxDesk ¶ 569,605), plus AMT (Code Sec. 25A(i)(5)(A)), over

... the sum of the credits allowable under Subpart A of Subtitle A, Chapter 1, Subchapter A, Part IV of the Code (the nonrefundable personal tax credits) (other than the Code Sec. 23 adoption credit, see FTC 2d/FIN ¶ A-4401; USTR ¶ 234; TaxDesk ¶ 569,501, the Code Sec. 25D residential energy efficiency property [REEP] credit, see FTC 2d/FIN ¶ A-4781; USTR ¶ 25D4; TaxDesk ¶ 569,553, and the Code Sec. 30D new qualified plug-in electric drive motor vehicle [NQPEDMV] credit, see FTC 2d/FIN ¶ L-18031; USTR ¶ 30D4; TaxDesk ¶ 397,131), and the Code Sec. 27 foreign tax credit, see FTC 2d/FIN ¶ O-4001; USTR ¶ 274. (Code Sec. 25A(i)(5)(B))

Thus, the modified Hope credit may be claimed against a taxpayer's AMT liability. (Com Rept, see ¶ 5004)

> **observation:** That is, for 2009, the modified Hope credit may be claimed against AMT liability under the rules of Code Sec. 26(a)(2), as discussed in detail at ¶ 204, and for 2010 under Code Sec. 25A(i)(5), as discussed above.

Any reference in Code Sec. 25A (the Hope and Lifetime Learning credit rules), Code Sec. 24 (the child tax credit rules), Code Sec. 25 (the residential mortgage interest credit rules), Code Sec. 26 (the general tax liability limitation for nonrefundable personal credits), Code Sec. 25B (the "saver's credit" for elective deferrals and IRA contributions rules), Code Sec. 904 (the foreign tax credit rules), or Code Sec. 1400C (the first-time D.C. homebuyer's credit rules) to a credit allowable under Code Sec. 25A(i) (i.e., the 2009 and 2010 modified Hope credit) will be treated as a reference to so much of the credit allowable

FTC 2d References are to Federal Tax Coordinator 2d
FIN References are to RIA's Analysis of Federal Taxes: Income
USTR References are to United States Tax Reporter: Income
PE References are to Pension Explanations

under Code Sec. 25A(a)—i.e., the allowable higher education credit (the sum of the taxpayer's Hope and Lifetime Learning credit for the year) as is attributable to the Hope credit. (Code Sec. 25A(i)(5))

observation: Specifically, the effect of the amendment to Code Sec. 26(a)(1) (above) and the rules of Code Sec. 25A(i)(5) (above) are to make the modified Hope credit generally allowable to the full extent of a taxpayer's regular income tax and AMT liabilities, reduced only by certain other credits.

Coordination with other personal credits. References to Code Sec. 25A(i) are added to the series of credits referred to respectively in Code Sec. 24(b)(3)(B), Code Sec. 25(e)(1)(C)(ii), Code Sec. 25B(g)(2), Code Sec. 904(i), and Code Sec. 1400C(d)(2). (Code Sec. 24(b)(3)(B) as amended by 2009 Recovery Act §1004(b)(1)) (Code Sec. 25(e)(1)(C)(ii) as amended by 2009 Recovery Act §1004(b)(2)) (Code Sec. 25B(g)(2) as amended by 2009 Recovery Act §1004(b)(4)) (Code Sec. 904(i) as amended by 2009 Recovery Act §1004(b)(5)) (Code Sec. 1400C(d)(2) as amended by 2009 Recovery Act §1004(b)(6)).

observation: The added references to Code Sec. 25A(i) conform the following rules to the rules of Code Sec. 25A(i)(5): Code Sec. 24(b)(3)(B) (part of the tax liability limit rule for the child tax credit, see FTC 2d/FIN ¶ A-4054; USTR ¶ 244.01; TaxDesk ¶ 569,104), Code Sec. 25(e)(1)(C)(ii) (part of the carryover rule for the residential mortgage interest credit, see FTC 2d/FIN ¶ A-4010; USTR ¶ 254; TaxDesk ¶ 568,509), Code Sec. 25B(g)(2) (part of the tax liability limit rule for the saver's credit for certain elective deferrals and IRA contributions, see FTC 2d/FIN ¶ A-4455; USTR ¶ 25B4; TaxDesk ¶ 569,205), Code Sec. 904(i) (part of the tax liability limit rule for the foreign tax credit, see FTC 2d/FIN ¶ O-4411; USTR ¶ 9044.01; TaxDesk ¶ 393,001), and Code Sec. 1400C(d)(2) (part of the carryover rule for the first-time D.C. homebuyer credit, see FTC 2d/FIN ¶ A-4255; USTR ¶ 14,00C4; TaxDesk ¶ 568,805).

Code Sec. 25A(i)(5) as described above provides that the Code Sec. 25A(i) modified Hope credit offsets tax liabilities (regular and AMT) only to the extent that the credit exceeds most other personal credits, and the foreign tax credit. Thus, the effect of Code Sec. 25A(i)(5), combined with the conforming changes to other Code sections discussed above, is that the modified Hope credit is applied against tax liabilities only after most other personal credits are applied against tax liabilities. These ordering rules benefit taxpayers entitled to claim a modified Hope credit because as to any part of the credit that can't be applied to offset tax liability (because of other personal credits the taxpayer can claim), as described below, a portion of that excess amount can be refunded to the taxpayer.

Portion of the credit made refundable. For 2009 and 2010, except as otherwise described below, 40% of so much of the higher education credit allowed under Code Sec. 25A(a) as is attributable to the modified Hope credit (determined after application of the Code Sec. 25A(i)(4) phase out rules above, and without regard to this refundability rule and the tax liability limitation rules under Code Sec. 26(a)(2) or Code Sec. 25A(i)(5) above, as applicable) will be treated as a credit allowable under Subpart C of Subtitle A, Chapter 1, Subchapter A, Part IV of the Code—i.e., as a refundable credit (and not as a nonrefundable personal credit allowed under Code Sec. 25A(a)). (Code Sec. 25A(i)(6)) (2009 Recovery Act §1004(b)(8)) (But see exception to application of the refundability rule for bona fide residents of U.S. possessions, below.)

That is, under the above rule, 40% of a taxpayer's otherwise allowable modified Hope credit is refundable. (Com Rept, see ¶ 5004)

> ⏺ *illustration (2):* For 2009, H and W (married joint filers) are eligible for a $2,500 modified Hope credit. They have modified AGI of less than $160,000 and so their credit isn't subject to any phase out. However, other credits the couple is claiming are applied first to offset their tax liability for the year, and result in reducing that liability to zero. Under the 2009 Recovery Act, 40% of the $2,500 credit, i.e., $1,000 (.4 × $2,500), may nevertheless be claimed by H and W as a refund.
>
> Because no special rule under Code Sec. 25A(i) provides for the carryback or carryforward of any excess modified Hope credit amounts, H and W lose the benefit of the remaining $1,500 (.6 × $2,500) of the credit.

> ⏺ *illustration (3):* If, in *RIA illustration (2),* H and W had modified AGI of $170,000, the Code Sec. 25A(i)(4) phase out rules would require that they reduce their allowable modified Hope credit by 50%, i.e., to $1,250. Because the refundability rules apply after application of the phase out rules, H and W's refund would equal only 40% of that $1,250 credit, i.e., $500 (.4 × $1,250).
>
> And if H and W's modified AGI was $180,000 or more, resulting in the complete phase out of their modified Hope credit, there would be no refundable credit amount.

FTC 2d References are to Federal Tax Coordinator 2d
FIN References are to RIA's Analysis of Federal Taxes: Income
USTR References are to United States Tax Reporter: Income
PE References are to Pension Explanations

The refundability rules above, however, won't apply to any taxpayer for any tax year if that taxpayer is a child to whom the Code Sec. 1(g) "kiddie tax" rules apply for that tax year (Code Sec. 25A(i)(6)) (i.e., generally, any child under age 18 or any child under age 24 who is a student providing less than one-half of his or her support, who has at least one living parent, and does not file a joint return). (Com Rept, see ¶ 5004)

> **◉ observation:** The above rule appears to make any child to whom the kiddie tax rules may apply (i.e., a child as described in the Committee Report, above) ineligible to claim a refund of the modified Hope credit. The rule does not appear to require that the kiddie tax rules be triggered with respect to that child, i.e., requiring that he or she pay tax at his or her parent's highest tax rate on unearned income (see FTC 2d/FIN ¶ A-1301; USTR ¶ 14.09; TaxDesk ¶ 568,301).

Coordination with Midwestern disaster area benefits. An expanded Hope credit applies to individuals who attend an eligible educational institution located in the Midwestern disaster area in any tax year beginning in 2009, which permits a maximum Hope credit of $3,600 for the year (see FTC 2d/FIN ¶ A-4523.2; USTR ¶ 14,00O4.02; TaxDesk ¶ 568,923.2). The 2009 Recovery Act provides that for a taxpayer eligible for this expanded Hope credit, the taxpayer may elect to waive application of the modified Hope credit for that year. (Code Sec. 25A(i)(7))

Residents of U.S. possessions. Bona fide residents of U.S. possessions can't claim the refundable portion of the modified Hope credit in the U.S. Instead, they claim the refundable portion of the credit in the possession in which they reside. The U.S. Treasury will reimburse the possessions for the credits allowed to their residents under their internal laws. (Com Rept, see ¶ 5004) The Commonwealth of Puerto Rico and the Commonwealth of the Northern Mariana Islands are treated as U.S. possessions for this purpose. (2009 Recovery Act §1004(c)(3)(A))

The treatment of each possession depends on whether it has a "mirror code tax system." A U.S. possession has a mirror code tax system if the income tax liability of the possession's residents under the possession's income tax system is determined by reference to the U.S. income tax laws as if the possession were the U.S. (2009 Recovery Act §1004(c)(3)(B))

Mirror code possessions. For U.S. possessions that have mirror code tax systems (2009 Recovery Act §1004(c)(1)(A))—i.e., the U.S. Virgin Islands, Guam, and the Northern Mariana Islands (Com Rept, see ¶ 5004)—the U.S. Treasury will make payments to that possession equal to that possession's loss for tax years 2009 and 2010 by reason of the application of Code Sec. 25A(i)(6) (the provision permitting a portion of the modified Hope credit to be refunded, see above). Treasury will determine these amounts based on information provided by the possession's government. (2009 Recovery Act §1004(c)(1)(A)) (2009 Recovery Act §1004(c)(1)(C))

Non-mirror code possessions. For U.S. possessions that don't have mirror code tax systems (2009 Recovery Act §1004(c)(1)(B))—i.e., Puerto Rico and American Samoa (Com Rept, see ¶ 5004)—the U.S. Treasury will make payments to the possession in an amount that it estimates to be equal to the aggregate benefits that would have been provided to that possession's residents for tax years 2009 and 2010 by reason of the application of Code Sec. 25A(i)(6) if a mirror code tax system had been in effect in the possession. But a possession won't receive the payments unless it has a plan, approved by the U.S. Treasury, under which it will promptly distribute the payment to its residents. (2009 Recovery Act §1004(c)(1)(B)) (2009 Recovery Act §1004(c)(1)(C)) Thus, bona fide residents of non-mirror code possession can claim the refundable portion of the credit in the possession in which the individual is a resident, but only if the possession establishes a plan for permitting the claim under its internal law. (Com Rept, see ¶ 5004)

Coordination with credit allowed against U.S. income taxes. Code Sec. 25A(i)(6), the provision permitting a portion of the modified Hope credit to be refunded, won't apply to a bona fide resident of any U.S. possession. (2009 Recovery Act §1004(c)(2))

Modified Hope credit treated as negative tax in deficiency computation. Any excess of the modified Hope credit over the income tax is taken into account as a negative amount of tax in computing a taxpayer's tax deficiency. (Code Sec. 6211(b)(4)(A) as amended by 2009 Recovery Act §1004(b)(7)) For how deficiencies are computed, see FTC 2d/FIN ¶ T-1501; USTR ¶ 62,114; TaxDesk ¶ 822,501.

Sunset provision. The amendment made by 2009 Recovery Act § 1004(b)(1) (to Code Sec. 24(b)(3)(B) as discussed above) is subject to title IX of the 2001 Economic Growth and Tax Relief Reconciliation Act of 2001—i.e., the EGTRRA sunset provision, see 2001 EGTRRA § 901 (Sec. 901, PL 107-16, 6/7/2001)—in the same manner as the provision of 2001 EGTRRA to which the amendment relates. (2009 Recovery Act §1004(e))

> *observation:* 2001 EGTRRA § 901 requires that amendments made by 2001 EGTRRA will not be effective for tax years beginning after Dec. 31, 2010.

> *observation:* All of Code Sec. 24(b)(3) (which provides the tax liability limit rule for the child tax credit of which Code Sec. 24(b)(3)(B) is part) is subject to the EGTRRA sunset provision. Thus, without 2009

FTC 2d References are to Federal Tax Coordinator 2d
FIN References are to RIA's Analysis of Federal Taxes: Income
USTR References are to United States Tax Reporter: Income
PE References are to Pension Explanations

Recovery Act § 1004(e), there would be a technical inconsistency in which the amendment to Code Sec. 24(b)(3)(B) made by 2009 Recovery Act § 1004(b)(1) would survive the post-2010 termination of Code Sec. 24(b)(3).

Treasury study and report regarding education incentives. The 2009 Recovery Act requires the Secretary of the Treasury and the Secretary of Education, or their delegates, to: (1) study (i) how to coordinate the Code Sec. 25A higher education credit with the Federal Pell Grant program under § 401 of the Higher Education Act of 1965 to maximize their effectiveness at promoting college affordability (2009 Recovery Act §1004(f)(1)(A)), (ii) ways to expedite the delivery of the Code Sec. 25A higher education credit (2009 Recovery Act §1004(f)(1)(B)), and (iii) the feasibility of requiring community service as a condition of taking tuition and related expenses into account under Code Sec. 25A (2009 Recovery Act §1004(f)(2)); and (2) report the results to Congress not later than one year after Feb. 17, 2009 (i.e., not later than Feb. 17, 2010). (2009 Recovery Act §1004(f)(3))

☐ **Effective:** For changes to the Hope credit, for tax years beginning after Dec. 31, 2008 (2009 Recovery Act §1004(d)), but only for tax years beginning in 2009 and 2010. (Code Sec. 25A(i)) For required Treasury studies and report, as described immediately above.

¶ 108. Computer technology and equipment, and Internet access and related services, qualify as higher education expenses under 529 plans for 2009 and 2010

Code Sec. 529(e)(3)(A), as amended by 2009 Recovery Act § 1005(a)
Generally effective: Expenses paid or incurred after Dec. 31, 2008
Committee Reports, see ¶ 5005

Code Sec. 529 provides specified income tax and transfer tax rules for the treatment of accounts and contracts established under qualified tuition programs (QTPs, or 529 plans). A 529 plan is a program established and maintained by a state or agency or instrumentality thereof, or by one or more eligible educational institutions, which satisfies certain requirements and under which a person may purchase tuition credits or certificates on behalf of a designated beneficiary that entitle the beneficiary to the waiver or payment of qualified higher education expenses of the beneficiary (a "prepaid tuition program"). In the case of a program established and maintained by a state or agency or instrumentality thereof, a 529 plan also includes a program under which a person may make contributions to an account that is established for the purpose of satisfying the qualified higher education expenses of the designated beneficiary of the account, if it satisfies certain specified requirements (a "savings account program"). Under both types of 529 plans, a contributor establishes an account for the benefit of a particular designated beneficiary to provide for that beneficiary's higher education expenses.

Under pre-2009 Recovery Act law, qualified higher education expenses included tuition, books, supplies, and equipment required for the enrollment or attendance of a designated beneficiary at an eligible education institution, and expenses for special needs services in the case of a special needs beneficiary that are incurred in connection with this enrollment or attendance. (FTC 2d/FIN ¶ A-4700, ¶ A-4711; USTR ¶ 5294; TaxDesk ¶ 672,310)

New Law. Under the 2009 Recovery Act, expenses paid or incurred in 2009 or 2010 for the purchase of any computer technology or equipment (as defined under Code Sec. 170(e)(6)(F)(i), see FTC 2d/FIN ¶ K-3243; USTR ¶ 1704.42; TaxDesk ¶ 331,743), or Internet access and related services, are qualified higher education expenses for purposes of the rules for 529 plans. However, the technology, equipment, or services must be used by the beneficiary and the beneficiary's family during any of the years that the beneficiary is enrolled at an eligible educational institution. (Code Sec. 529(e)(3)(A)(iii) as amended by 2009 Recovery Act §1005(a)) And expenses for computer software designed for sports, games, or hobbies are excluded from qualified higher education expenses unless the software is predominantly educational in nature. (Code Sec. 529(e)(3)(A)) Thus, the 2009 Recovery Act expands the definition of qualified higher education expenses for 529 plans to include computer technology and equipment. (Com Rept, see ¶ 5005)

☐ **Effective:** For expenses paid or incurred after Dec. 31, 2008 (2009 Recovery Act §1005(b)) but only in 2009 or 2010. (Code Sec. 529(e)(3)(A)(iii))

¶ 109. Refundable portion of child tax credit is increased for 2009 and 2010

Code Sec. 24(d)(4), as amended by 2009 Recovery Act § 1003(a)
Generally effective: Tax years beginning in 2009 and 2010
Committee Reports, see ¶ 5003

The amount of the child tax credit is $1,000 per qualifying dependent child under age 17 through 2010 (and $500 thereafter). The credit is phased out for taxpayers with modified adjusted gross income above certain levels. (FTC 2d/FIN ¶ A-4050; USTR ¶ 244; TaxDesk ¶ 569,100)

FTC 2d References are to Federal Tax Coordinator 2d
FIN References are to RIA's Analysis of Federal Taxes: Income
USTR References are to United States Tax Reporter: Income
PE References are to Pension Explanations

The child tax credit is, generally, refundable to the extent of 15% of the taxpayer's earned income in excess of $10,000, adjusted for inflation for the applicable tax year (under pre-2009 Recovery Act law, $12,550 for 2009). But for taxpayers with three or more qualifying children, the child tax credit is refundable to the extent the taxpayer's social security taxes exceed the taxpayer's earned income credit (EIC), if the refundable amount, computed under this rule, exceeds the refundable amount computed under the 15%-of-the-excess-over-$10,000-as adjusted for inflation ($12,550 for 2009) rule. (FTC 2d/FIN ¶ A-4055; USTR ¶ 244.02; TaxDesk ¶ 569,105)

> *observation:* With a refundable credit, if the amount of a credit exceeds the amount of the taxpayer's income tax liability, the excess is payable to the taxpayer as a direct transfer payment.

New Law. The 2009 Recovery Act modifies the above-described earned income formula for determining the refundable child tax credit to apply to 15% of earned income in excess of $3,000 for tax years 2009 and 2010. (Com Rept, see ¶ 5003) Specifically, the 2009 Recovery Act provides that notwithstanding Code Sec. 24(d)(3) (i.e., the inflation adjustment of the statutory $10,000 amount), for any tax year beginning in 2009 or 2010, the dollar amount in effect for that tax year for purposes of Code Sec. 24(d)(1)(B)(i) (i.e., the 15%-of-the-excess-over-$10,000 [as adjusted for inflation] rule) is $3,000. (Code Sec. 24(d)(4) as amended by 2009 Recovery Act §1003(a))

> *observation:* That is, under the 2009 Recovery Act, for 2009 and 2010, the child tax credit is refundable to the extent of 15% of the taxpayer's earned income that's in excess of $3,000. For taxpayers with three or more qualifying children, as under pre-2009 Recovery Act law, the credit is also refundable to the extent the taxpayer's social security taxes exceed the taxpayer's EIC, if that produces a greater refundable amount.

> *illustration (1):* In 2009, H and W, joint filers, have earned income of $12,500 and two qualifying children. They have no income tax liability for 2009 and so none of the $2,000 child tax credit for which they're eligible is used to offset income tax liability. But, under the 2009 Recovery Act, H and W may claim a refundable child tax credit of $1,425—i.e., 15% of their earned income in excess of $3,000 (.15 × $9,500 [$12,500 − $3,000]). (Under pre-2009 Recovery Act law, H and W wouldn't have been entitled to claim any refundable child tax credit because their earned income didn't exceed the then applicable inflation-adjusted amount for 2009 of $12,550. That is, they would have gotten no benefit from the child tax credit.)

illustration (2): If, in *RIA illustration (1)*, H and W have earned income of $17,000, under the 2009 Recovery Act, they may claim the entire $2,000 child tax credit as a refundable credit. That is, H and W may claim their child tax credit as a refundable credit to the extent of 15% of their earned income that's in excess of $3,000, and because 15% of their earned income in excess of $3,000 is $2,100 (.15 × $14,000 [$17,000 − $3,000]), they can claim the full $2,000 of credit for which they're eligible. (Under pre-2009 Recovery Act law, H and W would have been entitled to claim a refundable credit of only $667.50—i.e., 15% of their earned income in excess of $12,550 [.15 × $4,450 ($17,000 − $12,500)].)

observation: Under the 2009 Recovery Act, for 2009 and 2010, a taxpayer with one qualifying child, who earns as little as $9,667 but has no income tax liability, may nevertheless claim a full $1,000 refundable child tax credit.

observation: The maximum additional refundable child tax credit any taxpayer may claim for 2009 as a result of the 2009 Recovery Act changes is $1,432.50 (i.e., 15% [.15] × $9,550 [$12,550 − $3,000]).

☐ **Effective:** Tax years beginning after Dec. 31, 2008 (2009 Recovery Act §1003(b)), but only for tax years beginning in 2009 or 2010. (Code Sec. 24(d)(4))

¶ 110. EIC credit percentage is increased for families with three or more qualifying children for 2009 and 2010

Code Sec. 32(b)(3)(A), as amended by 2009 Recovery Act § 1002(a)
Generally effective: Tax years beginning in 2009 and 2010
Committee Reports, see ¶ 5002

Certain low-income workers are allowed a refundable earned income credit ("EIC," also called the earned income tax credit, or "EITC").

observation: With a refundable credit, if the amount of the credit exceeds the taxpayer's income tax liability, the excess is payable to the taxpayer as a direct transfer payment.

The EIC, generally, is computed by multiplying the specified credit percentage by the individual's earned income, up to a maximum earned income dollar

---

FTC 2d References are to Federal Tax Coordinator 2d
FIN References are to RIA's Analysis of Federal Taxes: Income
USTR References are to United States Tax Reporter: Income
PE References are to Pension Explanations

amount (which is adjusted for inflation) for the tax year. The credit percentage and the earned income amount, and therefore the maximum EIC, depend on the number of "qualifying children" the taxpayer has. Under pre-2009 Recovery Act law, for 2009, these amounts (as increased for inflation) were:

Qualifying children	Credit percentage	Earned income amount	Maximum credit
None	7.65%	$ 5,970	$ 457
One	34%	$ 8,950	$3,043
Two or more	40%	$12,570	$5,028

However, the EIC phases out for taxpayers whose income levels exceed a specified phaseout amount. For discussion of the phaseout rules, including the 2009 Recovery Act's increase to the beginning point of the phaseout range for joint filers for 2009 and 2010, see ¶ 111.

No EIC is allowed if the taxpayer's disqualified income (generally, investment income) exceeds a specified inflation-adjusted dollar amount for the year ($3,100 for 2009). (FTC 2d/FIN ¶ A-4200, ¶ A-4201; USTR ¶ 324.01; TaxDesk ¶ 569,001)

New Law. To provide larger families with additional tax relief, the 2009 Recovery Act increases the EIC credit percentage for families with three or more qualifying children. (Com Rept, see ¶ 5002) Specifically, the 2009 Recovery Act provides that for any tax year beginning in 2009 or 2010 (Code Sec. 32(b)(3) as amended by 2009 Recovery Act §1002(a)), in the case of a taxpayer with three or more qualifying children, the EIC credit percentage is 45%. (Code Sec. 32(b)(3)(A))

> *observation:* The 2009 Recovery Act doesn't also increase the maximum earned income dollar amount for families with three or more children for tax years 2009 and 2010. Thus, the maximum (inflation-adjusted) earned income dollar amount that's in effect for 2009 (and the inflation-adjusted amount that will be in effect for 2010) for taxpayers with *two or more qualifying children* is (as Congress illustrates below), the same dollar amount that applies for families with three or more qualified children.

Thus, for example, in 2009, taxpayers with three or more qualifying children may claim an EIC equal to 45% of earnings up to $12,570 (i.e., .45 × $12,570), resulting in a maximum EIC of $5,656.50. (Com Rept, see ¶ 5002)

> *observation:* Under pre-2009 Recovery Act law, the maximum EIC allowable for 2009 for a taxpayer with three or more qualifying children (as reflected in the table above) would have been $5,028 (the same maximum for a taxpayer with two qualifying children). Thus, the 2009 Recovery Act change discussed above results in a maximum additional

EIC credit for 2009 for a taxpayer with three or more qualifying children of $628.50 ($5,656.50 − $5,028).

🅥 *observation:* The 2009 Recovery Act doesn't otherwise change the applicable EIC credit percentages in effect for 2009 and 2010. Thus, reflecting the 2009 Recovery Act change, for 2009, the credit percentage, earned income amount, and maximum EIC are:

Qualifying children	Credit percentage	Earned income amount	Maximum credit
None	7.65%	$ 5,970	$ 457
One	34%	$ 8,950	$3,043
Two	40%	$12,570	$5,028
Three or more	45%	$12,570	$,656.50

🅥 *observation:* A taxpayer who qualifies for the refundable EIC and has at least one qualifying child can receive advance payment of a portion of the EIC by having the employer add it to his or her paycheck each pay period. Other than for agricultural workers paid on a daily basis, an employer paying wages must pay in advance a ratable portion of the EIC to an employee who has filed an earned income eligibility certificate (a Form W-5) showing his or her entitlement to the advance payment. The amount of the credit to be reflected in each paycheck is computed from tables provided by IRS in IRS Publication No. 15. (See FTC 2d/FIN ¶ H-4855; USTR ¶ 35,074; TaxDesk ¶ 569,028.)

☐ **Effective:** For tax years beginning after Dec. 31, 2008 (2009 Recovery Act §1002(b)), but only for tax years beginning in 2009 or 2010. (Code Sec. 32(b)(3))

¶ 111. Beginning point of EIC phaseout range is increased for joint filers for 2009 and 2010

Code Sec. 32(b)(3)(B), as amended by 2009 Recovery Act § 1002(a)
Generally effective: Tax years beginning in 2009 or 2010
Committee Reports, see ¶ 5002

As described at ¶ 110, certain low-income workers are allowed a refundable earned income credit (EIC). However, that EIC is phased out for taxpayers whose earned income (or adjusted gross income (AGI), if greater) exceeds a phaseout amount. For these individuals, the maximum credit amount is reduced by the phaseout percentage multiplied by the earned income (or AGI) in excess

---

FTC 2d References are to Federal Tax Coordinator 2d
FIN References are to RIA's Analysis of Federal Taxes: Income
USTR References are to United States Tax Reporter: Income
PE References are to Pension Explanations

of the phaseout amount (as adjusted for inflation). The EIC phaseout percentage differs depending on the number of "qualifying children" while the EIC phaseout amount differs depending on both the number of qualifying children, and whether the eligible individual files a joint return with his or her spouse.

An individual who is married must, generally, file a joint return in order to claim the EIC (an exception applies for certain separated taxpayers). When a married individual who files a joint return claims the EIC, the credit is calculated based on the couple's combined income. This may penalize some individuals who end up receiving a smaller EIC credit when they marry, than if they had not married. To provide some relief from this "marriage penalty," the 2001 Economic Growth and Tax Relief Act (PL 107-16, 6/7/2001) phased in an increase in the EIC phaseout amounts for married couples filing a joint return. Under pre-2009 Recovery Act law, the credit phaseout amounts for married couples filing a joint return for 2009 were increased by $3,000, as adjusted for inflation ($3,120 for 2009) (i.e., the beginning and ending points of the credit phaseout were increased by this amount).

Under pre-2009 Recovery Act law, for 2009, the phaseout percentage, phaseout amounts, and completed phaseout level (the level at which the credit is reduced to zero) (as adjusted for inflation) were as follows:

Qualifying children	Phaseout percentage	Other than Joint Filers		Joint Filers	
		Threshold phaseout amount	Completed phaseout level	Threshold phaseout amount	Completed phaseout level
None	7.65%	$ 7,470	$13,440	$10,590	$16,560
One	15.98%	$16,420	$35,463	$19,540	$38,583
Two or more	21.06%	$16,420	$40,295	$19,540	$43,415

(FTC 2d/FIN ¶ A-4200, ¶ A-4202; USTR ¶ 324.01; TaxDesk ¶ 569,002)

New Law. To provide additional marriage penalty relief, the 2009 Recovery Act provides higher threshold phaseout amounts for married couples filing joint returns. (Com Rept, see ¶ 5002) Specifically, the 2009 Recovery Act provides that for tax years beginning in 2009 or 2010 (Code Sec. 32(b)(3) as amended by 2009 Recovery Act §1002(a)), the threshold EIC credit phaseout amounts for married couples filing a joint return are increased by $5,000 (Code Sec. 32(b)(3)(B)(i)) (plus an inflation adjustment for 2010, as described below). That is, the threshold phaseout amounts for married couples filing joint returns is increased to $5,000 above the threshold phaseout amounts for singles, surviving spouses, and heads of household, for 2009 and 2010. (Com Rept, see ¶ 5002)

observation: Thus, reflecting the 2009 Recovery Act changes above, for 2009, and the increased maximum credit permitted for taxpayers with three of more children discussed at ¶ 110, the phaseout percentage, phaseout amount, and completed phaseout level (the level at which the credit is reduced to zero) are as follows:

| | | Other than Joint Filers | | Joint Filers | |
Qualifying children	Phaseout percentage	Threshold phaseout amount	Completed phaseout level	Threshold phaseout amount	Completed phaseout level
None	7.65%	$ 7,470	$13,440	$12,470	$18,440
One	15.98%	$16,420	$35,463	$21,420	$40,463
Two	21.06%	$16,420	$40,295	$21,420	$45,295
Three or more	21.06%	$16,420	$43,281	$21,420	$48,281

For example, for 2009, the maximum EIC for a taxpayer with one qualifying child is $3,043 (see ¶ 110) and the EIC is available to such a taxpayer if the taxpayer's earnings are between $8,950 (the maximum earned income dollar amount for these taxpayers, see ¶ 110) and $16,420 ($21,420 for married filing jointly, see the table in the *RIA observation* above). The credit begins to phase down at a rate of 15.98% of earnings above $16,420 ($21,420 if married filing jointly). And, the credit is phased down to $0 at $35,463 of earnings ($40,463 if married filing jointly). (Com Rept, see ¶ 5002)

For a tax year beginning in 2010, the above $5,000 amount is adjusted for inflation. (Com Rept, see ¶ 5002) Specifically, the $5,000 amount is increased by an amount equal to (Code Sec. 32(b)(3)(B)(ii)):

(a) $5,000, multiplied by (Code Sec. 32(b)(3)(B)(ii)(I))

(b) the cost of living adjustment determined under Code Sec. 1(f)(3) (relating to inflation adjustments for the tax rate brackets, see FTC 2d/FIN ¶ A-1103; TaxDesk ¶ 568,203), for the calendar year in which the tax year begins, but determined by substituting "calendar year 2008" for "calendar year 1992" in Code Sec. 1(f)(3)(B) (Code Sec. 32(b)(3)(B)(ii)(II))—i.e., the adjustment for 2010 is to be the percentage (if any) by which the consumer price index (CPI) for 2009 exceeds the CPI for 2008.

After determining the increased amount under the above rules, if any amount is not a multiple of $10, it is to be rounded to the nearest multiple of $10. (Code Sec. 32(b)(3)(B)(iii))

☐ **Effective:** For tax years beginning after Dec. 31, 2008 (2009 Recovery Act §1002(b)), but only for tax years beginning in 2009 or 2010. (Code Sec. 32(b)(3))

FTC 2d References are to Federal Tax Coordinator 2d
FIN References are to RIA's Analysis of Federal Taxes: Income
USTR References are to United States Tax Reporter: Income
PE References are to Pension Explanations

¶ 200. AMT Provisions

¶ 201. AMT exemption amounts for 2009 are increased to $46,700 for unmarrieds, to $70,950 for joint filers, and to $35,475 for marrieds filing separately

Code Sec. 55(d)(1)(A), as amended by 2009 Recovery Act § 1012(a)(1)
Code Sec. 55(d)(1)(B), as amended by 2009 Recovery Act § 1012(a)(2)
Generally effective: Tax years beginning in 2009
Committee Reports, see ¶ 5010

In computing the alternative minimum tax (AMT) for individuals, the AMT tax rate is applied against the taxpayer's alternative minimum taxable income (AMTI), as reduced by the taxpayer's exemption amount (which phases out for AMTI above certain threshold levels). Pre-2009 Recovery Act law provided the following AMT exemption amounts for tax years beginning in 2009:

. . . $33,750 for unmarried individuals who aren't surviving spouses;

. . . $45,000 for married couples filing jointly and surviving spouses; and

. . . $22,500 (technically, 50% of the joint return/surviving spouse amount) for married individuals filing separately.

For tax years beginning in 2008, the AMT exemption amounts were:

• $46,200 for unmarried individuals who weren't surviving spouses;

• $69,950 for married couples filing jointly and surviving spouses; and

• $34,975 for marrieds filing separately.

The higher amounts for 2008 reflected the temporary increases provided by the 2008 Extenders Act (Sec. 102DivC, PL 110-343, 10/3/2008) as part of an AMT "patch" to reduce the number of individuals who otherwise would be subject to the AMT. (Similar patches were enacted by the 2007 Tax Increase Prevention Act (Sec. 2, PL 110-166, 12/26/2007), 2005 Tax Increase Prevention Act (Sec. 301, PL 109-222, 5/17/2006), 2001 Economic Growth and Tax Relief Reconciliation Act (Sec. 701, PL 107-16, 6/7/2001), as amended by the 2003 Jobs and Growth Act (Sec. 106, PL 108-27, 5/28/2003), and 2004 Working Families Act (Sec. 103, PL 108-311, 10/4/2004).) Under pre-2009 Recovery Act law, the temporary increases expired after 2008. (FTC 2d/FIN ¶ A-8160, ¶ A-8162; USTR ¶ 554.01; TaxDesk ¶ 691,302)

FTC 2d References are to Federal Tax Coordinator 2d
FIN References are to RIA's Analysis of Federal Taxes: Income
USTR References are to United States Tax Reporter: Income
PE References are to Pension Explanations

New Law. For tax years beginning in 2009, the 2009 Recovery Act (the Act) increases the AMT exemption amounts as follows (rather than allowing them to decrease to pre-"patch" levels):

. . . to $70,950 (up from $69,950 in 2008) for married couples filing a joint return and surviving spouses (Code Sec. 55(d)(1)(A) as amended by 2009 Recovery Act §1012(a)(1));

. . . to $46,700 (up from $46,200 in 2008) for an individual who isn't married or a surviving spouse (Code Sec. 55(d)(1)(B) as amended by 2009 Recovery Act §1012(a)(2));

. . . to $35,475 (up from $34,975 in 2008) for married individuals filing separate returns.

> *observation:* The Act doesn't change the rule that the AMT exemption amount for married individuals filing separately is 50% of the AMT exemption amount for joint filers and surviving spouses (see FTC 2d/FIN ¶ A-8162; USTR ¶ 554.01; TaxDesk ¶ 691,302). Thus, although the Act doesn't provide a specific increase for married individuals filing separately in 2009, the exemption amount for those individuals is effectively increased for 2009, because the joint return/surviving spouse exemption amount is increased to $70,950. That is, the AMT exemption amount for married individuals filing separately is increased to $35,475 (50% × $70,950) for 2009. Under pre-Act law, the AMT exemption amount for marrieds filing separately would have dropped to $22,500 in 2009.

> *observation:* In addition to increasing the individual AMT exemption amounts for 2009, the one-year "patch" provided by Act § 1012 also has the effect of postponing for one year the reductions in those amounts that, under pre-Act law, were scheduled to go into effect for tax years beginning after 2008. Thus, these reductions are now scheduled to go into effect for tax years beginning after 2009, i.e., for 2010 and later years.

For the one-year extension of the rule allowing nonrefundable personal credits to offset AMT (as well as regular tax), see ¶ 204.

> *observation:* Individuals may be entitled to further AMT-related tax relief under the AMT refundable credit rules. Those rules, enacted by the 2006 Tax Relief Act, allow individuals with unused minimum tax credits that are more than three years old to get a partial refund (instead of a credit). See FTC 2d/FIN ¶ A-8808; USTR ¶ 534; TaxDesk ¶ 691,508.

The impact of Act § 1012 can be seen in the following table:

AMT Exemption Amount

	2009 Recovery Act			Pre-2009 Recovery Act		
	Unmarried	Joint	Married Filing Separate	Unmarried	Joint	Married Filing Separate
2008	$46,200	$69,950	$34,975	$46,200	$69,950	$34,975
2009	$46,700	$70,950	$35,475	$33,750	$45,000	$22,500
2010	$33,750	$45,000	$22,500	$33,750	$45,000	$22,500

observation: Congress's intent in enacting the "patch" is to minimize the "spread" of AMT liability to increasing numbers of taxpayers. However, given the enormous complexity of the AMT, the determination as to whether an individual has AMT liability still must be made on an individual basis.

Kiddie tax AMT exemption amount. For a child subject to the "kiddie tax" (i.e., certain children with unearned income over $1,900 for 2009, see FTC 2d/FIN ¶ A-1300 *et seq.*; USTR ¶ 14.09; TaxDesk ¶ 568,300 *et seq.*), the AMT exemption amount can't exceed the sum of the child's earned income plus $6,700 in 2009. In addition, the kiddie tax AMT exemption can't be more than the child's regular AMT exemption (the unmarried individual's exemption amount, discussed above). (FTC 2d/FIN ¶ A-8163; USTR ¶ 594; TaxDesk ¶ 691,303)

observation: As stated above, the unmarried individual's AMT exemption amount is $46,700 for tax years beginning in 2009. Thus, a child subject to the kiddie tax is entitled to a maximum AMT exemption of $46,700 in 2009 but only if he has earned income of $40,000 ($6,700 + $40,000 = $46,700) or more before taking the phaseout for unmarried individuals into account.

AMT exemption amount for estates and trusts.

observation: The Act doesn't change the $22,500 exemption amount for an estate or trust (see FTC 2d/FIN ¶ A-8164; USTR ¶ 554.01; TaxDesk ¶ 691,304).

Phase-out of AMT exemption amount.

observation: The Act doesn't change the phase-out rules for the AMT exemption amount. Under those rules, the AMT exemption amount is reduced by an amount equal to 25% of the amount by which

---

FTC 2d References are to Federal Tax Coordinator 2d
FIN References are to RIA's Analysis of Federal Taxes: Income
USTR References are to United States Tax Reporter: Income
PE References are to Pension Explanations

the individual's AMTI exceeds the following threshold amounts (FTC 2d/FIN ¶ A-8162; USTR ¶ 554.01; TaxDesk ¶ 691,302):

... $112,500 for unmarried individuals who aren't surviving spouses,

... $150,000 for married individuals filing a joint return and surviving spouses, and

... $75,000 for married individuals filing separate returns.

observation: Under these rules, the exemption is completely phased-out at an AMTI dollar amount equal to:

Applicable phase-out threshold + (4 × applicable exemption amount).

observation: Thus, the AMT exemption for 2009 completely phases-out (i.e., the taxpayer is subject to AMT on *all* of his AMTI), at the following AMTI levels:

- $299,300 ($112,500 + $186,800 [4 × $46,700]) for an individual who isn't married and isn't a surviving spouse,
- $433,800 ($150,000 + $283,800 [4 × $70,950]) for married individuals filing jointly or for a surviving spouse, and
- $216,900 ($75,000 + $141,900 [4 × $35,475]) for a married individual filing separately.

Post-2009 AMT exemption amounts.

observation: Absent future legislation (e.g., another one-year AMT "patch"), the reduction in the AMT exemption amounts that, under pre-Act law, was scheduled to apply to tax years beginning after 2009, will apply to tax years beginning after 2009. This means that in 2010, without further "patches," or broader changes to the AMT generally, the AMT exemption amounts will drop as follows:

... to $33,750 for unmarried individuals who aren't surviving spouses;

... to $45,000 for married couples filing jointly and surviving spouses; and

... to $22,500 for marrieds filing separately.

☐ **Effective:** Tax years beginning after Dec. 31, 2008 (2009 Recovery Act §1012(b)), but only tax years beginning in 2009. (Code Sec. 55(d)(1))

observation: Although Act § 1012(b) provides that the increased AMT exemption amounts apply for "tax years beginning after Dec. 31, 2008," Act § 1012(a) amends Code Sec. 55(d)(1) so that the increased exemptions apply for only 2009. That is, the AMT exemption amounts the Act prescribes for 2009 don't apply in tax years beginning after 2009.

observation: Act § 1012 increases the AMT exemption amounts for 2009, and so applies retroactively to tax years beginning on or after Jan. 1, 2009.

¶ 202. Interest on tax-exempt bonds issued in 2009 or 2010 isn't subject to AMT

Code Sec. 57(a)(5)(C)(vi), as amended by 2009 Recovery Act § 1503(a)
Generally effective: Bonds issued after Dec. 31, 2008 and before Jan. 1, 2011
Committee Reports, see ¶ 5062

Private activity bonds—i.e., state and local bonds issued to provide financing for private purposes—are exempt from federal income tax if they belong to one of seven categories of "qualified bonds" and meet certain other requirements. See FTC 2d/FIN ¶ J-3150; USTR ¶ 1414; TaxDesk ¶ 158,010.

The exemption doesn't apply for purposes of the alternative minimum tax (AMT, see FTC 2d/FIN ¶ A-8100 *et seq.*; USTR ¶ 554; TaxDesk ¶ 691,000 *et seq.*). Tax-exempt interest on "specified private activity bonds," reduced by any deduction that would have been allowable if the interest were taxable, is a preference item that is included in alternative minimum taxable income (AMTI). This limits the marketability of these bonds and, therefore, forces state and local governments to issue these bonds at higher interest rates. (Com Rept, see ¶ 5062)

"Specified private activity bonds" are "qualified" private activity bonds issued after Aug. 7, '86, with limited exceptions. There is an exception for certain tax-exempt housing bonds issued after July 30, 2008, but pre-2009 Recovery Act law didn't except other categories of private activity bonds, or provide a specific exception for bonds issued in 2009 or 2010. As a result, the tax-exempt interest on those bonds was subject to AMT. (FTC 2d/FIN ¶ A-8201; USTR ¶ 574; TaxDesk ¶ 696,501)

New Law. The 2009 Recovery Act (the Act) provides an exception for bonds issued in 2009 and 2010 (Code Sec. 57(a)(5)(C)(vi) as amended by 2009 Recovery Act §1503(a)) by providing that bonds issued after Dec. 31, 2008 and before Jan. 1, 2011 are not "specified private activity bonds." (Code Sec. 57(a)(5)(C)(vi)(I)) In other words, tax-exempt interest on private activity bonds

---

FTC 2d References are to Federal Tax Coordinator 2d
FIN References are to RIA's Analysis of Federal Taxes: Income
USTR References are to United States Tax Reporter: Income
PE References are to Pension Explanations

issued in 2009 and 2010 is not an item of tax preference for AMT purposes. (Com Rept, see ¶ 5062)

The Act thus excludes the remaining categories of private activity bonds (i.e., private activity bonds that aren't tax-exempt housing bonds) from the AMT if the bond is issued in 2009 or 2010. (Com Rept, see ¶ 5062)

For this purpose, a refunding bond—i.e., a bond issued to refund (pay the principal or interest on) another bond—is (except as provided below) treated as issued on the date the refunded bond was issued. If there has been a series of refundings, the refunding is treated as issued on the date the original bond was issued. This applies to both current and advance refundings. (Code Sec. 57(a)(5)(C)(vi)(II))

> *observation:* This means that the tax-exempt interest on a refunding bond issued after 2010 will be be exempt from AMT if the bond it refunds (or the original bond, if the refunding is part of a series of refundings) is issued in 2009 or 2010.

The issue date rule described above for refunding bonds doesn't apply to a refunding bond issued to refund a bond that was issued after Dec. 31, 2003, and before Jan. 1, 2009. (Code Sec. 57(a)(5)(C)(vi)(III)) This allows AMT relief for current refunding of private activity bonds issued after 2003, that are refunded during 2009 and 2010. (Com Rept, see ¶ 5062)

> *observation:* In other words, a refunding bond issued to refund a bond that was issued in 2004-2008 is treated as issued on the date of its issuance, for purposes of the AMT exemption for tax-exempt interest on bonds issued in 2009 or 2010. Without this rule, the AMT relief would not have applied to a refunding bond issued in 2009 or 2010 unless the bond it refunded (or the original bond, if the refunding was part of a series) was issued in 2009 or 2010 (or another exception applied).

> *observation:* If the refunded bond (or the original bond, if the refunding is part of a series) was issued before 2004, the Code Sec. 57(a)(5)(C)(vi)(III) exception won't apply. Thus, the refunding bond won't qualify for the AMT relief even if it's issued in 2009 or 2010.

For a similar rule relating to a corporation's AMT adjustment for adjusted current earnings (ACE), see ¶ 203.

☐ **Effective:** Bonds issued after Dec. 31, 2008 (2009 Recovery Act §1503(c))—i.e., interest on bonds issued after Dec. 31, 2008 (Com Rept, see ¶ 5062) and before Jan. 1, 2011. (Code Sec. 57(a)(5)(C)(vi)(I))

¶ 203. Corporate ACE adjustment isn't required for tax-exempt bonds issued in 2009 or 2010

Code Sec. 56(g)(4)(B)(iv), as amended by 2009 Recovery Act § 1503(b)
Generally effective: Bonds issued after Dec. 31, 2008 and before Jan. 1, 2011
Committee Reports, see ¶ 5062

The alternative minimum tax (AMT) is imposed if tentative minimum tax exceeds regular income tax. The tentative minimum tax is computed on alternative minimum taxable income (AMTI), which is taxable income modified to take into account certain preferences and adjustments. See FTC 2d ¶ A-8100 *et seq.*; USTR ¶ 554; TaxDesk ¶ 691,000 *et seq.*

Corporations must make an AMT adjustment based on current earnings. Any item that is excluded from gross income in computing AMTI, but taken into account in computing earnings and profits (E&P) for regular tax purposes, is included in adjusted current earnings (ACE). If ACE exceeds AMTI, as determined without the ACE adjustment itself and the AMT net operating loss deduction (ATNOLD), 75% of the excess is added to AMTI. See FTC 2d ¶ A-8400 *et seq.*; USTR ¶ 564.01; TaxDesk ¶ 698,000 *et seq.*

Tax-exempt interest is one of the items requiring an ACE adjustment. There is an exception for certain tax-exempt housing bonds issued after July 30, 2008, but pre-2009 Recovery Act law didn't provide an exception for tax-exempt bonds generally. An ACE adjustment was required for the tax-exempt interest on "qualified" state or local bonds, including private activity bonds. (FTC 2d/FIN ¶ A-8406; USTR ¶ 564.03; TaxDesk ¶ 698,006)

New Law. The 2009 Recovery Act (the Act) provides that interest on tax-exempt bonds issued in 2009 or 2010 is not included in the adjustment based on corporate earnings (the ACE adjustment). (Com Rept, see ¶ 5062) Specifically, for purposes of Code Sec. 56(g)(4)(B)(i) (requiring amounts taken into account in computing E&P to be included in AMTI), a "private activity bond" doesn't include any bond issued after Dec. 31, 2008 and before Jan. 1, 2011. (Code Sec. 56(g)(4)(B)(iv)(I) as amended by 2009 Recovery Act §1503(b))

> **observation:** The Act provides that interest on tax-exempt bonds issued in 2009 or 2010 isn't subject to AMT (see ¶ 202). However, because the ACE adjustment would otherwise require tax-exempt bond interest to be included in AMTI, new Code Sec. 56(g)(4)(B)(iv) is needed

FTC 2d References are to Federal Tax Coordinator 2d
FIN References are to RIA's Analysis of Federal Taxes: Income
USTR References are to United States Tax Reporter: Income
PE References are to Pension Explanations

to make the full AMT exemption for the bond interest apply to corporations.

For this purpose, a refunding bond—i.e., a bond issued to refund (pay the principal or interest on) another bond—is (except as provided below) treated as issued on the date the refunded bond was issued. If there has been a series of refundings, the refunding is treated as issued on the date the original bond was issued. This applies to both current and advance refundings. (Code Sec. 56(g)(4)(B)(iv)(II))

> **observation:** This means that an ACE adjustment won't be required for a refunding bond issued after 2010 if the bond it refunds (or the original bond, if the refunding is part of a series of refundings) was issued in 2009 or 2010.

The issue date rule described above for refunding bonds doesn't apply to a refunding bond issued to refund a bond that was issued after Dec. 31, 2003, and before Jan. 1, 2009. (Code Sec. 56(g)(4)(B)(iv)(III)) This allows AMT relief for current refunding of private activity bonds issued after 2003, that are refunded during 2009 and 2010. (Com Rept, see ¶ 5062)

> **observation:** In other words, a refunding bond issued to refund a bond that was issued in 2004-2008 is treated as issued on the date of its issuance, for purposes of the exception to the ACE adjustment for tax-exempt bond interest, for bonds issued in 2009 or 2010. Without this rule, the exception would not have applied to a refunding bond issued in 2009 or 2010—i.e., the ACE adjustment would have been required for the tax-exempt interest—unless the bond it refunded (or the original bond, if the refunding was part of a series) was issued in 2009 or 2010 (or another exception applied).

> **observation:** If the refunded bond (or the original bond, if the refunding is part of a series) was issued before 2004, the Code Sec. 56(g)(4)(B)(iv)(III) exception won't apply. Thus, the ACE adjustment is required even if the refunding bond is issued in 2009 or 2010.

☐ **Effective:** Bonds issued after Dec. 31, 2008 (2009 Recovery Act §1503(c))—i.e., interest on bonds issued after Dec. 31, 2008 (Com Rept, see ¶ 5062) and before Jan. 1, 2011. (Code Sec. 56(g)(4)(B)(iv)(I))

¶ 204. Nonrefundable personal credits can offset AMT through 2009 (instead of 2008)

Code Sec. 26(a)(2), as amended by 2009 Recovery Act § 1011(a)(1)
Code Sec. 23(b)(4), 2009 Recovery Act § 1011(a)(1)
Code Sec. 24(b)(3), 2009 Recovery Act § 1011(a)(1)
Code Sec. 25(e)(1)(C), 2009 Recovery Act § 1011(a)(1)
Code Sec. 25A(i)(5), 2009 Recovery Act § 1011(a)(1)
Code Sec. 25B(g), 2009 Recovery Act § 1011(a)(1)
Code Sec. 25D(c), 2009 Recovery Act § 1011(a)(1)
Code Sec. 30D(d)(2)(B), 2009 Recovery Act § 1011(a)(1)
Code Sec. 904(i), 2009 Recovery Act § 1011(a)(1)
Code Sec. 1400C(d), 2009 Recovery Act § 1011(a)(1)
Generally effective: Tax years beginning in 2009
Committee Reports, see ¶ 5010

Individuals may qualify for a number of nonrefundable personal tax credits (as listed below). However, for tax years beginning in 2000-2008, the nonrefundable personal tax credits listed below are subject to a limitation based on tax liability. Under Code Sec. 26(a)(2), these credits are allowed only to the extent that the aggregate amount of the credits doesn't exceed the sum of:

. . . the taxpayer's regular tax liability (FTC 2d/FIN ¶ A-4905; USTR ¶ 264.01; TaxDesk ¶ 569,605) for the tax year, reduced by the foreign tax credit allowable under Code Sec. 27(a), and

. . . the alternative minimum tax (AMT) imposed by Code Sec. 55(a) for the tax year (i.e., the excess of the tentative minimum tax over the regular tax, see FTC 2d/FIN ¶ A-8801; USTR ¶ 554.01; TaxDesk ¶ 691,001).

The Code Sec. 26(a)(2) AMT offset rule described above means that the nonrefundable personal credits may offset both the regular tax and the AMT. In other words, individual taxpayers may offset their entire regular tax liability and AMT tax liability by the nonrefundable personal credits.

The nonrefundable personal credits affected by the Code Sec. 26(a)(2) rule are:

(1) the Code Sec. 21 child and dependent care credit (see FTC 2d/FIN ¶ A-4300 *et seq.*; USTR ¶ 214; TaxDesk ¶ 569,300 *et seq.*);

(2) the Code Sec. 22 credit for the elderly and disabled (see FTC 2d/FIN ¶ A-4100 *et seq.*; USTR ¶ 224; TaxDesk ¶ 568,700 *et seq. et seq.*);

FTC 2d References are to Federal Tax Coordinator 2d
FIN References are to RIA's Analysis of Federal Taxes: Income
USTR References are to United States Tax Reporter: Income
PE References are to Pension Explanations

(3) the Code Sec. 23 adoption expense credit (see FTC 2d/FIN ¶ A-4400 *et seq.*; USTR ¶ 234; TaxDesk ¶ 569,500 *et seq.*);

(4) the Code Sec. 24 child tax credit (see FTC 2d/FIN ¶ A-4050 *et seq.*; USTR ¶ 214; TaxDesk ¶ 569,100 *et seq.*);

(5) the Code Sec. 25 credit for interest paid or accrued on certain home mortgages of low-income persons (the mortgage credit certificate [MCC] credit), see FTC 2d/FIN ¶ A-4008; USTR ¶ 254.01; TaxDesk ¶ 568,507);

(6) the Code Sec. 25A credit for higher education expenses (the Hope credit and the Lifetime Learning credit, see FTC 2d/FIN ¶ A-4500 *et seq.*; USTR ¶ 25A4; TaxDesk ¶ 568,900 *et seq.*) (the Hope credit is modified and made partially refundable for 2009 and 2010, see ¶ 107);

(7) the Code Sec. 25B credit for elective deferrals and IRA contributions (the saver's credit, see FTC 2d/FIN ¶ A-4450 *et seq.*; USTR ¶ 25B4; TaxDesk ¶ 569,200 *et seq.*);

(8) the Code Sec. 25C nonbusiness energy property credit for energy-efficient improvements to a principal residence (see FTC 2d/FIN ¶ A-4750 *et seq.*; USTR ¶ 25C4; TaxDesk ¶ 569,550 *et seq.*);

(9) the Code Sec. 25D residential energy efficient property (REEP) credit for photovoltaic, solar hot water, and fuel cell property added to a residence (see FTC 2d/FIN ¶ A-4780 *et seq.*; USTR ¶ 25D4; TaxDesk ¶ 569,560 *et seq.*);

(10) the nonbusiness portion (i.e., any portion that doesn't relate to depreciable property) of the Code Sec. 30D new qualified plug-in electric drive motor vehicle (NQPEDMV) credit (see FTC 2d/FIN ¶ L-18030 *et seq.*; USTR ¶ 30D4; TaxDesk ¶ 397,130 *et seq.*); and

(11) the Code Sec. 1400C first-time homebuyer credit for the District of Columbia (the "first-time D.C. homebuyer credit," see FTC 2d/FIN ¶ A-4250 *et seq.*; USTR ¶ 1400C4; TaxDesk ¶ 568,800 *et seq.*).

(FTC 2d/FIN ¶ A-4902; USTR ¶ 264; TaxDesk ¶ 569,602)

Under pre-2009 Recovery Act law, the Code Sec. 26(a)(2) AMT offset rule was scheduled to cease to apply for tax years beginning after 2008. Instead, for those tax years, the nonrefundable personal tax credits listed above (other than the "specified personal credits" listed below) were to be subject to a limitation prescribed by Code Sec. 26(a)(1) which would not have allowed them to offset AMT. The credits subject to Code Sec. 26(a)(1)—collectively, the "Code Sec. 26(a)(1) limitation credits"—were to be allowed to the extent that the aggregate amount of those credits didn't exceed the excess of:

. . . the taxpayer's regular tax liability (FTC 2d/FIN ¶ A-4905; USTR ¶ 264.01; TaxDesk ¶ 569,604) for the tax year, over

. . . the taxpayer's tentative minimum tax for the tax year, determined under Code Sec. 55(b)(1) (FTC 2d/FIN ¶ A-8801; USTR ¶ 554.01; TaxDesk

¶ 691,001), but without regard to the AMT foreign tax credit (FTC 2d/FIN ¶ A-8181 *et seq.*; USTR ¶ 594; TaxDesk ¶ 691,401 *et seq.*).

(FTC 2d/FIN ¶ A-4900, ¶ A-4901; USTR ¶ 264; TaxDesk ¶ 569,601)

> *observation:* Under the post-2008 rule discussed above, the AMT could indirectly limit a taxpayer's nonrefundable personal tax credits even in situations where the taxpayer wasn't liable for the AMT. See FTC 2d/FIN ¶ A-8320; USTR ¶ 264.

The "specified personal credits" that are excepted from the Code Sec. 26(a)(1) limitation are the Code Sec. 23 adoption expense credit (item (3) above), the Code Sec. 24 child tax credit (item (4) above), the Code Sec. 25B saver's credit (item (7) above), the Code Sec. 25D REEP credit (item (9) above), and the nonbusiness portion of the Code Sec. 30D NQPEDMV credit (item (10) above). (FTC 2d/FIN ¶ A-4903; USTR ¶ 264; TaxDesk ¶ 569,603)

Under pre-2009 Recovery Act law, for tax years beginning after 2008, each of the "specified personal credits" was to be subject to separate limitations that would allow those credits to offset both regular tax and AMT. (FTC 2d/FIN ¶ A-4400, ¶ A-4405, ¶ A-4050, ¶ A-4054, ¶ A-4450, ¶ A-4455, ¶ A-4780, ¶ A-4781.1, ¶ L-18030, ¶ L-18034.1, ¶ A-8300, ¶ A-8320; USTR ¶ 234, ¶ 244.01, ¶ 25B4, ¶ 25D4, ¶ 30D4.07; TaxDesk ¶ 569,505, ¶ 569,104, ¶ 569,205, ¶ 569,561.1, ¶ 397,143)

New Law. The 2009 Recovery Act ("the Act") extends the Code Sec. 26(a)(2) AMT offset rule to apply to tax years beginning during 2009. (Code Sec. 26(a)(2) as amended by 2009 Recovery Act §1011(a)(1))

> *observation:* This means that for tax years beginning in 2009, the nonrefundable personal credits may offset AMT as well as regular tax.

Specifically, for tax years beginning in 2009 (as well as 2000 through 2008), the aggregate amount of nonrefundable personal credits may not exceed the sum of:

. . . the taxpayer's regular tax liability (FTC 2d/FIN ¶ A-4905; USTR ¶ 264.01; TaxDesk ¶ 569,604) for the tax year, reduced by the foreign tax credit allowable under Code Sec. 27(a), and

. . . the tax imposed by Code Sec. 55(a) (Code Sec. 26(a)(2))—i.e., the AMT (see FTC 2d/FIN ¶ A-8101; USTR ¶ 554.01; TaxDesk ¶ 691,002).

> *observation:* This means that in 2009 (as was the case in 2008), all of the otherwise allowable nonrefundable personal credits—i.e., not just

---

FTC 2d References are to Federal Tax Coordinator 2d
FIN References are to RIA's Analysis of Federal Taxes: Income
USTR References are to United States Tax Reporter: Income
PE References are to Pension Explanations

the "specified personal credits"—may be used to reduce AMT (as well as regular tax). This is because the maximum amount of total nonrefundable personal credits that a taxpayer may claim in 2009 can't exceed the sum of: (1) his regular tax liability (reduced by the foreign tax credit) for 2009, plus (2) his AMT liability for 2009. Under this rule, the taxpayer may claim up to the amount of that sum (i.e., regular tax plus AMT) as nonrefundable personal credits.

observation: Act § 1011 thus provides a one-year extension for the Code Sec. 26(a)(2) AMT offset, as part of the one-year "patch" provided for individual AMT relief. The Act also increases the AMT exemption amounts for 2009, see ¶ 201.

observation: A taxpayer is subject to the AMT if his tentative minimum tax liability for the tax year is greater than his regular tax liability for the tax year. The AMT equals the amount of that excess, if any (see FTC 2d/FIN ¶ A-8101; USTR ¶ 554.01; TaxDesk ¶ 691,002).

illustration (1): In 2009, Taxpayer's regular tax is $8,000, and her tentative minimum tax is $7,200. Thus, she is liable for $8,000 regular tax, but no AMT. Taxpayer can claim up to $8,000 of nonrefundable personal credits for 2009. Under pre-Act law, the amount of nonrefundable personal credits Taxpayer could claim for 2009 would have been limited to $800—i.e., the excess of $8,000 regular tax over $7,200 tentative minimum tax.

illustration (2): In 2009, Taxpayer's regular tax is $5,000, and his tentative minimum tax is $5,500. Thus, Taxpayer must pay a regular tax of $5,000, plus an AMT of $500 (excess of $5,500 tentative minimum tax over $5,000 regular tax). Taxpayer can claim up to $5,500 of nonrefundable personal credits for 2009 (the sum of his $5,000 regular tax and $500 AMT). Under pre-Act law, the Taxpayer couldn't have claimed any nonrefundable personal credits for 2009, because his regular tax ($5,000) didn't exceed his tentative minimum tax ($5,500).

observation: The rule allowing the nonrefundable personal credits to reduce the AMT (as well as regular tax) benefits middle income individuals who:

. . . have low taxable income (and thus a low regular tax), e.g., because of a large number of personal exemptions;

. . . are subject to the AMT because personal exemptions (as well as the standard deduction and certain itemized deductions) generally are not allowed in computing the AMT (see FTC 2d/FIN ¶s A-8305, A-8315; USTR ¶ 564.02; TaxDesk ¶s 697,005, 697,015); and

... have substantial nonrefundable personal credits such as the child tax credit.

⚫*observation:* By extending the Code Sec. 26(a)(2) AMT offset rule for one year, Act § 1011 provides a one-year postponement of the effective date for the limitations that, under pre-Act law, applied after 2008. Absent another extension, those postponed limitations will apply after 2009 (see "Tax liability limitations on nonrefundable personal credits after 2009," below).

How extension of Code Sec. 26(a)(2) through 2009 affects other credit limitations and carryover rules.

⚫*observation:* The statutory rules that provide for the limitations on and carryover of certain unused personal credits and the foreign tax credit include two sets of rules: (1) rules for tax years in which the personal credits are allowed against the AMT—i.e., tax years when Code Sec. 26(a)(2) applies, and (2) rules for tax years in which the credits are not so allowed—i.e., non-Code Sec. 26(a)(2) tax years. Thus, the one-year extension of the period in which the Code Sec. 26(a)(2) AMT offset rule applies to include 2009 also affects the carryover rules for certain credits in 2009.

Adoption credit (Code Sec. 23). The adoption credit is subject to the tax liability limitation prescribed by Code Sec. 23(b)(4) in tax years when Code Sec. 26(a)(2) doesn't apply (see FTC 2d/FIN ¶ A-4405; USTR ¶ 234; TaxDesk ¶ 569,505). The extension of Code Sec. 26(a)(2) so that it applies in 2009 means that the adoption credit is subject to that limitation in 2009. (Code Sec. 26(a)(2))

⚫*observation:* As noted above, the separate tax liability limitation on the adoption credit lets taxpayers use the credit to offset AMT as well as regular tax. Thus, the one-year extension of the Code Sec. 26(a)(2) limitation (which lets *all* the nonrefundable personal credits offset AMT as well as regular tax) doesn't affect the AMT offset allowance for the adoption credit in 2009. However, Code Sec. 23(b)(4) has specific ordering rules which, under pre-Act law, could have reduced the amount of the allowable adoption credit.

Child tax credit (Code Sec. 24). The child tax credit is subject to the tax liability limitation prescribed by Code Sec. 24(b)(3) in tax years when Code

FTC 2d References are to Federal Tax Coordinator 2d
FIN References are to RIA's Analysis of Federal Taxes: Income
USTR References are to United States Tax Reporter: Income
PE References are to Pension Explanations

Sec. 26(a)(2) doesn't apply (see FTC 2d/FIN ¶ A-4054; USTR ¶ 244.01; TaxDesk ¶ 569,104). The extension of Code Sec. 26(a)(2) so that it applies in 2009 means that the child tax credit is subject to that limitation in 2009. (Code Sec. 26(a)(2))

> **☑️ observation:** As noted above, the separate tax liability limitation on the child tax credit lets taxpayers use the credit to offset AMT as well as regular tax. Thus, the one-year extension of Code Sec. 26(a)(2) (which lets *all* the nonrefundable personal credits offset AMT as well as regular tax) doesn't affect the AMT offset allowance for the child tax credit in 2009. However, Code Sec. 24(b)(3) has specific ordering rules which, under pre-Act law, could have reduced the amount of the allowable child tax credit for 2009.

MCC credit (Code Sec. 25). If the MCC credit for a tax year exceeds the "applicable limitation" for the year, the excess is carried over to each of the next three years. The "applicable limitation" is: (a) the Code Sec. 26(a)(2) limitation for the tax year, reduced by the nonrefundable personal credits (other than the MCC credit, adoption credit, REEP credit, D.C. first-time homebuyer credit) for the year, or (b) for non-Code Sec. 26(a)(2) tax years, the limitation under Code Sec. 26(a)(1) reduced by the nonrefundable personal credits (other than the MCC credit, D.C. first-time homebuyer credit, or "specified personal credits") for the year. (FTC 2d/FIN ¶ A-4010; USTR ¶ 254.01; TaxDesk ¶ 380,502) (The Act adds the new qualified plug-in electric drive vehicle [QPEV] credit and the alternative motor vehicle [AMV] credit to these computations, see ¶ 1003 and ¶ 205, respectively.)

> **☑️ observation:** The extension of Code Sec. 26(a)(2) so that it applies in 2009 means that the Code Sec. 26(a)(2) limitation is the starting point for determining the MCC credit carryover for 2009.

American Opportunity tax credit (Code Sec. 25A). The Act modifies the Hope credit (which, as modified, is renamed the "American Opportunity tax credit," and herein referred to as the "modified Hope credit"), and allows a portion of it to be refundable, for tax years beginning in 2009 and 2010. The modified Hope credit is subject to the tax liability limitation prescribed by new Code Sec. 25A(i)(5) in tax years when Code Sec. 26(a)(2) doesn't apply (see ¶ 107). The extension of Code Sec. 26(a)(2) so that it applies in 2009 means that the modified Hope credit is subject to that limitation in 2009. (Code Sec. 26(a)(2))

> **☑️ observation:** The Code Sec. 26(a)(2) limitation is the starting point for determining the refundable portion of the modified Hope credit for 2009 (see ¶ 107).

Saver's credit (Code Sec. 25B). The saver's credit is subject to the tax liability limitation prescribed by Code Sec. 25B(g) in tax years when Code Sec. 26(a)(2) doesn't apply (see FTC 2d/FIN ¶ A-4455; USTR ¶ 25B4; TaxDesk ¶ 569,205). The extension of Code Sec. 26(a)(2) so that it applies in 2009 means that the saver's credit is subject to that limitation in 2009. (Code Sec. 26(a)(2))

> **🄰 *observation:*** As noted above, the separate tax liability limitation on the saver's credit lets taxpayers use the credit to offset AMT as well as regular tax. Thus, the one-year extension of the Code Sec. 26(a)(2) rule doesn't change the AMT offset allowance for the saver's credit in 2009. However, Code Sec. 25B(g) has specific ordering rules which, under pre-Act law, could have reduced the amount of the allowable saver's credit for 2009.

Residential energy efficient property (REEP) credit (Code Sec. 25D). If the REEP credit for a tax year exceeds the "applicable limitation" for the year, the excess is carried over to the next tax year. The applicable limitation is: (a) the Code Sec. 26(a)(2) limitation for the tax year, reduced by the nonrefundable personal credits (other than the REEP credit) for the year, or (b) for non-Code Sec. 26(a)(2) tax years, the sum of regular tax liability plus AMT, reduced by the nonrefundable personal credits (other than the REEP credit) and the foreign tax credit for the year. (FTC 2d/FIN ¶ A-4781.1; USTR ¶ 25D4; TaxDesk ¶ 569,561.1) The extension of Code Sec. 26(a)(2) so that it applies in 2009 means that the REEP credit is subject to that limitation in 2009. (Code Sec. 26(a)(2))

> **🄰 *observation:*** As noted above, the separate tax liability limitation on the REEP credit lets taxpayers use the credit to offset AMT as well as regular tax. Thus, the one-year extension of Code Sec. 26(a)(2) doesn't affect the AMT offset allowance for the REEP credit in 2009. It also means that the Code Sec. 26(a)(2) limitation is the starting point for determining the REEP credit carryover for 2009.

Qualified plug-in electric vehicle (QPEV) credit (Code Sec. 30). The Act provides a new QPEV credit for certain low-speed vehicles and 2- or 3-wheeled vehicles acquired after Feb. 17, 2009. The nonbusiness portion of the QPEV credit is treated as a nonrefundable personal credit subject to the tax liability limitation in Code Sec. 26(a)(2), see ¶ 1003. The extension of Code Sec. 26(a)(2) so that it applies in 2009 means that the nonbusiness portion of the QPEV credit is subject to that limitation in 2009. (Code Sec. 26(a)(2))

FTC 2d References are to Federal Tax Coordinator 2d
FIN References are to RIA's Analysis of Federal Taxes: Income
USTR References are to United States Tax Reporter: Income
PE References are to Pension Explanations

Alternative motor vehicle (AMV) credit (Code Sec. 30B). The Act provides new rules treating the nonbusiness portion of the AMV credit (see FTC 2d/FIN ¶ L-18020 *et seq.*; USTR ¶ 30B4; TaxDesk ¶ 397,100 *et seq.*) as a nonrefundable personal credit subject to the tax liability limitation in Code Sec. 26(a)(2), see ¶ 205. The extension of Code Sec. 26(a)(2) so that it applies in 2009 means that the nonbusiness portion of the AMV credit is subject to that limitation in 2009. (Code Sec. 26(a)(2))

New qualified plug-in electric drive motor vehicle (NQPEDMV) credit (Code Sec. 30D). The nonbusiness portion of the NQPEDMV credit is subject to the tax liability limitation prescribed by Code Sec. 30D(d)(2)(B) in tax years when Code Sec. 26(a)(2) doesn't apply (see FTC 2d/FIN ¶ L-18034.1; USTR ¶ 30D4; TaxDesk ¶ 397,143). The extension of Code Sec. 26(a)(2) so that it applies in 2009 means that the nonbusiness portion of the NQPEDMV credit is subject to that limitation in 2009. (Code Sec. 26(a)(2))

> *observation:* As noted above, the separate tax liability limitation on the nonbusiness portion of the NQPEDMV credit lets taxpayers use the credit to offset AMT as well as regular tax. Thus, the one-year extension of the Code Sec. 26(a)(2) limitation doesn't affect the AMT offset allowance for the NQPEDMV credit in 2009. However, Code Sec. 30D(d)(2)(B) has specific ordering rules which, under pre-Act law, could have reduced the amount of the allowable NQPEDMV credit for 2009.

D.C. first-time homebuyer credit (Code Sec. 1400C). If the D.C. first-time homebuyer credit exceeds the "applicable limitation" for the tax year, the excess is carried over to the next tax year. The "applicable limitation" is: (a) the Code Sec. 26(a)(2) limitation for the tax year, reduced by the nonrefundable personal credits (other than the D.C. first-time homebuyer credit and the REEP credit) for the year, or (b) for non-Code Sec. 26(a)(2) tax years, the limitation under Code Sec. 26(a)(1) reduced by the nonrefundable personal credits (other than the "specified personal credits") for the year. (FTC 2d/FIN ¶ A-4255; USTR ¶ 14,00C4; TaxDesk ¶ 568,805) (The Act adds the new QPEV credit and the AMV credit to these computations, see ¶ 1003 and ¶ 205, respectively.)

> *observation:* The extension of Code Sec. 26(a)(2) so that it applies in 2009 means that the Code Sec. 26(a)(2) limitation is the starting point for determining the D.C. first-time homebuyer credit carryover for 2009.

Foreign tax credit (Code Sec. 904). For tax years to which Code Sec. 26(a)(2) doesn't apply (i.e., tax years to which Code Sec. 26(a)(1) applies), the U.S. tax liability against which an individual's foreign tax credit is taken is reduced by the sum of the nonrefundable personal credits (other than the adoption credit, child tax credit, and saver's credit) allowable for the year. (FTC 2d/FIN

¶ O-4401; USTR ¶ 9044.01; TaxDesk ¶ 393,001) (The Act adds the modified Hope credit, the new QPEV credit, and the AMV credit to these computations, see ¶ 107, ¶ 1003, and ¶ 205, respectively.)

observation: The extension of Code Sec. 26(a)(2) so that it applies in 2009 means that the above-described reduction isn't made in computing the foreign tax credit for 2009. Thus, in computing the foreign tax credit for 2009, an individual doesn't reduce his U.S. tax liability by the personal credits (other than the adoption credit, child tax credit, saver's credit, modified Hope credit, QPEV credit, or AMV credit). This, in turn, results in a larger foreign tax credit for 2009.

observation: Code Sec. 904(i), which provides the rules for the above-described reduction, generally reflects the exceptions under Code Sec. 26(a)(1) limitation. That is, the credits that aren't counted in the Code Sec. 904(i) reduction are included in the "specified personal credits" that are excepted from the Code Sec. 26(a)(1) limitation. For example, the Act adds the new Code Sec. 25A(i) modified Hope Credit to the "specified personal credits" excepted from Code Sec. 26(a)(1), and makes a corresponding addition to the credits excluded from the Code Sec. 904(i) reduction (see ¶ 107). The 2008 Energy Act added the Code Sec. 25D REEP credit and the Code Sec. 30D NQPEDMV credit to the "specified personal credits," but didn't make the corresponding change to Code Sec. 904(i). This omission appears to reflect a drafting error.

AMT not offset by qualified alternative vehicle fuel (QAFV) refueling property credit. The Code Sec. 26(a) limitations don't apply to the Code Sec. 30C refueling property credit (see FTC 2d/FIN ¶ L-18040 *et seq.*; USTR ¶ 30C4; TaxDesk ¶ 397,200 *et seq.*). The separate tax liability limitation that applies to this credit doesn't permit the use of the nonbusiness portion of the credit (i.e., any portion that doesn't relate to depreciable property) as an offset against AMT in 2009 (see FTC 2d/FIN ¶ L-18022; L-18042; USTR ¶ 30B4; 30C4; TaxDesk ¶ 397,102; 397,202).

observation: Although the Act provides new rules treating the nonbusiness portion of the AMV credit as a nonrefundable personal credit allowed against AMT (see ¶ 205), it doesn't make any changes to the tax liability limitations applicable to the QAFV refueling property credit generally (see FTC 2d/FIN ¶ L-18042; USTR ¶ 30C4; TaxDesk ¶ 397,202), or otherwise provide for the credits to be used to offset AMT in 2009 (e.g., by making it subject to Code Sec. 26(a)(2)). Thus, as under pre-Act law, the nonbusiness portions of the credit can't be

FTC 2d References are to Federal Tax Coordinator 2d
FIN References are to RIA's Analysis of Federal Taxes: Income
USTR References are to United States Tax Reporter: Income
PE References are to Pension Explanations

used to reduce AMT in 2009. However, the increased AMT exemption amounts that Act § 1012 provides for 2009 (see ¶ 201) will allow some previously ineligible taxpayers to claim a larger portion of the credit in 2009.

Tax liability limitations on the nonrefundable personal credits after 2009. As discussed above, Act § 1011(a)(1) extends the Code Sec. 26(a)(2) AMT off-set rule so that it applies through 2009 (instead of through 2008).

> 🅡🅐 *observation:* Absent another extension, for tax years beginning after 2009, the nonrefundable personal credits—*other than the "specified personal credits"*—will be subject to the limitation under Code Sec. 26(a)(1). The aggregate amount of those credits—collectively, the "Code Sec. 26(a)(1) limitation credits"—can't exceed the excess of: (a) the individual's regular tax liability, over (b) the individual's tenta-tive minimum tax, determined without regard to the AMT foreign tax credit (see FTC 2d/FIN ¶ A-4901; USTR ¶ 264; TaxDesk ¶ 569,604).

> 🅡🅐 *illustration (3):* In 2010, Taxpayers' regular tax is $7,400, their ten-tative minimum tax is $6,500, and they have a $1,200 Code Sec. 26(a)(1) limitation credit. Although they don't owe AMT, they are able to claim only $900 of the credits ($7,400 regular tax liability – $6,500 tentative minimum tax).

> 🅡🅐 *observation:* The Act excepts the modified Hope credit, the nonbusi-ness portion of the new QPEV credit, and the nonbusiness portion of the AMV credit from the Code Sec. 26(a)(1) limitation, see ¶ 107, ¶ 1003, and ¶ 205. These credits are included in the "specified personal credits" that are allowed against AMT.

> 🅡🅐 *observation:* Absent another extension of Code Sec. 26(a)(2), for tax years beginning after 2009, the "specified person credits" will be lim-ited as follows:

(1) The *adoption credit* can't exceed the excess of: (a) the sum of regular tax liability plus AMT liability, over (b) the sum of nonrefund-able personal credits (other than the adoption credit and the REEP credit) plus the foreign tax credit (see FTC 2d/FIN ¶ A-4405; USTR ¶ 234; TaxDesk ¶ 569,505).

(2) The *child tax credit* can't exceed the excess of: (a) the sum of regular tax liability plus AMT liability, over (b) the sum of nonrefund-able personal credits (other than the "specified personal credits") plus the foreign tax credit (see ¶ 107, ¶ 1003, ¶ 205, and FTC 2d/FIN ¶ A-4054; USTR ¶ 244.01; TaxDesk ¶ 569,104).

(3) The *saver's credit* can't exceed the excess of: (a) the sum of nonrefundable personal credits (other than the saver's credit, adoption credit, REEP credit, NQPEDMV credit, modified Hope credit, QPEV credit, and AMV credit) plus the foreign tax credit (see ¶ 107, ¶ 1003, ¶ 205, and FTC 2d/FIN ¶ A-4455; USTR ¶ 25B4; TaxDesk ¶ 569,205).

(4) The *REEP credit* can't exceed the sum of regular tax liability plus AMT, reduced by the nonrefundable personal credits (other than the REEP credit) and the foreign tax credit for the year (see (FTC 2d/FIN ¶ A-4781.1; USTR ¶ 25D4; TaxDesk ¶ 569,561.1).

(5) The nonbusiness portion of the *NQPEDMV credit* can't exceed the sum of regular tax liability plus AMT, reduced by the nonrefundable personal credits (other than the NQPEDMV credit, the adoption credit, and the REEP credit), plus the foreign tax credit (see FTC 2d/FIN ¶ L-18034.1; USTR ¶ 30D4; TaxDesk ¶ 397,143).

(6) The *modified Hope credit* (which applies only through 2010) can't exceed the excess of (a) the sum of regular tax liability plus AMT, over (b) the sum of the nonrefundable personal credits (other than the modified Hope credit itself, the adoption credit, the REEP credit, and the NQPEDMV credit) plus the foreign tax credit, for the year (for refundability of excess, see ¶ 107).

(7) The nonbusiness portion of the *AMV credit* will be subject to the separate tax liability limitation discussed at ¶ 205.

(8) The nonbusiness portion of the *QPEV credit* will be subject to the separate tax liability limitation discussed at ¶ 1003.

illustration (4): For 2010, H and W, married taxpayers, have a regular tax liability of $2,100 and no AMT liability. Without taking into account any credit limitations, they are entitled to a $1,200 child tax credit and a $1,000 Code Sec. 26(a)(1) limitation credit. The sum of their regular tax plus AMT exceeds the sum of their nonrefundable personal credits other than the child credit by $1,100 ($2,100 − $1,000). They are thus entitled to claim only $1,100 of the child tax credit. They may claim the full amount of the Code Sec. 26(a)(1) limitation credit.

observation: In other words, the adoption credit, child tax credit, saver's credit, REEP credit, nonbusiness NQPEDMV credit, modified Hope credit, nonbusiness AMV credit, and nonbusiness QPEV credit are the only nonrefundable personal credits that can reduce AMT (as well as regular tax) in tax years beginning after 2009.

FTC 2d References are to Federal Tax Coordinator 2d
FIN References are to RIA's Analysis of Federal Taxes: Income
USTR References are to United States Tax Reporter: Income
PE References are to Pension Explanations

⚫/ *illustration* (5): In 2010, Taxpayers' regular tax is $4,000, and their tentative minimum tax is $4,500. They have a $1,000 Code Sec. 26(a)(1) limitation credit and a $1,000 child credit. Because their tentative minimum tax exceeds their regular tax liability, they can't claim any Code Sec. 26(a)(1) limitation credit for the year. However, they can use the full $1,000 child tax credit. Thus, their total tax after the child credit is $3,500 ($4,000 regular tax, plus $500 AMT, reduced by the $1,000 child credit).

⚫/ *observation*: The Code Sec. 26(a)(1) limitation that will be in effect after 2009 may reduce a taxpayer's nonrefundable personal tax credits even if the taxpayer has no AMT liability, see FTC 2d/FIN ¶ A-8320; USTR ¶ 264.

⚫/ *observation*: The specific limitations on each of the "specified personal credits" that will apply after 2009 are similar to the Code Sec. 26(a)(2) limitation that, as a result of the Act extension, applies through 2009. Each of the specific limitations allows individuals to use the specific credit to offset their AMT liability. However, the post-2009 limitations for each credit have specific ordering rules which may reduce the amount allowable for these credits.

☐ **Effective:** Tax years beginning after Dec. 31, 2008 (2009 Recovery Act §1011(b)), but only for tax years beginning during 2009. (Code Sec. 26(a)(2))

¶ 205. Alternative motor vehicle credit (AMVC) is treated as a personal credit allowed against AMT for tax years beginning after 2008

Code Sec. 30B(g)(2), as amended by 2009 Recovery Act § 1144(a)
Code Sec. 24(b)(3)(B), as amended by 2009 Recovery Act § 1144(b)(1)(A)
Code Sec. 25(e)(1)(C)(ii), as amended by 2009 Recovery Act
§ 1144(b)(1)(B)
Code Sec. 25B(g)(2), as amended by 2009 Recovery Act § 1144(b)(1)(C)
Code Sec. 26(a)(1), as amended by 2009 Recovery Act § 1144(b)(1)(D)
Code Sec. 904(i), as amended by 2009 Recovery Act § 1144(b)(1)(E)
Code Sec. 1400C(d)(2), as amended by 2009 Recovery Act § 1144(b)(1)(F)
Code Sec. 30C(d)(2)(A), as amended by 2009 Recovery Act § 1144(b)(2)
Code Sec. 55(c)(3), as amended by 2009 Recovery Act § 1144(b)(3)
Generally effective: Tax years beginning after Dec. 31, 2008
Committee Reports, see ¶ 5027

Under pre-2009 Recovery Act law, the alternative motor vehicle credit (AMVC) under Code Sec. 30B had four components:

. . . the qualified fuel cell motor vehicle credit (see FTC 2d/FIN ¶ L-18024; USTR ¶ 30B4.01; TaxDesk ¶ 397,104).

. . . the advanced lean-burn technology motor vehicle credit (see FTC 2d/FIN ¶ L-18025; USTR ¶ 30B4.02; TaxDesk ¶ 397,105).

. . . the qualified hybrid motor vehicle credit (see FTC 2d/FIN ¶ L-18026; USTR ¶ 30B4.03; TaxDesk ¶ 397,106).

. . . the qualified alternative fuel motor vehicle credit (see FTC 2d/FIN ¶ L-18029.1; USTR ¶ 30B4.06; TaxDesk ¶ 397,110). (FTC 2d/FIN ¶ L-18020; USTR ¶ 30B4; TaxDesk ¶ 397,101)

The portion of the AMVC attributable to a vehicle that is depreciable is treated as part of the general business credit, see FTC 2d/FIN ¶s L-15201, L-18022; USTR ¶s 30B4, 384.01; TaxDesk ¶s 380,501, 397,102. Under pre-2009 Recovery Act law, the remainder of the AMVC was a personal credit that could offset the excess of the regular tax liability (reduced by the sum of the credits allowed under Code Sec. 21 through Code Sec. 26 (nonrefundable personal credits), Code Sec. 27 (foreign tax credit), and Code Sec. 30 (qualified electric vehicles credit), over the tentative minimum tax for the tax year. (FTC 2d/FIN ¶ L-18020, ¶ L-18021; USTR ¶ 30B4; TaxDesk ¶ 397,101) As a result, under pre-2009 Recovery Act law, even a person who wasn't subject to the alternative minimum tax (AMT) might not have been able to claim the maximum allowable AMVC, or any AMVC, for a qualified vehicle. If a taxpayer's regular tax liability was zero, the amount of the AMVC taken as a personal credit was zero. (FTC 2d/FIN ¶ L-18022; USTR ¶ 30B4; TaxDesk ¶ 397,106)

New Law. For income tax purposes, the AMVC for any tax year (determined after the application of the rules under Code Sec. 30B(g)(1) that treat the portion of the AMVC that is attributable to depreciable property as a general business credit) is treated as a credit allowable under Subtitle A, Chapter 1, Subchapter A, Part IV, Subpart A of the Code (also known as a personal credit) for the tax year. (Code Sec. 30B(g)(2)(A) as amended by 2009 Recovery Act §1144(a))

However, the credit allowed under Code Sec. 30B isn't subject to the rule that provides that personal credits can't exceed the excess (if any) of the taxpayer's regular tax liability for the tax year over the tentative minimum tax for the tax year (determined without regard to the AMT foreign tax credit). (Code Sec. 26(a)(1) as amended by 2009 Recovery Act §1144(b)(1)(D)) Instead, for a tax year to which Code Sec. 26(a)(2) (under which specified nonrefundable personal tax credits may offset both regular and AMT liability) doesn't apply (i.e., any tax year beginning after 2009, as modified by the 2009 Recovery Act, see

FTC 2d References are to Federal Tax Coordinator 2d
FIN References are to RIA's Analysis of Federal Taxes: Income
USTR References are to United States Tax Reporter: Income
PE References are to Pension Explanations

69

¶ 204), the credit allowed under Code Sec. 30B(a) for any tax year (determined after the application of Code Sec. 30B(g)(1)) can't exceed the excess of: (Code Sec. 30B(g)(2)(B))

(1) the sum of the regular tax liability (as defined in Code Sec. 26(b), see ¶ 204) *plus* the tax imposed by Code Sec. 55, *over* (Code Sec. 30B(g)(2)(B)(i))

(2) the sum of the personal credits allowable under subpart A (other than the AMVC under Code Sec. 30B and the adoption credit under Code Sec. 23 (see FTC 2d/FIN ¶ A-4401; USTR ¶ 234; TaxDesk ¶ 569,501), the residential energy efficient credit under Code Sec. 25D (see FTC 2d/FIN ¶ A-4781; USTR ¶ 25D4; TaxDesk ¶ 569,553), the electric vehicle credit under Code Sec. 30 (see FTC 2d/FIN ¶ L-18011; USTR ¶ 304; TaxDesk ¶ 569,553), and the new qualified plug-in electric drive motor vehicle credit under Code Sec. 30D (see FTC 2d/FIN ¶ L-18031; USTR ¶ 30D4; TaxDesk ¶ 397,001), and the foreign tax credit under Code Sec. 27 (see FTC 2d/FIN ¶ O-4000; USTR ¶ 274; TaxDesk ¶ 569,601)) for the tax year. (Code Sec. 30B(g)(2)(B)(ii))

Thus, the AMVC is a personal credit allowed against the AMT. (Com Rept, see ¶ 5027)

> **✪** *observation:* The effect of the amendments to Code Sec. 26(a)(1) and Code Sec. 30B(g)(2) (discussed above) is that the non-depreciable property portion of the AMVC is generally allowable to the extent of a taxpayer's regular income tax and AMT liabilities, reduced only by certain other credits.

For plug-in conversion credit added to the AMVC under the 2009 Recovery Act, see ¶ 1004.

Coordination with other personal credits. References to the AMVC under Code Sec. 30B are added to the series of credits referred to in the following conforming changes:

. . . Code Sec. 24(b)(3)(B) (part of the tax liability limit rule for the child tax credit, see FTC 2d/FIN ¶ A-4054; USTR ¶ 244.01; TaxDesk ¶ 569,104 and ¶ 107). (Code Sec. 24(b)(3)(B) as amended by 2009 Recovery Act §1144(b)(1)(A))

. . . Code Sec. 25(e)(1)(C)(ii) (part of the carryover rule for the residential mortgage interest credit, see FTC 2d/FIN ¶ A-4010; USTR ¶ 254; TaxDesk ¶ 568,509 and ¶ 107). (Code Sec. 25(e)(1)(C)(ii) as amended by 2009 Recovery Act §1144(b)(1)(B))

. . . Code Sec. 25B(g)(2) (part of the tax liability limit rule for the saver's credit for certain elective deferrals and IRA contributions, see FTC 2d/FIN ¶ A-4455; USTR ¶ 25B4; TaxDesk ¶ 569,205 and ¶ 107). (Code Sec. 25B(g)(2) as amended by 2009 Recovery Act §1144(b)(1)(C))

. . . Code Sec. 904(i) (part of the tax liability limit rule for the foreign tax credit, see FTC 2d/FIN ¶ O-4411; USTR ¶ 9044.01; TaxDesk ¶ 393,001 and ¶ 107). (Code Sec. 904(i) as amended by 2009 Recovery Act §1144(b)(1)(E)).

. . . Code Sec. 1400C(d)(2) (part of the carryover rule for the first-time D.C. homebuyer credit, see FTC 2d/FIN ¶ A-4255; USTR ¶ 14,00C4; TaxDesk ¶ 568,805 and ¶ 107). (Code Sec. 1400C(d)(2) as amended by 2009 Recovery Act §1144(b)(1)(F))

> *observation:* Code Sec. 30B(g)(2) (discussed above) provides that the AMVC offsets tax liabilities (regular and AMT) only to the extent that the AMVC exceeds certain personal credits and the foreign tax credit. Thus, the effect of the Code Sec. 30B(g)(2) and the conforming changes (listed above) is that the AMVC is applied against tax liabilities (regular and AMT).

References to Code Sec. 30B were stricken in the following series of credits referred to in:

. . . Code Sec. 30C(d)(2)(A) (application of alternative fuel vehicle refueling (QAFV) credit with other credits, see ¶ 1003 and FTC 2d/FIN ¶ L-18042; USTR ¶ 30C4.01; TaxDesk ¶ 397,202), and (Code Sec. 30C(d)(2)(A) as amended by 2009 Recovery Act §1144(b)(2))

. . . Code Sec. 55(c)(3) (a list of certain credits that are *not* allowable against the AMT). (Code Sec. 55(c)(3) as amended by 2009 Recovery Act §1144(b)(3))

Sunset provision. The amendment made by 2009 Recovery Act § 1144(b)(1)(A) (to Code Sec. 24(b)(3)(B) as discussed above) is subject to title IX of the 2001 Economic Growth and Tax Relief Reconciliation Act of 2001— i.e., the EGTRRA sunset provision, see 2001 EGTRRA § 901 (Sec. 901, PL 107-16, 6/7/2001)—in the same manner as the provision of 2001 EGTRRA to which the amendment relates. (2009 Recovery Act §1144(d))

> *observation:* 2001 EGTRRA § 901 requires that amendments made by 2001 EGTRRA will not be effective for tax years beginning after Dec. 31, 2010.

> *observation:* All of Code Sec. 24(b)(3) (which provides the tax liability limit rule for the child tax credit of which Code Sec. 24(b)(3)(B) is part) is subject to the EGTRRA sunset provision. Thus, without 2009 Recovery Act § 1144(d), there would be a technical inconsistency in which the amendment to Code Sec. 24(b)(3)(B) made by 2009 Recov-

---

FTC 2d References are to Federal Tax Coordinator 2d
FIN References are to RIA's Analysis of Federal Taxes: Income
USTR References are to United States Tax Reporter: Income
PE References are to Pension Explanations

ery Act § 1144(b)(1)(A) would survive the post-2010 termination of Code Sec. 24(b)(3).

☐ **Effective:** Tax years beginning after Dec. 31, 2008. (2009 Recovery Act §1144(c))

¶ 300. Subsidized COBRA Coverage

¶ 301. COBRA premium subsidy provided for 9 months to workers involuntarily terminated between Sept. 10, 2008 through Dec. 31, 2009

Code Sec. NONE, 2009 Recovery Act § 3001
Generally effective: For periods of COBRA coverage provided beginning on or after Feb. 17, 2009
Committee Reports, see ¶ 5082

Under the so-called COBRA continuation rules added by the Consolidated Omnibus Budget Reconciliation Act of 1985, employees and their dependents who are covered under group health insurance plans maintained by employers that have at least 20 employees, must be allowed to elect to continue their coverage at their own expense, plus a 2% administrative fee. This coverage can continue for at least 18 months after the date that their health plan coverage is lost due to an employee's termination of employment i.e., due to a "qualifying event." (FTC 2d/FIN ¶ H-1250 *et seq.*; USTR ¶ 49,80B4.01; PE ¶ 4980B-4.01.)

All "qualified beneficiaries" must be allowed to continue the same coverage that they had immediately before the occurrence of the qualifying event that caused the loss of coverage. (FTC 2d/FIN ¶ H-1303; USTR ¶ 49,80B4.08; PE ¶ 4980B-4.08)

Following the occurrence of a qualifying event that causes the loss of coverage under a group health plan, the plan administrator must, within 14 days of being provided notice of the qualifying event, provide each qualified beneficiary with a notice that explains the beneficiaries' right to elect COBRA continuation coverage, the coverage that may be elected, the duration of the coverage, and how much the coverage will cost and how and when it must be paid. (FTC 2d/FIN ¶ H-1313; USTR ¶ 49,80B-4.10; PE ¶ 4980B-4.10)

> *observation:* Nothing in the law requires the plan to charge qualified beneficiaries for their continuation coverage. The COBRA rules merely set the upper limit for the premiums a plan is allowed to charge, i.e., 102% of the employee's cost.

(FTC 2d/FIN ¶ H-1250; USTR ¶ 49,80B4.04; PE ¶ 4980B-4.04)

New Law. The 2009 Recovery Act provides that, for a period not more than nine months, an "assistance eligible individual" (AEI) is treated as having paid any premium required for COBRA continuation coverage under a group

FTC 2d References are to Federal Tax Coordinator 2d
FIN References are to RIA's Analysis of Federal Taxes: Income
USTR References are to United States Tax Reporter: Income
PE References are to Pension Explanations

health plan if the individual pays 35% of the premium (2009 Recovery Act §3001(a)(1)(A)). Thus, if the AEI pays 35% of the of the premium, the group health plan must treat that individual as having paid the full premium required for COBRA continuation coverage, and the individual is effectively entitled to a "subsidy" for 65% of the premium. (Com Rept, see ¶ 5082)

For purposes of these rules, "COBRA continuation coverage" means continuation coverage provided under:

(a) ERISA §601 *et seq.* (other than ERISA §609);

(b) Title XXII of the Public Health Service Act;

(c) Code Sec. 4980B (other than Code Sec. 4980B(f)(1), to the extent it relates to pediatric vaccines);

(d) 5 USC §8905a (i.e., under the Federal Employees Health Benefit Plan (FEHBP); or

(e) under a state program that provides comparable continuation coverage.

However, COBRA continuation coverage does not include coverage under a flexible spending account under a cafeteria plan within the meaning of Code Sec. 125. (2009 Recovery Act §3001(a)(10)(B))

Payment of a premium by an AEI includes payment by another individual paying on behalf of the AEI, e.g., a parent or guardian, or an entity paying on behalf of the AEI, e.g., a state agency or charity. ((Com Rept, see ¶ 5082))

The base amount that is used to calculate the employee's reduced COBRA premium under the Act is the premium that the employee would have been required to pay for COBRA continuation coverage under pre-Act law, generally 102% of the employer's premium. ((Com Rept, see ¶ 5082))

> *illustration:* John is laid off from work and is eligible to elect COBRA continuation coverage. The cost to his employer for the coverage while John was employed was $100 per month. Under pre-Act law, John's COBRA premium for that coverage was $102 per month (i.e., 102% of the employer's premium). Under the Act, John has to pay only 35% of the $102 premium, i.e., $35.70. The $66.30 balance is the "subsidy" that the Act provides.

Who is an assistance eligible individual. For purposes of these rules, an "assistance eligible individual" (AEI) is any qualified beneficiary if:

• at any time from Sept. 1, 2008 through Dec. 31, 2009, the qualified beneficiary is eligible for COBRA continuation coverage;

• the beneficiary elects COBRA continuation coverage; and

• the qualifying event giving rise to a beneficiary's COBRA eligibility consists of the involuntary termination of the covered employee's employment during this period. (2009 Recovery Act §3001(a)(3))

An AEI can be any qualified beneficiary who's associated with the relevant covered employee (e.g., a dependent of an employee who is covered immediately before a qualifying event). As under pre-Act law, the qualified beneficiary can independently elect COBRA and under the Act can independently receive a subsidy. (Com Rept, see ¶ 5082)

> *Illustration:* John is a covered employee married to Jane. Both are qualified beneficiaries and AEIs who have elected COBRA continuation coverage and receive the subsidy for the required COBRA premiums. John dies during the subsidy period. Jane continues to be eligible for the subsidy after John's death. (Com Rept, see ¶ 5082)

When assistance eligible individual's (AEI's) eligibility for COBRA premium subsidy ends. The Act provides that an AEI's eligibility for a COBRA premium assistance subsidy will end for months of coverage beginning on or after the *earlier* of

- the first date that the AEI is eligible for coverage under: any other group health plan (other than coverage consisting of only dental, vision, counseling, or referral services, or a combination thereof), coverage under a health reimbursement arrangement or a health flexible spending arrangement, or coverage of treatment that is furnished in an on-site medical facility maintained by the employer and that consists primarily of first-aid services, prevention and wellness care, or similar care (or a combination thereof); or the first date that the AEI is eligible for benefits under title XVIII of the Social Security Act; or

- the earliest of—

(i) the date that is nine months after the first day of the first month that the subsidy becomes available to the individual,

(ii) the date following the expiration of the maximum period of continuation coverage required under the applicable COBRA continuation coverage provision, or

(iii) the date following the expiration of the period of the continuation coverage allowed under the rules at ¶ 302. (2009 Recovery Act §3001(a)(2)(A))

Thus, the maximum period for which the subsidy can be provided is nine months. (Com Rept, see ¶ 5082)

Expedited DOL review of plan's denial of premium assistance eligibility. The Act includes an expedited 15-day review process under which an individual may request review of a group health plan's denial of treatment as an assistance

---

FTC 2d References are to Federal Tax Coordinator 2d
FIN References are to RIA's Analysis of Federal Taxes: Income
USTR References are to United States Tax Reporter: Income
PE References are to Pension Explanations

eligible individual. For plans subject to ERISA's parallel continuation coverage requirements, The Department of Labor (DOL) will set the form and manner of the review process in consultation with IRS. (Plans that must provide continuation coverage under other provisions of the law will be provided the form and manner of the review process by the secretary of Health and Human Services (HHS). (2009 Recovery Act §3001(a)(5))

Required safeguards. The Act directs IRS to provide whatever rules, regulations, and other guidance may be necessary to prevent fraud and abuse of the COBRA premium assistance provided by the Act. (2009 Recovery Act §3001(a)(8))

Outreach and guidance provisions. The Act directs DOL, in consultation with IRS and the Department of Health and Human Services (HHS) to provide an outreach program involving public education and enrollment assistance as to the premium reduction provided by the Act. This program is to be directed toward employers, group health plan administrators, public assistance programs, states, insurers, and other entities such as these three agencies determine. The outreach effort, which the agencies will make available on their Websites, must initially focus on those individuals who are AEIs and other qualified beneficiaries referred to in 2009 Recovery Act §3001(a)(7)(C) who became eligible for COBRA coverage before Feb. 17, 2009 (see ¶ 302). (2009 Recovery Act §3001(a)(9))

Additional rules. Workers who were involuntarily terminated between September 1, 2008 and Feb. 17, 2009, but initially failed to elect COBRA because it was unaffordable, are given an additional 60 days to elect COBRA and receive the subsidy, see ¶ 302.

COBRA-subsidized individuals may elect to change COBRA continuation coverage to a different plan where the employer so permits, see ¶ 303.

COBRA premium assistance provided to high income taxpayers can be recaptured, see ¶ 304.

The COBRA subsidy is excluded from income, see ¶ 305.

COBRA-subsidized individuals are not eligible for the refundable federal health coverage tax credit, see ¶ 306.

Terminated workers must be notified of their right to the COBRA continuation benefits subsidy, see ¶ 307.

There is a reimbursement mechanism provided to plans for COBRA premiums that are not paid by COBRA-subsidized individuals, see ¶ 308.

For the penalty imposed on COBRA-subsidized individuals who fail to notify their group health plan when they become eligible for other health coverage, see ¶ 309.

☐ **Effective:** For COBRA premiums to which 2009 Recovery Act §3001(a)(1)(A) applies , i.e., for premiums provided for periods of coverage beginning on or after Feb. 17, 2009. (2009 Recovery Act §3001(a)(1)(A))

¶ 302. Certain unemployed workers have an extended 60-day period to elect subsidized COBRA continuation coverage

Code Sec. None, 2009 Recovery Act § 3001(a)(4)
Generally effective: For periods of COBRA continuation coverage beginning after Feb. 17, 2009
Committee Reports, see ¶ 5082

Group health plans are required to offer certain individuals (e.g., employees and certain dependents, referred to as "qualified beneficiaries") the opportunity to continue to participate ("continuation coverage") for a specified period of time (generally, up to 18 months) in the group health plan after the occurrence of certain events (referred to as "qualifying events," like involuntary termination of employment) that otherwise would have terminated plan participation. These continuation coverage rules are often referred to as "COBRA continuation coverage," see FTC 2d/FIN ¶ H-1251; USTR ¶ 49,80B4; PE ¶ 4980B-4.

The COBRA rules specify a minimum election period under which a qualified beneficiary is entitled to elect continuation coverage. The election period (referred to as the "standard election period") must be at least 60 days long, and ends not earlier than 60 days after the later of:

. . . the date on which coverage terminates under the group health plan due to a qualifying event; or

. . . the date of any notice by the plan administrator. (FTC 2d/FIN ¶ H-1250, ¶ H-1293; USTR ¶ 49,80B4.09; PE ¶ 4980B-4.09)

Under pre-2009 Recovery Act law, only the standard election period applied.

Group health plans may impose a pre-existing condition exclusion for no more than 12 months after a participant or beneficiary's enrollment date. The 12-month period must be reduced by the aggregate period of creditable coverage (which includes periods of coverage under another group health plan). A period of creditable coverage can be disregarded if, after the coverage period, and before the enrollment date, there was a 63-day period during which the individual was not covered under any creditable coverage, see FTC 2d/FIN ¶ H-1325.6; USTR ¶ 98,014; PE ¶ 9801-4.

FTC 2d References are to Federal Tax Coordinator 2d
FIN References are to RIA's Analysis of Federal Taxes: Income
USTR References are to United States Tax Reporter: Income
PE References are to Pension Explanations

New Law. As part of its overhaul of the COBRA rules, the 2009 Recovery Act provides that an "assistance eligible individual" (AEI) who elects COBRA coverage under the employer's group health plan, is required to pay no more than 35% of the applicable premium for COBRA coverage, and that IRS will provide a "subsidy" for the remaining 65%, see ¶ 301.

For purposes of the COBRA continuation coverage election period, a special 60-day *extended* election period is provided for certain qualified beneficiaries who are eligible for subsidized COBRA coverage. Specifically, an individual who does *not* have a COBRA continuation coverage election in effect on Feb. 17, 2009, but who *would* be an AEI *if* the election were in effect, is permitted to elect COBRA continuation coverage during the period:

. . . beginning on Feb. 17, 2009; and

. . . ending 60 days after the date on which the notice regarding the extended election period is provided to him (as required under 2009 Recovery Act §3001(a)(7)(C), see ¶ 307). (2009 Recovery Act §3001(a)(4)(A))

A qualified beneficiary who elected COBRA coverage *before* Feb. 17, 2009, but who is no longer enrolled *on* Feb. 17, 2009 (e.g., because the qualified beneficiary was unable to continue paying the premium), is entitled to elect COBRA coverage during this extended election period. (Com Rept, see ¶ 5082)

Any COBRA continuation coverage elected by a qualified beneficiary during the extended election period must:

(a) begin with the first period of coverage (see ¶ 301) beginning on or after Feb. 17, 2009; and

(b) not extend beyond the period of COBRA continuation coverage that would otherwise have been required if the coverage had been elected under the *standard* (i.e., not extended) election period. (2009 Recovery Act §3001(a)(4)(B))

Thus, the extended election period does *not* extend the period of COBRA continuation coverage beyond the original maximum required period (generally, 18 months after a qualifying event). (Com Rept, see ¶ 5082)

Preexisting conditions. For a qualified beneficiary who elects COBRA continuation coverage under the extended election period, above, the period that (i) begins on the date of the qualifying event (e.g., involuntary termination of employment), and (ii) ends with the beginning of the period described in item (a), above, is disregarded for purposes of determining the 63-day period under the rules that limit group health plans from imposing pre-existing condition limitations. (2009 Recovery Act §3001(a)(4)(C))

The 60-day extended election period applies to any group health plan that is subject to the COBRA continuation coverage requirements of the Code, ERISA, the Public Health Service Act (PHSA), and title 10 of the US Code (relating to plans maintained by the federal government). (Com Rept, see ¶ 5082)

☐ **Effective:** For periods of COBRA continuation coverage beginning after Feb. 17, 2009. (Com Rept, see ¶ 5082)

¶ 303. COBRA-subsidized individuals may elect to change COBRA continuation coverage to a different plan where employer so permits

Code Sec. None, 2009 Recovery Act § 3001(a)(1)(B)
Generally effective: For periods of COBRA continuation coverage beginning after Feb. 17, 2009
Committee Reports, see ¶ 5082

As part of its overhaul of the COBRA rules, the 2009 Recovery Act provides that an "assistance eligible individual" (AEI) who elects COBRA coverage under the employer's group health plan, is required to pay no more than 35% of the applicable premium for COBRA coverage, and that IRS will provide a "subsidy" for the remaining 65%, see ¶ 301. (FTC 2d/FIN ¶ H-1250; USTR ¶ 49,80B4.04; PE ¶ 4980B-4.04)

New Law. Under the 2009 Recovery Act, regardless of other COBRA continuation provisions, an AEI may, within 90 days after the date of notice of the plan enrollment option described below, elect to enroll in coverage under a plan offered by the employer involved, or the employee organization involved (including a joint board of trustees of a multiemployer trust affiliated with one or more multiemployer plans), that differs from the coverage under the plan in which the AEI was enrolled at the time the qualifying event occurred. This other coverage is treated as COBRA continuation coverage for purposes of the applicable COBRA continuation coverage provisions. (2009 Recovery Act §3001(a)(1)(B)(i))

Thus, an AEI is permitted to *change* coverage options under the plan in conjunction with electing COBRA continuation coverage. However, once the election of the other coverage is made, it becomes COBRA continuation coverage, and must be continued for the required period (generally 18 or 36 months) even though the premium subsidy for AEIs only lasts for nine months. (Com Rept, see ¶ 5082)

> **✔ observation:** The 90-day time limit on changing enrollment from one plan to another does not appear to affect the 60-day time limit applicable to electing COBRA coverage generally.

FTC 2d References are to Federal Tax Coordinator 2d
FIN References are to RIA's Analysis of Federal Taxes: Income
USTR References are to United States Tax Reporter: Income
PE References are to Pension Explanations

An AEI may elect to enroll in different coverage only if:

(1) the employer involved has determined that it will permit AEIs to enroll in different coverage;

(2) the premium for the different coverage isn't more than the premium for coverage in which the individual was enrolled at the time the qualifying event occurred;

(3) the different coverage elected is coverage that also is offered to the active employees of the employer at the time the election is made; and

(4) the different coverage isn't—

(i) coverage that provides only dental, vision, counseling, or referral services (or a combination of such services);

(ii) a health flexible spending account (FSA); or

(iii) coverage that provides benefits for services or treatments furnished in an on-site medical facility maintained by the employer and that consists primarily of first-aid services, prevention and wellness care, or similar care (or a combination of such care). (2009 Recovery Act §3001(a)(1)(B)(ii))

☐ **Effective:** For periods of COBRA continuation coverage beginning after Feb. 17, 2009. (Com Rept, see ¶ 5082)

¶ 304. Recapture of COBRA premium assistance provided to high income taxpayers

Code Sec. None, 2009 Recovery Act § 3001(b)
Generally effective: Tax years ending after Feb. 17, 2009
Committee Reports, see ¶ 5082

As part of its overhaul of the COBRA rules, the 2009 Recovery Act provides that an "assistance eligible individual" (AEI) who elects COBRA coverage under the employer's group health plan, is required to pay no more than 35% of the applicable premium for COBRA coverage, and that IRS will provide a "subsidy" for the remaining 65%, see ¶ 301.

New Law. The 2009 Recovery Act provides a recapture provision for premium assistance provided to high-income taxpayers. Under this provision, if: (a) premium assistance is provided for any COBRA continuation coverage which covers the taxpayer, the taxpayer's spouse, or any dependent of the taxpayer (as defined below) during any portion of the tax year, and (b) the taxpayer's modified adjusted gross income (MAGI; as defined below) for the tax year exceeds $125,000 ($250,000 in the case of a joint return), the taxpayer's income tax for the tax year is increased by the amount of the premium assistance (subject to a graduated phaseout, see below). (2009 Recovery Act §3001(b)(1))

⚠️ *observation:* Although the 2009 Recovery Act does not impose income limits for individuals receiving COBRA premium assistance, the premium assistance recapture provision effectively imposes a cap of $145,000 of MAGI ($290,000 for joint returns) on participants in the premium assistance program, as any premium assistance received by taxpayers with MAGI of $145,000 ($290,000 for joint returns) or over is fully recaptured.

⚠️ *illustration:* John, who is single, works as a bond trader at an investment bank. John is laid off from work on Aug. 31, 2009 and begins receiving COBRA continuation coverage effective Sept. 1, 2009. Despite his high income (2009 MAGI of $1.2 million), John is eligible for COBRA premium assistance for the period Sept. 1, 2009 through June 30, 2010. However, all of the COBRA premium assistance John receives in 2009 will be recaptured.

Due to the difficult job market, John can only find free-lance work (without benefits) in 2010, so his MAGI falls below $125,000. Thus, the COBRA premium assistance John receives in 2010 will not be subject to recapture.

For purposes of the premium assistance recapture rules, "dependent" is defined in Code Sec. 152, but without regard to:

... Code Sec. 152(b)(1) (the requirement that a taxpayer's dependent cannot claim a dependent on his or her own return for the tax year),

... Code Sec. 152(b)(2) (the requirement that an individual filing a joint return with his or her spouse for a tax year not be claimed as a dependent of another taxpayer for that same year), and

... Code Sec. 152(d)(1)(B) (the requirement that the gross income of a relative qualifying as a dependent not exceed the exemption amount for the year). (2009 Recovery Act §3001(b)(1))

For purposes of the premium assistance recapture rules, MAGI means the taxpayer's adjusted gross income (as determined in Code Sec. 62) for the tax year, increased by any amount excluded from his gross income under:

... the Code Sec. 911 foreign earned income exclusion,

... the Code Sec. 931 exclusion for income from U.S. possessions, or

... the Code Sec. 933 exclusion for income from Puerto Rico. (2009 Recovery Act §3001(b)(4))

FTC 2d References are to Federal Tax Coordinator 2d
FIN References are to RIA's Analysis of Federal Taxes: Income
USTR References are to United States Tax Reporter: Income
PE References are to Pension Explanations

Phase-in of recapture. For taxpayers whose MAGI for the tax year is less than $145,000 ($290,000 for joint returns), the increase in the tax imposed by the premium assistance recapture rules must not exceed the phase-in percentage of such increase (determined without regard to this phase-in rule). "Phase-in percentage" means the ratio (expressed as a percentage) obtained by dividing—

(i) the excess of the taxpayer's MAGI over $125,000 ($250,000 for joint returns), by

(ii) $20,000 ($40,000 for joint returns). (2009 Recovery Act §3001(b)(2))

> 🔴 *illustration:* Ima Ponzi, who is single, worked as a bond rating analyst at the firm AAA-R-Us. Due to loss of business caused by AAA's inappropriately high ratings of dodgy investment vehicles, Ima is laid off from work on March 31, 2009 and begins receiving COBRA continuation coverage effective April 1, 2009. Ima is eligible for, and accepts $2,000 in COBRA premium assistance for the period April 1, 2009 through November 30, 2010. However, due to the income generated by Ima's new career as an expert witness in lawsuits brought against her former employer, some (or all) of the COBRA premium assistance she receives in 2009 may be recaptured as follows, if Ima's 2009 MAGI is
>
> - $125,000, there will be no recapture amount [$125,000 − $125,000 = 0; 0 ÷ $20,000 = 0%; $2,000 × 0% = $0];
> - $130,000, the recapture amount will be $500 [$130,000 − $125,000 = $5,000; $5,000 ÷ $20,000 = 25%; $2,000 × 25% = $500];
> - $135,000, the recapture amount will be $1,000 [$135,000 − $125,000 = $10,000; $10,000 ÷ $20,000 = 50%; $2,000 × 50% = $1,000];
> - $140,000, the recapture amount will be $1,500 [$140,000 − $125,000 = $15,000; $15,000 ÷ $20,000 = 75%; $2,000 × 75% = $2,000]
> - $145,000 or more, all $2,000 is recaptured.

Despite the definition of "assistance eligible individual" provided in Sec. 3001(a)(3) of the 2009 Recovery Act (see ¶ 301) an individual will not be treated as an AEI for purposes of the COBRA premium assistance rules of the Act and Code Sec. 6432 (see ¶ 308) if the individual—

(1) makes a permanent election (in the manner to be set out by IRS) to waive the right to premium assistance, and

(2) notifies the entity to whom premiums are reimbursed under Code Sec. 6432—typically, the employer maintaining the group health plan, or the insurer providing coverage for the plan—of the waiver election. (2009 Recovery Act §3001(b)(3))

In determining a taxpayer's regular tax liability under Code Sec. 26(b), the tax increase resulting from the premium assistance recapture rules will not be treated as a tax imposed under chapter 1 of the Code. (2009 Recovery Act §3001(b)(5))

> **⊘** *observation:* A taxpayer's regular tax liability for the tax year is the tax imposed by chapter 1 of the Code, and specifically excludes certain other taxes, such as the alternative minimum tax. As nonrefundable tax credits typically only offset a taxpayer's regular tax liability, the increase in taxes resulting from the premium assistance recapture rules cannot be offset by these credits.

Finally, IRS is required to issue regulations or other guidance as necessary or appropriate to carry out the premium assistance recapture rules, including requirements that the entity to whom premiums are reimbursed under Code Sec. 6432(a) (see above) report to IRS, and to each assistance eligible individual, the amount of premium assistance provided for each such individual. (2009 Recovery Act §3001(b)(6))

☐ **Effective:** Tax years ending after Feb. 17, 2009. (2009 Recovery Act §3001(b)(7))

¶ 305. COBRA subsidy excluded from income

Code Sec. 139C, as added by 2009 Recovery Act § 3001(a)(15)(A)
Generally effective: Tax years ending after Feb. 17, 2009
Committee Reports, see ¶ 5082

As part of its overhaul of the COBRA rules, the 2009 Recovery Act provides that an "assistance eligible individual" (AEI) who elects COBRA coverage under the employer's group health plan, is required to pay no more than 35% of the applicable premium for COBRA coverage, and that IRS will provide a "subsidy" for the remaining 65%, see ¶ 301.

New Law. The 2009 Recovery Act establishes that any premium reduction provided is excluded from the gross income of assistance eligible individuals, as defined in Sec. 3002(a) of the "Health Insurance Assistance for the Unemployed Act of 2009" [sic]. (Code Sec. 139C as added by 2009 Recovery Act §3001(a)(15)(A))

> **⊘** *observation:* The reference to Sec. 3002(a) of the of the Health Insurance Assistance for the Unemployed Act of 2009 for the definition of assistance eligible individuals is a drafting error that should refer to

FTC 2d References are to Federal Tax Coordinator 2d
FIN References are to RIA's Analysis of Federal Taxes: Income
USTR References are to United States Tax Reporter: Income
PE References are to Pension Explanations

83

Sec. 3001(a) of the 2009 Recovery Act. This will most likely be fixed when technical corrections to the Act are issued.

observation: Thus, a taxpayer's receipt of the subsidy for COBRA continuation coverage is not subject to federal income tax.

For the recapture of premium assistance for high income taxpayers, see ¶ 304.

However, for purposes of determining the gross income of the employer and the welfare benefit plan of which the group health plan is a part, the amount of the premium reduction is to be treated as an employee contribution to the group health plan. (Com Rept, see ¶ 5082)

Further, despite any other provision of law to the contrary, the subsidy may not be considered as income or resources in determining the recipient's eligibility for, or the amount of, any public benefits provided under federal or state law, including that of any political subdivision. (Com Rept, see ¶ 5082)

☐ **Effective:** Tax years ending after Feb. 17, 2009.
(2009 Recovery Act §3001(a)(15)(C))

¶ 306. Eligible individuals receiving COBRA premium assistance cannot claim the health coverage tax credit

Code Sec. 35(g)(9), as amended by 2009 Recovery Act § 3001(a)(14)(A)
Generally effective: Tax years ending after Feb. 17, 2009
Committee Reports, see ¶ 5082

To help taxpayers cope with the loss of their jobs due to increased imports from, or a shift in production to, foreign countries, the Trade Act of 1974 (as amended) provides certain benefits, such as job development or referrals. In addition, the 2002 Trade Act provides for a refundable tax credit (the Health Coverage Tax Credit, or HCTC) of 65% of the amount paid for their coverage and that of "qualifying family members" under COBRA continuation coverage and various state-based group health coverage for eligible coverage months beginning in the tax year. To be eligible for the HCTC, a taxpayer must be an "eligible individual." (FTC 2d/FIN ¶ A-4230, ¶ A-4231 *et seq.*; USTR ¶ 354; TaxDesk ¶ 569,400 *et seq.*)

IRS was required to establish a program for making payment of the HCTC in advance (i.e., before the filing of the taxpayer's return), on behalf of "certified individuals" to providers of qualified health insurance (i.e., COBRA continuation coverage, certain state-based coverage and certain individual health insurance) for those individuals. For this purpose, a certified individual is anyone for whom a qualified health insurance costs credit eligibility certificate is in effect (FTC 2d/FIN ¶ H-4870, ¶ H-4871; USTR ¶ 75,274; TaxDesk ¶ 569,401)

As part of its overhaul of the COBRA rules, the 2009 Recovery Act provides that an "assistance eligible individual" (AEI) who elects COBRA coverage under the employer's group health plan, is required to pay no more than 35% of the applicable premium for COBRA coverage, and that IRS will provide a "subsidy" for the remaining 65%, see ¶ 301.

New Law. The 2009 Recovery Act provides that for any month for which an assistance eligible individual receives a COBRA premium reduction under Sec. 3002(a) of the "Health Insurance Assistance for the Unemployed Act of 2009"[sic]—the subsidy described above—he will not be an eligible individual, a certified individual, or a qualifying family member for purposes of the HCTC and the advance payment of the HCTC. (Code Sec. 35(g)(9) as amended by 2009 Recovery Act §3001(a)(14)(A))

> *observation:* The reference to Sec. 3002(a) of the of the Health Insurance Assistance for the Unemployed Act of 2009 for the COBRA premium reduction provision is a drafting error that should refer to Sec. 3001(a) of the 2009 Recovery Act. This will most likely be fixed when technical corrections to the Act are issued.

> *observation:* Thus, a taxpayer receiving the premium reduction subsidy for COBRA continuation coverage provided under the 2009 Act is not eligible for the HCTC or the advance payment of the HCTC.

☐ **Effective:** Tax years ending after Feb. 17, 2009.
(2009 Recovery Act §3001(a)(14)(B))

¶ 307. Terminated workers must be notified of right to COBRA continuation benefits subsidy

Code Sec. 4980B(f)(6)(D), 2009 Recovery Act § 3001(a)(7)
ERISA § 606(4), 2009 Recovery Act § 3001(a)(7)
Generally effective: Feb. 17, 2009
Committee Reports, see ¶ 5082

Under the COBRA provisions of the Internal Revenue Code and ERISA, following the qualifying event of a covered employee's termination of service or reduction of hours that causes the loss of coverage under a group health plan, the group health plan administrator must, within 14 days of being provided notice of the qualifying event, provide each qualified beneficiary with a notice that explains the beneficiaries' right to elect COBRA continuation coverage, the coverage that may be elected, the duration of the coverage, and how much the

FTC 2d References are to Federal Tax Coordinator 2d
FIN References are to RIA's Analysis of Federal Taxes: Income
USTR References are to United States Tax Reporter: Income
PE References are to Pension Explanations

coverage will cost and how and when it must be paid. FTC 2d/FIN ¶ H-1313; USTR ¶ 49,80B4.10; PE ¶ 49,80B4.10.

As part of its overhaul of the COBRA rules, the 2009 Recovery Act provides that an "assistance eligible individual" (AEI) who elects COBRA coverage under the employer's group health plan is required to pay no more than 35% of the applicable premium for COBRA coverage, and that IRS will provide a "subsidy" for the remaining 65%, see ¶ 301. (FTC 2d/FIN ¶ H-1250; USTR ¶ 49,80B4.04; PE ¶ 49,80B4.04)

New Law. The Act provides that the requirement to provide a notice of COBRA continuation coverage will not be treated as met unless the notice includes an additional notification about the availability of the premium reduction subsidy with respect to that COBRA coverage, and a description of the option to enroll in different coverage offered if so permitted by the employer (see ¶ 303). (2009 Recovery Act §3001(a)(7)(A)(i)) The Act clarifies that a violation of this additional notice provision is also a violation of the notice requirements of the underlying COBRA provision. (Com Rept, see ¶ 5082)

For COBRA continuation to which the notice provision does *not* apply, DOL, in consultation with IRS and the Department of Health and Human Services must, in coordination with administrators of the group health plans or other entities that provide or administer the COBRA coverage involved, provide rules requiring such a notice. (2009 Recovery Act §3001(a)(7)(A)(ii))

> *observation:* By covering plans to which the COBRA provisions do not apply, the Act is requiring that plans exempt from COBRA, such as plans maintained by the Federal government, will be subject to similar rules to the Act's requirements for additional notification.

The additional notification requirement may be met either by amending existing notice forms, or by including a separate document with the notice otherwise required. (2009 Recovery Act §3001(a)(7)(A)(iii))

Each required additional notification must include:

(1) the forms necessary for establishing eligibility for premium reduction;

(2) the name, address, and telephone number needed to contact the plan administrator and any other person maintaining relevant information in connection with the premium reduction;

(3) a description of the extended election period discussed at ¶ 302;

(4) a description of the obligation of the qualified beneficiary to notify the plan providing continuation coverage of eligibility for subsequent coverage under another group health plan or Medicare, and the penalty for failure to do so (see ¶ 309);

(5) a description, displayed in a prominent manner, of the qualified beneficiary's right to a reduced premium and any conditions on entitlement to the reduced premium; and

(6) a description of the option of the qualified beneficiary to enroll in different coverage offered, if so permitted by the employer (see ¶ 303). (2009 Recovery Act §3001(a)(7)(B))

In addition to providing the additional notice to persons who become eligible for COBRA coverage during the subsidy period, the plan administrator (or other entity) involved with a group health plan must, by Apr. 18, 2009, also provide the additional notification to any AEI who had elected COBRA coverage as of Feb. 17, 2009, and to any individual eligible to take advantage of the extended election period (see ¶ 302). Failure to provide such notice is treated as a failure to meet the COBRA notice requirements. (2009 Recovery Act §3001(a)(7)(C))

No later than Mar. 19, 2009, DOL, in consultation with IRS and the Department of Health and Human Services, must prescribe models for the required additional notification (other than the notification for federal employees described below). (2009 Recovery Act §3001(a)(7)(D)(i))

No later than Mar. 19, 2009, the Office of Personnel Management must prescribe a model for the required additional notification required to be provided to federal employees. (2009 Recovery Act §3001(a)(7)(D)(ii))

☐ **Effective:** Feb. 17, 2009

¶ 308. Reimbursement mechanism provided to plans for COBRA premiums that are not paid by COBRA subsidized individuals

Code Sec. 6432, as added by 2009 Recovery Act § 3001(a)(12)(A)
Generally effective: For COBRA premiums provided for periods of coverage beginning on or after Feb. 17, 2009.
Committee Reports, see ¶ 5082

As part of its overhaul of the COBRA rules, the 2009 Recovery Act provides that an "assistance eligible individual" (AEI) who elects COBRA coverage under the employer's group health plan is required to pay no more than 35% of the applicable premium for COBRA coverage, and that IRS will provide a "subsidy" for the remaining 65%, see ¶ 301. (FTC 2d/FIN ¶ H-1250; USTR ¶ 4980B4.04; PE ¶ 4980B-4.04)

FTC 2d References are to Federal Tax Coordinator 2d
FIN References are to RIA's Analysis of Federal Taxes: Income
USTR References are to United States Tax Reporter: Income
PE References are to Pension Explanations

New Law. The Act provides a mechanism for reimbursing the person to which premiums are payable for the difference between the full premium and the amount paid by an AEI. Specifically, the person to which premiums are payable under COBRA continuation coverage must be reimbursed for the amount of the premiums that are not paid by AEIs on account of the 65% premium reduction. (Code Sec. 6432(a) as added by 2009 Recovery Act §3001(a)(12)(A))

The person to whom premiums are payable will be, except as IRS provides otherwise, either the plan, the employer, or the insurer. Specifically, the person entitled to reimbursement is:

(1) in the case of a group health plan that is a multiemployer plan (as defined by ERISA §3(37)), the plan;

(2) in the case of a group health plan which is not a multiemployer plan and which is subject to the COBRA continuation provisions contained in the Code, ERISA, Public Health Service Act, or civil service provisions of the U.S. Code, and under which some or all of the coverage is not provided by insurance, the employer; and

(3) in the case of any group health plan not described in (1) or (2) above, the insurer providing the coverage under the plan. (Code Sec. 6432(b))

A person entitled to reimbursement and who files a claim for reimbursement at such time and in such manner as IRS may require will be treated as having paid to IRS, on the date that the AEI's premium payment is received, payroll taxes in an amount equal to the portion of the reimbursement relating to that premium. To the extent that the amount treated as paid exceeds the amount of the person's liability for payroll taxes, IRS will credit or refund the excess in the same manner as if it were an overpayment of payroll taxes. (Code Sec. 6432(c)(1))

Any overstatement of the reimbursement to which the person is entitled and any amount paid by IRS as a result of an overstatement will be treated as an underpayment of payroll taxes by that person and may be assessed and collected by IRS in the same manner as payroll taxes. (Code Sec. 6432(c)(2))

Thus, IRS can assert appropriate penalties for failing to truthfully account for the reimbursement. However, it is not intended that any portion of the reimbursement is taken into account when determining the amount of any penalty to be imposed against any person, required to collect, truthfully account for, and pay over any tax under Code Sec. 6672 (dealing with penalties for failure to collect and pay over tax). (Com Rept, see ¶ 5082)

No person is eligible for this reimbursement, however, until the person has received the reduced premium payment from the AEI. (Code Sec. 6432(c)(3))

For purposes of determining a person's payroll tax liability, "payroll taxes" includes amounts deducted and withheld for a payroll period for an employee's federal income and FICA taxes, and amounts imposed for a payroll period for the employer's share of FICA taxes. (Code Sec. 6432(d)(1))

A "person" includes any governmental entity. (Code Sec. 6432(d)(2))

Any person entitled to reimbursement for any period must submit reports, at such time and in such manner as IRS may require, including (1) an attestation of the involuntary termination of employment of each covered employee on the basis of whose termination entitlement to reimbursement of premiums is claimed, (2) a report of the amount of payroll taxes offset for a reporting period and the estimated offsets of such taxes for the subsequent reporting period, and (3) a report containing the TINs of all covered employees, the amount of subsidy reimbursed with respect to each covered employee and qualified beneficiaries, and a designation with respect to each covered employee as to whether the subsidy reimbursement is for coverage of one individual or of two or more individuals. (Code Sec. 6432(e))

IRS is authorized to issue regulations or other guidance as may be necessary or appropriate to carry out the reimbursement provisions, including the reporting requirement or the establishment of other methods for verifying the correct payments and credits. In addition, IRS must issue regulations or guidance with respect to applying the reimbursement provisions to group health plans that are multiemployer plans. (Code Sec. 6432(f))

In the case of an AEI who pays the full premium amount required for CO-BRA for the first period to which the subsidy applies or the immediately subsequent period, the person to whom the payment is made must:

(1) make a reimbursement payment to the AEI for the amount of the premium paid in excess of the amount required to be paid; or

(2) provide credit to the AEI for that amount in a manner that reduces one or more subsequent premium payments that the AEI is required to pay for the coverage involved.

The person reimbursing or crediting the individual will in turn be reimbursed as provided for above.

Unless it is reasonable to believe that the credit for excess payment described in (2) above will be used by the AEI within 180 days of the date on which the person paid received the full premium payment, that person must make the payment required to the AEI within 60 days of that full payment. However, if, as of any day within the 180-day period, it is no longer reasonable to believe that the credit will be used during that period, payment equal to the remainder of the

FTC 2d References are to Federal Tax Coordinator 2d
FIN References are to RIA's Analysis of Federal Taxes: Income
USTR References are to United States Tax Reporter: Income
PE References are to Pension Explanations

credit outstanding must be made to the AEI within 60 days of that day. (2009 Recovery Act §S3001(b)(12)(E))

It is intended that the reimbursement arrangements not be mirrored in the U.S. possessions that have mirror income tax codes (the Commonwealth of the Northern Mariana Islands, Guam, and the Virgin Islands). Rather, Congress intends that reimbursement have direct application to persons in those possessions. Moreover, it is intended that income tax withholding payable to the government of any possession (American Samoa, the Commonwealth of the Northern Mariana Islands, the Commonwealth of Puerto Rico, Guam, or the Virgin Islands) will not be reduced. A person liable for both federal FICA withholding and income tax withholding payable to a possession government will be credited or refunded any excess of (1) the amount of FICA taxes treated as paid under the reimbursement rule of the provision over (2) the amount of the person's liability for those FICA taxes. (Com Rept, see ¶ 5082)

☐ **Effective:** For COBRA premiums to which 2009 Recovery Act §3001(a)(1)(A) applies (2009 Recovery Act §3001(a)(12)(D)), i.e., for premiums provided for periods of coverage beginning on or after Feb. 17, 2009, see ¶ 301.

¶ 309. Penalty imposed on COBRA-subsidized individuals who fail to notify group health plan when they become eligible for other health coverage

Code Sec. None, 2009 Recovery Act § 3001(a)(2)(C)
Code Sec. 6720C, as added by 2009 Recovery Act § 3001(a)(13)(A)
Generally effective: Feb. 17, 2009
Committee Reports, see ¶ 5082

As part of its overhaul of the COBRA rules, the 2009 Recovery Act provides that an "assistance eligible individual" (AEI) who elects COBRA coverage under the employer's group health plan is required to pay no more than 35% of the applicable premium for COBRA coverage, and that IRS will provide a "subsidy" for the remaining 65%, see ¶ 301.

The Act also provides that eligibility ends when an AEI becomes eligible for coverage under another group health plan—other than a plan that provides certain limited or specified coverage, i.e., dental-only or vision-only coverage, health flexible spending arrangements, health reimbursement arrangements, etc.—or Medicare, see ¶ 301. (FTC 2d/FIN ¶ H-1250; USTR ¶ 49,80B4.04; PE ¶ 4980B4.04)

New Law. Under the Act, an AEI who is no longer eligible for the subsidized COBRA premium because of eligibility for coverage under another group health plan or Medicare (see ¶ 301) must notify the group health plan providing the subsidized COBRA coverage. The notice must be in writing and be provided in the time and manner that DOL may specify. (2009 Recovery Act §3001(a)(2)(C))

The notice must inform the group health plan providing COBRA coverage of the eligibility under the other plan or Medicare. (Com Rept, see ¶ 5082)

> **observation:** No notice need be given where an AEI receiving a CO-BRA subsidy becomes eligible for coverage that provides only certain limited or specified coverage (see above and at ¶ 301).

Penalty for failure to provide notice. Any person who is required to notify the group health plan providing subsidized COBRA coverage of eligibility for other health coverage (as described above), but fails to provide the notice in the time and manner required by DOL, must pay a penalty of 110% of the premium reduction (i.e., the subsidy described above) after termination of eligibility for the subsidized COBRA coverage. (Code Sec. 6720C(a) as added by 2009 Recovery Act §3001(a)(13)(A))

> **illustration:** John is laid off from work in January of 2009, and is eligible to elect COBRA continuation coverage. The cost to his employer for the coverage is $100 per month. Under pre-Act law, John's COBRA premium for that coverage was $102 per month (i.e., 102% of the regular premium). Under the Act, John has to pay only 35% of the $102 premium, i.e., $35.70. The $66.30 balance is the "subsidy" that the Act provides.
>
> On June 1, 2009, John is hired by an employer that provides group health plan coverage, for which John is immediately eligible. This ends John's eligibility for the COBRA premium subsidy. John continues to pay for coverage under his former employer's group health plan, because his COBRA coverage is more comprehensive than his new employer's plan's coverage. John fails to notify his former employer's group health plan of his eligibility for other group health plan coverage, and continues to pay only $35.70 per month for this COBRA coverage, until the end of 2009.
>
> The penalty on John for failure to notify the group health plan providing COBRA coverage is $510.51 (i.e., 110% × ($102 − $35.70) × 7 months, June through December of 2009).

No penalty will be imposed if it is shown that the failure to provide the required notice is due to reasonable cause and not to willful neglect. (Code Sec. 6720C(b))

FTC 2d References are to Federal Tax Coordinator 2d
FIN References are to RIA's Analysis of Federal Taxes: Income
USTR References are to United States Tax Reporter: Income
PE References are to Pension Explanations

The penalty applies only if the subsidy in the form of the premium reduction is actually provided to a qualified beneficiary (i.e., to an AEI receiving COBRA benefits) for a month that he is not eligible for the reduction. If, for example, the beneficiary becomes eligible for other coverage and stops paying the reduced COBRA continuation premium, the penalty generally will not apply. If, however, the beneficiary continues to pay the reduced premium and does not notify the group health plan of his other eligibility, the penalty will generally arise. (Com Rept, see ¶ 5082)

☐ **Effective:** Feb. 17, 2009. However, the penalty provision is effective for notification failures occurring after Feb. 17, 2009. (2009 Recovery Act §3001(a)(13)(C))

¶ 400. Compensation & Benefits

¶ 401. Scope of $500,000 compensation deduction limit on TARP recipients is broadened; other non-tax executive compensation restrictions are imposed

Code Sec. 162(m)(5), 2009 Recovery Act § 7001
Code Sec. None, 2009 Recovery Act § 7002
Generally effective: Feb. 17, 2009
Committee Reports, see ¶ 5084

A publicly held corporation can't deduct more than $1 million per year of applicable employee remuneration (defined below) paid to a covered employee. (FTC 2d/FIN ¶ H-3776; USTR ¶ 1624.009; TaxDesk ¶ 276,001.1) "Covered employee" means the principal executive officer (PEO) or someone acting in that capacity and the three highest paid officers other than the PEO or principal financial officer (PFO). (FTC 2d/FIN ¶ H-3780; USTR ¶ 1624.009; TaxDesk ¶ 276,001.1)

"Applicable employee remuneration" means a covered employee's aggregate remuneration for services performed (during the deduction year or another tax year) that would be deductible entirely for the tax year if the $1 million limit didn't apply. But it doesn't include commissions generated directly by the executive's performance, certain other performance-based compensation, certain grandfathered contracts, qualified plan contributions, and certain excludable employee fringe benefits. (FTC 2d/FIN ¶ H-3781; USTR ¶ 1624.009; TaxDesk ¶ 276,001.1)

Under Code Sec. 162(m)(5), the $1 million deduction limit is reduced to $500,000 for remuneration paid to covered executives—generally, the chief executive officer (CEO), chief financial officer (CFO), and the three highest paid other officers of an "applicable employer." (FTC 2d/FIN ¶ H-3775, ¶ H-3821; USTR ¶ 1624.009; TaxDesk ¶ 276,001.2) The $500,000 limit applies to the covered executive's applicable employee remuneration, but without the exclusions for commissions, performance-based compensation, and grandfathered contracts. (FTC 2d/FIN ¶ H-3823; USTR ¶ 1624.009; TaxDesk ¶ 276,001.8)

Under pre-2009 Recovery Act law, an "applicable employer" meant a financial institution (even if not publicly held or not incorporated) from whom troubled assets were acquired under the Troubled Assets Relief Program (TARP) established by the 2008 Economic Stabilization Act, if the aggregate amount of acquired assets exceeded $300 million. Assets acquired through direct purchase

FTC 2d References are to Federal Tax Coordinator 2d
FIN References are to RIA's Analysis of Federal Taxes: Income
USTR References are to United States Tax Reporter: Income
PE References are to Pension Explanations

by the Treasury Department were taken into account in meeting the $300 million threshold. However, if all the acquisitions were direct purchases, the $500,000 limit didn't apply. (FTC 2d/FIN ¶ H-3821.1; USTR ¶ 1624.009; TaxDesk ¶ 276,001.3)

The $500,000 limit applied for any "applicable tax year," i.e., the first employer tax year that included any part of the TARP authorities period in which the $300 million amount (excluding direct purchases) was cumulatively exceeded, and any later employer tax year that included any part of the TARP authorities period. The "TARP authorities period" was the period from Oct. 3, 2008 to Dec. 31, 2009, but could be extended until Oct. 3, 2010. (FTC 2d/FIN ¶ H-3821.3; USTR ¶ 1624.009; TaxDesk ¶ 276,001.5)

2008 Economic Stabilization Act § 111 also included a set of executive compensation and corporate governance requirements that applied to financial institutions selling troubled assets under TARP.

New Law. The 2009 Recovery Act provides that each TARP recipient is subject to the $500,000 compensation deduction limit of Code Sec. 162(m)(5), as applicable, during the period in which any obligation arising from financial assistance provided under TARP remains outstanding. (2008 Economic Stabilization Act § 111(b)(1) (Sec. 111(b)(1), PL 110-343, 10/3/2008) as amended by 2009 Recovery Act §7001)

For this purpose, "TARP recipient" means any entity that has received or will receive financial assistance under TARP. (2008 Economic Stabilization Act § 111(a)(3) as amended by § 7001)

> *observation:* The term "TARP" means the Troubled Asset Relief Program established under 2008 Economic Stabilization Act § 101. (2008 Economic Stabilization Act § 3(8))

The period in which any obligation arising from financial assistance provided under TARP remains outstanding doesn't include any period during which the federal government only holds warrants to purchase the TARP recipient's common stock. (2008 Economic Stabilization Act § 111(a)(5) as amended by § 7001)

> *observation:* The 2009 Recovery Act expands the scope of the $500,000 compensation deduction limit in the following ways:
>
> . . . The $500,000 limit applies to "any entity," not just to financial institutions.
>
> . . . The $500,000 limit applies to all entities that have received or will receive TARP financial assistance of any type or amount. It isn't restricted to institutions from which more than $300 million of troubled assets were acquired, and there is no exception for institutions from which assets were acquired only through direct purchase.

... The $500,000 limit will remain in effect as long as any obligation arising from TARP financial assistance remains outstanding (with the exception of warrants to purchase common stock). It isn't restricted to employer tax years that include any part of the "TARP authorities period," which would have ended by Oct. 3, 2010.

Non-tax executive compensation and corporate governance rules for TARP recipients broadened. In addition to the above tax rules, the 2009 Recovery Act also expands the non-tax executive compensation and corporate governance rules that apply to TARP recipients.

Treasury standards for executive compensation and corporate governance. The Secretary must require each TARP recipient to meet appropriate standards for executive compensation and corporate governance. (2008 Economic Stabilization Act § 111(b)(2) as amended by § 7001) Each TARP recipient is subject to those standards during the period in which any obligation arising from financial assistance provided under TARP remains outstanding. (2008 Economic Stabilization Act § 111(b)(1)(A) as amended by § 7001)

> ⓡ *observation:* The term "Secretary" means the Secretary of the Treasury. (2008 Economic Stabilization Act § 3(7))

The standards to be established by the Treasury Secretary must include the following (2008 Economic Stabilization Act § 111(b)(3) as amended by § 7001):

Exclusion of incentives for excessive risk-taking. The Treasury standards must set limits on compensation that exclude incentives for the TARP recipient's senior executive officers to take unnecessary and excessive risks that threaten the recipient's value during the period in which any obligation arising from TARP assistance is outstanding. (2008 Economic Stabilization Act § 111(b)(3)(A) as amended by § 7001)

The term "senior executive officer" means one of the top five most highly paid executives of a public company whose compensation must be disclosed under the Securities Exchange Act of 1934, and any regulations under that Act, and the counterparts of those executives in non-public companies. (2008 Economic Stabilization Act § 111(a)(1) as amended by § 7001)

Clawback of compensation based on inaccurate statements. The Treasury standards must provide for the TARP recipient to recover any bonus, retention award, or incentive compensation paid to a senior executive officer and any of the next 20 most highly-compensated employees of the TARP recipient based

FTC 2d References are to Federal Tax Coordinator 2d
FIN References are to RIA's Analysis of Federal Taxes: Income
USTR References are to United States Tax Reporter: Income
PE References are to Pension Explanations

on statements of earnings, revenues, gains, or other criteria that are later found to be materially inaccurate. (2008 Economic Stabilization Act § 111(b)(3)(B) as amended by § 7001) Under pre-2009 Recovery Act law, this requirement applied to only the five senior executive officers. (Com Rept, see ¶ 5084)

"Golden parachute payments" prohibited. The Treasury standards must prohibit a TARP recipient from making any golden parachute payment to a senior executive officer or any of the next five most highly-compensated employees of the TARP recipient during the period in which any obligation arising from TARP assistance is outstanding. (2008 Economic Stabilization Act § 111(b)(3)(C) as amended by § 7001) Under pre-2009 Recovery Act law, this prohibition applied only to the five senior executive officers. (Com Rept, see ¶ 5084)

The term "golden parachute payment" means any payment to a senior executive officer for departure from a company for any reason, except for payments for services performed or benefits accrued. (2008 Economic Stabilization Act § 111(a)(2) as amended by § 7001)

> **🅡🅘🅐** *observation:* Thus, this rule prohibits making any severance payment in any amount to the 10 most highly-compensated employees, except for payments for services performed or benefits accrued. In contrast, the golden parachute rules of Code Sec. 280G apply to only "parachute payments" as specifically defined and "excess" payments above a base amount (see FTC 2d/FIN ¶ H-3825; USTR ¶ 280G4; TaxDesk ¶ 279,000).

> In addition, the golden parachute rules of Code Sec. 280G don't prohibit excess parachute payments, though they do disallow a deduction to the payor and impose a 20% excise tax on the recipient. The rule discussed above prohibits any golden parachute payment during the relevant period.

> **🅡🅘🅐** *observation:* This statute appears to contain a technical problem. While 2008 Economic Stabilization Act § 111(b)(3)(C) prohibits golden parachute payments to senior executive officers *and* the next five most highly-compensated employees, 2008 Economic Stabilization Act § 111(a)(2) defines a "golden parachute payment" as a payment to a senior executive officer, with no mention of the next five employees.

Prohibition on bonuses and incentive compensation. The Treasury standards must prohibit TARP recipients from paying or accruing any bonus, retention award, or incentive compensation during the period in which any obligation arising from financial assistance provided under TARP is outstanding. (2008 Economic Stabilization Act § 111(b)(3)(D)(i) as amended by § 7001)

However, compensation may be paid in the form of restricted stock. (Com Rept, see ¶ 5084) Specifically, any prohibition developed under this rule won't apply to the payment of long-term restricted stock by the TARP recipient, if the long-term restricted stock (2008 Economic Stabilization Act § 111(b)(3)(D)(i) as amended by § 7001):

. . . doesn't fully vest during the period in which any obligation arising from financial assistance provided to that TARP recipient remains outstanding (2008 Economic Stabilization Act § 111(b)(3)(D)(i)(I) as amended by § 7001);

. . . has a value not greater than ⅓ of the total annual compensation of the employee receiving the stock (2008 Economic Stabilization Act § 111(b)(3)(D)(i)(II) as amended by § 7001); and

. . . is subject to any other terms and conditions that the Treasury Secretary determines are in the public interest. (2008 Economic Stabilization Act § 111(b)(3)(D)(i)(III) as amended by § 7001)

The restriction is phased in by the amount of TARP financial assistance received by the entity. (Com Rept, see ¶ 5084) Thus, if a financial institution received TARP financial assistance equal to:

. . . less than $25 million, the prohibition will apply to only the institution's most highly compensated employee. (2008 Economic Stabilization Act § 111(b)(3)(D)(ii)(I) as amended by § 7001)

. . . at least $25 million, but less than $250 million, the prohibition will apply to at least the five most highly-compensated employees of the institution, or to a higher number that the Secretary determines for any TARP recipient is in the public interest. (2008 Economic Stabilization Act § 111(b)(3)(D)(ii)(II) as amended by § 7001)

. . . at least $250 million, but less than $500 million, the prohibition will apply to the senior executive officers and at least the 10 next most highly-compensated employees, or to a higher number that the Secretary determines for any TARP recipient is in the public interest. (2008 Economic Stabilization Act § 111(b)(3)(D)(ii)(III) as amended by § 7001)

. . . $500 million or more, the prohibition will apply to the senior executive officers and at least the 20 next most highly-compensated employees, or to a higher number that the Secretary determines for any TARP recipient is in the public interest. (2008 Economic Stabilization Act § 111(b)(3)(D)(ii)(IV) as amended by § 7001)

The prohibition won't apply to any bonus payment required to be paid under a written employment contract executed on or before Feb. 11, 2009, as those

FTC 2d References are to Federal Tax Coordinator 2d
FIN References are to RIA's Analysis of Federal Taxes: Income
USTR References are to United States Tax Reporter: Income
PE References are to Pension Explanations

valid employment contracts are determined by the Treasury Secretary or the Secretary's designee. (2008 Economic Stabilization Act § 111(b)(3)(D)(iii) as amended by § 7001)

> **⊘** *observation:* This prohibition will require a departure from Wall Street's usual pattern of paying relatively low base salaries and large bonuses. An unintended consequence may be a sharp increase in the base salaries of top employees, which unlike bonuses will be payable regardless of the employee's performance for the year.

> **⊘** *observation:* Regulations may be needed to clarify how to determine the most highly-compensated employees. Because employees in the prohibited group are barred from receiving bonuses, employees with lower base salaries who aren't subject to the prohibition on bonuses may end up with higher total compensation. Those employees may themselves become subject to the prohibition on bonuses, either for the current year or the next year.

Prohibition on compensation plans that encourage manipulation. The Treasury standards must prohibit any compensation plan that would encourage manipulation of the TARP recipient's reported earnings to enhance the compensation of any of its employees. (2008 Economic Stabilization Act § 111(b)(3)(E) as amended by § 7001)

Compensation committee requirement. The Treasury standards must require TARP recipients to establish a Board Compensation Committee that meets the requirements of 2008 Economic Stabilization Act § 111(c) as amended by § 7001 (see below under "Board Compensation Committee"). (2008 Economic Stabilization Act § 111(b)(3)(F) as amended by § 7001)

Certification of compliance. The CEO and CFO (or their equivalents) of each TARP recipient must provide a written certification of compliance by the TARP recipient with the executive compensation and corporate governance requirements of 2008 Economic Stabilization Act § 111. (2008 Economic Stabilization Act § 111(b)(4) as amended by § 7001)

TARP recipients whose securities are publicly traded must provide the certification to the Securities and Exchange Commission (SEC), together with annual filings required by the securities laws. (2008 Economic Stabilization Act § 111(b)(4)(A) as amended by § 7001) Other TARP recipients must provide the certification to the Treasury Secretary. (2008 Economic Stabilization Act § 111(b)(4)(B) as amended by § 7001)

Board Compensation Committee. Each TARP recipient must establish a Board Compensation Committee, comprised entirely of independent directors, to review employee compensation plans. (2008 Economic Stabilization Act § 111(c)(1) as amended by § 7001) This committee must meet at least semiannually to discuss and evaluate employee compensation plans in light of an assessment of any risk that those plans pose to the TARP recipient. (2008 Economic Stabilization Act § 111(c)(2) as amended by § 7001)

For a TARP recipient whose common or preferred stock isn't registered under the Securities Exchange Act of 1934, and that has received $25 million or less of TARP assistance, the TARP recipient's board of directors will carry out the Board Compensation Committee's duties. (2008 Economic Stabilization Act § 111(c)(3) as amended by § 7001)

Limit on luxury expenditures. A TARP recipient's board of directors must have in place a company-wide policy regarding excessive or luxury expenditures, as identified by the Treasury Secretary. (2008 Economic Stabilization Act § 111(d) as amended by § 7001) These may include excessive expenditures on:

. . . entertainment or events (2008 Economic Stabilization Act § 111(d)(1) as amended by § 7001);

. . . office and facility renovations (2008 Economic Stabilization Act § 111(d)(2) as amended by § 7001);

. . . aviation or other transportation services (2008 Economic Stabilization Act § 111(d)(3) as amended by § 7001); or

. . . other activities or events that aren't reasonable expenditures for staff development, reasonable performance incentives, or other similar measures conducted in the normal course of the TARP recipient's business operations. (2008 Economic Stabilization Act § 111(d)(4) as amended by § 7001)

Say-on-pay. During the period in which any obligation arising from financial assistance provided under TARP remains outstanding, any proxy or consent or authorization for an annual or other meeting of the shareholders of any TARP recipient must permit a separate shareholder vote to approve the compensation of executives, as disclosed under the SEC's compensation disclosure rules. The disclosure must include the compensation discussion and analysis (CD&A), the compensation tables, and any related material. (2008 Economic Stabilization Act §§ 111(e)(1) and 111(a)(4) as amended by § 7001)

Vote is non-binding. The shareholder vote isn't binding on the TARP recipient's board of directors. It may not be construed as:

. . . overruling a decision by the board,

. . . creating or implying any additional fiduciary duty by the board, or

---

FTC 2d References are to Federal Tax Coordinator 2d
FIN References are to RIA's Analysis of Federal Taxes: Income
USTR References are to United States Tax Reporter: Income
PE References are to Pension Explanations

... restricting or limiting the shareholders' ability to make proposals for inclusion in proxy materials related to executive compensation. (2008 Economic Stabilization Act § 111(e)(2) as amended by § 7001)

SEC rules. The SEC must issue any final rules and regulations required by the above say-on-pay provisions no later than one year after Feb. 17, 2009, i.e., by Feb. 17, 2010. (2008 Economic Stabilization Act § 111(e)(3) as amended by § 7001)

Review and reimbursement of pre-Feb. 17, 2009 executive compensation. The Treasury Secretary must review bonuses, retention awards, and other compensation paid to senior executive officers and the next 20 most highly compensated employees of each entity receiving TARP assistance before Feb. 17, 2009, to determine whether any payments were inconsistent with the purposes of 2008 Economic Stabilization Act § 111 or TARP or otherwise contrary to the public interest. (2008 Economic Stabilization Act § 111(f)(1) as amended by § 7001)

If the Treasury Secretary determines that payments were inconsistent, etc., he must seek to negotiate with the TARP recipient and the employee for appropriate reimbursements to the federal government of compensation or bonuses. (2008 Economic Stabilization Act § 111(f)(2) as amended by § 7001)

Withdrawal from TARP permitted. The Treasury Secretary, in consultation with the appropriate federal banking agency, will permit a TARP recipient to repay any assistance previously provided under TARP, without regard to whether the funds have been replaced from any other source or to any waiting period. When the assistance is repaid, the Secretary will liquidate warrants associated with that assistance at the current market price. (2008 Economic Stabilization Act § 111(g) as amended by § 7001)

> *observation:* Once the TARP recipient has repaid its TARP assistance, it will no longer be subject to the executive compensation and corporate governance requirements described above.

Regulations. The Treasury Secretary is to promulgate regulations to implement 2008 Economic Stabilization Act § 111. (2008 Economic Stabilization Act § 111(h) as amended by § 7001)

Executive compensation rules don't apply to loan modifications. The Treasury Secretary isn't required to apply the above executive compensation restrictions solely in connection with any loan modification under 2008 Economic Stabilization Act § 109 (which authorizes the Secretary to facilitate loan modifications to prevent avoidable foreclosures). (2008 Economic Stabilization Act § 109(a)(2) (Sec. 109(a)(2), PL 110-343, 10/3/2008) as amended by 2009 Recovery Act §7002)

☐ **Effective:** Feb. 17, 2009.

¶ 402. Monthly exclusion for employer-provided transit passes and vanpooling benefits increased to same level as employer-provided parking, for the rest of 2009 and 2010

Code Sec. 132(f)(2), as amended by 2009 Recovery Act § 1151(a)
Generally effective: Months beginning on or after Feb. 17, 2009
Committee Reports, see ¶ 5032

An employer may exclude from an employee's income an inflation-adjusted amount of up to $120 a month (for 2009) for qualified transportation fringe benefits that the employer provides through transit passes and vanpooling.

An employer may also exclude from an employee's income up to $230 a month (for 2009) for qualified transportation fringe benefits that the employer provides through employer-provided parking. (FTC 2d/FIN ¶ H-2217; USTR ¶ 1324.08; TaxDesk ¶ 134,591; PE ¶ 132-4.08)

New Law. The 2009 Recovery Act increases the monthly exclusion for employer-provided transit passes and vanpooling to the same level as the exclusion for employer-provided parking. (Com Rept, see ¶ 5032) Specifically, the Act provides that, for any month beginning on or after the Feb. 17, 2009 and before Jan. 1, 2011, the monthly exclusion limitation for employer-provided transit and vanpooling benefits is the same as for employer-provided parking. (Code Sec. 132(f)(2) as amended by 2009 Recovery Act §1151(a))

> *observation:* Thus, if an employer provides benefits on a calendar month basis, for January and February 2009, the employer may exclude the aggregate of transit passes and vanpooling benefits from an employee's income at the rate of up to $120 a month. For March through December 2009, the employer may exclude up to $230 a month. For 2010, an employer will be able to exclude up to whatever the inflation-adjusted amount for employer-provided parking for 2010 turns out to be.

☐ **Effective:** Months beginning on or after Feb. 17, 2009. (2009 Recovery Act §1151(b))

FTC 2d References are to Federal Tax Coordinator 2d
FIN References are to RIA's Analysis of Federal Taxes: Income
USTR References are to United States Tax Reporter: Income
PE References are to Pension Explanations

¶ 403. Special enrollment and notification requirements for group health plans for Medicaid- or CHIP-eligible employees or dependents

Code Sec. 9801(f)(3), as amended by 2009 Children's Health Insurance Act § 311(a)

ERISA § 701(f)(3), as amended by 2009 Children's Health Insurance Act § 311(b)(1)(A)

ERISA § 102(b), as amended by 2009 Children's Health Insurance Act § 311(b)(1)(B)

ERISA § 502, as amended by 2009 Children's Health Insurance Act § 311(b)(1)(E)

Generally effective: April 1, 2009

Committee Reports, see ¶ 5102

Under the Children's Health Insurance Program ("CHIP") as reauthorized by the Children's Health Insurance Program Reauthorization Act of 2009 (PL 111-3), the federal Centers for Medicare and Medicaid Services (CMS) administers a program under which federal matching funds help states expand health care coverage to uninsured children. In addition, CMS oversees the Medicaid program under Title XIX of the Social Security Act, which subsidizes state provision of health care benefits to certain low-income individuals and families who fit into an eligibility group that is recognized by federal and state law. (FTC 2d/FIN ¶ H-1325; USTR ¶ 98,014; PE ¶ 9801-4)

New Law. The Children's Health Insurance Program Reauthorization Act of 2009 ("2009 CHIP") provides that group health plans must permit special enrollment arrangements for employees regarding eligibility under either Medicaid or CHIP. Specifically, a group health plan must permit an employee, or his dependent, who is eligible, but not enrolled, for coverage under the employer's group health plan, to enroll for coverage in the employer's plan if either:

(1) the employee or dependent is covered under a Medicaid plan or state CHIP, and (a) coverage of the employee or dependent is terminated as a result of loss of eligibility, and (b) the employee requests coverage under the group health plan no later than 60 days after the date coverage terminates; or

(2) the employee or dependent becomes eligible for assistance under a Medicaid plan or state CHIP (including under any waiver or demonstration project conducted under or in relation to those plans), and the employee requests coverage under the group health plan no later than 60 days after the date the employee or dependent is determined to be eligible for assistance.

(Code Sec. 9801(f)(3)(A) as amended by 2009 Children's Health Insurance Act §311(a))

In order to facilitate reaching out to employees and communicating the relationship between Medicaid and CHIP coverage and group health plan coverage, the 2009 CHIP also provides that each employer that maintains a group health plan in a state in which the Medicaid or CHIP plan provides benefits in the form of premium assistance for the purchase of coverage under a group health plan must provide each employee a written notice informing the employee of those potential opportunities for the employee or the employee's dependents then currently available in the state in which the employee resides. For purposes of complying with this provision, an employer may use a state-specific model notice (see below). (Code Sec. 9801(f)(3)(B)(i)(I)) An employer may provide this notice to employees when notifying them of health plan eligibility, concurrent with the material provided to employees in connection with an open season or election process conducted under the plan, or concurrent with the furnishing of the summary plan description. (Code Sec. 9801(f)(3)(B)(i)(II)) ERISA is amended to permit the inclusion of the model notice in the summary plan description. (ERISA §102(b) as amended by 2009 Children's Health Insurance Act § 311(b)(1)(B))

In addition to these notice requirements, the plan administrator of any group health plan that has a participant or beneficiary who is covered under Medicaid or CHIP must disclose to the state, upon request, information about the benefits available under the plan in "sufficient specificity" so that the state may make a determination concerning the cost-effectiveness of the state providing assistance through purchasing coverage, and in order for the state to provide supplemental benefits required under section 2105(c)(10)(E) of the Social Security Act. What constitutes "sufficient specificity" for these purposes will be determined under regulations issued by the Department of Health and Human Services (HHS), in consultation with IRS and DOL, that require use of the model coverage coordination disclosure form (see below). (Code Sec. 9801(f)(3)(B)(ii))

Similar changes are made to the parallel ERISA provision. (ERISA §701(f)(3) as amended by 2009 Children's Health Insurance Act § 311(b)(1)(A))

Model employee notices. The 2009 CHIP amends ERISA to provide that, not later than April 1, 2010, DOL and HHS must, in consultation with the directors of state Medicaid agencies and directors of state CHIP agencies, jointly develop national and state-specific model notices for employers to provide their employees. DOL must provide employers with the model notices so as to enable employers to comply in a timely manner with the employer notice requirements. The model notices must include information regrading how an employee may contact the state in which the employee resides for additional information

---

FTC 2d References are to Federal Tax Coordinator 2d
FIN References are to RIA's Analysis of Federal Taxes: Income
USTR References are to United States Tax Reporter: Income
PE References are to Pension Explanations

regarding potential opportunities for premium assistance, including how to apply for such assistance. (ERISA §701(f)(3)(B)(i)(II))

DOL and HHS must develop an initial model notice, and DOL must provide the notices to employers, no later than April 1, 2010. Each employer must provide the initial annual notice to its employees, beginning with the first plan year that begins after the date on which the initial model notices are first issued. (2009 Children's Health Insurance Act §311(b)(1)(D))

Noncompliance penalties. The 2009 CHIP also provides for civil penalties for violations of the notification requirements. Specifically, DOL may assess an employer a civil penalty of up to $100 a day from the date of the employer's failure to meet the requirement to provide an employee notice of the availability of state assistance. Each violation to any single employee will be treated as a separate violation. (ERISA §502(c)(9)(A) as amended by 2009 Children's Health Insurance Act § 311(b)(1)(E)(ii))

In addition, DOL may assess a plan administrator a civil penalty of up to $100 a day from the date of the plan administrator's failure to timely provide to any state the information required to be disclosed concerning participants or beneficiaries eligible for state assistance. Each violation with respect to any single participant or beneficiary will be treated as a separate violation. (ERISA §502(c)(9)(B))

Model coverage coordination disclosure form. In order to develop the model notice, DOL and HHS must, no later than June 1, 2009, jointly establish a "Medicaid, CHIP, and Employer-Sponsored Coverage Coordination Working Group" to develop a model coverage coordination disclosure form, and to identify the impediments to the effective coordination of coverage available to families that include employees of employers that maintain group health plans and members who are eligible for Medicaid or CHIP assistance or other health benefits coverage under title XXI of the Social Security Act. (2009 Children's Health Insurance Act §311(b)(1)(C)(i)(I))

To this end, the 2009 CHIP also describes what should be contained in the model disclosure form, (2009 Children's Health Insurance Act §311(b)(1)(C)(i)(II)) the makeup of the Working Group, (2009 Children's Health Insurance Act §311(b)(1)(C)(ii)) and the requirement that the Working Group issue a report no later than October 1, 2010. (2009 Children's Health Insurance Act §311(b)(1)(C)(v)).

The model coverage coordination disclosure form developed by DOL and HHS will apply for requests made by states beginning with the first plan year that begins after the date on which the model form is first issued. (2009 Children's Health Insurance Act §311(b)(1)(D))

☐ **Effective:** Except for the dates applicable to the use and development of model notices, discussed above, April 1, 2009. (2009 Children's Health Insurance Act §3(a))

FTC 2d References are to Federal Tax Coordinator 2d
FIN References are to RIA's Analysis of Federal Taxes: Income
USTR References are to United States Tax Reporter: Income
PE References are to Pension Explanations

105

¶ 500. Health Coverage Tax Credit

¶ 501. Overview of the health coverage tax credit (HCTC)

To help taxpayers cope with the loss of their jobs due to increased imports from, or a shift in production to, foreign countries, the Trade Act of 1974 (as amended) provides certain benefits, such as job development or referrals. The Trade Act of 2002 provided that "TAA-eligible individuals" are eligible for a health coverage tax credit (HCTC). (Com Rept, see ¶ 5078)

The HCTC is a refundable income tax credit based on the amount a taxpayer pays for qualified health insurance for the taxpayer and qualifying family members (spouse and dependents) for each eligible coverage month beginning in the tax year. Under pre-2009 Recovery Act law, eligible individuals could receive an HCTC of 65% of the individual's premiums for qualified health insurance of the individual and qualifying family members. (FTC 2d/FIN ¶ A-4230, ¶ A-4231; USTR ¶ 354; TaxDesk ¶ 569,401)

Qualified health insurance is continuation coverage under the Consolidated Omnibus Reconciliation Act of 1985 (COBRA), certain state-based coverage, and individual health insurance (as specially defined). An otherwise eligible individual isn't eligible for the credit for a month if the individual has "other specified coverage" (employer paid coverage and coverage under certain governmental health plans), see FTC 2d/FIN ¶ A-4230; USTR ¶ 354; TaxDesk ¶ 569,400.

The HCTC is available on an advance basis. An individual is eligible for the advance payment of the HCTC once a credit eligibility certificate is in effect, see FTC 2d/FIN ¶ H-4871; USTR ¶ 354; TaxDesk ¶ 569,408

Under pre-2009 Recovery Act law, the advance payment of the HCTC couldn't exceed 65% of the amount paid by the taxpayer for coverage of the taxpayer and qualifying family members under qualified health insurance for eligible coverage months beginning in the tax year. (FTC 2d/FIN ¶ H-4870; USTR ¶ 354; TaxDesk ¶ 569,408)

New Law. The 2009 Recovery Act modifies the HCTC to make it more favorable to eligible individuals and their qualifying family members.

• For the refundable HCTC for eligible individuals' health insurance costs being increased from 65% to 80%, see ¶ 502;

• For IRS being required to pay premiums due before the start of advance payments of the HCTC in 2009 and 2010, see ¶ 503;

FTC 2d References are to Federal Tax Coordinator 2d
FIN References are to RIA's Analysis of Federal Taxes: Income
USTR References are to United States Tax Reporter: Income
PE References are to Pension Explanations

- For eligible TAA recipients not enrolled in training programs becoming eligible for the HCTC, see ¶ 504;

- For the TAA pre-certification period rule for purposes of determining whether there's a 63-day lapse in creditable coverage, see ¶ 505;

- For family members continuing to qualify for the HCTC after certain events for coverage months beginning in 2010, see ¶ 506;

- For extension of COBRA benefits for certain TAA-eligible individuals and Pension Benefit Guaranty Corporation (PBGC) recipients, see ¶ 507;

- For the HCTC for voluntary employees' beneficiary association (VEBA) coverage before 2011, see ¶ 508;

- For the information that must be included on an HCTC cost eligibility certificate, see ¶ 509.

¶ 502. Refundable HCTC for eligible individuals' health insurance costs is increased from 65% to 80% through 2010

Code Sec. 35(a), as amended by 2009 Recovery Act § 1899A(a)(1)
Code Sec. 7527(b), as amended by 2009 Recovery Act § 1899A(a)(2)
Generally effective: Coverage months beginning on or after May 1, 2009
  and before Jan. 1, 2011
Committee Reports, see ¶ 5078

Under pre-2009 Recovery Act law, eligible individuals could receive a refundable health coverage tax credit (HCTC) of 65% of the individual's premiums for qualified health insurance of the individual and qualifying family members for eligible coverage months beginning in the tax year. (FTC 2d/FIN ¶ A-4231; USTR ¶ 354; TaxDesk ¶ 569,401) Qualifying family members are the individual's spouse and any dependents for whom the individual is entitled to claim a dependency exemption, see FTC 2d/FIN ¶ A-4235; USTR ¶ 354; TaxDesk ¶ 569,402. The credit is available on an advance basis. (FTC 2d/FIN ¶ H-4871; USTR ¶ 75,274; TaxDesk ¶ 569,401)

For a general overview of the HCTC, see ¶ 501.

New Law. The 2009 Recovery Act increases the amount of the HCTC to 80% of the amount paid by the taxpayer for coverage of the taxpayer and qualifying family members under qualified health insurance for eligible coverage months beginning before Jan. 1, 2011. (Code Sec. 35(a) as amended by 2009 Recovery Act §1899A(a)(1))

Correspondingly, the 2009 Recovery Act requires IRS to make advance payments of the HCTC only to the extent the total amount of the payments made on behalf of any individual during the tax year doesn't exceed 80% of the amount paid by the taxpayer for coverage of the taxpayer and qualifying family members under qualified health insurance for eligible coverage months beginning before Jan. 1, 2011. (Code Sec. 7527(b) as amended by 2009 Recovery Act §1899A(a)(2))

> **⊘** *observation:* Thus, under the 2009 Recovery Act, both the HCTC amount and the advance payment of the HCTC that is available from IRS are increased from 65% to 80% of the taxpayer's premiums for qualified health insurance.

☐ **Effective:** Coverage months beginning on or after the first day of the first month beginning 60 days after Feb. 17, 2009 (i.e., May 1, 2009) (2009 Recovery Act §1899A(b)) and before Jan. 1, 2011. (Code Sec. 35(a)) (Code Sec. 7527(b))

¶ 503. IRS is required to pay premiums due before start of HCTC advance payments in 2009 and 2010

Code Sec. 7527(e), as amended by 2009 Recovery Act § 1899B(a)
Generally effective: For coverage months beginning after Dec. 31, 2008 and before Jan. 1, 2011
Committee Reports, see ¶ 5078

IRS makes payments of the health coverage tax credit (HCTC) in advance (i.e., before the filing of the taxpayer's return) (see ¶ 502), on behalf of individuals who have filed the required certificate (certified individuals), to providers of qualified health insurance, i.e., continuation coverage under the Consolidated Omnibus Budget Reconciliation Act of 1985 (COBRA), certain state-based coverage and certain individual health insurance, for those individuals. (FTC 2d/ FIN ¶ H-4871; USTR ¶ 75,274; TaxDesk ¶ 569,408) Under pre-2009 Recovery Act law, there was no provision for retroactive payments of premiums for qualified individuals.

For a general overview of the HCTC, see ¶ 501.

New Law. The 2009 Recovery Act require IRS to make, under its advance payment program, one or more retroactive payments on behalf of certified individuals in an aggregate amount equal to 80% of the premiums for coverage of the taxpayer and qualifying family members under qualified health insurance for eligible coverage months occurring before the first month for which an advance payment is made on behalf of that individual. (Code Sec. 7527(e)(1) as amended by 2009 Recovery Act §1899B(a)) The amount of any retroactive pay-

FTC 2d References are to Federal Tax Coordinator 2d
FIN References are to RIA's Analysis of Federal Taxes: Income
USTR References are to United States Tax Reporter: Income
PE References are to Pension Explanations

ment must be reduced by the amount of any payment made to the taxpayer for purchase of qualified health insurance under a national emergency grant under Sec. 173(f) of the Workforce Investment Act of 1998 for a tax year including the eligible coverage months occurring before the first month for which an advance payment is made on behalf of that individual. (Code Sec. 7527(e)(2))

This provision applies for eligible coverage months beginning before Jan. 1, 2011. (Code Sec. 7527(e)) Thus, it doesn't apply to months beginning after Dec. 31, 2010. (Com Rept, see ¶ 5078)

☐ **Effective:** For coverage months beginning after Dec. 31, 2008 (2009 Recovery Act §1899B(b)) and before Jan. 1, 2011. (Code Sec. 7527(e)) But IRS isn't required to make any payments until after the date that is six months after Feb. 17, 2009 (i.e., Aug. 18, 2009). (2009 Recovery Act §1899B(c))

¶ 504. Eligible TAA recipients not enrolled in training programs are eligible for the HCTC

Code Sec. 35(c)(2)(B), as amended by 2009 Recovery Act § 1899C(a)
Generally effective: Coverage months beginning after Feb. 17, 2009 and before Jan. 1, 2011
Committee Reports, see ¶ 5078

To qualify for the health coverage tax credit (HCTC), a taxpayer must be an eligible individual, which includes an eligible TAA recipient. An eligible TAA recipient means, with respect to any month, any individual who:

(1) is receiving for any day of that month a trade adjustment allowance (TAA) under chapter 2 or Title II of the Trade Act of 1974 (the Trade Act) or who would be eligible to receive that allowance if Sec. 231 of that Act were applied without regard to Sec. 231(a)(3)(B), that is, without regard to the requirement that the individual exhaust unemployment benefits before being eligible to receive an allowance; and

(2) with respect to that allowance, is covered under a certification issued under subchapter A or D of chapter 2 of title II of the Trade Act.

An individual will continue to be treated as an eligible TAA recipient during the first month the individual would otherwise cease to be an eligible TAA by reason of the above rule. (FTC 2d/FIN ¶ A-4230, ¶ A-4232; USTR ¶ 354; TaxDesk ¶ 569,401)

For a general overview of the HCTC, see ¶ 501.

New Law. The 2009 Recovery Act modifies the definition of an eligible TAA recipient to eliminate the requirement that an individual receiving unemployment compensation be enrolled in training. (Com Rept, see ¶ 5078) Under the 2009 Recovery Act, for any coverage month beginning after Feb. 17, 2009 and before Jan. 1, 2011, the term "eligible TAA recipient" means, with respect to any month, any individual who (Code Sec. 35(c)(2)(B) as amended by 2009 Recovery Act §1899C(a)):

(A) is receiving for any day of that month a TAA under chapter 2 of title II of the Trade Act (Code Sec. 35(c)(2)(B)(i));

(B) would be eligible to receive a TAA except that the individual is in a break in training provided under a training program under Sec. 236 of the Trade Act that exceeds a period specified in Sec. 233(c) of the Trade Act, but is within the period for receiving those allowances provided under Sec. 233(a) of the Trade Act (Code Sec. 35(c)(2)(B)(ii)); or

(C) is receiving unemployment compensation (as defined in Code Sec. 85(b), see FTC 2d/FIN ¶ H-3008; USTR ¶ 854.01; TaxDesk ¶ 132,507) for any day of that month and who would be eligible to receive a TAA for that month if Sec. 231 of the Trade Act were applied without regard to Sec. 231(a)(3)(B) and Sec. 231(a)(5). (Code Sec. 35(c)(2)(B)(iii))

> **🅡 observation:** As noted above, Sec. 231(a)(3)(B) of the Trade Act requires TAA recipients to have exhausted their unemployment benefits. Sec. 231(a)(5) of the Trade Act contains the requirement that TAA recipients be enrolled in training programs, which is the requirement that the 2009 Recovery Act is waiving.

In addition, an individual continues to be treated as an eligible TAA recipient during the first month that the individual would otherwise cease to be an eligible TAA recipient by reason of the above rule. (Code Sec. 35(c)(2)(B))

Thus, the 2009 Recovery Act clarifies that the definition of an eligible TAA recipient includes an individual who would be eligible to receive a TAA except that the individual is in a break in training that exceeds the period specified in Sec. 233(c) of the Trade Act, but within the period for receiving the allowance. (Com Rept, see ¶ 5078)

☐ **Effective:** Coverage months beginning after Feb. 17, 2009 (2009 Recovery Act §1899C(b)), and before Jan. 1, 2011. (Code Sec. 35(c)(2)(B))

FTC 2d References are to Federal Tax Coordinator 2d
FIN References are to RIA's Analysis of Federal Taxes: Income
USTR References are to United States Tax Reporter: Income
PE References are to Pension Explanations

111

¶ 505. Pre-certification period after TAA-related loss of health coverage is temporarily ignored for certain HIPAA and HCTC purposes

Code Sec. 9801(c)(2)(D), as amended by 2009 Recovery Act § 1899D(a)
ERISA § 701(c)(2)(C), as amended by 2009 Recovery Act § 1899D(b)
Generally effective: Plan years beginning after Feb. 17, 2009 and before Jan. 1, 2011
Committee Reports, see ¶ 5078

Group health plans are subject to certain requirements intended to foster access, portability, and renewability of coverage. These requirements limit preexisting condition exclusions, prohibit the exclusion of certain individuals based on health status, and guarantee the renewability of health insurance coverage. These requirements were added by the Health Insurance Portability and Accountability Act of 1996 ("HIPAA") and so are often referred to as "the HIPAA rules."

Under the HIPAA rules, a group health plan may impose a "preexisting condition exclusion" only if: (1) the exclusion relates to a condition (whether physical or mental), regardless of cause, for which medical advice, diagnosis, care, or treatment was recommended or received within the six-month period ending on the enrollment date; (2) the exclusion does not extend for more than 12 months (18 months in the case of a "late enrollee") after the enrollment date; and (3) the period of any preexisting condition exclusion is reduced by the length of the aggregate of the periods of any "creditable coverage" applicable to the participant or beneficiary as of the enrollment date.

Under the HIPAA rules, days of "creditable coverage" that occur before a 63-day break in creditable coverage need not be counted for purposes of reducing the preexisting condition exclusion period. Thus, under this rule, a significant break in coverage means a 63-day period during all of which the individual was not covered under any creditable coverage. (FTC 2d/FIN ¶ H-1325, ¶ H-1325.5 *et seq.*; USTR ¶ 98,014)

Health Coverage Tax Credit (HCTC). To help taxpayers cope with the loss of their jobs due to increased imports from, or a shift in production to, foreign countries, the Trade Act of 1974 (as amended) provides certain benefits, such as job development or referrals. The Trade Act of 2002 provided that "TAA-eligible individuals" are eligible for the HCTC, see ¶ 501.

To qualify for the HCTC, an eligible individual must be covered by qualified health insurance, not have other specified coverage, and not be imprisoned. "Qualified health insurance" includes COBRA continuation coverage, various forms of state-based coverage, and certain individual health insurance. State-based coverage is qualified health insurance if the state so elects and provides that each "qualifying individual" is guaranteed enrollment if he pays the premium, or provides a certificate (see below) and pays the remainder of the premium, and certain other requirements are met.

A "qualifying individual" is an eligible individual who seeks to enroll in a state-based coverage and who (a) has aggregate periods of "creditable coverage" of three months or longer, (b) does not have other specified coverage, and (c) is not imprisoned. In general, "creditable coverage," which is determined under the Code Sec. 9801(c) HIPAA rules, includes health care coverage without a gap of more than 63 days. Therefore, if an individual's qualifying coverage were terminated more than 63 days before the individual enrolled in the state-based coverage, the individual would not be a qualifying individual and would not be entitled to the state-based protections. A qualifying individual also includes his qualified family members. (FTC 2d/FIN ¶ A-4230, ¶ A-4231 et seq., ¶ H-4237; USTR ¶ 354; TaxDesk ¶ 569,400 et seq.)

IRS has a program for making payment of the HCTC in advance (i.e., before the filing of the taxpayer's return) on behalf of "certified individuals" to providers of qualified health insurance for those individuals. For this purpose, a certified individual is anyone for whom a "qualified health insurance costs credit eligibility certificate" is in effect. (FTC 2d/FIN ¶ H-4870, ¶ H-4871; USTR ¶ 75,274; TaxDesk ¶ 569,401)

New Law. Under the 2009 Recovery Act, in determining if there has been a 63-day lapse in coverage for a TAA-eligible individual, the period (i) beginning on the date the individual has a TAA-related loss of coverage, and (ii) ending on the date which is 7 days after the date of IRS's issuance of a qualified health insurance costs credit eligibility certificate (under Code Sec. 7527) for that individual, is not taken into account. (Code Sec. 9801(c)(2)(D)(i) as amended by 2009 Recovery Act §1899D(a)) This provision applies only for plan years beginning before Jan. 1, 2011. (Code Sec. 9801(c)(2)(D)(i))

> *observation:* This provision coordinates (i) the determination as to whether an individual has had no creditable coverage for a continuous 63-day period, with (ii) the pre-certification period rule (under Code Sec. 7527(d)(2)(C), see ¶ 509), which provides that a TAA-eligible individual has 63 days from the date that is 7 days after the date of the certificate's issuance, to enroll in insurance without a lapse in creditable coverage.

The terms "TAA-eligible individual" and "TAA-related loss of coverage" have the meanings provided in Code Sec. 4980B(f)(5)(C)(iv). (Code Sec. 9801(c)(2)(D)(ii))

FTC 2d References are to Federal Tax Coordinator 2d
FIN References are to RIA's Analysis of Federal Taxes: Income
USTR References are to United States Tax Reporter: Income
PE References are to Pension Explanations

The Act also amends ERISA (and the Public Health Services Act) to include provisions parallel to the Code provisions described above. (ERISA §701(c)(2)(C) as amended by 2009 Recovery Act § 1899D(b))

☐ **Effective:** Plan years beginning after Feb. 17, 2009 (2009 Recovery Act §1899D(d)), and before Jan. 1, 2011. (Code Sec. 9801(c)(2)(D)(i))

¶ 506. Family members will continue to qualify for the HCTC after certain events for coverage months beginning in 2010

Code Sec. 35(g)(9), as amended by 2009 Recovery Act § 1899E(a)
Generally effective: Coverage months beginning after Dec. 31, 2009 and
    before Jan. 1, 2011
Committee Reports, see ¶ 5078

An eligible individual is allowed a health coverage tax credit (HCTC) for amounts paid by that individual for qualified health insurance coverage for that individual and qualifying family members. For this purpose, the term qualifying family member means (1) the taxpayer's spouse, and (2) any dependent of the taxpayer with respect to whom the taxpayer is entitled to a deduction under the normal dependent exemption rules. (FTC 2d/FIN ¶s A-4230, A-4235; USTR ¶ 354; TaxDesk ¶ 569,402)

Rules similar to the rules defining marital status under the child and dependent care credit (see FTC 2d/FIN ¶ A-4310; USTR ¶ 214.07; TaxDesk ¶ 569,310) and the rules treating certain married individuals living apart as not married under the child and dependent care credit (see FTC 2d/FIN ¶ A-4311; USTR ¶ 214.07; TaxDesk ¶ 569,311) apply. (FTC 2d/FIN ¶ A-4235; USTR ¶ 354; TaxDesk ¶ 569,402) The spouse of the taxpayer isn't treated as a qualifying family member for purposes of the credit if:

- the taxpayer is married at the close of the tax year,
- the taxpayer and the taxpayer's spouse are both eligible individuals during the tax year, and
- the taxpayer files a separate return for the tax year. (FTC 2d/FIN ¶ A-4235; USTR ¶ 354; TaxDesk ¶ 569,402)

For a general overview of the HCTC, see ¶ 501.

New Law. The 2009 Recovery Act provides continued eligibility for the HCTC for family members after certain events. The rule applies in the case of (1) the eligible individual becoming entitled to Medicare, (2) divorce, and (3) death. (Com Rept, see ¶ 5078)

Eligibility if an individual qualifies for Medicare. For eligible coverage months beginning before Jan. 1, 2011 (Code Sec. 35(g)(9) as amended by 2009

Recovery Act §1899E(a)), in the case of any month that would be an eligible coverage month for an eligible individual except for Code Sec. 35(f)(2)(A) (Code Sec. 35(g)(9)(A))—i.e., the individual is entitled to benefits under Medicare Part A or is enrolled in Medicare Part B (Com Rept, see ¶ 5078)—that month is treated as an eligible coverage month for that individual solely to determine the amount of the HCTC under Code Sec. 35 for any qualifying family members of that individual, and any advance payment of the HCTC under Code Sec. 7527. (Code Sec. 35(g)(9)(A)) This means that the HCTC is allowed for expenses paid for qualifying family members after the eligible individual is eligible for Medicare. This treatment (Com Rept, see ¶ 5078) applies for only the first 24 months after the eligible individual is (Code Sec. 35(g)(9)(A)) first entitled to benefits under Medicare Part A or is enrolled in Medicare Part B. (Com Rept, see ¶ 5078)

Eligibility after divorce. For eligible coverage months beginning before Jan. 1, 2011 (Code Sec. 35(g)(9)), in the case of the finalization of a divorce between an eligible individual and the individual's spouse, the spouse is treated as an eligible individual for Code Sec. 35 and Code Sec. 7527 purposes for a period of 24 months beginning with the date the divorce is finalized. However, the only qualifying family members who may be taken into account with respect to the spouse are those family members who were qualifying family members immediately before the divorce was finalized. (Code Sec. 35(g)(9)(B))

Eligibility after death. For eligible coverage months beginning before Jan. 1, 2011 (Code Sec. 35(g)(9)), the following rules apply if an eligible individual dies.

That individual's spouse (determined at the time of death) is treated as an eligible individual for Code Sec. 35 and Code Sec. 7527 purposes for a period of 24 months beginning with the date of the individual's death. However, the only qualifying family members who may be taken into account with respect to the spouse are those individuals who were qualifying family members immediately before the death. (Code Sec. 35(g)(9)(C)(i))

Any individual who was a qualifying family member of the decedent immediately before the death is treated as an eligible individual for Code Sec. 35 and Code Sec. 7527 purposes for the 24-month period beginning with the date of death. If Code Sec. 35(g)(4) applies (which denies the HCTC to dependents, see FTC 2d/FIN ¶ A-4231; USTR ¶ 354; TaxDesk ¶ 569,401), the taxpayer to whom the Code Sec. 151 dependency deduction is allowable is an eligible individual. In determining the amount of the HCTC, only the qualifying family member may be taken into account. (Code Sec. 35(g)(9)(C)(ii)) In other words, any individual who was a qualifying family member of the decedent immedi-

FTC 2d References are to Federal Tax Coordinator 2d
FIN References are to RIA's Analysis of Federal Taxes: Income
USTR References are to United States Tax Reporter: Income
PE References are to Pension Explanations

ately before the decedent's death is treated as an eligible individual for a period of 24 months beginning with the date of death, except that in determining the amount of the HCTC, only the qualifying family member may be taken into account. For a dependent, the rule applies to the taxpayer to whom the personal exemption deduction under Code Sec. 151 is allowable. (Com Rept, see ¶ 5078)

☐ **Effective:** Coverage months beginning after Dec. 31, 2009 (2009 Recovery Act §1899E(c)) and before Jan. 1, 2011. (Code Sec. 35(g)(9))

¶ 507. Eligibility for COBRA continuation coverage extended up to Dec. 31, 2010 for PBGC recipients and TAA-eligible individuals who lose employment or work hours

Code Sec. 4980B(f)(2)(B)(i), as amended by 2009 Recovery Act § 1899F(b)
ERISA § 602(2)(A), as amended by 2009 Recovery Act § 1899F(a)
Generally effective: Coverage periods that would otherwise end on or after
Feb. 17, 2009; through Dec. 31, 2010
Committee Reports, see ¶ 5078

COBRA requires that a group health plan must offer continuation coverage for a specified period to each qualified beneficiary who would lose coverage under the plan as a result of a qualifying event. An excise tax applies on the group health plan's failure to meet this requirement.

Qualifying events include: the death of the covered employee, termination of the covered employee's employment (other than for gross misconduct) or the reduction of the covered employee's hours, divorce or legal separation of the covered employee, and certain bankruptcy proceedings of the employer.

A qualified beneficiary generally includes a covered employee, his spouse, and his dependent children, who are beneficiaries under a group health plan on the day before the covered employee's qualifying event.

For a termination of employment or a reduction of hours, COBRA continuation coverage must be extended for a period of not less than 18 months. For certain qualifying events that follow a termination of employment or a reduction of hours (other than the employer's bankruptcy), COBRA coverage must be for a period of not less than 36 months.

A plan may require the beneficiary to pay a premium of 102% of the applicable premium for a period of COBRA continuation coverage (see ¶ 301). (FTC 2d/FIN ¶ H-1250, ¶ H-1296 *et seq.*; USTR ¶ 49,80B4.07)

To help taxpayers cope with the loss of their jobs due to increased imports from, or a shift in production to, foreign countries, the Trade Act of 1974 and the Trade Act of 2002 provide certain benefits, such as job development or referrals. For the definition of a "TAA-eligible individual," and an overview of the health insurance tax credit, see ¶ 501.

New Law. Under the 2009 Recovery Act, the maximum required COBRA continuation period is extended for certain individuals whose qualifying event is a termination of employment or a reduction in hours.

PBGC recipients. For a covered employee (i) whose qualifying event was a termination of employment or a reduction in hours of employment, and (ii) who, as of that qualifying event, has a nonforfeitable right to a benefit any portion of which is to be paid by the Pension Benefit Guarantee Corporation (PBGC) under Title IV of ERISA, the period of COBRA continuation coverage must extend at least to:

(a) the date of death of the covered employee, or

(b) for the covered employee's surviving spouse or dependent children, 24 months after the covered employee's date of death. (Code Sec. 4980B(f)(2)(B)(i)(V) as amended by 2009 Recovery Act §1899F(b)(2))

The extension of the maximum COBRA continuation coverage period described above will not require any period of coverage to extend beyond Dec. 31, 2010. (Code Sec. 4980B(f)(2)(B)(i)(V))

> *observation:* For a PBGC recipient who, on or after Feb. 17, 2009, loses his job or whose hours are reduced, causing him to lose coverage under a group health plan, the COBRA continuation period must extend at least to Dec. 31, 2010 (unless he dies before then).

TAA-eligible individuals. For a covered employee (i) whose qualifying event was a termination of employment or a reduction in hours of employment, and (ii) who is a TAA-eligible individual as of the date that the COBRA continuation coverage period would otherwise terminate (as described in item (a), below), the period of COBRA continuation coverage will not terminate before the later of:

(a) (i) 18 months after the qualifying event (for a qualifying event that was the termination, or reduction of hours, of employment), or (ii) 36 months after a qualifying event described in item (a)(i), where another qualifying event (other than the employer's bankruptcy) occurs within 18 months of the prior qualifying event, or

(b) the date on which the covered employee ceases to be a TAA-eligible individual. (Code Sec. 4980B(f)(2)(B)(i)(VI))

FTC 2d References are to Federal Tax Coordinator 2d
FIN References are to RIA's Analysis of Federal Taxes: Income
USTR References are to United States Tax Reporter: Income
PE References are to Pension Explanations

The extension of the COBRA continuation coverage period described above also applies if the covered employee was a TAA-eligible individual as of the date that the COBRA continuation coverage period would otherwise have terminated, as described in (a) (above), but for the extension of COBRA continuation coverage because of the covered employee having become entitled to Medicare within 18 months after the termination, or reduction of hours, of his employment. (Code Sec. 4980B(f)(2)(B)(i)(VI))

The extension of the maximum COBRA continuation coverage period described above for TAA-eligible individuals will not require any period of coverage to extend beyond Dec. 31, 2010. (Code Sec. 4980B(f)(2)(B)(i)(VI))

ERISA. The Act amends ERISA to extend the COBRA continuation period in the same manner as the Code for TAA-eligible individuals. (The Act also amends the Public Health Services Act to extend the COBRA continuation period for TAA-eligible individuals, but does not contain such a provision for PBGC recipients.) (ERISA §602(2)(A) as amended by 2009 Recovery Act § 1899F(a)) .

☐ **Effective:** Coverage periods that (but for the extension described above) would end on or after Feb. 17, 2009; through Dec. 31, 2010. (2009 Recovery Act §1899F(d))

¶ 508. HCTC is allowed for VEBA coverage before 2011

Code Sec. 35(e)(1)(K), as amended by 2009 Recovery Act § 1899G(a)
Generally effective: Coverage months beginning after Feb. 17, 2009 and
  before Jan. 1, 2011
Committee Reports, see ¶ 5078

An individual is allowed a health coverage tax credit (HCTC) for a percentage of amounts the individual pays for coverage by qualified health insurance. The term qualified health insurance means any of the following:

(1) coverage under a continuation provision under the Consolidated Omnibus Reconciliation Act of 1985 (COBRA);

(2) state-based continuation coverage provided by the state under a state law that requires that coverage;

(3) coverage offered through a qualified state high risk pool (as defined in section 2744(c)(2) of the Public Health Service Act, 30 42 U.S.C. §300gg-44(c)(2));

(4) coverage under a health insurance program offered for state employees;

(5) coverage under a state-based health insurance program that is comparable to the health insurance program offered for state employees;

(6) coverage to HCTC eligible individuals through an arrangement entered into by a state with (a) an issuer of health insurance coverage, (b) an adminis-

trator, (c) an employer, or (d) a group health plan (including certain multiemployer plans);

(7) coverage offered through a state arrangement with a private sector health care coverage purchasing pool;

(8) coverage under a state-operated health plan that doesn't receive any federal financial participation;

(9) coverage under a group health plan that is available through the employment of the eligible individual's spouse;

(10) for any eligible individual and that individual's qualifying family members (¶ 506), coverage under individual health insurance if the eligible individual was covered under individual health insurance during the entire 30-day period that ends on the date that individual became separated from the employment that qualified that individual for (a) in the case of an eligible TAA recipient, the trade adjustment allowance (TAA), (b) in the case of an eligible alternative TAA recipient, the benefit under section 246(a) of the Trade Act of 1974, or (c) in the case of any eligible Pension Benefit Guaranty Corporation (PBGC) pension recipient, the pension benefit paid by the PBGC. (FTC 2d/FIN ¶ A-4236; USTR ¶ 354; TaxDesk ¶ 569,405)

Under pre-2009 Recovery Act law, qualified health insurance didn't include voluntary employee benefit plan (VEBA) coverage.

For a general overview of the HCTC, see ¶ 501.

New Law. The 2009 Recovery Act adds, to the above list of qualified health insurance, coverage under an employee benefit plan funded by a Code Sec. 501(c)(9) VEBA established under a bankruptcy court order or by an agreement with an authorized representative under 11 U.S.C. §1114. This provision applies for eligible coverage months beginning before Jan. 1, 2011. (Code Sec. 35(e)(1)(K) as amended by 2009 Recovery Act §1899G(a)) Thus, the provision won't apply for certificates of eligibility issued after Dec. 31, 2010. (Com Rept, see ¶ 5078)

☐ **Effective:** Coverage months beginning after Feb. 17, 2009 (2009 Recovery Act §1899G(b)) and before Jan. 1, 2011. (Code Sec. 35(e)(1)(K))

FTC 2d References are to Federal Tax Coordinator 2d
FIN References are to RIA's Analysis of Federal Taxes: Income
USTR References are to United States Tax Reporter: Income
PE References are to Pension Explanations

¶ 509. Additional information is required on qualified health insurance cost eligibility certificates issued before 2011

Code Sec. 7527(d), as amended by 2009 Recovery Act § 1899H(a)
Generally effective: For certificates issued on or after Aug. 18, 2009 and before Jan. 1, 2011
Committee Reports, see ¶ 5078

IRS can make advance payment of the health coverage tax credit (HCTC) on behalf of an individual for whom a qualified health insurance cost credit eligibility certificate is in effect. A qualified health insurance cost credit eligibility certificate means any written statement that an individual is an eligible individual for health insurance credit purposes—i.e., an eligible TAA recipient, an alternative TAA recipient, or an eligible Pension Benefit Guaranty Corporation (PBGC) pension recipient—if the statement provides the information that IRS may require for purposes of the advance payment rules. Form 8887 is filed for this purpose by an authorized representative of a state or the PBGC. (FTC 2d/FIN ¶ H-4872; USTR ¶ 75,274)

For a general overview of the HCTC, see ¶ 501.

New Law. Under the 2009 Recovery Act, a qualified health insurance cost credit eligibility certificate provided in connection with the advance payment of the HCTC must include the following information:

(1) the name, address, and telephone number of the state office or offices responsible for providing the individual with assistance with enrollment in qualified health insurance (Code Sec. 7527(d)(2)(A) as amended by 2009 Recovery Act §1899H(a)),

(2) a list of coverage options that are treated as qualified health insurance by the state in which the individual resides (Code Sec. 7527(d)(2)(B)),

(3) for a TAA-eligible individual, a statement informing the individual that the individual has 63 days from the date that is seven days after the issuance of the certificate to enroll in the insurance without a lapse in creditable coverage (Code Sec. 7527(d)(2)(C)), and

(4) any other information that IRS may require. (Code Sec. 7527(d)(1))

> ⊘ *observation:* IRS will have to revise Form 8887, Health Insurance Credit Eligibility Certificate, to include this additional information.

This provision applies to statements issued before Jan. 1, 2011. (Code Sec. 7527(d)(2)) Thus, it doesn't apply to months beginning after Dec. 31, 2010. (Com Rept, see ¶ 5078)

☐ **Effective:** For certificates issued after the date that is six months after Feb. 17, 2009 (i.e., Aug. 18, 2009) (2009 Recovery Act §1899H(b)) and before Jan. 1, 2011. (Code Sec. 7527(d)(2))

FTC 2d References are to Federal Tax Coordinator 2d
FIN References are to RIA's Analysis of Federal Taxes: Income
USTR References are to United States Tax Reporter: Income
PE References are to Pension Explanations

121

Health Coverage Tax Credit

¶ 600. Loss Carryback Provisions

¶ 601. Carryback period for 2008 NOLs is increased to three, four, or five years (from two years) for electing small businesses

Code Sec. 172(b)(1)(H), as amended by 2009 Recovery Act § 1211(a)
Code Sec. 172, 2009 Recovery Act § 1211(c)
Code Sec. 172, 2009 Recovery Act § 1211(d)(2)
Generally effective: NOLs arising in tax years ending after Dec. 31, 2007
Committee Reports, see ¶ 5037

A net operating loss (NOL) is the excess of business deductions (computed with certain modifications) over gross income in a particular tax year. The loss can be deducted, through an NOL carryback or carryover, in another tax year in which gross income exceeds business deductions. (See FTC 2d/FIN ¶ M-4000; USTR ¶ 1724; TaxDesk ¶ 354,001)

In general, NOLs may be carried back two years and forward 20 years. The NOL is first carried back to the earliest tax year for which it's allowable as a carryback or a carryover, and is then carried to the next earliest tax year. (FTC 2d/FIN ¶ M-4300, ¶ M-4301; USTR ¶ 1724.30; TaxDesk ¶ 356,000, ¶ 356,001) A taxpayer may elect to forego the entire carryback period for an NOL and instead carry it forward. (See FTC 2d/FIN ¶ M-4303; USTR ¶ 1724.33; TaxDesk ¶ 356,003)

Different rules apply for certain types of losses. For example, a three-year carryback is allowed for "eligible losses"—i.e., (a) individual losses from casualty or theft and (b) farm or small business (average annual gross receipts of $5 million or less) losses attributable to designated disasters. (See FTC 2d/FIN ¶s M-4305.1, M-4305.2; USTR ¶s 1724.434, 1724.436; TaxDesk ¶s 356,010, 356,011) A five-year carryback is allowed for "farming losses" (see FTC 2d/FIN ¶ M-4305.3; USTR ¶ 1724.437; TaxDesk ¶ 356,012), "qualified disaster losses" (see FTC 2d/FIN ¶ M-4305.6; USTR ¶ 1724.438; TaxDesk ¶ 356,013.1), and certain amounts related to specified disasters (see FTC 2d/FIN ¶s M-4342, M-4351, M-4354; USTR ¶ 14,00N4.06; TaxDesk ¶s 356,014, 356,021.1). Certain NOLs can't be carried back at all—e.g., so-called "excess interest losses," which are NOLs attributable to interest allocable to a corporate equity reduction transaction (CERT). (See FTC 2d/FIN ¶ M-4306 *et seq.*; USTR ¶ 1724.35; TaxDesk ¶ 356,005)

FTC 2d References are to Federal Tax Coordinator 2d
FIN References are to RIA's Analysis of Federal Taxes: Income
USTR References are to United States Tax Reporter: Income
PE References are to Pension Explanations

A special five-year carryback was provided for 2001 and 2002 NOLs (in response to the economic downturn following the events of Sept. 11, 2001), but taxpayers could elect to use the regular carryback instead. (See FTC 2d/FIN ¶ M-4301.1; USTR ¶ 1724.31; TaxDesk ¶ 356,001.1)

New Law. The 2009 Recovery Act (the Act) provides that if an "eligible small business" elects to apply Code Sec. 172(b)(1)(H) to an "applicable 2008 NOL" (or "applicable NOL") (Code Sec. 172(b)(1)(H)(i) as amended by 2009 Recovery Act §1211(a); 2009 Recovery Act §1211(b)), then Code Sec. 172(b)(1)(A)(i) (which provides the general two-year NOL carryback) is applied by replacing "two" with any whole number the taxpayer elects that is more than two and less than six. (Code Sec. 172(b)(1)(H)(i)(I))

> *observation:* In other words, an eligible business may elect a three-, four-, or five-year carryback period for the 2008 NOL, instead of the general two-year carryback period.

> *illustration (1):* Taxpayer, an eligible small business, incurs an NOL for its tax year ending Jan. 31, 2008. The NOL is an "applicable 2008 NOL" (see below). Taxpayer may elect to carry the loss back five years to its tax year that ended Jan. 31, 2003. Without the change in the law, Taxpayer could have carried the NOL back only two years, to its tax year that ended Jan. 31, 2006.

> *observation:* The Act doesn't change the allowable carryforward period for 2008 NOLs.

> *observation:* The NOL carryback and carryover rules are designed to allow taxpayers to smooth out swings in business income (and taxes on that income) that result from business cycle fluctuations. In a report accompanying an earlier version of this provision, Congress indicated it was concerned about the severity of the current economic downturn, which resulted in significant financial losses for many taxpayers. The temporary extension of the NOL carryback period provides taxpayers in all sectors of the economy that experience these losses with the ability to get refunds of income taxes paid in earlier years. The refunds can be used to fund capital investment or other expenses.

> *observation:* A carryback can generate a refund because it allows the taxpayer to offset income that has already been taxed. Under pre-Act law, a small business taxpayer couldn't have used the NOL to offset the taxable income for the fifth, fourth, and third tax years preceding the NOL year, years when the taxpayer was more likely to have had taxable income. Allowing the carryback to the earlier years thus increases the likelihood that the taxpayer will be entitled to a refund, and may increase the amount of the refund.

🅁 *illustration (2):* Taxpayer, an eligible small business, has an "applicable NOL" for 2008. Taxpayer had taxable income for 2005 (and paid the applicable federal income tax), but not for 2006 or 2007. Taxpayer elects a three-year carryback for the NOL, and carries it back to 2005. The NOL wipes outs Taxpayer's 2005 taxable income, entitling Taxpayer to a refund of the tax it paid on that income. Under pre-Act law, the NOL could have been carried back only two years, to 2006 and 2007. Because Taxpayer had no taxable income for either year, the carryback wouldn't have resulted in a refund. Taxpayer would have had to wait until later years when it had taxable income to get any tax benefit from the NOL.

🅁 *recommendation:* The taxpayer should use the tentative (or "quick") carryback procedures (under which taxpayers can recover a refund attributable to an NOL carryback before IRS processes the return filed for the year the NOL arises, see FTC 2d/FIN ¶ T-6501 *et seq.*; USTR ¶ 64,114; TaxDesk ¶ 804,001 *et seq.*) to expedite the recovery of the refund. That way, the taxpayer won't have to wait until IRS processes the return for the NOL year to get the refund. Presumably, the taxpayer will have to indicate the increased carryback election on the claim form (Form 1045 for individuals, Form 1139 for corporations).

🅁 *observation:* The increased carryback provision benefits small business manufacturers, retailers, and home builders that did well financially during the years when the economy was flourishing (e.g., during the housing boom), but that don't expect to report profits for the foreseeable future.

🅁 *observation:* The key factor in deciding whether to elect to carry an NOL back three, four, or five tax years should be which election will result in the largest tax savings. (Note that in determining the NOL amount carried back [or forward], the necessary computations involving any other year must be made under the law applicable to that other year, see FTC 2d/FIN ¶ M-4201; USTR ¶ 724.20; TaxDesk ¶ 357,001.) Thus, if the NOL is more or at least equal to the taxpayer's combined income for the third, fourth, and fifth years before the year in which it arose, then the loss should be carried back to the fifth year so that it can be used in all three years (see *RIA Illustration (3),* below). On the other hand, if the NOL is less than the combined income for those three years, the taxpayer should try to carry it back to the year(s) in which his income was taxed at the highest rate so as to get the highest refund

FTC 2d References are to Federal Tax Coordinator 2d
FIN References are to RIA's Analysis of Federal Taxes: Income
USTR References are to United States Tax Reporter: Income
PE References are to Pension Explanations

(see *RIA Illustration (4)*, below). In some cases, it may be better to not make the election because the largest tax savings will come from carrying the NOL back to the second year before the year in which the NOL arose (see *RIA Illustration (5)*, below). (Generally, if the taxpayer can get at least some tax savings from a carryback to a year before the first year before the year in which the NOL arose, the taxpayer would not want to carry the NOL back to that year because the income for that first year could be applied against an NOL the taxpayer might have in its succeeding tax year.)

illustration (3): Taxpayer, a C corporation and a calendar year taxpayer, has an NOL of $200,000 for its 2008 tax year. It had taxable income of $50,000 in 2003, $50,000 in 2004, and $100,000 in 2005. It had taxable income of $25,000 in both 2006 and 2007. Taxpayer paid federal income taxes of $7,500 on its 2003 income, $7,500 on its 2004 income, $22,250 on its 2005 income, and $3,750 on its income for both 2006 and 2007. If Taxpayer elects to carry its 2008 NOL back *five years*, the NOL will completely offset its income for 2003, 2004, and 2005 ($50,000 + $50,000 + $100,000 = $200,000), and it will be entitled to a refund of $37,250 (the sum of the taxes it paid for those three years).

If Taxpayer carries the NOL back only *four years*, it will completely offset its income for 2004, 2005, 2006, and 2007 ($50,000 + $100,000 + $25,000 + $25,000 = $200,000), and will also result in a refund of $37,250 (the sum of the taxes paid for those four years), but it will mean that the income for 2007 will not be available to offset any NOL taxpayer may possibly have in 2009.

If Taxpayer carries the NOL back only *three years*, it will completely offset its income for 2005, 2006, and 2007 ($100,000 + $25,000 + $25,000 = $150,000), and $50,000 ($200,000 − $150,000) of the loss can be carried forward to 2009. However, it will result in a refund of only $29,750 (the sum of the taxes paid in those three years).

illustration (4): Assume the same facts as in *RIA Illustration (3)*, except that in 2005, Taxpayer had taxable income of $300,000 on which it paid federal income taxes of $100,250. If Taxpayer elects to carry the NOL of $200,000 back *five years*, it will completely offset the income of $50,000 for 2003 and 2004, and $100,000 of the income for 2005. Because the income for 2005 above $100,000 is taxed at a rate of 39%, this will result in a refund of $39,000 (39% of $200,000 [$300,000 − $100,000]) for that year and a total refund of $54,000 ($7,500 for 2003, $7,500 for 2004, and $39,000 for 2005).

However, if Taxpayer carries the NOL back only *three years* to 2005, it will be entitled to a refund of $78,000 (39% of $200,000, the taxable income for 2005 over $100,000).

 observation: Because in *RIA Illustration (4),* the income for 2003, 2004, and 2005 will not be available to offset any NOL that might arise in 2009, there is no reason to carry the NOL back before 2005 if carrying it back to that year will result in the largest tax refund.

 illustration (5): Assume the same facts as in *RIA Illustration (3),* except that Taxpayer had taxable income of $300,000 in 2006. Taxpayer will get the largest refund if it *does not elect* to carry the NOL back beyond two years. By carrying it back to 2006, it will get a refund of $78,000 (39% of the taxable income for 2005 over $100,000). If Taxpayer elected to carry the NOL back *five years,* it would get a refund of only $37,250 as shown in *RIA Illustration (3).* If it carries the NOL back *four years,* it would get a refund of $49,250 ($7,500 for 2004, $22,250 for 2005, and $19,500 [39% of $50,000] for 2006). If it elected to carry the NOL back *three years,* it would get a refund of $61,250 ($22,250 for 2005 and $39,000 [39% of $100,000] for 2006).

 observation: Because in *RIA Illustration (5),* the income for 2006 will not be available to offset any NOL that might arise in 2009, there is no reason to carry the NOL back before 2006 if carrying it back to that year will result in the largest tax refund.

 viewpoint: Attorney-CPA Michael A. Spielman, author of WG&L's U.S. International Estate Planning treatise, and a Senior Manager in the Transaction Advisory Services Practice of Ernst & Young LLP, where he advises public and private companies and private equity firms on the tax aspects of mergers and acquisitions, notes that to the extent this provision enables an eligible small business to claim a tax refund for taxes paid in earlier years, the refund may result in increased equity in the business, or enable distributions or dividends to owners. This factor will need to be considered when valuing business interests for income, estate, gift, or generation-skipping transfer (GST) tax purposes.

 observation: The taxpayer must affirmatively elect the increased carryback. Absent any election, the regular NOL carryback period rules apply. Thus, even if a taxpayer qualifies as a "eligible small business" and the taxpayer's NOL qualifies as an "applicable NOL," the NOL

FTC 2d References are to Federal Tax Coordinator 2d
FIN References are to RIA's Analysis of Federal Taxes: Income
USTR References are to United States Tax Reporter: Income
PE References are to Pension Explanations

can't be carried back more than two years unless the taxpayer elects to apply Code Sec. 172(b)(1)(H) (or one of the other special carryback periods applies). By contrast, the special five-year carryback for 2001 and 2002 NOLs applied automatically; a taxpayer that wanted to use the regular carryback had to make an election "out" (see FTC 2d/FIN ¶ M-4301.1; USTR ¶ 1724.31; TaxDesk ¶ 356,001.1).

observation: The Act doesn't affect the taxpayer's ability to make a Code Sec. 172(b)(3) election to forego the entire carryback for the NOL and instead carry it forward (see FTC 2d/FIN ¶ M-4303; USTR ¶ 1724.33; TaxDesk ¶ 356,003).

"Eligible small business" defined. An "eligible small business" that may elect the increased carryback for a 2008 NOL is a "small business" as defined in Code Sec. 172(b)(1)(F)(iii) for purposes of the "eligible loss" carryback rule described above—i.e., a corporation or partnership that meets the gross receipts test of Code Sec. 448(c) (see FTC 2d/FIN ¶ G-2069; USTR ¶ 4484; TaxDesk ¶ 440,807) for the tax year in which the loss arose, or a sole proprietorship that would meet that test if it were a corporation (see FTC 2d/FIN ¶ M-4305.2; USTR ¶ 1724.436; TaxDesk ¶ 356,011), but using $15 million (instead of $5 million) in the Code Sec. 448(c) gross receipts test. (Code Sec. 172(b)(1)(H)(iv)) (For further coordination between the two carryback provisions, see below.)

observation: In other words, an "eligible small business" that may elect the increased carryback is any trade or business (including one conducted in or through a corporation, partnership, or sole proprietorship) whose average annual gross receipts (or the average annual gross receipts of any of its predecessors) for the three-tax-year period (or shorter period of existence) ending with the tax year before the year in which the loss arose are $15 million or less. Thus, a taxpayer can't elect the increased carryback for a 2008 NOL if the taxpayer's average annual gross receipts for 2005-2007 exceeded $15 million. The taxpayer can carry the NOL back only two years (unless another special carryback rule applies).

observation: Code Sec. 448(c) provides that the receipts of all related entities must be aggregated for purposes of applying the average annual gross receipts test. Entities are related if they would be treated as a single employer under Code Sec. 52(a) or Code Sec. 52(b) (dealing with commonly controlled businesses), or under Code Sec. 414(m) or Code Sec. 414(o) (dealing with affiliated service groups). (See FTC 2d/FIN ¶ G-2071; USTR ¶ 4484; TaxDesk ¶ 440,808) Thus, even if a taxpayer would be an "eligible small business" based on its own gross receipts, the taxpayer won't be able to make the increased carryback election for a 2008 loss if, taking into account the gross receipts of all related entities, the total average annual gross receipts for 2006-2008 exceeded $15 million.

"Applicable 2008 NOL" defined. An "applicable 2008 NOL" for purposes of the increased carryback election is: (Code Sec. 172(b)(1)(H)(ii))

(1) the taxpayer's NOL for any tax year *ending* in 2008, or (Code Sec. 172(b)(1)(H)(ii)(I))

(2) if the taxpayer so elects (see below), the taxpayer's NOL for any tax year *beginning* in 2008. (Code Sec. 172(b)(1)(H)(ii)(II))

> *observation:* Thus, the NOL for which an eligible small business may elect the three-, four-, or five-year carryback under Code Sec. 172(b)(1)(H) is the NOL for the taxpayer's tax year ending in 2008 (see 1, above). For a calendar year taxpayer, this means the NOL for calendar year 2008. For fiscal year taxpayers, it means the NOL for the tax year ending in 2008 (i.e., the tax year beginning in 2007). A taxpayer can elect to use the NOL for the tax year *beginning* in 2008 (see 2, above), in which case the increased carryback will apply to the NOL for tax year ending in 2009. Thus, for fiscal year taxpayers, "applicable NOLs" can include NOLs for tax years beginning as early as Feb. 1, 2007 or ending as late as Nov. 30, 2009 (see FTC 2d/FIN ¶ G-1004; USTR ¶ 4414; TaxDesk ¶ 431,006). Fiscal year taxpayers thus have more flexibility than calendar year taxpayers, who are limited to the NOL for calendar year 2008.

Making the election. Any election under Code Sec. 172(b)(1)(H) must be made in the manner prescribed by IRS. It must be made by the due date (including extensions) for filing the taxpayer's return for the tax year of the NOL. (Code Sec. 172(b)(1)(H)(iii)) For special transitional rules for NOLs for tax years ending before Feb. 17, 2009, see below.

> *observation:* Individual income tax returns must be filed on or before the 15th day of the fourth month after the end of the tax year (Apr. 15, for most individuals). (See FTC 2d/FIN ¶ S-4701; USTR ¶ 60,724; TaxDesk ¶ 570,219) Thus, absent an extension, any Code Sec. 172(b)(1)(H) election that a calendar year individual taxpayer wants to make for a 2008 NOL must be made by Apr. 15, 2009.

FTC 2d References are to Federal Tax Coordinator 2d
FIN References are to RIA's Analysis of Federal Taxes: Income
USTR References are to United States Tax Reporter: Income
PE References are to Pension Explanations

observation: Corporate income tax returns generally must be filed on or before the 15th day of the third month after the end of the tax year. (See FTC 2d/FIN ¶ S-4704; USTR ¶ 60,724) Thus, absent an extension, any Code Sec. 172(b)(1)(H) election that a calendar year corporation wants to make for a 2008 NOL must be made by Mar. 15, 2009.

observation: Code Sec. 172(b)(1)(H) provides for three elections:

(1) an election under Code Sec. 172(b)(1)(H)(i) to apply the increased carryback provision to an "applicable NOL"—the "Code Sec. 172(b)(1)(H) election";

(2) an election under Code Sec. 172(b)(1)(H)(i)(I) as to the length of the increased carryback (i.e., three, four, or five years). This election is part of the Code Sec. 172(b)(1)(H) election in (1), above, and is made when that election is made; and

(3) an election under Code Sec. 172(b)(1)(H)(ii)(II) to have the increased carryback apply to NOLs for tax years *beginning* in 2008 (instead of NOLs for tax years ending in 2008).

Once an election under Code Sec. 172(b)(1)(H) is made, it is irrevocable. (Code Sec. 172(b)(1)(H)(iii))

observation: Thus, if the taxpayer elects an increased carryback for a 2008 NOL, the taxpayer must carry the NOL back to the earliest tax year allowable under the election. The taxpayer can't change the length of the increased carryback period (e.g., from five years to four years), or revoke the election altogether if its circumstances improve so that it has taxable income in later years.

Any election under Code Sec. 172(b)(1)(H) may be made for only one tax year. (Code Sec. 172(b)(1)(H)(iii))

Consolidated returns. An affiliated group of corporations may elect to file a consolidated return in place of separate returns by each member (see FTC 2d/ FIN ¶ E-7500 *et seq.*; USTR ¶ 15,014; TaxDesk ¶ 603,601). All elections under Code Sec. 172(b)(1)(H) for a group of corporations filing a consolidated return are made by the common parent, and are binding on all the group members. (Com Rept, see ¶ 5037)

Coordination with other NOL carryback rules. The Act provides rules for coordinating the Code Sec. 172(b)(1)(H) increased carryback election with other special NOL carryback rules, see below.

"Excess interest losses." If a corporation has a CERT (i.e., a major stock acquisition or an excess distribution) and an "excess interest loss" (i.e., interest allocable to the CERT) for a "loss limitation year," the loss is an NOL. It's

subject to the regular NOL carryback and carryover rules, except that it can't be carried back to a tax year before the year in which the CERT occurred. (See FTC 2d/FIN ¶ M-4306 *et seq.*; USTR ¶ 1724.35; TaxDesk ¶ 356,005) The "loss limitation year" is generally the tax year in which the CERT occurred (the "CERT year") and each of the next two tax years. (FTC 2d/FIN ¶ M-4308)

Under the Act, if an eligible small business makes a Code Sec. 172(b)(1)(H) election to increase the carryback for an applicable 2008 NOL, then Code Sec. 172(b)(1)(E)(ii) (which defines "loss limitation year") is applied by using the whole number that is one less than the number of years the taxpayer elected as the carryback for the NOL instead of "two." (Code Sec. 172(b)(1)(H)(i)(II))

> *observation:* The number of "loss limitation years" that applies for an excess interest loss NOL is equal to the number of years in the carryback period the taxpayer elected for the NOL. For example, if a three-year carryback is elected, the loss limitation year is the CERT year and each of the next two (i.e., one less than three) tax years, for a total of three tax years. The increase in the number of loss limitation years where the taxpayer elects an increased carryback period is needed to permit the carryback over the increased period.

"Eligible losses." Code Sec. 172(b)(1)(F) (which provides the three-year carryback described above for "eligible losses" [including certain small business disaster losses], see FTC 2d/FIN ¶s M-4305.1, M-4305.2; USTR ¶s 1724.434, 1724.36; TaxDesk ¶s 356,010, 356,011) doesn't apply to an applicable 2008 NOL for which the taxpayer has made a Code Sec. 172(b)(1)(H) election. (Code Sec. 172(b)(1)(H)(i)(III))

> *observation:* In other words, if an eligible small business taxpayer makes a Code Sec. 172(b)(1)(H) election for an "applicable 2008 NOL" that also qualifies as an "eligible loss," the taxpayer must use the rules under Code Sec. 172(b)(1)(H), rather than those under Code Sec. 172(b)(1)(F), for the carryback. While both provisions allow a three-year carryback, Code Sec. 172(b)(1)(F) doesn't include the CERT modification described above (although any overlap between the two provisions is unlikely). Taxpayers that want a three-year carryback for an NOL should first determine whether Code Sec. 172(b)(1)(F) applies before making any Code Sec. 172(b)(1)(H) election. As stated above, the Code Sec. 172(b)(1)(H) election is irrevocable.

> *observation:* Taxpayers are more likely to qualify for relief under Code Sec. 172(b)(1)(H), which applies to any 2008 NOL and uses a

---

FTC 2d References are to Federal Tax Coordinator 2d
FIN References are to RIA's Analysis of Federal Taxes: Income
USTR References are to United States Tax Reporter: Income
PE References are to Pension Explanations

$15 million gross receipts test to determine eligibility, than under Code Sec. 172(b)(1)(F), which is limited to certain casualty, theft, and disaster losses, and uses a $5 million gross receipts test to define a "small business." Code Sec. 172(b)(1)(H) also allows a longer carryback period—the taxpayer can elect a three-, four-, or five-year carryback. Code Sec. 172(b)(1)(F) provides only a one-year extension, to three years.

Alternative tax net operating loss.   An alternative tax net operating loss deduction (ATNOLD or ATNOL deduction) is allowed for alternative minimum tax (AMT) purposes instead of the regular NOL deduction. (See FTC 2d/FIN ¶ A-8210 *et seq.*; USTR ¶ 564.01; TaxDesk ¶ 696,000 *et seq.*)

> *observation:* The regular tax NOL deduction and the ATNOLD are governed by a single carryback period (see FTC 2d/FIN ¶ A-8213; USTR ¶ 564.01; TaxDesk ¶ 696,509). Thus, the increased carryback elected for the 2008 NOL also applies for the ATNOLD in computing AMTI.

Anti-abuse rules.   IRS will prescribe the rules that are necessary to prevent the abuse of the purposes of Act § 1211, including anti-stuffing rules, anti-churning rules (including rules relating to sale-leasebacks), and rules similar to the Code Sec. 1091 rules relating to losses from wash sales. (2009 Recovery Act §1211(c))

> *observation:* An NOL may include losses that are subject to special carryover periods, in which case specific ordering rules apply. Any portion of an NOL that is attributable to specified types of losses is considered to be a separate NOL and is applied as a carryover after the remainder of the NOL for that year is applied. (See FTC 2d/FIN ¶ M-4302.1; USTR ¶ 1724.49; TaxDesk ¶ 356,002.1) The anti-abuse rules might include a similar rule for 2008 NOLs for which the taxpayer has elected the increased carryback.

Transitional rules for tax years ending before Feb. 17, 2009.   For an NOL for a tax year ending before Feb. 17, 2009 (2009 Recovery Act §1211(d)(2)), the Act provides three transitional rules (Com Rept, see ¶ 5037):

(1) An election made under Code Sec. 172(b)(3) (i.e., to waive the carryback altogether) for the loss may be revoked (notwithstanding that Code Sec. 172(b)(3) provides that the election is irrevocable) before the "applicable date" (2009 Recovery Act §1211(d)(2)(A)), which is the date that is 60 days after Feb. 17, 2009 (2009 Recovery Act §S1211(d)(2)) (i.e., Apr. 18, 2009).

> *observation:*   Thus, if a taxpayer that made a Code Sec. 172(b)(3) election to waive the carryback period for a 2008 NOL had taxable in-

come for 2003, 2004, or 2005, the taxpayer can revoke that election and make a Code Sec. 172(b)(1)(H) election to carry the NOL back three, four, or five years to offset the taxable income for those earlier years. The taxpayer has until Apr. 17, 2009 to revoke the Code Sec. 172(b)(3) election.

🅡🅐 *action alert:* The revocation of a Code Sec. 172(b)(3) election that was made for an NOL for a tax year ending before Feb. 17, 2009 must be made before Apr. 18, 2009.

(2) An election made under Code Sec. 172(b)(1)(H) for the loss will be treated as timely made (notwithstanding that Code Sec. 172(b)(1)(H)(iii) requires the election to be made by the return due date) if it's made before the "applicable date." (2009 Recovery Act §1211(d)(2)(B))

🅡🅐 *observation:* Thus, the taxpayer can make a Code Sec. 172(b)(1)(H) election to increase the carryback for an NOL for a tax year ending in 2008, even if the due date for filing the return for that year has passed. But the election must be made before Apr. 18, 2009.

🅡🅐 *action alert:* A Code Sec. 172(b)(1)(H) election for an NOL for a tax year for which the return due date has passed must be made before Apr. 18, 2009.

(3) An application under Code Sec. 6411(a) (i.e., a tentative carryback adjustment to get a "quick" refund attributable to an NOL) for the loss will be treated as timely filed if it's filed before the "applicable date." (2009 Recovery Act §1211(d)(2)(C))

🅡🅐 *observation:* The tentative carryback adjustment application generally must be filed within 12 months after the end of the tax year in which the NOL arose. (See FTC 2d ¶ T-6506; USTR ¶ 64,114; TaxDesk ¶ 804,005) The Act's increased carryback election is available for NOLs for tax years ending in 2008. For taxpayers with tax years ending early in the calendar year, the 12-month deadline for a 2008 NOL, the 12-month deadline for a 2008 NOL might already have passed. To remedy this, the Act gives taxpayers until Apr. 17, 2009 to file the quick carryback claim.

FTC 2d References are to Federal Tax Coordinator 2d
FIN References are to RIA's Analysis of Federal Taxes: Income
USTR References are to United States Tax Reporter: Income
PE References are to Pension Explanations

⚕️ action alert: An application for a tentative carryback adjustment with respect to an NOL for a tax year ending Jan. 31, 2008 must be made before Apr. 18, 2009.

⚕️ observation: As stated above, the "applicable NOLs" for which an eligible small business may elect the increased carryback period are NOLs for tax years ending in 2008 (or, if the taxpayer so elects, NOLs for tax years beginning in 2008). As tax years ending in 2008 necessarily ended before Feb. 17, 2009, the above transitional rules (which apply to NOLs for tax years ending before Feb. 17, 2009) appear to apply generally. However, the transitional rule for tentative carryback claims (see (3), above) only applies for fiscal years ending on or before Mar. 31, 2008. If the year ended on Apr. 30, 2008 or later, the taxpayer would have more time to make the tentative carryback election under the general rule than under the transitional rule. In earlier versions of this provision, the increased carryback period was also available for 2009 NOLs, which would not have qualified for the transitional relief.

☐ **Effective:** NOLs arising in tax years ending after Dec. 31, 2007 (2009 Recovery Act §1211(d)(1))—i.e., NOLs for tax years ending in 2008 (or, if the taxpayer so elects, NOLs for tax years beginning in 2008). (Code Sec. 172(b)(1)(H)(ii))

¶ 602. Revocation of IRS guidance exempting banks from loss limitation rules following an ownership change

Code Sec. None, 2009 Recovery Act § 1261(a)
Code Sec. 382(h), 2009 Recovery Act § 1261(b)
Generally effective: For ownership changes after Jan. 16, 2009
Committee Reports, see ¶ 5048

Code Sec. 382 limits the rate at which losses may be used to offset income generated after an ownership change which can occur as a result of acquisitions, certain capital infusions, or other changes in corporate ownership. The annual limitation is generally an amount equal to the value of the corporation immediately before the ownership change multiplied by the long-term tax exempt rate. The Code Sec. 382 loss limitation rules apply to net operating losses present at the time of the ownership change (the change date) and also apply to net unrealized built-in losses (NUBIL) on the change date to the extent that the built-in losses in the corporation's assets exceed the built-in gains in its assets. Under Code Sec. 382(h) a recognized built-in-loss (RBIL) for any tax year during the 5-year period following the ownership change (the recognition period) is subject to the section 382 limitation as if it were a pre-change net operating loss. In addition, an amount allowed as a deduction during the recognition period which is attributable to a pre-change date is treated as an RBIL. An ownership change is generally an increase of more than 50 percentage points (by value) in the percentage of loss corporation stock owned by one or more five percent (or greater) shareholders over a 3-year period. (FTC 2d/FIN ¶ F-7201; USTR ¶ 3824; TaxDesk ¶ 240,302)

IRS provides two alternative safe harbor approaches for the identification of built-in items for purposes of Code Sec. 382(h): the "1374 approach" and the "338 approach." The 1374 approach allows companies to treat the amount of gain or loss recognized on the sale of an asset during the recognition period as built-in to the extent that particular item of gain or loss accrued before the change date. The 1374 approach has an exception for bad debt deductions under Code Sec. 166 under which any deduction properly taken into account during the first 12 months of the recognition period as a bad debt deduction under Code Sec. 166 is treated as RBIL if the item arises from a debt owed to the loss corporation at the beginning of the recognition period (and deductions for these items properly taken into account after the first 12 months of the recognition period are not RBILs). The 338 approach identifies items of built-in gains and losses by comparing a corporation's actual items of income and deductions realized during the recognition period with the hypothetical items that would have resulted if the corporation had made a Code Sec. 338 election on the change date. This approach does not include an exception for bad debts under Code Sec. 166. (FTC 2d/FIN ¶s E-9066, E-9067, F-7342.1, F-7342.2, M-2401; USTR ¶s 3824.25, 1664; TaxDesk ¶s 240,319, 320,501)

Code Sec. 166 allows a deduction for worthless debt. In the case of a bank subject to federal and certain state authorities, a debt is presumed to be worthless to the extent that the debt is charged off under a specific order of that authority or in accordance with established policies of that authority. Banks can make a conformity election under which debts charged off for regulatory purposes during a tax year in accordance with an order are conclusively presumed to be worthless for tax purposes to the same extent. (FTC 2d/FIN ¶s E-3205, E-3208, E-3209; USTR ¶ 1664.225)

Under pre-2009 Recovery Act law, Notice 2008-83 provided that any deduction properly allowed after an ownership change to a bank (as defined in Code Sec. 581) for losses on loans or bad debts (including any deduction for a reasonable addition to a reserve for bad debts) would not be treated as a built-in loss or a deduction attributable to periods before the change date. Banks were permitted to rely on this rule until further guidance was provided.(FTC 2d/FIN ¶ F-7360, ¶ F-7383; USTR ¶ 3824.25)

FTC 2d References are to Federal Tax Coordinator 2d
FIN References are to RIA's Analysis of Federal Taxes: Income
USTR References are to United States Tax Reporter: Income
PE References are to Pension Explanations

observation: Thus, under Notice 2008-83, which was issued by IRS in conjunction with the bank bailout legislation passed in October 2008, banks were allowed to deduct unlimited losses on loans, bad debts or additions to bad debt reserves that were brought over by an acquired bank in a merger or acquisition.

New Law. The 2009 Recovery Act provides that IRS is not authorized under Code Sec. 382(m) to provide exemptions or special rules that are restricted to particular industries or classes of taxpayers, and that Notice 2008-83 is inconsistent with the Congressional intent in enacting Code Sec. 382(m). (2009 Recovery Act §1261(a))

Although IRS's legal authority to prescribe the Notice is doubtful, for taxpayers who have already relied upon its guidance, it is effective only for ownership changes (as defined in Code Sec. 382(g)) occurring on or before Jan. 16, 2009 (2009 Recovery Act §1261(b)(1)), except that the guidance is effective for ownership changes occurring after Jan. 16, 2009 that were made (i) under a written binding contract entered into on or before Jan 16, 2009, or (ii) under a written agreement entered into on or before Jan 16, 2009 if the agreement was described on or before that date in a public announcement or in a filing with the SEC required by reason of the ownership change. (2009 Recovery Act §1261(b)(2))

viewpoint: Stanley I. Langbein, author of WG&L's *Federal Income Taxation of Banks & Financial Institutions, Seventh Edition,* and a professor of law at the University of Miami School of Law, notes that the new law differs from earlier proposed legislation in two important aspects: first, the new law permits Notice 2008-83 to apply retroactively, that is, to transactions in which there is no reason to believe that the taxpayers involved "relied upon" any IRS guidance; second, it omits the directive of an investigation and report by the Inspector General of conflicts of interest surrounding issuance of the Notice.

For a discussion of when the loss limitation rules do not apply to restructurings made under 2008 EESA bail-out agreements, see ¶ 603.

☐ **Effective:**   Feb. 17, 2009 (Com Rept, see ¶ 5048)

observation: Thus, after Feb. 17, 2009, Notice 2008-83 will have no effect for ownership changes after Jan. 16, 2009 unless one of the exceptions under (i) or (ii) above applies.

¶ 603. Code Sec. 382 loss limitation rule doesn't apply where EESA bail-out agreement requires ownership restructuring

Code Sec. 382(n), as amended by 2009 Recovery Act § 1262(a)
Generally effective: Ownership changes made after Feb. 17, 2009
Committee Reports, see ¶ 5049

Code Sec. 382 limits the rate at which losses may be used to offset income generated after an ownership change, which can occur as a result of acquisitions, capital contributions, or other changes in corporate ownership. The annual limitation is generally an amount equal to the value of the corporation immediately before the ownership change multiplied by the long-term tax exempt rate. The Code Sec. 382 loss limitation rules also apply to net operating losses and net unrealized built-in losses present in the loss corporation at the time of the ownership change. An ownership change is generally an increase of more than 50 percentage points (by value) in the percentage of loss corporation stock owned by one or more five percent (or greater) shareholders over a 3-year period. (FTC 2d/FIN ¶ F-7201; USTR ¶ 3824; TaxDesk ¶ 240,302)

The Emergency Economic Stabilization Act of 2008 (2008 EESA) authorized the Treasury Secretary to establish the Troubled Asset Relief Program to purchase troubled assets from financial institutions in order to ameliorate the financial crisis. (Sec. 101DivA, PL 110-343, 10/03/2008) IRS issued guidance providing tax relief for business entities affected by the economic crisis and measures designed to ameliorate the crisis. In Notice 2008-76, IRS announced that it would issue regulations under Code Sec. 382(m) to provide that the Code Sec. 382 testing date did not include any date on or after the date on which the U.S. acquired in a "Housing Act Acquisition" stock or an option to acquire stock in a corporation. Thus, under this rule, U.S. government purchases of Fannie Mae and Freddie Mac obligations would be exempt from the Code Sec. 382 loss limitation rule. Unless additional guidance was issued, the regulations would apply after Sept. 6, 2008. (FTC 2d/FIN ¶ F-7443; USTR ¶ 3824.03)

In Notice 2009-14, IRS provided guidance on how the Code Sec. 382 loss limitation rule would apply to loss corporations (financial institutions and auto companies) whose instruments were acquired by the U.S. under 5 programs established under 2008 EESA: (1) the Capital Purchase Program for publicly-traded issuers (Public CPP); (2) the Capital Purchase Program for private issuers (Private CPP); (3) the Capital Purchase Program for S corporations (S Corp CPP); (4) the Targeted Investment Program (TARP TIP); and (5) the Au-

FTC 2d References are to Federal Tax Coordinator 2d
FIN References are to RIA's Analysis of Federal Taxes: Income
USTR References are to United States Tax Reporter: Income
PE References are to Pension Explanations

tomotive Industry Financing Program (TARP Auto). This Notice amplified and superseded Notice 2008-100, 2008-44, which provided guidance only for the acquisition of instruments in financial institutions under the CPP program. (FTC 2d/FIN ¶s F-7481, F-7617.1; USTR ¶s 3824.09, 3824.275)

IRS also issued Notice 2008-83, which provided guidance exempting banks from the loss limitation rules. (FTC 2d/FIN ¶ F-7383; USTR ¶ 3824.25) The 2009 Recovery Act revokes that Notice, see ¶ 602.

New Law. The 2009 Recovery Act provides that the Code Sec. 382 loss limitation rules do not apply to an ownership change (i) occurring under a restructuring plan required under a loan agreement or a commitment for a line of credit entered into with the U.S. under the 2008 EESA, and (ii) intended to result in a rationalization of the costs, capitalization, and capacity with regard to the manufacturing workforce of, and suppliers to, the taxpayer and its subsidiaries. (Code Sec. 382(n)(1) as amended by 2009 Recovery Act §1262(a)) This rule, however, does not apply to a later ownership change, unless that ownership change also is described above. (Code Sec. 382(n)(2))

In addition, this rule does not apply to an ownership change if, immediately after the ownership change, any person (other than a voluntary employees' beneficiary association under Code Sec. 501(c)(9) owns stock of the old loss corporation possessing 50% or more of the total combined voting power of all classes of stock entitled to vote, or of the total value of the stock of that corporation. For these purposes, related persons are treated as a single person. A person is treated as related to another person if the person bears a relationship to the other person described in Code Sec. 267(b) or Code Sec. 707(b), or the persons are members of a group of persons acting in concert. (Code Sec. 382(n)(3))

> ⓡ *observation:* The law exempts certain companies, possibly only General Motors, from the Code Sec. 382 loss limitation rule when a company is forced to restructure as part of an agreement for a federal loan.

This exception from the application of the Code Sec. 382 loss limitation rule does not change the fact that an ownership change has occurred for other purposes of Code Sec. 382 (e.g., an ownership change for purposes of determining the testing period under Code Sec. 382(i)(2)). (Com Rept, see ¶ 5049)

For a discussion of related person rules, see FTC 2d/FIN ¶s G-2707, B-2016; USTR ¶s 2674, 7074; TaxDesk ¶s 227,900, 584,514.

☐ **Effective:** For ownership changes after Feb. 17, 2009. (2009 Recovery Act §1262(b))

¶ 700. Withholding & Estimated Tax

¶ 701. Decreased required estimated tax payments in 2009 for certain small businesses

Code Sec. 6654(d)(1)(D), as amended by 2009 Recovery Act § 1212
Generally effective: Tax years beginning in 2009
Committee Reports, see ¶ 5038

Generally, the required annual payment for individual estimated income tax is the lesser of (i) 90% of the tax shown on the return for the tax year (or, if no return is filed, 90% of the tax for that year), or (ii) under pre-2009 Recovery Act law, 100% of the tax shown on the return of the individual for the preceding tax year. (FTC 2d/FIN ¶ S-5200, ¶ S-5204, ¶ S-5233; USTR ¶ 66,544.03; TaxDesk ¶ 571,304, ¶ 571,328, ¶ 666,005) However, if the adjusted gross income (AGI) shown on the return of the individual for the preceding tax year exceeds $150,000 ($75,000 for a married individual who files a separate return), higher percentages than 100% of the tax shown on the return of the individual for the preceding tax year (option (ii), above) apply. (FTC 2d/FIN ¶ S-5200, ¶ S-5203, ¶ S-5204.1, ¶ S-5301; USTR ¶ 66,544.03; TaxDesk ¶ 571,303, ¶ 571,305, ¶ 571,328, ¶ 658,501, ¶ 666,006)

> *observation:* Thus, in the case of individuals whose AGI exceeded the above mentioned amounts in the preceding year, the option to base the estimated tax payments on the previous year's tax return required them to pay a higher percentage of the previous year's tax as estimated tax.

New Law. The 2009 Recovery Act provides that, notwithstanding Code Sec. 6654(d)(1)(C) (the rules imposing higher percentages than 100% of the tax shown on the return of the individual for the preceding tax year, see FTC 2d/FIN ¶ S-5200, ¶ S-5203, ¶ S-5204.1, ¶ S-5301; USTR ¶ 66,544.03; TaxDesk ¶ 571,303, ¶ 571,305, ¶ 571,328, ¶ 658,501, ¶ 666,006), for any tax year beginning in 2009, in computing the amount of the required annual installments of estimated income tax of any "qualified individual" (defined below), the term "required annual payment" means the lesser of (1) 90% of the tax shown on the return for the tax year, or (2) *90% of the tax shown on the return of the individual for the preceding tax year.* (Code Sec. 6654(d)(1)(D)(i) as amended by 2009 Recovery Act §1212)

FTC 2d References are to Federal Tax Coordinator 2d
FIN References are to RIA's Analysis of Federal Taxes: Income
USTR References are to United States Tax Reporter: Income
PE References are to Pension Explanations

⚫ *observation:* Thus, for tax years beginning in 2009, 100% of the tax shown on the individual's return for the preceding tax year in the computation under Code Sec. 6654(d)(1)(B)(ii) is reduced to 90% of the tax so shown.

Thus, the 2009 Recovery Act provides that the required annual estimated tax payments of a qualified individual for tax years beginning in 2009 is not greater than 90 percent of the tax liability shown on the tax return for the preceding tax year. (Com Rept, see ¶ 5038)

For purposes of this special rule for 2009 tax years, "qualified individual" means any individual if— (Code Sec. 6654(d)(1)(D)(ii))

(I) the adjusted gross income shown on the return of that individual for the preceding tax year is less than $500,000, and (Code Sec. 6654(d)(1)(D)(ii)(I))

(II) that individual certifies that more than 50 percent of the gross income shown on the return of that individual for the preceding tax year was income from a small business. (Code Sec. 6654(d)(1)(D)(ii)(II))

A certification under (II), above, must be in the form and manner, and filed at a time, as IRS may prescribe by regulations. (Code Sec. 6654(d)(1)(D)(ii))

A married individual (within the meaning of Code Sec. 7703, see FTC 2d/ FIN ¶ A-1601; USTR ¶ 77,034.01; TaxDesk ¶ 566,501) who files a separate return for the tax year for which the amount of the installment is being determined, is a "qualified individual" if the adjusted gross income shown on the return of that individual for the preceding tax year is less than *$250,000,* and that individual meets the certification requirement of Code Sec. 6654(d)(1)(D)(ii)(II) discussed above. (Code Sec. 6654(d)(1)(D)(iv))

Thus, the 2009 Recovery Act provides that a qualified individual means any individual if the adjusted gross income shown on the tax return for the preceding tax year is less than $500,000 ($250,000 if married filing separately) and the individual certifies that at least 50 percent of the gross income shown on the return for the preceding tax year was income from a small trade or business. (Com Rept, see ¶ 5038)

For purposes of the definition of "qualified individual," income from a small business means, with respect to any individual, income from a trade or business the average number of employees of which was less than 500 employees for the calendar year ending with or within the preceding tax year of the individual. (Code Sec. 6654(d)(1)(D)(iii))

⚫ *observation:* The Conference Report indicates that a small trade or business means any trade or business that employed *no more than 500 persons,* effectively setting the average-number-of-employees limit at 500. (Com Rept, see ¶ 5038) This contradicts the controlling statutory language that effectively sets the limit at 499. Thus, if Congress intended to set the limit for a small trade or business at 500 rather than at 499, a technical correction will be required.

For an estate or trust, adjusted gross income is determined as provided in Code Sec. 67(e) (see FTC 2d/FIN ¶s C-2202, C-2206, C-7202; USTR ¶ 6424.01; TaxDesk ¶s 653,001, 653,004, 663,001). (Code Sec. 6654(d)(1)(D)(v))

☐ **Effective:** Feb. 17, 2009 (Com Rept, see ¶ 5038), for tax years beginning in 2009. (Code Sec. 6654(d)(1)(D)(i))

¶ 702. Estimated tax payments due from corporations with assets of $1 billion or more are increased for installments due in July, Aug., Sept. 2013

Code Sec. 6655, 2009 Children's Health Insurance Act § 704
Generally effective: Feb. 4, 2009
Committee Reports, see ¶ 5101

Generally, corporations are required to pay estimated income tax for each tax year in 4 equal installments due on the 15th day of the 4th, 6th, 9th, and 12th month of the tax year. See FTC 2d/FIN ¶ S-5353; USTR ¶ 66,554; TaxDesk ¶ 609,201.

illustration (1): Corp T uses a tax year beginning on Jan. 1. The due dates for its installments are: April 15, June 15, Sept. 15, and Dec. 15.

The 2005 Tax Increase Prevention Act (TIPRA) §401(1)(C) (Sec. 401(1)(C), PL 109-222, 5/17/2006, as amended by Sec. 4, PL 110-191, 2/29/2008, Sec. 3, PL 110-287, 7/29/2008, Sec. 3094(b), PL 110-289, 7/30/2008, and Sec. 6, PL 110-436, 10/16/2008) provides that, in the case of a corporation with assets of at least $1 billion (determined as of the end of the preceding tax year) the amount of any required installment of corporate estimated tax which is otherwise due in July, Aug., or Sept. 2013 is 120.00% of that amount. TIPRA §401(1)(D) (Sec. 401(1)(D), PL 109-222, 5/17/2006) provides that the amount of the next required installment after an installment referred to in §401(1)(C) is appropriately reduced to reflect the amount of the increase required by §401(1)(C). (FTC 2d/FIN ¶ S-5353; USTR ¶ 66,554; TaxDesk ¶ 609,201)

illustration (2): Corp X, a calender-year taxpayer with assets of at least $1 billion, calculates its estimated tax payment otherwise due in Sept. 2013 to be $100,000,000. Instead, X must make a payment of

FTC 2d References are to Federal Tax Coordinator 2d
FIN References are to RIA's Analysis of Federal Taxes: Income
USTR References are to United States Tax Reporter: Income
PE References are to Pension Explanations

141

$120,000,000 ($100,000,000 × 120.00%) by the due date in Sept. 2013. X calculates its estimated tax payment otherwise due in Dec. 2013 to be $100,000,000. X reduces the estimated tax payment otherwise due in Dec. 2013 by $20,000,000 ($120,000,000 − $100,000,000). Therefore, X must make a payment of $80,000,000 ($100,000,000 − $20,000,000) by the due date in Dec. 2013.

New Law. The 2009 Children's Health Insurance Act provides that the percentage under 2005 TIPRA §401(1)(C) in effect on Feb. 4, 2009 is increased by 0.5 percentage point. (2009 Children's Health Insurance Act §704).

> ⊘ *observation:* Accordingly, the 2009 Children's Health Insurance Act increases the corporate estimated tax payment due in July, Aug., or Sept. 2013 from 120.00% to 120.50% of the payment otherwise due. However, considering that there have been numerous pre-2009 Children's Health Insurance Act statutory amendments changing the percentages provided for in §401(1) 2005 TIPRA, it is likely that the percentages will be further amended by post-2009 Children's Health Insurance Act legislation.

> ⊘ *observation:* The 2009 Children's Health Insurance Act accelerates government revenue for one estimated tax installment in the government's 2013 fiscal year (Oct. 1, 2012 through Sept. 30, 2013), but the next required installment payment is reduced in the same amount as the amount of the accelerated payment. However, the reduced payment applies for the government's 2014 fiscal year (Oct. 1, 2013 through Sept. 30, 2014). The result of this is to shift revenue from the government's fiscal year ending Sept. 30, 2014 into the government's fiscal year ending Sept. 30, 2013.

> ⊘ *illustration (3):* Corp X (see illustration (2) above) calculates its estimated tax payment otherwise due in Sept. 2013 to be $100,000,000. Instead, X must make a payment of $120,500,000 ($100,000,000 × 120.50%) by the due date in Sept. 2013. X calculates its estimated tax payment otherwise due in Dec. 2013 to be $100,000,000. X reduces the estimated tax payment otherwise due in Dec. 2013 by $20,500,000 ($120,500,000 − $100,000,000). Therefore, X must make a payment of $79,500,000 ($100,000,000 − $20,500,000) by the due date in Dec. 2013. The accelerated payment is due during the government's 2013 fiscal year (Oct. 1, 2012 through Sept. 30, 2013), and the reduced payment is due during the government's 2014 fiscal year (Oct. 1, 2013 through Sept. 30, 2014).

🅡✍ *observation:* Corporations with a fiscal year that begins July 1 will not be affected by the above rule because they do not have any estimated tax payments due in July, Aug., or Sept.

🅡✍ *illustration (4):* Corp Z uses a tax year beginning on July 1. For Z's year beginning July 1, 2013, the due dates for its installments are: Oct. 15, 2013, Dec. 15, 2013, March 15, 2014, and June 15, 2014.

☐ **Effective:** Feb. 4, 2009. (Com Rept, see ¶ 5101)

¶ 703. Withholding tax on government contractors is delayed for one year until 2012

Code Sec. 3402(t), 2009 Recovery Act § 1511
Generally effective: Feb. 17, 2009
Committee Reports, see ¶ 5065

Under pre-2009 Recovery Act law, for payments made after 2010, the federal government and the government of every state, political subdivision of a state, and instrumentality of a state or state subdivision (including multi-state agencies) making certain payments to a person providing any property or services would have been required to deduct and withhold tax from that payment in an amount equal to 3% of the payment. This withholding requirement also applied to a payment made in connection with a government voucher or certificate program that functioned as a payment for property or services. For example, payments to a commodity producer under a government commodity support program were subject to the withholding requirement. The rule also imposed information reporting requirements.

Political subdivisions of states (or any instrumentality thereof) with less than $100 million of annual expenditures for property or services that would otherwise have been subject to withholding under this rule were exempt from the withholding requirement. In addition, the 3% withholding requirement did not apply to (i) any payments made through a federal, state, or local government public assistance or public welfare program for which eligibility was determined by a needs or income test; (ii) payments to which mandatory (e.g., U.S. source income of foreign taxpayers) or voluntary (e.g., unemployment benefits) withholding applied; (iii) payments from which amounts were actually being withheld under backup withholding rules; (iv) payments of interest; (v) payments for real property; (vi) payments to tax-exempt entities or foreign governments; (vii) intra-governmental payments; (viii) payments made under a classified or confi-

---

FTC 2d References are to Federal Tax Coordinator 2d
FIN References are to RIA's Analysis of Federal Taxes: Income
USTR References are to United States Tax Reporter: Income
PE References are to Pension Explanations

dential contract (as defined in Code Sec. 6050M(e)(3)); and (ix) payments to government employees for their services as employees, which were not otherwise excludable from these withholding rules. (FTC 2d/FIN ¶ J-8700; USTR ¶ 34,024.29; TaxDesk ¶ 554,101)

New Law. The 2009 Recovery Act delays the implementation of the 3% withholding requirement by one year to apply to payments made after Dec. 31, 2011. (2005 Tax Increase Prevention Act § 511(b) (Sec. 511(b), PL 109-222, 5/17/2006 as amended by 2009 Recovery Act §1511)

☐ **Effective:** Feb. 17, 2009. (Com Rept, see ¶ 5065)

¶ 800. Depreciation Provisions

¶ 801. 50% bonus depreciation and AMT depreciation relief are extended one year through Dec. 31, 2009 (Dec. 31, 2010 for certain property)

Code Sec. 168(k)(2)(A)(iii), as amended by 2009 Recovery Act § 1201(a)(1)(B)

Code Sec. 168(k)(2)(A)(iv), as amended by 2009 Recovery Act § 1201(a)(1)

Code Sec. 168(k)(2)(B)(ii), as amended by 2009 Recovery Act § 1201(a)(1)(B)

Code Sec. 168(k)(2)(E)(i), as amended by 2009 Recovery Act § 1201(a)(1)(B)

Generally effective: Property placed in service before Jan. 1, 2010 and after Dec. 31, 2008

Committee Reports, see ¶ 5034

Under Code Sec. 168(k), "qualified property" (see below) is allowed 50% depreciation (bonus depreciation) in the year that the property is placed in service (with corresponding reductions in basis and, thus, reductions of the regular depreciation deductions otherwise allowed in the placed-in-service year and in later years). (FTC 2d/FIN ¶ L-9310 *et seq.*; USTR ¶ 1684.025; TaxDesk ¶ 269,341)

Additionally, qualified property is exempt from the alternative minimum tax (AMT) depreciation adjustment, see FTC 2d/FIN ¶ A-8221; USTR ¶ 1684.029; TaxDesk ¶ 696,514, which is the adjustment that requires that certain property depreciated on the 200% declining balance method for regular income tax purposes must be depreciated on the 150% declining balance method for AMT purposes, see FTC 2d/FIN ¶ A-8220; USTR ¶ 564.01; TaxDesk ¶ 696,513.

Also, qualified property is allowed an $8,000 increase in the otherwise-applicable dollar limit on first-year depreciation for passenger cars, see FTC 2d/FIN ¶ L-10004.1A; USTR ¶s 1684.0281, 280F4; TaxDesk ¶ 267,602.2.

The rules discussed above for qualified property don't apply to classes of property for which, under Code Sec. 168(k)(2)(D)(iii), the taxpayer elects to not apply Code Sec. 168(k) (an "election-out"), see FTC 2d/FIN ¶ L-9318; USTR ¶ 1684.0291; TaxDesk ¶ 269,348.

The following are the requirements for qualified property under Code Sec. 168(k)(2):

FTC 2d References are to Federal Tax Coordinator 2d
FIN References are to RIA's Analysis of Federal Taxes: Income
USTR References are to United States Tax Reporter: Income
PE References are to Pension Explanations

... the property must be of a qualifying type; i.e., generally, most machinery, equipment or other tangible personal property; most computer software; and certain leasehold improvements;

... the property must not be either property that must be depreciated under the alternative depreciation system or "qualified New York Liberty Zone leasehold improvement property");

... the property must not be the subject of certain disqualifying transactions involving users other than the taxpayer or persons related to the taxpayer or the other users;

... the property's original use generally must begin with the taxpayer after Dec. 31, 2007;

... the property must meet a timely-placed-in-service requirement (see below)

... the property must meet a timely acquisition requirement (see below), see FTC 2d/FIN ¶ L-9312 *et seq.*; USTR ¶ 1684.026 *et seq.*; TaxDesk ¶ 269,342 *et seq.*

Under pre-2009 Recovery Act law, the timely-placed-in-service requirement was that the property had to be placed in service by the taxpayer before Jan. 1, 2009, except for certain aircraft and certain long-production-period property that had to be placed in service before Jan. 1, 2010. (FTC 2d/FIN ¶ L-9310, ¶ L-9312, ¶ L-9316 *et seq.*; USTR ¶ 1684.026, ¶ 1684.027; TaxDesk ¶ 269,342, ¶ 269,346 *et seq.*) However, long-production-period property could qualify for the Dec. 31, 2009 placed-in-service deadline only to the extent of adjusted basis attributable to manufacture, construction or production before Jan. 1, 2009 (the progress expenditure rule). (FTC 2d/FIN ¶ L-9310, ¶ L-9316.1; USTR ¶ 1684.027; TaxDesk ¶ 269,346.1)

Under pre-2009 Recovery Act law, the timely acquisition requirement was satisfied if the property was acquired by the taxpayer either (1) after Dec. 31, 2007 and before Jan. 1, 2009, but only if no written binding contract for the acquisition was in effect before Jan. 1, 2008, or (2) under a written binding contract entered into after Dec. 31, 2007 and before Jan. 1, 2009. For a taxpayer manufacturing, constructing or producing property for its own use, the timely acquisition requirement was treated as met if the taxpayer began the manufacture, construction or production before Jan. 1, 2009. (FTC 2d/FIN ¶ L-9310, ¶ L-9312, ¶ L-9315 *et seq.*; USTR ¶ 1684.026; TaxDesk ¶ 269,342, ¶ 269,345 *et seq.*)

Under Code Sec. 168(k)(4), a corporation can elect, subject to certain limitations, to forego bonus and accelerated depreciation for "eligible qualified property" in exchange for the present allowance, as refundable tax credits, of otherwise-deferred "pre-2006 credits" (research credits from tax years beginning before 2006 and credits for AMT paid that is attributable to tax years beginning before 2006), see FTC 2d/FIN ¶ L-15213 *et seq.*; USTR ¶ 1684.0293; TaxDesk ¶ 580,511 *et seq.*

New Law. The 2009 Recovery Act changes the timely-placed-in-service requirement (above) to provide that qualified property has to be placed in service by the taxpayer before *Jan. 1, 2010*, except that the aircraft and long-production-period property discussed above have to be placed in service before *Jan. 1, 2011*. (Code Sec. 168(k)(2)(A)(iv) as amended by 2009 Recovery Act §1201(a)(1))

> 🅡🅘🅐 *observation:* In addition to extending the eligibility period for bonus depreciation, the extension of the placed-in-service deadline for qualified property also extends the eligibility period for obtaining the exemption, discussed above, from the AMT depreciation adjustment. For the extension of eligibility for the $8,000 increase in the first-year depreciation limit for passenger automobiles (above), see ¶ 803. For the optional extension of the Code Sec. 168(k)(4) election, see ¶ 804. For an election, available to certain taxpayers, to apply Code Sec. 168(k)(4) only to tax years ending after Dec. 31, 2008, see ¶ 805. For technical corrections to the binding contract and tax deficiency rules for the Code Sec. 168(k)(4) election, see ¶ 806.

Also, the 2009 Recovery Act changes the progress expenditure rule to provide that long-production-period property can qualify for the Dec. 31, 2010 placed-in-service deadline only to the extent of adjusted basis attributable to manufacture, construction or production after Dec. 31, 2007 and before *Jan. 1, 2010* (Code Sec. 168(k)(2)(B)(ii) as amended by 2009 Recovery Act §1201(a)(1)(B))

> 🅡🅘🅐 *observation:* Because the above change to the progress expenditure rule applies to property placed in service after Dec. 31, 2008 (see "Effective" below), presumably the change applies *both* to long-production-period property placed in service during calendar year 2010 (long-production-period property which meets the Dec. 31, 2010 placed-in-service deadline provided by the 2009 Recovery Act) *and* during calendar year 2009 (long-production-period property which meets the Dec. 31, 2009 placed-in-service deadline provided under pre-2009 Recovery Act law). Thus, the entire adjusted basis of the long-production-period property placed in service during calendar year 2009 can qualify for bonus depreciation and AMT depreciation relief.

Changes to the timely-acquisition rules. Under the 2009 Recovery Act, the timely acquisition requirement is satisfied if the property is acquired by the taxpayer either (1) after Dec. 31, 2007 and before *Jan. 1, 2010*, but only if no writ-

FTC 2d References are to Federal Tax Coordinator 2d
FIN References are to RIA's Analysis of Federal Taxes: Income
USTR References are to United States Tax Reporter: Income
PE References are to Pension Explanations

ten binding contract for the acquisition was in effect before Jan. 1, 2008, or (2) under a written binding contract entered into after Dec. 31, 2007 and before *Jan. 1, 2010.* (Code Sec. 168(k)(2)(A)(iii) as amended by 2009 Recovery Act §1201(a)(1)(B)) For a taxpayer manufacturing, constructing or producing property for its own use, the timely acquisition requirement is treated as met if the taxpayer began the manufacture, construction or production before *Jan. 1, 2010* (the self-constructed property rule). (Code Sec. 168(k)(2)(E)(i) as amended by 2009 Recovery Act §1201(a)(1)(B))

⚫ *observation:* The italicized dates of "before Jan. 1, 2010" above (and the "before Jan. 1, 2009" dates that they replace) are relevant only for the aircraft and long-production-period property discussed above that are subject to separate treatment under the placed-in-service rules.

⚫ *observation:* Because the above changes to dates in the timely acquisition rules apply to property placed in service after Dec. 31, 2008 (see "Effective" below), presumably the changes apply *both* to qualifying aircraft and long-production-period property placed in service during calendar year 2010 (qualifying aircraft and long-production-period property which meet the Dec. 31, 2010 placed-in-service deadline provided by the 2009 Recovery Act) *and* during calendar year 2009 (qualifying aircraft and long-production-period property which meet the Dec. 31, 2009 placed-in-service deadline provided under pre-2009 Recovery Act law). Thus, qualifying aircraft and long-production-period property placed in service during calendar year 2009 can qualify for bonus depreciation and AMT depreciation relief even if they aren't acquired before Jan. 1, 2009 (taking into account the self-constructed property rule) nor under a written binding contract entered into before Jan. 1, 2009.

☐ **Effective:** Property placed in service before Jan. 1, 2010 (before Jan. 1, 2011 for the aircraft and long-production-period property discussed above) (Code Sec. 168(k)(2)(A)(iv)) and after Dec. 31, 2008 in tax years ending after Dec. 31, 2008. (2009 Recovery Act §1201(c)(1))

¶ 802. Regular Code Sec. 179 deduction limit of $250,000 and beginning of phaseout amount of $800,000 for 2008 are each extended to apply to tax years beginning in 2009

Code Sec. 179(b)(7), as amended by 2009 Recovery Act § 1202(a)
Generally effective: Tax years beginning in 2009
Committee Reports, see ¶ 5035

Generally, many taxpayers can elect to treat the cost of any section 179 property placed in service during the tax year as an expense which is not chargeable to capital account, and any cost so treated is allowed as a deduction for the tax year in which the section 179 property is placed in service, see FTC 2d/FIN ¶ L-9900 *et seq.*; USTR ¶ 1794 *et seq.*; TaxDesk ¶ 268,400 *et seq.*

For tax years beginning in 2008, the deductible Code Sec. 179 expense cannot exceed $250,000, and the maximum deductible expense must be reduced (i.e., phased out) by the amount by which the cost of section 179 property placed in service during the 2008 tax year exceeds $800,000 (i.e., the "beginning-of-phaseout amount"), see FTC 2d/FIN ¶ L-9907; USTR ¶ 1794.01; TaxDesk ¶ 268,411. The $250,000 and $800,000 amounts are not adjusted for inflation, see FTC 2d/FIN ¶ L-9907.1; USTR ¶ 1794.01; TaxDesk ¶ 268,411.

Under pre-2009 Recovery Act law, for tax years beginning in 2009, the deductible Code Sec. 179 expense could not exceed $125,000, and the maximum deductible expense had to be reduced by the amount by which the cost of section 179 property placed in service during the 2009 tax year exceeds $500,000. (FTC 2d/FIN ¶ L-9900, ¶ L-9907; USTR ¶ 1794.01; TaxDesk ¶ 268,400, ¶ 268,411) The $125,000 and $500,000 amounts were each adjusted for inflation. Thus, under pre-2009 Recovery Act law, for tax years beginning in 2009, the $125,000 maximum expense and the $500,000 "beginning-of-phaseout" amounts were inflation-adjusted to $133,000 and $530,000, respectively. (FTC 2d/FIN ¶ L-9900, ¶ L-9907.1; USTR ¶ 1794.01; TaxDesk ¶ 268,411).

illustration: T, a calendar-year taxpayer, places into service section 179 property with a cost of $660,000 during 2009. Under pre-2009 Recovery Act law, T could have elected to expense $3,000: $133,000 [maximum expense for 2009] − $130,000 [the amount by which the cost of section 179 property placed in service, $660,000, exceeds the "beginning-of-phaseout amount" for 2009, $530,000].

FTC 2d References are to Federal Tax Coordinator 2d
FIN References are to RIA's Analysis of Federal Taxes: Income
USTR References are to United States Tax Reporter: Income
PE References are to Pension Explanations

There are certain concepts and computations affected by the amount of the Code Sec. 179 deduction limit, and the beginning of phaseout amount, for a particular tax year. These concepts and computations are: 50% bonus depreciation for "qualified disaster assistance property" (FTC 2d/FIN ¶ L-9365, ¶ L-9366; USTR ¶ 1684.085); computing the expense deduction ceiling amount for partnerships and partners, S corporations and their shareholders (FTC 2d/FIN ¶ L-9900, ¶ L-9909; USTR ¶ 1794.01; TaxDesk ¶ 268,414); the maximum Code Sec. 179 expense deduction and phaseout amount for enterprise zone businesses (FTC 2d/FIN ¶ L-9950, ¶ L-9951, ¶ L-9952; USTR ¶ 13,97A4; TaxDesk ¶ 268,413); the amount of Code Sec. 179 expensing and phaseout for renewal community businesses (FTC 2d/FIN ¶ L-9985, ¶ L-9986, ¶ L-9988.1; USTR ¶ 14,00J4; TaxDesk ¶ 268,704); and the Code Sec. 179 expensing and phaseout amounts for qualified section 179 Gulf Opportunity Zone (GO Zone) property (FTC 2d/FIN ¶ L-9995, ¶ L-9996, ¶ L-9996.1; USTR ¶ 14,00N4.025; TaxDesk ¶ 268,600).

New Law. The 2009 Recovery Act provides that: (Code Sec. 179(b)(7) as amended by 2009 Recovery Act §1202(a))

. . . a $250,000 limitation on the Code Sec. 179 expense deduction applies for tax years beginning in 2009, (Code Sec. 179(b)(7)(A))

. . . an $800,000 beginning-of-phaseout amount applies for tax years beginning in 2009, and (Code Sec. 179(b)(7)(B))

. . . neither the $250,000 amount nor the $800,000 amount (above) is subject to adjustment for inflation. (Code Sec. 179(b)(7)(C))

Thus, the 2009 Recovery Act extends the $250,000 and $800,000 amounts to tax years beginning in 2009. (Com Rept, see ¶ 5035)

> *illustration:* A, a calendar-year taxpayer, places into service section 179 property with a cost of $660,000 during 2009. A can elect to expense $250,000: $250,000 [maximum expense for 2009] − $0 [the amount by which the cost of section 179 property placed in service, $660,000, exceeds the "beginning-of-phaseout amount" for 2009, $800,000].

> *observation:* Presumably, the use of the phrase "any tax year beginning in 2008, or 2009," in the body of Code Sec. 179(b)(7) is not intended to compel a taxpayer to choose between applying the higher dollar limitations for *either* its tax year beginning in 2008 *or* its tax year beginning in 2009. It seems clear that the intention of the 2009 Recovery Act is to allow the taxpayer to elect the higher dollar limitations for *either* or *both* years.

> *illustration:* B, a calendar-year taxpayer, places into service section 179 property with a cost of $660,000 during each of 2008 and 2009. B

can elect to expense $250,000 for each of 2008 and 2009: $250,000 [maximum expense for 2008 and 2009] − $0 [the amount by which the cost of section 179 property placed in service, $660,000, exceeds the "beginning-of-phaseout amount" for 2008 and 2009, $800,000].

☐ **Effective:** Tax years beginning after Dec. 31, 2008. (2009 Recovery Act §1202(b))

> 🔵*observation:* Although 2009 Recovery Act §1202(b) provides that the amendments made by 2009 Recovery Act §1202 apply to tax years beginning after Dec. 31, 2008, 2009 Recovery Act §1202(a) only adds the tax year 2009 to Code Sec. 179(b)(7). Therefore, other tax years beginning after Dec. 31, 2008 (2010, 2011, etc.) are not affected by this provision of the 2009 Recovery Act.

¶ 803. $8,000 increase in first-year depreciation limit for passenger automobiles that are "qualified property" is extended through Dec. 31, 2009

Code Sec. 168(k)(2)(A)(iv), as amended by 2009 Recovery Act § 1201(a)
Generally effective: Property placed in service before Jan. 1, 2010 and after Dec. 31, 2008
Committee Reports, see ¶ 5034

Code Sec. 280F(a) imposes dollar limits on the depreciation deductions (including deductions under the Code Sec. 179 expensing election) that can be claimed with respect to "passenger automobiles," see FTC 2d/FIN ¶ L-10003; USTR ¶ 280F4; TaxDesk ¶ 267,603. The dollar limits are adjusted annually from a base amount to reflect changes in the automobile component of the Consumer Price Index (CPI). Generally, for passenger automobiles placed in service in 2008, the adjusted first-year limit was $2,960, see FTC 2d/FIN ¶ L-10004; USTR ¶ 280F4; TaxDesk ¶ 267,601. For passenger automobiles built on a truck chassis ("qualifying trucks and vans") a different CPI component is used, and for 2008 the adjusted first-year limit was $3,160, see FTC 2d/FIN ¶ L-10004.4; USTR ¶ 280F4; TaxDesk ¶ 267,602.3.

For any passenger automobile that is "qualified property" and which *isn't* subject to a taxpayer election to *decline* the 50% bonus depreciation and AMT depreciation relief otherwise available for "qualified property" under Code Sec. 168(k) (see ¶ 801), the above rules apply, except that the applicable first-year depreciation limit is increased by $8,000 (not indexed for inflation),

FTC 2d References are to Federal Tax Coordinator 2d
FIN References are to RIA's Analysis of Federal Taxes: Income
USTR References are to United States Tax Reporter: Income
PE References are to Pension Explanations

see FTC 2d/FIN ¶ L-10004.1A; USTR ¶s 1684.021, 280F4; TaxDesk ¶ 267,602.2. Thus, for passenger automobiles that were qualified property placed in service in 2008, the adjusted first-year depreciation limit was $10,960 ($11,160 if the passenger automobiles that were qualified property were "qualifying trucks and vans" (see above)). (FTC 2d/FIN ¶ L-10000, ¶ L-10004.1A; USTR ¶ 1684.0281, ¶ 280F4; TaxDesk ¶ 267,602.2)

Under pre-2009 Recovery Act law, qualified property didn't include property placed in service after Dec. 31, 2008, except for certain aircraft and certain long-production-period property that had, instead, a Dec. 31, 2009 placed-in-service deadline. (FTC 2d/FIN ¶ L-9310, ¶ L-9312, ¶ L-9316 *et seq.*; USTR ¶ 1684.026, ¶ 1684.027; TaxDesk ¶ 269,342, ¶ 269,346 *et seq.*)

> ℝ⟋*observation:* The Dec. 31, 2009 deadline provided under pre-2009 Recovery Act law for certain aircraft and long-production period property wasn't available for passenger automobiles. Clearly, passenger automobiles couldn't qualify as aircraft. Additionally, passenger automobiles couldn't qualify as long-production-period property because one of the requirements for being long-production-period property was that the property either have at least a 10 year MACRS recovery period or be used in the trade or business of transporting persons or property. However, passenger automobiles have a recovery period of only five years, see FTC 2d/FIN ¶ L-8205; USTR ¶ 1684.01; TaxDesk ¶ 266,205, and a vehicle used in the trade or business of transporting persons or property isn't treated as a passenger automobile, see FTC 2d/FIN ¶ L-10003; USTR ¶ 280F4; TaxDesk ¶ 267,602.2. Thus, under pre-2009 Recovery Act law, passenger automobiles placed in service after Dec. 31, 2008 couldn't be qualified property and, thus, couldn't qualify for the $8,000 increase in the first-year depreciation limit.

New Law. The 2009 Recovery Act provides that the placed-in-service deadline for "qualified property" is Dec. 31, 2009 (Dec. 31, 2010 for the aircraft and long-production-period property discussed above) (Code Sec. 168(k)(2)(A)(iv) as amended by 2009 Recovery Act §1201(a)) For the changed placed-in-service deadline as it applies to the availability of bonus depreciation and AMT depreciation relief for "qualified property," see ¶ 801.

> ℝ⟋*observation:* Thus, for a passenger automobile that satisfies the other requirements (see below) for qualified property (and isn't subject to the election discussed above to decline bonus depreciation and AMT depreciation relief), the 2009 Recovery Act extends the placed-in-service deadline for the $8,000 increase in the first-year depreciation limit from Dec, 31, 2008 to Dec. 31, 2009. The Dec. 31, 2010 deadline that applies to the aircraft and long-production-period property discussed above isn't available for passenger automobiles for the reasons dis-

cussed above concerning the Dec. 31, 2009 deadline under pre-2009 Recovery Act law.

observation: For each calendar year, IRS calculates the CPI adjustments discussed above and, based on the calculation, announces the automobile depreciation limits that apply to vehicles placed in service in that calendar year. IRS announced the limits for calendar year 2008 (see above), but has yet to do so for 2009. Thus, strictly for purposes of illustration, the illustrations below assume that the first-year depreciation limits for 2009 will be the same as for 2008.

observation: Property is "qualified property" if it satisfies the definitional requirements and isn't subject to certain ineligibility rules, see ¶ 801. As applied to passenger automobiles, the effect of these requirements and ineligibility rules is that in most instances a passenger automobile that satisfies the Dec. 31, 2009 placed-in-service deadline will be eligible for the $8,000 increase in the first-year depreciation limit if (1) the automobile's original use begins with the taxpayer after Dec. 31, 2007, (2) the automobile is predominantly used by the taxpayer in his business and (3) the automobile is acquired by the taxpayer after Dec. 31, 2007.

illustration (1): On Oct. 15, 2009, T, a calendar year taxpayer, places a new passenger automobile into service in his business. Assume that the vehicle is "qualified property" (and an election to decline bonus depreciation and AMT depreciation relief doesn't apply to the vehicle). T is allowed first-year depreciation for 2009 of no more than $10,960 ($2,960 plus $8,000).

illustration (2): The facts are the same as in illustration (1) except that the passenger automobile that T places into service is a "qualifying truck or van" (see above). T is allowed first-year depreciation for 2009 of no more than $11,160 ($3,160 plus $8,000).

illustration (3): The facts are the same as in illustration (1), except that in 2009 T uses the passenger automobile 80% for business and 20% for personal activities. Because the passenger auto depreciation limits are proportionally reduced to the extent that a vehicle isn't exclusively used in business, see FTC 2d/FIN ¶ L-10004; USTR ¶ 280F4; TaxDesk ¶ 267,601, T is allowed first-year depreciation for 2009 of no more than $8,768 (80% × $10,960).

FTC 2d References are to Federal Tax Coordinator 2d
FIN References are to RIA's Analysis of Federal Taxes: Income
USTR References are to United States Tax Reporter: Income
PE References are to Pension Explanations

☐ **Effective:** Property placed in service before Jan. 1, 2010 (Code Sec. 168(k)(2)(A)(iv)) and after Dec. 31, 2008 in tax years ending after Dec. 31, 2008. (2009 Recovery Act §1201(c)(1))

¶ 804. Election to trade bonus and accelerated depreciation for otherwise-deferred credits is optionally extended through Dec. 31, 2009 (Dec. 31, 2010 for certain property)

Code Sec. 168(k)(2)(A)(iv), as amended by 2009 Recovery Act § 1201(a)(1)
Code Sec. 168(k)(4)(D)(ii), as amended and redesignated by 2009 Recovery Act § 1201
Code Sec. 168(k)(4)(H), as amended by 2009 Recovery Act § 1201(b)(1)(B)
Generally effective: Property placed in service before Jan. 1, 2010 and after Dec. 31, 2008
Committee Reports, see ¶ 5034

A corporation can, under an election that is made for its first tax year ending after Mar. 31, 2008, but also covers all later tax years (a Code Sec. 168(k)(4) election), choose to forego bonus and accelerated depreciation for "eligible qualified property" (see below) in exchange for the present allowance, as refundable tax credits, of otherwise-deferred "pre-2006 credits" (research credits from tax years beginning before 2006 and credits for alternative minimum tax (AMT) paid that is attributable to tax years beginning before 2006). (FTC 2d/ FIN ¶ L-15200, ¶ L-15213 *et seq.*; USTR ¶ 1684.0293; TaxDesk ¶ 580,511 *et seq.*) The amount of otherwise-deferred pre-2006 credits presently allowed for a tax year is determined by the bonus depreciation amount for the tax year, which is limited to 20% of the difference between (1) depreciation allowed for "eligible qualified property" if bonus depreciation is allowed and (2) depreciation allowed for "eligible qualified property" if bonus depreciation isn't allowed. Additionally, the bonus depreciation amount for a tax year can't exceed the "maximum amount," which is the lesser of $30 million or 6% of the taxpayer's pre-2006 credits (the maximum increase amount) decreased by the bonus depreciation amount for all preceding tax years, see FTC 2d/FIN ¶ L-15213.1; USTR ¶ 1684.0293; TaxDesk ¶ 380,512.

"Eligible qualified property" is, generally, defined by reference to "qualified property" as defined for bonus depreciation purposes, but with differences in some, but not all, relevant dates, see FTC 2d/FIN ¶s L-9312 *et seq.*, L-15213.2; USTR ¶s 1684.026 *et seq.*, 1684.0293; TaxDesk ¶s 268,342 *et seq.*, 380,513.

Thus, under pre-2009 Recovery Act law, both qualified property and eligible qualified property didn't include property placed in service after Dec. 31, 2008, except for certain aircraft and certain long-production-period property that had, instead, a Dec. 31, 2009 placed-in-service deadline (the placed-in-service rule).

(FTC 2d/FIN ¶ L-9310, ¶ L-9312, ¶ L-9316 *et seq.*, ¶ L-15200, ¶ L-15213.2; USTR ¶ 1684.026, ¶ 1684.027, ¶ 1684.0293; TaxDesk ¶ 269,342, ¶ 269,346 *et seq.*, ¶ 380,513)

On the other hand, in "progress expenditure rules" (see immediately below) that are related to the placed-in-service rule, the relevant dates for qualified property and eligible qualified property were different. Under the progress expenditure rule for qualified property, long-production-period property could qualify for the Dec. 31, 2009 placed-in-service deadline only to the extent of adjusted basis attributable to manufacture, construction or production before Jan. 1, 2009. (FTC 2d/FIN ¶ L-9310, ¶ L-9316.1; USTR ¶ 1684.027; TaxDesk ¶ 269,346.1) Under the progress expenditure rule for eligible qualified property, long-production-period property could qualify for the Dec. 31, 2009 placed-in-service deadline only to the extent of adjusted basis attributable to manufacture, construction or production before Jan. 1, 2009 and after Mar. 31, 2008. (FTC 2d/FIN ¶ L-15200, ¶ L-15213.2; USTR ¶ 1684.0293; TaxDesk ¶ 580,513)

New Law. The 2009 Recovery Act changes:

(1) the placed-in-service deadline for "qualified property" to Dec. 31, 2009, but, for the aircraft and long-production-period property discussed above, to Dec. 31, 2010, (Code Sec. 168(k)(2)(A)(iv) as amended by 2009 Recovery Act §1201(a)(1))

(2) changes the progress expenditure rule for eligible qualified property (see above) to provide that long-production-period property can qualify for the Dec. 31, 2010 placed-in-service deadline only to the extent of adjusted basis attributable to manufacture, construction or production before Jan. 1, 2010 and after Mar. 31, 2008. (Code Sec. 168(k)(4)(D)(iii) as amended by 2009 Recovery Act §1201(b)(1)(A); Code Sec. 168(k)(4)(D)(iii) as redesignated by 2009 Recovery Act §1201(a)(3)(A)(ii))

Additionally, the 2009 Recovery Act defines "extension property" as property which is "eligible qualified property" solely because of the extension of the application of the special allowance under Code Sec. 168(k)(1) (i.e., bonus depreciation) under the amendments made by 2009 Recovery Act §1201(a) (see item (1)), and the application of that extension to the Code Sec. 168(k)(4) election by 2009 Recovery Act §1201(b)(1)(A) (see item (2) above). (Code Sec. 168(k)(4)(H)(iii) as amended by 2009 Recovery Act §1201(b)(1)(B))

> **✔ *observation:*** The effects of the above changes are (1) to extend the Code Sec. 168(k)(4) election to cover property placed in service by Dec. 31, 2009 (Dec. 31, 2010 for the aircraft and

---

FTC 2d References are to Federal Tax Coordinator 2d
FIN References are to RIA's Analysis of Federal Taxes: Income
USTR References are to United States Tax Reporter: Income
PE References are to Pension Explanations

long-production-period property discussed above) instead of, as under pre-2009 Recovery Act law, property placed in service by Dec. 31, 2008 (Dec. 31, 2009 for the aircraft and long-production-period property discussed above) and (2) define extension property, in substance, as property to which the extension applies. However, as discussed below under **"Option to decline extension,"** taxpayers can decline the extension.

Separate computations for extension property. If a taxpayer doesn't make the election (discussed below) to decline the extension of the Code Sec. 168(k)(4) election, a separate bonus depreciation amount (see above), maximum amount (see above) and maximum increase amount (see above) are computed and applied for eligible qualified property that is extension property and eligible qualified property that isn't extension property. (Code Sec. 168(k)(4)(H)(i)(II)) Thus, in computing the maximum amount, the maximum increase amount for extension property is reduced by bonus depreciation amounts for preceding tax years only with respect to extension property. (Com Rept, see ¶ 5034)

> *observation:* An effect of separate computations for eligible qualified property that is and isn't extension property would appear to be the possibility of cumulatively doubling the amount of otherwise deferred pre-2006 credits (see above) that are presently allowed as refundable credits under the election.

Option to decline the extension. A taxpayer that made the Code Sec. 168(k)(4) election for the first tax year ending after Mar. 31, 2008 (as described above) may elect to not have Code Sec. 168(k)(4) apply to "extension property." (Code Sec. 168(k)(4)(H)(i); Code Sec. 168(k)(4)(H)(i)(I))

> *observation:* Thus, a taxpayer that made the Code Sec. 168(k)(4) election for the first tax year ending after Mar. 31, 2008 (as described above) has the option of not applying the election to eligible qualified property placed in service before Jan. 1, 2010 and after Dec. 31, 2008 (before Jan. 1, 2011 and after Dec. 31, 2009 if the property is aircraft or long-production-period property discussed above).

> *observation:* To decide whether to decline the extension of the election, the taxpayer must decide whether the benefits of bonus and accelerated depreciation for "extension property" outweigh the cost of not being presently allowed the otherwise-deferred "pre-2006 credits," the present allowance of which would be attributable to bonus depreciation amounts (see above) attributable to the extension property. Generally, the decision will, at the least, (1) require predictions of (a) whether, and in what amounts, the taxpayer will have regular tax or AMT liabilities

in future years and (b) the taxpayer's marginal tax rates in future years and (2) require that the taxpayer do a "present value" analysis that compares (a) the value of the credits if allowed immediately against the value of the credits if allowed in future years and (b) the value of depreciation deductions allowed under an accelerated method that also includes bonus depreciation against the value of depreciation deductions allowed under a straight-line method with no bonus depreciation.

observation: Code Sec. 168(k)(4)(H)(i) doesn't specify when or how the make the election to not apply Code Sec. 168(k)(4) to extension property. Presumably, IRS will provide guidance, as it has with regard to the initial making of an election to apply Code Sec. 168(k)(4), see FTC 2d/FIN ¶ L-15213 *et seq.*; USTR ¶ 1684.0293; TaxDesk ¶ 380,511 *et seq.*

For an election, available to certain taxpayers, to apply Code Sec. 168(k)(4) *only* to extension property and only for tax years ending after Dec. 31, 2008, see ¶ 805.

For a correction of the definition of eligible qualified property, see ¶ 806.

For the changed placed-in-service deadline for qualified property as it applies to the availability of bonus depreciation and AMT depreciation relief for "qualified property," see ¶ 801.

☐ **Effective:** Property placed in service before Jan. 1, 2010 (before Jan. 1, 2011 for the aircraft and long-production-period property discussed above) (Code Sec. 168(k)(2)(A)(iv)) and after Dec. 31, 2008 in tax years ending after Dec. 31, 2008. (2009 Recovery Act §1201(c)(1))

¶ 805. Post-Dec. 31, 2008 election to trade bonus and accelerated depreciation for otherwise-deferred credits is allowed if an earlier election wasn't made

Code Sec. 168(k)(4)(H)(ii), as amended by 2009 Recovery Act § 1201(b)(1)(B)
Generally effective: Property placed in service before Jan. 1, 2010 and after Dec. 31, 2008
Committee Reports, see ¶ 5034

Under Code Sec. 168(k)(4), a corporation can elect, subject to certain limitations, to forego bonus and accelerated depreciation for "eligible qualified prop-

FTC 2d References are to Federal Tax Coordinator 2d
FIN References are to RIA's Analysis of Federal Taxes: Income
USTR References are to United States Tax Reporter: Income
PE References are to Pension Explanations

157

erty" (see below) in exchange for the present allowance, as refundable tax credits, of otherwise-deferred "pre-2006 credits" (research credits from tax years beginning before 2006 and credits for AMT paid that is attributable to tax years beginning before 2006), see FTC 2d/FIN ¶ L-15213 *et seq.*; USTR ¶ 1684.0293; TaxDesk ¶ 580,511 *et seq.*

"Eligible qualified property" is "qualified property" as defined for bonus depreciation purposes, but with differences in some, but not all, relevant dates, see FTC 2d/FIN ¶s L-9312 *et seq.*, L-15213.2; USTR ¶s 1684.026 *et seq.*, 1684.0293; TaxDesk ¶s 268,342 *et seq.*, 380,513.

Under pre-2009 Recovery Act law, the election had to be made for the tax year ending after Mar. 31, 2008, but also applied to all later tax years. (FTC 2d/FIN ¶ L-15200, ¶ L-15213.1; USTR ¶ 1684.0293; TaxDesk ¶ 580,512)

New Law. The 2009 Recovery Act provides that if a taxpayer didn't make the Code Sec. 168(k)(4) election for its first tax year ending after Mar. 31, 2008 (see above)— (Code Sec. 168(k)(4)(H)(ii) as amended by 2009 Recovery Act §1201(b)(1)(B))

... the taxpayer may make the Code Sec. 168(k)(4) election for its first tax year ending after Dec. 31, 2008 and each later year, and (Code Sec. 168(k)(4)(H)(ii)(I))

... in that case, the election applies only to eligible qualified property that is "extension property" (as defined at ¶ 804 and in the observation immediately below). (Code Sec. 168(k)(4)(H)(ii)(II))

> *observation:* As discussed at ¶ 804, the 2009 Recovery Act extended the Code Sec. 168(k)(4) election to cover property placed in service by Dec. 31, 2009 (Dec. 31, 2010 for certain aircraft and long-production-period property) instead of, as under pre-2009 Recovery Act law, property placed in service by Dec. 31, 2008 (Dec. 31, 2009 for certain aircraft and long-production-period property). Thus, as discussed at ¶ 804, extension property is eligible qualified property placed in service before Jan. 1, 2010 and after Dec. 31, 2008 (before Jan. 1, 2011 and after Dec. 31, 2009 if the property is certain aircraft or long-production-period property).

For a correction of the definition of eligible qualified property, see ¶ 806.

For the changed placed-in-service deadline for qualified property as it applies to the availability of bonus depreciation and AMT depreciation relief for "qualified property," see ¶ 801.

☐ **Effective:** Property placed in service before Jan. 1, 2010 (before Jan. 1, 2011 for certain aircraft and long-production-period property, see ¶ 804) (Code Sec. 168(k)(2)(A)(iv)) and after Dec. 31, 2008 in tax years ending after Dec. 31, 2008. (2009 Recovery Act §1201(c)(1))

¶ 806. Binding contract rule and tax deficiency rule for the election to trade bonus and accelerated depreciation for certain otherwise-deferred credits are corrected

Code Sec. 168(k)(4)(D)(ii), as amended by 2009 Recovery Act § 1201(a)(3)(A)(iii)
Code Sec. 6211(b)(4)(A), as amended by 2009 Recovery Act § 1201(a)(3)(B)
Code Sec. 6211(b)(4)(A), as amended by 2009 Recovery Act § 1201(b)(2)
Generally effective: Tax years ending after Mar. 31, 2008
Committee Reports, see ¶ 5034

A corporation can, under an election that is made for its first tax year ending after Mar. 31, 2008, but also covers all later tax years (a Code Sec. 168(k)(4) election), choose to forego bonus and accelerated depreciation for "eligible qualified property" (see below) in exchange for the present allowance, as refundable credits, of otherwise-deferred "pre-2006 credits" (research credits from tax years beginning before 2006 and credits for alternative minimum tax (AMT) paid that is attributable to tax years beginning before 2006), see FTC 2d/FIN ¶ L-15213 *et seq.*; USTR ¶ 1684.0293; TaxDesk ¶ 380,511 *et seq.* The amount of otherwise-deferred pre-2006 credits presently allowed for a tax year is determined by the bonus depreciation amount for the tax year, which is limited to 20% of the difference between (1) depreciation allowed for "eligible qualified property" if bonus depreciation is allowed and (2) depreciation allowed for "eligible qualified property" if bonus depreciation isn't allowed. Additionally, the bonus depreciation amount for a tax year can't exceed the "maximum amount," which is the lesser of $30 million or 6% of the taxpayer's pre-2006 credits (the maximum increase amount) decreased by the bonus depreciation amount for all preceding tax years, see FTC 2d/FIN ¶ L-15213.1; USTR ¶ 1684.0293; TaxDesk ¶ 380,512.

"Eligible qualified property" is, generally, defined by reference to "qualified property" as defined for bonus depreciation purposes, but with differences in certain relevant dates, see FTC 2d/FIN ¶s L-9312 *et seq.*, L-15213.2; USTR ¶s 1684.026 *et seq.*, 1684.0293; TaxDesk ¶s 268,342 *et seq.*, 380,513. Thus, for example, qualified property must be acquired after Dec. 31, 2007 (the acquisition rule), but eligible qualified property must be acquired after Mar. 31, 2008, see FTC 2d/FIN ¶ L-15213.2; USTR ¶ 1684.0293; TaxDesk ¶ 380,513. However, the 2008 Housing Act, which provided the election under Code Sec. 168(k)(4), didn't provide a date adjustment in a rule closely related to the acquisition rule. Specifically, the 2008 Housing Act didn't, for purposes of de-

FTC 2d References are to Federal Tax Coordinator 2d
FIN References are to RIA's Analysis of Federal Taxes: Income
USTR References are to United States Tax Reporter: Income
PE References are to Pension Explanations

159

fining "eligible qualified property," adjust the date in the "written binding contract rule" that requires that qualified property not be acquired under a written binding contract entered into before Jan. 1, 2008. In Rev Proc 2008-65, 2008-44 IRB 1082, which provided guidance concerning the Code Sec. 168(k)(4) election, IRS followed the 2008 Housing Act in not adjusting the Jan. 1, 2008 date in the written binding contract rule for purposes of defining "eligible qualified property." (FTC 2d/FIN ¶ L-15200, ¶ L-15213.2; USTR ¶ 1684.0293; TaxDesk ¶ 580,513)

Generally, Code Sec. 6211(a) defines a tax "deficiency" as the amount by which taxes imposed by the Code exceed the excess of (1) the sum of (A) the amount shown as the tax by the taxpayer upon his return, if a return was made by the taxpayer and an amount was shown as the tax by the taxpayer on the return, plus (B) the amounts previously assessed (or collected without assessment) as a deficiency *over* (2) the amount of rebates, see FTC 2d/FIN ¶ T-1501; USTR ¶ 62,114; TaxDesk ¶ 822,501. Code Sec. 6211(b)(4)(A) lists most refundable credits provided by the Code and states that, for purposes of the definition of tax "deficiency," the listed credits, to the extent allowable, are taken into account as negative amounts of tax. Under pre-2009 Recovery Act law, credits allowable under Code Sec. 168(k)(4) (see above) weren't included in the list of refundable credits provided in Code Sec. 6211(b)(4)(A). (FTC 2d/FIN ¶ T-1500, ¶ T-1505; USTR ¶ 62,114; TaxDesk ¶ 822,501)

New Law. The 2009 Recovery Act changes the date in the written binding contract rule, for purposes of defining eligible qualified property, from "Jan. 1, 2008" to "Apr. 1, 2008." (Code Sec. 168(k)(4)(D)(ii) as amended by 2009 Recovery Act §1201(a)(3)(A)(iii)) Thus, the change is a technical amendment which provides that no written binding contract for the acquisition of eligible qualified property may be in effect before Apr. 1, 2008. (Com Rept, see ¶ 5034)

> *observation:* The effect of changing, for purposes of defining eligible qualified property, the date in the written binding contract rule from Jan. 1, 2008 to Apr. 1, 2008 is to restrict the property that qualifies as eligible qualified property. The change reduces the property for which a taxpayer must forego bonus and accelerated bonus depreciation, but may also reduce the amount of otherwise-deferred pre-2006 credits that the taxpayer is presently allowed.

For the extension of bonus depreciation through Dec. 31, 2009 (and, for some property, through Dec. 31, 2010), see ¶ 801.

For the optional extension of the Code Sec. 168(k)(4) election to cover property placed in service before Jan. 1, 2010 (and, in some instances, before Jan. 1, 2011), see ¶ 804.

For an election, available to certain taxpayers, to apply Code Sec. 168(k)(4) only to tax years ending after Dec. 31, 2008, see ¶ 805.

Tax deficiency rule. The 2009 Recovery Act adds credits allowable under Code Sec. 168(k)(4) to the list of allowable credits that, as discussed above, are treated as a negative amount of tax for purposes of the definition of tax "deficiency." (Code Sec. 6211(b)(4)(A) as amended by 2009 Recovery Act §1201(a)(3)(B); Code Sec. 6211(b)(4)(A) as amended by 2009 Recovery Act §1201(b)(2))

> **RIA** *observation:* In what is presumably an unintended duplication, both 2009 Recovery Act §1201(a)(3)(B) and 2009 Recovery Act §1201(b)(2) provide the rule, described immediately above, concerning credits allowable under Code Sec. 168(k)(4).

Redesignation. Pre-2009 Recovery Act Code Sec. 168(k)(4)(D)(ii) is redesignated as Code Sec. 168(k)(4)(D)(iii). (Code Sec. 168(k)(4)(D)(iii) as redesignated by 2009 Recovery Act §1201(a)(3)(A)(ii))

☐ **Effective:** Tax years ending after Mar. 31, 2008. (2009 Recovery Act §1201(c)(2))

> **RIA** *observation:* Because the 2008 Housing Act provided that the Code Sec. 168(k)(4) election is allowed only for tax years ending after Mar. 31, 2008, the above change has the effect of retroactively repealing the Jan. 1, 2008 date as if that date never applied. Thus, taxpayers that have already filed returns reflecting a Code Sec. 168(k)(4) election and that are affected by the change must file amended returns, resulting in some instances in a refund (if the effect of decreased depreciation is outweighed by increased credits) and in other instances in an additional payment of tax (if the effect of decreased depreciation outweighs increased credits).

FTC 2d References are to Federal Tax Coordinator 2d
FIN References are to RIA's Analysis of Federal Taxes: Income
USTR References are to United States Tax Reporter: Income
PE References are to Pension Explanations

¶ 900. Other Business Provisions

¶ 901. Income from reacquisitions of business debt at a discount in 2009 and 2010 is deferred for up to five years, then included ratably over five years

Code Sec. 108(i), as amended by 2009 Recovery Act § 1231(a)

Generally effective: Discharges in tax years ending after Dec. 31, 2008, for reacquisitions after Dec. 31, 2008, and before Jan. 1, 2011

Committee Reports, see ¶ 5041

A discharge of indebtedness generally results in income to the debtor. (FTC 2d/FIN ¶ J-7000; USTR ¶ 614.114; TaxDesk ¶ 186,000) The amount of income generally equals the difference between the debt's adjusted issue price—i.e., the outstanding amount of the debt just before the discharge—and any amount paid to satisfy the debt. (FTC 2d/FIN ¶ J-7200; USTR ¶ 1084.04; TaxDesk ¶ 186,002)

However, a discharge of indebtedness doesn't give rise to gross income if it: (1) occurs in a Title 11 bankruptcy case; (2) occurs when the taxpayer is insolvent; (3) is a discharge of "qualified farm indebtedness"; (4) is a discharge of "qualified real property business indebtedness"; or (5) is a discharge of up to $2 million of mortgage debt on the taxpayer's main home. (FTC 2d/FIN ¶ J-7400; USTR ¶ 1084.01; TaxDesk ¶ 188,010) Where these exclusions apply, taxpayers generally reduce certain tax attributes, including loss and credit carryovers and basis in property, by the amount of the excluded income. (FTC 2d/FIN ¶ J-7404; USTR ¶ 1084.02; TaxDesk ¶ 188,016)

Repurchase at discount. An issuer realizes debt discharge income on the repurchase of a debt instrument for less than its adjusted issue price. The amount of income equals the excess of the adjusted issue price over the repurchase price. A repurchase includes the retirement of a debt instrument, conversion of a debt instrument into stock of the issuer, or exchange of a newly issued debt instrument for an existing debt instrument.

Under pre-2009 Recovery Act law, the debt discharge income realized on the repurchase of a debt instrument had to be recognized in the year of repurchase. (FTC 2d/FIN ¶ J-7204.1; USTR ¶ 1084.04; TaxDesk ¶ 186,002)

Debt-for-debt exchanges. If a debtor issues a new debt instrument in satisfaction of an outstanding indebtedness, the debtor is treated as having satisfied the indebtedness with an amount of money equal to the issue price of the new

---

FTC 2d References are to Federal Tax Coordinator 2d
FIN References are to RIA's Analysis of Federal Taxes: Income
USTR References are to United States Tax Reporter: Income
PE References are to Pension Explanations

debt instrument. The issue price of the new debt instrument is determined under the original issue discount (OID) rules of Code Sec. 1273 and Code Sec. 1274. Thus, debt discharge income in a debt-for-debt exchange is measured by the excess of the adjusted issue price of the old obligation over the issue price of the new obligation, and the issue price of the new obligation is determined under the OID rules. (FTC 2d/FIN ¶ J-7205; USTR ¶ 1084.04; TaxDesk ¶ 186,004)

Acquisition by related person. Under Code Sec. 108(e)(4), a debtor is treated as having acquired its indebtedness if a person related to the debtor acquires the indebtedness from an unrelated third party. The acquisition results in debt discharge income to the extent required under the debt discharge rules.

For example, if a corporation's wholly-owned subsidiary buys the parent's debt from an unrelated third party for less than its adjusted issue price, the subsidiary's purchase is treated as an acquisition by the parent. As a result, the parent realizes debt discharge income. (FTC 2d/FIN ¶ J-7016; USTR ¶ 1084.04; TaxDesk ¶ 186,022)

A person related to the debtor is defined by reference to Code Sec. 267(b) (loss disallowance in transactions between related taxpayers, see FTC 2d/FIN ¶ G-2707; USTR ¶ 2674.03; TaxDesk ¶ 227,904) and Code Sec. 707(b)(1) (loss disallowance in transactions with controlled partnerships, see FTC 2d/FIN ¶ B-2016; USTR ¶ 7074.03; TaxDesk ¶ 584,514). However, family members who are treated as related are the individual's spouse, children, grandchildren, parent, and any spouse of the individual's children and grandchildren. (FTC 2d/FIN ¶ J-7019; USTR ¶ 1084.04; TaxDesk ¶ 186,024)

> *observation:* For this purpose, an individual's family doesn't include brothers or sisters. Hence, there would be no debt discharge income where a brother or sister of an individual debtor acquires the debt at a discount from an unrelated third party-creditor.

In addition, entities are treated as related if they are treated as a single employer under:

. . . Code Sec. 414(b) (controlled group of corporations, see FTC 2d/FIN ¶ H-7901; USTR ¶ 4144.02; TaxDesk ¶ 584,514) or

. . . Code Sec. 414(c) (trades or businesses under common control, see FTC 2d/FIN ¶ H-7902; USTR ¶ 4144.01; TaxDesk ¶ 584,514). (FTC 2d/FIN ¶ J-7019; USTR ¶ 1084.04; TaxDesk ¶ 186,024)

New Law. Under the 2009 Recovery Act, at the taxpayer's election, debt discharge income from the reacquisition of an applicable debt instrument after Dec. 31, 2008, and before Jan. 1, 2011, is includible in gross income ratably over a period of five tax years beginning with (Code Sec. 108(i)(1) as amended by 2009 Recovery Act §1231(a)):

(1) for reacquisitions occurring in 2009, the fifth tax year following the tax year in which the reacquisition occurs (Code Sec. 108(i)(1)(A)), and

(2) for reacquisitions occurring in 2010, the fourth tax year following the tax year in which the reacquisition occurs. (Code Sec. 108(i)(1)(B))

> *illustration (1):* In 2009, Taxpayer reacquires for $6 million notes that it issued with an adjusted issue price of $10 million. Taxpayer elects to include the income over a five-year period.
>
> Taxpayer realizes $4 million of debt discharge income, but doesn't recognize that income in 2009. Instead, it recognizes $800,000 of debt discharge income ($4 million ÷ 5) in each of the five tax years from 2014 to 2018, inclusive.

> *illustration (2):* The facts are the same as in RIA illustration (1), except that the reacquisition occurred in 2010. Taxpayer recognizes no debt discharge income in 2010, but recognizes $800,000 of debt discharge income ($4 million ÷ 5) in each of the five tax years from 2014 to 2018, inclusive.

> *observation:* This provision will help companies that buy back their troubled debt at a discount. It will enable those companies to restructure their balance sheets and possibly avoid bankruptcy.
>
> Although all of the deferred debt discharge income will eventually be recognized, the taxpayer benefits from having the tax deferred to later years. None of the taxpayer's tax attributes have to be reduced.

> *observation:* A taxpayer might choose not to make the deferral election if, for example, it has a net operating loss (NOL) carryover that it can use to offset the debt discharge income and that otherwise would expire unused.
>
> A taxpayer might also choose not to make the deferral election if the debt discharge income qualifies for one of the exclusions and the taxpayer determines that the exclusion (with the required tax attribute reduction) is more beneficial than the deferral. See below under "Coordination with other exclusions."

"Applicable debt instrument" defined. The term "applicable debt instrument" means any debt instrument that was issued by (Code Sec. 108(i)(3)(A)):

. . . a C corporation (Code Sec. 108(i)(3)(A)(i)), or

FTC 2d References are to Federal Tax Coordinator 2d
FIN References are to RIA's Analysis of Federal Taxes: Income
USTR References are to United States Tax Reporter: Income
PE References are to Pension Explanations

... any other person in connection with the conduct of a trade or business by that person. (Code Sec. 108(i)(3)(A)(ii))

"Debt instrument" defined. The term "debt instrument" is broadly defined to include (Com Rept, see ¶ 5041) a bond, debenture, note, certificate, or any other instrument or contractual arrangement constituting indebtedness within the meaning of Code Sec. 1275(a)(1) (see FTC 2d/FIN ¶ J-4054; USTR ¶ 12,714; TaxDesk ¶ 153,002). (Code Sec. 108(i)(3)(B))

"Reacquisition" defined. The term "reacquisition" means any acquisition of an applicable debt instrument by (Code Sec. 108(i)(4)(A)):

... the debtor that issued (or is otherwise the obligor under) the debt instrument (Code Sec. 108(i)(4)(A)(i)), or

... a related person to that debtor. (Code Sec. 108(i)(4)(A)(ii))

"Acquisition" defined. The term "acquisition" for any applicable debt instrument includes:

... an acquisition of the debt instrument for cash,

... the exchange of the debt instrument for another debt instrument (including an exchange resulting from a modification of the debt instrument),

... the exchange of the debt instrument for corporate stock or a partnership interest,

... the contribution of the debt instrument to capital, and

... the complete forgiveness of the indebtedness by the holder of the debt instrument. (Code Sec. 108(i)(4)(B))

Who is a related person. Whether a person is related to another person is determined in the same manner as under the related-person acquisition rules of Code Sec. 108(e)(4). (Code Sec. 108(i)(5)(A)) See FTC 2d/FIN ¶ J-7019; USTR ¶ 1084.04; TaxDesk ¶ 186,024.

> *illustration (3):* A C corporation's wholly-owned subsidiary buys the parent's debt from an unrelated third party for less than its adjusted issue price. The parent can elect to defer the resulting debt discharge income and include it ratably over five years.

> *illustration (4):* An individual's debt issued in connection with a trade or business is bought by the individual's spouse for less than its adjusted issue price. The individual can elect to defer the resulting debt discharge income and include it ratably over five years.

> *illustration (5):* An individual's debt that was issued in connection with a trade or business is bought by the individual's brother for less than its adjusted issue price. Here, there is no debt discharge income,

because a brother or sister isn't a related person under the related-party acquisition rules.

Election. An election to defer debt discharge income from a reacquisition of an applicable debt instrument is made by including with the income tax return for the tax year in which the debt instrument is reacquired a statement that (Code Sec. 108(i)(5)(B)(i)) clearly identifies the instrument (Code Sec. 108(i)(5)(B)(i)(I)) and includes the amount of deferred income and any other information required by IRS. (Code Sec. 108(i)(5)(B)(i)(II))

The election is made on an instrument-by-instrument basis. (Com Rept, see ¶ 5041) Once made, the election is irrevocable. (Code Sec. 108(i)(5)(B)(ii))

For partnerships, S corporations, or other pass-through entities, the election is made by the partnership, corporation, or other entity. (Code Sec. 108(i)(5)(B)(iii))

IRS may issue regs requiring reporting of the election (and other information required by IRS) on tax returns for later tax years. (Code Sec. 108(i)(7)(B))

Coordination with other exclusions. If a taxpayer elects to defer debt discharge income from a reacquisition of an applicable debt instrument, the exclusions for title 11 bankruptcy, insolvency, qualified farm indebtedness, and qualified real property business indebtedness won't apply to the debt discharge income for the tax year of the election or any later tax year. (Code Sec. 108(i)(5)(C))

Thus, for example, an insolvent taxpayer may elect under the provision to defer debt discharge income rather than excluding that income and reducing tax attributes by a corresponding amount. (Com Rept, see ¶ 5041)

Deferral of OID deductions in debt-for-debt exchanges. Where a debt instrument having OID, as determined under Code Sec. 1271 through Code Sec. 1275, is issued in exchange for an applicable debt instrument that is reacquired (or is treated as reacquired under the related-person acquisition rules of Code Sec. 108(e)(4) and its regs) as part of a reacquisition to which the income-deferral rule applies (Code Sec. 108(i)(2)(A)), the issuer of the debt instrument can't deduct the portion of the OID that (Code Sec. 108(i)(2)(A)(i)):

. . . accrues before the first tax year in the five-tax-year period in which the debt discharge income attributable to the reacquisition of the debt instrument is includible (Code Sec. 108(i)(2)(A)(i)(I)), and

. . . doesn't exceed the debt discharge income from the debt instrument being reacquired. (Code Sec. 108(i)(2)(A)(i)(II))

FTC 2d References are to Federal Tax Coordinator 2d
FIN References are to RIA's Analysis of Federal Taxes: Income
USTR References are to United States Tax Reporter: Income
PE References are to Pension Explanations

However, the aggregate amount of deductions disallowed under the above rule is deductible ratably over the five-tax-year period in which the debt discharge income attributable to the reacquisition of the debt instrument is includible. (Code Sec. 108(i)(2)(A)(ii))

Thus, if a taxpayer makes the deferral election for a debt-for-debt exchange in which the newly issued debt instrument issued (or deemed issued, including by operation of Reg §1.108-2(g)) in satisfaction of an outstanding debt instrument of the debtor has OID, any otherwise allowable OID deduction for the newly issued debt instrument that (1) accrues before the first year of the five-tax-year period in which the related, deferred debt discharge income is included in the taxpayer's gross income and (2) doesn't exceed the related, deferred debt discharge income, is deferred and allowed as a deduction ratably over the same five-tax-year period in which the deferred debt discharge income is included in gross income. (Com Rept, see ¶ 5041)

> *observation:* The issuer of a debt instrument with OID can generally deduct a portion of the OID as interest in each tax year that the debt instrument is outstanding, even though the OID isn't paid until maturity. See FTC 2d/FIN ¶ K-5701; USTR ¶ 1634.051; TaxDesk ¶ 319,701.

> In the case of a debt-for-debt exchange to which the income-deferral rule applies, however, the OID deduction is deferred in order to match the timing of the deduction to the inclusion of debt discharge income.

If the amount of the OID accruing before the first tax year in the five-tax-year period exceeds the debt discharge income from the reacquisition of the applicable debt instrument, the deductions are disallowed in the order in which the OID is accrued. (Code Sec. 108(i)(2)(A))

Rule applies to certain debt-for-cash exchanges. The OID deferral rule can also apply in certain cases when a debtor reacquires its debt for cash. (Com Rept, see ¶ 5041) If the issuer of a debt instrument uses the proceeds directly or indirectly to reacquire an applicable debt instrument of the issuer, the debt instrument that was issued is treated as issued for the debt instrument being reacquired. (Code Sec. 108(i)(2)(B))

If the newly issued debt instrument has OID, the OID deferral rule applies. Thus, all or a portion of the interest deductions for OID on the newly issued debt instrument are deferred into the five-tax-year period in which the debt discharge income is recognized. (Com Rept, see ¶ 5041)

If only a portion of the proceeds from a debt instrument are used to reacquire an applicable debt instrument of the issuer, the OID deferral rule applies to the portion of any OID on the newly issued debt instrument that is equal to the portion of the proceeds from that instrument used to reacquire the outstanding instrument. (Code Sec. 108(i)(2)(B))

Acceleration of deferred items. In the case of the taxpayer's death, the liquidation or sale of substantially all the taxpayer's assets (including in a Title 11 or similar case), the cessation of business by the taxpayer, or similar circumstances, any item of income or deduction that is deferred under the above rules (and hasn't previously been taken into account) is taken into account in the tax year in which that event occurs (or in a Title 11 case, the day before the petition is filed). (Code Sec. 108(i)(5)(D)(i))

Deferred items are accelerated in a Title 11 case where the taxpayer liquidates, sells substantially all of its assets, or ceases to do business, but not where a taxpayer reorganizes and emerges from the Title 11 case. (Com Rept, see ¶ 5041)

This acceleration rule also applies in the case of the sale or exchange or redemption of an interest in a partnership, S corporation, or other pass-through entity by a partner, shareholder, or other person holding an ownership interest in the entity. (Code Sec. 108(i)(5)(D)(ii))

IRS may issue regs extending the application of the rules on acceleration of deferred items to other circumstances where appropriate. (Code Sec. 108(i)(7)(A))

Partnership allocations. In the case of a partnership, any deferred debt discharge income is allocated to the partners immediately before the discharge in the manner those amounts would have been included in the distributive shares of the partners under Code Sec. 704 (see FTC 2d/FIN ¶ B-2400; USTR ¶ 7044; TaxDesk ¶ 586,100) if the income or deduction were recognized at that time. (Code Sec. 108(i)(6))

Any decrease in a partner's share of partnership liabilities as a result of the discharge isn't taken into account for purposes of Code Sec. 752 partnership liability rules (see FTC 2d/FIN ¶ B-1600; USTR ¶ 7524; TaxDesk ¶ 582,000) to the extent it would cause the partner to recognize gain under Code Sec. 731 (see FTC 2d/FIN ¶ B-3600; USTR ¶ 7314; TaxDesk ¶ 589,500). (Code Sec. 108(i)(6)) Thus, the deemed distribution under Code Sec. 752 is deferred for a partner to the extent it exceeds the partner's basis. (Com Rept, see ¶ 5041)

Any decrease in partnership liabilities that is deferred under this rule will be taken into account by the partner at the same time, and to the same extent, as the deferred income is recognized. (Code Sec. 108(i)(6))

Regulatory authority. IRS may prescribe any regs that are necessary or appropriate for applying the above rules. (Code Sec. 108(i)(7)) The regs may provide rules for the application of the above provisions to partnerships, S corpora-

FTC 2d References are to Federal Tax Coordinator 2d
FIN References are to RIA's Analysis of Federal Taxes: Income
USTR References are to United States Tax Reporter: Income
PE References are to Pension Explanations

tions, and other pass through entities, including rules for the allocation of deferred deductions. (Code Sec. 108(i)(7)(C))

☐ **Effective:** Discharges in tax years ending after Dec. 31, 2008. (2009 Recovery Act §1231(b)) The provision applies to reacquisitions after Dec. 31, 2008, and before Jan. 1, 2011. (Code Sec. 108(i)(1))

¶ 902. Noncorporate taxpayers can exclude 75% (rather than 50% or 60%) of gain on the sale or exchange of QSBS held for more than 5 years and acquired after Feb. 17, 2009 and before Jan. 1, 2011

Code Sec. 1202(a)(3), as amended by 2009 Recovery Act § 1241(a)
Generally effective: Stock acquired after Feb. 17, 2009 and before Jan. 1, 2011
Committee Reports, see ¶ 5044

Under pre-2009 Recovery Act law, noncorporate taxpayers can exclude 50% of any gain realized on the sale or exchange of "qualified small business stock" (QSBS) held for more than five years. (FTC 2d/FIN ¶ I-9100, ¶ I-9100.1; USTR ¶ 12,024; TaxDesk ¶ 246,601)

The portion of the gain includible in taxable income is taxed at a maximum rate of 28% under the regular tax. A percentage of the excluded gain is an alternative minimum tax (AMT) preference. The portion of the gain includible in AMTI is taxed at a maximum rate of 28% under the AMT. Thus, under pre-2009 Recovery Act law, gain from the sale of QSBS is taxed at effective rates of (1) 14% under the regular tax, (2) 14.98% under the AMT for dispositions before Jan. 1, 2011, (3) 19.98% under the AMT for dispositions after Dec. 31, 2010 for stock acquired before Jan. 1, 2001, and (5) 17.92% under the AMT for dispositions after Dec. 31, 2010 for stock acquired after Dec. 31, 2000 (Com Rept, see ¶ 5044), see FTC 2d/FIN ¶ A-8304; USTR ¶ 574; TaxDesk ¶ 697,004.

Generally, for gain on the sale or exchange of any QSBS to be excludible, the taxpayer has to acquire the stock at original issue. The amount of gain eligible for exclusion by any individual for any QSBS is the greater of: (1) ten times the taxpayer's basis in the QSBS issued by the corporation and disposed of by the taxpayer in the tax year, or (2) $10 million ($5 million if married filing separately), less the total amount of eligible gain taken into account by the taxpayer on dispositions of QSBS issued by the corporation in all earlier tax years. To qualify as a small business, when the stock is issued, the corporation's gross assets cannot exceed $50 million, and the issuer must also meet certain active trade or business requirements, see FTC 2d/FIN ¶ I-9101 *et seq.*; USTR ¶ 12,024 *et seq.*; TaxDesk ¶ 246,601 *et seq.*

Under pre-2009 Recovery Act law, for QSBS in a corporation that is a "qualified business entity" (QBE) during substantially all of the taxpayer's holding period, noncorporate taxpayers can exclude 60% of the gain realized on the sale or exchange of that QSBS, if held for more than five years. This rule does not apply to gain attributable to periods after Dec. 31, 2014. A QBE is a corporation that meets the requirements of a qualified business under the empowerment zone rules, see FTC 2d/FIN ¶ L-9955; USTR ¶ 13,97A4; TaxDesk ¶ 268,431, during substantially all of the taxpayer's holding period. (FTC 2d/FIN ¶ I-9100.1A; USTR ¶ 12,024; TaxDesk ¶ 246,602)

Under pre-2009 Recovery Act law, for purposes of the 60% gain exclusion for QBE QSBS, the District of Columbia Enterprise Zone is not treated as an empowerment zone. Further, if the designation of the enterprise zone in which the QBE was an enterprise zone business is terminated, the termination is disregarded in determining whether property is QBE QSBS. If the corporation issuing the stock is not a QBE during substantially all of the taxpayer's holding period in the stock, the stock continues to be treated as QBE QSBS, but the gain exclusion is limited. (FTC 2d/FIN ¶ I-9100.1A; USTR ¶ 12,024; TaxDesk ¶ 246,602)

> *observation:* Under pre-2009 Recovery Act law, there were no rules that (1) permitted 75% gain exclusion on the sale or exchange of QSBS acquired after Feb. 17, 2009 and before Jan. 1, 2011, and (2) disregarded all the 60% gain exclusion rules for QBE QSBS if that stock was acquired during that same temporary timeframe.

New Law. The 2009 Recovery Act provides that, for QSBS acquired after Feb. 17, 2009 and before Jan. 1, 2011— (Code Sec. 1202(a)(3) as amended by 2009 Recovery Act §1241(a))

. . . the 50% gain exclusion is increased to 75%, and (Code Sec. 1202(a)(3)(A))

. . . none of the 60% gain exclusion rules for QBE QSBS apply. (Code Sec. 1202(a)(3)(B))

Thus, under the 2009 Recovery Act, the percentage exclusion for QSBS sold by an individual is increased to 75% for stock issued after Feb. 17, 2009 and before Jan. 1, 2011. In addition, as a result of the increased exclusion, gain from the sale of QSBS to which 2009 Recovery Act §1241 applies is taxed at effective rates of 7% under the regular tax and 12.88% under the AMT. (Com Rept, see ¶ 5044)

> *observation:* Presumably, the increased gain exclusion will encourage investment in QSBS during the above statutory period.

observation: Tax return preparers will have to ascertain that QSBS sold or exchanged was purchased within the above statutory period and held for more than 5 years, for it to qualify for the 75% gain exclusion.

illustration (1): L, an unmarried individual filing an individual return, acquired 100 shares of non-QBE QSBS in 2008 at a total cost of $100,000. This is the only QSBS L has ever owned. L sells all the shares in 2017 for $1.1 million. L can exclude $500,000, i.e., 50% of the $1 million gain, on her 2017 individual return.

illustration (2): The facts are the same as in illustration 1, except that L acquired the QSBS in 2010. L can exclude $750,000, i.e., 75% of the $1 million gain, on her 2017 individual return.

illustration (3): The facts are the same as in illustration 2, except that L sold all the QSBS in 2017 for $20.1 million. The maximum gain eligible for exclusion is the greater of (1) $1 million, i.e., 10 times L's $100,000 total basis in the 100 shares, or (2) $10 million. Thus, L, on her 2017 individual return, can exclude $7.5 million of the gain, i.e., 75% × the $10 million cap, not 75% of $20 million.

observation: If, in illustration 3, L is married filing separately in 2017, the amount she could exclude would be $3.75 million, i.e., 75% × $5 million cap for married filing separately.

observation: For QSBS acquired after Feb. 17, 2009 and before Jan. 1, 2011, there is no distinction between 50% gain exclusion non-QBE QSBS and 60% gain exclusion QBE QSBS. Thus, 60% gain exclusion QBE QSBS, which, under pre-2009 Recovery Act law would have been eligible for only 50% gain exclusion on post-2014 appreciation, is eligible for 75% gain exclusion on all sale or exchange gain if purchased during the statutory period and held for more than 5 years.

illustration (4): J, an unmarried individual who is filing an individual return each year, acquired 100 shares of QBE QSBS in 2008 at a total cost of $200,000. This is the only QSBS J has ever owned. The stock was worth $5.2 million on Dec. 31, 2014. J sold all 100 shares on Dec. 31, 2015, when the stock was worth $6.2 million. J can exclude $3.5 million total gain on the sale, i.e., 60% × $5 million pre-2015 appreciation + 50% × $1 million post-2014 appreciation, on her 2015 individual return.

illustration (5): The facts are the same as in illustration 4, except that J acquired the stock in 2010. J can exclude $4 million of the total gain on the sale, i.e., 75% × $6 million, on her 2015 individual return.

> **🅡 *observation:*** Unless Congress extends the statutory purchase period of QSBS eligible for the 75% gain exclusion, for QSBS purchased after Dec. 31, 2010, the 50% and 60% gain exclusion regimes will again be in effect.

☐ **Effective:** Stock acquired after Feb. 17, 2009 (2009 Recovery Act §1241(b)) and before Jan. 1, 2011 (Code Sec. 1202(a)(3) as amended by 2009 Recovery Act §1241(a)).

¶ 903. S Corp built-in gain holding period shortened for 2009 and 2010

Code Sec. 1374(d)(7), as amended by 2009 Recovery Act § 1251(a)
Generally effective: Tax years beginning after Dec. 31, 2008
Committee Reports, see ¶ 5046

An S corporation is generally not subject to tax, but passes through its items to its shareholders, who pay tax on their pro-rata shares of the S corporation's income. Where a corporation that was formed as a C corporation elected to become an S corporation (or where an S corporation receives property from a C corporation in a nontaxable carryover basis transfer), the S corporation was taxed at the highest corporate rate (currently 35%) on all gains that were built-in at the time of the election if the gains are recognized during the recognition period, i.e., the first ten S corporation years (or during the ten-period after the transfer). Under a special exception, the recognition period was unlimited for distributions by thrift institutions that were deemed to be out of pre-'88 reserves. Gains are not built-in gains to the extent they are shown to have arisen while the S election was in effect or are offset by losses. (FTC 2d/FIN ¶ D-1640, ¶ D-1643, ¶ D-1655; USTR ¶ 13,744.01; TaxDesk ¶ 615,002, ¶ 615,014)

New Law. The 2009 Recovery Act provides that, for S corporation tax years beginning in 2009 and 2010, no tax is imposed on the net unrecognized built-in gain of an S corporation if the seventh tax year in the recognition period preceded the 2009 and 2010 tax years. This rule applies separately for property acquired from C corporations in carryover basis transactions. (Code Sec. 1374(d)(7)(B) as amended by 2009 Recovery Act §1251(a)) Thus, for the 2009 and 2010 tax years, the recognition period is reduced to seven years. For property acquired from C corporations in carryover basis transactions, the recognition period is reduced to seven years from the date the property was acquired. (Com Rept, see ¶ 5046)

FTC 2d References are to Federal Tax Coordinator 2d
FIN References are to RIA's Analysis of Federal Taxes: Income
USTR References are to United States Tax Reporter: Income
PE References are to Pension Explanations

observation: Thus, the recognition period will end at the beginning of the 2009 tax year if the S corporation election was made for the 2002 tax year and the recognition period will end at the beginning of the 2010 tax year if the S corporation election was made for the 2003 tax year.

The unlimited recognition period for distributions by thrift institutions that are deemed to be out of pre-'88 reserves is amended to provide that the 2009 and 2010 seven-year period also does not apply. (Code Sec. 1374(d)(7)(C))

observation: Thus, the unlimited recognition period for distributions by thrift institutions that are deemed to be out of pre-'88 reserves remains.

☐ **Effective:** Tax years beginning after Dec. 31, 2008. (2009 Recovery Act §1251(b))

¶ 904. Work opportunity credit is expanded to apply to new target group of unemployed veterans and disconnected youth who begin work in 2009 or 2010

Code Sec. 51(d)(14), as amended by 2009 Recovery Act § 1221(a)
Generally effective: Individuals who begin work for the employer after Dec. 31, 2008 and before Jan. 1, 2011
Committee Reports, see ¶ 5039

A work opportunity tax credit (WOTC) is available on an elective basis to employers for qualified first-year wages paid to members of one or more of nine "targeted groups" (including qualified veterans). Subject to lower limits for wages paid to summer youth employees or to employees who work less than 400 hours, the maximum credit is $2,400 per employee (40% of up to a maximum of $6,000 of qualified first-year wages), see FTC 2d/FIN ¶ L-17775, ¶ L-17776; USTR ¶ 514; TaxDesk ¶ 380,700. Higher credit limits apply to qualified veterans (see FTC 2d/FIN ¶ L-17779.2; USTR ¶ 514; TaxDesk ¶ 380,702.2) and long-term family assistance recipients (see FTC 2d/FIN ¶ L-17779.1; USTR ¶ 514; TaxDesk ¶ 380,702.1).

For these purposes, a "qualified veteran" is an individual who is a veteran (defined below) and who is certified by a designated local agency (defined as a state employment security agency, see FTC 2d/FIN ¶ L-17784.1; USTR ¶ 514; TaxDesk ¶ 380,708) as meeting either the food stamp test or the disability test. Under the food stamp test, the individual must be a member of a family receiving assistance under a food stamp program under the Food Stamp Act of '77 for at least 3 months all or part of which is during the 12-month period ending on the hiring date. FTC 2d/FIN ¶ L-17785.1; USTR ¶ 514; TaxDesk ¶ 380,711.

Under the disability test, the individual must be entitled to compensation for a service-connected disability and:

. . . have a hiring date that isn't more than one year after having been discharged or released from active duty in the U.S. Armed Forces, or

. . . have aggregate periods of unemployment during the one-year period ending on the hiring date that equal or exceed six months. FTC 2d/FIN ¶ L-17785.1; USTR ¶ 514; TaxDesk ¶ 380,711.

A "veteran" for these purposes is an individual certified as either having served on active duty (other than for training) in the U.S. Armed Forces for more than 180 days, or having been discharged or released from active duty in the U.S. Armed Forces for a service-connected disability. However, individuals serving on active duty for more than 90 days (other than for training), must be further certified as not having served any of the active duty during the 60-day period ending on the hiring date. FTC 2d/FIN ¶ L-17785.1; USTR ¶ 514; TaxDesk ¶ 380,711.

Qualified first-year wages are certain wages attributable to service during the one-year period beginning with the day the individual begins work for the employer, see FTC 2d/FIN ¶ L-17783; USTR ¶ 514; TaxDesk ¶ 380,707.

The WOTC isn't available for wages paid to an employee in any of the targeted groups if the employee begins work for the taxpayer after Aug. 31, 2011, see FTC 2d/FIN ¶ L-17775; USTR ¶ 514; TaxDesk ¶ 380,700.

New Law. The 2009 Recovery Act creates a new targeted group for the WOTC. (Com Rept, see ¶ 5039) Specifically, any unemployed veteran (defined below) or disconnected youth (defined below) who begins work for the employer during 2009 or 2010 is treated as a member of a targeted group for purposes of the rules for computing the WOTC. (Code Sec. 51(d)(14)(A) as amended by 2009 Recovery Act §1221(a))

> *observation:* Thus, there are now ten targeted groups for the WOTC (rather than nine, as under pre-2009 Recovery Act law).

> *illustration:* Employer hires an unemployed veteran in 2009. The veteran works 500 hours for the employer at $10 per hour, thus earning $5,000 in 2009. Employer is entitled to a credit of 40% of $5,000, or $2,000.

FTC 2d References are to Federal Tax Coordinator 2d
FIN References are to RIA's Analysis of Federal Taxes: Income
USTR References are to United States Tax Reporter: Income
PE References are to Pension Explanations

"Unemployed veteran" defined. For purposes of the above rule (Code Sec. 51(d)(14)(B)), an "unemployed veteran" is any veteran (defined below) who is certified by the designated local agency as (Code Sec. 51(d)(14)(B)(i)):

. . . having been discharged or released from active duty in the Armed Forces at any time during the five-year period ending on the hiring date (Code Sec. 51(d)(14)(B)(i)(I)), and

. . . being in receipt of unemployment compensation under state or federal law for not less than four weeks during the one-year period ending on the hiring date. (Code Sec. 51(d)(14)(B)(i)(II))

A veteran, for these purposes, is an individual certified as either having served on active duty (other than for training) in the U.S. Armed Forces for more than 180 days, or having been discharged or released from active duty in the U.S. Armed Forces for a service-connected disability. (Code Sec. 51(d)(14)(B)(i))

> *observation:* There is no requirement that, to be considered a veteran for these purposes, individuals serving on active duty for more than 90 days (other than for training), must be further certified as not having served any of the active duty during the 60-day period ending on the hiring date. The definition of an *unemployed* veteran for purposes of this provision is thus broader than the definition of a *qualified* veteran under pre-2009 Recovery Act law.

"Disconnected youth" defined. For purposes of the rule treating certain disconnected youth as members of a targeted group for WOTC purposes (Code Sec. 51(d)(14)(B)), a "disconnected youth" is any individual who is certified by the designated local agency (Code Sec. 51(d)(14)(B)(ii)):

. . . as having attained age 16 but not age 25 on the hiring date (Code Sec. 51(d)(14)(B)(ii)(I)),

. . . as not regularly attending any secondary, technical, or post-secondary school during the six-month period preceding the hiring date (Code Sec. 51(d)(14)(B)(ii)(II)),

. . . as not regularly employed during that 6-month period (Code Sec. 51(d)(14)(B)(ii)(III)), and

. . . as not readily employable by reason of lacking a sufficient number of basic skills. (Code Sec. 51(d)(14)(B)(ii)(IV))

For these purposes, Congress intends that a low level of formal education may satisfy the requirement that an individual is not readily employable by reason of lacking a sufficient number of skills. (Com Rept, see ¶ 5039)

Congress also intends that IRS, when providing general guidance regarding the various new criteria (discussed above), will take into account the administrability of the program by state agencies. (Com Rept, see ¶ 5039)

> **⊘** *observation:* Presumably, the state agencies referred to here are the designated local agencies discussed above.

☐ **Effective:** Individuals who begin work for the employer after Dec. 31, 2008 (2009 Recovery Act §1221(b)) and before Jan. 1, 2011 (Code Sec. 51(d)(14)(A) as amended by 2009 Recovery Act §1221(a)).

¶ 905. New markets tax credit national limit is raised for 2008 and 2009 with a preferential allocation rule for the 2008 increase

Code Sec. 45D(f)(1), as amended by 2009 Recovery Act § 1403(a)(3)
Code Sec. 45D(f)(2), 2009 Recovery Act § 1403(b)
Generally effective: Feb. 17, 2009
Committee Reports, see ¶ 5057

Code Sec. 45D provides a new markets tax credit for qualified equity investments in a qualified community development entity (CDE, see FTC 2d/FIN ¶ L-17923; USTR ¶ 45D4; TaxDesk ¶ 384,703), see FTC 2d/FIN ¶ L-17921; USTR ¶ 45D4; TaxDesk ¶ 384,701. A qualified equity investment is any equity investment in a CDE for which the CDE has received an allocation from IRS if, among other requirements, the CDE uses substantially all of the cash from the investment to make qualified low-income community investments (the investment requirement), see FTC 2d/FIN ¶ L-17924; USTR ¶ 45D4; TaxDesk ¶ 384,704. The credit is available through calendar year 2009 subject to a nationwide credit limitation on qualified equity investments for each calendar year. Under pre-2009 Recovery Act law, the nationwide credit limitations on qualified equity investments for each calendar year were as follows:

. . . $1 billion for 2001,

. . . $1.5 billion for 2002 and 2003,

. . . $2 billion for 2004 and 2005, and

. . . $3.5 billion for 2006, 2007, 2008 and 2009. (FTC 2d/FIN ¶ L-17920, ¶ L-17927; USTR ¶ 45D4; TaxDesk ¶ 384,711)

Under Code Sec. 45D(f)(2), the nationwide credit limitations are allocated to CDEs by IRS under an allocation rule that gives priority to any entity (1) with a

FTC 2d References are to Federal Tax Coordinator 2d
FIN References are to RIA's Analysis of Federal Taxes: Income
USTR References are to United States Tax Reporter: Income
PE References are to Pension Explanations

record of having successfully provided capital or technical assistance to disadvantaged businesses or communities, or (2) which intends to satisfy the "investment requirement" (see above) by making qualified low-income community investments in one or more businesses in which persons unrelated to the entity hold the majority equity interest. (FTC 2d/FIN ¶ L-17920, ¶ L-17927; USTR ¶ 45D4; TaxDesk ¶ 384,711)

New Law. The 2009 Recovery Act provides that the nationwide credit limitations for calendar years 2008 and 2009 are each $5 billion. (Code Sec. 45D(f)(1)(E) as amended by 2009 Recovery Act §1403(a)(3)), (Code Sec. 45D(f)(1)(F) as amended by 2009 Recovery Act §1403(a)(3)) Thus, the maximum amount of qualified equity investments is raised by $1.5 billion for both 2008 and 2009. (Com Rept, see ¶ 5057)

The $1.5 billion increase in the credit limitation for calendar year 2008 must be allocated in accordance with the allocation rule in Code Sec. 45D(f)(2) (see above), but to CDEs (see above) which— (2009 Recovery Act §1403(b))

(1) submitted an allocation application for calendar year 2008, *and* (2009 Recovery Act §1403(b)(1))

(2) either—

(A) didn't receive an allocation for calendar year 2008, or (2009 Recovery Act §1403(b)(2)(A))

(B) received an allocation for calendar year 2008 in an amount less than the amount requested in the allocation application. (2009 Recovery Act §1403(b)(2)(B))

☐ **Effective:** Feb. 17, 2009. (Com Rept, see ¶ 5057)

¶ 906. States can elect grants, instead of tax credits, to finance low-income housing for 2009, but tax credit allocations are reduced

Code Sec. 42(i)(9), as amended by 2009 Recovery Act § 1404
Code Sec. None, 2009 Recovery Act § 1602
Generally effective: Feb. 17, 2009
Committee Reports, see ¶ 5058

The low-income housing credit, which is a type of business tax credit that may be used to offset taxable income, can be claimed over a 10-year period by owners of certain residential rental property for the cost of rental housing occupied by tenants having incomes below specified levels, see FTC 2d/FIN ¶ L-15701; USTR ¶ 424; TaxDesk ¶ 383,001.

Any building eligible for the low-income housing credit which is not financed with the proceeds of tax-exempt bonds subject to certain volume limitation rules must, in order to claim the credit, receive an allocation of the low-income housing credit from a state or local credit agency, see FTC 2d/FIN ¶ L-16001; USTR ¶ 424.70; TaxDesk ¶ 383,004.

The aggregate dollar amount of low-income housing credit which a state has available to allocate in any year is limited. (FTC 2d/FIN ¶ L-16000, ¶ L-16006; USTR ¶ 424.70; TaxDesk ¶ 383,012) A state's low-income housing credit ceiling amount for any calendar year is the sum of the following four amounts:

(1) an unused carryforward component (i.e., any unused state housing credit ceiling for the preceding calendar year);

(2) a population component (i.e., the greater of (i) $2.30 multiplied by the state population, or (ii) $2,665,000);

(3) a returned credit component (i.e., the amount of the state housing credit ceiling returned in the calendar year); and

(4) a national pool component (i.e., the amount, if any, allocated to the state from other states by IRS), see FTC 2d/FIN ¶s L-16006.1, L-16006.2, L-16006.3, L-16006.8; USTR ¶ 424.76; TaxDesk ¶ 383,012.

> *observation:* Under pre-2009 Recovery Act law, the low-income housing tax credit allocations that states are entitled to for 2009 could not be substituted with grant money.

New Law. Because the current economic downturn has reduced the attractiveness of low-income housing tax credits (since some potential investors have reduced, or no, taxable income to offset with tax credits), states may *elect* to receive *grants* for low-income housing projects *instead of* the low-income housing tax *credit* allocations that those states would otherwise be entitled to for 2009. Specifically, the 2009 Recovery Act directs IRS (or its delegate, see below) to grant to each state's housing credit agency an amount equal to each state's "low-income housing grant election amount" (defined below). (2009 Recovery Act §1602(a)) The option to elect low-income housing grant money, instead of credit allocations for 2009, is intended to give state allocating agencies added flexibility, and to encourage the building of more low-income housing in the short term until investors can again make use of the tax credits. (Com Rept, see ¶ 5058)

Low-income housing grant election amount. A state's "low-income housing grant election amount" is an amount elected by the state, subject to certain lim-

---

FTC 2d References are to Federal Tax Coordinator 2d
FIN References are to RIA's Analysis of Federal Taxes: Income
USTR References are to United States Tax Reporter: Income
PE References are to Pension Explanations

its. A state's maximum low-income housing grant election amount may not exceed 85% of the product of— (2009 Recovery Act §1602(b))

(I) the sum of— (2009 Recovery Act §1602(b)(1))

(A) 100% of the state's 2009 housing credit ceiling attributable to the amounts described in items (1) and (3), above, and (2009 Recovery Act §1602(b)(1)(A))

(B) 40% of the state's 2009 housing credit ceiling attributable to the amounts described in items (2) and (4), above, multiplied by (2009 Recovery Act §1602(b)(1)(B))

(II) 10. (2009 Recovery Act §1602(b)(2))

Thus, the low-income housing grant election amount for a state is an amount elected by the state subject to certain limits. The maximum low-income housing grant election amount for a state cannot exceed 85% of the product of ten and the sum of the state's: (1) unused housing credit ceiling for 2008; (2) any returns to the state during 2009 of credit allocations previously made by the state; (3) 40% of the state's 2009 credit allocation; and (4) 40% of the state's share of the national pool allocated in 2009 (if any). (Com Rept, see ¶ 5058)

An award of a low-income housing grant is *not* taxable income to the recipient. (Com Rept, see ¶ 5058)

Subawards for low-income buildings. A state housing credit agency receiving a grant as described above must use the grant to make subawards to finance the construction, or acquisition and rehabilitation, of qualified low-income buildings. A subaward may be made to finance a qualified low-income building regardless of whether the building has an allocation of low-income housing credit. However, for qualified low-income buildings with*out* allocations of the low-income housing credit, the state housing credit agency *must* make a determination that the subaward for the building will increase the *total* funds available to the state to build and rehabilitate affordable housing. In complying with this determination requirement, the state housing credit agency must establish a process in which applicants that are allocated credits are required to demonstrate good faith efforts to obtain investment commitments for the credits *before* the agency makes the subawards. (2009 Recovery Act §1602(c)(1))

Any subaward, for any qualified low-income building, must be made in the same manner, and be subject to the same limitations (including rent, income, and use restrictions on the building), as an allocation of housing credit dollar amount allocated by the state housing credit agency under the low-income housing credit rules. However, the subawards are *not* limited by, and do not otherwise affect ("except as provided in Code Sec. 42(h)(3)(J)" [sic]), the state's housing credit ceiling applicable to the agency. (2009 Recovery Act §1602(c)(2)) *observation:* Code Sec. 42(h)(3)(J), mentioned above, does not exist. A technical correction apparently is required to correct what appears to be a drafting error.

The state's housing credit agency is required to perform asset management functions to ensure compliance with the low-income housing credit rules and the long-term viability of buildings funded by any subaward. The agency can collect reasonable fees from subaward recipients to cover the expenses of the agency's asset management duties. The agency may also retain an agent, or other private contractor, to perform these asset management duties. (2009 Recovery Act §1602(c)(3))

The state's housing credit agency must impose conditions or restrictions, including a requirement providing for recapture, on any subaward to assure that a building for which a subaward is made remains a qualified low-income building during the compliance period. Any recapture is payable to IRS for deposit in IRS's general fund, and can be enforced by means of liens or other methods as IRS determines appropriate. (2009 Recovery Act §1602(c)(4))

Return of unused grant funds. Any grant funds not used to make subawards before Jan. 1, 2011, must be returned to IRS on that date. Any subawards returned to a state's housing credit agency on or after Jan. 1, 2011 must be promptly returned to IRS. All amounts returned to IRS must be deposited in IRS's general fund. (2009 Recovery Act §1602(d))

Definitions. Any term described above that is also used in the Code Sec. 42 low-income housing credit rules has the same meaning as when used in Code Sec. 42. Any reference above to "IRS" is treated as including the IRS's delegate. (2009 Recovery Act §1602(e))

Appropriations. All monies necessary to carry out the low-income housing grants described above are appropriated by Congress to IRS. (2009 Recovery Act §1602(f))

Coordination of low-income housing credit and low-income housing grants. A state electing to receive low-income housing grants in 2009, as described above, must reduce its low-income housing credit ceiling by the amount taken into account in determining the low-income housing grant election amount. (Com Rept, see ¶ 5058) Specifically, the amounts described in items (1) through (4), above, for any state for 2009, must each be reduced by the amount that is taken into account in determining the amount of any low-income housing grant to that state. (Code Sec. 42(i)(9)(A) as amended by 2009 Recovery Act §1404)

FTC 2d References are to Federal Tax Coordinator 2d
FIN References are to RIA's Analysis of Federal Taxes: Income
USTR References are to United States Tax Reporter: Income
PE References are to Pension Explanations

The basis of a qualified low-income building is *not* reduced by the amount of a low-income housing grant. (Code Sec. 42(i)(9)(B))

☐ **Effective:** Feb. 17, 2009. (Com Rept, see ¶ 5058)

¶ 907. Rules for high-yield OID obligations are suspended for obligations issued from Sept. 1, 2008 to Dec. 31, 2009

Code Sec. 163(e)(5)(F), as amended by 2009 Recovery Act § 1232(a)
Generally effective: Obligations issued after Aug. 31, 2008 and before Jan. 1, 2010, in tax years ending after Aug. 31, 2008
Committee Reports, see ¶ 5042

Original issue discount (OID) on obligations (bonds, notes, debentures, certificates and other evidences of indebtedness) is generally deductible by the issuer as interest. The discount must be amortized over the life of the obligation. (FTC 2d/FIN ¶s K-5700, K-5701; USTR ¶ 1634.051; TaxDesk ¶ 319,701)

Unlike the deduction for regular OID, the yield on certain high-yield OID obligations is divided into two parts: an interest element which is deductible only when paid and a return on equity element that isn't deductible as interest, but that may qualify for the dividends received deduction. These rules apply to any "applicable high-yield discount obligation" (AHYDO) issued by a corporation (other than during periods when it's an S corporation). A debt instrument is an AHYDO if: (1) its maturity date is more than five years from the issue date, (2) the yield to maturity equals or exceeds the sum of the applicable federal rate (AFR) in effect under Code Sec. 1274(d) (FTC 2d/FIN ¶ J-4181; USTR ¶ 12,714.04; TaxDesk ¶ 153,030) for the calendar month the obligation is issued plus five percentage points (high yield to maturity), and (3) it has "significant OID." (FTC 2d/FIN ¶ K-5763; USTR ¶ 1634.051; TaxDesk ¶ 319,734)

A debt instrument has "significant OID" if the aggregate amount that would be includable in gross income with respect to the instrument for periods before the close of any accrual period (as defined in Code Sec. 1272(a)(5), see FTC 2d/FIN ¶ J-4301; USTR ¶ 1634.051; TaxDesk ¶ 153,008) ending after the date five years after the issue date exceeds the sum of the aggregate amount of interest to be paid under the instrument before the close of the accrual period plus the product of the issue price of the instrument (as defined in Code Sec. 1273(b) and Code Sec. 1274(a), see FTC 2d/FIN ¶s J-4130, J-4151; USTR ¶ 12,714.03; TaxDesk ¶ 153,025) and its yield to maturity. The issuer's choice of accrual periods to determine OID accruals is also used to determine if a debt instrument has significant OID. (FTC 2d/FIN ¶ K-5764; USTR ¶ 1634.051; TaxDesk ¶ 319,735)

The rules give special treatment to a portion of the OID on an AHYDO. The issuer gets no deduction on this disqualified portion, and the remainder of the OID isn't deductible until paid. The holder is entitled to a dividends received deduction for the part of the disqualified portion that would have been treated as a dividend if the issuing corporation had distributed it with respect to stock. This is the dividend equivalent portion. (FTC 2d/FIN ¶ K-5754; USTR ¶ 1634.051; TaxDesk ¶ 319,730)

The disqualified portion of OID is generally the portion of the total return on the obligation that bears the same ratio to the total return as the disqualified yield bears to the total yield to maturity. The disqualified yield is the portion of the yield that exceeds the AFR for the month in which the obligation is issued plus six percentage points. If the yield to maturity determined by disregarding the OID exceeds the AFR plus six percentage points, the disqualified portion is the entire amount of the OID. (FTC 2d/FIN ¶ K-5765, ¶ K-5766, ¶ K-5768; USTR ¶ 1634.051; TaxDesk ¶ 319,736, ¶ 319,737, ¶ 319,738)

Under pre-2009 Recovery Act law, IRS provided exceptions from the AHYDO rules in certain cases where market conditions worsened after a lender made a financing commitment, causing the issue price of the debt instrument to be significantly less than the amount of money the borrowing corporation received, see Rev Proc 2008-51. (FTC 2d/FIN ¶ K-5755.1; USTR ¶ 1634.051; TaxDesk ¶ 319,731)

New Law. The 2009 Recovery Act suspends the AHYDO rules so that the rules do not apply to any AHYDO issued during the period beginning on Sept. 1, 2008 and ending on Dec. 31, 2009 in exchange (including an exchange resulting from a modification of the debt instrument) for an obligation that is not an AHYDO and the issuer (or obligor) of which is the same as the issuer (or obligor) of the applicable high yield discount obligation. (Code Sec. 163(e)(5)(F)(i) as amended by 2009 Recovery Act §1232(a)) Thus, the 2009 Recovery Act suspends the Code Sec. 163(e)(5) rules for certain obligations issued in a debt-for-debt exchange, including an exchange resulting from a significant modification of a debt instrument, after Aug. 31, 2008 and before Jan. 1, 2010. (Com Rept, see ¶ 5042)

This Code Sec. 163(e)(5)(F)(i) exception does not apply to any obligation the interest on which is interest described in Code Sec. 871(h)(4) (without regard to Code Sec. 871(h)(4)(D)) (contingent interest, see FTC 2d/FIN ¶ O-10216.1; USTR ¶ 8714.02; TaxDesk ¶ 630,124) or to any obligation issued to a related person (within the meaning of Code Sec. 108(e)(4), the related party acquisition rules that apply to cancellations of indebtedness, see FTC 2d/FIN ¶ J-7019; USTR ¶ 1084.04; TaxDesk ¶ 186,024). (Code Sec. 163(e)(5)(F)(i))

FTC 2d References are to Federal Tax Coordinator 2d
FIN References are to RIA's Analysis of Federal Taxes: Income
USTR References are to United States Tax Reporter: Income
PE References are to Pension Explanations

Exception continues with new obligation. Any obligation to which Code Sec. 163(e)(5)(F)(i) applies is not treated as an AHYDO for purposes of applying Code Sec. 163(e)(5)(F) to any other obligation issued in exchange for that obligation. (Code Sec. 163(e)(5)(F)(ii))

Thus, for example, if a new debt instrument that would be an AHYDO under pre-2009 Recovery Act law is issued in exchange for a debt instrument that is not an AHYDO, and the 2009 Recovery Act provision suspends application of Code Sec. 163(e)(5), then another new debt instrument that is issued during the suspension period in exchange for the instrument with respect to which the rule in Code Sec. 163(e)(5) was suspended, would be eligible for the relief provided by this provision despite the fact that it is issued for an instrument that is an AHYDO under pre-2009 Recovery Act law. (Com Rept, see ¶ 5042)

IRS can extend the suspension beyond Dec. 31, 2009. If IRS determines that continued distressed conditions in the debt capital markets necessitate applying the suspension of the rules to debt instruments issued in periods after Dec. 31, 2009, it has the authority to continue to suspend the rules. (Code Sec. 163(e)(5)(F)(iii))

☐ **Effective:** Obligations issued after Aug. 31, 2008 and before Jan. 1, 2010 (Code Sec. 163(e)(5)(F)(i)), in tax years ending after Aug. 31, 2008. (2009 Recovery Act §1232(c)(1))

¶ 908. Beginning in 2010, IRS will be able to apply a higher rate to determine whether an obligation is an applicable high-yield discount obligation

Code Sec. 163(i)(1), as amended by 2009 Recovery Act § 1232(b)
Generally effective: Obligations issued after Dec. 31, 2009, in tax years
*   ending after Dec. 31, 2009*
Committee Reports, see ¶ 5042

Under the original issue discount (OID) rules, a debt instrument is an applicable high-yield discount obligation (AHYDO, i.e., an obligation subject to certain interest deduction limitations) if: (1) its maturity date is more than five years from the issue date, (2) the yield to maturity equals or exceeds the sum of the applicable federal rate (AFR) in effect under Code Sec. 1274(d) for the calendar month the obligation is issued plus five percentage points (high yield to maturity), and (3) it has significant OID. For a complete description of these rules and an exception to them provided by the 2009 Recovery Act, see ¶ 907.

IRS may issue regs permitting a rate higher than the AFR to be used to test a debt instrument's yield to maturity if the taxpayer establishes to IRS's satisfaction that the higher rate is based on the same principles as the AFR and was appropriate for the term of the instrument. Under this regulatory authority, IRS may allow a rate that "more exactly establishes the average market yield" on outstanding marketable U.S. obligations for the same time of issue and maturity as the tested obligation. (FTC 2d/FIN ¶ K-5700, ¶ K-5763; USTR ¶ 1634.051; TaxDesk ¶ 319,734)

New Law. Under 2009 Recovery Act law, for obligations issued after Dec. 31, 2009, for purposes of determining whether a debt obligation is an AHYDO, IRS will be able to permit, on a temporary basis, a rate to be used for any debt instrument that is higher than the AFR if IRS determines that this rate is appropriate in light of distressed conditions in the debt capital markets. (Code Sec. 163(i)(1) as amended by 2009 Recovery Act §1232(b))

> *observation:* The new regulatory authority given to IRS under the 2009 Recovery Act is in addition to its authority (see above) to issue regs allowing a higher rate if it is based on the same principles as the AFR and is appropriate for the term of the instrument, which continues to be in effect.

☐ **Effective:** Obligations issued after Dec. 31, 2009, in tax years ending after Dec. 31, 2009. (2009 Recovery Act §1232(c)(2))

FTC 2d References are to Federal Tax Coordinator 2d
FIN References are to RIA's Analysis of Federal Taxes: Income
USTR References are to United States Tax Reporter: Income
PE References are to Pension Explanations

185

¶ 1000. Credits for Energy Saving Vehicles

¶ 1001. Credit for QAFV refueling property is increased for property placed in service in tax years beginning in 2009 or 2010

Code Sec. 30C(e)(6), as amended by 2009 Recovery Act § 1123(a)
Generally effective: Tax years beginning after Dec. 31, 2008
Committee Reports, see ¶ 5023

Under pre-2009 Recovery Act law, taxpayers were entitled to a 30% income tax credit for the cost of installing qualified alternative fuel vehicle (QAFV) refueling property to be used in a taxpayer's trade or business or at the taxpayer's principal residence. The credit couldn't exceed $30,000 per tax year, per location, in the case of depreciable QAFV refueling property used in a trade or business, and $1,000 per tax year per location for any other QAFV refueling property installed on property used as a principal residence. (FTC 2d/FIN ¶ L-18040, ¶ L-18041; USTR ¶ 30C4; TaxDesk ¶ 397,201)

QAFV refueling property is property (not including a building or its structural components) for the storage or dispensing of a clean-burning fuel or electricity into the fuel tank or battery of a motor vehicle propelled by such fuel or electricity, but only if the storage or dispensing of the fuel or electricity is at the point of delivery into the fuel tank or battery of the motor vehicle. The use of QAFV refueling property must begin with the taxpayer, see FTC 2d/FIN ¶ L-18043; USTR ¶ 30C4.02; TaxDesk ¶ 397,203.

The credit is available for property placed in service after Dec. 31, 2005, and (except in the case of hydrogen refueling property) before Jan. 1, 2011. For hydrogen refueling property, the property has to be placed in service before Jan. 1, 2015, see FTC 2d/FIN ¶ L-18041; USTR ¶ 30C4; TaxDesk ¶ 397,201.

> **🅡 observation:** An example of hydrogen refueling property would be hydrogen refueling pumps (i.e., fuel pumps that dispense hydrogen).

New Law. The 2009 Recovery Act provides that, for property placed in service in tax years beginning after Dec. 31, 2008 and before Jan. 1, 2011— (Code Sec. 30C(e)(6) as amended by 2009 Recovery Act §1123(a))

. . . for any QAFV refueling property not relating to hydrogen, the credit is 50% of the cost of the property placed in service by the taxpayer in the tax year (Code Sec. 30C(e)(6)(A)(i)),

---

FTC 2d References are to Federal Tax Coordinator 2d
FIN References are to RIA's Analysis of Federal Taxes: Income
USTR References are to United States Tax Reporter: Income
PE References are to Pension Explanations

... up to a maximum credit of $50,000 for depreciable QAFV refueling property (Code Sec. 30C(e)(6)(A)(ii)), and

... up to a maximum credit of $2,000 for nondepreciable QAFV refueling property installed on property used as a principal residence. (Code Sec. 30C(e)(6)(A)(iii))

Congress believes that widespread adoption of advanced technology and alternative-fuel vehicles is needed to transform automotive transportation in the U.S. to be cleaner, more fuel efficient, and less reliant on petroleum fuels. Congress further believes that one important method to encourage this trend is to provide additional tax incentives for the development and installation of the infrastructure needed to deliver clean fuels to drivers of clean-fuel vehicles. Thus, for property placed in service in tax years beginning in 2009 or 2010, the 2009 Recovery Act increases the maximum credit available for business property to $50,000 for qualified refueling property not related to hydrogen. For nonbusiness property, the maximum credit is increased to $2,000. In addition, the credit rate is increased from 30% to 50%, except in the case of hydrogen refueling property (discussed below). (Com Rept, see ¶ 5023)

> *observation:* For depreciable QAFV refueling property, this is a 66⅔% increase in the maximum credit (from $30,000 to $50,000). For nondepreciable QAFV refueling property, this is a 100% increase in the maximum credit (from $1,000 to $2,000).

> *illustration (1):* In 2008, T, a calendar-year taxpayer, installed several items of depreciable QAFV refueling property, with a total cost of $160,000, at one location. T is allowed a $30,000 credit for the property (30% × $160,000, but capped at $30,000) for 2008.

> *illustration (2):* The facts are the same as in Illustration 1, except T places all the items in service in 2009. None of the property placed in service is related to hydrogen. T is allowed a $50,000 credit for the property (50% × $160,000, but capped at $50,000) for 2009.

> *observation:* Thus, where the credit for QAFV refueling property is 50% of the cost of the property up to a $50,000 maximum credit for the tax year, cost in excess of $100,000 will not result in a tax benefit for purposes of the credit. Where the QAFV refueling property credit is 50% of the cost of the property up to a $2,000 maximum credit for the tax year, cost in excess of $4,000 will not result in a tax benefit for purposes of the credit.

If the QAFV refueling property is related to hydrogen, the credit is 30% of the cost of the QAFV refueling property, capped at $200,000. (Code Sec. 30C(e)(6)(B))

Thus, for property placed in service in tax years beginning in 2009 or 2010, the 2009 Recovery Act increases the maximum credit available for *business* property to $200,000 for qualified hydrogen refueling property. (Com Rept, see ¶ 5023)

> **observation:** For *nondepreciable* qualified hydrogen refueling property placed in service in tax years beginning in 2009 or 2010, the credit percentage remains at 30%, and the maximum dollar amount of the credit remains at $1,000.

> **observation:** While the credit percentage remains at 30% for QAFV refueling property related to hydrogen, the increase in the maximum credit from $30,000 to $200,000 for business property is a 666% increase and, presumably, will encourage taxpayers to place into service in 2009 and 2010 depreciable QAFV refueling property related to hydrogen.

> **illustration (3):** In 2008, V, a calendar-year taxpayer, placed in service $500,000 of depreciable QAFV refueling property related to hydrogen. V's QAFV refueling property credit for 2008 is $30,000 (30% × $500,000, but capped at $30,000).

> **illustration (4):** The facts are the same as in Illustration 3, except that V places the property in service in 2009. V's QAFV refueling property credit for 2009 is $150,000 (30% × $500,000).

> **illustration (5):** In 2010, V places in service $1,000,000 of depreciable QAFV refueling property related to hydrogen. V's QAFV refueling property credit for 2010 is $200,000 (30% × $1,000,000, but capped at $200,000).

> **observation:** Thus, where the QAFV refueling property credit is 30% of the cost of the property up to a $200,000 maximum credit for the year, cost in excess of $666,666 will not result in a tax benefit for purposes of the credit.

☐ **Effective:** Tax years beginning after Dec. 31, 2008. (2009 Recovery Act §1123(b))

FTC 2d References are to Federal Tax Coordinator 2d
FIN References are to RIA's Analysis of Federal Taxes: Income
USTR References are to United States Tax Reporter: Income
PE References are to Pension Explanations

¶ 1002. "New qualified plug-in electric drive motor vehicle credit" will be modified for vehicles acquired after Dec. 31, 2009

Code Sec. 30D, as amended by 2009 Recovery Act § 1141(a)
Code Sec. 30B(d)(3)(D), as amended by 2009 Recovery Act § 1141(b)(1)
Code Sec. 38(b)(35), as amended by 2009 Recovery Act § 1141(b)(2)
Code Sec. 904(i), as amended by 2009 Recovery Act § 1142(b)(1)(E)
Code Sec. 1016(a)(25), as amended by 2009 Recovery Act § 1141(b)(3)
Code Sec. 6501(m), as amended by 2009 Recovery Act § 1141(b)(4)
Generally effective: Vehicles acquired after Dec. 31, 2009
Committee Reports, see ¶ 5027

Code Sec. 30D provides a credit for the purchase of certain battery powered vehicles called "qualified plug-in electric drive motor vehicles" (NQPEDMVs)). (FTC 2d/FIN ¶ L-18030 *et seq.*; USTR ¶ 30D4 *et seq.*; TaxDesk ¶ 397,130 *et seq.*)

New Law. The 2009 Recovery Act provides a credit, as described below, for NQPEDMVs. (Code Sec. 30D as amended by 2009 Recovery Act §1141(a)). For the separate credit, provided by the 2009 Recovery Act, under Code Sec. 30 for certain low-speed and 2- or 3-wheeled plug-in vehicles, see ¶ 1003. For the addition, by the 2009 Recovery Act, to the alternative motor vehicle credit (AMVC) under Code Sec. 30B of a credit for certain costs of converting vehicles to plug-in vehicles, see ¶ 1004.

> ✒ *observation:* The credit provided by Code Sec. 30D for NQPEDMVs as described below will, as noted below, differ in significant respects from the credit provided, under pre-2009 Recovery Act law, by Code Sec. 30D for NQPEDMVs (the pre-2009 Recovery Act credit). For vehicles acquired before Jan. 1, 2010 (see "Effective" below), the pre-2009 Recovery Act credit for NQPEDMVs remains in effect.

> ✒ *observation:* Under pre-2009 Recovery Act law, no credit for NQPEDMVs was available for vehicles purchased after Dec. 31, 2014, see FTC 2d/FIN ¶ L-18030 *et seq.*, USTR ¶ 30D4, TaxDesk ¶ 397,130 *et seq.* As modified by the 2009 Recovery Act, the credit will be subject, as under pre-2009 Recovery Act law, to a phase-out (see below), but won't be subject to the Dec. 31, 2014 termination date, or any other termination date.

Under the 2009 Recovery Act, the amount of the credit will be the sum described immediately below for *each* NQPEDMV placed in service by the taxpayer during the tax year (the per-vehicle credit). (Code Sec. 30D(a)(1)). For rules that may limit the amount or availability of the credit even though a vehicle meets the requirements for being a NQPEDMV, see "Phaseout rules," "Tax liability limit for depreciable property," "Tax liability limit for non-depreciable property" and "Property used outside of the U.S." below.

The per-vehicle credit will be the sum of the following: (Code Sec. 30D(b)(1))

(1) $2,500; plus (Code Sec. 30D(b)(2))

(2) for a vehicle which draws propulsion energy from a battery with not less than 5 kilowatt hours of capacity, $417 for each kilowatt hour of capacity in excess of 5 kilowatt hours, but not in excess of $5,000. (Code Sec. 30D(b)(3)) For this purpose, capacity, with respect to any battery is the quantity of electricity that the battery is capable of storing, expressed in kilowatt hours, as measured from a 100% state of charge to a zero percent state of charge. (Code Sec. 30D(d)(4)) Thus, the maximum credit is $7,500, regardless of weight. (Com Rept, see ¶ 5027)

> **☑️ observation:** Under pre-2009 Recovery Act law, the per-vehicle amount of the credit for NQPEDMVs is determined as follows:
>
> . . . Code Sec. 30D(a)(2) provides that the per-vehicle credit equals $2,500, plus $417 for each kilowatt hour of traction battery capacity in excess of 4 kilowatt hours;
>
> . . . Code Sec. 30D(b)(1) provides that the per-vehicle amount determined under Code Sec. 30D(a)(2) can't exceed amounts that increase from $7,500 to $15,000 as the gross vehicle weight rating (GVWR (loaded weight)) of the vehicle increases. (FTC 2d/FIN ¶ L-18030, ¶ L-18031.1; USTR ¶ 30D4.01; TaxDesk ¶ 397,132)

> **☑️ observation:** Because of the complexities of the credit for NQPEDMVs, presumably IRS will provide procedures for issuing certifications, on which taxpayers can rely, as to the eligibility of a specific vehicle for the credit and as to the amount of the credit for that vehicle. For certification procedures under the credit for alternative motor vehicles under Code Sec. 30B, see, for example, FTC 2d/FIN ¶ L-18025.1 *et seq.*, USTR ¶ 30B4.02, TaxDesk ¶ 397,105.1 *et seq.*

Phaseout rules.

> **☑️ observation:** Unlike the phase-out rules for the pre-2009 Recovery Act credit, which count all U.S. sales of NQPEDMVs against a single

---

FTC 2d References are to Federal Tax Coordinator 2d
FIN References are to RIA's Analysis of Federal Taxes: Income
USTR References are to United States Tax Reporter: Income
PE References are to Pension Explanations

limit, the phaseout rules below are applied with per-manufacturer limits. Also, under the pre-2009 Recovery Act credit, the number of vehicles that triggers the phase-out is 250,000, instead of 200,000 (see below), and the vehicles taken into account are those sold after Dec. 31, 2008, instead of after Dec. 31, 2009 (see below) (FTC 2d/FIN ¶ L-18030, ¶ L-18031.2; USTR ¶ 30D4.02; TaxDesk ¶ 397,133).

For an NQPEDMV sold during the "phaseout period" (defined below), only the "applicable percentage" (defined below) of the otherwise allowable credit will be allowed. (Code Sec. 30D(e)(1))

The "phaseout period" will be the period beginning with the second calendar quarter following the calendar quarter that includes the first date on which *the number of NQPEDMVs manufactured by the manufacturer of the NQPEDMV and sold for use in the U.S. after Dec. 31, 2009 is at least 200,000.* (Code Sec. 30D(e)(2))

The "applicable percentage" will be: (Code Sec. 30D(e)(3))

. . . 50% for the first two calendar quarters of the phaseout period, (Code Sec. 30D(e)(3)(A))

. . . 25% for the third and fourth calendar quarters of the phaseout period, and (Code Sec. 30D(e)(3)(B))

. . . 0% for each later calendar quarter. (Code Sec. 30D(e)(3)(C))

For purposes of Code Sec. 30D(e), rules similar to the rules in Code Sec. 30B(f)(4) will apply. (Code Sec. 30D(e)(4))

> *observation:* Code Sec. 30B(f)(4) treats as one manufacturer certain related or otherwise-affiliated manufacturers in determining if and when phaseout of the new qualified hybrid motor vehicle and new advanced lean burn technology portions of the AMVC occurs, see FTC 2d/FIN ¶s L-18028, E-10626, H-5612, H-7953, L-17787; USTR ¶s 30B4.04, 514, 4144.05, 15,634; TaxDesk ¶s 380,719, 397,108, 607,513. Thus, under Code Sec. 30D(e)(4), certain related or otherwise-affiliated manufacturers will be added together in determining whether the 200,000 per-manufacturer level is reached.

Tax liability limit for depreciable property.

> *observation:* The rules below concerning the tax liability limit for depreciable property are the same as those that apply to the pre-2009 Recovery Act credit.

The portion of the credit for NQPEDMVs that is attributable to property of a character subject to an allowance for depreciation (generally, property used in a trade or business or for the production of income, see FTC 2d/FIN ¶ L-7901;

USTR ¶ 1674.006; TaxDesk ¶ 265,401) will be treated as a credit listed under Code Sec. 38(b) for the tax year (i.e., a credit that is part of the general business credit for the tax year, see FTC 2d/FIN ¶ L-15201; USTR ¶ 384.01; TaxDesk ¶ 380,501) and not as a credit allowed under Code Sec. 30D(a) (discussed above). (Code Sec. 30D(c)(1); Code Sec. 38(b)(35) as amended by 2009 Recovery Act §1141(b)(2))

> *observation:* Thus, as part of the general business credit provided by Code Sec. 38, the portion of the credit for NQPEDMVs that is attributable to depreciable property (the depreciable property portion) won't be allowed to offset any of a taxpayer's alternative minimum tax (AMT), and may be limited in its offset of a taxpayer's regular income tax, see FTC 2d/FIN ¶ L-15202; USTR ¶ 384.02; TaxDesk ¶ 380,502. However, depreciable property portions disallowed because of the tax liability limits are carried back or forward to the extent provided in Code Sec. 39, see FTC 2d/FIN ¶ L-15209; USTR ¶ 394; TaxDesk ¶ 380,509.

Tax liability limit for non-depreciable property.

> *observation:* The rules below concerning the tax liability limit for non-depreciable property are the same as those that apply to the pre-2009 Recovery Act credit, except that Code Sec. 26(a)(2) never applied to the non-depreciable property portion of the pre-2009 Recovery Act credit because, under pre-2009 Recovery Act law, Code Sec. 26(a)(2) terminated before the pre-2009 Recovery Act credit became effective. See FTC 2d/FIN ¶ L-18034.1; USTR ¶ 30D4.07; TaxDesk ¶ 397,143 and ¶ 204.

The portion of the credit for NQPEDMVs that isn't attributable to depreciable property (the non-depreciable property portion) will be treated as a credit allowed under Subtitle A, Chapter 1, Subchapter A, Part IV, Subpart A of the Code (also known as a Subpart A credit or personal credit). (Code Sec. 30D(c)(2)(A) as amended by 2009 Recovery Act §1141(a))

However, the credit allowed under Code Sec. 30D *won't be subject* to the rule that provides that Subpart A credits can't exceed the excess (if any) of the taxpayer's regular tax liability for the tax year over the tentative minimum tax for the tax year (determined without regard to the AMT foreign tax credit). (Code Sec. 26(a)(1)) Instead, for tax years to which Code Sec. 26(a)(2) doesn't apply (see the first observation below), the non-depreciable property portion can't exceed for any tax year an amount equal to the following:

FTC 2d References are to Federal Tax Coordinator 2d
FIN References are to RIA's Analysis of Federal Taxes: Income
USTR References are to United States Tax Reporter: Income
PE References are to Pension Explanations

... the *excess* of (Code Sec. 30D(c)(2)(B)) the sum of the taxpayer's AMT and "regular tax liability" as defined in Code Sec. 26(b) (i.e., a taxpayer's income tax, not including the AMT and other special taxes, see FTC 2d/FIN ¶ A-4905; USTR ¶ 264.01; TaxDesk ¶ 569,603), *over* (Code Sec. 30D(c)(2)(B)(i))

... the sum of the allowable credit provided by Code Sec. 27 (the foreign tax credit, see FTC 2d/FIN ¶ O-4000; USTR ¶ 274; TaxDesk ¶ 569,601) and the allowable Subpart A credits (other than the adoption credit provided by Code Sec. 23, see FTC 2d/FIN ¶ A-4401; USTR ¶ 234; TaxDesk ¶ 569,501, the residential energy efficiency credit provided by Code Sec. 25D, see FTC 2d/FIN ¶ A-4781; USTR ¶ 25D4; TaxDesk ¶ 569,553, and the credit for NQPEDMVs), see FTC 2d/FIN ¶ A-4902; USTR ¶ 264; TaxDesk ¶ 569,602. (Code Sec. 30D(c)(2)(B)(ii))

> **⊘** *observation:* Code Sec. 26(a)(2) provides, with respect to all Subpart A credits, as discussed at ¶ 204, credit limitation and "ordering" rules that are similar but not the same as those provided by Code Sec. 30D(c)(2) (immediately above) specifically for the non-depreciable property portion of the NQPEDMV credit as modified by the 2009 Recovery Act (the modified credit). Code Sec. 26(a)(2) is effective for tax years beginning before calendar year 2010, and the modified credit is effective for vehicles acquired after calendar year 2009. Thus, it is possible that a taxpayer with a fiscal tax year beginning in calendar year 2009 and ending in calendar year 2010 (fiscal tax year 2010) could place into service (during the part of calendar year 2010 that is in fiscal tax year 2010) an NQPEDMV that is subject to both the modified credit and, regarding the non-depreciable property portion of the credit, Code Sec. 26(a)(2). In that case, the rules provided by Code Sec. 26(a)(2) would apply instead of the rules, discussed immediately above, provided by Code Sec. 30D(c)(2).

> **⊘** *observation:* When Code Sec. 26(a)(2) doesn't apply, the effect of Code Sec. 26(a)(1) and of Code Sec. 30D(c)(2) (immediately above) is that the non-depreciable property portion of the credit for NQPEDMVs will be generally allowable to the full extent of a taxpayer's regular income tax and AMT liabilities, reduced by the foreign tax credit and any allowable Subpart A credits (including credits treated as if they are Subpart A credits), other than the adoption credit and the residential energy efficiency credit.

> **⊘** *observation:* Subpart A credits that are disallowed because of the tax liability limits can't be carried forward or back, except where the Code section that provides a specific credit expressly allows carryforwards or carrybacks. Code Sec. 30D (see above) does *not* provide for carryfor-

wards or carrybacks of the non-depreciable property portion of the credit for NQPEDMVs.

Coordination with foreign tax credit. In years in which Code Sec. 26(a)(2) doesn't apply (see above), the non-depreciable property portion of the credit for NQPEDMVs is applied against the AMT and regular tax liabilities after the foreign tax credit. (Code Sec. 904(i) as amended by 2009 Recovery Act §1142(b)(1)(E))

> **◆ *observation:*** The amendment to Code Sec. 904(i) by the 2009 Recovery Act conforms Code Sec. 904 (FTC 2d/FIN ¶ O-4400, ¶ O-4401; USTR ¶ 9044.01; TaxDesk ¶ 393,001) to the priority given the foreign tax credit under Code Sec. 30D(c)(2)(B)(ii) (discussed above). The following are previously enacted provisions that similarly coordinate the non-depreciable property portion of the credit for NQPEDMVs with certain other Subpart A credits (or credits treated as Subpart A credits): Code Sec. 24(b)(3)(B) (the child tax credit, see FTC 2d/FIN ¶ A-4054; USTR ¶ 244.01; TaxDesk ¶ 569,104), Code Sec. 25(e)(1)(C)(ii) (the residential mortgage interest credit, see FTC 2d/FIN ¶ A-4010; USTR ¶ 254.01; TaxDesk ¶ 568,509), Code Sec. 25B(g)(2) (the credit for certain elective deferrals and IRS contributions, see FTC 2d/FIN ¶ A-4455; USTR ¶ 25B4; TaxDesk ¶ 569,205) and Code Sec. 1400C(d)(2) (the first-time D.C. homebuyer credit, see FTC 2d/FIN ¶ A-4255; USTR ¶ 14,00C4; TaxDesk ¶ 568,805).

Property used outside of the U.S.

> **◆ *observation:*** In addition to the prohibition for foreign-use property discussed immediately below, the pre-2009 Recovery Act credit is prohibited for property expensed under Code Sec. 179 (which, subject to various limits, permits taxpayers to expense, rather than capitalize and depreciate, the cost of most personal depreciable property, see FTC 2d/FIN ¶ L-9900; USTR ¶ 1794; TaxDesk ¶ 268,400).

The credit for NQPEDMVs won't be allowed for any property referred to in Code Sec. 50(b)(1) (subject to certain exceptions, property used predominantly outside of the U.S., see FTC 2d/FIN ¶ L-16501; USTR ¶ 504.01; TaxDesk ¶ 381,401). (Code Sec. 30D(f)(4))

> **◆ *observation:*** One of the exceptions to the prohibition on property used predominantly outside of the U.S. is an exception for vehicles operated to and from the U.S. by U.S. persons, see FTC 2d/FIN

FTC 2d References are to Federal Tax Coordinator 2d
FIN References are to RIA's Analysis of Federal Taxes: Income
USTR References are to United States Tax Reporter: Income
PE References are to Pension Explanations

¶s L-16501, L-9406; USTR ¶s 504.01, 1684.03; TaxDesk ¶s 381,401, 267,504.

Property sold to certain tax-exempt persons.

observation: The rules below concerning property sold to tax-exempt persons are the same as the rules that apply to the pre-2009 Recovery Act credit.

In the case of a motor vehicle the use of which is described in Code Sec. 50(b)(3) or Code Sec. 50(b)(4) (see observation below) and isn't subject to a lease, the person who sold the vehicle (the seller) to the person or entity using the vehicle (the buyer) will be treated as the taxpayer that placed the vehicle in service, but only if the seller clearly discloses to the buyer in a document the amount of any NQPEDMV credit allowable for the vehicle (determined without the tax liability limits discussed above). (Code Sec. 30D(f)(3))

observation: Code Sec. 50(b)(3) or Code Sec. 50(b)(4) generally apply, respectively, to property used by a tax-exempt organization (other than certain cooperatives), unless the property is used in an unrelated trade or business or is debt-financed, and to property used by the U.S., any state, possession or political subdivision (or any agency or instrumentality of any of these entities) or by certain foreign persons.

Basis reduction.

observation: The rules below concerning basis reduction are the same as the rules that apply to the pre-2009 Recovery Act credit.

The basis of any property for which the credit for NQPEDMVs is allowable will be reduced by the amount of the credit allowed. (Code Sec. 30D(f)(1))

Also, the basis reduction under Code Sec. 30D(f)(1) is included on the list of proper basis adjustments that must be made under Code Sec. 1016(a), see FTC 2d/FIN ¶ P-1700; USTR ¶ 10,164; TaxDesk ¶ 213,000. (Code Sec. 1016(a)(25) as amended by 2009 Recovery Act §1141(b)(3))

caution: The amendment, discussed immediately above, to Code Sec. 1016(a)(25) by 2009 Recovery Act §1141(b)(3) literally provides that "Code Sec. 1016(a)(25) is amended by striking 'section 30D(e)(4)' and inserting 'section 30D(f)(1).'" Thus, the amendment is intended to conform Code Sec. 1016 to the replacement of pre-2009 Recovery Act Code Sec. 30D(e)(4) by Code Sec. 30D(f)(1) as the source of the basis reduction rule for NQPEDMVs. However, it is pre-2009 Recovery Act Code Sec. 1016(a)(37), not pre-2009 Recovery Act Code Sec. 1016(a)(25), that refers to pre-2009 Recovery Act Code Sec.

30D(e)(4). Thus, it can be presumed that 2009 Recovery Act §1141(b)(3) was intended to amend Code Sec. 1016(a)(37), instead of, as reflected above, Code Sec. 1016(a)(25).

observation: Code Sec. 1016(a)(1) doesn't cause the reduction in basis made under Code Sec. 30D(f)(1) to be repeated under Code Sec. 1016. Instead, the main effect of being included on the list of items requiring basis adjustments in Code Sec. 1016(a) is to make the reduction under Code Sec. 30D(f)(1) subject to Code provisions that cross-refer to Code Sec. 1016 and require that adjustments be made under Code Sec. 1016. For example, Code Sec. 1011 clarifies that adjustments under Code Sec. 1016 are taken into account in determining the adjusted basis of property for purposes of determining gain or loss upon sale or other disposition of the property.

Reduction of other tax benefits.

observation: The rule below concerning other tax benefits is the same as the rule that applies to the pre-2009 Recovery Act credit.

The amount of any other income tax deduction or credit allowable for a NQPEDMV will be reduced by the amount of NQPEDMV credit allowed for that NQPEDMV for the tax year. (Code Sec. 30D(f)(2))

Prohibition of AMVC.

observation: The rule below concerning the alternative motor vehicle credit is the same as the rule that applies to the pre-2009 Recovery Act credit.

Any vehicle for which the credit for NQPEDMVs is allowable won't be taken into account under Code Sec. 30B (which provides the AMVC). (Code Sec. 30B(d)(3)(D) as amended by 2009 Recovery Act §1141(b)(1)))

Recapture.

observation: The rule below concerning recapture is the same as the rule that applies to the pre-2009 Recovery Act credit, except that the rule for the pre-2009 Recovery Act credit included a specific direction to issue regs addressing recapture in the case of a lease period of less than the economic life of a vehicle. (FTC 2d/FIN ¶ L-18030, ¶ L-18033.1; USTR ¶ 30D4; TaxDesk ¶ 397,139) Under pre-2009 Recovery Act law, Code Sec. 30D also directed IRS to issue all regs nec-

---

FTC 2d References are to Federal Tax Coordinator 2d
FIN References are to RIA's Analysis of Federal Taxes: Income
USTR References are to United States Tax Reporter: Income
PE References are to Pension Explanations

essary to carry out Code Sec. 30D, whether or not concerning recapture. (FTC 2d/FIN ¶ L-18030, ¶ L-18034.7; USTR ¶ 30D4; TaxDesk ¶ 397,149)

IRS will be required to issue regs that provide for recapturing the benefit of any credit allowable for NQPEDMVs with respect to any property that stops being property eligible for the credit. (Code Sec. 30D(f)(5))

Election-out.

> *observation:* The rules below concerning an election-out are the same as the ones that applied to the pre-2009 Recovery Act credit.

The credit for NQPEDMVs won't be allowed for a vehicle if the taxpayer elects to not have the credit apply to that vehicle (an election-out). (Code Sec. 30D(f)(6)) The period for assessing a deficiency attributable to an election-out (or a revocation of an election-out) won't expire before the date one year after the date that IRS is notified of the election-out (or revocation of the election-out). (Code Sec. 6501(m) as amended by 2009 Recovery Act §1141(b)(4))

"New qualified plug-in electric drive motor vehicle" (NQPEDMV) defined. For purposes of the above rules (Code Sec. 30D(d)), a "new qualified plug-in electric drive motor vehicle" (NQPEDMV, see above) is a "motor vehicle" (defined below) that satisfies the requirements listed below: (Code Sec. 30D(d)(1))

> *observation:* Requirements (1) through (3) listed below are the same as the requirements that applied under the pre-2009 Recovery Act credit.

(1) the original use of the vehicle begins with the taxpayer. (Code Sec. 30D(d)(1)(A))

(2) the vehicle is acquired for use or lease by the taxpayer and not for resale. (Code Sec. 30D(d)(1)(B))

(3) the vehicle is made by a "manufacturer" (defined below). (Code Sec. 30D(d)(1)(C))

> *observation:* Requirement (4) below, concerning title II of the Clean Air Act, didn't apply under the pre-2009 Recovery Act credit and has the effect of barring low-speed motor vehicles from the credit available under Code Sec. 30D. However, vehicles that can't qualify as motor vehicles for purposes of Code Sec. 30D because they are low-speed may qualify for credit under Code Sec. 30, as provided by the 2009 Recovery Act, see ¶ 1003.

(4) the vehicle is treated as a motor vehicle for purposes of title II of the Clean Air Act. (Code Sec. 30D(d)(1)(D))

observation: Requirement (5) below didn't apply under the pre-2009 Recovery Act credit.

(5) the vehicle has a gross vehicle weight rating (GVWR (loaded weight)) of less than 14,000 pounds. (Code Sec. 30D(d)(1)(E))

observation: Instead of requirement (6) below, the pre-2009 Recovery Act credit required that NQPEDMVs draw propulsion using a traction battery with at least 4 kilowatt hours of capacity and use an off-board source of energy to recharge the battery. (FTC 2d/FIN ¶ L-18030, ¶ L-18032; USTR ¶ 30D4.03; TaxDesk ¶ 397,134)

(6) the vehicle is propelled to a significant extent by an electric motor that draws electricity from a battery that (Code Sec. 30D(d)(1)(F)) has a capacity of at least 4 kilowatt hours, and (Code Sec. 30D(d)(1)(F)(i)) is capable of being recharged from an external source of electricity. (Code Sec. 30D(d)(1)(F)(ii))

observation: Another definitional requirement not imposed on NQPEDMVs by the 2009 Recovery Act, but imposed under pre-2009 Recovery Act law, was that passenger automobiles and light trucks with a gross vehicle weight rating of no more than 8,500 pounds meet certain emission standards. (FTC 2d/FIN ¶ L-18030, ¶ L-18032; USTR ¶ 30D4.03; TaxDesk ¶ 397,134)

observation: The rules below concerning compliance are the same as the rules that applied to the pre-2009 Recovery Act credit, except that compliance wasn't required if, elsewhere, Code Sec. 30D provided otherwise. (FTC 2d/FIN ¶ L-18030, ¶ L-18032.1; USTR ¶ 30D4.04; TaxDesk ¶ 397,135)

Also, a motor vehicle isn't considered eligible for the credit for NQPEDMVs unless the vehicle is in compliance with: (Code Sec. 30D(f)(7))

... the applicable provisions of the Clean Air Act for the applicable make and model year of the vehicle (or applicable air quality provisions of state law in the case of a state which had adopted the provision under a waiver under section 209(b) of the Clean Air Act), and (Code Sec. 30D(f)(7)(A))

... the motor vehicle safety provisions of 49 USC §30101 through 49 USC §30169. (Code Sec. 30D(f)(7)(B))

observation: The definitions of "motor vehicle" and "manufacturer" below are the same as the definitions that applied to the pre-2009 Recovery Act credit.

FTC 2d References are to Federal Tax Coordinator 2d
FIN References are to RIA's Analysis of Federal Taxes: Income
USTR References are to United States Tax Reporter: Income
PE References are to Pension Explanations

A "motor vehicle" is any vehicle manufactured primarily for use on public streets, roads and highways (not including a vehicle operated exclusively on a rail or rails) and that has at least four wheels. (Code Sec. 30D(d)(2))

> **☻️ observation:** The above definition of motor vehicle is the same as the definition provided by pre-2009 Recovery Act Code Sec. 30 for qualified electric vehicles placed in service before Jan. 1, 2007 (the pre-2007 QEV credit). For IRS guidance regarding the definition for pre-2007 QEV credit purposes, see FTC 2d/FIN ¶ L-18018; USTR ¶ 304.

> **☻️ observation:** Vehicles that can't qualify as motor vehicles for purposes of Code Sec. 30D because they have only two or three wheels may qualify for credit under Code Sec. 30, as provided by the 2009 Recovery Act, see ¶ 1003.

A "manufacturer" has the meaning given that term in regs prescribed by the Administrator of the EPA for purposes of the administration of title II of the Clean Air Act (42 U.S.C. 7521 *et seq.*). (Code Sec. 30D(d)(3))

☐ **Effective:** Vehicles acquired after Dec. 31, 2009. (2009 Recovery Act §1141(c))

¶ 1003. Qualified plug-in electric vehicle credit is provided for certain low-speed vehicles and 2- or 3-wheeled vehicles acquired before Jan. 1, 2012

Code Sec. 24(b)(3)(B), as amended by 2009 Recovery Act § 1142(b)(1)(A)
Code Sec. 25(e)(1)(C)(ii), as amended by 2009 Recovery Act
§ 1142(b)(1)(B)
Code Sec. 25B(g)(2), as amended by 2009 Recovery Act § 1142(b)(1)(C)
Code Sec. 26(a)(1), as amended by 2009 Recovery Act § 1142(b)(1)(D)
Code Sec. 30, as amended by 2009 Recovery Act § 1142(a)
Code Sec. 30B(h)(1), as amended by 2009 Recovery Act § 1142(b)(2)
Code Sec. 30C(d)(2)(A), as amended by 2009 Recovery Act § 1142(b)(3)
Code Sec. 53(d)(1)(B)(iii), as amended by 2009 Recovery Act
§ 1142(b)(4)(A)
Code Sec. 904(i), as amended by 2009 Recovery Act § 1142(b)(1)(E)
Code Sec. 1016(a)(25), as amended by 2009 Recovery Act § 1142(b)(6)
Code Sec. 1400C(d)(2), as amended by 2009 Recovery Act § 1142(b)(1)(F)
Code Sec. 6501(m), as amended by 2009 Recovery Act § 1142(b)(7)
Generally effective: Vehicles acquired before Jan. 1, 2012 and after Feb. 17, 2009
Committee Reports, see ¶ 5027

Code Sec. 30D provides a credit for the purchase of new qualified plug-in electric drive motor vehicles (certain battery powered vehicles (NQPEDMVs)). (FTC 2d/FIN ¶ L-18030; USTR ¶ 30D4; TaxDesk ¶ 397,130) Under pre-2009 Recovery Act law, (1) credit for low-speed vehicles was provided as part of the credit for NQPEDMVs under Code Sec. 30D (and, not as part of a separate credit) and (2) vehicles with less than four wheels weren't eligible for credit as part of the credit for NQPEDMVs under Code Sec. 30D or as part of a separate credit, see ¶ 1002.

New Law. The 2009 Recovery Act provides a credit equal to 10% percent of the cost of any qualified plug-in electric vehicle ("QPEV" defined below) placed in service by the taxpayer during the tax year. (Code Sec. 30(a) as amended by 2009 Recovery Act §1142(a))

> *observation:* In amending Code Sec. 30 to provide the credit for QPEVs, the 2009 Recovery Act struck from the text of Code Sec. 30 all of the provisions of the pre-2007 credit that were available for qualified electric vehicles. (FTC 2d/FIN ¶ L-18010 *et seq.*; USTR ¶ 304; TaxDesk ¶ 397,000 *et seq.*)

The amount of the credit can't exceed $2,500 per vehicle. (Code Sec. 30(b)) The credit isn't available for any vehicle acquired after Dec. 31, 2011. (Code Sec. 30(f)) For rules that may limit the amount or availability of the credit even though a vehicle meets the requirements for being a QPEV, see "Tax liability limit for depreciable property," "Tax liability limit for non-depreciable property" and "Property used outside of the U.S." below.

For the modification of the credit for NQPEDMVs under Code Sec. 30D by the 2009 Recovery Act, see ¶ 1002. For the addition, by the 2009 Recovery Act, to the alternative motor vehicle credit (AMVC) under Code Sec. 30B of a credit for certain costs of converting vehicles to plug-in vehicles, see ¶ 1004.

Tax liability limit for depreciable property. The portion of the credit for QPEVs that is attributable to property of a character subject to an allowance for depreciation (generally, property used in a trade or business or for the production of income, see FTC 2d/FIN ¶ L-7901; USTR ¶ 1674.006; TaxDesk ¶ 265,401) is treated as a credit listed under Code Sec. 38(b) for the tax year (i.e., a credit that is part of the general business credit for the tax year, see FTC 2d/FIN ¶ L-15201; USTR ¶ 384.01; TaxDesk ¶ 380,501) and not as a credit allowed under Code Sec. 30(a) (discussed above). (Code Sec. 30(c)(1))

> *observation:* Thus, as part of the general business credit provided by Code Sec. 38, the portion of the credit for QPEVs that is attributable to

---

FTC 2d References are to Federal Tax Coordinator 2d
FIN References are to RIA's Analysis of Federal Taxes: Income
USTR References are to United States Tax Reporter: Income
PE References are to Pension Explanations

depreciable property (the depreciable property portion) isn't allowed to offset any of a taxpayer's alternative minimum tax (AMT) and may be limited in its offset of a taxpayer's regular income tax, see FTC 2d/FIN ¶ L-15202; USTR ¶ 384.02; TaxDesk ¶ 380,502. However, depreciable property portions disallowed because of the tax liability limits are carried back or forward to the extent provided in Code Sec. 39, see FTC 2d/FIN ¶ L-15209; USTR ¶ 394; TaxDesk ¶ 380,509.

Tax liability limit for non-depreciable property. The portion of the credit for QPEVs that isn't attributable to depreciable property (the non-depreciable property portion) is treated as a credit allowed under Subtitle A, Chapter 1, Subchapter A, Part IV, Subpart A of the Code (also known as a Subpart A credit or personal credit). (Code Sec. 30(c)(2)(A))

However, the credit allowed under Code Sec. 30 isn't subject to the rule that provides that Subpart A credits can't exceed the excess (if any) of the taxpayer's regular tax liability for the tax year over the tentative minimum tax for the tax year (determined without regard to the AMT foreign tax credit). (Code Sec. 26(a)(1) as amended by 2009 Recovery Act §1142(b)(1)(D)) Instead, for tax years to which Code Sec. 26(a)(2) (see the first observation below) doesn't apply (any tax year beginning after 2009, see ¶ 204), the non-depreciable property portion can't exceed for any tax year an amount equal to the following:

. . . the *excess* of (Code Sec. 30(c)(2)(B)) the sum of the taxpayer's AMT and "regular tax liability" as defined in Code Sec. 26(b) (i.e., a taxpayer's income tax, not including the AMT and other special taxes, see FTC 2d/FIN ¶ L-18103; USTR ¶ 264.01; TaxDesk ¶ 569,603), *over* (Code Sec. 30(c)(2)(B)(i))

. . . the sum of the allowable credit provided by Code Sec. 27 (the foreign tax credit, see FTC 2d/FIN ¶s L-18101, O-4000; USTR ¶ 274; TaxDesk ¶ 569,601) and the allowable Subpart A credits (other than the adoption credit provided by Code Sec. 23, see FTC 2d/FIN ¶ A-4401; USTR ¶ 234; TaxDesk ¶ 569,501, the residential energy efficiency credit provided by Code Sec. 25D, see FTC 2d/FIN ¶ A-4781; USTR ¶ 25D4; TaxDesk ¶ 569,553, the credit for NQPEDMVs and the QPEV credit), see FTC 2d/FIN ¶ L-18102; USTR ¶ 264; TaxDesk ¶ 569,602. (Code Sec. 30(c)(2)(B)(ii))

> *observation:* Code Sec. 26(a)(2) provides, with respect to all Subpart A credits as discussed at ¶ 204, credit limitation and "ordering" rules that are similar but not the same as those provided by Code Sec. 30(c)(2) (immediately above) specifically for the non-depreciable property portion of the QPEV.

> *observation:* When Code Sec. 26(a)(2) doesn't apply, the effect of Code Sec. 26(a)(1) and of Code Sec. 30(c)(2)(B) (above) is that the non-depreciable property portion of the credit for QPEVs will be gener-

ally allowable to the full extent of a taxpayer's regular income tax and AMT liabilities, reduced only by certain other credits (including credits treated as if they are Subpart A credits), other than the adoption credit, residential energy efficiency credit and credit for NQPEDMVs.

🅡 *observation:* Subpart A credits that are disallowed because of the tax liability limits can't be carried forward or back, except where the Code section that provides a specific credit expressly allows carryforwards or carrybacks. Code Sec. 30 (see above) does *not* provide for carryforwards or carrybacks of the non-depreciable property portion of the credit for QPEVs.

Coordination with other personal credits.

🅡 *observation:* The amendments immediately below conform treatment of the listed credits to the ordering rule provided by Code Sec. 30(c)(2)(B)(ii) (discussed above).

In years in which Code Sec. 26(a)(2) doesn't apply (see above), the non-depreciable property portion of the credit for NQPEDMVs is applied against the AMT and regular tax liabilities after the following Subpart A credits (or credits treated as Subpart A credits):

. . . the child tax credit (FTC 2d/FIN ¶ A-4050, ¶ A-4054; USTR ¶ 244.01; TaxDesk ¶ 569,101); (Code Sec. 24(b)(3)(B) as amended by 2009 Recovery Act §1142(b)(1)(A))

. . . the residential mortgage interest credit (FTC 2d/FIN ¶ A-4000, ¶ A-4010; USTR ¶ 254.01; TaxDesk ¶ 568,509); (Code Sec. 25(e)(1)(C)(ii) as amended by 2009 Recovery Act §1142(b)(1)(B))

. . . the credit for certain elective deferrals and IRA contributions (FTC 2d/FIN ¶ A-4450, ¶ A-4455; USTR ¶ 25B4; TaxDesk ¶ 569,205); (Code Sec. 25B(g)(2) as amended by 2009 Recovery Act §1142(b)(1)(C))

. . . the foreign tax credit (FTC 2d/FIN ¶ O-4400, ¶ O-4401; USTR ¶ 9044.01; TaxDesk ¶ 393,001); and (Code Sec. 904(i) as amended by 2009 Recovery Act §1142(b)(1)(E))

. . . the first-time D.C. homebuyer's credit (FTC 2d/FIN ¶ A-4250, ¶ A-4255; USTR ¶ 14,00C4; TaxDesk ¶ 568,805). (Code Sec. 1400C(d)(2) as amended by 2009 Recovery Act §1142(b)(1)(F))

Sunset provision. The amendment made by 2009 Recovery Act §1142(b)(1)(A) (to Code Sec. 24(b)(3) as discussed above) is subject to title IX

FTC 2d References are to Federal Tax Coordinator 2d
FIN References are to RIA's Analysis of Federal Taxes: Income
USTR References are to United States Tax Reporter: Income
PE References are to Pension Explanations

of the 2001 Economic Growth and Tax Relief Reconciliation Act of 2001 (i.e.,
the EGTRRA sunset provision, see 2001 EGTRRA §901 (Sec. 901, PL 107-16,
6/7/2001)) in the same manner as the provision of 2001 EGTRRA to which the
amendment relates. (2009 Recovery Act §1142(e))

> *observation:* Generally, 2001 EGTRRA §901 requires that amend-
> ments made by 2001 EGTRRA will not be effective for tax years be-
> ginning after Dec. 31, 2010.

> *observation:* All of Code Sec. 24(b)(3) (which provides the tax lia-
> bility limit rule of which Code Sec. 24(b)(3)(B) (above) is part) is sub-
> ject to the EGTRRA sunset provision. Thus, without 2009 Recovery
> Act §1142(e), there would be a technical inconsistency in which the
> amendment to Code Sec. 24(b)(3) made by 2009 Recovery Act
> §1142(b)(1)(A) would survive the post-2010 termination of Code
> Sec. 24(b)(3).

Property used outside the U.S.   The credit for QPEVs isn't allowed for any
property referred to in Code Sec. 50(b)(1) (generally, property used predominantly outside of the U.S., see FTC 2d/FIN ¶ L-16501; USTR ¶ 504.01;
TaxDesk ¶ 381,401). (Code Sec. 30(e)(4))

> *observation:* One of the exceptions to the prohibition on property
> used predominantly outside of the U.S. is for vehicles operated to and
> from the U.S. by U.S. persons, see FTC 2d/FIN ¶s L-16501, L-9406;
> USTR ¶s 504.01, 1684.03; TaxDesk ¶s 381,401, 267,504.

Property sold to certain tax-exempt persons.   In the case of a motor vehicle the use of which is described in Code Sec. 50(b)(3) or Code Sec. 50(b)(4)
(see observation below) and isn't subject to a lease, the person who sold the vehicle (the seller) to the person or entity using the vehicle (the buyer) is treated
as the taxpayer that placed the vehicle in service, but only if the seller clearly
discloses to the buyer in a document the amount of any QPEV credit allowable
for the vehicle (determined without the tax liability limits discussed above).
(Code Sec. 30(e)(3))

> *observation:* Code Sec. 50(b)(3) or Code Sec. 50(b)(4) generally ap-
> ply, respectively, to property used by a tax-exempt organization (other
> than certain cooperatives), unless the property is used in an unrelated
> trade or business or is debt-financed, and to property used by the U.S.,
> any state, possession or political subdivision (or any agency or instru-
> mentality of any of these entities) or by certain foreign persons.

Basis reduction. The basis of any property for which the credit for QPEVs is allowable is reduced by the amount of the credit allowed. (Code Sec. 30(e)(1))

Also, the basis reduction under Code Sec. 30(e)(1) is included on the list of proper basis adjustments that must be made under Code Sec. 1016(a), see FTC 2d/FIN ¶ P-1700; USTR ¶ 10,164; TaxDesk ¶ 213,000. (Code Sec. 1016(a)(25) as amended by 2009 Recovery Act §1142(b)(6))

> **⚓** *observation:* Code Sec. 1016(a)(1) doesn't cause the reduction in basis made under Code Sec. 30(e)(1) to be repeated under Code Sec. 1016. Instead, the main effect of being included on the list of items requiring basis adjustments in Code Sec. 1016(a) is to make the reduction under Code Sec. 30(e)(1) subject to Code provisions that cross-refer to Code Sec. 1016 and require that adjustments be made under Code Sec. 1016. For example, Code Sec. 1011 clarifies that adjustments under Code Sec. 1016 are taken into account in determining the adjusted basis of property for purposes of determining gain or loss upon sale or other disposition of the property.

Reduction of other tax benefits. The amount of any other income tax deduction or credit allowable for a QPEV is reduced by the amount of QPEV credit allowed for that QPEV. (Code Sec. 30(e)(2))

Recapture. IRS is required to issue regs that provide for recapturing the benefit of any credit allowable for QPEVs with respect to any property that stops being property eligible for the credit. (Code Sec. 30(e)(5))

Election-out. The credit for QPEVs isn't allowed for a vehicle if the taxpayer elects to not have the credit apply to that vehicle (an election-out). (Code Sec. 30(e)(6)) The period for assessing a deficiency attributable to an election-out (or a revocation of an election-out) won't expire before the date one year after the date that IRS is notified of the election-out (or revocation of the election-out). (Code Sec. 6501(m) as amended by 2009 Recovery Act §1142(b)(7))

"Qualified plug-in electric vehicle" (QPEV) defined. For purposes of the above rules (Code Sec. 30(d)), a "qualified plug-in electric vehicle" (QPEV see above) is a "specified vehicle" (defined below) that satisfies the requirements listed below: (Code Sec. 30(d)(1))

(1) the original use of the vehicle begins with the taxpayer; (Code Sec. 30(d)(1)(A))

FTC 2d References are to Federal Tax Coordinator 2d
FIN References are to RIA's Analysis of Federal Taxes: Income
USTR References are to United States Tax Reporter: Income
PE References are to Pension Explanations

(2) the vehicle is acquired for use or lease by the taxpayer and not for resale; (Code Sec. 30(d)(1)(B))

(3) the vehicle is made by a "manufacturer" (defined below); (Code Sec. 30(d)(1)(C))

(4) the vehicle is manufactured (see below) primarily for use on public streets, roads and highways; (Code Sec. 30(d)(1)(D))

(5) the vehicle has a gross vehicle weight rating (GVWR (loaded weight)) of less than 14,000 pounds; and (Code Sec. 30(d)(1)(E))

(6) the vehicle is propelled to a significant extent by an electric motor that draws electricity from a battery that (Code Sec. 30(d)(1)(F)) has a capacity (defined immediately below) of at least 4 kilowatt hours (at least 2.5 kilowatt hours in the case of a 2- or-3-wheeled vehicle, and (Code Sec. 30(d)(1)(F)(i)) is capable of being recharged from an external source of electricity. (Code Sec. 30(d)(1)(F)(ii)) "Capacity," with respect to any battery is the quantity of electricity that the battery is capable of storing, expressed in kilowatt hours, as measured from a 100 percent state of charge to a zero percent state of charge. (Code Sec. 30(d)(4))

A specified vehicle means any vehicle that— (Code Sec. 30(d)(2))

. . . is a "low-speed vehicle" within the meaning of section 571.3 of title 49 of the Code of Federal Regulations (CFR) (as in effect on Feb. 17, 2009) (see the observation below), or (Code Sec. 30(d)(2)(A))

. . . has two or three wheels. (Code Sec. 30(d)(2)(B))

> **⚡ observation:** Section 571.3 of title 49 of the CFR defines a low-speed motor vehicle as a 4-wheeled vehicle with a gross vehicle weight rating (GVWR) of no more than 3,000 pounds with a capability of attaining speeds of no less than 20 mph and no more than 25 mph.

A "manufacturer" has the meaning given that term in regs prescribed by the Administrator of the EPA for purposes of the administration of title II of the Clean Air Act (42 USC §7521 *et seq.*). (Code Sec. 30(d)(3))

Changes related to termination of the pre-2007 electric vehicle credit. The 2009 Recovery Act provides that, for purposes of the alternative motor vehicle credit (AMVC) provided by Code Sec. 30B, a "motor vehicle" is any vehicle that is manufactured primarily for use on public streets, roads, and highways (not including a vehicle operated exclusively on a rail or rails) and which has at least four wheels. (Code Sec. 30B(h)(1) as amended by 2009 Recovery Act §1142(b)(2))

> **⚡ observation:** Under pre-2009 Recovery Act law, Code Sec. 30B(h)(1) defined a motor vehicle as defined in pre-2009 Recovery Act Code Sec. 30(c)(2) (which defined motor vehicle for purposes

of the pre-2007 qualified electric vehicle credit). (FTC 2d/FIN ¶ L-18020, ¶ L-18021; USTR ¶ 30B4; TaxDesk ¶ 397,101) However, that definition was eliminated as part of the 2009 Recovery Act's amendment to Code Sec. 30 in which the credit for QPEVs replaced the pre-2007 credit for qualified electric vehicles (see above).

The 2009 Recovery Act eliminates the rule that provides that the pre-2007 qualified electric vehicle credit (see above) is applied against income tax liabilities before the credit for qualified alternative fuel vehicle refueling property provided by Code Sec. 30C (FTC 2d/FIN ¶ L-18040, ¶ L-18042; USTR ¶ 30C4.01; TaxDesk ¶ 397,202). (Code Sec. 30C(d)(2)(A) as amended by 2009 Recovery Act §1142(b)(3)

The 2009 Recovery Act eliminates the rule that increases adjusted net minimum tax, for purposes of the credit for AMT under Code Sec. 53, by the amount of pre-2007 qualified electric vehicle credit not allowed because of tax liability limitations. (FTC 2d/FIN ¶ A-8800, ¶ A-8802; USTR ¶ 534; TaxDesk ¶ 397,202). (Code Sec. 53(d)(1)(B)(iii) as amended by 2009 Recovery Act §1142(b)(4)(A))

Redesignation. Pre-2009 Recovery Act Code Sec. 53(d)(1)(B)(iv) is redesignated as Code Sec. 53(d)(1)(B)(iii). (Code Sec. 53(d)(1)(B)(iii) as redesignated by 2009 Recovery Act §1142(b)(4)(A))

☐ **Effective:** Vehicles acquired before Jan. 1, 2012 (Code Sec. 30(f)) and after Feb. 17, 2009. (2009 Recovery Act §1142(c)) However, for a vehicle acquired after Feb. 17, 2009 and before Jan. 1, 2010, no QPEV credit under Code Sec. 30 is allowed if a credit for new qualified plug-in electric drive motor vehicles (NQPEDMVs) under Code Sec. 30D is allowed with respect to the vehicle. (2009 Recovery Act §1142(d))

> **⦿ observation:** The credit under Code Sec. 30D for NQPEDMVs acquired before Jan. 1, 2010 is the credit available under Code Sec. 30D for NQPEDMVs before the changes made by the 2009 Recovery Act, as described at ¶ 1002.

FTC 2d References are to Federal Tax Coordinator 2d
FIN References are to RIA's Analysis of Federal Taxes: Income
USTR References are to United States Tax Reporter: Income
PE References are to Pension Explanations

¶ 1004. Alternative motor vehicle credit (AMVC) is expanded to include a plug-in conversion credit for property placed in service after Feb. 17, 2009 and before Jan. 1, 2012

Code Sec. 30B(i), as amended by 2009 Recovery Act § 1143(a)
Code Sec. 30B(a)(5), as amended by 2009 Recovery Act § 1143(b)
Code Sec. 30B(h)(8), as amended by 2009 Recovery Act § 1143(c)
Generally effective: Property placed in service after Feb. 17, 2009 and conversions made before Jan. 1, 2012
Committee Reports, see ¶ 5027

Under pre-2009 Recovery Act law, the alternative motor vehicle credit (AMVC) under Code Sec. 30B had four components:

... the qualified fuel cell motor vehicle credit (see FTC 2d/FIN ¶ L-18024; USTR ¶ 30B4.01; TaxDesk ¶ 397,104).

... the advanced lean-burn technology motor vehicle credit (see FTC 2d/FIN ¶ L-18025; USTR ¶ 30B4.02; TaxDesk ¶ 397,105).

... the qualified hybrid motor vehicle credit (see FTC 2d/FIN ¶ L-18026; USTR ¶ 30B4.03; TaxDesk ¶ 397,106).

... the qualified alternative fuel motor vehicle credit (see FTC 2d/FIN ¶ L-18029.1; USTR ¶ 30B4.06; TaxDesk ¶ 397,110). (FTC 2d/FIN ¶ L-18020; USTR ¶ 30B4; TaxDesk ¶ 397,101)

New Law. The 2009 Recovery Act adds the plug-in conversion credit determined under Code Sec. 30B(i) to the list of credits that are components of the AMVC. (Code Sec. 30B(a)(5) as amended by 2009 Recovery Act §1143(b)) For 2009 Recovery Act changes making the AMVC a personal credit that can be used against the alternative minimum tax (AMT) in tax years beginning after Dec. 31, 2008, see ¶ 205.

For purposes of the AMVC, the plug-in conversion credit determined with respect to any motor vehicle that is converted to a qualified plug-in electric drive motor vehicle (QPEDM) is 10% of so much of the cost of converting the vehicle as does not exceed $40,000. (Code Sec. 30B(i)(1) as amended by 2009 Recovery Act §1143(a))

observation: A motor vehicle doesn't have to be used in a trade or business or for the production of income in order to qualify for the plug-in conversion credit. Thus, a personal use motor vehicle can qualify for the plug-in conversion credit.

⚡ *illustration (1):* T converts a motor vehicle into a qualified plug-in electric drive motor vehicle. The cost of converting the vehicle is $39,000. T's plug-in conversion credit is $3,900 ($39,000 × 10%).

⚡ *observation:* Since the cost of converting a vehicle in excess of $40,000 isn't taken into account in computing the amount of the plug-in conversion credit under Code Sec. 30B(i)(1), the maximum amount that can be claimed as a plug-in conversion credit for any vehicle is $4,000 ($40,000 × 10%).

⚡ *illustration (2):* The facts are the same as in illustration (1) except the cost of the conversion of the vehicle is $55,000. Since the cost of converting the vehicle exceeds $40,000, T's plug-in conversion credit is limited to $4,000 ($40,000 × 10%).

Qualified plug-in electric drive motor vehicle defined. For purposes of the plug-in conversion credit, a QPEDM vehicle is any new qualified plug-in electric drive motor vehicle (NQPEDMV as defined in Code Sec. 30D (see ¶ 1002 and FTC 2d/FIN ¶ L-18032; USTR ¶ 30D4.03; TaxDesk ¶ 397,134) determined *without regard* to whether the vehicle is made by a manufacturer (as defined in ¶ 1002 and FTC 2d/FIN ¶ L-18034.6; USTR ¶ 30D4.03; TaxDesk ¶ 397,148), or whether the original use of the vehicle commences with the taxpayer). (Code Sec. 30B(i)(2)) To be eligible for the credit, the minimum capacity of a qualified battery module has to be four kilowatt hours. Lessors of battery modules can't claim the plug-in conversion credit. (Com Rept, see ¶ 5027)

⚡ *observation:* Since the original use of the vehicle doesn't have to commence with the taxpayer, a used car that is converted into a QPEDM presumably can qualify for the plug-in conversion credit.

⚡ *observation:* For vehicles acquired *after* Dec. 31, 2009, the 2009 Recovery Act changed the definition of a NQPEDMV (as defined in Code Sec. 30D), see ¶ 1002. Since the plug-in conversion credit incorporates the definition of a NQPEDMV by reference in Code Sec. 30B(i)(2), QPEDMs placed in service *after* Feb. 17, 2009 and *before* the 2009 Recovery Act definition of a NQPEDMV becomes effective presumably would have to meet the requirements provided in the definition of NQPEDMV that was in effect before the amendments made by the 2009 Recovery Act (see ¶ 1002).

FTC 2d References are to Federal Tax Coordinator 2d
FIN References are to RIA's Analysis of Federal Taxes: Income
USTR References are to United States Tax Reporter: Income
PE References are to Pension Explanations

Coordination with other credits. The plug-in conversion credit allowed under Code Sec. 30B(i) is allowed with respect to a motor vehicle notwithstanding whether a credit has been allowed with respect to the motor vehicle under Code Sec. 30B (other than the plug-in conversion credit under Code Sec. 30B(i)) in any preceding tax year. (Code Sec. 30B(i)(3))

> ⚑ *observation:* Thus, the plug-in conversion credit can be allowed for a vehicle that previously qualified for one of the other components of the AMVC in an earlier tax year.

Recapture. IRS is to issue regs providing for the recapture of any AMVC for any property that ceases to be eligible for that credit (including recapture in the case of a lease period of less than the economic life of a vehicle), *except that no benefit is recaptured if the property ceases to be eligible for the credit by reason of conversion to a QPEDM vehicle.* (Code Sec. 30B(h)(8) as amended by 2009 Recovery Act §1143(c))

> ⚑ *observation:* 2009 Recovery Act §1143(c) adds the italicized language above to existing Code Sec. 30B(h)(8).

Sunset. Code Sec. 30B(i) doesn't apply to conversions made after Dec. 31, 2011. (Code Sec. 30B(i)(4))

Redesignations. Pre-2009 Recovery Act Code Sec. 30B(i) (relating to IRS's issuance of regs relating to the AMVC) and Code Sec. 30B(j) (termination provisions for the AMVC) are redesignated as Code Sec. 30B(j) and Code Sec. 30B(k). (2009 Recovery Act §1143(a))

☐ **Effective:** Property placed in service after Feb. 17, 2009 (2009 Recovery Act §1143(a)) and conversions made before Jan. 1, 2012. (Code Sec. 30B(i)(4))

¶ 1100. Nonbusiness Energy Credits

¶ 1101. Nonbusiness energy property credit is increased from 10% to 30% and extended for one year

Code Sec. 25C(a), as amended by 2009 Recovery Act § 1121(a)
Code Sec. 25C(b), as amended by 2009 Recovery Act § 1121(a)
Code Sec. 25C(g)(2), as amended by 2009 Recovery Act § 1121(e)
Generally effective: Tax years beginning after Dec. 31, 2008
Committee Reports, see ¶ 5021

Individual taxpayers are allowed a personal tax credit, known as the nonbusiness energy property credit, for energy efficient improvements to a dwelling unit in the U.S. owned and used by the taxpayer as the taxpayer's principal residence. Under pre-2009 Recovery Act law, this credit was equal to the sum of:

(1) 10% of the amount paid or incurred by the taxpayer for qualified energy efficiency improvements (i.e., building envelope components meeting certain requirements) installed during the tax year, and

(2) the amount of residential energy property expenditures (i.e., $50 for each advanced main air circulating fan, $150 for each qualified natural gas, propane, or oil furnace or hot water boiler, and $300 for "qualified energy efficient property," including heat pumps, water heaters, central air conditioners, and biomass fuel stoves) paid or incurred by the taxpayer during the tax year. (FTC 2d/FIN ¶ A-4750; USTR ¶ 25C4; TaxDesk ¶ 569,550)

Under pre-2009 Recovery Act law, the credit was subject to a lifetime cap. The total credit for all tax years couldn't exceed $500, no more than $200 of which could be for expenditures on windows. (FTC 2d/FIN ¶ A-4751; USTR ¶ 25C4; TaxDesk ¶ 569,551)

Under pre-2009 Recovery Act law, expenditures made from subsidized energy financing weren't taken into account for purposes of the credit. (FTC 2d/ FIN ¶ A-4756; USTR ¶ 25C4; TaxDesk ¶ 569,556)

The credit is allowed for property placed in service in calendar years 2006, 2007, and 2009. Under pre-2009 Recovery Act law, the credit wasn't available for property placed in service after Dec. 31, 2009. (FTC 2d/FIN ¶ A-4751; USTR ¶ 25C4; TaxDesk ¶ 569,551)

New Law. The 2009 Recovery Act modifies and extends the nonbusiness energy property credit in the following ways:

FTC 2d References are to Federal Tax Coordinator 2d
FIN References are to RIA's Analysis of Federal Taxes: Income
USTR References are to United States Tax Reporter: Income
PE References are to Pension Explanations

... the 10% credit rate is increased to 30%;

... all energy property that was previously eligible for the $50, $150, and $300 credits is instead eligible for a 30% credit on expenditures for that property;

... the $500 lifetime cap ($200 for windows) is eliminated and replaced with an aggregate $1,500 cap for 2009 and 2010; and

... the credit is extended for one year, through Dec. 31, 2010. (Com Rept, see ¶ 5021)

For changes to the requirements for certain types of property to qualify for the credit, see ¶ 1102.

For allowance of the credit for expenditures from subsidized energy financing, see ¶ 1103.

> *viewpoint:* Attorney-CPA Michael A. Spielman, author of WG&L's U.S. International Estate Planning treatise, and a Senior Manager in the Transaction Advisory Services Practice of Ernst & Young LLP, where he advises public and private companies and private equity firms on the tax aspects of mergers and acquisitions, notes that taxpayers and their advisors should not overlook the potential applicability of this credit to donors that have established a qualified personal residence trust (QPRT). Because these trusts are grantor trusts, the donor should be able to claim the nonbusiness energy property credit to the extent that the credit would be available to the donor as an individual.

Amount of credit. The 2009 Recovery Act provides that individuals are allowed a credit for the tax year equal to 30% of the sum of (Code Sec. 25C(a) as amended by 2009 Recovery Act §1121(a)):

(1) the amount paid or incurred by the taxpayer during the tax year for qualified energy efficiency improvements (Code Sec. 25C(a)(1)), and

(2) the amount of the residential energy property expenditures paid or incurred by the taxpayer during the tax year. (Code Sec. 25C(a)(2))

The dollar limitations on residential energy property expenditures—$50 for each advanced main air circulating fan, $150 for each qualified natural gas, propane, or oil furnace or hot water boiler, $300 for each item of qualified energy efficient property—have been eliminated. (Code Sec. 25C(b))

Credit cap. The aggregate amount of credits allowed to a taxpayer for tax years beginning in 2009 and 2010 may not exceed $1,500. (Code Sec. 25C(b))

The lifetime limitation of $500 ($200 for windows) has been eliminated. (Code Sec. 25C(b))

✔️observation: Taxpayers who had exhausted their $500 lifetime limitation in 2006 and 2007 can now claim an additional $1,500 of aggregate credits in 2009 and 2010.

Termination. The credit won't be available for property placed in service after Dec. 31, 2010. (Code Sec. 25C(g)(2) as amended by 2009 Recovery Act §1121(e))

☐ **Effective:** Tax years beginning after Dec. 31, 2008. (2009 Recovery Act §1121(f)(1)) The credit won't be available for property placed in service after Dec. 31, 2010. (Code Sec. 25C(g)(2))

¶ 1102. Standards are modified for property qualifying for the nonbusiness energy property credit

Code Sec. 25C(c)(2)(A), as amended by 2009 Recovery Act § 1121(d)(2)
Code Sec. 25C(c)(4), as amended by 2009 Recovery Act § 1121(d)(1)
Code Sec. 25C(d)(2)(A)(ii), as amended by 2009 Recovery Act § 1121(c)(2)
Code Sec. 25C(d)(3)(B), as amended by 2009 Recovery Act § 1121(b)(1)
Code Sec. 25C(d)(3)(C), as amended by 2009 Recovery Act § 1121(b)(2)
Code Sec. 25C(d)(3)(D), as amended by 2009 Recovery Act § 1121(b)(3)
Code Sec. 25C(d)(3)(E), as amended by 2009 Recovery Act § 1121(b)(4)
Code Sec. 25C(d)(4), as amended by 2009 Recovery Act § 1121(c)(1)
Generally effective: Property placed in service after Feb. 17, 2009
Committee Reports, see ¶ 5021

Individual taxpayers are allowed a personal tax credit, known as the nonbusiness energy property credit, for energy-efficient improvements to a dwelling unit in the U.S. owned and used by the taxpayer as the taxpayer's principal residence. The credit is available for: (1) amounts paid or incurred for qualified energy efficiency improvements (i.e., building envelope components meeting certain requirements) installed during the tax year and (2) residential energy property expenditures (i.e., expenditures for qualified energy property) paid or incurred during the tax year. (FTC 2d/FIN ¶ A-4750; USTR ¶ 25C4; TaxDesk ¶ 569,550)

For changes to the credit percentages and limits made by the 2009 Recovery Act, see ¶ 1101.

Building envelope components. The "building envelope components" for which the credit is allowed include:

FTC 2d References are to Federal Tax Coordinator 2d
FIN References are to RIA's Analysis of Federal Taxes: Income
USTR References are to United States Tax Reporter: Income
PE References are to Pension Explanations

... any insulation material or system specifically and primarily designed to reduce the dwelling unit's heat loss or gain when installed in or on the dwelling unit;

... exterior windows and skylights;

... exterior doors; and

... any metal roof or asphalt roof installed on a dwelling unit, but only if the roof has appropriate pigmented coatings or cooling granules that are specifically and primarily designed to reduce the dwelling unit's heat gain. (FTC 2d/FIN ¶ A-4753; USTR ¶ 25C4; TaxDesk ¶ 569,553)

Qualified energy property. "Qualified energy property" means: (1) energy-efficient building property, including (a) electric heat pump water heaters, (b) electric heat pumps, (c) central air conditioners, (d) natural gas, propane, or oil water heaters, and (e) biomass fuel stoves; (2) qualified natural gas, propane, or oil furnaces or hot water boilers; and (3) advanced main air circulating fans.

Under pre-2009 Recovery Act law, the credit was available for:

... electric heat pumps that had a heating seasonal performance factor (HSPF) of at least 9, a seasonal energy efficiency ratio (SEER) of at least 15, and an energy efficiency ratio (EER) of at least 13. (FTC 2d/FIN ¶ A-4753; USTR ¶ 25C4; TaxDesk ¶ 569,553)

... central air conditioners that achieved the highest efficiency tier established by the Consortium for Energy Efficiency, as in effect on Jan. 1, 2006. (FTC 2d/ FIN ¶ A-4753; USTR ¶ 25C4; TaxDesk ¶ 569,553)

... natural gas, propane, or oil water heaters that had an energy factor of at least 0.80 or a thermal efficiency of at least 90%. (FTC 2d/FIN ¶ A-4753; USTR ¶ 25C4; TaxDesk ¶ 569,553)

... biomass fuel stoves that burned biomass fuel (i.e., a renewable plant-derived fuel such as wood) to heat a dwelling unit that the taxpayer used as a residence, or to heat water for use in the residence, and that had a thermal efficiency rating of at least 75%. (FTC 2d/FIN ¶ A-4753; USTR ¶ 25C4; TaxDesk ¶ 569,553)

... natural gas, propane, or oil furnaces or hot water boilers that achieved an annual fuel utilization efficiency rate of not less than 95. (FTC 2d/FIN ¶ A-4753; USTR ¶ 25C4; TaxDesk ¶ 569,553)

New Law. The 2009 Recovery Act modifies the efficiency standards for property qualifying for the nonbusiness energy property credit. The new efficiency standards, other than those for biomass fuel stoves, apply to property placed in service after Feb. 17, 2009. (Com Rept, see ¶ 5021)

Building envelope components. *Insulation.* The 2009 Recovery Act updates the building insulation requirements to follow the prescriptive criteria of the 2009 International Energy Conservation Code. (Com Rept, see ¶ 5021) An insulation material or system doesn't qualify for the credit unless it meets the prescriptive criteria for that material or system established by the 2009 International Energy Conservation Code (including supplements), as in effect on Feb. 17, 2009. (Code Sec. 25C(c)(2)(A) as amended by 2009 Recovery Act §1121(d)(2))

Exterior windows, skylights, and doors. The 2009 Recovery Act provides that exterior windows, skylights, and doors don't qualify for the credit unless the component is equal to or below a U factor of 0.30 and an SHGC of 0.30. (Code Sec. 25C(c)(4) as amended by 2009 Recovery Act §1121(d)(1)) The acronym "SHGC" stands for solar heat gain coefficient. (Com Rept, see ¶ 5021)

> *observation:* The U factor measures how well a component prevents heat from escaping. U factors generally fall between 0.20 and 1.20. A low U Factor means that the product is efficient at keeping heat inside.
>
> The SHGC measures how well a component blocks solar heat from entering. SHGCs fall between 0 and 1. The lower the SHGC, the more heat the product blocks.

Qualified energy property. *Electric heat pumps.* Under the 2009 Recovery Act, the credit is available for electric heat pumps that achieve the highest efficiency tier established by the Consortium for Energy Efficiency, as in effect on Jan. 1, 2009. (Code Sec. 25C(d)(3)(B) as amended by 2009 Recovery Act §1121(b)(1))

These standards are:

. . . a seasonal energy efficiency ratio (SEER) greater than or equal to 15, energy efficiency ratio (EER) greater than or equal to 12.5, and heating seasonal performance factor (HSPF) greater than or equal to 8.5 for split heat pumps, and

. . . a SEER greater than or equal to 14, EER greater than or equal to 12, and HSPF greater than or equal to 8.0 for packaged heat pumps. (Com Rept, see ¶ 5021)

Central air conditioners. Under the 2009 Recovery Act, the credit is available for central air conditioners that achieve the highest efficiency tier established by the Consortium for Energy Efficiency, as in effect on Jan. 1, 2009 (rather than 2006). (Code Sec. 25C(d)(3)(C) as amended by 2009 Recovery Act §1121(b)(2))

These standards are:

FTC 2d References are to Federal Tax Coordinator 2d
FIN References are to RIA's Analysis of Federal Taxes: Income
USTR References are to United States Tax Reporter: Income
PE References are to Pension Explanations

. . . a SEER greater than or equal to 16 and EER greater than or equal to 13 for split systems, and

. . . a SEER greater than or equal to 14 and EER greater than or equal to 12 for packaged systems. (Com Rept, see ¶ 5021)

Natural gas, propane, or oil water heaters. Under the 2009 Recovery Act, the credit is available for natural gas, propane, or oil water heaters that have either an energy factor of at least 0.82 or a thermal efficiency of at least 90%. (Code Sec. 25C(d)(3)(D) as amended by 2009 Recovery Act §1121(b)(3))

Biomass fuel stoves. Under the 2009 Recovery Act, the credit is available for biomass fuel stoves that burn biomass fuel to heat a dwelling unit that the taxpayer uses as a residence, or to heat water for use in the residence, and that has a thermal efficiency rating of at least 75%, *as measured using a lower heating value.* (Code Sec. 25C(d)(3)(E) as amended by 2009 Recovery Act §1121(b)(4))

> **🅡🅙** *caution:* The above change regarding biomass fuel stoves is effective for tax years beginning after Dec. 31, 2008. See the effective date discussion, below.

Furnaces and boilers. The 2009 Recovery Act establishes six separate categories for qualified natural gas furnaces, qualified propane furnaces, qualified oil furnaces, qualified natural gas hot water boilers, qualified propane hot water boilers, and qualified oil hot water boilers. (Code Sec. 25C(d)(2)(A)(ii) as amended by 2009 Recovery Act §1121(c)(2)) Under the 2009 Recovery Act:

. . . a "qualified natural gas furnace" means any natural gas furnace that achieves an annual fuel utilization efficiency rate of not less than 95. (Code Sec. 25C(d)(4)(A) as amended by 2009 Recovery Act §1121(c)(1))

. . . a "qualified propane furnace" means any propane furnace that achieves an annual fuel utilization efficiency rate of not less than 95. (Code Sec. 25C(d)(4)(C))

. . . a "qualified oil furnace" means any oil furnace that achieves an annual fuel utilization efficiency rate of not less than 90. (Code Sec. 25C(d)(4)(E))

. . . a "qualified natural gas hot water boiler" means any natural gas hot water boiler that achieves an annual fuel utilization efficiency rate of not less than 90. (Code Sec. 25C(d)(4)(B))

. . . a "qualified propane hot water boiler" means any propane hot water boiler that achieves an annual fuel utilization efficiency rate of not less than 90. (Code Sec. 25C(d)(4)(D))

. . . a "qualified oil hot water boiler" means any oil hot water boiler that achieves an annual fuel utilization efficiency rate of not less than 90. (Code Sec. 25C(d)(4)(F))

☑ *observation:* The annual fuel utilization efficiency rate is the rate at which a furnace or boiler converts fuel into heat. A rate of 90 means that the item converts 90% of the fuel into heat, while the other 10% is lost.

☑ *observation:* The standards for qualified natural gas furnaces and qualified propane furnaces remain the same under the 2009 Recovery Act.

In the case of qualified oil furnaces, qualified natural gas hot water boilers, qualified propane hot water boilers, and qualified oil hot water boilers, the minimum annual fuel utilization efficiency rate is reduced from 95 to 90.

☐ **Effective:** Property placed in service after Feb. 17, 2009 (2009 Recovery Act §1121(f)(2)), except that the change regarding biomass fuel stoves takes effect for tax years beginning after Dec. 31, 2008. (2009 Recovery Act §1121(f)(1))

☑ *observation:* Thus, the change regarding biomass fuel stoves applies to expenditures paid or incurred in tax years beginning after Dec. 31, 2008, even if the stove was placed in service before Feb. 18, 2009.

¶ 1103. Expenditures from subsidized energy financing can qualify for REEP credit and nonbusiness energy property credit

Code Sec. 25C(e)(1), as amended by 2009 Recovery Act § 1103(b)(2)(A)
Code Sec. 25D(e)(9), as amended by 2009 Recovery Act § 1103(b)(2)(B)
Generally effective: Tax years beginning after Dec. 31, 2008
Committee Reports, see ¶ 5021, 5022

Individual taxpayers are allowed a nonrefundable personal tax credit, known as the residential energy efficient property (REEP) credit, for 30% of expenditures for qualified solar water heating, geothermal heat pump, fuel cell, small wind energy, and solar electric property made during the tax year. (FTC 2d/FIN ¶ A-4780; USTR ¶ 25D4; TaxDesk ¶ 569,560)

Individual taxpayers are also allowed a nonrefundable personal tax credit, known as the nonbusiness energy property credit, for energy efficient improvements to a dwelling unit in the U.S. owned and used by the taxpayer as the taxpayer's principal residence. (FTC 2d/FIN ¶ A-4750; USTR ¶ 25C4; TaxDesk ¶ 569,550)

FTC 2d References are to Federal Tax Coordinator 2d
FIN References are to RIA's Analysis of Federal Taxes: Income
USTR References are to United States Tax Reporter: Income
PE References are to Pension Explanations

Under pre-2009 Recovery Act law, expenditures made from subsidized energy financing (as defined in Code Sec. 48(a)(4)(C)) weren't taken into account for purposes of the REEP credit. (FTC 2d/FIN ¶ A-4782; USTR ¶ 25D4; TaxDesk ¶ 569,562)

> **⊘** *observation:* Under Code Sec. 48(a)(4)(C), "subsidized energy financing" means financing provided under a federal, state, or local program, a principal purpose of which is to provide subsidized financing for projects designed to conserve or produce energy.

A similar rule applied for purposes of the nonbusiness energy property credit. Thus, expenditures made from subsidized energy financing weren't taken into account for purposes of that credit. (FTC 2d/FIN ¶ A-4756; USTR ¶ 25C4; TaxDesk ¶ 569,556)

New Law. The 2009 Recovery Act eliminates the rules under which expenditures made from subsidized energy financing weren't taken into account for purposes of:

. . . the REEP credit (Code Sec. 25D(e)(9) as amended by 2009 Recovery Act §1103(b)(2)(B)) and

. . . the nonbusiness energy property credit. (Code Sec. 25C(e)(1) as amended by 2009 Recovery Act §1103(b)(2)(A))

> **⊘** *observation:* Thus, expenditures made from subsidized energy financing can qualify for the REEP credit and the nonbusiness energy property credit, if they otherwise meet the requirements for those credits.

For repeal of the basis-reduction rule under the business energy tax credit for property financed with subsidized energy financing, see ¶ 1206.

☐ **Effective:** Tax years beginning after Dec. 31, 2008. (2009 Recovery Act §1103(c)(2))

¶ 1104. Dollar caps on REEP credit are eliminated for solar hot water, geothermal, and wind property expenditures

Code Sec. 25D(b)(1), as amended by 2009 Recovery Act § 1122(a)(1)
Code Sec. 25D(e)(4), as amended by 2009 Recovery Act § 1122(a)(2)
Generally effective: Tax years beginning after Dec. 31, 2008
Committee Reports, see ¶ 5022

Individual taxpayers are allowed a nonrefundable personal tax credit, known as the residential energy efficient property (REEP) credit, for 30% of expenditures made during the tax year for qualified solar water heating, geothermal heat pump, fuel cell, small wind energy, and solar electric property. (FTC 2d/FIN ¶ A-4780; USTR ¶ 25D4; TaxDesk ¶ 569,560)

The REEP credit for a tax year was limited to:

. . . under pre-2009 Recovery Act law, $2,000 for qualified solar water heating property;

. . . under pre-2009 Recovery Act law, $2,000 for qualified geothermal heat pump property;

. . . $500 for each 0.5 kilowatt of capacity of qualified fuel cell property; and

. . . under pre-2009 Recovery Act law, $500 for each 0.5 kilowatt of capacity (not to exceed $4,000) of qualified small wind energy property.

There is no dollar limit for solar electric property after 2008. (FTC 2d/FIN ¶ A-4781; USTR ¶ 25D4; TaxDesk ¶ 569,561)

Rules are provided for allocating the credit where two or more individuals jointly occupy a dwelling unit and use it as a residence. The maximum amount of expenditures taken into account by all the individuals during the calendar year was:

. . . under pre-2009 Recovery Act law, $6,667 for qualified solar water heating property expenditures;

. . . under pre-2009 Recovery Act law, $6,667 for qualified geothermal heat pump property expenditures;

. . . $1,667 for each 0.5 kilowatt of capacity of qualified fuel cell property for which qualified fuel cell property expenditures are made; and

. . . under pre-2009 Recovery Act law, $1,667 for each 0.5 kilowatt of capacity (not to exceed $13,333) of wind turbines for which qualified small wind energy property expenditures are made. (FTC 2d/FIN ¶ A-4785; USTR ¶ 25D4; TaxDesk ¶ 569,565)

> **🅡🅘🅐 observation:** Those amounts ($6,667, $1,667, and $13,333) were the maximum amounts of expenditures that qualified for the credit—30% of $6,667 is $2,000; 30% of $1,667 is $500; and 30% of $13,333 is $4,000.

New Law. The 2009 Recovery Act eliminates the REEP credit caps for qualified solar water heating, geothermal heat pump, and small wind energy property (Com Rept, see ¶ 5022), while retaining the credit cap for qualified fuel cell property. Thus, for any qualified fuel cell property expenditure, the

---

FTC 2d References are to Federal Tax Coordinator 2d
FIN References are to RIA's Analysis of Federal Taxes: Income
USTR References are to United States Tax Reporter: Income
PE References are to Pension Explanations

REEP credit for any tax year can't exceed $500 for each 0.5 kilowatt of capacity of the qualified fuel cell property to which the expenditure relates. (Code Sec. 25D(b)(1) as amended by 2009 Recovery Act §1122(a)(1))

Joint occupancy. The rules for allocating the credit among joint occupants are revised to conform to this change. Where two or more individuals jointly occupy a dwelling unit and use it as a residence, the maximum amount of qualified fuel cell property expenditures that may be taken into account by all of the individuals for the calendar year is $1,667 for each 0.5 kilowatt of capacity of qualified fuel cell property to which the expenditures relate. The allocation rules for other types of qualified expenditures are eliminated. (Code Sec. 25D(e)(4) as amended by 2009 Recovery Act §1122(a)(2))

For allowance of the credit for expenditures from subsidized energy financing, see ¶ 1103.

☐ **Effective:** Tax years beginning after Dec. 31, 2008. (2009 Recovery Act §1122(b))

¶ 1200. Alternative Energy Provisions

¶ 1201. $4,000 annual limitation on business energy tax credit for qualified small wind energy property is repealed for periods after Dec. 31, 2008

Code Sec. 48(c)(4)(B), as amended by 2009 Recovery Act § 1103(a)
Generally effective: Periods after Dec. 31, 2008
Committee Reports, see ¶ 5015

The nonrefundable business energy credit for any tax year is the energy percentage of the basis of each energy property placed in service during the tax year, see FTC 2d/FIN ¶ L-16401; USTR ¶ 484; TaxDesk ¶ 381,601. The energy percentage is 30% for "qualified small wind energy property," which is property that uses a qualifying small wind turbine (defined below) to generate electricity, see FTC 2d/FIN ¶ L-16436.4; USTR ¶ 484; TaxDesk ¶ 381,602.

A "qualifying small wind turbine" is a wind turbine that has a nameplate capacity of not more than 100 kilowatts, see FTC 2d/FIN ¶ L-16436.4; USTR ¶ 484; TaxDesk ¶ 381,602.

"Qualified small wind energy property" doesn't include any property for any period after Dec. 31, 2016, see FTC 2d/FIN ¶ L-16436.4; USTR ¶ 484; TaxDesk ¶ 381,602.

Under pre-2009 Recovery Act law, for qualified small wind energy property placed in service during the tax year, the credit otherwise determined under Code Sec. 48(a)(1) (the energy percentage of the basis of each energy property placed in service during that tax year, see FTC 2d/FIN ¶ L-16401; USTR ¶ 484; TaxDesk ¶ 381,601) for all that property of the taxpayer for that tax year couldn't exceed $4,000. (FTC 2d/FIN ¶ L-16400, ¶ L-16436.4; USTR ¶ 484)

New Law. The 2009 Recovery Act specifically repeals the per taxpayer $4,000 annual limitation on the energy credit for qualified small wind energy property (Code Sec. 48(c)(4)(B) as amended by 2009 Recovery Act §1103(a)). Thus, the 2009 Recovery Act eliminates the credit cap applicable to qualified small wind energy property. (Com Rept, see ¶ 5015)

> *observation:* Thus, subject to the project expenditure rules discussed under "Effective" below, qualified small wind energy property is eligible for an uncapped 30% credit if placed in service after 2008.

FTC 2d References are to Federal Tax Coordinator 2d
FIN References are to RIA's Analysis of Federal Taxes: Income
USTR References are to United States Tax Reporter: Income
PE References are to Pension Explanations

illustration (1): In 2008, J Corp., a calendar year taxpayer, places into service $40,000 of qualified small wind energy property. J's energy credit for 2008 for that property is $4,000 ($40,000 × 30%, capped at $4,000).

illustration (2): The facts are the same as in Illustration 1, except that J places the property in service in 2009. Thus, subject to the project expenditure rules discussed under "Effective" below, J's credit for 2009 is $12,000 ($40,000 × 30%).

observation: Code Sec. 48(a)(1) defines the energy credit for any tax year as the energy percentage of the basis of each energy property placed in service during the tax year, with certain exceptions, including the $4,000 limitation on the credit for qualified small wind energy property placed in service in a tax year by a taxpayer, see FTC 2d/FIN ¶ L-16401; USTR ¶ 484. Because Congress repealed the $4,000 limitation contained in Code Sec. 48(c)(4)(B), a technical correction may be necessary to remove the language in Code Sec. 48(a)(1) that refers to Code Sec. 48(c)(4)(B).

Redesignations. The 2009 Recovery Act redesignates pre-2009 Recovery Act Code Sec. 48(c)(4)(C) as Code Sec. 48(c)(4)(B) and pre-2009 Recovery Act Code Sec. 48(c)(4)(D) as Code Sec. 48(c)(4)(C). (2009 Recovery Act §1103(a))

For the availability under the 2009 Recovery Act of a taxpayer election to receive grants instead of energy credits for specific energy property placed in service in 2009 and 2010, see ¶ 1204.

For retroactive termination of the rule reducing the basis of property for purposes of claiming the energy credit if the property is financed in whole or in part by subsidized energy financing or with proceeds from private activity bonds, see ¶ 1206.

For the availability under the 2009 Recovery Act of an irrevocable election to treat qualified investment credit facilities placed in service after 2008 and before 2014 (before 2013 for wind facilities) as property eligible for the 30% business energy credit, see ¶ 1203.

☐ **Effective:** Periods after Dec. 31, 2008, under rules (progress expenditure rules) similar to the rules of former Code Sec. 48(m) as in effect on Nov. 4, '90. (2009 Recovery Act §1103(c)(1))

observation: 2009 Recovery Act §1103(c)(1) provides that the above provision is effective under rules similar to the rules of former Code Sec. 48(m) (as in effect on the day before the date of enactment of the '90 Revenue Act (PL 101-508, 11/5/1990)). The '90 Revenue Act was enacted on Nov. 5, '90.

❤️observation: Former Code Sec. 48(m) provided that when the application of former Code Sec. 48(m)(1), former Code Sec. 46(b) (amount of credit percentage), or former Code Sec. 46(c)(3) (qualified investment in public utility property) is expressed in terms of a time period, and the construction, reconstruction, or erection of that property is completed after the beginning of that period, only the portion of the basis which is properly attributable to construction, reconstruction, or erection after the beginning of that period qualifies for the credit. Thus, the repeal of the $4,000 limitation applies only to the portion of the basis of qualified small wind energy property that is constructed, reconstructed, or erected after Dec. 31, 2008.

Also, in the case of property acquired and placed in service by the taxpayer during the period (rather than constructed by the taxpayer), only property acquired and placed in service after the beginning of that period will qualify for the credit. Thus, the repeal of the $4,000 limitation applies only to qualified small wind energy property acquired and placed in service after Dec. 31, 2008.

¶ 1202. 30% credit is allowed for investment in qualified property used in a qualified advanced energy manufacturing project

Code Sec. 46(5), as amended by 2009 Recovery Act § 1302(a)
Code Sec. 48C, as added by 2009 Recovery Act § 1302(b)
Code Sec. 49(a)(1)(C)(v), as amended by 2009 Recovery Act § 1302(c)(1)
Generally effective: Periods after Feb. 17, 2009
Committee Reports, see ¶ 5052

Under pre-2009 Recovery Act law, taxpayers were allowed an investment credit equal to the sum of:

. . . the rehabilitation credit,

. . . the energy credit,

. . . the qualifying advanced coal project credit, and

. . . the qualifying gasification project credit.

(FTC 2d/FIN ¶ L-16500, ¶ L-16501; USTR ¶ 464; TaxDesk ¶ 381,401).

The term "credit base," for purposes of certain nonrecourse financing excluded under the at-risk rules, meant:

FTC 2d References are to Federal Tax Coordinator 2d
FIN References are to RIA's Analysis of Federal Taxes: Income
USTR References are to United States Tax Reporter: Income
PE References are to Pension Explanations

- the portion of the basis of any qualified rehabilitated building attributable to qualified rehabilitation expenditures,

- the basis of any energy property,

- the basis of any property which is part of a qualifying advanced coal project, and

- the basis of any property which is part of a qualifying gasification project.

(FTC 2d/FIN ¶ P-1600, ¶ P-1611; USTR ¶ 494; TaxDesk ¶ 381,402).

New Law. The 2009 Recovery Act provides that the qualifying energy project credit (defined below) is included in the credits composing the Code Sec. 46 investment credit. (Code Sec. 46(5) as amended by 2009 Recovery Act §1302(a))

> *observation:* Thus, the investment credit will consist of:
>
> . . . the rehabilitation credit,
>
> . . . the energy credit,
>
> . . . the qualifying advanced coal project credit,
>
> . . . the qualifying gasification project credit, *and*
>
> . . . the qualifying energy project credit.

For purposes of Code Sec. 46 (which enumerates the items composing the investment credit), the qualifying advanced energy project credit for any tax year is an amount equal to 30% of the qualified investment (defined below) for that tax year with respect to any qualifying advanced energy project (defined below) of the taxpayer. (Code Sec. 48C(a) as added by 2009 Recovery Act §1302(b))

Qualified investment. For these purposes, the qualified investment for any tax year is the basis of eligible property that is placed in service by the taxpayer during that tax year and that is part of a qualifying advanced energy project. (Code Sec. 48C(b)(1))

The basis of qualified property must be reduced by the amount of credit received. (Com Rept, see ¶ 5052)

Rules similar to the rules relating to the treatment of qualified progress expenditures under Code Sec. 46(c)(4) and Code Sec. 46(d) before repeal by the '90 Revenue Act (Sec. 11813(a), PL 101-508, 11/5/1990) also apply. (Code Sec. 48C(b)(2))

> *observation:* The '90 Revenue Act was enacted on Nov. 5, '90.

Limitation. The amount which is treated for all tax years with respect to any qualifying advanced energy project will not exceed the amount designated by IRS as eligible for the credit under Code Sec. 48C. (Code Sec. 48C(b)(3))

🅡🅘🅐 *observation:* Presumably, this means that the amount which is treated *as qualified investment* for all tax years with respect to any qualifying advanced energy project will not exceed the amount designated by IRS as eligible for the credit under these rules. A technical correction may be needed to clarify this point.

Qualified advanced energy project. A qualifying advanced energy project is a project: (Code Sec. 48C(c)(1)(A))

(i) which re-equips, expands, or establishes a manufacturing facility for the production of: (Code Sec. 48C(c)(1)(A)(i))

(I) property designed to be used to produce energy from the sun, wind, geothermal deposits (within the meaning of Code Sec. 613(e)(2)), or other renewable resources, (Code Sec. 48C(c)(1)(A)(i)(I))

(II) fuel cells, microturbines, or an energy storage system for use with electric or hybrid-electric motor vehicles, (Code Sec. 48C(c)(1)(A)(i)(II))

(III) electric grids to support the transmission of intermittent sources of renewable energy, including storage of that energy, (Code Sec. 48C(c)(1)(A)(i)(III))

(IV) property designed to capture and sequester carbon dioxide emissions, (Code Sec. 48C(c)(1)(A)(i)(IV))

(V) property designed to refine or blend renewable fuels (Code Sec. 48C(c)(1)(A)(i)(V)), other than fossil fuels (Com Rept, see ¶ 5052)), to produce energy conservation technologies (including energy-conserving lighting technologies and smart grid technologies), (Code Sec. 48C(c)(1)(A)(i)(V))

(VI) new qualified plug-in electric drive motor vehicles (as defined by Code Sec. 30D), qualified plug-in electric vehicles (as defined by Code Sec. 30(d)), or components which are designed specifically for use with those vehicles, including electric motors, generators, and power control units, or (Code Sec. 48C(c)(1)(A)(i)(VI))

(VII) other advanced energy property designed to reduce greenhouse gas emissions as may be determined by IRS, and (Code Sec. 48C(c)(1)(A)(i)(VII))

(ii) any portion of the qualified investment of which is certified by IRS under Code Sec. 48C(d) (discussed below) as eligible for a credit under Code Sec. 48C. (Code Sec. 48C(c)(1)(A)(ii))

However, a qualifying advanced energy project does not include any portion of a project for the production of any property which is used in the refining or blending of any transportation fuel (other than renewable fuels). (Code Sec. 48C(c)(1)(B))

Eligible property. Eligible property is any property: (Code Sec. 48C(c)(2))

(A) which is necessary for the production of property described in Code Sec. 48C(c)(1)(A)(i) (see item (i) under "Qualified advanced energy project," above), (Code Sec. 48C(c)(2)(A))

(B) which is: (Code Sec. 48C(c)(2)(B))

(i) tangible personal property, or (Code Sec. 48C(c)(2)(B)(i))

(ii) other tangible property (not including a building or its structural components), but only if that property is used as an integral part of the qualified investment credit facility, and (Code Sec. 48C(c)(2)(B)(ii))

(C) with respect to which depreciation (or amortization in lieu of depreciation) is allowable. (Code Sec. 48C(c)(2)(C))

Qualifying advanced energy project program. Not later than Aug. 17, 2009, IRS, in consultation with the Secretary of Energy, is to establish a qualifying advanced energy project program to consider and award certifications for qualified investments eligible for credits under Code Sec. 48C to qualifying advanced energy project sponsors. (Code Sec. 48C(d)(1)(A)) The total amount of credits that may be allocated under the program cannot exceed $2,300,000,000. (Code Sec. 48C(d)(1)(B))

Each applicant for certification must submit an application containing whatever information IRS may require during the 2-year period beginning on the date IRS establishes the qualifying advanced energy project program. (Code Sec. 48C(d)(2)(A))

Each applicant will have one year from the date IRS accepts the application during which to provide to IRS evidence that the requirements of the certification have been met. (Code Sec. 48C(d)(2)(B))

An applicant receiving a certification has three years from the date of issuance of the certification to place the project in service. If the project is not placed in service by that time period, the certification is no longer valid. (Code Sec. 48C(d)(2)(C))

Selection criteria. In determining which qualifying advanced energy projects to certify under these rules, IRS (Code Sec. 48C(d)(3)) will take into consideration only those projects where there is a reasonable expectation of commercial viability, (Code Sec. 48C(d)(3)(A)) and will take into consideration which projects: (Code Sec. 48C(d)(3)(B))

(i) will provide the greatest domestic job creation (both direct and indirect) during the credit period, (Code Sec. 48C(d)(3)(B)(i))

(ii) will provide the greatest net impact in avoiding or reducing air pollutants or anthropogenic emissions of greenhouse gases, (Code Sec. 48C(d)(3)(B)(ii))

(iii) have the greatest potential for technological innovation and commercial deployment, (Code Sec. 48C(d)(3)(B)(iii))

(iv) have the lowest levelized cost of generated or stored energy, or of measured reduction in energy consumption or greenhouse gas emission (based on costs of the full supply chain), and (Code Sec. 48C(d)(3)(B)(iv))

(v) have the shortest project time from certification to completion. (Code Sec. 48C(d)(3)(B)(v))

Review and redistribution. Not later than Feb. 17, 2013, IRS is to review the credits allocated under these rules as of that date. (Code Sec. 48C(d)(4)(A))

IRS can reallocate credits awarded under these rules if it determines that: (Code Sec. 48C(d)(4)(B))

(i) there is an insufficient quantity of qualifying applications for certification pending at the time of the review, or (Code Sec. 48C(d)(4)(B)(i))

(ii) any certification made under these rules has been revoked under the two-year rule of Code Sec. 48C(d)(2)(B) (above) because the project subject to the certification has been delayed as a result of third party opposition or litigation to the proposed project. (Code Sec. 48C(d)(4)(B)(ii))

If IRS determines that credits under these rules are available for reallocation under the requirements set forth in Code Sec. 48C(d)(2) (discussed above), it is authorized to conduct an additional program for applications for certification. (Code Sec. 48C(d)(4)(C))

Disclosure of allocations. IRS must, upon making a certification under Code Sec. 48C(d), publicly disclose the identity of the applicant and the amount of the credit with respect to that applicant. (Code Sec. 48C(d)(5))

No double benefit. A credit is not allowed under Code Sec. 48C for any qualified investment for which a credit is allowed under Code Sec. 48 (the energy credit), Code Sec. 48A (the qualifying advanced coal project credit), or Code Sec. 48B (the qualifying gasification project credit). (Code Sec. 48C(e))

Credit base for purposes of certain nonrecourse financing excluded under the at-risk rules. For purposes of certain nonrecourse financing excluded under the at-risk rules, the term credit base includes the basis of any property which is part of a qualifying advanced energy project under the above rules. (Code Sec. 49(a)(1)(C)(v) as amended by 2009 Recovery Act §1302(c)(1))

FTC 2d References are to Federal Tax Coordinator 2d
FIN References are to RIA's Analysis of Federal Taxes: Income
USTR References are to United States Tax Reporter: Income
PE References are to Pension Explanations

observation: Thus, the credit base consists of:

- the portion of the basis of any qualified rehabilitated building attributable to qualified rehabilitation expenditures,

- the basis of any energy property,

- the basis of any property which is part of a qualifying advanced coal project,

- the basis of any property which is part of a qualifying gasification project, *and*

- the basis of any property which is part of a qualifying advanced energy project under the Code Sec. 48C rules discussed above.

☐ **Effective:** Periods after Feb. 17, 2009, under rules similar to the rules of former Code Sec. 48(m) (as in effect on Nov. 4, '90). (2009 Recovery Act §1302(d))

observation: 2009 Recovery Act §1302(d) provides that the above provision is effective under rules similar to the rules of former Code Sec. 48(m) (as in effect on the day before the date of enactment of the '90 Revenue Act (PL 101-508, 11/5/1990)). The '90 Revenue Act was enacted on Nov. 5, '90.

observation: Former Code Sec. 48(m) provided that when the application of former Code Sec. 48(m)(1), former Code Sec. 46(b) (amount of credit percentage), or former Code Sec. 46(c)(3) (qualified investment in public utility property) is expressed in terms of a time period, and the construction, reconstruction, or erection of that property is completed after the beginning of that period, only the portion of the basis which is properly attributable to construction, reconstruction, or erection after the beginning of that period qualifies for the credit. Thus, the increased credit limit applies only to the portion of the basis of qualified property used in a qualified advanced energy manufacturing project that was constructed, reconstructed, or erected after Feb. 17, 2009.

Also, in the case of property acquired and placed in service by the taxpayer during the period (rather than constructed by the taxpayer), only property acquired and placed in service after the beginning of that period will qualify for the credit. Thus, the increased credit limit applies only to qualified property used in a qualified advanced energy manufacturing project property acquired and placed in service after Feb. 17, 2009.

¶ 1203. Taxpayers can irrevocably elect 30% business energy credit instead of electricity production credit for qualified property that is part of qualified investment credit facilities placed in service after 2008 and before 2014 (2013 for wind facilities)

Code Sec. 48(a)(5), as amended by 2009 Recovery Act § 1102(a)
Generally effective: Facilities placed in service after Dec. 31, 2008 and
*   before Jan. 1, 2014 (2013 for wind facilities)*
Committee Reports, see ¶ 5014

In general, for any tax year, an income tax credit for electricity produced from certain renewable resources (electricity production credit) is available for electricity produced from qualified energy resources and refined coal and Indian coal produced at a qualified facility. The electricity produced must be sold by the taxpayer to an unrelated person during the tax year. The credit is available at a reduced rate for electricity produced and sold from certain types of qualified facilities, see FTC 2d/FIN ¶s L-17750, L-17751, L-17770; USTR ¶s 454, 454.01, 454.09 *et seq.*; TaxDesk ¶s 384,054, 384,054.1.

The electricity production credit is generally available for a ten-year period beginning on the placed-in-service date of the qualifying facility for electricity produced during that period, see FTC 2d/FIN ¶ L-17752; USTR ¶ 454.055; TaxDesk ¶ 384,055.

Subject to certain exceptions and limitations, the non-refundable business energy credit for any tax year is the energy percentage of the basis of each energy property placed in service during the tax year. The energy percentage is 30% for (1) qualified fuel cell property, (2) energy property described in Code Sec. 48(a)(3)(A)(i) (equipment using solar energy to generate electricity, to heat or cool (or provide hot water for use in) a structure, or to provide solar process heat, excepting property used to generate energy for the purpose of heating a swimming pool), but only for periods ending before Jan. 1, 2017; (3) energy property described in Code Sec. 48(a)(3)(A)(ii) (equipment that uses solar energy to illuminate the inside of a structure using fiber-optic distributed sunlight), but only for periods ending before Jan. 1, 2017; and (4) qualified small wind energy property. A 10% business energy credit applies to certain other types of property. (FTC 2d/FIN ¶ L-16400, ¶ L-16401; USTR ¶ 484; TaxDesk ¶ 381,601)

FTC 2d References are to Federal Tax Coordinator 2d
FIN References are to RIA's Analysis of Federal Taxes: Income
USTR References are to United States Tax Reporter: Income
PE References are to Pension Explanations

observation: Under pre-2009 Recovery Act law, there was no provision allowing a taxpayer to irrevocably elect the business energy credit instead of the electricity production credit for qualified investment credit facilities.

New Law. The 2009 Recovery Act provides that, for any qualified property (defined below) that is part of a "qualified investment credit facility" (defined below)— (Code Sec. 48(a)(5)(A) as amended by 2009 Recovery Act §1102(a))

... that property can be treated as energy property for purposes of the election to treat qualified facilities as energy property, and (Code Sec. 48(a)(5)(A)(i))

... the energy percentage for that property is 30%. (Code Sec. 48(a)(5)(A)(ii))

"Qualified property" defined. For purposes of the election, "qualified property" means property —(Code Sec. 48(a)(5)(D))

... that is (Code Sec. 48(a)(5)(D)(i)) tangible personal property, or (Code Sec. 48(a)(5)(D)(i)(I)) other tangible property (not including a building or its structural components), but only if that property is used as an integral part of the qualified investment credit facility, and (Code Sec. 48(a)(5)(D)(i)(II))

... for which depreciation (or amortization in lieu of depreciation) is allowable. (Code Sec. 48(a)(5)(D)(ii))

Thus, for a wind facility, Congress intends that only property eligible for 5-year depreciation under Code Sec. 168(e)(3)(b)(vi) is treated as credit-eligible energy property under the election. (Com Rept, see ¶ 5014)

"Qualified investment credit facility" defined. For purposes of the election, "qualified investment credit facility" means (Code Sec. 48(a)(5)(C)) any qualified facility within the meaning of Code Sec. 45 that is: (Code Sec. 48(a)(5)(C)(i); Code Sec. 48(a)(5)(C)(ii))

... a wind facility described in Code Sec. 45(d)(1), see FTC 2d/FIN ¶ L-17771.5; USTR ¶ 454.14; TaxDesk ¶ 384,054.1, if the facility is placed in service in 2009, 2010, 2011, or 2012 (Code Sec. 48(a)(5)(C)(i)); and,

... a closed-loop biomass facility described in Code Sec. 45(d)(2), see FTC 2d/FIN ¶ L-17771; USTR ¶ 454.09; TaxDesk ¶ 384,054.1;

... an open-loop biomass facility described in Code Sec. 45(d)(3), see FTC 2d/FIN ¶ L-17771.1; USTR ¶ 454.10; TaxDesk ¶ 384,054.1;

... a geothermal energy facility described in Code Sec. 45(d)(4), see FTC 2d/FIN ¶ L-17771.2; USTR ¶ 454.11; TaxDesk ¶ 384,054.1;

... a landfill gas facility described in Code Sec. 45(d)(6), see FTC 2d/FIN ¶ L-17771.4; USTR ¶ 454.13; TaxDesk ¶ 384,054.1;

... a trash facility described in Code Sec. 45(d)(7), see FTC 2d/FIN ¶ L-17771.4; USTR ¶ 454.13; TaxDesk ¶ 384,054.1;

. . . a qualified hydropower facility described in Code Sec. 45(d)(9), see FTC 2d/FIN ¶ L-17771.6; USTR ¶ 454.15; TaxDesk ¶ 384,054.1; and

. . . a marine and hydrokinetic renewable energy facility described in Code Sec. 45(d)(11), see FTC 2d/FIN ¶ L-17771.9; USTR ¶ 454.18, if the facility described in Code Sec. 45(d)(2), Code Sec. 45(d)(3), Code Sec. 45(d)(4), Code Sec. 45(d)(6), Code Sec. 45(d)(7), Code Sec. 45(d)(9), or Code Sec. 45(d)(11) is placed in service in 2009, 2010, 2011, 2012, or 2013, (Code Sec. 48(a)(5)(C)(ii))

if no electricity production credit under Code Sec. 45 has been allowed for that facility and the taxpayer irrevocably elects the business energy credit for that facility. (Code Sec. 48(a)(5)(C))

Thus, for purposes of the election, qualified facilities are facilities otherwise eligible for the Code Sec. 45 production tax credit (other than refined coal, Indian coal, and solar facilities) for which no credit under Code Sec. 45 has been allowed. (Com Rept, see ¶ 5014)

> *observation:* Essentially, the 2009 Recovery Act allows taxpayers that place qualified investment facilities (other than wind facilities) in service in 2009, 2010, 2011, 2012, or 2013 to irrevocably elect to take the 30% business energy credit in the year the facility is placed in service, instead of the electricity production tax credit, which is taken for ten years. Taxpayers have to place qualified investment facilities that are wind facilities in service in 2009, 2010, 2011, or 2012 to be able to irrevocably elect the 30% business energy credit instead of the electricity production credit.

> *illustration:* V Corp., a calendar year taxpayer, places into service in 2011 a trash facility with a depreciable basis of $500,000. V irrevocably elects to take the business energy credit for the facility. V's 2011 business energy credit for the facility is $150,000 (30% × $500,000).

Electricity production credit denied for property subject to the election. No electricity production credit under Code Sec. 45 is allowed for any tax year for any qualified investment credit facility. (Code Sec. 48(a)(5)(B)) That is, a taxpayer electing to treat a facility as energy property may not claim the production credit under Code Sec. 45. (Com Rept, see ¶ 5014)

> *observation:* Thus, in the illustration above, V Corp. cannot take the Code Sec. 45 electricity production credit for that facility, nor later file an amended return to revoke the business energy credit election.

FTC 2d References are to Federal Tax Coordinator 2d
FIN References are to RIA's Analysis of Federal Taxes: Income
USTR References are to United States Tax Reporter: Income
PE References are to Pension Explanations

231

🖉 *observation:* Presumably, IRS will issue guidance on how to make the irrevocable election to take the business energy credit instead of the electricity production credit, since none is provided in the 2009 Recovery Act.

☐ **Effective:** Facilities placed in service after Dec. 31, 2008 (2009 Recovery Act §1102(b)) and before Jan. 1, 2014 (2013 for wind facilities) (Code Sec. 48(a)(5)(C)(ii) as amended by 2009 Recovery Act §1102(a); Code Sec. 48(a)(5)(C)(i)).

¶ 1204. Grants in lieu of Code Sec. 45 electricity production credit and Code Sec. 48 energy credit for specified energy property placed in service or under construction in 2009 or 2010

Code Sec. 45, 2009 Recovery Act § 1603
Code Sec. 48, 2009 Recovery Act § 1603
Code Sec. 50, 2009 Recovery Act § 1603
Generally effective: Feb. 17, 2009
Committee Reports, see ¶ 5016

Under pre-2009 Recovery Act law, grants in lieu of tax credits under Code Sec. 45 (see FTC 2d/FIN ¶ L-17750 *et seq.*; USTR ¶ 454 *et seq.*; TaxDesk ¶ 384,054 *et seq.*) and Code Sec. 48 (see FTC 2d/FIN ¶ L-16400 *et seq.*; USTR ¶ 484 *et seq.*; TaxDesk ¶ 381,600 *et seq.*) for specified energy property placed in service were not available.

A limitation on the energy credit applies to qualified fuel cell property. For property placed in service during the tax year, the energy credit can't exceed an amount equal to $1,500 for each 0.5 kilowatt of capacity of the property. The $1,500 per one-half kilowatt limitation can also be expressed (at least where fractional kilowatts aren't involved) as a $3,000 per kilowatt limitation (see FTC 2d/FIN ¶ L-16436; USTR ¶ 484; TaxDesk ¶ 381,601).

A limitation on the energy credit applies to qualified microturbine property placed in service during the tax year. The energy credit for the tax year with respect to that property can't exceed an amount equal to $200 for each kilowatt of capacity of the property (see FTC 2d/FIN ¶ L-16437; USTR ¶ 484; TaxDesk ¶ 381,601).

A limitation on the energy credit applies for combined heat and power system (CHP) property placed in service during the tax year that has an electrical capacity in excess of the "applicable capacity" (defined below). The energy credit for CHP property for a tax year is equal to an amount that bears the same ratio to the credit as the applicable capacity bears to the capacity of the property (see FTC 2d/FIN ¶ L-16436.3B; USTR ¶ 484; TaxDesk ¶ 381,601). The term "applicable capacity" means 15 megawatts, or a mechanical energy capacity of more than 20,000 horsepower, or an equivalent combination of electrical and mechanical energy capacities (see FTC 2d/FIN ¶ L-16436.3C; USTR ¶ 484; TaxDesk ¶ 381,601). (FTC 2d/FIN ¶ L-16400, ¶ L-17750; USTR ¶ 454, ¶ 484; TaxDesk ¶ 381,601, ¶ 384,054)

Under the recapture rules of Code Sec. 50, an energy credit recapture determination is required if the energy property is disposed of or otherwise ceases to be energy property to the taxpayer before the end of its recapture period. This means that for purposes of recapture, a disposition or cessation occurring five years or more after the date the property is placed in service doesn't cause any recapture. For example, if the energy credit is 10%, the credit allowed is 2% for each year the property is held. If 5-year property that was allowed the credit were disposed of during the fifth year, the recapture amount would be 2%. No credit is recaptured after the fifth full year (see FTC 2d/FIN ¶s L-16418, L-17312; USTR ¶ 504.02; TaxDesk ¶ 381,405).

New Law. Each person can apply to the Treasury Secretary for a grant when they place in service specified energy property (defined below) in order to reimburse that person for part of the expense of the facility. The Treasury Secretary must provide a grant to an applicant who meets the requirements discussed below. (2009 Recovery Act §1603(a))

In order to receive a grant with respect to any property, the applicant must either:

(1) place the property in service during 2009 or 2010, or (2009 Recovery Act §1603(a)(1))

(2) place the property in service after 2010 and before the credit termination date (discussed below) with respect to that property, but only if the construction of the property began during 2009 or 2010. (2009 Recovery Act §1603(a)(2))

Thus, the 2009 Recovery Act authorizes the Treasury Secretary to provide a grant to each person who places in service in 2009 or 2010 energy property that is either (1) an electricity production facility otherwise eligible for the renewable electricity production credit or (2) qualifying property otherwise eligible for the energy credit. (Com Rept, see ¶ 5016)

Conversely, nonbusiness property and property that would not otherwise be eligible for credit under Code Sec. 48 or part of a facility that would be eligible for credit under Code Sec. 45 is not eligible for a grant under 2009 Recovery Act §1603. The grant may be paid to whichever party would have been entitled to a credit under Code Sec. 48 or Code Sec. 45, as the case may be. (Com Rept, see ¶ 5016)

FTC 2d References are to Federal Tax Coordinator 2d
FIN References are to RIA's Analysis of Federal Taxes: Income
USTR References are to United States Tax Reporter: Income
PE References are to Pension Explanations

observation: In order to receive the grant, the taxpayer must meet the requirements discussed below, including timely filing of the application, placing qualifying property in service, and satisfying the rules under Code Sec. 45, Code Sec. 48 and Code Sec. 50, as applicable.

observation: Presumably, the Treasury Secretary will provide guidance on how to elect a grant instead of a credit, and will issue the forms for applying for the grant.

Congress understands that some investors in renewable energy projects have suffered economic losses that prevent them from benefiting from the Code Sec. 45 renewable electricity credit and the Code Sec. 48 energy credit. Congress further believes that this situation, combined with current economic conditions, has the potential to jeopardize investment in renewable energy facilities. Congress therefore believes that, in the short term, allowing renewable energy developers to elect to receive direct grants in lieu of the renewable electricity credit and the energy credit is necessary for continued growth in this important industry. (Com Rept, see ¶ 5016)

For prohibition on taxpayers both claiming a credit and receiving a grant with respect to the same property, see ¶ 1205.

Time for payment of grant. The Treasury Secretary is to make payment of any grant under 2009 Recovery Act §1603(a) during the 60-day period beginning on the *later* of: (2009 Recovery Act §1603(c))

(1) the date of the application for the grant, or (2009 Recovery Act §1603(c)(1))

(2) the date the specified energy property for which the grant is being made is placed in service. (2009 Recovery Act §1603(c)(2))

Credit termination date. For purposes of 2009 Recovery Act §1603, the term "credit termination date" means: (2009 Recovery Act §1603(e))

... Jan. 1, 2013, for any specified energy property that is part of a wind facility described in Code Sec. 45(d)(1), (2009 Recovery Act §1603(e)(1))

... Jan. 1, 2014, for any specified energy property that is part of a closed-loop biomass, open-loop biomass, geothermal energy, landfill gas, trash, qualified hydropower or marine and hydrokinetic renewable energy facility described in Code Sec. 45(d)(2), Code Sec. 45(d)(3), Code Sec. 45(d)(4), Code Sec. 45(d)(6), Code Sec. 45(d)(7), Code Sec. 45(d)(9), or Code Sec. 45(d)(11), and (2009 Recovery Act §1603(e)(2))

... Jan. 1, 2017, for any specified energy property described in Code Sec. 48. (2009 Recovery Act §1603(e)(3))

For any property described in 2009 Recovery Act §1603(e)(3) and also in either 2009 Recovery Act §1603(e)(1) or 2009 Recovery Act §1603(e)(2), for purposes of the credit termination date, 2009 Recovery Act §1603(e)(3) applies with respect to that property. (2009 Recovery Act §1603(e))

> **⟪RIA⟫** *observation:* Thus, if any specified energy property qualifies for the energy credit under Code Sec. 48, and also qualifies under one of the electricity production credit categories under Code Sec. 45 that are immediately enumerated above, the property is treated as Code Sec. 48 property for purposes of the credit termination date, which, in this case, would be Jan. 1, 2017.

How to compute the amount of the grant. The amount of the grant with respect to any specified energy property (defined below) is the applicable percentage (defined below) of the basis of the property. (2009 Recovery Act §1603(b)(1))

Applicable percentage. The term "applicable percentage," for purposes of determining the amount of a grant, means: (2009 Recovery Act §1603(b)(2))

... 30% for the following types of "specified energy property" that are described in paragraphs (1) through (4) of 2009 Recovery Act §1603(d): (2009 Recovery Act §1603(b)(2)(A))

(1) qualified facilities for purposes of the Code Sec. 45 electricity production credit using wind, closed-loop biomass, open-loop biomass, geothermal energy, landfill gas, trash, qualified hydropower and marine and hydrokinetic renewables (see FTC 2d/FIN ¶ L-17771 *et seq.*; USTR ¶ 454 *et seq.*; TaxDesk ¶ 384,054 *et seq.*) (2009 Recovery Act §1603(d)(1))

(2) qualified fuel cell property as defined in Code Sec. 48(c)(1) (see FTC 2d/FIN ¶ L-16436.1; USTR ¶ 484; TaxDesk ¶ 381,602); (2009 Recovery Act §1603(d)(2))

(3) solar property as defined in Code Sec. 48(a)(3)(A)(i) or Code Sec. 48(a)(3)(A)(ii) (see FTC 2d/FIN ¶ L-16424; USTR ¶ 484; TaxDesk ¶ 381,602); and (2009 Recovery Act §1603(d)(3))

(4) qualified small wind energy property as defined in Code Sec. 48(c)(4) (see FTC 2d/FIN ¶ L-16436.4; USTR ¶ 484; TaxDesk ¶ 381,602). (2009 Recovery Act §1603(d)(4))
and

... 10% for any other property. (2009 Recovery Act §1603(b)(2)(B))

FTC 2d References are to Federal Tax Coordinator 2d
FIN References are to RIA's Analysis of Federal Taxes: Income
USTR References are to United States Tax Reporter: Income
PE References are to Pension Explanations

"Specified energy property" doesn't include property for which depreciation (or amortization in lieu of depreciation) isn't allowable. (2009 Recovery Act §1603(d))

Thus, in general, the grant amount is 30% of the basis of the depreciable (or amortizable) property that would (1) be eligible for credit under Code Sec. 48 or (2) comprise a Code Sec. 45 credit-eligible facility. For qualified microturbine, combined heat and power system, and geothermal heat pump property, the amount is 10% of the basis of the property. (Com Rept, see ¶ 5016)

> *observation:* Thus, "any other property" for purposes of the 10% energy percentage rule (above) presumably means the following types of specified energy property defined in 2009 Recovery Act §1603(d):
>
> • geothermal property (any property described in Code Sec. 48(a)(3)(A)(iii), see FTC 2d/FIN ¶ L-16426; USTR ¶ 484; TaxDesk ¶ 381,602;); (2009 Recovery Act §1603(d)(5))
>
> • qualified microturbine property (as defined in Code Sec. 48(c)(2), see FTC 2d/FIN ¶ L-16437.1; USTR ¶ 484; TaxDesk ¶ 381,601); (2009 Recovery Act §1603(d)(6))
>
> • combined heat and power (CHP) system property (as defined in Code Sec. 48(c)(3), see FTC 2d/FIN ¶ L-16436.3A; USTR ¶ 484; TaxDesk ¶ 381,601); and (2009 Recovery Act §1603(d)(7))
>
> • geothermal heat pump property (any property described in Code Sec. 48(a)(3)(A)(vii), see FTC 2d/FIN ¶ L-16426; USTR ¶ 484; TaxDesk ¶ 381,602). (2009 Recovery Act §1603(d)(8))

> *observation:* Thus, certain *facilities* eligible for the electricity production credit are instead eligible for a grant of 30% of the basis of the facility, if the taxpayer elects. Some *property* eligible for the energy credit is eligible for a grant of 30% of the basis of the facility, and other property eligible for the energy credit is eligible for a grant of 10% of the basis of the facility.

Dollar limitations on amount of grant. For qualified fuel cell property as defined in Code Sec. 48(c)(1), qualified microturbine property as defined in Code Sec. 48(c)(2) or combined heat and power system (CHP) property as defined in Code Sec. 48(c)(3), the amount of any grant under 2009 Recovery Act §1603 with respect to that property can't exceed the limitations (discussed above) under Code Sec. 48(c)(1)(B), Code Sec. 48(c)(2)(B) or Code Sec. 48(c)(3)(B) respectively, with regard to that property. (2009 Recovery Act §1603(b)(3))

Code Sec. 50 rules, including recapture. In making grants, the Treasury Secretary is to apply rules similar to those of Code Sec. 50 (see FTC 2d/FIN ¶s L-16418, L-17301 *et seq.*, L-17312, P-2007; USTR ¶ 504.02; TaxDesk ¶ 381,405). In applying these rules, if the property is disposed of, or otherwise ceases to be specified energy property, the Treasury Secretary is to provide for the recapture of the appropriate percentage of the grant amount in the manner as the Treasury Secretary deems appropriate. (2009 Recovery Act §1603(f))

> *observation:* Code Sec. 50, among other provisions, contains the rules for recapture of the investment tax credit if property is disposed of or ceases to qualify as investment credit property.

Some or all of each grant is subject to recapture if the grant-eligible property is disposed of by the grant recipient within five years of being placed in service. (Com Rept, see ¶ 5016)

> *observation:* The statement in the Committee Report (above) is consistent with the Code Sec. 50 rules with respect to the five-year recapture period.

For basis reduction rules with respect to grant-eligible property under Code Sec. 50, see ¶ 1205.

Coordination of terms with terms used in Code Sec. 45 and Code Sec. 48. Terms used in 2009 Recovery Act §1603 that are also used in Code Sec. 45 or Code Sec. 48 have the same meaning as used in those Code sections. (2009 Recovery Act §1603(h))

Nontaxpayers ineligible for grants. The following nontaxpayers are not eligible for grants: (2009 Recovery Act §1603(g))

... federal, state or local governments and any of their political subdivisions, agencies or instrumentalities, (2009 Recovery Act §1603(g)(1))

... Code Sec. 501(c) tax-exempt organizations, (2009 Recovery Act §1603(g)(2))

... any entity referred to in Code Sec. 54(j)(4) (a clean renewable energy bond lender, a cooperative electric company or a governmental body, see FTC 2d/FIN ¶ L-16489; USTR ¶ 544.02), or (2009 Recovery Act §1603(g)(3))

... any partnership or other pass-through entity any partner (or other holder of an equity or profits interest) of which is described elsewhere in 2009 Recovery Act §1603(g) (above). (2009 Recovery Act §1603(g)(4))

FTC 2d References are to Federal Tax Coordinator 2d
FIN References are to RIA's Analysis of Federal Taxes: Income
USTR References are to United States Tax Reporter: Income
PE References are to Pension Explanations

Treasury Secretary includes Secretary's delegate. Any reference in 2009 Recovery Act §1603 to the Treasury Secretary includes the Treasury Secretary's delegate. (2009 Recovery Act §1603(h))

For exclusion of grants from the recipient's gross income, see ¶ 1205.

Termination. The Treasury Secretary cannot make a grant to any person under 2009 Recovery Act §1603 unless that person's application for a grant is received before Oct. 1, 2011. (2009 Recovery Act §1603(j))

> ℰ *observation:* Presumably, the applications must be received by the Treasury Secretary or his delegate before Oct. 1, 2011.

☐ **Effective:** Feb. 17, 2009. (Com Rept, see ¶ 5016)

¶ 1205. Coordination of Code Sec. 48 energy credit and Code Sec. 45 electricity production credit with renewable energy grants

Code Sec. 48(d), as amended by 2009 Recovery Act § 1104
Generally effective: Feb. 17, 2009
Committee Reports, see ¶ 5016

Under pre-2009 Recovery Act law, there were no grants (see ¶ 1204) available to taxpayers in lieu of the Code Sec. 48 energy credit (see FTC 2d/FIN ¶ L-16400 *et seq.*; USTR ¶ 484 *et seq.*; TaxDesk ¶ 381,600 *et seq.*) or the Code Sec. 45 electricity production credit (see FTC 2d/FIN ¶ L-17750 *et seq.*; USTR ¶ 454 *et seq.*; TaxDesk ¶ 384,054 *et seq.*). (FTC 2d/FIN ¶ L-16400, ¶ L-17750; USTR ¶ 454, ¶ 484; TaxDesk ¶ 381,601, ¶ 384,054)

For purposes of computing depreciation, and gain or loss on disposition, the basis of Code Sec. 38 property for which the Code Sec. 48 business energy credit is allowed must be reduced by 50% of the energy credit allowed, see FTC 2d ¶ P-2005; USTR ¶ 504.03; TaxDesk ¶ 213,006.

New Law. For specified energy property with respect to which a grant is made by the Treasury Secretary under 2009 Recovery Act §1603 (see ¶ 1204), no energy credit is allowed under Code Sec. 48, and no electricity production credit is allowed under Code Sec. 45, with respect to specified energy property for the tax year in which the grant is made or any later tax year. (Code Sec. 48(d)(1) as amended by 2009 Recovery Act §1104)

Congress says that nonbusiness property and property that would not otherwise be eligible for credit under Code Sec. 48 or part of a facility that would be eligible for credit under Code Sec. 45 is not eligible for a grant under 2009 Recovery Act §1603 (see ¶ 1204). The grant may be paid to whichever party would have been entitled to a credit under Code Sec. 48 or Code Sec. 45, as the case may be. (Com Rept, see ¶ 5016)

☞ *observation:* Thus, a taxpayer can elect to take either a tax credit or a grant for a qualifying specified energy property placed in service in a tax year, but not both.

☞ *observation:* A taxpayer should consider whether it is more advantageous to take a credit or a grant for a particular energy property in a tax year. For example, a taxpayer may have no tax liability for a tax year, and thus won't be able to use the credit in that tax year.

If an energy credit was determined under Code Sec. 48 with respect to property for which a grant is made under 2009 Recovery Act §1603 (see ¶ 1204) for any tax year ending before the grant was made: (Code Sec. 48(d)(2))

. . . the income tax on the taxpayer for the tax year in which the grant is made is increased by so much of the credit allowed under the Code Sec. 38 general business credit (see FTC 2d/FIN ¶ L-15201 *et seq.*; USTR ¶ 384 *et seq.*; TaxDesk ¶ 380,500 *et seq.*); (Code Sec. 48(d)(2)(A))

. . . the general business carryforwards under Code Sec. 39, see FTC 2d/FIN ¶ L-15209; USTR ¶ 394 *et seq.*; TaxDesk ¶ 380,509, are adjusted to recapture the portion of the credit that was not allowed; and (Code Sec. 48(d)(2)(B))

. . . the amount of the grant is determined without regard to any reduction in the basis of the specified energy property by reason of that credit. (Code Sec. 48(d)(2)(C))

Congress intends that the grant under 2009 Recovery Act §1603 mimic the operation of the Code Sec. 48 credit. (Com Rept, see ¶ 5016)

Thus, the amount of the grant is not includible in the taxpayer's gross income. (Code Sec. 48(d)(3)(A)). However, the grant is taken into account in determining the basis of the energy property to which the grant relates, except that the basis of that property must be reduced under Code Sec. 50(c) in the same manner as a credit allowed under Code Sec. 48(a). (Code Sec. 48(d)(3)(B)). Thus, the basis of the energy property is reduced by 50% of the amount of the grant. (Com Rept, see ¶ 5016)

☞ *observation:* Code Sec. 50(c)(1) provides that if an investment credit is allowed with respect to qualifying investment credit property, the basis of that property is reduced by the amount of the credit, see FTC 2d/FIN ¶ P-2011; USTR ¶ 504.03; TaxDesk ¶ 213,006. But Code Sec. 50(c)(3)(A) provides that only 50% of the credit is taken into account under Code Sec. 50(c)(1), see FTC 2d/FIN ¶ P-2005; USTR

FTC 2d References are to Federal Tax Coordinator 2d
FIN References are to RIA's Analysis of Federal Taxes: Income
USTR References are to United States Tax Reporter: Income
PE References are to Pension Explanations

¶ 504.03; TaxDesk ¶ 213,006. Thus, "in the same manner," the basis of the energy property is reduced by 50% of the amount of the grant.

🖋 *illustration:* Taxpayer A receives a grant of $30,000 for qualifying 30% energy property with a basis of $100,000. Taxpayer A does not claim an energy credit for this property for the tax year. The basis of the property is reduced by 50% of the grant amount ($30,000 × .5, or $15,000). The basis after the reduction is $85,000.

☐ **Effective:** Feb. 17, 2009. (Com Rept, see ¶ 5016)

¶ 1206. Business energy tax credit basis reduction rule for property financed by tax-exempt government subsidies or private activity bonds is retroactively terminated for periods after Dec. 31, 2008

Code Sec. 48(a)(4)(D), as amended by 2009 Recovery Act § 1103(b)(1)
Code Sec. 48A(b)(2), as amended by 2009 Recovery Act § 1103(b)(2)(C)
Code Sec. 48B(b)(2), as amended by 2009 Recovery Act § 1103(b)(2)(D)
Generally effective: Periods after Dec. 31, 2008
Committee Reports, see ¶ 5015

Subject to certain exceptions and limitations, the non-refundable business energy credit for any tax year is the energy percentage of the basis of each energy property placed in service during the tax year. The energy percentage is 30% for (1) qualified fuel cell property, (2) energy property described in Code Sec. 48(a)(3)(A)(i) (equipment using solar energy to generate electricity, to heat or cool (or provide hot water for use in) a structure, or to provide solar process heat, excepting property used to generate energy for the purpose of heating a swimming pool), but only for periods ending before Jan. 1, 2017; (3) energy property described in Code Sec. 48(a)(3)(A)(ii) (equipment that uses solar energy to illuminate the inside of a structure using fiber-optic distributed sunlight), but only for periods ending before Jan. 1, 2017; and (4) qualified small wind energy property. The credit is 10% of the basis of any energy property not listed at (1) through (4), above. Thus, a 10% credit applies to geothermal property, qualified microturbine property, solar energy property for periods after Dec. 31, 2016 (unless Congress extends the 30% credit applicable to solar energy property), and combined heat and power system property, see FTC 2d/FIN ¶s L-16401, L-16402; USTR ¶ 484; TaxDesk ¶s 381,601, 381,602.

For the availability under the 2009 Recovery Act of an irrevocable election to treat qualified investment credit facilities (including certain geothermal facilities) placed in service in 2009 through 2013 (2009 through 2012 for wind facilities) as property eligible for the 30% business energy credit, see ¶ 1203.

Under pre-2009 Recovery Act law, where property was financed in whole or in part by subsidized financing or tax-exempt private activity bonds, the amount taken into account as qualified investment for purposes of the energy credit was a fraction which was 1 (one), reduced by a fraction the numerator of which was that portion of the qualified investment in the property which was allocable to such financing or proceeds, and the denominator of which was the qualified investment in the property. This fraction was determined by dividing that portion of qualified investment in the property which was allocable to subsidized financing or from proceeds of tax-exempt private activity bonds by qualified investment in the property and subtracting this quotient from one. (FTC 2d/FIN ¶ L-16400, ¶ L-16415; USTR ¶ 484; TaxDesk ¶ 381,603)

Under pre-2009 Recovery Act law, "subsidized energy financing" meant financing provided under a Federal, State, or local program, a principal purpose of which was to provide subsidized financing for projects designed to conserve or produce energy. Subsidized financing included, but wasn't limited to, the direct or indirect use of tax-exempt bonds for providing funds under such a program. Subsidized financing didn't include loan guarantees. (FTC 2d/FIN ¶ L-16400, ¶ L-16415; USTR ¶ 484; TaxDesk ¶ 381,603)

New Law. The 2009 Recovery Act provides that the special basis reduction rule for property financed by subsidized energy financing or private activity bonds does not apply to periods after Dec. 31, 2008, under rules similar to the rules of Code Sec. 48(m) as in effect on Nov. 4, '90. (Code Sec. 48(a)(4)(D) as amended by 2009 Recovery Act §1103(b)(1))

Thus, the 2009 Recovery Act removes the rule that reduces the basis of the property for purposes of claiming the business energy tax credit if the property is financed in whole or in part by subsidized energy financing or with proceeds from private activity bonds. (Com Rept, see ¶ 5015)

> *illustration (1):* In 2008, G Corp., a calendar year taxpayer, placed into service $100,000 of qualified solar energy property. The property's purchase was 40% financed by private activity bonds. Thus, only 60% of the basis qualified for the business energy credit (1 − ($40,000/$100,000)). G's business energy credit for 2008 was limited to $18,000 (30% × (60% × $100,000)).

> *illustration (2):* The facts are the same as in Illustration 1, except that G places the property into service in 2009. G's business energy credit for 2009 is $30,000 (30% × $100,000).

FTC 2d References are to Federal Tax Coordinator 2d
FIN References are to RIA's Analysis of Federal Taxes: Income
USTR References are to United States Tax Reporter: Income
PE References are to Pension Explanations

For the repeal of a similar rule that applies for purposes of the residential energy efficient property (REEP) credit and the nonbusiness energy property credit, see ¶ 1103.

For the repeal of the per taxpayer annual $4,000 limitation on the business energy tax credit for qualified small wind energy property, see ¶ 1201.

Coordination with other credits. For purposes of the Code Sec. 48A qualifying advanced coal project credit and the Code Sec. 48B qualifying gasification project credit, both of which use the Code Sec. 48(a)(4) special basis reduction rule for property financed by subsidized energy financing or private activity bonds, that rule will continue to be applied without regard to Code Sec. 48(a)(4)(D). (Code Sec. 48A(b)(2) as amended by 2009 Recovery Act §1103(b)(2)(C); Code Sec. 48B(b)(2) as amended by 2009 Recovery Act §1103(b)(2)(D))

> *observation:* Thus, for purposes of the Code Sec. 48A qualifying advanced coal project credit and the Code Sec. 48B qualifying gasification project credit, the special basis reduction rule for property financed by subsidized energy financing or private activity bonds continues to apply and does not terminate for periods after Dec. 31, 2008.

☐ **Effective:** Periods after Dec. 31, 2008, under rules similar to the rules of former Code Sec. 48(m) as in effect on Nov. 4, '90. (2009 Recovery Act §1103(c)(1))

> *observation:* 2009 Recovery Act §1103(c)(1) provides that the termination of the special basis reduction rule is effective under rules similar to the rules of former Code Sec. 48(m) (as in effect on the day before the date of the enactment of the '90 Revenue Act (PL 101-508, 11/5/1990)). The '90 Revenue Act was enacted on Nov. 5, '90.

> *observation:* Former Code Sec. 48(m) provided that when the application of former Code Sec. 48(m)(1), former Code Sec. 46(b) (amount of credit percentage), or former Code Sec. 46(c)(3) (qualified investment in public utility property) is expressed in terms of a time period, and the construction, reconstruction, or erection of that property is completed after the beginning of that period, only the portion of the basis which is properly attributable to construction, reconstruction, or erection after the beginning of that period qualifies for the credit. Thus, the repeal of the basis reduction rule applies only to energy property that is constructed, reconstructed, or erected after Dec. 31, 2008.

> Also, in the case of property acquired and placed in service by the taxpayer during the period (rather than constructed by the taxpayer), only property acquired and placed in service after the beginning of that period will qualify for the credit. Thus, the repeal of the basis reduction

rule applies only to energy property acquired and placed in service after Dec. 31, 2008.

¶ 1207. Placed-in-service end date is extended for three years through Dec. 31, 2013 for certain qualified facilities for purposes of the electricity production credit

Code Sec. 45(d)(2), as amended by 2009 Recovery Act § 1101(a)(2)
Code Sec. 45(d)(3), as amended by 2009 Recovery Act § 1101(a)(2)
Code Sec. 45(d)(4), as amended by 2009 Recovery Act § 1101(a)(2)
Code Sec. 45(d)(6), as amended by 2009 Recovery Act § 1101(a)(2)
Code Sec. 45(d)(7), as amended by 2009 Recovery Act § 1101(a)(2)
Code Sec. 45(d)(9), as amended by 2009 Recovery Act § 1101(a)(2)
Generally effective: Property placed in service after Feb. 17, 2009
Committee Reports, see ¶ 5013

Under pre-2009 Recovery Act law, a facility using closed-loop biomass (FTC 2d/FIN ¶ L-17750, ¶ L-17771; USTR ¶ 454.09), open-loop biomass (FTC 2d/FIN ¶ L-17750, ¶ L-17771.1; USTR ¶ 454.10), geothermal energy (FTC 2d/FIN ¶ L-17750, ¶ L-17771.2; USTR ¶ 454.11), landfill gas (FTC 2d/FIN ¶ L-17750, ¶ L-17771.4; USTR ¶ 454.13), trash (FTC 2d/FIN ¶ L-17750, ¶ L-17771.4; USTR ¶ 454.13), or qualified hydropower (FTC 2d/FIN ¶ L-17750, ¶ L-17771.6; USTR ¶ 454.15) had to be originally placed in service before Jan. 1, 2011 in order to be a "qualified facility", see FTC 2d/FIN ¶ L-17771 *et seq.*; USTR ¶ 454 *et seq.*; TaxDesk ¶ 384,054, for purposes of the electricity production credit.

New Law. The 2009 Recovery Act provides that the originally placed-in-service end date for the following qualified energy facilities is Jan. 1, 2014:

. . . closed-loop biomass (Code Sec. 45(d)(2) as amended by 2009 Recovery Act §1101(a)(2)),

. . . open-loop biomass (Code Sec. 45(d)(3)),

. . . geothermal energy (Code Sec. 45(d)(4)),

. . . landfill gas (Code Sec. 45(d)(6)),

. . . trash (Code Sec. 45(d)(7)), and

. . . qualified hydropower. (Code Sec. 45(d)(9))

FTC 2d References are to Federal Tax Coordinator 2d
FIN References are to RIA's Analysis of Federal Taxes: Income
USTR References are to United States Tax Reporter: Income
PE References are to Pension Explanations

Thus, the 2009 Recovery Act extends for three years (through 2013) the period during which qualified facilities producing electricity from closed-loop biomass, open-loop biomass, geothermal energy, municipal solid waste, and qualified hydropower may be placed in service for purposes of the electricity production credit. (Com Rept, see ¶ 5013)

> **⊘** *observation:* Accordingly, under the 2009 Recovery Act, a closed-loop biomass, open-loop biomass, geothermal energy, landfill gas, trash or qualified hydropower facility originally placed in service through Dec. 31, 2013 can be a qualified facility for purposes of the electricity production credit.

Congress believes that additional incentives for the production of electricity from renewable resources will help limit the environmental consequences of continued reliance on power generated using fossil fuels. Congress also believes that a multi-year extension of the pre-2009 Recovery Act electricity production credit will encourage the development of renewable energy projects that will create new jobs for workers. (Com Rept, see ¶ 5013)

☐ **Effective:** Property placed in service after Feb. 17, 2009. (2009 Recovery Act §1101(c)(1))

¶ 1208. Placed-in-service end date is extended for three years through Dec. 31, 2012 for qualified wind facilities for purposes of the electricity production credit

Code Sec. 45(d)(1), as amended by 2009 Recovery Act § 1101(a)(1)
Generally effective: Property placed in service after Feb. 17, 2009
Committee Reports, see ¶ 5013

Under pre-2009 Recovery Act law, a facility using wind to produce electricity had to be originally placed in service before Jan. 1, 2010 in order to be a "qualified facility," see FTC 2d/FIN ¶ L-17771 *et seq.*; USTR ¶ 454 *et seq.*; TaxDesk ¶ 384,054, for purposes of the electricity production credit. (FTC 2d/FIN ¶ L-17750, ¶ L-17771.5; USTR ¶ 454.14)

New Law. The 2009 Recovery Act provides that the originally placed-in-service end date for wind facilities is Jan. 1, 2013. (Code Sec. 45(d)(1) as amended by 2009 Recovery Act §1101(a)(1))

Thus, the 2009 Recovery Act extends for three years (through 2012) the period during which qualified facilities producing electricity from wind may be placed in service for purposes of the electricity production credit. (Com Rept, see ¶ 5013) *observation:* Accordingly, under the 2009 Recovery Act, a wind facility placed in service through Dec. 31, 2012 can be a qualified facility for purposes of the electricity production credit.

Congress believes that additional incentives for the production of electricity from renewable resources will help limit the environmental consequences of continued reliance on power generated using fossil fuels. Congress also believes that a multi-year extension of the pre-2009 Recovery Act electricity production credit will encourage the development of renewable energy projects that will create new jobs for workers. (Com Rept, see ¶ 5013)

☐ **Effective:** Property placed in service after Feb. 17, 2009. (2009 Recovery Act §1101(c)(1))

¶ 1209. Placed-in-service end date is extended for two years through Dec. 31, 2013 for qualified marine and hydrokinetic renewable energy facilities for purposes of the electricity production credit

Code Sec. 45(d)(11)(B), as amended by 2009 Recovery Act § 1101(a)(3)
Generally effective: Property placed in service after Feb. 17, 2009
Committee Reports, see ¶ 5013

Under pre-2009 Recovery Act law, a facility using marine and hydrokinetic renewable energy to produce electricity had to be originally placed in service before Jan. 1, 2012 in order to be a qualified facility, see FTC 2d/FIN ¶ L-17771 *et seq.*; USTR ¶ 454.09 *et seq.*; TaxDesk ¶ 384,054, for purposes of the electricity production credit. (FTC 2d/FIN ¶ L-17750, ¶ L-17771.9; USTR ¶ 454.18)

New Law. The 2009 Recovery Act provides that the originally placed-in-service end date for marine and hydrokinetic renewable energy facilities is Jan. 1, 2014. (Code Sec. 45(d)(11)(B) as amended by 2009 Recovery Act §1101(a)(3))

Thus, the 2009 Recovery Act extends for two years (through 2013) the placed-in-service period for marine and hydrokinetic renewable energy resources. (Com Rept, see ¶ 5013)

observation: Accordingly, under the 2009 Recovery Act, a marine and hydrokinetic renewable energy facility placed in service through

---

FTC 2d References are to Federal Tax Coordinator 2d
FIN References are to RIA's Analysis of Federal Taxes: Income
USTR References are to United States Tax Reporter: Income
PE References are to Pension Explanations

Dec. 31, 2013 can be a qualified facility for purposes of the electricity production credit.

observation: The placed-in-service end date of a small irrigation power facility as a *separate category* of qualified facility is Oct. 3, 2008, see FTC 2d/FIN ¶ L-17771.3; USTR ¶ 454.12. After that date, small irrigation power facilities qualify for the electricity production credit as marine and hydrokinetic renewable energy facilities. Thus, the category of marine and hydrokinetic renewable energy facilities subsumes that of small irrigation power facilities.

Congress believes that additional incentives for the production of electricity from renewable resources will help limit the environmental consequences of continued reliance on power generated using fossil fuels. Congress also believes that a multi-year extension of the pre-2009 Recovery Act electricity production credit will encourage the development of renewable energy projects that will create new jobs for workers. (Com Rept, see ¶ 5013)

☐ **Effective:** Property placed in service after Feb. 17, 2009. (2009 Recovery Act §1101(c)(1))

¶ 1210. National bond volume limitation for new CREBs is increased by up to $1.6 billion

Code Sec. 54C(c)(4), as amended by 2009 Recovery Act § 1111
Generally effective: Bonds issued after Feb. 17, 2009
Committee Reports, see ¶ 5018

A new clean renewable energy bond ("new CREB") is a type of qualified tax credit bond. A new CREB is any bond issued as part of an issue if:

(1) 100% of the issue's available project proceeds are to be used for capital expenditures incurred by government bodies, public power providers, or cooperative electric companies for one or more qualified renewable energy facilities;

(2) the bond is issued by a qualified user; and

(3) the issuer designates the bond as a new CREB. (FTC 2d/FIN ¶ L-15561; USTR ¶ 54C4)

The maximum aggregate face amount of tax credit bonds that can be designated as new CREBs by any issuer can't exceed the amount allocated to the issuer by IRS. IRS must allocate the national bond volume limitation for new CREBs (a specified amount, see below) as follows:

(i) not more than one-third to qualified projects of public power providers;

(ii) not more than one-third to qualified projects of government bodies; and

(iii) not more than one-third to cooperative electric companies.

Additional rules prescribe the method of allocation. (FTC 2d/FIN ¶ L-15564; USTR ¶ 54C4.02)

Under pre-2009 Recovery Act law, the national bond volume limitation for new CREBs was $800,000 million. (FTC 2d/FIN ¶ L-15560, ¶ L-15564; USTR ¶ 54C4.02)

New Law. The 2009 Recovery Act increases the national bond volume limitation for new CREBs by $1.6 billion. (Code Sec. 54C(c)(4) as amended by 2009 Recovery Act §1111) Thus, the 2009 Recovery Act expands the new CREBs program by authorizing the issuance of up to an additional $1.6 billion of new CREBS. (Com Rept, see ¶ 5018) IRS must allocate the increase consistent with the rules referred to above. (Code Sec. 54C(c)(4))

> **🔴 *observation:*** The 2009 Recovery Act increases the maximum amount that IRS can allocate to qualified projects of public power providers, or qualified projects of government bodies, or cooperative electric companies, from $266.7 million (1/3 × $800,000 million) to $800,000 million (1/3 × $2.4 billion [$800,000 million + $1.6 billion]). The Act doesn't change the allocation rules themselves.

☐ **Effective:** Bonds issued after Feb. 17, 2009. (Com Rept, see ¶ 5018)

¶ 1211. National bond volume limitation for qualified energy conservation bonds is increased by $2.4 billion; bonds for green community programs can fund loans or grants to individuals

Code Sec. 54D(d), as amended by 2009 Recovery Act § 1112(a)
Code Sec. 54D(e)(4), as amended by 2009 Recovery Act § 1112(b)(2)
Code Sec. 54D(f)(1)(A)(ii), as amended by 2009 Recovery Act § 1112(b)(1)
Generally effective: Bonds issued after Feb. 17, 2009
Committee Reports, see ¶ 5019

Qualified energy conservation bonds are qualified tax credit bonds entitling the holder to a nonrefundable credit on specified dates during the year. The credit is includible in gross income, and is treated as interest income. (FTC 2d/FIN ¶ L-15570; USTR ¶ 54D4; TaxDesk ¶ 568,521)

FTC 2d References are to Federal Tax Coordinator 2d
FIN References are to RIA's Analysis of Federal Taxes: Income
USTR References are to United States Tax Reporter: Income
PE References are to Pension Explanations

A qualified energy conservation bond is any bond issued as part of an issue that meets the qualified tax credit bond requirements (expenditures, reporting, arbitrage, maturity, and financial conflicts of interest) if:

- 100% of the issue's available project proceeds are to be used for one or more qualified conservation purposes (defined below);
- the bond is issued by a state or local government; and
- the issuer designates the bond as a qualified energy conservation bond. (FTC 2d/FIN ¶ L-15571; USTR ¶ 54D4)

A qualified conservation purpose is any of the following:

(A) Capital expenditures incurred for purposes of: (1) reducing energy consumption in publicly owned buildings by at least 20%; (2) implementing green community programs; (3) rural development involving the production of electricity from renewable energy resources; or (4) any qualified facility (as determined under Code Sec. 45(d) without regard to refined coal production or Indian coal production facilities and without regard to any placed in service date).

(B) Expenditures with respect to research facilities and research grants that support research in: (1) the development of cellulosic ethanol or other nonfossil fuels; (2) technologies for the capture and sequestration of carbon dioxide produced through the use of fossil fuels; (3) increasing the efficiency of existing technologies for producing nonfossil fuels; (4) automobile battery technologies and other technologies to reduce fossil fuel consumption in transportation; or (5) technologies to reduce energy use in buildings.

(C) Mass commuting facilities and related facilities that reduce the consumption of energy, including expenditures to reduce pollution from vehicles used for mass commuting.

(D) Demonstration projects designed to promote the commercialization of: (1) green building technology; (2) conversion of agricultural waste for use in the production of fuel or otherwise; (3) advanced battery manufacturing technologies; (4) technologies to reduce peak use of electricity; or (5) technologies for the capture and sequestration of carbon dioxide emitted from combusting fossil fuels in order to produce electricity.

(E) Public education campaigns to promote energy efficiency. (FTC 2d/FIN ¶ L-15572; USTR ¶ 54D4)

Under pre-2009 Recovery Act law, the national bond volume limitation for qualified energy conservation bonds was $800 million, which IRS had to allocate among the states in proportion to their populations. (FTC 2d/FIN ¶ L-15573; USTR ¶ 54D4.01) Under these allocation rules, for any state in which there is a large local government (i.e., any municipality or county with a population of 100,000 or more), each government will be allocated a portion of that state's allocation that bears the same ratio to the state's allocation (determined without regard to this rule) as the government's population bears to the state's population. Any unused limitation amount may be allocated back to the state. However, any allocation to issuers within a state or large local government must be made in a manner that results in not less than 70% of the allocation to that state or large local government being used to designate bonds that aren't private activity bonds. See FTC 2d/FIN ¶ L-15573; USTR ¶ 54D4.01.

New Law. Under the 2009 Recovery Act, the national energy conservation bond limitation is increased to $3.2 billion. (Code Sec. 54D(d) as amended by 2009 Recovery Act §1112(a)) This means that an additional $2.4 billion of national energy conservation bonds may be issued each year. (Com Rept, see ¶ 5019)

Loans and grants for green community programs. The 2009 Recovery Act clarifies that capital expenditures to implement green community programs (see (A)(2), above) include loans, grants, and other repayment mechanisms to implement those programs (Com Rept, see ¶ 5019), by amending the definition of qualified conservation purpose in Code Sec. 54D(f)(1)(A)(ii) to provide that green community programs include the use of loans, grants, or other repayment mechanisms to implement the programs. (Code Sec. 54D(f)(1)(A)(ii) as amended by 2009 Recovery Act §1112(b)(1)) An example of a permitted use of proceeds from the bonds under this expanded definition includes using the funds to finance retrofits of existing private buildings using loans or grants to individual homeowners or businesses, or through other repayment mechanisms. (Com Rept, see ¶ 5019)

The 2009 Recovery Act also provides that, for purposes of the rule that any allocation to issuers within a state or large local government must be made in a manner that results in not less than 70% of the allocation to that state or large local government being used to designate bonds that aren't private activity bonds, these bonds are not treated as private activity bonds. (Code Sec. 54D(e)(4) as amended by 2009 Recovery Act §1112(b)(2)) Thus, any bond used to provide loans and grants or other repayment mechanisms for capital expenditures to implement any green community program is not treated as a private activity bond for purposes of determining whether the requirement that not less than 70% of the allocations within a state or large local government be used to designate bonds that are not private activity bonds has been satisfied. (Com Rept, see ¶ 5019)

☐ **Effective:** Bonds issued after Feb. 17, 2009. (Com Rept, see ¶ 5019)

FTC 2d References are to Federal Tax Coordinator 2d
FIN References are to RIA's Analysis of Federal Taxes: Income
USTR References are to United States Tax Reporter: Income
PE References are to Pension Explanations

¶ 1212. Secure geological storage disposal requirement to apply to the $10 per metric ton component of the carbon dioxide sequestration credit

Code Sec. 45Q(a)(2)(C), as amended by 2009 Recovery Act § 1131(a)
Code Sec. 45Q(d)(2), as amended by 2009 Recovery Act § 1131(b)(1)(A)
Code Sec. 45Q(d)(2), as amended by 2009 Recovery Act § 1131(b)(1)(B)
Code Sec. 45Q(d)(2), as amended by 2009 Recovery Act § 1131(b)(1)(C)
Code Sec. 45Q(a)(1)(B), as amended by 2009 Recovery Act § 1131(b)(2)
Code Sec. 45Q(e), as amended by 2009 Recovery Act § 1131(b)(3)
Generally effective: Carbon dioxide captured after Feb. 17, 2009
Committee Reports, see ¶ 5025

Under pre-2009 Recovery Act law, a credit of $20 per metric ton is available for qualified carbon dioxide captured by a taxpayer at a qualified facility and disposed of by that taxpayer in secure geological storage (including storage at deep saline formations and unminable coal seams under conditions determined by IRS). (FTC 2d/FIN ¶ L-18400, ¶ L-18401; USTR ¶ 45Q4).

IRS, in consultation with the Administrator of the Environmental Protection Agency (EPA), is to issue regs for determining adequate security measures for the geological storage of carbon dioxide under the rule providing for the $20 per metric ton component of the credit to ensure that the carbon dioxide does not escape into the atmosphere. Geological storage includes storage at deep saline formations and unminable coal seams under conditions IRS may determine under the regs. (FTC 2d/FIN ¶ L-18400, ¶ L-18401; USTR ¶ 45Q4).

In addition to the $20 per metric ton component of the carbon dioxide sequestration credit, under pre-2009 Recovery Act law, taxpayers could take a credit of $10 per metric ton of qualified carbon dioxide that was captured by the taxpayer at a qualified facility and used by the taxpayer as a tertiary injectant (including carbon dioxide augmented waterflooding and immiscible carbon dioxide displacement) in a qualified enhanced oil or natural gas recovery project. (FTC 2d/FIN ¶ L-18400, ¶ L-18401; USTR ¶ 45Q4).

> **🅡ᴬobservation:** Thus, under pre-2009 Recovery Act law, there was no requirement that qualified carbon dioxide had to be disposed of in secure geological storage in order to be eligible for the $10 per metric ton carbon dioxide sequestration credit.

Under pre-2009 Recovery Act law, the carbon dioxide sequestration credit was to apply with respect to qualified carbon dioxide before the end of the calendar year in which IRS, in consultation with the Administrator of the Environmental Protection Agency (EPA), certifies that 75,000,000 metric tons of qualified carbon dioxide have been captured and disposed of or used as a tertiary injectant. (FTC 2d/FIN ¶ L-18400, ¶ L-18405; USTR ¶ 45Q4).

New Law. The 2009 Recovery Act provides that qualified carbon dioxide used as a tertiary injectant and otherwise eligible for the $10 per metric ton credit component of the carbon dioxide sequestration credit must be disposed of by the taxpayer in secure geological storage. (Code Sec. 45Q(a)(2)(C) as amended by 2009 Recovery Act §1131(a)) The geologic storage must also be permanent. (Com Rept, see ¶ 5025)

> *observation:* Thus, the 2009 Recovery Act extends to the $10 per metric ton component of the carbon dioxide sequestration credit the secure geological storage requirement that under pre-2009 Recovery Act law only applied to the $20 per metric ton component of the credit.

The statutory direction to IRS to issue regs for determining adequate security measures for the geological storage of carbon dioxide to ensure it doesn't escape into the atmosphere is extended to also apply to the $10 per metric ton component of the credit. (Code Sec. 45Q(d)(2) as amended by 2009 Recovery Act §1131(b)(1)(A))

> *observation:* Thus, the direction to issue regs, which under pre-2009 Recovery Act law applied only to the $20 per metric ton component of the credit, is extended to the $10 per metric ton component of the credit by the 2009 Recovery Act.

The regs are to be issued in consultation with the Administrator of the EPA, the Secretary of Energy, and the Secretary of the Interior. (Code Sec. 45Q(d)(2) as amended by 2009 Recovery Act §1131(b)(1)(C))

In addition, secure geological storage includes storage at oil and gas reservoirs. (Code Sec. 45Q(d)(2) as amended by 2009 Recovery Act §1131(b)(1)(B))

> *observation:* Thus, under the 2009 Recovery Act, secure geological storage for the 10% and 20% per metric ton credit components includes storage at oil and gas reservoirs as well as storage at deep saline formations and unminable coal seams.

The 2009 Recovery Act provides that carbon dioxide qualifying for the $20 per metric ton component of the credit must not be used by the taxpayer as described in Code Sec. 45Q(a)(2)(B). (Code Sec. 45Q(a)(1)(B) as amended by 2009 Recovery Act §1131(b)(2))

FTC 2d References are to Federal Tax Coordinator 2d
FIN References are to RIA's Analysis of Federal Taxes: Income
USTR References are to United States Tax Reporter: Income
PE References are to Pension Explanations

⊘ *observation:* Thus, carbon dioxide qualifying for the $20 per ton component must not be used by the taxpayer as a tertiary injectant in a qualified enhanced oil or natural gas recovery project.

The 2009 Recovery Act replaces the "captured and disposed of or used as a tertiary injectant" language that was in pre-2009 Recovery Act Code Sec. 45Q(e) with "taken into account in accordance with Code Sec. 45Q(a)" so that the carbon dioxide sequestration credit will apply with respect to qualified carbon dioxide before the end of the calendar year in which IRS, in consultation with the Administrator of the Environmental Protection Agency (EPA), certifies that 75,000,000 metric tons of qualified carbon dioxide have been *taken into account in accordance with Code Sec. 45Q(a)*. (Code Sec. 45Q(e) as amended by 2009 Recovery Act §1131(b)(3))

⊘ *observation:* Thus, the conforming change to Code Sec. 45Q(e) reflects the 2009 Recovery Act's expanded disposal in secure geological storage requirement for the availability of the 10% per metric ton credit component, and the 2009 Recovery Act's expanded definition of secure geological storage to include storage at oil and gas reservoirs for purposes of both the 10% and 20% per metric ton components of the credit.

☐ **Effective:** Carbon dioxide captured after Feb. 17, 2009. (2009 Recovery Act §1131(c))

¶ 1300. Tax-Exempt Bond Provisions

¶ 1301. New tax credit bond option is added for "Build America Bonds" issued in 2009 and 2010; issuer may claim alternative, refundable credit for "qualified bonds"

Code Sec. 54(c)(2), as amended by 2009 Recovery Act § 1531(c)(3)
Code Sec. 54A(c)(1)(B), as amended by 2009 Recovery Act § 1531(c)(2)
Code Sec. 54AA, as added by 2009 Recovery Act § 1531(a)
Code Sec. 54AA, 2009 Recovery Act § 1531(d)
Code Sec. 1397E(c)(2), as amended by 2009 Recovery Act § 1531(c)(3)
Code Sec. 1400N(l)(3)(B), as amended by 2009 Recovery Act § 1531(c)(3)
Code Sec. 6211(b)(4)(A), as amended by 2009 Recovery Act § 1531(c)(4)
Code Sec. 6401(b)(1), as amended by 2009 Recovery Act § 1531(c)(5)
Code Sec. 6431, as added by 2009 Recovery Act § 1531(b)
Code Sec. 6431, 2009 Recovery Act § 1531(c)(1)
Generally effective: Obligations issued after Feb. 17, 2009 and before Jan. 1, 2011
Committee Reports, see ¶ 5070

Under Code Sec. 103, interest on state or local bonds is exempt (excluded) from federal income tax. This rule doesn't apply to interest on private activity bonds (other than specified "qualified" private activity bonds), arbitrage bonds, or bonds that fail to satisfy the technical requirements of Code Sec. 149. (FTC 2d/FIN ¶ J-3000, ¶ J-3001; USTR ¶ 1034; TaxDesk ¶ 158,001)

As an alternative to traditional tax-exempt bonds, state and local governments may issue qualified tax credit bonds (e.g., qualified forestry conservation bonds, see FTC 2d/FIN ¶ L-15551 *et seq.*; USTR ¶ 54B4 *et seq.*, or new clean renewable energy bonds (new CREBS), see FTC 2d/FIN ¶ L-15561 *et seq.*; USTR ¶ 54C4 *et seq.*). Unlike tax-exempt bonds, qualified tax credit bonds aren't interest-bearing obligations. Rather, the taxpayer holding the bond on a credit allowance date is entitled to a credit against regular income tax and alternative minimum tax (AMT) liability. The credit accrues quarterly and is includible in gross income as if it were an interest payment on the bond. The amount of the credit is determined by multiplying the bond's credit rate by the face amount of the bond. The credit rate is determined by IRS and is a rate that permits the bonds to be issued without discount and interest cost to the issuer.

FTC 2d References are to Federal Tax Coordinator 2d
FIN References are to RIA's Analysis of Federal Taxes: Income
USTR References are to United States Tax Reporter: Income
PE References are to Pension Explanations

Code Sec. 54A sets forth general rules applicable to qualified tax credit bonds, including requirements regarding credit allowance dates, the expenditure of available project proceeds, reporting, arbitrage, maturity limitations, and financial conflicts of interest, among other rules. (See FTC 2d/FIN ¶ L-15531 et seq.; USTR ¶ 54A4 et seq.; TaxDesk ¶ 568,521.)

New Law. For 2009 and 2010, the 2009 Recovery Act ("the Act") permits an issuer to elect to have an otherwise tax-exempt bond treated as a new type of tax credit bond—a "Build America Bond." The holder of these bonds will accrue a tax credit equal to 35% of the interest payable on the interest payment dates of the bond during the calendar year. In addition, under a special rule for certain "qualified bonds," in lieu of the tax credit to the holder, the Act permits the issuer to claim a credit equal to 35% of each interest payment made under the bond. (Com Rept, see ¶ 5070)

Tax credit for holder of Build America Bond ("Code Sec. 54AA credit"). Specifically, the Act adds new Subpart J (Build America Bonds) to Subtitle A, Chapter 1, Subchapter A, Part IV of the Code (Credits against tax). Under Subpart J, a new provision provides that if a taxpayer holds a Build America Bond (as defined below) on one or more interest payment dates of the bond (see below) during any tax year, a credit is allowed against federal income tax for the tax year in an amount equal to the sum of the credits determined under Code Sec. 54AA(b) (see below) with respect to those interest payment dates. (Code Sec. 54AA(a) as added by 2009 Recovery Act §1531(a))

> **observation:** The Act doesn't add the Code Sec. 54AA credit as part of Subpart C of Part IV of Subchapter A, Chapter 1, Subtitle A, which allows the *refundable* credits (see FTC 2d/FIN ¶ A-4001; TaxDesk ¶ 568,501). Therefore, the Code Sec. 54AA credit is a nonrefundable credit (i.e., a credit that can reduce tax liability to zero, but can't result in a refund). As described below, a specific limitation on this credit based on tax liability, and a credit carryover rule, apply to the Code Sec. 54AA credit.

The amount of the Code Sec. 54AA(a) credit for any interest payment date for a Build America Bond is 35% of the amount of interest payable by the issuer with respect to that date. (Code Sec. 54AA(b))

That is, unlike under the general rules of Code Sec. 54A for qualified tax credit bonds (which provide that the credit rate is to be calculated by IRS), the Code Sec. 54AA credit rate is set by law at 35%. (Com Rept, see ¶ 5070)

The actual Code Sec. 54AA(a) credit that a taxpayer may claim is determined by multiplying the interest payment that the taxpayer receives from the issuer (i.e., the bond coupon payment) by 35%. (Com Rept, see ¶ 5070)

Original issue discount (OID) isn't treated as a payment of interest for purposes of determining the credit under Code Sec. 54AA. OID is the excess of an obligation's stated redemption price at maturity over the obligation's issue price. (Com Rept, see ¶ 5070)

For regulated investment company's (RIC's) and real estate investment company's (REIT's) permitted pass through of the Code Sec. 54AA tax credit to shareholders, see ¶ 1308.

Limitation based on amount of tax liability. The credit allowed under Code Sec. 54AA(a) for any tax year can't exceed the excess of (Code Sec. 54AA(c)(1)):

(1) the sum of the regular tax liability (as defined in Code Sec. 26(b), i.e., a taxpayer's income tax, not including AMT and other special taxes, see FTC 2d/ FIN ¶ A-4905; USTR ¶ 264.01; TaxDesk ¶ 569,605) plus the tax imposed by Code Sec. 55 (i.e., AMT) (Code Sec. 54AA(c)(1)(A)), over

(2) the sum of the credits allowable under Subtitle A, Chapter 1, Subchapter A, Part IV of the Code (other than the subpart C refundable credits (i.e., Code Sec. 31 through Code Sec. 37), and new subpart J (i.e., Code Sec. 54AA)). (Code Sec. 54AA(c)(1)(B))

Thus, the sum of the accrued credits under Code Sec. 54AA(a) is allowed against regular tax and AMT. (Com Rept, see ¶ 5070)

Carryover of unused Code Sec. 54AA credit. If the Code Sec. 54AA(a) credit exceeds the above limitation for the tax year, the excess is carried to the next tax year and added to the credit allowable under Code Sec. 54AA(a) for that tax year (determined before the application of the above limitation to that tax year). (Code Sec. 54AA(c)(2)) That is, an unused credit may be carried forward to later tax years. (Com Rept, see ¶ 5070)

Build America Bond defined. For purposes of the Code Sec. 54AA(a) credit, the term "Build America Bond" means any obligation (other than a private activity bond) if (Code Sec. 54AA(d)(1)):

(A) the interest on the obligation would (but for Code Sec. 54AA) be excludable from gross income under Code Sec. 103 (Code Sec. 54AA(d)(1)(A));

(B) the obligation is issued before Jan. 1, 2011 (Code Sec. 54AA(d)(1)(B)); and

(C) the issuer makes an irrevocable election to have Code Sec. 54AA apply. (Code Sec. 54AA(d)(1)(C))

In applying the definition above (Code Sec. 54AA(d)(2)):

(i) for purposes of Code Sec. 149(b) (rule providing that state and local bonds aren't tax-exempt if bond is federally guaranteed, see FTC 2d/FIN

FTC 2d References are to Federal Tax Coordinator 2d
FIN References are to RIA's Analysis of Federal Taxes: Income
USTR References are to United States Tax Reporter: Income
PE References are to Pension Explanations

¶ J-3656; USTR ¶ 1494.02; TaxDesk ¶ 158,001), a Build America Bond won't be treated as federally guaranteed by reason of the credit allowed under Code Sec. 54AA or Code Sec. 6431 (the alternative issuer's credit, described below) (Code Sec. 54AA(d)(2)(A));

(ii) for purposes of Code Sec. 148 (the arbitrage bond requirements, see FTC 2d/FIN ¶ J-3403 *et seq.*; USTR ¶ 1484 *et seq.*; TaxDesk ¶ 158,013), the yield on a Build America Bond is to be determined without regard to the Code Sec. 54AA(a) credit (Code Sec. 54AA(d)(2)(B)); and

(iii) a bond won't be treated as a Build America Bond if the issue price has more than a de minimis amount (determined under rules similar to the Code Sec. 1273(a)(3) rules relating to the de minimis exception applied in determining OID on a debt instrument, see FTC 2d/FIN ¶ J-4102; USTR ¶ 12,714; TaxDesk ¶ 153,004) of premium over the stated principal amount of the bond. (Code Sec. 54AA(d)(2)(C))

Interest payment date for Code Sec. 54AA credit. For purposes of the Code Sec. 54AA credit, the term "interest payment date" means any date on which the holder of record of the Build America Bond is entitled to a payment of interest under the bond. (Code Sec. 54AA(e))

Interest on taxable governmental bonds includible in gross income. For federal income tax purposes, interest on any Build America Bond is includible in gross income. (Code Sec. 54AA(f)(1))

As discussed above, the credit the taxpayer may claim equals the interest payment the taxpayer receives from the issuer (the bond coupon payment) times 35%. Because the credit is also included in income, Congress anticipates that state and local issuers will issue bonds paying interest at rates approximately equal to 74.1% of comparable taxable bonds. Congress anticipates that if an issuer issued a Build America Bond with coupons at 74.1% of a comparable taxable bond's coupon, then the issuer's bond should sell at par. (Com Rept, see ¶ 5070)

> ***Illustration (1):*** If a taxable bond of comparable risk pays a $1,000 coupon and sells at par, then if a state or local issuer issues an equal-sized bond with a coupon of $741, that bond should also sell at par. The taxpayer who acquires the $741 coupon bond will receive an interest payment of $741 and may claim a credit of $259 (35% × $741). The credit and interest payment are both included in the taxpayer's income. Thus, the taxpayer's taxable income from this instrument would be $1,000. This is the same taxable income that the taxpayer would recognize from holding the comparable taxable bond (i.e., the $1,000 coupon bond). Thus, the issuer's bond should sell at the same price as would the taxable bond. (Com Rept, see ¶ 5070)

Application of certain qualified tax credit bond credit rules to the Code Sec. 54AA credit. Rules similar to the general rules for qualified tax credit bonds under Code Sec. 54A(f), Code Sec. 54A(g), Code Sec. 54A(h), and Code Sec. 54A(i) apply for purposes of the Code Sec. 54AA(a) credit for Build America Bonds. (Code Sec. 54AA(f)(2))

> *observation:* That is, Code Sec. 54AA Build America Bonds are subject to rules similar to the following Code Sec. 54A rules:
>
> ... Code Sec. 54A(f), which provides that the credit for qualified tax credit bonds is treated as interest includable in gross income (see FTC 2d/FIN ¶ L-15533; USTR ¶ 54A4; TaxDesk ¶ 568,521);
>
> ... Code Sec. 54A(g), which provides that for a qualified tax credit bond held by an S corporation or partnership that the allocation of the credit to the shareholders or the partners, as applicable, is treated as a distribution (see FTC 2d/FIN ¶ L-15532; USTR ¶ 54A4.01);
>
> ... Code Sec. 54A(h), which provides rules for qualified tax credit bonds held by regulated investment companies and real estate investment trusts (see FTC 2d/FIN ¶ L-15532; USTR ¶ 54A4.01); and
>
> ... Code Sec. 54A(i), which provides that qualified tax credit bonds may be stripped, i.e., there may be a separation of the ownership of the bond and the entitlement to the credit for the bond (see FTC 2d/FIN ¶ L-15538; USTR ¶ 54A4.02).

Code Sec. 54AA credit won't reduce tax liability under the tax liability limitation rules applicable to certain credits. The following tax liability limitation rules—under which the amount of the applicable credit that may be claimed for the tax year is limited to the amount of the taxpayer's regular tax and AMT liability, reduced by specified credits—are amended to add the Code Sec. 54AA credit as a credit that's disregarded in applying the limitations:

... Code Sec. 54A(c)(1)(B) (part of the tax liability limitation rule for the qualified tax credit bond credit, see FTC 2d/FIN ¶ L-15537; USTR ¶ 54A4; TaxDesk ¶ 568,521) (Code Sec. 54A(c)(1)(B) as amended by 2009 Recovery Act §1531(c)(2));

... Code Sec. 54(c)(2) (part of the tax liability limitation rule for the clean renewable energy bond (CREB) credit, see FTC 2d/FIN ¶ L-16487; USTR ¶ 544.01; TaxDesk ¶ 384,807) (Code Sec. 54(c)(2) as amended by 2009 Recovery Act §1531(c)(3));

... Code Sec. 1397E(c)(2) (part of the tax liability limitation rule for the qualified zone academy bond (QZAB) credit, see FTC 2d/FIN ¶ L-15645.1; USTR

FTC 2d References are to Federal Tax Coordinator 2d
FIN References are to RIA's Analysis of Federal Taxes: Income
USTR References are to United States Tax Reporter: Income
PE References are to Pension Explanations

¶ 13,97E4; TaxDesk ¶ 384,752) (Code Sec. 1397E(c)(2) as amended by 2009 Recovery Act §1531(c)(3)); and

... Code Sec. 1400N(l)(3)(B) (part of the tax liability limitation rule for the Gulf Opportunity tax credit bond credit, see FTC 2d/FIN ¶ L-17884.1; USTR ¶ 14,00N4.065; TaxDesk ¶ 382,155). (Code Sec. 1400N(l)(3)(B) as amended by 2009 Recovery Act §1531(c)(3))

> **(RIA) *observation:*** That is, in applying the tax liability limitation rules listed above, the Code Sec. 54AA credit won't reduce the amount of the taxpayer's tax liability against which the above-described applicable credits may be offset for the tax year.

Code Sec. 54AA credit increases amount of refundable credits that may actually be refunded. Under pre-2009 Recovery Act law, if the amount allowable as refundable credits under subpart C of Part IV of Subchapter A of Chapter 1 of Subtitle A of the Code exceeded the income tax imposed for the tax year, as reduced by the nonrefundable credits allowable under subparts A, B, D, G, H and I of that Part IV, the amount of the excess was an overpayment that could be refunded. (FTC 2d/FIN ¶ T-5500, ¶ T-5511; USTR ¶ 64,014; TaxDesk ¶ 801,008) The Act adds the Code Sec. 54AA credit allowable under subpart J of that Part IV to those nonrefundable credits that reduce the "income tax imposed for the tax year" in determining the amount of an overpayment under the above rule. (Code Sec. 6401(b)(1) as amended by 2009 Recovery Act §1531(c)(5))

> **(RIA) *observation:*** Because the Code Sec. 54AA credit reduces the taxpayer's income tax for the tax year, it may increase the amount by which the taxpayer's refundable credits exceed his or her tax liability for the tax year, increasing the amount that can be refunded to the taxpayer.

Special rule for "qualified bonds" issued in 2009 and 2010—election of issuer's credit in lieu of bond holder's credit. For a "qualified bond" (defined below) issued before Jan. 1, 2011 (Code Sec. 54AA(g)), in lieu of any above-described credit allowed under Code Sec. 54AA (to the bond holder) for the bond, the *issuer* of the bond is allowed a credit as provided in Code Sec. 6431 (see below). (Code Sec. 54AA(g)(1))

For purposes of this rule, the term "qualified bond" means any Build America Bond issued as part of an issue if (Code Sec. 54AA(g)(2)):

(I) 100% of the excess of (Code Sec. 54AA(g)(2)(A)):

(i) the available project proceeds (as defined in Code Sec. 54A, see FTC 2d/FIN ¶ L-15540; USTR ¶ 54A4.03) of the issue (Code Sec. 54AA(g)(2)(A)(i)), over

(ii) the amounts in a reasonably required reserve (within the meaning of Code Sec. 150(a)(3), see FTC 2d/FIN ¶ J-3004) (Code Sec. 54AA(g)(2)(A)(ii)), are to be used for capital expenditures (Code Sec. 54AA(g)(2)(A)); and

(II) the issuer makes an irrevocable election to have the special rule (i.e., the Code Sec. 6431 issuer's credit) apply. (Code Sec. 54AA(g)(2)(B))

Under Code Sec. 148(d)(2), a bond is an arbitrage bond if the amount of the proceeds from the sale of the issue that is part of any reserve or replacement fund exceeds 10% of the proceeds. As such, the interest on these bonds would not be tax-exempt under Code Sec. 103 and thus would not be qualified bonds for purposes of the rule above. (Com Rept, see ¶ 5070)

> *observation:* Reg § 150-1(b) defines capital expenditure as any cost of a type that's properly chargeable to capital account (or would be so chargeable with a proper election, or if the placed-in-service rule described in Reg § 150-2(c) applied) under general federal income tax principles. For example, costs incurred to acquire, construct, or improve land, buildings, and equipment generally are capital expenditures. (See FTC 2d/FIN ¶ J-3451; USTR ¶ 1504.04.)

Congress provides as an example of a capital expenditure, expenditures made for the purchase of fiber-optic cable to provide municipal broadband service. (Com Rept, see ¶ 5070)

Issuer's credit for qualified bonds ("Code Sec. 6431 credit") issued in 2009 and 2010. For a qualified bond issued before Jan. 1, 2011, the issuer of the bond is allowed a refundable credit for each interest payment under the bond. The credit is payable by IRS as provided in Code Sec. 6431(b) (see below). (Code Sec. 6431(a) as added by 2009 Recovery Act §1531(b); 2009 Recovery Act §1521(c)(1))

IRS will pay (contemporaneously with each interest payment date under the bond) to the bond's issuer (or to any person who makes the interest payments on behalf of the issuer), 35% of the interest payable under the bond on that date. (Code Sec. 6431(b))

OID isn't treated as a payment of interest for purposes of calculating the refundable credit under Code Sec. 6431. (Com Rept, see ¶ 5070)

> *Illustration (2):* If in *illustration (1),* above, the issuer elects to receive the Code Sec. 6431 credit, then, for the state and local issuer's bond to sell at par, the issuer would have to issue the bond with a $1,000 interest coupon. The taxpayer who holds this bond would include $1,000 of

FTC 2d References are to Federal Tax Coordinator 2d
FIN References are to RIA's Analysis of Federal Taxes: Income
USTR References are to United States Tax Reporter: Income
PE References are to Pension Explanations

interest in his or her income. From the taxpayer's (i.e., the holder's) perspective, the bond is the same as the taxable bond in *illustration (1)*, above, and the taxpayer would be willing to pay par for the bond. However, under Code Sec. 6431, the state or local issuer would receive a payment of $350 for each $1,000 coupon paid (i.e. 35% of $1,000). (The net interest cost to the issuer would be $650.) (Com Rept, see ¶ 5070)

Application of arbitrage rules. For purposes of the Code Sec. 148 arbitrage rules, the yield on a qualified bond is reduced by the issuer's payment/credit allowed under Code Sec. 6431. (Code Sec. 6431(c)) (Com Rept, see ¶ 5070)

> ✒ *observation:* A bond is an arbitrage bond (to which the Code Sec. 103 interest exclusion won't apply) if its proceeds are reasonably expected to be used, or intentionally are used, to acquire investments with a "materially higher yield" than the bond itself or to replace funds used to acquire those investments. An arbitrage bond loses its tax-exempt status unless a required rebate is paid to the U.S. Treasury. (See FTC 2d/FIN ¶ J-3403; USTR ¶ 1484; TaxDesk ¶ 158,013.)

Interest payment date for Code Sec. 6431 credit. For purposes of Code Sec. 6431, the term "interest payment date" means each date on which interest is payable by the issuer under the terms of the bond. (Code Sec. 6431(d))

"Qualified bond" defined for Code Sec. 6431 credit. For purposes of Code Sec. 6431, the term "qualified bond" has the meaning given that term in Code Sec. 54AA(g) above. (Code Sec. 6431(e))

> ✒ *observation:* The 2009 Recovery Act provides that a new category of bonds—"recovery zone economic development bonds"—are qualified bonds for purposes of Code Sec. 6431, but the Act applies an increased payment to the issuer (or other payor of interest) of 45% of the interest paid for these bonds, see ¶ 1306.

Code Sec. 6431 credit treated as negative tax in deficiency computation. Any excess of the Code Sec. 6431 credit over the income tax is taken into account as a negative amount of tax in computing a taxpayer's tax deficiency. (Code Sec. 6211(b)(4)(A) as amended by 2009 Recovery Act §1531(c)(4)) For how deficiencies are computed, see FTC 2d/FIN ¶ T-1501; USTR ¶ 62,114; TaxDesk ¶ 822,501.

IRS authorized to issue regs, other guidance. IRS is authorized to prescribe regs and other guidance as may be necessary or appropriate to carry out the rules of Code Sec. 54AA and Code Sec. 6431. (Code Sec. 54AA(h))

Transitional coordination with state law. Except as otherwise provided by a state after Feb. 17, 2009, the interest on any Build America Bond (as defined in Code Sec. 54AA above) and the amount of any credit determined under that provision with respect to the bond will be treated for purposes of the income tax laws of the state as being exempt from federal income tax. (2009 Recovery Act §1531(d))

That is, until a state provides otherwise, interest on any Build America Bond and the amount of any credit determined with respect to that bond will be treated as being exempt from federal income tax for purposes of state income tax laws. (Com Rept, see ¶ 5070)

☐ **Effective:** For obligations issued after Feb. 17, 2009 (2009 Recovery Act §1531(e)) and before Jan. 1, 2011. (Code Sec. 54AA(d)(1)(B))

¶ 1302. Qualified school construction bond is a new type of tax credit bond

Code Sec. 54F, as added by 2009 Recovery Act § 1521(a)
Code Sec. 54A(d)(1)(E), as amended by 2009 Recovery Act § 1521(b)(1)
Code Sec. 54A(d)(2)(C)(v), as amended by 2009 Recovery Act § 1521(b)(2)
Generally effective: Bonds issued after Feb. 17, 2009
Committee Reports, see ¶ 5067

Taxpayers who hold "qualified tax credit bonds" on specified dates during the year are entitled to a nonrefundable credit equal to a portion of the bonds' outstanding face amount. The credit is includible in gross income, and is treated as interest income. (FTC 2d/FIN ¶ L-15530; USTR ¶ 54A4)

Qualified tax credit bonds must meet certain requirements:

(i) expenditure: 100% or more of the available project proceeds must be spent for one or more qualified purposes within the three-years beginning on the date of issuance, and a binding commitment with a third party to spend at least 10% of the available project proceeds will be incurred in the six-month period beginning on the date of issuance (FTC 2d/FIN ¶ L-15540; USTR ¶ 54A4.03);

(ii) reporting: issuer must submit reports similar to those required for state and local bonds under Code Sec. 149(e) (FTC 2d/FIN ¶ L-15543; USTR ¶ 54A4.04;

(iii) arbitrage: issuer must satisfy the Code Sec. 148 arbitrage requirements with respect to the proceeds of the issue (FTC 2d/FIN ¶ L-15544; USTR ¶ 54A4.05);

FTC 2d References are to Federal Tax Coordinator 2d
FIN References are to RIA's Analysis of Federal Taxes: Income
USTR References are to United States Tax Reporter: Income
PE References are to Pension Explanations

(iv) maturity: the maturity of any bond that is part of the issue can't exceed the maximum term determined by IRS (FTC 2d/FIN ¶ L-15545; USTR ¶ 54A4.06); and

(v) conflicts of interest: the issuer must certify that the bonds meet certain conflicts of interest requirements (FTC 2d/FIN ¶ L-15546; USTR ¶ 54A4.07).

Under pre-2009 Recovery Act law, there were four different types of tax credit bonds:

(i) qualified forestry conservation bonds (FTC 2d/FIN ¶ L-15551; USTR ¶ 54B4);

(ii) new clean renewable energy bonds (FTC 2d/FIN ¶ L-15561; USTR ¶ 54C4);

(iii) qualified energy conservation bonds (FTC 2d/FIN ¶ L-15571; USTR ¶ 54D4); and

(iv) qualified zone academy bonds (FTC 2d/FIN ¶ L-15581; USTR ¶ 54E4).

Qualified zone academy bonds (above), which provide funds for repairing and renovating schools as well as for school equipment and teacher training, have been extended through 2010, see ¶ 1303.

New Law. The 2009 Recovery Act creates a new category of tax credit bonds—qualified school construction bonds. (Code Sec. 54A(d)(1)(E) as amended by 2009 Recovery Act §1521(b)(1))

The term "qualified school construction bond" means any bond issued as part of an issue (Code Sec. 54F(a) as added by 2009 Recovery Act §1521(a)), if:

. . . 100% of the available project proceeds of the bond issue are to be used for the construction, rehabilitation, or repair of a public school facility or for the acquisition of land on which a facility is to be constructed with part of the proceeds of the issue (Code Sec. 54F(a)(1)),

. . . the bond is issued by a state or local government within the jurisdiction of which the school is located (Code Sec. 54F(a)(2)), and

. . . the issuer designates the bond as a qualified school construction bond. (Code Sec. 54F(a)(3))

Thus, in order to qualify as a "qualified school construction bond," a bond must meet each of the three requirements listed above. (Com Rept, see ¶ 5067)

"Qualified purpose" defined. For purposes of these rules, a "qualified purpose" means a purpose specified in Code Sec. 54F(a)(1), i.e., 100% of the available project proceeds of the bond issue are to be used for the construction, rehabilitation, or repair of a public school facility or for the acquisition of land on which a facility is to be constructed. (Code Sec. 54A(d)(2)(C)(v))

● *observation:* There is also an expenditure requirement that must be met for any qualified tax credit bond issue. The expenditure requirement is met if, as of the date of issuance, the issuer reasonably expects that 100% or more of the available project proceeds will be spent on one or more qualified purposes within the three-year period beginning on the date of issuance. In addition to the expenditure requirement, a qualified tax credit bond must meet other requirements relating to reporting, arbitrage, maturity, and financial conflicts of interest, as discussed above.

$11 billion limitation for 2009 and 2010. The national qualified school construction bond limitation is ((Code Sec. 54F(c)):

... $11 billion for 2009 (Code Sec. 54F(c)(1)),

... $11 billion for 2010 (Code Sec. 54F(c)(2)), and

... except as provided under the carryover of unused limitation rules (below), $0 after 2010. (Code Sec. 54F(c)(3))

The maximum aggregate face amount of bonds that may be designated as qualified school construction bonds by any issuer cannot exceed the limitation amount allocated under Code Sec. 54F(d) (below) for that calendar year to that issuer. (Code Sec. 54F(b)))

Allocation of national bond volume limitation to the states. Except as provided in Code Sec. 54F(d)(2)(C) (relating to reductions in state allocation, below), the Code Sec. 54F(c) limitation for any calendar year most be allocated by IRS among the states in proportion to the respective amounts each state is eligible to receive under section 1124 of the Elementary and Secondary Education Act of 1965 (20 U.S.C. 6333) for the most recent fiscal year ending before that calendar year. The limitation amount allocated to any state is to be allocated by the state to issuers within that state. (Code Sec. 54F(d)(1))

For allocation purposes, a state includes the District of Columbia and any U.S. possession (discussed below). (Com Rept, see ¶ 5067)

● *observation:* The Elementary and Secondary Education Act of 1965 provides for funding for primary and secondary education, specifically for professional development, instructional materials, resources to support educational groups, and parental involvement promotion.

40% of overall national bond volume limitation allocated to large school districts. 40% of the national limitation on the amounts of qualified school

---

FTC 2d References are to Federal Tax Coordinator 2d
FIN References are to RIA's Analysis of Federal Taxes: Income
USTR References are to United States Tax Reporter: Income
PE References are to Pension Explanations

263

construction bonds designated for any calendar year is to be allocated by IRS, under the rules for minimum allocations to states (described above), among local educational agencies which are considered large local educational agencies (defined below) for that year. (Code Sec. 54F(d)(2)(A))

The amounts to be allocated under the preceding paragraph for any calendar year are to be allocated among large local educational agencies in proportion to the respective amounts each agency received under section 1124 of the Elementary and Secondary Education Act of 1965 (20 U.S.C. 6333) for the most recent fiscal year ending before that calendar year. (Code Sec. 54F(d)(2)(B))

The allocation to any state under Code Sec. 54F(d)(1) (above) is reduced by the aggregate amount of the allocations to large local educational agencies within that state. (Code Sec. 54F(d)(2)(C))

The amount allocated to a large local educational agency for any calendar year may be reallocated by that agency back to the state in which the agency is located. Any reallocated amount may be allocated as provided under Code Sec. 54F(d)(1) (above). (Code Sec. 54F(d)(2)(D))

In other words, if any amount allocated to a large local agency is unused, the agency may reallocate the amount to the state in which the agency is located. (Com Rept, see ¶ 5067)

"Large local educational agency"defined. A "large local educational agency" means, with respect to any calendar year, any local educational agency if that agency is (Code Sec. 54F(d)(2)(E)):

(a) among the 100 local educational agencies with the largest numbers of children aged 5 through 17 from families living below the poverty level, as determined by IRS using the most recent, satisfactory data available from the Department of Commerce (Code Sec. 54F(d)(2)(E)(i)), or

(b) one of not more than 25 local educational agencies (other than described in (a), above) that the Secretary of Education determines (based on the most recent, satisfactory data available to IRS) are in particular need of assistance, based on low level of resources for school construction, a high level of enrollment growth, or any other factors IRS deems appropriate. (Code Sec. 54F(d)(2)(E)(ii))

Allocations to certain possessions. The amount to be allocated under Code Sec. 54F(d)(1) to any U.S. possession other than Puerto Rico is the amount which would have been allocated if all allocations under that section were made on the basis of respective populations of individuals below the poverty line (as determined by the Office of Management and Budget). In making other allocations, the amount to be allocated is reduced by the aggregate amount allocated under these rules to U.S. possessions. (Code Sec. 54F(d)(3))

In other words, allocations to any U.S. possession other than Puerto Rico are made on the basis of the respective populations of individuals below the poverty line, *rather than* respective populations of children aged five through 17. This special allocation reduces the state allocation share of the national limitation otherwise available for allocation among the states. (Com Rept, see ¶ 5067)

Amounts allocated to Indian schools. In addition to the amounts otherwise allocated under Code Sec. 54F(d), i.e., the national bond volume limitation allocated to states, the Secretary of the Interior may allocate, for purposes of the construction, rehabilitation, and repair of schools funded by the Bureau of Indian Affairs:

. . . $200 million of qualified school construction bonds for 2009; and

. . . $200 million of qualified school construction bonds for 2010. (Code Sec. 54F(d)(4))

For purposes of the allocation rules, Indian tribal governments (as defined under Code Sec. 7701(a)(40), see FTC 2d/FIN ¶ J-1540; USTR ¶ 77,014.01; TaxDesk ¶ 158,007) are treated as qualified issuers of qualified school construction bonds. (Code Sec. 54F(d)(4))

The special allocation to Indian schools (described above) doesn't reduce the state allocation share of the national limitation otherwise available for allocation among the states. (Com Rept, see ¶ 5067)

Carryover of unused limitation permitted. Carryovers of unused limitation amounts are permitted. In general, if, for any calendar year (Code Sec. 54F(e))—the limitation amount for any state exceeds (Code Sec. 54F(e)(1)) the amount of bonds issued during the year which are designated as qualified school construction bonds, then the limitation amount for the state for the following calendar year is increased by the amount of the excess. (Code Sec. 54F(e)(2))

A similar rule applies to the amounts allocated to Indian schools under Code Sec. 54F(d)(4). (Code Sec. 54F(e)(2))

☐ **Effective:** Bonds issued after Feb. 17, 2009. (2009 Recovery Act §1521(c)))

FTC 2d References are to Federal Tax Coordinator 2d
FIN References are to RIA's Analysis of Federal Taxes: Income
USTR References are to United States Tax Reporter: Income
PE References are to Pension Explanations

¶ 1303. Credit for QZABs is extended through 2010; national bond volume limitation is increased to $1.4 billion for 2009 and 2010

Code Sec. 54E(c)(1), as amended by 2009 Recovery Act § 1522(a)
Generally effective: Bonds issued after Dec. 31, 2008
Committee Reports, see ¶ 5068

Qualified zone academy bonds (QZABs) are a type of qualified tax credit bond entitling the holder to a nonrefundable tax credit. (FTC 2d/FIN ¶ L-15580; USTR ¶ 54E4) A QZAB is any bond issued as part of an issue if:

(1) 100% of the available project proceeds of the issue are to be used for a qualified purpose with respect to a qualified zone academy established by an eligible local education agency;

(2) the bond is issued by a state or local government within the jurisdiction of which the academy is located; and

(3) the issuer designates the bond for purposes of the QZAB rules, certifies that it has written assurances that the private business contribution requirement will be satisfied, and certifies that it has the written approval of the eligible local education agency for the bond issuance. See FTC 2d/FIN ¶ L-15582; USTR ¶ 54E4.

Under pre-2009 Recovery Act law, a total of $400 million of QZABs could be issued each year from '98 through 2009; the amount after 2009 was zero, subject to a state's carryover. (FTC 2d/FIN ¶ L-15586; USTR ¶ 54E4.01) This amount is allocated by IRS among the states (including the District of Columbia and possessions) based on the percentage of their respective populations of individuals below the poverty line (as defined by the Office of Management and Budget). See FTC 2d/FIN ¶ L-15586; USTR ¶ 54E4.01.

New Law. The 2009 Recovery Act extends and expands the QZAB program by authorizing the issuance of up to $1.4 billion of QZABs annually for 2009 and 2010. (Com Rept, see ¶ 5068) Under the 2009 Recovery Act, the national bond volume limitation under Code Sec. 54E(c)(1) is changed to provide that the limitation is "$1,400,000,000 for 2009 and 2010." (Code Sec. 54E(c)(1) as amended by 2009 Recovery Act §1522(a))

> *observation:* Thus, under the 2009 Recovery Act, the QZAB national bond volume limitation amount for 2009 is increased from $400 million to $1.4 billion, and the program is extended through 2010 with the same $1.4 billion national bond volume limitation.

Congress wants to expand and extend the QZAB program because it believes that this category of tax credit bond is an efficient mechanism for renovating, providing equipment to, providing course materials for use at, training teachers and other personnel at, qualified zone academies. (Com Rept, see ¶ 5068)

☐ **Effective:** Bonds issued after Dec. 31, 2008. (2009 Recovery Act §1522(b))

¶ 1304. Overview of national limits on two new categories of recovery zone bonds issued in 2009 and 2010 which are allocated among states based on 2008 employment declines subject to a minimum allocation

Gross income doesn't include interest on state or local bonds. State bonds and local bonds are classified generally as either governmental bonds or private activity bonds. Governmental bond proceeds are primarily used to finance governmental functions or are repaid with governmental funds. Private activity bonds are bonds for which a state or local government acts as a conduit, providing financing to nongovernmental persons (e.g., private businesses or individuals).

Private activity bonds. A private activity bond is a bond that satisfies either (1) a private business test or (2) a private loan financing test. Under the private business test, a bond is a private activity bond if it is part of an issue in which:

(i) more than 10% of the issue proceeds (including use of the bond-financed property) are to be used in a trade or business other than that of a governmental unit (private business use); and

(ii) more than 10% of the payment of the issue's principal or interest is, directly or indirectly, secured by property used or to be used for a private business use or to be derived from payments from the property or borrowed money used or to be used for a private business use (private payment test).

Both item (i) and item (ii) of the above list must be satisfied for a bond to be a private activity bond under the private business test.

A bond is a private activity bond under the private loan financing test if proceeds exceeding the lesser of $5 million or 5% of the proceeds are used directly or indirectly to finance loans to one or more nongovernmental persons. Private loans include both business and other (e.g., personal) uses and payments to private persons. However, in the case of business uses and payments, all private loans are private business uses and payments are subject to the private business test. The 10% private business test is reduced to 5% for private business uses

FTC 2d References are to Federal Tax Coordinator 2d
FIN References are to RIA's Analysis of Federal Taxes: Income
USTR References are to United States Tax Reporter: Income
PE References are to Pension Explanations

(and payments for those uses) that are unrelated to any governmental use being financed by the issue.

> 📝 *observation:* The low percentages of private use in the above tests flush out private uses, so that bonds financing more than minimal private use can be subject to requirements discussed below to be tax-exempt.

Interest on a state or local private activity bond isn't exempt from federal income taxation unless it is a qualified bond. A qualified bond must:

- satisfy any applicable "volume cap" requirement (see below);
- satisfy the technical requirements of Code Sec. 147 including rules:

. . . proscribing the holding of the bond by a substantial user,

. . . limiting average maturity to 120% of the reasonably expected economic life of facilities being financed,

. . . limiting use for land acquisitions and the acquisition of existing property (with an exception for certain rehabilitations),

. . . limiting issuance costs (e.g., bond counsel and underwriter fees);

. . . satisfy the Code Sec. 148 arbitrage requirements;

- be one of the seven following types of bonds:

. . . an exempt facility bond,

. . . qualified mortgage bond,

. . . qualified veterans' mortgage bond,

. . . qualified small issue bond,

. . . qualified student loan bond,

. . . qualified redevelopment bond; or a

. . . qualified 501(c)(3) bond.

Under pre-2009 Recovery Act law, an exempt facility bond (first item on the immediately preceding list) included bonds issued to finance certain transportation facilities (airports, docks and wharves, mass commuting); qualified residential rental projects; privately owned and/or operated utility facilities (sewage, water, solid waste disposal, and local district heating and cooling facilities, certain private electric and gas facilities); qualified green building and sustainable design projects; and qualified highway or surface freight transfer facilities.

In most cases, the total volume of qualified private activity bonds is restricted by annual limits imposed on bonds issued by issuers within each state ("state volume cap"). For calendar year 2007, the state volume cap, was the greater of $85 per state resident, or $256.24 million. Exceptions to the cap applied for certain exempt facility bonds used to finance government-owned airports, docks and wharves, environmental enhancements of hydroelectric generating facilities, qualified public educational facilities, and solid waste disposal facilities; and bonds subject to separate local, state, or national volume limits (e.g., public/private educational facility bonds, enterprise zone facility bonds, qualified green building bonds, and qualified highway or surface freight transfer facility bonds).

An issue of exempt facility bonds is limited to an average life of not more than 120% of the average reasonably expected economic life of the facilities being financed.

In addition, qualified private activity bonds generally are subject to restrictions on the use of proceeds to finance certain specified facilities (e.g., airplanes, skyboxes, other luxury boxes, health club facilities, gambling facilities, underwriter fees). Small issue and redevelopment bonds also are subject to additional restrictions on the use of proceeds for certain facilities (e.g., golf courses and massage parlors and liquor stores). Also, certain public approval requirements (similar to requirements that typically apply under state law to issuance of governmental debt) apply to issuance of private activity bonds. (FTC 2d/FIN ¶ J-3150, ¶ J-3153, ¶ J-3252FTC 2d ¶ J-3253FTC 2d/FIN ¶ J-3274; USTR ¶ 1424.01, ¶ 1464.01; TaxDesk ¶ 158,010) (FTC 2d/FIN ¶ J-3101; FTC 2d/FIN ¶ J-3104; FTC 2d ¶ J-3110; FTC 2d/FIN ¶ J-3115; FTC 2d/FIN ¶ J-3150;FTC 2d/FIN ¶ J-3259; FTC 2d/FIN ¶ J-3260; FTC 2d/FIN ¶ J-3266FTC 2d/FIN ¶ J-3267;FTC 2d/FIN ¶ J-3277;FTC 2d/FIN ¶ J-3401; USTR ¶ 1414.01; USTR ¶ 1414.02; USTR ¶ 1474; USTR ¶ 1474.03)

Qualified tax credit bonds. Qualified tax credit bonds provide the holder with a tax credit instead of interest. Under pre-2009 recovery Act law, there were four types of qualified tax credit bonds: qualified forestry conservation bonds, new clean renewable energy bonds, qualified energy conservation bonds, and qualified zone academy bonds.

The holder of a qualified tax credit bond on a credit allowance date is entitled to a tax credit against the holder's income tax. Generally, the credit amount for any credit allowance date is 25% of the annual credit determined for the bond. (With the possible exception of the first or last year there will be four credit allowance dates during a year.) The annual credit amount is determined by multiplying the applicable credit rate by the outstanding face amount of the bond. The applicable credit rate is the rate that IRS estimates will permit the issuance of the bond with a specified maturity or redemption date without discount and without interest cost to the qualified issuer, based on assumptions about credit quality of the class of potential eligible issuers and other factors IRS thinks appropriate. The maturity is the term IRS estimates will result in the present value of the obligation to repay the principal on the bonds equaling 50% of the face amount of the bonds, using as a discount rate the average annual in-

FTC 2d References are to Federal Tax Coordinator 2d
FIN References are to RIA's Analysis of Federal Taxes: Income
USTR References are to United States Tax Reporter: Income
PE References are to Pension Explanations

terest rate of tax-exempt obligations having a term of ten years or more that are issued during the month the qualified tax credit bonds are issued.

The amount allowed as a credit is included in gross income. Regs can provide for the credit to be separated from the bond.

Code Sec. 54A provides the above rules and other general applicable requirements, including a requirement for the expenditure of 100% of available project proceeds within the three-year period that begins on the date of issuance. Available project proceeds are proceeds from the sale of the bond issue less issuance costs (not to exceed two percent) and any investment earnings on the sale proceeds. To the extent less than 100% of the available project proceeds are used to finance qualified projects during the three-year spending period, the bonds remain qualified if unspent proceeds are used within 90 days from the end of the three-year period to redeem bonds. IRS may extend the three-year period at the issuer's request on a showing that the failure is due to reasonable cause and the projects will proceed with due diligence.

Qualified tax credit bonds generally are subject to the arbitrage requirements, but available project proceeds invested during the three-year spending period are not subject to these yield restriction and rebate requirements. Also, amounts invested in a reserve fund are not subject to the arbitrage restrictions to the extent: (1) the fund is funded at a rate not more rapid than equal annual installments; (2) the fund is funded in a manner reasonably expected to result in an amount not greater than an amount necessary to repay the issued and (3) the yield on the fund is not greater than the average annual interest rate of tax-exempt obligations having a term of ten years or more issued during the month the qualified tax credit bonds are issued. There are also maturity limitations, and a rule for avoiding financial conflicts of interest. FTC 2d/FIN ¶ L-15530; FTC 2d/FIN ¶ L-15531 *et seq.*; USTR ¶ 54A4.

New Law. The 2009 Recovery Act provides for the issuance of two new types of government bonds in 2009 and 2010:

. . . Recovery zone economic development bonds, (Code Sec. 1400U-2 as added by 2009 Recovery Act §1401(a)) and

. . . Recovery zone facility bonds. (Code Sec. 1400U-3 as added by 2009 Recovery Act §1401(a))

For an introduction and a summary of these provisions, see below. For detailed discussions of these provisions, see ¶ 1306 for recovery zone economic development bonds and ¶ 1307 for recovery zone facility bonds. For limits on the issuance of these bonds, see ¶ 1305.

Congress provided for the issuance of these bonds because it believes that additional incentives are needed to assist communities most affected by the current economic crisis and that state and local governments often are in the best position to determine economic development needs. Thus, the 2009 Recovery Act provides state and local governments with access to subsidized financing to promote economic development in communities affected by job losses and to provide needed infrastructure. (Com Rept, see ¶ 5054)

Recovery zone economic development bonds and recovery zone facility bonds are subject respectively to $10 billion and $15 billion national limitations. (Code Sec. 1400U-1(a)(4))

Each limit is allocated to the states in proportion to their respective declines in employment in 2008, subject to each state receiving an allocation of at least nine tenths of one percent (.9%) of the national limit. (Code Sec. 1400U-1(a)(1)) Each state then reallocates its limit to counties and large municipalities in proportion to their respective declines in 2008 employment. (Code Sec. 1400U-1(a)(3))

Recovery zone economic development bonds. Recovery zone economic development bonds, which may be issued by a local government before Jan. 1, 2011, are subsidized by the U.S. Treasury which makes an interest payment to the issuer (or other interest payor) equal to 45% of the interest paid on each interest payment date. (Code Sec. 1400U-2(a)) All interest paid on the bond is taxable to the holder. (Code Sec. 1400U-2(b)(1))

> *observation:* The 2009 Recovery Act expands the issuance of tax credit bonds beyond the four categories provided for under pre 2009 Recovery Act. One of these provisions, Code Sec. 54AA, permits an issuer of a bond that qualifies as a tax exempt bond other than a private activity bond and is issued before Jan. 1, 2011 to irrevocably designate the bond as a build America bond. The holder then receives a 35% tax credit on the bond interest, but must include the interest in income. If a build America bond is to be used entirely for capital expenditures, the issuer may irrevocably elect to receive a payment from Treasury of 35% of the interest paid on the bond, instead of the holder receiving a tax credit, by applying new Code Sec. 6431, see ¶ 1301.
>
> The 2009 Recovery Act treats a recovery zone economic development bond as qualifying under Code Sec. 6431 but increases the payment to the issuer (or other payor of the interest) to 45% of the interest paid on the bond.

The bond must be designated by the issuer as a recovery zone economic development bond and all "available project proceeds" must be used in the zone for:

. . . capital expenditures,

FTC 2d References are to Federal Tax Coordinator 2d
FIN References are to RIA's Analysis of Federal Taxes: Income
USTR References are to United States Tax Reporter: Income
PE References are to Pension Explanations

... construction of public infrastructure and public facilities, and

... expenditures for job training and educational programs.

Recovery zone facility bonds. A Recovery zone facility bond is a tax exempt facilities bond if::

... at least 95% of the net proceeds are to be used for recovery zone property,

... it is issued before Jan. 1, 2011, and

... it is designated as a recovery zone economic development bond by the issuer. (Code Sec. 1400U-3(b)(1))

Property is recovery zone property if:

... it is depreciable tangible property (even if the taxpayer elects to expense it) constructed, reconstructed, renovated or purchased by the taxpayer (from an unrelated party that is not a member of the taxpayer's control group) after the effective date of the zone designation;

... the original use of the property in the recovery zone commences with the taxpayer; and

... substantially all the use of the property is in the recovery zone and in the taxpayer's active conduct of a qualified business (see ¶ 1307) in the zone. (Code Sec. 1400U-3(c)(1))

An issuer is limited to issuing an amount of bonds that doesn't exceed the amount of the ($15 billion) national limitation allocated to it. (Code Sec. 1400U-3(b)(2))

For special rules, see ¶ 1307.

A recovery zone is:

(1) any area designated by the issuer as having significant poverty, unemployment, home foreclosures, or general distress, (Code Sec. 1400U-1(b)(1))

(2) any area designated by the issuer as distressed by reason of the closure or realignment or a military installation, see ¶ 1305, (Code Sec. 1400U-1(b)(2)) and

(3) any area for which a designation as an empowerment zone or renewal community is in effect. (Code Sec. 1400U-1(b)(3)) see ¶ 1305.

☐ **Effective:** Obligations issued after Feb. 17, 2009 (2009 Recovery Act §1401(c)) and before Jan. 1, 2011. (Code Sec. 1400U-2(b)); (Code Sec. 1400U-3(b)(1)(B))

¶ 1305. National limits for recovery zone economic development bonds and recovery zone facility bonds issued in 2009 and 2010 are allocated among states based on their 2008 employment declines subject to a minimum allocation

Code Sec. 1400U-1, as added by 2009 Recovery Act § 1401(a)
Generally effective: Obligations issued after Feb. 17, 2009 and before 2011
Committee Reports, see ¶ 5054

For an overview of the background and 2009 Recovery Act changes regarding recovery zone economic development bonds and recovery zone facility bonds that are authorized under the rules discussed below, see ¶ 1304. For a complete discussion of recovery zone economic development bonds, see ¶ 1306. For a complete discussion of recovery zone facility bonds, see ¶ 1307.

New Law. The 2009 Recovery Act permits an issuer (which will be a government body under the rules discussed below) to designate an area as a recovery zone by reason of (1) its having significant poverty, unemployment, rate or home foreclosures, or general distress or (2) its being distressed by the closure or realignment or a military installation under the Defense Base Closure and Realignment Act of 1990. A recovery zone also includes any area for which a designation as an empowerment zone or renewal community is in effect. Issuers may issue recovery zone economic development bonds (see ¶ 1306) and recovery zone facility bonds (see ¶ 1307) for these zones. (Com Rept, see ¶ 5054)

IRS must allocate the national recovery zone economic development bond limitation (see below) and the national recovery zone facility bond limitation (see below) as follows:

(1) Allocate each limitation among the states in the proportion that each State's 2008 state employment decline bears to the total of the 2008 state employment declines for all the states. (Code Sec. 1400U-1(a)(1)(A) as added by 2009 Recovery Act §1401(a))

(2) Adjust the allocation for each state for any calendar year to the extent necessary to ensure that no state receives less than nine tenths of one percent (.9%) of the national recovery zone economic development bond limitation and nine tenths of one percent (.9%) of the national recovery zone facility bond limitation. (Code Sec. 1400U-1(a)(1)(B))

The 2008 state employment decline for any state is the excess if any of:

FTC 2d References are to Federal Tax Coordinator 2d
FIN References are to RIA's Analysis of Federal Taxes: Income
USTR References are to United States Tax Reporter: Income
PE References are to Pension Explanations

(1) the number of individuals employed in that state as determined for Dec. 2007, (Code Sec. 1400U-1(a)(2)(A)) over

(2) the number of individuals employed in the that state as determined for Dec. 2008. (Code Sec. 1400U-1(a)(2)(B))

> *observation:* The number of individuals employed in Dec. 2007 and in Dec. 2008, is presumably used because the number of persons employed in Dec. 2008, is available not too long after the end of the year. Thus, the fact that these numbers may be affected by out migration is presumably outweighed by the difficulty of securing that information without census numbers. Also, using the number of persons employed is probably preferable to using an unemployment rate since that raises an issue as to how to treat persons not seeking work because they have abandoned hope of landing a job.

The provision does not specify how may hours of work a week is required for a person to be considered employed (see observation (above)), and how self-employed persons are treated for purposes of this rule, but the legislative history mentions that Bureau of Labor Statistics data on state employment is available thus indicating that the Bureau's standards are expected to be followed. (Com Rept, see ¶ 5054)

Each state for which an allocation is made must reallocate the amount allocated to it among the counties and "large" municipalities in that state in the proportion that each county's or large municipality's 2008 employment decline bears to the total employment declines for all the counties and municipalities in the state. A county or municipality may waive any portion of this allocation. (Code Sec. 1400U-1(a)(3)(A))

> *observation:* The 2009 Recovery Act doesn't say what happens to the amount that is waived. Presumably the county or municipality that waives an allocation can't designate where the allocation goes and it is subject to reallocation as if the waived amount hadn't been allocated to the waiving county or municipality in the first place. An allocation might be waived, because the local government wishes to avoid responsibility for repaying a bond issue.

A large municipality is a municipality with a population of more than 100,000. (Code Sec. 1400U-1(a)(3)(B))

> *observation:* It is not entirely clear if the more than 100,000 population test for a large municipality is made in Dec. 2007 or Dec. 2008, although it is arguable that this should be determined when the allocation is made. Thus, if a municipality has a population of 101,000 in Dec. 2007 and a population of 95,000 in Dec. 2008, is it a large municipality? It is also not entirely clear as to who is included in the population,

(e.g., only legal residents?) and where the population information comes from years after the last census. But these questions will probably arise in only a handful of cases.

The employment decline of any municipality or county is determined in the same manner as determining the state employment decline under the immediately preceding list, except that if a portion of a municipality is in a county, that portion is treated as part of the municipality and not as part of the county. (Code Sec. 1400U-1(a)(3)(C))

> ⓇⒾⒶ *observation:* If one or more states did not suffer a decline in 2008 employment and there was no decline in employment in any county or large municipality the allocation formula doesn't work. Also, if one or more states did not suffer a decline in 2008 employment and there was only a small decline in employment in one or two sparsely populated counties, the per capital allocation could be quite large, since each state is guaranteed at least a $90 million limitation for recovery zone economic development bonds and a $135 million limitation for recovery zone facility bonds (see immediately below). Thus, there can be a large disparity between the amount allocated per capita of increased unemployment. To some degree this is consistent with the designation of Empowerment zones and enterprise communities which include in each case a designated percentage of rural communities, see FTC 2d/FIN ¶ J-3375 *et seq.*

A $10 billion national limitation applies to recovery zone economic development bonds, (Code Sec. 1400U-1(a)(4)(A)) and a $15 billion national limitation applies to recovery zone facility bonds. (Code Sec. 1400U-1(a)(4)(B))

> ⓇⒾⒶ *observation:* Recovery zone economic development bonds and recovery zone facility bonds must be issued before Jan. 1, 2011 (see ¶ 1306 and ¶ 1307) and after Feb. 17, 2009 (see below). Thus, they are part of a two year stimulus package.

For purposes of the rules discussed above and at ¶ 1304, ¶ 1306 and ¶ 1307, a recovery zone is:

(1) any area designated by the issuer as having significant poverty, unemployment, home foreclosures, or general distress, (Code Sec. 1400U-1(b)(1))

(2) any area designated by the issuer as distressed by reason of the closure or realignment or a military installation under the Defense Base Closure and Realignment Act of 1990, (Code Sec. 1400U-1(b)(2)) and

---

FTC 2d References are to Federal Tax Coordinator 2d
FIN References are to RIA's Analysis of Federal Taxes: Income
USTR References are to United States Tax Reporter: Income
PE References are to Pension Explanations

(3) any area for which a designation as an empowerment zone or renewal community (see FTC 2d/FIN ¶ J-3375 *et seq.*) is in effect. (Code Sec. 1400U-1(b)(3))

☐ **Effective:** Obligations issued after Feb. 17, 2009. (2009 Recovery Act §1401(c)) and before Jan. 1, 2011. (Code Sec. 1400U-2(b)); (Code Sec. 1400U-3(b)(1)(B))

¶ 1306. U.S. Treasury will pay the issuer 45% of the interest the issuer pays to the holder of a taxable recovery zone economic development bond issued before 2011

Code Sec. 1400U-2, as added by 2009 Recovery Act § 1401(a)
Generally effective: Obligations issued after Feb. 17, 2009 and before 2011
Committee Reports, see ¶ 5054

For an overview of the background and 2009 Recovery Act changes regarding the recovery zone economic development bonds that are discussed below, see ¶ 1304. For a complete discussion of the allocation of the national limit on the issuance of recovery zone economic development bonds and the statutory definition of a recovery zone, see ¶ 1305. For a complete discussion of recovery zone facility bonds, see ¶ 1307.

New Law. As discussed at ¶ 1305, the 2009 Recovery Act authorizes the issuance of $10 billion of recovery zone economic development bonds before Jan. 1, 2011. The governmental issuer (or other payor) receives a payment equal to 45% of the interest it pays on the bond under the immediately following list.

A recovery zone economic development bond (see definition below):

(1) is treated as a qualified bond for purposes of Code Sec. 6431 as added by 2009 Recovery Act §1531(b), see ¶ 1301. (Code Sec. 1400U-2(a)(1) as added by 2009 Recovery Act §1401(a)) and

(2) on each interest payment date the issuer of the bond (or any person who makes a payment under the bond for the issuer) receives a payment from the U.S. Treasury equal to 45% of the interest payable under the bond on that date. (Code Sec. 1400U-2(a)(2))

> *observation:* 2009 Recovery Act §1531(a) adds Code Sec. 54AA, which expands the category of taxable government bonds providing a tax credit to the holder (from the four types of bonds qualifying for this treatment under pre-2009 Recovery Act law) to include a new category, of bonds referred to as build America bonds. A build America bond is a bond (i) that would otherwise qualify as tax exempt, (ii) is not a private activity bond, (iii) is issued before Jan. 1, 2011 and (iv)

for which the issuer makes an irrevocably election. The holder of a build America bond receives a tax credit equal to 35% of the interest payable on each bond on each interest payment date. If a build America bond is part of an issue 100% of whose "available project proceeds" (over amounts in a "required reserve") are to be used for capital expenditures, the issuer can irrevocably elect to have the bond treated as a "qualified bond." If this election is made, new Code Sec. 6431 will apply and the issuer will receive a payment from the U.S. Treasury equal to 35% of the interest it pays (instead of the holder receiving a tax credit). The Treasury's payment is contemporaneous with the interest payment made by the issuer, and it may be made to a person making the interest payment on behalf of the issuer. For a complete discussion of new Code Sec. 54AA, and new Code Sec. 6431, see ¶ 1301.

Item (1) of the above list makes new Code Sec. 6431 applicable, so the issuer of a recovery zone economic development bond qualifies to receive a payment from Treasury. Item (2) provides that, for a recovery zone economic development bond, the payment from Treasury is 45% of the interest payable under the bond, instead of the 35% that would otherwise apply under Code Sec. 6431.

A recovery zone economic development bond is any build America bond (as defined in Code Sec. 54AA(d) (see observation (above) and ¶ 1301) issued before Jan. 1, 2011, as part of an issue if:

(1) 100% of the available project proceeds (as defined in Code Sec. 54A, i.e., the excess of the proceeds from the sale of the issue over the (i) issuance costs financed by the issue (not to exceed 2% of the proceeds) and (ii) the proceeds from any investment of that excess (see FTC 2d/FIN ¶ L-15540) of the issue, are to be used for one or more qualified economic development purposes, (see below) (Code Sec. 1400U-2(b)(1)(A)) and

(2) the issuer designates the bond for purposes of Code Sec. 1400U-2. (Code Sec. 1400U-2(b)(1)(B))

observation: Since these bonds are government bonds, the restrictions applicable to private activity bonds won't apply.

The maximum total of bonds which may be designated by any issuer under item (2) of the immediately preceding list may not exceed the amount of the recovery zone economic development bond limitation allocated to that issuer under Code Sec. 1400U-1, see ¶ 1305. (Code Sec. 1400U-2(b)(2))

FTC 2d References are to Federal Tax Coordinator 2d
FIN References are to RIA's Analysis of Federal Taxes: Income
USTR References are to United States Tax Reporter: Income
PE References are to Pension Explanations

observation: Thus, the issuer is limited to its share of the $10 billion national limitation allocated to it.

A qualified economic development purpose (item (1) of the immediately preceding list) means expenditures for purposes of promoting development or other economic activity in a recovery zone, including:

(A) capital expenditures paid or incurred with respect to property located in the zone, (Code Sec. 1400U-2(c)(1))

(B) expenditures for public infrastructure and construction of public facilities, (Code Sec. 1400U-2(c)(2)) and

(C) expenditures for job training and educational programs. (Code Sec. 1400U-2(c)(3))

A recovery zone is:

(1) any area designated by the issuer as having significant poverty, unemployment, home foreclosures, or general distress, (Code Sec. 1400U-1(b)(1))

(2) any area designated by the issuer as distressed by reason of the closure or realignment or a military installation under the Defense Base Closure and Realignment Act of 1990, (Code Sec. 1400U-1(b)(2)) and

(3) any area for which a designation as an empowerment zone or renewal community (see FTC 2d/FIN ¶ J-3375 *et seq.*) is in effect. (Code Sec. 1400U-1(b)(3))

observation: As compared to other Code Sec. 6431 bonds, recovery zone economic development bonds pay 45% of the interest paid instead of 35%. This greater subsidy is likely provided because the bonds are perceived as satisfying the gold standard of both relieving distress and also promoting economic development through useful expenditures (particularly item (B) of the second preceding list). Another factor may be a perceived need to encourage cash-strapped local governments to act. Although these bonds can only be issued in 2009 and 2110, Treasury will continue to make interest payment for well into the future. On the other hand, the issuer, and not Treasury, is responsible for paying the principal and 55% of the interest, so the issuer may be expected to choose projects with some care.

observation: Recovery zone economic development bonds are subject to the Davis-Bacon Act requirements that the minimum wage paid must be the average local wage (the prevailing wage), see ¶ 1311.

☐ **Effective:** Obligations issued after Feb. 17, 2009 (2009 Recovery Act §1401(c)) and before Jan. 1, 2011. (Code Sec. 1400U-2(b)(1))

¶ 1307. Recovery zone facility bonds are authorized for issuance in 2009 and 2010

Code Sec. 1400U-3, as added by 2009 Recovery Act § 1401(a)
Generally effective: Obligations issued after Feb. 17, 2009 and before 2011
Committee Reports, see ¶ 5054

For an overview of the background and 2009 Recovery Act changes regarding the recovery zone facility bonds that are discussed below, see ¶ 1304. For a complete discussion of the allocation of the national limit on the issuance of recovery zone facility bonds and the statutory definition of a recovery zone, see ¶ 1305. For a complete discussion of recovery zone economic development bonds, see ¶ 1306.

New Law. Recovery zone facility bonds are treated as exempt facility bonds. (Code Sec. 1400U-3(a) as added by 2009 Recovery Act §1401(a)). Thus, the 2009 Recovery Act creates a new category of exempt facility bonds. (Com Rept, see ¶ 5054)

> **RIA** *observation:* Thus, they may qualify as tax-exempt, qualified private activity bonds, see FTC 2d/FIN ¶ J-3153; USTR ¶ 1424; TaxDesk ¶ 158,010.

A recovery zone facility bond must be:

(1) part of an issue 95% or more of whose net proceeds (i.e., issue proceeds less amounts in a reasonably required reserve or replacement fund) are to be used for recovery zone property (see below); (Code Sec. 1400U-3(b)(1)(A))

(2) issued before Jan. 1, 2011; (Code Sec. 1400U-3(b)(1)(B)) and

(3) designated by the issuer as a recovery zone facility bond. (Code Sec. 1400U-3(b)(1)(C))

The total face amount of bonds that may be designated by the issuer (item (3) on the above list) must not exceed the amount of the recovery zone facility bond limitation allocated to the issuer under the rules at ¶ 1305. (Code Sec. 1400U-3(b)(2))

Recovery zone property (item (1) on the above list) is tangible property depreciable under Code Sec. 168 (even if the taxpayer elects to expense it under Code Sec. 179), if:

(1) the property was constructed, reconstructed, renovated, or acquired by purchase (as defined in Code Sec. 179(d)(2), see FTC 2d/FIN ¶ L-9925 *et seq.*)

FTC 2d References are to Federal Tax Coordinator 2d
FIN References are to RIA's Analysis of Federal Taxes: Income
USTR References are to United States Tax Reporter: Income
PE References are to Pension Explanations

by the taxpayer after the effective date of the zone designation; (Code Sec. 1400U-3(c)(1)(A))

(2) the original use of the property in the recovery zone commences with the taxpayer; (Code Sec. 1400U-3(c)(1)(B)) and

(3) substantially all the use of the property is in the recovery zone and in the active conduct of a qualified business (see below) by the taxpayer in the zone. (Code Sec. 1400U-3(c)(1)(C))

> *observation:* The Code Sec. 179(d)(2) definition of a purchase in item (1) of the immediately preceding list will exclude property acquired from a "related" party, a decedent, another member of a controlled group, or in a carryover basis transaction.

> *observation:* The rules of the immediately preceding list track certain Code Sec. 1397D rules for empowerment zones. The property only has to be (i) new *to the zone* with the taxpayer, as the first user *in the zone,* and (ii) used in an active (qualified) business in the zone. The qualified business restriction (immediately below) doesn't narrow this broad scope significantly. Thus, the perceived need to promote economic activity in recovery zones may be seen to trump the economic policy of encouraging the production of new property.

A qualified business (item (3) above) is any trade or business other than:

... the rental to others of residential real property as defined in Code Sec. 168(e)(2), see FTC 2d/FIN ¶ L-8203; USTR ¶ 1684.02; TaxDesk ¶ 266,202; (Code Sec. 1400U-3(c)(2)(A)) or

... the operation of a facility described in Code Sec. 144(c)(6)(B) (including the provision of land for) any private or commercial golf course, country club, massage parlor, hot tub facility, suntan facility, racetrack or other facility used for gambling, or any store the principal business of which is the sale of alcoholic beverages for consumption off premises, see FTC 2d/FIN ¶ L-9960; USTR ¶ 14,00N4.005; TaxDesk ¶ 268,432. (Code Sec. 1400U-3(c)(2)(B))

Rules similar to the rules of Code Sec. 1397D(a)(2) (defining substantially renovated property and including it as qualified zone property, see FTC 2d/FIN ¶ L-9953; USTR ¶ 1397A4) and Code Sec. 1397D(b) (providing that property sold and leased back by the taxpayer within three months after it was originally placed in service is treated as originally placed in service not earlier than the date on which it is used under the lease back) apply in determining if property is recovery zone property. (Code Sec. 1400U-3(c)(3))

> *observation:* Under Code Sec. 1397D(a)(2) property is treated as substantially renovated by the taxpayer if additions to basis in the hands of the taxpayer during any 24 month period beginning on the date the

designation of the zone took effect exceed the greater of the adjusted basis at the beginning of the period or $5,000. Since under the 2009 Act, a recovery zone includes any area designated by the issuer as having significant poverty, unemployment, home foreclosures, or general distress (see item (1) on the second list at ¶ 1305), a new area may be designated some months into 2009. Thus, under the 24 month rule, expenditures made in 2011, presumably beyond the time stimulus is hoped to be effective, would qualify. However, the possible delay allowed in getting the impact of expenditures is not unique to this rule.

Code Sec. 146 (relating to the total annual state private activity bond volume limits on certain exempt facility bonds FTC 2d/FIN ¶ J-3252 (FTC 2d/FIN ¶ J-3253; USTR ¶ 1464.01) and Code Sec. 147(d) (not permitting the acquisition of existing property) do not apply to recovery zone facility bonds. (Code Sec. 1400U-3(d)) However, subject to these two exceptions, issuance of recovery zone facility bonds is subject to the general rules applicable to issuance of qualified private activity bonds. (Com Rept, see ¶ 5054)

> **🅡🅐** *observation:* Thus, it appears that recovery zone facility bonds are subject to the bond maturity requirement applicable to other exempt facility bonds, i.e., that the average life of the bonds must not be more than 120% of the average reasonably expected economic life of the facilities being financed. See FTC 2d/FIN ¶s J-3266, J-3267. But whereas other exempt facility bonds finance infrastructure of a specific type (such as airports, residential rental projects; sewage facilities, and solid waste disposal facilities), recovery zone facility bonds can potentially finance a bewildering variety of depreciable property, including used property that is new to the zone. Thus, it will at best be difficult, and perhaps impossible, to apply the bond maturity requirement.

☐ **Effective:** Obligations issued after Feb. 17, 2009 (2009 Recovery Act §1401(c)) and before Jan. 1, 2011. (Code Sec. 1400U-3(b)(1)(B))

¶ 1308. Pass-through of tax credit bond credits by RICs and REITs is modified and expanded

Code Sec. 853A, as added by 2009 Recovery Act § 1541(a)
Code Sec. 54A(h), as amended by 2009 Recovery Act § 1541(b)
Generally effective: Tax years ending after Feb. 17, 2009
Committee Reports, see ¶ 5072

FTC 2d References are to Federal Tax Coordinator 2d
FIN References are to RIA's Analysis of Federal Taxes: Income
USTR References are to United States Tax Reporter: Income
PE References are to Pension Explanations

Regulated investment companies (RICs) and real estate investment trusts (REITs) that distribute the required percentage of their income and satisfy other requirements are allowed to deduct the dividends they pay. Thus, they are allowed to pass through their income to their shareholders without a tax at the entity level. In addition, RICs can pass through the character of certain items, such as capital gains, qualified dividends, tax-exempt interest, dividends eligible for the corporate dividends-received deduction, and foreign taxes paid to shareholders by RICs. (FTC 2d/FIN ¶ E-6150, ¶ E-6151 *et seq.*; USTR ¶ 8524.02; TaxDesk ¶ 173,000.1)

REITs are able to pass through the character of capital gains dividends and qualifying dividends to shareholders, but are not able to pass through the character of other items. (FTC 2d/FIN ¶ E-6600, ¶ E-6616 *et seq.*; USTR ¶ 8574.02; TaxDesk ¶ 173,006)

Holders of tax credit bonds receive tax credits in lieu of interest. The holders of the bonds must include the amount of the credits in income as interest. In addition to the pass-through of the items described above, the 2005 Energy Act (Sec. 1303, PL 109-58, 8/8/2005) added a provision that allowed RICs to pass through of the tax credit relating to clean renewable energy bonds (CREBs) to their shareholders under procedures to be prescribed by IRS. (FTC 2d/FIN ¶ L-16480, ¶ L-16482, ¶ L-16483; USTR ¶ 544) The 2008 Farm Act (Sec. 15316, PL 110-246, 6/18/2008) added a provision that allowed both RICs and REITs to pass through credits generated by other tax credit bonds to their shareholders under procedures to be prescribed by IRS. Under the 2008 Farm Act rules, the tax credits for the following bonds could be passed through:

. . . qualified forestry conservation bonds,

. . . new clean renewable energy bonds (new CREBs),

. . . qualified energy conservation bonds, and

. . . qualified zone academy bonds (QZABs).

However, IRS has not issued any procedures for the pass-through of the credit. (FTC 2d/FIN ¶ L-15530, ¶ L-15532, ¶ L-15533; USTR ¶ 54A4.01)

New Law. The 2009 Recovery Act modifies the pass-through rules to allow the pass-through of the credit from tax credit bonds to shareholders of both RIC and REITs.

Accordingly, the RIC provisions are amended so that a RIC that (i) holds (directly or indirectly) one or more tax credit bonds (see below) on one or more applicable dates (defined below) during the tax year (Code Sec. 853A(a)(1) as added by 2009 Recovery Act §1541(a)) and (ii) satisfies its distribution requirements and other pass-through requirements for the tax year may elect to pass through the credits allowable to the RIC during the tax year for the bonds. (Code Sec. 853A(a)(2))

If the election is in effect for the tax year:

(1) the RIC itself may not take any of the credits that it elects to pass through to its shareholders for the tax year (Code Sec. 853A(b)(1));

(2) the RIC (i) must include in gross income (as interest) for the tax year an amount equal to the amount that the RIC would have included in gross income relating to the credits if the election had not been made (Code Sec. 853A(b)(2)(A)) and (ii) must increase the amount of its dividends paid deduction for the tax year by the amount of the income (Code Sec. 853A(b)(2)(B)); and

(3) each shareholder of the RIC (a) must include in gross income an amount equal to the shareholder's proportionate share of the interest income attributable to the credits (Code Sec. 853A(b)(3)(A)) and (b) may take its proportionate share of the credits against its taxes. (Code Sec. 853A(b)(3)(B))

A shareholder's proportionate share of the credits passed through to the shareholder (Code Sec. 853A(c)(1)) and the gross income relating to the credits passed through (Code Sec. 853A(c)(2)) may not exceed the amounts designated by the RIC in a written notice mailed to its shareholders not later than 60 days after the close of its tax year. (Code Sec. 853A(c))

The election to pass through the credits and the notice to shareholders must be made in the manner prescribed by IRS. (Code Sec. 853A(d))

Tax credit bonds for which credits may be passed through include the following:

. . . qualified tax credit bonds described at Code Sec. 54A(d) (i.e., qualified forestry conservation bonds, new CREBs, qualified energy conservation bonds, qualified zone academy bonds, and qualified school construction bonds, see ¶ 1302) (Code Sec. 853A(e)(1)(A)(i)),

. . . Build America Bonds (a new type of bond provided under the 2009 Recovery Act, see ¶ 1301) (Code Sec. 853A(e)(1)(A)(ii)),

. . . any other bonds for which a credit is allowed under subpart H of part IV of subchapter A of the Code (i.e., CREBs). (Code Sec. 853A(e)(1)(A)(iii))

The applicable date means (i) in the case of qualified tax credit bonds or CREBs, any credit allowance date as defined in Code Sec. 54A(e)(1) (Code Sec. 853A(e)(1)(B)(i)) and (ii) in the case of a Build America Bond, any interest payment date, as defined in Code Sec. 54AA(e)(see ¶ 1301). (Code Sec. 853A(e)(1)(B)(ii))

FTC 2d References are to Federal Tax Coordinator 2d
FIN References are to RIA's Analysis of Federal Taxes: Income
USTR References are to United States Tax Reporter: Income
PE References are to Pension Explanations

observation: The credit allowance dates are defined in Code Sec. 54A(e)(1) as Mar. 15, June 15, Sep. 15, Dec. 15, and the last day on which a bond is outstanding, see FTC 2d/FIN ¶ L-15535; USTR ¶ 54A4.

If the ownership of a tax credit bond is "stripped" (i.e., separated from the credit relating to the bond), the election to pass through the credit applies by reference to the instruments evidencing the entitlement to the credit rather than the tax credit bond. (Code Sec. 853A(e)(2))

REITs are also allowed to pass through credits for qualified tax credit bonds (together with the income that relates to the credits) under procedures to be prescribed by IRS. (Code Sec. 54A(h) as amended by 2009 Recovery Act §1541(b)(2))

observation: Thus, REITs will not be allowed to pass through the credit for CREBs and build America bonds. Presumably, IRS will prescribe REIT pass-thorough rules that are similar to the RIC pass-through rules.

IRS is directed to issue regs or other guidance that may be necessary or appropriate to carry out the purposes of these rules, including methods for determining a shareholder's proportionate share of credits. (Code Sec. 853A(f))

As a conforming change, the pre-2009 Recovery Act credit pass-through rules are repealed. (Code Sec. 54(l) as amended by 2009 Recovery Act §1541(b)(1)) (Code Sec. 54A(h))

☐ **Effective:** Tax years ending after Feb. 17, 2009. (2009 Recovery Act §1541(c))

¶ 1309. Tax-exempt interest expense safe harbors for banks and small issuers are expanded for obligations issued in 2009 and 2010

Code Sec. 265(b)(7), as amended by 2009 Recovery Act § 1501(a)
Code Sec. 291(e)(1)(B)(iv), as amended by 2009 Recovery Act § 1501(b)
Code Sec. 265(b)(3)(G), as amended by 2009 Recovery Act § 1502(a)
Generally effective: Obligations issued after Dec. 31, 2008
Committee Reports, see ¶ 5060

The interest deduction is disallowed for interest on debt incurred or continued to purchase or carry obligations the interest on which is tax exempt. The disallowance applies only if the taxpayer has a purpose of using borrowed funds to purchase or carry tax-exempt obligations. IRS ordinarily takes the position that it will not infer that a taxpayer's borrowing had a purpose to purchase or carry tax-exempt obligations if the taxpayer's investment in tax-exempt obligations is insubstantial. In the case of an individual, the holdings of tax-exempt obligations are presumed to be insubstantial if during the tax year the average adjusted basis of the individual's tax-exempt obligations is 2% or less of the average adjusted basis of the individual's portfolio investments and assets held by the individual in the active conduct of a trade or business. In the case of a corporation, a similar 2% test is applied to the adjusted basis of the corporation's assets. (FTC 2d/FIN ¶ K-5520, ¶ K-5522.1; USTR ¶ 2654; TaxDesk ¶ 316,009 *et seq.*)

In the case of a financial institution, the disallowance applies to the portion of the interest expense that bears the same ratio to the interest expense as the average adjusted bases of tax-exempt obligations acquired after Aug. 7, '86, bears to the average adjusted bases of all assets of the taxpayer. An exception to the disallowance rule for financial institutions applies for interest expenses allocable under the pro rata rule to qualified tax-exempt obligations, for which only 20% of the interest expense is disallowed, as described below. (FTC 2d/FIN ¶ E-3100, ¶ E-3111, ¶ E-3112)

A qualified tax-exempt obligation is a tax-exempt obligation that (1) is issued after Aug. 7, '86 by a qualified small issuer, (2) is not a private activity bond, and (3) is designated by the issuer as qualifying for the exception.

A qualified small issuer is an issuer that reasonably anticipates that the amount of tax-exempt obligations that it will issue during the calendar year will be $10 million or less. For purposes of the $10 million limitation, (i) an issuer and all entities that issue obligations on behalf of such issuer are treated as one issuer, (ii) issuers and all obligations issued by a subordinate entity are treated as being issued by the parent entity, and (iii) an entity formed (or availed of) to avoid the $10 million limitation and all entities benefiting from the device are treated as one issuer.

Composite issues (i.e., combined issues of bonds for different entities) qualify for the qualified tax-exempt obligation exception only if certain requirements of the exception are met regarding (a) the composite issue as a whole (determined by treating the composite issue as a single issue) and (b) each separate lot of obligations that is part of the issue (determined by treating each separate lot of obligations as a separate issue). Thus, a composite issue may qualify for the exception only if the composite issue itself does not exceed $10 million and each issuer benefitting from the composite issue reasonably anticipates that it will not issue more than $10 million of tax-exempt obligations during the calendar year, including through the composite arrangement.

FTC 2d References are to Federal Tax Coordinator 2d
FIN References are to RIA's Analysis of Federal Taxes: Income
USTR References are to United States Tax Reporter: Income
PE References are to Pension Explanations

The amount allowable as a deduction to a financial institution for interest incurred to carry a qualified tax-exempt obligation is treated in the same manner as the interest on debt incurred to carry tax-exempt obligations acquired after Dec. 31, '82, and before Aug. 8, '86. Accordingly, the amount allowable is treated as a financial institution preference item, with the result that the deduction is reduced by 20%. (FTC 2d/FIN ¶ E-3124, ¶ E-3127, ¶ E-3128, ¶ E-3131, ¶ E-3133; USTR ¶ 2654)

New Law. The 2009 Recovery Act provides that tax-exempt obligations issued in 2009 and 2010 are not taken into account in determining the pro rata portion of interest incurred by a financial institution that is disallowed. (Code Sec. 265(b)(7)(A) as amended by 2009 Recovery Act §1501(a)) This exception applies for up to 2% of the average adjusted bases of all assets of the taxpayer. (Code Sec. 265(b)(7)(B))

For this purpose, a refunding bond (whether a current or advance refunding) is treated as issued on the issue date of the refunded bond (or in the case of a series of refundings, the original bond). (Code Sec. 265(b)(7)(C))

> **RIA** *observation:* This means that the qualified tax-exempt obligation exception won't apply to a refunding bond unless the bond it refunds (or the original bond, if the refunding is part of a series of refundings) is issued in 2009 or 2010 (or another exception applies). On the other hand, the exception will apply to a refunding bond issued after 2010 if the bond it refunds (or the original bond, if the refunding is part of a series of refundings) is issued in 2009 or 2010.

The portion of any obligation not taken into account under the above rule is treated as acquired on Aug. 7, '86 (Code Sec. 291(e)(1)(B)(iv) as amended by 2009 Recovery Act §1501(b)), with the result that it is treated as a financial institution preference item. Thus, the interest allowable as a deduction for interest incurred to carry that item is reduced by 20%. (Com Rept, see ¶ 5060)

The 2009 Recovery Act also amends the small issuer exception so that the annual limit for tax-exempt obligations issued in 2009 and 2010 is $30 million (rather than $10 million). (Code Sec. 265(b)(3)(G)(i) as amended by 2009 Recovery Act §1502(a)) For purposes of the exemption for tax-exempt obligations, a qualified Code Sec. 501(c)(3) bond (defined under Code Sec. 145, see FTC 2d/FIN ¶ J-3248; USTR ¶ 1454), issued during 2009 or 2010 for the benefit of a Code Sec. 501(c)(3) organization is treated as issued by the tax-exempt organization for whose benefit the bond was issued (Code Sec. 265(b)(3)(G)(ii)), rather than the actual issuer. Thus, the amount that may be issued for the benefit of a Code Sec. 501(c)(3) organization is limited to $30 million. (Com Rept, see ¶ 5060)

An exception from the composite issue rules described above applies for qualified financing issues issued during 2009 or 2010, under which the above rules limiting the amount of the composite issue do not apply. (Code Sec. 265(b)(3)(G)(iii)(I)) Instead, any obligation issued as a part of the issue is treated as a qualified tax-exempt obligation if the relevant requirements are met for each qualified portion of the issue (determined by treating each qualified portion as a separate issue which is issued by the qualified borrower for which the portion relates). (Code Sec. 265(b)(3)(G)(iii)(II))

For this purpose, a qualified financing issue is any composite, pooled, or other conduit financing issue for which the proceeds are used directly or indirectly to make or finance loans to one or more ultimate borrowers each of whom is a qualified borrower. (Code Sec. 265(b)(3)(G)(iv)). The qualified portion is the portion of the proceeds that are used for each qualified borrower under the issue. (Code Sec. 265(b)(3)(G)(v)) A qualified borrower is a borrower that is a state or political subdivision thereof or a tax-exempt Code Sec. 501(c)(3) organization. (Code Sec. 265(b)(3)(G)(vi))

> *Illustration:* A $100 million pooled financing issue that was issued in 2009 may qualify for the exception if the proceeds of the issue are used to make four equal loans of $25 million to four qualified borrowers. However, if (1) more than $30 million is loaned to any qualified borrower, (2) any borrower is not a qualified borrower, or (3) any borrower would, if it were the issuer of a separate issue in an amount equal to the amount loaned to that borrower, fail to meet any of the other requirements of the small issue exception, the entire $100 million pooled financing issue will fail to qualify for the exception. (Com Rept, see ¶ 5060)

☐ **Effective:** Obligations issued after Dec. 31, 2008. (2009 Recovery Act §1501(c)); (2009 Recovery Act §1502(b))

¶ 1310. IDBs issued before 2011 may finance facilities used to create intangible property

Code Sec. 144(a)(12)(C), as amended by 2009 Recovery Act § 1301(a)
Generally effective: Bonds issued after Feb. 17, 2009 and before Jan. 1, 2011
Committee Reports, see ¶ 5051

The Code grants tax-exempt status to certain "small issues" of state or local bonds that would otherwise be taxable private activity bonds or taxable industrial development bonds (IDBs). Qualified small issue bonds may be issued to

---

FTC 2d References are to Federal Tax Coordinator 2d
FIN References are to RIA's Analysis of Federal Taxes: Income
USTR References are to United States Tax Reporter: Income
PE References are to Pension Explanations

finance manufacturing facilities. (FTC 2d/FIN ¶ J-3150, ¶ J-3277, ¶ J-3233.3; USTR ¶ 1444.01)

Under pre-2009 Recovery Act law, a manufacturing facility was one that was used to produce *tangible* personal property, including the processing that resulted in a change in the condition of the property. It included facilities that were directly related and ancillary to a manufacturing facility if (1) the facilities were on the same site as the manufacturing facility, and (2) not more than 25% of the net proceeds of the qualified issue were used to provide those facilities. There was a distinction between core manufacturing and activities directly related and ancillary to manufacturing. All ancillary activities had to occur at the same site as the core manufacturing activity, and the core manufacturing activity had to constitute substantially all of the on-site economic activity. (FTC 2d/FIN ¶ J-3233.3; USTR ¶ 1444.01)

New Law. The 2009 Recovery Act expands the definition of facilities to mean any facility that is used in manufacturing, creating, or producing either tangible property *or* intangible property within the meaning of Code Sec. 197(d)(1)(C)(iii) (i.e., a patent, copyright, formula, process, design, pattern, knowhow, format, or similar item, see FTC 2d/FIN ¶ L-7957; USTR ¶ 1974; TaxDesk ¶ 269,004). (Com Rept, see ¶ 5051) Specifically, for bonds issued after Feb. 17, 2009 and before Jan. 1, 2011, the net proceeds from a bond are considered to be used to provide a manufacturing facility if the proceeds are used to provide (Code Sec. 144(a)(12)(C)(iii) as amended by 2009 Recovery Act §1301(a)) a facility that's used in the creation or production of intangible property as described in Code Sec. 197(d)(1)(C)(iii). (Code Sec. 144(a)(12)(C)(iii)(I))

The 2009 Recovery Act also provides that facilities that are functionally related and subordinate to a manufacturing facility are treated as a manufacturing facility, and the 25% net proceeds restriction doesn't apply to these facilities. However, functionally related and subordinate facilities must still be located on the same site as the manufacturing facility. (Com Rept, see ¶ 5051) Specifically, also for bonds issued after Feb. 17, 2009 and before Jan. 1, 2011, the 25% net proceeds restriction doesn't apply for purposes of the definition of manufacturing facility. In addition, the net proceeds from a bond are considered to be used to provide such a manufacturing facility if the proceeds are used to provide (Code Sec. 144(a)(12)(C)(iii)) a facility that's functionally related and subordinate to a manufacturing facility (determined without regard to this new Code Sec. 144(a)(12)(C)(iii)(II)) if the facility is located on the same site as the manufacturing facility. (Code Sec. 144(a)(12)(C)(iii)(II))

☐ **Effective:** Bonds issued after Feb. 17, 2009 (2009 Recovery Act §1301(b)) and before Jan. 1, 2011. (Code Sec. 144(a)(12)(C)(iii))

¶ 1311. Prevailing wage requirements are applied to projects financed with specified bonds

Code Sec. 54C, 2009 Recovery Act § 1601(1)
Code Sec. 54D, 2009 Recovery Act § 1601(2)
Code Sec. 54E, 2009 Recovery Act § 1601(3)
Code Sec. 54F, 2009 Recovery Act § 1601(4)
Code Sec. 1400U-2, 2009 Recovery Act § 1601(5)
Generally effective: Bonds issued after Feb. 17, 2009
Committee Reports, see ¶ 5074

Subchapter IV of Chapter 31 of Title 40 of the U.S. Code (Sec. 3141 *et seq.*, often referred to as the Davis-Bacon Act) requires that an average local wage (the prevailing wage) is the minimum wage that can be paid on certain contracts to which the federal government is a party. This prevailing wage requirement applies to contractors and subcontractors on contracts in excess of $2,000 for the construction, alteration, or repair (including painting and decorating) of public buildings or public works. Related statutes have added prevailing wage requirements for other construction projects.

Taxpayers who hold "qualified tax credit bonds" on specified dates during the year are entitled to a nonrefundable credit equal to a portion of the bond's outstanding face amount. The credit is includable in gross income, and is treated as interest income. A qualified tax credit bond is a specified type of bond that is part of an issue that meets certain requirements. Under pre-2009 Recovery Act law, the types of bonds that can be qualified tax credit bonds were:

(A) qualified forestry conservation bonds,

(B) new clean renewable energy bonds (new CREBs) defined in Code Sec. 54C,

(C) qualified energy conservation bonds defined in Code Sec. 54D, and

(D) qualified zone academy bonds (QZABs) defined in Code Sec. 54E. (FTC 2d/FIN ¶ L-15530; USTR ¶ 54A4; TaxDesk ¶ 568,521)

New Law. The 2009 Recovery Act provides that the requirements of Subchapter IV of Chapter 31 of Title 40 of the U.S. Code, discussed above, will apply to projects financed with the proceeds of:

(1) any new clean renewable energy bond (as defined in Code Sec. 54C) issued after Feb. 17, 2009,

---

FTC 2d References are to Federal Tax Coordinator 2d
FIN References are to RIA's Analysis of Federal Taxes: Income
USTR References are to United States Tax Reporter: Income
PE References are to Pension Explanations

(2) any qualified energy conservation bond (as defined in Code Sec. 54D) issued after Feb. 17, 2009,

(3) any qualified zone academy bond (as defined in Code Sec. 54E) issued after Feb. 17, 2009,

(4) any qualified school construction bond (as defined in Code Sec. 54F) (see ¶ 1302), and

(5) any recovery zone economic development bond (as defined in Code Sec. 1400U-2) (see ¶ 1304 *et seq.*). (2009 Recovery Act §1601)

> *observation:* Thus, the prevailing wage requirements will apply to a broader class of contracts including those financed by the bonds listed above.

> *observation:* As indicated in the discussion of pre-2009 Recovery Act law, items (1) through (3) relate to bonds that existed before the 2009 Recovery Act. The Code sections authorizing each of those bonds were enacted in 2008 effective for bonds issued after Oct. 3, 2008. In contrast, items (4) and (5) above are based on provisions that were added to the Code by the 2009 Recovery Act. Qualified school construction bonds (item (4)) were added to the list of tax credit bonds described at (A) through (D) above, see ¶ 1302. For a discussion of recovery zone economic development bonds (item (5)), see ¶ 1304 *et seq.*

☐ **Effective:** Bonds issued after Feb. 17, 2009. (2009 Recovery Act §1601), (Com Rept, see ¶ 5074)

> *observation:* 2009 Recovery Act §1601 does not contain an effective date provision, but its references to the bonds listed in items (1) through (3) above specify that the new prevailing wage requirement applies to those bonds if they are issued after Feb. 17, 2009. No such reference exists, however, for qualified school construction bonds (item (4) above) and recovery zone economic development bonds (item (5) above), both of which were added by the 2009 Recovery Act, The new qualified school construction bond provision was added to the Code effective for bonds issued after Feb. 17, 2009. The new recovery zone economic development bond provision was added to the Code effective for obligations issued after Feb. 17, 2009. The prevailing wage requirement presumably applies to items (4) and (5) for bonds issued after Feb. 17, 2009.

¶ 1312. Vehicles must be capable of attaining a maximum speed in excess of 150 m.p.h. under amended definition of high-speed intercity rail facilities

Code Sec. 142(i)(1), as amended by 2009 Recovery Act § 1504(a)
Generally effective: Bonds issued after Feb. 17, 2009
Committee Reports, see ¶ 5063

A private activity bond that is part of an issue, 95% or more of the net proceeds of which are used to finance a high-speed intercity rail facility, qualifies as an exempt facility bond. A high-speed intercity rail facility is a facility, not including rolling stock, which uses a fixed guideway rail system to transport passengers and their baggage between metropolitan statistical areas. Under pre-2009 Recovery Act law, to be a qualified facility, the trains were reasonably expected to operate at speeds in excess of 150 miles per hour (m.p.h.) between scheduled stops. In addition, the facility must be available to the general public or passengers. (FTC 2d/FIN ¶ J-3150, ¶ J-3177; USTR ¶ 1424.04)

New Law. The 2009 Recovery Act modifies the requirement that high-speed intercity rail transportation facilities use vehicles that are reasonably expected to operate at speeds in excess of 150 m.p.h., instead requiring that the facilities use vehicles reasonably expected to attain a top speed in excess of 150 m.p.h. (Com Rept, see ¶ 5063) Thus, the 2009 Recovery Act amends the definition of high-speed intercity rail facility in Code Sec. 142(i)(1) to provide that it means any facility using vehicles that are reasonably expected to be capable of attaining a maximum speed in excess of 150 m.p.h. between scheduled stops. (Code Sec. 142(i)(1) as amended by 2009 Recovery Act §1504(a))

☐ **Effective:** Bonds issued after Feb. 17, 2009. (2009 Recovery Act §1504(b))

¶ 1313. Indian tribal governments can issue $2 billion of tribal economic development bonds

Code Sec. 7871(f), as amended by 2009 Recovery Act § 1402(a)
Generally effective: Bonds issued after Feb. 17, 2009
Committee Reports, see ¶ 5056

Bonds issued by tribal governments are tax-exempt if substantially all the proceeds will be used in the exercise of an essential government function. Essential government functions do not include any functions that aren't customarily performed by state or local governments with general taxing powers (that

FTC 2d References are to Federal Tax Coordinator 2d
FIN References are to RIA's Analysis of Federal Taxes: Income
USTR References are to United States Tax Reporter: Income
PE References are to Pension Explanations

is, items such as schools, roads, government buildings, park and recreation buildings, and the like). FTC 2d/FIN ¶ J-3008; USTR ¶ 78,714.02

Tribal governments can issue private activity bonds to finance tribal manufacturing facilities. The requirements that must be met by bonds issued under the manufacturing exception include:

(1) the bonds must be issued by an Indian tribal government or a subdivision, and no other person may use the bond proceeds or be responsible for the debt service in a manner that violates the business use and private payment tests that generally determine whether a bond is a private activity bond (see FTC 2d/FIN ¶ J-3101; USTR ¶ 1414.01; TaxDesk ¶ 158,009) or be a principal user of bond proceeds or bond financed property in a manner that violates franchiser restrictions on participation in qualified small issue bonds (see FTC 2d/FIN ¶ J-3227; USTR ¶ 1444.01; TaxDesk ¶ 158,010).

(2) at least 95% of the bonds' net proceeds must be used to finance acquisition, construction, reconstruction or improvement of depreciable property which is a part of a manufacturing facility.

(3) at least 95% of the net proceeds must be used to finance property that is (a) located on Indian tribal land that has been held in trust by the U.S. for the issuing tribe for at least five years immediately preceding issuance, and while the bonds are outstanding; and that is (b) owned and operated by the issuer (or a wholly-owned Indian corporation on its behalf or a joint venture between tribal governments).

(4) an employment test (requiring at least $1 of wages to be paid to members of the tribe for each $20 of bonds outstanding) must be met. (FTC 2d/FIN ¶ J-3241, ¶ J-3242; USTR ¶ 78,714.02)

Under pre-2009 Recovery Act law, Indian tribes could not issue tax-exempt bonds for any other non-essential governmental function besides financing tribal manufacturing facilities. (FTC 2d/FIN ¶ J-3150, ¶ J-3241; USTR ¶ 78,714.02)

New Law. Under the 2009 Recovery Act, Indian tribal governments are permitted to issue tribal economic development bonds. (Com Rept, see ¶ 5056) A tribal economic bond is any bond issued by an Indian tribal government (Code Sec. 7871(f)(3)(A) as amended by 2009 Recovery Act §1402(a)):

(1) the interest on which would be exempt from tax under Code Sec. 103 (state and local bonds tax exemption, see FTC 2d/FIN ¶ J-3001; USTR ¶ 1034; TaxDesk ¶ 158,001) if issued by a state or local government (Code Sec. 7871(f)(3)(A)(i)); and

(2) which is designated by the Indian tribal government as a tribal economic development bond for purposes of Code Sec. 7871(f). (Code Sec. 7871(f)(3)(A)(ii))

⚫️ *observation:* Neither the statute nor the committee report contains a definition of Indian tribal government. However, it is defined elsewhere in the Code. Under Code Sec. 7701(a)(40)(A), Indian tribal government means the governing body of any tribe, band, community, village, or group of Indians, or (if applicable) Alaska Natives, which is determined by IRS, after consulting with the Secretary of the Interior, to exercise substantial governmental functions, see FTC 2d/FIN ¶ J-1540; USTR ¶ 77,014.01; TaxDesk ¶ 158,007.

Bonds treated as exempt from tax. In the case of a tribal economic development bond (Code Sec. 7871(f)(2)):

• notwithstanding Code Sec. 7871(c) (tax-exemption only for bonds funding essential government functions), the bond is treated as if it had been issued by a state (Code Sec. 7871(f)(2)(A));

• the Indian tribal government issuing the bond and any instrumentality of the Indian tribal government are treated as a state for purposes of Code Sec. 141 (the private activity bond rules, see FTC 2d/FIN ¶ J-3100; USTR ¶ 1414; TaxDesk ¶ 158,009) (Code Sec. 7871(f)(2)(B)); and

• Code Sec. 146 (volume caps on private activity bonds, see FTC 2d/FIN ¶ J-3252; USTR ¶ 1464) does not apply. (Code Sec. 7871(f)(2)(C))

Congress believes that, in the current economic crisis, tribes should be given the flexibility to use tax-exempt financing for economic development. Thus, the 2009 Recovery Act permits Indian tribes to issue tax-exempt bonds for purposes not permitted under pre-2009 Recovery Act law, if the bonds would have been tax-exempt if issued by a state. (Com Rept, see ¶ 5056)

National limitation. There is a $2 billion national tribal economic development bond volume limitation. (Code Sec. 7871(f)(1)(B))

Allocation of limitation. IRS must allocate the national tribal economic bond volume limitation among the Indian tribal governments in the manner IRS, in consultation with the Secretary of the Interior, determines appropriate. (Code Sec. 7871(f)(1)(A)) The maximum face amount of bonds that may be designated under Code Sec. 7871(f)(3)(A) by any Indian tribal government must not exceed the amount of the national bond volume limitation allocated to the government under Code Sec. 7871(f)(1). (Code Sec. 7871(f)(3)(C))

Exceptions. A tribal economic bond does not include any bond issued as part of an issue if any portion of the proceeds of the issue are used to finance (Code Sec. 7871(f)(3)(B)):

FTC 2d References are to Federal Tax Coordinator 2d
FIN References are to RIA's Analysis of Federal Taxes: Income
USTR References are to United States Tax Reporter: Income
PE References are to Pension Explanations

293

- any portion of a building in which class II or class III gaming (as defined in section 4 of the Indian Gaming Regulatory Act) is conducted or housed or any other property actually used in the conduct of the gaming (Code Sec. 7871(f)(3)(B)(i)),

> ☑ *observation:*   Class I gaming means social games solely for prizes of minimal value or traditional forms of Indian gaming engaged in by individuals as a part of, or in connection with, tribal ceremonies or celebrations. The term class II gaming includes bingo (including electronic or computer aided) that is played for prizes, including monetary prizes, and card games. The term class II gaming does not include any banking card games, including baccarat, chemin de fer, or blackjack (21), or electronic or electromechanical facsimiles of any game of chance or slot machines of any kind. The term class III gaming means all forms of gaming that are not class I gaming or class II gaming.

or

- any facility located outside the Indian reservation (as defined in Code Sec. 168(j)(6)). (Code Sec. 7871(f)(3)(B)(ii))

> ☑ *observation:* Code Sec. 168(j)(6) defines "Indian reservation" as defined in Section 3(d) of the '74 Indian Financing Act (25 USC 1452(d)) and Section 4(10) of the '78 Indian Child Welfare Act (25 USC 1903(10)), see FTC 2d/FIN ¶ L-8807; USTR ¶ 1684.01. Section 3(d) provides that reservation includes Indian reservations, public domain Indian allotments, former Indian reservations in Oklahoma, and land held by incorporated Native groups, regional corporations, and village corporations under the provisions of the Alaska Native Claims Settlement Act. Section 4(10) provides that reservation means Indian country as defined in section 1151 of title 18 and any lands, not covered under that section, title to which is either held by the U.S. in trust for the benefit of any Indian tribe or individual or held by any Indian tribe or individual subject to a restriction by the U.S. against alienation.

Study.   IRS must conduct a study of the effects of this new bond provision, and, not later than one year after Feb. 17, 2009, report the results of the study (2009 Recovery Act §1402(b)), including its recommendation whether the Code Sec. 7871(c) restrictions should be eliminated or otherwise modified. (Com Rept, see ¶ 5056)

☐ **Effective:** Bonds issued after Feb. 17, 2009. (2009 Recovery Act §1402(c))

¶ 1400. Client Letters and Interoffice Memos

¶ 1401. Tax changes affecting individuals and families in the American Recovery and Reinvestment Act of 2009

> **To the practitioner:** You can use the following letter to provide clients with an overview of these tax provisions in the American Recovery and Reinvestment Act of 2009. For analysis of the making work pay credit, see ¶ 101. For analysis of the economic recovery payment, see ¶ 102. For analysis of the unemployment compensation exclusion, see ¶ 106. For analysis of the expanded earned income tax credit, see ¶ 110. For analysis of the expanded higher education credit, see ¶ 107. For analysis of the provision permitting computers to qualify as education expenses in 529 education plans, see ¶ 108. For analysis of the expanded credit for first-time homebuyers, see ¶ 104. For analysis of the sales tax deduction for new car purchasers, see ¶ 105. For analysis of the increased AMT exemption amounts for 2009, see ¶ 201. For analysis of the provision allowing the personal credits against the AMT, see ¶ 204.

Dear Client,

The recently enacted "American Recovery and Reinvestment Act of 2009" contains a wide-ranging tax package that includes tax relief for low and moderate-income wage earners, individuals and families with college expenses, and home and car purchasers. I'm writing to give you an overview of the more widely applicable tax changes affecting individuals and families in the new law. Please call our offices for details of how the new changes may affect you and your family.

"Making Work Pay" credit. The new law provides an individual tax credit in the amount of 6.2% of earned income not to exceed $400 for single returns and $800 for joint returns in 2009 and 2010. The credit is phased out at adjusted gross income (AGI) in excess of $75,000 ($150,000 for married couples filing jointly). The credit can be claimed as a reduction in the amount of income tax that is withheld from a paycheck, or through a credit on a tax return. Under the credit, workers can expect to see perhaps $13 a week less withheld from their paychecks starting around June. Next year, the extra take-home pay will go down to around $7.70 per week.

Economic recovery payment. The new law provides for a one-time payment of $250 to retirees, disabled individuals and Social Security beneficiaries and SSI recipients receiving benefits from the Social Security Administration and Railroad Retirement beneficiaries, and to veterans receiving disability compensation and pension benefits from the U.S. Department of Veterans' Affairs. The one-time payment is a reduction to any allowable Making Work Pay credit.

FTC 2d References are to Federal Tax Coordinator 2d
FIN References are to RIA's Analysis of Federal Taxes: Income
USTR References are to United States Tax Reporter: Income
PE References are to Pension Explanations

Refundable credit for certain federal and state pensioners. The new law provides a one-time refundable tax credit of $250 in 2009 to certain government retirees who are not eligible for Social Security benefits. This one-time credit is a reduction to any allowable Making Work Pay credit.

Unemployment compensation exclusion. A provision temporarily suspends federal income tax on the first $2,400 of unemployment benefits received by a recipient in 2009.

Expanded earned income tax credit. The new law provides tax relief to families with three or more children and increases marriage penalty relief. The changes apply for 2009 and 2010.

Expanded child tax credit. A measure increases the eligibility for the refundable child tax credit in 2009 and 2010 by lowering the earned income threshold to $3,000 (from $8,500 in 2008).

Expanded and revised higher education tax credit. The new law creates a $2,500 higher education tax credit that is available for the first four years of college. The credit is based on 100% of the first $2,000 of tuition and related expenses (including books) paid during the tax year and 25% of the next $2,000 of tuition and related expenses paid during the tax year, subject to a phase-out for AGI in excess of $80,000 ($160,000 for married couples filing jointly). 40% of the credit is refundable. The new credit temporarily replaces the Hope credit.

Computers as an education expense. A provision permits computers and computer technology to qualify as qualified education expenses in 529 education plans for tax years beginning in 2009 and 2010.

Expanded credit for first-time home buyers. Last year, Congress provided taxpayers with a refundable tax credit that was equivalent to an interest-free loan equal to 10% of the purchase of a home (up to $7,500) by first-time home buyers. The provision applied to homes purchased on or after April 9, 2008 and before July 1, 2009. Taxpayers receiving this tax credit were required to repay any amount received under this provision back to the government over 15 years in equal installments (or earlier if the home was sold). The credit phases out for taxpayers with AGI in excess of $75,000 ($150,000 in the case of a joint return). The new law enhances the credit by eliminating the repayment obligation for taxpayers that purchase homes on or after January 1, 2009. It also extends the credit through the end of November 2009, and bumps up the maximum value of the credit from $7,500 to $8,000.

Tax break for new car purchasers. The new law allows taxpayers to deduct State and local sales taxes paid on the purchase of a new automobile, including light trucks, SUVs, motorcycles, and motor homes. The tax break phases out starting with taxpayers earning $125,000 per year ($250,000 for joint returns). The deduction is allowed to both those who itemize their deductions as well as to nonitemizers. However, the deduction cannot be taken by a taxpayer who elects to deduct state and local sales taxes in lieu of state and local income taxes.

Alternative minimum tax (AMT) patch. To hold the number of taxpayers subject to the AMT at bay, the new law increases the AMT exemption amounts for 2009 to $46,700 for unmarried individuals, to $70,950 for joint returns, and to $35,475 for married individuals filing separate returns, and allows the personal credits against the AMT.

I hope this information is helpful. If you would like more details about this or any other aspect of the new law, please do not hesitate to call.

Very truly yours,

FTC 2d References are to Federal Tax Coordinator 2d
FIN References are to RIA's Analysis of Federal Taxes: Income
USTR References are to United States Tax Reporter: Income
PE References are to Pension Explanations

¶ 1402. "Making Work Pay" tax credit in the American Recovery and Reinvestment Act of 2009

To the practitioner: You can use the following letter to provide clients with an overview of this tax provision in the American Recovery and Reinvestment Act of 2009. For analysis of the Making Work Pay tax credit, see ¶ 101. For analysis of the economic recovery payment, see ¶ 102.

Dear Client,

The recently enacted "American Recovery and Reinvestment Act of 2009" contains a wide-ranging tax package that includes tax relief for low and moderate-income wage earners, individuals and families with college expenses, and home and car purchasers. The centerpiece of the tax package—and at $115 billion its single largest component—is a "Making Work Pay" tax credit of up to $400 per year for individuals, or $800 per year for couples. Here are the details of this new credit:

• Eligible individuals will receive an income tax credit for two years (tax years beginning in 2009 and 2010). The new credit, like other tax credits, will reduce a person's tax liability on a dollar-for-dollar basis. Wage earners who don't earn enough to pay income taxes will be able to claim the difference as a tax refund.

• The new credit is the lesser of (1) 6.2% of an individual's earned income or (2) $400 ($800 in the case of a joint return). In other words, for individuals with earned income above roughly $6,451 ($12,902 for couples), the credit maxes out at $400 ($800 for couples). For the last half of 2009, workers can expect to see perhaps $13 a week less withheld from their paychecks starting around June. That reduction goes down to about $7.70 per week next year.

• Nonresident aliens do not qualify for this credit. Neither do estates, trusts, or individuals who can be claimed as a dependent on someone else's return.

• The credit is available in full only if AGI (adjusted gross income, with some modifications for highly specialized income) doesn't exceed $75,000 for an individual ($150,000 if you file a joint return). The credit is phased out at a rate of 2% of the eligible individual's AGI above $75,000 ($150,000 in the case of a joint return). So no credit is allowed for individuals with AGI of $100,000 or more, or for joint filers with AGI of $200,000 or more.

FTC 2d References are to Federal Tax Coordinator 2d
FIN References are to RIA's Analysis of Federal Taxes: Income
USTR References are to United States Tax Reporter: Income
PE References are to Pension Explanations

• Unlike the $600 per worker lump-sum rebates issued last year, the credit can be received as a reduction in the amount of income tax that is withheld from a paycheck, or through a credit on a tax return.

• Since the credit is based on taxable wages and thus unavailable to many retired people and others whose income does not come from wages, the new law includes a one-time payment of $250 to retirees, disabled individuals and SSI recipients receiving benefits from the Social Security Administration, and Railroad Retirement beneficiaries, and to veterans receiving disability compensation and pension benefits from the U.S. Department of Veterans' Affairs. The one-time payment is a reduction to any allowable Making Work Pay credit. Similarly, a one-time refundable tax credit of $250 is provided in 2009 to certain government retirees who are not eligible for Social Security benefits. This one-time credit is a reduction to any allowable Making Work Pay credit.

I hope this information is helpful. If you would like more details about this or any other aspect of the new law, please do not hesitate to call..

Very truly yours,

¶ 1403. Enhanced first-time homebuyer credit in the American Recovery and Reinvestment Act of 2009

> **To the practitioner:** You can use the following letter to provide clients with an overview of this tax provision in the American Recovery and Reinvestment Act of 2009. For analysis of the first-time homebuyer credit, see ¶ 104.

Dear Client,

In hopes of spurring the housing industry, the recently enacted "American Recovery and Reinvestment Act of 2009" includes an enhanced tax credit for first-time homebuyers. Here are the details.

You may remember that last year's Housing Act included a tax credit giving first-time homebuyers up to a $7,500 (actually, $7,500 or 10% of the purchase price, whichever is less) credit for buying a home between April 8, 2008, and July 1, 2009, with single taxpayers with incomes up to $75,000 and married couples with incomes up to $150,000 qualifying for the full tax credit. However, despite high hopes that the credit would be effective in getting people to buy homes and thereby reduce the excessive inventory on the market, the credit is widely acknowledged to have failed in its objective. The problem, according to realtors and industry officials, was that buyers were turned off by the odd way the credit worked. While the credit functioned initially like other tax credits, reducing a person's tax liability on a dollar-for-dollar basis, it was unusual in that, unlike other federal tax credits (for example, the child credit), the credit for first-time homebuyers had to be paid back to the government ratably over a period of 15 years (or earlier if the house is sold). So, as a practical matter, the credit was the equivalent of an interest-free loan from the government. It was the payback requirement that many in the industry felt kept potential buyers on the sidelines. Now, Congress has beefed up the credit in renewed optimism of enticing more first-time homebuyers to take the plunge. First and foremost, the new legislation scuttles the repayment requirement for homes purchased on or after January 1, 2009. The new law also extends the credit through the end of November 2009, and bumps up the maximum credit amount from $7,500 to $8,000. However, the new law retains the recapture provisions if the house is sold within three years of purchase.

I hope this information is helpful. If you would like more details about this or any other aspect of the new law, please do not hesitate to call.

FTC 2d References are to Federal Tax Coordinator 2d
FIN References are to RIA's Analysis of Federal Taxes: Income
USTR References are to United States Tax Reporter: Income
PE References are to Pension Explanations

Very truly yours,

¶ 1404. Tax break for new car buyers in the American Recovery and Reinvestment Act of 2009

> **To the practitioner:** You can use the following letter to provide clients with an overview of this tax provision in the American Recovery and Reinvestment Act of 2009. For analysis of the sales tax deduction for new car purchasers, see ¶ 105.

Dear Client,

In hopes of spurring the overall economy in general, and the automobile industry in particular, the recently enacted "American Recovery and Reinvestment Act of 2009" includes a new tax break for purchasers of new cars: a deduction for state and local sales and excise taxes paid on new vehicle purchases. Here are the details.

Sales tax is generally not a deductible item for individuals. A limited exception allows taxpayers who itemize their deductions to claim either state and local income taxes or state and local general sales taxes, which mainly benefits taxpayers with a state or local sales tax but no income tax. Under the new law, buyers can claim an income tax deduction for the sales or excise tax they pay on a vehicle purchase. Key details of this new tax incentive include:

• The tax break applies to purchases of passenger cars, minivans, light trucks, motorcycles, and motor homes, but it only applies on $49,500 of the vehicle's price and it only applies to new vehicles.

• The tax break covers new vehicles purchased between Feb. 17, 2009 and the end of 2009.

• You do not have to itemize your deductions to be able to claim the deduction. However, the deduction cannot be taken by a taxpayer who elects to deduct state and local sales taxes in lieu of state and local income taxes.

• Only couples making less than $250,000 a year, or individuals making less than $125,000 annually, qualify for the full deduction.

I hope this information is helpful. If you would like more details about this or any other aspect of the new law, please do not hesitate to call..

Very truly yours,

FTC 2d References are to Federal Tax Coordinator 2d
FIN References are to RIA's Analysis of Federal Taxes: Income
USTR References are to United States Tax Reporter: Income
PE References are to Pension Explanations

¶ 1405. Expanded tax credit for college in the American Recovery and Reinvestment Act of 2009

> **To the practitioner:** You can use the following letter to provide clients with an overview of this tax provision in the American Recovery and Reinvestment Act of 2009. For analysis of the expanded college credit, see ¶ 107.

Dear Client,

The recently enacted "American Recovery and Reinvestment Act of 2009" includes a measure aimed at making college more affordable for low and moderate-income students. The new provision temporarily enlarges the Hope tax credit (renamed the American Opportunity tax credit) for students from middle-income families and partially extends this tax credit for the first time to students from lower-income families. Here are the details.

• The new law creates a new American Opportunity tax credit for 2009 and 2010, replacing and expanding the Hope tax credit for those years.

• The maximum amount of the American Opportunity tax credit is $2,500 (up from a maximum credit of $1,800 under the Hope credit). The credit is 100% of the first $2,000 of qualifying expenses and 25% of the next $2,000, so the maximum credit of $2,500 is reached when a student has qualifying expenses of $4,000 or more.

• While the Hope credit was only available for the first two years of undergraduate education, the American Opportunity tax credit is available for up to four years.

• Under the Hope credit, qualifying expenses were narrowly defined to include just tuition and fees required for the student's enrollment. Textbooks were excluded, despite their escalating cost in recent years. The American Opportunity tax credit expands the list of qualifying expenses to include textbooks.

• The Hope credit was nonrefundable, i.e, it could reduce your regular tax bill to zero but could not result in a refund. This meant that if a family didn't owe any taxes it couldn't benefit from the credit, which prompted critics to argue that the credit was thus denied to the very families most in need of help affording college. The American Opportunity tax credit addresses this criticism to a degree by providing that 40% of the credit is refundable. This means that someone who has at least $4,000 in qualified expenses and who would thus qualify for the maximum credit of $2,500,

FTC 2d References are to Federal Tax Coordinator 2d
FIN References are to RIA's Analysis of Federal Taxes: Income
USTR References are to United States Tax Reporter: Income
PE References are to Pension Explanations

but who has no tax liability to offset that credit against, would qualify for a $1,000 (40% of $2,500) refund from the government.

• The Hope credit was not available to someone with higher than moderate income. Under the credit's "phaseout" provision, taxpayers with adjusted gross income (AGI) over $50,000 (for 2009) saw their credits reduced, and the credit was completely eliminated for AGIs over $60,000 (twice those amounts for joint filers). Under the American Opportunity tax credit, taxpayers with somewhat higher incomes can qualify, as the phaseout of the credit begins at AGI in excess of $80,000 ($160,000 for joint filers).

I hope this information is helpful. If you would like more details about this or any other aspect of the new law, please do not hesitate to call..

Very truly yours,

¶ 1406. Business tax changes in the American Recovery and Reinvestment Act of 2009

> **To the practitioner:** You can use the following letter to provide business clients with an overview of these tax provisions in the American Recovery and Reinvestment Act of 2009. For analysis of the extension of bonus depreciation, see ¶ 801. For analysis of the extension of enhanced small business expensing, see ¶ 802. For analysis of the provision expanding the loss carryback period for small businesses, see ¶ 601. For analysis of the provision expanding the work opportunity credit, see ¶ 904. For analysis of the provision extending monetization of accumulated AMT and R&D credits in lieu of bonus depreciation, see ¶ 805. For analysis of the provision delaying recognition of certain cancellation of debt income, see ¶ 901. For analysis of the provision increasing the exclusion for gain from the sale of certain small business stock, see ¶ 902. For analysis of the provision temporarily shortening the holding period of assets subject to the built-in gains tax, see ¶ 903. For analysis of the provision repealing IRS's built-in loss rules, see ¶ 602.

Dear Client,

I'm writing to give you an overview of the key tax changes affecting business in the recently enacted "American Recovery and Reinvestment Act of 2009" (the 2009 economic stimulus act). Please call our offices for details of how the new changes may affect your specific business.

Extension of bonus depreciation. Last year, Congress temporarily allowed business to recover the costs of capital expenditures made in 2008 faster than the ordinary depreciation schedule would allow by permitting these businesses to immediately write off 50% of the cost of depreciable property acquired in 2008 for use in the United States. The new law extends this temporary benefit for qualifying property purchased and placed into service in 2009.

Extension of enhanced small business expensing (Section 179). In order to help small businesses quickly recover the cost of certain capital expenses, small business taxpayers may elect to write off the cost of these expense in the year of acquisition in lieu of recovering these costs over time through depreciation. Last year, Congress temporarily increased the amount that small businesses could write off for capital expenditures incurred in 2008 to $250,000 and increased the phase-out threshold for 2008 to $800,000. The new law extends these temporary increases for capital expenditures incurred in 2009.

Expanded loss carryback of net operating losses for small businesses. Under pre-Act law, net operating losses (NOLs) may be carried back to the two years before the year that the loss arises and carried forward to

FTC 2d References are to Federal Tax Coordinator 2d
FIN References are to RIA's Analysis of Federal Taxes: Income
USTR References are to United States Tax Reporter: Income
PE References are to Pension Explanations

each of the succeeding twenty years after the year that the loss arises. For 2008, the new law extends the maximum NOL carryback period from two years to five years for small businesses with gross receipts of $15 million or less.

Incentives to hire unemployed veterans and disconnected youth. Businesses are allowed to claim a work opportunity tax credit equal to 40% of the first $6,000 of wages paid to employees of one of nine targeted groups. The new law expands the work opportunity tax credit to include two new targeted groups: (1) unemployed veterans; and (2) disconnected youth. Individuals qualify as unemployed veterans if they were discharged or released from active duty from the Armed Forces during 2008, 2009 or 2010 and received unemployment compensation for more than four weeks during the year before being hired. Individuals qualify as disconnected youths if they are between the ages of 16 and 25 and have not been regularly employed or attended school in the past 6 months.

Extension of monetization of accumulated AMT and R&D credits in lieu of bonus depreciation. The new law extends the provision contained in the Foreclosure Prevention Act of 2008 and allows AMT and loss taxpayers in 2009 to receive 20% of the value of their old AMT or research and development (R&D) credits to the extent such taxpayers invest in assets that qualify for bonus depreciation.

Delayed recognition of certain cancellation of debt income. To benefit certain businesses that buy their own debt at a discount, the new law lets the businesses recognize cancellation of debt income ("CODI") over 10 years (defer tax on CODI for the first four or five years and recognize this income ratably over the following five tax years) for specified types of business debt repurchased by the business in 2009 or 2010.

Qualified small business stock. The new law increases the exclusion for gain from the sale of certain small business stock held for more than five years from 50% to 75% for stock issued after the enactment date and before 2011.

S corp holding period. The new law temporarily shortens the holding period of assets subject to the built-in gains tax from 10 years to seven years..

Repeal of IRS's built-in loss rules. The new law provides a prospective repeal of Notice 2008-83, the controversial IRS guidance which provided that if a bank recognizes a loss from the disposition of a loan or takes a bad debt deduction under the specific charge-off or reserve methods of accounting after a change in ownership, that loss or deduction will not be treated as a built in loss attributable to the pre-acquisition period.

I hope this information is helpful. If you would like more details about these or any other aspects of the new law, please do not hesitate to call..

Very truly yours,

FTC 2d References are to Federal Tax Coordinator 2d
FIN References are to RIA's Analysis of Federal Taxes: Income
USTR References are to United States Tax Reporter: Income
PE References are to Pension Explanations

309

¶ 1407. Energy tax incentives in the American Recovery and Reinvestment Act of 2009

> **To the practitioner:** You can use the following letter to provide clients with an overview of these tax provisions in the American Recovery and Reinvestment Act of 2009. For analysis of the provision extending and modifying the renewable energy production credit, see ¶ 1207. For analysis of the temporary election to claim the investment tax credit in lieu of the production tax credit, see ¶ 1203. For analysis of the provision enhancing the business energy credit, see ¶ 1201. For analysis of changes to the credit for improvements to energy-efficient homes, see ¶ 1101. For analysis of the changes to the residential energy property credit, see ¶ 1104. For analysis of the changes to the tax credits for alternative fuel pumps, see ¶ 1101. For analysis of the provision establishing the credit for investment in advanced energy facilities, see ¶ 1202. For analysis of the revisions to the tax credit for plug-in electric vehicles, see ¶ 1102.

Dear Client,

The recently enacted "American Recovery and Reinvestment Act of 2009" (the 2009 economic stimulus act) includes a package of tax incentives to encourage investments in renewable energy projects or more-efficient technologies. I'm writing to give you an overview of these new provisions. Please call our offices for details of how the new changes may affect you, your investments, or your business.

Long-term extension and modification of renewable energy production tax credit. The new legislation extends the placed-in-service date for wind facilities for three years (through December 31, 2012). It also extends the placed-in-service date through December 31, 2013 for certain other qualifying facilities: closed-loop biomass; open-loop biomass; geothermal; small irrigation; hydropower; landfill gas; waste-to-energy; and marine renewable facilities.

Temporary election to claim the investment tax credit in lieu of the production tax credit. Facilities that produce electricity from solar facilities are eligible to take a 30% investment tax credit in the year the facility is placed in service. Facilities that produce electricity from wind, closed-loop biomass, open-loop biomass, geothermal, small irrigation, hydropower, landfill gas, waste-to-energy, and marine renewable facilities are eligible for a production tax credit, payable over a ten-year period. The Act provides a temporary election to claim the investment tax credit in lieu of the production tax credit.

FTC 2d References are to Federal Tax Coordinator 2d
FIN References are to RIA's Analysis of Federal Taxes: Income
USTR References are to United States Tax Reporter: Income
PE References are to Pension Explanations

Business energy credit. The new law enhances the business energy credit by eliminating the cap on small wind property and repealing the basis reduction requirement for subsidized energy financing.

Energy-efficient existing homes. The new law extends the tax credit for improvements to energy-efficient existing homes through 2010. For 2009 and 2010, the amount of the tax credit is increased from 10% to 30% of the amount paid or incurred by the taxpayer for qualified energy efficiency improvements during the tax year. The property-by-property dollar caps on the tax credit are also eliminated, and an aggregate $1,500 cap applies to all property qualifying for the credit.

Residential energy property. The new law removes the dollar limitations on certain energy credits, e.g, for qualified small wind energy property ($4,000 cap); for qualified solar water heating property ($2,000 cap); and qualified geothermal heat pumps ($2,000).

Tax credits for alternative fuel pumps. The new law provides an increase for 2009 and 2010 in the 30% alternative refueling property credit for businesses (capped at $30,000) to 50% (capped at $50,000).

Credit for investment in advanced energy facilities. The new law establishes a new manufacturing investment tax credit for investment in advanced energy facilities, such as facilities that manufacture components for the production of renewable energy, advanced battery technology, and other innovative next-generation green technologies.

Grants in lieu of electricity production credit and energy credit. Under current law, taxpayers are allowed to claim a production tax credit for electricity produced by certain renewable energy facilities and an investment tax credit for certain renewable energy property. These tax credits help attract private capital to invest in renewable energy projects. Current economic conditions have severely undermined the effectiveness of these tax credits. As a result, the new law allows taxpayers to receive a grant from the Treasury Department in lieu of tax credits. Most facilities are eligible for a 30% grant, but some (geothermal, qualified microturbine, combined heat and power, and geothermal heat pump) qualify only for a smaller, 10% grant. To earn a grant, the facility must be placed in service in 2009 or 2010, or construction must begin in either of those years and must be completed prior to the termination of the credit.

Vehicles. The new law provides a tax credit for purchases of plug-in electric drive vehicles ranging from $2,500 to $7,500 depending on battery capacity. The new law also restores and updates the electric vehicle credit for plug-in electric vehicles that would not otherwise qualify for the larger plug-in electric drive vehicle credit and provides a tax credit for plug-in electric drive conversion kits.

More funding for bonds. The new law authorizes additional funds for new clean renewable energy bonds and qualified energy conservation bonds.

I hope this information is helpful. If you would like more details about these or any other aspects of the new law, please do not hesitate to call..

Very truly yours,

FTC 2d References are to Federal Tax Coordinator 2d
FIN References are to RIA's Analysis of Federal Taxes: Income
USTR References are to United States Tax Reporter: Income
PE References are to Pension Explanations

313

¶ 1408. AMT relief in the American Recovery and Reinvestment Act of 2009

To the practitioner: You can use the following letter to provide clients with an overview of these tax provisions in the American Recovery and Reinvestment Act of 2009. For analysis of the increased AMT exemption amounts for 2009, see ¶ 201. For analysis of the provision allowing the personal credits against the AMT, see ¶ 204.

Dear Client,

I am writing to provide details regarding two key provisions in the recently enacted "American Recovery and Reinvestment Act of 2009" (the 2009 economic stimulus act). The provisions extend partial relief to individual taxpayers from the alternative minimum tax, or AMT. Earlier temporary measures to deal with the unintended creep of the AMT's reach expired at the end of 2008, meaning that more than 20 million additional taxpayers would have faced paying the tax on their 2009 returns without the new relief.

Brief overview of the AMT.

The AMT is a parallel tax system which does not permit several of the deductions permissible under the regular tax system, such as property tax. Taxpayers who may be subject to the AMT must calculate their tax liability under the regular federal tax system and under the AMT system taking into account certain "preferences" and "adjustments." If their liability is found to be greater under the AMT system, that's what they owe the federal government. Originally enacted to make sure that wealthy Americans did not escape paying taxes, the AMT has started to apply to more middle-income taxpayers, due in part to the fact that the AMT parameters are not indexed for inflation.

In recent years, Congress has provided a measure of relief from the AMT by raising the AMT "exemption amounts"—allowances that reduce the amount of alternative minimum taxable income (AMTI), reducing or eliminating AMT liability. (However, these exemption amounts are phased out for taxpayers whose AMTI exceeds specified amounts.) For 2008, the AMT exemption amounts were $69,950 for married couples filing jointly and surviving spouses; $46,200 for single taxpayers; and $34,975 for married filing separately. However, for 2009, those amounts were scheduled to fall back to the amounts that applied in 2000: $45,000, $33,750, and $22,500, respectively. This would have brought millions of additional mid-

FTC 2d References are to Federal Tax Coordinator 2d
FIN References are to RIA's Analysis of Federal Taxes: Income
USTR References are to United States Tax Reporter: Income
PE References are to Pension Explanations

315

dle-income Americans under the AMT system, resulting in higher federal tax bills for many of them, along with higher compliance costs associated with filling out and filing the complicated AMT tax form.

New law provides one-year stopgap fix.

To prevent the unintended result of having millions of middle-income taxpayers fall prey to the AMT, Congress has once again relied on a temporary "patch" to the problem, this time a one-year extension of the 2008 exemption amounts, increased slightly. Under the new law, for tax years beginning in 2009, the AMT exemption amounts are increased to: (1) $70,950 in the case of married individuals filing a joint return and surviving spouses; (2) $46,700 in the case of unmarried individuals other than surviving spouses; and (3) $35,475 in the case of married individuals filing a separate return.

Personal credits may be used to offset AMT through 2009.

Another provision in the new law provides AMT relief for taxpayers claiming personal tax credits. The tax liability limitation rules generally provide that certain nonrefundable personal credits (including the dependent care credit and the elderly and disabled credit) are allowed only to the extent that a taxpayer has regular income tax liability in excess of the tentative minimum tax, which has the effect of disallowing these credits against the AMT. Temporary provisions had been enacted which permitted these credits to offset the entire regular and AMT liability through the end of 2008. The new law extends this temporary provision to tax years beginning in 2009.

I hope this information is helpful. If you would like more details about this or any other aspect of the new law, please do not hesitate to call..

Very truly yours,

¶ 1409. Expanded work opportunity credit in the American Recovery and Reinvestment Act of 2009

> **To the practitioner:** This letter may be sent to employers who hire individuals in the targeted groups. For analysis of the provision expanding the work opportunity credit, see ¶ 904.

Dear Client,

I am writing to provide details regarding a key provision in the recently enacted "American Recovery and Reinvestment Act of 2009" (the 2009 economic stimulus act) which expands the categories of new-hires that are creditable under the work opportunity credit.

As you know, businesses are allowed to claim a work opportunity tax credit equal to 40% of the first $6,000 of wages paid to employees of one of nine targeted groups. These groups are: (1) qualified members of families receiving assistance under the Temporary Assistance for Needy Families (TANF) program, (2) qualified veterans, (3) qualified ex-felons, (4) designated community residents, (5) vocational rehabilitation referrals, (6) qualified summer youth employees, (7) qualified members of families receiving Food Stamp assistance, (8) qualified Supplemental Security Income recipients, and (9) long-term family assistance recipients.

The new law expands the work opportunity tax credit to include two new targeted groups: (1) unemployed veterans; and (2) disconnected youth. Individuals qualify as unemployed veterans if they were discharged or released from active duty from the Armed Forces during 2008, 2009 or 2010 and received unemployment compensation for more than four weeks during the year before being hired. Individuals qualify as disconnected youths if they are between the ages of 16 and 25 and have not been regularly employed or attended school in the past 6 months.

I welcome your questions about any of the above discussion, and, should you be interested, I would be pleased to work with you on the application of the credit to your situation.

Very truly yours,

FTC 2d References are to Federal Tax Coordinator 2d
FIN References are to RIA's Analysis of Federal Taxes: Income
USTR References are to United States Tax Reporter: Income
PE References are to Pension Explanations

¶ 1410. Up to five-year carryback of 2008 net operating losses for small businesses in the American Recovery and Reinvestment Act of 2009

> **To the practitioner:** You can use the following letter to provide business clients with an overview of this tax provision in the American Recovery and Reinvestment Act of 2009. For analysis of the provision expanding the loss carryback period for small businesses, see ¶ 601.

Dear Client,

As you no doubt know, Congress recently passed the "American Recovery and Reinvestment Act of 2009" (the Act) which is intended to jump-start our economy, in part through tax incentives aimed at encouraging businesses to increase investment. A key provision in the new law which is designed to help struggling businesses cope with the business downturn and spur new investment is a temporary extension of the carryback period for certain net operating losses (NOLs) from two years to up to five years for small businesses. I'm writing to give you an overview of the new carryback provision. Please call our offices for details of how the new changes may affect your specific business.

Background on business losses.

Businesses calculate taxable income by subtracting expenses from revenues. While net income is taxed immediately, net operating losses do not qualify for immediate refunds on current tax returns. However, businesses may effectively receive a refund to the extent that they can be "carried back" against income taxed in previous years. Under pre-Act law, businesses may use current losses to offset only the past two years of profits. Losses that exceed the sum of the previous two years of positive income may be "carried forward" and used to offset taxable income earned in future years. Losses can currently be carried forward for twenty years.

New provision

The new law extends the maximum NOL carryback period from two years to up to five years. In other words, an eligible business may elect a three-, four-, or five-year carryback period. The extended carryback period is subject to two important conditions: (1) it only applies to 2008 NOLs, and (2) it only applies to small businesses, defined as those with gross receipts of $15 million or less.

FTC 2d References are to Federal Tax Coordinator 2d
FIN References are to RIA's Analysis of Federal Taxes: Income
USTR References are to United States Tax Reporter: Income
PE References are to Pension Explanations

For those businesses that qualify, the extended carryback provision could be very helpful in two ways. First, a carryback can generate a refund because it allows the taxpayer to offset income that has already been taxed. Under pre-Act law, a small business taxpayer couldn't have used the NOL to offset the taxable income for the fifth, fourth, and third tax years preceding the NOL year, years when the taxpayer was more likely to have had taxable income. Allowing the carryback to the earlier years thus increases the likelihood that the taxpayer will be entitled to a refund, and may increase the amount of the refund. A second positive effect of the extended carryback period is that it will make temporary investment incentives such as bonus depreciation and expensing more effective. That is because businesses that are unable to absorb their current losses with past tax payments do not receive immediate benefits from investment tax incentives such as expensing or bonus depreciation. Unused deductions can't be used until future years. Because this blunts any stimulus provided by investment tax incentives, extending the carryback period enhance these incentives. The more generous carryback period can allow a company to benefit immediately from temporary investment incentives.

I should note, as a caveat, that the taxpayer must affirmatively elect the increased carryback. Absent any election, the regular NOL carryback period rules apply. Thus, even if a taxpayer qualifies as an eligible small business and the taxpayer's 2008 NOL otherwise qualifies for the increased carryback, the NOL can't be carried back more than two years unless the taxpayer elects to apply the extended carryback provision or one of the other special carryback periods applies.

I hope this information is helpful. If you would like more details about this or any other aspect of the new law, please do not hesitate to call..

Very truly yours,

¶ 1411. Expanded nonbusiness energy property credit in the American Recovery and Reinvestment Act of 2009

> **To the practitioner:** You can use the following letter to provide clients with an overview of these tax provisions in the American Recovery and Reinvestment Act of 2009. For analysis of changes to the credit for improvements to energy-efficient homes, see ¶ 1101.

Dear Client,

Unlike past efforts by Congress to use taxes to spur energy efficiency by homeowners, provisions in the recently enacted "American Recovery and Reinvestment Act of 2009" (the Act) are substantial. These include an increased credit of 30% of the cost of residential energy-efficient improvements such as more efficient furnaces, heat pumps and air conditioners, as well as energy-tight windows and more insulation, and a tripling of the maximum credit for a household to $1,500. Here are the details.

Background.

Individual taxpayers are allowed a personal tax credit, known as the nonbusiness energy property credit, for energy efficient improvements to a dwelling unit in the U.S. owned and used by the taxpayer as the taxpayer's principal residence. Under pre-Act law, this credit was equal to the sum of:

(1) 10% of the amount paid or incurred by the taxpayer for qualified energy efficiency improvements (i.e., building envelope components meeting certain requirements) installed during the tax year, and

(2) the amount of residential energy property expenditures (i.e., $50 for each advanced main air circulating fan, $150 for each qualified natural gas, propane, or oil furnace or hot water boiler, and $300 for qualified energy efficient property, including heat pumps, water heaters, and central air conditioners) paid or incurred by the taxpayer during the tax year.

Under pre-Act law, the credit was subject to a lifetime cap. The total credit for all tax years couldn't exceed $500, no more than $200 of which could be for expenditures on windows.

The credit was also set to expire at the end of this year.

New law.

The new legislation modifies and extends the nonbusiness energy property credit in the following ways:

FTC 2d References are to Federal Tax Coordinator 2d
FIN References are to RIA's Analysis of Federal Taxes: Income
USTR References are to United States Tax Reporter: Income
PE References are to Pension Explanations

... the 10% credit rate is increased to 30%;

... the dollar limitations on residential energy property expenditures have been eliminated; instead, all energy property that was previously eligible for the $50, $150, and $300 credits is instead eligible for a 30% credit;

... the $500 lifetime cap ($200 for windows) is eliminated and replaced with an aggregate $1,500 cap for 2009 and 2010; and

... the credit is extended for one year, through Dec. 31, 2010.

I hope this information is helpful. If you would like more details about this or any other aspect of the new law, please do not hesitate to call.

Very truly yours,

¶ 1412. Qualified tuition programs—"529 plans"— enhanced in the American Recovery and Reinvestment Act of 2009

> **To the practitioner:** You can use the following letter to provide clients with an overview of this tax provision in the American Recovery and Reinvestment Act of 2009. For analysis of the provision permitting computers to qualify as education expenses in 529 education plans, see ¶ 108.

Dear Client,

If you have a child (or a grandchild) who is going to attend college in the future you have probably heard about qualified tuition programs, also known as 529 plans (for the Internal Revenue Code section that provides for them), which allow prepayment of higher education costs on a tax-favored basis. I am writing regarding a provision in the recently enacted "American Recovery and Reinvestment Act of 2009" (the Act) which enhances the flexibility of 529 plans.

Under 529 plan rules, distributions from the program are tax-free if they don't exceed the student's qualified higher education expenses. These include tuition, fees, books, supplies, room and board (if the student is enrolled at least half-time), and required equipment. Under pre-Act rules, the cost of a computer doesn't qualify as an eligible expense unless the computer is required by the college or by a specific degree program or course. The new law changes that rule to allow money from 529 plans to be used to purchase computers and related technology. The change applies for 2009 and 2010.

I hope this information is helpful. If you would like more details about this or any other aspect of the new law, please do not hesitate to call.

Very truly yours,

FTC 2d References are to Federal Tax Coordinator 2d
FIN References are to RIA's Analysis of Federal Taxes: Income
USTR References are to United States Tax Reporter: Income
PE References are to Pension Explanations

¶ 1413. Expanded child tax credit in the American Recovery and Reinvestment Act of 2009

> **To the practitioner:** You can use the following letter to provide clients with an overview of this tax provision in the American Recovery and Reinvestment Act of 2009. For analysis of the provision expanding the child tax credit, see ¶ 109.

Dear Client,

I am writing regarding a provision in the recently enacted "American Recovery and Reinvestment Act of 2009" which expands the child tax credit for millions of children in low-income working families. Here are the details.

Currently, a taxpayer receives a $1,000 tax credit for each qualifying child under the age of 17. To the extent the child credit exceeds the taxpayer's tax liability, the taxpayer is eligible for a refundable credit (the additional child tax credit) equal to 15% of earned income in excess of a threshold dollar amount. The threshold dollar amount was $8,500 in 2008.

The new law increases the eligibility for the refundable child tax credit in 2009 and 2010 by lowering the earned income threshold to $3,000. This means that working families with earnings above $3,000 may qualify for at least a partial credit.

This change is significant because families with earnings just above the threshold qualify for a very small credit, because eligibility phases in slowly, at a rate of 15 cents per dollar of earnings above the threshold level. As a result, where the threshold is set has a large effect on families with incomes thousands of dollars above the threshold. For example, under the $8,500 threshold that applied for tax year 2008, a family with two children did not qualify for the full credit of $1,000 per child unless it had earnings of at least $21,833. Under the new law, such a family will qualify for the full credit when its earnings reach $16,333.

As a result of the change under the new law, an estimated 2.9 million more children will qualify for the credit than would have qualified under last year's $8,500 earnings threshold, and an estimated 10 million children who would have received a partial credit under the $8,500 threshold will receive a larger one under the new legislation.

If you would like more details about this or any other aspect of the new law, please do not hesitate to call.

FTC 2d References are to Federal Tax Coordinator 2d
FIN References are to RIA's Analysis of Federal Taxes: Income
USTR References are to United States Tax Reporter: Income
PE References are to Pension Explanations

Very truly yours,

¶ 1414. Changes to plug-in electric vehicle credit in the American Recovery and Reinvestment Act of 2009

> **To the practitioner:** You can use the following letter to provide clients with an overview of this tax provision in the American Recovery and Reinvestment Act of 2009. For analysis of the revisions to the tax credit for plug-in electric vehicles, see ¶ 1102.

Dear Client,

I am writing regarding changes in the recently enacted "American Recovery and Reinvestment Act of 2009" (the 2009 economic stimulus act) to the plug-in electric vehicle tax credit. While the changes are perhaps not of immediate concern, since the plug-in electric vehicles covered by the credit are still a couple of years away from reaching showrooms, the credit may affect your car-buying plans in the future.

Under the plug-in electric drive motor vehicle credit program, which was established last year, the base amount of the credit is $2,500, plus another $417 for each kilowatt hour of battery capacity in excess of four kilowatt hours. (By way of comparison, the current Toyota Prius stores 1.3 kilowatt hours.) The maximum credit for qualified vehicles weighing 10,000 pounds or less is $7,500. (Thus, a light-duty vehicle with a 16-kilowatt hour battery pack, such as the prospective Chevrolet Vol, would get the maximum credit, which may help ease the burden of the expected steep sticker prices of plug-in electric vehicles.) This maximum amount increases to $10,000 for vehicles weighing more than 10,000 pounds but not more than 14,000 pounds, to $12,500 for vehicles weighing more than 14,000 pounds but not more than 26,000 pounds, and to $15,000 for vehicles weighing more than 26,000 pounds. Once a total of 250,000 credit eligible vehicles had been sold for use in the United States, the credit was to be phased out over four calendar quarters.

The new law makes the following changes: (1) the maximum credit is limited to $7,500 regardless of vehicle weight, (2) the credit is eliminated for plug-in vehicles weighing 14,000 pounds or more, and (3) the 250,000 total plug-in vehicle imitation is replaced with a 200,000 plug-in vehicle per manufacturer limitation. These changes are effective for vehicles acquired after December 31, 2009.

FTC 2d References are to Federal Tax Coordinator 2d
FIN References are to RIA's Analysis of Federal Taxes: Income
USTR References are to United States Tax Reporter: Income
PE References are to Pension Explanations

I should also note that the new law provides a separate credit for certain low-speed and 2- or 3-wheeled plug-in vehicles, as well as a credit for certain costs of converting vehicles to plug-in vehicles.

I hope this information is helpful. If you would like more details about this or any other aspect of the new law, please do not hesitate to call..

Very truly yours,

¶ 1415. Interoffice memo on tax changes affecting individuals and families in the American Recovery and Reinvestment Act of 2009

> **To the practitioner:** You can use the following interoffice memo to provide upper management and other internal clients with an overview of these tax provisions in the American Recovery and Reinvestment Act of 2009.

To:

From:

CC:

Re: Tax Changes Affecting Individuals and Families in the American Recovery and Reinvestment Act of 2009

Date:

The recently enacted "American Recovery and Reinvestment Act of 2009" contains a wide-ranging tax package that includes tax relief for low and moderate-income wage earners, individuals and families with college expenses, and home and car purchasers.

This interoffice memo provides an overview of the more widely applicable tax changes affecting individuals and families in the new law.

• *"Making Work Pay" credit.* The new law provides an individual tax credit in the amount of 6.2% of earned income not to exceed $400 for single returns and $800 for joint returns in 2009 and 2010. The credit is phased out at adjusted gross income (AGI) in excess of $75,000 ($150,000 for married couples filing jointly). The credit can be claimed as a reduction in the amount of income tax that is withheld from a paycheck, or through a credit on a tax return. Under the credit, workers can expect to see perhaps $13 a week less withheld from their paychecks starting around June. Next year, the extra take-home pay will go down to around $7.70 per week.

• *Economic recovery payment.* The new law provides for a one-time payment of $250 to retirees, disabled individuals and Social Security beneficiaries and SSI recipients receiving benefits from the Social Security Administration and Railroad Retirement beneficiaries, and to veterans receiving disability compensation and pension benefits from the U.S. De-

---

FTC 2d References are to Federal Tax Coordinator 2d
FIN References are to RIA's Analysis of Federal Taxes: Income
USTR References are to United States Tax Reporter: Income
PE References are to Pension Explanations

partment of Veterans' Affairs. The one-time payment is a reduction to any allowable Making Work Pay credit.

• *Refundable credit for certain federal and state pensioners.* The new law provides a one-time refundable tax credit of $250 in 2009 to certain government retirees who are not eligible for Social Security benefits. This one-time credit is a reduction to any allowable Making Work Pay credit.

• *Unemployment compensation exclusion.* A provision temporarily suspends federal income tax on the first $2,400 of unemployment benefits received by a recipient in 2009.

• *Expanded earned income tax credit.* The new law provides tax relief to families with three or more children and increases marriage penalty relief. The changes apply for 2009 and 2010.

• *Expanded child tax credit.* A measure increases the eligibility for the refundable child tax credit in 2009 and 2010 by lowering the earned income threshold to $3,000 (from $8,500 in 2008).

• *Expanded and revised higher education tax credit.* The new law creates a $2,500 higher education tax credit that is available for the first four years of college. The credit is based on 100% of the first $2,000 of tuition and related expenses (including books) paid during the tax year and 25% of the next $2,000 of tuition and related expenses paid during the tax year, subject to a phase-out for AGI in excess of $80,000 ($160,000 for married couples filing jointly). 40% of the credit is refundable. The new credit temporarily replaces the Hope credit.

• *Computers as an education expense.* A provision permits computers and computer technology to qualify as qualified education expenses in 529 education plans for tax years beginning in 2009 and 2010.

• *Expanded credit for first-time home buyers.* Last year, Congress provided taxpayers with a refundable tax credit that was equivalent to an interest-free loan equal to 10% of the purchase of a home (up to $7,500) by first-time home buyers. The provision applied to homes purchased on or after April 9, 2008 and before July 1, 2009. Taxpayers receiving this tax credit were required to repay any amount received under this provision back to the government over 15 years in equal installments (or earlier if the home was sold). The credit phases out for taxpayers with AGI in excess of $75,000 ($150,000 in the case of a joint return). The new law enhances the credit by eliminating the repayment obligation for taxpayers that purchase homes on or after January 1, 2009. It also extends the credit through the end of November 2009, and bumps up the maximum value of the credit from $7,500 to $8,000.

• *Tax break for new car purchasers.* The new law allows taxpayers to deduct State and local sales taxes paid on the purchase of a new automobile, including light trucks, SUVs, motorcycles, and motor homes. The tax break phases out starting with taxpayers earning $125,000 per year ($250,000 for joint returns). The deduction is allowed to both those who itemize their deductions as well as to nonitemizers. However, the deduction cannot be taken by a taxpayer who elects to deduct state and local sales taxes in lieu of state and local income taxes.

• *Alternative minimum tax (AMT) patch.* To hold the number of taxpayers subject to the AMT at bay, the new law increases the AMT exemption amounts for 2009 to $46,700 for unmarried individuals, to $70,950 for joint returns, and to $35,475 for unmarried individuals filing separate returns, and allows the personal credits against the AMT.

Please keep in mind that this is only a summary of these new provisions.

FTC 2d References are to Federal Tax Coordinator 2d
FIN References are to RIA's Analysis of Federal Taxes: Income
USTR References are to United States Tax Reporter: Income
PE References are to Pension Explanations

¶ 1416. Interoffice memo on the "Making Work Pay" tax credit in the American Recovery and Reinvestment Act of 2009

> **To the practitioner:** You can use the following interoffice memo to provide upper management and other internal clients with an overview of this important provision in the American Recovery and Reinvestment Act of 2009.

To:

From:

CC:

Re: "Making Work Pay" Tax Credit in the American Recovery and Reinvestment Act of 2009

Date:

The recently enacted "American Recovery and Reinvestment Act of 2009" contains a wide-ranging tax package that includes tax relief for low and moderate-income wage earners, individuals and families with college expenses, and home and car purchasers. The centerpiece of the tax package—and at $115 billion its single largest component—is a "Making Work Pay" tax credit of up to $400 per year for individuals, or $800 per year for couples.

This interoffice memo provides an overview of this new provision.:

• Eligible individuals will receive an income tax credit for two years (tax years beginning in 2009 and 2010). The new credit, like other tax credits, will reduce a person's tax liability on a dollar-for-dollar basis. Wage earners who don't earn enough to pay income taxes will be able to claim the difference as a tax refund.

• The new credit is the lesser of (1) 6.2% of an individual's earned income or (2) $400 ($800 in the case of a joint return). In other words, for individuals with earned income above roughly $6,451 ($12,902 for couples), the credit maxes out at $400 ($800 for couples). For the last half of 2009, workers can expect to see perhaps $13 a week less withheld from their paychecks starting around June. That reduction goes down to about $7.70 per week next year.

FTC 2d References are to Federal Tax Coordinator 2d
FIN References are to RIA's Analysis of Federal Taxes: Income
USTR References are to United States Tax Reporter: Income
PE References are to Pension Explanations

• Nonresident aliens do not qualify for this credit. Neither do estates, trusts, or individuals who can be claimed as a dependent on someone else's return.

• The credit is available in full only if AGI (adjusted gross income, with some modifications for highly specialized income) doesn't exceed $75,000 for an individual ($150,000 if you file a joint return). The credit is phased out at a rate 2% of the eligible individual's AGI above $75,000 ($150,000 in the case of a joint return). So no credit is allowed for individuals with AGI of $100,000 or more, or for joint filers with AGI of $200,000 or more.

• Unlike the $600 per worker lump-sum rebates issued last year, the credit can be received as a reduction in the amount of income tax that is withheld from a paycheck, or through a credit on a tax return.

• Since the credit is based on taxable wages and thus unavailable to many retired people and other whose income does not come from wages, the new law includes a one-time payment of $250 to retirees, disabled individuals and SSI recipients receiving benefits from the Social Security Administration, and Railroad Retirement beneficiaries, and to veterans receiving disability compensation and pension benefits from the U.S Department of Veterans' Affairs. The one-time payment is a reduction to any allowable Making Work Pay credit. Similarly, a one-time refundable tax credit of $250 is provided in 2009 to certain government retirees who are not eligible for Social Security benefits. This one-time credit is a reduction to any allowable Making Work Pay credit.

Please keep in mind that this is only a summary of these new provisions.

¶ 1417. Interoffice memo on the enhanced first-time homebuyer credit in the American Recovery and Reinvestment Act of 2009

> **To the practitioner:** You can use the following interoffice memo to provide upper management and other internal clients with an overview of this important provision in the American Recovery and Reinvestment Act of 2009.

To:

From:

CC:

Re: Enhanced First-time Homebuyer Credit in the American Recovery and Reinvestment Act of 2009

Date:

In hopes of spurring the housing industry, the recently enacted "American Recovery and Reinvestment Act of 2009" includes an enhanced tax credit for first-time homebuyers.

This interoffice memo provides an overview of this new provision.

You may remember that last year's Housing Act included a tax credit giving first-time homebuyers up to a $7,500 (actually, 10% of the purchase price, or $7,500, whichever is less) credit for buying a home between April 8, 2008, and July 1, 2009, with single taxpayers with incomes up to $75,000 and married couples with incomes up to $150,000 qualifying for the full tax credit. However, despite high hopes that the credit would be effective in getting people to buy homes and thereby reduce the excessive inventory on the market, the credit is widely acknowledged to have failed in its objective. The problem, according to realtors and industry officials, was that buyers were turned off by the odd way the credit worked. While the credit functioned initially like other tax credits, reducing a person's tax liability on a dollar-for-dollar basis, it was unusual in that, unlike other federal tax credits (for example, the child credit), the credit for first-time homebuyers had to be paid back to the government ratably over a period of 15 years (or earlier if the house is sold). So, as a practical matter, the credit was the equivalent of an interest-free loan from the government. It was the payback requirement that many in the industry felt kept potential buyers on the sidelines. Now, Congress has beefed up the credit in renewed optimism of enticing more

FTC 2d References are to Federal Tax Coordinator 2d
FIN References are to RIA's Analysis of Federal Taxes: Income
USTR References are to United States Tax Reporter: Income
PE References are to Pension Explanations

first-time homebuyers to take the plunge. First and foremost, the new legislation scuttles the repayment requirement for homes purchased on or after January 1, 2009. The new law also extends the credit through the end of November 2009, and bumps up the maximum credit amount from $7,500 to $8,000. However, the new law retains the recapture provisions if the house is sold within three years of purchase.

Please keep in mind that this is only a summary of these new provisions.

¶ 1418. Interoffice memo on the tax break for new car buyers in the American Recovery and Reinvestment Act of 2009

> **To the practitioner:** You can use the following interoffice memo to provide upper management and other internal clients with an overview of this important provision in the American Recovery and Reinvestment Act of 2009.

To:

From:

CC:

Re: Tax Break for New Car Buyers in the American Recovery and Reinvestment Act of 2009

Date:

In hopes of spurring the overall economy in general, and the automobile industry in particular, the recently enacted "American Recovery and Reinvestment Act of 2009" includes a new tax break for purchasers of new cars: a deduction for state and local sales and excise taxes paid on new vehicle purchases.

This interoffice memo provides an overview of this new provision.

Sales tax is generally not a deductible item for individuals. A limited exception allows taxpayers who itemize their deductions to claim either state and local income taxes or state and local general sales taxes, which mainly benefits taxpayers with a state or local sales tax but no income tax. Under the new law, buyers can claim an income tax deduction for the sales or excise tax they pay on a vehicle purchase. Key details of this new tax incentive include:

• The tax break applies to purchases of passenger cars, minivans, light trucks, motorcycles, and motor homes, but it only applies on $49,500 of the vehicle's price and it only applies to new vehicles.

• The tax break covers new vehicles purchased between Feb. 17, 2009 and the end of 2009.

• You do not have to itemize your deductions to be able to claim the deduction. However, the deduction cannot be taken by a taxpayer who elects

---

FTC 2d References are to Federal Tax Coordinator 2d
FIN References are to RIA's Analysis of Federal Taxes: Income
USTR References are to United States Tax Reporter: Income
PE References are to Pension Explanations

to deduct state and local sales taxes in lieu of state and local income taxes.

• Only couples making less than $250,000 a year, or individuals making less than $125,000 annually, qualify for the full deduction.

Please keep in mind that this is only a summary of this new provision.

¶ 1419. Interoffice memo on the expanded tax credit for college in the American Recovery and Reinvestment Act of 2009

> **To the practitioner:** You can use the following interoffice memo to provide upper management and other internal clients with an overview of this important provision in the American Recovery and Reinvestment Act of 2009.

To:

From:

CC:

Re: Expanded Tax Credit for College in the American Recovery and Reinvestment Act of 2009

Date:

The recently enacted "American Recovery and Reinvestment Act of 2009" includes a measure aimed at making college more affordable for low and moderate-income students. The new provision temporarily enlarges the Hope tax credit (renamed the American Opportunity tax credit) for students from middle-income families and partially extends this tax credit for the first time to students from lower-income families.

This interoffice memo provides an overview of this new provision.

• The new law creates a new American Opportunity tax credit for 2009 and 2010, replacing and expanding the Hope tax credit for those years.

• The maximum amount of the American Opportunity tax credit is $2,500 (up from a maximum credit of $1,800 under the Hope credit). The credit is 100% of the first $2,000 of qualifying expenses and 25% of the next $2,000, so the maximum credit of $2,500 is reached when a student has qualifying expenses of $4,000 or more.

• While the Hope credit was only available for the first two years of undergraduate education, the American Opportunity tax credit is available for up to four years.

• Under the Hope credit, qualifying expenses were narrowly defined to include just tuition and fees required for the student's enrollment. Textbooks were excluded, despite their escalating cost in recent years. The

FTC 2d References are to Federal Tax Coordinator 2d
FIN References are to RIA's Analysis of Federal Taxes: Income
USTR References are to United States Tax Reporter: Income
PE References are to Pension Explanations

American Opportunity tax credit expands the list of qualifying expenses to include textbooks.

• The Hope credit was nonrefundable, i.e, it could reduce your regular tax bill to zero but could not result in a refund. This meant that if a family didn't owe any taxes it couldn't benefit from the credit, which prompted critics to argue that the credit was thus denied to the very families most in need of help affording college. The American Opportunity tax credit addresses this criticism to a degree by providing that 40% of the credit is refundable. This means that someone who has at least $4,000 in qualified expenses and who would thus qualify for the maximum credit of $2,500, but who has no tax liability to offset that credit against, would qualify for a $1,000 (40% of $2,500) refund from the government.

• The Hope credit was not available to someone with higher than moderate income. Under the credit's "phaseout" provision, taxpayers with adjusted gross income (AGI) over $50,000 (for 2009) saw their credits reduced, and the credit was completely eliminated for AGIs over $60,000 (twice those amounts for joint filers). Under the American Opportunity tax credit, taxpayers with somewhat higher incomes can qualify, as the phaseout of the credit begins at AGI in excess of $80,000 ($160,000 for joint filers).

Please keep in mind that this is only a summary of these new provisions.

¶ 1420. Interoffice memo on business tax changes in the American Recovery and Reinvestment Act of 2009

> **To the practitioner:** You can use the following interoffice memo to provide upper management and other internal clients with an overview of these tax provisions in the American Recovery and Reinvestment Act of 2009.

To:

From:

CC:

Re: Business Tax Changes in the American Recovery and Reinvestment Act of 2009

Date:

This interoffice memo provides an overview of the key tax changes affecting business in the recently enacted "American Recovery and Reinvestment Act of 2009" (the 2009 economic stimulus act).

• *Extension of bonus depreciation.* Last year, Congress temporarily allowed business to recover the costs of capital expenditures made in 2008 faster than the ordinary depreciation schedule would allow by permitting these businesses to immediately write off 50% of the cost of depreciable property acquired in 2008 for use in the United States. The new law extends this temporary benefit for qualifying property purchased and placed into service in 2009. *Extension of enhanced small business expensing (Section 179).* In order to help small businesses quickly recover the cost of certain capital expenses, small business taxpayers may elect to write off the cost of these expense in the year of acquisition in lieu of recovering these costs over time through depreciation. Last year, Congress temporarily increased the amount that small businesses could write off for capital expenditures incurred in 2008 to $250,000 and increased the phase-out threshold for 2008 to $800,000. The new law extends these temporary increases for capital expenditures incurred in 2009.

• *Expanded loss carryback of net operating losses for small businesses.* Under pre-Act law, net operating losses (NOLs) may be carried back to the two years before the year that the loss arises and carried forward to each of the succeeding twenty years after the year that the loss arises. For 2008, the new law extends the maximum NOL carryback period from two

---

FTC 2d References are to Federal Tax Coordinator 2d
FIN References are to RIA's Analysis of Federal Taxes: Income
USTR References are to United States Tax Reporter: Income
PE References are to Pension Explanations

years to five years for small businesses with gross receipts of $15 million or less.

• *Incentives to hire unemployed veterans and disconnected youth.* Businesses are allowed to claim a work opportunity tax credit equal to 40% of the first $6,000 of wages paid to employees of one of nine targeted groups. The new law expands the work opportunity tax credit to include two new targeted groups: (1) unemployed veterans; and (2) disconnected youth. Individuals qualify as unemployed veterans if they were discharged or released from active duty from the Armed Forces during 2008, 2009 or 2010 and received unemployment compensation for more than four weeks during the year before being hired. Individuals qualify as disconnected youths if they are between the ages of 16 and 25 and have not been regularly employed or attended school in the past 6 months.

• *Extension of monetization of accumulated AMT and R&D credits in lieu of bonus depreciation.* The new law extends the provision contained in the Foreclosure Prevention Act of 2008 and allows AMT and loss taxpayers in 2009 to receive 20% of the value of their old AMT or research and development (R&D) credits to the extent such taxpayers invest in assets that qualify for bonus depreciation.

• *Delayed recognition of certain cancellation of debt income.* To benefit certain businesses that buy their own debt at a discount, the new law lets the businesses recognize cancellation of debt income ("CODI") over 10 years (defer tax on CODI for the first four or five years and recognize this income ratably over the following five tax years) for specified types of business debt repurchased by the business in 2009 or 2010.

• *Qualified small business stock.* The new law increases the exclusion for gain from the sale of certain small business stock held for more than five years from 50% to 75% for stock issued after the enactment date and before 2011. *S corp holding period.* The new law temporarily shortens the holding period of assets subject to the built-in gains tax from 10 years to seven years..

• *Repeal of IRS's built-in loss rules.* The new law provides a prospective repeal of Notice 2008-83, the controversial IRS guidance which provided that if a bank recognizes a loss from the disposition of a loan or takes a bad debt deduction under the specific charge-off or reserve methods of accounting after a change in ownership, that loss or deduction will not be treated as a built in loss attributable to the pre-acquisition period.

Please keep in mind that this is only a summary of these new provisions.

¶ 1421. Interoffice memo on energy tax incentives in the American Recovery and Reinvestment Act of 2009

> **To the practitioner:** You can use the following interoffice memo to provide upper management and other internal clients with an overview of these tax provisions in the American Recovery and Reinvestment Act of 2009.

To:

From:

CC:

Re: Energy Tax Incentives in the American Recovery and Reinvestment Act of 2009

Date:

The recently enacted "American Recovery and Reinvestment Act of 2009" (the 2009 economic stimulus act) includes a package of tax incentives to encourage investments in renewable energy projects or more-efficient technologies.

This interoffice memo provides an overview of these new provisions.

• *Long-term extension and modification of renewable energy production tax credit.* The new legislation extends the placed-in-service date for wind facilities for three years (through December 31, 2012). It also extends the placed-in-service date through December 31, 2013 for certain other qualifying facilities: closed-loop biomass; open-loop biomass; geothermal; small irrigation; hydropower; landfill gas; waste-to-energy; and marine renewable facilities.

• *Temporary election to claim the investment tax credit in lieu of the production tax credit.* Facilities that produce electricity from solar facilities are eligible to take a 30% investment tax credit in the year the facility is placed in service. Facilities that produce electricity from wind, closed-loop biomass,open-loop biomass, geothermal, small irrigation, hydropower, landfill gas, waste-to-energy, and marine renewable facilities are eligible for a production tax credit, payable over a ten-year period. The Act provides a temporary election to claim the investment tax credit in lieu of the production tax credit.

FTC 2d References are to Federal Tax Coordinator 2d
FIN References are to RIA's Analysis of Federal Taxes: Income
USTR References are to United States Tax Reporter: Income
PE References are to Pension Explanations

• *Business energy credit.* The new law enhances the business energy credit by eliminating the cap on small wind property and repealing the basis reduction requirement for subsidized energy financing.

• *Energy-efficient existing homes.* The new law extends the tax credit for improvements to energy-efficient existing homes through 2010. For 2009 and 2010, the amount of the tax credit is increased from 10% to 30% of the amount paid or incurred by the taxpayer for qualified energy efficiency improvements during the tax year. The property-by-property dollar caps on the tax credit are also eliminated, and an aggregate $1,500 cap applies to all property qualifying for the credit.

• *Residential energy property.* The new law removes the dollar limitations on certain energy credits, e.g, for qualified small wind energy property ($4,000 cap); for qualified solar water heating property ($2,000 cap); and qualified geothermal heat pumps ($2,000).

• *Tax credits for alternative fuel pumps.* The new law provides an increase for 2009 and 2010 in the 30% alternative refueling property credit for businesses (capped at $30,000) to 50% (capped at $50,000).

• *Credit for investment in advanced energy facilities.* The new law establishes a new manufacturing investment tax credit for investment in advanced energy facilities, such as facilities that manufacture components for the production of renewable energy, advanced battery technology, and other innovative next-generation green technologies.

•

   Grants in lieu of electricity production credit and energy credit. Under current law, taxpayers are allowed to claim a production tax credit for electricity produced by certain renewable energy facilities and an investment tax credit for certain renewable energy property. These tax credits help attract private capital to invest in renewable energy projects. Current economic conditions have severely undermined the effectiveness of these tax credits. As a result, the new law allows taxpayers to receive a grant from the Treasury Department in lieu of tax credits. Most facilities are eligible for a 30% grant, but some (geothermal, qualified microturbine, combined heat and power, and geothermal heat pump) qualify only for a smaller, 10% grant. To earn a grant, the facility must be placed in service in 2009 or 2010, or construction must begin in either of those years and must be completed prior to the termination of the credit.

• *Vehicles.* The new law provides a tax credit for purchases of plug-in electric drive vehicles ranging from $2,500 to $7,500 depending on battery capacity. The new law also restores and updates the electric vehicle credit for plug-in electric vehicles that would not otherwise qualify for the larger plug-in electric drive vehicle credit and provides a tax credit for plug-in electric drive conversion kits.

• *More funding for bonds.* The new law authorizes additional funds for new clean renewable energy bonds and qualified energy conservation bonds.

Please keep in mind that this is only a summary of these new provisions.

FTC 2d References are to Federal Tax Coordinator 2d
FIN References are to RIA's Analysis of Federal Taxes: Income
USTR References are to United States Tax Reporter: Income
PE References are to Pension Explanations

¶ 1422. Interoffice memo on AMT relief in the American Recovery and Reinvestment Act of 2009

> **To the practitioner:** You can use the following interoffice memo to provide upper management and other internal clients with an overview of these tax provisions in the American Recovery and Reinvestment Act of 2009.

To:

From:

CC:

Re: AMT Relief in the American Recovery and Reinvestment Act of 2009

Date:

This interoffice memo provides an overview of two key provisions in the recently enacted "American Recovery and Reinvestment Act of 2009." The provisions extend partial relief to individual taxpayers from the alternative minimum tax, or AMT. Earlier temporary measures to deal with the unintended creep of the AMT's reach expired at the end of 2008, meaning that more than 20 million additional taxpayers would have faced paying the tax on their 2009 returns without the new relief.

Brief overview of the AMT.

The AMT is a parallel tax system which does not permit several of the deductions permissible under the regular tax system, such as property tax. Taxpayers who may be subject to the AMT must calculate their tax liability under the regular federal tax system and under the AMT system taking into account certain "preferences" and "adjustments." If their liability is found to be greater under the AMT system, that's what they owe the federal government. Originally enacted to make sure that wealthy Americans did not escape paying taxes, the AMT has started to apply to more middle-income taxpayers, due in part to the fact that the AMT parameters are not indexed for inflation.

In recent years, Congress has provided a measure of relief from the AMT by raising the AMT "exemption amounts"—allowances that reduce the amount of alternative minimum taxable income (AMTI), reducing or eliminating AMT liability. (However, these exemption amounts are phased

FTC 2d References are to Federal Tax Coordinator 2d
FIN References are to RIA's Analysis of Federal Taxes: Income
USTR References are to United States Tax Reporter: Income
PE References are to Pension Explanations

out for taxpayers whose AMTI exceeds specified amounts.) For 2008, the AMT exemption amounts were $69,950 for married couples filing jointly and surviving spouses; $46,200 for single taxpayers; and $34,975 for married filing separately. However, for 2009, those amounts were scheduled to fall back to the amounts that applied in 2000: $45,000, $33,750, and $22,500, respectively. This would have brought millions of additional middle-income Americans under the AMT system, resulting in higher federal tax bills for many of them, along with higher compliance costs associated with filling out and filing the complicated AMT tax form.

New law provides one-year stopgap fix.

To prevent the unintended result of having millions of middle-income taxpayers fall prey to the AMT, Congress has once again relied on a temporary "patch" to the problem, this time a one-year extension of the 2008 exemption amounts, increased slightly. Under the new law, for tax years beginning in 2009, the AMT exemption amounts are increased to: (1) $70,950 in the case of married individuals filing a joint return and surviving spouses; (2) $46,700 in the case of unmarried individuals other than surviving spouses; and (3) $35,475 in the case of married individuals filing a separate return.

Personal credits may be used to offset AMT through 2009.

Another provision in the new law provides AMT relief for taxpayers claiming personal tax credits. The tax liability limitation rules generally provide that certain nonrefundable personal credits (including the dependent care credit and the elderly and disabled credit) are allowed only to the extent that a taxpayer has regular income tax liability in excess of the tentative minimum tax, which has the effect of disallowing these credits against the AMT. Temporary provisions had been enacted which permitted these credits to offset the entire regular and AMT liability through the end of 2008. The new law extends this temporary provision to tax years beginning in 2009.

Please keep in mind that this is only a summary of these new provisions.

¶ 1423. Interoffice memo on the expanded work opportunity credit in the American Recovery and Reinvestment Act of 2009

> **To the practitioner:** You can use the following interoffice memo to provide upper management and other internal clients with an overview of this important provision in the American Recovery and Reinvestment Act of 2009.

To:

From:

CC:

Re: Expanded Work Opportunity Credit in the American Recovery and Reinvestment Act of 2009

Date:

This interoffice memo provides an overview of a key provision in the recently enacted "American Recovery and Reinvestment Act of 2009" (the 2009 economic stimulus act) which expands the categories of new-hires that are creditable under the work opportunity credit.

As you know, businesses are allowed to claim a work opportunity tax credit equal to 40% of the first $6,000 of wages paid to employees of one of nine targeted groups. These groups are: (1) qualified members of families receiving assistance under the Temporary Assistance for Needy Families (TANF) program, (2) qualified veterans, (3) qualified ex-felons, (4) designated community residents, (5) vocational rehabilitation referrals, (6) qualified summer youth employees, (7) qualified members of families receiving Food Stamp assistance, (8) qualified Supplemental Security Income recipients, and (9) long-term family assistance recipients.

The new law expands the work opportunity tax credit to include two new targeted groups: (1) unemployed veterans; and (2) disconnected youth. Individuals qualify as unemployed veterans if they were discharged or released from active duty from the Armed Forces during 2008, 2009 or 2010 and received unemployment compensation for more than four weeks during the year before being hired. Individuals qualify as disconnected youths if they are between the ages of 16 and 25 and have not been regularly employed or attended school in the past 6 months.

FTC 2d References are to Federal Tax Coordinator 2d
FIN References are to RIA's Analysis of Federal Taxes: Income
USTR References are to United States Tax Reporter: Income
PE References are to Pension Explanations

Please keep in mind that this is only a summary of this new provision.

¶ 1424. Interoffice memo on the up to five-year carryback of net operating losses for small businesses in the American Recovery and Reinvestment Act of 2009

> **To the practitioner:** You can use the following interoffice memo to provide upper management and other internal clients with an overview of this tax provision in the American Recovery and Reinvestment Act of 2009.

To:

From:

CC:

Re: Up to five-year Carryback of Net Operating Losses for Small Businesses in the American Recovery and Reinvestment Act of 2009

Date:

As you no doubt know, Congress recently passed the "American Recovery and Reinvestment Act of 2009," which is intended to jump-start our economy, in part through tax incentives aimed at encouraging businesses to increase investment. A key provision in the new law which is designed to help struggling businesses cope with the business downturn and spur new investment is a temporary extension of the carryback period for certain net operating losses (NOLs) from two years to up to five years for small businesses.

This interoffice memo provides an overview of the new carryback provision.

Background on business losses.

Businesses calculate taxable income by subtracting expenses from revenues. While net income is taxed immediately, net operating losses do not qualify for immediate refunds on current tax returns. However, businesses may effectively receive a refund to the extent that they can be "carried back" against income taxed in previous years. Under pre-Act law, businesses may use current losses to offset only the past two years of profits. Losses that exceed the sum of the previous two years of positive income may be "carried forward" and used to offset taxable income earned in future years. Losses can currently be carried forward for twenty years.

New law.

FTC 2d References are to Federal Tax Coordinator 2d
FIN References are to RIA's Analysis of Federal Taxes: Income
USTR References are to United States Tax Reporter: Income
PE References are to Pension Explanations

The new law extends the maximum NOL carryback period from two years to up to five years. In other words, an eligible small business may elect a three-, four-, or five-year carryback period. The extended carryback period is subject to two important conditions: (1) it only applies to 2008 NOLs, and (2) it only applies to small businesses, defined as those with gross receipts of $15 million or less.

For those businesses that qualify, the extended carryback provision could be very helpful in two ways. First, a carryback can generate a refund because it allows the taxpayer to offset income that has already been taxed. Under pre-Act law, a small business taxpayer couldn't have used the NOL to offset the taxable income for the fifth, fourth, and third tax years preceding the NOL year, years when the taxpayer was more likely to have had taxable income. Allowing the carryback to the earlier years thus increases the likelihood that the taxpayer will be entitled to a refund, and may increase the amount of the refund. A second positive effect of the extended carryback period is that it will make temporary investment incentives such as bonus depreciation and expensing more effective. That is because businesses that are unable to absorb their current losses with past tax payments do not receive immediate benefits from investment tax incentives such as expensing or bonus depreciation. Unused deductions can't be used until future years. Because this blunts any stimulus provided by investment tax incentives, extending the carryback period enhance these incentives. The more generous carryback period can allow a company to benefit immediately from temporary investment incentives.

I should note, as a caveat, that the taxpayer must affirmatively elect the increased carryback. Absent any election, the regular NOL carryback period rules apply. Thus, even if a taxpayer qualifies as an eligible small business and the taxpayer's 2008 NOL otherwise qualifies for the increased carryback, the NOL can't be carried back more than two years unless the taxpayer elects to apply the extended carryback provision or one of the other special carryback periods applies.

Please keep in mind that this is only a summary of this new provision.

¶ 1425. Interoffice memo on the expanded nonbusiness energy property credit in the American Recovery and Reinvestment Act of 2009

> **To the practitioner:** You can use the following interoffice memo to provide upper management and other internal clients with an overview of these tax provisions in the American Recovery and Reinvestment Act of 2009.

To:

From:

CC:

Re: Expanded Nonbusiness Energy Property Credit in the American Recovery and Reinvestment Act of 2009

Date:

Unlike past efforts by Congress to use taxes to spur energy efficiency by homeowners, provisions in the recently enacted "American Recovery and Reinvestment Act of 2009" (the Act) are substantial. These include an increased credit of 30% of the cost of residential energy-efficient improvements such as more efficient furnaces, heat pumps and air conditioners, as well as energy-tight windows and more insulation, and a tripling of the maximum credit for a household to $1,500.

This interoffice memo provides an overview of these new provisions.

Background.

Individual taxpayers are allowed a personal tax credit, known as the nonbusiness energy property credit, for energy efficient improvements to a dwelling unit in the U.S. owned and used by the taxpayer as the taxpayer's principal residence. Under pre-Act law, this credit was equal to the sum of:

(1) 10% of the amount paid or incurred by the taxpayer for qualified energy efficiency improvements (i.e., building envelope components meeting certain requirements) installed during the tax year, and

(2) the amount of residential energy property expenditures (i.e., $50 for each advanced main air circulating fan, $150 for each qualified natural gas, propane, or oil furnace or hot water boiler, and $300 for qualified energy efficient property, including heat pumps, water heaters, and central air conditioners) paid or incurred by the taxpayer during the tax year.

FTC 2d References are to Federal Tax Coordinator 2d
FIN References are to RIA's Analysis of Federal Taxes: Income
USTR References are to United States Tax Reporter: Income
PE References are to Pension Explanations

Under pre-Act law, the credit was subject to a lifetime cap. The total credit for all tax years couldn't exceed $500, no more than $200 of which could be for expenditures on windows.

The credit was also set to expire at the end of this year.

New law.

The new legislation modifies and extends the nonbusiness energy property credit in the following ways:

. . . the 10% credit rate is increased to 30%;

. . . the dollar limitations on residential energy property expenditures have been eliminated; instead, all energy property that was previously eligible for the $50, $150, and $300 credits is instead eligible for a 30% credit;

. . . the $500 lifetime cap ($200 for windows) is eliminated and replaced with an aggregate $1,500 cap for 2009 and 2010; and

. . . the credit is extended for one year, through Dec. 31, 2010.

Please keep in mind that this is only a summary of these new provisions.

¶ 1426. Interoffice memo on how qualified tuition programs—"529 plans"—are enhanced in the American Recovery and Reinvestment Act of 2009

> **To the practitioner:** You can use the following interoffice memo to provide upper management and other internal clients with an overview of this tax provision in the American Recovery and Reinvestment Act of 2009.

To:

From:

CC:

Re: How Qualified Tuition Programs—"529 plans"—Are Enhanced in the American Recovery and Reinvestment Act of 2009

Date:

If you have a child (or a grandchild) who is going to attend college in the future you have probably heard about qualified tuition programs, also known as 529 plans (for the Internal Revenue Code section that provides for them), which allow prepayment of higher education costs on a tax-favored basis.

This interoffice memo provides an overview of a provision in the recently enacted "American Recovery and Reinvestment Act of 2009" (the Act) which enhances the flexibility of 529 plans.

Under 529 plan rules, distributions from the program are tax-free if they don't exceed the student's qualified higher education expenses. These include tuition, fees, books, supplies, room and board (if the student is enrolled at least half-time), and required equipment. Under pre-Act rules, the cost of a computer doesn't qualify as an eligible expense unless the computer is required by the college or by a specific degree program or course. The new law changes that rule to allow money from 529 plans to be used to purchase computers and related technology. The change applies for 2009 and 2010.

Please keep in mind that this is only a summary of this new provision.

FTC 2d References are to Federal Tax Coordinator 2d
FIN References are to RIA's Analysis of Federal Taxes: Income
USTR References are to United States Tax Reporter: Income
PE References are to Pension Explanations

¶ 1427. Interoffice memo on the expanded child tax credit in the American Recovery and Reinvestment Act of 2009

To the practitioner: You can use the following interoffice memo to provide upper management and other internal clients with an overview of this tax provision in the American Recovery and Reinvestment Act of 2009.

To:

From:

CC:

Re: Expanded Child Tax Credit in the American Recovery and Reinvestment Act of 2009

Date:

This interoffice memo provides an overview of a provision in the recently enacted "American Recovery and Reinvestment Act of 2009," which expands the child tax credit for millions of children in low-income working families.

Currently, a taxpayer receives a $1,000 tax credit for each qualifying child under the age of 17. To the extent the child credit exceeds the taxpayer's tax liability, the taxpayer is eligible for a refundable credit (the additional child tax credit) equal to 15% of earned income in excess of a threshold dollar amount. The threshold dollar amount was $8,500 in 2008.

The new law increases the eligibility for the refundable child tax credit in 2009 and 2010 by lowering the earned income threshold to $3,000. This means that working families with earnings above $3,000 may qualify for at least a partial credit.

This change is significant because families with earnings just above the threshold qualify for a very small credit, because eligibility phases in slowly, at a rate of 15 cents per dollar of earnings above the threshold level. As a result, where the threshold is set has a large effect on families with incomes thousands of dollars above the threshold. For example, under the $8,500 threshold that applied for tax year 2008, a family with two children did not qualify for the full credit of $1,000 per child unless it had earnings

---

FTC 2d References are to Federal Tax Coordinator 2d
FIN References are to RIA's Analysis of Federal Taxes: Income
USTR References are to United States Tax Reporter: Income
PE References are to Pension Explanations

of at least $21,833. Under the new law, such a family will qualify for the full credit when its earnings reach $16,333.

As a result of the change under the new law, an estimated 2.9 million more children will qualify for the credit than would have qualified under last year's $8,500 earnings threshold, and an estimated 10 million children who would have received a partial credit under the $8,500 threshold will receive a larger one under the new legislation.

Please keep in mind that this is only a summary of this new provision.

¶ 1428. Interoffice memo on changes to the plug-in electric vehicle credit in the American Recovery and Reinvestment Act of 2009

> **To the practitioner:** You can use the following interoffice memo to provide upper management and other internal clients with an overview of this tax provision in the American Recovery and Reinvestment Act of 2009.

To:

From:

CC:

Re: Changes to the Plug-in Electric Vehicle Credit in the American Recovery and Recovery and Reinvestment Act of 2009

Date:

This interoffice memo provides an overview of changes in the recently enacted "American Recovery and Reinvestment Act of 2009" (the 2009 economic stimulus act) to the plug-in electric vehicle tax credit. While the changes are perhaps not of immediate concern, since the plug-in electric vehicles covered by the credit are still a couple of years away from reaching showrooms, the credit may affect your car-buying plans in the future.

Under the plug-in electric drive motor vehicle credit program, which was established last year, the base amount of the credit is $2,500, plus another $417 for each kilowatt hour of battery capacity in excess of four kilowatt hours. (By way of comparison, the current Toyota Prius stores 1.3 kilowatt hours.) The maximum credit for qualified vehicles weighing 10,000 pounds or less is $7,500. (Thus, a light-duty vehicle with a 16-kilowatt hour battery pack, such as the prospective Chevrolet Vol, would get the maximum credit, which may help ease the burden of the expected steep sticker prices of plug-in electric vehicles.) This maximum amount increases to $10,000 for vehicles weighing more than 10,000 pounds but not more than 14,000 pounds, to $12,500 for vehicles weighing more than 14,000 pounds but not more than 26,000 pounds, and to $15,000 for vehicles weighing more than 26,000 pounds. Once a total of 250,000 credit eligible vehicles had been sold for use in the United States, the credit was to be phased out over four calendar quarters.

The new law makes the following changes:

FTC 2d References are to Federal Tax Coordinator 2d
FIN References are to RIA's Analysis of Federal Taxes: Income
USTR References are to United States Tax Reporter: Income
PE References are to Pension Explanations

(1) the maximum credit is limited to $7,500 regardless of vehicle weight;

(2) the credit is eliminated for plug-in vehicles weighing 14,000 pounds or more; and

(3) the 250,000 total plug-in vehicle imitation is replaced with a 200,000 plug-in vehicle per manufacturer limitation.

These changes are effective for vehicles acquired after December 31, 2009.

It should also be note that the new law provides a separate credit for certain low-speed and 2- or 3-wheeled plug-in vehicles, as well as a credit for certain costs of converting vehicles to plug-in vehicles.

Please keep in mind that this is only a summary of these new provisions.

[¶ 3000]   Code as Amended

This section reproduces Code as Amended by P.L. 111-5, the American Recovery and Reinvestment Tax Act of 2009. Code Sections appear in order, as amended, added or repealed. New matter is shown in *italics*. All changes and effective dates are shown in the endnotes.

[¶ 3001]   Code Sec. 24.   Child tax credit.

* * * * * * * * * * * *

(b)   Limitations.

(1)   Limitation based on adjusted gross income. The amount of the credit allowable under subsection (a) shall be reduced (but not below zero) by $50 for each $1,000 (or fraction thereof) by which the taxpayer's modified adjusted gross income exceeds the threshold amount. For purposes of the preceding sentence, the term "modified adjusted gross income" means adjusted gross income increased by any amount excluded from gross income under section 911, 931, or 933.

(2)   Threshold amount. For purposes of paragraph (1), the term "threshold amount" means—

(A) $110,000 in the case of a joint return,

(B) $75,000 in the case of an individual who is not married, and

(C) $55,000 in the case of a married individual filing a separate return.

For purposes of this paragraph, marital status shall be determined under section 7703.

(3)   Limitation based on amount of tax. In the case of a taxable year to which section 26(a)(2) does not apply, the credit allowed under subsection (a) for any taxable year shall not exceed the excess of—

(A) the sum of the regular tax liability (as defined in section 26(b)) plus the tax imposed by section 55, over

(B) the sum of the credits allowable under this subpart (other than this section and sections 23, [1]25A(i), 25B, 25D, [2]30, [3]30B, and 30D) and section 27 for the taxable year.

* * * * * * * * * * * *

(d)   Portion of credit refundable.

(1)   In general. The aggregate credits allowed to a taxpayer under subpart C shall be increased by the lesser of—

(A) the credit which would be allowed under this section without regard to this subsection and the limitation under section 26(a)(2) or subsection (b)(3), as the case may be, or

(B) the amount by which the aggregate amount of credits allowed by this subpart (determined without regard to this subsection) would increase if the limitation imposed by section 26(a)(2) or subsection (b)(3), as the case may be, were increased by the greater of—

(i) 15 percent of so much of the taxpayer's earned income (within the meaning of section 32) which is taken into account in computing taxable income for the taxable year as exceeds $10,000, or

(ii) in the case of a taxpayer with 3 or more qualifying children, the excess (if any) of—

(I) the taxpayer's social security taxes for the taxable year, over

(II) the credit allowed under section 32 for the taxable year.

The amount of the credit allowed under this subsection shall not be treated as a credit allowed under this subpart and shall reduce the amount of credit otherwise allowable under subsection (a) without regard to section 26(a)(2) or subsection (b)(3), as the case may be. For purposes of subparagraph (B), any amount excluded from gross income by reason of section 112 shall be treated as earned income which is taken into account in computing taxable income for the taxable year.

401

(2) Social security taxes. For purposes of paragraph (1)—

(A) In general. The term "social security taxes" means, with respect to any taxpayer for any taxable year—

(i) the amount of the taxes imposed by sections 3101 and 3201(a) on amounts received by the taxpayer during the calendar year in which the taxable year begins,

(ii) 50 percent of the taxes imposed by section 1401 on the self-employment income of the taxpayer for the taxable year, and

(iii) 50 percent of the taxes imposed by section 3211(a) on amounts received by the taxpayer during the calendar year in which the taxable year begins.

(B) Coordination with special refund of social security taxes. The term "social security taxes" shall not include any taxes to the extent the taxpayer is entitled to a special refund of such taxes under section 6413(c).

(C) Special rule. Any amounts paid pursuant to an agreement under section 3121(l) (relating to agreements entered into by American employers with respect to foreign affiliates) which are equivalent to the taxes referred to in subparagraph (A)(i) shall be treated as taxes referred to in such subparagraph.

(3) Inflation adjustment. In the case of any taxable year beginning in a calendar year after 2001, the $10,000 amount contained in paragraph (1)(B) shall be increased by an amount equal to—

(A) such dollar amount, multiplied by

(B) the cost-of-living adjustment determined under section 1(f)(3) for the calendar year in which the taxable year begins, determined by substituting "calendar year 2000" for "calendar year 1992" in subparagraph (B) thereof.

Any increase determined under the preceding sentence shall be rounded to the nearest multiple of $50.

[4]*(4) Special rule for 2009 and 2010. Notwithstanding paragraph (3), in the case of any taxable year beginning in 2009 or 2010, the dollar amount in effect for such taxable year under paragraph (1)(B)(i) shall be $3,000.*

* * * * * * * * * * *

[For Analysis, see ¶ 107, ¶ 109, ¶ 204 and ¶ 205. For Committee Reports, see ¶ 5003, ¶ 5004, ¶ 5010 and ¶ 5027.]

[Endnote Code Sec. 24]

Code Sec. 24(b)(3)(B) was amended by Sec. 1004(b)(1) of the American Recovery and Reinvestment Tax Act of 2009, P.L. 111-5, 2/17/2009, as detailed below:

1. added "25A(i)," after "23," in subpara. (b)(3)(B)

Effective Date (Sec. 1004(d), P.L. 111-5, 2/17/2009) effective for tax. yrs. begin. after 12/31/2008.

Sec. 1004(e) of this Act, provides:

"(e) Application of EGTRRA sunset. The amendment made by subsection (b)(1) shall be subject to title IX of the Economic Growth and Tax Relief Reconciliation Act of 2001 in the same manner as the provision of such Act to which such amendment relates."

Code Sec. 24(b)(3)(B) was amended by Sec. 1142(b)(1)(A), P.L. 111-5, 2/17/2009, as detailed below:

2. added "30," after "25D," in subpara. (b)(3)(B) [as amended by Sec. 1004(b)(1) of this Act, see above]

Effective Date (Sec. 1142(c), P.L. 111-5, 2/17/2009) effective for vehicles acquired after 2/17/2009.

Sec. 1142(e) of this Act, provides:

"(e) Application of EGTRRA sunset. The amendment made by subsection (b)(1)(A) shall be subject to title IX of the Economic Growth and Tax Relief Reconciliation Act of 2001 in the same manner as the provision of such Act to which such amendment relates."

Code Sec. 24(b)(3)(B) was amended by Sec. 1144(b)(1)(A), P.L. 111-5, 2/17/2009, as detailed below:

3. added "30B," after "30," in subpara. (b)(3)(B) [as amended by Secs. 1004(b)(1) and 1142(b)(1)(A) of this Act, see above]

Effective Date (Sec. 1144(c), P.L. 111-5, 2/17/2009) effective for tax. yrs. begin. after 12/31/2008.

Sec. 1144(d) of this Act, provides:

"(d) Application of EGTRRA sunset. The amendment made by subsection (b)(1)(A) shall be subject to title IX of the Economic Growth and Tax Relief Reconciliation Act of 2001 in the same manner as the provision of such Act to which such amendment relates."

Code Sec. 24(d)(4) was amended by Sec. 1003(a), P.L. 111-5, 2/17/2009, as detailed below:

4. Prior to amendment, para. (d)(4) read as follows:

"(4) Special rule for 2008. Notwithstanding paragraph (3), in the case of any taxable year beginning in 2008, the dollar amount in effect for such taxable year under paragraph (1)(B)(i) shall be $8,500."

Effective Date (Sec. 1003(b), P.L. 111-5, 2/17/2009) effective for tax. yrs. begin. after 12/31/2008.

[¶3002]   Code Sec. 25.   Interest on certain home mortgages.

* * * * * * * * * * * *

(e) Special rules and definitions. For purposes of this section—

(1) Carryforward of unused credit.

(A) In general. If the credit allowable under subsection (a) for any taxable year exceeds the applicable tax limit for such taxable year, such excess shall be a carryover to each of the 3 succeeding taxable years and, subject to the limitations of subparagraph (B), shall be added to the credit allowable by subsection (a) for such succeeding taxable year.

(B) Limitation. The amount of the unused credit which may be taken into account under subparagraph (A) for any taxable year shall not exceed the amount (if any) by which the applicable tax limit for such taxable year exceeds the sum of—

(i) the credit allowable under subsection (a) for such taxable year determined without regard to this paragraph, and

(ii) the amounts which, by reason of this paragraph, are carried to such taxable year and are attributable to taxable years before the unused credit year.

(C) Applicable tax limit. For purposes of this paragraph, the term "applicable tax limit" means—

(i) in the case of a taxable year to which section 26(a)(2) applies, the limitation imposed by section 26(a)(2) for the taxable year reduced by the sum of the credits allowable under this subpart (other than this section and sections 23, 25D, and 1400C), and

(ii) in the case of a taxable year to which section 26(a)(2) does not apply, the limitation imposed by section 26(a)(1) for the taxable year reduced by the sum of the credits allowable under this subpart (other than this section and sections 23, 24, [1]25A(i), 25B, 25D, [2]30, [3]30B, 30D, and 1400C).

(2) Indebtedness not treated as certified where certain requirements not in fact met. Subsection (a) shall not apply to any indebtedness if all the requirements of subsections (c)(1), (d), (e), (f), and (i) of section 143 and clauses (iv), (v), and (vii) of subsection (c)(2)(A), were not in fact met with respect to such indebtedness. Except to the extent provided in regulations, the requirements described in the preceding sentence shall be treated as met if there is a certification, under penalty of perjury, that such requirements are met.

(3) Period for which certificate in effect.

(A) In general. Except as provided in subparagraph (B), a mortgage credit certificate shall be treated as in effect with respect to interest attributable to the period—

(i) beginning on the date such certificate is issued, and

(ii) ending on the earlier of the date on which—

(I) the certificate is revoked by the issuing authority, or

(II) the residence to which such certificate relates ceases to be the principal residence of the individual to whom the certificate relates.

(B) Certificate invalid unless indebtedness incurred within certain period. A certificate shall not apply to any indebtedness which is incurred after the close of the second calendar year following the calendar year for which the issuing authority made the applicable election under subsection (c)(2)(A)(ii).

(C) Notice to secretary when certificate revoked. Any issuing authority which revokes any mortgage credit certificate shall notify the Secretary of such revocation at such time and in such manner as the Secretary shall prescribe by regulations.

(4) Reissuance of mortgage credit certificates. The Secretary may prescribe regulations which allow the administrator of a mortgage credit certificate program to reissue a mortgage credit certificate specifying a certified mortgage indebtedness that replaces the outstanding balance of the certified mortgage indebtedness specified on the original certificate to any taxpayer to whom the original certificate was issued, under such terms and conditions as the Secretary determines are necessary to ensure that the amount of the credit allowable under subsection (a) with respect to such reissued certificate is equal to or less than the amount of credit which would be allowable under subsection (a) with respect to the original certificate for any taxable year ending after such reissuance.

(5) Public notice that certificates will be issued. At least 90 days before any mortgage credit certificate is to be issued after a qualified mortgage credit certificate program, the issuing authority shall provide reasonable public notice of—

(A) the eligibility requirements for such certificate,

(B) the methods by which such certificates are to be issued, and

(C) such other information as the Secretary may require.

(6) Interest paid or accrued to related persons. No credit shall be allowed under subsection (a) for any interest paid or accrued to a person who is a related person to the taxpayer (within the meaning of section 144(a)(3)(A)).

(7) Principal residence. The term "principal residence" has the same meaning as when used in section 121.

(8) Qualified rehabilitation and home improvement.

(A) Qualified rehabilitation. The term "qualified rehabilitation" has the meaning given such term by section 143(k)(5)(B).

(B) Qualified home improvement. The term "qualified home improvement" means an alteration, repair, or improvement described in section 143(k)(4).

(9) Qualified mortgage bond. The term "qualified mortgage bond" has the meaning given such term by section 143(a)(1).

(10) Manufactured housing. For purposes of this section, the term "single family residence" includes any manufactured home which has a minimum of 400 square feet of living space and a minimum width in excess of 102 inches and which is of a kind customarily used at a fixed location. Nothing in the preceding sentence shall be construed as providing that such a home will be taken into account in making determinations under section 143.

* * * * * * * * * * *

[For Analysis, see ¶ 107, ¶ 204 and ¶ 205. For Committee Reports, see ¶ 5004, ¶ 5010 and ¶ 5027.]

[Endnote Code Sec. 25]

Code Sec. 25(e)(1)(C)(ii) was amended by Sec. 1004(b)(2) of the American Recovery and Reinvestment Tax Act of 2009, P.L. 111-5, 2/17/2009, as detailed below:

1. Sec. 1004(b)(2) added "25A(i)," after "24," in clause (e)(1)(C)(ii)

Effective Date (Sec. 1004(d), P.L. 111-5, 2/17/2009) effective for tax. yrs. begin. after 12/31/2008.

Code Sec. 25(e)(1)(C)(ii) was amended by Sec. 1142(b)(1)(B), P.L. 111-5, 2/17/2009, as detailed below:

2. Sec. 1142(b)(1)(B) added "30," after "25D," in clause (e)(1)(C)(ii) [as amended by Sec. 1004(b)(2) of this Act, see above]

Effective Date (Sec. 1142(c), P.L. 111-5, 2/17/2009) effective for vehicles acquired after 2/17/2009.

Code Sec. 25(e)(1)(C)(ii) was amended by Sec. 1144(b)(1)(B), P.L. 111-5, 2/17/2009, as detailed below:

3. Sec. 1144(b)(1)(B) added "30B," after "30," in clause (e)(1)(C)(ii) [as amended by Sec. 1004(b)(2) and 1142(b)(1)(B) of this Act, see above]

Effective Date (Sec. 1144(c), P.L. 111-5, 2/17/2009) effective for tax. yrs. begin. after 12/31/2008.

[¶ 3003]   Code Sec. 25A.   Hope and Lifetime Learning Credits.

* * * * * * * * * * *

[1]*(i)* *American opportunity tax credit.* In the case of any taxable year beginning in 2009 or 2010—

(1) *Increase in credit.* The Hope Scholarship Credit shall be an amount equal to the sum of—

(A) 100 percent of so much of the qualified tuition and related expenses paid by the taxpayer during the taxable year (for education furnished to the eligible student during any academic period beginning in such taxable year) as does not exceed $2,000, plus

(B) 25 percent of such expenses so paid as exceeds $2,000 but does not exceed $4,000.

(2) *Credit allowed for first 4 years of post-secondary education.* Subparagraphs (A) and (C) of subsection (b)(2) shall be applied by substituting "4" for "2".

(3) *Qualified tuition and related expenses to include required course materials.* Subsection (f)(1)(A) shall be applied by substituting "tuition, fees, and course materials" for "tuition and fees".

(4) *Increase in AGI limits for hope scholarship credit.* In lieu of applying subsection (d) with respect to the Hope Scholarship Credit, such credit (determined without regard to this paragraph) shall be reduced (but not below zero) by the amount which bears the same ratio to such credit (as so determined) as—

(A) the excess of—

(i) the taxpayer's modified adjusted gross income (as defined in subsection (d)(3)) for such taxable year, over

(ii) $80,000 ($160,000 in the case of a joint return), bears to

(B) $10,000 ($20,000 in the case of a joint return).

(5) *Credit allowed against alternative minimum tax.* In the case of a taxable year to which section 26(a)(2) does not apply, so much of the credit allowed under subsection (a) as is attributable to the Hope Scholarship Credit shall not exceed the excess of—

(A) the sum of the regular tax liability (as defined in section 26(b)) plus the tax imposed by section 55, over

(B) the sum of the credits allowable under this subpart (other than this subsection and sections 23, 25D, and 30D) and section 27 for the taxable year.

Any reference in this section or section 24, 25, 26, 25B, 904, or 1400C to a credit allowable under this subsection shall be treated as a reference to so much of the credit allowable under subsection (a) as is attributable to the Hope Scholarship Credit.

(6) *Portion of credit made refundable.* 40 percent of so much of the credit allowed under subsection (a) as is attributable to the Hope Scholarship Credit (determined after application of paragraph (4) and without regard to this paragraph and section 26(a)(2) or paragraph (5), as the case may be) shall be treated as a credit allowable under subpart C (and not allowed under subsection (a)). The preceding sentence shall not apply to any taxpayer for any taxable year if such taxpayer is a child to whom subsection (g) of section 1 applies for such taxable year.

(7) *Coordination with midwestern disaster area benefits.* In the case of a taxpayer with respect to whom section 702(a)(1)(B) of the Heartland Disaster Tax Relief Act of 2008 applies for any taxable year, such taxpayer may elect to waive the application of this subsection to such taxpayer for such taxable year.

[2]*(j)* *Regulations.* The Secretary may prescribe such regulations as may be necessary or appropriate to carry out this section, including regulations providing for a recapture of the credit allowed under this section in cases where there is a refund in a subsequent taxable year of any amount which was taken into account in determining the amount of such credit.

[For Analysis, see ¶ 107 and ¶ 204. For Committee Reports, see ¶ 5004 and ¶ 5010.]

[Endnote Code Sec. 25A]

    Code Sec. 25A(i) and Code Sec. 25A(j) was amended by Sec. 1004(a) of the American Recovery and Reinvestment Tax Act of 2009, P.L. 111-5, 2/17/2009, as detailed below:

    1. Sec. 1004(a) added subsec. (i)

    2. Sec. 1004(a) redesignated subsec. (i) as subsec. (j)

Effective Date (Sec. 1004(d), P.L. 111-5, 2/17/2009) effective for tax. yrs. begin. after 12/31/2008. Sec. 1004(c) and (f) of this Act, reads as follows:

"(c) Treatment of possessions.

"(1) Payments to possessions.

"(A) Mirror code possession. The Secretary of the Treasury shall pay to each possession of the United States with a mirror code tax system amounts equal to the loss to that possession by reason of the application of section 25A(i)(6) of the Internal Revenue Code of 1986 (as added by this section) with respect to taxable years beginning in 2009 and 2010. Such amounts shall be determined by the Secretary of the Treasury based on information provided by the government of the respective possession.

"(B) Other possessions. The Secretary of the Treasury shall pay to each possession of the United States which does not have a mirror code tax system amounts estimated by the Secretary of the Treasury as being equal to the aggregate benefits that would have been provided to residents of such possession by reason of the application of section 25A(i)(6) of such Code (as so added) for taxable years beginning in 2009 and 2010 if a mirror code tax system had been in effect in such possession. The preceding sentence shall not apply with respect to any possession of the United States unless such possession has a plan, which has been approved by the Secretary of the Treasury, under which such possession will promptly distribute such payments to the residents of such possession.

"(2) Coordination with credit allowed against United States income taxes. Section 25A(i)(6) of such Code (as added by this section) shall not apply to a bona fide resident of any possession of the United States.

"(3) Definitions and special rules.

"(A) Possession of the United States. For purposes of this subsection, the term 'possession of the United States' includes the Commonwealth of Puerto Rico and the Commonwealth of the Northern Mariana Islands.

"(B) Mirror code tax system. For purposes of this subsection, the term 'mirror code tax system' means, with respect to any possession of the United States, the income tax system of such possession if the income tax liability of the residents of such possession under such system is determined by reference to the income tax laws of the United States as if such possession were the United States.

"(C) Treatment of payments. For purposes of section 1324(b)(2) of title 31, United States Code, the payments under this subsection shall be treated in the same manner as a refund due from the credit allowed under section 25A of the Internal Revenue Code of 1986 by reason of subsection (i)(6) of such section (as added by this section).

* * * * * * *

"(f) Treasury studies regarding education incentives.

"(1) Study regarding coordination with non-tax student financial assistance. The Secretary of the Treasury and the Secretary of Education, or their delegates, shall—

"(A) study how to coordinate the credit allowed under section 25A of the Internal Revenue Code of 1986 with the Federal Pell Grant program under section 401 of the Higher Education Act of 1965 to maximize their effectiveness at promoting college affordability, and

"(B) examine ways to expedite the delivery 2 of the tax credit.

"(2) Study regarding inclusion of community service requirements.The Secretary of the Treasury and the Secretary of Education, or their delegates, shall study the feasibility of requiring including community service as a condition of taking their tuition and related expenses into account under section 25A of the Internal Revenue Code of 1986.

"(3) Report. Not later than 1 year after the date of the enactment of this Act, the Secretary of the Treasury, or the Secretary's delegate, shall report to Congress on the results of the studies conducted under this paragraph."

[¶ 3004]   Code Sec. 25B.   Elective deferrals and IRA contributions by certain individuals.

* * * * * * * * * * * *

(g) Limitation based on amount of tax. In the case of a taxable year to which section 26(a)(2) does not apply, the credit allowed under subsection (a) for the taxable year shall not exceed the excess of—

(1) the sum of the regular tax liability (as defined in section 26(b)) plus the tax imposed by section 55, over

(2) the sum of the credits allowable under this subpart (other than this section and sections 23, ¹25A(i), 25D, ²30, ³30B, and 30D) and section 27 for the taxable year.

[For Analysis, see ¶ 107, ¶ 204 and ¶ 205. For Committee Reports, see ¶ 5004, ¶ 5010 and ¶ 5027.]

[Endnote Code Sec. 25B]

Code Sec. 25B(g)(2) was amended by Sec. 1004(b)(4) of the American Recovery and Reinvestment Tax Act of 2009, P.L. 111-5, 2/17/2009, as detailed below:

1. Sec. 1004(b)(4) added "25A(i)," after "23," in para. (g)(2)

Effective Date (Sec. 1004(d), P.L. 111-5, 2/17/2009) effective for tax. yrs. begin. after 12/31/2008.

Code Sec. 25B(g)(2) was amended by Sec. 1142(b)(1)(C), P.L. 111-5, 2/17/2009, as detailed below:

2. Sec. 1142(b)(1)(C) added "30," after "25D," in para. (g)(2) [as amended by Sec. 1004(b)(4) of this Act, see above]
Effective Date (Sec. 1142(c), P.L. 111-5, 2/17/2009) effective for vehicles acquired after 2/17/2009.

Code Sec. 25B(g)(2) was amended by Sec. 1144(b)(1)(C), P.L. 111-5, 2/17/2009, as detailed below:
3. Sec. 1144(b)(1)(C) added "30B," after "30," in para. (g)(2) [as amended by Secs. 1004(b)(4) and 1142(b)(1)(C) of this Act, see above]
Effective Date (Sec. 1144(c), P.L. 111-5, 2/17/2009) effective for tax. yrs. begin. after 12/31/2008.

[¶ 3005]   Code Sec. 25C.   Nonbusiness energy property.

[1]*(a)   Allowance of credit. In the case of an individual, there shall be allowed as a credit against the tax imposed by this chapter for the taxable year an amount equal to 30 percent of the sum of—*

(1) the amount paid or incurred by the taxpayer during such taxable year for qualified energy efficiency improvements, and

(2) the amount of the residential energy property expenditures paid or incurred by the taxpayer during such taxable year.

(b)   Limitation. *The aggregate amount of the credits allowed under this section for taxable years beginning in 2009 and 2010 with respect to any taxpayer shall not exceed $1,500.*

(c)   Qualified energy efficiency improvements. For purposes of this section—

(1)   In general. The term "qualified energy efficiency improvements" means any energy efficient building envelope component which meets the prescriptive criteria for such component established by the 2000 International Energy Conservation Code, as such Code (including supplements) is in effect on the date of the enactment of this section (or, in the case of a metal roof with appropriate pigmented coatings, or an asphalt roof with appropriate cooling granules, which meet the Energy Star program requirements), if—

(A) such component is installed in or on a dwelling unit located in the United States and owned and used by the taxpayer as the taxpayer's principal residence (within the meaning of section 121),

(B) the original use of such component commences with the taxpayer, and

(C) such component reasonably can be expected to remain in use for at least 5 years.

(2)   Building envelope component. The term "building envelope component" means—

(A) any insulation material or system which is specifically and primarily designed to reduce the heat loss or gain of a dwelling unit when installed in or on such dwelling unit, [2]*and meets the prescriptive criteria for such material or system established by the 2009 International Energy Conservation Code, as such Code (including supplements) is in effect on the date of the enactment of the American Recovery and Reinvestment Tax Act of 2009.*

(B) exterior windows (including skylights),

(C) exterior doors, and

(D) any metal roof or asphalt roof installed on a dwelling unit, but only if such roof has appropriate pigmented coatings or cooling granules which are specifically and primarily designed to reduce the heat gain of such dwelling unit.

(3)   Manufactured homes included. The term "dwelling unit" includes a manufactured home which conforms to Federal Manufactured Home Construction and Safety Standards (part 3280 of title 24, Code of Federal Regulations).

[3]*(4)   Qualifications for exterior windows, doors, and skylights. Such term shall not include any component described in subparagraph (B) or (C) of paragraph (2) unless such component is equal to or below a U factor of 0.30 and SHGC of 0.30.*

(d)   Residential energy property expenditures. For purposes of this section—

(1)   In general. The term "residential energy property expenditures" means expenditures made by the taxpayer for qualified energy property which is—

407

(A) installed on or in connection with a dwelling unit located in the United States and owned and used by the taxpayer as the taxpayer's principal residence (within the meaning of section 121), and

(B) originally placed in service by the taxpayer.

Such term includes expenditures for labor costs properly allocable to the onsite preparation, assembly, or original installation of the property.

(2) Qualified energy property.

(A) In general. The term "qualified energy property" means—

(i) energy-efficient building property,

[4]*(ii) any qualified natural gas furnace, qualified propane furnace, qualified oil furnace, qualified natural gas hot water boiler, qualified propane hot water boiler, or qualified oil hot water boiler, or*

(iii) an advanced main air circulating fan.

(B) Performance and quality standards. Property described under subparagraph (A) shall meet the performance and quality standards, and the certification requirements (if any), which—

(i) have been prescribed by the Secretary by regulations (after consultation with the Secretary of Energy or the Administrator of the Environmental Protection Agency, as appropriate), and

(ii) are in effect at the time of the acquisition of the property, or at the time of the completion of the construction, reconstruction, or erection of the property, as the case may be.

(C) Requirements and standards for air conditioners and heat pumps. The standards and requirements prescribed by the Secretary under subparagraph (B) with respect to the energy efficiency ratio (EER) for central air conditioners and electric heat pumps—

(i) shall require measurements to be based on published data which is tested by manufacturers at 95 degrees Fahrenheit, and

(ii) may be based on the certified data of the Air Conditioning and Refrigeration Institute that are prepared in partnership with the Consortium for Energy Efficiency.

(3) Energy-efficient building property. The term "energy–efficient building property" means—

(A) an electric heat pump water heater which yields an energy factor of at least 2.0 in the standard Department of Energy test procedure,

[5]*(B) an electric heat pump which achieves the highest efficiency tier established by the Consortium for Energy Efficiency, as in effect on January 1, 2009.*

(C) a central air conditioner which achieves the highest efficiency tier established by the Consortium for Energy Efficiency, as in effect on January 1, [6]*2009,*

[7]*(D) a natural gas, propane, or oil water heater which has either an energy factor of at least 0.82 or a thermal efficiency of at least 90 percent.*

(E) a stove which uses the burning of biomass fuel to heat a dwelling unit located in the United States and used as a residence by the taxpayer, or to heat water for use in such a dwelling unit, and which has a thermal efficiency rating of at least 75 percent [8], *as measured using a lower heating value.*

[9]**(4) *Qualified natural gas, propane, and oil furnaces and hot water boilers.***

(A) Qualified natural gas furnace. The term "qualified natural gas furnace" means any natural gas furnace which achieves an annual fuel utilization efficiency rate of not less than 95.

(B) Qualified natural gas hot water boiler. The term "qualified natural gas hot water boiler" means any natural gas hot water boiler which achieves an annual fuel utilization efficiency rate of not less than 90.

(C) Qualified propane furnace. The term "qualified propane furnace" means any propane furnace which achieves an annual fuel utilization efficiency rate of not less than 95.

(D) *Qualified propane hot water boiler.* The term "qualified propane hot water boiler" means any propane hot water boiler which achieves an annual fuel utilization efficiency rate of not less than 90.

(E) *Qualified oil furnaces.* The term "qualified oil furnace" means any oil furnace which achieves an annual fuel utilization efficiency rate of not less than 90.

(F) *Qualified oil hot water boiler.* The term "qualified oil hot water boiler" means any oil hot water boiler which achieves an annual fuel utilization efficiency rate of not less than 90.

(5) Advanced main air circulating fan. The term "advanced main air circulating fan" means a fan used in a natural gas, propane, or oil furnace and which has an annual electricity use of no more than 2 percent of the total annual energy use of the furnace (as determined in the standard Department of Energy test procedures).

> • *Caution:* Code Sec. 25C(d)(6), following, is effective for expenditures made after 12/31/2009.

(6) Biomass fuel. The term "biomass fuel" means any plant-derived fuel available on a renewable or recurring basis, including agricultural crops and trees, wood and wood waste and residues (including wood pellets), plants (including aquatic plants), grasses, residues, and fibers.

(e) Special rules. For purposes of this section—

(1) Application of rules. Rules similar to the rules under paragraphs (4), (5), (6), (7), [10]*and (8)* of section 25D(e) shall apply.

(2) Joint ownership of energy items.

(A) *In general.* Any expenditure otherwise qualifying as an expenditure under this section shall not be treated as failing to so qualify merely because such expenditure was made with respect to 2 or more dwelling units.

(B) *Limits applied separately.* In the case of any expenditure described in subparagraph (A), the amount of the credit allowable under subsection (a) shall (subject to paragraph (1)) be computed separately with respect to the amount of the expenditure made for each dwelling unit.

(f) Basis adjustments. For purposes of this subtitle, if a credit is allowed under this section for any expenditure with respect to any property, the increase in the basis of such property which would (but for this subsection) result from such expenditure shall be reduced by the amount of the credit so allowed.

(g) Termination. This section shall not apply with respect to any property placed in service—

(1) after December 31, 2007, and before January 1, 2009, or

(2) after [11]*December 31, 2010.*

[For Analysis, see ¶ 1101, ¶ 1102 and ¶ 1103. For Committee Reports, see ¶ 5021, ¶ 5022 and ¶ 5027.]

[Endnote Code Sec. 25C]

Code Sec. 25C(a) and Code Sec. 25C(b) are amended by Sec. 1121(a) of the American Recovery and Reinvestment Tax Act of 2009, P.L. 111-5, 2/17/2009, as detailed below:

1. Prior to amendment, subsecs. (a) and (b) read as follows:

"(a) Allowance of credit. In the case of an individual, there shall be allowed as a credit against the tax imposed by this chapter for the taxable year an amount equal to the sum of—

"(1) 10 percent of the amount paid or incurred by the taxpayer for qualified energy efficiency improvements installed during such taxable year, and

"(2) the amount of the residential energy property expenditures paid or incurred by the taxpayer during such taxable year.

"(b) Limitations.

"(1) Lifetime limitation. The credit allowed under this section with respect to any taxpayer for any taxable year shall not exceed the excess (if any) of $500 over the aggregate credits allowed under this section with respect to such taxpayer for all prior taxable years.

"(2) Windows. In the case of amounts paid or incurred for components described in subsection (c)(2)(B) by any taxpayer for any taxable year, the credit allowed under this section with respect to such amounts for such year shall not exceed the excess (if any) of $200 over the aggregate credits allowed under this section with respect to such amounts for all prior taxable years.

"(3) Limitation on residential energy property expenditures. The amount of the credit allowed under this section by reason of subsection (a)(2) shall not exceed—

"(A) $50 for any advanced main air circulating fan,

"(B) $150 for any qualified natural gas, propane, or oil furnace or hot water boiler, and

"(C) $300 for any item of energy-efficient building property."

Effective Date (Sec. 1121(f)(1), P.L. 111-5, 2/17/2009) effective for tax. yrs. begin. after 12/31/2008.

Code Sec. 25C(c)(2)(A), Code Sec. 25C(c)(4), Code Sec. 25C(d)(2)(A)(ii), Code Sec. 25C(d)(3)(B), Code Sec. 25C(d)(3)(C), and Code Sec. 25C(d)(3)(D) are amended by Secs. 1121(b)(1)-(3), (c)(2), and (d)(1)-(2), P.L. 111-5, 2/17/2009, as detailed below:

2. Sec. 1121(d)(2) added "and meets the prescriptive criteria for such material or system established by the 2009 International Energy Conservation Code, as such Code (including supplements) is in effect on the date of the enactment of the American Recovery and Reinvestment Tax Act of 2009" after "such dwelling unit" in subpara. (c)(2)(A)

3. Sec. 1121(d)(1) added para. (c)(4)

4. Prior to amendment, clause (d)(2)(A)(ii) read as follows:

"(ii) a qualified natural gas, propane, or oil furnace or hot water boiler, or

5. Prior to amendment, subpara. (d)(3)(B) read as follows:

"(B) an electric heat pump which has a heating seasonal performance factor (HSPF) of at least 9, a seasonal energy efficiency ratio (SEER) of at least 15, and an energy efficiency ratio (EER) of at least 13,"

6. Sec. 1121(b)(2) substituted "2009" for "2006" in subpara. (d)(3)(C)

7. Prior to amendment, subpara. (d)(3)(D) read as follows:

"(D) a natural gas, propane, or oil water heater which has an energy factor of at least 0.80 or a thermal efficiency of at least 90 percent, and"

Effective Date (Sec. 1121(f)(2), P.L. 111-5, 2/17/2009) effective for property placed in service after 2/17/2009.

Code Sec. 25C(d)(3)(E) is amended by Sec. 1121(b)(4), P.L. 111-5, 2/17/2009, as detailed below:

8. Sec. 1121(b)(4) added ", as measured using a lower heating value" after "75 percent" in subpara. (d)(3)(E)

Effective Date (Sec. 1121(f)(1), P.L. 111-5, 2/17/2009) effective for tax. yrs. begin. after 12/31/2008.

Code Sec. 25C(d)(4) is amended by Sec. 1121(c)(1), P.L. 111-5, 2/17/2009, as detailed below:

9. Prior to amendment, para. (d)(4) read as follows:

"(4) Qualified natural gas, propane, or oil furnace or hot water boiler. The term 'qualified natural gas, propane, or oil furnace or hot water boiler' means a natural gas, propane, or oil furnace or hot water boiler which achieves an annual fuel utilization efficiency rate of not less than 95."

Effective Date (Sec. 1121(f)(2), P.L. 111-5, 2/17/2009) effective for property placed in service after 2/17/2009.

Code Sec. 25C(e)(1) is amended by Sec. 1103(b)(2)(A), P.L. 111-5, 2/17/2009, as detailed below:

10. Sec. 1103(b)(2)(A) substituted "and (8)" for "(8), and (9)" in para. (e)(1)

Effective Date (Sec. 1103(c)(2), P.L. 111-5, 2/17/2009) effective for tax. yrs. begin. after 12/31/2008.

Code Sec. 25C(g)(2) is amended by Sec. 1121(e), P.L. 111-5, 2/17/2009, as detailed below:

11. substituted "December 31, 2010" for "December 31, 2009" in para. (g)(2)

Effective Date (Sec. 1121(f)(1), P.L. 111-5, 2/17/2009) effective for tax. yrs. begin. after 12/31/2008.

[¶ 3006]   Code Sec. 25D.   Residential energy efficient property.

* * * * * * * * * * *

(b) Limitations.

[1]*(1) Maximum credit for fuel cells. In the case of any qualified fuel cell property expenditure, the credit allowed under subsection (a) (determined without regard to subsection (c)) for any taxable year shall not exceed $500 with respect to each half kilowatt of capacity of the qualified fuel cell property (as defined in section 48(c)(1)) to which such expenditure relates.*

(2) Certification of solar water heating property. No credit shall be allowed under this section for an item of property described in subsection (d)(1) unless such property is certified for performance by the non-profit Solar Rating Certification Corporation or a comparable entity endorsed by the government of the State in which such property is installed.

* * * * * * * * * * *

(e) Special rules. For purposes of this section—

(1) Labor costs. Expenditures for labor costs properly allocable to the onsite preparation, assembly, or original installation of the property described in subsection (d) and for piping or wiring to interconnect such property to the dwelling unit shall be taken into account for purposes of this section.

(2) Solar panels. No expenditure relating to a solar panel or other property installed as a roof (or portion thereof) shall fail to be treated as property described in paragraph (1) or (2) of subsection (d) solely because it constitutes a structural component of the structure on which it is installed.

(3) Swimming pools, etc., used as storage medium. Expenditures which are properly allocable to a swimming pool, hot tub, or any other energy storage medium which has a function other than the function of such storage shall not be taken into account for purposes of this section.

²*(4) Fuel cell expenditure limitations in case of joint occupancy. In the case of any dwelling unit with respect to which qualified fuel cell property expenditures are made and which is jointly occupied and used during any calendar year as a residence by two or more individuals, the following rules shall apply:*

(A) Maximum expenditures for fuel cells. The maximum amount of such expenditures which may be taken into account under subsection (a) by all such individuals with respect to such dwelling unit during such calendar year shall be $1,667 in the case of each half kilowatt of capacity of qualified fuel cell property (as defined in section 48(c)(1)) with respect to which such expenditures relate.

(B) Allocation of expenditures. The expenditures allocated to any individual for the taxable year in which such calendar year ends shall be an amount equal to the lesser of—

(i) the amount of expenditures made by such individual with respect to such dwelling during such calendar year, or

(ii) the maximum amount of such expenditures set forth in subparagraph (A) multiplied by a fraction—

(I) the numerator of which is the amount of such expenditures with respect to such dwelling made by such individual during such calendar year, and

(II) the denominator of which is the total expenditures made by all such individuals with respect to such dwelling during such calendar year.

³*(C) [Deleted.]*

(5) Tenant–stockholder in cooperative housing corporation. In the case of an individual who is a tenant-stockholder (as defined in section 216) in a cooperative housing corporation (as defined in such section), such individual shall be treated as having made his tenant-stockholder's proportionate share (as defined in section 216(b)(3)) of any expenditures of such corporation.

(6) Condominiums.

(A) In general. In the case of an individual who is a member of a condominium management association with respect to a condominium which the individual owns, such individual shall be treated as having made the individual's proportionate share of any expenditures of such association.

(B) Condominium management association. For purposes of this paragraph, the term "condominium management association" means an organization which meets the requirements of paragraph (1) of section 528(c) (other than subparagraph (E) thereof) with respect to a condominium project substantially all of the units of which are used as residences.

(7) Allocation in certain cases. If less than 80 percent of the use of an item is for nonbusiness purposes, only that portion of the expenditures for such item which is properly allocable to use for nonbusiness purposes shall be taken into account.

(8) When expenditure made; amount of expenditure.

(A) In general. Except as provided in subparagraph (B), an expenditure with respect to an item shall be treated as made when the original installation of the item is completed.

(B) Expenditures part of building construction. In the case of an expenditure in connection with the construction or reconstruction of a structure, such expenditure shall be treated as made when the original use of the constructed or reconstructed structure by the taxpayer begins.

⁴*(9) Repealed.*

* * * * * * * * * * * *

[For Analysis, see ¶ 204, ¶ 1103 and ¶ 1104. For Committee Reports, see ¶ 5010, ¶ 5021 and ¶ 5022.]

[Endnote Code Sec. 25D]

Code Sec. 25D(b)(1), Code Sec. 25D(e)(4) opening para., Code Sec. 25D(e)(4)(A), and Code Sec. 25D(e)(4)(C) was amended by Sec. 1122(a)(1)-(a)(2)(A)-(B) of the American Recovery and Reinvestment Tax Act of 2009, P.L. 111-5, 2/17/2009, as detailed below:

1. Prior to amendment, para. (b)(1) read as follows:

"(1) Maximum credit. The credit allowed under subsection (a) (determined without regard to subsection (c)) for any taxable year shall not exceed—

"(A) $2,000 with respect to any qualified solar water heating property expenditures,

"(B) $500 with respect to each half kilowatt of capacity of qualified fuel cell property (as defined in section 48(c)(1)) for which qualified fuel cell property expenditures are made

"(C) $500 with respect to each half kilowatt of capacity (not to exceed $4,000) of wind turbines for which qualified small wind energy property expenditures are made, and

"(D) $2,000 with respect to any qualified geothermal heat pump property expenditures."

2. Prior to amendment, para. (e)(4) opening paragraph, and subpara. (e)(4)(A) read as follows:

"(4) Dollar amounts in case of joint occupancy. In the case of any dwelling unit which is jointly occupied and used during any calendar year as a residence by 2 or more individuals the following rules shall apply:

"(A) Maximum expenditures. The maximum amount of expenditures which may be taken into account under subsection (a) by all such individuals with respect to such dwelling unit during such calendar year shall be—

"(i) $6,667 in the case of any qualified solar water heating property expenditures,

"(ii) $1,667 in the case of each half kilowatt of capacity of qualified fuel cell property (as defined in section 48(c)(1)) for which qualified fuel cell property expenditures are made

"(iii) $1,667 in the case of each half kilowatt of capacity (not to exceed $13,333) of wind turbines for which qualified small wind energy property expenditures are made, and

"(iv) $6,667 in the case of any qualified geothermal heat pump property expenditures."

3. Prior to deletion, subpara. (e)(4)(C) read as follows;

"(C) Subparagraphs (A) and (B) shall be applied separately with respect to expenditures described in paragraphs (1), (2), and (3) of subsection (d)."

Effective Date (Sec. 1122(b), P.L. 111-5, 2/17/2009) effective for tax. yrs. begin. after 12/31/2008.

Code Sec. 25D(e)(9) was deleted by Sec. 1103(b)(2)(B), P.L. 111-5, 2/17/2009, as detailed below:

4. Prior to deletion, para. (e)(9) read as follows;

"(9) Property financed by subsidized energy financing. For purposes of determining the amount of expenditures made by any individual with respect to any dwelling unit, there shall not be taken into account expenditures which are made from subsidized energy financing (as defined in section 48(a)(4)(C))."

Effective Date (Sec. 1103(c)(2), P.L. 111-5, 2/17/2009) effective for tax. yrs. begin. after 12/31/2008.

[¶ 3007]   *Code Sec. 26.*   *Limitation based on tax liability; definition of tax liability.*

(a) Limitation based on amount of tax.

(1) In general. The aggregate amount of credits allowed by this subpart (other than sections 23, 24, ¹25A(i), 25B, 25D, ²30, ³30B, and 30D) for the taxable year shall not exceed the excess (if any) of—

(A) the taxpayer's regular tax liability for the taxable year, over

(B) the tentative minimum tax for the taxable year (determined without regard to the alternative minimum tax foreign tax credit).

For purposes of subparagraph (B), the taxpayer's tentative minimum tax for any taxable year beginning during 1999 shall be treated as being zero.

(2)   Special rule for taxable years 2000 through [4]***2009.*** For purposes of any taxable year beginning during 2000, 2001, 2002, 2003, 2004, 2005, 2006, 2007, [5]*2008, or 2009* the aggregate amount of credits allowed by this subpart for the taxable year shall not exceed the sum of—

(A) the taxpayer's regular tax liability for the taxable year reduced by the foreign tax credit allowable under section 27(a), and

(B) the tax imposed by section 55(a) for the taxable year.

* * * * * * * * * * * *

[For Analysis, see ¶ 107, ¶ 204 and ¶ 205. For Committee Reports, see ¶ 5004, ¶ 5010 and ¶ 5027.]

[Endnote Code Sec. 26]

Code Sec. 26(a)(1) was amended by Sec. 1004(b)(3) of the American Recovery and Reinvestment Tax Act of 2009, P.L. 111-5, 2/17/2009, as detailed below:

1. Sec. 1004(b)(3) added "25A(i)," after "24," in para. (a)(1)

Effective Date (Sec. 1004(d), P.L. 111-5, 2/17/2009) effective for tax. yrs. begin. after 12/31/2008.

Code Sec. 26(a)(1) was amended by Sec. 1142(b)(1)(D), P.L. 111-5, 2/17/2009, as detailed below:

2. Sec. 1142(b)(1)(D) added "30," after "25D," in para. (a)(1) [as amended by Sec. 1004(b)(3) of this Act, see above]

Effective Date (Sec. 1142(c), P.L. 111-5, 2/17/2009) effective for vehicles acquired after 2/17/2009.

Code Sec. 26(a)(1) was amended by Sec. 1144(b)(1)(D), P.L. 111-5, 2/17/2009, as detailed below:

3. Sec. 1144(b)(1)(D) added "30B," after "30," in para. (a)(1) [as amended by Secs. 1004(b)(3) and 1142(b)(1)(D) of this Act, see above]

Effective Date (Sec. 1144(c), P.L. 111-5, 2/17/2009) effective for tax. yrs. begin. after 12/31/2008.

Code Sec. 26(a)(2) heading and Code Sec. 26(a)(2) was amended by Sec. 1011(a)(1)-(2), P.L. 111-5, 2/17/2009, as detailed below:

4. Sec. 1011(a)(1) substituted "2009" for "2008" in the heading of para. (a)(2)

5. Sec. 1011(a)(2) substituted '2008, or 2009' for 'or 2008' in para. (a)(2)

Effective Date (Sec. 1011(b), P.L. 111-5, 2/17/2009) effective for tax. yrs. begin. after 12/31/2008.

[¶ 3008]   Code Sec.[1] **30.**   *Certain plug-in electric vehicles.*

*(a)   **Allowance of credit.*** *There shall be allowed as a credit against the tax imposed by this chapter for the taxable year an amount equal to 10 percent of the cost of any qualified plug-in electric vehicle placed in service by the taxpayer during the taxable year.*

*(b)   **Per vehicle dollar limitation.*** *The amount of the credit allowed under subsection (a) with respect to any vehicle shall not exceed $2,500.*

*(c)   **Application with other credits.***

*(1)   **Business credit treated as part of general business credit.*** *So much of the credit which would be allowed under subsection (a) for any taxable year (determined without regard to this subsection) that is attributable to property of a character subject to an allowance for depreciation shall be treated as a credit listed in section 38(b) for such taxable year (and not allowed under subsection (a)).*

*(2)   **Personal credit.***

(A) In general. For purposes of this title, the credit allowed under subsection (a) for any taxable year (determined after application of paragraph (1)) shall be treated as a credit allowable under subpart A for such taxable year.

(B) Limitation based on amount of tax. In the case of a taxable year to which section 26(a)(2) does not apply, the credit allowed under subsection (a) for any taxable year (determined after application of paragraph (1)) shall not exceed the excess of—

(i) the sum of the regular tax liability (as defined in section 26(b)) plus the tax imposed by section 55, over

(ii) the sum of the credits allowable under subpart A (other than this section and sections 23, 25D, and 30D) and section 27 for the taxable year.

413

(d) Qualified plug-in electric vehicle. *For purposes of this section—*

(1) **In general.** *The term "qualified plug-in electric vehicle" means a specified vehicle—*

   (A) the original use of which commences with the taxpayer,

   (B) which is acquired for use or lease by the taxpayer and not for resale,

   (C) which is made by a manufacturer,

   (D) which is manufactured primarily for use on public streets, roads, and highways,

   (E) which has a gross vehicle weight rating of less than 14,000 pounds, and

   (F) which is propelled to a significant extent by an electric motor which draws electricity from a battery which—

      (i) has a capacity of not less than 4 kilowatt hours (2.5 kilowatt hours in the case of a vehicle with 2 or 3 wheels), and

      (ii) is capable of being recharged from an external source of electricity.

(2) **Specified vehicle.** *The term "specified vehicle" means any vehicle which—*

   (A) is a low speed vehicle within the meaning of section 571.3 of title 49, Code of Federal Regulations (as in effect on the date of the enactment of the American Recovery and Reinvestment Tax Act of 2009), or

   (B) has 2 or 3 wheels.

(3) **Manufacturer.** *The term "manufacturer" has the meaning given such term in regulations prescribed by the Administrator of the Environmental Protection Agency for purposes of the administration of title II of the Clean Air Act (42 U.S.C. 7521 et seq.).*

(4) **Battery capacity.** *The term "capacity" means, with respect to any battery, the quantity of electricity which the battery is capable of storing, expressed in kilowatt hours, as measured from a 100 percent state of charge to a 0 percent state of charge.*

(e) Special rules.

(1) **Basis reduction.** *For purposes of this subtitle, the basis of any property for which a credit is allowable under subsection (a) shall be reduced by the amount of such credit so allowed.*

(2) **No double benefit.** *The amount of any deduction or other credit allowable under this chapter for a new qualified plug-in electric drive motor vehicle shall be reduced by the amount of credit allowable under subsection (a) for such vehicle.*

(3) **Property used by tax-exempt entity.** *In the case of a vehicle the use of which is described in paragraph (3) or (4) of section 50(b) and which is not subject to a lease, the person who sold such vehicle to the person or entity using such vehicle shall be treated as the taxpayer that placed such vehicle in service, but only if such person clearly discloses to such person or entity in a document the amount of any credit allowable under subsection (a) with respect to such vehicle (determined without regard to subsection (c)).*

(4) **Property used outside United States not qualified.** *No credit shall be allowable under subsection (a) with respect to any property referred to in section 50(b)(1).*

(5) **Recapture.** *The Secretary shall, by regulations, provide for recapturing the benefit of any credit allowable under subsection (a) with respect to any property which ceases to be property eligible for such credit.*

(6) **Election not to take credit.** *No credit shall be allowed under subsection (a) for any vehicle if the taxpayer elects to not have this section apply to such vehicle.*

(f) Termination. *This section shall not apply to any vehicle acquired after December 31, 2011.*

[For Analysis, see ¶ 1103. For Committee Reports, see ¶ 5027.]

[Endnote Code Sec. 30]

Code Sec. 30 was amended by Sec. 1142(a) of the American Recovery and Reinvestment Tax Act of 2009, P.L. 111-5, 2/17/2009, as detailed below:

1. Prior to amendment, Code Sec. 30 read as follows:

"SEC. 30. CREDIT FOR QUALIFIED ELECTRIC VEHICLES.

"(a) Allowance of credit. There shall be allowed as a credit against the tax imposed by this chapter for the taxable year an amount equal to 10 percent of the cost of any qualified electric vehicle placed in service by the taxpayer during the taxable year.

"(b) Limitations.

"(1) Limitation per vehicle. The amount of the credit allowed under subsection (a) for any vehicle shall not exceed $4,000.

"(2) Phaseout. In the case of any qualified electric vehicle placed in service after December 31, 2005, the credit otherwise allowable under subsection (a) (determined after the application of paragraph (1)) shall be reduced by 75 percent.

"(3) Application with other credits. The credit allowed by subsection (a) for any taxable year shall not exceed the excess (if any) of—

"(A) the regular tax for the taxable year reduced by the sum of the credits allowable under subpart A and section 27, over—

"(B) the tentative minimum tax for the taxable year.

"(c) Qualified electric vehicle. For purposes of this section—

"(1) In general. The term 'qualified electric vehicle' means any motor vehicle—

"(A) which is powered primarily by an electric motor drawing current from rechargeable batteries, fuel cells, or other portable sources of electrical current,

"(B) the original use of which commences with the taxpayer, and

"(C) which is acquired for use by the taxpayer and not for resale.

"(2) Motor vehicle. For purposes of paragraph (1), the term 'motor vehicle' means any vehicle which is manufactured primarily for use on public streets, roads, and highways (not including a vehicle operated exclusively on a rail or rails) and which has at least 4 wheels.

"(d) Special rules.

"(1) Basis reduction. The basis of any property for which a credit is allowable under subsection (a) shall be reduced by the amount of such credit (determined without regard to subsection (b)(3)).

"(2) Recapture. The Secretary shall, by regulations, provide for recapturing the benefit of any credit allowable under subsection (a) with respect to any property which ceases to be property eligible for such credit.

"(3) Property used outside United States, etc., not qualified. No credit shall be allowed under subsection (a) with respect to any property referred to in section 50(b) or with respect to the portion of the cost of any property taken into account under section 179.

"(4) Election to not take credit. No credit shall be allowed under section (a) for any vehicle if the taxpayer elects to not have this section apply to such vehicle.

"(e) Termination. This section shall not apply to any property placed in service after December 31, 2006."

Effective Date (Sec. 1142(c), P.L. 111-5, 2/17/2009) effective for vehicles acquired after 2/17/2009.

[¶ 3009]   Code Sec. 30B.   Alternative motor vehicle credit.

(a) Allowance of credit. There shall be allowed as a credit against the tax imposed by this chapter for the taxable year an amount equal to the sum of—

(1) the new qualified fuel cell motor vehicle credit determined under subsection (b),

(2) the new advanced lean burn technology motor vehicle credit determined under subsection (c),

(3) the new qualified hybrid motor vehicle credit determined under subsection (d), [1]

(4) the new qualified alternative fuel motor vehicle credit determined under subsection (e)[2], *and*

[3]*(5) the plug-in conversion credit determined under subsection (i).*

* * * * * * * * * * * *

(d) New qualified hybrid motor vehicle credit.

(1) In general. For purposes of subsection (a), the new qualified hybrid motor vehicle credit determined under this subsection for the taxable year is the credit amount determined under paragraph (2) with respect to a new qualified hybrid motor vehicle placed in service by the taxpayer during the taxable year.

(2) Credit amount.

(A) Credit amount for passenger automobiles and light trucks. In the case of a new qualified hybrid motor vehicle which is a passenger automobile or light truck and which has a gross vehicle weight rating of not more than 8,500 pounds, the amount determined under this paragraph is the sum of the amounts determined under clauses (i) and (ii).

(i) Fuel economy. The amount determined under this clause is the amount which would be determined under subsection (c)(2)(A) if such vehicle were a vehicle referred to in such subsection.

(ii) Conservation credit. The amount determined under this clause is the amount which would be determined under subsection (c)(2)(B) if such vehicle were a vehicle referred to in such subsection.

415

(B) Credit amount for other motor vehicles.

(i) In general. In the case of any new qualified hybrid motor vehicle to which subparagraph (A) does not apply, the amount determined under this paragraph is the amount equal to the applicable percentage of the qualified incremental hybrid cost of the vehicle as certified under clause (v).

(ii) Applicable percentage. For purposes of clause (i), the applicable percentage is—

(I) 20 percent if the vehicle achieves an increase in city fuel economy relative to a comparable vehicle of at least 30 percent but less than 40 percent,

(II) 30 percent if the vehicle achieves such an increase of at least 40 percent but less than 50 percent, and

(III) 40 percent if the vehicle achieves such an increase of at least 50 percent.

(iii) Qualified incremental hybrid cost. For purposes of this subparagraph, the qualified incremental hybrid cost of any vehicle is equal to the amount of the excess of the manufacturer's suggested retail price for such vehicle over such price for a comparable vehicle, to the extent such amount does not exceed—

(I) $7,500, if such vehicle has a gross vehicle weight rating of not more than 14,000 pounds,

(II) $15,000, if such vehicle has a gross vehicle weight rating of more than 14,000 pounds but not more than 26,000 pounds, and

(III) $30,000, if such vehicle has a gross vehicle weight rating of more than 26,000 pounds.

(iv) Comparable vehicle. For purposes of this subparagraph, the term "comparable vehicle" means, with respect to any new qualified hybrid motor vehicle, any vehicle which is powered solely by a gasoline or diesel internal combustion engine and which is comparable in weight, size, and use to such vehicle.

(v) Certification. A certification described in clause (i) shall be made by the manufacturer and shall be determined in accordance with guidance prescribed by the Secretary. Such guidance shall specify procedures and methods for calculating fuel economy savings and incremental hybrid costs.

(3) New qualified hybrid motor vehicle. For purposes of this subsection—

(A) In general. The term "new qualified hybrid motor vehicle" means a motor vehicle—

(i) which draws propulsion energy from onboard sources of stored energy which are both—

(I) an internal combustion or heat engine using consumable fuel, and

(II) a rechargeable energy storage system,

(ii) which, in the case of a vehicle to which paragraph (2)(A) applies, has received a certificate of conformity under the Clean Air Act and meets or exceeds the equivalent qualifying California low emission vehicle standard under section 243(e)(2) of the Clean Air Act for that make and model year, and

(I) in the case of a vehicle having a gross vehicle weight rating of 6,000 pounds or less, the Bin 5 Tier II emission standard established in regulations prescribed by the Administrator of the Environmental Protection Agency under section 202(i) of the Clean Air Act for that make and model year vehicle, and

(II) in the case of a vehicle having a gross vehicle weight rating of more than 6,000 pounds but not more than 8,500 pounds, the Bin 8 Tier II emission standard which is so established,

(iii) which has a maximum available power of at least—

(I) 4 percent in the case of a vehicle to which paragraph (2)(A) applies,

(II) 10 percent in the case of a vehicle which has a gross vehicle weight rating of more than 8,500 pounds and not more than 14,000 pounds, and

(III) 15 percent in the case of a vehicle in excess of 14,000 pounds,

(iv) which, in the case of a vehicle to which paragraph (2)(B) applies, has an internal combustion or heat engine which has received a certificate of conformity under the Clean Air Act as meeting the emission standards set in the regulations prescribed by the Administrator of the Environmental Protection Agency for 2004 through 2007 model year diesel heavy duty engines or ottocycle heavy duty engines, as applicable,

(v) the original use of which commences with the taxpayer,

(vi) which is acquired for use or lease by the taxpayer and not for resale, and

(vii) which is made by a manufacturer.

Such term shall not include any vehicle which is not a passenger automobile or light truck if such vehicle has a gross vehicle weight rating of less than 8,500 pounds.

(B) Consumable fuel. For purposes of subparagraph (A)(i)(I), the term "consumable fuel" means any solid, liquid, or gaseous matter which releases energy when consumed by an auxiliary power unit.

(C) Maximum available power.

(i) Certain passenger automobiles and light trucks. In the case of a vehicle to which paragraph (2)(A) applies, the term "maximum available power" means the maximum power available from the rechargeable energy storage system, during a standard 10 second pulse power or equivalent test, divided by such maximum power and the SAE net power of the heat engine.

(ii) Other motor vehicles. In the case of a vehicle to which paragraph (2)(B) applies, the term "maximum available power" means the maximum power available from the rechargeable energy storage system, during a standard 10 second pulse power or equivalent test, divided by the vehicle's total traction power. For purposes of the preceding sentence, the term "total traction power" means the sum of the peak power from the rechargeable energy storage system and the heat engine peak power of the vehicle, except that if such storage system is the sole means by which the vehicle can be driven, the total traction power is the peak power of such storage system.

(D) Exclusion of plug-in vehicles. Any vehicle with respect to which a credit is allowable under section 30D (determined without regard to [4]*subsection (c) thereof*) shall not be taken into account under this section.

* * * * * * * * * * * *

(g) Application with other credits.

(1) Business credit treated as part of general business credit. So much of the credit which would be allowed under subsection (a) for any taxable year (determined without regard to this subsection) that is attributable to property of a character subject to an allowance for depreciation shall be treated as a credit listed in section 38(b) for such taxable year (and not allowed under subsection (a)).

[5]*(2) Personal credit.*

(A) In general. For purposes of this title, the credit allowed under subsection (a) for any taxable year (determined after application of paragraph (1)) shall be treated as a credit allowable under subpart A for such taxable year.

(B) Limitation based on amount of tax. In the case of a taxable year to which section 26(a)(2) does not apply, the credit allowed under subsection (a) for any taxable year (determined after application of paragraph (1)) shall not exceed the excess of—

(i) the sum of the regular tax liability (as defined in section 26(b)) plus the tax imposed by section 55, over

(ii) the sum of the credits allowable under subpart A (other than this section and sections 23, 25D, 30, and 30D) and section 27 for the taxable year.

(h) Other definitions and special rules. For purposes of this section—

[6]*(1) Motor vehicle. The term "motor vehicle" means any vehicle which is manufactured primarily for use on public streets, roads, and highways (not including a vehicle operated exclusively on a rail or rails) and which has at least 4 wheels.*

(2) City fuel economy. The city fuel economy with respect to any vehicle shall be measured in a manner which is substantially similar to the manner city fuel economy is measured in accordance with procedures under part 600 of subchapter Q of chapter I of title 40, Code of Federal Regulations, as in effect on the date of the enactment of this section.

(3) Other terms. The terms "automobile", "passenger automobile", "medium duty passenger vehicle", "light truck", and "manufacturer" have the meanings given such terms in regulations prescribed by the Administrator of the Environmental Protection Agency for purposes of the administration of title II of the Clean Air Act (42 U.S.C. 7521 *et seq.*).

(4) Reduction in basis. For purposes of this subtitle, the basis of any property for which a credit is allowable under subsection (a) shall be reduced by the amount of such credit so allowed (determined without regard to subsection (g)).

(5) No double benefit. The amount of any deduction or other credit allowable under this chapter—

(A) for any incremental cost taken into account in computing the amount of the credit determined under subsection (e) shall be reduced by the amount of such credit attributable to such cost, and

(B) with respect to a vehicle described under subsection (b) or (c), shall be reduced by the amount of credit allowed under subsection (a) for such vehicle for the taxable year.

(6) Property used by tax-exempt entity. In the case of a vehicle whose use is described in paragraph (3) or (4) of section 50(b) and which is not subject to a lease, the person who sold such vehicle to the person or entity using such vehicle shall be treated as the taxpayer that placed such vehicle in service, but only if such person clearly discloses to such person or entity in a document the amount of any credit allowable under subsection (a) with respect to such vehicle (determined without regard to subsection (g)). For purposes of subsection (g), property to which this paragraph applies shall be treated as of a character subject to an allowance for depreciation.

(7) Property used outside United States, etc., not qualified. No credit shall be allowable under subsection (a) with respect to any property referred to in section 50(b)(1) or with respect to the portion of the cost of any property taken into account under section 179.

(8) Recapture. The Secretary shall, by regulations, provide for recapturing the benefit of any credit allowable under subsection (a) with respect to any property which ceases to be property eligible for such credit (including recapture in the case of a lease period of less than the economic life of a vehicle).[7], *except that no benefit shall be recaptured if such property ceases to be eligible for such credit by reason of conversion to a qualified plugin electric drive motor vehicle.*

(9) Election to not take credit. No credit shall be allowed under subsection (a) for any vehicle if the taxpayer elects to not have this section apply to such vehicle.

(10) Interaction with air quality and motor vehicle safety standards. Unless otherwise provided in this section, a motor vehicle shall not be considered eligible for a credit under this section unless such vehicle is in compliance with—

(A) the applicable provisions of the Clean Air Act for the applicable make and model year of the vehicle (or applicable air quality provisions of State law in the case of a State which has adopted such provision under a waiver under section 209(b) of the Clean Air Act), and

(B) the motor vehicle safety provisions of sections 30101 through 30169 of title 49, United States Code.

[8]*(i) Plug-in conversion credit.*

(1) In general. For purposes of subsection (a), the plug-in conversion credit determined under this subsection with respect to any motor vehicle which is converted to a qualified plug-in electric drive motor vehicle is 10 percent of so much of the cost of the converting such vehicle as does not exceed $40,000.

(2) Qualified plug-in electric drive motor vehicle. For purposes of this subsection, the term "qualified plug-in electric drive motor vehicle" means any new qualified plug-in

electric drive motor vehicle (as defined in section 30D, determined without regard to whether such vehicle is made by a manufacturer or whether the original use of such vehicle commences with the taxpayer).

(3) Credit allowed in addition to other credits. The credit allowed under this subsection shall be allowed with respect to a motor vehicle notwithstanding whether a credit has been allowed with respect to such motor vehicle under this section (other than this subsection) in any preceding taxable year.

(4) Termination. This subsection shall not apply to conversions made after December 31, 2011.

[9](j) Regulations.

(1) In general. Except as provided in paragraph (2), the Secretary shall promulgate such regulations as necessary to carry out the provisions of this section.

(2) Coordination in prescription of certain regulations. The Secretary of the Treasury, in coordination with the Secretary of Transportation and the Administrator of the Environmental Protection Agency, shall prescribe such regulations as necessary to determine whether a motor vehicle meets the requirements to be eligible for a credit under this section.

[10](k) Termination. This section shall not apply to any property purchased after—

(1) in the case of a new qualified fuel cell motor vehicle (as described in subsection (b)), December 31, 2014,

(2) in the case of a new advanced lean burn technology motor vehicle (as described in subsection (c)) or a new qualified hybrid motor vehicle (as described in subsection (d)(2)(A)), December 31, 2010,

(3) in the case of a new qualified hybrid motor vehicle (as described in subsection (d)(2)(B)), December 31, 2009, and

(4) in the case of a new qualified alternative fuel vehicle (as described in subsection (e)), December 31, 2010.

[For Analysis, see ¶ 205, ¶ 1102 and ¶ 1104. For Committee Reports, see ¶ 5027.]

[Endnote Code Sec. 30B]

Code Sec. 30B(a)(3), Code Sec. 30B(a)(4) and Code Sec. 30B(a)(5) was amended by Sec. 1143(b) of the American Recovery and Reinvestment Act of 2009, P.L. 111-5, 2/17/2009, as detailed below:
1. Sec. 1143(b) deleted "and" at the end of paragraph (a)(3),
2. substituted ", and" for the period at the end of para. (a)(4)
3. added para. (a)(5)
Effective Date (Sec. 1143(d), P.L. 111-5, 2/17/2009) effective for property placed in service after 2/17/2009.

Code Sec. 30B(d)(3)(D) was amended by Sec. 1141(b)(1), P.L. 111-5, 2/17/2009, as detailed below:
4. Sec. 1141(b)(1) substituted "subsection (c) thereof" for "subsection (d) thereof" in subpara. (d)(3)(D)
Effective Date (Sec. 1141(c), P.L. 111-5, 2/17/2009) effective for vehicles acquired after 12/31/2008.

Code Sec. 30B(g)(2) was amended by Sec. 1144(a), P.L. 111-5, 2/17/2009, as detailed below:
5. Prior to amendment, para. (g)(2) read as follows:
"(2) Personal credit. The credit allowed under subsection (a) (after the application of paragraph (1)) for any taxable year shall not exceed the excess (if any) of—
"(A) the regular tax liability (as defined in section 26(b)) reduced by the sum of the credits allowable under subpart A and sections 27 and 30, over
"(B) the tentative minimum tax for the taxable year."
Effective Date (Sec. 1144(c), P.L. 111-5, 2/17/2009) effective for tax. yrs. begin. after 12/31/2008.

Code Sec. 30B(h)(1) was amended by Sec. 1142(b)(2), P.L. 111-5, 2/17/2009, as detailed below:
6. Prior to amendment, para. (h)(1) read as follows:
"(1) Motor vehicle. The term 'motor vehicle' has the meaning given such term by section 30(c)(2)."
Effective Date (Sec. 1142(c), P.L. 111-5, 2/17/2009) effective for vehicles acquired after 2/17/2009.

Code Sec. 30B(h)(8) and Code Sec. 30B(i), Code Sec. 30B(j) and Code Sec. 30B(k) was amended by Sec. 1143(a) and (c), P.L. 111-5, 2/17/2009, as detailed below:
7. Sec. 1143(c) added ", except that no benefit shall be recaptured if such property ceases to be eligible for such credit by reason of conversion to a qualified plugin electric drive motor vehicle." at the end of para. (h)(8)

8. Sec. 1143(a) added subsec. (i)
9. Sec. 1143(a) redesignated subsec. (i) as subsec. (j)
10. Sec. 1143(a) redesignated subsec. (j) as subsec. (k)
Effective Date (Sec. 1143(d), P.L. 111-5, 2/17/2009) effective for property placed in service after 2/17/2009.

[¶ 3010]   **Code Sec. 30C.**   **Alternative fuel vehicle refueling property credit.**

* * * * * * * * * * * *

(c)   Qualified alternative fuel vehicle refueling property. For purposes of this section, the term "qualified alternative fuel vehicle refueling property" has the same meaning as the term "qualified clean-fuel vehicle refueling property" would have under section 179A if—

    (1) paragraph (1) of section 179A(d) did not apply to property installed on property which is used as the principal residence (within the meaning of section 121) of the taxpayer, and

    (2) only the following were treated as clean-burning fuels for purposes of section 179A(d):

       (A) Any fuel at least 85 percent of the volume of which consists of one or more of the following: ethanol, natural gas, compressed natural gas, liquefied natural gas, liquefied petroleum gas, or hydrogen.

       (B) Any mixture—

          (i) which consists of two or more of the following: biodiesel (as defined in section 40A(d)(1)), diesel fuel (as defined in section 4083(a)(3)), or kerosene, and

          (ii) at least 20 percent of the volume of which consists of biodiesel (as so defined) determined without regard to any kerosene in such mixture.

       (C) Electricity.

(d)   Application with other credits.

    (1)   Business credit treated as part of general business credit. So much of the credit which would be allowed under subsection (a) for any taxable year (determined without regard to this subsection) that is attributable to property of a character subject to an allowance for depreciation shall be treated as a credit listed in section 38(b) for such taxable year (and not allowed under subsection (a)).

    (2)   Personal credit. The credit allowed under subsection (a) (after the application of paragraph (1)) for any taxable year shall not exceed the excess (if any) of—

       (A) the regular tax liability (as defined in section 26(b)) reduced by the sum of the credits allowable under subpart A and [1], [2]*section 27*, over

       (B) the tentative minimum tax for the taxable year.

(e)   Special rules. For purposes of this section—

    (1)   Basis reduction. The basis of any property shall be reduced by the portion of the cost of such property taken into account under subsection (a).

    (2)   Property used by tax-exempt entity. In the case of any qualified alternative fuel vehicle refueling property the use of which is described in paragraph (3) or (4) of section 50(b) and which is not subject to a lease, the person who sold such property to the person or entity using such property shall be treated as the taxpayer that placed such property in service, but only if such person clearly discloses to such person or entity in a document the amount of any credit allowable under subsection (a) with respect to such property (determined without regard to subsection (d)). For purposes of subsection (d), property to which this paragraph applies shall be treated as of a character subject to an allowance for depreciation.

    (3)   Property used outside United States not qualified. No credit shall be allowable under subsection (a) with respect to any property referred to in section 50(b)(1) or with respect to the portion of the cost of any property taken into account under section 179.

    (4)   Election not to take credit. No credit shall be allowed under subsection (a) for any property if the taxpayer elects not to have this section apply to such property.

(5) Recapture rules. Rules similar to the rules of section 179A(e)(4) shall apply.

³*(6) Special rule for property placed in service during 2009 and 2010. In the case of property placed in service in taxable years beginning after December 31, 2008, and before January 1, 2011—*

    (A) in the case of any such property which does not relate to hydrogen—

        (i) subsection (a) shall be applied by substituting "50 percent" for "30 percent",

        (ii) subsection (b)(1) shall be applied by substituting "$50,000" for "$30,000", and

        (iii) subsection (b)(2) shall be applied by substituting "$2,000" for "$1,000", and

    (B) in the case of any such property which relates to hydrogen, subsection (b)(1)shall be applied by substituting "$200,000" for "$30,000".

(f) Regulations. The Secretary shall prescribe such regulations as necessary to carry out the provisions of this section.

(g) Termination. This section shall not apply to any property placed in service—

    (1) in the case of property relating to hydrogen, after December 31, 2014, and

    (2) in the case of any other property, after December 31, 2010.

[For Analysis, see ¶ 205 and ¶ 1101. For Committee Reports, see ¶ 5023 and ¶ 5027.]

[Endnote Code Sec. 30C]
  Code Sec. 30C(d)(2)(A) was amended by Sec. 1142(b)(3) of the American Recovery and Reinvestment Act of 2009, P.L. 111-5, 2/17/2009, as detailed below:
    1. Sec. 1142(b)(3) deleted ", 30," after "sections 27" in subpara. (d)(2)(A)
Effective Date (Sec. 1142(c), P.L. 111-5, 2/17/2009) effective for vehicles acquired after 2/17/2009.

  Code Sec. 30C(d)(2)(A) was amended by Sec. 1144(b)(2), P.L. 111-5, 2/17/2009, as detailed below:
    2. Sec. 1144(b)(2) substituted "section 27" for "sections 27 and 30B" in subpara. (d)(2)(A) [as amended by Sec. 1142(b)(3) of this Act, see above]
Effective Date (Sec. 1144(c), P.L. 111-5, 2/17/2009) effective for tax. yrs. begin. after 12/31/2008.

  Code Sec. 30C(e)(6) was added by Sec. 1123(a), P.L. 111-5, 2/17/2009, as detailed below:
    3. Sec. 1123(a) added para. (e)(6)
Effective Date (Sec. 1123(b), P.L. 111-5, 2/17/2009) effective for tax. yrs. begin. after 12/31/2008.

[¶ 3011]   Code Sec.¹ 30D. *New qualified plug-in electric drive motor vehicles.*

  (a) Allowance of credit. There shall be allowed as a credit against the tax imposed by this chapter for the taxable year an amount equal to the sum of the credit amounts determined under subsection (b) with respect to each new qualified plug-in electric drive motor vehicle placed in service by the taxpayer during the taxable year.

  (b) Per vehicle dollar limitation.

    (1) In general. The amount determined under this subsection with respect to any new qualified plug-in electric drive motor vehicle is the sum of the amounts determined under paragraphs (2) and (3) with respect to such vehicle.

    (2) Base amount. The amount determined under this paragraph is $2,500.

    (3) Battery capacity. In the case of a vehicle which draws propulsion energy from a battery with not less than 5 kilowatt hours of capacity, the amount determined under this paragraph is $417, plus $417 for each kilowatt hour of capacity in excess of 5 kilowatt hours. The amount determined under this paragraph shall not exceed $5,000.

  (c) Application with other credits.

    (1) Business credit treated as part of general business credit. So much of the credit which would be allowed under subsection (a) for any taxable year (determined without regard to this subsection) that is attributable to property of a character subject to an allowance for depreciation shall be treated as a credit listed in section 38(b) for such taxable year (and not allowed under subsection (a)).

421

(2) Personal credit.

(A) In general. For purposes of this title, the credit allowed under subsection (a) for any taxable year (determined after application of paragraph (1)) shall be treated as a credit allowable under subpart A for such taxable year.

(B) Limitation based on amount of tax. In the case of a taxable year to which section 26(a)(2) does not apply, the credit allowed under subsection (a) for any taxable year (determined after application of paragraph (1)) shall not exceed the excess of—

(i) the sum of the regular tax liability (as defined in section 26(b)) plus the tax imposed by section 55, over

(ii) the sum of the credits allowable under subpart A (other than this section and sections 23 and 25D) and section 27 for the taxable year.

(d) New qualified plug-in electric drive motor vehicle. For purposes of this section—

(1) In general. The term "new qualified plug-in electric drive motor vehicle" means a motor vehicle—

(A) the original use of which commences with the taxpayer,

(B) which is acquired for use or lease by the taxpayer and not for resale,

(C) which is made by a manufacturer,

(D) which is treated as a motor vehicle for purposes of title II of the Clean Air Act,

(E) which has a gross vehicle weight rating of less than 14,000 pounds, and

(F) which is propelled to a significant extent by an electric motor which draws electricity from a battery which—

(i) has a capacity of not less than 4 kilowatt hours, and

(ii) is capable of being recharged from an external source of electricity.

(2) Motor vehicle. The term "motor vehicle" means any vehicle which is manufactured primarily for use on public streets, roads, and highways (not including a vehicle operated exclusively on a rail or rails) and which has at least 4 wheels.

(3) Manufacturer. The term "manufacturer" has the meaning given such term in regulations prescribed by the Administrator of the Environmental Protection Agency for purposes of the administration of title II of the Clean Air Act (42 U.S.C. 7521 et seq.).

(4) Battery capacity. The term "capacity" means, with respect to any battery, the quantity of electricity which the battery is capable of storing, expressed in kilowatt hours, as measured from a 100 percent state of charge to a 0 percent state of charge.

(e) Limitation on number of new qualified plug-in electric drive motor vehicles eligible for credit.

(1) In general. In the case of a new qualified plug-in electric drive motor vehicle sold during the phaseout period, only the applicable percentage of the credit otherwise allowable under subsection (a) shall be allowed.

(2) Phaseout period. For purposes of this subsection, the phaseout period is the period beginning with the second calendar quarter following the calendar quarter which includes the first date on which the number of new qualified plug-in electric drive motor vehicles manufactured by the manufacturer of the vehicle referred to in paragraph (1) sold for use in the United States after December 31, 2009, is at least 200,000.

(3) Applicable percentage. For purposes of paragraph (1), the applicable percentage is—

(A) 50 percent for the first 2 calendar quarters of the phaseout period,

(B) 25 percent for the 3d and 4th calendar quarters of the phaseout period, and

(C) 0 percent for each calendar quarter thereafter.

(4) Controlled groups. Rules similar to the rules of section 30B(f)(4) shall apply for purposes of this subsection.

(f) Special rules.

(1) Basis reduction. For purposes of this subtitle, the basis of any property for which a credit is allowable under subsection (a) shall be reduced by the amount of such credit so allowed.

(2)   No double benefit. The amount of any deduction or other credit allowable under this chapter for a new qualified plug-in electric drive motor vehicle shall be reduced by the amount of credit allowed under subsection (a) for such vehicle.

(3)   Property used by tax-exempt entity. In the case of a vehicle the use of which is described in paragraph (3) or (4) of section 50(b) and which is not subject to a lease, the person who sold such vehicle to the person or entity using such vehicle shall be treated as the taxpayer that placed such vehicle in service, but only if such person clearly discloses to such person or entity in a document the amount of any credit allowable under subsection (a) with respect to such vehicle (determined without regard to subsection (c)).

(4)   Property used outside united states not qualified. No credit shall be allowable under subsection (a) with respect to any property referred to in section 50(b)(1).

(5)   Recapture. The Secretary shall, by regulations, provide for recapturing the benefit of any credit allowable under subsection (a) with respect to any property which ceases to be property eligible for such credit.

(6)   Election not to take credit. No credit shall be allowed under subsection (a) for any vehicle if the taxpayer elects to not have this section apply to such vehicle.

(7)   Interaction with air quality and motor vehicle safety standards. A motor vehicle shall not be considered eligible for a credit under this section unless such vehicle is in compliance with—

(A) the applicable provisions of the Clean Air Act for the applicable make and model year of the vehicle (or applicable air quality provisions of State law in the case of a State which has adopted such provision under a waiver under section 209(b) of the Clean Air Act), and

(B) the motor vehicle safety provisions of sections 30101 through 30169 of title 49, United States Code.

[For Analysis, see ¶ 204 and ¶ 1102. For Committee Reports, see ¶ 5027 and ¶ 5010.]

[Endnote Code Sec. 30D]

Code Sec. 30D was amended by Sec. 1141(a) of the American Recovery and Reinvestment Tax Act of 2009, P.L. 111-5, 2/17/2009, as detailed below:

1. Prior to amendment, Code Sec. 30D read as follows:

"SEC. 30D. NEW QUALIFIED PLUG-IN ELECTRIC DRIVE MOTOR VEHICLES.

"(a) Allowance of credit.

"(1) In general. There shall be allowed as a credit against the tax imposed by this chapter for the taxable year an amount equal to the applicable amount with respect to each new qualified plug-in electric drive motor vehicle placed in service by the taxpayer during the taxable year.

"(2) Applicable amount. For purposes of paragraph (1), the applicable amount is sum of—

"(A) $2,500, plus

"(B) $417 for each kilowatt hour of traction battery capacity in excess of 4 kilowatt hours.

"(b) Limitations.

"(1) Limitation based on weight. The amount of the credit allowed under subsection (a) by reason of subsection (a)(2) shall not exceed—

"(A) $7,500, in the case of any new qualified plug-in electric drive motor vehicle with a gross vehicle weight rating of not more than 10,000 pounds,

"(B) $10,000, in the case of any new qualified plug-in electric drive motor vehicle with a gross vehicle weight rating of more than 10,000 pounds but not more than 14,000 pounds,

"(C) $12,500, in the case of any new qualified plug-in electric drive motor vehicle with a gross vehicle weight rating of more than 14,000 pounds but not more than 26,000 pounds, and

"(D) $15,000, in the case of any new qualified plug-in electric drive motor vehicle with a gross vehicle weight rating of more than 26,000 pounds.

"(2) Limitation on number of passenger vehicles and light trucks eligible for credit.

"(A) In general. In the case of a new qualified plug-in electric drive motor vehicle sold during the phaseout period, only the applicable percentage of the credit otherwise allowable under subsection (a) shall be allowed.

"(B) Phaseout period. For purposes of this subsection , the phaseout period is the period beginning with the second calendar quarter following the calendar quarter which includes the first date on which the total number of such new qualified plug-in electric drive motor vehicles sold for use in the United States after December 31, 2008, is at least 250,000.

"(C) Applicable percentage. For purposes of subparagraph (A) , the applicable percentage is—

"(i) 50 percent for the first 2 calendar quarters of the phaseout period,

"(ii) 25 percent for the 3d and 4th calendar quarters of the phaseout period, and

"(iii) 0 percent for each calendar quarter thereafter.

"(D) Controlled groups. Rules similar to the rules of section 30B(f)(4) shall apply for purposes of this subsection.

"(c) New qualified plug-in electric drive motor vehicle. For purposes of this section, the term 'new qualified plug-in electric drive motor vehicle' means a motor vehicle—

"(1) which draws propulsion using a traction battery with at least 4 kilowatt hours of capacity,

"(2) which uses an offboard source of energy to recharge such battery,

"(3) which, in the case of a passenger vehicle or light truck which has a gross vehicle weight rating of not more than 8,500 pounds, has received a certificate of conformity under the Clean Air Act and meets or exceeds the equivalent qualifying California low emission vehicle standard under section 243(e)(2) of the Clean Air Act for that make and model year, and

"(A) in the case of a vehicle having a gross vehicle weight rating of 6,000 pounds or less, the Bin 5 Tier II emission standard established in regulations prescribed by the Administrator of the Environmental Protection Agency under section 202(i) of the Clean Air Act for that make and model year vehicle, and

"(B) in the case of a vehicle having a gross vehicle weight rating of more than 6,000 pounds but not more than 8,500 pounds, the Bin 8 Tier II emission standard which is so established,

"(4) the original use of which commences with the taxpayer,

"(5) which is acquired for use or lease by the taxpayer and not for resale, and

"(6) which is made by a manufacturer.

"(d) Application with other credits.

"(1) Business credit treated as part of general business credit. So much of the credit which would be allowed under subsection (a) for any taxable year (determined without regard to this subsection) that is attributable to property of a character subject to an allowance for depreciation shall be treated as a credit listed in section 38(b) for such taxable year (and not allowed under subsection (a)).

"(2) Personal credit.

"(A) In general. For purposes of this title, the credit allowed under subsection (a) for any taxable year (determined after application of paragraph (1)) shall be treated as a credit allowable under subpart A for such taxable year.

"(B) Limitation based on amount of tax. In the case of a taxable year to which section 26(a)(2) does not apply, the credit allowed under subsection (a) for any taxable year (determined after application of paragraph (1)) shall not exceed the excess of—

"(i) the sum of the regular tax liability (as defined in section 26(b)) plus the tax imposed by section 55, over

"(ii) the sum of the credits allowable under subpart A (other than this section and sections 23 and 25D) and section 27 for the taxable year.

"(e) Other definitions and special rules. For purposes of this section—

"(1) Motor vehicle. The term 'motor vehicle' has the meaning given such term by section 30(c)(2).

"(2) Other terms. The terms 'passenger automobile', 'light truck', and 'manufacturer' have the meanings given such terms in regulations prescribed by the Administrator of the Environmental Protection Agency for purposes of the administration of title II of the Clean Air Act (42 U.S.C. 7521 et seq.).

"(3) Traction battery capacity. Traction battery capacity shall be measured in kilowatt hours from a 100 percent state of charge to a zero percent state of charge.

"(4) Reduction in basis. For purposes of this subtitle, the basis of any property for which a credit is allowable under subsection (a) shall be reduced by the amount of such credit so allowed.

"(5) No double benefit. The amount of any deduction or other credit allowable under this chapter for a new qualified plug-in electric drive motor vehicle shall be reduced by the amount of credit allowed under subsection (a) for such vehicle for the taxable year.

"(6) Property used by tax-exempt entity. In the case of a vehicle the use of which is described in paragraph (3) or (4) of section 50(b) and which is not subject to a lease, the person who sold such vehicle to the person or entity using such vehicle shall be treated as the taxpayer that placed such vehicle in service, but only if such person clearly discloses to such person or entity in a document the amount of any credit allowable under subsection (a) with respect to such vehicle (determined without regard to subsection (b)(2)).

"(7) Property used outside United States, etc., not qualified. No credit shall be allowable under subsection (a) with respect to any property referred to in section 50(b)(1) or with respect to the portion of the cost of any property taken into account under section 179.

"(8) Recapture. The Secretary shall, by regulations, provide for recapturing the benefit of any credit allowable under subsection (a) with respect to any property which ceases to be property eligible for such credit (including recapture in the case of a lease period of less than the economic life of a vehicle).

"(9) Election to not take credit. No credit shall be allowed under subsection (a) for any vehicle if the taxpayer elects not to have this section apply to such vehicle.

"(10) Interaction with air quality and motor vehicle safety standards. Unless otherwise provided in this section , a motor vehicle shall not be considered eligible for a credit under this section unless such vehicle is in compliance with—

"(A) the applicable provisions of the Clean Air Act for the applicable make and model year of the vehicle (or applicable air quality provisions of State law in the case of a State which has adopted such provision under a waiver under section 209(b) of the Clean Air Act), and

"(B) the motor vehicle safety provisions of sections 30101 through 30169 of title 49, United States Code.

"(f) Regulations.

"(1) In general. Except as provided in paragraph (2) , the Secretary shall promulgate such regulations as necessary to carry out the provisions of this section.

"(2) Coordination in prescription of certain regulations. The Secretary of the Treasury, in coordination with the Secretary of Transportation and the Administrator of the Environmental Protection Agency, shall prescribe such regulations as necessary to determine whether a motor vehicle meets the requirements to be eligible for a credit under this section.

"(g) Termination. This section shall not apply to property purchased after December 31, 2014."

Effective Date (Sec. 1141(c), P.L. 111-5, 2/17/2009) effective for vehicles acquired after 12/31/2009. Sec. 1142(d) of this Act, provides:

"(d) Transitional rule. In the case of a vehicle acquired after the date of the enactment of this Act and before January 1, 2010, no credit shall be allowed under section 30 of the Internal Revenue Code of 1986, as added by this section, if credit is allowable under section 30D of such Code with respect to such vehicle."

[¶ 3012]   Code Sec. 32.   Earned income.

* * * * * * * * * * * *

(b)   Percentages and amounts. For purposes of subsection (a)—

(1)   Percentages. The credit percentage and the phaseout percentage shall be determined as follows:

(A) In general. In the case of taxable years beginning after 1995:

In the case of an eligible individual with:	The credit percentage is:	The phaseout percentage is:
1 qualifying child	34	15.98
2 or more qualifying children	40	21.06
No qualifying children	7.65	7.65

(B) Transitional percentages for 1995. In the case of taxable years beginning in 1995:

In the case of an eligible individual with:	The credit percentage is:	The phaseout percentage is:
1 qualifying child	34	15.98
2 or more qualifying children	36	20.22
No qualifying children	7.65	7.65

(C) Transitional percentages for 1994. In the case of a taxable year beginning in 1994:

In the case of an eligible individual with:	The credit percentage is:	The phaseout percentage is:
1 qualifying child	26.3	15.98
2 or more qualifying children	30	17.68
No qualifying children	7.65	7.65

(2)   Amounts.

(A) In general. Subject to subparagraph (B), the earned income amount and the phaseout amount shall be determined as follows:

In the case of an eligible individual with:	The earned income amount is:	The phaseout amount is:
1 qualifying child	$6,330	$11,610
2 or more qualifying children	$8,890	$11,610
No qualifying children	$4,220	$ 5,280

(B) Joint returns. In the case of a joint return filed by an eligible individual and such individual's spouse, the phaseout amount determined under subparagraph (A) shall be increased by—

(i) $1,000 in the case of taxable years beginning in 2002, 2003, and 2004,

(ii) $2,000 in the case of taxable years beginning in 2005, 2006, and 2007, and

(iii) $3,000 in the case of taxable years beginning after 2007.

[1]*(3)   Special rules for 2009 and 2010.* In the case of any taxable year beginning in 2009 or 2010—

(A) Increased credit percentage for 3 or more qualifying children. In the case of a taxpayer with 3 or more qualifying children, the credit percentage is 45 percent.

(B) Reduction of marriage penalty.

(i) In general. The dollar amount in effect under paragraph (2)(B) shall be $5,000.

(ii) *Inflation adjustment.* In the case of any taxable year beginning in 2010, the $5,000 amount in clause (i) shall be increased by an amount equal to—

(I) such dollar amount, multiplied by

(II) the cost of living adjustment determined under section 1(f)(3) for the calendar year in which the taxable year begins determined by substituting "calendar year 2008" for "calendar year 1992" in subparagraph (B) thereof.

(iii) *Rounding.* Subparagraph (A) of subsection (j)(2) shall apply after taking into account any increase under clause (ii).

* * * * * * * * * * * *

[For Analysis, see ¶ 110 and ¶ 111. For Committee Reports, see ¶ 5002.]

[Endnote Code Sec. 32]
Code Sec. 32(b)(3) was added by Sec. 1002(a) of the American Recovery and Reinvestment Tax Act of 2009, P.L. 111-5, 2/17/2009, as detailed below:
1. Sec. 1002(a) added para. (b)(3).
Effective Date (Sec. 1002(b), P.L. 111-5, 2/17/2009) effective for tax. yrs. begin. after 12/31/2008.

[¶ 3013]   Code Sec. 35.   Health insurance costs of eligible individuals.

(a)   **In general.** In the case of an individual, there shall be allowed as a credit against the tax imposed by subtitle A an amount equal to 65 percent [1]*(80 percent in the case of eligible coverage months beginning before January 1, 2011)* of the amount paid by the taxpayer for coverage of the taxpayer and qualifying family members under qualified health insurance for eligible coverage months beginning in the taxable year.

* * * * * * * * * * * *

(c)   **Eligible individual.** For purposes of this section—

(1)   **In general.** The term "eligible individual" means—

(A) an eligible TAA recipient,

(B) an eligible alternative TAA recipient, and

(C) an eligible PBGC pension recipient.

[2]*(2)   Eligible TAA recipient.*

(A) In general. Except as provided in subparagraph (B), the term "eligible TAA recipient" means, with respect to any month, any individual who is receiving for any day of such month a trade readjustment allowance under chapter 2 of title II of the Trade Act of 1974 or who would be eligible to receive such allowance if section 231 of such Act were applied without regard to subsection (a)(3)(B) of such section. An individual shall continue to be treated as an eligible TAA recipient during the first month that such individual would otherwise cease to be an eligible TAA recipient by reason of the preceding sentence.

(B) Special rule. In the case of any eligible coverage month beginning after the date of the enactment of this paragraph and before January 1, 2011, the term "eligible TAA recipient" means, with respect to any month, any individual who—

(i) is receiving for any day of such month a trade readjustment allowance under chapter 2 of title II of the Trade Act of 1974,

(ii) would be eligible to receive such allowance except that such individual is in a break in training provided under a training program approved under section 236 of such Act that exceeds the period specified in section 233(e) of such Act, but is within the period for receiving such allowances provided under section 233(a) of such Act, or

(iii) is receiving unemployment compensation (as defined in section 85(b)) for any day of such month and who would be eligible to receive such allowance for such month if section 231 of such Act were applied without regard to subsections (a)(3)(B) and (a)(5) thereof.

An individual shall continue to be treated as an eligible TAA recipient during the first month that such individual would otherwise cease to be an eligible TAA recipient by reason of the preceding sentence.

(3) Eligible alternative TAA recipient. The term "eligible alternative TAA recipient" means, with respect to any month, any individual who—

(A) is a worker described in section 246(a)(3)(B) of the Trade Act of 1974 who is participating in the program established under section 246(a)(1) of such Act, and

(B) is receiving a benefit for such month under section 246(a)(2) of such Act.

An individual shall continue to be treated as an eligible alternative TAA recipient during the first month that such individual would otherwise cease to be an eligible alternative TAA recipient by reason of the preceding sentence.

(4) Eligible PBGC pension recipient. The term "eligible PBGC pension recipient" means, with respect to any month, any individual who—

(A) has attained age 55 as of the first day of such month, and

(B) is receiving a benefit for such month any portion of which is paid by the Pension Benefit Guaranty Corporation under title IV of the Employee Retirement Income Security Act of 1974.

* * * * * * * * * * * *

(e) Qualified health insurance. For purposes of this section—

(1) In general. The term "qualified health insurance" means any of the following:

(A) Coverage under a COBRA continuation provision (as defined in section 9832(d)(1)).

(B) State-based continuation coverage provided by the State under a State law that requires such coverage.

(C) Coverage offered through a qualified State high risk pool (as defined in section 2744(c)(2) of the Public Health Service Act).

(D) Coverage under a health insurance program offered for State employees.

(E) Coverage under a State-based health insurance program that is comparable to the health insurance program offered for State employees.

(F) Coverage through an arrangement entered into by a State and—

(i) a group health plan (including such a plan which is a multiemployer plan as defined in section 3(37) of the Employee Retirement Income Security Act of 1974),

(ii) an issuer of health insurance coverage,

(iii) an administrator, or

(iv) an employer.

(G) Coverage offered through a State arrangement with a private sector health care coverage purchasing pool.

(H) Coverage under a State-operated health plan that does not receive any Federal financial participation.

(I) Coverage under a group health plan that is available through the employment of the eligible individual's spouse.

(J) In the case of any eligible individual and such individual's qualifying family members, coverage under individual health insurance if the eligible individual was covered under individual health insurance during the entire 30-day period that ends on the date that such individual became separated from the employment which qualified such individual for—

(i) in the case of an eligible TAA recipient, the allowance described in subsection (c)(2),

(ii) in the case of an eligible alternative TAA recipient, the benefit described in subsection (c)(3)(B), or

(iii) in the case of any eligible PBGC pension recipient, the benefit described in subsection (c)(4)(B).

For purposes of this subparagraph, the term "individual health insurance" means any insurance which constitutes medical care offered to individuals other than in connection with a group health plan and does not include Federal or State-based health insurance coverage.

[3](K) *In the case of eligible coverage months beginning before January 1, 2011, coverage under an employee benefit plan funded by a voluntary employees' beneficiary association (as defined in section 501(c)(9)) established pursuant to an order of a bankruptcy court, or by agreement with an authorized representative, as provided in section 1114 of title 11, United States Code.*

(2) Requirements for State-based coverage.

(A) In general. The term "qualified health insurance" does not include any coverage described in subparagraphs (B) through (H) of paragraph (1) unless the State involved has elected to have such coverage treated as qualified health insurance under this section and such coverage meets the following requirements:

(i) Guaranteed issue. Each qualifying individual is guaranteed enrollment if the individual pays the premium for enrollment or provides a qualified health insurance costs credit eligibility certificate described in section 7527 and pays the remainder of such premium.

(ii) No imposition of pre-existing condition exclusion. No pre-existing condition limitations are imposed with respect to any qualifying individual.

(iii) Nondiscriminatory premium. The total premium (as determined without regard to any subsidies) with respect to a qualifying individual may not be greater than the total premium (as so determined) for a similarly situated individual who is not a qualifying individual.

(iv) Same benefits. Benefits under the coverage are the same as (or substantially similar to) the benefits provided to similarly situated individuals who are not qualifying individuals.

(B) Qualifying individual. For purposes of this paragraph, the term "qualifying individual" means—

(i) an eligible individual for whom, as of the date on which the individual seeks to enroll in the coverage described in subparagraphs (B) through (H) of paragraph (1), the aggregate of the periods of creditable coverage (as defined in section 9801(c)) is 3 months or longer and who, with respect to any month, meets the requirements of clauses (iii) and (iv) of subsection (b)(1)(A); and

(ii) the qualifying family members of such eligible individual.

(3) Exception. The term "qualified health insurance" shall not include—

(A) a flexible spending or similar arrangement, and

(B) any insurance if substantially all of its coverage is of excepted benefits described in section 9832(c).

* * * * * * * * * * * *

(g) Special rules.

(1) Coordination with advance payments of credit. With respect to any taxable year, the amount which would (but for this subsection) be allowed as a credit to the taxpayer under subsection (a) shall be reduced (but not below zero) by the aggregate amount paid on behalf of such taxpayer under section 7527 for months beginning in such taxable year.

(2) Coordination with other deductions. Amounts taken into account under subsection (a) shall not be taken into account in determining any deduction allowed under section 162(l) or 213.

(3) Medical and health savings accounts. Amounts distributed from an Archer MSA (as defined in section 220(d)) or from a health savings account (as defined in section 223(d)) shall not be taken into account under subsection (a).

(4) Denial of credit to dependents. No credit shall be allowed under this section to any individual with respect to whom a deduction under section 151 is allowable to another taxpayer for a taxable year beginning in the calendar year in which such individual's taxable year begins.

(5) Both spouses eligible individuals. The spouse of the taxpayer shall not be treated as a qualifying family member for purposes of subsection (a), if—

(A) the taxpayer is married at the close of the taxable year,

(B) the taxpayer and the taxpayer's spouse are both eligible individuals during the taxable year, and

(C) the taxpayer files a separate return for the taxable year.

(6) Marital status; certain married individuals living apart. Rules similar to the rules of paragraphs (3) and (4) of section 21(e) shall apply for purposes of this section.

(7) Insurance which covers other individuals. For purposes of this section, rules similar to the rules of section 213(d)(6) shall apply with respect to any contract for qualified health insurance under which amounts are payable for coverage of an individual other than the taxpayer and qualifying family members.

(8) Treatment of payments. For purposes of this section—

(A) Payments by Secretary. Payments made by the Secretary on behalf of any individual under section 7527 (relating to advance payment of credit for health insurance costs of eligible individuals) shall be treated as having been made by the taxpayer on the first day of the month for which such payment was made.

(B) Payments by taxpayer. Payments made by the taxpayer for eligible coverage months shall be treated as having been made by the taxpayer on the first day of the month for which such payment was made.

• **Caution:** Code Sec. 35(g)(9), following, was added by Sec. 1899E(a) of P.L. 111-5, the American Recovery and Reinvestment Act, 2/17/2009, effective for months begin. after 12/31/2009. For Code Sec. 35(g)(9) as added by Sec. 3001(a)(14)(A) of such Act, see below.

---

[4]*(9) Continued qualification of family members after certain events. In the case of eligible coverage months beginning before January 1, 2011—*

(A) Medicare eligibility. In the case of any month which would be an eligible coverage month with respect to an eligible individual but for subsection (f)(2)(A), such month shall be treated as an eligible coverage month with respect to such eligible individual solely for purposes of determining the amount of the credit under this section with respect to any qualifying family members of such individual (and any advance payment of such credit under section 7527). This subparagraph shall only apply with respect to the first 24 months after such eligible individual is first entitled to the benefits described in subsection (f)(2)(A).

(B) Divorce. In the case of the finalization of a divorce between an eligible individual and such individual's spouse, such spouse shall be treated as an eligible individual for purposes of this section and section 7527 for a period of 24 months beginning with the date of such finalization, except that the only qualifying family members who may be taken into account with respect to such spouse are those individuals who were qualifying family members immediately before such finalization.

(C) Death. In the case of the death of an eligible individual—

(i) any spouse of such individual (determined at the time of such death) shall be treated as an eligible individual for purposes of this section and section 7527 for a period of 24 months beginning with the date of such death, except that the only qualifying family members who may be taken into account with respect to such spouse are those individuals who were qualifying family members immediately before such death, and

(ii) any individual who was a qualifying family member of the decedent immediately before such death (or, in the case of an individual to whom paragraph (4) applies, the taxpayer to whom the deduction under section 151 is allowable) shall be treated as an eligible individual for purposes of this section and section 7527 for a pe-

riod of 24 months beginning with the date of such death, except that in determining the amount of such credit only such qualifying family member may be taken into account.

> • **Caution:** Code Sec. 35(g)(9), following, was added by Sec. 3001(a)(14)(A) of P.L. 111-5, the American Recovery and Reinvestment Act, 2/17/2009, effective for tax. yrs. end. after 2/17/2009. For Code Sec. 35(g)(9) as added by Sec. 1899E(a) of such Act, see above.

[5]*(9)* ***COBRA premium assistance.*** *In the case of an assistance eligible individual who receives premium reduction for COBRA continuation coverage under section 3002(a) of the Health Insurance Assistance for the Unemployed Act of 2009 for any month during the taxable year, such individual shall not be treated as an eligible individual, a certified individual, or a qualifying family member for purposes of this section or section 7527 with respect to such month.*

[6]*(10)* **Regulations.** The Secretary may prescribe such regulations and other guidance as may be necessary or appropriate to carry out this section, section 6050T, and section 7527.

[Endnote Code Sec. 35]

Code Sec. 35(a) was amended by Sec. 1899A(a)(1) of the American Recovery and Reinvestment Act of 2009, P.L. 111-5, 2/17/2009, as detailed below:

1. Sec. 1899A(a)(1) added "(80 percent in the case of eligible coverage months beginning before January 1, 2011)" after "65 percent" in subsec. (a)

Effective Date (Sec. 1899A(b), P.L. 111-5, 2/17/2009) effective for coverage months beginning on or after the first day of the first month begin. 60 days after 2/17/2009.

Code Sec. 35(c)(2) was amended by Sec. 1899C(a), P.L. 111-5, 2/17/2009, as detailed below:

2. Sec. 1899C(a) amended para. (c)(2). Prior to amendment, para. (c)(2) read as follows:

"(2) Eligible TAA recipient. The term 'eligible TAA recipient' means, with respect to any month, any individual who is receiving for any day of such month a trade readjustment allowance under chapter 2 of title II of the Trade Act of 1974 or who would be eligible to receive such allowance if section 231 of such Act were applied without regard to subsection (a)(3)(B) of such section. An individual shall continue to be treated as an eligible TAA recipient during the first month that such individual would otherwise cease to be an eligible TAA recipient by reason of the preceding sentence."

Effective Date (Sec. 1899C(b), P.L. 111-5, 2/17/2009) effective for coverage months begin. after 2/17/2009.

Code Sec. 35(e)(1)(K) was amended by Sec. 1899G(a), P.L. 111-5, 2/17/2009, as detailed below:

3. Sec. 1899G(a) added subpara. (e)(1)(K)

Effective Date (Sec. 1899G(d), P.L. 111-5, 2/17/2009) effective for months begin. after 2/17/2009.

Code Sec. 35(g)(9) was added by Sec. 1899E(a), P.L. 111-5, 2/17/2009, as detailed below:

4. Sec. 1899E(a) added para. (g)(9) and redesignated para. (g)(9) as para. (g)(10)

Effective Date (Sec. 1899E(c), P.L. 111-5, 2/17/2009) effective for months begin. after 12/31/2009.

Code Sec. 35(g)(9) was added by Sec. 3001(a)(14)(A), P.L. 111-5, 2/17/2009, as detailed below:

5. Sec. 3001(a)(14)(A) added para. (g)(9) [Editor's note: Sec. 3001(a)(14)(A) of this Act also redesignated para. (g)(9) as para. (g)(10), however, this amendment was previously made by Sec. 1899E(a) of this Act, see above.]

Effective Date (Sec. 3001(a)(14)(B), P.L. 111-5, 2/17/2009) effective for tax. yrs. end. after 2/17/2009.

Code Sec. 35(g)(10) was amended by Sec. 3001(a)(14)(A), P.L. 111-5, 2/17/2009, as detailed below:

6. Sec. 3001(a)(14)(A) redesignated para. (g)(9) as para. (g)(10)

Effective Date (Sec. 3001(a)(14)(B), P.L. 111-5, 2/17/2009) effective for tax. yrs. end. after 2/17/2009.

Sec. 1899I and Sec. 1899L, P.L. 111-5, 2/17/2009, provide:

"SEC. 1899I. SURVEY AND REPORT ON ENHANCED HEALTH COVERAGE TAX CREDIT PROGRAM.

"(a) Survey.

" (1) In general. The Secretary of the Treasury shall conduct a biennial survey of eligible individuals (as defined in section 35(c) of the Internal Revenue Code of 1986) relating to the health coverage tax credit under section 35 of the Internal Revenue Code of 1986 (hereinafter in this section referred to as the 'health coverage tax credit').

"(2) Information obtained. The survey conducted under subsection (a) shall obtain the following information:

" HCTC participants. In the case of eligible individuals receiving the health coverage tax credit (including individuals participating in the health coverage tax credit program under section 7527 of such Code, hereinafter in this section referred to as the 'HCTC program')—

"(i) demographic information of such individuals, including income and education levels,

"(ii) satisfaction of such individuals with the enrollment process in the HCTC program,

"(iii) satisfaction of such individuals with available health coverage options under the credit, including level of premiums, benefits, deductibles, cost-sharing requirements, and the adequacy of provider networks, and

"(iv) any other information that the Secretary determines is appropriate.

"(B) Non-HCTC participants. In the case of eligible individuals not receiving the health coverage tax credit—

"(i) demographic information of each individual, including income and education levels,

"(ii) whether the individual was aware of the health coverage tax credit or the HCTC program,

"(iii) the reasons the individual has not enrolled in the HCTC program, including whether such reasons include the burden of the process of enrollment and the affordability of coverage,

"(iv) whether the individual has health insurance coverage, and, if so, the source of such coverage, and

"(v) any other information that the Secretary determines is appropriate.

"(3) Report. Not later than December 31 of each year in which a survey is conducted under paragraph (1) (beginning in 2010), the Secretary of the Treasury shall report to the Committee on Finance and the Committee on Health, Education, Labor, and Pensions of the Senate and the Committee on Ways and Means, the Committee on Education and Labor, and the Committee on Energy and Commerce of the House of Representatives the findings of the most recent survey conducted under paragraph (1).

"(b) Report. Not later than October 1 of each year (beginning in 2010), the Secretary of the Treasury (after consultation with the Secretary of Health and Human Services, and, in the case of the information required under paragraph (7), the Secretary of Labor) shall report to the Committee on Finance and the Committee on Health, Education, Labor, and Pensions of the Senate and the Committee on Ways and Means, the Committee on Education and Labor, and the Committee on Energy and Commerce of the House of Representatives the following information with respect to the most recent taxable year ending before such date:

"(1) In each State and nationally—

"(A) the total number of eligible individuals (as defined in section 35(c) of the Internal Revenue Code of 1986) and the number of eligible individuals receiving the health coverage tax credit,

"(B) the total number of such eligible individuals who receive an advance payment of the health coverage tax credit through the HCTC program, (C) the average length of the time period of the participation of eligible individuals in the HCTC program, and

"(D) the total number of participating eligible individuals in the HCTC program who are enrolled in each category of coverage as described in section 35(e)(1) of such Code, with respect to each category of eligible individuals described in section 35(c)(1) of such Code.

"(2) In each State and nationally, an analysis of—

"(A) the range of monthly health insurance premiums, for self-only coverage and for family coverage, for individuals receiving the health coverage tax credit, and

"(B) the average and median monthly health insurance premiums, for self-only coverage and for family coverage, for individuals receiving the health coverage tax credit, with respect to each category of coverage as described in section 35(e)(1) of such Code.

"(3) In each State and nationally, an analysis of the following information with respect to the health insurance coverage of individuals receiving the health coverage tax credit who are enrolled in coverage described in subparagraphs (B) through (H) of section 35(e)(1) of such Code:

"(A) Deductible amounts.

"(B) Other out-of-pocket cost-sharing amounts.

"(C) A description of any annual or lifetime limits on coverage or any other significant limits on coverage services, or benefits.

"The information required under this paragraph shall be reported with respect to each category of coverage described in such subparagraphs.

"(4) In each State and nationally, the gender and average age of eligible individuals (as defined in section 35(c) of such Code) who receive the health coverage tax credit, in each category of coverage described in section 35(e)(1) of such Code, with respect to each category of eligible individuals described in such section.

"(5) The steps taken by the Secretary of the Treasury to increase the participation rates in the HCTC program among eligible individuals, including outreach and enrollment activities.

"(6) The cost of administering the HCTC program by function, including the cost of subcontractors, and recommendations on ways to reduce administrative costs, including recommended statutory changes.

"(7) The number of States applying for and receiving national emergency grants under section 173(f) of the Workforce Investment Act of 1998 (29 U.S.C. 2918(f)), the activities funded by such grants on a State-by-State basis, and the time necessary for application approval of such grants."

     *   *   *   *   *

"SEC. 1899L. GAO STUDY AND REPORT.

"(a) Study. The Comptroller General of the United States shall conduct a study regarding the health insurance tax credit allowed under section 35 of the Internal Revenue Code of 1986.

"(b) Report. Not later than March 1, 2010, the Comptroller General shall submit a report to Congress regarding the results of the study conducted under subsection (a). Such report shall include an analysis of—

"(1) the administrative costs—

"(A) of the Federal Government with respect to such credit and the advance payment of such credit under section 7527 of such Code, and

"(B) of providers of qualified health insurance with respect to providing such insurance to eligible individuals and their qualifying family members,

"(2) the health status and relative risk status of eligible individuals and qualifying family members covered under such insurance,

"(3) participation in such credit and the advance payment of such credit by eligible individuals and their qualifying family members, including the reasons why such individuals did or did not participate and the effect of the amendments made by this part on such participation, and

"(4) the extent to which eligible individuals and their qualifying family members—

"(A) obtained health insurance other than qualifying health insurance, or

"(B) went without health insurance coverage.

"(c) Access to records. For purposes of conducting the study required under this section, the Comptroller General and any of his duly authorized representatives shall have access to, and the right to examine and copy, all documents, records, and other recorded information—

"(1) within the possession or control of providers of qualified health insurance, and

"(2) determined by the Comptroller General (or any such representative) to be relevant to the study.

"The Comptroller General shall not disclose the identity of any provider of qualified health insurance or any eligible individual in making any information obtained under this section available to the public.

"(d) Definitions. Any term which is defined in section 35 of the Internal Revenue Code of 1986 shall have the same meaning when used in this section."

[¶ 3014]   Code Sec. 36.   First-time homebuyer credit.

* * * * * * * * * * * *

(b) Limitations.

(1) Dollar limitation.

(A) In general. Except as otherwise provided in this paragraph, the credit allowed under subsection (a) shall not exceed [1]*$8,000.*

(B) Married individuals filing separately. In the case of a married individual filing a separate return, subparagraph (A) shall be applied by substituting "[2]*$4,000*" for "[3]*$8,000*".

(C) Other individuals. If two or more individuals who are not married purchase a principal residence, the amount of the credit allowed under subsection (a) shall be allocated among such individuals in such manner as the Secretary may prescribe, except that the total amount of the credits allowed to all such individuals shall not exceed [4]*$8,000.*

(2) Limitation based on modified adjusted gross income.

(A) In general. The amount allowable as a credit under subsection (a) (determined without regard to this paragraph) for the taxable year shall be reduced (but not below zero) by the amount which bears the same ratio to the amount which is so allowable as—

(i) the excess (if any) of—

(I) the taxpayer's modified adjusted gross income for such taxable year, over

(II) $75,000 ($150,000 in the case of a joint return), bears to

(ii) $20,000.

(B) Modified adjusted gross income. For purposes of subparagraph (A), the term "modified adjusted gross income" means the adjusted gross income of the taxpayer for the taxable year increased by any amount excluded from gross income under section 911, 931, or 933.

* * * * * * * * * * * *

(d) Exceptions. No credit under subsection (a) shall be allowed to any taxpayer for any taxable year with respect to the purchase of a residence if—

[5]*(1) Repealed.*

[6]*(2) Repealed.*

[7]*(1)* the taxpayer is a nonresident alien, or

[8]*(2)* the taxpayer disposes of such residence (or such residence ceases to be the principal residence of the taxpayer (and, if married, the taxpayer's spouse)) before the close of such taxable year.

* * * * * * * * * * * *

(f) Recapture of credit.

(1) In general. Except as otherwise provided in this subsection, if a credit under subsection (a) is allowed to a taxpayer, the tax imposed by this chapter shall be increased by 6⅔ percent of the amount of such credit for each taxable year in the recapture period.

(2) Acceleration of recapture. If a taxpayer disposes of the principal residence with respect to which a credit was allowed under subsection (a)(or such residence ceases to be the principal residence of the taxpayer (and, if married, the taxpayer's spouse)) before the end of the recapture period.

(A) the tax imposed by this chapter for the taxable year of such disposition or cessation shall be increased by the excess of the amount of the credit allowed over the amounts of tax imposed by paragraph (1) for preceding taxable years, and

(B) paragraph (1) shall not apply with respect to such credit for such taxable year or any subsequent taxable year.

(3) Limitation based on gain. In the case of the sale of the principal residence to a person who is not related to the taxpayer, the increase in tax determined under paragraph (2) shall not exceed the amount of gain (if any) on such sale. Solely for purposes of the preceding sentence, the adjusted basis of such residence shall be reduced by the amount of the credit allowed under subsection (a) to the extent not previously recaptured under paragraph (1).

(4) Exceptions.

(A) Death of taxpayer. Paragraphs (1) and (2) shall not apply to any taxable year ending after the date of the taxpayer's death.

(B) Involuntary conversion. Paragraph (2) shall not apply in the case of a residence which is compulsorily or involuntarily converted (within the meaning of section 1033(a)) if the taxpayer acquires a new principal residence during the 2-year period beginning on the date of the disposition or cessation referred to in paragraph (2). Paragraph (2)shall apply to such new principal residence during the recapture period in the same manner as if such new principal residence were the converted residence.

(C) Transfers between spouses or incident to divorce. In the case of a transfer of a residence to which section 1041(a) applies—

(i) paragraph (2) shall not apply to such transfer, and

(ii) in the case of taxable years ending after such transfer, paragraphs (1) and (2) shall apply to the transferee in the same manner as if such transferee were the transferor (and shall not apply to the transferor).

[9]*(D) Waiver of recapture for purchases in 2009. In the case of any credit allowed with respect to the purchase of a principal residence after December 31, 2008, and before December 1, 2009—*

(i) paragraph (1) shall not apply, and

(ii) paragraph (2) shall apply only if the disposition or cessation described in paragraph (2) with respect to such residence occurs during the 36-month period beginning on the date of the purchase of such residence by the taxpayer.

(5) Joint returns. In the case of a credit allowed under subsection (a) with respect to a joint return, half of such credit shall be treated as having been allowed to each individual filing such return for purposes of this subsection.

(6) Return requirement. If the tax imposed by this chapter for the taxable year is increased under this subsection, the taxpayer shall, notwithstanding section 6012, be required to file a return with respect to the taxes imposed under this subtitle.

(7) Recapture period. For purposes of this subsection, the term "recapture period" means the 15 taxable years beginning with the second taxable year following the taxable year in which the purchase of the principal residence for which a credit is allowed under subsection (a) was made.

(g) Election to treat purchase in prior year. In the case of a purchase of a principal residence after December 31, 2008, and before [10]*December 1, 2009*, a taxpayer may elect to treat such purchase as made on December 31, 2008, for purposes of this section (other than [11]*subsections (c) and (f)(4)(D))*.

(h) Application of section. This section shall only apply to a principal residence purchased by the taxpayer on or after April 9, 2008, and before [12]*December 1, 2009*.

[For Analysis, see ¶ 104. For Committee Reports, see ¶ 5006.]

[Endnote Code Sec. 36]

Code Sec. 36 was amended by Secs. 1006(a)(1) and (2), (b)(1) and (2), (c)(1) and (2), (d)(2) and (e) of The American Recovery and Reinvestment Act of 2009, P.L. 111-5, d.o.e, as detailed below:

1. Sec. 1006(b)(1) substituted "$8,000" for "$7,500" each place it appears in subsec. (b)
2. Sec. 1006(b)(2) substituted "$4,000" for "$3,500" in subpara. (b)(1)(B)
3. Sec. 1006(b)(1) substituted "$8,000" for "$7,500" each place it appears in subsec. (b)
4. Sec. 1006(b)(1) substituted "$8,000" for "$7,500" each place it appears in subsec. (b)
5. Sec. 1006(d)(2) repealed para. (d)(1)
6. Sec. 1006(e) repealed para. (d)(2)
Prior to repeal, paras. (d)(1) and (2) read as follows:
"(1) a credit under section 1400C (relating to first-time homebuyer in the District of Columbia) is allowable to the taxpayer (or the taxpayer's spouse) for such taxable year or any prior taxable year,
"(2) the residence is financed by the proceeds of a qualified mortgage issue the interest on which is exempt from tax under section 103"
7. Sec. 1006(e) redesignated para. (d)(3) as (d)(1)
8. Sec. 1006(e) redesignated para. (d)(4) as (d)(2)
9. Sec. 1006(c)(1) added subpara. (f)(4)(D)
10. Sec. 1006(a)(2) substituted "December 1, 2009" for "July 1, 2009" in subsec. (g)
11. Sec. 1006(c)(2) substituted "subsections (c) and (f)(4)(D)" for "subsection (c)" in subsec. (g)
12. Sec. 1006(a)(1) substituted "December 1, 2009" for "July 1, 2009" in subsec. (h)
Effective Date (Sec. 1006(f), P.L. 111-5, 2/17/2009) effective for residences purchased after 12/31/2008.

[¶ 3015]   *Code Sec.*[1] *36A.   Making work pay credit.*

*(a) **Allowance of credit.** In the case of an eligible individual, there shall be allowed as a credit against the tax imposed by this subtitle for the taxable year an amount equal to the lesser of—*

(1) 6.2 percent of earned income of the taxpayer, or

(2) $400 ($800 in the case of a joint return).

*(b) **Limitation based on modified adjusted gross income.***

*(1) **In general.** The amount allowable as a credit under subsection (a) (determined without regard to this paragraph and subsection (c)) for the taxable year shall be reduced (but not below zero) by 2 percent of so much of the taxpayer's modified adjusted gross income as exceeds $75,000 ($150,000 in the case of a joint return).*

*(2) **Modified adjusted gross income.** For purposes of subparagraph (A), the term "modified adjusted gross income" means the adjusted gross income of the taxpayer for the taxable year increased by any amount excluded from gross income under section 911, 931, or 933.*

*(c) **Reduction for certain other payments.** The credit allowed under subsection (a) for any taxable year shall be reduced by the amount of any payments received by the taxpayer during such taxable year under section 2201, or any credit allowed to the taxpayer under section 2202, of the American Recovery and Reinvestment Tax Act of 2009.*

*(d) **Definitions and special rules.** For purposes of this section—*

*(1) **Eligible individual.***

(A) In general. The term "eligible individual" means any individual other than—

(i) any nonresident alien individual,

(ii) any individual with respect to whom a deduction under section 151 is allowable to another taxpayer for a taxable year beginning in the calendar year in which the individual's taxable year begins, and

(iii) an estate or trust.

(B) Identification number requirement. Such term shall not include any individual who does not include on the return of tax for the taxable year—

(i) such individual's social security account number, and

(ii) in the case of a joint return, the social security account number of one of the taxpayers on such return. For purposes of the preceding sentence, the social security account number shall not include a TIN issued by the Internal Revenue Service.

(2) Earned income. The term "earned income" has the meaning given such term by section 32(c)(2), except that such term shall not include net earnings from self-employment which are not taken into account in computing taxable income. For purposes of the preceding sentence, any amount excluded from gross income by reason of section 112 shall be treated as earned income which is taken into account in computing taxable income for the taxable year.

(e) Termination. This section shall not apply to taxable years beginning after December 31, 2010.

[For Analysis, see ¶ 101 and ¶ 103. For Committee Reports, see ¶ 5001 and ¶ 5080.]

[Endnote Code Sec. 36A]

Code Sec. 36A was added by Sec. 1001(a) of the American Recovery and Reinvestment Act of 2009, P.L. 111-5, 2/17/2009, as detailed below:

1. added Code Sec. 36A

Effective Date (Sec. 1001(f), P.L. 111-5, 2/17/2009) effective for tax. yrs. begin. after 12/31/2008.

Sec. 1001(b)-(c) of this Act, provides:

"(b) Treatment of possessions.

"(1) Payments to possessions.

"(A) Mirror code possession. The Secretary of the Treasury shall pay to each possession of the United States with a mirror code tax system amounts equal to the loss to that possession by reason of the amendments made by this section with respect to taxable years beginning in 2009 and 2010. Such amounts shall be determined by the Secretary of the Treasury based on information provided by the government of the respective possession.

"(B) Other possessions. The Secretary of the Treasury shall pay to each possession of the United States which does not have a mirror code tax system amounts estimated by the Secretary of the Treasury as being equal to the aggregate benefits that would have been provided to residents of such possession by reason of the amendments made by this section for taxable years beginning in 2009 and 2010 if a mirror code tax system had been in effect in such possession. The preceding sentence shall not apply with respect to any possession of the United States unless such possession has a plan, which has been approved by the Secretary of the Treasury, under which such possession will promptly distribute such payments to the residents of such possession.

"(2) Coordination with credit allowed against United States income taxes. No credit shall be allowed against United States income taxes for any taxable year under section 36A of the Internal Revenue Code of 1986 (as added by this section) to any person—

"(A) to whom a credit is allowed against taxes imposed by the possession by reason of the amendments made by this section for such taxable year, or

"(B) who is eligible for a payment under a plan described in paragraph (1)(B) with respect to such taxable year.

"(3) Definitions and special rules.

"(A) Possession of the United States. For purposes of this subsection, the term 'possession of the United States' includes the Commonwealth of Puerto Rico and the Commonwealth of the Northern Mariana Islands.

"(B) Mirror code tax system. For purposes of this subsection, the term 'mirror code tax system' means, with respect to any possession of the United States, the income tax system of such possession if the income tax liability of the residents of such possession under such system is determined by reference to the income tax laws of the United States as if such possession were the United States.

"(C) Treatment of payments. For purposes of section 1324(b)(2) of title 31, United States Code, the payments under this subsection shall be treated in the same manner as a refund due from the credit allowed under section 36A of the Internal Revenue Code of 1986 (as added by this section).

"(c) Refunds disregarded in the administration of federal programs and federally assisted programs. Any credit or refund allowed or made to any individual by reason of section 36A of the Internal Revenue Code of 1986 (as added by this section) or by reason of subsection (b) of this section shall not be taken into account as income and shall not be taken into account as resources for the month of receipt and the following 2 months, for purposes of determining the eligibility of such individual or any other individual for benefits or assistance, or the amount or extent of benefits or assistance, under any Federal program or under any State or local program financed in whole or in part with Federal funds."

[¶ 3016]   Code Sec. 38.   General business credit.

(b)   Current year business credit. For purposes of this subpart, the amount of the current year business credit is the sum of the following credits determined for the taxable year:

* * * * * * * * * * * *

(35) the portion of the new qualified plug-in electric drive motor vehicle credit to which ¹*section 30D(c)(1)* applies.

* * * * * * * * * * * *

[For Analysis, see ¶ 1002. For Committee Reports, see ¶ 5027.]

[Endnote Code Sec. 38]

Code Sec. 38(b)(35) was amended by Sec. 1141(b)(2) of the American Recovery and Reinvestment Tax Act of 2009, P.L. 111-5, 2/17/2009, as detailed below:

1. Sec. 1141(b)(2) substituted "30D(c)(1)" for "30D(d)(1)" in para. (b)(35).

Effective Date (Sec. 1141(c), P.L. 111-5, 2/17/2009) effective for vehicles acquired after 12/31/2009.

[¶ 3017]   Code Sec. 42.   Low-income housing credit.

* * * * * * * * * * * *

(i)   Definitions and special rules. For purposes of this section—

(1)   Compliance period. The term "compliance period" means, with respect to any building, the period of 15 taxable years beginning with the 1st taxable year of the credit period with respect thereto.

(2)   Determination of whether building is federally subsidized.

(A) In general. Except as otherwise provided in this paragraph, for purposes of subsection (b)(1), a new building shall be treated as federally subsidized for any taxable year if, at any time during such taxable year or any prior taxable year, there is or was outstanding any obligation the interest on which is exempt from tax under section 103 the proceeds of which are or were used (directly or indirectly) with respect to such building or the operation thereof.

(B) Election to reduce eligible basis by proceeds of obligations. A tax-exempt obligation shall not be taken into account under subparagraph (A) if the taxpayer elects to exclude from the eligible basis of the building for purposes of subsection (d) the proceeds of such obligation.

(C) Special rule for subsidized construction financing. Subparagraph (A) shall not apply to any tax-exempt obligation used to provide construction financing for any building if—

(i) such obligation (when issued) identified the building for which the proceeds of such obligation would be used, and

(ii) such obligation is redeemed before such building is placed in service.

(3)   Low-income unit.

(A) In general. The term "low-income unit" means any unit in a building if—

(i) such unit is rent-restricted (as defined in subsection (g)(2)), and

(ii) the individuals occupying such unit meet the income limitation applicable under subsection (g)(1) to the project of which such building is a part.

(B) Exceptions.

(i) In general. A unit shall not be treated as a low-income unit unless the unit is suitable for occupancy and used other than on a transient basis.

(ii) Suitability for occupancy. For purposes of clause (i), the suitability of a unit for occupancy shall be determined under regulations prescribed by the Secretary taking into account local health, safety, and building codes.

(iii) Transitional housing for homeless. For purposes of clause (i), a unit shall be considered to be used other than on a transient basis if the unit contains sleeping accommodations and kitchen and bathroom facilities and is located in a building—

(I) which is used exclusively to facilitate the transition of homeless individuals (within the meaning of section 103 of the Stewart B. McKinney Homeless Assistance Act (42 U.S.C. 11302), as in effect on the date of the enactment of this clause) to independent living within 24 months, and

(II) in which a governmental entity or qualified nonprofit organization (as defined in subsection (h)(5)) provides such individuals with temporary housing and supportive services designed to assist such individuals in locating and retaining permanent housing.

(iv) Single-room occupancy units. For purposes of clause (i), a single-room occupancy unit shall not be treated as used on a transient basis merely because it is rented on a month-by-month basis.

(C) Special rule for buildings having 4 or fewer units. In the case of any building which has 4 or fewer residential rental units, no unit in such building shall be treated as a low-income unit if the units in such building are owned by—

(i) any individual who occupies a residential unit in such building, or

(ii) any person who is related (as defined in subsection (d)(2)(D)(iii)) to such individual.

(D) Certain students not to disqualify unit. A unit shall not fail to be treated as a low-income unit merely because it is occupied—

(i) by an individual who is—

(I) a student and receiving assistance under title IV of the Social Security Act,

(II) a student who was previously under the care and placement responsibility of the State agency responsible for administering a plan under part B or part E of title IV of the Social Security Act, or

(III) enrolled in a job training program receiving assistance under the Job Training Partnership Act or under other similar Federal, State, or local laws, or

(ii) entirely by full-time students if such students are—

(I) single parents and their children and such parents are not dependents (as defined in section 152, determined without regard to subsections (b)(1), (b)(2), and (d)(1)(B) thereof) of another individual and such children are not dependents (as so defined) of another individual other than a parent of such children, or. [sic ,]

(II) married and file a joint return.

(E) Owner-occupied buildings having 4 or fewer units eligible for credit where development plan.

(i) In general. Subparagraph (C) shall not apply to the acquisition or rehabilitation of a building pursuant to a development plan of action sponsored by a State or local government or a qualified nonprofit organization (as defined in subsection (h)(5)(C)).

(ii) Limitation on credit. In the case of a building to which clause (i) applies, the applicable fraction shall not exceed 80 percent of the unit fraction.

(iii) Certain unrented units treated as owner-occupied. In the case of a building to which clause (i) applies, any unit which is not rented for 90 days or more shall be treated as occupied by the owner of the building as of the 1st day it is not rented.

(4) New building. The term "new building" means a building the original use of which begins with the taxpayer.

(5) Existing building. The term "existing building" means any building which is not a new building.

(6) Application to estates and trusts. In the case of an estate or trust, the amount of the credit determined under subsection (a) and any increase in tax under subsection (j) shall be apportioned between the estate or trust and the beneficiaries on the basis of the income of the estate or trust allocable to each.

(7) Impact of tenant's right of 1st refusal to acquire property.

(A) In general. No Federal income tax benefit shall fail to be allowable to the taxpayer with respect to any qualified low-income building merely by reason of a right of 1st refusal held by the tenants (in cooperative form or otherwise) or resident management corporation of such building or by a qualified nonprofit organization (as defined in subsection (h)(5)(C)) or government agency to purchase the property after the close of the compliance period for a price which is not less than the minimum purchase price determined under subparagraph (B).

(B) Minimum purchase price. For purposes of subparagraph (A), the minimum purchase price under this subparagraph is an amount equal to the sum of—

(i) the principal amount of outstanding indebtedness secured by the building (other than indebtedness incurred within the 5-year period ending on the date of the sale to the tenants), and

(ii) all Federal, State, and local taxes attributable to such sale.

Except in the case of Federal income taxes, there shall not be taken into account under clause (ii) any additional tax attributable to the application of clause (ii).

(8) **Treatment of rural projects.** For purposes of this section, in the case of any project for residential rental property located in a rural area (as defined in section 520 of the Housing Act of 1949), any income limitation measured by reference to area median gross income shall be measured by reference to the greater of area median gross income or national non-metropolitan median income. The preceding sentence shall not apply with respect to any building if paragraph (1) of section 42(h) does not apply by reason of paragraph (4) thereof to any portion of the credit determined under this section with respect to such building.

[1]*(9) Coordination with low-income housing grants.*

(A) Reduction in state housing credit ceiling for low-income housing grants received in 2009. For purposes of this section, the amounts described in clauses (i) through (iv) of subsection (h)(3)(C) with respect to any State for 2009 shall each be reduced by so much of such amount as is taken into account in determining the amount of any grant to such State under section 1602 of the American Recovery and Reinvestment Tax Act of 2009.

(B) Special rule for basis. Basis of a qualified low-income building shall not be reduced by the amount of any grant described in subparagraph (A).

* * * * * * * * * * * *

[For Analysis, see ¶ 906. For Committee Reports, see ¶ 5058.]

[Endnote Code Sec. 42]
Code Sec. 42(i)(9) was added by Sec. 1404 of the American Recovery and Reinvestment Tax Act of 2009, P.L. 111-5, 2/17/2009, as detailed below:
1. Sec. 1404 added para. (i)(9).
Effective Date enacted 2/17/2009.
Sec. 1602 of this Act , reads as follows:
"Sec. 1602. Grants to states for low-income housing projects in lieu of low-income housing credit allocations for 2009.
"(a) In general. The Secretary of the Treasury shall make a grant to the housing credit agency of each State in an amount equal to such State's low-income housing grant election amount.
"(b) Low-income housing grant election amount. For purposes of this section, the term 'low-income housing grant election amount' means, with respect to any State, such amount as the State may elect which does not exceed 85 percent of the product of—
"(1) the sum of—
"(A) 100 percent of the State housing credit ceiling for 2009 which is attributable to amounts described in clauses (i) and (iii) of section 42(h)(3)(C) of the Internal Revenue Code of 1986, and
"(B) 40 percent of the State housing credit ceiling for 2009 which is attributable to amounts described in clauses (ii) and (iv) of such section, multiplied by
"(2) 10.
"(c) Subawards for low-income buildings.
"(1) In general. A State housing credit agency receiving a grant under this section shall use such grant to make subawards to finance the construction or acquisition and rehabilitation of qualified low-income buildings. A subaward under this section may be made to finance a qualified low-income building with or without an allocation under section 42 of the Internal Revenue Code of 1986, except that a State housing credit agency may make subawards to finance qualified low-income buildings without an allocation only if it makes a determination that such use will increase the total funds available to the State to build and rehabilitate affordable housing. In complying with such determination requirement, a State housing credit agency shall establish a process in which applicants that are allocated credits are required to demonstrate good faith efforts to obtain investment commitments for such credits before the agency makes such subawards.

"(2) Subawards subject to same requirements as low-income housing credit allocations. Any such subaward with respect to any qualified low-income building shall be made in the same manner and shall be subject to the same limitations (including rent, income, and use restrictions on such building) as an allocation of housing credit dollar amount allocated by such State housing credit agency under section 42 of the Internal Revenue Code of 1986, except that such subawards shall not be limited by, or otherwise affect (except as provided in subsection (h)(3)(J) of such section), the State housing credit ceiling applicable to such agency.

"(3) Compliance and asset management. The State housing credit agency shall perform asset management functions to ensure compliance with section 42 of the Internal Revenue Code of 1986 and the long-term viability of buildings funded by any subaward under this section. The State housing credit agency may collect reasonable fees from a subaward recipient to cover expenses associated with the performance of its duties under this paragraph. The State housing credit agency may retain an agent or other private contractor to satisfy the requirements of this paragraph.

"(4) Recapture. The State housing credit agency shall impose conditions or restrictions, including a requirement providing for recapture, on any subaward under this section so as to assure that the building with respect to which such subaward is made remains a qualified low-income building during the compliance period. Any such recapture shall be payable to the Secretary of the Treasury for deposit in the general fund of the Treasury and may be enforced by means of liens or such other methods as the Secretary of the Treasury determines appropriate.

"(d) Return of unused grant funds. Any grant funds not used to make subawards under this section before January 1, 2011, shall be returned to the Secretary of the Treasury on such date. Any subawards returned to the State housing credit agency on or after such date shall be promptly returned to the Secretary of the Treasury. Any amounts returned to the Secretary of the Treasury under this subsection shall be deposited in the general fund of the Treasury.

"(e) Definitions. Any term used in this section which is also used in section 42 of the Internal Revenue Code of 1986 shall have the same meaning for purposes of this section as when used in such section 42. Any reference in this section to the Secretary of the Treasury shall be treated as including the Secretary's delegate.

"(f) Appropriations. There is hereby appropriated to the Secretary of the Treasury such sums as may be necessary to carry out this section."

[¶ 3018]   Code Sec. 45.   Electricity produced from certain renewable resources, etc.

* * * * * * * * * * *

(d) **Qualified facilities.** For purposes of this section—

(1) **Wind facility.** In the case of a facility using wind to produce electricity, the term "qualified facility" means any facility owned by the taxpayer which is originally placed in service after December 31, 1993, and before January 1, [1]*2013.* Such term shall not include any facility with respect to which any qualified small wind energy property expenditure (as defined in subsection (d)(4) of section 25D) is taken into account in determining the credit under such section.

(2) **Closed-loop biomass facility.**

(A) In general. In the case of a facility using closed-loop biomass to produce electricity, the term "qualified facility" means any facility—

(i) owned by the taxpayer which is originally placed in service after December 31, 1992, and before January 1, [2]*2014,* or

(ii) owned by the taxpayer which before January 1, [3]*2014,* is originally placed in service and modified to use closed-loop biomass to co-fire with coal, with other biomass, or with both, but only if the modification is approved under the Biomass Power for Rural Development Programs or is part of a pilot project of the Commodity Credit Corporation as described in 65 Fed. Reg. 63052.

(B) Expansion of facility. Such term shall include a new unit placed in service after the date of the enactment of this subparagraph in connection with a facility described in subparagraph (A)(i), but only to the extent of the increased amount of electricity produced at the facility by reason of such new unit.

(C) Special rules. In the case of a qualified facility described in subparagraph (A)(ii)—

(i) the 10-year period referred to in subsection (a) shall be treated as beginning no earlier than the date of the enactment of this clause, and

(ii) if the owner of such facility is not the producer of the electricity, the person eligible for the credit allowable under subsection (a) shall be the lessee or the operator of such facility.

439

(3) Open-loop biomass facilities.

(A) In general. In the case of a facility using open-loop biomass to produce electricity, the term "qualified facility" means any facility owned by the taxpayer which—

(i) in the case of a facility using agricultural livestock waste nutrients—

(I) is originally placed in service after the date of the enactment of this subclause and before January 1, [4]*2014*, and

(II) the nameplate capacity rating of which is not less than 150 kilowatts, and

(ii) in the case of any other facility, is originally placed in service before January 1, [5]*2014*.

(B) Expansion of facility. Such term shall include a new unit placed in service after the date of the enactment of this subparagraph in connection with a facility described in subparagraph (A), but only to the extent of the increased amount of electricity produced at the facility by reason of such new unit.

(C) Credit eligibility. In the case of any facility described in subparagraph (A), if the owner of such facility is not the producer of the electricity, the person eligible for the credit allowable under subsection (a) shall be the lessee or the operator of such facility.

(4) Geothermal or solar energy facility. In the case of a facility using geothermal or solar energy to produce electricity, the term "qualified facility" means any facility owned by the taxpayer which is originally placed in service after the date of the enactment of this paragraph and before January 1, [6]*2014* (January 1, 2006, in the case of a facility using solar energy). Such term shall not include any property described in section 48(a)(3) the basis of which is taken into account by the taxpayer for purposes of determining the energy credit under section 48.

(5) Small irrigation power facility. In the case of a facility using small irrigation power to produce electricity, the term "qualified facility" means any facility owned by the taxpayer which is originally placed in service after the date of the enactment of this paragraph [7]*and before October 3, 2008*.

(6) Landfill gas facilities. In the case of a facility producing electricity from gas derived from the biodegradation of municipal solid waste, the term "qualified facility" means any facility owned by the taxpayer which is originally placed in service after the date of the enactment of this paragraph and before January 1, [8]*2014*.

(7) Trash facilities. In the case of a facility (other than a facility described in paragraph (6)) which uses municipal solid waste to produce electricity, the term "qualified facility" means any facility owned by the taxpayer which is originally placed in service after the date of the enactment of this paragraph and before January 1, [9]*2014*. Such term shall include a new unit placed in service in connection with a facility placed in service on or before the date of the enactment of this paragraph, but only to the extent of the increased amount of electricity produced at the facility by reason of such new unit.

(8) Refined coal production facility. In the case of a facility that produces refined coal, the term "refined coal production facility" means—

(A) with respect to a facility producing steel industry fuel, any facility (or any modification to a facility) which is placed in service before January 1, 2010, and

(B) with respect to any other facility producing refined coal, any facility placed in service after the date of the enactment of the American Jobs Creation Act of 2004 and before January 1, 2010.

(9) Qualified hydropower facility. In the case of a facility producing qualified hydroelectric production described in subsection (c)(8), the term "qualified facility" means—

(A) in the case of any facility producing incremental hydropower production, such facility but only to the extent of its incremental hydropower production attributable to efficiency improvements or additions to capacity described in subsection (c)(8)(B) placed in service after the date of the enactment of this paragraph and before January 1, [10]*2014*, and

(B) any other facility placed in service after the date of the enactment of this paragraph and before January 1, [11]*2014*.

(C) Credit period. In the case of a qualified facility described in subparagraph (A), the 10-year period referred to in subsection (a) shall be treated as beginning on the date the efficiency improvements or additions to capacity are placed in service.

(10) Indian coal production facility. In the case of a facility that produces Indian coal, the term "Indian coal production facility" means a facility which is placed in service before January 1, 2009.

(11) Marine and hydrokinetic renewable energy facilities. In the case of a facility producing electricity from marine and hydrokinetic renewable energy, the term "qualified facility" means any facility owned by the taxpayer—

(A) which has a nameplate capacity rating of at least 150 kilowatts, and

(B) which is originally placed in service on or after the date of the enactment of this paragraph and before January 1, [12]*2014*.

* * * * * * * * * * * *

[For Analysis, see ¶ 1204, ¶ 1207, ¶ 1208 and ¶ 1209. For Committee Reports, see ¶ 5013 and ¶ 5016.]

[Endnote Code Sec. 45]
Code Sec. 45(d)(1), Code Sec. 45(d)(2), Code Sec. 45(d)(3), and Code Sec. 45(d)(4), were amended by Sec. 1101(a)(1)-(2) of the American Recovery and Reinvestment Act of 2009, P.L. 111-5, 2/17/2009, as detailed below:
  1. Sec. 1101(a)(1) substituted "2013" for "2010" in para. (d)(1).
  2. Sec. 1101 (a)(2) substituted "2014" for "2011" in para. (d)(2)(A)(i).
  3. Sec. 1101(a)(2) substituted "2014" for "2011" in para. (d)(2)(A)(ii).
  4. Sec. 1101(a)(2) substituted "2014" for "2011" in para. (d)(3)(A)(i)(I).
  5. Sec. 1101(a)(2) substituted "2014" for "2011" in para (d)(3)(A)(ii).
  6. Sec. 1101(a)(2) substituted "2014" for "2011" in para (d)(4).
Effective Date (Sec. 1101(c)(1), P.L. 111-5, 2/17/2009) effective for property placed in service after 2/17/2009.

Code Sec. 45(d)(5) was amended by Sec. 1101(b) of the American Recovery and Reinvestment Tax Act of 2009, P.L. 111-5, 2/17/2009, as detailed below:
  7. Subsec. (b) substituted "and before October 3, 2008" for "and before the date of the enactment of paragraph (11)" in para (d)(5).
Effective Date (Sec. 1101(c)(2), P.L. 111-5, 2/17/2009) effective for electricity produced and sold after 10/3/2008, in tax. yrs. ending after 10/3/2008 (as stated in Sec. 102 Div. B of P.L. 110-343).

Code Sec. 45(d)(6), Code Sec. 45(d)(7), Code Sec. 45(d)(9), and Code Sec. 45(d)(11)(B) were amended by Sec. 1101(a)(2) and (a)(3), P.L. 111-5, 2/17/2009, as detailed below:
  8. Sec. 1101(a)(2) substituted "2014" for "2011" in para (d)(6).
  9. Sec. 1101(a)(2) substituted "2014" for "2011" in para (d)(7).
  10. Sec. 1101(a)(2) substituted "2014" for "2011" in para (d)(9)(A).
  11. Sec. 1101(a)(2) substituted "2014" for "2011" in para (d)(9)(B).
  12. Sec. 1101(a)(3) substituted "2014" for "2011" in subpara (d)(11)(B).
Effective Date (Sec. 1101(c)(1), P.L. 111-5, 2/17/2009) effective for property placed in service after 2/17/2009.
"Sec. 1603. Grants for specified energy property in lieu of tax credits.
"(a) In general. Upon application, the Secretary of the Treasury shall, subject to the requirements of this section, provide a grant to each person who places in service specified energy property to reimburse such person for a portion of the expense of such property as provided in subsection (b). No grant shall be made under this section with respect to any property unless such property—
"(1) is placed in service during 2009 or 2010, or
"(2) is placed in service after 2010 and before the credit termination date with respect to such property, but only if the construction of such property began during 2009 or 2010.
"(b) Grant amount.
"(1) In general. The amount of the grant under subsection (a) with respect to any specified energy property shall be the applicable percentage of the basis of such property.
"(2) Applicable percentage. For purposes of paragraph (1), the term 'applicable percentage' means—
"(A) 30 percent in the case of any property described in paragraphs (1) through (4) of subsection (d), and
"(B) 10 percent in the case of any other property.
"(3) Dollar limitations. In the case of property described in paragraph (2), (6), or (7) of subsection (d), the amount of any grant under this section with respect to such property shall not exceed the limitation described in section 48(c)(1)(B), 48(c)(2)(B), or 48(c)(3)(B) of the Internal Revenue Code of 1986, respectively, with respect to such property.
"(c) Time for payment of grant. The Secretary of the Treasury shall make payment of any grant under subsection (a) during the 60-day period beginning on the later of—
"(1) the date of the application for such grant, or
"(2) the date the specified energy property for which the grant is being made is placed in service.

"(d) Specified energy property. For purposes of this section, the term 'specified energy property' means any of the following:

"(1) Qualified facilities.—Any qualified property (as defined in section 48(a)(5)(D) of the Internal Revenue Code of 1986) which is part of a qualified facility (within the meaning of section 45 of such Code) described in paragraph (1), (2), (3), (4), (6), (7), (9), or (11) of section 45(d) of such Code.

"(2) Qualified fuel cell property. Any qualified fuel cell property (as defined in section 48(c)(1) of such Code).

"(3) Solar property. Any property described in clause (i) or (ii) of section 48(a)(3)(A) of such Code.

"(4) Qualified small wind energy property. Any qualified small wind energy property (as defined in section 48(c)(4) of such Code.

"(5) Geothermal property. Any property described in clause (iii) of section 48(a)(3)(A) of such Code.

"(6) Qualified microturbine property. Any qualified microturbine property (as defined in section 48(c)(2) of such Code).

"(7) Combined heat and power system property. Any combined heat and power system property (as defined in section 48(c)(3) of such Code).

"(8) Geothermal heat pump property. Any property described in clause (vii) of section 48(a)(3)(A) of such Code.

"Such term shall not include any property unless depreciation (or amortization in lieu of depreciation) is allowable with respect to such property.

"(e) Credit termination date. For purposes of this section, the term 'credit termination date' means—

"(1) in the case of any specified energy property which is part of a facility described in paragraph (1) of section 45(d) of the Internal Revenue Code of 1986, January 1, 2013,

"(2) in the case of any specified energy property which is part of a facility described in paragraph (2), (3), (4), (6), (7), (9), or (11) of section 45(d) of such Code, January 1, 2014, and

"(3) in the case of any specified energy property described in section 48 of such Code, January 1, 2017.

"In the case of any property which is described in paragraph (3) and also in another paragraph of this subsection, paragraph (3) shall apply with respect to such property.

"(f) Application of certain rules. In making grants under this section, the Secretary of the Treasury shall apply rules similar to the rules of section 50 of the Internal Revenue Code of 1986. In applying such rules, if the property is disposed of, or otherwise ceases to be specified energy property, the Secretary of the Treasury shall provide for the recapture of the appropriate percentage of the grant amount in such manner as the Secretary of the Treasury determines appropriate.

"(g) Exception for certain non-taxpayers. The Secretary of the Treasury shall not make any grant under this section to—

"(1) any Federal, State, or local government (or any political subdivision, agency, or instrumentality thereof),

"(2) any organization described in section 501(c) of the Internal Revenue Code of 1986 and exempt from tax under section 501(a) of such Code,

"(3) any entity referred to in paragraph (4) of section 54(j) of such Code, or

"(4) any partnership or other pass-thru entity any partner (or other holder of an equity or profits interest) of which is described in paragraph (1), (2) or (3).

"(h) Definitions. Terms used in this section which are also used in section 45 or 48 of the Internal Revenue Code of 1986 shall have the same meaning for purposes of this section as when used in such section 45 or 48. Any reference in this section to the Secretary of the Treasury shall be treated as including the Secretary's delegate.

"(i) Appropriations. There is hereby appropriated to the Secretary of the Treasury such sums as may be necessary to carry out this section.

"(j) Termination. The Secretary of the Treasury shall not make any grant to any person under this section unless the application of such person for such grant is received before October 1, 2011."

[¶ 3019]   Code Sec. 45D.   New markets tax credit.

* * * * * * * * * * * *

(f)   National limitation on amount of investments designated.

(1)   In general. There is a new markets tax credit limitation for each calendar year. Such limitation is—

(A) $1,000,000,000 for 2001,

(B) $1,500,000,000 for 2002 and 2003,

(C) $2,000,000,000 for 2004 and 2005,[1]

(D) $3,500,000,000 for 2006 [2]*and 2007,*

[3]*(E) $5,000,000,000 for 2008, and*

[4]*(F) $5,000,000,000 for 2009.*

(2)   Allocation of limitation. The limitation under paragraph (1) shall be allocated by the Secretary among qualified community development entities selected by the Secretary. In making allocations under the preceding sentence, the Secretary shall give priority to any entity—

(A) with a record of having successfully provided capital or technical assistance to disadvantaged businesses or communities, or

(B) which intends to satisfy the requirement under subsection (b)(1)(B) by making qualified low-income community investments in 1 or more businesses in which persons unrelated to such entity (within the meaning of section 267(b) or 707(b)(1)) hold the majority equity interest.

(3) Carryover of unused limitation. If the new markets tax credit limitation for any calendar year exceeds the aggregate amount allocated under paragraph (2) for such year, such limitation for the succeeding calendar year shall be increased by the amount of such excess. No amount may be carried under the preceding sentence to any calendar year after 2014.

* * * * * * * * * * * *

[For Analysis, see ¶ 905. For Committee Reports, see ¶ 5057.]

[Endnote Code Sec. 45D]
Code Sec. 45D(f)(1)(C), Code Sec. 45D(f)(1)(D), Code Sec. 45D(f)(1)(E), and Code Sec. 45D(f)(1)(F) were amended by Sec. 1403(a)(1)-(3) of the American Recovery and Reinvestment Act of 2009, P.L. 111-5, 2/17/2009, as detailed below:
  1. Sec. 1403(a)(1) deleted "and" at the end of subpara. (f)(1)(C).
  2. Sec. 1403(a)(2) substituted "and 2007" for ", 2007, 2008, and 2009." in subpara. (f)(1)(D).
  3. Sec. 1403(a)(3) added subpara. (f)(1)(E).
  4. Sec. 1403(a)(3) added subpara. (f)(1)(F).
Effective Date Enacted 2/17/2009.

Sec. 1403(b), P.L. 111-5, 2/17/2009, provides:
"(b) Special rule for allocation of increased 2008 limitation. The amount of the increase in the new markets tax credit limitation for calendar year 2008 by reason of the amendments made by subsection (a) shall be allocated in accordance with section 45D(f)(2) of the Internal Revenue Code of 1986 to qualified community development entities (as defined in section 45D(c) of such Code) which—
"(1) submitted an allocation application with respect to calendar year 2008, and
"(2)(A) did not receive an allocation for such calendar year, or
"(B) received an allocation for such calendar year in an amount less than the amount requested in the allocation application.

[¶ 3020]   Code Sec. 45Q.   Credit for carbon dioxide sequestration.

(a) General rule. For purposes of section 38, the carbon dioxide sequestration credit for any taxable year is an amount equal to the sum of—

(1) $20 per metric ton of qualified carbon dioxide which is—

(A) captured by the taxpayer at a qualified facility, and

(B) disposed of by the taxpayer in secure geological storage [1]*and not used by the taxpayer as described in paragraph (2)(B), and*

(2) $10 per metric ton of qualified carbon dioxide which is—

(A) captured by the taxpayer at a qualified facility,[2]

(B) used by the taxpayer as a tertiary injectant in a qualified enhanced oil or natural gas recovery project[3], *and*

[4]*(C) disposed of by the taxpayer in secure geological storage.*

* * * * * * * * * * * *

(d) Special rules and other definitions. For purposes of this section—

(1) Only carbon dioxide captured and disposed of or used within the United States taken into account. The credit under this section shall apply only with respect to qualified carbon dioxide the capture and disposal or use of which is within—

(A) the United States (within the meaning of section 638(1)), or

(B) a possession of the United States (within the meaning of section 638(2)).

(2) Secure geological storage. The Secretary, in consultation with the Administrator of the Environmental Protection Agency [5]*the Secretary of Energy, and the Secretary of the Interior,* shall establish regulations for determining adequate security measures for the geological storage of carbon dioxide under [6]*paragraph (1)(B) or (2)(C) of subsection (a)* such that the carbon dioxide does not escape into the atmosphere. Such term shall include storage at deep saline formations[7], *oil and gas reservoirs, and unminable coal seams* under such conditions as the Secretary may determine under such regulations.

(3) Tertiary injectant. The term "tertiary injectant" has the same meaning as when used within section 193(b)(1).

(4) Qualified enhanced oil or natural gas recovery project. The term "qualified enhanced oil or natural gas recovery project" has the meaning given the term "qualified enhanced oil recovery project" by section 43(c)(2), by substituting "crude oil or natural gas" for "crude oil" in subparagraph (A)(i) thereof.

(5) Credit attributable to taxpayer. Any credit under this section shall be attributable to the person that captures and physically or contractually ensures the disposal of or the use as a tertiary injectant of the qualified carbon dioxide, except to the extent provided in regulations prescribed by the Secretary.

(6) Recapture. The Secretary shall, by regulations, provide for recapturing the benefit of any credit allowable under subsection (a) with respect to any qualified carbon dioxide which ceases to be captured, disposed of, or used as a tertiary injectant in a manner consistent with the requirements of this section.

(7) Inflation adjustment. In the case of any taxable year beginning in a calendar year after 2009, there shall be substituted for each dollar amount contained in subsection (a) an amount equal to the product of—

(A) such dollar amount, multiplied by

(B) the inflation adjustment factor for such calendar year determined under section 43(b)(3)(B) for such calendar year, determined by substituting "2008" for "1990".

(e) Application of section. The credit under this section shall apply with respect to qualified carbon dioxide before the end of the calendar year in which the Secretary, in consultation with the Administrator of the Environmental Protection Agency, certifies that 75,000,000 metric tons of qualified carbon dioxide have been [8]*taken into account in accordance with subsection (a).*

[For Analysis, see ¶ 1212. For Committee Reports, see ¶ 5025.]

[Endnote Code Sec. 45Q]

Code Sec. 45Q(a)(1)(B), Code Sec. 45Q(a)(2)(A), Code Sec. 45Q(a)(2)(B), Code Sec. 45Q(a)(2)(C), Code Sec. 45Q(d)(2) and Code Sec. 45Q(e) was amended by Sec. 1131 of the American Recovery and Reinvestment Act of 2009, P.L. 111-5, 2/17/2009, as detailed below:

1. Sec. 1131(b)(2) added "and not used by the taxpayer as described in paragraph (2)(B)" after "storage" in subpara. (a)(1)(B).

2. Sec. 1131(a) deleted "and" at the end of subpara. (a)(2)(A).

3. Sec. 1131(a) substituted ", and" for the period in subpara. (a)(2)(B).

4. Sec. 1131(a) added subpara. (a)(2)(C).

5. Sec. 1131(b)(1)(C) added "the Secretary of Energy, and the Secretary of the Interior," after "Environmental Protection Agency" in para. (d)(2).

6. Sec. 1131(b)(1)(A) substituted "paragraph (1)(B) or (2)(C) of subsection (a)" for "subsection (a)(1)(B)" in para. (d)(2).

7. Sec. 1131(b)(1)(B) substituted ", oil and gas reservoirs, and unminable coal seams" for "and unminable coal seems" in para. (d)(2).

8. Sec. 1131(b)(3) substituted "taken into account in accordance with subsection (a)" for "captured and disposed of or used as a tertiary injectant" in subsec. (e).

Effective Date (Sec. 1131(c), P.L. 111-5, 2/17/2009) effective for carbon dioxide captured after 2/17/2009.

[¶ 3021]   Code Sec. 46.   Amount of credit.

For purposes of section 38, the amount of the investment credit determined under this section for any taxable year shall be the sum of—

(1) the rehabilitation credit,

(2) the energy credit[,]

(3) the qualifying advanced coal project credit,[1]

(4) the qualifying gasification project credit[2]

[3]*(5) the qualifying advanced energy project credit.*

[For Analysis, see ¶ 1202. For Committee Reports, see ¶ 5052.]

[Endnote Code Sec. 46]

Code Sec. 46(3), Code Sec. 46(4) and Code Sec. 46(5) were amended by Sec. 1302(a) of the American Recovery and Reinvestment Act of 2009, P.L. 111-5, 2/17/2009, as detailed below:

1. Sec. 1302(a) deleted 'and' at the end of para. (3).
2. Sec. 1302(a) deleted the period at the end of para. (4).
3. Sec. 1302(a) added para. (5).

Effective Date (Sec. 1302(d), P.L. 111-5, 2/17/2009) effective for periods after 2/17/2009, under rules similar to the rules of Code Sec. 48(m) (as in effect on the day before the date of the enactment of the Revenue Reconciliation Act of 1990 [enacted 11/5/90]).

[¶ 3022]   Code Sec. 48.   Energy credit.

(a)   Energy credit.

(1)   In general. For purposes of section 46, except as provided in paragraphs (1)(B), and (2)(B), (3)(B), and (4)(B) of subsection (c), the energy credit for any taxable year is the energy percentage of the basis of each energy property placed in service during such taxable year.

(2)   Energy percentage.

(A) In general. The energy percentage is—

(i) 30 percent in the case of—

(I) qualified fuel cell property,

(II) energy property described in paragraph (3)(A)(i) but only with respect to periods ending before January 1, 2017,

(III) energy property described in paragraph (3)(A)(ii), and

(IV) qualified small wind energy property, and

(ii) in the case of any energy property to which clause (i) does not apply, 10 percent.

(B) Coordination with rehabilitation credit. The energy percentage shall not apply to that portion of the basis of any property which is attributable to qualified rehabilitation expenditures.

(3)   Energy property. For purposes of this subpart, the term "energy property" means any property—

(A) which is—

(i) equipment which uses solar energy to generate electricity, to heat or cool (or provide hot water for use in) a structure, or to provide solar process heat, excepting property used to generate energy for the purposes of heating a swimming pool,

(ii) equipment which uses solar energy to illuminate the inside of a structure using fiber-optic distributed sunlight but only with respect to periods ending before January 1, 2017,

(iii) equipment used to produce, distribute, or use energy derived from a geothermal deposit (within the meaning of section 613(e)(2)), but only, in the case of electricity generated by geothermal power, up to (but not including) the electrical transmission stage,

(iv) qualified fuel cell property or qualified microturbine property,

(v) combined heat and power system property,

(vi) qualified small wind energy property, or

(vii) equipment which uses the ground or ground water as a thermal energy source to heat a structure or as a thermal energy sink to cool a structure, but only with respect to periods ending before January 1, 2017,

(B)

(i) the construction, reconstruction, or erection of which is completed by the tax-payer, or

(ii) which is acquired by the taxpayer if the original use of such property commences with the taxpayer,

(C) with respect to which depreciation (or amortization in lieu of depreciation) is allowable, and

(D) which meets the performance and quality standards (if any) which—

(i) have been prescribed by the Secretary by regulations (after consultation with the Secretary of Energy), and

(ii) are in effect at the time of the acquisition of the property.

Such term shall not include any property which is part of a facility the production from which is allowed as a credit under section 45 for the taxable year or any prior taxable year.

(4) Special rule for property financed by subsidized energy financing or industrial development bonds.

(A) Reduction of basis. For purposes of applying the energy percentage to any property, if such property is financed in whole or in part by—

(i) subsidized energy financing, or

(ii) the proceeds of a private activity bond (within the meaning of section 141) the interest on which is exempt from tax under section 103,

the amount taken into account as the basis of such property shall not exceed the amount which (but for this subparagraph) would be so taken into account multiplied by the fraction determined under subparagraph (B).

(B) Determination of fraction. For purposes of subparagraph (A), the fraction determined under this subparagraph is 1 reduced by a fraction—

(i) the numerator of which is that portion of the basis of the property which is allocable to such financing or proceeds, and

(ii) the denominator of which is the basis of the property.

(C) Subsidized energy financing. For purposes of subparagraph (A), the term "subsidized energy financing" means financing provided under a Federal, State, or local program a principal purpose of which is to provide subsidized financing for projects designed to conserve or produce energy.

[1]*(D) Termination. This paragraph shall not apply to periods after December 31, 2008, under rules similar to the rules of section 48(m) (as in effect on the day before the date of the enactment of the Revenue Reconciliation Act of 1990).*

[2]*(5) Election to treat qualified facilities as energy property.*

(A) In general. In the case of any qualified property which is part of a qualified investment credit facility—

(i) such property shall be treated as energy property for purposes of this section, and

(ii) the energy percentage with respect to such property shall be 30 percent.

(B) Denial of production credit. No credit shall be allowed under section 45 for any taxable year with respect to any qualified investment credit facility.

(C) Qualified investment credit facility. For purposes of this paragraph, the term "qualified investment credit facility" means any of the following facilities if no credit has been allowed under section 45 with respect to such facility and the taxpayer makes an irrevocable election to have this paragraph apply to such facility:

(i) Wind facilities. Any qualified facility (within the meaning of section 45) described in paragraph (1) of section 45(d) if such facility is placed in service in 2009, 2010, 2011, or 2012.

(ii) Other facilities. Any qualified facility (within the meaning of section 45) described in paragraph (2), (3), (4), (6), (7), (9), or (11) of section 45(d) if such facility is placed in service in 2009, 2010, 2011, 2012, or 2013.

(D) Qualified property. For purposes of this paragraph, the term "qualified property" means property—

(i) which is—

(I) tangible personal property, or

(II) other tangible property (not including a building or its structural components), and

(ii) with respect to which depreciation (or amortization in lieu of depreciation) is allowable but only if such property is used as an integral part of the qualified investment credit facility.

* * * * * * * * * * * *

(c) Definitions. *For purposes of this section—*

(1) Qualified fuel cell property.

(A) In general. The term *"qualified fuel cell property" means a fuel cell power plant which—*

(i) has a nameplate capacity of at least 0.5 kilowatt of electricity using an electrochemical process, and

(ii) has an electricity-only generation efficiency greater than 30 percent.

(B) Limitation. In the case of qualified fuel cell property placed in service during the taxable year, the credit otherwise determined under subsection (a) for such year with respect to such property shall not exceed an amount equal to $1,500 for each 0.5 kilowatt of capacity of such property.

(C) Fuel cell power plant. The term *"fuel cell power plant" means an integrated system comprised of a fuel cell stack assembly and associated balance of plant components which converts a fuel into electricity using electrochemical means.*

(D) Termination. The term *"qualified fuel cell property" shall not include any property for any period after December 31, 2016.*

(2) Qualified microturbine property.

(A) In general. The term *"qualified microturbine property" means a stationary microturbine power plant which—*

(i) has a nameplate capacity of less than 2,000 kilowatts, and

(ii) has an electricity-only generation efficiency of not less than 26 percent at International Standard Organization conditions.

(B) Limitation. In the case of qualified microturbine property placed in service during the taxable year, the credit otherwise determined under subsection (a) for such year with respect to such property shall not exceed an amount equal $200 for each kilowatt of capacity of such property.

(C) Stationary microturbine power plant. The term *"stationary microturbine power plant" means an integrated system comprised of a gas turbine engine, a combustor, a recuperator or regenerator, a generator or alternator, and associated balance of plant components which converts a fuel into electricity and thermal energy. Such term also includes all secondary components located between the existing infrastructure for fuel delivery and the existing infrastructure for power distribution, including equipment and controls for meeting relevant power standards, such as voltage, frequency, and power factors.*

(D) Termination. The term *"qualified microturbine property" shall not include any property for any period after December 31, 2016.*

(3) Combined heat and power system property.

(A) Combined heat and power system property. The term *"combined heat and power system property" means property comprising a system—*

(i) which uses the same energy source for the simultaneous or sequential generation of electrical power, mechanical shaft power, or both, in combination with the generation of steam or other forms of useful thermal energy (including heating and cooling applications),

(ii) which produces—

(I) at least 20 percent of its total useful energy in the form of thermal energy which is not used to produce electrical or mechanical power (or combination thereof), and

(II) at least 20 percent of its total useful energy in the form of electrical or mechanical power (or combination thereof),

(iii) the energy efficiency percentage of which exceeds 60 percent, and

(iv) which is placed in service before January 1, 2017.

(B) Limitation.

(i) In general. In the case of combined heat and power system property with an electrical capacity in excess of the applicable capacity placed in service during the taxable year, the credit under subsection (a)(1) (determined without regard to this paragraph) for such year shall be equal to the amount which bears the same ratio to such credit as the applicable capacity bears to the capacity of such property.

(ii) Applicable capacity. For purposes of clause (i), the term "applicable capacity" means 15 megawatts or a mechanical energy capacity of more than 20,000 horsepower or an equivalent combination of electrical and mechanical energy capacities.

(iii) Maximum capacity. The term "combined heat and power system property" shall not include any property comprising a system if such system has a capacity in excess of 50 megawatts or a mechanical energy capacity in excess of 67,000 horsepower or an equivalent combination of electrical and mechanical energy capacities.

(C) Special rules.

(i) Energy efficiency percentage. For purposes of this paragraph, the energy efficiency percentage of a system is the fraction—

(I) the numerator of which is the total useful electrical, thermal, and mechanical power produced by the system at normal operating rates, and expected to be consumed in its normal application, and

(II) the denominator of which is the lower heating value of the fuel sources for the system.

(ii) Determinations made on Btu basis. The energy efficiency percentage and the percentages under subparagraph (A)(ii) shall be determined on a Btu basis.

(iii) Input and output property not included. The term "combined heat and power system property" does not include property used to transport the energy source to the facility or to distribute energy produced by the facility.

(D) Systems using biomass. If a system is designed to use biomass (within the meaning of paragraphs (2) and (3) of section 45(c) without regard to the last sentence of paragraph (3)(A)) for at least 90 percent of the energy source—

(i) subparagraph (A)(iii) shall not apply, but

(ii) the amount of credit determined under subsection (a) with respect to such system shall not exceed the amount which bears the same ratio to such amount of credit (determined without regard to this subparagraph) as the energy efficiency percentage of such system bears to 60 percent.

(4) Qualified small wind energy property.

(A) In general. The term "qualified small wind energy property" means property which uses a qualifying small wind turbine to generate electricity.

[3, 4](B) Qualifying small wind turbine. The term "qualifying small wind turbine" means a wind turbine which has a nameplate capacity of not more than 100 kilowatts.

(C) Termination. The term "qualified small wind energy property" shall not include any property for any period after December 31, 2016.

[5]**(d) Coordination with department of treasury grants.** In the case of any property with respect to which the Secretary makes a grant under section 1603 of the American Recovery and Reinvestment Tax Act of 2009—

(1) Denial of production and investment credits. No credit shall be determined under this section or section 45 with respect to such property for the taxable year in which such grant is made or any subsequent taxable year.

(2) Recapture of credits for progress expenditures made before grant. If a credit was determined under this section with respect to such property for any taxable year ending before such grant is made—

(A) the tax imposed under subtitle A on the taxpayer for the taxable year in which such grant is made shall be increased by so much of such credit as was allowed under section 38,

(B) the general business carryforwards under section 39 shall be adjusted so as to recapture the portion of such credit which was not so allowed, and

(C) the amount of such grant shall be determined without regard to any reduction in the basis of such property by reason of such credit.

(3) Treatment of grants. Any such grant shall—

(A) not be includible in the gross income of the taxpayer, but

(B) shall be taken into account in determining the basis of the property to which such grant relates, except that the basis of such property shall be reduced under section 50(c) in the same manner as a credit allowed under subsection (a).

[For Analysis, see ¶ 1201, ¶ 1203, ¶ 1204, ¶ 1205 and ¶ 1206. For Committee Reports, see ¶ 5014, ¶ 5015 and ¶ 5016.]

[Endnote Code Sec. 48]

Code Sec. 48(a)(4)(D) was amended by Sec. 1103(b)(1) of the American Recovery and Reinvestment Act of 2009, P.L. 111-5, 2/17/2009, as detailed below:

1. Sec. 1103(b)(1) added subpara. (a)(4)(D)

Effective Date (Sec. 1103(c)(1), P.L. 111-5, 2/17/2009) effective for periods after 12/31/2008, under rules similar to the rules of section 48(m) of the Internal Revenue Code of 1986 (as in effect on the day before the date of the enactment of the Revenue Reconciliation Act of 1990 [enacted 11/5/90]).

Code Sec. 48(a)(5) was amended by Sec. 1102(a), P.L. 111-5, 2/17/2009, as detailed below:

2. Sec. 1102(a) added para. (a)(5)

Effective Date (Sec. 1102(b), P.L. 111-5, 2/17/2009) effective for facilities placed in service after 12/31/2008.

Code Sec. 48(c)(4)(B) and Code Sec. 48(c)(4)(C) was amended by Sec. 1103(a), P.L. 111-5, 2/17/2009, as detailed below:

3. Sec. 1103(a) deleted subpara. (c)(4)(B). Prior to deletion, subpara. (c)(4)(B) read as follows:

"(B) Limitation. In the case of qualified small wind energy property placed in service during the taxable year, the credit otherwise determined under subsection (a)(1) for such year with respect to all such property of the taxpayer shall not exceed $4,000."

4. Sec. 1103(a) redesignated subparas. (c)(4)(C)-(D) as (c)(4)(B)-(C)

Effective Date (Sec. 1103(c)(1), P.L. 111-5, 2/17/2009) effective for periods after 12/31/2008, under rules similar to the rules of section 48(m) of the Internal Revenue Code of 1986 (as in effect on the day before the date of the enactment of the Revenue Reconciliation Act of 1990 [enacted 11/5/90]).

Code Sec. 48(d) was amended by Sec. 1104, P.L. 111-5, 2/17/2009, as detailed below:

5. Sec. 1104 added subsec. (d)

Effective Date Enacted 2/17/2009.

Sec. 1603, P.L. 111-5, 2/17/2009, provides:

"Sec. 1603. Grants for specified energy property in lieu of tax credits.

"(a) In general. Upon application, the Secretary of the Treasury shall, subject to the requirements of this section, provide a grant to each person who places in service specified energy property to reimburse such person for a portion of the expense of such property as provided in subsection (b). No grant shall be made under this section with respect to any property unless such property—

"(1) is placed in service during 2009 or 2010, or

"(2) is placed in service after 2010 and before the credit termination date with respect to such property, but only if the construction of such property began during 2009 or 2010.

"(b) Grant amount.

"(1) In general. The amount of the grant under subsection (a) with respect to any specified energy shall be the applicable percentage of the basis of such property.

"(2) Applicable percentage. For purposes of paragraph (1), the term 'applicable percentage' means—

"(A) 30 percent in the case of any property described in paragraphs (1) through (4) of subsection (d), and

"(B) 10 percent in the case of any other property.

"(3) Dollar limitations. In the case of property described in paragraph (2), (6), or (7) of subsection (d), the amount of any grant under this section with respect to such property shall not exceed the limitation described in section 48(c)(1)(B), 48(c)(2)(B), or 48(c)(3)(B) of the Internal Revenue Code of 1986, respectively, with respect to such property.

"(c) Time for payment of grant. The Secretary of the Treasury shall make payment of any grant under subsection (a) during the 60-day period beginning on the later of—

"(1) the date of the application for such grant, or

"(2) the date the specified energy property for which the grant is being made is placed in service.

"(d) Specified energy property. For purposes of this section, the term 'specified energy property' means any of the following:

"(1) QUALIFIED FACILITIES. Any qualified property (as defined in section 48(a)(5)(D)) which is part of a qualified facility (within the meaning of section 45) described in paragraph (1), (2), (3), (4), (6), (7), (9), or (11) of section 45(d) of the Internal Revenue Code of 1986.

"(2) Qualified fuel cell property. Any qualified fuel cell property (as defined in section 48(c)(1) of such Code).

"(3) Solar property. Any property described in clause (i) or (ii) of section 48(a)(3)(A) of such Code.

"(4) Qualified small wind energy property. Any qualified small wind energy property (as defined in section 48(c)(4) of such Code).

"(5) Geothermal property. Any property described in clause (iii) of section 48(a)(3)(A) of such Code.

"(6) Qualified microturbine property. Any qualified microturbine property (as defined in section 48(c)(2) of such Code).

"(7) Combined heat and power system property. Any combined heat and power system property (as defined in section 48(c)(3) of such Code).

"(8) Geothermal heat pump property. Any property described in clause (vii) of section 48(a)(3)(A) of such Code.

"Such term shall not include any property unless depreciation (or amortization in lieu of depreciation) is allowable with respect to such property.

"(e) Credit termination date. For purposes of this section, the term 'credit termination date' means—

"(1) in the case of any specified energy property which is part of a facility described in paragraph (1) of section 45(d) of the Internal Revenue Code of 1986, January 1, 2013,

"(2) in the case of any specified energy property which is part of a facility described in paragraph (2), (3), (4), (6), (7), (9), or (11) of section 45(d) of the Internal Revenue Code of 1986, January 1, 2014, and

"(3) in the case of any specified energy property described in section 48, January 1, 2017.

"In the case of any property which is described in paragraph (3) and also in another paragraph of this subsection, paragraph (3) shall apply with respect to such property.

"(f) Application of certain rules. In making grants under this section, the Secretary of the Treasury shall apply rules similar to the rules of section 50 of the Internal Revenue Code of 1986. In applying such rules, if the property is disposed of, or otherwise ceases to be specified energy property, the Secretary of the Treasury shall provide for the recapture of the appropriate percentage of the grant amount in such manner as the Secretary of the Treasury determines appropriate.

"(g) Exception for certain non-taxpayers. The Secretary of the Treasury shall not make any grant under this section to—

"(1) any Federal, State, or local government (or any political subdivision, agency, or instrumentality thereof),

"(2) any organization described in section 501(c) of the Internal Revenue Code of 1986 and exempt from tax under section 501(a) of such Code,

"(3) any entity referred to in paragraph (4) of section 54(j) of such Code, or

"(4) any partnership or other pass-thru entity any partner (or other holder of an equity or profits interest) of which is described in paragraph (1), (2) or (3).

"(h) Definitions. Terms used in this section which are also used in section 45 or 48 of the Internal Revenue Code of 1986 shall have the same meaning for purposes of this section as when used in such section 45 or 48. Any reference in this section to the Secretary of the Treasury shall be treated as including the Secretary's delegate.

"(i) Appropriations. There is hereby appropriated to the Secretary of the Treasury such sums as may be necessary to carry out this section.

"(j) Termination. The Secretary of the Treasury shall not make any grant to any person under this section unless the application of such person for such grant is received before October 1, 2011."

[¶ 3023]   Code Sec. 48A.   Qualifying advanced coal project credit.

* * * * * * * * * * * *

(b)   Qualified investment.

(1)   In general. For purposes of subsection (a), the qualified investment for any taxable year is the basis of eligible property placed in service by the taxpayer during such taxable year which is part of a qualifying advanced coal project—

    (A)   (i) the construction, reconstruction, or erection of which is completed by the taxpayer, or

      (ii) which is acquired by the taxpayer if the original use of such property commences with the taxpayer, and

    (B) with respect to which depreciation (or amortization in lieu of depreciation) is allowable.

(2) Special rule for certain subsidized property. Rules similar to section 48(a)(4) [1]*(without regard to subparagraph (D) thereof)* shall apply for purposes of this section.

(3) Certain qualified progress expenditures rules made applicable. Rules similar to the rules of subsections (c)(4) and (d) of section 46 (as in effect on the day before the enactment of the Revenue Reconciliation Act of 1990) shall apply for purposes of this section.

* * * * * * * * * * *

[For Analysis, see ¶ 1206. For Committee Reports, see ¶ 5015.]

[Endnote Code Sec. 48A]
    Code Sec. 48A(b)(2) was amended by Sec. 1103(b)(2)(C) of the American Recovery and Reinvestment Tax Act of 2009, P.L. 111-5, 2/17/2009, as detailed below:
    1. Sec. 1103(b)(2)(C) added "(without regard to subparagraph (D) thereof)" after "section 48(a)(4)" in para. (b)(2)
Effective Date (Sec. 1103(c)(1), P.L. 111-5, 2/17/2009) effective for periods after 12/31/2008, under rules similar to the rules of section 48(m) of the Internal Revenue Code of 1986 (as in effect on the day before the date of the enactment of the Revenue Reconciliation Act of 1990 [enacted 11/5/90]).

[¶ 3024]   Code Sec. 48B.   Qualifying gasification project credit.

* * * * * * * * * * *

(b) Qualified investment.

(1) In general. For purposes of subsection (a), the qualified investment for any taxable year is the basis of eligible property placed in service by the taxpayer during such taxable year which is part of a qualifying gasification project—

    (A) (i) the construction, reconstruction, or erection of which is completed by the taxpayer, or

    (ii) which is acquired by the taxpayer if the original use of such property commences with the taxpayer, and

    (B) with respect to which depreciation (or amortization in lieu of depreciation) is allowable.

(2) Special rule for certain subsidized property. Rules similar to section 48(a)(4) [1]*(without regard to subparagraph (D) thereof)* shall apply for purposes of this section.

(3) Certain qualified progress expenditures rules made applicable. Rules similar to the rules of subsections (c)(4) and (d) of section 46 (as in effect on the day before the enactment of the Revenue Reconciliation Act of 1990) shall apply for purposes of this section.

* * * * * * * * * * *

[For Analysis, see ¶ 1206. For Committee Reports, see ¶ 5015.]

[Endnote Code Sec. 48B]
    Code Sec. 48B(b)(2) was amended by Sec. 1103(b)(2)(D) of the American Recovery and Reinvestment Tax Act of 2009, P.L. 111-5, 2/17/2009, as detailed below:
    1. Sec. 1103(b)(2)(D) added "(without regard to subparagraph (D) thereof)" after "section 48(a)(4)" in para. (b)(2)
Effective Date (Sec. 1103(c)(1), P.L. 111-5, 2/17/2009) effective for periods after 12/31/2008, under rules similar to the rules of section 48(m) of the Internal Revenue Code of 1986 (as in effect on the day before the date of the enactment of the Revenue Reconciliation Act of 1990).

[¶ 3025]   Code Sec.[1] 48C.   Qualifying advanced energy project credit.

    (a) In general. For purposes of section 46, the qualifying advanced energy project credit for any taxable year is an amount equal to 30 percent of the qualified investment for such taxable year with respect to any qualifying advanced energy project of the taxpayer.

(b)   Qualified investment.

(1)   In general. For purposes of subsection (a), the qualified investment for any taxable year is the basis of eligible property placed in service by the taxpayer during such taxable year which is part of a qualifying advanced energy project.

(2)   Certain qualified progress expenditures rules made applicable. Rules similar to the rules of subsections (c)(4) and (d) of section 46 (as in effect on the day before the enactment of the Revenue Reconciliation Act of 1990) shall apply for purposes of this section.

(3)   Limitation. The amount which is treated for all taxable years with respect to any qualifying advanced energy project shall not exceed the amount designated by the Secretary as eligible for the credit under this section.

(c)   Definitions.

(1)   Qualifying advanced energy project.

(A) In general. The term "qualifying advanced energy project" means a project—

(i) which re-equips, expands, or establishes a manufacturing facility for the production of—

(I) property designed to be used to produce energy from the sun, wind, geothermal deposits (within the meaning of section 613(e)(2)), or other renewable resources,

(II) fuel cells, microturbines, or an energy storage system for use with electric or hybrid-electric motor vehicles,

(III) electric grids to support the transmission of intermittent sources of renewable energy, including storage of such energy,

(IV) property designed to capture and sequester carbon dioxide emissions,

(V) property designed to refine or blend renewable fuels or to produce energy conservation technologies (including energy-conserving lighting technologies and smart grid technologies),

(VI) new qualified plug-in electric drive motor vehicles (as defined by section 30D), qualified plug-in electric vehicles (as defined by section 30(d)), or components which are designed specifically for use with such vehicles, including electric motors, generators, and power control units, or

(VII) other advanced energy property designed to reduce greenhouse gas emissions as may be determined by the Secretary, and

(ii) any portion of the qualified investment of which is certified by the Secretary under subsection (d) as eligible for a credit under this section.

(B) Exception. Such term shall not include any portion of a project for the production of any property which is used in the refining or blending of any transportation fuel (other than renewable fuels).

(2)   Eligible property. The term "eligible property" means any property—

(A) which is necessary for the production of property described in paragraph (1)(A)(i),

(B) which is—

(i) tangible personal property, or

(ii) other tangible property (not including a building or its structural components), but only if such property is used as an integral part of the qualified investment credit facility, and

(C) with respect to which depreciation (or amortization in lieu of depreciation) is allowable.

(d)   Qualifying advanced energy project program.

(1)   Establishment.

(A) In general. Not later than 180 days after the date of enactment of this section, the Secretary, in consultation with the Secretary of Energy, shall establish a qualifying advanced energy project program to consider and award certifications for qualified investments eligible for credits under this section to qualifying advanced energy project sponsors.

(B) *Limitation.* The total amount of credits that may be allocated under the program shall not exceed $2,000,000,000.

(2) Certification.

(A) *Application period.* Each applicant for certification under this paragraph shall submit an application containing such information as the Secretary may require during the 2-year period beginning on the date the Secretary establishes the program under paragraph (1).

(B) *Time to meet criteria for certification.* Each applicant for certification shall have 1 year from the date of acceptance by the Secretary of the application during which to provide to the Secretary evidence that the requirements of the certification have been met.

(C) *Period of issuance.* An applicant which receives a certification shall have 3 years from the date of issuance of the certification in order to place the project in service and if such project is not placed in service by that time period, then the certification shall no longer be valid.

(3) Selection criteria. In determining which qualifying advanced energy projects to certify under this section, the Secretary—

(A) shall take into consideration only those projects where there is a reasonable expectation of commercial viability, and

(B) shall take into consideration which projects—

(i) will provide the greatest domestic job creation (both direct and indirect) during the credit period,

(ii) will provide the greatest net impact in avoiding or reducing air pollutants or anthropogenic emissions of greenhouse gases,

(iii) have the greatest potential for technological innovation and commercial deployment,

(iv) have the lowest levelized cost of generated or stored energy, or of measured reduction in energy consumption or greenhouse gas emission (based on costs of the full supply chain), and

(v) have the shortest project time from certification to completion.

(4) Review and redistribution.

(A) *Review.* Not later than 4 years after the date of enactment of this section, the Secretary shall review the credits allocated under this section as of such date.

(B) *Redistribution.* The Secretary may reallocate credits awarded under this section if the Secretary determines that—

(i) there is an insufficient quantity of qualifying applications for certification pending at the time of the review, or

(ii) any certification made pursuant to paragraph (2) has been revoked pursuant to paragraph (2)(B) because the project subject to the certification has been delayed as a result of third party opposition or litigation to the proposed project.

(C) *Reallocation.* If the Secretary determines that credits under this section are available for reallocation pursuant to the requirements set forth in paragraph (2), the Secretary is authorized to conduct an additional program for applications for certification.

(5) Disclosure of allocations. The Secretary shall, upon making a certification under this subsection, publicly disclose the identity of the applicant and the amount of the credit with respect to such applicant.

(e) Denial of double benefit. A credit shall not be allowed under this section for any qualified investment for which a credit is allowed under section 48, 48A, or 48B.

[For Analysis, see ¶ 1202. For Committee Reports, see ¶ 5052.]

[Endnote Code Sec. 48C]

Code Sec. 48C was added by Sec. 1302(b) of the American Recovery and Reinvestment Act of 2009, P.L. 111-5, 2/17/2009, as detailed below:

1. Sec. 1302(b) added Code Sec. 48C

Effective Date (Sec. 1302(d), P.L. 111-5, 2/17/2009) effective for periods after 2/17/2009, under rules similar to the rules of section 48(m) of the Internal Revenue Code of 1986 (as in effect on the day before the date of the enactment of the Revenue Reconciliation Act of 1990 [enacted 11/5/90]).

[¶ 3026]   Code Sec. 49.   At-risk rules.

(a) General rule.

(1) Certain nonrecourse financing excluded from credit base.

(A) Limitation. The credit base of any property to which this paragraph applies shall be reduced by the nonqualified nonrecourse financing with respect to such credit base (as of the close of the taxable year in which placed in service).

(B) Property to which paragraph applies. This paragraph applies to any property which—

(i) is placed in service during the taxable year by a taxpayer described in section 465(a)(1), and

(ii) is used in connection with an activity with respect to which any loss is subject to limitation under section 465.

(C) Credit base defined. For purposes of this paragraph, the term "credit base" means—

(i) the portion of the basis of any qualified rehabilitated building attributable to qualified rehabilitation expenditures,

(ii) the basis of any energy property,

(iii) the basis of any property which is part of a qualifying advanced coal project under section 48A, [1]

(iv) the basis of any property which is part of a qualifying gasification project under section 48B[2], *and*

[3]*(v) the basis of any property which is part of a qualifying advanced energy project under section 48C.*

* * * * * * * * * * * *

[For Analysis, see ¶ 1202. For Committee Reports, see ¶ 5052.]

[Endnote Code Sec. 49]

Code Sec. 49(a)(1)(C)(iii), Code Sec. 49(a)(1)(C)(iv), and Code Sec. 49(a)(1)(C)(v) was added by Sec. 1302(c)(1) of the American Recovery and Reinvestment Tax Act of 2009, P.L. 111-5, 2/17/2009, as detailed below:

1. Sec. 1302(c)(1) deleted "and" at the end of clause (a)(1)(C)(iii)
2. Sec. 1302(c)(1) substituted ", and" for the period at the end of clause (a)(1)(C)(iv)
3. Sec. 1302(c)(1) added clause (a)(1)(C)(v)

Effective Date (Sec. 1302(d), P.L. 111-5, 2/17/2009) effective for periods after 2/17/2009, under rules similar to the rules of section 48(m) of the Internal Revenue Code of 1986 (as in effect on the day before the date of enactment of the Revenue Reconciliation Act of 1990 [enacted 11/5/90]).

[¶ 3027]   Code Sec. 51.   Amount of credit.

* * * * * * * * * * * *

(d) Members of targeted groups. For purposes of this subpart—

[1]*(14) Credit allowed for unemployed veterans and disconnected youth hired in 2009 or 2010.*

(A) In general. Any unemployed veteran or disconnected youth who begins work for the employer during 2009 or 2010 shall be treated as a member of a targeted group for purposes of this subpart.

(B) Definitions. For purposes of this paragraph—

(i) Unemployed veteran. The term "unemployed veteran" means any veteran (as defined in paragraph (3)(B), determined without regard to clause (ii) thereof) who is certified by the designated local agency as—

(I) having been discharged or released from active duty in the Armed Forces at any time during the 5-year period ending on the hiring date, and

(II) being in receipt of unemployment compensation under State or Federal law for not less than 4 weeks during the 1-year period ending on the hiring date.

(ii) Disconnected youth. The term *"disconnected youth"* means any individual who is certified by the designated local agency—

(I) as having attained age 16 but not age 25 on the hiring date,

(II) as not regularly attending any secondary, technical, or post-secondary school during the 6-month period preceding the hiring date,

(III) as not regularly employed during such 6-month period, and

(IV) as not readily employable by reason of lacking a sufficient number of basic skills.

* * * * * * * * * * * *

[For Analysis, see ¶ 904. For Committee Reports, see ¶ 5039.]

[Endnote Code Sec. 51]

Code Sec. 51(d)(14) was amended by Sec. 1221(a) of the American Recovery and Reinvestment Tax Act of 2009, P.L. 111-5, 2/17/2009, as detailed below:

1. Sec. 1221(a) added para. (d)(14)

Effective Date (Sec. 1221(b), P.L. 111-5, 2/17/2009) effective for individuals who begin work for the employer after 12/31/2008.

[¶ 3028]   **Code Sec. 53.**   **Credit for prior year minimum tax liability.**

* * * * * * * * * * * *

(d) **Definitions.** For purposes of this section—

(1) **Net minimum tax.**

(A) In general. The term "net minimum tax" means the tax imposed by section 55.

(B) Credit not allowed for exclusion preferences.

(i) Adjusted net minimum tax. The adjusted net minimum tax for any taxable year is—

(I) the amount of the net minimum tax for such taxable year, reduced by

(II) the amount which would be the net minimum tax for such taxable year if the only adjustments and items of tax preference taken into account were those specified in clause (ii).

(ii) Specified items. The following are specified in this clause—

(I) the adjustments provided for in subsection (b)(1) of section 56, and

(II) the items of tax preference described in paragraphs (1), (5) and (7) of section 57(a).

[1, 2]*(iii) Credit allowable for exclusion preferences of corporations. In the case of a corporation—*

(I) the preceding provisions of this subparagraph shall not apply, and

(II) the adjusted net minimum tax for any taxable year is the amount of the net minimum tax for such year[3].

(2) Tentative minimum tax. The term "tentative minimum tax" has the meaning given to such term by section 55(b).

[Endnote Code Sec. 53]

Code Sec. 53(d)(1)(B)(iii) and Code Sec. 53(d)(1)(B)(iii)(II) were amended by Sec. 1142(b)(4) of the American Recovery and Reinvestment Tax Act of 2009, P.L. 111-5, 2/17/2009, as detailed below:

1. Sec. 1142(b)(4)(A) deleted clause (d)(1)(B)(iii). Prior to deletion, clause (d)(1)(B)(iii) read as follows:

"(iii) Special rule. The adjusted net minimum tax for the taxable year shall be increased by the amount of the credit not allowed under section 30 solely by reason of the application of section 30(b)(3)(B)."

2. Sec. 1142(b)(4)(B) deleted "increased in the manner provided in clause (iii)" in subclause (d)(1)(B)(iii)(II) [as redesignated]

3. Sec. 1142(b)(4)(A) redesignated clause (d)(1)(B)(iv) as clause (d)(1)(B)(iii)

Effective Date (Sec. 1142(c), P.L. 111-5, 2/17/2009) effective for vehicles acquired after 2/17/2009.

[¶ 3029]   Code Sec. 54.   Credit to holders of clean renewable energy bonds.

* * * * * * * * * * * *

(c)   Limitation based on amount of tax. The credit allowed under subsection (a) for any taxable year shall not exceed the excess of—

(1) the sum of the regular tax liability (as defined in section 26(b)) plus the tax imposed by section 55, over

(2) the sum of the credits allowable under this part (other than subparts C[1], *I, and J,* section 1400N(l), and this section).

* * * * * * * * * * * *

(l)   Other definitions and special rules. For purposes of this section—

(1)   Bond. The term "bond" includes any obligation.

(2)   Pooled financing bond. The term "pooled financing bond" shall have the meaning given such term by section 149(f)(6)(A).

(3)   Partnership; S corporation; and other pass-thru entities.

(A) In general. Under regulations prescribed by the Secretary, in the case of a partnership, trust, S corporation, or other pass-thru entity, rules similar to the rules of section 41(g) shall apply with respect to the credit allowable under subsection (a).

(B) No basis adjustment. In the case of a bond held by a partnership or an S corporation, rules similar to the rules under section 1397E(l) shall apply.

[2]**(4)   Repealed.**

[3]*(4)*   **Ratable principal amortization required.** A bond shall not be treated as a clean renewable energy bond unless it is part of an issue which provides for an equal amount of principal to be paid by the qualified issuer during each calendar year that the issue is outstanding.

[4]*(5)*   **Reporting.** Issuers of clean renewable energy bonds shall submit reports similar to the reports required under section 149(e).

(m)   Termination. This section shall not apply with respect to any bond issued after December 31, 2009.

[For Analysis, see ¶ 1301. For Committee Reports, see ¶ 5070.]

[Endnote Code Sec. 54]

  Code Sec. 54(c)(2) was amended by Sec. 1531(c)(3) of the American Recovery and Reinvestment Act of 2009, P.L. 111-5, 2/17/2009, as detailed below:

  1. Sec. 1531(c)(3) substituted ", I, and J" for "and I"

Effective Date (Sec. 1531(e), P.L. 111-5, 2/17/2009) effective for obligations issued after 2/17/2009.

  Code Sec. 54(l)(4), Code Sec. 54(l)(5) and Code Sec. 54(l)(6) were amended by Sec. 1541(b)(1), P.L. 111-5, 2/17/2009, as detailed below:

  2. Sec. 1541(b)(1) repealed para. (l)(4)

  3. Sec. 1541(b)(1) redesignated para. (l)(5) as para. (l)(4)

  4. Sec. 1541(b)(1) redesignated para. (l)(6) as para. (l)(5)

Effective Date (Sec. 1541(c), P.L. 111-5, 2/17/2009) effective for tax. yrs. end. after 2/17/2009.

[¶ 3030]   Code Sec. 54A.   Credit to holders of qualified tax credit bonds.

* * * * * * * * * * * *

(c)   Limitation based on amount of tax.

(1)   In general. The credit allowed under subsection (a) for any taxable year shall not exceed the excess of—

(A) the sum of the regular tax liability (as defined in section 26(b)) plus the tax imposed by section 55, over

(B) the sum of the credits allowable under this part (other than [1]*subparts C and J* and this subpart).

(2) Carryover of unused credit. If the credit allowable under subsection (a) exceeds the limitation imposed by paragraph (1) for such taxable year, such excess shall be carried to the succeeding taxable year and added to the credit allowable under subsection (a) for such taxable year (determined before the application of paragraph (1) for such succeeding taxable year).

(d) Qualified tax credit bond. For purposes of this section—

  (1) Qualified tax credit bond. The term "qualified tax credit bond" means—

    (A) a qualified forestry conservation bond,

    (B) a new clean renewable energy bond,

    (C) a qualified energy conservation bond, [2]

    (D) a qualified zone academy bond, [3]*or*

    [4]*(E) a qualified school construction bond,*

  which is part of an issue that meets requirements of paragraphs (2), (3), (4), (5), and (6).

  (2) Special rules relating to expenditures.

    (A) In general. An issue shall be treated as meeting the requirements of this paragraph if, as of the date of issuance, the issuer reasonably expects—

      (i) 100 percent or more of the available project proceeds to be spent for 1 or more qualified purposes within the 3-year period beginning on such date of issuance, and

      (ii) a binding commitment with a third party to spend at least 10 percent of such available project proceeds will be incurred within the 6-month period beginning on such date of issuance.

    (B) Failure to spend required amount of bond proceeds within 3 years.

      (i) In general. To the extent that less than 100 percent of the available project proceeds of the issue are expended by the close of the expenditure period for 1 or more qualified purposes, the issuer shall redeem all of the nonqualified bonds within 90 days after the end of such period. For purposes of this paragraph, the amount of the nonqualified bonds required to be redeemed shall be determined in the same manner as under section 142.

      (ii) Expenditure period. For purposes of this subpart, the term "expenditure period" means, with respect to any issue, the 3-year period beginning on the date of issuance. Such term shall include any extension of such period under clause (iii).

      (iii) Extension of period. Upon submission of a request prior to the expiration of the expenditure period (determined without regard to any extension under this clause), the Secretary may extend such period if the issuer establishes that the failure to expend the proceeds within the original expenditure period is due to reasonable cause and the expenditures for qualified purposes will continue to proceed with due diligence.

    (C) Qualified purpose. For purposes of this paragraph, the term "qualified purpose" means—

      (i) in the case of a qualified forestry conservation bond, a purpose specified in section 54B(e),

      (ii) in the case of a new clean renewable energy bond, a purpose specified in section 54C(a)(1),

      (iii) in the case of a qualified energy conservation bond, a purpose specified in section 54D(a)(1), [5]

      (iv) in the case of a qualified zone academy bond, a purpose specified in section 54E(a)(1)[6], *and*

      [7]*(v) in the case of a qualified school construction bond, a purpose specified in section 54F(a)(1).*

    (D) Reimbursement. For purposes of this subtitle, available project proceeds of an issue shall be treated as spent for a qualified purpose if such proceeds are used to reimburse the issuer for amounts paid for a qualified purpose after the date that the Secretary makes an allocation of bond limitation with respect to such issue, but only if—

(i) prior to the payment of the original expenditure, the issuer declared its intent to reimburse such expenditure with the proceeds of a qualified tax credit bond,

(ii) not later than 60 days after payment of the original expenditure, the issuer adopts an official intent to reimburse the original expenditure with such proceeds, and

(iii) the reimbursement is made not later than 18 months after the date the original expenditure is paid.

(3) Reporting. An issue shall be treated as meeting the requirements of this paragraph if the issuer of qualified tax credit bonds submits reports similar to the reports required under section 149(e).

(4) Special rules relating to arbitrage.

(A) In general. An issue shall be treated as meeting the requirements of this paragraph if the issuer satisfies the requirements of section 148 with respect to the proceeds of the issue.

(B) Special rule for investments during expenditure period. An issue shall not be treated as failing to meet the requirements of subparagraph (A) by reason of any investment of available project proceeds during the expenditure period.

(C) Special rule for reserve funds. An issue shall not be treated as failing to meet the requirements of subparagraph (A) by reason of any fund which is expected to be used to repay such issue if—

(i) such fund is funded at a rate not more rapid than equal annual installments,

(ii) such fund is funded in a manner reasonably expected to result in an amount not greater than an amount necessary to repay the issue, and

(iii) the yield on such fund is not greater than the discount rate determined under paragraph (5)(B) with respect to the issue.

(5) Maturity limitation.

(A) In general. An issue shall be treated as meeting the requirements of this paragraph if the maturity of any bond which is part of such issue does not exceed the maximum term determined by the Secretary under subparagraph (B).

(B) Maximum term. During each calendar month, the Secretary shall determine the maximum term permitted under this paragraph for bonds issued during the following calendar month. Such maximum term shall be the term which the Secretary estimates will result in the present value of the obligation to repay the principal on the bond being equal to 50 percent of the face amount of such bond. Such present value shall be determined using as a discount rate the average annual interest rate of tax-exempt obligations having a term of 10 years or more which are issued during the month. If the term as so determined is not a multiple of a whole year, such term shall be rounded to the next highest whole year.

(6) Prohibition on financial conflicts of interest. An issue shall be treated as meeting the requirements of this paragraph if the issuer certifies that—

(A) applicable State and local law requirements governing conflicts of interest are satisfied with respect to such issue, and

(B) if the Secretary prescribes additional conflicts of interest rules governing the appropriate Members of Congress, Federal, State, and local officials, and their spouses, such additional rules are satisfied with respect to such issue.

* * * * * * * * * * * *

[8]*(h) Bonds held by real estate investment trusts. If any qualified tax credit bond is held by a real estate investment trust, the credit determined under subsection (a) shall be allowed to beneficiaries of such trust (and any gross income included under subsection (f) with respect to such credit shall be distributed to such beneficiaries) under procedures prescribed by the Secretary.*

(i) Credits may be stripped. Under regulations prescribed by the Secretary—

(1) In general. There may be a separation (including at issuance) of the ownership of a qualified tax credit bond and the entitlement to the credit under this section with respect to such bond. In case of any such separation, the credit under this section shall be allowed to the person who on the credit allowance date holds the instrument evidencing the entitlement to the credit and not to the holder of the bond.

(2) Certain rules to apply. In the case of a separation described in paragraph (1), the rules of section 1286 shall apply to the qualified tax credit bond as if it were a stripped bond and to the credit under this section as if it were a stripped coupon.

[For Analysis, see ¶ 1301, ¶ 1302 and ¶ 1308. For Committee Reports, see ¶ 5067, ¶ 5070 and ¶ 5072.]

[Endnote Code Sec. 54A]

Code Sec. 54A(c)(1)(B) was amended by Sec. 1531(c)(2) of the American Recovery and Reinvestment Act of 2009, P.L. 111-5, 2/17/2009, as detailed below:

1. Sec. 1531(c)(2) substituted ";subparts C and J"; for ";subpart C";

Effective Date (Sec. 1531(e), P.L. 111-5, 2/17/2009) effective for obligations issued after 2/17/2009.

Code Sec. 54A(d)(1)(C), Code Sec. 54A(d)(1)(D), Code Sec. 54A(d)(1)(E), Code Sec. 54A(d)(2)(C)(iii), Code Sec. 54A(d)(2)(C)(iv) and Code Sec. 54A(d)(2)(C)(v) was amended by Sec. 1521(b)(1) and (2), P.L. 111-5, 2/17/2009, as detailed below:

2. Sec. 1521(b)(1) deleted ";or"; at the end of subpara. (d)(1)(C)
3. Sec. 1521(b)(1) added ";or"; at the end of subpara. (d)(1)(D)
4. Sec. 1521(b)(1) added subpara. (d)(1)(E)
5. Sec. 1521(b)(2) deleted ";and"; at the end of clause (d)(2)(C)(iii)
6. Sec. 1521(b)(2) deleted the period at the end of clause (d)(2)(C)(iv)
7. Sec. 1521(b)(2) added clause (d)(2)(C)(v),

Effective Date (Sec. 1521(c), P.L. 111-5, 2/17/2009) effective for obligations issued after 2/17/2009.

Code Sec. 54A(h) was added by Sec. 1541(b)(2), P.L. 111-5, 2/17/2009.

8. Sec. 1541(b)(2) added subsec. (h)

Effective Date (Sec. 1541(c), P.L. 111-5, 2/17/2009) effective for tax. yrs. ending after 2/17/2009.

[¶ 3031]   Code Sec. 54C.   New clean renewable energy bonds.

(a) New clean renewable energy bonds.

* * * * * * * * * * * *

(c) Limitation on amount of bonds designated.

(1) In general. The maximum aggregate face amount of bonds which may be designated under subsection (a) by any issuer shall not exceed the limitation amount allocated under this subsection to such issuer.

(2) National limitation on amount of bonds designated. There is a national new clean renewable energy bond limitation of $800,000,000 which shall be allocated by the Secretary as provided in paragraph (3), except that—

(A) not more than 33⅓ percent thereof may be allocated to qualified projects of public power providers,

(B) not more than 33⅓ percent thereof may be allocated to qualified projects of governmental bodies, and

(C) not more than 33⅓ percent thereof may be allocated to qualified projects of cooperative electric companies.

(3) Method of allocation.

(A) Allocation among public power providers. After the Secretary determines the qualified projects of public power providers which are appropriate for receiving an allocation of the national new clean renewable energy bond limitation, the Secretary shall, to the maximum extent practicable, make allocations among such projects in such manner that the amount allocated to each such project bears the same ratio to the cost of such project as the limitation under paragraph (2)(A) bears to the cost of all such projects.

(B) Allocation among governmental bodies and cooperative electric companies. The Secretary shall make allocations of the amount of the national new clean renewable energy bond limitation described in paragraphs (2)(B) and (2)(C) among qualified projects of governmental bodies and cooperative electric companies, respectively, in such manner as the Secretary determines appropriate.

¹*(4) Additional limitation. The national new clean renewable energy bond limitation shall be increased by $1,600,000,000. Such increase shall be allocated by the Secretary consistent with the rules of paragraphs (2) and (3).*

(d) **Definitions.** For purposes of this section—

(1) **Qualified renewable energy facility.** The term "qualified renewable energy facility" means a qualified facility (as determined under section 45(d) without regard to paragraphs (8) and (10) thereof and to any placed in service date) owned by a public power provider, a governmental body, or a cooperative electric company.

(2) **Public power provider.** The term "public power provider" means a State utility with a service obligation, as such terms are defined in section 217 of the Federal Power Act (as in effect on the date of the enactment of this paragraph).

(3) **Governmental body.** The term "governmental body" means any State or Indian tribal government, or any political subdivision thereof.

(4) **Cooperative electric company.** The term "cooperative electric company" means a mutual or cooperative electric company described in section 501(c)(12) or section 1381(a)(2)(C).

(5) **Clean renewable energy bond lender.** The term "clean renewable energy bond lender" means a lender which is a cooperative which is owned by, or has outstanding loans to, 100 or more cooperative electric companies and is in existence on February 1, 2002, and shall include any affiliated entity which is controlled by such lender.

(6) **Qualified issuer.** The term "qualified issuer" means a public power provider, a cooperative electric company, a governmental body, a clean renewable energy bond lender, or a not-for-profit electric utility which has received a loan or loan guarantee under the Rural Electrification Act.

[For Analysis, see ¶ 1210 and ¶ 1311. For Committee Reports, see ¶ 5018 and ¶ 5074.]

[Endnote Code Sec. 54C]

Code Sec. 54C(c)(4) was added by Sec. 1111 of the American Recovery and Reinvestment Act of 2009, P.L. 111-5, 2/17/2009.

1. Sec. 1111 added para. (c)(4).

Effective Date Effective 2/17/2009.

Sec. 1601 of this Act provides:

"SEC. 1601. APPLICATION OF CERTAIN LABOR STANDARDS TO PROJECTS FINANCED WITH CERTAIN TAX FAVORED BONDS.

"Subchapter IV of chapter 31 of the title 40, United States Code, shall apply to projects financed with the proceeds of—

"(1) any new clean renewable energy bond (as defined in section 54C of the Internal Revenue Code of 1986) issued after the date of the enactment of this Act,

"(2) any qualified energy conservation bond (as defined in section 54D of the Internal Revenue Code of 1986) issued after the date of the enactment of this Act,

"(3) any qualified zone academy bond (as defined in section 54E of the Internal Revenue Code of 1986) issued after the date of the enactment of this Act,

"(4) any qualified school construction bond (as defined in section 54F of the Internal Revenue Code of 1986), and

"(5) any recovery zone economic development bond (as defined in section 1400U-2 of the Internal Revenue Code of 1986)."

[¶ 3032]   Code Sec. 54D.   Qualified energy conservation bonds.

* * * * * * * * * * * *

(d) **National limitation on amount of bonds designated.** There is a national qualified energy conservation bond limitation of ¹*$3,200,000,000.*

(e) Allocations.

(1) In general. The limitation applicable under subsection (d) shall be allocated by the Secretary among the States in proportion to the population of the States.

(2) Allocations to largest local governments.

(A) In general. In the case of any State in which there is a large local government, each such local government shall be allocated a portion of such State's allocation which bears the same ratio to the State's allocation (determined without regard to this subparagraph) as the population of such large local government bears to the population of such State.

(B) Allocation of unused limitation to state. The amount allocated under this subsection to a large local government may be reallocated by such local government to the State in which such local government is located.

(C) Large local government. For purposes of this section, the term "large local government" means any municipality or county if such municipality or county has a population of 100,000 or more.

(3) Allocation to issuers; restriction on private activity bonds. Any allocation under this subsection to a State or large local government shall be allocated by such State or large local government to issuers within the State in a manner that results in not less than 70 percent of the allocation to such State or large local government being used to designate bonds which are not private activity bonds.

²*(4) Special rules for bonds to implement green community programs. In the case of any bond issued for the purpose of providing loans, grants, or other repayment mechanisms for capital expenditures to implement green community programs, such bond shall not be treated as a private activity bond for purposes of paragraph (3).*

(f) Qualified conservation purpose. For purposes of this section—

(1) In general. The term "qualified conservation purpose" means any of the following:

(A) Capital expenditures incurred for purposes of—

(i) reducing energy consumption in publicly-owned buildings by at least 20 percent,

(ii) implementing green community programs ³*(including the use of loans, grants, or other repayment mechanisms to implement such programs),*

(iii) rural development involving the production of electricity from renewable energy resources, or

(iv) any qualified facility (as determined under section 45(d) without regard to paragraphs (8) and (10) thereof and without regard to any placed in service date).

(B) Expenditures with respect to research facilities, and research grants, to support research in—

(i) development of cellulosic ethanol or other nonfossil fuels,

(ii) technologies for the capture and sequestration of carbon dioxide produced through the use of fossil fuels,

(iii) increasing the efficiency of existing technologies for producing nonfossil fuels,

(iv) automobile battery technologies and other technologies to reduce fossil fuel consumption in transportation, or

(v) technologies to reduce energy use in buildings.

(C) Mass commuting facilities and related facilities that reduce the consumption of energy, including expenditures to reduce pollution from vehicles used for mass commuting.

(D) Demonstration projects designed to promote the commercialization of—

(i) green building technology,

(ii) conversion of agricultural waste for use in the production of fuel or otherwise,

(iii) advanced battery manufacturing technologies,

(iv) technologies to reduce peak use of electricity, or

(v) technologies for the capture and sequestration of carbon dioxide emitted from combusting fossil fuels in order to produce electricity.

461

(E) Public education campaigns to promote energy efficiency.

(2) Special rules for private activity bonds. For purposes of this section, in the case of any private activity bond, the term "qualified conservation purposes" shall not include any expenditure which is not a capital expenditure.

* * * * * * * * * * * *

[For Analysis, see ¶ 1211 and ¶ 1311. For Committee Reports, see ¶ 5019 and ¶ 5074.]

[Endnote Code Sec. 54D]
Code Sec. 54D(d), Code Sec. 54D(e)(4) and Code Sec. 54D(f)(1)(A)(ii) were amended by Sec. 1112(a), (b)(1) and (2) of the American Recovery and Reinvestment Tax Act of 2009, P.L. 111-5, 2/17/2009, as detailed below:
1. Sec. 1112(a) substituted "$3,200,000,000" for "$800,000,000" in subsec. (d)
2. Sec. 1112(b)(2) added para. (a)(4)
3. Sec. 1112(b)(1) added "(including the use of loans, grants, or other repayment mechanisms to implement such programs)" after "green community programs" in clause (f)(1)(A)(ii).
Effective Date Effective 2/17/2009.
Sec. 1601 of this Act provides:
"Application of certain labor standards to projects financed with certain tax favored bonds.
"Subchapter IV of chapter 31 of the title 40, United States Code, shall apply to projects financed with the proceeds of—
"(1) any new clean renewable energy bond (as defined in section 54C of the Internal Revenue Code of 1986) issued after the date of the enactment of this Act,
"(2) any qualified energy conservation bond (as defined in section 54D of the Internal Revenue Code of 1986) issued after the date of the enactment of this Act,
"(3) any qualified zone academy bond (as defined in section 54E of the Internal Revenue Code of 1986) issued after the date of the enactment of this Act,
"(4) any qualified school construction bond (as defined in section 54F of the Internal Revenue Code of 1986), and
"(5) any recovery zone economic development bond (as defined in section 1400U-2 of the Internal Revenue Code of 1986)."

[¶ 3033]   Code Sec. 54E.   Qualified zone academy bonds.

* * * * * * * * * * * *

(c) Limitation on amount of bonds designated.

(1) national limitation. There is a national zone academy bond limitation for each calendar year. Such limitation is $400,000,000 for 2008 ¹*and $1,400,000,000 for 2009 and 2010*, and, except as provided in paragraph (4), zero thereafter.

(2) Allocation of limitation. The national zone academy bond limitation for a calendar year shall be allocated by the Secretary among the States on the basis of their respective populations of individuals below the poverty line (as defined by the Office of Management and Budget). The limitation amount allocated to a State under the preceding sentence shall be allocated by the State education agency to qualified zone academies within such State.

(3) Designation subject to limitation amount. The maximum aggregate face amount of bonds issued during any calendar year which may be designated under subsection (a) with respect to any qualified zone academy shall not exceed the limitation amount allocated to such academy under paragraph (2) for such calendar year.

(4) Carryover of unused limitation.

(A) In general. If for any calendar year—

(i) the limitation amount for any State, exceeds

(ii) the amount of bonds issued during such year which are designated under subsection (a) with respect to qualified zone academies within such State, the limitation amount for such State for the following calendar year shall be increased by the amount of such excess.

(B) Limitation on carryover. Any carryforward of a limitation amount may be carried only to the first 2 years following the unused limitation year. For purposes of the preceding sentence, a limitation amount shall be treated as used on a first-in first-out basis.

(C) Coordination with section 1397E. Any carryover determined under section 1397E(e)(4) (relating to carryover of unused limitation) with respect to any State to calendar year 2008 or 2009 shall be treated for purposes of this section as a carryover with respect to such State for such calendar year under subparagraph (A), and the limitation of subparagraph (B) shall apply to such carryover taking into account the calendar years to which such carryover relates.

[For Analysis, see ¶ 1303 and ¶ 1311. For Committee Reports, see ¶ 5068 and ¶ 5074.]

[Endnote Code Sec. 54E]

Code Sec. 54E(c)(1) was amended by Sec. 1522(a) of the American Recovery and Reinvestment Act of 2009, P.L. 111-5, 2/17/2009, as detailed below:

1. Sec. 1522(a) substituted "and $1,400,000,000 for 2009 and 2010" for "and 2009" in para. (c)(1).

Effective Date (Sec. 1522(b), P.L. 111-5, 2/17/2009) effective for obligations issued after 12/31/2008.

Sec. 1601 of this Act provides:

"SEC. 1601. APPLICATION OF CERTAIN LABOR STANDARDS TO PROJECTS FINANCED WITH CERTAIN TAX FAVORED BONDS.

"Subchapter IV of chapter 31 of the title 40, United States Code, shall apply to projects financed with the proceeds of—

"(1) any new clean renewable energy bond (as defined in section 54C of the Internal Revenue Code of 1986) issued after the date of the enactment of this Act,

"(2) any qualified energy conservation bond (as defined in section 54D of the Internal Revenue Code of 1986) issued after the date of the enactment of this Act,

"(3) any qualified zone academy bond (as defined in section 54E of the Internal Revenue Code of 1986) issued after the date of the enactment of this Act,

"(4) any qualified school construction bond (as defined in section 54F of the Internal Revenue Code of 1986), and

"(5) any recovery zone economic development bond (as defined in section 1400U-2 of the Internal Revenue Code of 1986)."

[¶ 3034]   Code Sec.[1] 54F.   Qualified school construction bonds.

(a) Qualified school construction bond. For purposes of this subchapter, the term "qualified school construction bond" means any bond issued as part of an issue if—

(1) 100 percent of the available project proceeds of such issue are to be used for the construction, rehabilitation, or repair of a public school facility or for the acquisition of land on which such a facility is to be constructed with part of the proceeds of such issue,

(2) the bond is issued by a State or local government within the jurisdiction of which such school is located, and

(3) the issuer designates such bond for purposes of this section.

(b) Limitation on amount of bonds designated. The maximum aggregate face amount of bonds issued during any calendar year which may be designated under subsection (a) by any issuer shall not exceed the limitation amount allocated under subsection (d) for such calendar year to such issuer.

(c) National limitation on amount of bonds designated. There is a national qualified school construction bond limitation for each calendar year. Such limitation is—

(1) $11,000,000,000 for 2009,

(2) $11,000,000,000 for 2010, and

(3) except as provided in subsection (e), zero after 2010.

(d) Allocation of limitation.

(1) Allocation among states. Except as provided in paragraph (2)(C), the limitation applicable under subsection (c) for any calendar year shall be allocated by the Secretary among the States in proportion to the respective amounts each such State is eligible to receive under section 1124 of the Elementary and Secondary Education Act of 1965 (20 U.S.C. 6333) for the most recent fiscal year ending before such calendar year. The limitation amount allocated to a State under the preceding sentence shall be allocated by the State to issuers within such State.

(2)　40 percent of limitation allocated among largest school districts.

(A) In general. 40 percent of the limitation applicable under subsection (c) for any calendar year shall be allocated under subparagraph (B) by the Secretary among local educational agencies which are large local educational agencies for such year.

(B) Allocation formula. The amount to be allocated under subparagraph (A) for any calendar year shall be allocated among large local educational agencies in proportion to the respective amounts each such agency received under section 1124 of the Elementary and Secondary Education Act of 1965 (20 U.S.C. 6333) for the most recent fiscal year ending before such calendar year.

(C) Reduction in state allocation. The allocation to any State under paragraph (1) shall be reduced by the aggregate amount of the allocations under this paragraph to large local educational agencies within such State.

(D) Allocation of unused limitation to state. The amount allocated under this paragraph to a large local educational agency for any calendar year may be reallocated by such agency to the State in which such agency is located for such calendar year. Any amount reallocated to a State under the preceding sentence may be allocated as provided in paragraph (1).

(E) Large local educational agency. For purposes of this paragraph, the term "large local educational agency" means, with respect to a calendar year, any local educational agency if such agency is—

(i) among the 100 local educational agencies with the largest numbers of children aged 5 through 17 from families living below the poverty level, as determined by the Secretary using the most recent data available from the Department of Commerce that are satisfactory to the Secretary, or

(ii) 1 of not more than 25 local educational agencies (other than those described in clause (i)) that the Secretary of Education determines (based on the most recent data available satisfactory to the Secretary) are in particular need of assistance, based on a low level of resources for school construction, a high level of enrollment growth, or such other factors as the Secretary deems appropriate.

(3)　Allocations to certain possessions. The amount to be allocated under paragraph (1) to any possession of the United States other than Puerto Rico shall be the amount which would have been allocated if all allocations under paragraph (1) were made on the basis of respective populations of individuals below the poverty line (as defined by the Office of Management and Budget). In making other allocations, the amount to be allocated under paragraph (1) shall be reduced by the aggregate amount allocated under this paragraph to possessions of the United States.

(4)　Allocations for Indian schools. In addition to the amounts otherwise allocated under this subsection, $200,000,000 for calendar year 2009, and $200,000,000 for calendar year 2010, shall be allocated by the Secretary of the Interior for purposes of the construction, rehabilitation, and repair of schools funded by the Bureau of Indian Affairs. In the case of amounts allocated under the preceding sentence, Indian tribal governments (as defined in section 7701(a)(40)) shall be treated as qualified issuers for purposes of this subchapter.

(e)　Carryover of unused limitation. If for any calendar year—

(1) the amount allocated under subsection (d) to any State, exceeds

(2) the amount of bonds issued during such year which are designated under subsection (a) pursuant to such allocation,　the limitation amount under such subsection for such State for the following calendar year shall be increased by the amount of such excess. A similar rule shall apply to the amounts allocated under subsection (d)(4).

[For Analysis, see ¶ 1302 and ¶ 1311. For Committee Reports, see ¶ 5067 and ¶ 5074.]

[Endnote Code Sec. 54F]

Code Sec. 54F was added by Sec. 1521(a) of the American Recovery and Reinvestment Act of 2009, P.L. 111-5, 2/17/2009.

1. Sec. 1521(a) added Code Sec. 54F.

Effective Date (Sec. 1521(c), P.L. 111-5, 2/17/2009) effective for obligations issued after 2/17/2009.

Sec. 1601 of this Act provides:

"Application of certain labor standards to projects financed with certain tax favored bonds.

"Subchapter IV of chapter 31 of the title 40, United States Code, shall apply to projects financed with the proceeds of—

"(1) any new clean renewable energy bond (as defined in section 54C of the Internal Revenue Code of 1986) issued after the date of the enactment of this Act,

"(2) any qualified energy conservation bond (as defined in section 54D of the Internal Revenue Code of 1986) issued after the date of the enactment of this Act,

"(3) any qualified zone academy bond (as defined in section 54E of the Internal Revenue Code of 1986) issued after the date of the enactment of this Act,

"(4) any qualified school construction bond (as defined in section 54F of the Internal Revenue Code of 1986), and

"(5) any recovery zone economic development bond (as defined in section 1400U-2 of the Internal Revenue Code of 1986)."

[¶ 3035]   Code Sec.[1] 54AA.   Build America bonds.

(a) In general. If a taxpayer holds a build America bond on one or more interest payment dates of the bond during any taxable year, there shall be allowed as a credit against the tax imposed by this chapter for the taxable year an amount equal to the sum of the credits determined under subsection (b) with respect to such dates.

(b) Amount of credit. The amount of the credit determined under this subsection with respect to any interest payment date for a build America bond is 35 percent of the amount of interest payable by the issuer with respect to such date.

(c) Limitation based on amount of tax.

(1) In general. The credit allowed under subsection (a) for any taxable year shall not exceed the excess of—

(A) the sum of the regular tax liability (as defined in section 26(b)) plus the tax imposed by section 55, over

(B) the sum of the credits allowable under this part (other than subpart C and this subpart).

(2) Carryover of unused credit. If the credit allowable under subsection (a) exceeds the limitation imposed by paragraph (1) for such taxable year, such excess shall be carried to the succeeding taxable year and added to the credit allowable under subsection (a) for such taxable year (determined before the application of paragraph (1) for such succeeding taxable year).

(d) Build America bond.

(1) In general. For purposes of this section, the term "build America bond" means any obligation (other than a private activity bond) if—

(A) the interest on such obligation would (but for this section) be excludable from gross income under section 103,

(B) such obligation is issued before January 1, 2011, and

(C) the issuer makes an irrevocable election to have this section apply.

(2) Applicable rules. For purposes of applying paragraph (1)—

(A) for purposes of section 149(b), a build America bond shall not be treated as federally guaranteed by reason of the credit allowed under subsection (a) or section 6431,

(B) for purposes of section 148, the yield on a build America bond shall be determined without regard to the credit allowed under subsection (a), and

(C) a bond shall not be treated as a build America bond if the issue price has more than a de minimis amount (determined under rules similar to the rules of section 1273(a)(3)) of premium over the stated principal amount of the bond.

(e) Interest payment date. For purposes of this section, the term "interest payment date" means any date on which the holder of record of the build America bond is entitled to a payment of interest under such bond.

(f)   Special rules.

(1)   Interest on build America bonds includible in gross income for federal income tax purposes. For purposes of this title, interest on any build America bond shall be includible in gross income.

(2)   Application of certain rules. Rules similar to the rules of subsections (f), (g), (h), and (i) of section 54A shall apply for purposes of the credit allowed under subsection (a).

(g)   Special rule for qualified bonds issued before 2011. In the case of a qualified bond issued before January 1, 2011—

(1)   Issuer allowed refundable credit. In lieu of any credit allowed under this section with respect to such bond, the issuer of such bond shall be allowed a credit as provided in section 6431.

(2)   Qualified bond. For purposes of this subsection, the term "qualified bond" means any build America bond issued as part of an issue if—

(A) 100 percent of the excess of—

(i) the available project proceeds (as defined in section 54A) of such issue, over

(ii) the amounts in a reasonably required reserve (within the meaning of section 150(a)(3)) with respect to such issue,

are to be used for capital expenditures, and

(B) the issuer makes an irrevocable election to have this subsection apply.

(h)   Regulations. The Secretary may prescribe such regulations and other guidance as may be necessary or appropriate to carry out this section and section 6431.

[For Analysis, see ¶ 1301. For Committee Reports, see ¶ 5070.]

[Endnote Code Sec. 54AA]

Code Sec. 54AA was added by Sec. 1531(a) of the American Recovery and Reinvestment Act of 2009, P.L. 111-5, 2/17/2009.

1. Sec. 1531(a) added Code Sec. 54AA

Effective Date (Sec. 1531(e), P.L. 111-5, 2/17/2009) effective for obligations issued after 2/17/2009.

Sec. 1531(d), of this Act, provides:

"(d) TRANSITIONAL COORDINATION WITH STATE LAW.

"Except as otherwise provided by a State after the date of the enactment of this Act, the interest on any build America bond (as defined in section 54AA of the Internal Revenue Code of 1986, as added by this section) and the amount of any credit determined under such section with respect to such bond shall be treated for purposes of the income tax laws of such State as being exempt from Federal income tax."

[¶ 3036]   Code Sec. 55.   Alternative minimum tax imposed.

* * * * * * * * * * * *

(c)   Regular tax.

(1)   In general. For purposes of this section, the term "regular tax" means the regular tax liability for the taxable year (as defined in section 26(b)) reduced by the foreign tax credit allowable under section 27(a), the section 936 credit allowable under section 27(b), and the Puerto Rico economic activity credit under section 30A. Such term shall not include any increase in tax under section 45(e)(11)(C), 49(b) or 50(a) or subsection (j) or (k) of section 42.

(2)   Coordination with income averaging for farmers and fishermen. Solely for purposes of this section, section 1301 (relating to averaging of farm and fishing income) shall not apply in computing the regular tax liability.

(3)   Cross references. For provisions providing that certain credits are not allowable against the tax imposed by this section, see sections 26(a), ¹30C(d)(2), and 38(c).

(d)   Exemption amount. For purposes of this section—

(1)   Exemption amount for taxpayers other than corporations. In the case of a taxpayer other than a corporation, the term "exemption amount" means—

(A) \$45,000 [3]*(\$70,950 in the case of taxable years beginning in 2009)* in the case of—

    (i) a joint return, or

    (ii) a surviving spouse,

(B) \$33,750 [4]*(\$46,700 in the case of taxable years beginning in 2009)* in the case of an individual who—

    (i) is not a married individual, and

    (ii) is not a surviving spouse,

(C) 50 percent of the dollar amount applicable under paragraph (1)(A) in the case of a married individual who files a separate return, and

(D) \$22,500 in the case of an estate or trust.

For purposes of this paragraph, the term "surviving spouse" has the meaning given to such term by section 2(a), and marital status shall be determined under section 7703.

(2) Corporations. In the case of a corporation, the term "exemption amount" means \$40,000.

(3) Phase-out of exemption amount. The exemption amount of any taxpayer shall be reduced (but not below zero) by an amount equal to 25 percent of the amount by which the alternative minimum taxable income of the taxpayer exceeds—

(A) \$150,000 in the case of a taxpayer described in paragraph (1)(A) or (2),

(B) \$112,500 in the case of a taxpayer described in paragraph (1)(B), and

(C) \$75,000 in the case of a taxpayer described in subparagraph (C) or (D) of paragraph (1).

In the case of a taxpayer described in paragraph (1)(C), alternative minimum taxable income shall be increased by the lesser of (i) 25 percent of the excess of alternative minimum taxable income (determined without regard to this sentence) over the minimum amount of such income (as so determined) for which the exemption amount under paragraph (1)(C) is zero, or (ii) such exemption amount (determined without regard to this paragraph).

* * * * * * * * * * *

[For Analysis, see ¶ 201 and ¶ 205. For Committee Reports, see ¶ 5010 and ¶ 5027.]

[Endnote Code Sec. 55]

Code Sec. 55(c)(3) was amended by Sec. 1142(b)(5) the American Recovery and Reinvestment Act of 2009, P.L. 111-5, 2/17/2009, as detailed below:

1. Sec. 1142(b)(5) deleted "30(b)(3)," in para. (c)(3)

Effective Date (Sec. 1142(c), P.L. 111-5, d.o.e) effective for vehicles acquired after 2/17/2009

Code Sec. 55(c)(3) was amended by Sec. 1144(b)(3), P.L. 111-5, 2/17/2009, as detailed below:

2. Sec. 1144(b)(3) deleted "30B(g)(2)," in para. (c)(3)

Effective Date (Sec. 1144(c), P.L. 111-5, 2/17/2009) effective for tax. yrs. begin. after 12/31/2008.

Code Sec. 55(d)(1)(A) and Code Sec. 55(d)(1)(B) were amended by Sec. 1012(a)(1) and (2), P.L. 111-5, 2/17/2009, as detailed below:

3. Sec. 1012(a)(1) substituted "(\$70,950 in the case of taxable years beginning in 2009)" for "(\$69,950 in the case of taxable years beginning in 2008)" in subpara. (d)(1)(A)

4. Sec. 1012(a)(2) substituted "(\$46,700 in the case of taxable years beginning in 2009)" for "(\$46,200 in the case of taxable years beginning in 2008)" in subpara. (d)(1)(B)

Effective Date (Sec. 1012(b), P.L. 111-5, 2/17/2009) effective for tax. yrs. begin. after 12/31/2008.

[¶ 3037] **Code Sec. 56.** **Adjustments in computing alternative minimum taxable income.**

* * * * * * * * * * *

(b) Adjustments applicable to individuals. In determining the amount of the alternative minimum taxable income of any taxpayer (other than a corporation), the following treatment shall apply (in lieu of the treatment applicable for purposes of computing the regular tax):

(1) Limitation on deductions.

(A) In general. No deduction shall be allowed—

(i) for any miscellaneous itemized deduction (as defined in section 67(b)), or

(ii) for any taxes described in paragraph (1), (2), or (3) of section 164(a) or clause (ii) of section 164(b)(5)(A).

Clause (ii) shall not apply to any amount allowable in computing adjusted gross income.

(B) Medical expenses. In determining the amount allowable as a deduction under section 213, subsection (a) of section 213 shall be applied by substituting "10 percent" for "7.5 percent".

(C) Interest. In determining the amount allowable as a deduction for interest, subsections (d) and (h) of section 163 shall apply, except that—

(i) in lieu of the exception under section 163(h)(2)(D), the term "personal interest" shall not include any qualified housing interest (as defined in subsection (e)),

(ii) sections 163(d)(6) and 163(h)(5) (relating to phase-ins) shall not apply,

(iii) interest on any specified private activity bond (and any amount treated as interest on a specified private activity bond under section 57(a)(5)(B)), and any deduction referred to in section 57(a)(5)(A), shall be treated as includible in gross income (or as deductible) for purposes of applying section 163(d),

(iv) in lieu of the exception under section 163(d)(3)(B)(i), the term "investment interest" shall not include any qualified housing interest (as defined in subsection (e)), and

(v) the adjustments of this section and sections 57 and 58 shall apply in determining net investment income under section 163(d).

(D) Treatment of certain recoveries. No recovery of any tax to which subparagraph (A)(ii) applied shall be included in gross income for purposes of determining alternative minimum taxable income.

(E) Standard deduction and deduction for personal exemptions not allowed. The standard deduction under section 63(c), the deduction for personal exemptions under section 151, and the deduction under section 642(b) shall not be allowed. The preceding sentence shall not apply to so much of the standard deduction as is determined under [1]*subparagraphs (D) and (E) of section 63(c)(1).*

(F) Section 68 not applicable. Section 68 shall not apply.

(2) Circulation and research and experimental expenditures.

(A) In general. The amount allowable as a deduction under section 173 or 174(a) in computing the regular tax for amounts paid or incurred after December 31, 1986, shall be capitalized and—

(i) in the case of circulation expenditures described in section 173, shall be amortized ratably over the 3-year period beginning with the taxable year in which the expenditures were made, or

(ii) in the case of research and experimental expenditures described in section 174(a), shall be amortized ratably over the 10-year period beginning with the taxable year in which the expenditures were made.

(B) Loss allowed. If a loss is sustained with respect to any property described in subparagraph (A), a deduction shall be allowed for the expenditures described in subparagraph (A) for the taxable year in which such loss is sustained in an amount equal to the lesser of—

(i) the amount allowable under section 165(a) for the expenditures if they had remained capitalized, or

(ii) the amount of such expenditures which have not previously been amortized under subparagraph (A).

(C) Special rule for personal holding companies. In the case of circulation expenditures described in section 173, the adjustments provided in this paragraph shall apply also to a personal holding company (as defined in section 542).

(D) Exception for certain research and experimental expenditures. If the taxpayer materially participates (within the meaning of section 469(h)) in an activity, this paragraph shall not apply to any amount allowable as a deduction under section 174(a) for expenditures paid or incurred in connection with such activity.

(3) Treatment of incentive stock options. Section 421 shall not apply to the transfer of stock acquired pursuant to the exercise of an incentive stock option (as defined in section 422). Section 422(c)(2) shall apply in any case where the disposition and the inclusion for purposes of this part are within the same taxable year and such section shall not apply in any other case. The adjusted basis of any stock so acquired shall be determined on the basis of the treatment prescribed by this paragraph.

* * * * * * * * * * * *

(g) Adjustments based on adjusted current earnings.

(1) In general. The alternative minimum taxable income of any corporation for any taxable year shall be increased by 75 percent of the excess (if any) of—

(A) the adjusted current earnings of the corporation, over

(B) the alternative minimum taxable income (determined without regard to this subsection and the alternative tax net operating loss deduction).

(2) Allowance of negative adjustments.

(A) In general. The alternative minimum taxable income for any corporation of any taxable year, shall be reduced by 75 percent of the excess (if any) of—

(i) the amount referred to in subparagraph (B) of paragraph (1), over

(ii) the amount referred to in subparagraph (A) of paragraph (1).

(B) Limitation. The reduction under subparagraph (A) for any taxable year shall not exceed the excess (if any) of—

(i) the aggregate increases in alternative minimum taxable income under paragraph (1) for prior taxable years, over

(ii) the aggregate reductions under subparagraph (A) of this paragraph for prior taxable years.

(3) Adjusted current earnings. For purposes of this subsection, the term "adjusted current earnings" means the alternative minimum taxable income for the taxable year—

(A) determined with the adjustments provided in paragraph (4), and

(B) determined without regard to this subsection and the alternative tax net operating loss deduction.

(4) Adjustments. In determining adjusted current earnings, the following adjustments shall apply:

(A) Depreciation.

(i) Property placed in service after 1989. The depreciation deduction with respect to any property placed in service in a taxable year beginning after 1989 shall be determined under the alternative system of section 168(g). The preceding sentence shall not apply to any property placed in service after December 31, 1993, and the depreciation deduction with respect to such property shall be determined under the rules of subsection (a)(1)(A).

(ii) Property to which new ACRS system applies. In the case of any property to which the amendments made by section 201 of the Tax Reform Act of 1986 apply and which is placed in service in a taxable year beginning before 1990, the depreciation deduction shall be determined—

(I) by taking into account the adjusted basis of such property (as determined for purposes of computing alternative minimum taxable income) as of the close of the last taxable year beginning before January 1, 1990, and

(II) by using the straight-line method over the remainder of the recovery period applicable to such property under the alternative system of section 168(g).

(iii) Property to which original ACRS system applies. In the case of any property to which section 168 (as in effect on the day before the date of the enactment [10/22/86] of the Tax Reform Act of 1986 and without regard to subsection (d)(1)(A)(ii) thereof) applies and which is placed in service in a taxable year beginning before 1990, the depreciation deduction shall be determined—

(I) by taking into account the adjusted basis of such property (as determined for purposes of computing the regular tax) as of the close of the last taxable year beginning before January 1, 1990, and

(II) by using the straight line method over the remainder of the recovery period which would apply to such property under the alternative system of section 168(g).

(iv) Property placed in service before 1981. In the case of any property not described in clause (i), (ii), or (iii), the amount allowable as depreciation or amortization with respect to such property shall be determined in the same manner as for purposes of computing taxable income.

(v) Special rule for certain property. In the case of any property described in paragraph (1), (2), (3), or (4) of section 168(f), the amount of depreciation allowable for purposes of the regular tax shall be treated as the amount allowable under the alternative system of section 168(g).

(B) Inclusion of items included for purposes of computing earnings and profits.

(i) In general. In the case of any amount which is excluded from gross income for purposes of computing alternative minimum taxable income but is taken into account in determining the amount of earnings and profits—

(I) such amount shall be included in income in the same manner as if such amount were includible in gross income for purposes of computing alternative minimum taxable income, and

(II) the amount of such income shall be reduced by any deduction which would have been allowable in computing alternative minimum taxable income if such amount were includible in gross income.

The preceding sentence shall not apply in the case of any amount excluded from gross income under section 108 (or the corresponding provisions of prior law) or under section 139A or 1357. In the case of any insurance company taxable under section 831(b), this clause shall not apply to any amount not described in section 834(b).

(ii) Inclusion of buildup in life insurance contracts. In the case of any life insurance contract—

(I) the income on such contract (as determined under section 7702(g)) for any taxable year shall be treated as includible in gross income for such year, and

(II) there shall be allowed as a deduction that portion of any premium which is attributable to insurance coverage.

(iii) Tax exempt interest on certain housing bonds. Clause (i) shall not apply in the case of any interest on a bond to which section 57(a)(5)(C)(iii) applies.

²(iv) Tax exempt interest on bonds issued in 2009 and 2010.

(I) In general. Clause (i) shall not apply in the case of any interest on a bond issued after December 31, 2008, and before January 1, 2011.

(II) Treatment of refunding bonds. For purposes of subclause (I), a refunding bond (whether a current or advance refunding) shall be treated as issued on the date of the issuance of the refunded bond (or in the case of a series of refundings, the original bond).

(III) Exception for certain refunding bonds. Subclause (II) shall not apply to any refunding bond which is issued to refund any bond which was issued after December 31, 2003, and before January 1, 2009.

(C) Disallowance of items not deductible in computing earnings and profits.

(i) In general. A deduction shall not be allowed for any item if such item would not be deductible for any taxable year for purposes of computing earnings and profits.

(ii) Special rule for certain dividends.

(I) In general. Clause (i) shall not apply to any deduction allowable under section 243 or 245 for any dividend which is a 100-percent dividend or which is received from a 20-percent owned corporation (as defined in section 243(c)(2)), but only to the extent such dividend is attributable to income of the paying corporation which is subject to tax under this chapter (determined after the application of sections 30A, 936 (including subsections (a)(4), (i), and (j) thereof) and 921 (as in effect before its repeal by the FSC Repeal and Extraterritorial Income Exclusion Act of 2000)).

(II) 100-percent dividend. For purposes of subclause (I), the term "100 percent dividend" means any dividend if the percentage used for purposes of determining the amount allowable as a deduction under section 243 or 245 with respect to such dividend is 100 percent.

(iii) Treatment of taxes on dividends from 936 corporations.

(I) In general. For purposes of determining the alternative minimum foreign tax credit, 75 percent of any withholding or income tax paid to a possession of the United States with respect to dividends received from a corporation eligible for the credit provided by section 936 shall be treated as a tax paid to a foreign country by the corporation receiving the dividend.

(II) Limitation. If the aggregate amount of the dividends referred to in subclause (I) for any taxable year exceeds the excess referred to in paragraph (1), the amount treated as tax paid to a foreign country under subclause (I) shall not exceed the amount which would be so treated without regard to this subclause multiplied by a fraction the numerator of which is the excess referred to in paragraph (1) and the denominator of which is the aggregate amount of such dividends.

(III) Treatment of taxes imposed on 936 corporation. For purposes of this clause, taxes paid by any corporation eligible for the credit provided by section 936 to a possession of the United States shall be treated as a withholding tax paid with respect to any dividend paid by such corporation to the extent such taxes would be treated as paid by the corporation receiving the dividend under rules similar to the rules of section 902 (and the amount of any such dividend shall be increased by the amount so treated).

(IV) Separate application of foreign tax credit limitations. In determining the alternative minimum foreign tax credit, section 904(d) shall be applied as if dividends from a corporation eligible for the credit provided by section 936 were a separate category of income referred to in a subparagraph of section 904(d)(1).

(V) Coordination with limitation on 936 credit. Any reference in this clause to a dividend received from a corporation eligible for the credit provided by section 936 shall be treated as a reference to the portion of any such dividend for which the dividends received deduction is disallowed under clause (i) after the application of clause (ii)(I).

(VI) Application to section 30A corporations. References in this clause to section 936 shall be treated as including references to section 30A.

(iv) Special rule for certain dividends received by certain cooperatives. In the case of an organization to which part I of subchapter T (relating to tax treatment of cooperatives) applies which is engaged in the marketing of agricultural or horticultural products, clause (i) shall not apply to any amount allowable as a deduction under section 245(c). [Sec. 11(g)(2), P.L. 110-172, 12/29/2007, directs that Code Sec. 54(g)(4)(C)(iv) be amended. It appears as if the amendment should be made to Code Sec. 56(g)(4)(C)(iv) and is in place here. See notes following this Code Sec.]

(v) Deduction for domestic production. Clause (i) shall not apply to any amount allowable as a deduction under section 199.

(vi) Special rule for certain distributions from controlled foreign corporations. Clause (i) shall not apply to any deduction allowable under section 965.

(D) Certain other earnings and profits adjustments.

(i) Intangible drilling costs. The adjustments provided in section 312(n)(2)(A) shall apply in the case of amounts paid or incurred in taxable years beginning after December 31, 1989. In the case of a taxpayer other than an integrated oil company (as defined in section 291(b)(4)), in the case of any oil or gas well, this clause shall not apply in the case of amounts paid or incurred in taxable years beginning after December 31, 1992.

(ii) Certain amortization provisions not to apply. Sections 173 and 248 shall not apply to expenditures paid or incurred in taxable years beginning after December 31, 1989.

(iii) LIFO inventory adjustments. The adjustments provided in section 312(n)(4) shall apply, but only with respect to taxable years beginning after December 31, 1989.

(iv) Installment sales. In the case of any installment sale in a taxable year beginning after December 31, 1989, adjusted current earnings shall be computed as if the corporation did not use the installment method. The preceding sentence shall not apply to the applicable percentage (as determined under section 453A) of the gain from any installment sale with respect to which section 453A(a)(1) applies.

(E) Disallowance of loss on exchange of debt pools. No loss shall be recognized on the exchange of any pool of debt obligations for another pool of debt obligations having substantially the same effective interest rates and maturities.

(F) Depletion.

(i) In general. The allowance for depletion with respect to any property placed in service in a taxable year beginning after December 31, 1989, shall be cost depletion determined under section 611.

(ii) Exception for independent oil and gas producers and royalty owners. In the case of any taxable year beginning after December 31, 1992, clause (i) (and subparagraph (C)(i)) shall not apply to any deduction for depletion computed in accordance with section 613A(c).

(G) Treatment of certain ownership changes. If—

(i) there is an ownership change (within the meaning of section 382) in a taxable year beginning after 1989 with respect to any corporation, and

(ii) there is a net unrealized built-in loss (within the meaning of section 382(h)) with respect to such corporation,

then the adjusted basis of each asset of such corporation (immediately after the ownership change) shall be its proportionate share (determined on the basis of respective fair market values) of the fair market value of the assets of such corporation (determined under section 382(h)) immediately before the ownership change.

(H) Adjusted basis. The adjusted basis of any property with respect to which an adjustment under this paragraph applies shall be determined by applying the treatment prescribed in this paragraph.

(I) Treatment of charitable contributions. Notwithstanding subparagraphs (B) and (C), no adjustment related to the earnings and profits effects of any charitable contribution shall be made in computing adjusted current earnings.

(5) Other definitions. For purposes of paragraph (4)—

(A) Earnings and profits. The term "earnings and profits" means earnings and profits computed for purposes of subchapter C.

(B) Treatment of alternative minimum taxable income. The treatment of any item for purposes of computing alternative minimum taxable income shall be determined without regard to this subsection.

(6) Exception for certain corporations. This subsection shall not apply to any S corporation, regulated investment company, real estate investment trust, or REMIC.

[For Analysis, see ¶ 105 and ¶ 203. For Committee Reports, see ¶ 5008 and ¶ 5062.]

[Endnote Code Sec. 56]

Code Sec. 56(b)(1)(E) was added by Sec. 1008(d) of the American Recovery and Reinvestment Tax Act of 2009, P.L. 111-5, 2/17/2009, as detailed below:

1. Sec. 1008(d) substituted "subparagraphs (D) and (E) of section 63(c)(1)" for "section 63(c)(1)(D)" in subpara. (b)(1)(E)

Effective Date (Sec. 1008(e), P.L. 111-5, 2/17/2009) effective for purchases on or after 2/17/2009 in tax. yrs. end. after 2/17/2009.

Code Sec. 56(g)(4)(B)(iv) was added by Sec. 1503(b), P.L. 111-5, 2/17/2009, as detailed below:

2. Sec. 1503(b) added clause (g)(4)(B)(iv)
Effective Date (Sec. 1503(c), P.L. 111-5, 2/17/2009) effective for obligations issued after 12/31/2008.

[¶ 3038]   Code Sec. 57.   Items of tax preference.

(a)   General rule. For purposes of this part, the items of tax preference determined under this section are—

(1)   Depletion. With respect to each property (as defined in section 614), the excess of the deduction for depletion allowable under section 611 for the taxable year over the adjusted basis of the property at the end of the taxable year (determined without regard to the depletion deduction for the taxable year). Effective with respect to taxable years beginning after December 31, 1992, this paragraph shall not apply to any deduction for depletion computed in accordance with section 613A(c).

(2)   Intangible drilling costs.

(A) In general. With respect to all oil, gas, and geothermal properties of the taxpayer, the amount (if any) by which the amount of the excess intangible drilling costs arising in the taxable year is greater than 65 percent of the net income of the taxpayer from oil, gas, and geothermal properties for the taxable year.

(B) Excess intangible drilling costs. For purposes of subparagraph (A), the amount of the excess intangible drilling costs arising in the taxable year is the excess of—

(i) the intangible drilling and development costs paid or incurred in connection with oil, gas, and geothermal wells (other than costs incurred in drilling a nonproductive well) allowable under section 263(c) or 291(b) for the taxable year, over

(ii) the amount which would have been allowable for the taxable year if such costs had been capitalized and straight line recovery of intangibles (as defined in subsection (b)) had been used with respect to such costs.

(C) Net income from oil, gas, and geothermal properties. For purposes of subparagraph (A), the amount of the net income of the taxpayer from oil, gas, and geothermal properties for the taxable year is the excess of—

(i) the aggregate amount of gross income (within the meaning of section 613(a)) from all oil, gas, and geothermal properties of the taxpayer received or accrued by the taxpayer during the taxable year, over

(ii) the amount of any deductions allocable to such properties reduced by the excess described in subparagraph (B) for such taxable year.

(D) Paragraph applied separately with respect to geothermal properties and oil and gas properties. This paragraph shall be applied separately with respect to—

(i) all oil and gas properties which are not described in clause (ii), and

(ii) all properties which are geothermal deposits (as defined in section 613(e)(2)).

(E) Exception for independent producers. In the case of any oil or gas well—

(i) In general. In the case of any taxable year beginning after December 31, 1992, this paragraph shall not apply to any taxpayer which is not an integrated oil company (as defined in section 291(b)(4)).

(ii) Limitation on benefit. The reduction in alternative minimum taxable income by reason of clause (i) for any taxable year shall not exceed 40 percent (30 percent in case of taxable years beginning in 1993) of the alternative minimum taxable income for such year determined without regard to clause (i) and the alternative tax net operating loss deduction under section 56(a)(4).

(3)   Repealed.

(4)   Repealed.

(5)   Tax-exempt interest.

(A) In general. Interest on specified private activity bonds reduced by any deduction (not allowable in computing the regular tax) which would have been allowable if such interest were includible in gross income.

473

(B) Treatment of exempt-interest dividends. Under regulations prescribed by the Secretary, any exempt-interest dividend (as defined in section 852(b)(5)(A)) shall be treated as interest on a specified private activity bond to the extent of its proportionate share of the interest on such bonds received by the company paying such dividend.

(C) Specified private activity bonds.

(i) In general. For purposes of this part, the term "specified private activity bond" means any private activity bond (as defined in section 141) which is issued after August 7, 1986, and the interest on which is not includible in gross income under section 103.

(ii) Exception for qualified 501(c)(3) bonds. For purposes of clause (i), the term "private activity bond" shall not include any qualified 501(c)(3) bond (as defined in section 145).

(iii) Exception for certain housing bonds. For purposes of clause (i), the term "private activity bond" shall not include any bond issued after the date of the enactment of this clause if such bond is—

(I) an exempt facility bond issued as part of an issue 95 percent or more of the net proceeds of which are to be used to provide qualified residential rental projects (as defined in section 142(d)),

(II) a qualified mortgage bond (as defined in section 143(a)), or

(III) a qualified veterans' mortgage bond (as defined in section 143(b)).

The preceding sentence shall not apply to any refunding bond unless such preceding sentence applied to the refunded bond (or in the case of a series of refundings, the original bond).

(iv) Exception for refundings. For purposes of clause (i), the term "private activity bond" shall not include any refunding bond (whether a current or advance refunding) if the refunded bond (or in the case of a series of refundings, the original bond) was issued before August 8, 1986.

(v) Certain bonds issued before September 1, 1986. For purposes of this subparagraph, a bond issued before September 1, 1986, shall be treated as issued before August 8, 1986, unless such bond would be a private activity bond if—

(I) paragraphs (1) and (2) of section 141(b) were applied by substituting "25 percent" for "10 percent" each place it appears,

(II) paragraphs (3), (4), and (5) of section 141(b) did not apply, and

(III) subparagraph (B) of section 141(c)(1) did not apply.

¹*(vi) Exception for bonds issued in 2009 and 2010.*

(I) In general. For purposes of clause (i), the term "private activity bond" shall not include any bond issued after December 31, 2008, and before January 1, 2011.

(II) Treatment of refunding bonds. For purposes of subclause (I), a refunding bond (whether a current or advance refunding) shall be treated as issued on the date of the issuance of the refunded bond (or in the case of a series of refundings, the original bond).

(III) Exception for certain refunding bonds. Subclause (II) shall not apply to any refunding bond which is issued to refund any bond which was issued after December 31, 2003, and before January 1, 2009.

(6) Accelerated depreciation or amortization on certain property placed in service before January 1, 1987. The amounts which would be treated as items of tax preference with respect to the taxpayer under paragraphs (2), (3), (4), and (12) of this subsection (as in effect on the day before the date of the enactment [10/22/86] of the Tax Reform Act of 1986). The preceding sentence shall not apply to any property to which section 56(a)(1) or (5) applies.

(7) Exclusion for gains on sale of certain small business stock. An amount equal to 7 percent of the amount excluded from gross income for the taxable year under section 1202.

* * * * * * * * * * * *

[For Analysis, see ¶ 202. For Committee Reports, see ¶ 5062.]

[Endnote Code Sec. 57]

Code Sec. 57(a)(5)(C)(vi) was added by Sec. 1503(a) of the American Recovery and Reinvestment Tax Act of 2009, P.L. 111-5, 2/17/2009.

1. added clause (a)(5)(C)(vi)

Effective Date (Sec. 1503(c), P.L. 111-5, 2/17/2009) effective for obligations issued after 12/31/2008.

[¶ 3039]   **Code Sec. 63.**   **Taxable income defined.**

* * * * * * * * * * * *

(c) Standard deduction. For purposes of this subtitle—

(1) In general. Except as otherwise provided in this subsection, the term "standard deduction" means the sum of—

(A) the basic standard deduction,

(B) the additional standard deduction,

(C) in the case of any taxable year beginning in 2008 or 2009, the real property tax deduction, [1]

(D) the disaster loss deduction[2], *and*

[3]*(E) the motor vehicle sales tax deduction.*

(2) Basic standard deduction. For purposes of paragraph (1), the basic standard deduction is—

(A) 200 percent of the dollar amount in effect under subparagraph (C) for the taxable year in the case of—

   (i) a joint return, or

   (ii) a surviving spouse (as defined in section 2(a)),

(B) $4,400 in the case of a head of household (as defined in section 2(b)), or

(C) $3,000 in any other case.

(3) Additional standard deduction for aged and blind. For purposes of paragraph (1), the additional standard deduction is the sum of each additional amount to which the taxpayer is entitled under subsection (f).

(4) Adjustments for inflation. In the case of any taxable year beginning in a calendar year after 1988, each dollar amount contained in paragraph (2)(B), (2)(C), or (5) or subsection (f) shall be increased by an amount equal to—

(A) such dollar amount, multiplied by

(B) the cost-of-living adjustment determined under section 1(f)(3) for the calendar year in which the taxable year begins, by substituting for "calendar year 1992" in subparagraph (B) thereof—

   (i) "calendar year 1987" in the case of the dollar amounts contained in paragraph (2)(B), (2)(C), or (5)(A) or subsection (f), and

   (ii) "calendar year 1997" in the case of the dollar amount contained in paragraph (5)(B).

(5) Limitation on basic standard deduction in the case of certain dependents. In the case of an individual with respect to whom a deduction under section 151 is allowable to another taxpayer for a taxable year beginning in the calendar year in which the individual's taxable year begins, the basic standard deduction applicable to such individual for such individual's taxable year shall not exceed the greater of—

(A) $500, or

(B) the sum of $250 and such individual's earned income.

(6) Certain individuals, etc., not eligible for standard deduction. In the case of—

(A) a married individual filing a separate return where either spouse itemizes deductions,

(B) a nonresident alien individual,

(C) an individual making a return under section 443(a)(1) for a period of less than 12 months on account of a change in his annual accounting period, or

(D) an estate or trust, common trust fund, or partnership,
the standard deduction shall be zero.

(7) Real property tax deduction. For purposes of paragraph (1), the real property tax deduction is the lesser of—

(A) the amount allowable as a deduction under this chapter for State and local taxes described in section 164(a)(1), or

(B) $500 ($1,000 in the case of a joint return).

Any taxes taken into account under section 62(a) shall not be taken into account under this paragraph.

(8) Disaster loss deduction. For the purposes of paragraph (1), the term "disaster loss deduction" means the net disaster loss (as defined in section 165(h)(3)(B)).

[4]*(9) Motor vehicle sales tax deduction. For purposes of paragraph (1), the term "motor vehicle sales tax deduction" means the amount allowable as a deduction under section 164(a)(6). Such term shall not include any amount taken into account under section 62(a).*

* * * * * * * * * * * *

[For Analysis, see ¶ 105. For Committee Reports, see ¶ 5008.]

[Endnote Code Sec. 63]

Code Sec. 63(c)(1)(C), Code Sec. 63(c)(1)(D), Code Sec. 63(c)(1)(E) and Code Sec. 63(c)(9) were amended by Secs. 1008(c)(1) and (2) of the American Recovery and Reinvestment Tax Act of 2009, P.L. 111-5, 2/17/2009, as detailed below:

1. Sec. 1008(c)(1) deleted "and" at the end of subpara. (c)(1)(C)
2. Sec. 1008(c)(1) substituted ", and" for the period at the end of subpara. (c)(1)(D)
3. Sec. 1008(c)(1) added subpara. (c)(1)(E)
4. Sec. 1008(c)(2) added para. (c)(9)

Effective Date (Sec. 1008(e), P.L. 111-5, 2/17/2009) effective for purchases on or after 2/17/2009 in tax. yrs. end. after 2/17/2009.

[¶ 3040]   Code Sec. 85.   Unemployment compensation.

* * * * * * * * * * * *

[1]*(c) Special rule for 2009. In the case of any taxable year beginning in 2009, gross income shall not include so much of the unemployment compensation received by an individual as does not exceed $2,400.*

[For Analysis, see ¶ 106. For Committee Reports, see ¶ 5007.]

[Endnote Code Sec. 85]

Code Sec. 85(c) was added by Sec. 1007(a) of the American Recovery and Reinvestment Tax Act of 2009, P.L. 111-5, 2/17/2009.

1. Sec. 1007(a) added subsec. (c)

Effective Date (Sec. 1007(b), P.L. 111-5, 2/17/2009) effective for tax. yrs. begin. after 12/31/2008.

[¶ 3041]   Code Sec. 108.   Income from discharge of indebtedness.

* * * * * * * * * * * *

[1]*(i) Deferral and ratable inclusion of income arising from business indebtedness discharged by the reacquisition of a debt instrument.*

(1) In general. At the election of the taxpayer, income from the discharge of indebtedness in connection with the reacquisition after December 31, 2008, and before January 1,

2011, of an applicable debt instrument shall be includible in gross income ratably over the 5-taxable-year period beginning with—

(A) in the case of a reacquisition occurring in 2009, the fifth taxable year following the taxable year in which the reacquisition occurs, and

(B) in the case of a reacquisition occurring in 2010, the fourth taxable year following the taxable year in which the reacquisition occurs.

(2) Deferral of deduction for original issue discount in debt for debt exchanges.

(A) In general. If, as part of a reacquisition to which paragraph (1) applies, any debt instrument is issued for the applicable debt instrument being reacquired (or is treated as so issued under subsection (e)(4) and the regulations thereunder) and there is any original issue discount determined under subpart A of part V of subchapter P of this chapter with respect to the debt instrument so issued—

(i) except as provided in clause (ii), no deduction otherwise allowable under this chapter shall be allowed to the issuer of such debt instrument with respect to the portion of such original issue discount which—

(I) accrues before the 1st taxable year in the 5-taxable-year period in which income from the discharge of indebtedness attributable to the reacquisition of the debt instrument is includible under paragraph (1), and

(II) does not exceed the income from the discharge of indebtedness with respect to the debt instrument being reacquired, and

(ii) the aggregate amount of deductions disallowed under clause (i) shall be allowed as a deduction ratably over the 5-taxable-year period described in clause (i)(I).

If the amount of the original issue discount accruing before such 1st taxable year exceeds the income from the discharge of indebtedness with respect to the applicable debt instrument being reacquired, the deductions shall be disallowed in the order in which the original issue discount is accrued.

(B) Deemed debt for debt exchanges. For purposes of subparagraph (A), if any debt instrument is issued by an issuer and the proceeds of such debt instrument are used directly or indirectly by the issuer to reacquire an applicable debt instrument of the issuer, the debt instrument so issued shall be treated as issued for the debt instrument being reacquired. If only a portion of the proceeds from a debt instrument are so used, the rules of subparagraph (A) shall apply to the portion of any original issue discount on the newly issued debt instrument which is equal to the portion of the proceeds from such instrument used to reacquire the outstanding instrument.

(3) Applicable debt instrument. For purposes of this subsection—

(A) Applicable debt instrument. The term "applicable debt instrument" means any debt instrument which was issued by—

(i) a C corporation, or

(ii) any other person in connection with the conduct of a trade or business by such person.

(B) Debt instrument. The term "debt instrument" means a bond, debenture, note, certificate, or any other instrument or contractual arrangement constituting indebtedness (within the meaning of section 1275(a)(1)).

(4) Reacquisition. For purposes of this subsection—

(A) In general. The term "reacquisition" means, with respect to any applicable debt instrument, any acquisition of the debt instrument by—

(i) the debtor which issued (or is otherwise the obligor under) the debt instrument, or

(ii) a related person to such debtor.

(B) Acquisition. The term "acquisition" shall, with respect to any applicable debt instrument, include an acquisition of the debt instrument for cash, the exchange of the debt instrument for another debt instrument (including an exchange resulting from a modification of the debt instrument), the exchange of the debt instrument for corporate stock or a partnership interest, and the contribution of the debt instrument to capital.

Such term shall also include the complete forgiveness of the indebtedness by the holder of the debt instrument.

(5) Other definitions and rules. For purposes of this subsection—

(A) *Related person.* The determination of whether a person is related to another person shall be made in the same manner as under subsection (e)(4).

(B) *Election.*

(i) *In general.* An election under this subsection with respect to any applicable debt instrument shall be made by including with the return of tax imposed by chapter 1 for the taxable year in which the reacquisition of the debt instrument occurs a statement which—

(I) clearly identifies such instrument, and

(II) includes the amount of income to which paragraph (1) applies and such other information as the Secretary may prescribe.

(ii) *Election irrevocable.* Such election, once made, is irrevocable.

(iii) *Pass through entities.* In the case of a partnership, S corporation, or other pass through entity, the election under this subsection shall be made by the partnership, the S corporation, or other entity involved.

(C) *Coordination with other exclusions.* If a taxpayer elects to have this subsection apply to an applicable debt instrument, subparagraphs (A), (B), (C), and (D) of subsection (a)(1) shall not apply to the income from the discharge of such indebtedness for the taxable year of the election or any subsequent taxable year.

(D) *Acceleration of deferred items.*

(i) *In general.* In the case of the death of the taxpayer, the liquidation or sale of substantially all the assets of the taxpayer (including in a title 11 or similar case), the cessation of business by the taxpayer, or similar circumstances, any item of income or deduction which is deferred under this subsection (and has not previously been taken into account) shall be taken into account in the taxable year in which such event occurs (or in the case of a title 11 case, the day before the petition is filed).

(ii) *Special rule for pass thru entities.* The rule of clause (i) shall also apply in the case of the sale or exchange or redemption of an interest in a partnership, S corporation, or other pass through entity by a partner, shareholder, or other person holding an ownership interest in such entity.

(6) Special rule for partnerships. In the case of a partnership, any income or deduction deferred under this subsection shall be allocated to the partners in the partnership immediately before the discharge in the manner such amounts would have been included in the distributive shares of such partners under section 704 if such income were recognized at such time. Any decrease in a partner's share of partnership liabilities as a result of such discharge shall not be taken into account for purposes of section 752 at the time of the discharge to the extent it would cause the partner to recognize gain under section 731. Any decrease in partnership liabilities deferred under the preceding sentence shall be taken into account by such partner at the same time, and to the extent remaining in the same amount, as income deferred under this subsection is recognized.

(7) Secretarial authority. The Secretary may prescribe such regulations, rules, or other guidance as may be necessary or appropriate for purposes of applying this subsection, including—

(A) extending the application of the rules of paragraph (5)(D) to other circumstances where appropriate,

(B) requiring reporting of the election (and such other information as the Secretary may require) on returns of tax for subsequent taxable years, and

(C) rules for the application of this subsection to partnerships, S corporations, and other pass-thru entities, including for the allocation of deferred deductions.

[For Analysis, see ¶ 901. For Committee Reports, see ¶ 5041.]

[**Endnote Code Sec. 108**]

Code Sec. 108(i) was added by Sec. 1231(a) of The American Recovery and Reinvestment Act of 2009, P.L. 111-5, 2/17/2009, as detailed below:

1. Sec. 1231(a) added subsec. (i)
Effective Date (Sec. 1231(b) P.L. 111-5, 2/17/2009) effective for discharges in tax. yrs. end. after 12/31/2008.

[¶ 3042]   Code Sec. 132.   Certain fringe benefits.

* * * * * * * * * * *

(f) Qualified transportation fringe.

(1) In general. For purposes of this section, the term "qualified transportation fringe" means any of the following provided by an employer to an employee:

(A) Transportation in a commuter highway vehicle if such transportation is in connection with travel between the employee's residence and place of employment.

(B) Any transit pass.

(C) Qualified parking.

(D) Any qualified bicycle commuting reimbursement.

(2) Limitation on exclusion. The amount of the fringe benefits which are provided by an employer to any employee and which may be excluded from gross income under subsection (a)(5) shall not exceed—

(A) $100 per month in the case of the aggregate of the benefits described in subparagraphs (A) and (B) of paragraph (1),

(B) $175 per month in the case of qualified parking, and

(C) the applicable annual limitation in the case of any qualified bicycle commuting reimbursement.

¹*In the case of any month beginning on or after the date of the enactment of this sentence and before January 1, 2011, subparagraph (A) shall be applied as if the dollar amount therein were the same as the dollar amount in effect for such month under subparagraph (B).*

(3) Cash reimbursements. For purposes of this subsection, the term "qualified transportation fringe" includes a cash reimbursement by an employer to an employee for a benefit described in paragraph (1). The preceding sentence shall apply to a cash reimbursement for any transit pass only if a voucher or similar item which may be exchanged only for a transit pass is not readily available for direct distribution by the employer to the employee.

(4) No constructive receipt. No amount shall be included in the gross income of an employee solely because the employee may choose between any qualified transportation fringe (other than a qualified bicycle commuting reimbursement) and compensation which would otherwise be includible in gross income of such employee.

(5) Definitions. For purposes of this subsection—

(A) Transit pass. The term "transit pass" means any pass, token, farecard, voucher, or similar item entitling a person to transportation (or transportation at a reduced price) if such transportation is—

(i) on mass transit facilities (whether or not publicly owned), or

(ii) provided by any person in the business of transporting persons for compensation or hire if such transportation is provided in a vehicle meeting the requirements of subparagraph (B)(i).

(B) Commuter highway vehicle. The term "commuter highway vehicle" means any highway vehicle—

(i) the seating capacity of which is at least 6 adults (not including the driver), and

(ii) at least 80 percent of the mileage use of which can reasonably be expected to be—

(I) for purposes of transporting employees in connection with travel between their residences and their place of employment, and

(II) on trips during which the number of employees transported for such purposes is at least ½ of the adult seating capacity of such vehicle (not including the driver).

(C) Qualified parking. The term "qualified parking" means parking provided to an employee on or near the business premises of the employer or on or near a location from which the employee commutes to work by transportation described in subparagraph (A), in a commuter highway vehicle, or by carpool. Such term shall not include any parking on or near property used by the employee for residential purposes.

(D) Transportation provided by employer. Transportation referred to in paragraph (1)(A) shall be considered to be provided by an employer if such transportation is furnished in a commuter highway vehicle operated by or for the employer.

(E) Employee. For purposes of this subsection, the term "employee" does not include an individual who is an employee within the meaning of section 401(c)(1).

(F) Definitions related to bicycle commuting reimbursement.

(i) Qualified bicycle commuting reimbursement. The term "qualified bicycle commuting reimbursement" means, with respect to any calendar year, any employer reimbursement during the 15-month period beginning with the first day of such calendar year for reasonable expenses incurred by the employee during such calendar year for the purchase of a bicycle and bicycle improvements, repair, and storage, if such bicycle is regularly used for travel between the employee's residence and place of employment.

(ii) Applicable annual limitation. The term "applicable annual limitation" means, with respect to any employee for any calendar year, the product of $20 multiplied by the number of qualified bicycle commuting months during such year.

(iii) Qualified bicycle commuting month. The term "qualified bicycle commuting month" means, with respect to any employee, any month during which such employee—

(I) regularly uses the bicycle for a substantial portion of the travel between the employee's residence and place of employment, and

(II) does not receive any benefit described in subparagraph (A), (B), or (C) of paragraph (1).

(6) Inflation adjustment.

(A) In general. In the case of any taxable year beginning in a calendar year after 1999, the dollar amounts contained in subparagraphs (A) and (B) of paragraph (2) shall be increased by an amount equal to—

(i) such dollar amount, multiplied by

(ii) the cost-of-living adjustment determined under section 1(f)(3) for the calendar year in which the taxable year begins, by substituting "calendar year 1998" for "calendar year 1992".

In the case of any taxable year beginning in a calendar year after 2002, clause (ii) shall be applied by substituting "calendar year 2001" for "calendar year 1998" for purposes of adjusting the dollar amount contained in paragraph (2)(A).

(B) Rounding. If any increase determined under subparagraph (A) is not a multiple of $5, such increase shall be rounded to the next lowest multiple of $5.

(7) Coordination with other provisions. For purposes of this section, the terms "working condition fringe" and "de minimis fringe" shall not include any qualified transportation fringe (determined without regard to paragraph (2)).

* * * * * * * * * * * *

[For Analysis, see ¶ 402. For Committee Reports, see ¶ 5032.]

[Endnote Code Sec. 132]

Code Sec. 132(f)(2) was added by Sec. 1151(a) of The American Recovery and Reinvestment Act of 2009, P.L. 111-5, 2/17/2009, as detailed below:

1. Sec. 1151(a) added a flush sentence at the end para. (f)(2)

Effective Date (Sec. 1151(b) P.L. 111-5, 2/17/2009) effective for months begin. on or after 2/17/2009.

[¶ 3043]   *Code Sec.[1] 139C.   COBRA premium assistance.*
In the case of an assistance eligible individual (as defined in section 3002 of the Health Insurance Assistance for the Unemployed Act of 2009), gross income does not include any premium reduction provided under subsection (a) of such section.
[For Analysis, see ¶ 305. For Committee Reports, see ¶ 5082.]

[Endnote Code Sec. 139C]
   Code Sec. 139C was added by Sec. 3001(a)(15)(A) of The American Recovery and Reinvestment Act of 2009, P.L. 111-5, 2/17/2009, as detailed below:
   1. added Code Sec. 139C
Effective Date (Sec. 3001(a)(15)(C), P.L. 111-5, 2/17/2009) effective for tax. yrs. end. after 2/17/2009.

[¶ 3044]   Code Sec. 142.   Exempt facility bond.

* * * * * * * * * * *

   (i)   High-speed intercity rail facilities.
   (1)   In general. For purposes of subsection (a)(11), the term "high-speed intercity rail facilities" means any facility (not including rolling stock) for the fixed guideway rail transportation of passengers and their baggage between metropolitan statistical areas (within the meaning of section 143(k)(2)(B)) using vehicles that are reasonably expected to [1]*be capable of attaining a maximum speed in excess of* 150 miles per hour between scheduled stops, but only if such facility will be made available to members of the general public as passengers.
   (2)   Election by nongovernmental owners. A facility shall be treated as described in subsection (a)(11) only if any owner of such facility which is not a governmental unit irrevocably elects not to claim—
      (A) any deduction under section 167 or 168, and
      (B) any credit under this subtitle, with respect to the property to be financed by the net proceeds of the issue.
   (3)   Use of proceeds. A bond issued as part of an issue described in subsection (a)(11) shall not be considered an exempt facility bond unless any proceeds not used within a 3-year period of the date of the issuance of such bond are used (not later than 6 months after the close of such period) to redeem bonds which are part of such issue.

* * * * * * * * * * *

[For Analysis, see ¶ 1312. For Committee Reports, see ¶ 5063.]

[Endnote Code Sec. 142]
   Code Sec. 142(i)(1) was amended by Sec. 1504(a) of The American Recovery and Reinvestment Act of 2009, P.L. 111-5, 2/17/2009, as detailed below:
   1. Sec. 1504(a) substituted "be capable of attaining a maximum speed in excess of" for "operate at speeds in excess of" in para (i)(1)
Effective Date (Sec. 1504(b) P.L. 111-5, 2/17/2009) effective for obligations issued after the date of the enactment of this Act.

[¶ 3045]   Code Sec. 144.   Qualified small issue bond; qualified student loan bond; qualified redevelopment bond.
   (a)   Qualified small issue bond.

* * * * * * * * * * *

(12) Termination dates.

(A) In general. This subsection shall not apply to—

(i) any bond (other than a bond described in clause (ii)) issued after December 31, 1986, or

(ii) any bond (or series of bonds) issued to refund a bond issued on or before such date unless—

(I) the average maturity date of the issue of which the refunding bond is a part is not later than the average maturity date of the bonds to be refunded by such issue,

(II) the amount of the refunding bond does not exceed the outstanding amount of the refunded bond, and

(III) the net proceeds of the refunding bond are used to redeem the refunded bond not later than 90 days after the date of the issuance of the refunding bond.

For purposes of clause (ii)(I), average maturity shall be determined in accordance with section 147(b)(2)(A).

(B) Bonds issued to finance manufacturing facilities and farm property. Subparagraph (A) shall not apply to any bond issued as part of an issue 95 percent or more of the net proceeds of which are to be used to provide—

(i) any manufacturing facility, or

(ii) any land or property in accordance with section 147(c)(2).

(C) Manufacturing facility. ¹*For purposes of this paragraph—*

(i) In general. The term "manufacturing facility" *means any facility which is used in the manufacturing or production of tangible personal property (including the processing resulting in a change in the condition of such property). A rule similar to the rule of section 142(b)(2) shall apply for purposes of the preceding sentence. For purposes of the 1st sentence of this subparagraph, the term* "manufacturing facility" *includes facilities which are directly related and ancillary to a manufacturing facility (determined without regard to this sentence) if—*

²*(ii) Certain facilities included. Such term includes facilities which are directly related and ancillary to a manufacturing facility (determined without regard to this clause) if—*

(I) such facilities are located on the same site as the manufacturing facility, and

(II) not more than 25 percent of the net proceeds of the issue are used to provide such facilities.

(iii) Special rules for bonds issued in 2009 and 2010. In the case of any issue made after the date of enactment of this clause and before January 1, 2011, clause (ii) shall not apply and the net proceeds from a bond shall be considered to be used to provide a manufacturing facility if such proceeds are used to provide—

(I) a facility which is used in the creation or production of intangible property which is described in section 197(d)(1)(C)(iii), or

(II) a facility which is functionally related and subordinate to a manufacturing facility (determined without regard to this subclause) if such facility is located on the same site as the manufacturing facility.

* * * * * * * * * * * *

[For Analysis, see ¶ 1310. For Committee Reports, see ¶ 5051.]

[Endnote Code Sec. 144]

Code Sec. 144(a)(12)(C), Code Sec. 144(a)(12)(C)(i), Code Sec. 144(a)(12)(C)(ii), and Code Sec. 144(a)(12)(C)(iii) was amended by Secs. 1301(a)(1)-(2) of The American Recovery and Reinvestment Act of 2009, P.L. 111-5, 2/17/2009, as detailed below:

1. Sec. 1301(a)(1) substituted "For purposes of this paragraph—(i) In general. The term" for "For purposes of this paragraph, the term" in subpara. (a)(12)(C)

2. deleted the last sentence in subpara (a)(12)(C) and added clauses (ii) and (iii), prior to amendment clauses (i) and (ii) read as follows:

"(i) such facilities are located on the same site as the manufacturing facility, and

"(ii) not more than 25 percent of the net proceeds of the issue are used to provide such facilities."

Effective Date (Sec. 1301(b) P.L. 111-5, 2/17/2009) effective for obligations issued after 2/17/2009.

[¶ 3046]   Code Sec. 163.   Interest.

* * * * * * * * * * * *

(e) Original issue discount.

* * * * * * * * * * * *

(5) Special rules for original issue discount on certain high yield obligations.

(A) In general. In the case of an applicable high yield discount obligation issued by a corporation—

(i) no deduction shall be allowed under this chapter for the disqualified portion of the original issue discount on such obligation, and

(ii) the remainder of such original issue discount shall not be allowable as a deduction until paid.

For purposes of this paragraph, rules similar to the rules of subsection (i)(3)(B) shall apply in determining the amount of the original issue discount and when the original issue discount is paid.

(B) Disqualified portion treated as stock distribution for purposes of dividend received deduction.

(i) In general. Solely for purposes of sections 243, 245, 246, and 246A, the dividend equivalent portion of any amount includible in gross income of a corporation under section 1272(a) in respect of an applicable high yield discount obligation shall be treated as a dividend received by such corporation from the corporation issuing such obligation.

(ii) Dividend equivalent portion. For purposes of clause (i), the dividend equivalent portion of any amount includible in gross income under section 1272(a) in respect of an applicable high yield discount obligation is the portion of the amount so includible—

(I) which is attributable to the disqualified portion of the original issue discount on such obligation, and

(II) which would have been treated as a dividend if it had been a distribution made by the issuing corporation with respect to stock in such corporation.

(C) Disqualified portion.

(i) In general. For purposes of this paragraph, the disqualified portion of the original issue discount on any applicable high yield discount obligation is the lesser of—

(I) the amount of such original issue discount, or

(II) the portion of the total return on such obligation which bears the same ratio to such total return as the disqualified yield on such obligation bears to the yield to maturity on such obligation.

(ii) Definitions. For purposes of clause (i), the term "disqualified yield" means the excess of the yield to maturity on the obligation over the sum referred to subsection (i)(1)(B) plus 1 percentage point, and the term "total return" is the amount which would have been the original issue discount on the obligation if interest described in the parenthetical in section 1273(a)(2) were included in the stated redemption price at maturity.

(D) Exception for S corporations. This paragraph shall not apply to any obligation issued by any corporation for any period for which such corporation is an S corporation.

(E) Effect on earnings and profits. This paragraph shall not apply for purposes of determining earnings and profits; except that, for purposes of determining the dividend equivalent portion of any amount includible in gross income under section 1272(a) in respect of an applicable high yield discount obligation, no reduction shall be made for any amount attributable to the disqualified portion of any original issue discount on such obligation.

[1](F) *Suspension of application of paragraph.*

(i) *Temporary suspension. This paragraph shall not apply to any applicable high yield discount obligation issued during the period beginning on September 1, 2008, and ending on December 31, 2009, in exchange (including an exchange resulting from a modification of the debt instrument) for an obligation which is not an applicable high yield discount obligation and the issuer (or obligor) of which is the same as the issuer (or obligor) of such applicable high yield discount obligation. The preceding sentence shall not apply to any obligation the interest on which is interest described in section 871(h)(4) (without regard to subparagraph (D) thereof) or to any obligation issued to a related person (within the meaning of section 108(e)(4)).*

(ii) *Successive application. Any obligation to which clause (i) applies shall not be treated as an applicable high yield discount obligation for purposes of applying this subparagraph to any other obligation issued in exchange for such obligation.*

(iii) *Secretarial authority to suspend application. The Secretary may apply this paragraph with respect to debt instruments issued in periods following the period described in clause (i) if the Secretary determines that such application is appropriate in light of distressed conditions in the debt capital markets.*

[2](G) Cross reference. For definition of applicable high yield discount obligation, see subsection (i).

* * * * * * * * * * * *

(i) Applicable high yield discount obligation.

(1) In general. For purposes of this section, the term "applicable high yield discount obligation" means any debt instrument if—

(A) the maturity date of such instrument is more than 5 years from the date of issue,

(B) the yield to maturity on such instrument equals or exceeds the sum of—

(i) the applicable Federal rate in effect under section 1274(d) for the calendar month in which the obligation is issued, plus

(ii) 5 percentage points, and

> • *Caution:* Subpara. (i)(1)(C), following is effective before obligations issued after 12/31/2009, in tax. yrs. end. after such date. For subpara. (i)(1)(C), effective for obligations issued after 12/31/2009, in tax. yrs. end. after such date, see below.

(C) such instrument has significant original issue discount.

For purposes of subparagraph (B)(i), the Secretary may by regulation permit a rate to be used with respect to any debt instrument which is higher than the applicable Federal rate if the taxpayer establishes to the satisfaction of the Secretary that such higher rate is based on the same principles as the applicable Federal rate and is appropriate for the term of the instrument.

> • *Caution:* Subpara. (i)(1)(C), following is effective for obligations issued after 12/31/2009, in tax. yrs. end. after such date. For subpara. (i)(1)(C), effective before obligations issued after 12/31/2009, in tax. yrs. end. after such date, see above.

(C) such instrument has significant original issue discount.

For purposes of subparagraph (B)(i), the Secretary may by regulation

[3](i) permit a rate to be used with respect to any debt instrument which is higher than the applicable Federal rate if the taxpayer establishes to the satisfaction of the Secretary that such higher rate is based on the same principles as the applicable Federal rate and is appropriate for the term of the instrument [4], *or*

(ii) *permit, on a temporary basis, a rate to be used with respect to any debt instrument which is higher than the applicable Federal rate if the Secretary determines that such rate is appropriate in light of distressed conditions in the debt capital markets.*

(2) Significant original issue discount. For purposes of paragraph (1)(C), a debt instrument shall be treated as having significant original issue discount if—

(A) the aggregate amount which would be includible in gross income with respect to such instrument for periods before the close of any accrual period (as defined in section 1272(a)(5)) ending after the date 5 years after the date of issue, exceeds

(B) the sum of—

(i) the aggregate amount of interest to be paid under the instrument before the close of such accrual period, and

(ii) the product of the issue price of such instrument (as defined in sections 1273(b) and 1274(a)) and its yield to maturity.

(3) Special rules. For purposes of determining whether a debt instrument is an applicable high yield discount obligation—

(A) any payment under the instrument shall be assumed to be made on the last day permitted under the instrument, and

(B) any payment to be made in the form of another obligation of the issuer (or a related person within the meaning of section 453(f)(1)) shall be assumed to be made when such obligation is required to be paid in cash or in property other than such obligation.

Except for purposes of paragraph (1)(B), any reference to an obligation in subparagraph (B) of this paragraph shall be treated as including a reference to stock.

(4) Debt instrument. For purposes of this subsection, the term "debt instrument" means any instrument which is a debt instrument as defined in section 1275(a).

(5) Regulations. The Secretary shall prescribe such regulations as may be appropriate to carry out the purposes of this subsection and subsection (e)(5), including—

(A) regulations providing for modifications to the provisions of this subsection and subsection (e)(5) in the case of varying rates of interest, put or call options, indefinite maturities, contingent payments, assumptions of debt instruments, conversion rights, or other circumstances where such modifications are appropriate to carry out the purposes of this subsection and subsection (e)(5), and

(B) regulations to prevent avoidance of the purposes of this subsection and subsection (e)(5) through the use of issuers other than C corporations, agreements to borrow amounts due under the debt instrument, or other arrangements.

* * * * * * * * * * * *

[For Analysis, see ¶ 907 and ¶ 908. For Committee Reports, see ¶ 5042.]

[Endnote Code Sec. 163]

Code Sec. 163(e)(5)(F) and Code Sec. 163(e)(5)(G) were amended by Sec. 1232(a) of The American Recovery and Reinvestment Act of 2009, P.L. 111-5, 2/17/2009, as detailed below:

1. Sec. 1232(a) added subpara. (e)(5)(F)
2. Sec. 1232(a) redesignated subpara. (e)(5)(F) as subpara. (e)(5)(G)

Effective Date (Sec. 1232(c)(1), P.L. 111-5, 2/17/2009) effective for obligations issued after 8/31/2008, in tax. yrs. end. after such date.

Code Sec. 163(i)(1) was added by Sec. 1232(b)(1) and (2), P.L. 111-5, 2/17/2009, as detailed below:

3. Sec. 1232(b)(1) added "(i)" after "regulation" in subpara. (i)(1)(C)
4. Sec. 1232(b)(2) added clause (i)(1)(C)(ii) before the period in clause (i)(1)(C)(i)

Effective Date (Sec. 1232(c)(2), P.L. 111-5, 2/17/2009) effective for obligations issued after 12/31/2009, in tax. yrs. end. after such date.

[¶ 3047]   Code Sec. 164.   Taxes.

(a) General rule. Except as otherwise provided in this section, the following taxes shall be allowed as a deduction for the taxable year within which paid or accrued:

(1) State and local, and foreign, real property taxes.

(2) State and local personal property taxes.

(3) State and local, and foreign, income, war profits, and excess profits taxes.

(4) The GST tax imposed on income distributions.

(5) The environmental tax imposed by section 59A.

[1]*(6) Qualified motor vehicle taxes.* In addition, there shall be allowed as a deduction State and local, and foreign, taxes not described in the preceding sentence which are paid or accrued within the taxable year in carrying on a trade or business or an activity described in section 212 (relating to expenses for production of income). Notwithstanding the preceding sentence, any tax (not described in the first sentence of this subsection) which is paid or accrued by the taxpayer in connection with an acquisition or disposition of property shall be treated as part of the cost of the acquired property or, in the case of a disposition, as a reduction in the amount realized on the disposition.

(b) Definitions and special rules. For purposes of this section—

(1) Personal property taxes. The term "personal property tax" means an ad valorem tax which is imposed on an annual basis in respect of personal property.

(2) State or local taxes. A State or local tax includes only a tax imposed by a State, a possession of the United States, or a political subdivision of any of the foregoing, or by the District of Columbia.

(3) Foreign taxes. A foreign tax includes only a tax imposed by the authority of a foreign country.

(4) Special rules for GST tax.

(A) In general. The GST tax imposed on income distributions is—

(i) the tax imposed by section 2601, and

(ii) any State tax described in section 2604,

but only to the extent such tax is imposed on a transfer which is included in the gross income of the distributee and to which section 666 does not apply.

(B) Special rule for tax paid before due date. Any tax referred to in subparagraph (A) imposed with respect to a transfer occurring during the taxable year of the distributee (or, in the case of a taxable termination, the trust) which is paid not later than the time prescribed by law (including extensions) for filing the return with respect to such transfer shall be treated as having been paid on the last day of the taxable year in which the transfer was made.

(5) General sales taxes. For purposes of subsection (a)—

(A) Election to deduct State and local sales taxes in lieu of State and local income taxes. At the election of the taxpayer for the taxable year, subsection (a) shall be applied—

(i) without regard to the reference to State and local income taxes, and

(ii) as if State and local general sales taxes were referred to in a paragraph thereof.

(B) Definition of general sales tax. The term "general sales tax" means a tax imposed at one rate with respect to the sale at retail of a broad range of classes of items.

(C) Special rules for food, etc. In the case of items of food, clothing, medical supplies, and motor vehicles—

(i) the fact that the tax does not apply with respect to some or all of such items shall not be taken into account in determining whether the tax applies with respect to a broad range of classes of items, and

(ii) the fact that the rate of tax applicable with respect to some or all of such items is lower than the general rate of tax shall not be taken into account in determining whether the tax is imposed at one rate.

(D) Items taxed at different rates. Except in the case of a lower rate of tax applicable with respect to an item described in subparagraph (C), no deduction shall be allowed under this paragraph for any general sales tax imposed with respect to an item at a rate other than the general rate of tax.

(E) Compensating use taxes. A compensating use tax with respect to an item shall be treated as a general sales tax. For purposes of the preceding sentence, the term "compensating use tax" means, with respect to any item, a tax which—

(i) is imposed on the use, storage, or consumption of such item, and

(ii) is complementary to a general sales tax, but only if a deduction is allowable under this paragraph with respect to items sold at retail in the taxing jurisdiction which are similar to such item.

(F) Special rule for motor vehicles. In the case of motor vehicles, if the rate of tax exceeds the general rate, such excess shall be disregarded and the general rate shall be treated as the rate of tax.

(G) Separately stated general sales taxes. If the amount of any general sales tax is separately stated, then, to the extent that the amount so stated is paid by the consumer (other than in connection with the consumer's trade or business) to the seller, such amount shall be treated as a tax imposed on, and paid by, such consumer.

(H) Amount of deduction may be determined under tables.

(i) In general. At the election of the taxpayer for the taxable year, the amount of the deduction allowed under this paragraph for such year shall be—

(I) the amount determined under this paragraph (without regard to this subparagraph) with respect to motor vehicles, boats, and other items specified by the Secretary, and

(II) the amount determined under tables prescribed by the Secretary with respect to items to which subclause (I) does not apply.

(ii) Requirements for tables. The tables prescribed under clause (i)—

(I) shall reflect the provisions of this paragraph,

(II) shall be based on the average consumption by taxpayers on a State-by-State basis (as determined by the Secretary) of items to which clause (i)(I) does not apply, taking into account filing status, number of dependents, adjusted gross income, and rates of State and local general sales taxation, and

(III) need only be determined with respect to adjusted gross incomes up to the applicable amount (as determined under section 68(b)).

(I) Application of paragraph. This paragraph shall apply to taxable years beginning after December 31, 2003, and before January 1, 2010.

²*(6) Qualified motor vehicle taxes.*

(A) In general. For purposes of this section, the term "qualified motor vehicle taxes" means any State or local sales or excise tax imposed on the purchase of a qualified motor vehicle.

(B) Limitation based on vehicle price. The amount of any State or local sales or excise tax imposed on the purchase of a qualified motor vehicle taken into account under subparagraph (A) shall not exceed the portion of such tax attributable to so much of the purchase price as does not exceed $49,500.

(C) Income limitation. The amount otherwise taken into account under subparagraph (A) (after the application of subparagraph (B)) for any taxable year shall be reduced (but not below zero) by the amount which bears the same ratio to the amount which is so treated as—

(i) the excess (if any) of—

(I) the taxpayer's modified adjusted gross income for such taxable year, over

(II) $125,000 ($250,000 in the case of a joint return), bears to

(ii) $10,000.

For purposes of the preceding sentence, the term "modified adjusted gross income" means the adjusted gross income of the taxpayer for the taxable year (determined without regard to sections 911, 931, and 933).

(D) Qualified motor vehicle. For purposes of this paragraph—

(i) In general. The term "qualified motor vehicle" means—

(I) a passenger automobile or light truck which is treated as a motor vehicle for purposes of title II of the Clean Air Act, the gross vehicle weight rating of which is not more than 8,500 pounds, and the original use of which commences with the taxpayer,

(II) a motorcycle the gross vehicle weight rating of which is not more than 8,500 pounds and the original use of which commences with the taxpayer, and

(III) a motor home the original use of which commences with the taxpayer.

(ii) *Other terms.* The terms "motorcycle" and "motor home" have the meanings given such terms under section 571.3 of title 49, Code of Federal Regulations (as in effect on the date of the enactment of this paragraph).

(E) *Qualified motor vehicle taxes not included in cost of acquired property.* The last sentence of subsection (a) shall not apply to any qualified motor vehicle taxes.

(F) *Coordination with general sales tax.* This paragraph shall not apply in the case of a taxpayer who makes an election under paragraph (5) for the taxable year.

(G) *Termination.* This paragraph shall not apply to purchases after December 31, 2009.

* * * * * * * * * * * *

[For Analysis, see ¶ 105. For Committee Reports, see ¶ 5008.]

[Endnote Code Sec. 164]
   Code Sec. 164(a)(6) and Code Sec. 164(b)(6) was added by Secs. 1008(a) and (b) of The American Recovery and Reinvestment Act of 2009, P.L. 111-5, 2/17/2009, as detailed below:
   1. Sec. 1008(a) added para. (a)(6)
   2. Sec. 1008(b) added para. (b)(6)
Effective Date (Sec. 1008(e), P.L. 111-5, 2/17/2009) effective for purchases on or after 2/17/2009 in tax. yrs. end. after 2/17/2009.

[¶ 3048]   **Code Sec. 168.   Accelerated cost recovery system.**

* * * * * * * * * * * *

   (k)   Special allowance for certain property acquired after December 31, 2007, and before [1]***January 1, 2010.***

   (1)   Additional allowance. In the case of any qualified property—

   (A) the depreciation deduction provided by section 167(a) for the taxable year in which such property is placed in service shall include an allowance equal to 50 percent of the adjusted basis of the qualified property, and

   (B) the adjusted basis of the qualified property shall be reduced by the amount of such deduction before computing the amount otherwise allowable as a depreciation deduction under this chapter for such taxable year and any subsequent taxable year.

   (2)   Qualified property. For purposes of this subsection—

   (A) In general. The term "qualified property" means property—

      (i)   (I) to which this section applies which has a recovery period of 20 years or less,

      (II) which is computer software (as defined in section 167(f)(1)(B)) for which a deduction is allowable under section 167(a) without regard to this subsection,

      (III) which is water utility property, or

      (IV) which is qualified leasehold improvement property,

   (ii) the original use of which commences with the taxpayer after December 31, 2007,

   (iii) which is—

      (I) acquired by the taxpayer after December 31, 2007, and before [2]*January 1, 2010,* but only if no written binding contract for the acquisition was in effect before January 1, 2008, or

      (II) acquired by the taxpayer pursuant to a written binding contract which was entered into after December 31, 2007, and before [3]*January 1, 2010,* and

      (iv) which is placed in service by the taxpayer before [4]*January 1, 2010,* or, in the case of property described in subparagraph (B) or (C), before [5]*January 1, 2011.*

   (B) Certain property having longer production periods treated as qualified property.

(i) In general. The term "qualified property" includes any property if such property—

(I) meets the requirements of clauses (i), (ii), (iii), and (iv) of subparagraph (A),

(II) has a recovery period of at least 10 years or is transportation property,

(III) is subject to section 263A, and

(IV) meets the requirements of clause (iii) of section 263A(f)(1)(B) (determined as if such clauses also apply to property which has a long useful life (within the meaning of section 263A(f))).

(ii) Only [6]pre-January 1, 2010, basis eligible for additional allowance. In the case of property which is qualified property solely by reason of clause (i), paragraph (1) shall apply only to the extent of the adjusted basis thereof attributable to manufacture, construction, or production before [7]January 1, 2010.

(iii) Transportation property. For purposes of this subparagraph, the term "transportation property" means tangible personal property used in the trade or business of transporting persons or property.

(iv) Application of subparagraph. This subparagraph shall not apply to any property which is described in subparagraph (C).

(C) Certain aircraft. The term "qualified property" includes property—

(i) which meets the requirements of clauses (ii) , (iii), and (iv) of subparagraph (A),

(ii) which is an aircraft which is not a transportation property (as defined in subparagraph (B)(iii)) other than for agricultural or firefighting purposes,

(iii) which is purchased and on which such purchaser, at the time of the contract for purchase, has made a nonrefundable deposit of the lesser of—

(I) 10 percent of the cost, or

(II) $100,000, and

(iv) which has—

(I) an estimated production period exceeding 4 months, and

(II) a cost exceeding $200,000.

(D) Exceptions.

(i) Alternative depreciation property. The term "qualified property" shall not include any property to which the alternative depreciation system under subsection (g) applies, determined—

(I) without regard to paragraph (7) of subsection (g) (relating to election to have system apply), and

(II) after application of section 280F(b) (relating to listed property with limited business use).

(ii) Qualified New York Liberty Zone leasehold improvement property. The term "qualified property" shall not include any qualified New York Liberty Zone leasehold improvement property (as defined in section 1400L(c)(2)).

(iii) Election out. If a taxpayer makes an election under this clause with respect to any class of property for any taxable year, this subsection shall not apply to all property in such class placed in service during such taxable year.

(E) Special rules.

(i) Self-constructed property. In the case of a taxpayer manufacturing, constructing, or producing property for the taxpayer's own use, the requirements of clause (iii) of subparagraph (A) shall be treated as met if the taxpayer begins manufacturing, constructing, or producing the property after December 31, 2007, and before [8]January 1, 2010.

(ii) Sale-leasebacks. For purposes of clause (iii) and subparagraph (A)(ii), if property is—

(I) originally placed in service after December 31, 2007, by a person, and

(II) sold and leased back by such person within 3 months after the date such property was originally placed in service, such property shall be treated as originally placed in service not earlier than the date on which such property is used under the leaseback referred to in subclause (II).

(iii) Syndication. For purposes of subparagraph (A)(ii), if—

(I) property is originally placed in service after December 31, 2007, by the lessor of such property,

(II) such property is sold by such lessor or any subsequent purchaser within 3 months after the date such property was originally placed in service (or, in the case of multiple units of property subject to the same lease, within 3 months after the date the final unit is placed in service, so long as the period between the time the first unit is placed in service and the time the last unit is placed in service does not exceed 12 months), and

(III) the user of such property after the last sale during such 3-month period remains the same as when such property was originally placed in service, such property shall be treated as originally placed in service not earlier than the date of such last sale.

(iv) Limitations related to users and related parties. The term "qualified property" shall not include any property if—

(I) the user of such property (as of the date on which such property is originally placed in service) or a person which is related (within the meaning of section 267(b) or 707(b)) to such user or to the taxpayer had a written binding contract in effect for the acquisition of such property at any time on or before December 31, 2007, or

(II) in the case of property manufactured, constructed, or produced for such user's or person's own use, the manufacture, construction, or production of such property began at any time on or before December 31, 2007.

(F) Coordination with section 280F. For purposes of section 280F—

(i) Automobiles. In the case of a passenger automobile (as defined in section 280F(d)(5)) which is qualified property, the Secretary shall increase the limitation under section 280F(a)(1)(A)(i) by $8,000.

(ii) Listed property. The deduction allowable under paragraph (1) shall be taken into account in computing any recapture amount under section 280F(b)(2).

(G) Deduction allowed in computing minimum tax. For purposes of determining alternative minimum taxable income under section 55, the deduction under subsection (a) for qualified property shall be determined under this section without regard to any adjustment under section 56.

(3) Qualified leasehold improvement property. For purposes of this subsection—

(A) In general. The term "qualified leasehold improvement property" means any improvement to an interior portion of a building which is nonresidential real property if—

(i) such improvement is made under or pursuant to a lease (as defined in subsection (h)(7))—

(I) by the lessee (or any sublessee) of such portion, or

(II) by the lessor of such portion,

(ii) such portion is to be occupied exclusively by the lessee (or any sublessee) of such portion, and

(iii) such improvement is placed in service more than 3 years after the date the building was first placed in service.

(B) Certain improvements not included. Such term shall not include any improvement for which the expenditure is attributable to—

(i) the enlargement of the building,

(ii) any elevator or escalator,

(iii) any structural component benefiting a common area, and

(iv) the internal structural framework of the building.

(C) Definitions and special rules. For purposes of this paragraph—

(i) Commitment to lease treated as lease. A commitment to enter into a lease shall be treated as a lease, and the parties to such commitment shall be treated as lessor and lessee, respectively.

(ii) Related persons. A lease between related persons shall not be considered a lease. For purposes of the preceding sentence, the term "related persons" means—

(I) members of an affiliated group (as defined in section 1504), and

(II) persons having a relationship described in subsection (b) of section 267; except that, for purposes of this clause, the phrase "80 percent or more" shall be substituted for the phrase "more than 50 percent" each place it appears in such subsection.

(4) Election to accelerate the amt and research credits in lieu of bonus depreciation.

(A) In general. If a corporation elects to have this paragraph apply for the first taxable year of the taxpayer ending after March 31, 2008, in the case of such taxable year and each subsequent taxable year—

(i) paragraph (1) shall not apply to any eligible qualified property placed in service by the taxpayer,

(ii) the applicable depreciation method used under this section with respect to such property shall be the straight line method, and

(iii) each of the limitations described in subparagraph (B) for any such taxable year shall be increased by the bonus depreciation amount which is—

(I) determined for such taxable year under subparagraph (C), and

(II) allocated to such limitation under subparagraph (E).

(B) Limitations to be increased. The limitations described in this subparagraph are—

(i) the limitation imposed by section 38(c), and

(ii) the limitation imposed by section 53(c).

(C) Bonus depreciation amount. For purposes of this paragraph—

(i) In general. The bonus depreciation amount for any taxable year is an amount equal to 20 percent of the excess (if any) of—

(I) the aggregate amount of depreciation which would be allowed under this section for eligible qualified property placed in service by the taxpayer during such taxable year if paragraph (1) applied to all such property, over

(II) the aggregate amount of depreciation which would be allowed under this section for eligible qualified property placed in service by the taxpayer during such taxable year if paragraph (1) did not apply to any such property.

The aggregate amounts determined under subclauses (I) and (II) shall be determined without regard to any election made under subsection (b)(2)(C), (b)(3)(D), or (g)(7) and without regard to subparagraph (A)(ii).

(ii) Maximum amount. The bonus depreciation amount for any taxable year shall not exceed the maximum increase amount under clause (iii), reduced (but not below zero) by the sum of the bonus depreciation amounts for all preceding taxable years.

(iii) Maximum increase amount. For purposes of clause (ii), the term "maximum increase amount" means, with respect to any corporation, the lesser of—

(I) $30,000,000, or

(II) 6 percent of the sum of the business credit increase amount, and the AMT credit increase amount, determined with respect to such corporation under subparagraph (E).

(iv) Aggregation rule. All corporations which are treated as a single employer under section 52(a) shall be treated—

(I) as 1 taxpayer for purposes of this paragraph, and

(II) as having elected the application of this paragraph if any such corporation so elects.

(D) Eligible qualified property. For purposes of this paragraph, the term "eligible qualified property" means qualified property under paragraph (2), except that in applying paragraph (2) for purposes of this paragraph—

(i) "March 31, 2008" shall be substituted for "December 31, 2007" each place it appears in subparagraph (A) and clauses (i) and (ii) of subparagraph (E) thereof, [9]

[10]*(ii) "April 1, 2008" shall be substituted for "January 1, 2008" in subparagraph (A)(iii)(I) thereof, and*

[11]*(iii)* only adjusted basis attributable to manufacture, construction, or production after March 31, 2008, and before January 1, [12]*2010,* shall be taken into account under subparagraph (B)(ii) thereof.

(E) Allocation of bonus depreciation amounts.

(i) in general. Subject to clauses (ii) and (iii), the taxpayer shall, at such time and in such manner as the Secretary may prescribe, specify the portion (if any) of the bonus depreciation amount for the taxable year which is to be allocated to each of the limitations described in subparagraph (B) for such taxable year.

(ii) Limitation on allocations. The portion of the bonus depreciation amount which may be allocated under clause (i) to the limitations described in subparagraph (B) for any taxable year shall not exceed—

(I) in the case of the limitation described in subparagraph (B)(i), the excess of the business credit increase amount over the bonus depreciation amount allocated to such limitation for all preceding taxable years, and

(II) in the case of the limitation described in subparagraph (B)(ii), the excess of the AMT credit increase amount over the bonus depreciation amount allocated to such limitation for all preceding taxable years.

(iii) Business credit increase amount. For purposes of this paragraph, the term "business credit increase amount" means the amount equal to the portion of the credit allowable under section 38 (determined without regard to subsection (c) thereof) for the first taxable year ending after March 31, 2008, which is allocable to business credit carryforwards to such taxable year which are—

(I) from taxable years beginning before January 1, 2006, and

(II) properly allocable (determined under the rules of section 38(d)) to the research credit determined under section 41(a).

(iv) AMT credit increase amount. For purposes of this paragraph, the term "AMT credit increase amount" means the amount equal to the portion of the minimum tax credit under section 53(b) for the first taxable year ending after March 31, 2008, determined by taking into account only the adjusted minimum tax for taxable years beginning before January 1, 2006. For purposes of the preceding sentence, credits shall be treated as allowed on a first-in, first-out basis.

(F) Credit refundable. For purposes of section 6401(b), the aggregate increase in the credits allowable under part IV of subchapter A for any taxable year resulting from the application of this paragraph shall be treated as allowed under subpart C of such part (and not any other subpart).

(G) Other rules.

(i) Election. Any election under this paragraph (including any allocation under subparagraph (E)) may be revoked only with the consent of the Secretary.

(ii) Partnerships with electing partners. In the case of a corporation making an election under subparagraph (A) and which is a partner in a partnership, for purposes of determining such corporation's distributive share of partnership items under section 702—

(I) paragraph (1) shall not apply to any eligible qualified property, and

(II) the applicable depreciation method used under this section with respect to such property shall be the straight line method.

(iii) Special rule for passenger aircraft. In the case of any passenger aircraft, the written binding contract limitation under paragraph (2)(A)(iii)(I) shall not apply for purposes of subparagraphs (C)(i)(I) and (D).

[13]*(H) Special rules for extension property.*

(i) *Taxpayers previously electing acceleration.* In the case of a taxpayer who made the election under subparagraph (A) for its first taxable year ending after March 31, 2008—

(I) the taxpayer may elect not to have this paragraph apply to extension property, but

(II) if the taxpayer does not make the election under subclause (I), in applying this paragraph to the taxpayer a separate bonus depreciation amount, maximum amount, and maximum increase amount shall be computed and applied to eligible qualified property which is extension property and to eligible qualified property which is not extension property.

(ii) *Taxpayers not previously electing acceleration.* In the case of a taxpayer who did not make the election under subparagraph (A) for its first taxable year ending after March 31, 2008—

(I) the taxpayer may elect to have this paragraph apply to its first taxable year ending after December 31, 2008, and each subsequent taxable year, and

(II) if the taxpayer makes the election under subclause (I), this paragraph shall only apply to eligible qualified property which is extension property.

(iii) *Extension property.* For purposes of this subparagraph, the term "extension property" means property which is eligible qualified property solely by reason of the extension of the application of the special allowance under paragraph (1) pursuant to the amendments made by section 1201(a) of the American Recovery and Reinvestment Tax Act of 2009 (and the application of such extension to this paragraph pursuant to the amendment made by section 1201(b)(1) of such Act).

(l)   Special allowance for cellulosic biofuel plant property.

(1)   Additional allowance. In the case of any qualified cellulosic biomass ethanol plant property—

(A) the depreciation deduction provided by section 167(a) for the taxable year in which such property is placed in service shall include an allowance equal to 50 percent of the adjusted basis of such property, and

(B) the adjusted basis of such property shall be reduced by the amount of such deduction before computing the amount otherwise allowable as a depreciation deduction under this chapter for such taxable year and any subsequent taxable year.

(2)   Qualified cellulosic biofuel plant property. The term "qualified cellulosic biofuel plant property" means property of a character subject to the allowance for depreciation—

(A) which is used in the United States solely to produce cellulosic biofuel ,

(B) the original use of which commences with the taxpayer after the date of the enactment of this subsection,

(C) which is acquired by the taxpayer by purchase (as defined in section 179(d)) after the date of the enactment of this subsection, but only if no written binding contract for the acquisition was in effect on or before the date of the enactment of this subsection, and

(D) which is placed in service by the taxpayer before January 1, 2013.

(3)   Cellulosic biofuel. The term "cellulosic biofuel" means any liquid fuel which is produced from any lignocellulosic or hemicellulosic matter that is available on a renewable or recurring basis.

(4)   Exceptions.

(A) Bonus depreciation property under subsection (k). Such term shall not include any property to which section 168(k) applies.

(B) Alternative depreciation property. Such term shall not include any property described in section 168(k)(2)(D)(i).

(C) Tax-exempt bond-financed property. Such term shall not include any property any portion of which is financed with the proceeds of any obligation the interest on which is exempt from tax under section 103.

(D) Election out. If a taxpayer makes an election under this subparagraph with respect to any class of property for any taxable year, this subsection shall not apply to all property in such class placed in service during such taxable year.

(5) Special rules. For purposes of this subsection, rules similar to the rules of subparagraph (E) of section 168(k)(2) shall apply, except that such subparagraph shall be applied—

(A) by substituting "the date of the enactment of subsection (l)" for "December 31, 2007" each place it appears therein,

(B) by substituting "January 1, 2013" for "[14]*January 1, 2010*" in clause (i) thereof, and

(C) by substituting "qualified cellulosic biofuel plant property" for "qualified property" in clause (iv) thereof.

(6) Allowance against alternative minimum tax. For purposes of this subsection, rules similar to the rules of section 168(k)(2)(G) shall apply.

(7) Recapture. For purposes of this subsection, rules similar to the rules under section 179(d)(10) shall apply with respect to any qualified cellulosic biofuel plant property which ceases to be qualified cellulosic biofuel plant property.

(8) Denial of double benefit. Paragraph (1) shall not apply to any qualified cellulosic biofuel plant property with respect to which an election has been made under section 179C (relating to election to expense certain refineries).

* * * * * * * * * * *

(n) Special allowance for qualified disaster assistance property.

(1) In general. In the case of any qualified disaster assistance property—

(A) the depreciation deduction provided by section 167(a) for the taxable year in which such property is placed in service shall include an allowance equal to 50 percent of the adjusted basis of the qualified disaster assistance property, and

(B) the adjusted basis of the qualified disaster assistance property shall be reduced by the amount of such deduction before computing the amount otherwise allowable as a depreciation deduction under this chapter for such taxable year and any subsequent taxable year.

(2) Qualified disaster assistance property. For purposes of this subsection-

(A) In general. The term "qualified disaster assistance property" means any property—

(i) (I) which is described in subsection (k)(2)(A)(i), or

(II) which is nonresidential real property or residential rental property,

(ii) substantially all of the use of which is—

(I) in a disaster area with respect to a federally declared disaster occurring before January 1, 2010, and

(II) in the active conduct of a trade or business by the taxpayer in such disaster area,

(iii) which—

(I) rehabilitates property damaged, or replaces property destroyed or condemned, as a result of such federally declared disaster, except that, for purposes of this clause, property shall be treated as replacing property destroyed or condemned if, as part of an integrated plan, such property replaces property which is included in a continuous area which includes real property destroyed or condemned, and

(II) is similar in nature to, and located in the same county as, the property being rehabilitated or replaced,

(iv) the original use of which in such disaster area commences with an eligible taxpayer on or after the applicable disaster date,

(v) which is acquired by such eligible taxpayer by purchase (as defined in section 179(d)) on or after the applicable disaster date, but only if no written binding contract for the acquisition was in effect be fore such date, and

(vi) which is placed in service by such eligible taxpayer on or before the date which is the last day of the third calendar year following the applicable disaster date the fourth calendar year in the case of nonresidential real property and residential rental property).

(B) Exceptions.

(i) Other bonus depreciation property. The term 'qualified disaster assistance property' shall not include-

(I) any property to which subsection (k) (determined without regard to paragraph (4)), (l), or (m) applies,

(II) any property to which section 1400N(d) applies, and

(III) any property described in section 1400N(p)(3).

(ii) Alternative depreciation property. The term "qualified disaster assistance property" shall not include any property to which the alternative depreciation system under subsection (g) applies, determined without regard to paragraph (7) of subsection (g) (relating to election to have system apply).

(iii) Tax-exempt bond financed property. Such term shall not include any property any portion of which is financed with the proceeds of any obligation the interest on which is exempt from tax under section 103.

(iv) Qualified revitalization buildings. Such term shall not include any qualified revitalization building with respect to which the taxpayer has elected the application of paragraph (1) or (2) of section 1400I(a).

(v) Election out. If a taxpayer makes an election under this clause with respect to any class of property for any taxable year, this subsection shall not apply to all property in such class placed in service during such taxable year.

(C) Special rules. For purposes of this subsection, rules similar to the rules of subparagraph (E) of subsection (k)(2) shall apply, except that such subparagraph shall be applied-

(i) by substituting "the applicable disaster date" for "December 31, 2007" each place it appears therein,

(ii) without regard to 'and before [15]*January 1, 2010*' in clause (i) thereof, and

(iii) by substituting "qualified disaster assistance property" for "qualified property" in clause (iv) thereof.

(D) Allowance against alternative minimum tax. For purposes of this subsection, rules similar to the rules of subsection (k)(2)(G) shall apply.

(3) Other definitions. For purposes of this subsection—

(A) Applicable disaster date. The term "applicable disaster date" means, with respect to any federally declared disaster, the date on which such federally declared disaster occurs.

(B) Federally declared disaster. The term "federally declared disaster" has the meaning given such term under section 165(h)(3)(C)(i).

(C) Disaster area. The term "disaster area" has the meaning given such term under section 165(h)(3)(C)(ii).

(D) Eligible taxpayer. The term "eligible taxpayer" means a taxpayer who has suffered an economic loss attributable to a federally declared disaster.

(4) Recapture. For purposes of this subsection, rules similar to the rules under section 179(d)(10) shall apply with respect to any qualified disaster assistance property which ceases to be qualified disaster assistance property.

[For Analysis, see ¶ 801, ¶ 803, ¶ 804, ¶ 805 and ¶ 806. For Committee Reports, see ¶ 5034.]

[Endnote Code Sec. 168]
Code Sec. 168(k), heading Code Sec. 168(k)(2), Code Sec. 168(k)(2)(B)(ii), heading were amended by Secs. 1201(a)(2)(A)-(B), (a)(1)(A)-(B) of The American Recovery and Reinvestment Act of 2009, P.L. 111-5, 2/17/2009, as detailed below:
1. Sec. 1201(a)(2)(A) substituted 'January 1, 2010' for 'January 1, 2009' in the heading of subsec. (k)
2. Sec. 1201(a)(1)(B) substituted 'January 1, 2010' for 'January 1, 2009' each place it appears in para. (k)(2)

3. Sec. 1201(a)(1)(B) substituted 'January 1, 2010' for 'January 1, 2009' each place it appears in para. (k)(2)

4. Sec. 1201(a)(1)(B) substituted 'January 1, 2010' for 'January 1, 2009' each place it appears in para. (k)(2)

5. Sec. 1201(a)(1)(A) substituted 'January 1, 2011' for 'January 1, 2010' in para. (k)(2)

6. Sec. 1201(a)(2)(B) substituted 'pre-January 1, 2010' for 'pre-January 1, 2009' in the heading of subsec. (k)(2)(B)(ii)

7. Sec. 1201(a)(1)(B) substituted 'January 1, 2010' for 'January 1, 2009' each place it appears in para. (k)(2)

8. Sec. 1201(a)(1)(B) substituted 'January 1, 2010' for 'January 1, 2009' each place it appears in para. (k)(2)

Effective Date (Sec. 1201(c)(1), P.L. 111-5, 2/17/2009) effective for property placed in service after 12/31/2008, in tax. yrs. end. after such date.

Code Sec. 168(k)(4)(D)(i), heading Code Sec. 168(k)(4)(D)(ii), Code Sec. 168(k)(4)(D)(iii) was amended by Secs. 1201(a)(3)(A)(i)-(iii), P.L. 111-5, 2/17/2009, as detailed below:

9. Sec. 1201(a)(3)(A)(i) deleted 'and' at the end of clause (k)(4)(D)(i)

10. Sec. 1201(a)(3)(A)(ii) redesignated clause (k)(4)(D)(ii) as (k)(4)(D)(iii)

11. Sec. 1201(a)(3)(A)(iii) added clause (k)(4)(D)(ii)

Effective Date (Sec. 1201(c)(2), P.L. 111-5, 2/17/2009) effective for tax. yrs. end. after 3/31/2008.

Code Sec. 168(k)(4)(D)(iii), as redesignated Code Sec. 168(k)(4)(H), Code Sec. 168(l)(5)(B), and Code Sec. 168(n)(2)(C) were amended by Secs. 1201(b)(1)(A)-(B) and (a)(2)(C)-(D), P.L. 111-5, 2/17/2009, as detailed below:

12. Sec. 1201(b)(1)(A) substituted '"2010" for "2009" in subpara. (k)(4)(D)(iii) as redesignated by Law. Sec. 1201(a)(3)(A)(ii)

13. Sec. 1201(b)(1)(B) added subpara. (k)(4)(H)

14. Sec. 1201(a)(2)(C) substituted "January 1, 2010" for "January 1, 2009" in subpara. (l)(5)(B)

15. Sec. 1201(a)(2)(D) substituted "January 1, 2010" for "January 1, 2009" in subpara. (n)(2)(C)

Effective Date (Sec. 1201(c)(1), P.L. 111-5, 2/17/2009) effective for property placed in service after 12/31/2008, in tax. yrs. end. after such date.

[¶ 3049]   Code Sec. 172.   Net operating loss deduction.

* * * * * * * * * * * *

(b)   Net operating loss carrybacks and carryovers.

   (1)   Years to which loss may be carried.

      (A) General rule. Except as otherwise provided in this paragraph, a net operating loss for any taxable year—

         (i) shall be a net operating loss carryback to each of the 2 taxable years preceding the taxable year of such loss, and

         (ii) shall be a net operating loss carryover to each of the 20 taxable years following the taxable year of the loss.

      (B) Special rules for REIT's.

         (i) In general. A net operating loss for a REIT year shall not be a net operating loss carryback to any taxable year preceding the taxable year of such loss.

         (ii) Special rule. In the case of any net operating loss for a taxable year which is not a REIT year, such loss shall not be carried back to any taxable year which is a REIT year.

         (iii) REIT year. For purposes of this subparagraph, the term "REIT year" means any taxable year for which the provisions of part II of subchapter M (relating to real estate investment trusts) apply to the taxpayer.

      (C) Specified liability losses. In the case of a taxpayer which has a specified liability loss (as defined in subsection (f)) for a taxable year, such specified liability loss shall be a net operating loss carryback to each of the 10 taxable years preceding the taxable year of such loss.

      (D) Bad debt losses of commercial banks. In the case of any bank (as defined in section 585(a)(2)), the portion of the net operating loss for any taxable year beginning after December 31, 1986, and before January 1, 1994, which is attributable to the deduction allowed under section 166(a) shall be a net operating loss carryback to each of the 10 taxable years preceding the taxable year of the loss and a net operating loss carryover to each of the 5 taxable years following the taxable year of such loss.

      (E) Excess interest loss.

(i) In general. If—

(I) there is a corporate equity reduction transaction, and

(II) an applicable corporation has a corporate equity reduction interest loss for any loss limitation year ending after August 2, 1989,

then the corporate equity reduction interest loss shall be a net operating loss carryback and carryover to the taxable years described in subparagraph (A), except that such loss shall not be carried back to a taxable year preceding the taxable year in which the corporate equity reduction transaction occurs.

(ii) Loss limitation year. For purposes of clause (i) and subsection (h), the term "loss limitation year" means, with respect to any corporate equity reduction transaction, the taxable year in which such transaction occurs and each of the 2 succeeding taxable years.

(iii) Applicable corporation. For purposes of clause (i), the term "applicable corporation" means—

(I) a C corporation which acquires stock, or the stock of which is acquired in a major stock acquisition,

(II) a C corporation making distributions with respect to, or redeeming, its stock in connection with an excess distribution, or

(III) a C corporation which is a successor of a corporation described in subclause (I) or (II).

(iv) Other definitions.

For definitions of terms used in this subparagraph, see subsection (h).

(F) Retention of 3-year carryback in certain cases.

(i) In general. Subparagraph (A)(i) shall be applied by substituting "3 taxable years" for "2 taxable years" with respect to the portion of the net operating loss for the taxable year which is an eligible loss with respect to the taxpayer.

(ii) Eligible loss. For purposes of clause (i), the term "eligible loss" means—

(I) in the case of an individual, losses of property arising from fire, storm, shipwreck, or other casualty, or from theft,

(II) in the case of a taxpayer which is a small business, net operating losses attributable to federally declared disasters (as defined by subsection (h)(3)(C)(i)), and

(III) in the case of a taxpayer engaged in the trade or business of farming (as defined in section 263A(e)(4)), net operating losses attributable to such federally declared disasters.

Such term shall not include any farming loss (as defined in subsection (i)) or or qualified disaster loss (as defined in subsection (j)).

(iii) Small business. For purposes of this subparagraph, the term "small business" means a corporation or partnership which meets the gross receipts test of section 448(c) for the taxable year in which the loss arose (or, in the case of a sole proprietorship, which would meet such test if such proprietorship were a corporation).

(iv) Coordination with paragraph (2). For purposes of applying paragraph (2), an eligible loss for any taxable year shall be treated in a manner similar to the manner in which a specified liability loss is treated.

(G) Farming losses. In the case of a taxpayer which has a farming loss (as defined in subsection (i)) for a taxable year, such farming loss shall be a net operating loss carryback to each of the 5 taxable years preceding the taxable year of such loss.

(H) ¹*Carryback for 2008 net operating losses of small businesses.*

(i) In general. If an eligible small business elects the application of this subparagraph with respect to an applicable 2008 net operating loss—

(I) subparagraph (A)(i) shall be applied by substituting any whole number elected by the taxpayer which is more than 2 and less than 6 for "2",

(II) subparagraph (E)(ii) shall be applied by substituting the whole number which is one less than the whole number substituted under subclause (I) for "2", and

(III) subparagraph (F) shall not apply.

(ii) Applicable 2008 net operating loss. For purposes of this subparagraph, the term "applicable 2008 net operating loss" means—

    (I) the taxpayer's net operating loss for any taxable year ending in 2008, or

    (II) if the taxpayer elects to have this subclause apply in lieu of subclause (I), the taxpayer's net operating loss for any taxable year beginning in 2008.

(iii) Election. Any election under this subparagraph shall be made in such manner as may be prescribed by the Secretary, and shall be made by the due date (including extension of time) for filing the taxpayer's return for the taxable year of the net operating loss. Any such election, once made, shall be irrevocable. Any election under this subparagraph may be made only with respect to 1 taxable year.

(iv) Eligible small business. For purposes of this subparagraph, the term "eligible small business" has the meaning given such term by subparagraph (F)(iii), except that in applying such subparagraph, section 448(c) shall be applied by substituting "$15,000,000" for "$5,000,000" each place it appears.

(I) Transmission property and pollution control investment.

    (i) In general. At the election of the taxpayer for any taxable year ending after December 31, 2005, and before January 1, 2009, in the case of a net operating loss for a taxable year ending after December 31, 2002, and before January 1, 2006, there shall be a net operating loss carryback to each of the 5 taxable years preceding the taxable year of such loss to the extent that such loss does not exceed 20 percent of the sum of the electric transmission property capital expenditures and the pollution control facility capital expenditures of the taxpayer for the taxable year preceding the taxable year for which such election is made.

    (ii) Limitations. For purposes of this subsection—

        (I) not more than one election may be made under clause (i) with respect to any net operating loss for a taxable year, and

        (II) an election may not be made under clause (i) for more than 1 taxable year beginning in any calendar year.

    (iii) Coordination with ordering rule. For purposes of applying subsection (b)(2), the portion of any loss which is carried back 5 years by reason of clause (i) shall be treated in a manner similar to the manner in which a specified liability loss is treated.

    (iv) Special rules relating to credit or refund. In the case of the portion of the loss which is carried back 5 years by reason of clause (i)—

        (I) an application under section 6411(a) with respect to such portion shall not fail to be treated as timely filed if filed within 24 months after the due date specified under such section, and

        (II) references in sections 6501(h), 6511(d)(2)(A), and 6611(f)(1) to the taxable year in which such net operating loss arises or results in a net operating loss carryback shall be treated as references to the taxable year for which such election is made.

    (v) Definitions. For purposes of this subparagraph—

        (I) Electric transmission property capital expenditures. The term "electric transmission property capital expenditures" means any expenditure, chargeable to capital account, made by the taxpayer which is attributable to electric transmission property used by the taxpayer in the transmission at 69 or more kilovolts of electricity for sale. Such term shall not include any expenditure which may be refunded or the purpose of which may be modified at the option of the taxpayer so as to cease to be treated as an expenditure within the meaning of such term.

        (II) Pollution control facility capital expenditures. The term "pollution control facility capital expenditures" means any expenditure, chargeable to capital account, made by an electric utility company (as defined in section 2(3) of the Public Utility Holding Company Act (15 U.S.C. 79b(3)), as in effect on the day before the date of the enactment of the Energy Tax Incentives Act of 2005) which is attributable to a facility which will qualify as a certified pollution control facility as determined under section 169(d)(1) by striking "before January 1, 1976," and by substituting "an identifiable" for "a new identifiable". Such term shall not include any expenditure which may be refunded or the purpose of which may be modified at the option of the taxpayer so as to cease to be treated as an expenditure within the meaning of such term.

(J) Certain losses attributable federally declared disasters. In the case of a taxpayer who has a qualified disaster loss (as defined in subsection (j)), such loss shall be a net operating loss carryback to each of the 5 taxable years preceding the taxable year of such loss.

(2) Amount of carrybacks and carryovers. The entire amount of the net operating loss for any taxable year (hereinafter in this section referred to as the "loss year") shall be carried to the earliest of the taxable years to which (by reason of paragraph (1)) such loss may be carried. The portion of such loss which shall be carried to each of the other taxable years shall be the excess, if any, of the amount of such loss over the sum of the taxable income for each of the prior taxable years to which such loss may be carried. For purposes of the preceding sentence, the taxable income for any such prior taxable year shall be computed—

(A) with the modifications specified in subsection (d) other than paragraphs (1), (4), and (5) thereof, and

(B) by determining the amount of the net operating loss deduction without regard to the net operating loss for the loss year or for any taxable year thereafter,

and the taxable income so computed shall not be considered to be less than zero.

(3) Election to waive carryback. Any taxpayer entitled to a carryback period under paragraph (1) may elect to relinquish the entire carryback period with respect to a net operating loss for any taxable year. Such election shall be made in such manner as may be prescribed by the Secretary, and shall be made by the due date (including extensions of time) for filing the taxpayer's return for the taxable year of the net operating loss for which the election is to be in effect. Such election, once made for any taxable year, shall be irrevocable for such taxable year.

* * * * * * * * * * * *

²**(k)** Cross references.

(1) For treatment of net operating loss carryovers in certain corporate acquisitions, see section 381.

(2) For special limitation on net operating loss carryovers in case of a corporate change of ownership, see section 382.

[For Analysis, see ¶ 601. For Committee Reports, see ¶ 5037.]

[Endnote Code Sec. 172]

Code Sec. 172(b)(1)(H), Code Sec. 172(k) and Code Sec. 172(l) was amended by Secs. 1211(a) and (b) of The American Recovery and Reinvestment Act of 2009, P.L. 111-5, 2/17/2009, as detailed below:

1. Sec. 1211(a) amended subpara. (b)(1)(H)

Prior to amendment subpara. (b)(1)(H) read as follows:

"(H) In the case of a net operating loss for any taxable year ending during 2001 or 2002, subparagraph (A)(i) shall be applied by substituting '5' for '2' and subparagraph (F) shall not apply."

2. Sec. 1211(b) deleted (k) and redesignated subsec. (l) as (k)

Prior to deletion, subsec. (k, read as follows:

"(k) Election to disregard 5-year carryback for certain net operating losses

"Any taxpayer entitled to a 5-year carryback under subsection (b)(1)(H) from any loss year may elect to have the carryback period with respect to such loss year determined without regard to subsection (b)(1)(H). Such election shall be made in such manner as may be prescribed by the Secretary and shall be made by the due date (including extensions of time) for filing the taxpayer's return for the taxable year of the net operating loss. Such election, once made for any taxable year, shall be irrevocable for such taxable year."

Effective Date (Sec. 1211(d) P.L. 111-5, 2/17/2009) effective for net operating losses arising in tax. yrs. end. after 12/31/2007.

[¶ 3050]   Code Sec. 179.   **Election to expense certain depreciable business assets.**

* * * * * * * * * * * *

(b) Limitations.

(1) Dollar limitation. The aggregate cost which may be taken into account under subsection (a) for any taxable year shall not exceed $25,000 ($125,000 in the case of taxable years beginning after 2006 and before 2011).

(2) Reduction in limitation. The limitation under paragraph (1) for any taxable year shall be reduced (but not below zero) by the amount by which the cost of section 179 property placed in service during such taxable year exceeds $200,000 ($500,000 in the case of taxable years beginning after 2006 and before 2011).

(3) Limitation based on income from trade or business.

(A) In general. The amount allowed as a deduction under subsection (a) for any taxable year (determined after the application of paragraphs (1) and (2)) shall not exceed the aggregate amount of taxable income of the taxpayer for such taxable year which is derived from the active conduct by the taxpayer of any trade or business during such taxable year.

(B) Carryover of disallowed deduction. The amount allowable as a deduction under subsection (a) for any taxable year shall be increased by the lesser of

(i) the aggregate amount disallowed under subparagraph (A) for all prior taxable years (to the extent not previously allowed as a deduction by reason of this subparagraph), or

(ii) the excess (if any) of—

(I) the limitation of paragraphs (1) and (2) (or if lesser, the aggregate amount of taxable income referred to in subparagraph (A)), over

(II) the amount allowable as a deduction under subsection (a) for such taxable year without regard to this subparagraph.

(C) Computation of taxable income. For purposes of this paragraph, taxable income derived from the conduct of a trade or business shall be computed without regard to the deduction allowable under this section.

(4) Married individuals filing separately. In the case of a husband and wife filing separate returns for the taxable year—

(A) such individuals shall be treated as 1 taxpayer for purposes of paragraphs (1) and (2), and

(B) unless such individuals elect otherwise, 50 percent of the cost which may be taken into account under subsection (a) for such taxable year (before application of paragraph (3)) shall be allocated to each such individual.

(5) Inflation adjustments.

(A) In general. In the case of any taxable year beginning in a calendar year after 2007 and before 2011, the $125,000 and $500,000 amounts in paragraphs (1) and (2) shall each be increased by an amount equal to—

(i) such dollar amount, multiplied by

(ii) the cost-of-living adjustment determined under section 1(f)(3) for the calendar year in which the taxable year begins, by substituting "calendar year 2006" for "calendar year 1992" in subparagraph (B) thereof.

(B) Rounding.

(i) Dollar limitation. If the amount in paragraph (1) as increased under subparagraph (A) is not a multiple of $1,000, such amount shall be rounded to the nearest multiple of $1,000.

(ii) Phaseout amount. If the amount in paragraph (2) as increased under subparagraph (A) is not a multiple of $10,000, such amount shall be rounded to the nearest multiple of $10,000.

(6) Limitation on cost taken into account for certain passenger vehicles.

(A) In general. The cost of any sport utility vehicle for any taxable year which may be taken into account under this section shall not exceed $25,000.

(B) Sport utility vehicle. For purposes of subparagraph (A)—

(i) In general. The term "sport utility vehicle" means any 4-wheeled vehicle—

(I) which is primarily designed or which can be used to carry passengers over public streets, roads, or highways (except any vehicle operated exclusively on a rail or rails),

(II) which is not subject to section 280F, and

(III) which is rated at not more than 14,000 pounds gross vehicle weight.

(ii) Certain vehicles excluded. Such term does not include any vehicle which—

(I) is designed to have a seating capacity of more than 9 persons behind the driver's seat,

(II) is equipped with a cargo area of at least 6 feet in interior length which is an open area or is designed for use as an open area but is enclosed by a cap and is not readily accessible directly from the passenger compartment, or

(III) has an integral enclosure, fully enclosing the driver compartment and load carrying device, does not have seating rearward of the driver's seat, and has no body section protruding more than 30 inches ahead of the leading edge of the windshield.

(7) Increase in limitations for ¹*2008, and 2009.* In the case of any taxable year beginning in ²*2008, or 2009—*

(A) the dollar limitation under paragraph (1) shall be $250,000,

(B) the dollar limitation under paragraph (2) shall be $800,000, and

(C) the amounts described in subparagraphs (A) and (B) shall not be adjusted under paragraph (5).

* * * * * * * * * * * *

[For Analysis, see ¶ 802. For Committee Reports, see ¶ 5035.]

[Endnote Code Sec. 179]

Code Sec. 179(b)(7) was amended by Secs. 1202(a)(1) and (2) of The American Recovery and Reinvestment Act of 2009, P.L. 111-5, 2/17/2009, as detailed below:

1. Sec. 1202(a)(1) substituted '2008, or 2009' for '2008' in para. (b)(7)

2. Sec. 1202(a)(2) substituted '2008, and 2009' for '2008' in the heading of para. (b)(7)

Effective Date (Sec. 1202(b) P.L. 111-5, 2/17/2009) effective for tax. yrs. begin. after 12/31/2008.

[¶ 3051]   Code Sec. 265.   Expenses and interest relating to tax-exempt income.

* * * * * * * * * * * *

(b) Pro rata allocation of interest expense of financial institutions to tax-exempt interest.

(1) In general. In the case of a financial institution, no deduction shall be allowed for that portion of the taxpayer's interest expense which is allocable to tax-exempt interest.

(2) Allocation. For purposes of paragraph (1), the portion of the taxpayer's interest expense which is allocable to tax-exempt interest is an amount which bears the same ratio to such interest expense as—

(A) the taxpayer's average adjusted bases (within the meaning of section 1016) of tax-exempt obligations acquired after August 7, 1986, bears to

(B) such average adjusted bases for all assets of the taxpayer.

(3) Exception for certain tax-exempt obligations.

(A) In general. Any qualified tax-exempt obligation acquired after August 7, 1986, shall be treated for purposes of paragraph (2) and section 291(e)(1)(B) as if it were acquired on August 7, 1986.

(B) Qualified tax-exempt obligation.

(i) In general. For purposes of subparagraph (A), the term "qualified tax-exempt obligation" means a tax-exempt obligation—

(I) which is issued after August 7, 1986, by a qualified small issuer,

(II) which is not a private activity bond (as defined in section 141), and

(III) which is designated by the issuer for purposes of this paragraph.

(ii) Certain bonds not treated as private activity bonds. For purposes of clause (i)(II), there shall not be treated as a private activity bond—

(I) any qualified 501(c)(3) bond (as defined in section 145), or

(II) any obligation issued to refund (or which is part of a series of obligations issued to refund) an obligation issued before August 8, 1986, which was not an industrial development bond (as defined in section 103(b)(2) as in effect on the day before the date of the enactment [10/22/86] of the Tax Reform Act of 1986) or a private loan bond (as defined in section 103(o)(2)(A), as so in effect, but without regard to any exemption from such definition other than section 103(o)(2)(A)).

(C) Qualified small issuer.

(i) In general. For purposes of subparagraph (B), the term "qualified small issuer" means, with respect to obligations issued during any calendar year, any issuer if the reasonably anticipated amount of tax-exempt obligations (other than obligations described in clause (ii)) which will be issued by such issuer during such calendar year does not exceed $10,000,000.

(ii) Obligations not taken into account in determining status as qualified small issuer. For purposes of clause (i), an obligation is described in this clause if such obligation is—

(I) a private activity bond (other than a qualified 501(c)(3) bond, as defined in section 145),

(II) an obligation to which section 141(a) does not apply by reason of section 1312, 1313, 1316(g), or 1317 of the Tax Reform Act of 1986 and which would (if issued on August 15, 1986) have been an industrial development bond (as defined in section 103(b)(2) as in effect on the day before the date of the enactment of such Act) or a private loan bond (as defined in section 103(o)(2)(A), as so in effect, but without regard to any exception from such definition other than section 103(o)(2)(A)), or

(III) an obligation issued to refund (other than to advance refund within the meaning of section 149(d)(5)) any obligation to the extent the amount of the refunding obligation does not exceed the outstanding amount of the refunded obligation.

(iii) Allocation of amount of issue in certain cases. In the case of an issue under which more than 1 governmental entity receives benefits, if—

(I) all governmental entities receiving benefits from such issue irrevocably agree (before the date of issuance of the issue) on an allocation of the amount of such issue for purposes of this subparagraph, and

(II) such allocation bears a reasonable relationship to the respective benefits received by such entities,

then the amount of such issue so allocated to an entity (and only such amount with respect to such issue) shall be taken into account under clause (i) with respect to such entity.

(D) Limitation on amount of obligations which may be designated.

(i) In general. Not more than $10,000,000 of obligations issued by an issuer during any calendar year may be designated by such issuer for purposes of this paragraph.

(ii) Certain refundings of designated obligations deemed designated.—Except as provided in clause (iii), in the case of a refunding (or series of refundings) of a qualified tax-exempt obligation, the refunding obligation shall be treated as a qualified tax-exempt obligation (and shall not be taken into account under clause (i)) if—

(I) the refunding obligation was not taken into account under subparagraph (C) by reason of clause (ii)(III) thereof,

(II) the average maturity date of the refunding obligations issued as part of the issue of which such refunding obligation is a part is not later than the average maturity date of the obligations to be refunded by such issue, and

(III) the refunding obligation has a maturity date which is not later than the date which is 30 years after the date the original qualified tax-exempt obligation was issued.

Subclause (II) shall not apply if the average maturity of the issue of which the original qualified tax-exempt obligation was a part (and of the issue of which the obligations to be refunded are a part) is 3 years or less. For purposes of this clause, average maturity shall be determined in accordance with section 147(b)(2)(A).

(iii) Certain obligations may not be designated or deemed designated. No obligation issued as part of an issue may be designated under this paragraph (or may be treated as designated under clause (ii)) if—

(I) any obligation issued as part of such issue is issued to refund another obligation, and

(II) the aggregate face amount of such issue exceeds $10,000,000.

(E) Aggregation of issuers. For purposes of subparagraphs (C) and (D)—

(i) an issuer and all entities which issue obligations on behalf of such issuer shall be treated as 1 issuer,

(ii) all obligations issued by a subordinate entity shall, for purposes of applying subparagraphs (C) and (D) to each other entity to which such entity is subordinate, be treated as issued by such other entity, and

(iii) an entity formed (or, to the extent provided by the Secretary, availed of) to avoid the purposes of subparagraph (C) or (D) and all entities benefiting thereby shall be treated as 1 issuer.

(F) Treatment of composite issues. In the case of an obligation which is issued as part of a direct or indirect composite issue, such obligation shall not be treated as a qualified tax-exempt obligation unless—

(i) the requirements of this paragraph are met with respect to such composite issue (determined by treating such composite issue as a single issue), and

(ii) the requirements of this paragraph are met with respect to each separate lot of obligations which are part of the issue (determined by treating each such separate lot as a separate issue).

[1](G) Special rules for obligations issued during 2009 and 2010.

(i) Increase in limitation. In the case of obligations issued during 2009 or 2010, subparagraphs (C)(i), (D)(i), and (D)(iii)(II) shall each be applied by substituting "$30,000,000" for "$10,000,000".

(ii) Qualified 501(c)(3) bonds treated as issued by exempt organization. In the case of a qualified 501(c)(3) bond (as defined in section 145) issued during 2009 or 2010, this paragraph shall be applied by treating the 501(c)(3) organization for whose benefit such bond was issued as the issuer.

(iii) Special rule for qualified financings. In the case of a qualified financing issue issued during 2009 or 2010—

(I) subparagraph (F) shall not apply, and

(II) any obligation issued as a part of such issue shall be treated as a qualified tax-exempt obligation if the requirements of this paragraph are met with respect to each qualified portion of the issue (determined by treating each qualified portion as a separate issue which is issued by the qualified borrower with respect to which such portion relates).

(iv) Qualified financing issue. For purposes of this subparagraph, the term "qualified financing issue" means any composite, pooled, or other conduit financing issue the proceeds of which are used directly or indirectly to make or finance loans to 1 or more ultimate borrowers each of whom is a qualified borrower.

(v) Qualified portion. For purposes of this subparagraph, the term "qualified portion" means that portion of the proceeds which are used with respect to each qualified borrower under the issue.

(vi) Qualified borrower. For purposes of this subparagraph, the term "qualified borrower" means a borrower which is a State or political subdivision thereof or an organization described in section 501(c)(3) and exempt from taxation under section 501(a).

(4) Definitions. For purposes of this subsection—

(A) Interest expense. The term "interest expense" means the aggregate amount allowable to the taxpayer as a deduction for interest for the taxable year (determined without regard to this subsection, section 264, and section 291). For purposes of the preceding sentence, the term "interest" includes amounts (whether or not designated as interest) paid in respect of deposits, investment certificates, or withdrawable or repurchasable shares.

(B) Tax-exempt obligation. The term "tax-exempt obligation" means any obligation the interest on which is wholly exempt from taxes imposed by this subtitle. Such term includes shares of stock of a regulated investment company which during the taxable year of the holder thereof distributes exempt-interest dividends.

(5) Financial institution. For purposes of this subsection, the term "financial institution" means any person who—

(A) accepts deposits from the public in the ordinary course of such person's trade or business, and is subject to Federal or State supervision as a financial institution, or

(B) is a corporation described in section 585(a)(2).

(6) Special rules.

(A) Coordination with subsection (a). If interest on any indebtedness is disallowed under subsection (a) with respect to any tax-exempt obligation—

(i) such disallowed interest shall not be taken into account for purposes of applying this subsection, and

(ii) for purposes of applying paragraph (2), the adjusted basis of such tax-exempt obligation shall be reduced (but not below zero) by the amount of such indebtedness.

(B) Coordination with section 263A. This section shall be applied before the application of section 263A (relating to capitalization of certain expenses where taxpayer produces property).

²*(7) De minimis exception for bonds issued during 2009 or 2010.*

(A) In general. In applying paragraph (2)(A), there shall not be taken into account tax-exempt obligations issued during 2009 or 2010.

(B) Limitation. The amount of tax-exempt obligations not taken into account by reason of subparagraph (A) shall not exceed 2 percent of the amount determined under paragraph (2)(B).

(C) Refundings. For purposes of this paragraph, a refunding bond (whether a current or advance refunding) shall be treated as issued on the date of the issuance of the refunded bond (or in the case of a series of refundings, the original bond).

[For Analysis, see ¶ 1309. For Committee Reports, see ¶ 5060.]

[Endnote Code Sec. 265]

Code Sec. 265(b)(3)(G) was added by Sec. 1502(a) of The American Recovery and Reinvestment Act of 2009, P.L. 111-5, 2/17/2009, as detailed below:

1. Sec. 1502(a) added subpara. (b)(3)(G)

Effective Date (Sec. 1502(b), P.L. 111-5, 2/17/2009) effective for obligations issued after 12/31/2008.

Code Sec. 265(b)(7) was added by Sec. 1501(a), P.L. 111-5, 2/17/2009, as detailed below:

2. Sec. 1501(a) added para. (b)(7)

Effective Date (Sec. 1501(c), P.L. 111-5, 2/17/2009) effective for obligations issued after 12/31/2008.

[¶ 3052]   **Code Sec. 291.**   **Special rules relating to corporate preference items.**

* * * * * * * * * * * *

(e) Definitions. For purposes of this section—

(1) Financial institution preference item. The term "financial institution preference item" includes the following:

(A) Repealed.

(B) Interest on debt to carry tax-exempt obligations acquired after December 31, 1982, and before August 8, 1986.

(i) In general. In the case of a financial institution which is a bank (as defined in section 585(a)(2)) , the amount of interest on indebtedness incurred or continued to purchase or carry obligations acquired after December 31, 1982, and before August 8, 1986, the interest on which is exempt from taxes for the taxable year, to the extent that a deduction would (but for this paragraph or section 265(b)) be allowable with respect to such interest for such taxable year.

(ii) Determination of interest allocable to indebtedness on tax-exempt obligations. Unless the taxpayer (under regulations prescribed by the Secretary) establishes otherwise, the amount determined under clause (i) shall be an amount which bears the same ratio to the aggregate amount allowable (determined without regard to this section and section 265(b)) to the taxpayer as a deduction for interest for the taxable year as —

(I) the taxpayer's average adjusted basis (within the meaning of section 1016) of obligations described in clause (i), bears to

(II) such average adjusted basis for all assets of the taxpayer.

(iii) Interest. For purposes of this subparagraph, the term "interest" includes amounts (whether or not designated as interest) paid in respect of deposits, investment certificates, or withdrawable or repurchasable shares.

(iv) Application of subparagraph to certain obligations issued after August 7, 1986. For application of this subparagraph to certain obligations issued after August 7, 1986, see section 265(b)(3). [1]*That portion of any obligation not taken into account under paragraph (2)(A) of section 265(b) by reason of paragraph (7) of such section shall be treated for purposes of this section as having been acquired on August 7, 1986.*

(2) **Section 1245 and 1250 property.** The terms "section 1245 property" and "section 1250 property" have the meanings given such terms by sections 1245(a)(3) and 1250(c), respectively.

[For Analysis, see ¶ 1309. For Committee Reports, see ¶ 5060.]

[Endnote Code Sec. 291]

Code Sec. 291(e)(1)(B)(iv) was amended by Sec. 1501(b) of The American Recovery and Reinvestment Act of 2009, P.L. 111-5, 2/17/2009, as detailed below:

1. Sec. 1501(b) added "That portion of any obligation not taken into account under paragraph (2)(A) of section 265(b) by reason of paragraph (7) of such section shall be treated for purposes of this section as having been acquired on August 7, 1986." at the end of clause (e)(1)(B)(iv).

Effective Date (Sec. 1501(c), P.L. 111-5, 2/17/2009) effective for obligations issued after 12/31/2008.

[¶ 3053]　　Code Sec. 382.　　Limitation on net operating loss carryforwards and certain built-in losses following ownership change.

* * * * * * * * * * * *

[1]*(n)　Special rule for certain ownership changes.*

(1)　In general. The limitation contained in subsection (a) shall not apply in the case of an ownership change which is pursuant to a restructuring plan of a taxpayer which —

(A) is required under a loan agreement or a commitment for a line of credit entered into with the Department of the Treasury under the Emergency Economic Stabilization Act of 2008, and

(B) is intended to result in a rationalization of the costs, capitalization, and capacity with respect to the manufacturing workforce of, and suppliers to, the taxpayer and its subsidiaries.

(2)　Subsequent acquisitions. Paragraph (1) shall not apply in the case of any subsequent ownership change unless such ownership change is described in such paragraph.

505

(3) Limitation based on control in corporation.

(A) *In general. Paragraph (1) shall not apply in the case of any ownership change if, immediately after such ownership change, any person (other than a voluntary employees' beneficiary association under section 501(c)(9)) owns stock of the old loss corporation possessing 50 percent or more of the total combined voting power of all classes of stock entitled to vote, or of the total value of the stock of such corporation.*

(B) *Treatment of related persons.*

(i) *In general. Related persons shall be treated as a single person for purposes of this paragraph.*

(ii) *Related persons. For purposes of clause (i), a person shall be treated as related to another person if—*

(I) *such person bears a relationship to such other person described in section 267(b) or 707(b), or*

(II) *such persons are members of a group of persons acting in concert.*

[For Analysis, see ¶ 602 and ¶ 603. For Committee Reports, see ¶ 5048 and ¶ 5049.]

[Endnote Code Sec. 382]

Code Sec. 382(n) was added by Sec. 1262(a) of The American Recovery and Reinvestment Act of 2009, P.L. 111-5, 2/17/2009, as detailed below:

1. Sec. 1262(a) added subsec. (n).

Effective Date (Sec. 1262(b), P.L. 111-5, 2/17/2009) effective for ownership changes after 2/17/2009. Sec. 1261, of this Act, provides:

"Sec. 1261. Clarification of regulations related to limitations on certain built-in losses following an ownership change.

"(a) Findings. Congress finds as follows:

"(1) The delegation of authority to the Secretary of the Treasury under section 382(m) of the Internal Revenue Code of 1986 does not authorize the Secretary to provide exemptions or special rules that are restricted to particular industries or classes of taxpayers.

"(2) Internal Revenue Service Notice 2008-83 is inconsistent with the congressional intent in enacting such section 382(m).

"(3) The legal authority to prescribe Internal Revenue Service Notice 2008-83 is doubtful.

"(4) However, as taxpayers should generally be able to rely on guidance issued by the Secretary of the Treasury legislation is necessary to clarify the force and effect of Internal Revenue Service Notice 2008-83 and restore the proper application under the Internal Revenue Code of 1986 of the limitation on built-in losses following an ownership change of a bank.

"(b) Determination of force and effect of internal revenue service notice 2008-83 exempting banks from limitation on certain built-in losses following ownership change.

"(1) In general. Internal Revenue Service Notice 2008-83—

"(A) shall be deemed to have the force and effect of law with respect to any ownership change (as defined in section 382(g) of the Internal Revenue Code of 1986) occurring on or before January 16, 2009, and

"(B) shall have no force or effect with respect to any ownership change after such date.

"(2) Binding contracts. Notwithstanding paragraph (1), Internal Revenue Service Notice 2008-83 shall have the force and effect of law with respect to any ownership change (as so defined) which occurs after January 16, 2009, if such change—

"(A) is pursuant to a written binding contract entered into on or before such date, or

"(B) is pursuant to a written agreement entered into on or before such date and such agreement was described on or before such date in a public announcement or in a filing with the Securities and Exchange Commission required by reason of such ownership change."

[¶ 3054]   Code Sec. 529.   Qualified tuition programs.

* * * * * * * * * * * *

(e) Other definitions and special rules. For purposes of this section—

(1) Designated beneficiary. The term "designated beneficiary" means—

(A) the individual designated at the commencement of participation in the qualified tuition program as the beneficiary of amounts paid (or to be paid) to the program,

(B) in the case of a change in beneficiaries described in subsection (c)(3)(C), the individual who is the new beneficiary, and

(C) in the case of an interest in a qualified tuition program purchased by a State or local government (or agency or instrumentality thereof) or an organization described in section 501(c)(3) and exempt from taxation under section 501(a) as part of a scholarship program operated by such government or organization, the individual receiving such interest as a scholarship.

(2) Member of family. The term "member of the family" means, with respect to any designated beneficiary—

(A) the spouse of such beneficiary;

(B) an individual who bears a relationship to such beneficiary which is described in subparagraphs (A) through (G) of section 152(d)(2);

(C) the spouse of any individual described in subparagraph (B); and

(D) any first cousin of such beneficiary.

(3) Qualified higher education expenses.

(A) In general. The term "qualified higher education expenses" means—

(i) tuition, fees, books, supplies, and equipment required for the enrollment or attendance of a designated beneficiary at an eligible educational institution; [1]

(ii) expenses for special needs services in the case of a special needs beneficiary which are incurred in connection with such enrollment or attendance[2]

[3]*(iii) expenses paid or incurred in 2009 or 2010 for the purchase of any computer technology or equipment (as defined in section 170(e)(6)(F)(i)) or Internet access and related services, if such technology, equipment, or services are to be used by the beneficiary and the beneficiary's family during any of the years the beneficiary is enrolled at an eligible educational institution.*

Clause (iii) shall not include expenses for computer software designed for sports, games, or hobbies unless the software is predominantly educational in nature.

(B) Room and board included for students who are at least half-time.

(i) In general. In the case of an individual who is an eligible student (as defined in section 25A(b)(3)) for any academic period, such term shall also include reasonable costs for such period (as determined under the qualified tuition program) incurred by the designated beneficiary for room and board while attending such institution. For purposes of subsection (b)(6), a designated beneficiary shall be treated as meeting the requirements of this clause.

(ii) Limitation. The amount treated as qualified higher education expenses by reason of clause (i) shall not exceed—

(I) the allowance (applicable to the student) for room and board included in the cost of attendance (as defined in section 472 of the Higher Education Act of 1965 (20 U.S.C. 1087ll), as in effect on the date of the enactment [6/7/2001] of the Economic Growth and Tax Relief Reconciliation Act of 2001) as determined by the eligible educational institution for such period, or

(II) if greater, the actual invoice amount the student residing in housing owned or operated by the eligible educational institution is charged by such institution for room and board costs for such period.

(4) Application of section 514. An interest in a qualified tuition program shall not be treated as debt for purposes of section 514.

(5) Eligible educational institution. The term "eligible educational institution" means an institution—

(A) which is described in section 481 of the Higher Education Act of 1965 (20 U.S.C. 1088), as in effect on the date of the enactment [6/7/2001] of this paragraph, and

(B) which is eligible to participate in a program under title IV of such Act.

(f) Regulations. Notwithstanding any other provision of this section, the Secretary shall prescribe such regulations as may be necessary or appropriate to carry out the purposes of this section and to prevent abuse of such purposes, including regulations under chapters 11, 12, and 13 of this title.

[For Analysis, see ¶ 108. For Committee Reports, see ¶ 5005.]

[Endnote Code Sec. 529]

Code Sec. 529(e)(3)(A), Code Sec. 529(e)(3)(A)(i), Code Sec. 529(e)(3)(A)(ii), Code Sec. 529(e)(3)(A)(iii) was amended by Sec. 1005(a) of The American Recovery and Reinvestment Act of 2009, P.L. 111-5, 2/17/2009, as detailed below:

1. Sec. 1005(a) deleted "and" at the end of subpara. (e)(3)(A)(i),
2. Sec. 1005(a) deleted the period at the end of subpara. (e)(3)(A)(ii)
3. Sec. 1005(a) added clause (e)(3)(A)(iii)

Effective Date (Sec. 1005(b) P.L. 111-5, 2/17/2009) effective for expenses paid or incurred after 12/31/2008.

[¶ 3055]   Code Sec.[1] 853A.   *Credits from tax credit bonds allowed to shareholders.*

(a) General rule. A regulated investment company—

(1) which holds (directly or indirectly) one or more tax credit bonds on one or more applicable dates during the taxable year, and

(2) which meets the requirements of section 852(a) for the taxable year,

may elect the application of this section with respect to credits allowable to the investment company during such taxable year with respect to such bonds.

(b) Effect of election. If the election provided in subsection (a) is in effect for any taxable year—

(1) the regulated investment company shall not be allowed any credits to which subsection (a) applies for such taxable year,

(2) the regulated investment company shall—

(A) include in gross income (as interest) for such taxable year an amount equal to the amount that such investment company would have included in gross income with respect to such credits if this section did not apply, and

(B) increase the amount of the dividends paid deduction for such taxable year by the amount of such income, and

(3) each shareholder of such investment company shall—

(A) include in gross income an amount equal to such shareholder's proportionate share of the interest income attributable to such credits, and

(B) be allowed the shareholder's proportionate share of such credits against the tax imposed by this chapter.

(c) Notice to shareholders. For purposes of subsection (b)(3), the shareholder's proportionate share of—

(1) credits described in subsection (a), and

(2) gross income in respect of such credits, shall not exceed the amounts so designated by the regulated investment company in a written notice mailed to its shareholders not later than 60 days after the close of its taxable year.

(d) Manner of making election and notifying shareholders. The election provided in subsection (a) and the notice to shareholders required by subsection (c) shall be made in such manner as the Secretary may prescribe.

(e) Definitions and special rules.

(1) Definitions. For purposes of this subsection—

(A) Tax credit bond. The term "tax credit bond" means—

(i) a qualified tax credit bond (as defined in section 54A(d)),

(ii) a build America bond (as defined in section 54AA(d)), and

(iii) any bond for which a credit is allowable under subpart H of part IV of subchapter A of this chapter.

(B) Applicable date. The term "applicable date" means—

(i) in the case of a qualified tax credit bond or a bond described in subparagraph (A)(iii), any credit allowance date (as defined in section 54A(e)(1)), and

    (ii) in the case of a build America bond (as defined in section 54AA(d)), any interest payment date (as defined in section 54AA(e)).

    (2)　Stripped tax credit bonds. *If the ownership of a tax credit bond is separated from the credit with respect to such bond, subsection (a) shall be applied by reference to the instruments evidencing the entitlement to the credit rather than the tax credit bond.*

    (f)　Regulations, etc. *The Secretary shall prescribe such regulations or other guidance as may be necessary or appropriate to carry out the purposes of this section, including methods for determining a shareholder's proportionate share of credits.*

    [For Analysis, see ¶ 1308. For Committee Reports, see ¶ 5072.]

[Endnote Code Sec. 853A]
    Code Sec. 853A was added by Sec. 1541(a) of The American Recovery and Reinvestment Act of 2009, P.L. 111-5, 2/17/2009, as detailed below:
    1. Sec. 1541(a) added Code Sec. 853A
Effective Date (Sec. 1541(c), P.L. 111-5, 2/17/2009) effective for tax. yrs end. after 2/17/2009.

[¶ 3056]　　Code Sec. 904.　　Limitation on credit.

* * * * * * * * * * * *

    (i)　Coordination with nonrefundable personal credits. In the case of any taxable year of an individual to which section 26(a)(2) does not apply, for purposes of subsection (a), the tax against which the credit is taken is such tax reduced by the sum of the credits allowable under subpart A of part IV of subchapter A of this chapter (other than sections 23, 24, [1]*25A(i)*, [2]25B, 30 [3]*30B*, and 30D).

* * * * * * * * * * * *

    [For Analysis, see ¶ 107, ¶ 204 and ¶ 205. For Committee Reports, see ¶ 5004, ¶ 5010 and ¶ 5027.]

[Endnote Code Sec. 904]
    Code Sec. 904(i) was amended by Sec. 1004(b)(5) of the American Recovery and Reinvestment Act of 2009, P.L. 111-5, 2/17/2009, as detailed below:
    1. Sec. 1004(b)(5) added "25A(i)," after "24," in subsec. (i)
Effective Date (Sec. 1004(d), P.L. 111-5, 2/17/2009) effective for tax. yrs. begin. after 12/31/2008.

    Code Sec. 904(i) was amended by Sec. 1142(b)(1)(E), P.L. 111-5, 2/17/2009, as detailed below:
    2. Sec. 1142(b)(1)(E) substituted "25B, 30, and 30D" for "and 25B" in subsec. (i) [as amended by Sec. 1004(b)(5) of this Act, see above]
Effective Date (Sec. 1142(c), P.L. 111-5, 2/17/2009) effective for vehicles acquired after 2/17/2009.

    Code Sec. 904(i) was amended by Sec. 1144(b)(1)(E), P.L. 111-5, 2/17/2009, as detailed below:
    3. Sec. 1144(b)(1)(E) added "30B," after "30" in subsec. (i) [as amended by Secs. 1004(b)(5) and 1142(b)(1)(E) of this Act, see above]
Effective Date (Sec. 1144(c), P.L. 111-5, 2/17/2009) effective for tax. yrs. begin. after 12/31/2008.

[¶ 3057]　　Code Sec. 1016.　　Adjustments to basis.

    (a)　General rule. Proper adjustment in respect of the property shall in all cases be made—

    (1) for expenditures, receipts, losses, or other items, properly chargeable to capital account, but no such adjustment shall be made—

    (A) for taxes or other carrying charges described in section 266, or

    (B) for expenditures described in section 173 (relating to circulation expenditures), for which deductions have been taken by the taxpayer in determining taxable income for the taxable year or prior taxable years;

    (2) in respect of any period since February 28, 1913, for exhaustion, wear and tear, obsolescence, amortization, and depletion, to the extent of the amount—

(A) allowed as deductions in computing taxable income under this subtitle or prior income tax laws, and

(B) resulting (by reason of the deductions so allowed) in a reduction for any taxable year of the taxpayer's taxes under this subtitle (other than chapter 2, relating to tax on self-employment income), or prior income, war-profits, or excess-profits tax laws,

but not less than the amount allowable under this subtitle or prior income tax laws. Where no method has been adopted under section 167 (relating to depreciation deduction), the amount allowable shall be determined under the straight line method. Subparagraph (B) of this paragraph shall not apply in respect of any period since February 28, 1913, and before January 1, 1952, unless an election has been made under section 1020 (as in effect before the date of the enactment of the Tax Reform Act of 1976). Where for any taxable year before the taxable year 1932 the depletion allowance was based on discovery value or a percentage of income, then the adjustment for depletion for such year shall be based on the depletion which would have been allowable for such year if computed without reference to discovery value or a percentage of income;

(3) in respect of any period—

(A) before March 1, 1913,

(B) since February 28, 1913, during which such property was held by a person or an organization not subject to income taxation under this chapter or prior income tax laws,

(C) since February 28, 1913, and before January 1, 1958, during which such property was held by a person subject to tax under part I of subchapter L (or the corresponding provisions of prior income tax laws), to the extent that paragraph (2) does not apply, and

(D) since February 28, 1913, during which such property was held by a person subject to tax under part II of subchapter L (or the corresponding provisions of prior income tax laws), to the extent that paragraph (2) does not apply,

for exhaustion, wear and tear, obsolescence, amortization, and depletion, to the extent sustained;

(4) in the case of stock (to the extent not provided for in the foregoing paragraphs) for the amount of distributions previously made which, under the law applicable to the year in which the distribution was made, either were tax-free or were applicable in reduction of basis (not including distributions made by a corporation which was classified as a personal service corporation under the provisions of the Revenue Act of 1918 (40 Stat. 1057), or the Revenue Act of 1921 (42 Stat. 227), out of its earnings or profits which were taxable in accordance with the provisions of section 218 of the Revenue Act of 1918 or 1921);

(5) in the case of any bond (as defined in section 171(d)) the interest on which is wholly exempt from the tax imposed by this subtitle, to the extent of the amortizable bond premium disallowable as a deduction pursuant to section 171(a)(2), and in the case of any other bond (as defined in section 171(d)) to the extent of the deductions allowable pursuant to section 171(a)(1) (or the amount applied to reduce interest payments under section 171(e)(2)) with respect thereto;

(6) in the case of any municipal bond (as defined in section 75(b)), to the extent provided in section 75(a)(2);

(7) in the case of a residence the acquisition of which resulted, under section 1034 (as in effect on the day before the date of enactment [8/5/97] of the Taxpayer Relief Act of 1997), in the nonrecognition of any part of the gain realized on the sale, exchange, or involuntary conversion of another residence, to the extent provided in section 1034(e) (as so in effect);

(8) in the case of property pledged to the Commodity Credit Corporation, to the extent of the amount received as a loan from the Commodity Credit Corporation and treated by the taxpayer as income for the year in which received pursuant to section 77, and to the extent of any deficiency on such loan with respect to which the taxpayer has been relieved from liability;

(9) for amounts allowed as deductions as deferred expenses under section 616(b) (relating to certain expenditures in the development of mines) and resulting in a reduction of the

taxpayer's taxes under this subtitle, but not less than the amounts allowable under such section for the taxable year and prior years;

(10) Repealed.

(11) for deductions to the extent disallowed under section 268 (relating to sale of land with unharvested crops), notwithstanding the provisions of any other paragraph of this subsection;

(12) to the extent provided in section 28(h) of the Internal Revenue Code of 1939 in the case of amounts specified in a shareholder's consent made under section 28 of such code;

(13) Repealed.

(14) for amounts allowed as deductions as deferred expenses under section 174(b)(1) (relating to research and experimental expenditures) and resulting in a reduction of the taxpayers' taxes under this subtitle, but not less than the amounts allowable under such section for the taxable year and prior years;

(15) for deductions to the extent disallowed under section 272 (relating to disposal of coal or domestic iron ore), notwithstanding the provisions of any other paragraph of this subsection;

(16) in the case of any evidence of indebtedness referred to in section 811(b) (relating to amortization of premium and accrual of discount in the case of life insurance companies), to the extent of the adjustments required under section 811(b) (or the corresponding provisions of prior income tax laws) for the taxable year and all prior taxable years;

(17) to the extent provided in section 1367 in the case of stock of, and indebtedness owed to, shareholders of an S corporation;

(18) to the extent provided in section 961 in the case of stock in controlled foreign corporations (or foreign corporations which were controlled foreign corporations) and of property by reason of which a person is considered as owning such stock;

(19) to the extent provided in section 50(c), in the case of expenditures with respect to which a credit has been allowed under section 38;

(20) for amounts allowed as deductions under section 59(e) (relating to optional 10-year writeoff of certain tax preferences);

(21) to the extent provided in section 1059 (relating to reduction in basis for extraordinary dividends);

(22) in the case of qualified replacement property the acquisition of which resulted under section 1042 in the nonrecognition of any part of the gain realized on the sale or exchange of any property, to the extent provided in section 1042(d),

(23) in the case of property the acquisition of which resulted under section 1043, 1044, 1045, or 1397B in the nonrecognition of any part of the gain realized on the sale of other property, to the extent provided in section 1043(c), 1044(d), 1045(b)(3), or 1397B(b)(4), as the case may be,

(24) to the extent provided in section 179A(e)(6)(A),

(25) to the extent provided in ¹section 30(e)(1), [Ed. Note: Sec. 1141(b)(3), P.L. 111-5, 2/17/2009, says to amend Code Sec. 1016(a)(25). However, this amendment cannot be made to Code Sec. 1016(a)(25). We believe the intention of Congress was to amend Code Sec. 1016(a)(37), see below.]

(26) to the extent provided in sections 23(g) and 137(e),

(27) in the case of a residence with respect to which a credit was allowed under section 1400C, to the extent provided in section 1400C(h),

(28) in the case of a facility with respect to which a credit was allowed under section 45F, to the extent provided in section 45F(f)(1),

(29) in the case of railroad track with respect to which a credit was allowed under section 45G, to the extent provided in section 45G(e)(3),

(30) to the extent provided in section 179B(c),

(31) to the extent provided in section 179D(e),

(32) to the extent provided in section 45L(e), in the case of amounts with respect to which a credit has been allowed under section 45L,

(33) to the extent provided in section 25C(f), in the case of amounts with respect to which a credit has been allowed under section 25C,

(34) to the extent provided in section 25D(f), in the case of amounts with respect to which a credit has been allowed under section 25D,

(35) to the extent provided in section 30B(h)(4),

(36) to the extent provided in section 30C(e)(1), and

(37) to the extent provided in section 30D(e)(4) [2]*[sic section 30D(f)(1)]* [Ed. Note. Sec. 1141(b)(3), P.L. 111-5, says to substitute "section 30D(f)(1)" for "section 30D(e)(4)" in Code Sec. 1016(a)(25). However, we believe it was the intent of Congress to make that amendment to Code Sec. 1016(a)(37). The amendment is effective for vehicles acquired after 12/31/2009.].

* * * * * * * * * * * *

[For Analysis, see ¶ 1002 and ¶ 1003. For Committee Reports, see ¶ 5027.]

[Endnote Code Sec. 1016]
Code Sec. 1016(a)(25) was amended by Sec. 1142(b)(6) of The American Recovery and Reinvestment Act of 2009, P.L. 111-5, 2/17/2009, as detailed below:
1. Sec. 1142(b)(6) substituted "section 30(e)(1)" for "section 30(d)(1)" in para. (a)(25)
Effective Date (Sec. 1142(c), P.L. 111-5, 2/17/2009) effective for vehicles acquired after 2/17/2009.

Sec. 1141(b)(3), P.L. 111-5, says to substitute "section 30D(f)(1)" for "section 30D(e)(4)" in Code Sec. 1016(a)(25). That amendment cannot be made to Code Sec. 1016(a)(25). We believe it was the intent of Congress to make that amendment to Code Sec. 1016(a)(37).
2. "section 30D(e)(4)"
Effective Date (Sec. 1141(c), P.L. 111-5, 2/17/2009) effective for vehicles acquired after 12/31/2009.

[¶ 3058]   **Code Sec. 1202.**   **Partial exclusion for gain from certain small business stock.**

(a) Exclusion.

(1) In general. In the case of a taxpayer other than a corporation, gross income shall not include 50 percent of any gain from the sale or exchange of qualified small business stock held for more than 5 years.

(2) Empowerment zone businesses.

(A) In general. In the case of qualified small business stock acquired after the date of the enactment of this paragraph in a corporation which is a qualified business entity (as defined in section 1397C(b)) during substantially all of the taxpayer's holding period for such stock, paragraph (1) shall be applied by substituting "60 percent" for "50 percent".

(B) Certain rules to apply. Rules similar to the rules of paragraphs (5) and (7) of section 1400B(b) shall apply for purposes of this paragraph.

(C) Gain after 2014 not qualified. Subparagraph (A) shall not apply to gain attributable to periods after December 31, 2014.

(D) Treatment of DC Zone. The District of Columbia Enterprise Zone shall not be treated as an empowerment zone for purposes of this paragraph.

[1]*(3) Special rules for 2009 and 2010. In the case of qualified small business stock acquired after the date of the enactment of this paragraph and before January 1, 2011.*

(A) paragraph (1) shall be applied by substituting "75 percent" for "50 percent", and

(B) paragraph (2) shall not apply.

* * * * * * * * * * * *

[For Analysis, see ¶ 902. For Committee Reports, see ¶ 5044.]

[Endnote Code Sec. 1202]
Code Sec. 1202(a)(3) was added by Sec. 1241(a) of The American Recovery and Reinvestment Act of 2009, P.L. 111-5, 2/17/2009, as detailed below:
1. Sec. 1241(a) added para. (a)(3).

Effective Date (Sec. 1241(b), P.L. 111-5, 2/17/2009) effective for stock acquired after 2/17/2009.

[¶ 3059]   Code Sec. 1374.   Tax imposed on certain built-in gains.

* * * * * * * * * * *

(d)   Definitions and special rules. For purposes of this section—

* * * * * * * * * * *

¹*(7)   Recognition period.*

(A) In general. The term "recognition period" means the 10-year period beginning with the 1st day of the 1st taxable year for which the corporation was an S corporation.

(B) Special rule for 2009 and 2010. In the case of any taxable year beginning in 2009 or 2010, no tax shall be imposed on the net recognized built-in gain of an S corporation if the 7th taxable year in the recognition period preceded such taxable year. The preceding sentence shall be applied separately with respect to any asset to which paragraph (8) applies.

(C) Special rule for distributions to shareholders. For purposes of applying this section to any amount includible in income by reason of distributions to shareholders pursuant to section 593(e)—

(i) subparagraph (A) shall be applied without regard to the phrase "10-year", and

(i) subparagraph (B) shall not apply.

* * * * * * * * * * *

[For Analysis, see ¶ 903. For Committee Reports, see ¶ 5046.]

[Endnote Code Sec. 1374]
  Code Sec. 1374(d)(7) was amended by Sec. 1251(a) of The American Recovery and Reinvestment Act of 2009, P.L. 111-5, 2/17/2009, as detailed below:
  1. Prior to amendment, para. (d)(7) read as follows:
  "(7) Recognition period.
  "The term 'recognition period' means the 10-year period beginning with the 1st day of the 1st taxable year for which the corporation was an S corporation. For purposes of applying this section to any amount includible in income by reason of section 593(e), the preceding sentence shall be applied without regard to the phrase '10-year'."
Effective Date (Sec. 1251(b), P.L. 111-5, 2/17/2009) effective for tax. yrs. begin. after 12/31/2008.

[¶ 3060]   Code Sec. 1397E.   Credit to holders of qualified zone academy bonds.

* * * * * * * * * * *

(c)   Limitation based on amount of tax. The credit allowed under subsection (a) for any taxable year shall not exceed the excess of—

(1) the sum of the regular tax liability (as defined in section 26(b)) plus the tax imposed by section 55, over

(2) the sum of the credits allowable under part IV of subchapter A (other than subpart C thereof, relating to refundable credits, and subparts H¹, *I, and J* thereof).

* * * * * * * * * * *

[For Analysis, see ¶ 1301. For Committee Reports, see ¶ 5070.]

[Endnote Code Sec. 1397E]
  Code Sec. 1397E(c)(2) was amended by Sec. 1531(c)(3) of The American Recovery and Reinvestment Act of 2009, P.L. 111-5, 2/17/2009, as detailed below:
  1. Sec. 1531(c)(3) substituted ", I, and J" for "and I" in para. (c)(2).
Effective Date (Sec. 1531(e), P.L. 111-5, 2/17/2009) effective for obligations issued after 2/17/2009.

[¶ 3061]   Code Sec. 1400C.   First-time homebuyer credit for District of Columbia.

* * * * * * * * * * * *

(d) Carryforward of unused credit.

(1) Rule for years in which all personal credits allowed against regular and alternative minimum tax. In the case of a taxable year to which section 26(a)(2) applies, if the credit allowable under subsection (a) exceeds the limitation imposed by section 26(a)(2) for such taxable year reduced by the sum of the credits allowable under subpart A of part IV of subchapter A (other than this section and section 25D), such excess shall be carried to the succeeding taxable year and added to the credit allowable under subsection (a) for such taxable year.

(2) Rule for other years. In the case of a taxable year to which section 26(a)(2) does not apply, if the credit allowable under subsection (a) exceeds the limitation imposed by section 26(a)(1) for such taxable year reduced by the sum of the credits allowable under subpart A of part IV of subchapter A (other than this section and sections 23, 24, [1]*25A(i)*, 25B, [2]*25D, [3]30, and 30B*, and 30D), such excess shall be carried to the succeeding taxable year and added to the credit allowable under subsection (a) for such taxable year.

(e) Special rules. For purposes of this section—

(1) Allocation of dollar limitation.

(A) Married individuals filing separately. In the case of a married individual filing a separate return, subsection (a) shall be applied by substituting "$2,500" for "$5,000".

(B) Other taxpayers. If 2 or more individuals who are not married purchase a principal residence, the amount of the credit allowed under subsection (a) shall be allocated among such individuals in such manner as the Secretary may prescribe, except that the total amount of the credits allowed to all such individuals shall not exceed $5,000.

(2) Purchase.

(A) In general. The term "purchase" means any acquisition, but only if—

(i) the property is not acquired from a person whose relationship to the person acquiring it would result in the disallowance of losses under section 267 or 707(b) (but, in applying section 267(b) and (c) for purposes of this section, paragraph (4) of section 267(c) shall be treated as providing that the family of an individual shall include only his spouse, ancestors, and lineal descendants), and

(ii) the basis of the property in the hands of the person acquiring it is not determined—

(I) in whole or in part by reference to the adjusted basis of such property in the hands of the person from whom acquired, or

(II) under section 1014(a) (relating to property acquired from a decedent).

(B) Construction. A residence which is constructed by the taxpayer shall be treated as purchased by the taxpayer on the date the taxpayer first occupies such residence.

(3) Purchase price. The term "purchase price" means the adjusted basis of the principal residence on the date such residence is purchased.

[4]**(4) *Coordination with national first-time homebuyers credit.*** *No credit shall be allowed under this section to any taxpayer with respect to the purchase of a residence after December 31, 2008 and before December 1, 2009, if a credit under section 36 is allowable to such taxpayer (or the taxpayer's spouse) with respect to such purchase.*

* * * * * * * * * * * *

[For Analysis, see ¶ 104, ¶ 107, ¶ 204 and ¶ 205. For Committee Reports, see ¶ 5004, ¶ 5006, ¶ 5010 and ¶ 5027.]

[Endnote Code Sec. 1400C]

Code Sec. 1400C(d)(2) was amended by Sec. 1004(b)(6) of the American Recovery and Reinvestment Act of 2009, P.L. 111-5, 2/17/2009, as detailed below:

1. Sec. 1004(b)(6) added '25A(i),' after '24,' in para. (d)(2)

Effective Date (Sec. 1004(d), P.L. 111-5, 2/17/2009) effective for tax. yrs. begin. after 12/31/2008.

Code Sec. 1400C(d)(2) was amended by Sec. 1142(b)(1)(F), P.L. 111-5, 2/17/2009, as detailed below:

2. Sec. 1142(b)(1)(F) substituted '25D, and 30' for 'and 25D' in para. (d)(2) [as amended by Sec. 1004(b)(6) of this Act, see above]
Effective Date (Sec. 1142(c), P.L. 111-5, 2/17/2009) effective for vehicles acquired after 2/17/2009.

Code Sec. 1400C(d)(2) was amended by Sec. 1144(b)(1)(F), P.L. 111-5, 2/17/2009, as detailed below:
3. Sec. 1144(b)(1)(F) substituted "30, and 30B" for "and 30" in para. (d)(2) [as amended by Secs. 1004(b)(6) and 1142(b)(1)(F) of this Act, see above]
Effective Date (Sec. 1144(c), P.L. 111-5, 2/17/2009) effective for tax. yrs. begin. after 12/31/2008.

Code Sec. 1400C(e)(4) was added by Sec. 1006(d)(1), P.L. 111-5, 2/17/2009, as detailed below:
4. Sec. 1006(d)(1) added para. (e)(4)
Effective Date (Sec. 1006(e), P.L. 111-5, 2/17/2009) effective for residences purchased after 12/31/2008.

[¶ 3062]   Code Sec. 1400N.   Tax benefits for Gulf Opportunity Zone.

* * * * * * * * * * * *

(d) Special allowance for certain property acquired on or after August 28, 2005.

(1) Additional allowance. In the case of any qualified Gulf Opportunity Zone property—

(A) the depreciation deduction provided by section 167(a) for the taxable year in which such property is placed in service shall include an allowance equal to 50 percent of the adjusted basis of such property, and

(B) the adjusted basis of the qualified Gulf Opportunity Zone property shall be reduced by the amount of such deduction before computing the amount otherwise allowable as a depreciation deduction under this chapter for such taxable year and any subsequent taxable year.

(2) Qualified Gulf Opportunity Zone property. For purposes of this subsection—

(A) In general. The term "qualified Gulf Opportunity Zone property" means property—

(i) (I) which is described in section 168(k)(2)(A)(i), or

(II) which is nonresidential real property or residential rental property,

(ii) substantially all of the use of which is in the Gulf Opportunity Zone and is in the active conduct of a trade or business by the taxpayer in such Zone,

(iii) the original use of which in the Gulf Opportunity Zone commences with the taxpayer on or after August 28, 2005,

(iv) which is acquired by the taxpayer by purchase (as defined in section 179(d)) on or after August 28, 2005, but only if no written binding contract for the acquisition was in effect before August 28, 2005, and

(v) which is placed in service by the taxpayer on or before December 31, 2007 (December 31, 2008, in the case of nonresidential real property and residential rental property).

(B) Exceptions.

(i) Alternative depreciation property. Such term shall not include any property described in section 168(k)(2)(D)(i).

(ii) Tax-exempt bond-financed property. Such term shall not include any property any portion of which is financed with the proceeds of any obligation the interest on which is exempt from tax under section 103.

(iii) Qualified revitalization buildings. Such term shall not include any qualified revitalization building with respect to which the taxpayer has elected the application of paragraph (1) or (2) of section 1400I(a).

(iv) Election out. If a taxpayer makes an election under this clause with respect to any class of property for any taxable year, this subsection shall not apply to all property in such class placed in service during such taxable year.

(3) **Special rules.** For purposes of this subsection, rules similar to the rules of subparagraph (E) of section 168(k)(2) shall apply, except that such subparagraph shall be applied—

(A) by substituting "August 27, 2005" for "December 31, 2007" each place it appears therein,

(B) without regard to "and before [1]*January 1, 2010*" in clause (i) thereof, and

(C) by substituting "qualified Gulf Opportunity Zone property" for "qualified property" in clause (iv) thereof.

(4) **Allowance against alternative minimum tax.** For purposes of this subsection, rules similar to the rules of section 168(k)(2)(G) shall apply.

(5) **Recapture.** For purposes of this subsection, rules similar to the rules under section 179(d)(10) shall apply with respect to any qualified Gulf Opportunity Zone property which ceases to be qualified Gulf Opportunity Zone property.

(6) **Extension for certain property.**

(A) In general. In the case of any specified Gulf Opportunity Zone extension property, paragraph (2)(A) shall be applied without regard to clause (v) thereof.

(B) Specified Gulf Opportunity Zone extension property. For purposes of this paragraph, the term "specified Gulf Opportunity Zone extension property" means property—

(i) substantially all of the use of which is in one or more specified portions of the GO Zone, and

(ii) which is—

(I) nonresidential real property or residential rental property which is placed in service by the taxpayer on or before December 31, 2010, or

(II) in the case of a taxpayer who places a building described in subclause (I) in service on or before December 31, 2010, property described in section 168(k)(2)(A)(i) if substantially all of the use of such property is in such building and such property is placed in service by the taxpayer not later than 90 days after such building is placed in service.

(C) Specified portions of the GO Zone. For purposes of this paragraph, the term "specified portions of the GO Zone" means those portions of the GO Zone which are in any county or parish which is identified by the Secretary as being a county or parish in which hurricanes occurring during 2005 damaged (in the aggregate) more than 60 percent of the housing units in such county or parish which were occupied (determined according to the 2000 Census).

(D) Only pre-January 1, 2010, basis of real property eligible for additional allowance. In the case of property which is qualified Gulf Opportunity Zone property solely by reason of subparagraph (B)(ii)(I), paragraph (1) shall apply only to the extent of the adjusted basis thereof attributable to manufacture, construction, or production before January 1, 2010.

(E) Exception for bonus depreciation property under section 168(k). The term "specified Gulf Opportunity Zone extension property" shall not include any property to which section 168(k) applies.

* * * * * * * * * * * *

(l) **Credit to holders of Gulf tax credit bonds.**

(1) **Allowance of credit.** If a taxpayer holds a Gulf tax credit bond on one or more credit allowance dates of the bond occurring during any taxable year, there shall be allowed as a credit against the tax imposed by this chapter for the taxable year an amount equal to the sum of the credits determined under paragraph (2) with respect to such dates.

(2) **Amount of credit.**

(A) In general. The amount of the credit determined under this paragraph with respect to any credit allowance date for a Gulf tax credit bond is 25 percent of the annual credit determined with respect to such bond.

(B) Annual credit. The annual credit determined with respect to any Gulf tax credit bond is the product of—

(i) the credit rate determined by the Secretary under subparagraph (C) for the day on which such bond was sold, multiplied by

(ii) the outstanding face amount of the bond.

(C) Determination. For purposes of subparagraph (B), with respect to any Gulf tax credit bond, the Secretary shall determine daily or cause to be determined daily a credit rate which shall apply to the first day on which there is a binding, written contract for the sale or exchange of the bond. The credit rate for any day is the credit rate which the Secretary or the Secretary's designee estimates will permit the issuance of Gulf tax credit bonds with a specified maturity or redemption date without discount and without interest cost to the issuer.

(D) Credit allowance date. For purposes of this subsection, the term "credit allowance date" means March 15, June 15, September 15, and December 15. Such term also includes the last day on which the bond is outstanding.

(E) Special rule for issuance and redemption. In the case of a bond which is issued during the 3-month period ending on a credit allowance date, the amount of the credit determined under this paragraph with respect to such credit allowance date shall be a ratable portion of the credit otherwise determined based on the portion of the 3-month period during which the bond is outstanding. A similar rule shall apply when the bond is redeemed or matures.

(3) Limitation based on amount of tax. The credit allowed under paragraph (1) for any taxable year shall not exceed the excess of—

(A) the sum of the regular tax liability (as defined in section 26(b)) plus the tax imposed by section 55, over

(B) the sum of the credits allowable under part IV of subchapter A (other than subparts C ˡI, and J and this subsection).

(4) Gulf tax credit bond. For purposes of this subsection—

(A) In general. The term "Gulf tax credit bond" means any bond issued as part of an issue if—

(i) the bond is issued by the State of Alabama, Louisiana, or Mississippi,

(ii) 95 percent or more of the proceeds of such issue are to be used to—

(I) pay principal, interest, or premiums on qualified bonds issued by such State or any political subdivision of such State, or

(II) make a loan to any political subdivision of such State to pay principal, interest, or premiums on qualified bonds issued by such political subdivision,

(iii) the Governor of such State designates such bond for purposes of this subsection,

(iv) the bond is a general obligation of such State and is in registered form (within the meaning of section 149(a)),

(v) the maturity of such bond does not exceed 2 years, and

(vi) the bond is issued after December 31, 2005, and before January 1, 2007.

(B) State matching requirement. A bond shall not be treated as a Gulf tax credit bond unless—

(i) the issuer of such bond pledges as of the date of the issuance of the issue an amount equal to the face amount of such bond to be used for payments described in subclause (I) of subparagraph (A)(ii), or loans described in subclause (II) of such subparagraph, as the case may be, with respect to the issue of which such bond is a part, and

(ii) any such payment or loan is made in equal amounts from the proceeds of such issue and from the amount pledged under clause (i).

The requirement of clause (ii) shall be treated as met with respect to any such payment or loan made during the 1-year period beginning on the date of the issuance (or any successor 1-year period) if such requirement is met when applied with respect to the aggregate amount of such payments and loans made during such period.

(C) Aggregate limit on bond designations. The maximum aggregate face amount of bonds which may be designated under this subsection by the Governor of a State shall not exceed—

(i) $200,000,000 in the case of the State of Louisiana,

(ii) $100,000,000 in the case of the State of Mississippi, and

(iii) $50,000,000 in the case of the State of Alabama.

(D) Special rules relating to arbitrage. A bond which is part of an issue shall not be treated as a Gulf tax credit bond unless, with respect to the issue of which the bond is a part, the issuer satisfies the arbitrage requirements of section 148 with respect to proceeds of the issue and any loans made with such proceeds.

(5) **Qualified bond.** For purposes of this subsection—

(A) In general. The term "qualified bond" means any obligation of a State or political subdivision thereof which was outstanding on August 28, 2005.

(B) Exception for private activity bonds. Such term shall not include any private activity bond.

(C) Exception for advance refundings. Such term shall not include any bond with respect to which there is any outstanding refunded or refunding bond during the period in which a Gulf tax credit bond is outstanding with respect to such bond.

(D) Use of proceeds requirement. Such term shall not include any bond issued as part of an issue if any portion of the proceeds of such issue was (or is to be) used to provide any property described in section 144(c)(6)(B).

(6) **Credit included in gross income.** Gross income includes the amount of the credit allowed to the taxpayer under this subsection (determined without regard to paragraph (3)) and the amount so included shall be treated as interest income.

(7) **Other definitions and special rules.** For purposes of this subsection—

(A) Bond. The term "bond" includes any obligation.

(B) Partnership; S corporation; and other pass-thru entities.

(i) In general. Under regulations prescribed by the Secretary, in the case of a partnership, trust, S corporation, or other pass-thru entity, rules similar to the rules of section 41(g) shall apply with respect to the credit allowable under paragraph (1).

(ii) No basis adjustment. In the case of a bond held by a partnership or an S corporation, rules similar to the rules under section 1397E(l) shall apply.

(C) Bonds held by regulated investment companies. If any Gulf tax credit bond is held by a regulated investment company, the credit determined under paragraph (1) shall be allowed to shareholders of such company under procedures prescribed by the Secretary.

(D) Reporting. Issuers of Gulf tax credit bonds shall submit reports similar to the reports required under section 149(e).

(E) Credit treated as nonrefundable bondholder credit. For purposes of this title, the credit allowed by this subsection shall be treated as a credit allowable under subpart H of part IV of subchapter A of this chapter.

* * * * * * * * * * * *

[For Analysis, see ¶ 1301. For Committee Reports, see ¶ 5070.]

[Endnote Code Sec. 1400N]

Code Sec. 1400N(d)(3)(B) was amended by Sec. 1201(a)(2)(E) of the American Recovery and Reinvestment Act of 2009, P.L. 111-5, 2/17/2009, as detailed below:

1. Sec. 1201(a)(2)(E) substituted "January 1, 2010" for "January 1, 2009" in subpara. (d)(3)(B)

Effective Date (Sec. 1201(c)(1), P.L. 111-5, 2/17/2009) effective for property placed in service after 12/31/2008, in tax. yrs. ending after such date.

Code Sec. 1400N(l)(3)(B) was amended by Sec. 1531(c)(3), P.L. 111-5, 2/17/2009, as detailed below:

2. Sec. 1531(c)(3) substituted ", I, and J" for "and I" in subpara. (l)(3)(B)

Effective Date (Sec. 1531(e), P.L. 111-5, 2/17/2009) effective for obligations issued after 2/17/2009.

[¶ 3063]   *Code Sec.[1] 1400U-1.*   *Allocation of recovery zone bonds.*

  (a) *Allocations.*

    (1) *In general.*

      (A) General allocation. The Secretary shall allocate the national recovery zone economic development bond limitation and the national recovery zone facility bond limitation among the States in the proportion that each such State's 2008 State employment decline bears to the aggregate of the 2008 State employment declines for all of the States.

      (B) Minimum allocation. The Secretary shall adjust the allocations under subparagraph (A) for any calendar year for each State to the extent necessary to ensure that no State receives less than 0.9 percent of the national recovery zone economic development bond limitation and 0.9 percent of the national recovery zone facility bond limitation.

    (2) *2008 State employment decline.* For purposes of this subsection, the term "2008 State employment decline" means, with respect to any State, the excess (if any) of—

      (A) the number of individuals employed in such State determined for December 2007, over

      (B) the number of individuals employed in such State determined for December 2008.

    (3) *Allocations by States.*

      (A) In general. Each State with respect to which an allocation is made under paragraph (1) shall reallocate such allocation among the counties and large municipalities in such State in the proportion to each such county's or municipality's 2008 employment decline bears to the aggregate of the 2008 employment declines for all the counties and municipalities in such State. A county or municipality may waive any portion of an allocation made under this subparagraph.

      (B) Large municipalities. For purposes of subparagraph (A), the term "large municipality" means a municipality with a population of more than 100,000.

      (C) Determination of local employment declines. For purposes of this paragraph, the employment decline of any municipality or county shall be determined in the same manner as determining the State employment decline under paragraph (2), except that in the case of a municipality any portion of which is in a county, such portion shall be treated as part of such municipality and not part of such county.

    (4) *National limitations.*

      (A) Recovery zone economic development bonds. There is a national recovery zone economic development bond limitation of $10,000,000,000.

      (B) Recovery zone facility bonds. There is a national recovery zone facility bond limitation of $15,000,000,000.

  (b) *Recovery zone.* For purposes of this part, the term "recovery zone" means—

    (1) any area designated by the issuer as having significant poverty, unemployment, rate of home foreclosures, or general distress,

    (2) any area designated by the issuer as distressed by reason of the closure or realignment of a military installation pursuant to the Defense Base Closure and Realignment Act of 1990, and

    (3) any area for which a designation as an empowerment zone or renewal community is in effect.

    [For Analysis, see ¶ 1304 and ¶ 1305. For Committee Reports, see ¶ 5054.]

[Endnote Code Sec. 1400U-1]

    Code Sec. 1400U-1 was added by Sec. 1401(a) of the American Recovery and Reinvestment Act of 2009, P.L. 111-5, 2/17/2009, as detailed below:

    1. Sec. 1401(a) added Code Sec. 1400U-1

Effective Date (Sec. 1401(c), P.L. 111-5, 2/17/2009) effective for obligations issued after 2/17/2009.

[¶ 3064]   Code Sec.[1] 1400U-2. *Recovery zone economic development bonds.*

(a) In general. In the case of a recovery zone economic development bond—

(1) such bond shall be treated as a qualified bond for purposes of section 6431, and

(2) subsection (b) of such section shall be applied by substituting "45 percent" for '35 percent".

(b) Recovery zone economic development bond.

(1) In general. For purposes of this section, the term "recovery zone economic development bond" means any build America bond (as defined in section 54AA(d)) issued before January 1, 2011, as part of issue if—

(A) 100 percent of the excess of—

(i) the available project proceeds (as defined in section 54A) of such issue, over

(ii) the amounts in a reasonably required reserve (within the meaning of section 150(a)(3)) with respect to such issue,

are to be used for one or more qualified economic development purposes, and

(B) the issuer designates such bond for purposes of this section.

(2) Limitation on amount of bonds designated. The maximum aggregate face amount of bonds which may be designated by any issuer under paragraph (1) shall not exceed the amount of the recovery zone economic development bond limitation allocated to such issuer under section 1400U-1.

(c) Qualified economic development purpose. For purposes of this section, the term "qualified economic development purpose" means expenditures for purposes of promoting development or other economic activity in a recovery zone, including—

(1) capital expenditures paid or incurred with respect to property located in such zone,

(2) expenditures for public infrastructure and construction of public facilities, and

(3) expenditures for job training and educational programs.

[For Analysis, see ¶ 1304, ¶ 1306 and ¶ 1311. For Committee Reports, see ¶ 5054 and ¶ 5074.]

[Endnote Code Sec. 1400U-2]

Code Sec. 1400U-2 was added by Sec. 1401(a) of the American Recovery and Reinvestment Act of 2009, P.L. 111-5, 2/17/2009, as detailed below:

1. Sec. 1401(a) added Code Sec. 1400U-2

Effective Date (Sec. 1401(c), P.L. 111-5, 2/17/2009) effective for obligations issued after 2/17/2009.

Sec. 1601(5), of this Act, provides:

"SEC. 1601. APPLICATION OF CERTAIN LABOR STANDARDS TO PROJECTS FINANCED WITH CERTAIN TAX-FAVORED BONDS.

"Subchapter IV of chapter 31 of the title 40, United States Code, shall apply to projects financed with the proceeds of—

* * * * * *

"(5) any recovery zone economic development bond (as defined in section 1400U-2 of the Internal Revenue Code of 1986)."

[¶ 3065]   Code Sec.[1] 1400U-3. *Recovery zone facility bonds.*

(a) In general. For purposes of part IV of subchapter B (relating to tax exemption requirements for State and local bonds), the term "exempt facility bond" includes any recovery zone facility bond.

(b) Recovery zone facility bond.

(1) In general. For purposes of this section, the term "recovery zone facility bond" means any bond issued as part of an issue if—

(A) 95 percent or more of the net proceeds (as defined in section 150(a)(3)) of such issue are to be used for recovery zone property,

(B) such bond is issued before January 1, 2011, and

(C) the issuer designates such bond for purposes of this section.

(2) Limitation on amount of bonds designated. The maximum aggregate face amount of bonds which may be designated by any issuer under paragraph (1) shall not ex-

ceed the amount of recovery zone facility bond limitation allocated to such issuer under section 1400U-1.

(c) Recovery zone property. For purposes of this section—

(1) In general. The term "recovery zone property" means any property to which section 168 applies (or would apply but for section 179) if—

(A) such property was constructed, reconstructed, renovated, or acquired by purchase (as defined in section 179(d)(2)) by the taxpayer after the date on which the designation of the recovery zone took effect,

(B) the original use of which in the recovery zone commences with the taxpayer, and

(C) substantially all of the use of which is in the recovery zone and is in the active conduct of a qualified business by the taxpayer in such zone.

(2) Qualified business. The term "qualified business" means any trade or business except that—

(A) the rental to others of real property located in a recovery zone shall be treated as a qualified business only if the property is not residential rental property (as defined in section 168(e)(2)), and

(B) such term shall not include any trade or business consisting of the operation of any facility described in section 144(c)(6)(B).

(3) Special rules for substantial renovations and sale-leaseback. Rules similar to the rules of subsections (a)(2) and (b) of section 1397D shall apply for purposes of this subsection.

(d) Nonapplication of certain rules. Sections 146 (relating to volume cap) and 147(d) (relating to acquisition of existing property not permitted) shall not apply to any recovery zone facility bond.

[For Analysis, see ¶ 1304 and ¶ 1307. For Committee Reports, see ¶ 5054.]

[Endnote Code Sec. 1400U-3]
Code Sec. 1400U-3 was added by Sec. 1401(a) of the American Recovery and Reinvestment Act of 2009, P.L. 111-5, 2/17/2009, as detailed below:
1. Sec. 1401(a) added Code Sec. 1400U-3
Effective Date (Sec. 1401(c), P.L. 111-5, 2/17/2009) effective for obligations issued after 2/17/2009.

[¶ 3066]   Code Sec. 4980B.   Failure to satisfy continuation coverage requirements of group health plans.

* * * * * * * * * * * *

(f) Continuation coverage requirements of group health plans.

(1) In general. A group health plan meets the requirements of this subsection only if the coverage of the costs of pediatric vaccines (as defined under section 2162 of the Public Health Service Act) is not reduced below the coverage provided by the plan as of May 1, 1993, and only if each qualified beneficiary who would lose coverage under the plan as a result of a qualifying event is entitled to elect, within the election period, continuation coverage under the plan.

(2) Continuation coverage. For purposes of paragraph (1), the term "continuation coverage" means coverage under the plan which meets the following requirements:

(A) Type of benefit coverage. The coverage must consist of coverage which, as of the time the coverage is being provided, is identical to the coverage provided under the plan to similarly situated beneficiaries under the plan with respect to whom a qualifying event has not occurred. If coverage under the plan is modified for any group of similarly situated beneficiaries, the coverage shall also be modified in the same manner for all individuals who are qualified beneficiaries under the plan pursuant to this subsection in connection with such group.

521

(B) Period of coverage. The coverage must extend for at least the period beginning on the date of the qualifying event and ending not earlier than the earliest of the following:

(i) Maximum required period.

(I) General rule for terminations and reduced hours. In the case of a qualifying event described in paragraph (3)(B), except as provided in subclause (II), the date which is 18 months after the date of the qualifying event.

(II) Special rule for multiple qualifying events. If a qualifying event (other than a qualifying event described in paragraph (3)(F)) occurs during the 18 months after the date of a qualifying event described in paragraph (3)(B), the date which is 36 months after the date of the qualifying event described in paragraph (3)(B).

(III) Special rule for certain bankruptcy proceedings. In the case of a qualifying event described in paragraph (3)(F) (relating to bankruptcy proceedings), the date of the death of the covered employee or qualified beneficiary (described in subsection (g)(1)(D)(iii)), or in the case of the surviving spouse or dependent children of the covered employee, 36 months after the date of the death of the covered employee.

(IV) General rule for other qualifying events. In the case of a qualifying event not described in paragraph (3)(B) or (3)(F), the date which is 36 months after the date of the qualifying event.

[1](V) Special rule for PBGC recipients. In the case of a qualifying event described in paragraph (3)(B) with respect to a covered employee who (as of such qualifying event) has a nonforfeitable right to a benefit any portion of which is to be paid by the Pension Benefit Guaranty Corporation under title IV of the Employee Retirement Income Security Act of 1974, notwithstanding subclause (I) or (II), the date of the death of the covered employee, or in the case of the surviving spouse or dependent children of the covered employee, 24 months after the date of the death of the covered employee. The preceding sentence shall not require any period of coverage to extend beyond December 31, 2010.

[2](VI) Special rule for TAA eligible individuals. In the case of a qualifying event described in paragraph (3)(B) with respect to a covered employee who is (as of the date that the period of coverage would, but for this subclause or subclause (VII), otherwise terminate under subclause (I) or (II)) a TAA-eligible individual (as defined in paragraph (5)(C)(iv)(II)), the period of coverage shall not terminate by reason of subclause (I) or (II), as the case may be, before the later of the date specified in such subclause or the date on which such individual ceases to be such a TAA-eligible individual. The preceding sentence shall not require any period of coverage to extend beyond December 31, 2010.

[3](VII) Medicare entitlement followed by qualifying event. In the case of a qualifying event described in paragraph (3)(B) that occurs less than 18 months after the date the covered employee became entitled to benefits under title XVIII of the Social Security Act, the period of coverage for qualified beneficiaries other than the covered employee shall not terminate under this clause before the close of the 36-month period beginning on the date the covered employee became so entitled.

[4](VIII) Special rule for disability. In the case of a qualified beneficiary who is determined, under title II or XVI of the Social Security Act, to have been disabled at any time during the first 60 days of continuation coverage under this section, any reference in subclause (I) or (II) to 18 months is deemed a reference to 29 months (with respect to all qualified beneficiaries), but only if the qualified beneficiary has provided notice of such determination under paragraph (6)(C) before the end of such 18 months.

(ii) End of plan. The date on which the employer ceases to provide any group health plan to any employee.

(iii) Failure to pay premium. The date on which coverage ceases under the plan by reason of a failure to make timely payment of any premium required under the plan with respect to the qualified beneficiary. The payment of any premium (other than any payment referred to in the last sentence of subparagraph (C)) shall be considered to be timely if made within 30 days after the date due or within such longer period as applies to or under the plan.

(iv) Group health plan coverage or medicare entitlement. The date on which the qualified beneficiary first becomes, after the date of the election—

(I) covered under any other group health plan (as an employee or otherwise), which does not contain any exclusion or limitation with respect to any preexisting condition of such beneficiary (other than such an exclusion or limitation which does not apply to (or is satisfied by) such beneficiary by reason of chapter 100 of this title, part 7 of subtitle B of title I of the Employee Retirement Income Security Act of 1974, or title XXVII of the Public Health Services Act), or

(II) in the case of a qualified beneficiary other than a qualified beneficiary described in subsection (g)(1)(D) entitled to benefits under title XVIII of the Social Security Act.

(v) Termination of extended coverage for disability. In the case of a qualified beneficiary who is disabled at any time during the first 60 days of continuation coverage under this section, the month that begins more than 30 days after the date of the final determination under title II or XVI of the Social Security Act that the qualified beneficiary is no longer disabled.

(C) Premium requirements. The plan may require payment of a premium for any period of continuation coverage, except that such premium—

(i) shall not exceed 102 percent of the applicable premium for such period, and

(ii) may, at the election of the payor, be made in monthly installments.

In no event may the plan require the payment of any premium before the day which is 45 days after the day on which the qualified beneficiary made the initial election for continuation coverage. In the case of an individual described in the last sentence of subparagraph (B)(i), any reference in clause (i) of this subparagraph to "102 percent" is deemed a reference to "150 percent" for any month after the 18th month of continuation coverage described in subclause (I) or (II) of subparagraph (B)(i).

(D) No requirement of insurability. The coverage may not be conditioned upon, or discriminate on the basis of lack of, evidence of insurability.

(E) Conversion option. In the case of a qualified beneficiary whose period of continuation coverage expires under subparagraph (B)(i), the plan must, during the 180-day period ending on such expiration date, provide to the qualified beneficiary the option of enrollment under a conversion health plan otherwise generally available under the plan.

(3) Qualifying event. For purposes of this subsection, the term "qualifying event" means, with respect to any covered employee, any of the following events which, but for the continuation coverage required under this subsection, would result in the loss of coverage of a qualified beneficiary—

(A) The death of the covered employee.

(B) The termination (other than by reason of such employee's gross misconduct), or reduction of hours, of the covered employee's employment.

(C) The divorce or legal separation of the covered employee from the employee's spouse.

(D) The covered employee becoming entitled to benefits under title XVIII of the Social Security Act.

(E) A dependent child ceasing to be a dependent child under the generally applicable requirements of the plan.

(F) A proceeding in a case under title 11, United States Code, commencing on or after July 1, 1986, with respect to the employer from whose employment the covered employee retired at any time.

In the case of an event described in subparagraph (F), a loss of coverage includes a substantial elimination of coverage with respect to a qualified beneficiary described in subsection (g)(1)(D) within one year before or after the date of commencement of the proceeding.

(4)　Applicable premium. For purposes of this subsection—

(A) In general. The term "applicable premium" means, with respect to any period of continuation coverage of qualified beneficiaries, the cost to the plan for such period of the coverage for similarly situated beneficiaries with respect to whom a qualifying event has not occurred (without regard to whether such cost is paid by the employer or employee).

(B) Special rule for self-insured plans. To the extent that a plan is a self-insured plan—

(i) In general. Except as provided in clause (ii), the applicable premium for any period of continuation coverage of qualified beneficiaries shall be equal to a reasonable estimate of the cost of providing coverage for such period for similarly situated beneficiaries which—

(I) is determined on an actuarial basis, and

(II) takes into account such factors as the Secretary may prescribe in regulations.

(ii) Determination on basis of past cost. If a plan administrator elects to have this clause apply, the applicable premium for any period of continuation coverage of qualified beneficiaries shall be equal to—

(I) the cost to the plan for similarly situated beneficiaries for the same period occurring during the preceding determination period under subparagraph (C), adjusted by

(II) the percentage increase or decrease in the implicit price deflator of the gross national product (calculated by the Department of Commerce and published in the Survey of Current Business) for the 12-month period ending on the last day of the sixth month of such preceding determination period.

(iii) Clause (ii) not to apply where significant change. A plan administrator may not elect to have clause (ii) apply in any case in which there is any significant difference between the determination period and the preceding determination period, in coverage under or in employees covered by, the plan. The determination under the preceding sentence for any determination period shall be made at the same time as the determination under subparagraph (C).

(C) Determination period. The determination of any applicable premium shall be made for a period of 12 months and shall be made before the beginning of such period.

(5)　Election. For purposes of this subsection

(A) Election period. The term "election period" means the period which—

(i) begins not later than the date on which coverage terminates under the plan by reason of a qualifying event,

(ii) is of at least 60 days' duration, and

(iii) ends not earlier than 60 days after the later of—

(I) the date described in clause (i), or

(II) in the case of any qualified beneficiary who receives notice under paragraph (6)(D), the date of such notice.

(B) Effect of election on other beneficiaries. Except as otherwise specified in an election, any election of continuation coverage by a qualified beneficiary described in subparagraph (A)(i) or (B) of subsection (g)(1) shall be deemed to include an election of continuation coverage on behalf of any other qualified beneficiary who would lose coverage under the plan by reason of the qualifying event. If there is a choice among types of coverage under the plan, each qualified beneficiary is entitled to make a separate selection among such types of coverage.

(C) Temporary extension of COBRA election period for certain individuals.

(i) In general. In the case of a nonelecting TAA-eligible individual and notwithstanding subparagraph (A), such individual may elect continuation coverage under this subsection during the 60-day period that begins on the first day of the month in which the individual becomes a TAA-eligible individual, but only if such election is made not later than 6 months after the date of the TAA-related loss of coverage.

(ii) Commencement of coverage; no reach-back. Any continuation coverage elected by a TAA-eligible individual under clause (i) shall commence at the beginning of the 60-day election period described in such paragraph and shall not include any period prior to such 60-day election period.

(iii) Preexisting conditions. With respect to an individual who elects continuation coverage pursuant to clause (i), the period—

(I) beginning on the date of the TAA-related loss of coverage, and

(II) ending on the first day of the 60-day election period described in clause (i),
shall be disregarded for purposes of determining the 63-day periods referred to in section 9801(c)(2), section 701(c)(2) of the Employee Retirement Income Security Act of 1974, and section 2701(c)(2) of the Public Health Service Act.

(iv) Definitions. For purposes of this subsection:

(I) Nonelecting TAA-eligible individual. The term "nonelecting TAA-eligible individual" means a TAA-eligible individual who has a TAA-related loss of coverage and did not elect continuation coverage under this subsection during the TAA-related election period.

(II) TAA-eligible individual. The term "TAA-eligible individual" means an eligible TAA recipient (as defined in paragraph (2) of section 35(c)) and an eligible alternative TAA recipient (as defined in paragraph (3) of such section).

(III) TAA-related election period. The term "TAA-related election period" means, with respect to a TAA-related loss of coverage, the 60-day election period under this subsection which is a direct consequence of such loss.

(IV) TAA-related loss of coverage. The term "TAA-related loss of coverage" means, with respect to an individual whose separation from employment gives rise to being an TAA-eligible individual, the loss of health benefits coverage associated with such separation.

(6) Notice requirement. In accordance with regulations prescribed by the Secretary—

(A) The group health plan shall provide, at the time of commencement of coverage under the plan, written notice to each covered employee and spouse of the employee (if any) of the rights provided under this subsection.

(B) The employer of an employee under a plan must notify the plan administrator of a qualifying event described in subparagraph (A), (B), (D), or (F) of paragraph (3) with respect to such employee within 30 days (or, in the case of a group health plan which is a multiemployer plan, such longer period of time as may be provided in the terms of the plan) of the date of the qualifying event.

(C) Each covered employee or qualified beneficiary is responsible for notifying the plan administrator of the occurrence of any qualifying event described in subparagraph (C) or (E) of paragraph (3) within 60 days after the date of the qualifying event and each qualified beneficiary who is determined, under title II or XVI of the Social Security Act, to have been disabled at any time during the first 60 days of continuation coverage under this section is responsible for notifying the plan administrator of such determination within 60 days after the date of the determination and for notifying the plan administrator within 30 days of the date of any final determination under such title or titles that the qualified beneficiary is no longer disabled.

(D) The plan administrator shall notify—

(i) in the case of a qualifying event described in subparagraph (A), (B), (D), or (F) of paragraph (3), any qualified beneficiary with respect to such event, and

(ii) in the case of a qualifying event described in subparagraph (C) or (E) of paragraph (3) where the covered employee notifies the plan administrator under subparagraph (C), any qualified beneficiary with respect to such event,
of such beneficiary's rights under this subsection.

The requirements of subparagraph (B) shall be considered satisfied in the case of a multiemployer plan in connection with a qualifying event described in paragraph (3)(B) if the plan provides that the determination of the occurrence of such qualifying event will be made by the plan administrator. For purposes of subparagraph (D), any notification shall be made within 14 days (or, in the case of a group health plan which is a multiemployer plan, such longer period of time as may be provided in the terms of the plan) of the date on which the plan administrator is notified under subparagraph (B) or (C), whichever is applicable, and any such notification to an individual who is a qualified beneficiary as the spouse of the covered employee shall be treated as notification to all other qualified beneficiaries residing with such spouse at the time such notification is made.

(7)   Covered employee. For purposes of this subsection, the term "covered employee" means an individual who is (or was) provided coverage under a group health plan by virtue of the performance of services by the individual for 1 or more persons maintaining the plan (including as an employee defined in section 401(c)(1)).

(8)   Optional extension of required periods. A group health plan shall not be treated as failing to meet the requirements of this subsection solely because the plan provides both—

(A) that the period of extended coverage referred to in paragraph (2)(B) commences with the date of the loss of coverage, and

(B) that the applicable notice period provided under paragraph (6)(B) commences with the date of the loss of coverage.

* * * * * * * * * * * *

[For Analysis, see ¶ 307, ¶ 501 and ¶ 507. For Committee Reports, see ¶ 5078 and ¶ 5082.]

[Endnote Code Sec. 4980B]

Code Sec. 4980B(f)(2)(B)(i) was amended by Sec. 1899F(b)(1) and (2) of The American Recovery and Reinvestment Act of 2009, P.L. 111-5, 2/17/2009, as detailed below:

1. Sec. 1899F(b)(2) added new subclause (f)(2)(B)(i)(V)
2. Sec. 1899F(b)(2) added new subclause (f)(2)(B)(i)(VI)
3. Sec. 1899F(b)(1) substituted "(VI) SPECIAL RULE FOR DISABILITY. In the case of a qualified beneficiary" for "In the case of a qualified beneficiary" in clause (f)(2)(B)(i)
4. Sec. 1899F(b)(2) redesignated subclause (f)(2)(B)(i)(VI) as (f)(2)(B)(i)(VIII)

Effective Date (Sec. 1899F(d), P.L. 111-5, 2/17/2009) effective for periods of coverage which would (without regard to the amendments made by this section) end on or after 2/17/2009.

[¶ 3067]   Code Sec. 6211.   Definition of a deficiency.

* * * * * * * * * * * *

(b)   Rules for application of subsection (a). For purposes of this section—

(1) The tax imposed by Subtitle A and the tax shown on the return shall both be determined without regard to payments on account of estimated tax, without regard to the credit under section 31, without regard to the credit under section 33, and without regard to any credits resulting from the collection of amounts assessed under section 6851 or 6852 (relating to termination assessments).

(2) The term "rebate" means so much of an abatement, credit, refund, or other repayment, as was made on the ground that the tax imposed by subtitle A or B or chapter 41, 42, 43, or 44 was less than the excess of the amount specified in subsection (a)(1) over the rebates previously made.

(3) The computation by the Secretary, pursuant to section 6014, of the tax imposed by chapter 1 shall be considered as having been made by the taxpayer and the tax so computed considered as shown by the taxpayer upon his return.

(4) For purposes of subsection (a)—

(A) any excess of the sum of the credits allowable under sections 24(d), *¹25A by reason of subsection (i)(6) thereof*, 32, 34, 35, 36, *²36A*, 53(e), *³168(k)(4)*,*⁴6428, and 6431* over the tax imposed by subtitle A (determined without regard to such credits), and

(B) any excess of the sum of such credits as shown by the taxpayer on his return over the amount shown as the tax by the taxpayer on such return (determined without regard to such credits), shall be taken into account as negative amounts of tax.

* * * * * * * * * * *

[For Analysis, see ¶ 101, ¶ 103, ¶ 107, ¶ 806 and ¶ 1301. For Committee Reports, see ¶ 5001, ¶ 5004, ¶ 5034, ¶ 5070 and ¶ 5080.]

[Endnote Code Sec. 6211]

Code Sec. 6211(b)(4)(A) was amended by Sec. 1004(b)(7) of the American Recovery and Reinvestment Act of 2009, P.L. 111-5, 2/17/2009, as detailed below:

1. Sec. 1004(b)(7) added "25A by reason of subsection (i)(6) thereof," after "24(d)," in subpara. (b)(4)(A)

Effective Date (Sec. 1004(d), P.L. 111-5, 2/17/2009) effective for tax. yrs. begin. after 12/31/2008.

Code Sec. 6211(b)(4)(A) was amended by Sec. 1001(e)(1), P.L. 111-5, 2/17/2009, as detailed below:

2. Sec. 1001(e)(1) added "36A," after "36," in subpara. (b)(4)(A)

Effective Date (Sec. 1001(f), P.L. 111-5, 2/17/2009) effective for tax. yrs. begin. after 12/31/2008.

Code Sec. 6211(b)(4)(A) was amended by Secs. 1201(a)(3)(B) and (b)(2), P.L. 111-5, 2/17/2009, as detailed below:

3. Sec. 1201(a)(3)(B) [Ed. Note: Sec. 1201(b)(2) makes the same amendment as Sec. 1201(a)(3)(B)] added "168(k)(4)," after "53(e)," in subpara. (b)(4)(A)

Effective Date (Sec. 1201(c)(2), P.L. 111-5, 2/17/2009) effective for tax. yrs. end. after 3/31/2008.

Code Sec. 6211(b)(4)(A) was amended by Sec. 1531(c)(4), P.L. 111-5, 2/17/2009, as detailed below:

4. Sec. 1531(c)(4) substituted "6428, and 6431" for "and 6428" in subpara. (b)(4)(A)

Effective Date (Sec. 1531(e), P.L. 111-5, 2/17/2009) effective for obligations issued after 2/17/2009.

[¶ 3068]   Code Sec. 6213.   Restrictions applicable to deficiencies; petition to Tax Court.

* * * * * * * * * * *

(g) Definitions. For purposes of this section—

(1) Return. The term "return" includes any return, statement, schedule, or list, and any amendment or supplement thereto, filed with respect to any tax imposed by subtitle A or B, or chapter 41, 42, 43, or 44.

(2) Mathematical or clerical error. The term "mathematical or clerical error" means—

(A) an error in addition, subtraction, multiplication, or division shown on any return,

(B) an incorrect use of any table provided by the Internal Revenue Service with respect to any return if such incorrect use is apparent from the existence of other information on the return,

(C) an entry on a return of an item which is inconsistent with another entry of the same or another item on such return,

(D) an omission of information which is required to be supplied on the return to substantiate an entry on the return,

(E) an entry on a return of a deduction or credit in an amount which exceeds a statutory limit imposed by subtitle A or B, or chapter 41, 42 43, or 44, if such limit is expressed—

(i) as a specified monetary amount, or

(ii) as a percentage, ratio, or fraction,

and if the items entering into the application of such limit appear on such return,

(F) an omission of a correct taxpayer identification number required under section 32 (relating to the earned income credit) to be included on a return,

(G) an entry on a return claiming the credit under section 32 with respect to net earnings from self-employment described in section 32(c)(2)(A) to the extent the tax imposed by section 1401 (relating to self-employment tax) on such net earnings has not been paid,

(H) an omission of a correct TIN required under section 21 (relating to expenses for household and dependent care services necessary for gainful employment) or section 151 (relating to allowance of deductions for personal exemptions),

(I) an omission of a correct TIN required under section 24(e) (relating to child tax credit) to be included on a return,

(J) an omission of a correct TIN required under section 25A(g)(1) (relating to higher education tuition and related expenses) to be included on a return,

(K) an omission of information required by section 32(k)(2) (relating to taxpayers making improper prior claims of earned income credit),

(L) the inclusion on a return of a TIN required to be included on the return under section 21, 24, 32, or 6428 if—

(i) such TIN is of an individual whose age affects the amount of the credit under such section, and

(ii) the computation of the credit on the return reflects the treatment of such individual as being of an age different from the individual's age based on such TIN, [1]

(M) the entry on the return claiming the credit under section 32 with respect to a child if, according to the Federal Case Registry of Child Support Orders established under section 453(h) of the Social Security Act, the taxpayer is a noncustodial parent of such child[2], *and*

[3]*(N) an omission of the reduction required under section 36A(c) with respect to the credit allowed under section 36A or an omission of the correct social security account number required under section 36A(d)(1)(B). A taxpayer shall be treated as having omitted a correct TIN for purposes of the preceding sentence if information provided by the taxpayer on the return with respect to the individual whose TIN was provided differs from the information the Secretary obtains from the person issuing the TIN.*

* * * * * * * * * * * *

[For Analysis, see ¶ 101 and ¶ 103. For Committee Reports, see ¶ 5001 and ¶ 5080.]

[Endnote Code Sec. 6213]

Code Sec. 6213(g)(2)(L)(ii), Code Sec. 6213(g)(2)(M) and Code Sec. 6213(g)(2)(N) were amended by Sec. 1001(d) of the American Recovery and Reinvestment Tax Act of 2009, P.L. 111-5, 2/17/2009, as detailed below:

1. Sec. 1001(d) deleted "and" at the end of clause (g)(2)(L)(ii)
2. Sec. 1001(d) substituted ", and" for the period at the end of subpara. (g)(2)(M)
3. Sec. 1001(d) added subpara. (g)(2)(N)

Effective Date (Sec. 1001(f), P.L. 111-5, 2/17/2009) effective for tax. yrs. begin. after 12/31/2008.

[¶ 3069]   Code Sec. 6401.   Amounts treated as overpayments.

* * * * * * * * * * * *

(b)   Excessive credits.

(1)   In general. If the amount allowable as credits under subpart C of part IV of subchapter A of chapter 1 (relating to refundable credits) exceeds the tax imposed by subtitle A (reduced by the credits allowable under subparts A, B, D, G, H, [1]*I, and J* of such part IV), the amount of such excess shall be considered an overpayment.

(2)   Special rule for credit under section 33. For purposes of paragraph (1), any credit allowed under section 33 (relating to withholding of tax on nonresident aliens and on foreign corporations) for any taxable year shall be treated as a credit allowable under subpart C of part IV of subchapter A of chapter 1 only if an election under subsection (g) or (h) of section 6013 is in effect for such taxable year. The preceding sentence shall not apply to any credit so allowed by reason of section 1446.

* * * * * * * * * * * *

[For Analysis, see ¶ 1301. For Committee Reports, see ¶ 5070.]

[Endnote Code Sec. 6401]

Code Sec. 6401(b)(1), was amended by Sec. 1531(c)(5) of the American Recovery and Reinvestment Tax Act of 2009, P.L. 111-5, 2/17/2009, as detailed below:

1. Sec. 1531(c)(5) substituted "I, and J" for "and I" in para. (b)(1)

Effective Date (Sec. 1531(e), P.L. 111-5, 2/17/2009) effective for obligations issued after 2/17/2009.

[¶ 3070]   Code Sec.¹ 6431.   Credit for qualified bonds allowed to issuer.

(a) In general. In the case of a qualified bond issued before January 1, 2011, the issuer of such bond shall be allowed a credit with respect to each interest payment under such bond which shall be payable by the Secretary as provided in subsection (b).

(b) Payment of credit. The Secretary shall pay (contemporaneously with each interest payment date under such bond) to the issuer of such bond (or to any person who makes such interest payments on behalf of the issuer) 35 percent of the interest payable under such bond on such date.

(c) Application of arbitrage rules. For purposes of section 148, the yield on a qualified bond shall be reduced by the credit allowed under this section.

(d) Interest payment date. For purposes of this subsection, the term "interest payment date" means each date on which interest is payable by the issuer under the terms of the bond.

(e) Qualified bond. For purposes of this subsection, the term "qualified bond" has the meaning given such term in section 54AA(g).

[For Analysis, see ¶ 1301. For Committee Reports, see ¶ 5070.]

[Endnote Code Sec. 6431]

Code Sec. 6431 was added by Sec. 1531(b) of the American Recovery and Reinvestment Tax Act of 2009, P.L. 111-5, 2/17/2009.

1. added Code Sec. 6431

Effective Date (Sec. 1531(e), P.L. 111-5, 2/17/2009) effective for obligations issued after 2/17/2009.

[¶ 3071]   Code Sec.¹ 6432.   COBRA premium assistance.

(a) In general. The person to whom premiums are payable under COBRA continuation coverage shall be reimbursed as provided in subsection (c) for the amount of premiums not paid by assistance eligible individuals by reason of section 3002(a) of the Health Insurance Assistance for the Unemployed Act of 2009.

(b) Person entitled to reimbursement. For purposes of subsection (a), except as otherwise provided by the Secretary, the person to whom premiums are payable under COBRA continuation coverage shall be treated as being—

(1) in the case of any group health plan which is a multiemployer plan (as defined in section 3(37) of the Employee Retirement Income Security Act of 1974), the plan,

(2) in the case of any group health plan not described in paragraph (1)—

(A) which is subject to the COBRA continuation provisions contained in—

(i) the Internal Revenue Code of 1986,

(ii) the Employee Retirement Income Security Act of 1974,

(iii) the Public Health Service Act, or

(iv) title 5, United States Code, or

(B) under which some or all of the coverage is not provided by insurance, the employer maintaining the plan, and

(3) in the case of any group health plan not described in paragraph (1) or (2), the insurer providing the coverage under the group health plan.

(c) Method of reimbursement. Except as otherwise provided by the Secretary—

(1) Treatment as payment of payroll taxes. Each person entitled to reimbursement under subsection (a) (and filing a claim for such reimbursement at such time and in such manner as the Secretary may require) shall be treated for purposes of this title and section 1324(b)(2) of title 31, United States Code, as having paid to the Secretary, on the date that the assistance eligible individual's premium payment is received, payroll taxes in an amount equal to the portion of such reimbursement which relates to such premium. To the extent that the amount treated as paid under the preceding sentence exceeds the amount of

such person's liability for such taxes, the Secretary shall credit or refund such excess in the same manner as if it were an overpayment of such taxes.

(2) Overstatements. *Any overstatement of the reimbursement to which a person is entitled under this section (and any amount paid by the Secretary as a result of such overstatement) shall be treated as an underpayment of payroll taxes by such person and may be assessed and collected by the Secretary in the same manner as payroll taxes.*

(3) Reimbursement contingent on payment of remaining premium. *No reimbursement may be made under this section to a person with respect to any assistance eligible individual until after the reduced premium required under section 3002(a)(1)(A) of such Act with respect to such individual has been received.*

(d) Definitions. *For purposes of this section—*

(1) Payroll taxes. *The term "payroll taxes" means—*

(A) *amounts required to be deducted and withheld for the payroll period under section 3402 (relating to wage withholding),*

(B) *amounts required to be deducted for the payroll period under section 3102 (relating to FICA employee taxes), and*

(C) *amounts of the taxes imposed for the payroll period under section 3111 (relating to FICA employer taxes).*

(2) Person. *The term "person" includes any governmental entity.*

(e) Reporting. *Each person entitled to reimbursement under subsection (a) for any period shall submit such reports (at such time and in such manner) as the Secretary may require, including—*

(1) *an attestation of involuntary termination of employment for each covered employee on the basis of whose termination entitlement to reimbursement is claimed under subsection (a),*

(2) *a report of the amount of payroll taxes offset under subsection (a) for the reporting period and the estimated offsets of such taxes for the subsequent reporting period in connection with reimbursements under subsection (a), and*

(3) *a report containing the TINs of all covered employees, the amount of subsidy reimbursed with respect to each covered employee and qualified beneficiaries, and a designation with respect to each covered employee as to whether the subsidy reimbursement is for coverage of 1 individual or 2 or more individuals.*

(f) Regulations. *The Secretary shall issue such regulations or other guidance as may be necessary or appropriate to carry out this section, including—*

(1) *the requirement to report information or the establishment of other methods for verifying the correct amounts of reimbursements under this section, and*

(2) *the application of this section to group health plans that are multiemployer plans (as defined in section 3(37) of the Employee Retirement Income Security Act of 1974).*

[For Analysis, see ¶ 308. For Committee Reports, see ¶ 5082.]

[Endnote Code Sec. 6432]

Code Sec. 6432, was added by Sec. 3001(a)(12)(A) of the American Recovery and Reinvestment Tax Act of 2009, P.L. 111-5, 2/17/2009, as detailed below:

1. Sec. 3001(a)(12)(A) added Code Sec. 6432

Effective Date (Sec. 3001(a)(12)(D), P.L. 111-5, 2/17/2009) effective for premiums to which subsec. (a)(1)(A) applies. Sec. 3001(a)(1)(A), P.L. 111-5, 2/17/2009, reads as follows:

"SEC. 3001. PREMIUM ASSISTANCE FOR COBRA BENEFITS.

"(a) Premium assistance for COBRA continuation coverage for individuals and their families.

"(1) Provision of premium assistance.

"(A) Reduction of premiums payable. In the case of any premium for a period of coverage beginning on or after the date of the enactment of this Act for COBRA continuation coverage with respect to any assistance eligible individual, such individual shall be treated for purposes of any COBRA continuation provision as having paid the amount of such premium if such individual pays (or a person other than such individual's employer pays on behalf of such individual) 35 percent of the amount of such premium (as determined without regard to this subsection)."

Sec. 3001(a)(12)(B), P.L. 111-5, 2/17/2009, provides:

"(B) Social security trust funds held harmless. In determining any amount transferred or appropriated to any fund under the Social Security Act, section 6432 of the Internal Revenue Code of 1986 shall not be taken into account."

Sec. 3001(a)(12)(E), P.L. 111-5, 2/17/2009, provides:

"(E) Special rule.

"(i) In general. In the case of an assistance eligible individual who pays, with respect to the first period of COBRA continuation coverage to which subsection (a)(1)(A) applies or the immediately subsequent period, the full premium amount for such coverage, the person to whom such payment is payable shall—

"(I) make a reimbursement payment to such individual for the amount of such premium paid in excess of the amount required to be paid under subsection (a)(1)(A); or

"(II) provide credit to the individual for such amount in a manner that reduces one or more subsequent premium payments that the individual is required to pay under such subsection for the coverage involved.

'(ii) Reimbursing employer. A person to which clause (i) applies shall be reimbursed as provided for in section 6432 of the Internal Revenue Code of 1986 for any payment made, or credit provided, to the employee under such clause.

"(iii) Payment of credits. Unless it is reasonable to believe that the credit for the excess payment in clause (i)(II) will be used by the assistance eligible individual within 180 days of the date on which the person receives from the individual the payment of the full premium amount, a person to which clause (i) applies shall make the payment required under such clause to the individual within 60 days of such payment of the full premium amount. If, as of any day within the 180-day period, it is no longer reasonable to believe that the credit will be used during that period, payment equal to the remainder of the credit outstanding shall be made to the individual within 60 days of such day."

[¶ 3072]   Code Sec. 6501.   Limitations on assessment and collection.

* * * * * * * * * * * *

> • **Caution:** Code Sec. 6501(m), following, is effective for vehicles acquired before 12/31/2009. For Code Sec. 6501(m) effective after 12/31/2009 see below.

(m)   Deficiencies attributable to election of certain credits. The period for assessing a deficiency attributable to any election under ¹*section 30(e)(6)*, 30B(h)(9), 30C(e)(5), 30D(e)(9), 40(f), 43, 45B, 45C(d)(4), 45H(g), or 51(j) (or any revocation thereof) shall not expire before the date 1 year after the date on which the Secretary is notified of such election (or revocation).

> • **Caution:** Code Sec. 6501(m), following, is effective for vehicles acquired after 12/31/2009. For Code Sec. 6501(m) effective before 12/31/2009 see above.

(m)   Deficiencies attributable to election of certain credits. The period for assessing a deficiency attributable to any election under section 30(e)(6), 30B(h)(9), 30C(e)(5), [**Ed. Note: See history for Code Sec. 6501] ²*30D(e)(4)*, 40(f), 43, 45B, 45C(d)(4), 45H(g), or 51(j) (or any revocation thereof) shall not expire before the date 1 year after the date on which the Secretary is notified of such election (or revocation).

* * * * * * * * * * * *

[For Analysis, see ¶ 1002. For Committee Reports, see ¶ 5027.]

[Endnote Code Sec. 6501]

Code Sec. 6501(m) was amended by Sec. 1142(b)(7) of The American Recovery and Reinvestment Act of 2009, P.L. 111-5, 2/17/2009, as detailed below:

1. Sec. 1142(b)(7) substituted "section 30(e)(6)" for "section 30(d)(4)" in subsec. (m)

Effective Date (Sec. 1142(c), P.L. 111-5, 2/17/2009) effective for vehicles acquired after 2/17/2009.

Code Sec. 6501(m) was amended by Sec. 1141(b)(4), P.L. 111-5, 2/17/2009, as detailed below:

2. Sec. 1141(b)(4) substituted "section 30D(e)(4)" for "section 30D(e)(9)" in subsec. (m) [**Ed. Note: See history of Code Sec. 6501]

Effective Date (Sec. 1141(c), P.L. 111-5, 2/17/2009) effective for vehicles acquired after 12/31/2009.

[¶ 3073]   Code Sec. 6654.   Failure by individual to pay estimated income tax.

* * * * * * * * * * * *

(d) Amount of required installments. For purposes of this section—

(1) Amount.

(A) In general. Except as provided in paragraph (2), the amount of any required installment shall be 25 percent of the required annual payment.

(B) Required annual payment. For purposes of subparagraph (A), the term "required annual payment" means the lesser of—

(i) 90 percent of the tax shown on the return for the taxable year (or, if no return is filed, 90 percent of the tax for such year), or

(ii) 100 percent of the tax shown on the return of the individual for the preceding taxable year.

Clause (ii) shall not apply if the preceding taxable year was not a taxable year of 12 months or if the individual did not file a return for such preceding taxable year.

(C) Limitation on use of preceding year's tax.

(i) In general. If the adjusted gross income shown on the return of the individual for the preceding taxable year beginning in any calendar year exceeds $150,000, clause (ii) of subparagraph (B) shall be applied by substituting the applicable percentage for "100 percent". For purposes of the preceding sentence, the applicable percentage shall be determined in accordance with the following table:

If the preceding taxable year begins in:	The applicable percentage is:
1998	105
1999	108.6
2000	110
2001	112
2002 or thereafter	110

This clause shall not apply in the case of a preceding taxable year beginning in calendar year 1997.

(ii) Separate returns. In the case of a married individual (within the meaning of section 7703) who files a separate return for the taxable year for which the amount of the installment is being determined, clause (i) shall be applied by substituting "$75,000" for "$150,000".

(iii) Special rule. In the case of an estate or trust, adjusted gross income shall be determined as provided in section 67(e).

¹*(D) Special rule for 2009.*

(i) In general. Notwithstanding subparagraph (C), in the case of any taxable year beginning in 2009, clause (ii) of subparagraph (B) shall be applied to any qualified individual by substituting "90 percent" for "100 percent".

(ii) Qualified individual. For purposes of this subparagraph, the term "qualified individual" means any individual if—

(I) the adjusted gross income shown on the return of such individual for the preceding taxable year is less than $500,000, and

(II) such individual certifies that more than 50 percent of the gross income shown on the return of such individual for the preceding taxable year was income from a small business.

A certification under subclause (II) shall be in such form and manner and filed at such time as the Secretary may by regulations prescribe.

(iii) Income from a small business. For purposes of clause (ii), income from a small business means, with respect to any individual, income from a trade or business the average number of employees of which was less than 500 employees for the calendar year ending with or within the preceding taxable year of the individual.

(iv) Separate returns. In the case of a married individual (within the meaning of section 7703) who files a separate return for the taxable year for which the amount of

the installment is being determined, clause (ii)(I) shall be applied by substituting "$250,000" for "$500,000".

(v) Estates and trusts. In the case of an estate or trust, adjusted gross income shall be determined as provided in section 67(e).

(2) Lower required installment where annualized income installment is less than amount determined under paragraph (1).

(A) In general. In the case of any required installment, if the individual establishes that the annualized income installment is less than the amount determined under paragraph (1)—

(i) the amount of such required installment shall be the annualized income installment, and

(ii) any reduction in a required installment resulting from the application of this subparagraph shall be recaptured by increasing the amount of the next required installment determined under paragraph (1) by the amount of such reduction (and by increasing subsequent required installments to the extent that the reduction has not previously been recaptured under this clause).

(B) Determination of annualized income installment. In the case of any required installment, the annualized income installment is the excess (if any) of—

(i) an amount equal to the applicable percentage of the tax for the taxable year computed by placing on an annualized basis the taxable income, alternative minimum taxable income, and adjusted self-employment income for months in the taxable year ending before the due date for the installment, over

(ii) the aggregate amount of any prior required installments for the taxable year.

(C) Special rules. For purposes of this paragraph—

(i) Annualization. The taxable income, alternative minimum taxable income, and adjusted self-employment income shall be placed on an annualized basis under regulations prescribed by the Secretary.

(ii) Applicable percentage.

In the case of the following required installments:	The applicable percentage is:
1st	22.5
2nd	45
3rd	67.5
4th	90.

(iii) Adjusted self-employment income. The term "adjusted self-employment income" means self-employment income (as defined in section 1402(b)); except that section 1402(b) shall be applied by placing wages (within the meaning of section 1402(b)) for months in the taxable year ending before the due date for the installment on an annualized basis consistent with clause (i).

(D) Treatment of subpart F and section 936 income.

(i) In general. Any amounts required to be included in gross income under section 936(h) or 951(a) (and credits properly allocable thereto) shall be taken into account in computing any annualized income installment under subparagraph (B) in a manner similar to the manner under which partnership income inclusions (and credits properly allocable thereto) are taken into account.

(ii) Prior year safe harbor. If a taxpayer elects to have this clause apply to any taxable year—

(I) clause (i) shall not apply, and

(II) for purposes of computing any annualized income installment for such taxable year, the taxpayer shall be treated as having received ratably during such taxable year items of income and credit described in clause (i) in an amount equal to the amount of such items shown on the return of the taxpayer for the preceding taxable year (the second preceding taxable year in the case of the first and second required installments for such taxable year).

* * * * * * * * * * * *

[For Analysis, see ¶ 701. For Committee Reports, see ¶ 5038.]

[Endnote Code Sec. 6654]

Code Sec. 6654(d)(1)(D) was added by Sec. 1212 of The American Recovery and Reinvestment Act of 2009, P.L. 111-5, 2/17/2009, as detailed below:

1. Sec. 1212 added subpara. (d)(1)(D), effective 2/17/2009.

Effective Date Enacted 2/17/2009

[¶ 3074]

Code Sec.[1] **6720C.**   *Penalty for failure to notify health plan of cessation of eligibility for COBRA premium assistance.*

*(a) **In general.** Any person required to notify a group health plan under section 3002(a)(2)(C)) of the Health Insurance Assistance for the Unemployed Act of 2009 who fails to make such a notification at such time and in such manner as the Secretary of Labor may require shall pay a penalty of 110 percent of the premium reduction provided under such section after termination of eligibility under such subsection.*

*(b) **Reasonable cause exception.** No penalty shall be imposed under subsection (a) with respect to any failure if it is shown that such failure is due to reasonable cause and not to willful neglect.*

[For Analysis, see ¶ 309. For Committee Reports, see ¶ 5082.]

[Endnote Code Sec. 6720C]

Code Sec. 6720C was added by Sec. 3001(a)(13)(A) of The American Recovery and Reinvestment Act of 2009, P.L. 111-5, 2/17/2009, as detailed below:

1. Sec. 3001(a)(13)(A) added Code Sec. 6720C

Effective Date (Sec. 3001(a)(13)(C), P.L. 111-5, 2/17/2009) effective for failures occurring after 2/17/2009.

[¶ 3075]   Code Sec. 7527.   Advance payment of credit for health insurance costs of eligible individuals.

(a)   General rule. Not later than August 1, 2003, the Secretary shall establish a program for making payments on behalf of certified individuals to providers of qualified health insurance (as defined in section 35(e)) for such individuals.

(b)   Limitation on advance payments during any taxable year. The Secretary may make payments under subsection (a) only to the extent that the total amount of such payments made on behalf of any individual during the taxable year does not exceed 65 percent [1]*(80 percent in the case of eligible coverage months beginning before January 1, 2011)* of the amount paid by the taxpayer for coverage of the taxpayer and qualifying family members under qualified health insurance for eligible coverage months beginning in the taxable year.

(c)   Certified individual. For purposes of this section, the term "certified individual" means any individual for whom a qualified health insurance costs credit eligibility certificate is in effect.

[2]*(d)   Qualified health insurance costs eligibility certificate.*

*(1)   **In general.** For purposes of this section, the term "qualified health insurance costs eligibility certificate" means any written statement that an individual is an eligible individual (as defined in section 35(c)) if such statement provides such information as the Secretary may require for purposes of this section and—*

(A) in the case of an eligible TAA recipient (as defined in section 35(c)(2)) or an eligible alternative TAA recipient (as defined in section 35(c)(3)), is certified by the Secretary of Labor (or by any other person or entity designated by the Secretary), or

534

(B) in the case of an eligible PBGC pension recipient (as defined in section 35(c)(4)), is certified by the Pension Benefit Guaranty Corporation (or by any other person or entity designated by the Secretary).

(2) **Inclusion of certain information.** *In the case of any statement described in paragraph (1) which is issued before January 1, 2011, such statement shall not be treated as a qualified health insurance costs credit eligibility certificate unless such statement includes—*

(A) the name, address, and telephone number of the State office or offices responsible for providing the individual with assistance with enrollment in qualified health insurance (as defined in section 35(e)),

(B) a list of the coverage options that are treated as qualified health insurance (as so defined) by the State in which the individual resides, and

(C) in the case of a TAA-eligible individual (as defined in section 4980B(f)(5)(C)(iv)(II)), a statement informing the individual that the individual has 63 days from the date that is 7 days after the date of the issuance of such certificate to enroll in such insurance without a lapse in creditable coverage (as defined in section 9801(c)).

[3]*(e)* **Payment for premiums due prior to commencement of advance payments.** *In the case of eligible coverage months beginning before January 1, 2011—*

(1) **In general.** *The program established under subsection (a) shall provide that the Secretary shall make 1 or more retroactive payments on behalf of a certified individual in an aggregate amount equal to 80 percent of the premiums for coverage of the taxpayer and qualifying family members under qualified health insurance for eligible coverage months (as defined in section 35(b)) occurring prior to the first month for which an advance payment is made on behalf of such individual under subsection (a).*

(2) **Reduction of payment for amounts received under national emergency grants.** *The amount of any payment determined under paragraph (1) shall be reduced by the amount of any payment made to the taxpayer for the purchase of qualified health insurance under a national emergency grant pursuant to section 173(f) of the Workforce Investment Act of 1998 for a taxable year including the eligible coverage months described in paragraph (1).*

[For Analysis, see ¶ 501, ¶ 502, ¶ 503 and ¶ 509. For Committee Reports, see ¶ 5078.]

[Endnote Code Sec. 7527]

Code Sec. 7527(b) was amended by Sec. 1899A(a)(2) of The American Recovery and Reinvestment Act of 2009, P.L. 111-5, 2/17/2009, as detailed below:

1. Sec. 1899A(a)(2) added "(80 percent in the case of eligible coverage months beginning before January 1, 2011)" after "65 percent" in subsec. (b)

Effective Date (Sec. 1899A(b), P.L. 111-5, 2/17/2009) effective for coverage months begin. on or after the first day of the first month begin. 60 days after 2/17/2009.

Code Sec. 7527(d) was amended by Sec. 1899H(a), P.L. 111-5, 2/17/2009, as detailed below:

2. Sec. 1899H(a) amended subsec. (d)

Effective Date (Sec. 1899H(b), P.L. 111-5, 2/17/2009) effective for certificates issued after the date that is 6 months after 2/17/2009.

Code Sec. 7527(e) was added by Sec. 1899B(a), P.L. 111-5, 2/17/2009.

3. Sec. 1899B(a) added subsec. (e).

Effective Date (Sec. 1899B(b), P.L. 111-5, 2/17/2009) effective for coverage months begin. after 12/31/2008.

Sec. 1899B(c) of this Act provides:

"(c) Transitional rule. The Secretary of the Treasury shall not be required to make any payments under section 7527(e) of the Internal Revenue Code of 1986, as added by this section, until after the date that is 6 months after the date of the enactment of this Act."

[¶ 3076]   Code Sec. 7871.   Indian tribal governments treated as states for certain purposes.

* * * * * * * * * * *

[1](f)   *Tribal economic development bonds.*

(1)   Allocation of limitation.

(A) In general. The Secretary shall allocate the national tribal economic development bond limitation among the Indian tribal governments in such manner as the Secretary, in consultation with the Secretary of the Interior, determines appropriate.

(B) National limitation. There is a national tribal economic development bond limitation of $2,000,000,000.

(2)   Bonds treated as exempt from tax. In the case of a tribal economic development bond —

(A) notwithstanding subsection (c), such bond shall be treated for purposes of this title in the same manner as if such bond were issued by a State,

(B) the Indian tribal government issuing such bond and any instrumentality of such Indian tribal government shall be treated as a State for purposes of section 141, and

(C) section 146 shall not apply.

(3)   Tribal economic development bond.

(A) In general. For purposes of this section, the term "tribal economic development bond" means any bond issued by an Indian tribal government —

(i) the interest on which would be exempt from tax under section 103 if issued by a State or local government, and

(ii) which is designated by the Indian tribal government as a tribal economic development bond for purposes of this subsection.

(B) Exceptions. Such term shall not include any bond issued as part of an issue if any portion of the proceeds of such issue are used to finance —

(i) any portion of a building in which class II or class III gaming (as defined in section 4 of the Indian Gaming Regulatory Act) is conducted or housed or any other property actually used in the conduct of such gaming, or

(ii) any facility located outside the Indian reservation (as defined in section 168(j)(6)).

(C) Limitation on amount of bonds designated. The maximum aggregate face amount of bonds which may be designated by any Indian tribal government under subparagraph (A) shall not exceed the amount of national tribal economic development bond limitation allocated to such government under paragraph (1).

[For Analysis, see ¶ 1313. For Committee Reports, see ¶ 5056.]

[Endnote Code Sec. 7871]

Code Sec. 7871(f) was added by section 1402(a) of the American Recovery and Reinvestment Act of 2009, P.L. 111-5, 2/17/2009.

1. Sec. 1402(a) added subsec. (f).

Effective Date (Sec. 1402(c), P.L. 111-5, 2/17/2009) effective for obligations issued after 2/17/2009.

Sec. 1402(b) of this Act provides:

"Study. The Secretary of the Treasury, or the Secretary's delegate, shall conduct a study of the effects of the amendment made by subsection (a). Not later than 1 year after the date of the enactment of this Act, the Secretary of the Treasury, or the Secretary's delegate, shall report to Congress on the results of the study conducted under this paragraph, including the Secretary's recommendations regarding such amendment."

[¶ 3077]

Code Sec. 9801.   Increased portability through limitation on preexisting condition exclusions.

* * * * * * * * * * * *

(c)   Rules relating to crediting previous coverage.

(1)   Creditable coverage defined. For purposes of this part, the term "creditable coverage" means, with respect to an individual, coverage of the individual under any of the following:

(A) A group health plan.

(B) Health insurance coverage.

(C) Part A or part B of title XVIII of the Social Security Act.

(D) Title XIX of the Social Security Act, other than coverage consisting solely of benefits under section 1928.

(E) Chapter 55 of title 10, United States Code.

(F) A medical care program of the Indian Health Service or of a tribal organization.

(G) A State health benefits risk pool.

(H) A health plan offered under chapter 89 of title 5, United States Code.

(I) A public health plan (as defined in regulations).

(J) A health benefit plan under section 5(e) of the Peace Corps Act (22 U.S.C. 2504(e)).

Such term does not include coverage consisting solely of coverage of excepted benefits (as defined in section 9832(c)).

(2)   Not counting periods before significant breaks in coverage.

(A) In general. A period of creditable coverage shall not be counted, with respect to enrollment of an individual under a group health plan, if, after such period and before the enrollment date, there was a 63-day period during all of which the individual was not covered under any creditable coverage.

(B) Waiting period not treated as a break in coverage. For purposes of subparagraph (A) and subsection (d)(4), any period that an individual is in a waiting period for any coverage under a group health plan or is in an affiliation period shall not be taken into account in determining the continuous period under subparagraph (A).

(C) Affiliation period.

(i) In general. For purposes of this section, the term "affiliation period" means a period which, under the terms of the health insurance coverage offered by the health maintenance organization, must expire before the health insurance coverage becomes effective. During such an affiliation period, the organization is not required to provide health care services or benefits and no premium shall be charged to the participant or beneficiary.

(ii) Beginning. Such period shall begin on the enrollment date.

(iii) Runs concurrently with waiting period. Any such affiliation period shall run concurrently with any waiting period under the plan.

[1]*(D) TAA-eligible individuals. In the case of plan years beginning before January 1, 2011—*

(i) TAA pre-certification period rule. In the case of a TAA-eligible individual, the period beginning on the date the individual has a TAA-related loss of coverage and ending on the date which is 7 days after the date of the issuance by the Secretary (or by any person or entity designated by the Secretary) of a qualified health insurance costs credit eligibility certificate for such individual for purposes of section 7527 shall not be taken into account in determining the continuous period under subparagraph (A).

(ii) Definitions. The terms "TAA eligible individual" and "TAA-related loss of coverage" have the meanings given such terms in section 4980B(f)(5)(C)(iv).

(3)   Method of crediting coverage.

(A) Standard method. Except as otherwise provided under subparagraph (B), for purposes of applying subsection (a)(3), a group health plan shall count a period of creditable coverage without regard to the specific benefits for which coverage is offered during the period.

(B) Election of alternative method. A group health plan may elect to apply subsection (a)(3) based on coverage of any benefits within each of several classes or categories of benefits specified in regulations rather than as provided under subparagraph (A). Such election shall be made on a uniform basis for all participants and beneficiaries. Under such election a group health plan shall count a period of creditable coverage with respect to any class or category of benefits if any level of benefits is covered within such class or category.

(C) Plan notice. In the case of an election with respect to a group health plan under subparagraph (B), the plan shall—

(i) prominently state in any disclosure statements concerning the plan, and state to each enrollee at the time of enrollment under the plan, that the plan has made such election, and

(ii) include in such statements a description of the effect of this election.

(4) Establishment of period. Periods of creditable coverage with respect to an individual shall be established through presentation of certifications described in subsection (e) or in such other manner as may be specified in regulations.

* * * * * * * * * * *

(f) Special enrollment periods.

* * * * * * * * * * *

[2]*(3)* *Special rules relating to Medicaid and CHIP.*

(A) In general. A group health plan shall permit an employee who is eligible, but not enrolled, for coverage under the terms of the plan (or a dependent of such an employee if the dependent is eligible, but not enrolled, for coverage under such terms) to enroll for coverage under the terms of the plan if either of the following conditions is met:

(i) Termination of Medicaid or CHIP coverage. The employee or dependent is covered under a Medicaid plan under title XIX of the Social Security Act or under a State child health plan under title XXI of such Act and coverage of the employee or dependent under such a plan is terminated as a result of loss of eligibility for such coverage and the employee requests coverage under the group health plan not later than 60 days after the date of termination of such coverage.

(ii) Eligibility for employment assistance under Medicaid or CHIP. The employee or dependent becomes eligible for assistance, with respect to coverage under the group health plan under such Medicaid plan or State child health plan (including under any waiver or demonstration project conducted under or in relation to such a plan), if the employee requests coverage under the group health plan not later than 60 days after the date the employee or dependent is determined to be eligible for such assistance.

(B) Employee outreach and disclosure.

(i) Outreach to employees regarding availability of Medicaid and CHIP coverage.

(I) In general. Each employer that maintains a group health plan in a State that provides medical assistance under a State Medicaid plan under title XIX of the Social Security Act, or child health assistance under a State child health plan under title XXI of such Act, in the form of premium assistance for the purchase of coverage under a group health plan, shall provide to each employee a written notice informing the employee of potential opportunities then currently available in the State in which the employee resides for premium assistance under such plans for health coverage of the employee or the employee's dependents. For purposes of compliance with this clause, the employer may use any State-specific model notice developed in accordance with section 701(f)(3)(B)(i)(II) of the Employee Retirement Income Security Act of 1974 (29 U.S.C. 1181(f)(3)(B)(i)(II)).

(II) Option to provide concurrent with provision of plan materials to employee. An employer may provide the model notice applicable to the State in which an employee resides concurrent with the furnishing of materials notifying the employee

of health plan eligibility, concurrent with materials provided to the employee in connection with an open season or election process conducted under the plan, or concurrent with the furnishing of the summary plan description as provided in section 104(b) of the Employee Retirement Income Security Act of 1974 (29 U.S.C. 1024).

(ii) Disclosure about group health plan benefits to States for Medicaid and CHIP eligible individuals. In the case of a participant or beneficiary of a group health plan who is covered under a Medicaid plan of a State under title XIX of the Social Security Act or under a State child health plan under title XXI of such Act, the plan administrator of the group health plan shall disclose to the State, upon request, information about the benefits available under the group health plan in sufficient specificity, as determined under regulations of the Secretary of Health and Human Services in consultation with the Secretary that require use of the model coverage coordination disclosure form developed under section 311(b)(1)(C) of the Children's Health Insurance Program Reauthorization Act of 2009, so as to permit the State to make a determination (under paragraph (2)(B), (3), or (10) of section 2105(c) of the Social Security Act or otherwise) concerning the cost-effectiveness of the State providing medical or child health assistance through premium assistance for the purchase of coverage under such group health plan and in order for the State to provide supplemental benefits required under paragraph (10)(E) of such section or other authority.

[For Analysis, see ¶ 403, ¶ 501 and ¶ 505. For Committee Reports, see ¶ 5078 and ¶ 5102.]

[Endnote Code Sec. 9801]

Code Sec. 9801(c)(2)(D) was added by Sec. 1899D(a) of The American Recovery and Reinvestment Act of 2009, P.L. 111-5, 2/17/2009, as detailed below:

1. Sec. 1899D(a) added subpara. (c)(2)(D)

Effective Date (Sec. 1899D(d), P.L. 111-5, 2/17/2009) effective for plan years begin. after 2/17/2009.

Code Sec. 9801(f)(3) was added by Sec. 311(a), P.L. 111-3.

2. Sec. 311(a) added subpara. (f)(3)

Effective Date (Sec. 3, P.L. 111-3) Sec. 3, P.L. 111-3 provides:

"Sec. 3. General effective date; exception for State legislation; contingent effective date; reliance on law.

"(a) General effective date. Unless otherwise provided in this Act, subject to subsections (b) through (d), this Act (and the amendments made by this Act) shall take effect on April 1, 2009, and shall apply to child health assistance and medical assistance provided on or after that date.

"(b) Exception for state legislation. In the case of a State plan under title XIX or State child health plan under XXI of the Social Security Act, which the Secretary of Health and Human Services determines requires State legislation in order for the respective plan to meet one or more additional requirements imposed by amendments made by this Act, the respective plan shall not be regarded as failing to comply with the requirements of such title solely on the basis of its failure to meet such an additional requirement before the first day of the first calendar quarter beginning after the close of the first regular session of the State legislature that begins after the date of enactment of this Act. For purposes of the previous sentence, in the case of a State that has a 2-year legislative session, each year of the session shall be considered to be a separate regular session of the State legislature.

"(c) Coordination of CHIP Funding for fiscal year 2009. Notwithstanding any other provision of law, insofar as funds have been appropriated under section 2104(a)(11), 2104(k), or 2104(l) of the Social Security Act, as amended by section 201 of Public Law 110-173, to provide allotments to States under CHIP for fiscal year 2009—

"(1) any amounts that are so appropriated that are not so allotted and obligated before April 1, 2009, are rescinded; and

"(2) any amount provided for CHIP allotments to a State under this Act (and the amendments made by this Act) for such fiscal year shall be reduced by the amount of such appropriations so allotted and obligated before such date.

"(d) Reliance on law. With respect to amendments made by this Act (other than title VII) that become effective as of a date—

"(1) such amendments are effective as of such date whether or not regulations implementing such amendments have been issued; and

"(2) Federal financial participation for medical assistance or child health assistance furnished under title XIX or XXI, respectively, of the Social Security Act on

" or after such date by a State in good faith reliance on such amendments before the date of promulgation of final regulations, if any, to carry out such amendments (or before the date of guidance, if any, regarding the implementation of such amendments) shall not be denied on the basis of the State's failure to comply with such regulations or guidance."

[¶ 3500]   ERISA As Amended
This section reproduces ERISA as Amended by P.L. 111-5, American Recovery and Reinvestment Act of 2009. ERISA sections appear in order, as amended, added or repealed. New matter is shown in *italics. All changes and effective dates are shown in the endnotes.*

[¶ 3501]
ERISA §102. [29 USC 1022]   Summary plan description.

* * * * * * * * * * * *

(b) The summary plan description shall contain the following information: The name and type of administration of the plan; in the case of a group health plan (as defined in section 733(a)(1)), whether a health insurance issuer (as defined in section 733(b)(2)) is responsible for the financing or administration (including payment of claims) of the plan and (if so) the name and address of such issuer; the name and address of the person designated as agent for the service of legal process, if such person is not the administrator; the name and address of the administrator; names, titles and addresses of any trustee or trustees (if they are persons different from the administrator); a description of the relevant provisions of any applicable collective bargaining agreement; the plan's requirements respecting eligibility for participation and benefits; a description of the provisions providing for nonforfeitable pension benefits; circumstances which may result in disqualification, ineligibility, or denial or loss of benefits; the source of financing of the plan and the identity of any organization through which benefits are provided; the date of the end of the plan year and whether the records of the plan are kept on a calendar, policy, or fiscal year basis; the procedures to be followed in presenting claims for benefits under the plan including the office at the Department of Labor through which participants and beneficiaries may seek assistance or information regarding their rights under this Act and the Health Insurance Portability and Accountability Act of 1996 with respect to health benefits that are offered through a group health plan (as defined in section 733(a)(1)) ¹, *the remedies* available under the plan for the redress of claims which are denied in whole or in part (including procedures required under section 503 of this Act [29 USC §1133])², *and if the employer so elects for purposes of complying with section 701(f)(3)(B)(i), the model notice applicable to the State in which the participants and beneficiaries reside.*
(Sept. 2, 1974, P.L. 93-406 §102, Title I, Subtitle B, Part 1, 88 Stat. 841; Aug. 21, 1996, P.L. 104-191, §101(c)(2), 110 Stat. 1951; Sept. 26, 1996, P.L. 104-204, § 603(b)(3)(C), 110 Stat. 2938; Aug. 5, 1997, P.L. 105-34, § 1503(b), Title XV, Subtitle A, 111 Stat. 1061; Feb. 4, 2009 P.L. 111-3, §§311(b)(1)(B)(i)-(ii), Title III, Subtitle B.)

[Endnote ERISA §1022]
29 USC 1022(b) was added by Sec. 311(b)(1)(B)(i) , P.L. 111-3, 2/4/2009, as detailed below:
1. Sec. 311(b)(1)(B)(i) substituted ", the remedies" for "and the remedies" in subsec. (b).
2. Sec. 311(b)(1)(B)(ii) added ", and if the employer so elects for purposes of complying with section 701(f)(3)(B)(i), the model notice applicable to the State in which the participants and beneficiaries reside" before the period in subsec. (b).
Effective Date (Sec. 3, P.L. 111-3, 2/4/2009) effective 4/1/2009, and shall apply to child health assistance and medical assistance provided on or after 4/1/2009.
Sec. 311(b)(1)(D), reads as follows:
"(D) Effective dates. The Secretary of Labor and the Secretary of Health and Human Services shall develop the initial model notices under section 701(f)(3)(B)(i)(II) of the Employee Retirement Income Security Act of 1974, and the Secretary of Labor shall provide such notices to employers, not later than the date that is 1 year after the date of enactment of this Act, and each employer shall provide the initial annual notices to such employer's employees beginning with the first plan year that begins after the date on which such initial model notices are first issued. The model coverage coordination disclosure form developed under subparagraph (C) shall apply with respect to requests made by States beginning with the first plan year that begins after the date on which such model coverage coordination disclosure form is first issued."

[¶ 3502]
ERISA §502. [29 USC 1132]　Civil enforcement.
　(a) **Persons empowered to bring a civil action.** A civil action may be brought—

　　　　　　* * * * * * * * * * * *

　(6) by the Secretary to collect any civil penalty under paragraph (2), (4), (5), (6), (7), [1](8), or (9) of subsection (c) or under subsection (i) or (l);

　　　　　　* * * * * * * * * * * *

　(b) **Plans qualified under Internal Revenue Code; maintenance of actions involving delinquent contributions.**

　　　　　　* * * * * * * * * * * *

　(c) **Administrator's refusal to supply requested information; penalty for failure to provide annual report in complete form.**

　　　　　　* * * * * * * * * * * *

　(9) **Secretarial enforcement authority relating to use of genetic information.**
　　(A) General rule. The Secretary may impose a penalty against any plan sponsor of a group health plan, or any health insurance issuer offering health insurance coverage in connection with the plan, for any failure by such sponsor or issuer to meet the requirements of subsection (a)(1)(F), (b)(3), (c), or (d) of section 702 or section 701 or 702(b)(1) with respect to genetic information, in connection with the plan.
　　(B) Amount.
　　　(i) In general. The amount of the penalty imposed by subparagraph (A) shall be $100 for each day in the noncompliance period with respect to each participant or beneficiary to whom such failure relates.
　　　(ii) Noncompliance period. For purposes of this paragraph, the term "noncompliance period" means, with respect to any failure, the period—
　　　　(I) beginning on the date such failure first occurs; and
　　　　(II) ending on the date the failure is corrected.
　　(C) Minimum penalties where failure discovered. Notwithstanding clauses (i) and (ii) of subparagraph (D):
　　　(i) In general. In the case of 1 or more failures with respect to a participant or beneficiary—
　　　　(I) which are not corrected before the date on which the plan receives a notice from the Secretary of such violation; and
　　　　(II) which occurred or continued during the period involved;
　　　the amount of penalty imposed by subparagraph (A) by reason of such failures with respect to such participant or beneficiary shall not be less than $2,500.
　　　(ii) Higher minimum penalty where violations are more than de minimis. To the extent violations for which any person is liable under this paragraph for any year are more than de minimis, clause (i) shall be applied by substituting "$15,000" for "$2,500" with respect to such person.
　　(D) Limitations.
　　　(i) Penalty not to apply where failure not discovered exercising reasonable diligence. No penalty shall be imposed by subparagraph (A) on any failure during any period for which it is established to the satisfaction of the Secretary that the person otherwise liable for such penalty did not know, and exercising reasonable diligence would not have known, that such failure existed.
　　　(ii) Penalty not to apply to failures corrected within certain periods. No penalty shall be imposed by subparagraph (A) on any failure if—
　　　　(I) such failure was due to reasonable cause and not to willful neglect; and

(II) such failure is corrected during the 30-day period beginning on the first date the person otherwise liable for such penalty knew, or exercising reasonable diligence would have known, that such failure existed.

(iii) Overall limitation for unintentional failures. In the case of failures which are due to reasonable cause and not to willful neglect, the penalty imposed by subparagraph (A) for failures shall not exceed the amount equal to the lesser of—

(I) 10 percent of the aggregate amount paid or incurred by the plan sponsor (or predecessor plan sponsor) during the preceding taxable year for group health plans; or

(II) $500,000.

(E) Waiver by secretary. In the case of a failure which is due to reasonable cause and not to willful neglect, the Secretary may waive part or all of the penalty imposed by subparagraph (A) to the extent that the payment of such penalty would be excessive relative to the failure involved.

(F) Definitions. Terms used in this paragraph which are defined in section 733 shall have the meanings provided such terms in such section.

> • *Caution:* Para. (c)(9), following, is effective 4/1/2009, and shall apply to child health assistance and medical assistance provided on or after that date, as amended by P.L. 111-3.

[2]*(9)* (A) The Secretary may assess a civil penalty against any employer of up to $100 a day from the date of the employer's failure to meet the notice requirement of section 701(f)(3)(B)(i)(I). For purposes of this subparagraph, each violation with respect to any single employee shall be treated as a separate violation.

(B) The Secretary may assess a civil penalty against any plan administrator of up to $100 a day from the date of the plan administrator's failure to timely provide to any State the information required to be disclosed under section 701(f)(3)(B)(ii). For purposes of this subparagraph, each violation with respect to any single participant or beneficiary shall be treated as a separate violation.

> • *Caution:* Para. (c)(10), following, is effective with respect to group health plans for plan yrs. begin. after 5/21/2009, as amended by P.L. 110-233.

(10) The Secretary and the Secretary of Health and Human Services shall maintain such ongoing consultation as may be necessary and appropriate to coordinate enforcement under this subsection with enforcement under section 1144(c)(8) of the Social Security Act.

> • *Caution:* Para. (c)(10), following, is effective 4/1/2009, and shall apply to child health assistance and medical assistance provided on or after that date, as redesignated by P.L. 111-3.

[3]*(10)* The Secretary and the Secretary of Health and Human Services shall maintain such ongoing consultation as may be necessary and appropriate to coordinate enforcement under this subsection with enforcement under section 1144(c)(8) of the Social Security Act.

* * * * * * * * * * * *

(Sept. 2, 1974, P.L. 93-406, Sec. 502, Title I, Subtitle B, Part 5, 88 Stat. 891; Sept. 26, 1980, P.L. 96-364, Sec. 306(b), Title III, 94 Stat. 1295; Apr. 7, 1986, P.L. 99-272, Sec. 10002(b), Title X, 100 Stat. 231; Dec. 22, 1987, P.L. 100-203, Title IX, Subtitle D, Part II, Subpart D,

§§9342(c), 9344, 101 Stat. 1330-372, 1330-373; Dec. 19, 1989, P.L. 101-239, Title II, Subpart B, §2101(a), (b), Title VII, Subtitle H, Part V, Subpart C, §7881(b)(5)(B), (j)(2), (3),
Subpart D, §§7891(a)(1), 7894(f)(1), 103 Stat. 2123, 2438, 2438, 2442, 2450; Nov. 5, 1990,
P.L. 101-508, Sec. 12012(d)(2), Title XII, Subtitle B, 104 Stat. 1388-573; Aug. 10, 1993,
P.L. 103-66, Sec. 4301(c)(1), Title IV, Subtitle D, (2), (3), 107 Stat. 312; Oct. 22, 1994, P.L.
103-401, §§2,3; Dec. 8, 1994, P.L. 103-465, Title VII, Subtitle F, Part I, Subpart B,
§761(a)(9)(B)(ii); Aug. 21, 1996, P.L. 104-191, Sec. 101(b), (e)(2)(A) and (B), 110 Stat.
1951, 1952; Sept. 26, 1996, P.L. 104-204, Sec. 603(b)(3)(E), 110 Stat. 2938; Aug. 5, 1997,
P.L. 105-34, Title XV, Subtitle A, §§1503(c)(2)(B), (d)(7); Jul. 30, 2002, P.L. 107-204, Sec.
306(b)(3), Title III; April 10, 2004, P.L. 108-218, Title I, §§102(d), 103(b), 104(a)(2); Aug.
17, 2006, P.L. 109-280, Sec. 103(b)(2), Title 1, Subtitle A, Title II, Subtitle A,
§202(b)(1)-(3), (c), Title V, §§502(a)(2), (b)(2), 507(b), 508(a)(2)(C), Title IX, §902(f)(2);
May 21, 2008, P.L. 110-233, Sec. 101(e), Title I; Dec. 23, 2008, P.L. 110-458
§§101(c)(1)(H), 102(b)(1)(H)-(I), Title I, Subtitle A; Feb. 4, 2009, P.L. 111-3
§§311(b)(1)(E)(i), 311(b)(1)(E)(ii), Title III, Subtitle B.)

[Endnote ERISA §1132]

29 USC 1132(a)(6) was added by Sec. 311(b)(1)(E)(i)-(ii), P.L. 111-3, 2/4/2009, as detailed below:

1. Sec. 311(b)(1)(E)(i) substituted "(8), or (9)" for "or (8)" in para. (a)(6)
2. Sec. 311(b)(1)(E)(ii) added para. (c)(9)
3. Sec. 311(b)(1)(E)(ii) redesignated para. (c)(9) as para. (c)(10)

Effective Date (Sec. 3, P.L. 111-3, 2/4/2009) effective 4/1/2009, and shall apply to child health assistance and medical assistance provided on or after 4/1/2009.

Sec. 311(b)(1)(D), reads as follows:

"(D) Effective dates. The Secretary of Labor and the Secretary of Health and Human Services shall develop the initial model notices under section 701(f)(3)(B)(i)(II) of the Employee Retirement Income Security Act of 1974, and the Secretary of Labor shall provide such notices to employers, not later than the date that is 1 year after the date of enactment of this Act, and each employer shall provide the initial annual notices to such employer's employees beginning with the first plan year that begins after the date on which such initial model notices are first issued. The model coverage coordination disclosure form developed under subparagraph (C) shall apply with respect to requests made by States beginning with the first plan year that begins after the date on which such model coverage coordination disclosure form is first issued."

[¶ 3503]
ERISA §602. [29 USC 1162]   Continuation coverage.
For purposes of section 601 [29 USC §1161], the term "continuation coverage" means coverage under the plan which meets the following requirements:

(1) Type of benefit coverage. The coverage must consist of coverage which, as of the time the coverage is being provided, is identical to the coverage provided under the plan to similarly situated beneficiaries under the plan with respect to whom a qualifying event has not occurred. If coverage is modified under the plan for any group of similarly situated beneficiaries, such coverage shall also be modified in the same manner for all individuals who are qualified beneficiaries under the plan pursuant to this part [29 USC §§1161 *et seq.*] in connection with such group.

(2) Period of coverage. The coverage must extend for at least the period beginning on the date of the qualifying event and ending not earlier than the earliest of the following:

(A) Maximum required period.

(i) General rule for terminations and reduced hours. In the case of a qualifying event described in section 603(2) [29 USC §1163(2)], except as provided in clause (ii), the date which is 18 months after the date of the qualifying event.

(ii) Special rule for multiple qualifying events. If a qualifying event (other than a qualifying event described in section 603(6) [29 USC §1163(6)] occurs during the 18 months after the date of a qualifying event described in section 603(2) [29 USC §1163(2)], the date which is 36 months after the date of the qualifying event described in section 603(2) [29 USC §1163(2)].

(iii) Special rule for certain bankruptcy proceedings. In the case of a qualifying event described in section 603(6) [29 USC §1163(6)] (relating to bankruptcy proceedings), the date of the death of the covered employee or qualified beneficiary (described in section 607(3)(C)(iii) [29 USC §1167(3)(C)(iii)]), or in the case of the surviving spouse or dependent children of the covered employee, 36 months after the date of the death of the covered employee.

(iv) General rule for other qualifying events. In the case of a qualifying event not described in section 603(2) or 603(6) [29 USC §1163(2) or (6)], the date which is 36 months after the date of the qualifying event.

[1]*(v) Special rule for PBGC recipients. In the case of a qualifying event described in section 603(2) with respect to a covered employee who (as of such qualifying event) has a nonforfeitable right to a benefit any portion of which is to be paid by the Pension Benefit Guaranty Corporation under title IV, notwithstanding clause (i) or (ii), the date of the death of the covered employee, or in the case of the surviving spouse or dependent children of the covered employee, 24 months after the date of the death of the covered employee. The preceding sentence shall not require any period of coverage to extend beyond December 31, 2010.*

[2]*(vi) Special rule for TAA-eligible individuals. In the case of a qualifying event described in section 603(2) with respect to a covered employee who is (as of the date that the period of coverage would, but for this clause or clause (vii), otherwise terminate under clause (i) or (ii)) a TAA-eligible individual (as defined in section 605(b)(4)(B)), the period of coverage shall not terminate by reason of clause (i) or (ii), as the case may be, before the later of the date specified in such clause or the date on which such individual ceases to be such a TAA-eligible individual. The preceding sentence shall not require any period of coverage to extend beyond December 31, 2010.*

[3]*(vii)* Medicare entitlement followed by qualifying event. In the case of a qualifying event described in section 603(2) [29 USC §1163(2)] that occurs less than 18 months after the date the covered employee became entitled to benefits under title XVIII of the Social Security Act [42 USC §§1395 et seq.], the period of coverage for qualified beneficiaries other than the covered employee shall not terminate under this subparagraph before the close of the 36-month period beginning on the date the covered employee became so entitled.

[4]*(viii)* [5]*Special rule for disability. In the case of a qualified beneficiary* who is determined, under title II [29 USC §§401 et seq.] or XVI of the Social Security Act [42 USC §§1381 et seq.], to have been disabled at any time during the first 60 days of continuation coverage under this part, any reference in clause (i) or (ii) to 18 months is deemed a reference to 29 months (with respect to all qualified beneficiaries), but only if the qualified beneficiary has provided notice of such determination under section 606(3) [29 USC §1166(3)] before the end of such 18 months.

(B) End of plan. The date on which the employer ceases to provide any group health plan to any employee.

(C) Failure to pay premium. The date on which coverage ceases under the plan by reason of a failure to make timely payment of any premium required under the plan with respect to the qualified beneficiary. The payment of any premium (other than any payment referred to in the last sentence of paragraph (3)) shall be considered to be timely if made within 30 days after the date due or within such longer period as applies to or under the plan.

(D) Group health plan coverage or Medicare entitlement. The date on which the qualified beneficiary first becomes, after the date of the election—

(i) covered under any other group health plan (as an employee or otherwise) which does not contain any exclusion or limitation with respect to any preexisting condition of such beneficiary (other than such an exclusion or limitation which does not apply to (or is satisfied by) such beneficiary by reason of chapter 100 of the Internal Revenue Code of 1986 [26 USC §§9801 et seq.], part 7 of this subtitle [29 USC §§1181 *et seq.*], or title XXVII of the Public Health Service Act) [42 USC §§300gg *et seq.*], or

(ii) in the case of a qualified beneficiary other than a qualified beneficiary described in section 607(3)(C) [29 USC §1167(3)(C)], entitled to benefits under title XVIII of the Social Security Act [42 USC §§1395 *et seq.*].

(E) Termination of extended coverage for disability. In the case of a qualified beneficiary who is disabled at any time during the first 60 days of continuation coverage under this part [29 USC §§1161 *et seq.*], the month that begins more than 30 days after the date of the final determination under title II [29 USC §401 *et seq.*] or XVI of the Social Security Act [42 USC §1381 *et seq.*] that the qualified beneficiary is no longer disabled.

(3) Premium requirements. The plan may require payment of a premium for any period of continuation coverage, except that such premium—

(A) shall not exceed 102 percent of the applicable premium for such period, and

(B) may, at the election of the payor, be made in monthly installments.

In no event may the plan require the payment of any premium before the day which is 45 days after the day on which the qualified beneficiary made the initial election for continuation coverage. In the case of an individual described in the last sentence of paragraph (2)(A), any reference in subparagraph (A) of this paragraph to "102 percent" is deemed a reference to "150 percent" for any month after the 18th month of continuation coverage described in clause (i) or (ii) of paragraph (2)(A).

(4) No requirement of insurability. The coverage may not be conditioned upon, or discriminate on the basis of lack of, evidence of insurability.

(5) Conversion option. In the case of a qualified beneficiary whose period of continuation coverage expires under paragraph (2)(A), the plan must, during the 180-day period ending on such expiration date, provide to the qualified beneficiary the option of enrollment under a conversion health plan otherwise generally available under the plan.

(Sept. 2, 1974, P.L. 93-406, Sec. 602, Title I, Subtitle B, Part 6, as added Apr. 7, 1986, P.L. 99-272, Sec. 10002(a), Title X in part, 100 Stat. 228; Oct. 21, 1986, P.L. 99-509, Sec. 9501(b)(1)(B), Title IX, Subtitle F, (2)(B) 100 Stat. 2076, 2077; Oct. 22, 1986, P.L. 99-514, Sec. 1895(d)(1)(B), Title XVIII, Subtitle C, Ch 1, (2)(B), (3)(B), (4)(B), 100 Stat. 2936-2938; Dec. 19, 1989, P.L. 101--239, Sec. 6703(a), Title VI, Subtitle E, Part 1, (b); Title VII, Subtitle H, Part V, Subpart A, §7862(c)(3)(B), (4)(A), (5)(B); Subpart B, §7871(c), 103 Stat. 2296, 2432, 2433, 2435; Aug 20, 1996, P.L. 104-188, 110 Stat. 1880; Aug 21, 1996, P.L. 104-191, Sec. 421(b), 110 Stat. 2088; Feb. 17, 2009, P.L. 111-5, Division B, Subtitle I, Part VI, §1899F(a)(1)-(3).)

[Endnote ERISA §1162]

29 USC 1162(2)(A)(v), (vi), (vii) and (viii) were amended by Sec. 1899F(a)(1)-(3) of the American Recovery and Reinvestment Act of 2009, P.L. 111-5, 2/17/09, as detailed below:

1. Sec. 1899F(a)(3) added clause (v)
2. Sec. 1899F(a)(3) added clause (vi)
3. Sec. 1899F(a)(3) redesignated clause (v) as (vii)
4. Sec. 1899F(a)(3) redesignated clause (vi) as (viii) [as amended by Sec. 1899F(a)(2) of this Act, see below]
5. Sec. 1899F(a)(2) substituted '(vi) Special rule for disability. In the case of a qualified beneficiary' for 'In the case of a qualified beneficiary' [subsequently redes. as clause (viii) by Sec. 1899F(a)(3) of this Act, see above]

Effective Date (Sec. 1899F(d), P.L. 111-5, 2/17/09) effective for periods of coverage which would (without regard to the amendments made by this section) end on or after 2/17/2009.

[¶ 3504]

ERISA §701. [29 USC 1181] Increased portability through limitation on preexisting condition exclusions.

* * * * * * * * * * * *

(c) Rules relating to crediting previous coverage.

(1) Creditable coverage defined. For purposes of this part, the term "creditable coverage" means, with respect to an individual, coverage of the individual under any of the following:

(A) A group health plan.

(B) Health insurance coverage.

(C) Part A [42 USC §§1395c *et seq.*] or part B [42 USC §§1395j *et seq.*] of title XVIII of the Social Security Act.

(D) Title XIX of the Social Security Act [42 USC §§1396 *et seq.*], other than coverage consisting solely of benefits under section 1928.

(E) Chapter 55 of title 10, United States Code [10 USC §§1071 *et seq.*]..

(F) A medical care program of the Indian Health Service or of a tribal organization.

(G) A State health benefits risk pool.

(H) A health plan offered under chapter 89 of title 5, United States Code [5 USC §§8901 *et seq.*].

(I) A public health plan (as defined in regulations).

(J) A health benefit plan under section 5(e) of the Peace Corps Act (22 USC 2504(e)).

Such term does not include coverage consisting solely of coverage of excepted benefits (as defined in section 733(c) [29 USC §1191b(c)]).

(2) Not counting periods before significant breaks in coverage.

(A) In general. A period of creditable coverage shall not be counted, with respect to enrollment of an individual under a group health plan, if, after such period and before the enrollment date, there was a 63-day period during all of which the individual was not covered under any creditable coverage.

(B) Waiting period not treated as a break in coverage. For purposes of subparagraph (A) and subsection (d)(4), any period that an individual is in a waiting period for any coverage under a group health plan (or for group health insurance coverage) or is in an affiliation period (as defined in subsection (g)(2)) shall not be taken into account in determining the continuous period under subparagraph (A).

[1]*(C) TAA-eligible individuals. In the case of plan years beginning before January 1, 2011 —*

(i) TAA pre-certification period rule. In the case of a TAA-eligible individual, the period beginning on the date the individual has a TAA-related loss of coverage and ending on the date that is 7 days after the date of the issuance by the Secretary (or by any person or entity designated by the Secretary) of a qualified health insurance costs credit eligibility certificate for such individual for purposes of section 7527 of the Internal Revenue Code of 1986 shall not be taken into account in determining the continuous period under subparagraph (A).

(ii) Definitions. The terms "TAA eligible individual" and "TAA-related loss of coverage" have the meanings given such terms in section 605(b)(4).

(3) Method of crediting coverage.

(A) Standard method. Except as otherwise provided under subparagraph (B), for purposes of applying subsection (a)(3), a group health plan, and a health insurance issuer offering group health insurance coverage, shall count a period of creditable coverage without regard to the specific benefits covered during the period.

(B) Election of alternative method. A group health plan, or a health insurance issuer offering group health insurance coverage, may elect to apply subsection (a)(3) based on coverage of benefits within each of several classes or categories of benefits specified in regulations rather than as provided under subparagraph (A). Such election shall be made on a uniform basis for all participants and beneficiaries. Under such election a group health plan or issuer shall count a period of creditable coverage with respect to any class or category of benefits if any level of benefits is covered within such class or category.

(C) Plan notice. In the case of an election with respect to a group health plan under subparagraph (B) (whether or not health insurance coverage is provided in connection with such plan), the plan shall—

(i) prominently state in any disclosure statements concerning the plan, and state to each enrollee at the time of enrollment under the plan, that the plan has made such election, and

(ii) include in such statements a description of the effect of this election.

(4) Establishment of period. Periods of creditable coverage with respect to an individual shall be established through presentation of certifications described in subsection (e) or in such other manner as may be specified in regulations.

* * * * * * * * * * * *

(f) Special enrollment periods.

(1) Individuals losing other coverage. A group health plan, and a health insurance issuer offering group health insurance coverage in connection with a group health plan, shall permit an employee who is eligible, but not enrolled, for coverage under the terms of the plan (or a dependent of such an employee if the dependent is eligible, but not enrolled, for coverage under such terms) to enroll for coverage under the terms of the plan if each of the following conditions is met:

(A) The employee or dependent was covered under a group health plan or had health insurance coverage at the time coverage was previously offered to the employee or dependent.

(B) The employee stated in writing at such time that coverage under a group health plan or health insurance coverage was the reason for declining enrollment, but only if the plan sponsor or issuer (if applicable) required such a statement at such time and provided the employee with notice of such requirement (and the consequences of such requirement) at such time.

(C) The employee's or dependent's coverage described in subparagraph (A)—

(i) was under a COBRA continuation provision and the coverage under such provision was exhausted; or

(ii) was not under such a provision and either the coverage was terminated as a result of loss of eligibility for the coverage (including as a result of legal separation, divorce, death, termination of employment, or reduction in the number of hours of employment) or employer contributions toward such coverage were terminated.

(D) Under the terms of the plan, the employee requests such enrollment not later than 30 days after the date of exhaustion of coverage described in subparagraph (C)(i) or termination of coverage or employer contribution described in subparagraph (C)(ii).

(2) For dependent beneficiaries.

(A) In general. If—

(i) a group health plan makes coverage available with respect to a dependent of an individual,

(ii) the individual is a participant under the plan (or has met any waiting period applicable to becoming a participant under the plan and is eligible to be enrolled under the plan but for a failure to enroll during a previous enrollment period), and

(iii) a person becomes such a dependent of the individual through marriage, birth, or adoption or placement for adoption,

the group health plan shall provide for a dependent special enrollment period described in subparagraph (B) during which the person (or, if not otherwise enrolled, the individual) may be enrolled under the plan as a dependent of the individual, and in the case of the birth or adoption of a child, the spouse of the individual may be enrolled as a dependent of the individual if such spouse is otherwise eligible for coverage.

(B) Dependent special enrollment period. A dependent special enrollment period under this subparagraph shall be a period of not less than 30 days and shall begin on the later of—

(i) the date dependent coverage is made available, or

(ii) the date of the marriage, birth, or adoption or placement for adoption (as the case may be) described in subparagraph (A)(iii).

(C) No waiting period. If an individual seeks to enroll a dependent during the first 30 days of such a dependent special enrollment period, the coverage of the dependent shall become effective—

(i) in the case of marriage, not later than the first day of the first month beginning after the date the completed request for enrollment is received;

(ii) in the case of a dependent's birth, as of the date of such birth; or

(iii) in the case of a dependent's adoption or placement for adoption, the date of such adoption or placement for adoption.

• **Caution:** Para. (f)(3), following, is effective not later than 2/4/2010. See the provisions of Sec. 311(b)(1)(D) of P.L.111-3, reproduced in the history of this section.

[1]**(3) Special rules for application in case of Medicaid and CHIP**

(A) In general. A group health plan, and a health insurance issuer offering group health insurance coverage in connection with a group health plan, shall permit an employee who is eligible, but not enrolled, for coverage under the terms of the plan (or a dependent of such an employee if the dependent is eligible, but not enrolled, for coverage under such terms) to enroll for coverage under the terms of the plan if either of the following conditions is met:

(i) Termination of Medicaid or CHIP coverage. The employee or dependent is covered under a Medicaid plan under title XIX of the Social Security Act or under a State child health plan under title XXI of such Act and coverage of the employee or dependent under such a plan is terminated as a result of loss of eligibility for such coverage and the employee requests coverage under the group health plan (or health insurance coverage) not later than 60 days after the date of termination of such coverage.

(ii) Eligibility for employment assistance under Medicaid or CHIP. The employee or dependent becomes eligible for assistance, with respect to coverage under the group health plan or health insurance coverage, under such Medicaid plan or State child health plan (including under any waiver or demonstration project conducted under or in relation to such a plan), if the employee requests coverage under the group health plan or health insurance coverage not later than 60 days after the date the employee or dependent is determined to be eligible for such assistance.

(B) Coordination with Medicaid and CHIP.

(i) Outreach to employees regarding availability of Medicaid and CHIP coverage.

(I) In general. Each employer that maintains a group health plan in a State that provides medical assistance under a State Medicaid plan under title XIX of the Social Security Act, or child health assistance under a State child health plan under title XXI of such Act, in the form of premium assistance for the purchase of coverage under a group health plan, shall provide to each employee a written notice informing the employee of potential opportunities then currently available in the State in which the employee resides for premium assistance under such plans for health coverage of the employee or the employee's dependents.

(II) Model notice. Not later than 1 year after the date of enactment of the Children's Health Insurance Program Reauthorization Act of 2009, the Secretary and the Secretary of Health and Human Services, in consultation with Directors of State Medicaid agencies under title XIX of the Social Security Act and Directors of State CHIP agencies under title XXI of such Act, shall jointly develop national and State-specific model notices for purposes of subparagraph (A). The Secretary shall provide employers with such model notices so as to enable employers to timely

709

comply with the requirements of subparagraph (A). Such model notices shall include information regarding how an employee may contact the State in which the employee resides for additional information regarding potential opportunities for such premium assistance, including how to apply for such assistance.

(III) Option to provide concurrent with provision of plan materials to employee. An employer may provide the model notice applicable to the State in which an employee resides concurrent with the furnishing of materials notifying the employee of health plan eligibility, concurrent with materials provided to the employee in connection with an open season or election process conducted under the plan, or concurrent with the furnishing of the summary plan description as provided in section 104(b).

(ii) Disclosure about group health plan benefits to states for Medicaid and CHIP eligible individuals. In the case of a participant or beneficiary of a group health plan who is covered under a Medicaid plan of a State under title XIX of the Social Security Act or under a State child health plan under title XXI of such Act, the plan administrator of the group health plan shall disclose to the State, upon request, information about the benefits available under the group health plan in sufficient specificity, as determined under regulations of the Secretary of Health and Human Services in consultation with the Secretary that require use of the model coverage coordination disclosure form developed under section 311(b)(1)(C) of the Children's Health Insurance Program Reauthorization Act of 2009, so as to permit the State to make a determination (under paragraph (2)(B), (3), or (10) of section 2105(c) of the Social Security Act or otherwise) concerning the cost-effectiveness of the State providing medical or child health assistance through premium assistance for the purchase of coverage under such group health plan and in order for the State to provide supplemental benefits required under paragraph (10)(E) of such section or other authority.

* * * * * * * * * * * *

(Aug. 21, 1996, P.L. 104-191, Sec. 101(a), Title I, Subtitle A, Part 1, 110 Stat. 1939; Sept. 26, 1996, P.L. 104-204, Sec. 603(b)(3)(H), 110 Stat. 2938; Feb. 4, 2009, P.L. 111-3, Sec. 311(b)(1)(A), Title III, Subtitle A; Feb. 17, 2009, P.L. 111-5, Div. B, Subtitle I, Part VI, Sec. 1899D(b).)

[Endnote ERISA §1181]

29 USC 1181(c)(2)(C) was added by Sec. 1899D(b) of the American Recovery and Reinvestment Act of 2009, P.L. 111-5, 2/17/09, as detailed below:

1. Sec. 1899D(b) added subpara. (c)(2)(C)

Effective Date (Sec. 1899D(d), P.L. 111-5, 2/17/09) effective for plan yrs. begin. after 2/17/09.

---

29 USC 1181(f)(3) was added by Sec. 311(b)(1)(A), P.L. 111-3, 2/4/2009, as detailed below:

2. Sec. 311(b)(1)(A) added para. (f)(3)

Effective Date (Sec. 3, P.L. 111-3, 2/4/2009) effective 4/1/2009, and shall apply to child health assistance and medical assistance provided on or after 4/1/2009.

Sec. 311(b)(1)(D), reads as follows:

"(D) Effective dates. The Secretary of Labor and the Secretary of Health and Human Services shall develop the initial model notices under section 701(f)(3)(B)(i)(II) of the Employee Retirement Income Security Act of 1974, and the Secretary of Labor shall provide such notices to employers, not later than the date that is 1 year after the date of enactment of this Act, and each employer shall provide the initial annual notices to such employer's employees beginning with the first plan year that begins after the date on which such initial model notices are first issued. The model coverage coordination disclosure form developed under subparagraph (C) shall apply with respect to requests made by States beginning with the first plan year that begins after the date on which such model coverage coordination disclosure form is first issued."

American Recovery and Reinvestment Act of 2009, P.L. 111-5

[¶ 4000] Act sections of the American Recovery and Reinvestment Act of 2009, P.L. 111-5, that do not amend specific Internal Revenue Code sections. Sections of the Internal Revenue Code as amended are reproduced at *Code as Amended.*

[¶ 4001] Sec. 1000. Short Title, etc.

(a) Short Title. This title may be cited as the "American Recovery and Reinvestment Tax Act of 2009".

(b) Reference. Except as otherwise expressly provided, whenever in this title an amendment or repeal is expressed in terms of an amendment to, or repeal of, a section or other provision, the reference shall be considered to be made to a section or other provision of the Internal Revenue Code of 1986.

[¶ 4001] Sec. 1001. Making work pay credit.
* * * * * * * * * * * *

(b) Treatment of possessions.
  (1) Payments to possessions.
    (A) Mirror code possession. The Secretary of the Treasury shall pay to each possession of the United States with a mirror code tax system amounts equal to the loss to that possession by reason of the amendments made by this section with respect to taxable years beginning in 2009 and 2010. Such amounts shall be determined by the Secretary of the Treasury based on information provided by the government of the respective possession.
    (B) Other possessions. The Secretary of the Treasury shall pay to each possession of the United States which does not have a mirror code tax system amounts estimated by the Secretary of the Treasury as being equal to the aggregate benefits that would have been provided to residents of such possession by reason of the amendments made by this section for taxable years beginning in 2009 and 2010 if a mirror code tax system had been in effect in such pos session. The preceding sentence shall not apply with respect to any possession of the United States unless such possession has a plan, which has been approved by the Secretary of the Treasury, under which such possession will promptly distribute such payments to the residents of such possession.
  (2) Coordination with credit allowed against United States income taxes. No credit shall be allowed against United States income taxes for any taxable year under section 36A of the Internal Revenue Code of 1986 (as added by this section) to any person —
    (A) to whom a credit is allowed against taxes imposed by the possession by reason of the amendments made by this section for such taxable year, or
    (B) who is eligible for a payment under a plan described in paragraph (1)(B) with respect to such taxable year.
  (3) Definitions and special rules.
    (A) Possession of the United States. For purposes of this subsection, the term "possession of the United States" includes the Commonwealth of Puerto Rico and the Commonwealth of the Northern Mariana Islands.
    (B) Mirror code tax system. For purposes of this subsection, the term "mirror code tax system" means, with respect to any possession of the United States, the income tax system of such possession if the income tax liability of the residents of such possession under such system is determined by reference to the income tax laws of the United States as if such possession were the United States.
    (C) Treatment of payments. For purposes of section 1324(b)(2) of title 31, United States Code, the payments under this subsection shall be treated in the same manner as a refund due from the credit allowed under section 36A of the Internal Revenue Code of 1986 (as added by this section).

751

(c) Refunds disregarded in the administration of federal programs and federally assisted programs. Any credit or refund allowed or made to any individual by reason of section 36A of the Internal Revenue Code of 1986 (as added by this section) or by reason of subsection (b) of this section shall not be taken into account as income and shall not be taken into account as resources for the month of receipt and the following 2 months, for purposes of determining the eligibility of such individual or any other individual for benefits or assistance, or the amount or extent of benefits or assistance, under any Federal program or under any State or local program financed in whole or in part with Federal funds.

* * * * * * * * * * * *

(f) Effective date. This section, and the amendments made by this section, shall apply to taxable years beginning after December 31, 2008.

[¶ 4003] Sec. 1002. Temporary increase in earned income tax credit.

* * * * * * * * * * * *

(b) Effective date. The amendments made by this section shall apply to taxable years beginning after December 31, 2008.

[¶ 4004] Sec. 1003. Temporary increase of refundable portion of child credit.

* * * * * * * * * * * *

(b) Effective date. The amendments made by this section shall apply to taxable years beginning after December 31, 2008.

[¶ 4005] Sec. 1004. American opportunity tax credit.

* * * * * * * * * * * *

(c) Treatment of possessions.

(1) Payments to possessions.

(A) Mirror code possession. The Secretary of the Treasury shall pay to each possession of the United States with a mirror code tax system amounts equal to the loss to that possession by reason of the application of section 25A(i)(6) of the Internal Revenue Code of 1986 (as added by this section) with respect to taxable years beginning in 2009 and 2010.

Such amounts shall be determined by the Secretary of the Treasury based on information provided by the government of the respective possession.

(B) Other possessions. The Secretary of the Treasury shall pay to each possession of the United States which does not have a mirror code tax system amounts estimated by the Secretary of the Treasury as being equal to the aggregate benefits that would have been provided to residents of such possession by reason of the application of section 25A(i)(6) of such Code (as so added) for taxable years beginning in 2009 and 2010 if a mirror code tax system had been in effect in such possession. The preceding sentence shall not apply with respect to any possession of the United States unless such possession has a plan, which has been approved by the Secretary of the Treasury, under which such possession will promptly distribute such payments to the residents of such possession.

(2) Coordination with credit allowed against United States income taxes. Section 25A(i)(6) of such Code (as added by this section) shall not apply to a bona fide resident of any possession of the United States.

(3) Definitions and special rules.

(A) Possession of the United States. For purposes of this subsection, the term "possession of the United States" includes the Commonwealth of Puerto Rico and the Commonwealth of the Northern Mariana Islands.

(B) Mirror code tax system. For purposes of this subsection, the term "mirror code tax system" means, with respect to any possession of the United States, the income tax system of such possession if the income tax liabil ity of the residents of such possession under such system is determined by reference to the income tax laws of the United States as if such possession were the United States.

(C) Treatment of payments. For purposes of section 1324(b)(2) of title 31, United States Code, the payments under this subsection shall be treated in the same manner as a refund due from the credit allowed under section 25A of the Internal Revenue Code of 1986 by reason of subsection (i)(6) of such section (as added by this section).

(d) Effective date. The amendments made by this section shall apply to taxable years beginning after December 31, 2008.

(e) Application of EGTRRA sunset. The amendment made by subsection (b)(1) shall be subject to title IX of the Economic Growth and Tax Relief Reconciliation Act of 2001 in the same manner as the provision of such Act to which such amendment relates.

(f) Treasury studies regarding education incentives.

(1) Study regarding coordination with non-tax student financial assistance. The Secretary of the Treasury and the Secretary of Education, or their delegates, shall—

(A) study how to coordinate the credit allowed under section 25A of the Internal Revenue Code of 1986 with the Federal Pell Grant program under section 401 of the Higher Education Act of 1965 to maximize their effectiveness at promoting college affordability, and

(B) examine ways to expedite the delivery of the tax credit.

(2) Study regarding inclusion of community service requirements. The Secretary of the Treasury and the Secretary of Education, or their delegates, shall study the feasibility of requiring including community service as a condition of taking their tuition and related expenses into account under section 25A of the Internal Revenue Code of 1986.

(3) Report. Not later than 1 year after the date of the enactment of this Act, the Secretary of the Treasury, or the Secretary's delegate, shall report to Congress on the results of the studies conducted under this paragraph.

[¶ 4006] Sec. 1005. Computer technology and equipment allowed as a qualified higher education expense for Section 529 accounts in 2009 and 2010.
* * * * * * * * * * * *

(b) Effective date. The amendments made by this section shall apply to expenses paid or incurred after December 31, 2008.

[¶ 4007] Sec. 1006. Extension of and increase in first-time homebuyer credit; waiver of requirement to repay.
* * * * * * * * * * * *

(f) Effective date. The amendments made by this section shall apply to residences purchased after December 31, 2008.

[¶ 4008] Sec. 1007. Suspension of tax on portion of unemployment compensation.
* * * * * * * * * * * *

(b) Effective date. The amendment made by this section shall apply to taxable years beginning after December 31, 2008.

[¶ 4009] Sec. 1008. Additional deduction for state sales tax and excise tax on the purchase of certain motor vehicles.
* * * * * * * * * * * *

(e) Effective date. The amendments made by this section shall apply to purchases on or after the date of the enactment of this Act in taxable years ending after such date.

[¶ 4010] Sec. 1011. Extension of A for nonrefundable personal credits.
* * * * * * * * * * * *

(b) Effective date. The amendments made by this section shall apply to taxable years beginning after December 31, 2008.

[¶ 4011] Sec. 1101. Extension of credit for electricity produced from certain renewable resources.

* * * * * * * * * * *

(c) Effective date.

(1) In general. The amendments made by subsection (a) shall apply to property placed in service after the date of the enactment of this Act.

(2) Technical Amendment. The amendment made by subsection (b) shall take effect as if included in section 102 of the Energy Improvement and Extension Act of 2008.

[¶ 4012] Sec. 1102. Election of investment credit in lieu of production credit.

* * * * * * * * * * *

(b) Effective date. The amendments made by this section shall apply to facilities placed in service after December 31, 2008.

[¶ 4013] Sec. 1103. Repeal of certain limitations on credit for renewable energy property.

* * * * * * * * * * *

(c) Effective date.

(1) In general. Except as provided in paragraph (2), the amendment made by this section shall apply to periods after December 31, 2008, under rules similar to the rules of section 48(m) of the Internal Revenue Code of 1986 (as in effect on the day before the date of the enactment of the Revenue Reconciliation Act of 1990).

(2) Conforming Amendments. The amendments made by subparagraphs (A) and (B) of section (b)(2) shall apply to taxable years beginning after December 31, 2008.

[¶ 4014] Sec. 1121. Extension and modification of credit for nonbusiness energy property.

* * * * * * * * * * *

(f) Effective dates.

(1) In general. Except as provided in paragraph (2), the amendments made by this section shall apply to taxable years beginning after December 31, 2008.

(2) Efficiency Standards. The amendments made by paragraphs (1), (2), and (3) of sub20 section (b) and subsections (c) and (d) shall apply to property placed in service after the date of the enactment of this Act.

[¶ 4015] Sec. 1122. Modification of credit for residential energy efficient property.

* * * * * * * * * * *

(b) Effective date. The amendments made by this section shall apply to taxable years beginning after December 31, 2008.

[¶ 4016] Sec. 1123. Temporary increase in credit for alternative fuel vehicle refueling property.

* * * * * * * * * * *

(b) Effective date. The amendment made by this section shall apply to taxable years beginning after December 31, 2008.

[¶ 4017] Sec. 1131. Application of monitoring requirements to carbon dioxide used as a tertiary injectant.

* * * * * * * * * * *

(c) Effective date. The amendments made by this section shall apply to carbon dioxide captured after the date of the enactment of this Act.

[¶ 4018] Sec. 1141. Credit for new qualified plug-in electric drive motor vehicles.
* * * * * * * * * * *

(c) Effective date. The amendments made by this section shall apply to vehicles acquired after December 31, 2009.

[¶ 4019] Sec. 1142. Credit for certain plug-in electric vehicles.
* * * * * * * * * * *

(c) Effective date. The amendments made by this section shall apply to vehicles acquired after the date of the enactment of this Act.

(d) Transitional rule. In the case of a vehicle acquired after the date of the enactment of this Act and before January 1, 2010, no credit shall be allowed under section 30 of the Internal Revenue Code of 1986, as added by this section, if credit is allowable under section 30D of such Code with respect to such vehicle.

(e) Application of EGTRRA Sunset. The amendment made by subsection (b)(1)(A) shall be subject to title IX of the Economic Growth and Tax Relief Reconciliation Act of 2001 in the same manner as the provision of such Act to which such amendment relates.

[¶ 4020] Sec. 1143. Conversion kits.
* * * * * * * * * * *

(d) Effective date. The amendments made by this section shall apply to property placed in service after the date of the enactment of this Act.

[¶ 4021] Sec. 1144. Treatment of alternative motor vehicle credit as a personal credit allowed against AMT.
* * * * * * * * * * *

(c) Effective date. The amendments made by this section shall apply to taxable years beginning after December 31, 2008.

(d) Application of EGTRRA sunset. The amendment made by subsection (b)(1)(A) shall be subject to title IX of the Economic Growth and Tax Relief Reconciliation Act of 2001 in the same manner as the provision of such Act to which such amendment relates.

[¶ 4022] Sec. 1151. Increased exclusion amount for commuter transit benefits and transit passes.
* * * * * * * * * * *

(b) Effective date. The amendment made by this section shall apply to months beginning on or after the date of the enactment of this section.

[¶ 4023] Sec. 1201. Special allowance for certain property acquired during 2009.
* * * * * * * * * * *

(c) Effective dates.
　　(1) In general. Except as provided in paragraph (2), the amendments made by this section shall apply to property placed in service after December 31, 2008, in taxable years ending after such date.
　　(2) Technical amendments. The amendments made by subsections (a)(3) and (b)(2) shall apply to taxable years ending after March 31, 2008.

[¶ 4024] Sec. 1202. Temporary increase in limitations on expensing of certain depreciable business assets.

* * * * * * * * * * *

(b) Effective date. The amendments made by this section shall apply to taxable years beginning after December 31, 2008.

[¶ 4025] Sec. 1211. 5-year carryback of operating losses of small businesses.

* * * * * * * * * * *

(c) Anti-abuse rules. The Secretary of Treasury or the Secretary's designee shall prescribe such rules as are necessary to prevent the abuse of the purposes of the amendments made by this section, including anti-stuffing rules, anti-churning rules (including rules relating to sale leasebacks), and rules similar to the rules under section 1091 of the Internal Revenue Code of 1986 relating to losses from wash sales.

(d) Effective date.
    (1) In general. Except as otherwise provided in this subsection, the amendments made by this section shall apply to net operating losses arising in taxable years ending after December 31, 2007.
    (2) Transitional rule. In the case of a net operating loss for a taxable year ending before the date of the enactment of this Act.
        (A) any election made under section 172(b)(3) of the Internal Revenue Code of 1986 with respect to such loss may (notwithstanding such section) be revoked before the applicable date,
        (B) any election made under section 172(b)(1)(H) of such Code with respect to such loss shall (notwithstanding such section) be treated as timely made if made before the applicable date, and
        (C) any application under section 6411(a) of such Code with respect to such loss shall be treated as timely filed if filed before the applicable date. For purposes of this paragraph, the term "applicable date" means the date which is 60 days after the date of the enactment of this Act.

* * * * * * * * * * *

[¶ 4026] Sec. 1221. Incentives to hire unemployed veterans and disconnected youth.

* * * * * * * * * * *

(b) Effective date. The amendments made by this section shall apply to individuals who begin work for the employer after December 31, 2008.

[¶ 4027] Sec. 1231. Deferral and ratable inclusion of income arising from business indebtedness discharged by the reacquisition of a debt instrument.

* * * * * * * * * * *

(b) Effective date. The amendments made by this section shall apply to discharges in taxable years ending after December 31, 2008.

[¶ 4028] Sec. 1232. Modifications of rules for original issue discount on certain high yield obligations.

* * * * * * * * * * *

(c) Effective date.
    (1) Suspension. The amendments made by subsection (a) shall apply to obligations issued after August 31, 2008, in taxable years ending after such date.
    (2) Interest rate authority. The amendments made by subsection (b) shall apply to obligations issued after December 31, 2009, in taxable years ending after such date.

[¶ 4029] Sec. 1241. Special rules applicable to qualified small business stock for 2009 and 2010.

* * * * * * * * * * *

(a) Effective date. The amendment made by this section shall apply to stock acquired after the date of the enactment of this Act.

[¶ 4030] Sec. 1251. Temporary reduction in recognition period for built-in gains tax.

* * * * * * * * * * *

(b) Effective date. The amendment made by this section shall apply to taxable years beginning after December 31, 2008.

[¶ 4031] Sec. 1261. Clarification of regulations related to limitations on certain built-in losses following an ownership change.

(a) Findings. Congress finds as follows:

(1) The delegation of authority to the Secretary of the Treasury under section 382(m) of the Internal Revenue Code of 1986 does not authorize the Secretary to provide exemptions or special rules that are restricted to particular industries or classes of taxpayers.

(2) Internal Revenue Service Notice 2008-83 is inconsistent with the congressional intent in enacting such section 382(m).

(3) The legal authority to prescribe Internal Revenue Service Notice 2008-83 is doubtful.

(2) However, as taxpayers should generally be able to rely on guidance issued by the Secretary of the Treasury legislation is necessary to clarify the force and effect of Internal Revenue Service Notice 2008-83 and restore the proper application under the Internal Revenue Code of 1986 of the limitation on built-in losses following an ownership change of a bank.

(b) Determination of force and effect of Internal Revenue Service Notice 2008-83 exempting banks from limitation on certain built-in losses following ownership change.

(1) In general. Internal Revenue Service Notice 2008-83—

(A) shall be deemed to have the force and effect of law with respect to any ownership change (as defined in section 382(g) of the Internal Revenue Code of 1986) occurring on or before January 16, 2009, and

(B)

(B) shall have no force or effect with respect to any ownership change after such date.

(2) Binding contracts. Notwithstanding paragraph (1), Internal Revenue Service Notice 2008-83 shall have the force and effect of law with respect to any ownership change (as so defined) which occurs after January 16, 2009, if such change—

(A) is pursuant to a written binding contract entered into on or before such date, or

(B) is pursuant to a written agreement entered into on or before such date and such agreement was described on or before such date in a public announcement or in a filing with the Securities and Exchange Commission required by reason of such ownership change.

[¶ 4032] Sec. 1262. Treatment of certain ownership changes for purposes of limitations on net operating loss carryforwards and certain built-in losses.

* * * * * * * * * * *

(b) Effective date. The amendment made by this section shall apply to ownership changes after the date of the enactment of this Act.

[¶ 4033] Sec. 1301. Temporary expansion of availability of industrial development bonds to facilities manufacturing intangible property.

757

* * * * * * * * * * *

(b) Effective date. The amendments made by this section shall apply to obligations issued after the date of the enactment of this Act.

[¶ 4034] Sec. 1302. Credit for investment in advanced energy facilities.

* * * * * * * * * * *

(d) Effective date. The amendments made by this section shall apply to periods after the date of the enactment of this Act, under rules similar to the rules of section 48(m) of the Internal Revenue Code of 1986 (as in effect on the day before the date of the enactment of the Revenue Reconciliation Act of 1990).

Subtitle E Economic Recovery Tools

[¶ 4035] Sec. 1401. Recovery zone bonds.

* * * * * * * * * * *

(c) Effective date. The amendments made by this section shall apply to obligations issued after the date of the enactment of this Act.

[¶ 4036] Sec. 1402. Tribal economic development bonds.

* * * * * * * * * * *

(b) Study. The Secretary of the Treasury, or the Secretary's delegate, shall conduct a study of the effects of the amendment made by subsection (a). Not later than 1 year after the date of the enactment of this Act, the Secretary of the Treasury, or the Secretary's delegate, shall report to Congress on the results of the study conducted under this paragraph, including the Secretary's recommendations regarding such amendment.

(c) Effective date. The amendment made by subsection (a) shall apply to obligations issued after the date of the enactment of this Act.

[¶ 4037] Sec. 1403. Increase in new markets tax credit.

* * * * * * * * * * *

(b) Special rule for allocation of increased 2008 limitation. The amount of the increase in the new markets tax credit limitation for calendar year 2008 by reason of the amendments made by subsection (a) shall be allocated in accordance with section 45D(f)(2) of the Internal Revenue Code of 1986 to qualified community development entities (as defined in section 45D(c) of such Code) which—

    (1) submitted an allocation application with respect to calendar year 2008, and

    (2)

      (A) did not receive an allocation for such calendar year, or

      (B) received an allocation for such calendar year in an amount less than the amount requested in the allocation application.

* * * * * * * * * * *

[¶ 4038] Sec. 1501. De minimis safe harbor exception for tax exempt interest expense of financial institutions.

* * * * * * * * * * *

(c) Effective date. The amendments made by this section shall apply to obligations issued after December 31, 2008.

[¶ 4039] Sec. 1502. Modification of small issuer exception to tax-exempt interest expense allocation rules for financial institutions.

* * * * * * * * * * *

(b) Effective date. The amendment made by this section shall apply to obligations issued after December 31, 2008.

[¶ 4040] Sec. 1503. Temporary modification of alternative minimum tax limitations on tax-exempt bonds.

* * * * * * * * * * *

(c) Effective date. The amendments made by this section shall apply to obligations issued after December 31, 2008.

[¶ 4041] Sec. 1504. Modification to high speed intercity rail facility bonds.

* * * * * * * * * * *

(b) Effective date. The amendment made by this section shall apply to obligations issued after the date of the enactment of this Act.

[¶ 4042] Sec. 1511. Delay in application of withholding tax on government contractors. Subsection (b) of section 511 of the Tax Increase Prevention and Reconciliation Act of 2005 is amended by striking ''December 31, 2010'' and inserting ''December 31, 2011''.

[¶ 4043] Sec. 1521. Qualified school construction bondS.

* * * * * * * * * * *

(c) Effective date. The amendments made by this section shall apply to obligations issued after the date of the enactment of this Act.

[¶ 4044] Sec. 1522. Extension and expansion of qualified zone academy bonds.

* * * * * * * * * * *

(b) Effective date. The amendment made by this section shall apply to obligations issued after December 31, 2008.

[¶ 4045] Sec. 1531. Build America bonds.

* * * * * * * * * * *

(d) Transitional coordination with state law. Except as otherwise provided by a State after the date of the enactment of this Act, the interest on any build America bond (as defined in section 54AA of the Internal Revenue Code of 1986, as added by this section) and the amount of any credit determined under such section with respect to such bond shall be treated for purposes of the income tax laws of such State as being exempt from Federal income tax.

(e) Effective date. The amendments made by this section shall apply to obligations issued after the date of the enactment of this Act.

[¶ 4046] Sec. 1541. Regulated investment companies allowed to pass-thru tax credit bond credits.

* * * * * * * * * * *

(c) Effective date. The amendments made by this section shall apply to taxable years ending after the date of the enactment of this Act.

[¶ 4047] Sec. 1601. Application of certain labor standards to projects financed with certain tax favored bonds. Subchapter IV of chapter 31 of the title 40, United States Code, shall apply to projects financed with the proceeds of—

(1) any new clean renewable energy bond (as defined in section 54C of the Internal Revenue Code of 1986) issued after the date of the enactment of this Act,

(2) any qualified energy conservation bond (as defined in section 54D of the Internal Revenue Code of 1986) issued after the date of the enactment of this Act,

(3) any qualified zone academy bond (as defined in section 54E of the Internal Revenue Code of 1986) issued after the date of the enactment of this Act,

(4) any qualified school construction bond (as defined in section 54F of the Internal Revenue Code of 1986), and

(5) any recovery zone economic development bond (as defined in section 1400U-2 of the Internal Revenue Code of 1986).

[¶ 4048] Sec. 1602. Grants to states for low-income housing projects in lieu of low-income housing credit allocations for 2009.

(a) In general. The Secretary of the Treasury shall make a grant to the housing credit agency of each State in an amount equal to such State's low-income housing grant election amount.

(b) Low-income housing grant election amount. For purposes of this section, the term "low income housing grant election amount" means, with respect to any State, such amount as the State may elect which does not exceed 85 percent of the product of—
    (1) the sum of—
        (A) 100 percent of the State housing credit ceiling for 2009 which is attributable to amounts described in clauses (i) and (iii) of section 42(h)(3)(C) of the Internal Revenue Code of 1986, and
        (B) 40 percent of the State housing credit ceiling for 2009 which is attributable to amounts described in clauses (ii) and (iv) of such section, multiplied by
    (2) 10.

(c) Subawards for low-income buildings.
    (1) In general. A State housing credit agency receiving a grant under this section shall use such grant to make subawards to finance the construction or acquisition and rehabilitation of qualified low-in come buildings. A subaward under this section may be made to finance a qualified low-income building with or without an allocation under section 42 of the Internal Revenue Code of 1986, except that a State housing credit agency may make subawards to finance qualified low-income buildings without an allocation only if it makes a determination that such use will increase the total funds available to the State to build and rehabilitate affordable housing. In complying with such determination requirement, a State housing credit agency shall establish a process in which applicants that are allocated credits are required to demonstrate good faith efforts to obtain investment commitments for such credits before the agency makes such subawards.
    (2) Subawards subject to same requirements as low-income housing credit allocations. Any such subaward with respect to any qualified low-income building shall be made in the same manner and shall be subject to the same limitations (including rent, income, and use

restrictions on such building) as an allocation of housing credit dollar amount allocated by such State housing credit agency under section 42 of the Internal Revenue Code of 1986, except that such subawards shall not be limited by, or otherwise affect (except as provided in subsection (h)(3)(J) of such section), the State housing credit ceiling applicable to such agency.

(3) Compliance and asset management. The State housing credit agency shall perform asset management functions to ensure compliance with section 42 of the Internal Revenue Code of 1986 and the long-term viability of buildings funded by any subaward under this section. The State housing credit agency may collect reasonable fees from a subaward recipient to cover expenses associated with the performance of its duties under this paragraph. The State housing credit agency may retain an agent or other private contractor to satisfy the requirements of this paragraph.

(4) Recapture. The State housing credit agency shall impose conditions or restrictions, including a requirement providing for recapture, on any subaward under this section so as to assure that the building with respect to which such subaward is made remains a qualified low-income building during the compliance period. Any such recapture shall be payable to the Secretary of the Treasury for deposit in the general fund of the Treasury and may be enforced by means of liens or such other methods as the Secretary of the Treasury determines appropriate.

(d) Return of unused grant funds. Any grant funds not used to make subawards under this section before January 1, 2011, shall be returned to the Secretary of the Treasury on such date. Any subawards returned to the State housing credit agency on or after such date shall be promptly returned to the Secretary of the Treasury. Any amounts returned to the Secretary of the Treasury under this subsection shall be deposited in the general fund of the Treasury.

(e) Definitions. Any term used in this section which is also used in section 42 of the Internal Revenue Code of 1986 shall have the same meaning for purposes of this section as when used in such section 42. Any reference in this section to the Secretary of the Treasury shall be treated as including the Secretary's delegate.

(f) Appropriations. There is hereby appropriated to the Secretary of the Treasury such sums as may be necessary to carry out this section.

[¶ 4049] Sec. 1603. Grants for specified energy property in lieu of tax credits.

(a) In general. Upon application, the Secretary of the Treasury shall, subject to the requirements of this section, provide a grant to each person who places in service specified energy property to reimburse such person for a portion of the expense of such property as provided in subsection (b). No grant shall be made under this section with respect to any property unless such property—

(1) is placed in service during 2009 or 2010, or

(2) is placed in service after 2010 and before the credit termination date with respect to such property, but only if the construction of such property began during 2009 or 2010.

(b) Grant amount.

(1) In general. The amount of the grant under subsection (a) with respect to any specified energy property shall be the applicable percentage of the basis of such property.

(2) Applicable percentage. For purposes of paragraph (1), the term "applicable percentage" means—

(A) 30 percent in the case of any property described in paragraphs (1) through (4) of subsection (d), and

(B) 10 percent in the case of any other property.

(3) Dollar limitations. In the case of property described in paragraph (2), (6), or (7) of subsection (d), the amount of any grant under this section with respect to such property

761

shall not exceed the limitation described in section 48(c)(1)(B), 48(c)(2)(B), or 48(c)(3)(B) of the Internal Revenue Code of 1986, respectively, with respect to such property.

(c) Time for payment of grant. The Secretary of the Treasury shall make payment of any grant under subsection (a) during the 60-day period beginning on the later of—

(1) the date of the application for such grant, or

(2) the date the specified energy property for which the grant is being made is placed in service.

(d) Specified energy property. For purposes of this section, the term "specified energy property" means any of the following:

(1) **Qualified facilities.** Any qualified property (as defined in section 48(a)(5)(D)) which is part of a qualified facility (within the meaning of section 45) described in paragraph (1), (2), (3), (4), (6), (7), (9), or (11) of section 45(d) of the Internal Revenue Code of 1986.

(2) **Qualified fuel cell property.** Any qualified fuel cell property (as defined in section 48(c)(1) of such Code).

(3) **Solar property.** Any property described in clause (i) or (ii) of section 48(a)(3)(A) of such Code.

(4) **Qualified small wind energy property.** Any qualified small wind energy property (as defined in section 48(c)(4) of such Code).

(5) **Geothermal property.** Any property described in clause (iii) of section 48(a)(3)(A) of such Code.

(6) **Qualified microturbine property.** Any qualified microturbine property (as defined in section 48(c)(2) of such Code).

(7) **Combined heat and power system property.** Any combined heat and power system property (as defined in section 48(c)(3) of such Code).

(8) **Geothermal heat pump property.** Any property described in clause (vii) of section 48(a)(3)(A) of such Code. Such term shall not include any property unless depreciation (or amortization in lieu of depreciation) is allowable with respect to such property.

(e) Credit termination date. For purposes of this section, the term ''credit termination date'' means-

(1) in the case of any specified energy property which is part of a facility described in paragraph (1) of section 45(d) of the Internal Revenue Code of 1986, January 1, 2013,

(2) in the case of any specified energy property which is part of a facility described in paragraph (2), (3), (4), (6), (7), (9), or (11) of section 45(d) of the Internal Revenue Code of 1986, January 1, 2014, and

(3) in the case of any specified energy property described in section 48, January 1, 2017. In the case of any property which is described in paragraph (3) and also in another paragraph of this subsection, paragraph (3) shall apply with respect to such property.

(f) Application of certain rules. In making grants under this section, the Secretary of the Treasury shall apply rules similar to the rules of section 50 of the Internal Revenue Code of 1986. In applying such rules, if the property is disposed of, or otherwise ceases to be specified energy property, the Secretary of the Treasury shall provide for the recapture of the appropriate percent age of the grant amount in such manner as the Secretary of the Treasury determines appropriate.

(g) Exception for certain non-taxpayers. The Secretary of the Treasury shall not make any grant under this section to—

(1) any Federal, State, or local government (or any political subdivision, agency, or instrumentality thereof),

(2) any organization described in section 501(c) of the Internal Revenue Code of 1986 and exempt from tax under section 501(a) of such Code,

(3) any entity referred to in paragraph (4) of section 54(j) of such Code, or

(4) any partnership or other pass-thru entity any partner (or other holder of an equity or profits interest) of which is described in paragraph (1), (2) or (3).

(h) Definitions. Terms used in this section which are also used in section 45 or 48 of the Internal Revenue Code of 1986 shall have the same meaning for purposes of this section as when used in such section 45 or 48. Any reference in this section to the Secretary of the Treasury shall be treated as including the Secretary's delegate.

(i) Appropriations. There is hereby appropriated to the Secretary of the Treasury such sums as may be necessary to carry out this section.

(j) Termination. The Secretary of the Treasury shall not make any grant to any person under this section unless the application of such person for such grant is received before October 1, 2011.

* * * * * * * * * * *

[¶ 4050] Sec. 1899. Short title. This part may be cited as the "TAA Health Coverage Improvement Act of 2009".

[¶ 4051] Sec. 1899A. Improvement of the affordability of the credit.

* * * * * * * * * * * *

(b) Effective date. The amendments made by this section shall apply to coverage months beginning on or after the first day of the first month beginning 60 days after the date of the enactment of this Act.

[¶ 4052] Sec. 1899B. Payment for monthly premiums paid prior to commencement of advance payments of credit.

* * * * * * * * * * * *

(b) Effective date. The amendments made by this section shall apply to coverage months beginning after December 31, 2008.

(c) Transitional rule. The Secretary of the Treasury shall not be required to make any payments under section 7527(e) of the Internal Revenue Code of 1986, as added by this section, until after the date that is 6 months after the date of the enactment of this Act.

[¶ 4053] Sec. 1899C. TAA recipients not enrolled in training programs eligible for credit.

* * * * * * * * * * * *

(b) Effective date. The amendment made by this section shall apply to coverage months beginning after the date of the enactment of this Act.

[¶ 4054] Sec. 1899D. TAA pre-certification period rule for purposes of determining whether there is a 63-day lapse in creditable coverage.

* * * * * * * * * * * *

(d) Effective date. The amendments made by this section shall apply to plan years beginning after the date of the enactment of this Act.

[¶ 4055] Sec. 1899E. Continued qualification of family members after certain events.

* * * * * * * * * * * *

(c) Effective date. The amendments made by this section shall apply to months beginning after December 31, 2009.

[¶ 4056] Sec. 1899F. Extension of COBRA benefits for certain TAA-eligible individuals and PBGC recipients.

* * * * * * * * * * * *

(d) Effective date. The amendments made by this section shall apply to periods of coverage which would (without regard to the amendments made by this section) end on or after the date of the enactment of this Act.

[¶ 4057] Sec. 1899G. Addition of coverage through voluntary employees' beneficiary associations.

* * * * * * * * * * * *

(b) Effective date. The amendments made by this section shall apply to coverage months beginning after the date of the enactment of this Act.

[¶ 4058] Sec. 1899H. Notice requirements.

* * * * * * * * * * * *

(b) Effective date. The amendment made by this section shall apply to certificates issued after the date that is 6 months after the date of the enactment of this Act.

[¶ 4059] Sec. 1899I. Survey and report on enhanced health coverage tax credit program. (a) Survey.

(1) In general. The Secretary of the Treasury shall conduct a biennial survey of eligible individuals (as defined in section 35(c) of the Internal Revenue Code of 1986) relating to the health coverage tax credit under section 35 of the Internal Revenue Code of 1986 (hereinafter in this section referred to as the "health coverage tax credit").

(2) Information obtained. The survey conducted under subsection (a) shall obtain the following information:

(A) HCTC participants. In the case of eligible individuals receiving the health coverage tax credit (including individuals participating in the health coverage tax credit program under section 7527 of such Code, hereinafter in this section referred to as the "HCTC program")—

(i) demographic information of such individuals, including income and edu9 cation levels,

(ii) satisfaction of such individuals with the enrollment process in the HCTC program,

(iii) satisfaction of such individuals with available health coverage options under the credit, including level of premiums, benefits, deductibles, cost-sharing requirements, and the adequacy of provider networks, and

(iv) any other information that the Secretary determines is appropriate.

(B) NON-HCTC participants. In the case of eligible individuals not receiving the health coverage tax credit—

(i) demographic information of each individual, including income and education levels,

(ii) whether the individual was aware of the health coverage tax credit or the HCTC program,

(iii) the reasons the individual has not enrolled in the HCTC program, including whether such reasons include the burden of the process of enrollment and the afford11 ability of coverage,

(iv) whether the individual has health insurance coverage, and, if so, the source of such coverage, and

(v) any other information that the Secretary determines is appropriate.

(3) Report. Not later than December 31 of each year in which a survey is conducted under paragraph (1) (beginning in 2010), the Secretary of the Treasury shall report to the Committee on Finance and the Committee on Health, Education, Labor, and Pensions of the Senate and the Committee on Ways and Means, the Committee on Education and Labor, and the Committee on Energy and Commerce of the House of Representatives the findings of the most recent survey conducted under paragraph (1).

(b) Report. Not later than October 1 of each year (beginning in 2010), the Secretary of the Treasury (after consultation with the Secretary of Health and Human Services, and, in the case of the information required under paragraph (7), the Secretary of Labor) shall report to the Committee on Finance and the Committee on Health, Education, Labor, and Pensions of the Senate and the Committee on Ways and Means, the Committee on Education and Labor, and the Committee on Energy and Commerce of the House of Representatives the following information with respect to the most recent taxable year ending before such date:

(1) In each State and nationally—

(A) the total number of eligible individuals (as defined in section 35(c) of the Internal Revenue Code of 1986) and the number of eligible individuals receiving the health coverage tax credit,

(B) the total number of such eligible individuals who receive an advance payment of the health coverage tax credit through the HCTC program,

(C) the average length of the time period of the participation of eligible individuals in the HCTC program, and

(D) the total number of participating eligible individuals in the HCTC program who are enrolled in each category of coverage as described in section 35(e)(1) of such Code, with respect to each category of eligible individuals described in section 35(c)(1) of such Code.

(2) In each State and nationally, an analysis of—

(A) the range of monthly health insurance premiums, for self-only coverage and for family coverage, for individuals receiving the health coverage tax credit, and

(B) the average and median monthly health insurance premiums, for self-only coverage and for family coverage, for individuals receiving the health coverage tax credit, with respect to each category of coverage as described in section 35(e)(1) of such Code.

(3) In each State and nationally, an analysis of the following information with respect to the health insurance coverage of individuals receiving the health coverage tax credit who are enrolled in coverage described in subparagraphs (B) through (H) of section 35(e)(1) of such Code:

(A) Deductible amounts.

(B) Other out-of-pocket cost-sharing amounts.

(C) A description of any annual or lifetime limits on coverage or any other significant limits on coverage services, or benefits.

The information required under this paragraph shall be reported with respect to each category of coverage described in such subparagraphs.

(4) In each State and nationally, the gender and average age of eligible individuals (as defined in section 35(c) of such Code) who receive the health coverage tax credit, in each category of coverage described in section 35(e)(1) of such Code, with respect to each category of eligible individuals described in such section.

(5) The steps taken by the Secretary of the Treasury to increase the participation rates in the HCTC program among eligible individuals, including outreach and enrollment activities. (6) The cost of administering the HCTC program by function, including the cost of subcontractors, and recommendations on ways to reduce administrative costs, including recommended statutory changes.

(7) The number of States applying for and receiving national emergency grants under section 173(f) of the Workforce Investment Act of 1998 (29 U.S.C. 2918(f)), the activities funded by such grants on a State-by-State basis, and the time necessary for application approval of such grants.

     * * * * * * * * * * * *

[¶ 4060] Sec. 1899L.   GAO study and report. (a) Study. The Comptroller General of the United States shall conduct a study regarding the health insurance tax credit allowed under section 35 of the Internal Revenue Code of 1986.

(b) Report. Not later than March 1, 2010, the Comptroller General shall submit a report to Congress re-garding the results of the study conducted under subsection (a). Such report shall include an analysis of—

(1) the administrative costs—

(A) of the Federal Government with respect to such credit and the advance payment of such credit under section 7527 of such Code, and

(B) of providers of qualified health insurance with respect to providing such insurance to eligible individuals and their qualifying family members,

(2) the health status and relative risk status of eligible individuals and qualifying family members covered under such insurance,

(3) participation in such credit and the advance payment of such credit by eligible individuals and their qualifying family members, including the reasons why such individuals did or did not participate and the effect of the amendments made by this part on such participation, and

(4) the extent to which eligible individuals and their qualifying family members—

(A) obtained health insurance other than qualifying health insurance, or

(B) went without health insurance cov2 erage.

(c) Access to records. For purposes of conducting the study required under this section, the Comptroller General and any of his duly authorized representatives shall have access to, and the right to examine and copy, all documents, records, and other recorded information—

(1) within the possession or control of providers of qualified health insurance, and

(2) determined by the Comptroller General (or any such representative) to be relevant to the study. The Comptroller General shall not disclose the identity of any provider of qualified health insurance or any eligible individual in making any information obtained under this section available to the public.

(d) Definitions. Any term which is defined in section 35 of the Internal Revenue Code of 1986 shall have the same meaning when used in this section.

[¶ 4061] Sec. 2201. Economic recovery payment to recipients of Social Security, Supplemental Security Income, Railroad Retirement Benefits, and Veterans Disability Compensation or Pension Benefits.

(a) **Authority to make payments.**

(1) **Eligibility.**

(A) In general. Subject to paragraph (5)(B), the Secretary of the Treasury shall disburse a $250 payment to each individual who, for any month during the 3-month period ending with the month which ends prior to the month that includes the date of the enactment of this Act, is entitled to a benefit payment described in clause (i), (ii), or (iii) of subparagraph (B) or is eligible for a SSI cash benefit described in subparagraph (C).

(B) Benefit payment described. For purposes of subparagraph (A):

(i) Title II benefit. A benefit payment described in this clause is a monthly insurance benefit payable (without regard to sections 202(j)(1) and 223(b) of the Social Security Act (42 U.S.C. 402(j)(1), 423(b)) under —

(I) section 202(a) of such Act (42 U.S.C. 402(a));

(II) section 202(b) of such Act (42 U.S.C. 402(b));

(III) section 202(c) of such Act (42 U.S.C. 402(c));

(IV) section 202(d)(1)(B)(ii) of such Act (42 U.S.C. 402(d)(1)(B)(ii));

(V) section 202(e) of such Act (42 U.S.C. 402(e));

(VI) section 202(f) of such Act (42 U.S.C. 402(f));

(VII) section 202(g) of such Act (42 U.S.C. 402(g));

(VIII) section 202(h) of such Act (42 U.S.C. 402(h));

(IX) section 223(a) of such Act (42 U.S.C. 423(a));

(X) section 227 of such Act (42 U.S.C. 427); or

(XI) section 228 of such Act (42 U.S.C. 428).

(ii) Railroad Retirement Benefit. A benefit payment described in this clause is a monthly annuity or pension payment payable (without regard to section 5(a)(ii) of the Railroad Retirement Act of 1974 (45 U.S.C. 231d(a)(ii))) under —

(I) section 2(a)(1) of such Act (45 U.S.C. 231a(a)(1));

(II) section 2(c) of such Act (45 U.S.C. 231a(c));

(III) section 2(d)(1)(i) of such Act (45 U.S.C. 231a(d)(1)(i));

(IV) section 2(d)(1)(ii) of such Act (45 U.S.C. 231a(d)(1)(ii));

(V) section 2(d)(1)(iii)(C) of such Act to an adult disabled child (45 U.S.C. 231a(d)(1)(iii)(C));

(VI) section 2(d)(1)(iv) of such Act (45 U.S.C. 231a(d)(1)(iv));

(VII) section 2(d)(1)(v) of such Act (45 U.S.C. 231a(d)(1)(v)); or

(VIII) section 7(b)(2) of such Act (45 U.S.C. 231f(b)(2)) with respect to any of the benefit payments described in clause (i) of this subparagraph.

(iii) Veterans benefit. A benefit payment described in this clause is a compensation or pension payment payable under —

(I) section 1110, 1117, 1121, 1131, 1141, or 1151 of title 38, United States Code;

(II) section 1310, 1312, 1313, 1315, 1316, or 1318 of title 38, United States Code;

(III) section 1513, 1521, 1533, 1536, 1537, 1541, 1542, or 1562 of title 38, United States Code; or

(IV) section 1805, 1815, or 1821 of title 38, United States Code, to a veteran, surviving spouse, child, or parent as described in paragraph (2), (3), (4)(A)(ii), or (5) of section 101, title 38, United States Code, who received that benefit during any month within the 3 month period ending with the month which ends prior to the month that includes the date of the enactment of this Act.

    (A) SSI cash benefit described. A SSI cash benefit described in this subparagraph is a cash benefit payable under section 1611 (other than under subsection (e)(1)(B) of such section) or 1619(a) of the Social Security Act (42 U.S.C. 1382, 1382h).

(2) Requirement. A payment shall be made under paragraph (1) only to individuals who reside in 1 of the 50 States, the District of Columbia, Puerto Rico, Guam, the United States Virgin Islands, American Samoa, or the Northern Mariana Islands. For purposes of the preceding sentence, the determination of the individual's residence shall be based on the current address of record under a program specified in paragraph (1).

(3) No double payments. An individual shall be paid only 1 payment under this section, regardless of whether the individual is entitled to, or eligible for, more than 1 benefit or cash payment described in paragraph (1).

(4) Limitation. A payment under this section shall not be made—

    (A) in the case of an individual entitled to a benefit specified in paragraph (1)(B)(i) or paragraph (1)(B)(ii)(VIII) if, for the most recent month of such individual's entitlement in the 3-month period described in paragraph (1), such individual's benefit under such paragraph was not payable by reason of subsection (x) or (y) of section 202 the Social Security Act (42 U.S.C. 402) or section 1129A of such Act (42 U.S.C. 1320a-8a);

    (B) in the case of an individual entitled to a benefit specified in paragraph (1)(B)(iii) if, for the most recent month of such individual's entitlement in the 3 month period described in paragraph (1), such individual's benefit under such paragraph was not payable, or was reduced, by reason of section 1505, 5313, or 5313B of title 38, United States Code;

    (C) in the case of an individual entitled to a benefit specified in paragraph (1)(C) if, for such most recent month, such individual's benefit under such paragraph was not payable by reason of subsection (e)(1)(A) or (e)(4) of section 1611 (42 U.S.C. 1382) or section 1129A of such Act (42 U.S.C. 1320a-8a); or

    (D) in the case of any individual whose date of death occurs before the date on which the individual is certified under subsection (b) to receive a payment under this section.

(5) Timing and manner of payments.

    (A) In general. —The Secretary of the Treasury shall commence disbursing payments under this section at the earliest practicable date but in no event later than 120 days after the date of enactment of this Act. The Secretary of the Treasury may disburse any payment electronically to an individual in such manner as if such payment was a benefit payment or cash benefit to such individual under the applicable program described in subparagraph (B) or (C) of paragraph (1).

    (B) Deadline. No payments shall be disbursed under this section after December 31, 2010, regardless of any determinations of entitlement to, or eligibility for, such payments made after such date.

(b) Identification of recipients. The Commissioner of Social Security, the Railroad Retirement Board, and the Secretary of Veterans Affairs shall certify the individuals entitled to receive payments under this section and provide the Secretary of the Treasury with the information needed to disburse such payments. A certification of an individual shall be unaffected by any subsequent determination or redetermination of the individual's entitlement to, or eligibility for, a benefit specified in subparagraph (B) or (C) of subsection (a)(1).

(c) Treatment of payments.

(1) Payment to be disregarded for purposes of all federal and federally assisted programs. A payment under subsection (a) shall not be regarded as income and shall not be regarded as a resource for the month of receipt and the following 9 months, for purposes of determining the eligibility of the recipient (or the recipient's spouse or family) for benefits or assistance, or the amount or extent of benefits or assistance, under any Federal program or under any State or local program financed in whole or in part with Federal funds.

(2) Payment not considered income for purposes of taxation. A payment under subsection (a) shall not be considered as gross income for purposes of the Internal Revenue Code of 1986.

(3) Payments protected from assignment. The provisions of sections 207 and 1631(d)(1) of the Social Security Act (42 U.S.C. 407, 1383(d)(1)), section 14(a) of the Railroad Retirement Act of 1974 (45 U.S.C. 231m(a)), and section 5301 of title 38, United States Code, shall apply to any payment made under subsection (a) as if such payment was a benefit payment or cash benefit to such individual under the applicable program described in subparagraph (B) or (C) of subsection (a)(1).

(4) Payments subject to offset. Notwithstanding paragraph (3), for purposes of section 3716 of title 31, United States Code, any payment made under this section shall not be considered a benefit payment or cash benefit made under the applicable program described in subparagraph (B) or (C) of subsection (a)(1) and all amounts paid shall be subject to offset to collect delinquent debts.

(d) Payment to representative payees and fiduciaries.

(1) In general. In any case in which an individual who is entitled to a payment under subsection (a) and whose benefit payment or cash benefit described in paragraph (1) of that subsection is paid to a representative payee or fiduciary, the payment under subsection (a) shall be made to the individual's representative payee or fiduciary and the entire payment shall be used only for the benefit of the individual who is entitled to the payment.

(2) Applicability.

(A) Payment on the basis of a title II or SSI benefit. Section 1129(a)(3) of the Social Security Act (42 U.S.C. 1320a-8(a)(3)) shall apply to any payment made on the basis of an entitlement to a benefit specified in paragraph (1)(B)(i) or (1)(C) of subsection (a) in the same manner as such section applies to a payment under title II or XVI of such Act.

(B) Payment on the basis of a Railroad Retirement Benefit. Section 13 of the Railroad Retirement Act (45 U.S.C. 231l) shall apply to any payment made on the basis of an entitlement to a benefit specified in paragraph (1)(B)(ii) of subsection (a) in the same manner as such section applies to a payment under such Act.

(C) Payment on the basis of a Veterans Benefit. Sections 5502, 6106, and 6108 of title 38, United States Code, shall apply to any payment made on the basis of an entitlement to a benefit specified in paragraph (1)(B)(iii) of subsection (a) in the same manner as those sections apply to a payment under that title.

(e) Appropriation. Out of any sums in the Treasury of the United States not otherwise appropriated, the following sums are appropriated for the period of fiscal years 2009 through 2011, to remain available until expended, to carry out this section:

(1) For the Secretary of the Treasury, $131,000,000 for administrative costs incurred in carrying out this section, section 2202, section 36A of the Internal Revenue Code of 1986 (as added by this Act), and other provisions of this Act or the amendments made by this Act relating to the Internal Revenue Code of 1986.

(2) For the Commissioner of Social Security—

(A) such sums as may be necessary for payments to individuals certified by the Commissioner of Social Security as entitled to receive a payment under this section; and

(B) $90,000,000 for the Social Security Administration's Limitation on Administrative Expenses for costs incurred in carrying out this section.

(3) For the Railroad Retirement Board—

(A) such sums as may be necessary for payments to individuals certified by the Railroad Retirement Board as entitled to receive a payment under this section; and

(B) $1,400,000 to the Railroad Retirement Board's Limitation on Administration for administrative costs incurred in carrying out this section.

(4)

(A) For the Secretary of Veterans Affairs—

(i) such sums as may be necessary for the Compensation and Pensions account, for payments to individuals certified by the Secretary of Veterans Affairs as entitled to receive a payment under this section; and

(i) $100,000 for the Information Systems Technology account and $7,100,000 for the General Operating Expenses account for administrative costs incurred in carrying out this section.

(B) The Department of Veterans Affairs Compensation and Pensions account shall hereinafter be available for payments authorized under subsection (a)(1)(A) to individuals entitled to a benefit payment described in subsection (a)(1)(B)(iii).

[¶ 4062] Sec. 2202. Special credit for certain government retirees.

(a) In general. In the case of an eligible individual, there shall be allowed as a credit against the tax imposed by subtitle A of the Internal Revenue Code of 1986 for the first taxable year beginning in 2009 an amount equal $250 ($500 in the case of a joint return where both spouses are eligible individuals).

(b) Eligible individual. For purposes of this section—

(1) In general. The term "eligible individual" means any individual—

(A) who receives during the first taxable year beginning in 2009 any amount as a pension or annuity for service performed in the employ of the United States or any State, or any instrumentality thereof, which is not considered employment for purposes of chapter 21 of the Internal Revenue Code of 1986, and

(B) who does not receive a payment under section 2201 during such taxable year.

(2) Identification number requirement. Such term shall not include any individual who does not include on the return of tax for the taxable year—

(A) such individual's social security account number, and

(B) in the case of a joint return, the social security account number of one of the taxpayers on such return.

For purposes of the preceding sentence, the social security account number shall not include a TIN (as defined in section 7701(a)(41) of the Internal Revenue Code of 1986) issued by the Internal Revenue Service. Any omission of a correct social security account number required under this subparagraph shall be treated as a mathematical or clerical error for purposes of applying section 6213(g)(2) of such Code to such omission.

(c) Treatment of credit.

(1) Refundable credit.

(A) In general. The credit allowed by subsection (a) shall be treated as allowed by subpart C of part IV of subchapter A of chapter 1 of the Internal Revenue Code of 1986.

(B) Appropriations. For purposes of section 1324(b)(2) of title 31, United States Code, the credit allowed by subsection (a) shall be treated in the same manner a refund from the credit allowed under section 36A of the Internal Revenue Code of 1986 (as added by this Act).

(2) Deficiency rules. For purposes of section 6211(b)(4)(A) of the Internal Revenue Code of 1986, the credit allowable by subsection (a) shall be treated in the same manner as the credit allowable under section 36A of the Internal Revenue Code of 1986 (as added by this Act).

770

(d) Refunds disregarded in the administration of federal programs and federally assisted programs. Any credit or refund allowed or made to any individual by reason of this section shall not be taken into account as income and shall not be taken into account as resources for the month of receipt and the following 2 months, for purposes of determining the eligibility of such individual or any other individual for benefits or assistance, or the amount or extent of benefits or assistance, under any Federal program or under any State or local program financed in whole or in part with Federal funds.

[¶ 4064] Sec. 3001. Premium assistance for COBRA benefits. (a) Premium assistance for cobra continuation coverage for individuals and their families.

(1) Provision of premium assistance.

(A) Reduction of premiums payable.In the case of any premium for a period of coverage beginning on or after the date of the enactment of this Act for COBRA continuation coverage with respect to any assistance eligible individual, such individual shall be treated for purposes of any COBRA continuation provision as having paid the amount of such premium if such individual pays (or a person other than such individual's employer pays on behalf of such individual) 35 percent of the amount of such premium (as determined without regard to this subsection).

(B) Plan enrollment option.

(i) In general. Notwithstanding the COBRA continuation provisions, an assistance eligible individual may, not later than 90 days after the date of notice of the plan enrollment option described in this subparagraph, elect to enroll in coverage under a plan offered by the employer involved, or the employee organization involved (including, for this purpose, a joint board of trustees of a multiemployer trust affiliated with one or more multiemployer plans), that is different than coverage under the plan in which such individual was enrolled at the time the qualifying event occurred, and such coverage shall be treated as COBRA continuation coverage for purposes of the applicable COBRA continuation coverage provision.

(ii) Requirements. An assistance eligible individual may elect to enroll in different coverage as described in clause (i) only if—

(I) the employer involved has made a determination that such employer will permit assistance eligible individuals to enroll in different coverage as provided for this subparagraph;

(II) the premium for such different coverage does not exceed the premium for coverage in which the individual was enrolled at the time the qualifying event occurred;

(III) the different coverage in which the individual elects to enroll is coverage that is also offered to the active employees of the employer at the time at which such election is made; and

(IV) the different coverage is not—

(aa) coverage that provides only dental, vision, counseling, or referral services (or a combination of such services);

(bb) a flexible spending arrangement (as defined in section 106(c)(2) of the Internal Revenue Code of 1986); or

(cc) coverage that provides coverage for services or treatments furnished in an on-site medical facility maintained by the employer and that consists primarily of first-aid services, prevention and wellness care, or similar care (or a combination of such care).

(C) Premium reimbursement. For provisions providing the balance of such premium, see section 6432 of the Internal Revenue Code of 1986, as added by paragraph (12).

(2) Limitation of period of premium assistance.

(A) In general. Paragraph (1)(A) shall not apply with respect to any assistance eligible individual for months of coverage beginning on or after the earlier of—

(i) the first date that such individual is eligible for coverage under any other group health plan (other than coverage consisting of only dental, vision, counseling, or referral services (or a combination thereof), coverage under a flexible spending arrangement (as defined in section 106(c)(2) of the Internal Revenue Code of 1986), or coverage of treatment that is furnished

771

in an on-site medical facility maintained by the employer and that consists primarily of first-aid services, prevention and wellness care, or similar care (or a combination thereof)) or is eligible for benefits under title XVIII of the Social Security Act, or

(ii) the earliest of—

(I) the date which is 9 months after the first day of the first month that paragraph (1)(A) applies with respect to such individual,

(II) the date following the expiration of the maximum period of continuation coverage required under the applicable COBRA continuation coverage provision, or

(III) the date following the expiration of the period of continuation coverage allowed under paragraph (4)(B)(ii).

(B) Timing of eligibility for additional coverage. For purposes of subparagraph (A)(i), an individual shall not be treated as eligible for coverage under a group health plan before the first date on which such individual could be covered under such plan.

(C) Notification requirement. An assistance eligible individual shall notify in writing the group health plan with respect to which paragraph (1)(A) applies if such paragraph ceases to apply by reason of subparagraph (A)(i). Such notice shall be provided to the group health plan in such time and manner as may be specified by the Secretary of Labor.

(3) Assistance eligible individual. For purposes of this section, the term "assistance eligible individual" means any qualified beneficiary if—

(A) at any time during the period that begins with September 1, 2008, and ends with December 31, 2009, such qualified beneficiary is eligible for COBRA continuation coverage,

(B) such qualified beneficiary elects such coverage, and

(C) the qualifying event with respect to the COBRA continuation coverage consists of the involuntary termination of the covered employee's employment and occurred during such period.

(4) Extension of election period and effect on coverage.

(A) In general. For purposes of applying section 605(a) of the Employee Retirement Income Security Act of 1974, section 4980B(f)(5)(A) of the Internal Revenue Code of 1986, section 2205(a) of the Public Health Service Act, and section 8905a(c)(2) of title 5, United States Code, in the case of an individual who does not have an election of COBRA continuation coverage in effect on the date of the enactment of this Act but who would be an assistance eligible individual if such election were so in effect, such individual may elect the COBRA continuation coverage under the COBRA continuation coverage provisions containing such sections during the period beginning on the date of the enactment of this Act and ending 60 days after the date on which the notification required under paragraph (7)(C) is provided to such individual.

(B) Commencement of coverage; no reach-back. Any COBRA continuation coverage elected by a qualified beneficiary during an extended election period under subparagraph (A)—

(i) shall commence with the first period of coverage beginning on or after the date of the enactment of this Act, and

(ii) shall not extend beyond the period of COBRA continuation coverage that would have been required under the applicable COBRA continuation coverage provision if the coverage had been elected as required under such provision.

(C) Preexisting conditions. With respect to a qualified beneficiary who elects COBRA continuation coverage pursuant to subparagraph (A), the period—

(i) beginning on the date of the qualifying event, and

(ii) ending with the beginning of the period described in subparagraph (B)(i), shall be disregarded for purposes of determining the 63-day periods referred to in section 701(c)(2) of the Employee Retirement Income Security Act of 1974, section 9801(c)(2) of the Internal Revenue Code of 1986, and section 2701(c)(2) of the Public Health Service Act.

(5) Expedited review of denials of premium assistance. In any case in which an individual requests treatment as an assistance eligible individual and is denied such treatment by the

group health plan, the Secretary of Labor (or the Secretary of Health and Human Services in connection with COBRA continuation coverage which is provided other than pursuant to part 6 of subtitle B of title I of the Employee Retirement Income Security Act of 1974), in consultation with the Secretary of the Treasury, shall provide for expedited review of such denial. An individual shall be entitled to such review upon application to such Secretary in such form and manner as shall be provided by such Secretary. Such Secretary shall make a determination regarding such individual's eligibility within 15 business days after receipt of such individual's application for review under this paragraph. Either Secretary's determination upon review of the denial shall be de novo and shall be the final determination of such Secretary. A reviewing court shall grant deference to such Secretary's determination. The provisions of this paragraph, paragraphs (1) through (4), and paragraph (7) shall be treated as provisions of title I of the Employee Retirement Income Security Act of 1974 for purposes of part 5 of subtitle B of such title.

(6) Disregard of subsidies for purposes of federal and state programs. Notwithstanding any other provision of law, any premium reduction with respect to an assistance eligible individual under this subsection shall not be considered income or resources in determining eligibility for, or the amount of assistance or benefits provided under, any other public benefit provided under Federal law or the law of any State or political subdivision thereof.

(7) Notices to individuals.

(A) General notice.

(i) In general. In the case of notices provided under section 606(a)(4) of the Employee Retirement Income Security Act of 1974 (29 U.S.C. 1166(4)), section 4980B(f)(6)(D) of the Internal Revenue Code of 1986, section 2206(4) of the Public Health Service Act (42 U.S.C. 300bb-6(4)), or section 8905a(f)(2)(A) of title 5, United States Code, with respect to individuals who, during the period described in paragraph (3)(A), become entitled to elect COBRA continuation coverage, the requirements of such sections shall not be treated as met unless such notices include an additional notification to the recipient of—

(I) the availability of premium reduction with respect to such coverage under this subsection, and

(II) the option to enroll in different coverage if the employer permits assistance eligible individuals to elect enrollment in different coverage (as described in paragraph (1)(B)).

(ii) Alternative notice. In the case of COBRA continuation coverage to which the notice provision under such sections does not apply, the Secretary of Labor, in consultation with the Secretary of the Treasury and the Secretary of Health and Human Services, shall, in consultation with administrators of the group health plans (or other entities) that provide or administer the COBRA continuation coverage involved, provide rules requiring the provision of such notice.

(iii) Form. The requirement of the additional notification under this subparagraph may be met by amendment of existing notice forms or by inclusion of a separate document with the notice otherwise required.

(B) Specific requirements. Each additional notification under subparagraph (A) shall include—

(i) the forms necessary for establishing eligibility for premium reduction under this subsection,

(ii) the name, address, and telephone number necessary to contact the plan administrator and any other person maintaining relevant information in connection with such premium reduction,

(iii) a description of the extended election period provided for in paragraph (4)(A),

(iv) a description of the obligation of the qualified beneficiary under paragraph (2)(C) to notify the plan providing continuation coverage of eligibility for subsequent coverage under another group health plan or eligibility for benefits under title XVIII of the Social Security Act and the penalty provided under section 6720C of the Internal Revenue Code of 1986 for failure to so notify the plan,

(v) a description, displayed in a prominent manner, of the qualified beneficiary's right to a reduced premium and any conditions on entitlement to the reduced premium, and

(vi) a description of the option of the qualified beneficiary to enroll in different coverage if the employer permits such beneficiary to elect to enroll in such different coverage under paragraph (1)(B).

(C) Notice in connection with extended election periods. In the case of any assistance eligible individual (or any individual described in paragraph (4)(A)) who became entitled to elect COBRA continuation coverage before the date of the enactment of this Act, the administrator of the group health plan (or other entity) involved shall provide (within 60 days after the date of enactment of this Act) for the additional notification required to be provided under subparagraph (A) and failure to provide such notice shall be treated as a failure to meet the notice requirements under the apalicable COBRA continuation provision.

(D) Model notices. Not later than 30 days after the date of enactment of this Act—

(i) the Secretary of the Labor, in consultation with the Secretary of the Treasury and the Secretary of Health and Human Services, shall prescribe models for the additional notification required under this paragraph (other than the additional notification described in clause (ii)), and

(ii) in the case of any additional notification provided pursuant to subparagraph (A) under section 8905a(f)(2)(A) of title 5, United States Code, the Office of Personnel Management shall prescribe a model for such additional notification.

(8) Regulations. The Secretary of the Treasury may prescribe such regulations or other guidance as may be necessary or appropriate to carry out the provisions of this subsection, including the prevention of fraud and abuse under this subsection, except that the Secretary of Labor and the Secretary of Health and Human Services may prescribe such regulations (including interim final regulations) or other guidance as may be necessary or appropriate to carry out the provisions of paragraphs (5), (7), and (9).

(9) Outreach. The Secretary of Labor, in consultation with the Secretary of the Treasury and the Secretary of Health and Human Services, shall provide outreach consisting of public education and enrollment assistance relating to premium reduction provided under this subsection. Such outreach shall target employers, group health plan administrators, public assistance programs, States, insurers, and other entities as determined appropriate by such Secretaries. Such outreach shall include an initial focus on those individuals electing continuation coverage who are referred to in paragraph (7)(C). Information on such premium reduction, including enrollment, shall also be made available on websites of the Departments of Labor, Treasury, and Health and Human Services.

(10) definitions. For purposes of this section—

(A) Administrator. The term "administrator" has the meaning given such term in section 3(16)(A) of the Employee Retirement Income Security Act of 1974.

(B) COBRA continuation coverage. The term "COBRA continuation coverage" means continuation coverage provided pursuant to part 6 of subtitle B of title I of the Employee Retirement Income Security Act of 1974 (other than under section 609), title XXII of the Public Health Service Act, section 4980B of the Internal Revenue Code of 1986 (other than subsection (f)(1) of such section insofar as it relates to pediatric vaccines), or section 8905a of title 5, United States Code, or under a State program that provides comparable continuation coverage. Such term does not include coverage under a health flexible spending arrangement under a cafeteria plan within the meaning of section 125 of the Internal Revenue Code of 1986.

(C) COBRA continuation provision. The term "COBRA continuation provision" means the provisions of law described in sub6 paragraph (B).

(D) Covered employee. The term "covered employee" has the meaning given such term in section 607(2) of the Employee Retirement Income Security Act of 1974.

(E) Qualified beneficiary. The term "qualified beneficiary" has the meaning given such term in section 607(3) of the Employee Retirement Income Security Act of 1974.

(F) Group health plan. The term "group health plan" has the meaning given such term in section 607(1) of the Employee Retirement Income Security Act of 1974.

(G) State. The term "State" includes the District of Columbia, the Commonwealth of Puerto Rico, the Virgin Islands, Guam, American Samoa, and the Commonwealth of the Northern Mariana Islands.

(H) Period of coverage. Any reference in this subsection to a period of coverage shall be treated as a reference to a monthly or shorter period of coverage with respect to which premiums are charged with respect to such coverage.

(11) Reports.

(A) Interim report. The Secretary of the Treasury shall submit an interim report to the Committee on Education and Labor, the Committee on Ways and Means, and the Committee on Energy and Commerce of the House of Representatives and the Committee on Health, Education, Labor, and Pensions and the Committee on Finance of the Senate regarding the premium reduction provided under this subsection that includes —

(i) the number of individuals provided such assistance as of the date of the report; and

(ii) the total amount of expenditures incurred (with administrative expenditures noted separately) in connection with such assistance as of the date of the report.

(B) Final report. As soon as practicable after the last period of COBRA continuation coverage for which premium reduction is provided under this section, the Secretary of the Treasury shall submit a final report to each Committee referred to in subparagraph (A) that includes —

(i) the number of individuals provided premium reduction under this section;

(ii) the average dollar amount (monthly and annually) of premium reductions provided to such individuals; and

(iii) the total amount of expenditures incurred (with administrative expenditures noted separately) in connection with premium reduction under this section.

* * * * * * * * * * * *

(B) Social security trust funds held harmless. In determining any amount transferred or appropriated to any fund under the Social Security Act, section 6432 of the Internal Revenue Code of 1986 shall not be taken into account.

* * * * * * * * * * * *

(D) Effective date. The amendments made by this paragraph shall apply to premiums to which subsection (a)(1)(A) applies.

(E) Special rule.

(i) In general. In the case of an assistance eligible individual who pays, with respect to the first period of COBRA continuation coverage to which subsection (a)(1)(A) applies or the immediately subsequent period, the full premium amount for such coverage, the person to whom such payment is payable shall —

(I) make a reimbursement payment to such individual for the amount of such premium paid in excess of the amount required to be paid under subsection (a)(1)(A); or

(II) provide credit to the individual for such amount in a manner that reduces one or more subsequent premium payments that the individual is required to pay under such subsection for the coverage involved.

(ii) Reimbursing employer. A person to which clause (i) applies shall be reimbursed as provided for in section 6432 of the Internal Revenue Code of 1986 for any payment made, or credit provided, to the employee under such clause.

(iii) Payment or credits. Unless it is reasonable to believe that the credit for the excess payment in clause (i)(II) will be used by the assistance eligible individual within 180 days of the date on which the person receives from the individual the payment of the full premium amount, a person to which clause (i) applies shall make the payment required under such clause to the individual within 60 days of such payment of the full premium amount.

If, as of any day within the 180-day period, it is no longer reasonable to believe that the credit will be used during that period, payment equal to the remainder of the credit outstanding shall be made to the individual within 60 days of such day.

* * * * * * * * * * * *

(C) Effective date. The amendments made by this paragraph shall apply to failures occurring after the date of the enactment of this Act.

(14) Coordination with HCTC.

(A) In general.

* * * * * * * * * * * *

(B) Effective date. The amendment made by subparagraph (A) shall apply to taxable years ending after the date of the enactment of this Act.

(15) Exclusion of cobra premium assistance from gross income.

* * * * * * * * * * * *

(C) Effective date. The amendments made by this paragraph shall apply to taxable years ending after the date of the enactment of this Act.

(b) Elimination of premium subsidy for high Income individuals.

(1) Recapture of subsidy for high-income individuals.

(A) If premium assistance is provided under this section with respect to any COBRA continuation coverage which covers the taxpayer, the taxpayer's spouse, or any dependent (within the meaning of section 152 of the Internal Revenue Code of 1986, determined without regard to subsections (b)(1), (b)(2), and (d)(1)(B) thereof) of the taxpayer during any portion of the taxable year, and

(B) the taxpayer's modified adjusted gross income for such taxable year exceeds $125,000 ($250,000 in the case of a joint return), then the tax imposed by chapter 1 of such Code with respect to the taxpayer for such taxable year shall be increased by the amount of such assistance.

(2) Phase-in of recapture.

(A) In general. In the case of a taxpayer whose modified adjusted gross income for the taxable year does not exceed $145,000 ($290,000 in the case of a joint return), the increase in the tax imposed under paragraph (1) shall not exceed the phase-in percentage of such increase (determined without regard to this paragraph).

(B) Phase-in percentage. For purposes of this subsection, the term "phase-in percentage" means the ratio (expressed as a percentage) obtained by dividing—

(i) the excess of described in subparagraph (B) of paragraph (1), by

(ii) $20,000 ($40,000 in the case of a joint return).

(3) Option for high-income individuals to waive assistance and avoid recapture. Notwithstanding subsection (a)(3), an individual shall not be treated as an assistance eligible individual for purposes of this section and section 6432 of the Internal Revenue Code of 1986 if such individual—

(A) makes a permanent election (at such time and in such form and manner as the Secretary of the Treasury may prescribe) to waive the right to the premium assistance provided under this section, and

(B) notifies the entity to whom premiums are reimbursed under section 6432(a) of such Code of such election.

(4) Modified adjusted gross income. For purposes of this subsection, the term "modified adjusted gross income" means the adjusted gross income (as defined in section 62 of the Internal Revenue Code of 1986) of the taxpayer for the taxable year increased by any amount excluded from gross income under section 911, 931, or 933 of such Code.

(5) Credits not allowed against tax, etc. For purposes determining regular tax liability under section 26(b) of such Code, the increase in tax under this subsection shall not be treated as a tax imposed under chapter 1 of such Code.

(6) Regulations. The Secretary of the Treasury shall issue such regulations or other guidance as are necessary or appropriate to carry out this subsection, including requirements that

the entity to whom premiums are reimbursed under section 6432(a) of the Internal Revenue Code of 1986 report to the Secretary, and to each assistance eligible individual, the amount of premium assistance provided under subsection (a) with respect to each such individual.

(7) Effective date. The provisions of this subsection shall apply to taxable years ending after the date of the enactment of this Act.

[¶ 4065] Sec. 7001. Executive compensation and corporate governance. Section 111 of the Emergency Economic Stabilization Act of 2008 (12 U.S.C. 5221) is amended to read as follows:

"Sec. 111. Executive compensation and corporate governance.

"(a) Definitions. For purposes of this section, the following definitions shall apply:

"(1) Senior executive officer. The term 'senior executive officer' means an individual who is 1 of the top 5 most highly paid executives of a public company, whose compensation is required to be disclosed pursuant to the Securities Exchange Act of 1934, and any regulations issued thereunder, and non-public company counterparts.

"(2) Golden parachute payment. The term 'golden parachute payment' means any payment to a senior executive officer for departure from a company for any reason, except for payments for services performed or benefits accrued.

"(3) TARP recipient. The term 'TARP recipient' means any entity that has received or will receive financial assistance under the financial as11 sistance provided under the TARP.

"(4) Commission. The term 'Commission' means the Securities and Exchange Commission.

"(5) Period in which obligation is outstanding; rule of construction. For purposes of this section, the period in which any obligation arising from financial assistance provided under the TARP remains outstanding does not include any period during which the Federal Government only holds warrants to purchase common stock of the TARP recipient.

"(b) Executive compensation and corporate governance.

"(1) Establishment of standards. During the period in which any obligation arising from financial assistance provided under the TARP remains outstanding, each TARP recipient shall be subject to—

"(A) the standards established by the Secretary under this section; and

"(B) the provisions of section 162(m)(5) of the Internal Revenue Code of 1986, as applicable.

"(2) Standards required. The Secretary shall require each TARP recipient to meet appropriate standards for executive compensation and corporate governance.

"(3) Specific requirements. The standards established under paragraph (2) shall include the following:

"(A) Limits on compensation that exclude incentives for senior executive officers of the TARP recipient to take unnecessary and excessive risks that threaten the value of such recipient during the period in which any obligation arising from financial assistance provided under the TARP remains outstanding.

"(B) A provision for the recovery by such TARP recipient of any bonus, retention award, or incentive compensation paid to a senior executive officer and any of the next 20 most highly-compensated employees of the TARP recipient based on statements of earnings, revenues, gains, or other criteria that are later found to be materially inaccurate.

"(C) A prohibition on such TARP recipient making any golden parachute payment to a senior executive officer or any of the next 5 most highly-compensated employees of the TARP recipient during the period in which any obligation arising from financial assistance provided under the TARP remains outstanding.

"(D)(i) A prohibition on such TARP recipient paying or accruing any bonus, retention award, or incentive compensation during the period in which any obligation arising from financial assistance provided under the TARP remains outstanding, except that any prohibition developed under this paragraph shall not apply to the payment of long-term restricted stock by such TARP recipient, provided that such longterm restricted stock—

"(I) does not fully vest during the period in which any obligation arising from financial assistance provided to that TARP recipient remains outstanding;

"(II) has a value in an amount that is not greater than 1?3 of the total amount of annual compensation of the employee receiving the stock; and

"(III) is subject to such other terms and conditions as the Secretary may determine is in the public interest.

"(ii) The prohibition required under clause

"(i) shall apply as follows:

"(I) For any financial institution that received financial assistance provided under the TARP equal to less than $25,000,000, the prohibition shall apply only to the most highly compensated employee of the financial institution.

"(II) For any financial institution that received financial assistance provided under the TARP equal to at least $25,000,000, but less than $250,000,000, the prohibition shall apply to at least the 5 most highly-compensated employees of the financial institution, or such higher number as the Secretary may determine is in the public interest with respect to any TARP recipient.

"(III) For any financial institution that received financial assistance provided under the TARP equal to at least$250,000,000, but less than $500,000,000, the prohibition shall apply to the senior executive officers and at least the 10 next most highly-compensated employees, or such higher number as the Secretary may determine is in the public interest with respect to any TARP recipient.

"(IV) For any financial institution that received financial assistance provided under the TARP equal to $500,000,000 or more, the prohibition shall apply to the senior executive officers and at least the 20 next most highly-compensated employees, or such higher number as the Secretary may determine is in the public interest with respect to any TARP recipient.

"(iii) The prohibition required under clause

(i) shall not be construed to prohibit any bonus payment required to be paid pursuant to a written employment contract executed on or before February 11, 2009, as such valid employment contracts are determined by the Secretary or the designee of the Secretary.

"(E) A prohibition on any compensation plan that would encourage manipulation of the reported earnings of such TARP recipient to enhance the compensation of any of its employees.

"(F) A requirement for the establishment of a Board Compensation Committee that meets the requirements of subsection (c).

"(4) Certification of compliance. The chief executive officer and chief financial officer (or the equivalents thereof) of each TARP recipient shall provide a written certification of compliance by the TARP recipient with the requirements of this section—

"(A) in the case of a TARP recipient, the securities of which are publicly traded, to the Securities and Exchange Commission, together with annual filings required under the securities laws; and

"(B) in the case of a TARP recipient that is not a publicly traded company, to the Secretary.

"(c) Board compensation committee.

"(1) Establishment of board required. Each TARP recipient shall establish a Board Compensation Committee, comprised entirely of independent directors, for the purpose of reviewing employee compensation plans.

"(2) Meetings. The Board Compensation Committee of each TARP recipient shall meet at least semiannually to discuss and evaluate employee compensation plans in light of an assessment of any risk posed to the TARP recipient from such plans.

"(3) Compliance by non-SEC registrants. In the case of any TARP recipient, the common or preferred stock of which is not registered pursuant to the Securities Exchange Act of 1934, and that has received $25,000,000 or less of TARP assistance, the duties of the Board Compensation Committee under this subsection shall be carried out by the board of directors of such TARP recipient.

"(d) Limitation on luxury expenditures. The board of directors of any TARP recipient shall have in place a company-wide policy regarding excessive or luxury expenditures, as identified by the Secretary, which may include excessive expenditures on—

"(1) entertainment or events;

"(2) office and facility renovations;

"(3) aviation or other transportation services; or

"(4) other activities or events that are not reasonable expenditures for staff development, reasonable performance incentives, or other similar measures conducted in the normal course of the business operations of the TARP recipient.

"(e) Shareholder approval of executive compensation.

"(1) Annual shareholder approval of executive compensation. Any proxy or consent or authorization for an annual or other meeting of the shareholders of any TARP recipient during the period in which any obligation arising from financial assistance provided under the TARP remains outstanding shall permit a separate shareholder vote to approve the compensation of executives, as disclosed pursuant to the compensation disclosure rules of the Commission (which disclosure shall include the compensation discussion and analysis, the compensation tables, and any related material).

"(2) Nonbinding vote. A shareholder vote escribed in paragraph (1) shall not be binding on the board of directors of a TARP recipient, and may not be construed as overruling a decision by such board, nor to create or imply any additional fiduciary duty by such board, nor shall such vote be construed to restrict or limit the ability of shareholders to make proposals for inclusion in proxy materials related to executive compensation.

"(3) Deadline for rulemaking. Not later than 1 year after the date of enactment of the American Recovery and Reinvestment Act of 2009, the Commission shall issue any final rules and regulations required by this subsection.

"(f) Review of prior payments to executives.

"(1) In general. The Secretary shall review bonuses, retention awards, and other compensation paid to the senior executive officers and the next 20 most highly-compensated employees of each entity receiving TARP assistance before the date of enactment of the American Recovery and Reinvestment Act of 2009, to determine whether any such payments were inconsistent with the purposes of this section or the TARP or were otherwise contrary to the public interest.

"(2) Negotiations for reimbursement. If the Secretary makes a determination described in paragraph (1), the Secretary shall seek to negotiate with the TARP recipient and the subject employee for appropriate reimbursements to the Federal Government with respect to compensation or bonuses.

"(g) No impediment to withdrawal by TARP recipients. Subject to consultation with the appropriate Federal banking agency (as that term is defined in section 3 of the Federal Deposit Insurance Act), if any, the Secretary shall permit a TARP recipient to repay any assistance previously provided under the TARP to such financial institution, without regard to whether the financial institution has replaced such funds from any other source or to any waiting period, and when such assistance is repaid, the Secretary shall liquidate warrants associated with such assistance at the current market price.

"(h) Regulations. The Secretary shall promulgate regulations to implement this section.''.

[¶ 4066] Sec. 7002. Applicability with respect to loan modifications. Section 109(a) of the Emergency Economic Stabilization Act of 2008 (12 U.S.C. 5219(a)) is amended—

(1) by striking ''To the extent'' and inserting the following:

"(1) In general. To the extent''; and

(2) by adding at the end the following:

"(2) Waiver of certain provisions in connection with loan modifications. The Secretary shall not be required to apply executive compensation restrictions under section 111, or to receive warrants or debt instruments under section 113, solely in connection with any loan modification under this section.".

Children's Health Insurance Program Reauthorization Act of 2009

[¶ 4067] Act sections of the Children's Health Insurance Program Reauthorization Act of 2009 that affect, but do not amend, the Internal Revenue Code or ERISA are reproduced here.

[¶ 4068] Sec. 311. Special enrollment period under group health plans in case of termination of MEDICAID or CHIP coverage or eligibility for assistance in purchase of employment-based coverage; coordination of coverage.

      * * * * * * * * * * * *

(b) Conforming Amendments.

  (1) Amendments to Employee Retirement Income Security Act—

    (C) Working group to develop model coverage coordination disclosure form—

      (i) MEDICAID, CHIP, and employer-sponsored coverage coordination working group.;

        (I) In general. Not later than 60 days after the date of enactment of this Act, the Secretary of Health and Human Services and the Secretary of Labor shall jointly establish a Medicaid, CHIP, and Employer-Sponsored Coverage Coordination Working Group (in this subparagraph referred to as the "Working Group"). The purpose of the Working Group shall be to develop the model coverage coordination disclosure form described in subclause (II) and to identify the impediments to the effective coordination of coverage available to families that include employees of employers that maintain group health plans and members who are eligible for medical assistance under title XIX of the Social Security Act or child health assistance or other health benefits coverage under title XXI of such Act.

        (II) Model coverage coordination disclosure form described. The model form described in this subclause is a form for plan administrators of group health plans to complete for purposes of permitting a State to determine the availability and cost-effectiveness of the coverage available under such plans to employees who have family members who are eligible for premium assistance offered under a State plan under title XIX or XXI of such Act and to allow for coordination of coverage for enrollees of such plans. Such form shall provide the following information in addition to such other information as the Working Group determines appropriate:

          (aa) A determination of whether the employee is eligible for coverage under the group health plan.

          (bb) The name and contract information of the plan administrator of the group health plan.

          (cc) The benefits offered under the plan.

          (dd) The premiums and cost-sharing required under the plan.

          (ee) Any other information relevant to coverage under the plan.

      (ii) Membership. The Working Group shall consist of not more than 30 members and shall be composed of representatives of—

        (I) the Department of Labor;

        (II) the Department of Health and Human Services;

        (III) State directors of the Medicaid program under title XIX of the Social Security Act;

        (IV) State directors of the State Children's Health Insurance Program under title XXI of the Social Security Act;

        (V) employers, including owners of small businesses and their trade or industry representatives and certified human resource and payroll professionals;

        (VI) plan administrators and plan sponsors of group health plans (as defined in section 607(1) of the Employee Retirement Income Security Act of 1974);

(VII) health insurance issuers; and

(VIII) children and other beneficiaries of medical assistance under title XIX of the Social Security Act or child health assistance or other health benefits coverage under title XXI of such Act.

(iii) Compensation. The members of the Working Group shall serve without compensation.

(iv) Administrative support. The Department of Health and Human Services and the Department of Labor shall jointly provide appropriate administrative support to the Working Group, including technical assistance. The Working Group may use the services and facilities of either such Department, with or without reimbursement, as jointly determined by such Departments.

(v) Report.

(I) Report by working group to the secretaries. Not later than 18 months after the date of the enactment of this Act, the Working Group shall submit to the Secretary of Labor and the Secretary of Health and Human Services the model form described in clause (i)(II) along with a report containing recommendations for appropriate measures to address the impediments to the effective coordination of coverage between group health plans and the State plans under titles XIX and XXI of the Social Security Act.

(I) Report by Secretaries to the Congress. Not later than 2 months after receipt of the report pursuant to subclause (I), the Secretaries shall jointly submit a report to each House of the Congress regarding the recommendations contained in the report under such subclause.

(vi) Termination. The Working Group shall terminate 30 days after the date of the issuance of its report under clause (v).

(D) Effective dates. The Secretary of Labor and the Secretary of Health and Human Services shall develop the initial model notices under section 701(f)(3)(B)(i)(II) of the Employee Retirement Income Security Act of 1974, and the Secretary of Labor shall provide such notices to employers, not later than the date that is 1 year after the date of enactment of this Act, and each employer shall provide the initial annual notices to such employer's employees beginning with the first plan year that begins after the date on which such initial model notices are first issued. The model coverage coordination disclosure form developed under subparagraph (C) shall apply with respect to requests made by States beginning with the first plan year that begins after the date on which such model coverage coordination disclosure form is first issued.

* * * * * * * * * * *

[¶ 4069] Sec. 704. Time for payment of corporate estimated taxes. The percentage under subparagraph (C) of section 401(1) of the Tax Increase Prevention and Reconciliation Act of 2005 in effect on the date of the enactment of this Act is increased by 0.5 percentage point.

[¶ 5000] Congressional Committee Reports Accompanying the American Recovery and Reinvestment Act of 2009

This section, in ¶ 5001 through ¶ 5084, reproduces all relevant parts of the Congressional Committee Reports relating to H.R. 1 (P.L. 111-5, 2/17/2009), the American Recovery and Reinvestment Act of 2009. The material comes from the House Report (H Rept No. 111-8 Part 2, 1/28/2009) related to H.R. 598, a predecessor bill to H.R. 1, the Joint Committee on Taxation Reports (JCX-10-09, 1/23/2009, and JCX-12-09, 1/27/2009) related to the Senate Finance Committee version of H.R. 1, and the Conference Report (Conf Rept No. 111-16, 2/12/2009) for Division B of H.R. 1.

[¶ 5001]   Section 1001.   Making work pay credit.

(Code Sec. 36A)

[Conference Report]

Present Law

Earned income tax credit

Low- and moderate-income workers may be eligible for the refundable earned income tax credit ("EITC"). Eligibility for the EITC is based on earned income, adjusted gross income, investment income, filing status, and immigration and work status in the United States. The amount of the EITC is based on the presence and number of qualifying children in the worker's family, as well as on adjusted gross income and earned income.

The EITC generally equals a specified percentage of earned income[1] up to a maximum dollar amount. The maximum amount applies over a certain income range and then diminishes to zero over a specified phaseout range. For taxpayers with earned income (or adjusted gross income ("AGI"), if greater) in excess of the beginning of the phaseout range, the maximum EITC amount is reduced by the phaseout rate multiplied by the amount of earned income (or AGI, if greater) in excess of the beginning of the phaseout range. For taxpayers with earned income (or AGI, if greater) in excess of the end of the phaseout range, no credit is allowed.

The EITC is a refundable credit, meaning that if the amount of the credit exceeds the taxpayer's Federal income tax liability, the excess is payable to the taxpayer as a direct transfer payment. Under an advance payment system, eligible taxpayers may elect to receive the credit in their paychecks, rather than waiting to claim a refund on their tax returns filed by April 15 of the following year.

Child credit

An individual may claim a tax credit for each qualifying child under the age of 17. The amount of the credit per child is $1,000 through 2010 and $500 thereafter. A child who is not a citizen, national, or resident of the United States cannot be a qualifying child.

The credit is phased out for individuals with income over certain threshold amounts. Specifically, the otherwise allowable child tax credit is reduced by $50 for each $1,000 (or fraction thereof) of modified adjusted gross income over $75,000 for single individuals or heads of households, $110,000 for married individuals filing joint returns, and $55,000 for married individuals filing separate returns. For purposes of this limitation,

1. Earned income is defined as (1) wages, salaries, tips, and other employee compensation, but only if such amounts are includible in gross income, plus (2) the amount of the individual's net self-employment earnings.

801

modified adjusted gross income includes certain otherwise excludible income earned by U.S. citizens or residents living abroad or in certain U.S. territories.

The credit is allowable against the regular tax and the alternative minimum tax. To the extent the child credit exceeds the taxpayer's tax liability, the taxpayer is eligible for a refundable credit (the additional child tax credit) equal to 15 percent of earned income in excess of a threshold dollar amount (the "earned income" formula). The threshold dollar amount is $12,550 (for 2009), and is indexed for inflation.

Families with three or more children may determine the additional child tax credit using the "alternative formula," if this results in a larger credit than determined under the earned income formula. Under the alternative formula, the additional child tax credit equals the amount by which the taxpayer's social security taxes exceed the taxpayer's earned income tax credit.

Earned income is defined as the sum of wages, salaries, tips, and other taxable employee compensation plus net self-employment earnings. Unlike the EITC, which also includes the preceding items in its definition of earned income, the additional child tax credit is based only on earned income to the extent it is included in computing taxable income. For example, some ministers' parsonage allowances are considered self-employment income, and thus are considered earned income for purposes of computing the EITC, but the allowances are excluded from gross income for individual income tax purposes, and thus are not considered earned income for purposes of the additional child tax credit.

House Bill

In general

The provision provides eligible individuals a refundable income tax credit for two years (taxable years beginning in 2009 and 2010).

The credit is the lesser of (1) 6.2 percent of an individual's earned income or (2) $500 ($1,000 in the case of a joint return). For these purposes, the earned income definition is the same as for the earned income tax credit with two modifications. First, earned income for these purposes does not include net earnings from self-employment which are not taken into account in computing taxable income. Second, earned income for these purposes includes combat pay excluded from gross income under section 112.[2]

The credit is phased out at a rate of two percent of the eligible individual's modified adjusted gross income above $75,000 ($150,000 in the case of a joint return). For these purposes an eligible individual's modified adjusted gross income is the eligible individual's adjusted gross income increased by any amount excluded from gross income under sections 911, 931, or 933. An eligible individual means any individual other than: (1) a nonresident alien; (2) an individual with respect to whom another individual may claim a dependency deduction for a taxable year beginning in 8 calendar year in which the eligible individual's taxable year begins; and (3) an estate or trust. Each eligible individual must satisfy identical taxpayer identification number requirements to those applicable to the earned income tax credit.

Treatment of the U.S. possessions

Mirror code possessions[3]

The U.S. Treasury will make payments to each mirror code possession in an amount equal to the aggregate amount of the credits allowable by reason of the provision to that possession's residents against its income tax. This amount will be determined by the

---

2. Unless otherwise stated, all section references are to the Internal Revenue Code of 1986, as amended (the "Code").
3. Possessions with mirror code tax systems are the United States Virgin Islands, Guam, and the Commonwealth of the Northern Mariana Islands.

Treasury Secretary based on information provided by the government of the respective possession. For purposes of these payments, a possession is a mirror code possession if the income tax liability of residents of the possession under that possession's income tax system is determined by reference to the U.S. income tax laws as if the possession were the United States.

Non-mirror code possessions[4]

To each possession that does not have a mirror code tax system, the U.S. Treasury will make two payments (for 2009 and 2010, respectively) in an amount estimated by the Secretary as being equal to the aggregate credits that would have been allowed to residents of that possession if a mirror code tax system had been in effect in that possession. Accordingly, the amount of each payment to a non-mirror Code possession will be an estimate of the aggregate amount of the credits that would be allowed to the possession's residents if the credit provided by the provision to U.S. residents were provided by the possession to its residents. This payment will not be made to any U.S. possession unless that possession has a plan that has been approved by the Secretary under which the possession will promptly distribute the payment to its residents.

General rules

No credit against U.S. income tax is permitted under the provision for any person to whom a credit is allowed against possession income taxes as a result of the provision (for example, under that possession's mirror income tax). Similarly, no credit against U.S. income tax is permitted for any person who is eligible for a payment under a non-mirror code possession's plan for distributing to its residents the payment described above from the U.S. Treasury.

For purposes of the payments to the possessions, the Commonwealth of Puerto Rico and the Commonwealth of the Northern Mariana Islands are considered possessions of the United States.

For purposes of the rule permitting the Treasury Secretary to disburse appropriated amounts for refunds due from certain credit provisions of the Internal Revenue Code of 1986, the payments required to be made to possessions under the provision are treated in the same manner us a refund due from the credit allowed under the provision.

Federal programs or Federally-assisted programs

Any credit or refund allowed or made to an individual under this provision (including to any resident of a U.S. possession) is not taken into account as income and shall not be taken into account as resources for the month of receipt and the following two months for purposes of determining eligibility of such individual or any other individual for benefits or assistance, or the amount or extent of benefits or assistance, under any Federal program or under any State or local program financed in whole or in part with Federal funds.

Income tax withholding

Taxpayers' reduced tax liability under the provision shall be expeditiously implemented through revised income tax withholding schedules produced by the Internal Revenue Service. These revised income tax withholding schedules should be designed to reduce taxpayers' income tax withheld for each remaining pay period in the remainder of 2009 by an amount equal to the amount that withholding would have been reduced had the provision been reflected in the income tax withholding schedules for the entire taxable year.

---

4. Possessions that do not have mirror code tax systems are Puerto Rico and American Samoa.

Senate Amendment

In general

The Senate is the same as the House bill, except that the credit is phased out at a rate of four percent (rather than two percent) of the eligible individual's modified adjusted gross income above $70,000 ($140,000 in the case of a joint return).

Also, the Senate amendment provides that the otherwise allowable credit allowed under the provision is reduced by the amount of any payment received by the taxpayer pursuant to the provisions of the bill providing economic recovery payments under the Veterans' Administration, Railroad Retirement Board, and the Social Security Administration. The provision treats the failure to reduce the credit by the amount of these payments, and the omission of the correct TIN, as clerical errors. This allows the IRS to assess any tax resulting from such failure or omission without the requirement to send the taxpayer a notice of deficiency allowing the taxpayer the right to file a petition with the Tax Court.

Income tax withholding

The Senate amendment also provides for a more accelerated delivery of the credit in 2009 through revised income tax withholding schedules produced by the Department of the Treasury. Under the Senate amendment, these revised income tax withholding schedules would be designed to reduce taxpayers' income tax withheld for the remainder of 2009 in such a manner that the full annual benefit of the provision is reflected in income tax withheld during the remainder of 2009.

Conference Agreement

In general

The provision provides eligible individuals a refundable income tax credit for two years (taxable years beginning in 2009 and 2010).

The credit is the lesser of (1) 6.2 percent of an individual's earned income or (2) $400 ($800 in the case of a joint return). For these purposes, the earned income definition is the same as for the earned income tax credit with two modifications. First, earned income for these purposes does not include net earnings from self-employment which are not taken into account in computing taxable income. Second, earned income for these purposes includes combat pay excluded from gross income under section 112.

The credit is phased out at a rate of two percent of the eligible individual's modified adjusted gross income above $75,000 ($150,000 in the case of a joint return). For these purposes an eligible individual's modified adjusted gross income is the eligible individual's adjusted gross income increased by any amount excluded from gross income under sections 911, 931, or 933. An eligible individual means any individual other than: (1) a nonresident alien; (2) an individual with respect to whom another individual may claim a dependency deduction for a taxable year beginning in a calendar year in which the eligible individual's taxable year begins; and (3) an estate or trust.

Also, the conference agreement provides that the otherwise allowable making work pay credit allowed under the provision is reduced by the amount of any payment received by the taxpayer pursuant to the provisions of the bill providing economic recovery payments under the Veterans Administration, Railroad Retirement Board, and the Social Security Administration and a temporary refundable tax credit for certain government retirees.[5] The conference agreement treats the failure to reduce the making work pay credit by the amount of such payments or credit, and the omission of the correct TIN, as clerical errors. This allows the IRS to assess any tax, resulting from such failure or omission without the requirement to send the taxpayer a notice of deficiency allowing the taxpayer the right to file a petition with the Tax Court.

Each tax return on which this credit is claimed must include the social security number of the taxpayer (in the case of it joint return, the social security number of at least one spouse).

Treatment of the U.S. possessions

The conference agreement follows the House bill and the Senate amendment.

Federal programs for Federally-assisted programs

The conference agreement follows the House bill and the Senate amendment.

Income tax withholding

The conference agreement follows the Senate amendment.

Effective Date

The provision applies to taxable years beginning after December 31, 2008.

[¶ 5002]   Section 1002.   Temporary increase in earned income tax credit.

(Code Sec. 32)

[Conference Report]

Present Law

Overview

Low- and moderate-income workers may be eligible for the refundable earned income tax credit ("EITC"). Eligibility for the EITC is based on earned income, adjusted gross income, investment income, filing status, and immigration and work status in the United States. The amount of the EITC is based on the presence and number of qualifying children in the worker's family, as well as on adjusted gross income and earned income.

The EITC generally equals a specified percentage of earned income[6] up to a maximum dollar amount. The maximum amount applies over a certain income range and then diminishes to zero over a specified phaseout range. For taxpayers with earned income (or adjusted gross income (AGI), if greater) in excess of the beginning of the phaseout range, the maximum EITC amount is reduced by the phaseout rate multiplied by the amount of earned income (or AGI, if greater) in excess of the beginning of the phaseout range. For taxpayers with earned income (or AGI, if greater) in excess of the end of the phaseout range, no credit is allowed.

An individual is not eligible for the EITC if the aggregate amount of disqualified income of the taxpayer for the taxable year exceeds $3,100 (for 2009). This threshold is indexed for inflation. Disqualified income is the sum of: (1) interest (taxable and tax exempt); (2) dividends; (3) net rent and royalty income (if greater than zero); (4) capital

---

5. The credit for certain government employees is available for 2009. The credit is $250 ($500 for a joint return where both spouses are eligible individuals). An eligible individual for these purposes is an individual: (1) who receives an amount as a pension or annuity for service performed in the employ of the United States or any State or any instrumentality thereof, which is not considered employment for purposes of Social Security taxes; and (2) who does not receive an economic recovery payment under the Veterans Administration, Railroad Retirement Board, or the Social Security Administration.

6. Earned income is defined as (1) wages, salaries, tips, and other employee compensation, but only if such amounts are includible in gross income, plus (2) the amount of the individual's net self-employment earnings.

gains net income; and (5) net passive income (if greater than zero) that is not self-employment income.

The EITC is a refundable credit, meaning that if the amount of the credit exceeds the taxpayer's Federal income tax liability, the excess is payable to the taxpayer as a direct transfer payment. Under an advance payment system, eligible taxpayers may elect to receive the credit in their paychecks, rather than waiting to claim a refund on their tax returns filed by April 15 of the following year.

Filing status

An unmarried individual may claim the EITC if he or she files as a single filer or as a head of household. Married individuals generally may not claim the EITC unless they file jointly. An exception to the joint return filing requirement applies to certain spouses who are separated. Under this exception, a married taxpayer who is separated from his or her spouse for the last six months of the taxable year shall not be considered as married (and, accordingly, may file a return as head of household and claim the EITC), provided that the taxpayer maintains a household that constitutes the principal place of abode for a dependent child (including a son, stepson, daughter, stepdaughter, adopted child, or a foster child) for over half the taxable year,[7] and pays over half the cost of maintaining the household in which he or she resides with the child during the year.

Presence of qualifying children and amount of the earned income credit

Three separate credit schedules apply: one schedule for taxpayers with no qualifying children, one schedule for taxpayers with one qualifying child, and one schedule for taxpayers with more than one qualifying child.[8]

Taxpayers with no qualifying children may claim a credit if they are over age 24 and below age 65. The credit is 7.65 percent of earnings up to $5,970, resulting in a maximum credit of $457 for 2009. The maximum is available for those with incomes between $5,970 and $7,470 ($10,590 if married filing jointly). The credit begins to phase down at a rate of 7.65 percent of earnings above $7,470 ($10,590 if married filing jointly) resulting in a $0 credit at $13,440 of earnings ($16,560 if married filing jointly).

Taxpayers with one qualifying child may claim a credit in 2009 of 34 percent of their earnings up to $8,950, resulting in a maximum credit of $3,043. The maximum credit is available for those with earnings between $8,950 and $16,420 ($19,540 if married filing jointly). The credit begins to phase down at a rate of 15.98 percent of earnings above $16,420 ($19,540 if married filing jointly). The credit is phased down to $0 at $35,463 of earnings ($38,583 if married filing jointly).

Taxpayers with more than one qualifying child may claim a credit in 2009 of 40 percent of earnings up to $12,570, resulting in a maximum credit of $5,028. The maximum credit is available for those with earnings between $12,570 and $16,420 ($19,540 if married filing jointly). The credit begins to phase down at a rate of 21.06 percent of earnings above $16,420 ($19,540 if married filing jointly). The credit is phased down to $0 at $40,295 of earnings ($43,415 if married filing jointly).

If more than one taxpayer lives with a qualifying child, only one of these taxpayers may claim the child for purposes of the EITC. If multiple eligible taxpayers actually claim the same qualifying child, then a tiebreaker rule determines which taxpayer is entitled to the EITC with respect to the qualifying child. Any eligible taxpayer with at least one qualifying child who does not claim the EITC with respect to qualifying children due to failure to meet certain identification requirements with respect to such children (i.e., providing the name, age and taxpayer identification number of each of such children) may not claim the EITC for taxpayers without qualifying children.

---

7. A foster child must reside with the taxpayer for the entire taxable year.
8. All income thresholds are indexed for inflation annually.

House Bill

Three or more qualifying children

The provision increases the EITC credit percentage for families with three or more qualifying children to 45 percent for 2009 and 2010. For example, in 2009 taxpayers with three or more qualifying children may claim a credit of 45 percent of earnings up to $12,570, resulting in a maximum credit of $5,656.50.

Provide additional marriage penalty relief through higher threshold phase-out amounts for married couples filing joint returns

The provision increases the threshold phase-out amounts for married couples filing joint returns to $5,000[9] above the threshold phase-out amounts for singles, surviving spouses, and heads of households) for 2009 and 2010. For example, in 2009 the maximum credit of $3,043 for one qualifying child is available for those with earnings between $8,950 and $16,420 ($21,420 if married filing jointly). The credit begins to phase down at a rate of 15.98 percent of earnings above $16,420 ($21,420 if married filing jointly). The credit is phased down to $0 at $35,463 of earnings ($40,463 if married filing jointly).

Senate Amendment

The Senate amendment is the same as the House bill.

Conference Agreement

The conference agreement follows the House bill and the Senate amendment.

Effective Date

The provision is effective for taxable years beginning after December 31, 2008.

[¶ 5003]　　Section 1003.　Temporary increase of refundable portion of child credit.

(Code Sec. 24)

[Conference Report]

Present Law

An individual may claim a tax credit for each qualifying child under the age of 17. The amount of the credit per child is $1,000 through 2010, and $500 thereafter. A child who is not a citizen, national, or resident of the United States cannot be a qualifying child.

The credit is phased out for individuals with income over certain threshold amounts. Specifically, the otherwise allowable child tax credit is reduced by $50 for each $1,000 (or fraction thereof) of modified adjusted gross income over $75,000 for single individuals or heads of households, $110,000 for married individuals filing joint returns, and $55,000 for married individuals filing separate returns. For purposes of this limitation, modified adjusted gross income includes certain otherwise excludable income earned by U.S. citizens or residents living abroad or in certain U.S. territories.

The credit is allowable against the regular tax and the alternative minimum tax. To the extent the child credit exceeds the taxpayer's tax liability, the taxpayer is eligible for a refundable credit (the additional child tax credit) equal to 15 percent of earned income in excess of a threshold dollar amount (the "earned income" formula). The threshold dollar amount is $12,550 (for 2009), and is indexed for inflation.

---

9. The $5,000 is indexed for inflation in the case of taxable years beginning in 2010.

Families with three or more children may determine the additional child tax credit using the "alternative formula," if this results in a larger credit than determined under the earned income formula. Under the alternative formula, the additional child tax credit equals the amount by which the taxpayer's social security taxes exceed the taxpayer's earned income tax credit ("EITC").

Earned income is defined as the sum of wages, salaries, tips, and other taxable employee compensation plus net self-employment earnings. Unlike the EITC, which also includes the preceding items in its definition of earned income, the additional child tax credit is based only on earned income to the extent it is included in computing taxable income. For example, some ministers' parsonage allowances are considered self-employment income and thus, are considered earned income for purposes of computing the EITC, but the allowances are excluded from gross income for individual income tax purposes and thus, are not considered earned income for purposes of the additional child tax credit.

Any credit or refund allowed or made to an individual under this provision (including to any resident of a U.S. possession) is not taken into account as income and shall not be taken into account as resources for the month of receipt and the following two months for purposes of determining eligibility of such individual or any other individual for benefits or assistance, or the amount or extent of benefits or assistance, under any Federal program or under any State or local program financed in whole or in part with Federal funds.

House Bill

The provision modifies the earned income formula for the determination of the refundable child credit to apply to 15 percent of earned income in excess of $0 for taxable years beginning in 2009 and 2010.

Senate Amendment

The Senate amendment is the same as the House bill except that the refundable child credit is calculated to apply to 15 percent of earned income in excess of $8,100 for taxable years beginning in 2009 and 2010.

Conference Agreement

The conference agreement follows the House bill and the Senate amendment except that the refundable child credit is calculated to apply to 15 percent of earned income in excess of $3,000 for taxable years beginning in 2009 and 2010.

Effective Date

The provision is effective for taxable years beginning after December 31, 2008.

[¶ 5004]   Section 1004.   American opportunity tax credit.

(Code Sec. 25A)

[Conference Report]

Present Law

Individual taxpayers are allowed to claim a nonrefundable credit, the Hope credit, against Federal income taxes of up to $1,800 (for 2009) per eligible student per year for qualified tuition and related expenses paid for the first two years of the student's post-secondary education in a degree or certificate program.[10] The Hope credit rate is

---

10. Sec. 25A. The Hope credit generally may not be claimed against a taxpayer's alternative minimum tax liability. However, the credit may be claimed against a taxpayer's alternative minimum tax liability for taxable years beginning prior to January 1, 2009.

100 percent on the first $1,200 of qualified tuition and related expenses, and 50 percent on the next $1,200 of qualified tuition and related expenses; these dollar amounts are indexed for inflation, with the amount rounded down to the next lowest multiple of $100. Thus, for example, a taxpayer who incurs $1,200 of qualified tuition and related expenses for an eligible student is eligible (subject to the adjusted gross income phaseout described below) for a $1,200 Hope credit. If a taxpayer incurs $2,400 of qualified tuition and related expenses for an eligible student, then he or she is eligible for a $1,800 Hope credit.

The Hope credit that a taxpayer may otherwise claim is phased out ratably for taxpayers with modified adjusted gross income between $50,000 and $60,000 ($100,000 and $120,000 for married taxpayers filing a joint return) for 2009. The adjusted gross income phaseout ranges are indexed for inflation, with the amount rounded down to the next lowest multiple of $1,000.

The qualified tuition and related expenses must be incurred on behalf of the taxpayer, the taxpayer's spouse, or a dependent of the taxpayer. The Hope credit is available with respect to an individual student for two taxable years, provided that the student has not completed the first two years of post-secondary education before the beginning of the second taxable year.

The Hope credit is available in the taxable year the expenses are paid, subject to the requirement that the education is furnished to the student during that year or during an academic period beginning during the first three months of the next taxable year. Qualified tuition and related expenses paid with the proceeds of a loan generally are eligible for the Hope credit. The repayment of a loan itself is not a qualified tuition or related expense.

A taxpayer may claim the Hope credit with respect to an eligible student who is not the taxpayer or the taxpayer's spouse (e.g., in cases in which the student is the taxpayer's child) only if the taxpayer claims the student as a dependent for the taxable year for which the credit is claimed. If a student is claimed as a dependent, the student is not entitled to claim a Hope credit for that taxable year on the student's own tax return. If a parent (or other taxpayer) claims a student as a dependent, any qualified tuition and related expenses paid by the student are treated as paid by the parent (or other taxpayer) for purposes of determining the amount of qualified tuition and related expenses paid by such parent (or other taxpayer) under the provision. In addition, for each taxable year, a taxpayer may elect either the Hope credit, the Lifetime Learning credit, or an above-the-line deduction for qualified tuition and related expenses with respect to an eligible student.

The Hope credit is available for "qualified tuition and related expenses," which include tuition and fees (excluding nonacademic fees) required to be paid to an eligible educational institution as a condition of enrollment or attendance of an eligible student at the institution. Charges and fees associated with meals, lodging, insurance, transportation, and similar personal, living, or family expenses are not eligible for the credit. The expenses of education involving sports, games, or hobbies are not qualified tuition and related expenses unless this education is part of the student's degree program.

Qualified tuition and related expenses generally include only out-of-pocket expenses. Qualified tuition and related expenses do not include expenses covered by employer-provided educational assistance and scholarships that are not required to be included in the gross income of either the student or the taxpayer claiming the credit. Thus, total qualified tuition and related expenses are reduced by any scholarship or fellowship grants excludable from gross income under section 117 and any other tax-free educational benefits received by the student (or the taxpayer claiming the credit) during the taxable year. The Hope credit is not allowed with respect to any education expense for which a deduction is claimed under section 162 or any other section of the Code.

An eligible student for purposes of the Hope credit is an individual who is enrolled in a degree, certificate, or other program (including a program of study abroad approved for credit by the institution at which such student is enrolled) leading to a recognized educational credential at an eligible educational institution. The student must pursue a course of study on at least a halftime basis. A student is considered to pursue a course of study on at least a half-time basis if the student carries at least one half the normal full-time work load for the course of study the student is pursuing for at least one academic period that begins during the taxable year. To be eligible for the Hope credit, a student must not have been convicted of a Federal or State felony consisting of the possession or distribution of a controlled substance.

Eligible educational institutions generally are accredited post-secondary educational institutions offering credit toward a bachelor's degree, an associate's degree, or another recognized post-secondary credential. Certain proprietary institutions and post-secondary vocational institutions also are eligible educational institutions. To qualify as an eligible educational institution, an institution must be eligible to participate in Department of Education student aid programs.

Effective for taxable years beginning after December 31, 2010, the changes to the Hope credit made by the Economic Growth and Tax Relief Reconciliation Act of 2001 ("EGTRRA") no longer apply. The principal EGTRRA change scheduled to expire is the change that permitted a taxpayer to claim a Hope credit in the same year that he or she claimed an exclusion from a Coverdell education savings account. Thus, after 2010, a taxpayer cannot claim a Hope credit in the same year he or she claims an exclusion from a Coverdell education savings account.

House Bill

The provision modifies the Hope credit for taxable years beginning in 2009 or 2010. The modified credit is referred to as the American Opportunity Tax credit. The allowable modified credit is up to $2,500 per eligible student per year for qualified tuition and related expenses paid for each of the first four years of the student's post-secondary education in a degree or certificate program. The modified credit rate is 100 percent on the first $2,000 of qualified tuition and related expenses, and 25 percent on the next $2,000 of qualified tuition and related expenses. For purposes of the modified credit, the definition of qualified tuition and related expenses is expanded to include course materials.

Under the provision, the modified credit is available with respect to an individual student for four years, provided that the student has not completed the first four years of post-secondary education before the beginning of the fourth taxable year. Thus, the modified credit, in addition to other modifications, extends the application of the Hope credit to two more years of post-secondary education.

The modified credit that a taxpayer may otherwise claim is phased out ratably for taxpayers with modified adjusted gross income between $80,000 and $90,000 ($160,000 and $180,000 for married taxpayers filing a joint return). The modified credit may be claimed against a taxpayer's alternative minimum tax liability.

Forty percent of a taxpayer's otherwise allowable modified credit is refundable. However, no portion of the modified credit is refundable if the taxpayer claiming the credit is a child to whom section 1(g) applies for such taxable year (generally, any child under age 18 or any child under age 24 who is a student providing less than one-half of his or her own support, who has at least one living parent and does not file a joint return).

In addition, the provision requires the Secretary of the Treasury to conduct two studies and submit a report to Congress on the results of those studies within one year after the date of enactment. The first study shall examine how to coordinate the Hope and Lifetime Learning credits with the Pell grant program. The second study shall examine requiring students to perform community service as a condition of taking their tuition and related expenses into account for purposes of the Hope and Lifetime Learning credits.

Senate Amendment

The Senate amendment is the same as the House bill, except that the Senate amendment provides that only 30 percent of a taxpayer's otherwise allowable modified credit is refundable.

Conference Agreement

The conference agreement follows the House bill, with the following modifications. Under the conference agreement, bona fide residents of the U.S. possessions (American Samoa, Commonwealth of the Northern Mariana Islands, Commonwealth of Puerto Rico, Guam, Virgin Islands) are not permitted to claim the refundable portion of the American opportunity credit in the United States. Rather, a bona fide resident of a mirror code possession (Commonwealth of the Northern Mariana Islands, Guam, Virgin Islands) may claim the refundable portion of the credit in the possession in which the individual is a resident. Similarly, a bona fide resident of a non-mirror code possession (Commonwealth of Puerto Rico, American Samoa) may claim the refundable portion of the credit in the possession in which the individual is a resident, but only if that possession establishes a plan for permitting the claim under its internal law.

The conference agreement provides that the U.S. Treasury will make payments to the possessions in respect of credits allowable to their residents under their internal laws. Specifically, the U.S. Treasury will make payments for to each mirror code possession in an amount equal to the aggregate amount of the refundable portion of the credits allowable by reason of the provision to that possession's residents against its income tax. This amount will be determined by the Treasury Secretary based on information provided by the government of the respective possession. To each possession that does not have a mirror code tax system, the U.S. Treasury will make two payments (for 2009 and 2010, respectively) in an amount estimated by the Secretary as being equal to the aggregate amount of the refundable portion of the credits that would have been allowed to residents of that possession if a mirror code tax system had been in effect in that possession. Accordingly, the amount of each payment to a non-mirror code. possession will be an estimate of the aggregate amount of the refundable portion of the credits that would be allowed to the possession's residents if the credit provided by the provision to U.S. residents were provided by the possession to its residents. This payment will not be made to any U.S. possession unless that possession has a plan that has been approved by the Secretary under which the possession will promptly distribute the payment to its residents.

Effective Date

The provision is effective with respect to taxable years beginning after December 31, 2008.

[¶ 5005]   Section 1005. Computer technology and equipment allowed as a qualified higher education expense for section 529 accounts in 2009 and 2010.

(Code Sec. 529)

[Conference Report]

Present Law

Section 529 provides specified income tax and transfer tax rules for the treatment of accounts and contracts established under qualified tuition programs.[11] A qualified tuition

---

11. For purposes of this description, the term "account" is used interchangeably to refer to a prepaid tuition benefit contract or a tuition savings account established pursuant to a qualified tuition program.

program is a program established and maintained by a State or agency or instrumentality thereof, or by one or more eligible educational institutions, which satisfies certain requirements and under which a person may purchase tuition credits or certificates on behalf of a designated beneficiary that entitle the beneficiary to the waiver or payment of qualified higher education expenses of the beneficiary (a "prepaid tuition program"). In the case of a program established and maintained by a State or agency or instrumentality thereof, a qualified tuition program also includes a program under which a person may make contributions to an account that is established for the purpose of satisfying the qualified higher education expenses of the designated beneficiary of the account, provided it satisfies certain specified requirements (a "savings account program"). Under both types of qualified tuition programs, a contributor establishes an account for the benefit of a particular designated beneficiary to provide for that beneficiary's higher education expenses.

For this purpose, qualified higher education expenses means tuition, fees, books, supplies, and equipment required for the enrollment or attendance of a designated beneficiary at an eligible educational institution, and expenses for special needs services in the case of a special needs beneficiary that are incurred in connection with such enrollment or attendance. Qualified higher education expenses generally also include room and board for students who are enrolled at least half-time.

Contributions to a qualified tuition program must be made in cash. Section 529 does not impose a specific dollar limit on the amount of contributions, account balances, or prepaid tuition benefits relating to a qualified tuition account; however, the program is required to have adequate safeguards to prevent contributions in excess of amounts necessary to provide for the beneficiary's qualified higher education expenses. Contributions generally are treated as a completed gift eligible for the gift tax annual exclusion. Contributions are not tax deductible for Federal income tax purposes, although they may be deductible for State income tax purposes. Amounts in the account accumulate on a tax-free basis (i.e., income on accounts in the plan is not subject to current income tax).

Distributions from a qualified tuition program are excludable from the distributee's gross income to the extent that the total distribution does not exceed the qualified higher education expenses incurred for the beneficiary. If a distribution from a qualified tuition program exceeds the qualified higher education expenses incurred for the beneficiary, the portion of the excess that is treated as earnings generally is subject to income tax and an additional 10-percent tax. Amounts in a qualified tuition program may be rolled over to another qualified tuition program for the same beneficiary or for a member of the family of that beneficiary without income tax consequences.

In general, prepaid tuition contracts and tuition savings accounts established under a qualified tuition program involve prepayments or contributions made by one or more individuals for the benefit of a designated beneficiary. with decisions with respect to the contract or account to be made by an individual who is not the designated beneficiary. Qualified tuition accounts or contracts generally require the designation of a person (generally referred to as an "account owner") whom the program administrator (oftentimes a third party administrator retained by the State or by the educational institution that established the program) may look to for decisions, recordkeeping, and reporting with respect to the account established for a designated beneficiary. The person or persons who make the contributions to the account need not be the same person who is regarded as the account owner for purposes of administering the account. Under many qualified tuition programs, the account owner generally has control over the account or contract, including the ability to change designated beneficiaries and to withdraw funds at any time and for any purpose. Thus, in practice, qualified tuition accounts or contracts generally involve a contributor, a designated beneficiary, an account owner (who oftentimes is not the contributor or the designated beneficiary), and an administrator of the account or contract.[12]

House Bill

No provision.

Senate Amendment

The provision expands the definition of qualified higher education expenses for expenses paid or incurred in 2009 and 2010 to include expenses for certain computer technology and equipment to be used by the designated beneficiary while enrolled at an eligible educational institution.

Conference Agreement

The conference agreement follows the Senate amendment.

Effective Date

The provision is effective for expenses paid or incurred after December 31, 2008.

[¶ 5006]   Section 1006.   Extension of and increase in first-time homebuyer credit; waiver of requirement to repay.

(Code Sec. 36, 1400C)

[Conference Report]

Present Law

A taxpayer who is a first-time homebuyer is allowed a refundable tax credit equal to the lesser of $7,500 ($3,750 for a married individual filing separately) or 10 percent of the purchase price of a principal residence. The credit is allowed for the tax year in which the taxpayer purchases the home unless the taxpayer makes an election as described below. The credit is allowed for qualifying home purchases on or after April 9, 2008 and before July 1, 2009 (without regard to whether there was a binding contract to purchase prior to April 9, 2008).

The credit phases out for individual taxpayers with modified adjusted gross income between $75,000 and $95,000 ($150,000 and $170,000 for joint filers) for the year of purchase.

A taxpayer is considered a first-time homebuyer if such individual had no ownership interest in a principal residence in the United States during the three-year period prior to the purchase of the home to which the credit applies.

No credit is allowed if the D.C. homebuyer credit is allowable for the taxable year the residence is purchased or a prior taxable year. A taxpayer is not permitted to claim the credit if the taxpayer's financing is from tax-exempt mortgage revenue bonds, if the taxpayer is a nonresident alien, or if the taxpayer disposes of the residence (or it ceases to be a principal residence) before the close of a taxable year for which a credit otherwise would be allowable.

The credit is recaptured ratably over fifteen years with no interest charge beginning in the second taxable year after the taxable year in which the home is purchased. For example, if the taxpayer purchases a home in 2008, the credit is allowed on the 2008 tax return, and repayments commence with the 2010 tax return. If the taxpayer sells the home (or the home ceases to be used as the principal residence of the taxpayer or the taxpayer's spouse) prior to complete repayment of the credit, any remaining credit re-

---

12. Section 529 refers to contributors and designated beneficiaries, but does not define or otherwise refer to the term account owner, which is a commonly used term among qualified tuition programs.

payment amount is due on the tax return for the year in which the home is sold (or ceases to be used as the principal residence). However, the credit repayment amount may not exceed the amount of gain from the sale of the residence to an unrelated person. For this purpose, gain is determined by reducing the basis of the residence by the amount of the credit to the extent not previously recaptured. No amount is recaptured after the death of a taxpayer. In the case of an involuntary conversion of the home, recapture is not accelerated if a new principal residence is acquired within a two year period. In the case of a transfer of the residence to a spouse or to a former spouse incident to divorce, the transferee spouse (and not the transferor spouse) will be responsible for any future recapture.

An election is provided to treat a home purchased in the eligible period in 2009 as if purchased on December 31, 2008 for purposes of claiming the credit on the 2008 tax return and for establishing the beginning of the recapture period. Taxpayers may amend their returns for this purpose.

House Bill

The provision waives the recapture of the credit for qualifying home purchases after December 31, 2008 and before July 1, 2009. This waiver of recapture applies without regard to whether the taxpayer elects to treat the purchase in 2009 as occurring on December 31, 2008. If the taxpayer disposes of the home or the home otherwise ceases to be the principal residence of the taxpayer within 36 months from the date of purchase, the present law rules for recapture of the credit will still apply.

Senate Amendment

The Senate amendment repeals the existing section 36 for purchases on or after the date of enactment of the American Recovery and Reinvestment Act of 2009.

A taxpayer is allowed a new nonrefundable tax credit equal to the lesser of $15,000 ($7,500 for a married individual filing separately) or 10 percent of the purchase price of a principal residence. The credit is allowed for the tax year in which the taxpayer purchases the home unless the taxpayer makes an election as described below. The credit is allowed for qualifying home purchases after the date of enactment of the American Recovery and Reinvestment Act and on or before the date that is one year after such date of enactment.

The credit is limited to the excess of regular tax liability plus alternative minimum tax liability over the sum of other nonrefundable personal credits.

No credit is allowed for any purchase for which the section 36 first-time homebuyer credit or the D.C. homebuyer credit is allowable. If a credit is allowed under this provision in the case of any individual (and such individual's spouse, if married) with respect to the purchase of any principal residence, no credit is allowed with respect to the purchase of any other principal residence by such individual or a spouse of such individual.

If the taxpayer disposes of the residence (or it ceases to be a principal residence) at any time within 24 months after the date on which the taxpayer purchased the residence, then the credit shall be subject to recapture for, the taxable year in which such disposition occurred (or in which the taxpayer failed to occupy the residence as a principal residence). No amount is recaptured after the death of a taxpayer or in the case of a member of the Armed Forces of the United States on active duty who fails to meet the residency requirement pursuant to a military order and incident to a permanent change of station. In the case of an involuntary conversion of the home, recapture is not accelerated if a new principal residence is acquired within a two year period. In the case of a transfer of the residence to a spouse or to a former spouse incident to divorce, the transferee spouse (and not the transferor spouse) will be responsible for any future recapture.

A further election is provided to treat a home purchased in the eligible period as if purchased on December 31, 2008 for purposes of claiming the credit on the 2008 tax return. Taxpayers may amend their returns for this purpose.

Conference Agreement

The conference agreement extends the existing homebuyer credit for qualifying home purchases before December 1, 2009. In addition, it increases the maximum credit amount to $8,000 ($4,000 for a married individual filing separately) and waives the recapture of the credit for qualifying home purchases after December 31, 2008 and before December 1, 2009. This waiver of recapture applies without regard to whether the taxpayer elects to treat the purchase in 2009 as occurring on December 31, 2008. If the taxpayer disposes of the home or the home otherwise ceases to be the principal residence of the taxpayer within 36 months from the date of purchase, the present law rules for recapture of the credit will apply.

The conference agreement modifies the coordination with the first-time homebuyer credit for residents of the District of Columbia under section 1400C. No credit under section 1400C shall be allowed to any taxpayer with respect to the purchase of a residence during 2009 if a credit under section 36 is allowable to such taxpayer (or the taxpayer's spouse) with respect to such purchase. Taxpayers thus qualify for the more generous national first-time homebuyer credit rather than the D.C. homebuyer credit for qualifying purchases in 2009. No credit under section 36 is allowed for a taxpayer who claimed the D.C. homebuyer credit in any prior taxable year.

The conference agreement removes the prohibition on claiming the credit if the residence is financed by the proceeds of a mortgage revenue bond, a qualified mortgage issue the interest on which is exempt from tax under section 103.

Effective Date

The provision applies to residences purchased after December 31, 2008.

[¶ 5007] Section 1007. Suspension of tax on portion of unemployment compensation.

(Code Sec. 85)

[Conference Report]

Present Law

An individual must include in gross income any unemployment compensation benefits received under the laws of the United States or any State.

House Bill

No provision.

Senate Amendment

The Senate amendment provides that up to $2,400 of unemployment compensation benefits received in 2009 are excluded from gross income by the recipient.

Conference Agreement

The conference agreement follows the Senate amendment.

Effective Date

The provision is effective for taxable years beginning after December 31, 2008.

[¶ 5008]   Section 1008.   Additional deduction for State sales tax and excise tax on the purchase of certain motor vehicles.

(Code Sec. 63, 164)

[Conference Report]

Present Law

In general, a deduction from gross income is allowed for certain taxes for the taxable year within which the taxes are paid or accrued. These include State and local, and foreign, real property taxes; State and local personal property taxes; State, local, and foreign income, war profits, and excess profit taxes; generation skipping transfer taxes; environmental taxes imposed by section 59A; and taxes paid or accrued within the taxable year in carrying on a trade or business or an activity described in section 212 (relating to the expenses for production of income). At the election of the taxpayer for the taxable year, a taxpayer may deduct State and local sales taxes in lieu of State and local income taxes. No deduction is allowed for any general sales tax imposed with respect to an item at a rate other than the general rate of tax, except in the case of a lower rate of tax applicable to items of food, clothing, medical supplies, and motor vehicles. In the case of motor vehicles, if the rate of tax exceeds the general rate, such excess shall be disregarded and the general rate shall be treated as the rate of tax.

House Bill

No provision.

Senate Amendment

The Senate amendment provides an above-the-line deduction for qualified motor vehicle taxes. Qualified motor vehicle taxes include any State or local sales or excise tax imposed on the purchase of a qualified motor vehicle. A qualified motor vehicle means a passenger automobile or light truck acquired for use by the taxpayer and not for resale after November 12, 2008 and before January 1, 2010, the original use of which commences with the taxpayer and which has a gross vehicle weight rating of not more than 8,500 pounds.

The deduction is limited to sales tax of up to $49,500.

The deduction is phased out for taxpayers with modified adjusted gross income between $125,000 and $135,000 ($250,000 and $260,000 in the case of a joint return).

Notwithstanding other provisions of present law, qualified motor vehicle taxes are not treated as part of the cost of acquired property or, in the case of a disposition, as a reduction in the amount realized on the disposition.

A taxpayer who makes an election to deduct State and local sales taxes for the taxable year shall not be allowed the above-the-line deduction for qualified motor vehicle taxes.

If the indebtedness described in section 163(h)(5)(A) includes the amounts of any State or local sales or excise taxes paid or accrued by the taxpayer in connection with the acquisition of a qualified motor vehicle, the aggregate amount of such indebtedness taken into account shall be reduced, but not below zero, by the amount of any such taxes for which a deduction is allowed.

Conference Agreement

The conference agreement does not include the House bill or the Senate amendment. The conference agreement provides a deduction for qualified motor vehicle taxes. It expands the definition of taxes allowed as a deduction to include qualified motor vehicle taxes paid or accrued within the taxable year. A taxpayer who itemizes and makes an election to deduct State and local sales taxes for qualified motor vehicles for the taxable year shall not be allowed the increased standard deduction for qualified motor vehicle taxes.

Qualified motor vehicle taxes include any State or local sales or excise tax imposed on the purchase of a qualified motor vehicle. A qualified motor vehicle means a passenger automobile, light truck, or motorcycle which has a gross vehicle weight rating of not more than 8,500 pounds, or a motor home acquired for use by the taxpayer after the date of enactment and before January 1, 2010, the original use of which commences with the taxpayer.

The deduction is limited to the tax on up to $49,500 of the purchase price of a qualified motor vehicle. The deduction is phased out for taxpayers with modified adjusted gross income between $125,000 and $135,000 ($250,000 and $260,000 in the case of a joint return).

Effective Date

The provision is effective for purchases on or after the date of enactment and before January 1, 2010.

[¶ 5010]   Section 1011; 1012.   Extension of alternative minimum tax relief for nonrefundable personal credits; Extension of increased alternative minimum tax exemption amount.

(Code Sec. 26, 55)

[Conference Report]

Present Law

Present law imposes an alternative minimum tax ("AMT") on individuals. The AMT is the amount by which the tentative minimum tax exceeds the regular income tax. An individual's tentative minimum tax is the sum of (1) 26 percent of so much of the taxable excess as does not exceed $175,000 ($87,500 in the case of a married individual filing a separate return) and (2) 28 percent of the remaining taxable excess. The taxable excess is so much of the alternative minimum taxable income ("AMTI") as exceeds the exemption amount. The maximum tax rates on net capital gain and dividends used in computing the regular tax are used in computing the tentative minimum tax. AMTI is the individual's taxable income adjusted to take account of specified preferences and adjustments.

The exemption amounts are: (1) $69,950 for taxable years beginning in 2008 and $45,000 in taxable years beginning after 2008 in the case of married individuals filing a joint return and surviving spouses; (2) $46,200 for taxable years beginning in 2008 and $33,750 in taxable years beginning after 2008 in the case of other unmarried individuals; (3) $34,975 for taxable years beginning in 2008 and $22,500 in taxable years beginning after 2008 in the case of married individuals filing separate returns: and (4) $22,500 in the case of an estate or trust. The exemption amount is phased out by an amount equal to 25 percent of the amount by which the individual's AMTI exceeds (1) $150,000 in the case of married individuals filing a joint return and surviving spouses, (2) $112,500 in the case of other unmarried individuals, and (3) $75,000 in the case of married individuals filing separate returns or an estate or a trust. These amounts are not indexed for inflation.

Present law provides for certain nonrefundable personal tax credits (i.e., the dependent care credit, the credit for the elderly and disabled, the adoption credit, the child credit, the credit for interest on certain home mortgages, the Hope Scholarship and Lifetime Learning credits, the credit for savers, the credit for certain nonbusiness energy property, the credit for residential energy efficient property, the credit for plug-in electric drive motor vehicles, and the D.C. first-time homebuyer credit).

For taxable years beginning before 2009, the nonrefundable personal credits are allowed to the extent of the full amount of the individual's regular tax and alternative minimum tax.

For taxable years beginning after 2008, the nonrefundable personal credits (other than the adoption credit, the child credit, the credit for savers, the credit for residential energy efficient property, and the credit for plug-in electric drive motor vehicles) are allowed only to the extent that the individual's regular income tax liability exceeds the individual's tentative minimum tax, determined without regard to the minimum tax foreign tax credit. The adoption credit, the child credit, the credit for savers, the credit for residential energy efficient property, and the credit for plug-in electric drive motor vehicles are allowed to the full extent of the individual's regular tax and alternative minimum tax.[18]

House Bill

No provision.

Senate Amendment

The Senate amendment provides that the individual AMT exemption amount for taxable years beginning in 2009 is $70,950, in the case of married individuals filing a joint return and surviving spouses; (2) $46,700 in the case of other unmarried individuals; and (3) $35,475 in the case of married individuals filing separate returns.

For taxable years beginning in 2009, the provision allows an individual to offset the entire regular tax liability and alternative minimum tax liability by the nonrefundable personal credits.

Conference Agreement

The conference agreement follows the Senate amendment.

Effective Date

The provision is effective for taxable years beginning in 2009.

[¶ 5013]   Section 1101.   Extension of credit for electricity produced from certain renewable resources.

(Code Sec. 45)

[Conference Report]

Present Law

In general

An income tax credit is allowed for the production of electricity from qualified energy resources at qualified facilities (the "renewable electricity production credit").[167] Qualified energy resources comprise wind, closed-loop biomass, open-loop biomass, geothermal energy, solar energy, small irrigation power, municipal solid waste, qualified hydropower production, and marine and hydrokinetic renewable energy. Qualified facilities are, generally, facilities that generate electricity using qualified energy resources. To be eligible for the credit, electricity produced from qualified energy resources at qualified facilities must be sold by the taxpayer to an unrelated person.

---

18. The rule applicable to the adoption credit and child credit is subject to the EGTRRA sunset.
167. Sec. 45. In addition to the renewable electricity production credit, section 45 also provides income tax credits for the production of Indian coal and refined coal at qualified facilities.

Credit amounts and credit period

In general

The base amount of the electricity production credit is 1.5 cents per kilowatt-hour. (indexed annually for inflation) of electricity produced. The amount of the credit was 2.1 cents per kilowatt-hour for 2008. A taxpayer may generally claim a credit during the 10-year period commencing with the date the qualified facility is placed in service. The credit is reduced for grants, tax-exempt bonds, subsidized energy financing, and other credits.

Credit phaseout

The amount of credit a taxpayer may claim is phased out as the market price of electricity exceeds certain threshold levels. The electricity production credit is reduced over a 3-cent phaseout range to the extent the annual average contract price per kilowatt-hour of electricity sold in the prior year from the same qualified energy resource exceeds 8 cents (adjusted for inflation; 11.8 cents for 2008).

Reduced credit periods and credit amounts

Generally, in the case of open-loop biomass facilities (including agricultural livestock waste nutrient facilities), geothermal energy facilities, solar energy facilities, small irrigation power facilities, landfill gas facilities, and trash combustion facilities placed in service before August 8, 2005, the 10-year credit period is reduced to five years, commencing on the date the facility was originally placed in service. However, for qualified open-loop biomass facilities (other than a facility described in section 45(d)(3)(A)(i) that uses agricultural livestock waste nutrients) placed in service before October 22, 2004, the five-year period commences on January 1, 2005. In the case of a closed-loop biomass facility modified to co-fire with coal, to co fire with other biomass, or to co-fire with coal and other biomass, the credit period begins no earlier than October 22, 2004.

In the case of open-loop biomass facilities (including agricultural livestock waste nutrient facilities), small irrigation power facilities, landfill gas facilities, trash combustion facilities, and qualified hydropower facilities the otherwise allowable credit amount is 0.75 cent per kilowatt-hour, indexed for inflation measured after 1992 (1 cent per kilowatt-hour for 2008).

Other limitations on credit claimants and credit amounts

In general, in order to claim the credit, a taxpayer must own the qualified facility and sell the electricity produced by the facility to an unrelated party. A lessee or operator may claim the credit in lieu of the owner of the qualifying facility in the case of qualifying open-loop biomass facilities and in the case of closed-loop biomass facilities modified to co-fire with coal, to co-fire with other biomass, or to co-fire with coal and other biomass. In the case of a poultry waste facility, the taxpayer may claim the credit as a lessee or operator of a facility owned by a governmental unit.

For all qualifying facilities, other than closed-loop biomass facilities modified to co-fire with coal, to co-fire with other biomass, or to co-fire with coal and other biomass, the amount of credit a taxpayer may claim is reduced by reason of grants, tax-exempt bonds, subsidized energy financing, and other credits, but the reduction cannot exceed 50 percent of the otherwise allowable credit. In the case of closed-loop biomass facilities modified to co-fire with coal, to co-fire with other biomass, or to co-fire with coal and other biomass, there is no reduction in credit by reason of grants, tax-exempt bonds, subsidized energy financing, and other credits.

The credit for electricity produced from renewable resources is a component of the general business credit.[168] Generally, the general business credit for any taxable year

---

168. Sec. 38(b)(8).

may not exceed the amount by which the taxpayer's net income tax exceeds the greater of the tentative minimum tax or 25 percent of so much of the net regular tax liability as exceeds $25,000. However, this limitation does not apply to section 45 credits for electricity or refined coal produced from a facility (placed in service after October 22, 2004) during the first four years of production beginning on the date the facility is placed in service.[169] Excess credits may be carried back one year and forward up to 20 years.

Qualified facilities

Wind energy facility

A wind energy facility is a facility that uses wind to produce electricity. To be a qualified facility, a wind energy facility must be placed in service after December 31, 1993, and before January 1, 2010.

Closed-loop biomass facility

A closed-loop biomass facility is a facility that uses any organic material from a plant which is planted exclusively for the purpose of being used at a qualifying facility to produce electricity. In addition, a facility can be a closed-loop biomass facility if it is a facility that is modified to use closed-loop biomass to co-fire with coal, with other biomass, or with both coal and other biomass, but only if the modification is approved under the Biomass Power for Rural Development Programs or is part of a pilot project of the Commodity Credit Corporation.

To be a qualified facility, a closed-loop biomass facility must be placed in service after December 31, 1992, and before January 1, 2011. In the case of a facility using closed-loop biomass but also co-firing the closed-loop biomass with coal, other biomass, or coal and other biomass, a qualified facility must be originally placed in service and modified to co-fire the closed-loop biomass at any time before January 1, 2011.

A qualified facility includes a new power generation unit placed in service after October 3, 2008, at an existing closed-loop biomass facility, but only to the extent of the increased amount of electricity produced at the existing facility by reason of such new unit.

Open-loop biomass (including agricultural livestock waste nutrients) facility

An open-loop biomass facility is a facility that uses open-loop biomass to produce electricity. For purposes of the credit, open-loop biomass is defined as (1) any agricultural livestock waste nutrients or (2) any solid, nonhazardous, cellulosic waste material or any lignin material that is segregated from other waste materials and which is derived from:

• forest-related resources, including mill and harvesting residues, pre-commercial thinnings, slash, and brush;

• solid wood waste materials, including waste pallets, crates, dunnage, manufacturing and construction wood wastes, and landscape or right-of-way tree trimmings; or

• agricultural sources, including orchard tree crops, vineyard, grain, legumes, sugar, and other crop by-products or residues.

Agricultural livestock waste nutrients are defined as agricultural livestock manure and litter, including bedding material for the disposition of manure. Wood waste materials do not qualify as open-loop biomass to the extent they are pressure treated, chemically treated, or painted. In addition, municipal solid waste, gas derived from the biodegradation of solid waste, and paper which is commonly recycled do not qualify as open-loop biomass. Open-loop biomass does not include closed-loop biomass or any biomass

---

169. Sec. 38(c)(4)(B)(ii).

burned in conjunction with fossil fuel (co-firing) beyond such fossil fuel required for start up and flame stabilization.

In the case of an open-loop biomass facility that uses agricultural livestock waste nutrients, a qualified facility is one that was originally placed in service after October 22, 2004, and before January 1, 2009, and has a nameplate capacity rating which is not less than 150 kilowatts. In the case of any other open-loop biomass facility, a qualified facility is one that was originally placed in service before January 1, 2011. A qualified facility includes a new power generation unit placed in service after October 3, 2008, at an existing open-loop biomass facility, but only to the extent of the increased amount of electricity produced at the existing facility by reason of such new unit.

Geothermal facility

A geothermal facility is a facility that uses geothermal energy to produce electricity. Geothermal energy is energy derived from a geothermal deposit that is a geothermal reservoir consisting of natural heat that is stored in rocks or in an aqueous liquid or vapor (whether or not under pressure). To be a qualified facility, a geothermal facility must be placed in service after October 22, 2004, and before January 1, 2011.

Solar facility

A solar facility is a facility that uses solar energy to produce electricity. To be a qualified facility, a solar facility must be placed in service after October 22, 2004, and before January 1, 2006.

Small irrigation facility

A small irrigation power facility is a facility that generates electric power through an irrigation system canal or ditch without any dam or impoundment of water. The installed capacity of a qualified facility must be at least 150 kilowatts but less than five megawatts. To be a qualified facility, a small irrigation facility must be originally placed in service after October 22, 2004, and before October 3, 2008. Marine and hydrokinetic renewable energy facilities, described below, subsume small irrigation power facilities after October 2, 2008.

Landfill gas facility

A landfill gas facility is a facility that uses landfill gas to produce electricity. Landfill gas is defined as methane gas derived from the biodegradation of municipal solid waste. To be a qualified facility, a landfill gas facility must be placed in service after October 22, 2004, and before January 1, 2011.

Trash combustion facility

Trash combustion facilities are facilities that use municipal solid waste (garbage) to produce steam to drive a turbine for the production of electricity. To be a qualified facility, a trash combustion facility must be placed in service after October 22, 2004, and before January 1, 2011. A qualified trash combustion facility includes a new unit, placed in service after October 22, 2004, that increases electricity production capacity at an existing trash combustion facility. A new unit generally would include a new burner/boiler and turbine. The new unit may share certain common equipment, such as trash handling equipment, with other pre-existing units at the same facility. Electricity produced at a new unit of an existing facility qualifies for the production credit only to the extent of the increased amount of electricity produced at the entire facility.

Hydropower facility

A qualifying hydropower facility is (1) a facility that produced hydroelectric power (a hydroelectric dam) prior to August 8, 2005, at which efficiency improvements or additions to capacity have been made after such date and before January 1, 2011, that enable the taxpayer to produce incremental hydropower or (2) a facility placed in service before August 8, 2005, that did not produce hydroelectric power (a nonhydroelectric dam) on such date, and to which turbines or other electricity generating equipment have been added after such date and before January 1, 2011.

At an existing hydroelectric facility, the taxpayer may claim credit only for the production of incremental hydroelectric power. Incremental hydroelectric power for any taxable year is equal to the percentage of average annual hydroelectric power produced at the facility attributable to the efficiency improvement or additions of capacity determined by using the same water flow information used to determine an historic average annual hydroelectric power production baseline for that facility. The Federal Energy Regulatory Commission will certify the baseline power production of the facility and the percentage increase due to the efficiency and capacity improvements.

Non-hydroelectric dams converted to produce electricity must be licensed by the Federal Energy Regulatory Commission and meet all other applicable environmental, licensing, and regulatory requirements.

For a nonhydroelectric dam converted to produce electric power before January 1, 2009, there must not be any enlargement of the diversion structure, construction or enlargement of a bypass channel, or the impoundment or any withholding of additional water from the natural stream channel.

For a nonhydroelectric dam converted to produce electric power after December 31, 2008, the nonhydroelectric dam must have been (1) placed in service before October 3, 2008, (2) operated for flood control, navigation, or water supply purposes and (3) did not produce hydroelectric power on October 3, 2008. In addition, the hydroelectric project must be operated so that the water surface elevation at any given location and time that would have occurred in the absence of the hydroelectric project is maintained, subject to any license requirements imposed under applicable law that change the water surface elevation for the purpose of improving environmental quality of the affected waterway. The Secretary, in consultation with the Federal Energy Regulatory Commission, shall certify if a hydroelectric project licensed at a nonhydroelectric dam meets this criteria.

Marine and hydrokinetic renewable energy facility

A qualified marine and hydrokinetic renewable energy facility is any facility that produces electric power from marine and hydrokinetic renewable energy, has a nameplate capacity rating of at least 150 kilowatts, and is placed in service after October 2, 2008, and before January 1, 2012. Marine and hydrokinetic renewable energy is defined as energy derived from (1) waves, tides, and currents in oceans, estuaries, and tidal areas; (2) free flowing water in rivers, lakes, and streams; (3) free flowing water in an irrigation system, canal, or other man-made channel, including projects that utilize nonmechanical structures to accelerate the flow of water for electric power production purposes; or (4) differentials in ocean temperature (ocean thermal energy conversion). The term does not include energy derived from any source that uses a dam, diversionary structure (except for irrigation systems, canals, and other man-made channels), or impoundment for electric power production.

Summary of credit rate and credit period by facility type

Table 1.—Summary of Section 45 Credit for Electricity Produced from Certain Renewable Resources

Eligible electricity production activity	Credit amount for 2008 (cents per kilowatt-hour)	Credit period for facilities placed in service on or before August 8, 2005 (years from placed-in-service date)	Credit period for facilities placed in service after August 8, 2005 (years from placed-in-service date)
Wind	2.1	10	10
Closed-loop biomass	2.1	10[1]	10
Open-loop biomass (including agricultural livestock waste nutrient facilities)	1.0	5[2]	10
Geothermal	2.1	5	10
Solar (pre-2006 facilities only)	2.1	5	10
Small irrigation power	1.0	5	10
Municipal solid waste (including landfill gas facilities and trash combustion facilities)	1.0	5	10
Qualified hydropower	1.0	N/A	10
Marine and hydrokinetic	1.0	N/A	10

[1] In the case of certain co-firing closed-loop facilities, the credit period begins no earlier than October 22, 2004.

[2] For certain facilities placed in service before October 22, 2004, the five-year period commences on January 1, 2005.

Taxation of cooperatives and their patrons

For Federal income tax purposes, a cooperative generally computes its income as if it were a taxable corporation, with one exception: the cooperative may exclude from its taxable income distributions of patronage dividends. Generally, a cooperative that is subject to the cooperative tax rules of subchapter T of the Code[170] is permitted a deduction for patronage dividends paid only to the extent of net income that is derived from transactions with patrons who are members of the cooperative.[171] The availability of such deductions from taxable income has the effect of allowing the cooperative to be treated like a conduit with respect to profits derived from transactions with patrons who are members of the cooperative.

Eligible cooperatives may elect to pass any portion of the credit through to their patrons. An eligible cooperative is defined as a cooperative organization that is owned more than 50 percent by agricultural producers or entities owned by agricultural producers. The credit may be apportioned among patrons eligible to share in patronage dividends on the basis of the quantity or value of business done with or for such patrons for the taxable year. The election must be made on a timely filed return for the taxable year and, once made, is irrevocable for such taxable year.

170. Secs. 1381-1383.
171. Sec. 1382.

House Bill

The provision extends for three years (generally, through 2013; through 2012 for wind facilities) the period during which qualified facilities producing electricity from wind, closed-loop biomass, open-loop biomass, geothermal energy, municipal solid waste, and qualified hydropower may be placed in service for purposes of the electricity production credit. The provision extends for two years (through 2013) the placed-in-service period for marine and hydrokinetic renewable energy resources.

The provision also makes a technical amendment to the definition of small irrigation power facility to clarify its integration into the definition of marine and hydrokinetic renewable energy facility.

Senate Amendment

The Senate amendment is the same as the House Bill.

Conference Agreement

The conference agreement follows the House bill and the Senate amendment.

Effective Date

The extension of the electricity production credit is effective for property placed in service after the date of enactment. The technical amendment is effective as if included in section 102 of the Energy Improvement and Extension Act of 2008.

[¶ 5014]   Section 1102.   Election of investment credit in lieu of production credit.

(Code Sec. 45, 48)

[Conference Report]

Present Law

Renewable electricity credit

An income tax credit is allowed for the production of electricity from qualified energy resources at qualified facilities.[172] Qualified energy resources comprise wind, closed-loop biomass, open-loop biomass, geothermal energy, solar energy, small irrigation power, municipal solid waste, qualified hydropower production, and marine and hydrokinetic renewable energy. Qualified facilities are, generally, facilities that generate electricity using qualified energy resources. To be eligible for the credit, electricity produced from qualified energy resources at qualified facilities must be sold by the taxpayer to an unrelated person. The credit amounts, credit periods, definitions of qualified facilities, and other rules governing this credit are described more fully in section D.1 of this document.

Energy credit

An income tax credit is also allowed for certain energy property placed in service. Qualifying property includes certain fuel cell property, solar property, geothermal power production property, small wind energy property, combined heat and power system property, and geothermal heat pump property.[173] The amounts of credit, definitions of qualifying property, and other rules governing this credit are described more fully in section D.3 of this document.

---

172. Sec. 45. In addition to the electricity production credit, section 45 also provides income tax credits for the production of Indian coal and refined coal at qualified facilities.
173. Sec. 48.

House Bill

The House bill allows the taxpayer to make an irrevocable election to have certain qualified facilities placed in service in 2009 and 2010 be treated as energy property eligible for a 30 percent investment credit under section 48. For this purpose, qualified facilities are facilities otherwise eligible for the section 45 production tax credit (other than refined coal, Indian coal, and solar facilities) with respect to which no credit under section 45 has been allowed. A taxpayer electing to treat a facility as energy property may not claim the production credit under section 45.

Senate Amendment

The Senate amendment is similar to the House bill, but with a modification with respect to the placed in service period that determines eligibility for the election. Under the Senate amendment, facilities are eligible if placed in service during the extension period of section 45 as provided in the Senate amendment (generally, through 2013; through 2012 for wind facilities), and with respect to which no credit under section 45 has been allowed.

Conference Agreement

The conference agreement generally follows the Senate amendment. Property eligible for the credit is tangible personal or other tangible property (not including a building or its structural components), and with respect to which depreciation or amortization is allowable but only if such property is used as an integral part of the qualified facility. For example, in the case of a wind facility, the conferees intend that only property eligible for five-year depreciation under section 168(e)(3)(b)(vi) is treated as credit-eligible energy property under the election.

Effective Date

The provision applies to facilities placed in service after December 31, 2008.

[¶ 5015]   Section 1103.   Repeal of certain limitations on credit for renewable energy property.

(Code Sec. 48)

[Conference Report]

Present Law

In general

A nonrefundable, 10-percent business energy credit[175] is allowed for the cost of new property that is equipment that either (1) uses solar energy to generate electricity, to heat or cool a structure, or to provide solar process heat, or (2) is used to produce, distribute, or use energy derived from a geothermal deposit, but only, in the case of electricity generated by geothermal power, up to the electric transmission stage. Property used to generate energy for the purposes of heating a swimming pool is not eligible solar energy property.

The energy credit is a component of the general business credit.[176] An unused general business credit generally may be carried back one year and earned forward 20 years.[177] The taxpayer's basis in the property is reduced by one-half of the amount of the credit claimed. For projects whose construction time is expected to equal or exceed two years, the credit may be claimed as progress expenditures are made on the project, rather than during the year the property is placed in service. The credit is allowed against the alter-

---

175. Sec. 48
176. Sec. 38(b)(1).
177. Sec. 39.

native minimum tax for credits determined in taxable years beginning after October 3, 2008.

Property financed by subsidized energy financing or with proceeds from private activity bonds is subject to a reduction in basis for purposes of claiming the credit. The basis reduction is proportional to the share of the basis of the property that is financed by the subsidized financing or proceeds. The term "subsidized energy financing" means financing provided under a Federal, State, or local program a principal purpose of which is to provide subsidized financing for projects designed to conserve or produce energy.

Special rules for solar energy property

The credit for solar energy property is increased to 30 percent in the case of periods prior to January 1, 2017. Additionally, equipment that uses fiber-optic distributed sunlight to illuminate the inside of a structure is solar energy property eligible for the 30-percent credit.

Fuel cells and microturbines

The energy credit applies to qualified fuel cell power plants, but only for periods prior to January 1, 2017. The credit rate is 30 percent.

A qualified fuel cell power plant is an integrated system composed of a fuel cell stack assembly and associated balance of plant components that (1) converts a fuel into electricity using electrochemical means, and (2) has an electricity-only generation efficiency of greater than 30 percent and a capacity of at least one-half kilowatt. The credit may not exceed $1,500 for each 0.5 kilowatt of capacity.

The energy credit applies to qualifying stationary microturbine power plants for periods prior to January 1, 2017. The credit is limited to the lesser of 10 percent of the basis of the property or $200 for each kilowatt of capacity.

A qualified stationary microturbine power plant is an integrated system comprised of a gas turbine engine, a combustor, a recuperator or regenerator; a generator or alternator, and associated balance of plant components that converts a fuel into electricity and thermal energy. Such system also includes all secondary components located between the existing infrastructure for fuel delivery and the existing infrastructure for power distribution, including equipment and controls for meeting relevant power standards, such as voltage, frequency and power factors. Such system must have an electricity-only generation efficiency of not less than 26 percent at International Standard Organization conditions and a capacity of less than 2,000 kilowatts.

Geothermal heat pump property

The energy credit applies to qualified geothermal heat pump property placed in service prior to January 1, 2017. The credit rate is 10 percent. Qualified geothermal heat pump property is equipment that uses the ground or ground water as a thermal energy source to heat a structure or as a thermal energy sink to cool a structure.

Small wind property

The energy credit applies to qualified small wind energy property placed in service prior to January 1, 2017. The credit rate is 30 percent. The credit is limited to $4,000 per year with respect to all wind energy property of any taxpayer. Qualified small wind energy property is property that uses a qualified wind turbine to generate electricity. A qualifying wind turbine means a wind turbine of 100 kilowatts of rated capacity or less.

Combined heat and power property

The energy credit applies to combined heat and power ("CHP") property placed in service prior to January 1, 2017. The credit rate is 10 percent.

CHP property is property: (1) that uses the same energy source for the simultaneous or sequential generation of electrical power, mechanical shaft power, or both, in combination with the generation of steam or other forms of useful thermal energy (including heating and cooling applications); (2) that has an electrical capacity of not more than 50 megawatts or a mechanical energy capacity of no more than 67,000 horsepower or an equivalent combination of electrical and mechanical energy capacities; (3) that produces at least 20 percent of its total useful energy in the form of thermal energy that is not used to produce electrical or mechanical power, and produces at least 20 percent of its total useful energy in the form of electrical or mechanical power (or a combination thereof); and (4) the energy efficiency percentage of which exceeds 60 percent. CHP property does not include property used to transport the energy source to the generating facility or to distribute energy produced by the facility.

The otherwise allowable credit with respect to CHP property is reduced to the extent the property has an electrical capacity or mechanical capacity in excess of any applicable limits. Property in excess of the applicable limit (15 megawatts or a mechanical energy capacity of more than 20,000 horsepower or an equivalent combination of electrical and mechanical energy capacities) is permitted to claim a fraction of the otherwise allowable credit. The fraction is equal to the applicable limit divided by the capacity of the property. For example, a 45 megawatt property would be eligible to claim 15/45ths, or one third, of the otherwise allowable credit. Again, no credit is allowed if the property exceeds the 50 megawatt or 67,000 horsepower limitations described above.

Additionally, the provision provides that systems whose fuel source is at least 90 percent open-loop biomass and that would qualify for the credit but for the failure to meet the efficiency standard are eligible for a credit that is reduced in proportion to the degree to which the system fails to meet the efficiency standard. For example, a system that would otherwise be required to meet the 60-percent efficiency standard, but which only achieves 30-percent efficiency, would be permitted a credit equal to one-half of the otherwise allowable credit (i.e., a 5-percent credit).

House Bill

The House bill eliminates the credit cap applicable to qualified small wind energy property. The House bill also removes the rule that reduces the basis of the property for purposes of claiming the credit if the property is financed in whole or in part by subsidized energy financing or with proceeds from private activity bonds.

Senate Amendment

The Senate amendment is the same as the House bill.

Conference Agreement

The conference agreement follows the House bill and the Senate amendment.

Effective Date

The provision applies to periods after December 31, 2008, under rules similar to the rules of section 48(m) of the Code (as in effect on the day before the enactment of the Revenue Reconciliation Act of 1990).

[¶ 5016]   Section 1603, 1604.   Coordination with renewable energy grants; Grants for specified energy property in lieu of tax credits.

(Code Sec. 45, 48)

[Conference Report]

Present Law

Renewable electricity production credit

An income tax credit is allowed for the production of electricity from qualified energy resources at qualified facilities (the "renewable electricity production credit").[178] Qualified energy resources comprise wind, closed-loop biomass, open-loop biomass, geothermal energy, solar energy, small irrigation power, municipal solid waste, qualified hydropower production, and marine and hydrokinetic renewable energy. Qualified facilities are, generally, facilities that generate electricity using qualified energy resources. To be eligible for the credit, electricity produced from qualified energy resources at qualified facilities must be sold by the taxpayer to an unrelated person. The credit amounts, credit periods, definitions of qualified facilities, and other rules governing this credit are described more fully in section D.1 of this document.

Energy credit

An income tax credit is also allowed for certain energy property placed in service. Qualifying property includes certain fuel cell property, solar property, geothermal power production property, small wind energy property, combined heat and power system property, and geothermal heat pump property.[179] The amounts of credit, definitions of qualifying property, and other rules governing this credit are described more fully in section D.3 of this document.

House Bill

The provision authorizes the Secretary of Energy to provide a grant to each person who places in service during 2009 or 2010 energy property that is either (1) an electricity production facility otherwise eligible for the renewable electricity production credit or (2) qualifying property otherwise eligible for the energy credit. In general, the grant amount is 30 percent of the basis of the property that would (1) be eligible for credit under section 48 or (2) comprise a section 45 credit-eligible facility. For qualified microturbine, combined heat and power system, and geothermal heat pump property, the amount is 10 percent of the basis of the property.

It is intended that the grant provision mimic the operation of the credit under section 48. For example, the amount of the grant is not includable in gross income. However, the basis of the property is reduced by fifty percent of the amount of the grant. In addition, some or all of each grant is subject to recapture if the grant eligible property is disposed of by the grant recipient within five years of being placed in service.[180]

Nonbusiness property and property that would not otherwise be eligible for credit under section 48 or part of a facility that would be eligible for credit under section 45 is not eligible for a grant under the provision. The grant may be paid to whichever party would have been entitled to a credit under section 48 or section 45, as the case may be.

Under the provision, if a grant is paid, no renewable electricity credit or energy credit may be claimed with respect to the grant eligible property. In addition, no grant may be awarded to any Federal, State, or local government (or any political subdivision, agency, or instrumentality thereof) or any section 501(c) tax-exempt entity.

---

178. Sec. 45. In addition to the renewable electricity production credit, section 45 also provides income tax credits for the production of Indian coal and refined coal at qualified facilities.

179. Sec. 48.

180. Section 1604 of the House bill.

The provision appropriates to the Secretary of Energy the funds necessary to make the grants. No grant may be made unless the application for the grant has been received before October 1, 2011.

Senate Amendment

No provision.

Conference Agreement

The conference agreement generally follows the House bill with the following modifications. The conference agreement clarifies that qualifying property must be depreciable or amortizable to be eligible for a grant. The conference agreement also permits taxpayers to claim the credit with respect to otherwise eligible property that is not placed in service in 2009 and 2010 so long as construction begins in either of those years and is completed prior to 2013 (in the case of wind facility property), 2014 (in the case of other renewable power facility property eligible for credit under section 45), or 2017 (in the case of any specified energy property described in section 48). The conference agreement also provides that the grant program be administered by the Secretary of the Treasury.

Effective Date

The provision is effective on date of enactment.

[¶ 5018]   Section 1111.   Increased limitation on issuance of new clean renewable energy bonds.

(Code Sec. 54C)

[Conference Report]

Present Law

New Clean Renewable Energy Bonds

New clean renewable energy bonds ("New CREBs") may be issued by qualified issuers to finance qualified renewable energy facilities.[181]   Qualified renewable energy facilities are facilities that: (1) qualify for the tax credit under section 45 (other than Indian coal and refined coal production facilities), without regard to the placed-in-service date requirements of that section; and (2) are owned by a public power provider, governmental body, or cooperative electric company.

The term "qualified issuers" includes: (1) public power providers; (2) a governmental body; (3) cooperative electric companies; (4) a not-for-profit electric utility that has received a loan or guarantee under the Rural Electrification Act; and (5) clean renewable energy bond lenders. The term "public power provider" means a State utility with a service obligation, as such terms are defined in section 217 of the Federal Power Act (as in effect on the date of the enactment of this paragraph). A "governmental body" means any State or Indian tribal government, or any political subdivision thereof. The term "cooperative electric company" means a mutual or cooperative electric company (described in section 501(c)(12) or section 1381(a)(2)(C)). A clean renewable energy bond lender means a cooperative that is owned by, or has outstanding loans to, 100 or more cooperative electric companies and is in existence on February 1, 2002 (including any affiliated entity which is controlled by such lender).

There is a national limitation for New CREBs of $800 million. No more than one third of the national limit may be allocated to projects of public power providers, governmental bodies, or cooperative electric companies. Allocations to governmental bodies

---

181. Sec. 54C.

and cooperative electric companies may be made in the manner the Secretary determines appropriate. Allocations to projects of public power providers shall be made, to the extent practicable, in such manner that the amount allocated to each such project bears the same ratio to the cost of such project as the maximum allocation limitation to projects of public power providers bears to the cost of all such projects.

New CREBs are a type of qualified tax credit bond for purposes of section 54A of the Code. As such, 100 percent of the available project proceeds of New CREBs must be used within the three-year period that begins on the date of issuance. Available project proceeds are proceeds from the sale of the bond issue less issuance costs (not to exceed two percent) and any investment earnings on such sale proceeds. To the extent less than 100 percent of the available project proceeds are used to finance qualified projects during the three-year spending period, bonds will continue to qualify as New CREBs if unspent proceeds are used within 90 days from the end of such three-year period to redeem bonds. The three-year spending period may be extended by the Secretary upon the qualified issuer's request demonstrating that the failure to satisfy the three-year requirement is due to reasonable cause and the projects will continue to proceed with due diligence.

New CREBs generally are subject to the arbitrage requirements of section 148. However, available project proceeds invested during the three-year spending period are not subject to the arbitrage restrictions (i.e., yield restriction and rebate requirements). In addition, amounts invested in a reserve fund are not subject to the arbitrage restrictions to the extent: (1) such fund is funded at a rate not more rapid than equal annual installments; (2) such fund is funded in a manner reasonably expected to result in an amount not greater than an amount necessary to repay the issue; and (3) the yield on such fund is not greater than the average annual interest rate of tax-exempt obligations having a term of 10 years or more that are issued during the month the New CREBs are issued.

As with other tax credit bonds, a taxpayer holding New CREBs on a credit allowance date is entitled to a tax credit. However, the credit rate on New CREBs is set by the Secretary at a rate that is 70 percent of the rate that would permit issuance of such bonds without discount and interest cost to the issuer.[182] The Secretary determines credit rates for tax credit bond based on general assumptions about credit quality of the class of potential eligible issuers and such other factors as the Secretary deems appropriate. The Secretary may determine credit rates based on general credit market yield indexes and credit ratings.[183]

The amount of the tax credit is determined by multiplying the bond's credit rate by the face amount of the holder's bond. The credit accrues quarterly, is includible in gross income (as if it were an interest payment on the bond), and can be claimed against regular income tax liability and alternative minimum tax liability. Unused credits may be carried forward to succeeding taxable years. In addition, credits may be separated from the ownership of the underlying bond similar to how interest coupons can be stripped for interest-bearing bonds.

An issuer of New CREBs is treated as meeting the "prohibition on financial conflicts of interest" requirement in section 54A(d)(6) if it certifies that it satisfies (i) applicable State and local law requirements governing conflicts of interest and (ii) any additional conflict of interest rules prescribed by the Secretary with respect to any Federal, State, or local government official directly involved with the issuance of New CREBs.

---

182. Given the differences in credit quality and other characteristics of individual issuers, the Secretary cannot set credit rates in a manner that will allow each issuer to issue tax credit bonds at par.
183. See Internal Revenue Service, Notice 2009-15, Credit Rates on Tax Credit Bonds, 2009-6 I.R.B. 1 (January 22, 2009).

House Bill

In general

The provision expands the New CREBs program. The provision authorizes issuance of up to an additional $1.6 billion of New CREBs.

Senate Amendment

The Senate amendment is the same as the House bill.

Conference Agreement

The conference agreement follows the House bill and the Senate amendment.

Effective Date

The provision applies to obligations issued after the date of enactment.

[¶ 5019]   Section 1112.   Increased limitation on issuance of qualified energy conservation bonds.

(Code Sec. 54D)

[Conference Report]

Present Law

Qualified energy conservation bonds may be used to finance qualified conservation purposes.

The term "qualified conservation purpose" means:

(1.) Capital expenditures incurred for purposes of reducing energy consumption in publicly owned buildings by at least 20 percent; implementing green community programs; rural development involving the production of electricity from renewable energy resources; or any facility eligible for the production tax credit under section 45 (other than Indian coal and refined coal production facilities);

(2.) Expenditures with respect to facilities or grants that support research in: (a) development of cellulosic ethanol or other nonfossil fuels; (b) technologies for the capture and sequestration of carbon dioxide produced through the use of fossil fuels; (c) increasing the efficiency of existing technologies for producing nonfossil fuels; (d) automobile battery technologies and other technologies to reduce fossil fuel consumption in transportation; and (E) technologies to reduce energy use in buildings;

(3.) Mass commuting facilities and related facilities that reduce the consumption of energy, including expenditures to reduce pollution from vehicles used for mass commuting;

(4.) Demonstration projects designed to promote the commercialization of: (a) green building technology; (b) conversion of agricultural waste for use in the production of fuel or otherwise; (c) advanced battery manufacturing technologies; (D) technologies to reduce peak-use of electricity; and (d) technologies for the capture and sequestration of carbon dioxide emitted from combusting fossil fuels in order to produce electricity; and

(5.) Public education campaigns to promote energy efficiency (other than movies, concerts, and other events held primarily for entertainment purposes).

There is a national limitation on qualified energy conservation bonds of $800 million. Allocations of qualified energy conservation bonds are made to the States with sub-allocations to large local governments. Allocations are made to the States according to their respective populations, reduced by any sub-allocations to large local governments (defined below) within the States. Sub-allocations to large local governments shall be an amount of the national qualified energy conservation bond limitation that bears the same ratio to the amount of such limitation that otherwise would be allocated to the State in which such large local government is located as the population of such large local government bears to the population of such State. The term "large local government" means: any municipality or county if such municipality or county has a population of 100,000 or more. Indian tribal governments also are treated as large local governments for these purposes (without regard to population).

Each State or large local government receiving an allocation of qualified energy conservation bonds may further allocate issuance authority to issuers within such State or large local government. However, any allocations to issuers within the State or large local government shall be made in a manner that results in not less than 70 percent of the allocation of qualified energy conservation bonds to such State or large local government being used to designate bonds that are not private activity bonds (i.e., the bond cannot meet the private business tests or the private loan test of section 141).

Qualified energy conservations bonds are a type of qualified tax credit bond for purposes of section 54A of the Code. As a result, 100 percent of the available project proceeds of qualified energy conservation bonds must be used for qualified conservation purposes. In the case of qualified conservation bonds issued as private activity bonds, 100 percent of the available project proceeds must be used for capital expenditures. In addition, qualified energy conservation bonds only may be issued by Indian tribal governments to the extent such bonds are issued for purposes that satisfy the present law requirements for tax-exempt bonds issued by Indian tribal governments (i.e., essential governmental functions and certain manufacturing purposes).

Under present law, 100 percent of the available project proceeds of qualified energy conservation bonds to be used within the three-year period that begins on the date of issuance. Available project proceeds are proceeds from the sale of the issue less issuance costs (not to exceed two percent) and any investment earnings on such sale proceeds. To the extent less than 100 percent of the available project proceeds are used to finance qualified conservation purposes during the three-year spending period, bonds will continue to qualify as qualified energy conservation bonds if unspent proceeds are used within 90 days from the end of such three-year period to redeem bonds. The three-year spending period may be extended by the Secretary upon the issuer's request demonstrating that the failure to satisfy the three-year requirement is due to reasonable cause and the projects will continue to proceed with due diligence.

Qualified energy conservation bonds generally are subject to the arbitrage requirements of section 148. However, available project proceeds invested during the three-year spending period are not subject to the arbitrage restrictions (i.e., yield restriction and rebate requirements). In addition, amounts invested in a reserve fund are not subject to the arbitrage restrictions to the extent: (1) such fund is funded at a rate not more rapid than equal annual installments; (2) such fund is funded in a manner reasonably expected to result in an amount not greater than an amount necessary to repay the issue; and (3) the yield on such fund is not greater than the average annual interest rate of tax-exempt obligations having a term of 10 years or more that are issued during the month the qualified energy conservation bonds are issued.

The maturity of qualified energy conservation bonds is the term that the Secretary estimates will result in the present value of the obligation to repay the principal on such bonds being equal to 50 percent of the face amount of such bonds, using as a discount rate the average annual interest rate of tax-exempt obligations having a term of 10 years or more that are issued during the month the qualified energy conservation bonds are issued.

As with other tax credit bonds, the taxpayer holding qualified energy conservation bonds on a credit allowance date is entitled to a tax credit. The credit rate on the bonds is set by the Secretary at a rate that is 70 percent of the rate that would permit issuance of such bonds without discount and interest cost to the issuer.[184] The Secretary deter-mines credit rates for tax credit bonds based on general assumptions about credit quality of the class of potential eligible issuers and such other factors as the Secretary deems appropriate. The Secretary may determine credit rates based on general credit market yield indexes and credit ratings.[185] The amount of the tax credit is determined by multi-plying the bond's credit rate by the face amount on the holder's bond. The credit ac-crues quarterly, is includible in gross income (as if it were an interest payment on the bond), and can be claimed against regular income tax liability and alternative minimum tax liability. Unused credits may be carried forward to succeeding taxable years. In addi-tion, credits may be separated from the ownership of the underlying bond similar to how interest coupons can be stripped for interest-bearing bonds.

Issuers of qualified energy conservation bonds are required to certify that the financial disclosure requirements that applicable State and local law requirements governing con-flicts of interest are satisfied with respect to such issue, as well as any other additional conflict of interest rules prescribed by the Secretary with respect to any Federal, State, or local government official directly involved with the issuance of qualified energy con-servation bonds.

House Bill

In general

The provision expands the present-law qualified energy conservation bond program. The provision authorizes issuance of an additional $2.4 billion of qualified energy con-servation bonds. The provision expands eligibility for these tax credit bonds to include loans and grants for capital expenditures as part of green community programs. For ex-ample, this expansion will enable States to issue these tax credit bonds to finance loans and/or grants to individual homeowners to retrofit existing housing. The use of bond proceeds for such loans and grants will not cause such bond to be treated as a private activity bond for purposes of the private activity bond restrictions contained in the quali-fied energy conservation bond provisions.

Senate Amendment

In general

The provision expands the present-law qualified energy conservation bond program. The provision authorizes issuance of an additional $2.4 billion of qualified energy con-servation bonds. The provision clarifies that capital expenditures to implement green community programs, includes grants, loans and other repayment mechanisms for capital expenditures to implement such programs.

Conference Agreement

In general

The provision expands the present-law qualified energy conservation bond program. The provision authorizes issuance of an additional $2.4 billion of qualified energy con-servation bonds. Also, the provision clarifies that capital expenditures to implement green community programs includes grants, loans and other repayment mechanisms to implement such programs. For example, this expansion will enable States to issue these tax credit bonds to finance retrofits of existing private buildings through loans and/or grants to individual homeowners or businesses, or through other repayment mechanisms. Other repayment mechanisms can include periodic fees assessed on a government bill or utility bill that approximates the energy savings of energy efficiency or conservation re-

---

184. Given the differences in credit quality and other characteristics of individual issuers, the Secretary cannot set credit rates in a manner that will allow each issuer to issue tax credit bonds at par.
185. See Internal Revenue Service, Notice 2009-15, *Credit Rates on Tax Credit Bonds*, 2009-6 I.R.B. 1 (January 22, 2009).

trofits. Retrofits can include heating, cooling, lighting, water-saving, storm water-reducing, or other efficiency measures.

Finally, the provision clarifies that any bond used for the purpose of providing grants, loans or other repayment mechanisms for capital expenditures to implement green community programs is not treated as a private activity bond for purposes of determining whether the requirement that not less than 70 percent of allocations within a State or large local government be used to designate bonds that are not private activity bonds (sec. 54D(e)(3)) has been satisfied.

Effective Date

The provision is effective for bonds issued after the date of enactment

[¶ 5021]   Section 1121.   Extension and modification of credit for nonbusiness energy property.

(Code Sec. 25C)

[Conference Report]

Present Law

Section 25C provides a 10-percent credit for the purchase of qualified energy efficiency improvements to existing homes. A qualified energy efficiency improvement is any energy efficiency building envelope component (1) that meets or exceeds the prescriptive criteria for such a component established by the 2000 International Energy Conservation Code as supplemented and as in effect on August 8, 2005 (or, in the case of metal roofs with appropriate, pigmented coatings, meets the Energy Star program requirements); (2) that is installed in or on a dwelling located in the United States and owned and used by the taxpayer as the taxpayer's principal residence; (3) the original use of which commences with the taxpayer; and (4) that reasonably can be expected to remain in use for at least five years. The credit is nonrefundable.

Building envelope components are: (1) insulation materials or systems which are specifically and primarily designed to reduce the heat loss or gain for a dwelling; (2) exterior windows (including skylights) and doors; and (3) metal or asphalt roofs with appropriate pigmented coatings or cooling granules that are specifically and primarily designed to reduce the heat gain for a dwelling.

Additionally, section 25C provides specified credits for the purchase of specific energy efficient property. The allowable credit for the purchase of certain property is (1) $50 for each advanced main air circulating fan, (2) $150 for each qualified natural gas, propane, or oil furnace or hot water boiler, and (3) $300 for each item of qualified energy efficient property.

An advanced main air circulating fan is a fan used in a natural gas, propane, or oil furnace originally placed in service by the taxpayer during the taxable year, and which has an annual electricity use of no more than two percent of the total annual energy use of the furnace (as determined in the standard Department of Energy test procedures).

A qualified natural gas, propane, or oil furnace or hot water boiler is a natural gas, propane, or oil furnace or hot water boiler with an annual fuel utilization efficiency rate of at least 95.

Qualified energy-efficient property is: (1) an electric heat pump water heater which yields an energy factor of at least 2.0 in the standard Department of Energy test procedure, (2) an electric heat pump which has a heating seasonal performance factor (HSPF) of at least 9, a seasonal energy efficiency ratio (SEER) of at least 15, and an energy efficiency ratio (EER) of at least 13, (3) a central air conditioner with energy efficiency of at least the highest efficiency tier established by the Consortium for Energy Efficiency as in effect on Jan. 1, 2006[186], (4) a natural gas, propane, or oil water heater which has an energy factor of at least 0.80 or thermal efficiency of at least 90 percent, and (5) biomass fuel property.

Biomass fuel property is a stove that bums biomass fuel to heat a dwelling unit located in the United States and used as a principal residence by the taxpayer, or to heat water for such dwelling unit, and that has a thermal efficiency rating of at least 75 percent. Biomass fuel is any plant-derived fuel available on a renewable or recurring basis, including agricultural crops and trees, wood and wood waste and residues (including wood pellets), plants (including aquatic plants, grasses, residues, and fibers).

Under section 25C the maximum credit for a taxpayer with respect to the same dwelling for all taxable years is $500, and no more than $200 of such credit may be attributable to expenditures on windows.

The taxpayer's basis in the property is reduced by the amount of the credit. Special proration rules apply in the case of jointly owned property, condominiums, and tenant-stockholders in cooperative housing corporations. If less than 80 percent of the property is used for nonbusiness purposes, only that portion of expenditures that is used for nonbusiness purposes is taken into account.

For purposes of determining the amount of expenditures made by any individual with respect to any dwelling unit, there shall not be taken into account expenditures which are made from subsidized energy financing. The term "subsidized energy financing" means financing provided under a Federal, State, or local program a principal purpose of which is to provide subsidized financing for projects designed to conserve or produce energy.

The credit applies to expenditures made after December 31, 2008 for property placed in service after December 31, 2008, and prior to January 1, 2010.

House Bill

The House bill raises the 10 percent credit rate to 30 percent. Additionally, all energy property otherwise eligible for the $50, $100, or $150 credits is instead eligible for a 30 percent credit on expenditures for such property.

The House bill additionally extends the provision for one year, through December 31, 2010. Finally, the $500 lifetime cap (and the $200 lifetime cap with respect to windows) is eliminated and replaced with an aggregate cap of $1,500 in the case of property placed in service after December 31, 2008 and prior to January 1, 2011.

The present law rule related to subsidized energy financing is eliminated.

Senate Amendment

The Senate amendment is similar to the House bill, but modifies the efficiency standards for qualifying property.

Specifically, the Senate amendment updates the building insulation requirements to follow the prescriptive criteria of the 2009 International Energy Conservation Code. Additionally, qualifying exterior windows, doors, and skylights must have a U-factor at or below 0.30 and a seasonal heat gain coefficient ("SHGC") at or below 0.30.

Electric heat pumps must achieve the highest efficiency tier of Consortium for Energy Efficiency, as in effect on January 1, 2009. These standards are a SEER greater than or equal to 15, EER greater than or equal to 12.5, and HSPF greater than or equal to 8.5

---

186. The highest tier in effect at this time was tier 2, requiring SEER of at least 15 and EER of at least 12.5 for split central air conditioning systems and SEER of at least 14 and EER of at least 12 for packaged central air conditioning systems.

for split heat pumps, and SEER greater than or equal to 14, EER greater than or equal to 12, and HSPF greater than or equal to 8.0 for packaged heat pumps.

Central air conditioners must achieve the highest efficiency tier of Consortium for Energy Efficiency, as in effect on January 1, 2009. These standards are a SEER greater than or equal to 16 and EER greater than or equal to 13 for split systems, and SEER greater than or equal to 14 and EER greater than or equal to 12 for packaged systems.

Natural gas, propane, or oil water heaters must have an energy factor greater than or equal to 0.82 or a thermal efficiency of greater than or equal to 90 percent. Natural gas, propane, or oil water boilers must achieve an annual fuel utilization efficiency rate of at least 90. Qualified oil furnaces must achieve an annual fuel utilization efficiency rate of at least 90.

Lastly, the requirement that biomass fuel property have a thermal efficiency rating of at least 75 percent is modified to be a thermal efficiency rating of at least 75 percent as measured using a lower heating value.

Conference Agreement

The conference agreement follows the Senate amendment, with the exception that the new efficiency standards for qualifying property, other than those for biomass fuel property, apply to property placed in service after the date of enactment.

Effective Date

The provision is generally effective for taxable years beginning after December 31, 2008. The provisions that alter the efficiency standards of qualifying property, other than biomass fuel property, apply to property placed in service after December 31, 2009. The modification with respect to biomass fuel property is effective for taxable years beginning after December 31, 2008.

[¶ 5022] Section 1122. Modification of credit for residential energy efficient property.

(Code Sec. 25D)

[Conference Report]

Present Law

Section 25D provides a personal tax credit for the purchase of qualified solar electric property and qualified solar water heating property that is used exclusively for purposes other than heating swimming pools and hot tubs. The credit is equal to 30 percent of qualifying expenditures, with a maximum credit of $2,000 with respect to qualified solar water heating property. There is no cap with respect to qualified solar electric property.

Section 25D also provides a 30 percent credit for the purchase of qualified geothermal heat pump property, qualified small wind energy property, and qualified fuel cell power plants. The credit for geothermal heat pump property is capped at $2,000, the credit for qualified small wind energy property is limited to $500 with respect to each half kilowatt of capacity, not to exceed $4,000, and the credit for any fuel cell may not exceed $500 for each 0.5 kilowatt of capacity.

The credit with respect to all qualifying property may be claimed against the alternative minimum tax.

Qualified solar electric property is property that uses solar energy to generate electricity for use in a dwelling unit. Qualifying solar water heating property is property used to heat water for use in a dwelling unit located in the United States and used as a residence if at least half of the energy used by such property for such purpose is derived from the sun.

A qualified fuel cell power plant is an integrated system comprised of a fuel cell stack assembly and associated balance of plant components that (1) converts a fuel into electricity using electrochemical means, (2) has an electricity-only generation efficiency of greater than 30 percent. The qualified fuel cell power plant must be installed on or in connection with a dwelling unit located in the United States and used by the taxpayer as a principal residence.

Qualified small wind energy property is property that uses a wind turbine to generate electricity for use in a dwelling unit located in the U.S. and used as a residence by the taxpayer.

Qualified geothermal heat pump property means any equipment which (1) uses the ground or ground water as a thermal energy source to heat the dwelling unit or as a thermal energy sink to cool such dwelling unit, (2) meets the requirements of the Energy Star program which are in effect at the time that the expenditure for such equipment is made, and (3) is installed on or in connection with a dwelling unit located in the United States and used as a residence by the taxpayer.

The credit is nonrefundable, and the depreciable basis of the property is reduced by the amount of the credit. Expenditures for labor costs allocable to onsite preparation, assembly, or original installation of property eligible for the credit are eligible expenditures.

Special proration rules apply in the case of jointly owned property, condominiums, and tenant-stockholders in cooperative housing corporations. If less than 80 percent of the property is used for nonbusiness purposes, only that portion of expenditures that is used for nonbusiness purposes is taken into account.

For purposes of determining the amount of expenditures made by any individual with respect to any dwelling unit, there shall not be taken into account expenditures which are made from subsidized energy financing. The term "subsidized energy financing" means financing provided under a Federal, State, or local program a principal purpose of which is to provide subsidized financing for projects designed to conserve or produce energy.

The credit applies to property placed in service prior to January 1, 2017.

House Bill

The House bill eliminates the credit caps for solar hot water, geothermal, and wind property and eliminates the reduction in credits for property using subsidized energy financing.

Senate Amendment

The Senate amendment is the same as the House bill.

Conference Agreement

The conference agreement follows the House bill and the Senate amendment.

Effective Date

The provision applies to taxable years beginning after December 31, 2008.

[¶ 5023]   Section 1123.   Temporary increase in credit for alternative fuel vehicle refueling property.

(Code Sec. 30C)

[Conference Report]

Present Law

Taxpayers may claim a 30-percent credit for the cost of installing qualified clean-fuel vehicle refueling property to be used in a trade or business of the taxpayer or installed at the principal residence of the taxpayer.[187] The credit may not exceed $30,000 per taxable year per location, in the case of qualified refueling property used in a trade or business and $1,000 per taxable year per location, in the case of qualified refueling property installed on property which is used as a principal residence.

Qualified refueling property is property (not including a building or its structural components) for the storage or dispensing of a clean-burning fuel or electricity into the fuel tank or battery of a motor vehicle propelled by such fuel or electricity, but only if the storage or dispensing of the fuel or electricity is at the point of delivery into the fuel tank or battery of the motor vehicle. The use of such property must begin with the taxpayer.

Clean-burning fuels are any fuel at least 85 percent of the volume of which consists of ethanol, natural gas, compressed natural gas, liquefied natural gas, liquefied petroleum gas, or hydrogen. In addition, any mixture of biodiesel and diesel fuel, determined without regard to any use of kerosene and containing at least 20 percent biodiesel, qualifies as a clean fuel.

Credits for qualified refueling property used in a trade or business are part of the general business credit and may be carried back for one year and forward for 20 years. Credits for residential qualified refueling property cannot exceed for any taxable year the difference between the taxpayer's regular tax (reduced by certain other credits) and the taxpayer's tentative minimum tax. Generally, in the case of qualified refueling property sold to a tax-exempt entity, the taxpayer selling the property may claim the credit.

A taxpayer's basis in qualified refueling property is reduced by the amount of the credit. In addition, no credit is available for property used outside the United States or for which an election to expense has been made under section 179.

The credit is available for property placed in service after December 31, 2005, and (except in the case of hydrogen refueling property) before January 1, 2011. In the case of hydrogen refueling property, the property must be placed in service before January 1, 2015.

[House Report]

Reasons for Change

The Committee believes that widespread adoption of advanced technology and alternative-fuel vehicles is necessary to transform automotive transportation in the United States to be cleaner, more fuel efficient, and less reliant on petroleum fuels. The Committee further believes that one important method to encourage this trend is to provide additional tax incentives for the development and installation of the infrastructure necessary to deliver clean fuels to drivers of clean-fuel vehicles.

---

187. Sec. 30C.

[Conference Report]

House Bill

For property placed in service in 2009 or 2010, the provision increases the maximum credit available for business property to $200,000 for qualified hydrogen refueling property and to $50,000 for other qualified refueling property. For nonbusiness property, the maximum credit is increased to $2,000. In addition, the credit rate is increased from 30 percent to 50 percent, except in the case of hydrogen refueling property.

Senate Amendment

The Senate amendment is the same as the House bill, except that it adds interoperability, public access, and other standards to qualified refueling property that is used for recharging electric or hybrid-electric motor vehicles.

Conference Agreement

The conference agreement follows the House bill.

Effective Date

The provision is effective for taxable years beginning after December 31, 2008.

[¶ 5025]   Section 1131.   Application of monitoring requirements to carbon dioxide used as a tertiary injection.

(Code Sec. 45Q)

[Conference Report]

Present Law

A credit of $20 per metric ton is available for qualified carbon dioxide captured by a taxpayer at a qualified facility and disposed of by such taxpayer in secure geological storage (including storage at deep saline formations and unminable coal seams under such conditions as the Secretary may determine).[208] In addition, a credit of $10 per metric ton is available for qualified carbon dioxide that is captured by the taxpayer at a qualified facility and used by such taxpayer as a tertiary injectant (including carbon dioxide augmented waterflooding and immiscible carbon dioxide displacement) in a qualified enhanced oil or natural gas recovery project. Both credit amounts are adjusted for inflation after 2009.

Qualified carbon dioxide is defined as carbon dioxide captured from an industrial source that (1) would otherwise be released into the atmosphere as an industrial emission of greenhouse gas, and (2) is measured at the source of capture and verified at the point or points of injection. Qualified carbon dioxide includes the initial deposit of captured carbon dioxide used as a tertiary injectant but does not include carbon dioxide that is recaptured, recycled, and re-injected as part of an enhanced oil or natural gas recovery project process. A qualified enhanced oil or natural gas recovery project is a project that would otherwise meet the definition of an enhanced oil recovery project under section 43, if natural gas projects were included within that definition.

A qualified facility means any industrial facility (1) which is owned by the taxpayer, (2) at which carbon capture equipment is placed in service, and (3) which captures not less than 500,000 metric tons of carbon dioxide during the taxable year. The credit applies only with respect to qualified carbon dioxide captured and sequestered or injected in the United States[209] or one of its possessions.[210]

---

208. Sec. 45Q.
209. Sec. 638(1).
210. Sec. 638(2).

Except as provided in regulations, credits are attributable to the person that captures and physically or contractually ensures the disposal, or use as a tertiary injectant, of the qualified carbon dioxide. Credits are subject to recapture, as provided by regulation, with respect to any qualified carbon dioxide that ceases to be recaptured, disposed of, or used as a tertiary injectant in a manner consistent with the rules of the provision.

The credit is part of the general business credit. The credit sunsets at the end of the calendar year in which the Secretary, in consultation with the Administrator of the Environmental Protection Agency, certifies that 75 million metric tons of qualified carbon dioxide have been captured and disposed of or used as a tertiary injectant.

House Bill

No provision.

Senate Amendment

The provision requires that carbon dioxide used as a tertiary injectant and otherwise eligible for a $10 per metric ton credit must be sequestered by the taxpayer in permanent geological storage in order to qualify for such credit. The Senate amendment also clarifies that the term permanent geological storage includes oil and gas reservoirs in addition to unminable coal seams and deep saline formations. In addition, the Senate amendment requires that the Secretary of the Treasury consult with the Secretary of Energy and the Secretary of the Interior, in addition to the Administrator of the Environmental Protection Agency, in promulgating regulations relating to the permanent geological storage of carbon dioxide.

Conference Agreement

The conference agreement follows the Senate amendment.

Effective Date

The provision is effective for carbon dioxide captured after the date of enactment.

[¶ 5027]   Section 1141, 1142, 1143, 1144.   Credit for new qualified plug-in electric drive motor vehicles; Credit for certain plug-in electric vehicles; Conversion kits; Treatment of alternative motor vehicle credit as a personal credit allowed against AMT.

(Code Sec. 30; 30B; 30D)

[Conference Report]

Present Law

Alternative motor vehicle credit

A credit is available for each new qualified fuel cell vehicle, hybrid vehicle, advanced lean burn technology vehicle, and alternative fuel vehicle placed in service by the taxpayer during the taxable year.[211] In general, the credit amount varies depending upon the type of technology used, the weight class of the vehicle, the amount by which the vehicle exceeds certain fuel economy standards, and, for some vehicles, the estimated lifetime fuel savings. The credit generally is available for vehicles purchased after 2005. The credit terminates after 2009, 2010, or 2014, depending on the type of vehicle. The alternative motor vehicle credit is not allowed against the alternative minimum tax.

Plug-in electric drive motor vehicle credit

A credit is available for each qualified plug-in electric drive motor vehicle placed in service. A qualified plug-in electric drive motor vehicle is a motor vehicle that has at

---

211. Sec. 30B.

least four wheels, is manufactured for use on public roads, meets certain emissions standards (except for certain heavy vehicles), draws propulsion using a traction battery with at least four kilowatt-hours of capacity, and is capable of being recharged from an external source of electricity.

The base amount of the plug-in electric drive motor vehicle credit is $2,500, plus another $417 for each kilowatt-hour of battery capacity in excess of four kilowatt-hours. The maximum credit for qualified vehicles weighing 10,000 pounds or less is $7,500. This maximum amount increases to $10,000 for vehicles weighing more than 10,000 pounds but not more than 14,000 pounds, to $12,500 for vehicles weighing more than 14,000 pounds but not more than 26,000 pounds, and to $15,000 for vehicle weighing more than 26,000 pounds.

In general, the credit is available to the vehicle owner, including the lessor of a vehicle subject to lease. If the qualified vehicle is used by certain tax-exempt organizations, governments, or foreign persons and is not subject to a lease, the seller of the vehicle may claim the credit so long as the seller clearly discloses to the user in a document the amount that is allowable as a credit. A vehicle must be used predominantly in the United States to qualify for the credit.

Once a total of 250,000 credit-eligible vehicles have been sold for use in the United States, the credit phases out over four calendar quarters. The phaseout period begins in the second calendar quarter following the quarter during which the vehicle cap has been reached. Taxpayers may claim one-half of the otherwise allowable credit during the first two calendar quarters of the phaseout period and twenty-five percent of the otherwise allowable credit during the next two quarters. After this, no credit is available. Regardless of the phase-out limitation, no credit is available for vehicles purchased after 2014.

The basis of any qualified vehicle is reduced by the amount of the credit. To the extent a vehicle is eligible for credit as a qualified plug-in electric drive motor vehicle, it is not eligible for credit as a qualified hybrid vehicle under section 30B. The portion of the credit attributable to vehicles of a character subject to an allowance for depreciation is treated as part of the general business credit; the nonbusiness portion of the credit is allowable to the extent of the excess of the regular tax over the alternative minimum tax (reduced by certain other credits) for the taxable year.

House Bill

No provision.

Senate Amendment

Credit for electric drive low-speed vehicles, motorcycles, and three-wheeled vehicles

The Senate amendment creates a new 10-percent credit for low-speed vehicles, motorcycles, and three-wheeled vehicles that would otherwise meet the criteria of a qualified plug-in electric drive motor vehicle but for the fact that they are low-speed vehicles or do not have at least four wheels. The maximum credit for such vehicles is $4,000. Basis reduction and other rules similar to those found in section 30 apply under the provision. The new credit is part of the general business credit. The new credit is not available for vehicles sold after December 31, 2011.

Credit for converting a vehicle into a plug-in electric drive motor vehicle

The Senate amendment also creates a new 10-percent credit, up to $4,000, for the cost of converting any motor vehicle into a qualified plug-in electric drive motor vehicle. To be eligible for the credit, a qualified plug-in traction battery module must have a capacity of at least 2.5 kilowatt-hours. In the case of a leased traction battery module, the credit may be claimed by the lessor but not the lessee. The credit is not available for conversions made after December 31, 2012.

Modification of plug-in electric drive motor vehicle credit

The Senate amendment modifies the plug-in electric drive motor vehicle credit by increasing the 250,000 vehicle limitation to 500,000. It also modifies the definition of qualified plug-in electric drive motor vehicle to exclude low-speed vehicles.

Conference Agreement

The conference agreement follows the Senate amendment with substantial modifications.

Credit for electric drive low-speed vehicles, motorcycles, and three-wheeled vehicles

With respect to electric drive low-speed vehicles, motorcycles, and thee-wheeled vehicles, the conference agreement follows the Senate amendment with the following modifications. Under the conference agreement, the maximum credit available is $2,500. The conference agreement also makes other technical changes.

Credit for converting a vehicle into a plug-in electric drive motor vehicle

With respect to plug-in vehicle conversions, the conference agreement follows the Senate amendment but increases the minimum capacity of a qualified battery module to four kilowatt-hours, changes the effective date to property placed in service after the date of enactment, and eliminates the credit for plug-in conversions made after December 31, 2011. The conference agreement also removes the rule permitting lessors of battery modules to claim the plug-in conversion credit.

Modification of the plug-in electric drive motor vehicle credit

The conference agreement modifies the plug-in electric drive motor vehicle credit by limiting the maximum credit to $7,500 regardless of vehicle weight. The conference agreement also eliminates the credit for low speed plug-in vehicles and for plug-in vehicles weighing 14,000 pounds or more.

The conference agreement replaces the 250,000 total plug-in vehicle limitation with a 200,000 plug-in vehicles per manufacturer limitation. The credit phases out over four calendar quarters beginning in the second calendar quarter following the quarter in which the manufacturer limit is reached. The conference agreement also makes other technical changes.

The changes to the plug-in electric drive motor vehicle credit are effective for vehicles acquired after December 31, 2009.

Treatment of alternative motor vehicle credit as a personal credit allowed against the alternative minimum tax

The conference agreement provides that the alternative motor vehicle credit is a personal credit allowed against the alternative minimum tax. The provision is effective for taxable years beginning after December 31, 2008.

Effective Date

The Senate amendment is generally effective for vehicles sold after December 31, 2009. The credit for plug-in vehicle conversion is effective for property placed in service after December 31, 2008, in taxable years beginning after such date.

[¶ 5032]   Section 1151.   Increased exclusion amount for commuter transit benefits and transit passes.

(Code Sec. 132)

[Conference Report]

Present Law

Qualified transportation fringe benefits provided by an employer are excluded from an employee's gross income for income tax purposes and from an employee's wages for payroll tax purposes.[212] Qualified transportation fringe benefits include parking, transit passes, vanpool benefits, and qualified bicycle commuting reimbursements. Up to $230 (for 2009) per month of employer-provided parking is excludable from income. Up to $120 (for 2009) per month of employer-provided transit and vanpool benefits are excludable from gross income. These amounts are indexed annually for inflation, rounded to the nearest multiple of $5. No amount is includible in the income of an employee merely because the employer offers the employee a choice between cash and qualified transportation fringe benefits. Qualified transportation fringe benefits also include a cash reimbursement by an employer to an employee. However, in the case of transit passes, a cash reimbursement is considered a qualified transportation fringe benefit only if a voucher or similar item which may be exchanged only for a transit pass is not readily available for direct distribution.by the employer to the employee.

House Bill

No provision.

Senate Amendment

The provision increases the monthly exclusion for employer-provided transit and vanpool benefits to the same level as the exclusion for employer-provided parking.

Conference Agreement

The conference agreement follows the Senate amendment.

Effective Date

The provision is effective for months beginning on or after date of enactment. The proposal does not apply to tax years beginning after December 31, 2010.

[¶ 5034]   Section 1201.   Special allowance for certain property acquired during 2009.

(Code Sec. 168)

[Conference Report]

Present Law

An additional first-year depreciation deduction is allowed equal to 50 percent of the adjusted basis of qualified property placed in service during 2008 (and 2009 for certain longer-lived and transportation property).[19] The additional first-year depreciation deduction is allowed for both regular tax and alternative minimum tax purposes for the taxable year in which the property is placed in service.[20] The basis of the property and the depreciation allowances in the year of purchase and later years are appropriately adjusted to reflect the additional first-year depreciation deduction. In addition, there are no adjust-

---

212. Code secs. 132(f), 3121(b)(2), 3306(b)(16), and 3401(a)(19).
19. Sec. 168(k). The additional first-year depreciation deduction is subject to the general rules regarding whether an item is deductible under section 162 or instead is subject to capitalization under section 263 or section 263A.
20. However, the additional first-year depreciation deduction is not allowed for purposes of computing earnings and profits.

843

ments to the allowable amount of depreciation for purposes of computing a taxpayer's alternative minimum taxable income with respect to property to which the provision applies. The amount of the additional first-year depreciation deduction is not affected by a short taxable year. The taxpayer may elect out of additional first-year depreciation for any class of property for any taxable year.

The interaction of the additional first-year depreciation allowance with the otherwise applicable depreciation allowance may be illustrated as follows. Assume that in 2008, a taxpayer purchases new depreciable property and places it in service.[21] The property's cost is $1,000, and it is five-year property subject to the half-year convention. The amount of additional first-year depreciation allowed is $500. The remaining $500 of the cost of the property is deductible under the rules applicable to 5-year property. Thus, 20 percent, or $100, is also allowed as a depreciation deduction in 2008. The total depreciation deduction with respect to the property for 2008 is $600. The remaining $400 cost of the property is recovered under otherwise applicable rules for computing depreciation.

In order for property to qualify for the additional first-year depreciation deduction it must meet all of the following requirements. First, the property must be (1) property to which MACRS applies with an applicable recovery period of 20 years or less, (2) water utility property (as defined in section 168(e)(5)), (3) computer software other than computer software covered by section 197, or (4) qualified leasehold improvement property (as defined in section 168(k)(3)).[22] Second, the original use[23] of the property must commence with the taxpayer after December 31, 2007.[24] Third, the taxpayer must purchase the property within the applicable time period. Finally, the property must be placed in service after December 31, 2007, and before January 1, 2009. An extension of the placed in service date of one year (i.e., to January 1, 2010) is provided for certain property with a recovery period of ten years or longer and certain transportation property.[25] Transportation property is defined as tangible personal property used in the trade or business of transporting persons or property.

The applicable time period for acquired property is (1) after December 31, 2007, and before January 1, 2009, but only if no binding written contract for the acquisition is in effect before January 1, 2008, or (2) pursuant to a binding written contract which was entered into after December 31, 2007, and before January 1, 2009.[26] With respect to property that is manufactured, constructed, or produced by the taxpayer for use by the taxpayer, the taxpayer must begin the manufacture, construction, or production of the property after December 31, 2007, and before January 1, 2009. Property that is manufactured, constructed, or produced for the taxpayer by another person under a contract that is entered into prior to the manufacture, construction, or production of the property is considered to be manufactured, constructed, or produced by the taxpayer. For property eligible for the extended placed in service date, a special rule limits the amount of costs

---

21. Assume that the cost of the property is not eligible for expensing under section 179.
22. A special rule precludes the additional first-year depreciation deduction for any property that is required to be depreciated under the alternative depreciation system of MACRS.
23. The term "original use" means the first use to which the property is put, whether or not such use corresponds to the use of such property by the taxpayer.

If in the normal course of its business a taxpayer sells fractional interests in property to unrelated third parties, then the original use of such property begins with the first user of each fractional interest (i.e., each fractional owner is considered the original user of its proportionate share of the property)

24. A special rule applies in the case of certain leased property. In the case of any property that is originally placed in service by a person and that is sold to the taxpayer and leased back to such person by the taxpayer within three months after the date that the property was placed in service, the property would be treated as originally placed in service by the taxpayer not earlier than the date that the property is used under the leaseback.

If property is originally placed in service by a lessor (including by operation of section 168(k)(2)(D)(i)) such property is sold within three months after the date that the property was placed in service, and the user of such property does not change, then the property is treated as originally placed in service by the taxpayer not earlier than the date of such sale.

25. In order for property to qualify for the extended placed in service date, the property is required to have an estimated production period exceeding one year and a cost exceeding $1 million.
26. Property does not fail to qualify for the additional first-year depreciation merely because a binding written contract to acquire a component of the property is in effect prior to January 1, 2008.

eligible for the additional first-year depreciation. With respect to such property, only the portion of the basis that is properly attributable to the costs incurred before January 2009 ("progress expenditures") is eligible for the additional first-year depreciation.[27]

Property does not qualify for the additional first-year depreciation deduction when the user of such property (or a related party) would not have been eligible for the additional first-year depreciation deduction if the user (or a related party) were treated as the owner. For example, if a taxpayer sells to a related party property that was under construction prior to January 1, 2008, the property does not qualify for the additional first-year depreciation deduction. Similarly, if a taxpayer sells to a related party property that was subject to a binding written contract prior to January 1, 2008, the property does not qualify for the additional first-year depreciation deduction. As a further example, if a taxpayer (the lessee) sells property in a sale-leaseback arrangement, and the property otherwise would not have qualified for the additional first-year depreciation deduction if it were owned by the taxpayer-lessee, then the lessor is not entitled to the additional first-year depreciation deduction.

The limitation on the amount of depreciation deductions allowed with respect to certain passenger automobiles (sec. 280F) is increased in the first year by $8,000 for automobiles that qualify (and do not elect out of the increased first year deduction). The $8,000 increase is not indexed for inflation.

Corporations otherwise eligible for additional first year depreciation under section 168(k) may elect to claim additional research or minimum tax credits in lieu of claiming depreciation under section 168(k) for "eligible qualified property" placed in service after March 31, 2008 and before December 31, 2008.[28] A corporation making the election forgoes the depreciation deductions allowable under section 168(k) and instead increases the limitation under section 38(c) on the use of research credits or section 53(c) on the use of minimum tax credits.[29] The increases in the allowable credits are treated as refundable for purposes of this provision. The depreciation for qualified property is calculated for both regular tax and AMT purposes using the straight-line method in place of the method that would otherwise be used absent the election under this provision.

The research credit or minimum tax credit limitation is increased by the bonus depreciation amount, which is equal to 20 percent of bonus depreciation[30] for certain eligible qualified property that could be claimed absent an election under this provision, Generally, eligible qualified property included in the calculation is bonus depreciation property that meets the following requirements: (1) the original use of the property must commence with the taxpayer after March 31, 2008; (2) the taxpayer must purchase the property either (a) after March 31, 2008, and before January 1, 2009, but only if no binding written contract for the acquisition is in effect before April 1, 2008[31] or (b) pursuant to a binding written contract which was entered into after March 31, 2008, and before January 1, 2009;[32] and (3) the property must be placed in service after March 31, 2008, and before January 1, 2009 (January 1, 2010 for certain longer-lived and transportation property).

The bonus depreciation amount is limited to the lesser of: (1) $30 million, or (2) six percent of the sum of research credit carry forwards from taxable years beginning before

---

27. For purposes of determining the amount of eligible progress expenditures, it is intended that rules similar to sec. 46(d)(3) as in effect prior to the Tax Reform Act of 1986 shall apply.
28. Sec. 168(k)(4). In the case of an electing corporation that is a partner in a partnership, the corporate partner's distributive share of partnership items is determined as if section 168(k) does not apply to any eligible qualified property and the straight line method is used to calculate depreciation of such property.
29. Special rules apply to an applicable partnership.
30. For this purpose, bonus depreciation is the difference between (i) the aggregate amount of depreciation for all eligible qualified property determined if section 168(k)(1) applied using the most accelerated depreciation method (determined without regard to this provision), and shortest life allowable for each property, and (ii) the amount of depreciation that would be determined if section 168(k)(1) did not apply using the same method and life for each property.
31. In the case of passenger aircraft, the written binding contract limitation does not apply.
32. Special rules apply to property manufactured, constructed, or produced by the taxpayer for use by the taxpayer.

January 1, 2006 and minimum tax credits allocable to the adjusted minimum tax imposed for taxable years beginning before January 1, 2006, All corporations treated as a single employer under section 52(a) are treated as one taxpayer for purposes of the limitation, as well as for electing the application of this provision.

House Bill

The provision extends the additional first-year depreciation deduction for one year, generally through 2009 (through 2010 for certain longer-lived and transportation property).[33]

Senate Amendment

The provision extends the additional first-year depreciation deduction for one year, generally through 2009 (through 2010 for certain longer-lived and transportation property).

The provision generally permits corporations to increase the research credit or minimum tax credit limitation by the bonus depreciation amount with respect to certain property placed in service in 2009 (2010 in the case of certain longer-lived and transportation property). The provision applies with respect to extension property, which is defined as property that is eligible qualified property solely because it meets the requirements under the extension of the special allowance for certain property acquired during 2009.

Under the provision, a taxpayer that has made an election to increase the research credit or minimum tax credit limitation for eligible qualified property for its first taxable year ending after March 31, 2008, may choose not to make this election for extension property. Further, the provision allows a taxpayer that has not made an election for eligible qualified property for its first taxable year ending after March 31, 2008, to make the election for extension property for its first taxable year ending after December 31, 2008, and for each subsequent year. In the case of a taxpayer electing to increase the research or minimum tax credit for both eligible qualified property and extension property, a separate bonus depreciation amount, maximum amount, and maximum increase amount is computed and applied to each group of property.[34]

Conference Agreement

The conference agreement follows the Senate amendment.

Effective Date

The extension of the additional first-year depreciation deduction is generally effective for property placed in service after December 31, 2008.

The extension of the election to accelerate AMT and research credits in lieu of bonus depreciation is effective for taxable years ending after December 31, 2008.

---

33. The provision does not modify the property eligible for the election to accelerate AMT and research credits in lieu of bonus depreciation under section 168(k)(4). However, the provision includes a technical amendment to section 168(k)(4)(D) providing that no written binding contract for the acquisition of eligible qualified property may be in effect before April 1, 2008 (effective for taxable years ending after March 31, 2008).
34. In computing the maximum amount, the maximum increase amount for extension property is reduced by bonus depreciation amounts for preceding taxable years only with respect to extension property.

[¶ 5035]   Section 1202.   Temporary increase in limitations on expensing of certain depreciable business assets.

(Code Sec. 179)

[Conference Report]

Present Law

In lieu of depreciation, a taxpayer with a sufficiently small amount of annual investment may elect to deduct (or "expense") such costs under section 179. Present law provides that the maximum amount a taxpayer may expense for taxable years beginning, in 2008 is $250,000 of the cost of qualifying property placed in service for the taxable year.[35] For taxable years beginning in 2009 and 2010, the limitation is $125,000. In general, qualifying property is defined as depreciable tangible personal property that is purchased for use in the active conduct of a trade or business. Off-the-shelf computer software placed in service in taxable years beginning before 2011 is treated as qualifying property. For taxable years beginning in 2008, the $250,000 amount is reduced (but not below zero) by the amount by which the cost of qualifying property placed in service during the taxable year exceeds $800,000. For taxable years beginning in 2009 and 2010, the $125,000 amount is reduced (but not below zero) by the amount by which the cost of qualifying property placed in service during the taxable year exceeds $500,000. The $125,000 and $500,000 amounts are indexed for inflation in taxable years beginning in 2009 and 2010.

The amount eligible to be expensed for a taxable year may not exceed the taxable income for a taxable year that is derived from the active conduct of a trade or business (determined without regard to this provision). Any amount that is not allowed as a deduction because of the taxable income limitation may be carried forward to succeeding taxable years (subject to similar limitations). No general business credit under section 38 is allowed with respect to any amount for which a deduction is allowed under section 179. An expensing election is made under rules prescribed by the Secretary.[36]

For taxable years beginning in 2011 and thereafter (or before 2003), the following rules apply. A taxpayer with a sufficiently small amount of annual investment may elect to deduct up to $25,000 of the cost of qualifying property placed in service for the taxable year. The $25,000 amount is reduced (but not below zero) by the amount by which the cost of qualifying property placed in service during the taxable year exceeds $200,000. The $25,000 and $200,000 amounts are not indexed for inflation. In general, qualifying property is defined as depreciable tangible personal property that is purchased for use in the active conduct of a trade or business (not including off-the-shelf computer software). An expensing election may be revoked only with consent of the Commissioner.[37]

House Bill

The provision extends the $250,000 and $800,000 amounts to taxable years beginning in 2009.

Senate Amendment

The Senate amendment is the same as the House bill.

---

35. Additional section 179 incentives are provided with respect to qualified property meeting applicable requirements that is used by a business in an empowerment zone (sec. 1397A) or a renewal community (sec. 1400J), qualified section 179 Gulf Opportunity Zone property (sec. 1400N(e), qualified Recovery Assistance property placed in service in the Kansas disaster area (Pub. L. No. 110-234, sec. 15345 (2008)), and qualified disaster assistance property (sec. 179(e)).
36. Sec. 179(c)(1). Under Treas. Reg. sec. 1.179-5, applicable to property placed in service in taxable years beginning after 2002 and before 2008, a taxpayer is permitted to make or revoke an election under section 179 without the consent of the Commissioner on an amended Federal tax return for that taxable year. This amended return must be filed within the time prescribed by law for filing an amended return for the taxable year. T.D. 9209, July 12, 2005.
37. Sec. 179(c)(2).

Conference Agreement

The conference agreement follows the House bill and the Senate amendment.

Effective Date

The provision is effective for taxable years beginning after December 31, 2008.

[¶ 5037]   Section 1211.   5-year carryback of operating losses of small businesses.

(Code Sec. 172)

[Conference Report]

Present Law

Under present law, a net operating loss ("NOL") generally means the amount by which a taxpayer's business deductions exceed its gross income. In general, an NOL may be carried back two years and carried over 20 years to offset taxable income in such years.[38] NOLs offset taxable income in the order of the taxable years to which the NOL may be carried.[39]

The alternative minimum tax rules provide that a taxpayer's NOL deduction cannot reduce the taxpayer's alternative minimum taxable income ("AMTI") by more than 90 percent of the AMTI.

Different rules apply with respect to NOLs arising in certain circumstances. A three-year carryback applies with respect to NOLs (1) arising from casualty or theft losses of individuals, or (2) attributable to Presidentially declared disasters for taxpayers engaged in a farming business or a small business. A five-year carryback applies to NOLs (1) arising from a farming loss (regardless of whether the loss was incurred in a Presidentially declared disaster area), (2) certain amounts related to Hurricane Katrina, Gulf Opportunity Zone, and Midwestern Disaster Area, or (3) qualified disaster losses.[40] Special rules also apply to real estate investment trusts (no carryback), specified liability losses (10-year carryback), and excess interest losses (no carryback to any year preceding a corporate equity reduction transaction). Additionally, a special rule applies to certain electric utility companies.

In the case of a life insurance company, present law allows a deduction for the operations loss carryovers and carrybacks to the taxable year, in lieu of the deduction for net operation losses allowed to other corporations.[41] A life insurance company is permitted to treat a loss from operations (as defined under section 810(c) for any taxable year as an operations loss carryback to each of the three taxable years preceding the loss year and an operations loss carryover to each of the 15 taxable years following the loss year.[42] Special rules apply to new life insurance companies.

House Bill

The House bill provides an election[43] to increase the present-law carryback period for an applicable 2008 or 2009 NOL from two years to any whole number of years elected by the taxpayer which is more than two and less than six. An applicable NOL is the taxpayer's NOL for any taxable year ending in 2008 or 2009, or if elected by the taxpayer, the NOL for any taxable year beginning in 2008 or 2009. If an election is made to increase the carryback period, the applicable NOL is permanently reduced by 10 percent.

---

38. Sec. 172(b)(1)(A).
39. Sec. 172(b)(2).
40. Sec. 172(b)(1)(J).
41. Secs. 810, 805(a)(5).
42. Sec. 810(b)(1)
43. For all elections under this provision, the common parent of a group of corporations filing a consolidated return makes the election, which is binding on all such corporations.

These provisions may be illustrated by the following example. Taxpayer incurs a $100 NOL for its taxable year ended January 31, 2008 and elects to carryback the NOL five years to its taxable year ended January 31, 2003. Under the provision, Taxpayer must first permanently reduce the NOL by 10 percent, or $10, and then may carryback the $90 NOL to its taxable year ended January 31, 2003.

The provision also suspends the 90-percent limitation on the use of any alternative tax NOL deduction attributable to carrybacks of losses from taxable years ending during 2008 or 2009, and carryovers of losses to such taxable years (this rule applies to taxable years beginning in 2008 or 2009 if an election is in place to use such years as applicable NOLs).

For life insurance companies, the provision provides an election to increase the Present law carryback period for an applicable loss from operations from three years to four or five years. An applicable loss from operations is the taxpayer's loss from operations for any taxable year ending in 2008 or 2009, or if elected by the taxpayer, the loss from operations for any taxable year beginning in 2008 or 2009. If an election is made to increase the carryback period, the applicable loss from operations is permanently reduced by 10 percent.

The provision does not apply to: (1) any taxpayer if (a) the Federal Government acquires, at any time,[44] an equity interest in the taxpayer pursuant to the Emergency Economic Stabilization Act of 2008, or (b) the Federal Government acquires, at any time, any warrant (or other right) to acquire any equity interest with respect to the taxpayer, pursuant to such Act; (2) the Federal National Mortgage Association and the Federal Home Loan Mortgage Corporation; or (3) any taxpayer that in 2008 or 2009[45] is a member of the same affiliated group (as defined in section 1504 without regard to subsection (b) thereof) as a taxpayer to which the provision does not otherwise apply.

Senate Amendment

The Senate amendment is generally the same as the House bill, except that the Senate amendment does not include the permanent reduction of the NOL for taxpayers electing to increase the carryback period.

Conference Agreement

The conference agreement provides an eligible small business with an election[47] to increase the present-law carryback period for an applicable 2008 NOL from two years to any whole number of years elected by the taxpayer that is more than two and less than six. An eligible small business is a taxpayer meeting a $15,000,000 gross receipts test.[48] An applicable NOL is the taxpayer's NOL for any taxable year ending in 2008, or if elected by the taxpayer, the NOL for any taxable year beginning in 2008. However, any election under this provision may be made only with respect to one taxable year.

Effective Date

The conference agreement provision is effective for net operating losses arising in taxable years ending after December 31, 2007.

---

44. For example, if the Federal government acquires an equity interest in the taxpayer during 2010, or in later years, the taxpayer is not entitled to the extended carryback rules under this provision. If the carryback has previously been claimed, amended filings may be necessary to reflect this disallowance.
45. For example, a taxpayer with an NOL in 2008 that in 2010 joins an affiliated group with a member in which the Federal Government has an equity interest pursuant to the Emergency Economic Stabilization Act of 2008 may not utilize the extended carryback rules under this provision with regard to the 2008 NOL. The taxpayer is required to amend prior filings to reflect the permitted carryback period.
47. For all elections under this provision, the common parent of a group of corporations filing a consolidated return makes the election, which is binding on all such corporations.
48. For this purpose, the gross receipt test of sec. 448(c) is applied by substituting $15,000,000 for $5,000,000 each place it appears.

For an NOL for a taxable year ending before the enactment of the provision, the provision includes the following transition rules: (1) any election to waive the carryback period under either section 172(b)(3) with respect to such loss may be revoked before the applicable date; (2) any election to increase the carryback period under this provision is treated as timely made if made before the applicable date; and (3) any application for a tentative carryback adjustment under section 6411(a) with respect to such loss is treated as timely filed if filed before the applicable date. For purposes of the transition rules, the applicable date is the date which is 60 days after the date of the enactment of the provision.

[¶ 5038]   Section 1212.   Decreased required estimated tax payments in 2009 for certain small businesses.

(Code Sec. 6654)

[Conference Report]

Present Law

Under present law, the income tax system is designed to ensure that taxpayers pay taxes throughout the year based on their income and deductions. To the extent that tax is not collected through withholding, taxpayers are required to make quarterly estimated payments of tax, the amount of which is determined by reference to the required annual payment. The required annual payment is the lesser of 90 percent of the tax shown on the return or 100 percent of the tax shown on the return for the prior taxable year (110 percent if the adjusted gross income for the preceding year exceeded $150,000). An underpayment results if the required payment exceeds the amount (if any) of the installment paid on or before the due date of the installment. The period of the underpayment runs from the due date of the installment to the earlier of (1) the 15th day of the fourth month following the close of the taxable year or (2) the date on which each portion of the underpayment is made. If a taxpayer fails to pay the required estimated tax payments under the rules, a penalty is imposed in an amount determined by applying the underpayment interest rate to the amount of the underpayment for the period of the underpayment. The penalty for failure to pay estimated tax is the equivalent of interest, which is based on the time value of money.

Taxpayers are not liable for a penalty for the failure to pay estimated tax in certain circumstances. The statute provides exceptions for U.S. persons who did not have a tax liability the preceding year, if the tax shown on the return for the taxable year (or, if no return is filed, the tax), reduced by withholding, is less than $1,000, or the taxpayer is a recently retired or disabled person who satisfies the reasonable cause exception.

House Bill

No provision.

Senate Amendment

No provision.

Conference Agreement

The conference agreement provides that the required annual estimated tax payments of a qualified individual for taxable years beginning in 2009 is not greater than 90 percent of the tax liability shown on the tax return for the preceding taxable year. A qualified individual means any individual if the adjusted gross income shown on the tax return for the preceding taxable year is less than $500,000 ($250,000 if married filing separately) and the individual certifies that at least 50 percent of the gross income shown on the return for the preceding taxable year was income from a small trade or business. For purposes of this provision, a small trade or business means any trade or business that employed no more than 500 persons, on average, during the calendar year ending in or with the preceding taxable year.

Effective Date

The proposal is effective on the date of enactment.

[¶ 5039]   Section 1221.   Incentives to hire unemployed veterans and disconnected youth.

(Code Sec. 51)

[Conference Report]

Present Law

In general

The work opportunity tax credit is available on an elective basis for employers hiring individuals from one or more of nine targeted groups. The amount of the credit available to an employer is determined by the amount of qualified wages paid by the employer. Generally, qualified wages consist of wages attributable to service rendered by a member of a targeted group during the one-year period beginning with the day the individual begins work for the employer (two years in the case of an individual in the long-term family assistance recipient category).

Targeted groups eligible for the credit

Generally an employer is eligible for the credit only for qualified wages paid to members of a targeted group.

(1) Families receiving TANF

An eligible recipient is an individual certified by a designated local employment agency (e.g., a State employment agency) as being a member of a family eligible to receive benefits under the Temporary Assistance for Needy Families Program ("TANF") for a period of at least nine months part of which is during the 18-month period ending on the hiring date. For these purposes, members of the family are defined to include only those individuals taken into account for purposes of determining eligibility for the TANF.

(2) Qualified veteran

There are two subcategories of qualified veterans related to eligibility for Food stamps and compensation for a service-connected disability.

Food stamps

A qualified veteran is a veteran who is certified by the designated local agency as a member of a family receiving assistance under a food stamp program under the Food Stamp Act of 1977 for a period of at least three months part of which is during the 12-month period ending on the hiring date. For these purposes, members of a family are, defined to include only those individuals taken into account for purposes of determining eligibility for a food stamp program under the Food Stamp Act of 1977.

Entitled to compensation for a service-connected disability

A qualified veteran also includes an individual who is certified as entitled to compensation for a service-connected disability and: (1) having a hiring date which is not more than one year after having been discharged or released from active duty in the Armed Forces of the United States; or (2) having been unemployed for six months or more (whether or not consecutive) during the one-year period ending on the date of hiring.

Definitions

For these purposes, being entitled to compensation for a service-connected disability is defined with reference to section 101 of Title 38, U.S. Code, which means having a disability rating of 10 percent or higher for service connected injuries.

For these purposes, a veteran is an individual who has served on active duty (other than for training) in the Armed Forces for more than 180 days or who has been discharged or released from active duty in the Armed Forces for a service-connected disability. However, any individual who has served for a period of more than 90 days during which the individual was on active duty (other than for training) is not a qualified veteran if any of this active duty occurred during the 60-day period ending on the date the individual was hired by the employer. This latter rule is intended to prevent employers who hire current members of the armed services (or those departed from service within the last 60 days) from receiving the credit.

(3) Qualified ex-felon

A qualified ex-felon is an individual certified as: (1) having been convicted of a felony under any State or Federal law; and (2) having a hiring date within one year of release from prison or the date of conviction.

(4) Designated community residents

A designated community resident is an individual certified as being at least age 18 but not yet age 40 on the hiring date and as having a principal place of abode within an . empowerment zone, enterprise community, renewal community or a rural renewal community. For these purposes, a rural renewal county is a county outside a metropolitan statistical area (as defined by the Office of Management and Budget) which had a net population loss during the five-year periods 1990-1994 and 1995-1999. Qualified wages do not include wages paid or incurred for services performed after the individual moves outside an empowerment zone, enterprise community, renewal community or a rural renewal community.

(5) Vocational rehabilitation referral

A vocational rehabilitation referral is an individual who is certified by a designated local agency as an individual who has a physical or mental disability that constitutes a substantial handicap to employment and who has been referred to the employer while receiving, or after completing: (a) vocational rehabilitation services under an individualized, written plan for employment under a State plan approved under the Rehabilitation Act of 1973; (b) under a rehabilitation plan for veterans carried out under Chapter 31 of Title 38, U.S. Code; or (c) an individual work plan developed and implemented by an employment network pursuant to subsection (g) of section 1148 of the Social Security Act. Certification will be provided by the designated local employment agency upon assurances from the vocational rehabilitation agency that the employee has met the above conditions.

(6) Qualified summer youth employee

A qualified summer youth employee is an individual: (a) who performs services during any 90-day period between May 1 and September 15; (b) who is certified by the designated local agency as being 16 or 17 years of age on the hiring date; (c) who has not been an employee of that employer before; and (d) who is certified by the designated local agency as having a principal place of abode within an empowerment zone, enterprise community, or renewal community (as defined under Subchapter U of Subtitle A, Chapter 1 of the Internal Revenue Code). As with designated community residents, no credit is available on wages paid or incurred for service performed after the qualified summer youth moves outside of an empowerment zone, enterprise community, or renewal community. If, after the end of the 90-day period, the employer continues to employ a youth who was certified during the 90-day period as a member of another targeted group, the limit on qualified first year wages will take into account wages paid to the youth while a qualified summer youth employee.

(7) Qualified food stamp recipient

A qualified food stamp recipient is an individual at least age 18 but not yet age 40 certified by a designated local employment agency as being a member of a family receiving assistance under a food stamp program under the Food Stamp Act of 1977 for a period of at least six months ending on the hiring date. In the case of families that cease to be eligible for food stamps under section 6(o) of the Food Stamp Act of 1977, the six-month requirement is replaced with a requirement that the family has been receiving food stamps for at least three of the five months ending on the date of hire. For these purposes, members of the family are defined to include only those individuals taken into account for purposes of determining eligibility for a food stamp program under the Food Stamp Act of 1977.

(8) Qualified SSI recipient

A qualified SSI recipient is an individual designated by a local agency as receiving supplemental security income ("SSI") benefits under Title XVI of the Social Security Act for any month ending within the 60-day period ending on the hiring date.

(9) Long-term family assistance recipients

A qualified long-term family assistance recipient is an individual certified by a designated local agency as being: (a) a member of a family that has received family assistance for at least 18 consecutive months ending on the hiring date; (b) a member of a family that has received such family assistance for a total of at least 18 months (whether or not consecutive) after August 5, 1997 (the date of enactment of the welfare-to-work tax credit)[49] if the individual is hired within two years after the date that the 18-month total is reached; or (c) a member of a family who is no longer eligible for family assistance because of either Federal or State time limits, if the individual is hired within two years after the Federal or State time limits made the family ineligible for family assistance.

Qualified wages

Generally, qualified wages are defined as cash wages paid by the employer to a member of a targeted group. The employer's deduction for wages is reduced by the amount of the credit.

For purposes of the credit, generally, wages are defined by reference to the FUTA definition of wages contained in sec. 3306(b) (without regard to the dollar limitation therein contained). Special rules apply in the case of certain agricultural labor and certain railroad labor.

Calculation of the credit

The credit available to an employer for qualified wages paid to members of all targeted groups except for long-term family assistance recipients equals 40 percent (25 percent for employment of 400 hours or less) of qualified first-year wages. Generally, qualified first-year wages are qualified wages (not in excess of $6,000) attributable to service rendered by a member of a targeted group during the one-year period beginning with the day the individual began work for the employer. Therefore, the maximum credit per employee is $2,400 (40 percent of the first $6,000 of qualified first-year wages). With respect to qualified summer youth employees, the maximum credit is $1,200 (40

---

49. The welfare-to-work tax credit was consolidated into the work opportunity tax credit in the Tax Relief and Health Care Act of 2006, for qualified individuals who begin to work for an employer after December 31, 2006.

percent of the first $3,000 of qualified first-year wages). Except for long-term family assistance recipients, no credit is allowed for second-year wages.

In the case of long-term family assistance recipients, the credit equals 40 percent (25 percent for employment of 400 hours or less) of $10,000 for qualified first-year wages and 50 percent of the first $10,000 of qualified second-year wages. Generally, qualified second-year wages are qualified wages (not in excess of $10,000) attributable to service rendered by a member of the long-term family assistance category during the one-year period beginning on the day after the one-year period beginning with the day the individual began work for the employer. Therefore, the maximum credit per employee is $9,000 (40 percent of the first $10,000 of qualified first-year wages plus 50 percent of the first $10,000 of qualified second-year wages).

In the case of a qualified veteran who is entitled to compensation for a service connected disability, the credit equals 40 percent of $12,000 of qualified first-year wages. This expanded definition of qualified first-year wages does not apply to the veterans qualified with reference to a food stamp program, as defined under present law.

Certification rules

An individual is not treated as a member of a targeted group unless: (1) on or before the day on which an individual begins work for an employer, the employer has received a certification from a designated local agency that such individual is a member of a targeted group; or (2) on or before the day an individual is offered employment with the employer, a pre-screening notice is completed by the employer with respect to such individual, and not later than the 28th day after the individual begins work for the employer. the employer submits such notice, signed by the employer and the individual under penalties of perjury, to the designated local agency as part of a written request for certification. For these purposes, a pre-screening notice is a document (in such form as the Secretary may prescribe) which contains information provided by the individual on the basis of which the employer believes that the individual is a member of a targeted group.

Minimum employment period

No credit is allowed for qualified wages paid to employees who work less than 120 hours in the first year of employment.

Other rules

The work opportunity tax credit is not allowed for wages paid to a relative or dependent of the taxpayer. No credit is allowed for wages paid to an individual who is a more than fifty-percent owner of the entity. Similarly, wages paid to replacement workers during a strike or lockout are not eligible for the work opportunity tax credit. Wages paid to any employee during any period for which the employer received on-the-job training program payments with respect to that employee are not eligible for the work opportunity tax credit. The work opportunity tax credit generally is not allowed for wages paid to individuals who had previously been employed by the employer. In addition, many other technical rules apply.

Expiration

The work opportunity tax credit is not available for individuals who begin work for an employer after August 31, 2011.

House Bill

In general

The provision creates a new targeted group for the work opportunity tax credit. That new category is unemployed veterans and disconnected youth who begin work for the employer in 2009 or 2010.

An unemployed veteran is defined as an individual certified by the designated local agency as someone who: (1) has served on active duty (other than for training) in the Armed Forces for more than 180 days or who has been discharged or released from active duty in the Armed Forces for a service-connected disability; (2) has been discharged or released from active duty in the Armed Forces during 2008, 2009, or 2010; and (3) has received unemployment compensation under State or federal law for not less than four weeks during the one-year period ending on the hiring date.

A disconnected youth is defined as an individual certified by the designated local agency as someone: (1) at least age 16 but not yet age 25 on the hiring date; (2) not regularly attending any secondary, technical, or post-secondary school during the six-month period preceding the hiring date; (3) not regularly employed during the six-month period preceding the hiring date; and (4) not readily employable by reason of lacking a sufficient number of skills.

Senate Amendment

The Senate amendment is the same as the House bill except that the otherwise applicable definition of unemployed veterans is expanded to include individuals who were discharged or released from active duty in the Armed Forces during the period beginning on September 1, 2001 and ending on December 31, 2010.

Conference Agreement

The conference agreement follows the House bill and the Senate amendment with one modification. Under this modification a unemployed veteran for purposes of this new targeted group is defined below:

An unemployed veteran is defined as an individual certified by the designated local agency as someone who: (1) has served on active duty (other than for training) in the Armed Forces for more than 180 days or who has been discharged or released from active duty in the Armed Forces for a service-connected disability; (2) has been discharged or released from active duty in the Armed Forces during the five-year period ending on the hiring date; and (3) has received unemployment compensation under State or Federal law for not less than four weeks during the one-year period ending on the hiring date.

For purposes of the disconnected youths, it is intended that a low-level of formal education may satisfy the requirement that an individual is not readily employable by reason of lacking a sufficient number of skills. Further, it is intended that the Internal Revenue Service, when providing general guidance regarding the various new criteria, shall take into account the administrability of the program by the State agencies.

Effective Date

The provisions are effective for individuals who begin work for an employer after December 31, 2008.

[¶ 5041]   Section 1231.   Deferral and ratable inclusion of income arising from indebtedness discharged by the reacquisition of a debt instrument.

(Code Sec. 108)

[Conference Report]

Present Law

In general, gross income includes income that is realized by a debtor from the discharge of indebtedness, subject to certain exceptions for debtors in title 11 bankruptcy cases, insolvent debtors, certain student loans, certain farm indebtedness, certain real property business indebtedness, and certain qualified principal residence indebtedness.[81] In cases involving discharges of indebtedness that are excluded from gross income under the exceptions to the general rule, taxpayers generally are required to reduce certain tax attributes, including net operating losses, general business credits, minimum tax credits, capital loss carryovers, and basis in property, by the amount of the discharge of indebtedness.[82]

The amount of discharge of indebtedness excluded from income by an insolvent debtor not in a title 11 bankruptcy case cannot exceed the amount by which the debtor is insolvent. In the case of a discharge in bankruptcy or where the debtor is insolvent any reduction in basis may not exceed the excess of the aggregate bases of properties held by the taxpayer immediately after the discharge over the aggregate of the liabilities of the taxpayer immediately after the discharge.[83]

For all taxpayers, the amount of discharge of indebtedness generally is equal to the excess of the adjusted issue price of the indebtedness being satisfied over the amount paid (or deemed paid) to satisfy such indebtedness.[84] This rule generally applies to (1) the acquisition by the debtor of its debt instrument in exchange for cash, (2) the issuance of a debt instrument by the debtor in satisfaction of its indebtedness, including a modification of indebtedness that is treated as an exchange (a debt-for-debt exchange), (3) the transfer by a debtor corporation of stock, or a debtor partnership of a capital or profits interest in such partnership, in satisfaction of its indebtedness (an equity-for-debt exchange), and (4) the acquisition by a debtor corporation of its indebtedness from a shareholder as a contribution to capital.

Debt-for-debt exchanges

If a debtor issues a debt instrument in satisfaction of its indebtedness, the debtor is treated as having satisfied the indebtedness with an amount of money equal to the issue price of the newly issued debt instrument.[85] The issue price of such newly issued debt instrument generally is determined under sections 1273 and 1274.[86] Similarly, a "significant modification" of a debt instrument, within the meaning of Treas. Reg. sec. 1.1001-3, results in an exchange of the original debt instrument for a modified instrument. In such cases, where the issue price of the modified debt instrument is less than the adjusted issue price of the original debt instrument, the debtor will have income from the cancellation of indebtedness.

If any new debt instrument is issued (including as a result of a significant modification to a debt instrument), such debt instrument will have original issue discount equal to the excess (if any) of such debt instrument's stated redemption price at maturity over its issue price.[87] In general, an issuer of a debt instrument with original issue discount may deduct for any taxable year, with respect to such debt instrument, an amount of original issue discount equal to the aggregate daily portions of the original issue discount for days during such taxable year.[88]

Equity-for-debt exchanges

If a corporation transfers stock, or a partnership transfers a capital or profits interest in such partnership, to a creditor in satisfaction of its indebtedness, then such corporation or partnership is treated as having satisfied its indebtedness with an amount of money equal to the fair market value of the stock or interest.[89]

81. See sections 61(a)(12) and 108. But see sec. 102 (a debt cancellation which constitutes a gift or bequest is not treated as income to the donee debtor).
82. Sec. 108(b).
83. Sec. 1017.
84. Treas. Reg. sec. 1.61-12(c)(2)(ii). Treas. Reg. sec. 1.1275-1(b) defines "adjusted issue price."
85. Sec. 108(e)(10)(A).
86. Sec. 108(e)(10)(B).
87. Sec. 1273.
88. Sec. 163(e).
89. Sec. 108(e)(8).

Related party acquisitions

Indebtedness directly or indirectly acquired by a person who bears a relationship to the debtor described in section 267(b) or section 707(b) is treated as if it were acquired by the debtor.[90] Thus, where a debtor's indebtedness is acquired for less than its adjusted issue price by a person related to the debtor (within the meaning of section 267(b) or 707(b), the debtor recognizes income from the cancellation of indebtedness. Regulations under section 108 provide that the indebtedness acquired by the related party is treated as new indebtedness issued by the debtor to the related holder on the acquisition date (the deemed issuance).[91] The new indebtedness is deemed issued with an issue price equal to the amount used under regulations to compute the amount of cancellation of indebtedness income realized by the debtor (i.e., either the holder's adjusted basis or the fair market value of the indebtedness, as the case may be).[92] The indebtedness deemed issued pursuant to the regulations has original issue discount to the extent its stated redemption price. at maturity exceeds its issue price.

In the case of a deemed issuance under Treas. Reg. sec. 1.108-2(g), the related holder does not recognize any gain or loss, and the related holder's adjusted basis in the indebtedness remains the same as it was immediately before the deemed issuance.[93] The deemed issuance is treated as a purchase of the indebtedness by the related holder for purposes of section 1272(a)(7) (pertaining to reduction of original issue discount where a subsequent holder pays acquisition premium) and section 1276 (pertaining to acquisitions of debt at a market discount).[94]

Contribution of a debt instrument to capital of a corporation

Where a debtor corporation acquires its indebtedness from a shareholder as a contribution to capital, section 118[95] does not apply, but the corporation is treated as satisfying such indebtedness with an amount of money equal to the shareholder's adjusted basis in the indebtedness.

House Bill

No provision.

Senate Amendment

The provision permits a taxpayer to elect to defer income from cancellation of indebtedness recognized by the taxpayer as a result of a repurchase by (1) the taxpayer or (2) a person who bears a relationship to the taxpayer described in section 267(b) or section 707(b), of a "debt instrument" that was issued by the taxpayer. The provision applies only to repurchases of debt that (1) occur after December 31, 2008, and prior to January 1, 2011, and (2) are repurchases for cash. Thus, for example, the provision does not apply to a debt-for-debt exchange or to any exchange of the taxpayer's equity for a debt instrument of the taxpayer. For purposes of the provision, a "debt instrument" is broadly defined to include any bond, debenture, note, certificate or any other instrument or contractual arrangement constituting indebtedness.

Income from the discharge of indebtedness in connection with the repurchase of a debt instrument in 2009 or 2010 must be included in the gross income of the taxpayer ratably in the eight taxable years beginning with (1) for repurchases in 2009, the second taxable year following the taxable year in which the repurchase occurs or (2) for repurchases in 2010, the taxable year following the taxable year in which the repurchase oc-

---

90. Sec. 108(e)(4).
91. Treas. Reg. sec. 1.108-2(g).
92. Id.
93. Treas. Reg. sec. 1.108-2(g)(2).
94. Id.
95. Section 118 provides, in general, that in the case of a corporation, gross income does not include any contribution to the capital of the taxpayer.

curs. The provision authorizes the Secretary of the Treasury to prescribe such regulations as may be necessary or appropriate for purposes of applying the provision.

Conference Agreement

The conference agreement follows the Senate amendment with modifications. The provision permits a taxpayer to elect to defer cancellation of indebtedness income arising from a "reacquisition" of "an applicable debt instrument" after December 31, 2008, and before January 1, 2011. Income deferred pursuant to the election must be included in the gross income of the taxpayer ratably in the five taxable years beginning with (1) for repurchases in 2009, the fifth taxable year following the taxable year in which the repurchase occurs or (2) for repurchases in 2010, the fourth taxable year following the taxable year in which the repurchase occurs.

An "applicable debt instrument" is any debt instrument issued by (1) a C corporation or (2) any other person in connection with the conduct of a trade or business by such person. For purposes of the provision, a "debt instrument" is broadly defined to include any bond, debenture, note, certificate or any other instrument or contractual arrangement constituting indebtedness (within the meaning of section 1275(a)(1)).

A "reacquisition" is any "acquisition" of an applicable debt instrument by (1) the debtor that issued (or is otherwise the obligor under) such debt instrument or (2) any person related to the debtor within the meaning of section 108(e)(4). For purposes of the provision, an "acquisition" includes, without limitation, (1) an acquisition of a debt instrument for cash, (2) the exchange of a debt instrument for another debt instrument (including an exchange resulting from a modification of a debt instrument), (3) the exchange of corporate stock or a partnership interest for a debt instrument, (4) the contribution of a debt instrument to the capital of the issuer, and (5) the complete forgiveness of a debt instrument by a holder of such instrument.

Special rules for debt-for-debt exchanges

If a taxpayer makes the election provided by the provision for a debt-for-debt exchange in which the newly issued debt instrument issued (or deemed issued, including by operation of the rules in Treas. Reg. sec. 1.108-2(g)) in satisfaction of an outstanding debt instrument of the debtor has original issue discount, then any otherwise allowable deduction for original issue discount with respect to such newly issued debt instrument that (1) accrues before the first year of the five-taxable-year period in which the related, deferred discharge of indebtedness income is included in the gross income of the taxpayer and (2) does not exceed such related, deferred discharge of indebtedness income, is deferred and allowed as a deduction ratably over the same five-taxable-year period in which the deferred discharge of indebtedness income is included in gross income.

This rule can apply also in certain cases when a debtor reacquires its debt for cash. If the taxpayer issues a debt instrument and the proceeds of such issuance are used directly or indirectly to reacquire a debt instrument of the taxpayer, the provision treats the newly issued debt instrument as if it were issued in satisfaction of the retired debt instrument. If the newly issued debt instrument has original issue discount, the rule described above applies. Thus, all or a portion of the interest deductions with respect to original issue discount on the newly issued debt instrument are deferred into the five-taxable-year period in which the discharge of indebtedness income is recognized. Where only a portion of the proceeds of a new issuance are used by a taxpayer to satisfy outstanding debt, then the deferral rule applies to the portion of the original issue discount on the newly issued debt instrument that is equal to the portion of the proceeds of such newly issued instrument used to retire outstanding debt of the taxpayer.

Acceleration of deferred items

Cancellation of indebtedness income and any related deduction for original issue discount that is deferred by an electing taxpayer (and has not previously been taken into account) generally is accelerated and taken into income in the taxable year in which the taxpayer: (1) dies, (2) liquidates or sells substantially all of its assets (including in a title 11 or similar case), (3) ceases to do business, or (4) or is in similar circumstances. In a case under title 11 or a similar case, any deferred items are taken into income as of the day before the petition is filed. Deferred items are accelerated in a case under Title 11 where the taxpayer liquidates, sells substantially all of its assets, or ceases to do business, but not where a taxpayer reorganizes and emerges from the Title 11 case. In the case of a pass thru entity, this acceleration rule also applies to the sale, exchange, or redemption of an interest in the entity by a holder of such interest.

Special rule for partnerships

In the case of a partnership, any income deferred under the provision is allocated to the partners in the partnership immediately before the discharge of indebtedness in the manner such amounts would have been included in the distributive shares of such partners under section 704 if such income were recognized at the time of the discharge. Any decrease in a partner's share of liabilities as a result of such discharge is not taken into account for purposes of section 752 at the time of the discharge to the extent the deemed distribution under section 752 would cause the partner to recognize gain under section 731. Thus, the deemed distribution under section 752 is deferred with respect to a partner to the extent it exceeds such partner's basis. Amounts so deferred are taken into account at the same time. and to the extent remaining in the same amount. as income deferred under the provision is recognized by the partner.

Coordination with section 108(a) and procedures for election

Where a taxpayer makes the election provided by the provision, the exclusions provided by section 108(a)(1)(A), (B), (C), and (D) shall not apply to the income from the discharge of indebtedness for the year in which the taxpayer makes the election or any subsequent year. Thus, for example, an insolvent taxpayer may elect under the provision to defer income from the discharge of indebtedness rather than excluding such income and reducing tax attributes by a corresponding amount. The election is to be made on an instrument by instrument basis; once made, the election is irrevocable. A taxpayer makes an election with respect to a debt instrument by including with its return for the taxable year in which the reacquisition of the debt instrument occurs a statement that (1) clearly identifies the debt instrument and (2) includes the amount of deferred income to which the provision applies and such other information as may be prescribed by the Secretary. The Secretary is authorized to require reporting of the election (and other information with respect to the reacquisition) for years subsequent to the year of the reacquisition.

Regulatory authority

The provision authorizes the Secretary of the Treasury to prescribe such regulations as may be necessary or appropriate for purposes of applying the provision, including rules extending the acceleration provisions to other circumstances where appropriate, rules requiring reporting of the election and such other information as the Secretary may require on returns of tax for subsequent taxable years, rules for the application of the provision to partnerships, S corporations, and other pass thru entities, including for the allocation of deferred deductions.

Effective Date

The provision is effective for discharges in taxable years ending after December 31, 2008.

[¶ 5042] Section 1232. Modifications of rules for original issue discount on certain high yield obligations.

(Code Sec. 163)

[Conference Report]

Present Law

In general, the issuer of a debt instrument with original issue discount may deduct the portion of such original issue discount equal to the aggregate daily portions of the original issue discount for days during the taxable year.[96] However, in the case of an applicable high-yield discount obligation (an "AHYDO") issued by a corporate issuer: (1) no deduction is allowed for the "disqualified portion" of the original issue discount on such obligation, and (2) the remainder of the original issue discount on any such obligation is not allowable as a deduction until paid by the issuer.[97]

An AHYDO is any debt instrument if (1) the maturity date on such instrument is more than five years from the date of issue; (2) the yield to maturity on such instrument exceeds the sum of (a) the applicable Federal rate in effect under section 1274(d) for the calendar month in which the obligation is issued and (b) five percentage points, and (3) such instrument has "significant original issue discount."[98] An instrument is treated as having "significant original issue discount" if the aggregate amount of interest that would be includible in the gross income of the holder with respect to such instrument for periods before the close of any accrual period (as defined in section 1272(a)(5) ending after the date five years after the date of issue, exceeds the sum of (1) the aggregate amount of interest to be paid under the instrument before the close of such accrual period, and (2) the product of the issue price of such instrument (as defined in sections 1273(b) and 1274(a) and its yield to maturity.[99]

The disqualified portion of the original issue discount on an AHYDO is the lesser of (1) the amount of original issue discount with respect to such obligation or (2) the portion of the "total return" on such obligation which bears the same ratio to such total return as the "disqualified yield" (i.e., the excess of the yield to maturity on the obligation over the applicable Federal rate plus six percentage points) on such obligation bears to the yield to maturity on such obligation.[100] The term "total return" means the amount which would have been the original issue discount of the obligation if interest described in section 1273(a)(2) were included in the stated redemption to maturity.[101] A corporate holder treats the disqualified portion of original issue discount as a stock distribution for purposes of the dividend received deduction.[102]

House Bill

No provision.

Senate Amendment

No provision.

Conference Agreement

The conference agreement adds a provision that suspends the rules in section 163(e)(5) for certain obligations issued in a debt-for-debt exchange, including an ex-

---

96. Sec. 163(e)(1). For purposes of section 163(e)(1), the daily portion of the original issue discount for any day is determined under section 1272(a) (without regard to paragraph (7) thereof and without regard to section 1273(a)(3).
97. Sec. 163(e)(5).
98. Sec. 163(i)(1).
99. Sec. 163(i)(2).
100. Sec. 163(e)(5)(C).
101. Sec. 163(e)(5)(C)(ii).
102. Sec. 163(e)(5)(B).

change resulting from a significant modification of a debt instrument, after August 31, 2008, and before January 1, 2010.

In general, the suspension does not apply to any newly issued debt instrument (including any debt instrument issued as a result of a significant modification of a debt instrument) that is issued for an AHYDO. However, any newly issued debt instrument (including any debt instrument issued as a result of a significant modification of a debt instrument) for which the AHYDO rules are suspended under the provision is not treated as an AHYDO for purposes of a subsequent application of the suspension rule. Thus, for example, if a new debt instrument that would be an AHYDO under present law is issued in exchange for a debt instrument that is not an AHYDO, and the provision suspends application of section 163(e)(5), another new debt instrument, issued during the suspension period in exchange for the instrument with respect to which the rule in section 163(e)(5) was suspended, would be eligible for the relief provided by the provision despite the fact that it is issued for an instrument that is an AHYDO under present law.

In addition, the suspension does not apply to any newly issued debt instrument (including any debt instrument issued as a result of a significant modification of a debt instrument) that is (1) described in section 871(h)(4) (without regard to subparagraph (D) thereof) (i.e., certain contingent debt) or (2) issued to a person related to the issuer (within the meaning of section 108(e)(4)).

The provision provides authority to the Secretary to apply the suspension rule to periods after December 31, 2009, where the Secretary determines that such application is appropriate in light of distressed conditions in the debt capital markets. In addition, the provision grants authority to the Secretary to use a rate that is higher than the applicable Federal rate for purposes of applying section 163(e)(5) for obligations issued after December 31, 2009, in taxable years ending after such date if the Secretary determines that such higher rate is appropriate in light of distressed conditions in the debt capital markets.

Effective Date

The temporary suspension of section 163(e)(5) applies to obligations issued after August 31, 2008, in taxable years ending after such date. The additional authority granted to the Secretary to use a rate higher than the applicable Federal rate for purposes of applying section 163(e)(5) applies to obligations issued after December 31, 2009, in taxable years ending after such date.

[¶ 5044]   Section 1241.   Special rules applicable to qualified small business stock for 2009 and 2010.

(Code Sec. 1202)

[Conference Report]

Present Law

Under present law, individuals may exclude 50 percent (60 percent for certain empowerment zone businesses) of the gain from the sale of certain small business stock acquired at original issue and held for at least five years.[103] The portion of the gain includible in taxable income is taxed at a maximum rate of 28 percent under the regular tax.[104] A percentage of the excluded gain is an alternative minimum tax preference;[105]

---

103. Sec. 1202.
104. Sec. 1(h).
105. Sec. 57(a)(7). In the case of qualified small business stock, the percentage of gain excluded from gross income which is an alternative minimum tax preference is (i) seven percent in the case of stock disposed of in a taxable year beginning before 2011; (ii) 42 percent in the case of stock acquired before January 1, 2001, and disposed of in a taxable year beginning after 2010; and (iii) 28 percent in the case of stock acquired after December 31, 2000, and disposed of in a taxable year beginning after 2010.

the portion of the gain includible in alternative minimum taxable income is taxed at a maximum rate of 28 percent under the alternative minimum tax.

Thus, under present law, gain from the sale of qualified small business stock is taxed at effective rates of 14 percent under the regular tax[106] and (i) 14.98 percent under the alternative minimum tax for dispositions before January 1, 2011; (ii) 19.98 percent under the alternative minimum tax for dispositions after December 31, 2010, in the case of stock acquired before January 1, 2001; and (iii) 17.92 percent under the alternative minimum tax for dispositions after December 31, 2010, in the case of stock acquired after December 31, 2000.[107]

The amount of gain eligible for the exclusion by an individual with respect to any corporation is the greater of (1) ten times the taxpayer's basis in the stock or (2) $10 million. In order to qualify as a small business, when the stock is issued, the gross assets of the corporation may not exceed $50 million. The corporation also must meet certain active trade or business requirements.

House Bill

No provision.

Senate Amendment

Under the Senate amendment, the percentage exclusion for qualified small business stock sold by an individual is increased from 50 percent (60 percent for certain empowerment zone businesses) to 75 percent.

As a result of the increased exclusion, gain from the sale of qualified small business stock to which the provision applies is taxed at effective rates of seven percent under the regular tax[108] and 12.88 percent under the alternative minimum tax.[109]

Conference Agreement

The conference agreement follows the Senate amendment

Effective Date

The provision is effective for stock issued after the date of enactment and before January 1, 2011.

[¶ 5046]   Section 1251.   Temporary reduction in recognition period for built-in gains tax.

(Code Sec. 1374)

[Conference Report]

Present Law

A "small business corporation" (as defined in section 1361(b)) may elect to be treated as an S corporation. Unlike C corporations, S corporations generally pay no corporate-level tax. Instead, items of income and loss of an S corporation pass though to its shareholders. Each shareholder takes into account separately its share of these items on its individual income tax return.[110]

---

106. The 50 percent of gain included in taxable income is taxed at a maximum rate of 28 percent.
107. The amount of gain included in alternative minimum tax is taxed at a maximum rate of 28 percent. The amount so included is the sum of (i) 50 percent (the percentage included in taxable income) of the total gain and (ii) the applicable preference percentage of the one-half gain that is excluded from taxable income.
108. The 25 percent of gain included in taxable income is taxed at a maximum rate of 28 percent.
109. The 46 percent of gain included in alternative minimum tax is taxed at a maximum rate of 28 percent. Forty-six percent is the sum of 25 percent (the percentage of total gain included in taxable income) plus 21 percent (the percentage of total gain which is an alternative minimum tax preference).
110. Sec. 1366.

A corporate level tax, at the highest marginal rate applicable to corporations (currently 35 percent) is imposed on an S corporation's gain that arose prior to the conversion of the C corporation to an S corporation and is recognized by the S corporation during the recognition period, i.e., the first 10 taxable years that the S election is in effect.[111]

Gains recognized in the recognition period are not built-in gains to the extent they are shown to have arisen while the S election was in effect or are offset by recognized built-in losses. The built-in gains tax also applies to gains with respect to net recognized built-in gain attributable to property received by an S corporation from a C corporation in a carryover basis transaction.[112] The amount of the built-in gains tax is treated as a loss taken into account by the shareholders in computing their individual income tax.[113]

House Bill

No provision.

Senate Amendment

The Senate amendment provides that, for any taxable year beginning in 2009 and 2010, no tax is imposed on an S corporation under section 1374 if the seventh taxable year in the corporation's recognition period preceded such taxable year. Thus, with respect to gain that arose prior to the conversion of a C corporation to an S corporation, no tax will be imposed under section 1374 after the seventh taxable year the S corporation election is in effect. In the case of built-in gain attributable to an asset received by an S corporation from a C corporation in a carryover basis transaction, no tax will be imposed under section 1374 if such gain is recognized after the date that is seven years following the date on which such asset was acquired.[114]

Conference Agreement

The conference agreement follows the Senate amendment.

Effective Date

The provision applies to taxable years beginning after December 31, 2008.

[¶ 5048]   Section 1261.   Clarification of regulations related to limitations on certain built-in losses following an ownership change.

(Code Sec. 382)

[Conference Report]

Present Law

Section 382 limits the extent to which a "loss corporation" that experiences an "ownership change" may offset taxable income in any post-change taxable year by pre-change net operating losses, certain built-in losses, and deductions attributable to the pre-change period.[50] In general, the amount of income in any post-change year that may be offset by such net operating losses, built-in losses and deductions is limited to an amount (referred to as the "Section 382 limitation") determined by multiplying the value of the loss

---

111. Sec. 1374.
112. Sec. 1374(d)(8). With respect to such assets, the recognition period runs from the day on which such assets were acquired (in lieu of the beginning of the first taxable year for which the corporation was an S corporation). Sec. 1374(d)(8)(B).
113. Sec. 1366(f)(2)
114. Shareholders will continue to take into account all items of gain and loss under section 1366.
50. Sec. 383 imposes similar limitations, under regulations, on the use of carryforwards of general business credits, alternative minimum tax credits, foreign tax credits, and net capital loss carryforwards. Sec. 383 generally refers to section 382 for the meanings of its terms, but requires appropriate adjustments to take account of its application to credits and net capital losses.

corporation immediately before the ownership change by the long-term tax-exempt interest rate.[51]

A "loss corporation" is defined as a corporation entitled to use a net operating loss carryover or having a net operating loss carryover for the taxable year in which the ownership change occurs. Except to the extent provided in regulations, such term includes any corporation with a "net unrealized built-in loss" (or NUBIL),[52] defined as the amount by which the fair market value of the assets of the corporation immediately before an ownership change is less than the aggregate adjusted basis of such assets at such time. However, if the amount of the NUBIL does not exceed the lesser of (i) 15 percent of the fair market value of the corporation's assets or (ii) $10,000,000, then the amount of the NUBIL is treated as zero.[53]

An ownership change is defined generally as an increase by more than 50-percentage points in the percentage of stock of a loss corporation that is owned by anyone or more five-percent (or greater) shareholders (as defined) within a three-year period.[54] Treasury regulations provide generally that this measurement is to be made as of any "testing date," which is any date on which the ownership of one or more persons who were or who become five-percent shareholders increases.[55]

Section 382(h) governs the treatment of certain built-in losses and built-in gains recognized with respect to assets held by the loss corporation at the time of the ownership

---

51. If the loss corporation had a "net unrealized built-in gain" (or NUBIG) at the time of the Ownership change, then the sec. 382 limitation for any taxable year may be increased by the amount of the "recognized built-in gains" (discussed further below) for that year. A NUBIG is defined as the amount by which the fair market value of the assets of the corporation immediately before an ownership change exceeds the aggregate adjusted basis of such assets at such time. However, if the amount of the NUBIG does not exceed the lesser of (i) 15 percent of the fair market value of the corporation's assets or (ii) $10,000,000, then the amount of the NUBIG is treated as zero. Sec. 382(h)(1).
52. Sec. 382(k)(1).
53. Sec. 382(h)(3).
54. Determinations of the percentage of stock of any corporation held by any person are made on the basis of value. Sec. 382(k)(6)(C).
55. See Treas. Reg. sec. 1.382-2(a)(4) (providing that "a loss corporation is required to determine whether an ownership change has occurred immediately after any owner shift, or issuance or transfer (including an issuance or transfer described in Treas. Reg. sec. 1.382-4(d)(8)(i) or (ii) of an option with respect to stock of the loss corporation that is treated as exercised under Treas. Reg. sec. 1.382-4(d)(2)" and defining a "testing date" as "each date on which a loss corporation is required to make a determination of whether an ownership change has occurred") and Temp. Treas. Reg. sec. 1.382-2T(e)(1) (defining an "owner shift" as "any change in the ownership of the stock of a loss corporation that affects the percentage of such stock owned by any 5-percent shareholder"). Treasury regulations under section 382 provide that, in computing stock ownership on specified testing dates, certain unexercised options must be treated as exercised if certain ownership, control, or income tests are met. These tests are met only if "a principal purpose of the issuance, transfer, or structuring of the option (alone or in combination with other arrangements) is to avoid or ameliorate the impact of an ownership change of the loss corporation." Treas. Reg. sec. 1.382-4(d). Compare prior temporary regulations, Temp. Reg. sec. 1.382-2T(h)(4) ("Solely for the purpose of determining whether there is an ownership change on any testing date, stock of the loss corporation that is subject to an option shall be treated as acquired on any such date, pursuant to an exercise of the option by its owner on that date, if such deemed exercise would result in an ownership change."). Internal Revenue Service Notice 2008-76, I.R.B. 2008-39 (September 29, 2008), released September 7, 2008, provides that the Treasury Department intends to issue regulations modifying the term "testing date" under sec. 382 to exclude any date on or after which the United States acquires stock or options to acquire stock in certain corporations with respect to which there is a "Housing Act Acquisition" pursuant to the Housing and Economic Recovery Act of 2008 (P.L. 110-289). The Notice states that the regulations will apply on and after September 7, 2008, unless and until there is additional guidance. Internal Revenue Service Notice 2008-84, I.R.B. 2008-41 (October 14, 2008), provides that the Treasury Department intends to issue regulations modifying the term "testing date" under sec. 382 to exclude any date as of the close of which the United States owns, directly or indirectly, a more than 50 percent interest in a loss corporation, which regulations will apply unless and until there is additional guidance. Internal Revenue Service Notice 2008-100, 2008-14 I.R.B. 1081 (released October 15, 2008) provides that the Treasury Department intends to issue regulations providing, among other things, that certain instruments acquired by the Treasury Department under the Capital Purchase Program (CPP) pursuant to the Emergency Economic Stabilization Act of 2008 (P.L. 100-343)("EESA") shall not be treated as stock for certain purposes. The Notice also provides that certain capital contributions made by Treasury pursuant to the CPP shall not be considered to have been made as part of a plan the principal purpose of which was to avoid or increase any sec. 382 limitation (for purposes of section 382(1)(1)). The Notice states that taxpayers may rely on the rules described unless and until there is further guidance; and that any contrary guidance will not apply to instruments (i) held by Treasury that were acquired pursuant to the CCP prior to publication of that guidance, or (ii) issued to Treasury pursuant to the CCP under written binding contracts entered into prior to the publication of that guidance. Internal Revenue Service Notice 2009-14, 2009-7 I.R.B. 1(January 30, 2009) amplifies and supersedes Notice 2008-100, and provides additional guidance regarding the application of sec. 382 and other provisions of law to corporations whose instruments are acquired by the Treasury Department under certain programs pursuant to EESA.

change. In the case of a loss corporation that has a NUBIL (measured immediately before an ownership change). section 382(h)(1) provides that any "recognized built-in loss" (or RBIL) for any taxable year during a "recognition period" (consisting of the five years beginning on the ownership change date) is subject to the section 382 limitation in the same manner as if it were a pre-change net operating loss.[56] An RBIL is defined for this purpose as any loss recognized during the recognition period on the disposition of any asset held by the loss corporation immediately before the ownership change date, to the extent that such loss is attributable to an excess of the adjusted basis of the asset on the change date over its fair market value on that date.[57] An RBIL also includes any amount allowable as depreciation, amortization or depletion during the recognition period, to the extent that such amount is attributable to the excess of the adjusted basis of the asset over its fair market value on the ownership change date.[58] In addition, any amount that is allowable as a deduction during the recognition period (determined without regard to any carryover) but which is attributable to periods before the ownership change date is treated as an RBIL for the taxable year in which it is allowable as a deduction.[59]

As indicated above, section 382(h)(1) provides in the case of a loss corporation that has a NUBIG that the section 382 limitation may be increased for any taxable year during the recognition period by the amount of recognized built-in gains (or RBIGs) for such taxable year.[60] An RBIG is defined for this purpose as any gain recognized during the recognition period on the disposition of any asset held by the loss corporation immediately before the ownership change date, to the extent that such gain is attributable to an excess of the fair market value of the asset on the change date over its adjusted basis on that date.[61] In addition, any item of income that is properly taken into account during the recognition period but which is attributable to periods before the ownership change date is treated as an RBIG for the taxable year in which it is properly taken into account.[62]

Internal Revenue Service Notice 2003-65[63] provides two alternative safe harbor approaches for the identification of built-in items for purposes of section 382(h): the "1374 approach" and the "338 approach."

Under the 1374 approach,[64] NUBIG or NUBIL is the net amount of gain or loss that would be recognized in a hypothetical sale of the assets of the loss corporation immediately before the ownership change.[65] The amount of gain or loss recognized during the recognition period on the sale or exchange of an asset held at the time of the ownership change is RBIG or RBIL. respectively, to the extent it is attributable to a difference between the adjusted basis and the fair market value of the asset on the change date, as described above. However, the 1374 approach generally relies on the accrual method of accounting to identify items of income or deduction as RBIG or RBIL, respectively. Generally, items of income or deduction properly included in income or allowed as a deduction during the recognition period are considered attributable to period before the

---

56. Sec. 382(h)(2). The total amount of the loss corporation's RBILs that are subject to the section 382 limitation cannot exceed the amount of the corporation's NUBIL.
57. Sec. 382(h)(2)(B).
58. Id.
59. Sec. 382(h)(6)(B).
60. The total amount of such increases cannot exceed the amount of the corporation's NUBIG.
61. Sec. 382(h)(2)(A).
62. Sec. 382(h)(6)(A).
63. 2003-2 C.B. 747.
64. The 1374 approach generally incorporates rules similar to those of section 1374(d) and the Treasury regulations thereunder in calculating NUBIG and NUBIL and identifying RBIG and RBIL.
65. More specifically, NUBIG or NUBIL is calculated by determining the amount that would be realized if immediately before the ownership change the loss corporation had sold all of its assets, including goodwill, at fair market value to a third party that assumed all of its liabilities, decreased by the sum of any deductible liabilities of the loss corporation that would be included in the amount realized on the hypothetical sale and the loss corporation's aggregate adjusted basis in all of its assets, increased or decreased by the corporation's section 481 adjustments that would be taken into account on a hypothetical sale, and increased by any RBIL that would not be allowed as a deduction under section 382, 383 or 384 on the hypothetical sale.

change date (and thus are treated as RBIG or RBIL. respectively). If a taxpayer using an accrual method of accounting would have included the item in income or been allowed a deduction for the item before the change date. However, the 1374 approach includes a number of exceptions to this general rule, including a special rule dealing with bad debt deductions under section 166. Under this special rule, any deduction item properly taken into account during the first 12 months of the recognition period as a bad debt deduction under section 166 is treated as RBIL if the item arises from a debt owed to the loss corporation at the beginning of the recognition period (and deductions for such items properly taken into account after the first 12 months of the recognition period are not RBILs).[66]

The 338 approach identifies items of RBIG and RBIL generally by comparing the loss corporation's actual items of income, gain, deduction and loss with those that would have resulted if a section 338 election had been made with respect to a hypothetical purchase of all of the outstanding stock of the loss corporation on the change date. Under the 338 approach, NUBIG or NUBIL is calculated in the same manner as it is under the 1374 approach.[67] The 338 approach identifies RBIG or RBIL by comparing the loss corporation's actual items of income, gain, deduction and loss with the items of income, gain, deduction and loss that would result if a section 338 election had been made for the hypothetical purchase. The loss corporation is treated for this purpose as using those accounting methods that the loss corporation actually uses. The 338 approach does not include any special rule with regard to bad debt deductions under section 166.

Section 166 generally allows a deduction in respect of any debt that becomes worthless, in whole or in part, during the taxable year.[68] The determination of whether a debt is worthless, in whole or in part, is a question of fact. However, in the case of a bank or other corporation that is subject to supervision by Federal authorities, or by State authorities maintaining substantially equivalent standards, the Treasury regulations under section 166 provide a presumption of worthlessness to the extent that a debt is charged off during the taxable year pursuant to a specific order of such an authority or in accordance with established policies of such an authority (and in the latter case, the authority confirms in writing upon the first subsequent audit of the bank or other corporation that the charge-off would have been required if the audit had been made at the time of the charge-off). The presumption does not apply if the taxpayer does not claim the amount so charged off as a deduction for the taxable year in which the charge-off takes place. In that case, the charge-off is treated as having been involuntary; however, in order to claim the section 166 deduction in a later taxable year, the taxpayer must produce sufficient evidence to show that the debt became partially worthless in the later year or became recoverable only in part subsequent to the taxable year of the charge-off, as the case may be, and to the extent that the deduction claimed in the later year for a partially worthless debt was not involuntarily charged off in prior taxable years, it was charged off in the later taxable year.[69]

The Treasury regulations also permit a bank (generally as defined for purposes of section 581, with certain modifications) that is subject to supervision by Federal authorities, or State authorities maintaining substantially equivalent standards, to make a "conformity election" under which debts charged off for regulatory purposes during a taxable year are conclusively presumed to be worthless for tax purposes to the same extent, provided that the charge-off results from a specific order of the regulatory authority or corre-

---

66. Notice 2003-65, section III.B.2.b.
67. Accordingly, unlike the case in which a section 338 election is actually made, contingent consideration (including a contingent liability) is taken into account in the initial calculation of NUBIG or NUBIL, and no further adjustments are made to reflect subsequent changes in deemed consideration.
68. Section 166 does not apply, however, to a debt which is evidenced by a security, defined for this purpose (by cross-reference to section 165(g)(2)(C)) as a bond, debenture, note or certificate or other evidence of indebtedness issued by a corporation or by a government or political subdivision thereof, with interest coupons or in registered form. Sec. 166(e).
69. See Treas. Reg. sec. 1.166-2(d)(1) and (2).

sponds to the institution's classification of the debt as a "loss asset" pursuant to loan loss classification standards that are consistent with those of certain specified bank regulatory authorities. The conformity election is treated as the adoption of a method of accounting.[70]

Internal Revenue Service Notice 2008-83,[71] released on October 1, 2008, provides that "[f]or purposes of section 382(h), any deduction properly allowed after an ownership change (as defined in section 382(g)) to a bank with respect to losses on loans or bad debts (including any deduction for a reasonable addition to a reserve for bad debts) shall not be treated as a built-in loss or a deduction that is attributable to periods before the change date.[72] The Notice further states that the Internal Revenue Service and the Treasury Department are studying the proper treatment under section 382(h) of certain items of deduction or loss allowed after an ownership change to a corporation that is a bank (as defined in section 581) both immediately before and after the change date, and that any such corporation may rely on the treatment set forth in Notice 2008-83 unless and until there is additional guidance.

House Bill

The provision states that Congress finds as follows: (1) The delegation of authority to the Secretary of the Treasury, or his delegate, under section 382(m) does not authorize the Secretary to provide exemptions or special rules that are restricted to particular industries or classes of taxpayers; (2) Internal Revenue Service Notice 2008-83 is inconsistent with the congressional intent in enacting such section 382(m); (3) the legal authority to prescribe Notice 2008-83 is doubtful; (4) however, as taxpayers should generally be able to rely on guidance issued by the Secretary of the Treasury, legislation is necessary to clarify the force and effect of Notice 2008-83 and restore the proper application under the Internal Revenue Code of the limitation on built-in losses following an ownership change of a bank.

Under the provision, Treasury Notice 2008-83 shall be deemed to have the force and effect of law with respect to any ownership change (as defined in section 382(g) occurring on or before January 16, 2009, and with respect to any ownership change (as so defined) which occurs after January 16, 2009, if such change (1) is pursuant to a written binding contract entered in to on or before such date or (2) is pursuant to a written agreement entered into on or before such date and such agreement was described on or before such date in a public announcement or in a filing with the Securities and Exchange Commission required by reason of such ownership change, but shall otherwise have no force or effect with respect to any ownership change after such date.

Senate Amendment

The Senate amendment is the same as the House bill.

Conference Agreement

The conference agreement follows the House bill and the Senate amendment.

Effective Date

The provision is effective on the date of enactment.

---

70. See Treas. Reg. sec. 1.166-2(d)(3); cf. Priv. Let. Rul. 9248048 (July 7,1992); Tech. Ad. Mem. 9122001 (Feb. 8,1991).
71. 2008-42 I.R.B. 2008-42 (Oct. 20, 2008).
72. Notice 2008-83, section 2.

[¶ 5049]   Section 1262.   Treatment of certain ownership changes for purposes of limitations on net operating loss carryforwards and certain built-in losses.

(Code Sec. 382)

[Conference Report]

Present Law

Section 382 limits the extent to which a "loss corporation" that experiences an "ownership change" may offset taxable income in any post-change taxable year by pre-change net operating losses, certain built-in losses, and deductions attributable to the pre-change period.[73] In general, the amount of income in any post-change year that may be offset by such net operating losses, built-in losses and deductions is limited to an amount (referred to as the "section 382 limitation") determined by multiplying the value of the loss corporation immediately before the ownership change by the long-term tax-exempt interest rate.[74]

A "loss corporation" is defined as a corporation entitled to use a net operating loss carryover or having a net operating loss carryover for the taxable year in which the ownership change occurs. Except to the extent provided in regulations, such term includes any corporation with a "net unrealized built-in loss" (or NUBIL),[75] defined as the amount by which the fair market value of the assets of the corporation immediately before an ownership change is less than the aggregate adjusted basis of such assets at such time. However, if the amount of the NUBIL does not exceed the lesser of (i) 15 percent of the fair market value of the corporation's assets or (ii) $10,000,000, then the amount of the NUBIL is treated as zero.[76]

An ownership change is defined generally as an increase by more than 50-percentage points in the percentage of stock of a loss corporation that is owned by anyone or more five-percent (or greater) shareholders (as defined) within a three year period.[77] Treasury regulations provide generally that this measurement is to be made as of any "testing

---

73. Section 383 imposes similar limitations, under regulations, on the use of carry forwards of general business credits, alternative minimum tax credits, foreign tax credits, and net capital loss carryforwards. Section 383 generally refers to section 382 for the meanings of its terms, but requires appropriate adjustments to take account of its application to credits and net capital losses.

74. If the loss corporation had a "net unrealized built in gain" (or NUBIG) at the time of the ownership change, then the section 382 limitation for any taxable year may be increased by the amount of the "recognized built-in gains" (discussed further below) for that year. A NUBIG is defined as the amount by which the fair market value of the assets of the corporation immediately before an ownership change exceeds the aggregate adjusted basis of such assets at such time. However, if the amount of the NUBIG does not exceed the lesser of (i) 15 percent of the fair market value of the corporation's assets or (ii) $10,000,000, then the amount of the NUBIG is treated as zero. Sec. 382(h)(1)

75. Sec. 382(k)(1).

76. Sec. 382(h)(3).

77. Determinations of the percentage of stock of any corporation held by any person are made on the basis of value. Sec. 382(k)(6)(C).

date," which is any date on which the ownership of one or more persons who were or who become five-percent shareholders increases.[78]

House Bill

No provision.

Senate Amendment

No provision.

Conference Agreement

The conference agreement amends section 382 of the Code to provide an exception from the application of the section 382 limitation. Under the provision, the section 382 limitation that would otherwise arise as a result of an ownership change shall not apply in the case of an ownership change that occurs pursuant to a restructuring plan of a taxpayer which is required under a loan agreement or commitment for a line of credit entered into with the Department of the Treasury under the Emergency Economic Stabilization Act of 2008, and is intended to result in a rationalization of the costs, capitalization, and capacity with respect to the manufacturing workforce of, and suppliers to, the taxpayer and its subsidiaries.[79]

However, an ownership change that would otherwise be excepted from the section 382 limitation under the provision will instead remain subject to the section 382 limitation if, immediately after such ownership change, any person (other than a voluntary employees' beneficiary association within the meaning of section 501(c)(9)) owns stock of the new loss corporation possessing 50 percent or more of the total combined voting power of all classes of stock entitled to vote or of the total value of the stock of such corporation. For purposes of this rule, persons who bear a relationship to one another

78. See Treas. Reg. sec. 1.382-2(a)(4) (providing that "a loss corporation is required to determine whether an ownership change has occurred immediately after any owner shift, or issuance or transfer (including an issuance or transfer described in Treas. Reg. sec. 1.382-4(d)(8)(i) or (ii)) of an option with respect to stock of the loss corporation that is treated as exercised under Treas. Reg. sec. 1.382-4(d)(2)" and defining a "testing date" as "each date on which a loss corporation is required to make a determination of whether an ownership change has occurred") and Temp. Treas. Reg. sec. 1.382-2T(e)(1)(defining an "owner shift" as "any change in the ownership of the stock of a loss corporation that affects the percentage of such stock owned by any 5-percent shareholder"). Treasury regulations under section 382 provide that, in computing stock ownership on specified testing dates, certain unexercised options must be treated as exercised if certain ownership, control, or income tests are met. These tests are met only if "a principal purpose of the issuance, transfer, or structuring of the option (alone or in combination with other arrangements) is to avoid or ameliorate the impact of an ownership change of the loss corporation." Treas. Reg. sec. 1.382-4(d). Compare prior temporary regulations, Temp. Reg. sec. 1.382-2T(h)(4) ("Solely for the purpose of determining whether there is an ownership change on any testing date, stock of the loss corporation that is subject to an option shall be treated as acquired on any such date, pursuant to an exercise of the option by its owner on that date, if such deemed exercise would result in an ownership change."). Internal Revenue Service Notice 2008-76, I.R.B. 2008-39 (September 29, 2008), released September 7, 2008, provides that the Treasury Department intends to issue regulations modifying the term "testing date" under section 382 to exclude any date on or after which the United States acquires stock or options to acquire stock in certain corporations with respect to which there is a "Housing Act Acquisition" pursuant to the Housing and Economic Recovery Act of 2008 (P.L. 110-289). The Notice states that the regulations will apply on and after September 7, 2008, unless and until there is additional guidance. Internal Revenue Service Notice 2008-84, I.R.B. 2008-41 (October 14, 2008), provides that the Treasury Department intends to issue regulations modifying the term "testing date" under section 382 to exclude any date as of the close of which the United States owns, directly or indirectly, a more than 50 percent interest in a loss corporation, which regulations will apply unless and until there is additional guidance. Internal Revenue Service Notice 2008-100, 2008-14 I.R.B. 1081 (released October 15, 2008) provides that the Treasury Department intends to issue regulations providing, among other things, that certain instruments acquired by the Treasury Department under the Capital Purchase Program (CPP) pursuant to the Emergency Economic Stabilization Act of 2008 (P.L. 100-343)("EESA")shall not be treated as stock for certain purposes. The Notice also provides that certain capital contributions made by Treasury pursuant to the CPP shall not be considered to have been made as part of a plan the principal purpose of which was to avoid or increase any section 382 limitation (for purposes of section 382(l)(1). The Notice states that taxpayers may rely on the rules described unless and until there is further guidance; and that any contrary guidance will not apply to instruments (i) held by Treasury that were acquired pursuant to the CCP prior to publication of that guidance, or (ii) issued to Treasury pursuant to the CCP under written binding contracts entered into prior to the publication of that guidance. Internal Revenue Service Notice 2009-14, 2009-7 I.R.B. 1 (January 30, 2009) amplifies and supersedes Notice 2008-100, and provides additional guidance regarding the application of section 382 and other provisions of law to corporations whose instruments are acquired by the Treasury Department under certain programs pursuant to EESA.
79. This exception shall not apply in the case of any subsequent ownership change unless such subsequent ownership change also meets the requirements of the exception.

described in section 267(b) or 707(b)(1), or who are members of a group of persons acting in concert, are treated as a single person.

The exception from the application of the section 382 limitation under the provision does not change the fact that an ownership change has occurred for other purposes of section 382.[80]

Effective Date

The conference agreement applies to ownership changes after the date of enactment.

[¶5051]   Section 1301.   Temporary expansion of availability of industrial development bonds to facilities manufacturing intangible property.

(Code Sec. 144)

[Conference Report]

Present Law

Qualified small issue bonds (commonly referred to as "industrial development bonds" or "small issue IDBs") are tax-exempt bonds issued by State and local governments to finance private business manufacturing facilities (including certain directly related and ancillary facilities) or the acquisition of land and equipment by certain farmers. In both instances, these bonds are subject to limits on the amount of financing that may be provided, both for a single borrowing and in the aggregate. In general, no more than $1 million of small-issue bond financing may be outstanding at any time for property of a business (including related parties) located in the same municipality or county. Generally, this $1 million limit may be increased to $10 million if, in addition to outstanding bonds, all other capital expenditures of the business (including related parties) in the same municipality or county are counted toward the limit over a six-year period that begins three years before the issue date of the bonds and ends three years after such date. Outstanding aggregate borrowing is limited to $40 million per borrower (including related parties) regardless of where the property is located.

The Code permits up to $10 million of capital expenditures to be disregarded, in effect increasing from $10 million to $20 million the maximum allowable amount of total capital expenditures by an eligible business in the same municipality or county. However, no more than $10 million of bond financing may be outstanding at any time for property of an eligible business (including related parties) located in the same municipality or county. Other limits (e.g., the $40 million per borrower limit) also continue to apply.

A manufacturing facility is any facility which is used in the manufacturing or production of tangible personal property (including the processing resulting in a change in the condition of such property). Manufacturing facilities include facilities that are directly related and ancillary to a manufacturing facility (as described in the previous sentence) if (1) such facilities are located on the same site as the manufacturing facility and (2) not more than 25 percent of the net proceeds of the issue are used to provide such facilities.[126]

---

80. For example, an ownership change has occurred for purposes of determining the testing period under section 382(i)(2).

126. The 25 percent restriction was enacted by the Technical and Miscellaneous Tax Act of 1988 because of concern over the scope of the definition of manufacturing facility. See H.R. Rpt. No. 100-795 (1988). The amendment was intended to clarify that while the manufacturing facility definition does not preclude the financing of ancillary activities, the 25 percent restriction was intended to limit the use of bond proceeds to finance facilities other than for "core manufacturing." The conference agreement followed the House bill, which the conference report described as follows: "The House bill clarifies that up to 25 percent of the proceeds of a qualified small issue may be used to finance ancillary activities which are carried out at the manufacturing site. All such ancillary activities must be subordinate and integral to the manufacturing process."

House Bill

No provision.

Senate Amendment

In general

For bonds issued after the date of enactment and before January 1, 2011, the provision expands the definition of manufacturing facilities to mean any facility that is used in the manufacturing, creation, or production of tangible property or intangible property (within the meaning of section 197(d)(1)(C)(iii)). For this purpose, intangible property means any patent, copyright, formula, process, design, knowhow, format, or other similar item. It is intended to include among other items, the creation of computer software, and intellectual property associated bio-tech and pharmaceuticals.

In lieu of the directly related and ancillary test of present law, the provision provides a special rule for bonds issued after the date of enactment and before January 1, 2011. For these bonds, the provision provides that facilities that are functionally related and subordinate to the manufacturing facility are treated as a manufacturing facility and the 25 percent of net proceeds restriction does not apply to such facilities.[127] Functionally related and subordinate facilities must be located on the same site as the manufacturing facility.

Conference Agreement

The conference follows the Senate amendment.

Effective Date

The provision is effective for bonds issued after date of enactment and before January 1, 2011.

[¶ 5052]   Section 1302.   Credit for investment in advanced energy facilities.

(Code Sec. 46, 48C)

[Conference Report]

Present Law

An income tax credit is allowed for the production of electricity from qualified energy resources at qualified facilities.[213] Qualified energy resources comprise wind, closed-loop biomass, open-loop biomass, geothermal energy, solar energy, small irrigation power, municipal solid waste, qualified hydropower production, and marine and hydrokinetic renewable energy. Qualified facilities are, generally, facilities that generate electricity using qualified energy resources.

An income tax credit is also allowed for certain energy property placed in service. Qualifying property includes certain fuel cell property, solar property, geothermal power production property, small wind energy property, combined heat and power system property, and geothermal heat pump property.[214]

In addition to these, numerous other credits are available to taxpayers to encourage renewable energy production and energy conservation, including, among others, credits for

---

127. The provision is based in part on a similar rule applicable to exempt facility bonds. Treas. Reg. sec. 1.103-8(a)(3) provides: "(3) Functionally related and subordinate. An exempt facility includes any land, building, or other property functionally related and subordinate to such facility. Property is not functionally related and subordinate to a facility if it is not of a character and size commensurate with the character and size of such facility."
213. Sec. 45. In addition to the electricity production credit, section 45 also provides income tax credits for the production of Indian coal and refined coal at qualified facilities.
214. Sec. 48.

certain biofuels, plug-in electric vehicles, and energy efficient appliances, and for improvements to heating, air conditioning, and insulation.

No credit is specifically designed under present law to encourage the development of a domestic manufacturing base to support the industries described above.

House Bill

No provision.

Senate Amendment

The Senate amendment establishes a 30 percent credit for investment in qualified property used in a qualified advanced energy manufacturing project. A qualified advanced energy project is a project that re-equips, expands, or establishes a manufacturing facility for the production: (1) property designed to be used to produce energy from the sun, wind, or geothermal deposits (within the meaning of section 613(e)(2)), or other renewable resources; (2) fuel cells, microturbines, or an energy storage system for use with electric or hybrid-electric motor vehicles; (3) electric grids to support the transmission of intermittent sources of renewable energy, including storage of such energy; (4) property designed to capture and sequester carbon dioxide; (5) property designed to refine or blend renewable fuels (but not fossil fuels) or to produce energy conservation technologies (including energy-conserving lighting technologies and smart grid technologies; or (6) other advanced energy property designed to reduce greenhouse gas emissions as may be determined by the Secretary.

Qualified property must be depreciable (or amortizable) property used in a qualified advanced energy project. Qualified property does not include property designed to manufacture equipment for use in the refining or blending of any transportation fuel other than renewable fuels. The basis of qualified property must be reduced by the amount of credit received.

Credits are available only for projects certified by the Secretary of Treasury, in consultation with the Secretary of Energy. The Secretary of Treasury must establish a certification program no later than 180 days after date of enactment, and may allocate up to $2 billion in credits.

In selecting projects, the Secretary may consider only those projects where there is a reasonable expectation of commercial viability. In addition, the Secretary must consider other selection criteria, including which projects (1) will provide the greatest domestic job creation; (2) will provide the greatest net impact in avoiding or reducing air pollutants or anthropogenic emissions of greenhouse gases; (3) have the greatest readiness for commercial employment, replication, and further commercial use in the United States, (4) will provide the greatest benefit in terms of newness in the commercial market; (5) have the lowest levelized cost of generated or stored energy, or of measured reduction in energy consumption or greenhouse gas emission; and (6) have the shortest project time from certification to completion.

Each project application must be submitted during the three-year period beginning on the date such certification program is established. An applicant for certification has two years from the date the Secretary accepts the application to provide the Secretary with evidence that the requirements for certification have been met. Upon certification, the applicant has five years from the date of issuance of the certification to place the project in service. Not later than six years after the date of enactment of the credit, the Secretary is required to review the credit allocations and redistribute any credits that were not used either because of a revoked certification or because of an insufficient quantity of credit applications.

872

Conference Agreement

The conference agreement follows the Senate amendment with the. following modifications. The conference agreement increases by $300 million (to $2.3 billion) the amount of credits that may be allocated by the Secretary. The conference agreement expands the list of qualifying advance energy projects to include projects designed to manufacture any new qualified plug-in electric drive motor vehicle (as defined by section 30D(c)), any specified vehicle (as defined by section 30D(f)(2)), or any component which is designed specifically for use with such vehicles, including any electric motor, generator, or power control unit. The conference agreement also replaces the third and fourth project selection criteria with a requirement that the Secretary, in addition to the remaining criteria, consider projects that have the greatest potential for technological innovation and commercial deployment.

In addition, the conference agreement shortens to two years the period during which project applications may be submitted, shortens to one year the period during which the project applicants must provide evidence that the certification requirements have been met, and shortens to three years the period during which certified projects must be placed in service. The conference agreement also shortens the period after which the Secretary must review the credit allocations from six to four years. Finally, the conference agreement clarifies that only tangible personal property and other tangible property (not including a building or its structural components) is credit-eligible.

Effective Date

The provision is effective on the date of enactment.

[¶ 5054]   Section 1401.   Recovery Zone Bonds.

(Code Sec. 1400U-1, 1400U-2, 1400U-3)

[Conference Report]

Present Law

In general

Under present law, gross income does not include interest on State or local bonds. State and local bonds are classified generally as either governmental bonds or private activity bonds. Governmental bonds are bonds the proceeds of which are primarily used to finance governmental functions or which are repaid with governmental funds. Private activity bonds are bonds in which the State or local government serves as a conduit providing financing to nongovernmental persons (e.g., private businesses or individuals). The exclusion from income for State and local bonds does not apply to private activity bonds unless the bonds are issued for certain permitted purposes ("qualified private activity bonds") and other Code requirements are met.

Private activity bonds

The Code defines a private activity bond as any bond that satisfies (1) the private business use test and the private security or payment test ("the private business test"); or (2) "the private loan financing test."[151]

Private business test

Under the private business test, a bond is a private activity bond if it is part of an issue in which:

---
151. Sec. 141.

(1.) More than 10 percent of the proceeds of the issue (including use of the bond-financed property) are to be used in the trade or business of any person other than a governmental unit ("private business use"); and

(2.) More than 10 percent of the payment of principal or interest on the issue is, directly or indirectly, secured by (a) property used or to be used for a private business use or (b) to be derived from payments in respect of property, or borrowed money, used or to be used for a private business use ("private payment test").[152]

A bond is not a private activity bond unless both parts of the private business test (i.e., the private business use test and the private payment test) are met. Thus, a facility that is 100 percent privately used does not cause the bonds financing such facility to be private activity bonds if the bonds are not secured by or paid with private payments. For example, land improvements that benefit a privately-owned factory may be financed with governmental bonds if the debt service on such bonds is not paid by the factory owner or other private parties and such bonds are not secured by the property.

Private loan financing test

A bond issue satisfies the private loan financing test if proceeds exceeding the lesser of $5 million or five percent of such proceeds are used directly or indirectly to finance loans to one or more nongovernmental persons. Private loans include both business and other (e.g., personal) uses and payments to private persons; however, in the case of business uses and payments, all private loans also constitute private business uses and payments subject to the private business test.

Arbitrage restrictions

The exclusion from income for interest on State and local bonds does not apply to any arbitrage bond.[153] An arbitrage bond is defined as any bond that is part of an issue if any proceeds of the issue are reasonably expected to be used (or intentionally are used) to acquire higher yielding investments or to replace funds that are used to acquire higher yielding investments.[154] In general, arbitrage profits may be earned only during specified periods (e.g., defined "temporary periods") before funds are needed for the purpose of the borrowing or on specified types of investments (e.g., "reasonably required reserve or replacement funds"). Subject to limited exceptions, investment profits that are earned during these periods or on such investments must be rebated to the Federal Government.

Qualified private activity bonds

Qualified private activity bonds permit States or local governments to act as conduits providing tax-exempt financing for certain private activities. The definition of qualified private activity bonds includes an exempt facility bond, or qualified mortgage, veterans' mortgage, small issue, redevelopment, 501(c)(3), or student loan bond (sec. 141(e)).

The definition of an exempt facility bond includes bonds issued to finance certain transportation facilities (airports, ports, mass commuting, and high-speed intercity rail facilities); qualified residential rental projects; privately owned and/or operated utility facilities (sewage, water, solid waste disposal, and local district heating and cooling facilities, certain private electric and gas facilities, and hydroelectric dam enhancements); public/private educational facilities; qualified green building and sustainable design projects; and qualified highway or surface freight transfer facilities (sec. 142(a)).

In most cases, the aggregate volume of qualified private activity bonds is restricted by annual aggregate volume limits imposed on bonds issued by issuers within each State

---

152. The 10 percent private business test is reduced to five percent in the case of private business uses (and payments with respect to such uses) that are unrelated to any governmental use being financed by the issue.
153. Sec. 103(a) and (b)(2).
154. Sec. 148.

("State volume cap"). For calendar year 2007, the State volume cap, which is indexed for inflation, equals $85 per resident of the State, or $256.24 million, if greater. Exceptions to the State volume cap are provided for bonds for certain governmentally owned facilities (e.g., airports, ports, high-speed intercity rail, and solid waste disposal) and bonds which are subject to separate local, State, or national volume limits (e.g., public/private educational facility bonds, enterprise zone facility bonds, qualified green building bonds, and qualified highway or surface freight transfer facility bonds).

Qualified private activity bonds generally are subject to restrictions on the use of proceeds for the acquisition of land and existing property. In addition, qualified private activity bonds generally are subject to restrictions on the use of proceeds to finance certain specified facilities (e.g., airplanes, skyboxes, other luxury boxes, health club facilities, gambling facilities, and liquor stores), and use of proceeds to pay costs of issuance (e.g., bond counsel and underwriter fees). Small issue and redevelopment bonds also are subject to additional restrictions on the use of proceeds for certain facilities (e.g., golf courses and massage parlors).

Moreover, the term of qualified private activity bonds generally may not exceed 120 percent of the economic life of the property being financed and certain public approval requirements (similar to requirements that typically apply under State law to issuance of governmental debt) apply under Federal law to issuance of private activity bonds.

Qualified tax credit bonds

In lieu of interest, holders of qualified tax credit bonds receive a tax credit that accrues quarterly. The following bonds are qualified tax credit bonds: qualified forestry conservation bonds, new clean renewable energy bonds, qualified energy conservation bonds, and qualified zone academy bonds.[155]

Section 54A of the Code sets forth general rules applicable to qualified tax credit bonds. These rules include requirements regarding the expenditure of available project proceeds, reporting, arbitrage, maturity limitations, and financial conflicts of interest, among other special rules.

A taxpayer who holds a qualified tax credit bond on one or more credit allowance dates of the bond during the taxable year shall be allowed a credit against the taxpayer's income tax for the taxable year. In general, the credit amount for any credit allowance date is 25 percent of the annual credit determined with respect to the bond. The annual credit is determined by multiplying the applicable credit rate by the outstanding face amount of the bond. The applicable credit rate for the bond is the rate that the Secretary estimates will permit the issuance of the qualified tax credit bond with a specified maturity or redemption date without discount and without interest cost to the qualified issuer.[156] The Secretary determines credit rates for tax credit bonds based on general assumptions about credit quality of the class of potential eligible issuers and such other factors as the Secretary deems appropriate. The Secretary may determine credit rates based on general credit market yield indexes and credit ratings. The credit is included in gross income and, under regulations prescribed by the Secretary, may be stripped.

Section 54A of the Code requires that 100 percent of the available project proceeds of qualified tax credit bonds must be used within the three-year period that begins on the date of issuance. Available project proceeds are proceeds from the sale of the bond issue less issuance costs (not to exceed two percent) and any investment earnings on such sale proceeds. To the extent less than 100 percent of the available project proceeds are used to finance qualified projects during the three-year spending period, bonds will continue to qualify as qualified tax credit bonds if unspent proceeds are used within 90 days from the end of such three-year period to redeem bonds. The three-year spending period may

---

155. See secs. 54B, 54C, 54D, and 54E.
156. Given the differences in credit quality and other characteristics of individual issuers, the Secretary cannot set credit rates in a manner that will allow each issuer to issue tax credit bonds at par.

be extended by the Secretary upon the issuer's request demonstrating that the failure to satisfy the three-year requirement is due to reasonable cause and the projects will continue to proceed with due diligence.

Qualified tax credit bonds generally are subject to the arbitrage requirements of section 148. However, available project proceeds invested during the three-year spending period are not subject to the arbitrage restrictions (i.e., yield restriction and rebate requirements). In addition, amounts invested in a reserve fund are not subject to the arbitrage restrictions to the extent: (1) such fund is funded at a rate not more rapid than equal annual installments; (2) such fund is funded in a manner reasonably expected to result in an amount not greater than an amount necessary to repay the issue; and (3) the yield on such fund is not greater than the average annual interest rate of tax-exempt obligations having a term of 10 years or more that are issued during the month the qualified tax credit bonds are issued.

The maturity of qualified tax credit bonds is the term that the Secretary estimates will result in the present value of the obligation to repay the principal on such bonds being equal to 50 percent of the face amount of such bonds, using as a discount rate the average annual interest rate of tax-exempt obligations having a term of 10 years or more that are issued during the month the qualified tax credit bonds are issued.

House Bill

In general

The provision permits an issuer to designate one or more areas as recovery zones. The area must have significant poverty, unemployment, general distress, or home foreclosures, or be any area for which a designation as an empowerment zone or renewal community is in effect. Issuers may issue recovery zone economic development bonds and recovery zone facility bonds with respect to these zones.

There is a national recovery zone economic development bond limitation of $10 billion. In addition, there is a separate national recovery zone facility bond limitation of $15 billion. The Secretary is to separately allocate the bond limitations among the States in the proportion that each State's employment decline bears to the national decline in employment (the aggregate 2008 State employment declines for all States). In turn each State is to reallocate its allocation among the counties (parishes) and large municipalities in such State in the proportion that each such county or municipality's 2008 employment decline bears to the aggregate employment declines for all counties and municipalities in such State. In calculating the local employment decline with respect to a county, the portion of such decline attributable to a large municipality is disregarded for purposes of determining the county's portion of the State employment decline and is attributable to the large municipality only.

For purposes of the provision "2008 State employment decline" means, with respect to any State, the excess (if any) of (i) the number of individuals employed in such State as determined for December 2007, over (ii) the number of individuals employed in such State as determined for December 2008. The term "large municipality" means a municipality with a population of more than 100,000.

Recovery Zone Economic Development Bonds

New section 54AA(h) of the House bill creates a special rule for qualified bonds (a type of taxable governmental bond) issued before January 1, 2011, that entitles the issuer of such bonds to receive an advance tax credit equal to 35 percent of the interest payable on an interest payment date. For taxable governmental bonds that are designated recovery zone economic development bonds, the applicable percentage is 55 percent.

A recovery zone economic development bond is a taxable governmental bond issued as part of an issue if 100 percent of the available project proceeds of such issue are to be used for one or more qualified economic development purposes and the issuer designates such bond for purposes of this section. A qualified economic development purpose means expenditures for purposes of promoting development or other economic activity in a recovery zone, including (1) capital expenditures paid or incurred with respect to property located in such zone, (2) expenditures for public infrastructure and construction of public facilities located in a recovery zone.

The aggregate face amount of bonds which may be designated by any issuer cannot exceed the amount of the recovery zone economic development bond limitation allocated to such issuer.

Recovery Zone Facility Bonds

The provision creates a new category of exempt facility bonds, "recovery zone facility bonds." A recovery zone facility bond means any bond issued as part of an issue if: (1) 95 percent or more of the net proceeds of such issue are to be used for recovery zone property and (2) such bond is issued before January 1, 2011, and (3) the issuer designates such bond as a recovery zone facility bond. The aggregate face amount of bonds which may be designated by any issuer cannot exceed the amount of the recovery zone facility bond limitation allocated to such issuer.

Under the provision, the term "recovery zone property" means any property subject to depreciation to which section 168 applies (or would apply but for section 179) if (1) such property was acquired by the taxpayer by purchase after the date on which the designation of the recovery zone took effect; (2) the original use of such property in the recovery zone commences with the taxpayer; and (3) substantially all of the use of such property is in the recovery zone and is in the active conduct of a qualified business by the taxpayer in such zone. The term "qualified business" means any trade or business except that the rental to others of real property located in a recovery zone shall be treated as a qualified business only if the property is not residential rental property (as defined in section 168(e)(2)) and does not include any trade or business consisting of the operation of any facility described in section 144(c)(6)(B) (i.e., any private or commercial golf course, country club, massage parlor, hot tub facility, suntan facility, racetrack or other facility used for gambling, or any store the principal purpose of which is the sale of alcoholic beverages for consumption off premises).

Subject to the following exceptions and modifications, issuance of recovery zone facility bonds is subject to the general rules applicable to issuance of qualified private activity bonds:

(1.) Issuance of the bonds is not subject to the aggregate annual State private activity bond volume limits (sec. 146);

(2.) The restriction on acquisition of existing property does not apply (sec. 147(d));

Senate Amendment

In general

The Senate amendment is the same as the House bill with a modification for allocating the bonds between the States. Under the Senate amendment each State receives a minimum allocation of one percent of the national recovery zone economic development bond limitation and one percent of the national recovery zone facility bond limitation. The remainder of each bond limitation is separately allocated among the States in the proportion that each State's employment decline bears to the national decline in employment (the aggregate 2008 State employment declines for all States).

Recovery Zone Economic Development Bonds

New section 54AA(g) of the Senate amendment creates a special rule for qualified bonds (a type of Build America Bond) issued before January 1, 2011, that entitles the issuer of such bonds to receive an advance tax credit equal to 35 percent of the interest payable on an interest payment date. For Build America Bonds that are designated recovery zone economic development bonds, the applicable percentage is 40 percent. In other respects the Senate amendment is the same as the House bill.

Recovery Zone Facility Bonds

The Senate amendment is the same as the House bill.

Conference Agreement

In general

The conference agreement follows the House bill, with a modification for allocating the bond limitations among the States. Under the conference agreement the national recovery zone economic development bond limitation and national recovery zone facility bond limitation are allocated among the States in the proportion that each State's employment decline bears to the national decline in employment (the aggregate 2008 State employment declines for all States).[157] The Secretary is to adjust each State's allocation for a calendar year such that no State receives less than 0.9 percent of the national recovery zone economic development bond limitation and no less than 0.9 percent of the national recovery zone facility bond limitation. The conference agreement also permits a county or large municipality to waive all or part of its allocation of the State bond limitations to allow further allocation within that State. With respect to all other aspects of the allocation of the bond limitations, the conference agreement follows the House bill.

The conference agreement also provides that a "recovery zone" includes any area designated by the issuer as economically distressed by reason of the closure or realignment of a military installation pursuant to the Defense Base Closure and Realignment Act of 1990.

Recovery Zone Economic Development Bonds

The conference agreement follows the House bill, except the issuer of recovery zone economic development bonds is entitled to receive an advance tax credit equal to 45 percent of the interest payable on an interest payment date and the conference agreement allows for a reasonably required reserve fund to be funded from the proceeds of a recovery zone economic development bond.

Recovery Zone Facility Bonds

The conference agreement follows the House bill, except "recovery zone property" is defined as any property subject to depreciation to which section 168 applies (or would apply but for section 179) if (1) such property was constructed, reconstructed, renovated, or acquired by purchase by the taxpayer after the date on which the designation of the recovery zone took effect; (2) the original use of such property in the recovery zone commences with the taxpayer; and (3) substantially all of the use of such property is in the recovery zone and is in the active conduct of a qualified business by the taxpayer in such zone.

Effective Date

The provision is effective for obligations issued after the date of enactment.

---

157. The Bureau of Labor Statistics prepares data on regional and State employment and unemployment. See e.g., Bureau of Labor Statistics, USDL 09-0093, *Regional and State Employment and Unemployment: December 2008* (January 27, 2009) ⟨http://www.bls.gov/news.release/laus.nr0.htm⟩.

[¶ 5056]   **Section 1402.**   **Tribal Economic Development Bonds.**

(Code Sec. 7871)

[Conference Report]

Present Law

Under present law, gross income does not include interest on State or local bonds.[158] State and local bonds are classified generally as either governmental bonds or private activity bonds. Governmental bonds are bonds the proceeds of which are primarily used to finance governmental facilities or the debt is repaid with governmental funds. Private activity bonds are bonds in which the State or local government serves as a conduit providing financing to nongovernmental persons. For these purposes, the term "nongovernmental person" includes the Federal government and all other individuals and entities other than States or local governments.[159] Interest on private activity bonds is taxable, unless the bonds are issued for certain purposes permitted by the Code and other requirements are met.[160]

Although not States or subdivisions of States, Indian tribal governments are provided with a tax status similar to State and local governments for specified purposes under the Code.[161] Among the purposes for which a tribal government is treated as a State is the issuance of tax-exempt bonds. Under section 7871(c), tribal governments are authorized to issue tax-exempt bonds only if substantially all of the proceeds are used for essential governmental functions.[162] The term essential governmental function does not include any function that is not customarily performed by State and local governments with general taxing powers. Section 7871(c) further prohibits Indian tribal governments from issuing tax-exempt private activity bonds (as defined in section 141(a)of the Code) with the exception of certain bonds for manufacturing facilities.

House Bill

Tribal Economic Development Bonds

The provision allows Indian tribal governments to issue "tribal economic development bonds." There is a national bond limitation of $2 billion, to be allocated as the Secretary determines appropriate, in consultation with the Secretary of the Interior. Tribal economic development bonds issued by an Indian tribal government are treated as if such bond were issued by a State except that section 146 (relating to State volume limitations) does not apply.

A tribal economic development bond is any bond issued by an Indian tribal government (1) the interest on which would be tax-exempt if issued by a State or local government but would be taxable under section 7871(c), and (2) that is designated by the Indian tribal government as a tribal economic development bond. The aggregate face amount of bonds that may be designated by any Indian tribal government cannot exceed the amount of national tribal economic development bond limitation allocated to such government.

Tribal economic development bonds cannot be used to finance any portion of a building in which class II or class III gaming (as defined in section 4 of the Indian Gaming Regulatory Act) is conducted, or housed, or any other property used in the conduct of such gaming. Nor can tribal economic development bonds be used to finance any facility located outside of the Indian reservation.

---

158. Sec. 103.
159. Sec. 141(b)(6); Treas. Reg. sec.1.141-1(b).
160. Secs. 103(b)(1) and 141.
161. Sec. 7871.
162. Sec. 7871(c).

Treasury study

The provision requires that the Treasury Department study the effects of tribal economic development bonds. One year after the date of enactment, a report is to be submitted to Congress providing the results of such study along with any recommendations, including whether the restrictions of section 7871(c) should be eliminated or otherwise modified.

Senate Amendment

The Senate amendment is the same as the House bill except the Senate amendment defines a tribal economic development bond as any bond issued by an Indian tribal government (1) the interest on which would be tax-exempt if issued by a State or local government, and (2) that is designated by the Indian tribal government as a tribal economic development bond.

The Senate amendment also clarifies that for purposes of section 141 of the Code, use of bond proceeds by an Indian tribe, or instrumentality thereof, is treated as use by a State.

Conference Agreement

The conference agreement follows the Senate amendment.

Effective Date

The provision applies to obligations issued after the date of enactment.

[¶ 5057]   Section 1403.   Increase in new markets tax credit.

(Code Sec. 45D)

[Conference Report]

Present Law

Section 45D provides a new markets tax credit for qualified equity investments made to acquire stock in a corporation, or a capital interest in a partnership, that is a qualified community development entity ("CDE").[165] The amount of the credit allowable to the investor (either the original purchaser or a subsequent holder) is (1) a five-percent credit for the year in which the equity interest is purchased from the CDE and for each of the following two years, and (2) a six-percent credit for each of the following four years. The credit is determined by applying the applicable percentage (five or six percent) to the amount paid to the CDE for the investment at its original issue, and is available for a taxable year to the taxpayer who holds the qualified equity investment on the date of the initial investment or on the respective anniversary date that occurs during the taxable year. The credit is recaptured if, at any time during the seven-year period that begins on the date of the original issue of the qualified equity investment, the issuing entity ceases to be a qualified CDE, the proceeds of the investment cease to be used as required, or the equity investment is redeemed.

A qualified CDE is any domestic corporation or partnership: (1) whose primary mission is serving or providing investment capital for low-income communities or low-income persons; (2) that maintains accountability to residents of low-income communities by providing them with representation on any governing board of or any advisory board to the CDE; and (3) that is certified by the Secretary as being a qualified CDE. A qualified equity investment means stock (other than nonqualified preferred stock) in a corporation or a capital interest in a partnership that is acquired directly from a CDE for cash, and includes an investment of a subsequent purchaser if such invest-

---

165. Section 45D was added by section 121(a) of the Community Renewal Tax Relief Act of 2000, Pub. L. No. 106-554 (2000).

ment was a qualified equity investment in the hands of the prior holder. Substantially all of the investment proceeds must be used by the CDE to make qualified low-income community investments. For this purpose, qualified low-income community investments include: (1) capital or equity investments in, or loans to, qualified active low-income community businesses; (2) certain financial counseling and other services to businesses and residents in low-income communities; (3) the purchase from another CDE of any loan made by such entity that is a qualified low-income community investment; or (4) an equity investment in, or loan to, another CDE.

A "low-income community" is a population census tract with either (1) a poverty rate of at least 20 percent or (2) median family income which does not exceed 80 percent of the greater of metropolitan area median family income or statewide median family income (for a non-metropolitan census tract, does not exceed 80 percent of statewide median family income). In the case of a population census tract located within a high migration rural county, low-income is defined by reference to 85 percent (rather than 80 percent) of statewide median family income. For this purpose, a high migration rural county is any county that, during the 20-year period ending with the year in which the most recent census was conducted, has a net out-migration of inhabitants from the county of at least 10 percent of the population of the county at the beginning of such period.

The Secretary has the authority to designate "targeted populations" as low-income communities for purposes of the new markets tax credit. For this purpose, a "targeted population" is defined by reference to section 103(20) of the Riegle Community Development and Regulatory Improvement Act of 1994 (12 U.S.C. 4702(20)) to mean individuals, or an identifiable group of individuals, including an Indian tribe, who (A) are low-income persons; or (B) otherwise lack adequate access to loans or equity investments. Under such Act, "low-income" means (1) for a targeted population within a metropolitan area, less than 80 percent of the area median family income; and (2) for a targeted population within a non-metropolitan area, less than the greater of 80 percent of the area median family income or 80 percent of the statewide non-metropolitan area median family income.[166] Under such Act, a targeted population is not required to be within any census tract. In addition, a population census tract with a population of less than 2,000 is treated as a low-income community for purposes of the credit if such tract is within an empowerment zone, the designation of which is in effect under section 1391, and is contiguous to one or more low-income communities.

A qualified active low-income community business is defined as a business that satisfies, with respect to a taxable year, the following requirements: (1) at least 50 percent of the total gross income of the business is derived from the active conduct of trade or business activities in any low-income community; (2) a substantial portion of the tangible property of such business is used in a low-income community; (3) a substantial portion of the services performed for such business by its employees is performed in a low-income community; and (4) less than five percent of the average of the aggregate unadjusted bases of the property of such business is attributable to certain financial property or to certain collectibles.

The maximum annual amount of qualified equity investments is capped at $3.5 billion per year for calendar years 2006 through 2009. Lower caps applied for calendar years 2001 through 2005.

House Bill

No provision.

---

166. 12 U.S.C. sec. 4702(17) (defines "low-income" for purposes of 12 U.S.C. sec. 4702(20)).

Senate Amendment

For calendar years 2008 and 2009, the Senate amendment increases the maximum amount of qualified equity investments by $1.5 billion (to $5 billion for each year). The Senate amendment requires that the additional amount for 2008 be allocated to qualified CDEs that submitted an allocation application with respect to calendar year 2008 and either (1) did not receive an allocation for such calendar year, or (2) received an allocation for such calendar year in an amount less than the amount requested in the allocation application. The Senate amendment also provides alternative minimum tax relief for equity investment allocations subject to the 2009 annual limitation.

Conference Agreement

The conference agreement generally follows the Senate amendment but does not provide for any alternative minimum tax relief

Effective Date

The provision is effective on the date of enactment.

[¶ 5058]   Section 1404, 1602.   Coordination of low-income housing credit and low-income housing grants; Grants to States for low-income housing projects in lieu of low-income housing credit allocations for 2009.

(Code Sec. 42)

[Conference Report]

Present Law

In general

The low-income housing credit may be claimed over a 10-year period by owners of certain residential rental property for the cost of rental housing occupied by tenants having incomes below specified levels.[13] The amount of the credit for any taxable year in the credit period is the applicable percentage of the qualified basis of each qualified low-income building. The qualified basis of any qualified low-income building for any taxable year equals the applicable fraction of the eligible basis of the building.

Volume limits

A low-income housing credit is allowable only if the owner of a qualified building receives a housing credit allocation from the State or local housing credit agency. Generally, the aggregate credit authority provided annually to each State for calendar year 2009 is $2.30 per resident, with a minimum annual cap of $2,665,000 for certain small population States.[14] These amounts are indexed for inflation. Projects that also receive financing with proceeds of tax-exempt bonds issued subject to the private activity bond volume limit do not require an allocation of the low-income housing credit.

Basic rule for Federal grants

The basis of a qualified building must be reduced by the amount of any federal granty [*sic:* grant] with respect to such building.

[House Report]

Reasons for Change

The current economic downturn has reduced the attractiveness of low-income housing tax credits to potential investors, in part, because some potential investors have reduced

---

13. Sec. 42.
14. Rev. Proc. 2008-66.

or no taxable income to offset with these tax credits. The Committee believes that this provision gives State allocating agencies added flexibility and will encourage the building of more low-income housing in the short-term until investors can again use these tax credits.

[Conference Report]

House Bill

Low-income housing grant election amount

The Secretary of the Treasury shall make a grant to the State housing credit agency of each State in an amount equal to the low-income housing grant election amount.

The low-income housing grant election amount for a State is an amount elected by the State subject to certain limits. The maximum low-income housing grant election amount for a State may not exceed 85 percent of the product of ten and the sum of the State's: (1) unused housing credit ceiling for 2008; (2) any returns to the State during 2009 of credit allocations previously made by the State; (3) 40 percent of the State's 2009 credit allocation; and (4) 40 percent of the State's share of the national pool allocated in 2009, if any).

Grants under this provision are not taxable income to recipients.

Subawards to low-income housing credit buildings

A State receiving a grant under this provision is to use these monies to make subawards to finance the construction, or acquisition and rehabilitation of qualified low-income buildings as defined under the low-income housing credit. A subaward may be made to finance a qualified low-income building regardless of whether the building has an allocation of low-income housing credit. However, in the case of qualified low-income buildings without allocations of the low-income housing credit, the State housing credit agency must make a determination that the sub award with respect to such building will increase the total funds available to the State to build and rehabilitate affordable housing. In conjunction with this determination the State housing credit agency must establish a process in which applicants for the subawards must demonstrate good faith efforts to obtain investment commitments before the agency makes such subawards.

Any building receiving grant money from a subaward is required to satisfy the low income housing credit rules. The State housing credit agency shall perform asset management functions to ensure compliance with the low-income housing credit rules and the long-term viability of buildings financed with these subawards.[15] Failure to satisfy the low-income housing credit rules will result in recapture enforced by means of liens or other methods that the Secretary of the Treasury (or delegate) deems appropriate. Any such recapture will be payable to the Secretary of the Treasury for deposit in the general fund of the Treasury.

Any grant funds not used to make subawards before January 1, 2011 and any grant monies from subawards returned on or after January 1, 2011 must be returned to the Secretary of the Treasury.

Basic rule for Federal grants

The grants received under this provision do not reduce tax basis of a qualified low-income building.

---

15. The State housing credit agency may collect reasonable fees from subaward recipients to cover the expenses of the agency's asset management duties. Alternatively, the State housing credit agency may retain a third-party to perform these asset management duties.

Reduction in low-income housing credit volume limit for 2009

The otherwise applicable low-income housing credit volume limit for any State for 2009 is reduced by the amount taken into account in determining the low-income housing grant election amount.

Appropriations

The provision appropriates to the Secretary of the Treasury such sums as may be necessary to carry out this provision.

Senate Amendment

No provision.

Conference Agreement

The conference agreement follows the House bill.

Effective Date

The provision is effective on the date of enactment.

[¶ 5060]   Section 1501.   De minimis safe harbor exception for tax-exempt interest expense of financial institutions; Modification of small issuer exception to tax-exempt interest expense allocation rules for financial institutions.

(Code Sec. 265, 291)

[Conference Report]

Present Law

Present law disallows a deduction for interest on indebtedness incurred or continued to purchase or carry obligations the interest on which is exempt from tax.[116] In general, an interest deduction is disallowed only if the taxpayer has a purpose of using borrowed funds to purchase or carry tax-exempt obligations; a determination of the taxpayer's purpose in borrowing funds is made based on all of the facts and circumstances.[117]

Two-percent rule for individuals and certain nonfinancial corporations

In the absence of direct evidence linking an individual taxpayer's indebtedness with the purchase or carrying of tax-exempt obligations, the Internal Revenue Service takes the position that it ordinarily will not infer that a taxpayer's purpose in borrowing money was to purchase or carry tax-exempt obligations if the taxpayer's investment in tax-exempt obligations is "insubstantial."[118] An individual's holdings of tax-exempt obligations are presumed to be insubstantial if during the taxable year the average adjusted basis of the individual's tax-exempt obligations is two percent or less of the average adjusted basis of the individual's portfolio investments and assets held by the individual in the active conduct of a trade or business.

Similarly, in the case of a corporation that is not a financial institution or a dealer in tax-exempt obligations, where there is no direct evidence of a purpose to purchase or carry tax-exempt obligations, the corporation's holdings of tax-exempt obligations are presumed to be insubstantial if the average adjusted basis of the corporation's tax-exempt obligations is two percent or less of the average adjusted basis of all assets held by the corporation in the active conduct of its trade or business.

116. Sec. 265(a).
117. See Rev. Proc. 72-18, 1972-1 C.B. 740.
118. *Id.*

Financial institutions

In the case of a financial institution, the Code generally disallows that portion of the taxpayer's interest expense that is allocable to tax-exempt interest.[119] The amount of interest that is disallowed is an amount which bears the same ratio to such interest expense as the taxpayer's average adjusted bases of tax-exempt obligations acquired after August 7, 1986, bears to the average adjusted bases for all assets of the taxpayer.

Exception for certain obligations of qualified small issuers

The general rule in section 265(b), denying financial institutions' interest expense deductions allocable to tax-exempt obligations, does not apply to "qualified tax-exempt obligations."[120] Instead, as discussed in the next section, only 20 percent of the interest expense allocable to "qualified tax-exempt obligations" is disallowed.[121] A "qualified tax-exempt obligation" is a tax-exempt obligation that (1) is issued after August 7, 1986, by a qualified small issuer, (2) is not a private activity bond, and (3) is designated by the issuer as qualifying for the exception from the general rule of section 265(b).

A "qualified small issuer" is an issuer that reasonably anticipates that the amount of tax-exempt obligations that it will issue during the calendar year will be $10 million or less.[122] The Code specifies, the circumstances under which an issuer and all subordinate entities are aggregated.[123] For purposes of the $10 million limitation, an issuer and all entities that issue obligations on behalf of such issuer, are treated as one issuer. All obligations issued by a subordinate entity are treated as being issued by the entity to which it is subordinate. An entity formed (or availed of) to avoid the $10 million limitation and all entities benefiting from the device are treated as one issuer.

Composite issues (i.e., combined issues of bonds for different entities) qualify for the "qualified tax-exempt obligation" exception only if the requirements of the exception are met with respect to (1) the composite issue as a whole (determined by treating the composite issue as a single issue) and (2) each separate lot of obligations that is part of the issue (determined by treating each separate lot of obligations as a separate issue).[124] Thus, a composite issue may qualify for the exception only if the composite issue itself does not exceed $10 million, and if each issuer benefitting from the composite issue reasonably anticipates that it will not issue more than $10 million of tax-exempt obligations during the calendar year, including through the composite arrangement.

Treatment of financial institution preference items

Section 291(a)(3) reduces by 20 percent the amount allowable as a deduction with respect to any financial institution preference item. Financial institution preference items include interest on debt to carry tax-exempt obligations acquired after December 31, 1982, and before August 8, 1986.[125] Section 265(b)(3) treats qualified tax-exempt obligations as if they were acquired on August 7, 1986. As a result, the amount allowable as a deduction by a financial institution with respect to interest incurred to carry a qualified tax-exempt obligation is reduced by 20 percent.

House Bill

Two-percent safe harbor for financial institutions

The provision provides that tax-exempt obligations issued during 2009 or 2010 and held by a financial institution, in an amount not to exceed two percent of the adjusted

---

119. Sec. 265(b)(1). A "financial institution" is any person that (1) accepts deposits from the public in the ordinary course of such person's trade or business and is subject to Federal or State supervision as a financial institution or (2) is a corporation described in section 585(a)(2). Sec. 265(b)(5).
120. Sec. 265(b)(3).
121. Secs. 265(b)(3)(A), 291(a)(3) and 291(e)(1).
122. Sec. 265(b)(3)(C).
123. Sec. 265(b)(3)(E).
124. Sec. 265(b)(3)(F).
125. Sec. 291(e)(1).

basis of the financial institution's assets, are not taken into account for the purpose of determining the portion of the financial institution's interest expense subject to the pro rata interest disallowance rule of section 265(b). For purposes of this rule, a refunding bond (whether a current or advance refunding) is treated as issued on the date of the issuance of the refunded bond (or in the case of a series of refundings, the original bond).

The provision also amends section 291(e) to provide that tax-exempt obligations issued during 2009 and 2010, and not taken into account for purposes of the calculation of a financial institution's interest expense subject to the pro rata interest disallowance rule, are treated as having been acquired on August 7, 1986. As a result, such obligations are financial institution preference items, and the amount allowable as a deduction by a financial institution with respect to interest incurred to carry such obligations is reduced by 20 percent.

Modifications to qualified small issuer exception

With respect to tax-exempt obligations issued during 2009 and 2010, the provision increases from $10 million to $30 million the annual limit for qualified small issuers.

In addition, in the case of "qualified financing issue" issued in 2009 or 2010, the provision applies the $30 million annual volume limitation at the borrower level (rather than at the level of the pooled financing issuer). Thus, for the purpose of applying the requirements of the section 265(b)(3) qualified small issuer exception, the portion of the proceeds of a qualified financing issue that are loaned to a "qualified borrower" that participates in the issue are treated as a separate issue with respect to which the qualified borrower is deemed to be the issuer.

A "qualified financing issue" is any composite, pooled or other conduit financing issue the proceeds of which are used directly or indirectly to make or finance loans to one or more ultimate borrowers all of whom are qualified borrowers. A "qualified borrower" means (1) a State or political subdivision of a State or (2) an organization described in section 501(c)(3) and exempt from tax under section 501(a). Thus, for example, a $100 million pooled financing issue that was issued in 2009 could qualify for the section 265(b)(3) exception if the proceeds of such issue were used to make four equal loans of $25 million to four qualified borrowers. However, if (1) more than $30 million were loaned to any qualified borrower, (2) any borrower were not a qualified borrower, or (3) any borrower would, if it were the issuer of a separate issue in an amount equal to the amount loaned to such borrower, fail to meet any of the other requirements of section 265(b)(3), the entire $100 million pooled financing issue would fail to qualify for the exception.

For purposes of determining whether an issuer meets the requirements of the small issuer exception, qualified 501(c)(3) bonds issued in 2009 or 2010 are treated as if they were issued by the 501(c)(3) organization for whose benefit they were issued (and not by the actual issuer of such bonds). In addition, in the case of an organization described in section 501(c)(3) and exempt from taxation under section 501(a), requirements for "qualified financing issues" shall be applied as if the section 501(c)(3) organization were the issuer. Thus, in any event, an organization described in section 501(c)(3) and exempt from taxation under section 501(a) shall be limited to the: $30 million per issuer cap for qualified tax-exempt obligations described in section 265(b)(3).

Senate Amendment

The Senate amendment is the same as the House bill.

Conference Agreement

The conference agreement follows the House bill and the Senate amendment.

Effective Date

The provisions are effective for obligations issued after December 31, 2008.

[¶ 5062]   Section 1503.   Temporary modification of alternative minimum tax limitations on tax-exempt bonds.

(Code Sec. 57, 56)

[Conference Report]

Present Law

Present law imposes an alternative minimum tax ("AMT") on individuals and corporations. AMT is the amount by which the tentative minimum tax exceeds the regular income tax. The tentative minimum tax is computed based upon a taxpayer's alternative minimum taxable income ("AMTI"). AMTI is the taxpayer's taxable income modified to take into account certain preferences and adjustments. One of the preference items is tax-exempt interest on certain tax-exempt bonds issued for private activities (sec. 57(a)(5)). Also, in the case of a corporation, an adjustment based on current earnings is determined, in part, by taking into account 75 percent of items, including tax-exempt interest, that are excluded from taxable income but included in the corporation's earnings and profits (sec. 56(g)(4)(B)).

House Bill

The House bill provides that tax-exempt interest on private activity bonds issued in 2009 and 2010 is not an item of tax preference for purposes of the alternative minimum tax and interest on tax exempt bonds issued in 2009 and 2010 is not included in the corporate adjustment based on current earnings. For these purposes, a refunding bond is treated as issued on the date of the issuance of the refunded bond (or in the case of a series of refundings, the original bond).

Senate Amendment

The Senate amendment is the same as the House bill.

Conference Agreement

The conference agreement provides that tax-exempt interest on private activity bonds issued in 2009 and 2010 is not an item of tax preference for purposes of the alternative minimum tax and interest on tax exempt bonds issued in 2009 and 2010 is not included in the corporate adjustment based on current earnings. For these purposes, a refunding bond is treated as issued on the date of the issuance of the refunded bond (or in the case of a series of refundings, the original bond).

The conference agreement also provides that tax-exempt interest on private activity bonds issued in 2009 and 2010 to currently refund a private activity bond issued after December 31, 2003, and before January 1, 2009, is not an item of tax preference for purposes of the alternative minimum tax. Also tax-exempt interest on bonds issued in 2009 and 2010 to currently refund a bond issued after December 31, 2003, and before January 1, 2009, is not included in the corporate adjustment based on current earnings.

Effective Date

The provision applies to interest on bonds issued after December 31, 2008.

[¶ 5063]   Section 1504.   Modification to high speed intercity rail facility bonds.

(Code Sec. 142)

[Conference Report]

Present Law

In general

Under present law, gross income does not include interest on State or local bonds. State and local bonds are classified generally as either governmental bonds or private activity bonds. Governmental bonds are bonds the proceeds of which are primarily used to finance governmental functions or which are repaid with governmental funds. Private activity bonds are bonds in which the State or local government serves as a conduit providing financing to nongovernmental persons (e.g., private businesses or individuals). The exclusion from income for State and local bonds does not apply to private activity bonds unless the bonds are issued for certain permitted purposes ("qualified private activity bonds") and other Code requirements are met.

High-speed rail

An exempt facility bond is a type of qualified private activity bond. Exempt facility bonds can be issued for high-speed intercity rail facilities. A facility qualifies as a high-speed intercity rail facility if it is a facility (other than rolling stock) for fixed guideway rail transportation of passengers and their baggage between metropolitan statistical areas. The facilities must use vehicles that are reasonably expected to operate at speeds in excess of 150 miles per hour between scheduled stops and the facilities must be made available to members of the general public as passengers. If the bonds are to be issued for a non-governmental owner of the facility, such owner must irrevocably elect not to claim depreciation or credits with respect to the property financed by the net proceeds of the issue.

The Code imposes a special redemption requirement for these types of bonds. Any proceeds not used within three years of the date of issuance of the bonds must be used within the following six months to redeem such bonds.

Seventy-five percent of the principal amount of the bonds issued for high-speed rail facilities is exempt from the volume limit. If all the property to be financed by the net proceeds of the issue is to be owned by a governmental unit, then such bonds are completely exempt from the volume limit.

House Bill

No provision.

Senate Amendment

In general

The provision modifies the requirement that high-speed intercity rail transportation facilities use vehicles that are reasonably expected to operate at speeds in excess of 150 miles per hour. Instead, under the provision such facilities must use vehicles capable of attaining a maximum speed in excess of 150 miles per hour.

Conference Agreement

The conference agreement follows the Senate amendment.

Effective Date

The provision is effective for obligations issued after the date of enactment.

[¶ 5065] Section 1511. Delay in application of withholding tax on government contractors.

(Code Sec. 3402)

[Conference Report]

Present Law

For payments made after December 31, 2010, the Code imposes a withholding requirement at a three-percent rate on certain payments to persons providing property or services made by the Government of the United States, every State, every political subdivision thereof, and every instrumentality of the foregoing (including multi-State agencies). The withholding requirement applies regardless of whether the government entity making such payment is the recipient of the property or services. Political subdivisions of States (or any instrumentality thereof) with less than $100 million of annual expenditures for property or services that would otherwise be subject to withholding are exempt from the withholding requirement.

Payments subject to the three-percent withholding requirement include any payment made in connection with a government voucher or certificate program which functions as a payment for property or services. For example, payments to a commodity producer under a government commodity support program are subject to the withholding requirement. Present law also imposes information reporting requirements on the payments that are subject to withholding requirement.

The three-percent withholding requirement does not apply to any payments made through a Federal, State, or local government public assistance or public welfare program for which eligibility is determined by a needs or income test. The three-percent withholding requirement also does not apply to payments of wages or to any other payment with respect to which mandatory (e.g., U.S.-source income of foreign taxpayers) or voluntary (e.g., unemployment benefits) withholding applies under present law. Although the withholding requirement applies to payments that are potentially subject to backup withholding under section 3406, it does not apply to those payments from which amounts are actually being withheld under backup withholding rules.

The three-percent withholding requirement also does not apply to the following: payments of interest; payments for real property; payments to tax-exempt entities or foreign governments; intra-governmental payments; payments made pursuant to a classified or confidential contract (as defined in section 6050M(e)(3); and payments to government employees that are not otherwise excludable from the new withholding proposal with respect to the employees' services as employees.

House Bill

The provision repeals the three-percent withholding requirement on government payments.

Senate Amendment

The provision delays the implementation of the three percent withholding requirement by one year to apply to payments after December 31, 2011.

Conference Agreement

The conference follows the Senate amendment.

Effective Date

The provision is effect on the date of enactment.

[¶ 5067]   Section 1521.   Qualified school construction bonds.

(Code Sec. 54F)

[Conference Report]

Present Law

Tax-exempt bonds

Interest on State and local governmental bonds generally is excluded from gross income for Federal income tax purposes if the proceeds of the bonds are used to finance direct activities of these governmental units or if the bonds are repaid with revenues of the governmental units. These can include tax-exempt bonds which finance public schools.[128] An issuer must file with the Internal Revenue Service certain information about the bonds issued in order for that bond issue to be tax-exempt.[129] Generally, this information return is required to be filed no later than the 15th day of the second month after the close of the calendar quarter in which the bonds were issued.

The tax exemption for State and local bonds does not apply to any arbitrage bond.[130] An arbitrage bond is defined as any bond that is part of an issue if any proceeds of the issue are reasonably expected to be used (or intentionally are used) to acquire higher yielding investments or to replace funds that are used to acquire higher yielding investments.[131] In general, arbitrage profits may be earned only during specified periods (e.g., defined "temporary periods") before funds are needed for the purpose of the borrowing or,on specified types of investments (e.g., "reasonably required reserve or replacement funds"). Subject to limited exceptions, investment profits that are earned during these periods or on such investments must be rebated to the Federal Government.

Qualified zone academy bonds

As an alternative to traditional tax-exempt bonds, States and local governments were given the authority to issue "qualified zone academy bonds."[132] A total of $400 million of qualified zone academy bonds is authorized to be issued annually in calendar years 1998 through 2009. The $400 million aggregate bond cap is allocated each year to the States according to their respective populations of individuals below the poverty line. Each State, in sum, allocates the credit authority to qualified zone academies within such State.

A taxpayer holding a qualified zone academy bond on the credit allowance date is entitled to a credit. The credit is includible in gross income (as if it were a taxable interest payment on the bond), and may be claimed against regular income tax and alternative minimum tax liability.

The Treasury Department the credit rate at a rate estimated to allow issuance of qualified zone academy bonds without discount and without interest cost to the issuer.[133] The Secretary determines credit rates for tax credit bonds based on general assumptions about credit quality of the class of potential eligible issuers and such other factors as the Secretary deems appropriate. The Secretary may determine credit rates based on general credit market yield indexes and credit ratings. The maximum term of the bond is determined by the Treasury Department, so that the present value of the obligation to repay the principal on the bond is 50 percent of the face value of the bond.

---

128. Sec. 103.
129. Sec. 149(e).
130. Sec. 103(a) and (b)(2).
131. Sec. 148.
132. Sec. 1397E.
133. Given the differences in credit quality and other characteristics of individual issuers, the Secretary cannot set credit rates in a manner that will allow each issuer to issue tax credit bonds at par.

"Qualified zone academy bonds" are defined as any bond issued by a State or local government, provided that (1) at least, 95 percent of the proceeds are used for the purpose of renovating, providing equipment to, developing course materials for use at, or training teachers and other school personnel in a "qualified zone academy" and (2) private entities have promised to contribute to the qualified zone academy certain equipment, technical assistance or training, employee services, or other property or services with a value equal to at least 10 percent of the bond proceeds.

A school is a "qualified zone academy" if (1) the school is a public school that provides education and training below the college level, (2) the school operates a special academic program in cooperation with businesses to enhance the academic curriculum and increase graduation and employment rates, and (3) either (a) the school is located in an empowerment zone or enterprise community designated under the Code, or (b) it is reasonably expected that at least 35 percent of the students at the school will be eligible for free or reduced-cost lunches under the school lunch program established under the National School Lunch Act.

The arbitrage requirements which generally apply to interest-bearing tax-exempt bonds also generally apply to qualified zone academy bonds. In addition, an issuer of qualified zone academy bonds must reasonably expect to and actually spend 100 percent of the proceeds of such bonds on qualified zone academy property within the three years period that begins on the date of issuance. To the extent less than 100 percent of the proceeds are used to finance qualified zone academy property during the three years spending period, bonds will continue to qualify as qualified zone academy bonds if unspent proceeds are used within 90 days from the end of such three years period to redeem any nonqualified bonds. The three years spending period may be extended by the Secretary if the issuer establishes that the failure to meet the spending requirement is due to reasonable cause and the related purposes for issuing the bonds will continue to proceed with due diligence.

Two special arbitrage rules apply to qualified zone academy bonds. First, available project proceeds invested during the three-year period beginning on the date of issue are not subject to the arbitrage restrictions (i.e., yield restriction and rebate requirements). Available project proceeds are proceeds from the sale of an issue of qualified zone academy bonds, less issuance costs (not to exceed two percent) and any investment earnings on such proceeds. Thus, available project proceeds invested during the three-year spending period may be invested at unrestricted yields, but the earnings on such investments must be spent on qualified zone academy property. Second, amounts invested in a reserve fund are not subject to the arbitrage restrictions to the extent: (1) such fund is funded at a rate not more rapid than equal annual installments; (2) such fund is funded in a manner reasonably expected to result in an amount not greater than an amount necessary to repay the issue; and (3) the yield on such fund is not greater than the average annual interest rate of tax-exempt obligations having a term of 10 years or more that are issued during the month the qualified zone academy bonds are issued.

Issuers of qualified zone academy bonds are required to report issuance to the Internal Revenue Service in a manner similar to the information returns required for tax-exempt bonds.

House Bill

In general

The provision creates a new category of tax-credit bonds: qualified school construction bonds. Qualified school construction bonds must meet three requirements: (1) 100 percent of the available project proceeds of the bond issue is used for the construction, rehabilitation, or repair of a public school facility or for the acquisition of land on which such a bond-financed facility is to be constructed; (2) the bond is issued by a State or local government within which such school is located; and (3) the issuer designates such bonds as a qualified school construction bond.

National limitation

There is a national limitation on qualified school construction bonds of $11 billion for calendar years 2009 and 2010, respectively. Allocations of the national limitation of qualified school construction bonds are divided between the States and certain large school districts. The States receive 60 percent of the national limitation for a calendar year and the remaining 40 percent of the national limitation for a calendar year is allocated to certain of the largest school districts.

Allocation to the States

Generally allocations are made to the States under the 60 percent allocation according to their respective populations of children aged five through seventeen. However, the Secretary of the Treasury shall adjust the annual allocations among the States to ensure that for each State the sum of its allocations under the 60 percent allocation plus any allocations to large educational agencies within the States is not less than a minimum percentage. A State's minimum percentage for a calendar year is a product of 1.68 and the minimum percentage described in section 1124(d) of the Elementary and Secondary Education Act of 1965 for such State for the most recent fiscal year ending before such calendar year.

For allocation purposes, a State includes the District of Columbia and any possession of the United States. The provision provides a special allocation for possessions of the United States other than Puerto Rico under the 60 percent share of the national limitation for States. Under this special rule an allocation to a possession other than Puerto Rico is made on the basis of the respective populations of individuals below the poverty line (as defined by the Office of Management and Budget) rather than respective populations of children aged five through seventeen. This special allocation reduces the State allocation share of the national limitation otherwise available for allocation among the States. Under another special rule the Secretary of the Interior may allocate $200 million of school construction bonds for 2009 and 2010, respectively, to Indian schools. This special allocation for Indian schools is to be used for purposes of the construction, rehabilitation, and repair of schools funded by the Bureau of Indian Affairs. For purposes of such allocations Indian tribal governments are qualified issuers. The special allocation for Indian schools does not reduce the State allocation share of the national limitation otherwise available for allocation among the States.

If an amount allocated under this allocation to the States is unused for a calendar year it may be carried forward by the State to the next calendar year.

Allocation to large school districts

The remaining 40 percent of the national limitation for a calendar year is allocated by the Secretary of the Treasury among local educational agencies which are large local educational agencies for such year. This allocation is made in proportion to the respective amounts each agency received for Basic Grants under subpart 2 of Part A of Title I of the Elementary and Secondary Education Act of 1965 for the most recent fiscal year ending before such calendar year. Any unused allocation of any agency within a State may be allocated by the agency to such State. With respect to a calendar year, the term large local educational agency means any local educational agency if such agency is: (1) among the 100 local educational agencies with the largest numbers of children aged 5 through 17 from families living below the poverty level, or (2) one of not more than 25 local educational agencies (other than in 1, immediately above) that the Secretary of Education determines are in particular need of assistance, based on a low level of resources for school construction, a high level of enrollment growth, or other such factors as the Secretary of Education deems appropriate. If any amount allocated to large local educational agency is unused for a calendar year the agency may reallocate such amount to the State in which the agency is located.

The provision makes qualified school construction bonds a type of qualified tax credit bond for purposes of section 54A. In addition, qualified school construction bonds may be issued by Indian tribal governments only to the extent such bonds are issued for purposes that satisfy the present law requirements for tax-exempt bonds issued by Indian tribal governments (i.e., essential governmental functions and certain manufacturing purposes).

The provision requires 100 percent of the available project proceeds of qualified school construction bonds to be used within the three-year period that begins on the date of issuance. Available project proceeds are proceeds from the sale of the issue less issuance costs (not to exceed two percent) and any investment earnings on such sale proceeds. To the extent less than 100 percent of the available project proceeds are used to finance qualified purposes during the three-year spending period, bonds will continue to qualify as qualified school construction bonds if unspent proceeds are used within 90 days from the end of such three-year period to redeem bonds. The three-year spending period may be extended by the Secretary upon the issuer's request demonstrating that the failure to satisfy the three-year requirement is due to reasonable cause and the projects will continue to proceed with due diligence.

Qualified school construction bonds generally are subject to the arbitrage requirements of section 148. However, available project proceeds invested during the three-year spending period are not subject to the arbitrage restrictions (i.e., yield restriction and rebate requirements). In addition, amounts invested in a reserve fund are not subject to the arbitrage restrictions to the extent: (1) such fund is funded at a rate not more rapid than equal annual installments; (2) such fund is funded in a manner reasonably expected to result in an amount not greater than an amount necessary to repay the issue; and (3) the yield on such fund is not greater than the average annual interest rate of tax-exempt obligations having a term of 10 years or more that are issued during the month the qualified school construction bonds are issued.

The maturity of qualified school construction bonds is the term that the Secretary estimates will result in the present value of the obligation to repay the principal on such bonds being equal to 50 percent of the face amount of such bonds, using as a discount rate the average annual interest rate of tax-exempt obligations having a term of 10 years or more that are issued during the month the qualified school construction bonds are issued.

As with present-law tax credit bonds, the taxpayer holding qualified school construction bonds on a credit allowance date is entitled to a tax credit. The credit rate on the bonds is set by the Secretary at a rate that is 100 percent of the rate that would permit issuance of such bonds without discount and interest cost to the issuer. The amount of the tax credit is determined by multiplying the bond's credit rate by the face amount on the holder's bond. The credit accrues quarterly, is includible in gross income (as if it were an interest payment on the bond), and can be claimed against regular income tax liability and alternative minimum tax liability. Unused credits may be carried forward to succeeding taxable years. In addition, credits may be separated from the ownership of the underlying bond in a manner similar to the manner in which interest coupons can be stripped from interest-bearing bonds.

Issuers of qualified school construction bonds are required to certify that the financial disclosure requirements and applicable State and local law requirements governing conflicts of interest are satisfied with respect to such issue, as well as any other additional conflict of interest rules prescribed by the Secretary with respect to any Federal, State, or local government official directly involved with the issuance of qualified school construction bonds.

Senate Amendment

In general

The Senate amendment is the same as the House bill.

National limitation

There is a national limitation on qualified school construction bonds of $5 billion for calendar years 2009 and 2010, respectively. Also, allocations of the national limitation of qualified school construction bonds are divided between the States with no special allocations to certain large school districts.

Allocation to the States

The allocations are made to the States according to their respective populations of children aged five through seventeen. However, the Secretary of the Treasury shall adjust the annual allocations among the States to ensure that for each State is not less than a minimum percentage. A State's minimum percentage for a calendar year is calculated by dividing (1) the amount the State is eligible to receive under section 1124(d) of the Elementary and Secondary Education Act of 1965 for such State for the most recent fiscal year ending before such calendar year by (2) the amount all States are eligible to received under section 1124(d) of the Elementary and Secondary Education Act of 1965 for such fiscal year, and then multiplying the result by 100.

Allocation to large school districts

No portion of the national limitation for a calendar year is allocated by the Secretary of the Treasury among local educational agencies which are large local educational agencies for such year.

Conference Agreement

In general

The provision creates a new category of tax-credit bonds: qualified school construction bonds. Qualified school construction bonds must meet three requirements: (1) 100 percent of the available project proceeds of the bond issue is used for the construction, rehabilitation, or repair of a public school facility or for the acquisition of land on which such a bond-financed facility is to be constructed; (2) the bond is issued by a State or local government within which such school is located; and (3) the issuer designates such bonds as a qualified school construction bond.

National limitation

There is a national limitation on qualified school construction bonds of $11 billion for calendar years 2009 and 2010, respectively.

Allocation to the States

The national limitation is tentatively allocated among the States in proportion to respective amounts each such State is eligible to receive under section 1124 of the Elementary and Secondary Education Act of 1965 for the most recent fiscal year ending before such calendar year. The amount each State is allocated under the above formula is then reduced by the amount received by any local large educational agency within the State.

For allocation purposes, a State includes the District of Columbia and any possession of the United States. The provision provides a special allocation for possessions of the United States other than Puerto Rico under the national limitation for States. Under this special rule an allocation to a possession other than Puerto Rico is made on the basis of the respective populations of individuals below the poverty line (as defined by the Office of Management and Budget) rather than respective populations of children aged five through seventeen. This special allocation reduces the State allocation share of the national limitation otherwise available for allocation among the States. Under another special rule the Secretary of the Interior may allocate $200 million of school construction bonds for 2009 and 2010, respectively, to Indian schools. This special allocation for Indian schools is to be used for purposes of the construction, rehabilitation, and repair of schools funded by the Bureau of Indian Affairs. For purposes of such allocations Indian tribal governments are qualified issuers. The special allocation for Indian schools does not reduce the State allocation share of the national limitation otherwise available for allocation among the States.

If an amount allocated under this allocation to the States is unused for a calendar year it may be carried forward by the State to the next calendar year.

Allocation to large school districts

Forty percent of the national limitation is allocated among large local educational agencies in proportion to the respective amounts each agency received under section 1124 of the Elementary and Secondary Education Act of 1965 for the most recent fiscal year ending before such calendar year. Any unused allocation of any agency within a State may be allocated by the agency to such State. With respect to a calendar year, the term large local educational agency means any local educational agency if such agency is: (1) among the 100 local educational agencies with the largest numbers of children aged 5 through 17 from families living below the poverty level, or (2) one of not more than 25 local educational agencies (other than in 1, immediately above) that the Secretary of Education determines are in particular need of assistance, based on a low level of resources for school construction, a high level of enrollment growth, or other such factors as the Secretary of Education deems appropriate. If any amount allocated to large local educational agency is unused for a calendar year the agency may reallocate such amount to the State in which the agency is located.

Application of qualified tax credit bond rules

The provision makes qualified school construction bonds a type of qualified tax credit bond for purposes of section 54A. In addition, qualified school construction bonds may be issued by Indian tribal governments only to the extent such bonds are issued for purposes that satisfy the present law requirements for tax-exempt bonds issued by Indian tribal governments (i.e., essential governmental functions and certain manufacturing purposes).

The provision requires 100 percent of the available project proceeds of qualified school construction bonds to be used within the three-year period that begins on the date of issuance. Available project proceeds are proceeds from the sale of the issue less issuance costs (not to exceed two percent) and any investment earnings on such sale proceeds. To the extent less than 100 percent of the available project proceeds are used to finance qualified purposes during the three-year spending period, bonds will continue to qualify as qualified school construction bonds if unspent proceeds are used within 90 days from the end of such three year period to redeem bonds. The three-year spending period may be extended by the Secretary upon the issuer's request demonstrating that the failure to satisfy the three-year requirement is due to reasonable cause and the projects will continue to proceed with due diligence.

Qualified school construction bonds generally are subject to the arbitrage requirements of section 148. However, available project proceeds invested during the three-year spending period are not subject to the arbitrage restrictions (i.e., yield restriction and rebate requirements). In addition, amounts invested in a reserve fund are not subject to the arbitrage restrictions to the extent: (1) such fund is funded at a rate not more rapid than equal annual installments; (2) such fund is funded in a manner reasonably expected to result in an amount not greater than an amount necessary to repay the issue; and (3) the yield on such fund is not greater than the average annual interest rate of tax-exempt obligations having a term of 10 years or more that are issued during the month the qualified school construction bonds are issued.

The maturity of qualified school construction bonds is the term that the Secretary estimates will result in the present value of the obligation to repay the principal on such bonds being equal to 50 percent of the face amount of such bonds, using as a discount rate the average annual interest rate of tax-exempt obligations having a term of 10 years or more that are issued during the month the qualified school construction bonds are issued.

As with present-law tax credit bonds, the taxpayer holding qualified school construction bonds on a credit allowance date is entitled to a tax credit. The credit rate on the bonds is set by the Secretary at a rate that is 100 percent of the rate that would permit issuance of such bonds without discount and interest cost to the issuer. The amount of the tax credit is determined by multiplying the bond's credit rate by the face amount on the holder's bond. The credit accrues quarterly, is includible in gross income (as if it were an interest payment on the bond), and can be claimed against regular income tax liability and alternative minimum tax liability. Unused credits may be carried forward to succeeding taxable years. In addition, credits may be separated from the ownership of the underlying bond in a manner similar to the manner in which interest coupons can be stripped from interest-bearing bonds.

Issuers of qualified school construction bonds are required to certify that the financial disclosure requirements and applicable State and local law requirements governing conflicts of interest are satisfied with respect to such issue, as well as any other additional conflict of interest rules prescribed by the Secretary with respect to any Federal, State, or local government official directly involved with the issuance of qualified school construction bonds.

Effective Date

The provision is effective for obligations issued after the date of enactment.

[¶ 5068]   Section 1522.   Extension and expansion of qualified zone academy bonds.

(Code Sec. 54E)

[Conference Report]

Present Law

Tax-exempt bonds

Interest on State and local governmental bonds generally is excluded from gross income for Federal income tax purposes if the proceeds of the bonds are used to finance direct activities of these governmental units or if the bonds are repaid with revenues of the governmental units. These can include tax-exempt bonds which finance public schools.[134] An issuer must file with the Internal Revenue Service certain information about the bonds issued in order for that bond issue to be tax-exempt.[135] Generally, this information return is required to be filed no later the 15th day of the second month after the close of the calendar quarter in which the bonds were issued.

The tax exemption for State and local bonds does not apply to any arbitrage bond.[136] An arbitrage bond is defined as any bond that is part of an issue if any proceeds of the issue are reasonably expected to be used (or intentionally are used) to acquire higher

---

134. Sec. 103.
135. Sec. 149(e).
136. Sec. 103(a) and (b)(2).

yielding investments or to replace funds that are used to acquire higher yielding investments.[137] In general, arbitrage profits may be earned only during specified periods (e.g., defined "temporary periods") before funds are needed for the purpose of the borrowing or on specified types of investments (e.g., "reasonably required reserve or replacement funds"). Subject to limited exceptions, investment profits that are earned during these periods or on such investments must be rebated to the Federal Government.

Qualified zone academy bonds

As an alternative to traditional tax-exempt bonds, States and local governments were given the authority to issue "qualified zone academy bonds."[138] A total of $400 million of qualified zone academy bonds is authorized to be issued annually in calendar years 1998 through 2009. The $400 million aggregate bond cap is allocated each year to the States according to their respective populations of individuals below the poverty line. Each State, in turn, allocates the credit authority to qualified zone academies within such State.

A taxpayer holding a qualified zone academy bond on the credit allowance date is entitled to a credit. The credit is includible in gross income (as if it were a taxable interest payment on the bond), and may be claimed against regular income tax and alternative minimum tax liability.

The Treasury Department sets the credit rate at a rate estimated to allow issuance of qualified zone academy bonds without discount and without interest cost to the issuer.[139] The Secretary determines credit rates for tax credit bonds based on general assumptions about credit quality of the class of potential eligible issuers and such other factors as the Secretary deems appropriate. The Secretary may determine credit rates based on general credit market yield indexes and credit ratings. The maximum term of the bond is determined by the Treasury Department, so that the present value of the obligation to repay the principal on the bond is 50 percent of the face value of the bond.

"Qualified zone academy bonds" are defined as any bond issued by a State or local government, provided that (1) at least 95 percent of the proceeds are used for the purpose of renovating, providing equipment to, developing course materials for use at, or training teachers and other school personnel in a "qualified zone academy" and (2) private entities have promised to contribute to the qualified zone academy certain equipment, technical assistance or training, employee services, or other property or services with a value equal to at least 10 percent of the bond proceeds.

A school is a "qualified zone academy" if (1) the school is a public school that provides education and training below the college level, (2) the school operates a special academic program in cooperation with businesses to enhance the academic curriculum and increase graduation and employment rates, and (3) either (a) the school is located in an empowerment zone or enterprise community designated under the Code, or (b) it is reasonably expected that at least 35 percent of the students at the school will be eligible for free or reduced-cost lunches under the school lunch program established under the National School Lunch Act.

The arbitrage requirements which generally apply to interest-bearing tax-exempt bonds also generally apply to qualified zone academy bonds. In addition, an issuer of qualified zone academy bonds must reasonably expect to and actually spend 100 percent or more of the proceeds of such bonds on qualified zone academy property within the three-year period that begins on the date of issuance. To the extent less than 100 percent of the proceeds are used to finance qualified zone academy property during the three-year spending period, bonds will continue to qualify as qualified zone academy bonds if un-

---

137. Sec. 148.
138. See secs. 54E and 1397E.
139. Given the differences in credit quality and other characteristics of individual issuers, the Secretary cannot set credit rates in a manner that will allow each issuer to issue tax credit bonds at par.

spent proceeds are used within 90 days from the end of such three-year period to redeem any nonqualified bonds. The three-year spending period may be extended by the Secretary if the issuer establishes that the failure to meet the spending requirement is due to reasonable cause and the related purposes for issuing the bonds will continue to proceed with due diligence.

Two special arbitrage rules apply to qualified zone academy bonds. First, available project proceeds invested during the three-year period beginning on the date of issue are not subject to the arbitrage restrictions (i.e., yield restriction and rebate requirements). Available project proceeds are proceeds from the sale of an issue of qualified zone academy bonds, less issuance costs (not to exceed two percent) and any investment earnings on such proceeds. Thus, available project proceeds invested during the three-year spending period may be invested at unrestricted yields, but the earnings on such investments must be spent on qualified zone academy property. Second, amounts invested in a reserve fund are not subject to the arbitrage restrictions to the extent: (1) such fund is funded at a rate not more rapid than equal annual installments; (2) such fund is funded in a manner reasonably expected to result in an amount not greater than an amount necessary to repay the issue; and (3) the yield on such fund is not greater than the average annual interest rate of tax-exempt obligations having a term of 10 years or more that are issued during the month the qualified zone academy bonds are issued.

Issuers of qualified zone academy bonds are required to report issuance to the Internal Revenue Service in a manner similar to the information returns required for tax-exempt bonds.

House Bill

In general

The provision extends and expands the present-law qualified zone academy bond program. The provision authorizes issuance of up to $1.4 billion of qualified zone academy bonds annually for 2009 and 2010, respectively.

Senate Amendment

The Senate amendment is the same as the House bill.

Conference Agreement

The conference agreement follows the House bill and the Senate amendment.

Effective Date

The provision applies to obligations issued after December 31, 2008.

[¶ 5070]   Section 1531.   Build America Bonds.

(Code Sec. 54AA)

[Conference Report]

Present Law

In general

Under present law, gross income does not include interest on State or local bonds. State and local bonds are classified generally as either governmental bonds or private activity bonds. Governmental bonds are bonds the proceeds of which are primarily used to finance governmental functions or which are repaid with governmental funds. Private activity bonds are bonds in which the State or local government serves as a conduit providing financing to nongovernmental persons (e.g., private businesses or individuals). The exclusion from income for State and local bonds does not apply to private activity bonds, unless the bonds are issued for certain permitted purposes ("qualified private activity bonds") and other Code requirements are met.

Private activity bonds

The Code defines a private activity bond as any bond that satisfies (1) the private business use test and the private security or payment test ("the private business test"); or (2) "the private loan financing test."[140]

Private business test

Under the private business test, a bond is a private activity bond if it is part of an issue in which:

(1) More than 10 percent of the proceeds of the issue (including use of the bond-financed property) are to be used in the trade or business of any person other than a governmental unit ("private business use"); and

(2) More than 10 percent of the payment of principal or interest on the issue is, directly or indirectly, secured by (a) property used or to be used for a private business use or (b) to be derived from payments in respect of property, or borrowed money, used or to be used for a private business use ("private payment test").[141]

A bond is not a private activity bond unless both parts of the private business test (i.e., the private business use test and the private payment test) are met. Thus, a facility that is 100 percent privately used does not cause the bonds financing such facility to be private activity bonds if the bonds are not secured by or paid with private payments. For example, land improvements that benefit a privately-owned factory may be financed with governmental bonds if the debt service on such bonds is not paid by the factory owner or other private parties.

Private loan financing test

A bond issue satisfies the private loan financing test if proceeds exceeding the lesser of $5 million or five percent of such proceeds are used directly or indirectly to finance loans to one or more nongovernmental persons. Private loans include both business and other (e.g., personal) uses and payments by private persons; however, in the case of business uses and payments, all private loans also constitute private business uses and payments subject to the private business test.

Arbitrage restrictions

The exclusion from income for interest on State and local bonds does not apply to any arbitrage bond.[142] An arbitrage bond is defined as any bond that is part of an issue if any proceeds of the issue are reasonably expected to be used (or intentionally are used) to acquire higher yielding investments or to replace funds that are used to acquire higher yielding investments.[143] In general, arbitrage profits may be earned only during specified periods (e.g., defined "temporary periods") before funds are needed for the purpose of the borrowing or on specified types of investments (e.g., "reasonably required reserve or replacement funds"). Subject to limited exceptions, investment profits that are earned during these periods or on such investments must be rebated to the Federal Government.

Qualified tax credit bonds

In lieu of interest, holders of qualified tax credit bonds receive a tax credit that accrues quarterly. The following bonds are qualified tax credit bonds: qualified forestry

---

140. Sec. 141.
141. The 10 percent private business test is reduced to five percent in the case of private business uses (and payments with respect to such uses) that are unrelated to any governmental use being financed by the issue.
142. Sec. 103(a) and (b)(2).
143. Sec. 148.

conservation bonds, new clean renewable energy bonds, qualified energy conservation bonds, and qualified zone academy bonds.[144]

Section 54A of the Code sets forth general rules applicable to qualified tax credit bonds. These rules include requirements regarding credit allowance dates, the expenditure of available project proceeds, reporting, arbitrage, maturity limitations, and financial conflicts of interest, among, other special rules.

A taxpayer who holds a qualified tax credit bond on one or more credit allowance dates of the bond during the taxable year shall be allowed a credit against the taxpayer's income tax for the taxable year. In general, the credit amount for any credit allowance date is 25 percent of the annual credit determined with respect to the bond. The annual credit is determined by multiplying the applicable credit rate by the outstanding face amount of the bond. The applicable credit rate for the bond is the rate that the Secretary estimates will permit the issuance of the qualified tax credit bond with a specified maturity or redemption date without discount and without interest cost to the qualified issuer.[145] The Secretary determines credit rates for tax credit bonds based on general assumptions about credit quality of the class of potential eligible issuers and such other factors as the Secretary deems appropriate. The Secretary may determine credit rates based on general credit market yield indexes and credit ratings.

The credit is included in gross income and, under regulations prescribed by the Secretary, may be stripped (a separation (including at issuance) of the ownership of a qualified tax credit bond and the entitlement to the credit with respect to such bond),

Section 54A of the Code requires that 100 percent of the available project proceeds of qualified tax credit bonds must be used within the three-year period that begins on the date of issuance. Available project proceeds are proceeds from the sale of the bond issue less issuance costs (not to exceed two percent) and any investment earnings on such sale proceeds. To the extent less than 100 percent of the available project proceeds are used to finance qualified projects during the three-year spending period, bonds will continue to qualify as qualified tax credit bonds if unspent proceeds are used within 90 days from the end of such three-year period to redeem bonds. The three-year spending period may be extended by the Secretary upon the issuer's request demonstrating that the failure to satisfy the three-year requirement is due to reasonable cause and the projects will continue to proceed with due diligence.

Qualified tax credit bonds generally are subject to the arbitrage requirements of section 148. However, available project proceeds invested during the three-year spending period are not subject to the arbitrage restrictions (i.e., yield restriction and rebate requirements). In addition, amounts invested in a reserve fund are not subject to the arbitrage restrictions to the extent: (1) such fund is funded at a rate not more rapid than equal annual installments; (2) such fund is funded in a manner reasonably expected to result in an amount not greater than an amount necessary to repay the issue; and (3) the yield on such fund is not greater than the average annual interest rate of tax-exempt obligations having a term of 10 years or more that are issued during the month the qualified tax credit bonds are issued.

The maturity of qualified tax credit bonds is the term that the Secretary estimates will result in the present value of the obligation to repay the principal on such bonds being equal to 50 percent of the face amount of such bonds, using as a discount rate the average annual interest rate of tax-exempt obligations having a term of 10 years or more that are issued during the month the qualified tax credit bonds are issued.

---

144. See secs. 54B, 54C, 54D, and 54E.
145. Given the differences in credit quality and other characteristics of individual issuers, the Secretary cannot set credit rates in a manner that will allow each issuer to issue tax credit bonds at par.

House Bill

In general

The provision permits an issuer to elect to have an otherwise tax-exempt bond treated as a "taxable governmental bond." A "taxable governmental bond" is any obligation (other than a private activity bond) if the interest on such obligation would be (but for this provision) excludable from gross income under section 103 and the issuer makes an irrevocable election to have the provision apply. In determining if an obligation would be tax-exempt under section 103, the credit (or the payment discussed below for qualified bonds) is not treated as a Federal guarantee. Further, the yield on a taxable governmental bond is determined without regard to the credit. A taxable governmental bond does not include any bond if the issue price has more than a de minimis amount of premium over the stated principal amount of the bond.

The holder of a taxable governmental bond will accrue a tax credit in the amount of 35 percent of the interest paid on the interest payment dates of the bond during the calendar year.[146] The interest payment date is any date on which the holder of record of the taxable governmental bond is entitled to a payment of interest under such bond. The sum of the accrued credits is allowed against regular and alternative minimum tax. Unused credit may be carried forward to succeeding taxable years. The credit, as well as the interest paid by the issuer, is included in gross income and the credit may be stripped under rules similar to those provided in section 54A regarding qualified tax credit bonds. Rules similar to those that apply for S corporations, partnerships and regulated investment companies with respect to qualified tax credit bonds also apply to the credit.

Unlike the tax credit for bonds issued under section 54A, the credit rate would not be calculated by the Secretary, but rather would be set by law at 35 percent. The actual credit that a taxpayer may claim is determined by multiplying the interest payment that the taxpayer receives from the issuer (i.e., the bond coupon payment) by 35 percent. Because the credit that the taxpayer claims is also included in income, the Committee anticipates that State and local issuers will issue bonds paying interest at rates approximately equal to 74.1 percent of comparable taxable bonds. The Committee anticipates that if an issuer issues a taxable governmental bond with coupons at 74.1 percent of a comparable taxable bond's coupon that the issuer's bond should sell at par. For example, if a taxable bond of comparable risk pays a $1,000 coupon and sells at par, then if a State or local issuer issues an equal-sized bond with coupon of $741.00, such a bond should also sell at par. The taxpayer who acquires the latter bond will receive an interest payment of $741 and may claim a credit of $259 (35 percent of $741). The credit and the interest payment are both included in the taxpayer's income. Thus, the taxpayer's taxable income from this instrument would be $1,000. This is the same taxable income that the taxpayer would recognize from holding the comparable taxable bond. Consequently the issuer's bond should sell at the same price as would the taxable bond.

Special rule for qualified bonds issued during 2009 and 2010

A "qualified bond" is any taxable governmental bond issued as part of an issue if 100 percent of the available project proceeds of such issue are to be used for capital expenditures.[147] The bond must be issued after the date of enactment of the provision and

---

146. Original issue discount (OID) is not treated as a payment of interest for purposes of determining the credit under the provision. OID is the excess of an obligation's stated redemption price at maturity over the obligation's issue price (sec. 1273(a)).

147. Under Treas. Reg. sec. 1.150-1(b), capital expenditure means any cost of a type that is properly chargeable to capital account (or would be so chargeable with a proper election or with the application of the definition of placed in service under Treas. Reg. sec. 1.150-2(c)) under general Federal income tax principles. For purposes of applying the "general Federal income tax principles" standard, an issuer should generally be treated as if it were a corporation subject to taxation under subchapter C of chapter 1 of the Code. An example of a capital expenditure would include expenditures made for the purchase of fiber-optic cable to provide municipal broadband service.

before January 1, 2011. The issuer must make an irrevocable election to have the special rule for qualified bonds apply.

Under the special rule for qualified bonds, in lieu of the tax credit to the holder, the issuer is allowed a credit equal to 35 percent of each interest payment made under such bond.[148] If in 2009 or 2010, the issuer elects to receive the credit, in the example above, for the State or local issuer's bond to sell at par, the issuer would have to issue the bond with a $1,000 interest coupon. The taxpayer who holds such a bond would include $1,000 on interest in his or her income. From the taxpayer's perspective the bond is the same the taxable bond in the example above and the taxpayer would be willing to pay par for the bond. However, under the provision the State or local issuer would receive a payment of $350 for each $1,000 coupon paid to bondholders. (The net interest cost to the issuer would be $650.)

The payment by the Secretary is to be made contemporaneously with the interest payment made by the issuer, and may be made either in advance or as reimbursement. In lieu of payment to the issuer, the payment may be made to a person making interest payments on behalf of the issuer. For purposes of the arbitrage rules, the yield on a qualified bond is reduced by the amount of the credit/payment.

Transitional coordination with State law

As noted above, interest on a taxable governmental bond and the related credit are includible in gross income to the holder for Federal tax purposes. The provision provides that until a State provides otherwise, the interest on any taxable governmental bond and the amount of any credit determined with respect to such bond shall be treated as being exempt from Federal income tax for purposes of State income tax laws.

Senate Amendment

In general

The Senate amendment is the same as the House bill except that it renames these bonds "Build America Bonds."

The Senate amendment also restricts these bonds to obligations issued before January 1, 2011.

For bonds issued by small issuers,[149] the credit rate is 40 percent instead of 35 percent.

Special rule for qualified bonds issued during 2009 and 2010

The Senate amendment is the same as the House bill, except for bonds issued by small issuers, the credit rate is 40 percent instead of 35 percent.

Transitional coordination with State law

The Senate amendment is the same as the House bill.

Conference Agreement

In general

The conference agreement follows the House bill except that it renames these bonds "Build America Bonds."

---

148. Original issue discount (OID) is not treated as a payment of interest for purposes of calculating the refundable credit under the provision.
149. Small issuer status is determined generally by reference to the rules of sec. 148(f)(4)(D) and increasing the aggregate face amount of all tax-exempt governmental bonds reasonably expected to be issued during the calendar year from $5 million to $30 million.

The conference agreement restricts these bonds to obligations issued before January 1, 2011.

Special rule for qualified bonds issued during 2009 and 2010

The conference agreement follows the House bill, except that it allows for a reasonably required reserve fund to be funded from bond proceeds.[150]

Transitional coordination with State law

The conference agreement follows the House bill and the Senate amendment.

Effective Date

The provision is effect for obligations issued after the date of enactment.

[¶ 5072]   Section 1541.   Regulated investment companies allowed to pass-thru tax credit bond credits.

(Code Sec. 853A)

[Conference Report]

Present Law

In lieu of interest, holders of qualified tax credit bonds receive a tax credit that accrues quarterly. The credit is treated as interest that is includible in gross income. The following bonds are qualified tax credit bonds: qualified forestry conservation bonds, new clean renewable energy bonds, qualified energy conservation bonds, and qualified zone academy bonds.[163] The Code provides that in the case of a qualified tax credit bond held by a regulated investment company, the credit is allowed to shareholders of such company (and any gross income included with respect to such credit shall be treated as distributed to such shareholders) under procedures prescribed by the Secretary.[164] The Secretary has not prescribed procedures for the pass through of the credit to regulated investment company shareholders.

House Bill

No provision.

Senate Amendment

No provision.

Conference Agreement

The conference agreement provides procedures for passing though credits on "tax credit bonds" to the shareholders of an electing regulated investment company. In general, an electing regulated investment company is not allowed any credits with respect to any tax credit bonds it holds during any year for which an election is in effect. The company is treated as having an amount of interest included in its gross income in an amount equal that which would have been included if no election were in effect, and a dividends paid deduction in the same amount is allowed to the company. Each shareholder of the electing regulated investment company is (1) required to include in gross income an amount equal to the shareholder's proportional share of the interest attributable to its credits and (2) allowed such proportional share as a credit against such shareholder's Federal income tax. In order to pass through tax credits to a shareholder, a regulated investment company is required to mail a written notice to such shareholder not

---

150. Under section 148(d)(2), a bond is an arbitrage bond if the amount of the proceeds from the sale of such issue that is part or any reserve or replacement fund exceeds 10 percent of the proceeds. As such the interest on such bond would not be tax-exempt under section 103 and thus would not be a qualified bond for purposes of the provision.
163. See secs. 54B, 54C, 54D, and 54E.
164. See sec. 54A(h), which also covers real estate investment trusts.

later than 60 days after the close of the regulated investment company's taxable year, designating the shareholder's proportionate share of passed-through credits and the shareholder's gross income in respect of such credits.

A tax credit bond means a qualified tax credit bond as defined in section 54A(d), a build America bond (as defined in section 54AA(d), and any other bond for which a credit is allowable under subpart H of part IV of subchapter A of the Code.

The provision gives the Secretary authority to prescribe the time and manner in which a regulated investment company makes the election to pass through credits on tax credit bonds. In addition, the provision requires the Secretary to prescribe such guidance as may be necessary to carry out the provision, including prescribing methods for determining a shareholder's proportionate share of tax credits.

Effective Date

The provision is applicable to taxable years ending after the date of enactment.

[¶ 5074]   Section 1601.   Application of certain labor standards to projects financed with certain tax-favored bonds.

(Code Sec. 54C, 54D, 54E, 54F)

[Conference Report]

Present Law

The United States Code (Subchapter IV of Chapter 31 of Title 40) applies a prevailing wage requirement to certain contracts to which the Federal Government is a party.

House Bill

The provision provides that Subchapter IV of Chapter 31 of Title 40 of the U.S. Code shall apply to projects financed with the proceeds of:

1. any qualified clean renewable energy bond (as defined in sec. 54C of the Code) issued after the date of enactment;

2. any qualified energy conservation bond (as defined in sec. 54D of the Code) issued after the date of enactment;

3. any qualified zone academy bond (as defined in sec. 54E of the Code) issued after the date of enactment;

4. any qualified school construction bond (as defined in sec. 54F of the Code); and

5. any recovery zone economic development bond (as defined in sec. 1400U-2 of the Code).

Senate Amendment

The Senate amendment is the same as the House bill except it makes a technical correction to change "qualified clean renewable energy bond" to "new clean renewable energy bond."

Conference Agreement

The conference agreement follows the Senate amendment.

Effective Date

The provision is effective on the date of enactment.

[¶ 5078]   Section 1899A through 1899H.   Improvement of the affordability of the credit; payment for monthly premiums paid prior to commencement of advance payments of credit; TAA recipients not enrolled in training programs eligible for credit; TAA pre-certification period rule for purposes of determining whether there is 63-day lapse in creditable coverage; Continued qualification of family members after certain events; Extension of Cobra benefits for certain TAA eligible individuals and PBGC recipients; Addition of coverage through voluntary employees' beneficiary associations; Notice requirements.

(Code Sec. 35, 7527, 4980, 9801)
(ERISA Sec. 602)

[Conference Report]

Present Law

In general

Under the Trade Act of 2002,[248] in the case of taxpayers who are eligible individuals, a refundable tax credit is provided for 65 percent of the taxpayer's premiums for qualified health insurance of the taxpayer and qualifying family members for each eligible coverage month beginning in the taxable year. The credit is commonly referred to as the health coverage tax credit ("HCTC"). The credit is available only with respect to amounts paid by the taxpayer. The credit is available on an advance basis.[249]

Qualifying family members are the taxpayer's spouse and any dependent of the taxpayer with respect to whom the taxpayer is entitled to claim a dependency exemption. Any individual who has other specified coverage is not a qualifying family member.

Persons eligible for the credit

Eligibility for the credit is determined on a monthly basis. In general, an eligible coverage month is any month if, as of the first day of the month, the taxpayer (1) is an eligible individual, (2) is covered by qualified health insurance, (3) does not have other specified coverage, and (4) is not imprisoned under Federal, State, or local authority.[250] In the case of a joint return, the eligibility requirements are met if at least one spouse satisfies the requirements.

An eligible individual is an individual who is (1) an eligible TAA recipient, (2) an eligible alternative Trade Adjustment Assistance ("TAA") recipient, or (3) an eligible Pension Benefit Guaranty Corporation ("PBGC") pension recipient.

An individual is an eligible TAA recipient during any month if the individual (1) is receiving for any day of such month a trade readjustment allowance[251] or who would be eligible to receive such an allowance but for the requirement that the individual exhaust unemployment benefits before being eligible to receive an allowance and (2) with respect to such allowance, is covered under a certification issued under subchapter A or D of chapter 2 of title II of the Trade Act of 1974. An individual is treated as an eligible TAA recipient during the first month that such individual would otherwise cease to be an eligible TAA recipient.

An individual is an eligible alternative TAA recipient during any month if the individual (1) is a worker described in section 246(a)(3)(B) of the Trade Act of 1974 who is

---

248. Pub. L. No. 107-210 (2002).
249. An individual is eligible for the advance payment of the credit once a qualified health insurance costs credit eligibility certificate is in effect. Sec. 7527. Unless otherwise indicated, all "section" references are to the Internal Revenue Code of 1986, as amended.
250. An eligible month must begin after November 4, 2002. This date is 90 days after the date of enactment of the Trade Act of 2002, which was August 6, 2002.
251. The eligibility rules and conditions for such an allowance are specified in chapter 2 of title II of the Trade Act of 1974. Among other requirements, payment of a trade readjustment allowance is conditioned upon the individual enrolling in certain training programs or receiving a waiver of training requirements.

participating in the program established under section 246(a)(1) of such Act, and (2) is receiving a benefit for such month under section 246(a)(2) of such Act. An individual is treated as an eligible alternative TAA recipient during the first month that such individual would otherwise cease to be an eligible TAA recipient.

An individual is a PBGC pension recipient for any month if he or she (1) is age 55 or over as of the first day of the month, and (2) is receiving a benefit any portion of which is paid by the PBGC. The IRS has interpreted the definition of PBGC pension recipient to also include certain alternative recipients and recipients who have received certain lump-sum payments on or after August 6, 2002. A person is not an eligible individual if he or she may be claimed as a dependent on another person's tax return.

An otherwise eligible taxpayer is not eligible for the credit for a month if, as of the first day of the month, the individual has other specified coverage. Other specified coverage is (1) coverage under any insurance which constitutes medical care (except for insurance substantially all of the coverage of which is for excepted benefits)[252] maintained by an employer (or former employer) if at least 50 percent of the cost of the coverage is paid by an employer[253] (or former employer) of the individual or his or her spouse or (2) coverage under certain governmental health programs. Specifically, an individual is not eligible for the credit if, as of the first day of the month, the individual is (1) entitled to benefits under Medicare Part A, enrolled in Medicare Part B, or enrolled in Medicaid or SCHIP, (2) enrolled in a health benefits plan under the Federal Employees Health Benefit Plan, or (3) entitled to receive benefits under chapter 55 of title 10 of the United States Code (relating to military personnel). An individual is not considered to be enrolled in Medicaid solely by reason of receiving immunizations.

A special rule applies with respect to alternative TAA recipients. For eligible alternative TAA recipients, an individual has other specified coverage if the individual is (1) eligible for coverage under any qualified health insurance (other than coverage under a COBRA continuation provision, State-based continuation coverage, or coverage through certain State arrangements) under which at least 50 percent of the cost of coverage is paid or incurred by an employer of the taxpayer or the taxpayer's spouse or (2) covered under any such qualified health insurance under which any portion of the cost of coverage is paid or incurred by an employer of the taxpayer or the taxpayer's spouse.

Qualified health insurance

Qualified health insurance eligible for the credit is: (1) COBRA continuation[254] coverage; (2) State-based continuation coverage provided by the State under a State law that requires such coverage; (3) coverage offered through a qualified State high risk pool; (4) coverage under a health insurance program offered to State employees or a comparable program; (5) coverage through an arrangement entered into by a State and a group health plan, an issuer of health insurance coverage, an administrator, or an employer; (6) coverage offered through a State arrangement with a private sector health care coverage purchasing pool; (7) coverage under a State-operated health plan that does not receive any Federal financial participation; (8) coverage under a group health plan that is available through the employment of the eligible individual's spouse; and (9) coverage under

---

252. Excepted benefits are: (1) coverage only for accident or disability income or any combination thereof; (2) coverage issued as a supplement to liability insurance; (3) liability insurance, including general liability insurance and automobile liability insurance; (4) worker's compensation or similar insurance; (5) automobile medical payment insurance; (6) credit-only insurance; (7) coverage for on-site medical clinics; (8) other insurance coverage similar to the coverages in (1)-(7) specified in regulations under which benefits for medical care are secondary or incidental to other insurance benefits; (9) limited scope dental or vision benefits; (10) benefits for long-term care, nursing home care, home health care, community-based care, or any combination thereof; and (11) other benefits similar to those in (9) and (10) as specified in regulations; (12) coverage only for a specified disease or illness; (13) hospital indemnity or other fixed indemnity insurance; and (14) Medicare supplemental insurance.
253. An amount is considered paid by the employer if it is excludable from income. Thus, for example, amounts paid for health coverage on a salary reduction basis under an employer plan are considered paid by the employer. A rule aggregating plans of the same employer applies in determining whether the employer pays at least 50 percent of the cost of coverage.
254. COBRA continuation is defined in section 9832(d)(1).

individual health insurance if the eligible individual was covered under individual health insurance during the entire 30-day period that ends on the date the individual became separated from the employment which qualified the individual for the TAA allowance, the benefit for an eligible alternative TAA recipient, or a pension benefit from the PBGC, whichever applies.[255]

Qualified health insurance does not include any State-based coverage (i.e., coverage described in (2)-(7) in the preceding paragraph), unless the State has elected to have such coverage treated as qualified health insurance and such coverage meets certain requirements.[256] Such State coverage must provide that each qualifying individual is guaranteed enrollment if the individual pays the premium for enrollment or provides a qualified health insurance costs eligibility certificate and pays the remainder of the premium. In addition, the State-based coverage cannot impose any pre-existing condition limitation with respect to qualifying individuals. State-based coverage cannot require a qualifying individual to pay a premium or contribution that is greater than the premium or contribution for a similarly situated individual who is not a qualified individual. Finally, benefits under the State-based coverage must be the same as (or substantially similar to) benefits provided to similarly situated individuals who are not qualifying individuals.

A qualifying individual is an eligible individual who seeks to enroll in the State-based coverage and who has aggregate periods of creditable coverage[257] of three months or longer, does not have other specified coverage, and who is not imprisoned. In general terms, creditable coverage includes health care coverage without a gap of more than 63 days. Therefore, if an individual's qualifying coverage were terminated more than 63 days before the individual enrolled in the State-based coverage, the individual would not be a qualifying individual and would not be entitled to the State-based protections. A qualifying individual also includes qualified family members of such an eligible individual.

Qualified health insurance does not include coverage under a flexible spending or similar arrangement or any insurance if substantially all of the coverage is for excepted benefits.

Other rules

Amounts taken into account in determining the credit may not be taken into account in determining the amount allowable under the itemized deduction for medical expenses or the deduction for health insurance expenses of self-employed individuals. Amounts distributed from a medical savings account or health savings accounts are not eligible for the credit. The amount of the credit available through filing a tax return is reduced by any credit received on an advance basis. Married taxpayers filing separate returns are eligible for the credit; however, if both spouses are eligible individuals and the spouses file separate returns, then the spouse of the taxpayer is not a qualifying family member.

The Secretary of the Treasury is authorized to prescribe such regulations and other guidance as may be necessary or appropriate to carry out the credit provision.

COBRA

The Consolidated Omnibus Reconciliation Act of 1985 ("COBRA") requires that a group health plan must offer continuation coverage to qualified beneficiaries in the case of a qualifying event. An excise tax under the Code applies on the failure of a group health plan to meet the requirement.[258] Qualifying events include the death of the cov-

---

255. For this purpose, "individual health insurance" means any insurance which constitutes medical care offered to individuals other than in connection with a group health plan. Such term does not include Federal- or State-based health insurance coverage.
256. For guidance on how a State elects a health program to be qualified health insurance for purposes of the credit, see Rev. Proc. 2004-12, 2004-1 C.B. 528.
257. Creditable coverage is determined under the Health Insurance Portability and Accountability Act. Sec. 9801(c).
258. Sec. 4980B.

ered employee, termination of the covered employee's employment, divorce or legal separation of the covered employee, and certain bankruptcy proceedings of the employer. In the case of termination from employment, the coverage must be extended for a period of not less than 18 months. In certain other cases, coverage must be extended for a period of not less than 36 months. Under such period of continuation coverage, the plan may require payment of a premium by the beneficiary of up to 102 percent of the applicable premium for the period.

House Bill

No provision.

Senate Amendment

No provision.[259]

Conference Agreement

Increase in credit percentage amount

The provision increases the amount of the HCTC to 80 percent of the taxpayer's premiums for qualified health insurance of the taxpayer and qualifying family members.

Effective date.-The provision is effective for coverage months beginning on or after the first day of the first month beginning 60 days after date of enactment. The increased credit rate does not apply to months beginning after December 31, 2010.

Payment for monthly premiums paid prior to commencement of advance payment of credit

The provision provides that the Secretary of Treasury shall make one or more retroactive payments on behalf of certified individuals equal to 80 percent of the premiums for coverage of the taxpayer and qualifying family members for qualified health insurance for eligible coverage months occurring prior to the first month for which an advance payment is made on behalf of such individual. The amount of the payment must be reduced by the amount of any payment made to the taxpayer under a national emergency grant pursuant to section 173(f) of the Workforce Investment Act of 1998 for a taxable year including such eligible coverage months.

Effective date.-The provision is effective for eligible coverage months beginning after December 31, 2008. The Secretary of the Treasury, however, is not required to make any payments under the provision until after the date that is six months after the date of enactment. The provision does not apply to months beginning after December 31, 2010.

TAA recipients not enrolled in training programs eligible for credit

The provision modifies the definition of an eligible TAA recipient to eliminate the requirement that an individual be enrolled in training in the case of an individual receiving unemployment compensation. In addition, the provision clarifies that the definition of an eligible TAA recipient includes an individual who would be eligible to receive a trade readjustment allowance except that the individual is in a break in training that exceeds the period specified in section 233(c) of the Trade Act of 1974, but is within the period for receiving the allowance.

Effective date.-The provision is effective for months beginning after the date of enactment in taxable years ending after such date, The provision does not apply to months beginning after December 31, 2010.

---

259. The Senate amendment did not amend the HCTC, but section 1701 of the Senate amendment provided for a temporary extension of the Trade Adjustment Assistance Program (generally until December 31, 2010). Certain beneficiaries of this program are eligible for the HCTC.

TAA pre-certification period rule for purposes of determining whether there is a 63-day lapse in creditable coverage

Under the provision, in determining if there has been a 63-day lapse in coverage (which determines, in part, if the State-based consumer protections apply), in the case of a TAA-eligible individual, the period beginning on the date the individual has a TAA-related loss of coverage and ending on the date which is seven days after the date of issuance by the Secretary (or by any person or entity designated by the Secretary) of a qualified health insurance costs credit eligibility certificate (under section 7527) for such individual is not taken into account.

Effective date.-The provision is effective for plan years beginning after the date of enactment. The provision does not apply to plan years beginning after December 31, 2010.

Continued qualification of family members after certain events

The provision provides continued eligibility for the credit for family members after certain events, The rule applies in the case of (1) the eligible individual becoming entitled to Medicare, (2) divorce and (3) death.

In the case of a month which would be an eligible coverage month with respect to an eligible individual except that the individual is entitled to benefits under Medicare Part A or enrolled in Medicare Part B, the month is treated as an eligible coverage month with respect to the individual solely for purposes of determining the amount of the credit with respect to qualifying family members (i.e. the credit is allowed for expenses paid for qualifying family members after the eligible individual is eligible for Medicare). Such treatment applies only with respect to the first 24 months after the eligible individual is first entitled to benefits under Medicare Part A or enrolled in Medicare Part B.

In the case of the finalization of a divorce between an eligible individual and the individual's spouse, the spouse is treated as an eligible individual for a period of 24 months beginning with the date of the finalization of the divorce. Under such rule, the only family members that may be taken into account with respect to the spouse as qualifying family members are those individuals who were qualifying family members immediately before such divorce finalization.

In the case of the death of an eligible individual, the spouse of such individual (determined at the time of death) is treated as an eligible individual for a period of 24 months beginning with the date of death. Under such rule, the only qualifying family members that may be taken into account with respect to the spouse are those individuals who were qualifying family members immediately before such death. In addition, any individual who was a qualifying family member of the decedent immediately before such death[260] is treated as an eligible individual for a period of 24 months beginning with the date of death, except that in determining the amount of the HCTC only such qualifying family member may be taken into account.

Effective date.-The provision is effective for months beginning oner December 31. 2009. The provision does not apply to months that begin after December 31, 2010.

Alignment of COBRA coverage

The maximum required COBRA continuation coverage period is modified by the provision with respect to certain individuals whose qualifying event is a termination of employment or a reduction in hours. First, in the case of such a qualifying event with respect to a covered employee who has a nonforfeitable right to a benefit any portion of which is paid by the PBGC, the maximum coverage period must end not earlier than the date of death of the covered employee (or in the case of the surviving spouse or dependent children of the covered employee, not earlier than 24 months after the date of death

---

260. In the case of a dependent, the rule applies to the taxpayer to whom the personal exemption deduction under section 151 is allowable.

of the covered employee). Second, in the case of such a qualifying event where the covered employee is a TAA eligible individual as of the date that the maximum coverage period would otherwise terminate, the maximum coverage period must extend during the period that the individual is a TAA eligible individual.

Effective date.-The provision is effective for periods of coverage that would, without regard to the provision, end on or after the date of enactment, provided that the provision does not extend any periods of coverage beyond December 31, 2010.

Addition of coverage through voluntary employees' beneficiary associations

The provision expands the definition of qualified health insurance by including coverage under an employee benefit plan funded by a voluntary employees' beneficiary association ("VEBA", as defined in section 501(c)(9)) established pursuant to an order of a bankruptcy court, or by agreement with an authorized representative, as provided in section 1114 of title 11, United States Code.

Effective date.-The provision is effective on the date of enactment. The provision does not apply with respect to certificates of eligibility issued after December 31, 2010.

Notice requirements

The provision requires that the qualified health insurance costs credit eligibility certificate provided in connection with the advance payment of the HCTC must include (1) the name, address, and telephone number of the State office or offices responsible for providing the individual with assistance with enrollment in qualified health insurance, (2) a list of coverage options that are treated as qualified health insurance by the State in which the individual resides, (3) in the case of a TAA-eligible individual, statement informing the individual that the individual has 63 days from the date that is seven days after the issuance of such certificate to enroll in such insurance without a lapse in creditable coverage, and (4) such other information as the Secretary may provide.

Effective date.-The provision is effective for certificates issued after the date that is six months after the date of enactment. The provision does not apply to months beginning after December 31, 2010.

Effective Date

The provision is generally effective upon the date of enactment, excepted as otherwise noted above.

[¶5079]   Section 2201.   Economic recovery payment to recipients of social security, supplemental security income, railroad retirement benefits, and veterans disability compensation or pension benefits.

(Code Sec. None)

[Conference Report]

Present Law

Title II of the Social Security Act authorizes cash benefits for retired and disabled workers and their dependents and survivors under the Old Age and Survivors Insurance (OASI) and Disability Insurance (DI) programs. Title XVI of the Social Security Act authorizes monthly cash benefits for blind and disabled persons and persons age 65 or over who have limited income and resources under the Supplemental Security Income (SSI) program.

The Railroad Retirement Act of 1974 authorizes cash benefits for retired and disabled railroad workers and their dependents and survivors.

Title 38 of the United States Code authorizes cash benefits for certain veterans and their dependents and survivors.

Current law does not authorize any one-time emergency payments for any of these programs. Under Title II of the Social Security Act, a person is eligible for Social Security benefits only if he or she has insured status as the result of sufficient employment that was covered by the Social Security system and for which Social Security payroll taxes were paid. Federal employees hired before 1983 were covered by the Civil Service Retirement System (CSRS) and, unless they were eligible for the CSRS-Offset or elected to enroll in the Federal Employees Retirement System (FERS), they are not eligible for Social Security benefits on the basis of their federal service. In addition, some state and local government employees are not covered by the Social Security system and thus are not eligible for Social Security benefits on the basis of their public service.

Current law does not authorize any one-time tax credit for government retirees who are not eligible for Social Security benefits.

House Bill

The House bill authorizes a one-time emergency payment to be made to SSI recipients. This payment must be made by the Social Security Administration (SSA) at the earliest practical date and no more than 120 days after enactment of the law. The amount of this one-time emergency payment would be equal to the average monthly amount of federal SSI benefits paid to an individual (approximately $456) or a married couple (approximately $637) in the most recent month for which data are available.

To be eligible for the one-time emergency payment, a person must be eligible for an SSI benefit, other than a personal needs allowance, for at least one day during the month of the payment. A person who was eligible for an SSI benefit, other than a personal needs allowance, for at least one day during the two-month period preceding the month of the emergency payment and their SSI eligibility ended during the two-month period solely because their income exceeded the SSI income guidelines is also eligible for the one-time emergency payment.

Only persons who are determined by the Commissioner of Social Security in calendar year 2009 to fall into one of the categories described above are eligible for the emergency payment. Thus, a person who is awarded SSI benefits anytime after 2009 would not be eligible for the emergency payment, even if he or she is awarded benefits retroactive to a date before the date of the emergency payment.

The one-time emergency payment would be protected from garnishment and assignment and would not be considered income in the month of receipt and the following 6 months for the purposes of determining eligibility of the recipient (or the recipient's spouse or family) for any means-tested program funded entirely or in part with federal funds.

The House bill provides an appropriation of such sums as may be necessary to carry out this section, including any administrative costs associated with the payment.

Senate Amendment

The Senate bill provides for a one-time economic recovery payment of $300 to adult Social Security (Old Age and Survivors Insurance and Disability Insurance) and Railroad Retirement beneficiaries, Supplemental Security Income (SSI) recipients, and veterans receiving compensation or pension benefits from the Department of Veterans Affairs.

The economic recovery payment would be made by the Secretary of the Treasury after eligible beneficiaries are identified by the Social Security Administration (SSA), the

Railroad Retirement Board, and the Department of Veteran Affairs. Payments are to be made at the earliest practicable date and in no event later than 120 days after enactment.

To be eligible for the economic recovery payment. a person must have been during the three month period prior to the month of the enactment: an adult Social Security Old Age and Survivors Insurance (OASI) or Disability Insurance (DI) beneficiary (including adults eligible for child's benefits on the basis of as disability that began before the age of 22, persons eligible under transitional insured status, and persons eligible under special rules for uninsured persons over the age of 72), an adult Railroad Retirement or disability beneficiary (including dependents, survivors, and disabled adult children), a veterans pension or compensation beneficiary, or an SSI recipient (excluding persons who only receive a personal needs allowance).

The Senate bill requires that economic recovery payment recipients live in the United States or its territories. The Senate bill prohibits any person from receiving more than one economic recovery payment regardless of whether the individual is entitled to, or eligible for, more than one benefit or cash payment under this section.

The Senate bill prohibits the payment of an economic recovery payment to any Social Security beneficiary or person eligible for Social Security benefits paid by the Railroad Retirement Board, or SSI recipient, if, for the most recent month of the three-month period prior to enactment the person's benefits were not payable due to his or her status as a prisoner, inmate in a public institute, illegal alien, or fugitive felon.

The bill prohibits an economic recovery payment to any veterans compensation or pension beneficiary if, for the most recent month of the three-month period prior to enactment, the person's benefits were not payable due to his or her status as a prisoner or fugitive felon. It also prohibits the payment of an economic recovery payment to any person who dies before the date he or she is certified as eligible to receive a payment.

The bill limits the applicability of the economic recovery payments to retroactive beneficiaries by providing that no payment may be made for any reason after December 31, 2010.

The economic recovery payment would not be considered income in the month of receipt and the following 9 months for the purposes of determining eligibility of the recipient (or the recipient's spouse or family) for any means-tested program funded entirely or in part with federal funds. The payment would not be considered income for the purposes of taxation and would be protected from garnishment and assignment. However, the payment could be used to collect debts owed to the federal government. Electronic payments and payments to representative payees and fiduciaries would be authorized.

The Senate bill provides additional appropriations for the period from fiscal year 2009 through fiscal year 2011 in the amounts of: $57,000,000 to the Department of the Treasury; $90,000,000 to the SSA; $1,000,000 to the Railroad Retirement Board; and $7,200,000 to the Department of Veterans Affairs for administrative expenses associated with the one-time economic recovery payment. Of the money appropriated to the Department of Veterans Affairs, $100,000 shall be for the Information Systems Technology Account and $7,100,000 for general expenses related to the administration of the economic recovery payment. It also appropriates to the Department of the Treasury such sums as may be necessary for making economic recovery payments. The Senate bill provides that the amount of a person's Making Work Pay tax credit authorized by Section 1001 of Division A of the Senate bill would be offset by the amount of any economic recovery payment that person receives.

Conference Agreement

The conference agreement follows the Senate bill, with some modifications. The conference agreement directs the Secretary of the Treasury to disburse a onetime Economic Recovery Payment of $250 to adults who were eligible for Social Security benefits,

Railroad Retirement benefits, or veteran's compensation or pension benefits; or individuals who were eligible for Supplemental Security Income (SSI) benefits (excluding individuals who receive SSI while in a Medicaid institution). Only individuals who were eligible for one of the four programs for any of the three months prior to the month of enactment shall receive an Economic Recovery Payment.

The provision stipulates that Economic Recovery Payments will only be made to individuals whose address of record is in 1 of the 50 states, the District of Columbia, Puerto Rico, Guam, the United States Virgin Islands, American Samoa, or the Northern Mariana Islands.

An individual shall only receive one $250 Economic Recovery Payment under this section regardless of whether the individual is eligible for a benefit from more than one of the four federal programs. If the individual is also eligible for the "Making Work Pay" credit from Section 1001, that credit shall be reduced by the Economic Recovery Payment made under this section.

Individuals who are otherwise eligible for an Economic Recovery Payment will not receive a payment if their federal program benefits have been suspended because they are in prison, a fugitive, a probation or parole violator, have committed fraud, or are no longer lawfully present in the United States.

The provision directs the Commissioner of Social Security, the Railroad Retirement Board, and the Secretary of Veterans Affairs to provide the Secretary of the Treasury with information and data to send the payments to eligible individuals and to disburse the payments.

The provision provides that the Economic Recovery Payments shall not be taken into account as income, or taken into account as resources for the month of receipt and the following 9 months, for purposes of determining the eligibility of such individual or any other individual for benefits or assistance, or the amount or extent of benefits or assistance, under any Federal program or under any State or local program financed in whole or in part with Federal funds.

The provision provides that Economic Recovery Payments shall not be considered gross income for income tax purposes and that the payments are protected by the assignment and garnishment provisions of the four federal benefit programs. The payments will be subject to the Treasury Offset Program.

The provision stipulates that if an individual who is eligible for an Economic Recovery Payment has a representative payee, the payment shall be made to the representative payee and the entire payment shall only be used for the benefit of the individual who is entitled to the Economic Recovery Payment.

The provision appropriates the following amounts for FY2009 through FY2011: to,the Secretary of the Treasury, $131 million for administrative costs to carry out the provisions of this section and the new Section 36A (the Making Work Pay credit); to the Commissioner of Social Security, such funds as are necessary to make the payments and $90 million to carry out the provisions of this section; to the Railroad Retirement Board, such funds as are necessary to make the payments and $1.4 million to carry out the provisions of this section; and to the Secretary of Veterans Affairs, such funds as are necessary to make the payments. $100,000 for the Information Systems Technology account and $7,100,000 to the General Operating Expenses account.

The Secretary of the Treasury shall commence making payments as soon as possible, but no later than 120 days after the date of enactment. No Economic Recovery Payments shall be made after December 31, 2010.

[¶ 5080]   Section 2202.   Special credit for certain government retirees.

(Code Sec. 6213; 6211)

[Conference Report]

Present Law

No provision.

House Bill

No provision.

Senate Amendment

No provision.

Conference Agreement

The conference agreement creates a $250 credit ($500 for a joint return where both spouses are eligible) against income taxes owed for tax year 2009 for individuals who receive a government pension or annuity from work not covered by Social Security, and were not eligible to receive a payment under section 2201. If the individual is also eligible for the "Making Work Pay" credit from Section 1001, that credit shall be reduced by the credit made under this section. Each tax return on which this credit is claimed must include the social security number of the taxpayer (in the case of a joint return, the social security number of at least one spouse). The provision states that the credit under this section shall be a refundable credit.

The provision provides that any credit or refund allowed or made by this provision shall not be taken into account as income and shall not be taken into account as resources for the month of receipt and the following two months for purposes of determining the eligibility of such individual or any other individual for benefits or assistance, or the amount or extent of benefits or assistance, under any Federal program or under any State or local program financed in whole or in part with Federal funds.

Effective Date

The provision is effective on the date of enactment.

[¶ 5082]   Section 3001.   Premium assistance for COBRA benefits.

(Code Sec. 4980B, 6432, 6720C, 139C, 35)

[Conference Report]

Present Law

In general

The Code contains rules that require certain group health plans to offer certain individuals ("qualified beneficiaries") the opportunity to continue to participate for a specified period of time in the group health plan ("continuation coverage") after the occurrence of certain events that otherwise would have terminated such participation ("qualifying events").[228] These continuation coverage rules are often referred to as "COBRA continuation coverage" or "COBRA," which is a reference to the acronym for the law that added the continuation coverage rules to the Code.[229]

---

228. Sec. 4980B.
229. The COBRA rules were added to the Code by the Consolidated Omnibus Budget Reconciliation Act of 1985, Pub. L. No. 99-272. The rules were originally added as Code sections 162(i) and (k). The rules were later restated as Code section 4980B, pursuant to the Technical and Miscellaneous Revenue Act of 1988, Pub. L. No. 100-647.

The Code imposes an excise tax on a group health plan if it fails to comply with the COBRA continuation coverage rules with respect to a qualified beneficiary. The excise tax with respect to a qualified beneficiary generally is equal to $100 for each day in the noncompliance period with respect to the failure. A plan's noncompliance period generally begins on the date the failure first occurs and ends when the failure is corrected. Special rules apply that limit the amount of the excise tax if the failure would not have been discovered despite the exercise of reasonable diligence or if the failure is due to reasonable cause and not willful neglect.

In the case of a multiemployer plan, the excise tax generally is imposed on the group health plan. A multiemployer plan is a plan to which more than one employer is required to contribute, that is maintained pursuant to one or more collective bargaining agreements between one or more employee organizations and more than one employer, and that satisfies such other requirements as the Secretary of Labor may prescribe by regulation. In the case of a plan other than a multiemployer plan (a "single employer plan"), the excise tax generally is imposed on the employer.

Plans subject to COBRA

A group health plan is defined as a plan of, or contributed to by, an employer (including a self-employed person) or employee organization to provide health care (directly or otherwise) to the employees. former employees, the employer, and others associated or formerly associated with the employer in a business relationship, or their families. A group health plan includes a self-insured plan. The term group health plan does not, however, include a plan under which substantially all of the coverage is for qualified long-term care services.

The following types of group health plans are not subject to the Code's COBRA rules: (1) a plan established and maintained for its employees by a church or by a convention or association of churches which is exempt from tax under section 501 (a "church plan"); (2) a plan established and maintained for its employees by the Federal government. the government of any State or political subdivision thereof, or by any instrumentality of the foregoing (a "governmental plan");[230] and (3) a plan maintained by an employer that normally employed fewer than 20 employees on a typical business day during the preceding calendar year[231] (a "small employer plan").

Qualifying events and qualified beneficiaries

A qualifying event that gives rise to COBRA continuation coverage includes, with respect to any covered employee, the following events which would result in a loss of coverage of a qualified beneficiary under a group health plan (but for COBRA continuation coverage): (1) death of the covered employee; (2) the termination (other than by reason of such employee's gross misconduct), or a reduction in hours, of the covered employee's employment; (3) divorce or legal separation of the covered employee; (4) the covered employee becoming entitled to Medicare benefits under title XVIII of the Social Security Act; (5) a dependent child ceasing to be a dependent child under the generally applicable requirements of the plan; and (6) a proceeding in a case under the U.S. Bankruptcy Code commencing on or after July 1, 1986, with respect to the employer from whose employment the covered employee retired at any time.

A "covered employee" is an individual who is (or was) provided coverage under the group health plan on account of the performance of services by the individual for one or more persons maintaining the plan and includes a self-employed individual. A "qualified beneficiary" means, with respect to a covered employee, any individual who on the day before the qualifying event for the employee is a beneficiary under the group health plan as the spouse or dependent child of the employee. The term qualified beneficiary also

---

230. A governmental plan also includes certain plans established by an Indian tribal government.
231. If the plan is a multi employer plan, then each of the employers contributing to the plan for a calendar year must normally employ fewer than 20 employees during the preceding calendar year.

includes the covered employee in the case of a qualifying event that is a termination of employment or reduction in hours.

Continuation coverage requirements

Continuation coverage that must be offered to qualified beneficiaries pursuant to CO-BRA must consist of coverage which, as of the time coverage is being provided, is identical to the coverage provided under the plan to similarly situated non-COBRA beneficiaries under the plan with respect to whom a qualifying event has not occurred. If coverage under a plan is modified for any group of similarly situated non-COBRA beneficiaries, the coverage must also be modified in the same manner for qualified beneficiaries. Similarly situated non-COBRA beneficiaries means the group of covered employees, spouses of covered employees, or dependent children of covered employees who (i) are receiving coverage under the group health plan for a reason other than pursuant to COBRA, and (ii) are the most similarly situated to the situation of the qualified beneficiary immediately before the qualifying event, based on all of the facts and circumstances.

The maximum required period of continuation coverage for a qualified beneficiary (i.e., the minimum period for which continuation coverage must be offered) depends upon a number of factors, including the specific qualifying event that gives rise to a qualified beneficiary's right to elect continuation coverage. In the case of a qualifying event that is the termination, or reduction of hours, of a covered employee's employment, the minimum period of coverage that must be offered to the qualified beneficiary is coverage for the period beginning with the loss of coverage on account of the qualifying event and ending on the date that is 18 months[232] after the date of the qualifying event. If coverage under a plan is lost on account of a qualifying event but the loss of coverage actually occurs at a later date, the minimum coverage period may be extended by the plan so that it is measured from the date when coverage is actually lost.

The minimum coverage period for a qualified beneficiary generally ends upon the earliest to occur of the following events: (1) the date on which the employer ceases to provide any group health plan to any employee, (2) the date on which coverage ceases under the plan by reason of a failure to make timely payment of any premium required with respect to the qualified beneficiary, and (3) the date on which the qualified beneficiary first becomes (after the date of election of continuation coverage) either (i) covered under any other group health plan (as an employee or otherwise) which does not include any exclusion or limitation with respect to any preexisting condition of such beneficiary or (ii) entitled to Medicare benefits under title XVIII of the Social Security Act. Mere eligibility for another group health plan or Medicare benefits is not sufficient to terminate the minimum coverage period. Instead, the qualified beneficiary must be actually covered by the other group health plan or enrolled in Medicare. Coverage under another group health plan or enrollment in Medicare does not terminate the minimum coverage period if such other coverage or Medicare enrollment begins on or before the date that continuation coverage is elected.

Election of continuation coverage

The COBRA rules specify a minimum election period under which a qualified beneficiary is entitled to elect continuation coverage. The election period begins not later than the date on which coverage under the plan terminates on account of the qualifying event, and ends not earlier than the later of 60 days or 60 days after notice is given to the qualified beneficiary of the qualifying event and the beneficiary's election rights.

---

232. In the case of a qualified beneficiary who is determined, under Title II or XVI of the Social Security Act, to have been disabled during the first 60 days of continuation coverage, the 18 month minimum coverage period is extended to 29 months with respect to all qualified beneficiaries if notice is given before the end of the initial 18 month continuation coverage period.

Notice requirements

A group health plan is required to give a general notice of COBRA continuation coverage rights to employees and their spouses at the time of enrollment in the group health plan.

An employer is required to give notice to the plan administrator of certain qualifying events (including a loss of coverage on account of a termination of employment or reduction in hours) generally within 30 days of the qualifying event. A covered employee or qualified beneficiary is required to give notice to the plan administrator of certain qualifying events within 60 days after the event. The qualifying events giving rise to an employee or beneficiary notification requirement are the divorce or legal separation of the covered employee or a dependent child ceasing to be a dependent child under the terms of the plan. Upon receiving notice of a qualifying event from the employer, covered employee, or qualified beneficiary, the plan administrator is then required to give notice of COBRA continuation coverage rights within 14 days to all qualified beneficiaries with respect to the event.

Premiums

A plan may require payment of a premium for any period of continuation coverage. The amount of such premium generally may not exceed 102 percent[233] of the "applicable premium" for such period and the premium must be payable, at the election of the payor, in monthly installments.

The applicable premium for any period of continuation coverage means the cost to the plan for such period of coverage for similarly situated non-COBRA beneficiaries with respect to whom a qualifying event has not occurred, and is determined without regard to whether the cost is paid by the employer or employee. The determination of any applicable premium is made for a period of 12 months (the "determination period") and is required to be made before the beginning of such 12 month period.

In the case of a self-insured plan, the applicable premium for any period of continuation coverage of qualified beneficiaries is equal to a reasonable estimate of the cost of providing coverage during such period for similarly situated non-COBRA beneficiaries which is determined on an actuarial basis and takes into account such factors as the Secretary of Treasury prescribes in regulations. A self-insured plan may elect to determine the applicable premium on the basis of an adjusted cost to the plan for similarly situated non-COBRA beneficiaries during the preceding determination period.

A plan may not require payment of any premium before the day which is 45 days after the date on which the qualified beneficiary made the initial election for continuation coverage. A plan is required to treat any required premium payment as timely if it is made within 30 days after the date the premium is due or within such longer period as applies to, or under, the plan.

Other continuation coverage rules

Continuation coverage rules which are parallel to the Code's continuation coverage rules apply to group health plans under the Employee Retirement Income Security Act of 1974 (ERISA).[234] ERISA generally permits the Secretary of Labor and plan participants to bring a civil action to obtain appropriate equitable relief to enforce the continuation coverage rules of ERISA and in the case of a plan administrator who fails to give timely notice to a participant or beneficiary with respect to COBRA continuation coverage. a court may hold the plan administrator liable to the participant or beneficiary in the amount of up to $110 a day from the date of such failure.

---

233. In the case of a qualified beneficiary whose minimum coverage period is extended to 29 months on account of a disability determination, the premium for the period of the disability extension may not exceed 150 percent of the applicable premium for the period.
234. Secs. 601 to 608 of ERISA.

Although the Federal government and State and local governments are not subject to the Code and ERISA's continuation coverage rules, other laws impose similar continuation coverage requirements with respect to plans maintained by such governmental employers.[235] In addition, many States have enacted laws or promulgated regulations that provide continuation coverage rights that are similar to COBRA continuation coverage rights in the case of a loss of group health coverage. Such State laws, for example, may apply in the case of a loss of coverage under a group health plan maintained by a small employer.

House Bill

Reduced COBRA premium

The provision provides that, for a period not exceeding 12 months, an assistance eligible individual is treated as having paid any premium required for COBRA continuation coverage under a group health plan if the individual pays 35 percent of the premium.[236] Thus, if the assistance eligible individual pays 35 percent of the premium, the group health plan must treat the individual as having paid the full premium required for COBRA continuation coverage, and the individual is entitled to a subsidy for 65 percent of the premium. An assistance eligible individual is any qualified beneficiary who elects COBRA continuation coverage and satisfies two additional requirements. First, the qualifying event with respect to the covered employee for that qualified beneficiary must be a loss of group health plan coverage on account of an involuntary termination of the covered employee's employment. However, a termination of employment for gross misconduct does not qualify (since such a termination under present law does not qualify for COBRA continuation coverage). Second, the qualifying event must occur during the period beginning September 1, 2008 and ending with December 31, 2009 and the qualified beneficiary must be eligible for COBRA continuation coverage during that period and elect such coverage.

An assistance eligible individual can be any qualified beneficiary associated with the relevant covered employee (e.g., a dependent of an employee who is covered immediately prior to a qualifying event), and such qualified beneficiary can independently elect COBRA (as provided under present law COBRA rules) and independently receive a subsidy. Thus, the subsidy for an assistance eligible individual continues after an intervening death of the covered employee.

Under the provision, any subsidy provided is excludible from the gross income of the covered employee and any assistance eligible individuals. However, for purposes of determining the gross income of the employer and any welfare benefit plan of which the group health plan is a part, the amount of the premium reduction is intended to be treated as an employee contribution to the group health plan. Finally, under the provision, notwithstanding any other provision of law, the subsidy is not permitted to be considered as income or resources in determining eligibility for, or the amount of assistance or benefits under, any public benefit provided under Federal or State law (including the law of any political subdivision).

---

235. Continuation coverage rights similar to COBRA continuation coverage rights are provided to individuals covered by health plans maintained by the Federal government. 5 U.S.C. sec. 8905a. Group health plans maintained by a State that receives funds under Chapter 6A of Title 42 of the United States Code (the Public Health Service Act) are required to provide continuation coverage rights similar to COBRA continuation coverage rights for individuals covered by plans maintained by such State (and plans maintained by political subdivisions of such State and agencies and instrumentalities of such State or political subdivision of such State). 42 U.S.C. sec. 300bb-1.

236. For this purpose, payment by an assistance eligible individual includes payment by another individual paying on behalf of the individual, such as a parent or guardian, or an entity paying on behalf of the individual, such as a State agency or charity. Further, the amount of the premium used to calculate the reduced premium is the premium amount that the employee would be required to pay for COBRA continuation coverage absent this premium reduction (e.g. 102 percent of the "applicable premium" for such period).

Eligible COBRA continuation coverage

Under the provision, continuation coverage that qualifies for the subsidy is not limited to coverage required to be offered under the Code's COBRA rules but also includes continuation coverage required under State law that requires continuation coverage comparable to the continuation coverage required under the Code's COBRA rules for group health plans not subject to those rules (e.g., a small employer plan) and includes continuation coverage requirements that apply to health plans maintained by the Federal government or a State government. Comparable continuation coverage under State law does not include every State law right to continue health coverage, such as a right to continue coverage with no rules that limit the maximum premium that can be charged with respect to such coverage. To be comparable, the right generally must be to continue substantially similar coverage as was provided under the group health plan (or substantially similar coverage as is provided to similarly situated beneficiaries) at a monthly cost that is based on a specified percentage of the group health plan's cost of providing such coverage.

The cost of coverage under any group health plan that is subject to the Code's COBRA rules (or comparable State requirements or continuation coverage requirement under health plans maintained by the Federal government or any State government) is eligible for the subsidy, except contributions to a health flexible spending account.

Termination of eligibility for reduced premiums

The assistance eligible individual's eligibility for the subsidy terminates with the first month beginning on or after the earlier of (1) the date which is 12 months after the first day of the first month for which the subsidy applies, (2) the end of the maximum required period of continuation coverage for the qualified beneficiary under the Code's COBRA rules or the relevant State or Federal law (or regulation), or (3) the date that the assistance eligible individual becomes eligible for Medicare benefits under title XVIII of the Social Security Act or health coverage under another group health plan (including, for example, a group health plan maintained by the new employer of the individual or a plan maintained by the employer of the individual's spouse). However, eligibility for coverage under another group health plan does not terminate eligibility for the subsidy if the other group health plan provides only dental, vision, counseling, or referral services (or a combination of the foregoing), is a health flexible spending account or health reimbursement arrangement, or is coverage for treatment that is furnished in an on-site medical facility maintained by the employer and that consists primarily of first-aid services, prevention and wellness care, or similar care (or a combination of such care).

If a qualified beneficiary paying a reduced premium for COBRA continuation coverage under this provision becomes eligible for coverage under another group health plan or Medicare, the provision requires the qualified beneficiary to notify, in writing, the group health plan providing the COBRA continuation coverage with the reduced premium of such eligibility under the other plan or Medicare. The notification by the assistance eligible individual must be provided to the group health plan in the time and manner as is specified by the Secretary of Labor. If an assistance eligible individual fails to provide this notification at the required time and in the required manner, and as a result the individual's COBRA continuation coverage continues to be subsidized after the termination of the individual's eligibility for such subsidy, a penalty is imposed on the individual equal to 110 percent of the subsidy provided after termination of eligibility.

This penalty only applies if the subsidy in the form of the premium reduction is actually provided to a qualified beneficiary for a month that the beneficiary is not eligible for the reduction. Thus, for example, if a qualified beneficiary becomes eligible for coverage under another group health plan and stops paying the reduced COBRA continuation premium, the penalty generally will not apply. As discussed below, under the provision, the group health plan is reimbursed for the subsidy for a month (65 percent of the amount of the premium for the month) only after receipt of the qualified beneficiary's portion (35 percent of the premium amount). Thus, the penalty generally will only arise when the qualified beneficiary continues to pay the reduced premium and does not notify the group health plan providing COBRA continuation coverage of the beneficiary's eligibility under another group health plan or Medicare.

Special COBRA election opportunity

The provision provides a special 60 day election period for a qualified beneficiary who is eligible for a reduced premium and who has not elected COBRA continuation coverage as of the date of enactment. The 60 day election period begins on the date that notice is provided to the qualified beneficiary of the special election period. However, this special election period does not extend the period of COBRA continuation coverage beyond the original maximum required period (generally 18 months after the qualifying event) and any COBRA continuation coverage elected pursuant to this special election period begins on the date of enactment and does not include any period prior to that date. Thus, for example, if a covered employee involuntarily terminated employment on September 10, 2008, but did not elect COBRA continuation coverage and was not eligible for coverage under another group health plan. the employee would have 60 days after date of notification of this new election right to elect the coverage and receive the subsidy. If the employee made the election, the coverage would begin with the date of enactment and would not include any period prior to that date. However, the coverage would not be required to last for 18 months. Instead the maximum required COBRA continuation coverage period would end not later than 18 months after September 10, 2008.

The special enrollment provision applies to a group health plan that is subject to the COBRA continuation coverage requirements of the Code, ERISA, Title 5 of the United States Code (relating to plans maintained by the Federal government), or the Public health Service Act ("PHSA").

With respect to an assistance eligible individual who elects coverage pursuant to the special election period, the period beginning on the date of the qualifying event and ending with the day before the date of enactment is disregarded for purposes of the rules that limit the group health plan from imposing pre-existing condition limitations with respect to the individual's coverage.[237]

Reimbursement of group health plans

The provision provides that the entity to which premiums are payable (determined under the applicable COBRA continuation coverage requirement)[238] shall be reimbursed by the amount of the premium for COBRA continuation coverage that is not paid by an assistance eligible individual on account of the premium reduction. An entity is not eligible for subsidy reimbursement, however, until the entity has received the reduced premium payment from the assistance eligible individual. To the extent that such entity has liability for income tax withholding from wages[239] or FICA taxes[240] with respect to its

---

237. Section 9801 provides that a group health plan may impose a pre-existing condition exclusion for no more than 12 months after a participant or beneficiary's enrollment date. Such 12-month period must be reduced by the aggregate period of creditable coverage (which includes periods of coverage under another group health plan). A period of creditable coverage can be disregarded if, after the coverage period and before the enrollment date, there was a 63-day period during which the individual was not covered under any creditable coverage. Similar rules are provided under ERISA and PHSA.
238. Applicable continuation coverage that qualifies for the subsidy and thus for reimbursement is not limited to coverage required to be offered under the Code's COBRA rules but also includes continuation coverage required under State law that requires continuation coverage comparable to the continuation coverage required under the Code's COBRA rules for group health plans not subject to those rules (e.g., a small employer plan) and includes continuation coverage requirements that apply to health plans maintained by the Federal government or a State government.
239. Sec. 3401.
240. Sec. 3102 (relating to FICA taxes applicable to employees) and sec. 3111 (relating to FICA taxes applicable to employers).

employees, the entity is reimbursed by treating the amount that is reimbursable to the entity as a credit against its liability for these payroll taxes.[241] To the extent that such amount exceeds the amount of the entity's liability for these payroll taxes, the Secretary shall reimburse the entity for the excess directly. The provision requires any entity entitled to such reimbursement to submit such reports as the Secretary of Treasury may require, including an attestation of the involuntary termination of employment of each covered employee on the basis of whose termination entitlement to reimbursement of premiums is claimed, and a report of the amount of payroll taxes offset for a reporting period and the estimated offsets of such taxes for the next reporting period. This report is required to be provided at the same time as the deposits of the payroll taxes would have been required, absent the offset, or such times as the Secretary specifics.

Notice requirements

The notice of COBRA continuation coverage that a plan administrator is required to provide to qualified beneficiaries with respect to a qualifying event under present law must contain, under the provision, additional information including, for example, information about the qualified beneficiary's right to the premium reduction (and subsidy) and the conditions on the subsidy, and a description of the obligation of the qualified beneficiary to notify the group health plan of eligibility under another group health plan or eligibility for Medicare benefits under title XVIII of the Social Security Act, and the penalty for failure to provide this notification. The provision also requires a new notice to be given to qualified beneficiaries entitled to a special election period after enactment. In the case of group health plans that are not subject to the COBRA continuation coverage requirements of the Code, ERISA, Title 5 of the United States Code (relating to plans maintained by the Federal government), or PHSA, the provision requires that notice be given to the relevant employees and beneficiaries as well, as specified by the Secretary of Labor. Within 30 days after enactment, the Secretary of Labor is directed to provide model language for the additional notification required under the provision. The provision also provides an expedited 10-day review process by the Department of Labor, under which an individual may request review of a denial of treatment as an assistance eligible individual by a group health plan.

Regulatory authority

The provision provides authority to the Secretary of the Treasury to issue regulations or other guidance as may be necessary or appropriate to carry out the provision, including any reporting requirements or the establishment of other methods for verifying the correct amounts of payments and credits under the provision. For example, the Secretary of the Treasury might require verification on the return of an assistance eligible individual who is the covered employee that the individual's termination of employment was involuntary. The provision directs the Secretary of the Treasury to issue guidance or regulations addressing the reimbursement of the subsidy in the case of a multiemployer group health plan. The provision also provides authority to the Secretary of the Treasury to promulgate rules, procedures, regulations, and other guidance as is necessary and appropriate to prevent fraud and abuse in the subsidy program, including the employment tax offset mechanism.

Reports

The provision requires the Secretary of the Treasury to submit an interim and a final report regarding the implementation of the premium reduction provision. The interim report is to include information about the number of individuals receiving assistance, and the total amount of expenditures incurred, as of the date of the report. The final report, to be issued as soon as practicable after the last period of COBRA continuation coverage for which premiums are provided, is to include similar information as provided in

---

241. In determining any amount transferred or appropriated to any fund under the Social Security Act, amounts credited against an employer's payroll tax obligations pursuant to the provision shall not be taken into account.

the interim report, with the addition of information about the average dollar amount (monthly and annually) of premium reductions provided to such individuals. The reports are to be given to the Committee on Ways and Means, the Committee on Energy and Commerce, the Committee on Health Education, Labor and Pensions and the Committee on Finance.

Senate Amendment

The Senate amendment is the same as the House bill with certain modifications. The amount of the COBRA the premium reduction (or subsidy) is 50 percent of the required premium under the Senate amendment (rather than 65 percent as provided under the House bill).

In addition, a group health plan is permitted to provide a special enrollment right to assistance-eligible individuals to allow them to change coverage options under the plan in conjunction with electing COBRA continuation coverage. Under this special enroll-ment right, the assistance eligible individual must only be offered the option to change to any coverage option offered to employed workers that provides the same or lower health insurance premiums than the individual's group health plan coverage as of the date of the covered employee's qualifying event. If the individual elects a different cov-erage option under this special enrollment right in conjunction with electing COBRA continuation coverage, this is the coverage that must be provided for purposes of satisfy-ing the COBRA continuation coverage requirement. However the coverage plan option into which the individual must be given the opportunity to enroll under this special en-rollment right does not include the following: a coverage option providing only dental, vision, counseling, or referral services (or a combination of the foregoing); a health flex-ible spending account or health reimbursement arrangement; or coverage for treatment that is furnished in an on-site medical facility maintained by the employer and that con-sists primarily of first-aid services, prevention and wellness care, or similar care (or a combination of such care).

Conference Agreement

In general

The conference agreement generally follows the House bill. Thus, as under the House bill, the rate of the premium subsidy is 65 percent of the premium for a period of cover-age. However, the period of the premium subsidy is limited to a maximum of 9 months of coverage (instead of a maximum of 12 months). As under the House bill and Senate amendment, the premium subsidy is only provided with respect to involuntary termina-tions that occur on or after September 1, 2008, and before January 1, 2010.

The conference agreement includes the provision in the Senate amendment that per-mits a group health plan to provide a special enrollment right to assistance eligible indi-viduals to allow them to change coverage options under the plan in conjunction with electing COBRA continuation coverage.[242] This provision only allows a group health plan to offer additional coverage options to assistance eligible individuals and does not change the basic requirement under Federal COBRA continuation coverage requirements that a group health plan must allow an assistance eligible individual to choose to con-tinue with the coverage in which the individual is enrolled as of the qualifying event.[243] However, once the election of the other coverage is made, it becomes COBRA continua-tion coverage under the applicable COBRA continuation provisions. Thus, for example, under the Federal COBRA continuation coverage provisions, if a covered employee chooses different coverage pursuant to being provided this option, the different coverage elected must generally be permitted to be continued for the applicable required period (generally 18 months or 36 months, absent an event that permits coverage to be termi-

---

242. An employer can make this option available to covered employees under current law.
243. All references to "Federal COBRA continuation coverage" mean the COBRA continuation coverage provisions of the Code, ERISA, and PHSA.

nated under the Federal COBRA continuation provisions) even though the premium subsidy is only for nine months.

The conference agreement adds an income threshold as an additional condition on an individual's entitlement to the premium subsidy during any taxable year. The income threshold applies based on the modified adjusted gross income for an individual income tax return for the taxable year in which the subsidy is received (i.e., either 2009 or 2010) with respect to which the assistance eligible individual is the taxpayer, the taxpayer's spouse or a dependent of the taxpayer (within the meaning of section 152 of the Code, determined without regard to sections 152(b)(1), (b)(2) and (d)(1)(B)). Modified adjusted gross income for this purpose means adjusted gross income as defined in section 62 of the Code increased by any amount excluded from gross income under section 911, 931, or 933 of the Code. Under this income threshold, if the premium subsidy is provided with respect to any COBRA continuation coverage which covers the taxpayer, the taxpayer's spouse, or any dependent of the taxpayer during a taxable year and the taxpayer's modified adjusted gross income exceeds $145,000 (or $290,000 for joint filers), then the amount of the premium subsidy for all months during the taxable year must be repaid. The mechanism for repayment is an increase in the taxpayer's income tax liability for the year equal to such amount. For taxpayers with adjusted gross income between $125,000 and $145,000 (or $250,000 and $290,000 for joint filers), the amount of the premium subsidy for the taxable year that must be repaid is reduced proportionately.

Under this income threshold, for example, an assistance eligible individual who is eligible for Federal COBRA continuation coverage based on the involuntary termination of a covered employee in August 2009 but who is not entitled to the premium subsidy for the periods of coverage during 2009 due to having income above the threshold, may nevertheless be entitled to the premium subsidy for any periods of coverage in the remaining period (e.g. 5 months of coverage) during 2010 to which the subsidy applies if the modified adjusted gross income for 2010 of the relevant taxpayer is not above the income threshold.

The conference report allows an individual to make a permanent election (at such time and in such form as the Secretary of Treasury may prescribe) to waive the right to the premium subsidy for all periods of coverage. For the election to take effect, the individual must notify the entity (to which premiums are reimbursed under section 6432(a) of the Code) of the election. This waiver provision allows an assistance eligible individual who is certain that the modified adjusted gross income limit prevents the individual from being entitled to any premium subsidy for any coverage period to decline the subsidy for all coverage periods and avoid being subject to the recapture tax. However, this waiver applies to all periods of coverage (regardless of the tax year of the coverage) for which the individual might be entitled to the subsidy. The premium subsidy for any period of coverage cannot later be claimed as a tax credit or otherwise be recovered, even if the individual later determines that the income threshold was not exceeded for a relevant tax year. This waiver is made separately by each qualified beneficiary (who could be an assistance eligible individual) with respect to a covered employee.

Technical changes

The conference agreement makes a number of technical changes to the COBRA premium subsidy provisions in the House bill. The conference agreement clarifies that a reference to a period of coverage in the provision is a reference to the monthly or shorter period of coverage with respect to which premiums are charged with respect to such coverage. For example, the provision is effective for a period of coverage beginning after the date of enactment. In the case of a plan that provides and charges for COBRA continuation coverage on a calendar month basis, the provision is effective for the first calendar month following date of enactment.

The conference agreement specifically provides that if a person other than the individual's employer pays on the individual's behalf then the individual is treated as paying 35 percent of the premium, as required to be entitled to the premium subsidy. Thus, the conference agreement makes clear that, for this purpose, payment by an assistance eligible individual includes payment by another individual paying on behalf of the individual, such as a parent or guardian, or an entity paying on behalf of the individual, such as a State agency or charity.

The conference agreement clarifies that, for the special 60 day election period for a qualified beneficiary who is eligible for a reduced premium and who has not elected COBRA continuation coverage as of the date of enactment provided in the House bill, the election period begins on the date of enactment and ends 60 days after the notice is provided to the qualified beneficiary of the special election period. In addition, the conference agreement clarifies that coverage elected under this special election right begins with the first period of coverage beginning on or after the date of enactment. The conference agreement also extends this special COBRA election opportunity to a qualified beneficiary who elected COBRA coverage but who is no longer enrolled on the date of enactment, for example, because the beneficiary was unable to continue paying the premium.

The conference agreement clarifies that a violation of the new notice requirements is also a violation of the notice requirements of the underlying COBRA provision. As under the House bill, a notice must be provided to all individuals who terminated employment during the applicable time period, and not just to individuals who were involuntarily terminated.

As under the House bill, coverage under a flexible spending account ("FSA") is not eligible for the subsidy. The conference agreement clarifies that a FSA is defined as a health flexible spending account offered under a cafeteria plan within the meaning of section 125 of the Code.[244]

As under the House bill, there is a provision for expedited review, by the Secretary of Labor or Health and Human Services (in consultation with the Secretary of the Treasury), of denials of the premium subsidy. Under the conference agreement, such reviews must be completed within 15 business days (rather than 10 business days as provided in the House bill) after receipt of the individual's application for review. The conference agreement is intended to give the Secretaries the flexibility necessary to make determinations within 15 business days based upon evidence they believe, in their discretion, to be appropriate. Additionally, the conference agreement intends that, if an individual is denied treatment as an assistance eligible individual and also submits a claim for benefits to the plan that would be denied by reason of not being eligible for Federal COBRA continuation coverage (or failure to pay full premiums), the individual would be eligible to proceed with expedited review irrespective of any claims for benefits that may be pending or subject to review under the provisions of ERISA 503. Under the conference agreement, either Secretary's determination upon review is de novo and is the final determination of such Secretary.

The conference agreement clarifies the reimbursement mechanism for the premium subsidy in several respects. First, it clarifies that the person to whom the reimbursement is payable is either (1) the multiemployer group health plan, (2) the employer maintaining the group health plan subject to Federal COBRA continuation coverage requirements, and (3) the insurer providing coverage under an insured plan. Thus, this is the person who is eligible to offset its payroll taxes for purposes of reimbursement. It also clarifies that the credit for the reimbursement is treated as a payment of payroll taxes. Thus, it clarifies that any reimbursement for an amount in excess of the payroll taxes

---

244. Other FSA coverage does not terminate eligibility for coverage. Coverage under another group Health Reimbursement Account ("HRA") will not terminate an individual's eligibility for the subsidy as long as the HRA is properly classified as an FSA under relevant IRS guidance. See Notice 2002-45, 2002-2 CB 93.

owed is treated in the same manner as a tax refund. Similarly, it clarifies that overstatement of reimbursement is a payroll tax violation. For example, IRS can assert appropriate penalties for failing to truthfully account for the reimbursement. However, it is not intended that any portion of the reimbursement is taken into account when determining the amount of any penalty to be imposed against any person, required to collect, truthfully account for, and pay over any tax under section 6672 of the Code.

It is intended that reimbursement not be mirrored in the U.S. possessions that have mirror income tax codes (the Commonwealth of the Northern Mariana Islands, Guam, and the Virgin Islands). Rather, the intent of Congress is that reimbursement will have direct application to persons in those possessions. Moreover, it is intended that income tax withholding payable to the government of any possession (American Samoa, the Commonwealth of the Northern Mariana Islands, the Commonwealth of Puerto Rico, Guam, or the Virgin Islands) (in contrast with FICA withholding payable to the U.S. Treasury) will not be reduced as a result of the application of this provision. A person liable for both FICA withholding payable to the U.S, Treasury and income tax withholding payable to a possession government will be credited or refunded any excess of (1) the amount of FICA taxes treated as paid under the reimbursement rule of the provision over (2) the amount of the person's liability for those FICA taxes.

Effective Date

The provision is effective for periods of coverage beginning after the date of enactment. In addition, specific rules are provided in the case of an assistance eligible individual who pays 100 percent of the premium required for COBRA continuation coverage for any coverage period during the 60-day period beginning on the first day of the first coverage period after the date of enactment. Such rules follow the Senate amendment.

[¶ 5084]   Section 7001.   Executive compensation and corporate governance.

(Code Sec. None)

[Conference Report]

Present Law

An employer generally may deduct reasonable compensation for personal services as an ordinary and necessary business expense. Section 162(m) (relating to remuneration expenses for certain executives that are in excess of $1 million) and section 280G (relating to excess parachute payments) provide explicit limitations on the deductibility of certain compensation expenses in the case of corporate employers, and section 4999 imposes an additional tax of 20 percent on the recipient of an excess parachute payment. The Emergency Economic Stabilization Act of 2008 ("EESA") limits the amount of payments that may be deducted as reasonable compensation by certain financial institutions ("TARP recipients") that receive financial assistance from the United States pursuant to the troubled asset relief program ("TARP") established under EESA by modifying the section 162(m) and section 280G limits. EESA also provided non-tax rules relating to the compensation that is payable by such a financial institution (the "TARP executive compensation rules").

House Bill

No provision.

Senate Amendment

The provision modifies and expands the present law non-tax TARP executive compensation rules. The modifications include: (1) expanding the requirement of recovery of a bonus, retention award, or incentive compensation paid to a senior executive officer based on statements of earnings, revenues, gains, or other criteria that are found to be materially inaccurate to the next 20 most highly compensated employees of a TARP recipient; (2) expanding the prohibition on the payment of golden parachute payments from senior executive officers to the next five most highly compensated employees of the TARP recipient, and defining the term "golden parachute payment" as any payment to a senior executive officer for departure from a company for any reason, except for payments for services performed or benefits accrued; and (3) prohibiting a TARP recipient from paying or accruing any bonus, retention award, or incentive compensation to at least the 25 most highly compensated employees; and (4) prohibiting any compensation plan that would encourage manipulation of the reported earnings of a TARP recipient to enhance the compensation of any of its employees. The provision also provides rules relating to the compensation committees of TARP recipients, nonbinding shareholder votes on executive compensation payable by a TARP recipient, and the adoption by TARP recipients of policies regarding luxury expenditures such as entertainment, aviation, and office renovation expenses.

Conference Agreement

The conference agreement follows the Senate amendment with several modifications. Among the modifications are (1) a rule that provides that financial assistance under TARP is not treated as outstanding for a period in which the United States only holds warrants to purchase common stock of the TARP recipient; (2) rules that phase-in the restriction on bonuses, retention awards, and other incentive compensation by the amount of financial assistance received by the entity receiving TARP assistance, and that permit compensation to be paid in the form of restricted stock; and (3) and a directive to the Secretary of the Treasury to review compensation paid to senior executive officers and the next 20 most highly compensated employees of an entity receiving TARP assistance before the date of enactment to determine whether such payments were inconsistent with the provision, the TARP, or public interest.

[¶ 5100] Joint Committee on Taxation Technical Explanation of the Children's Health Insurance Program Reauthorization Act of 2009

No official Committee Reports were issued to accompany H.R. 2, the Children's Health Insurance Program Reauthorization Act of 2009. Thus, this section, in ¶ 5101 and ¶ 5102, reproduces and treats as a Committee Report all relevant parts of the Joint Committee on Taxation Technical Explanation (JCX-3-09, 1/14/2009) of H.R. 2, the Children's Health Insurance Program Reauthorization Act of 2009 (P.L. 111-3, 2/4/ 2009).

[¶ 5101]   Section 704.   Time for payment of corporate estimated taxes.

(Code Sec. None)

[Joint Committee on Taxation Report]

Present Law

In general, corporations are required to make quarterly estimated tax payments of their income tax liability. For a corporation whose taxable year is a calendar year, these estimated payments must be made by April 15, June 15, September 15, and December 15. For tax years beginning on any date other than January 1, the payments are due in months of the fiscal year that correspond to the calendar year payment months.

Under the Tax Increase Prevention Act of 2005 ("TIPRA"), as amended, in the case of a corporation with assets of at least $1 billion, the payments due in July, August, and September, 2013, shall be increased to 120.00 percent of the payment otherwise due and the next required payment shall be reduced accordingly.

Explanation of Provision

The provision increases the otherwise applicable percentage for 2013 (120.00) by 1.00 percentage point.

Effective Date

The provision is effective on the date of enactment.

[¶ 5102]   Section 311.   Special enrollment period under group health plans in case of termination of Medicaid or CHIP coverage or eligibility for assistance in purchase of employment-based coverage; coordination of coverage.

(Code Sec. 9801)

[Joint Committee on Taxation Report]

Present Law

A group health plan is required to permit an employee who is eligible, but not enrolled, for coverage under the terms of the plan to enroll for coverage under the plan if certain conditions are satisfied.[31] Included among the conditions are (1) the employee was covered under a group health plan or had health insurance coverage at the time coverage was previously offered to the employee, and (2) such other coverage terminated as a result of loss of eligibility for such coverage. This special enrollment right must also be extended to a dependent of an employee if the dependent is eligible, but not enrolled, for coverage under the terms of the group health plan and the dependent satisfies the conditions for special enrollment. The special enrollment rights apply without regard to

---

31. Sec. 9801(f).

the dates on which the employee (or dependent) would otherwise be able to enroll under the plan. If a plan receives a request for special enrollment, coverage under the plan must generally begin no later than the first day of the first calendar month beginning after the date that notice of the request is received by the plan.

An excise tax is imposed if a group health plan fails to comply with the special enrollment rights requirement.[32] The rate of the tax on any failure is $100 for each day in the noncompliance period with respect to each individual to whom the failure relates. In the case of a single employer plan, the tax is imposed on the employer that maintains the plan.

Special enrollment rights that are parallel to the Code's rules are set forth in the Employee Retirement Income Security Act of 1974 ("ERISA") and the Public Health Service Act ("PHSA").

Explanation of Provision

Under the provision, a group health plan is required to permit an employee who is eligible, but not enrolled, for coverage under the plan to enroll for coverage if either (1) the employee is covered under a Medicaid plan or a State child health plan under titles XIX and XXI of the Social Security Act, respectively (a "Medicaid plan" or a "State child health plan"), and coverage is terminated as a result of loss of eligibility for the Medicaid plan or State child health plan and the employee requests coverage under the group health plan within 60 days of coverage loss; or (2) the employee becomes eligible for assistance with respect to coverage under the group health plan under a Medicaid plan or State child health plan, and the employee requests coverage not later than 60 days after the employee is determined to be eligible for such assistance. The special enrollment rights of the provision also apply to a dependent of an employee if the dependent is eligible, but not enrolled, for coverage under the terms of the group health plan and the dependent satisfies the conditions for special enrollment. The provision requires an employer to provide employees with written notice of the availability of premium assistance programs under Medicaid or State child health plans. In addition, the administrator of a group health plan must provide information upon request of a State regarding the benefits available under the plan with respect to a participant or beneficiary who is covered under a Medicaid or State child health plan. The provision makes parallel amendments to ERISA and PHSA.

Effective Date

The provision is effective on April 1, 2009.

---

32. Sec. 4980D.

¶ 6000. Act Section Cross Reference Table

Act § cites are to the 2009 American Recovery and Reinvestment Act unless otherwise indicated. * denotes 2009 Children's Health Insurance Program Reauthorization Act.

Act §	Code §	Topic	Generally effective date	Analysis ¶	Com Rep ¶
311(a)*	9801(f)(3)	Special enrollment and notification requirements for group health plans for Medicaid- or CHIP-eligible employees or dependents	April 1, 2009	403	5102
704*	6655	Estimated tax payments due from corporations with assets of $1 billion or more are increased for installments due in July, Aug., Sept. 2013	Feb. 4, 2009	702	5101
1001(a)	36A	Refundable "making work pay credit" of up to $400 ($800 on joint return) is allowed for 2009 and 2010	Tax years beginning after Dec. 31, 2008, and before Jan. 1, 2011	101	5001
1001(b)	36A	Refundable "making work pay credit" of up to $400 ($800 on joint return) is allowed for 2009 and 2010	Tax years beginning after Dec. 31, 2008, and before Jan. 1, 2011	101	5001
1001(c)	36A	Refundable "making work pay credit" of up to $400 ($800 on joint return) is allowed for 2009 and 2010	Tax years beginning after Dec. 31, 2008, and before Jan. 1, 2011	101	5001
1001(d)	6213(g)(2)(N)	Refundable "making work pay credit" of up to $400 ($800 on joint return) is allowed for 2009 and 2010	Tax years beginning after Dec. 31, 2008, and before Jan. 1, 2011	101	5001
1001(e)(1)	6211(b)(4)(A)	Refundable "making work pay credit" of up to $400 ($800 on joint return) is allowed for 2009 and 2010	Tax years beginning after Dec. 31, 2008, and before Jan. 1, 2011	101	5001

Act §	Code §	Topic	Generally effective date	Analysis ¶	Com Rep ¶
1002(a)	32(b)(3)(A)	EIC credit percentage is increased for families with three or more qualifying children for 2009 and 2010	Tax years beginning in 2009 and 2010	110	5002
1002(a)	32(b)(3)(B)	Beginning point of EIC phaseout range is increased for joint filers for 2009 and 2010	Tax years beginning in 2009 or 2010	111	5002
1003(a)	24(d)(4)	Refundable portion of child tax credit is increased for 2009 and 2010	Tax years beginning in 2009 and 2010	109	5003
1004(a)	25A(i)	Hope credit is increased and expanded (and re-named the "American Opportunity Tax Credit") for 2009 and 2010	Tax years beginning in 2009 and 2010	107	5004
1004(b)(1)	24(b)(3)(B)	Hope credit is increased and expanded (and re-named the "American Opportunity Tax Credit") for 2009 and 2010	Tax years beginning in 2009 and 2010	107	5004
1004(b)(2)	25(e)(1)(C)(ii)	Hope credit is increased and expanded (and re-named the "American Opportunity Tax Credit") for 2009 and 2010	Tax years beginning in 2009 and 2010	107	5004
1004(b)(3)	26(a)(1)	Hope credit is increased and expanded (and re-named the "American Opportunity Tax Credit") for 2009 and 2010	Tax years beginning in 2009 and 2010	107	5004
1004(b)(4)	25B(g)(2)	Hope credit is increased and expanded (and re-named the "American Opportunity Tax Credit") for 2009 and 2010	Tax years beginning in 2009 and 2010	107	5004
1004(b)(5)	904(i)	Hope credit is increased and expanded (and re-named the "American Opportunity Tax Credit") for 2009 and 2010	Tax years beginning in 2009 and 2010	107	5004
1004(b)(6)	1400C(d)(2)	Hope credit is increased and expanded (and re-named the "American Opportunity Tax Credit") for 2009 and 2010	Tax years beginning in 2009 and 2010	107	5004

Act §	Code §	Topic	Generally effective date	Analysis ¶	Com Rep ¶
1004(b)(7)	6211(b)(4)(A)	Hope credit is increased and expanded (and re-named the "American Opportunity Tax Credit") for 2009 and 2010	Tax years beginning in 2009 and 2010	107	5004
1004(b)(8)	25A	Hope credit is increased and expanded (and re-named the "American Opportunity Tax Credit") for 2009 and 2010	Tax years beginning in 2009 and 2010	107	5004
1004(c)	25A	Hope credit is increased and expanded (and re-named the "American Opportunity Tax Credit") for 2009 and 2010	Tax years beginning in 2009 and 2010	107	5004
1005(a)	529(e)(3)(A)	Computer technology and equipment, and Internet access and related services, qualify as higher education expenses under 529 plans for 2009 and 2010	Expenses paid or incurred after Dec. 31, 2008	108	5005
1006(a)(1)	36(h)	First-time homebuyer credit is extended to purchases before Dec. 1, 2009 and increased to $8,000 ($4,000 for marrieds filing separately); recapture is waived unless residence is sold or ceases to be a principal residence within 36 months of purchase	Residences purchased after Dec. 31, 2008 and before Dec. 1, 2009	104	5006
1006(a)(2)	36(g)	First-time homebuyer credit is extended to purchases before Dec. 1, 2009 and increased to $8,000 ($4,000 for marrieds filing separately); recapture is waived unless residence is sold or ceases to be a principal residence within 36 months of purchase	Residences purchased after Dec. 31, 2008 and before Dec. 1, 2009	104	5006

Act §	Code §	Topic	Generally effective date	Analysis ¶	Com Rep ¶
1006(b)(1)	36(b)	First-time homebuyer credit is extended to purchases before Dec. 1, 2009 and increased to $8,000 ($4,000 for marrieds filing separately); recapture is waived unless residence is sold or ceases to be a principal residence within 36 months of purchase	Residences purchased after Dec. 31, 2008 and before Dec. 1, 2009	104	5006
1006(b)(2)	36(b)(1)(B)	First-time homebuyer credit is extended to purchases before Dec. 1, 2009 and increased to $8,000 ($4,000 for marrieds filing separately); recapture is waived unless residence is sold or ceases to be a principal residence within 36 months of purchase	Residences purchased after Dec. 31, 2008 and before Dec. 1, 2009	104	5006
1006(c)(1)	36(f)(4)(D)	First-time homebuyer credit is extended to purchases before Dec. 1, 2009 and increased to $8,000 ($4,000 for marrieds filing separately); recapture is waived unless residence is sold or ceases to be a principal residence within 36 months of purchase	Residences purchased after Dec. 31, 2008 and before Dec. 1, 2009	104	5006
1006(c)(2)	36(g)	First-time homebuyer credit is extended to purchases before Dec. 1, 2009 and increased to $8,000 ($4,000 for marrieds filing separately); recapture is waived unless residence is sold or ceases to be a principal residence within 36 months of purchase	Residences purchased after Dec. 31, 2008 and before Dec. 1, 2009	104	5006

Act §	Code §	Topic	Generally effective date	Analysis ¶	Com Rep ¶
1006(d)(1)	1400C(e)(4)	First-time homebuyer credit is extended to purchases before Dec. 1, 2009 and increased to $8,000 ($4,000 for marrieds filing separately); recapture is waived unless residence is sold or ceases to be a principal residence within 36 months of purchase	Residences purchased after Dec. 31, 2008 and before Dec. 1, 2009	104	5006
1006(d)(1)	1400C(e)(4)	First-time homebuyer credit is extended to purchases before Dec. 1, 2009 and increased to $8,000 ($4,000 for marrieds filing separately); recapture is waived unless residence is sold or ceases to be a principal residence within 36 months of purchase	Residences purchased after Dec. 31, 2008 and before Dec. 1, 2009	104	5006
1006(e)	36(d)	First-time homebuyer credit is extended to purchases before Dec. 1, 2009 and increased to $8,000 ($4,000 for marrieds filing separately); recapture is waived unless residence is sold or ceases to be a principal residence within 36 months of purchase	Residences purchased after Dec. 31, 2008 and before Dec. 1, 2009	104	5006
1007(a)	85(c)	Up to $2,400 of unemployment compensation is excludible from recipient's gross income for 2009	Tax years beginning in 2009	106	5007
1008(a)	164(a)(6)	Standard or itemized deduction is allowed for sales and excise taxes imposed on most new vehicles purchased on or after Feb. 17, 2009 and before 2010	Purchases on or after Feb. 17, 2009 and before 2010	105	5008
1008(b)	164(b)(6)	Standard or itemized deduction is allowed for sales and excise taxes imposed on most new vehicles purchased on or after Feb. 17, 2009 and before 2010	Purchases on or after Feb. 17, 2009 and before 2010	105	5008

Act §	Code §	Topic	Generally effective date	Analysis ¶	Com Rep ¶
1008(c)(1)	63(c)(1)(E)	Standard or itemized deduction is allowed for sales and excise taxes imposed on most new vehicles purchased on or after Feb. 17, 2009 and before 2010	Purchases on or after Feb. 17, 2009 and before 2010	105	5008
1008(c)(2)	63(c)(9)	Standard or itemized deduction is allowed for sales and excise taxes imposed on most new vehicles purchased on or after Feb. 17, 2009 and before 2010	Purchases on or after Feb. 17, 2009 and before 2010	105	5008
1008(d)	56(b)(1)(E)	Standard or itemized deduction is allowed for sales and excise taxes imposed on most new vehicles purchased on or after Feb. 17, 2009 and before 2010	Purchases on or after Feb. 17, 2009 and before 2010	105	5008
1011(a)(1)	23(b)(4)	Nonrefundable personal credits can offset AMT through 2009 (instead of 2008)	Tax years beginning in 2009	204	5010
1011(a)(1)	24(b)(3)	Nonrefundable personal credits can offset AMT through 2009 (instead of 2008)	Tax years beginning in 2009	204	5010
1011(a)(1)	25(e)(1)(C)	Nonrefundable personal credits can offset AMT through 2009 (instead of 2008)	Tax years beginning in 2009	204	5010
1011(a)(1)	25A(i)(5)	Nonrefundable personal credits can offset AMT through 2009 (instead of 2008)	Tax years beginning in 2009	204	5010
1011(a)(1)	25B(g)	Nonrefundable personal credits can offset AMT through 2009 (instead of 2008)	Tax years beginning in 2009	204	5010
1011(a)(1)	25D(c)	Nonrefundable personal credits can offset AMT through 2009 (instead of 2008)	Tax years beginning in 2009	204	5010
1011(a)(1)	26(a)(2)	Nonrefundable personal credits can offset AMT through 2009 (instead of 2008)	Tax years beginning in 2009	204	5010

Act §	Code §	Topic	Generally effective date	Analysis ¶	Com Rep ¶
1011(a)(1)	30D(d)(2)(B)	Nonrefundable personal credits can offset AMT through 2009 (instead of 2008)	Tax years beginning in 2009	204	5010
1011(a)(1)	904(i)	Nonrefundable personal credits can offset AMT through 2009 (instead of 2008)	Tax years beginning in 2009	204	5010
1011(a)(1)	1400C(d)	Nonrefundable personal credits can offset AMT through 2009 (instead of 2008)	Tax years beginning in 2009	204	5010
1012(a)(1)	55(d)(1)(A)	AMT exemption amounts for 2009 are increased to $46,700 for unmarrieds, to $70,950 for joint filers, and to $35,475 for marrieds filing separately	Tax years beginning in 2009	201	5010
1012(a)(2)	55(d)(1)(B)	AMT exemption amounts for 2009 are increased to $46,700 for unmarrieds, to $70,950 for joint filers, and to $35,475 for marrieds filing separately	Tax years beginning in 2009	201	5010
1101(a)(1)	45(d)(1)	Placed-in-service end date is extended for three years through Dec. 31, 2012 for qualified wind facilities for purposes of the electricity production credit	Property placed in service after Feb. 17, 2009	1208	5013
1101(a)(2)	45(d)(2)	Placed-in-service end date is extended for three years through Dec. 31, 2013 for certain qualified facilities for purposes of the electricity production credit	Property placed in service after Feb. 17, 2009	1207	5013
1101(a)(2)	45(d)(3)	Placed-in-service end date is extended for three years through Dec. 31, 2013 for certain qualified facilities for purposes of the electricity production credit	Property placed in service after Feb. 17, 2009	1207	5013

Act §	Code §	Topic	Generally effective date	Analysis ¶	Com Rep ¶
1101(a)(2)	45(d)(4)	Placed-in-service end date is extended for three years through Dec. 31, 2013 for certain qualified facilities for purposes of the electricity production credit	Property placed in service after Feb. 17, 2009	1207	5013
1101(a)(2)	45(d)(6)	Placed-in-service end date is extended for three years through Dec. 31, 2013 for certain qualified facilities for purposes of the electricity production credit	Property placed in service after Feb. 17, 2009	1207	5013
1101(a)(2)	45(d)(7)	Placed-in-service end date is extended for three years through Dec. 31, 2013 for certain qualified facilities for purposes of the electricity production credit	Property placed in service after Feb. 17, 2009	1207	5013
1101(a)(2)	45(d)(9)	Placed-in-service end date is extended for three years through Dec. 31, 2013 for certain qualified facilities for purposes of the electricity production credit	Property placed in service after Feb. 17, 2009	1207	5013
1101(a)(3)	45(d)(11)(B)	Placed-in-service end date is extended for two years through Dec. 31, 2013 for qualified marine and hydrokinetic renewable energy facilities for purposes of the electricity production credit	Property placed in service after Feb. 17, 2009	1209	5013
1102(a)	48(a)(5)	Taxpayers can irrevocably elect 30% business energy credit instead of electricity production credit for qualified property that is part of qualified investment credit facilities placed in service after 2008 and before 2014 (2013 for wind facilities)	Facilities placed in service after Dec. 31, 2008 and before Jan. 1, 2014 (2013 for wind facilities)	1203	5014

Act §	Code §	Topic	Generally effective date	Analysis ¶	Com Rep ¶
1103(a)	48(c)(4)(B)	$4,000 annual limitation on business energy tax credit for qualified small wind energy property is repealed for periods after Dec. 31, 2008	Periods after Dec. 31, 2008	1201	5015
1103(b)(1)	48(a)(4)(D)	Business energy tax credit basis reduction rule for property financed by tax-exempt government subsidies or private activity bonds is retroactively terminated for periods after Dec. 31, 2008	Periods after Dec. 31, 2008	1206	5015
1103(b)(2)(A)	25C(e)(1)	Expenditures from subsidized energy financing can qualify for REEP credit and nonbusiness energy property credit	Tax years beginning after Dec. 31, 2008	1103	5021, 5022
1103(b)(2)(B)	25D(e)(9)	Expenditures from subsidized energy financing can qualify for REEP credit and nonbusiness energy property credit	Tax years beginning after Dec. 31, 2008	1103	5021, 5022
1103(b)(2)(C)	48A(b)(2)	Business energy tax credit basis reduction rule for property financed by tax-exempt government subsidies or private activity bonds is retroactively terminated for periods after Dec. 31, 2008	Periods after Dec. 31, 2008	1206	5015
1103(b)(2)(D)	48B(b)(2)	Business energy tax credit basis reduction rule for property financed by tax-exempt government subsidies or private activity bonds is retroactively terminated for periods after Dec. 31, 2008	Periods after Dec. 31, 2008	1206	5015
1104	48(d)	Coordination of Code Sec. 48 energy credit and Code Sec. 45 electricity production credit with renewable energy grants	Feb. 17, 2009	1205	5016
1111	54C(c)(4)	National bond volume limitation for new CREBs is increased by up to $1.6 billion	Bonds issued after Feb. 17, 2009	1210	5018

Act §	Code §	Topic	Generally effective date	Analysis ¶	Com Rep ¶
1112(a)	54D(d)	National bond volume limitation for qualified energy conservation bonds is increased by $2.4 billion; bonds for green community programs can fund loans or grants to individuals	Bonds issued after Feb. 17, 2009	1211	5019
1112(b)(1)	54D(f)(1)(A)(ii)	National bond volume limitation for qualified energy conservation bonds is increased by $2.4 billion; bonds for green community programs can fund loans or grants to individuals	Bonds issued after Feb. 17, 2009	1211	5019
1112(b)(2)	54D(e)(4)	National bond volume limitation for qualified energy conservation bonds is increased by $2.4 billion; bonds for green community programs can fund loans or grants to individuals	Bonds issued after Feb. 17, 2009	1211	5019
1121(a)	25C(a)	Nonbusiness energy property credit is increased from 10% to 30% and extended for one year	Tax years beginning after Dec. 31, 2008	1101	5021
1121(a)	25C(b)	Nonbusiness energy property credit is increased from 10% to 30% and extended for one year	Tax years beginning after Dec. 31, 2008	1101	5021
1121(b)(1)	25C(d)(3)(B)	Standards are modified for property qualifying for the nonbusiness energy property credit	Property placed in service after Feb. 17, 2009	1102	5021
1121(b)(2)	25C(d)(3)(C)	Standards are modified for property qualifying for the nonbusiness energy property credit	Property placed in service after Feb. 17, 2009	1102	5021
1121(b)(3)	25C(d)(3)(D)	Standards are modified for property qualifying for the nonbusiness energy property credit	Property placed in service after Feb. 17, 2009	1102	5021

Act §	Code §	Topic	Generally effective date	Analysis ¶	Com Rep ¶
1121(b)(4)	25C(d)(3)(E)	Standards are modified for property qualifying for the nonbusiness energy property credit	Tax years beginning after Dec. 31, 2008	1102	5021
1121(c)(1)	25C(d)(4)	Standards are modified for property qualifying for the nonbusiness energy property credit	Property placed in service after Feb. 17, 2009	1102	5021
1121(c)(2)	25C(d)(2)(A)(ii)	Standards are modified for property qualifying for the nonbusiness energy property credit	Property placed in service after Feb. 17, 2009	1102	5021
1121(d)(1)	25C(c)(4)	Standards are modified for property qualifying for the nonbusiness energy property credit	Property placed in service after Feb. 17, 2009	1102	5021
1121(d)(2)	25C(c)(2)(A)	Standards are modified for property qualifying for the nonbusiness energy property credit	Property placed in service after Feb. 17, 2009	1102	5021
1121(e)	25C(g)(2)	Nonbusiness energy property credit is increased from 10% to 30% and extended for one year	Tax years beginning after Dec. 31, 2008	1101	5021
1122(a)(1)	25D(b)(1)	Dollar caps on REEP credit are eliminated for solar hot water, geothermal, and wind property expenditures	Tax years beginning after Dec. 31, 2008	1104	5022
1122(a)(2)	25D(e)(4)	Dollar caps on REEP credit are eliminated for solar hot water, geothermal, and wind property expenditures	Tax years beginning after Dec. 31, 2008	1104	5022
1123(a)	30C(e)(6)	Credit for QAFV refueling property is increased for property placed in service in tax years beginning in 2009 or 2010	Tax years beginning after Dec. 31, 2008	1001	5023
1131(a)	45Q(a)(2)(C)	Secure geological storage disposal requirement to apply to the $10 per metric ton component of the carbon dioxide sequestration credit	Carbon dioxide captured after Feb. 17, 2009	1212	5025

Act §	Code §	Topic	Generally effective date	Analysis ¶	Com Rep ¶
1131(b)(1)(A)	45Q(d)(2)	Secure geological storage disposal requirement to apply to the $10 per metric ton component of the carbon dioxide sequestration credit	Carbon dioxide captured after Feb. 17, 2009	1212	5025
1131(b)(1)(B)	45Q(d)(2)	Secure geological storage disposal requirement to apply to the $10 per metric ton component of the carbon dioxide sequestration credit	Carbon dioxide captured after Feb. 17, 2009	1212	5025
1131(b)(1)(C)	45Q(d)(2)	Secure geological storage disposal requirement to apply to the $10 per metric ton component of the carbon dioxide sequestration credit	Carbon dioxide captured after Feb. 17, 2009	1212	5025
1131(b)(2)	45Q(a)(1)(B)	Secure geological storage disposal requirement to apply to the $10 per metric ton component of the carbon dioxide sequestration credit	Carbon dioxide captured after Feb. 17, 2009	1212	5025
1131(b)(3)	45Q(e)	Secure geological storage disposal requirement to apply to the $10 per metric ton component of the carbon dioxide sequestration credit	Carbon dioxide captured after Feb. 17, 2009	1212	5025
1141(a)	30D	"New qualified plug-in electric drive motor vehicle credit" will be modified for vehicles acquired after Dec. 31, 2009	Vehicles acquired after Dec. 31, 2009	1002	5027
1141(b)(1)	30B(d)(3)(D)	"New qualified plug-in electric drive motor vehicle credit" will be modified for vehicles acquired after Dec. 31, 2009	Vehicles acquired after Dec. 31, 2009	1002	5027
1141(b)(2)	38(b)(35)	"New qualified plug-in electric drive motor vehicle credit" will be modified for vehicles acquired after Dec. 31, 2009	Vehicles acquired after Dec. 31, 2009	1002	5027
1141(b)(3)	1016(a)(25)	"New qualified plug-in electric drive motor vehicle credit" will be modified for vehicles acquired after Dec. 31, 2009	Vehicles acquired after Dec. 31, 2009	1002	5027

Act §	Code §	Topic	Generally effective date	Analysis ¶	Com Rep ¶
1141(b)(4)	6501(m)	"New qualified plug-in electric drive motor vehicle credit" will be modified for vehicles acquired after Dec. 31, 2009	Vehicles acquired after Dec. 31, 2009	1002	5027
1142(a)	30	Qualified plug-in electric vehicle credit is provided for certain low-speed vehicles and 2- or 3-wheeled vehicles acquired before Jan. 1, 2012	Vehicles acquired before Jan. 1, 2012 and after Feb. 17, 2009	1003	5027
1142(b)(1)(A)	24(b)(3)(B)	Qualified plug-in electric vehicle credit is provided for certain low-speed vehicles and 2- or 3-wheeled vehicles acquired before Jan. 1, 2012	Vehicles acquired before Jan. 1, 2012 and after Feb. 17, 2009	1003	5027
1142(b)(1)(B)	25(e)(1)(C)(ii)	Qualified plug-in electric vehicle credit is provided for certain low-speed vehicles and 2- or 3 wheeled vehicles acquired before Jan. 1, 2012	Vehicles acquired before Jan. 1, 2012 and after Feb. 17, 2009	1003	5027
1142(b)(1)(C)	25B(g)(2)	Qualified plug-in electric vehicle credit is provided for certain low-speed vehicles and 2- or 3-wheeled vehicles acquired before Jan. 1, 2012	Vehicles acquired before Jan. 1, 2012 and after Feb. 17, 2009	1003	5027
1142(b)(1)(D)	26(a)(1)	Qualified plug-in electric vehicle credit is provided for certain low-speed vehicles and 2- or 3-wheeled vehicles acquired before Jan. 1, 2012	Vehicles acquired before Jan. 1, 2012 and after Feb. 17, 2009	1003	5027
1142(b)(1)(E)	904(i)	"New qualified plug-in electric drive motor vehicle credit" will be modified for vehicles acquired after Dec. 31, 2009	Vehicles acquired after Dec. 31, 2009	1002	5027
1142(b)(1)(E)	904(i)	Qualified plug-in electric vehicle credit is provided for certain low-speed vehicles and 2- or 3-wheeled vehicles acquired before Jan. 1, 2012	Vehicles acquired before Jan. 1, 2012 and after Feb. 17, 2009	1003	5027

Act §	Code §	Topic	Generally effective date	Analysis ¶	Com Rep ¶
1142(b)(1)(F)	1400C(d)(2)	Qualified plug-in electric vehicle credit is provided for certain low-speed vehicles and 2- or 3-wheeled vehicles acquired before Jan. 1, 2012	Vehicles acquired before Jan. 1, 2012 and after Feb. 17, 2009	1003	5027
1142(b)(2)	30B(h)(1)	Qualified plug-in electric vehicle credit is provided for certain low-speed vehicles and 2- or 3-wheeled vehicles acquired before Jan. 1, 2012	Vehicles acquired before Jan. 1, 2012 and after Feb. 17, 2009	1003	5027
1142(b)(3)	30C(d)(2)(A)	Qualified plug-in electric vehicle credit is provided for certain low-speed vehicles and 2- or 3-wheeled vehicles acquired before Jan. 1, 2012	Vehicles acquired before Jan. 1, 2012 and after Feb. 17, 2009	1003	5027
1142(b)(4)(A)	53(d)(1)(B)(iii)	Qualified plug-in electric vehicle credit is provided for certain low-speed vehicles and 2- or 3-wheeled vehicles acquired before Jan. 1, 2012	Vehicles acquired before Jan. 1, 2012 and after Feb. 17, 2009	1003	5027
1142(b)(6)	1016(a)(25)	Qualified plug-in electric vehicle credit is provided for certain low-speed vehicles and 2- or 3-wheeled vehicles acquired before Jan. 1, 2012	Vehicles acquired before Jan. 1, 2012 and after Feb. 17, 2009	1003	5027
1142(b)(7)	6501(m)	Qualified plug-in electric vehicle credit is provided for certain low-speed vehicles and 2- or 3-wheeled vehicles acquired before Jan. 1, 2012	Vehicles acquired before Jan. 1, 2012 and after Feb. 17, 2009	1003	5027
1143(a)	30B(i)	Alternative motor vehicle credit (AMVC) is expanded to include a plug-in conversion credit for property placed in service after Feb. 17, 2009 and before Jan. 1, 2012	Property placed in service after Feb. 17, 2009 and conversions made before Jan. 1, 2012	1004	5027

Act §	Code §	Topic	Generally effective date	Analysis ¶	Com Rep ¶
1143(b)	30B(a)(5)	Alternative motor vehicle credit (AMVC) is expanded to include a plug-in conversion credit for property placed in service after Feb. 17, 2009 and before Jan. 1, 2012	Property placed in service after Feb. 17, 2009 and conversions made before Jan. 1, 2012	1004	5027
1143(c)	30B(h)(8)	Alternative motor vehicle credit (AMVC) is expanded to include a plug-in conversion credit for property placed in service after Feb. 17, 2009 and before Jan. 1, 2012	Property placed in service after Feb. 17, 2009 and conversions made before Jan. 1, 2012	1004	5027
1144(a)	30B(g)(2)	Alternative motor vehicle credit (AMVC) is treated as a personal credit allowed against AMT for tax years beginning after 2008	Tax years beginning after Dec. 31, 2008	205	5027
1144(b)(1)(A)	24(b)(3)(B)	Alternative motor vehicle credit (AMVC) is treated as a personal credit allowed against AMT for tax years beginning after 2008	Tax years beginning after Dec. 31, 2008	205	5027
1144(b)(1)(B)	25(e)(1)(C)(ii)	Alternative motor vehicle credit (AMVC) is treated as a personal credit allowed against AMT for tax years beginning after 2008	Tax years beginning after Dec. 31, 2008	205	5027
1144(b)(1)(C)	25B(g)(2)	Alternative motor vehicle credit (AMVC) is treated as a personal credit allowed against AMT for tax years beginning after 2008	Tax years beginning after Dec. 31, 2008	205	5027
1144(b)(1)(D)	26(a)(1)	Alternative motor vehicle credit (AMVC) is treated as a personal credit allowed against AMT for tax years beginning after 2008	Tax years beginning after Dec. 31, 2008	205	5027
1144(b)(1)(E)	904(i)	Alternative motor vehicle credit (AMVC) is treated as a personal credit allowed against AMT for tax years beginning after 2008	Tax years beginning after Dec. 31, 2008	205	5027

Act §	Code §	Topic	Generally effective date	Analysis ¶	Com Rep ¶
1144(b)(1)(F)	1400C(d)(2)	Alternative motor vehicle credit (AMVC) is treated as a personal credit allowed against AMT for tax years beginning after 2008	Tax years beginning after Dec. 31, 2008	205	5027
1144(b)(2)	30C(d)(2)(A)	Alternative motor vehicle credit (AMVC) is treated as a personal credit allowed against AMT for tax years beginning after 2008	Tax years beginning after Dec. 31, 2008	205	5027
1144(b)(3)	55(c)(3)	Alternative motor vehicle credit (AMVC) is treated as a personal credit allowed against AMT for tax years beginning after 2008	Tax years beginning after Dec. 31, 2008	205	5027
1151(a)	132(f)(2)	Monthly exclusion for employer-provided transit passes and vanpooling benefits increased to same level as employer-provided parking, for the rest of 2009 and 2010	Months beginning on or after Feb. 17, 2009	402	5032
1201	168(k)(4)(D)(ii)	Election to trade bonus and accelerated depreciation for otherwise-deferred credits is optionally extended through Dec. 31, 2009 (Dec. 31, 2010 for certain property)	Property placed in service before Jan. 1, 2010 and after Dec. 31, 2008	804	5034
1201(a)	168(k)(2)(A)(iv)	$8,000 increase in first-year depreciation limit for passenger automobiles that are "qualified property" is extended through Dec. 31, 2009	Property placed in service before Jan. 1, 2010 and after Dec. 31, 2008	803	5034
1201(a)(1)	168(k)(2)(A)(iv)	50% bonus depreciation and AMT depreciation relief are extended one year through Dec. 31, 2009 (Dec. 31, 2010 for certain property)	Property placed in service before Jan. 1, 2010 and after Dec. 31, 2008	801	5034

Act §	Code §	Topic	Generally effective date	Analysis ¶	Com Rep ¶
1201(a)(1)	168(k)(2)(A)(iv)	Election to trade bonus and accelerated depreciation for otherwise-deferred credits is optionally extended through Dec. 31, 2009 (Dec. 31, 2010 for certain property)	Property placed in service before Jan. 1, 2010 and after Dec. 31, 2008	804	5034
1201(a)(1)(B)	168(k)(2)(A)(iii)	50% bonus depreciation and AMT depreciation relief are extended one year through Dec. 31, 2009 (Dec. 31, 2010 for certain property)	Property placed in service before Jan. 1, 2010 and after Dec. 31, 2008	801	5034
1201(a)(1)(B)	168(k)(2)(B)(ii)	50% bonus depreciation and AMT depreciation relief are extended one year through Dec. 31, 2009 (Dec. 31, 2010 for certain property)	Property placed in service before Jan. 1, 2010 and after Dec. 31, 2008	801	5034
1201(a)(1)(B)	168(k)(2)(E)(i)	50% bonus depreciation and AMT depreciation relief are extended one year through Dec. 31, 2009 (Dec. 31, 2010 for certain property)	Property placed in service before Jan. 1, 2010 and after Dec. 31, 2008	801	5034
1201(a)(3)(A)(iii)	168(k)(4)(D)(ii)	Binding contract rule and tax deficiency rule for the election to trade bonus and accelerated depreciation for certain otherwise-deferred credits are corrected	Tax years ending after Mar. 31, 2008	806	5034
1201(a)(3)(B)	6211(b)(4)(A)	Binding contract rule and tax deficiency rule for the election to trade bonus and accelerated depreciation for certain otherwise-deferred credits are corrected	Tax years ending after Mar. 31, 2008	806	5034
1201(b)(1)(B)	168(k)(4)(H)	Election to trade bonus and accelerated depreciation for otherwise-deferred credits is optionally extended through Dec. 31, 2009 (Dec. 31, 2010 for certain property)	Property placed in service before Jan. 1, 2010 and after Dec. 31, 2008	804	5034

Act §	Code §	Topic	Generally effective date	Analysis ¶	Com Rep ¶
1201(b)(1)(B)	168(k)(4)(H)(ii)	Post-Dec. 31, 2008 election to trade bonus and accelerated depreciation for otherwise-deferred credits is allowed if an earlier election wasn't made	Property placed in service before Jan. 1, 2010 and after Dec. 31, 2008	805	5034
1201(b)(2)	6211(b)(4)(A)	Binding contract rule and tax deficiency rule for the election to trade bonus and accelerated depreciation for certain otherwise-deferred credits are corrected	Tax years ending after Mar. 31, 2008	806	5034
1202(a)	179(b)(7)	Regular Code Sec. 179 deduction limit of $250,000 and beginning of phaseout amount of $800,000 for 2008 are each extended to apply to tax years beginning in 2009	Tax years beginning in 2009	802	5035
1211(a)	172(b)(1)(H)	Carryback period for 2008 NOLs is increased to three, four, or five years (from two years) for electing small businesses	NOLs arising in tax years ending after Dec. 31, 2007	601	5037
1211(c)	172	Carryback period for 2008 NOLs is increased to three, four, or five years (from two years) for electing small businesses	NOLs arising in tax years ending after Dec. 31, 2007	601	5037
1211(d)(2)	172	Carryback period for 2008 NOLs is increased to three, four, or five years (from two years) for electing small businesses	NOLs arising in tax years ending after Dec. 31, 2007	601	5037
1212	6654(d)(1)(D)	Decreased required estimated tax payments in 2009 for certain small businesses	Tax years beginning in 2009	701	5038
1221(a)	51(d)(14)	Work opportunity credit is expanded to apply to new target group of unemployed veterans and disconnected youth who begin work in 2009 or 2010	Individuals who begin work for the employer after Dec. 31, 2008 and before Jan. 1, 2011	904	5039

Act §	Code §	Topic	Generally effective date	Analysis ¶	Com Rep ¶
1231(a)	108(i)	Income from reacquisitions of business debt at a discount in 2009 and 2010 is deferred for up to five years, then included ratably over five years	Discharges in tax years ending after Dec. 31, 2008, for reacquisitions after Dec. 31, 2008, and before Jan. 1, 2011	901	5041
1232(a)	163(e)(5)(F)	Rules for high-yield OID obligations are suspended for obligations issued from Sept. 1, 2008 to Dec. 31, 2009	Obligations issued after Aug. 31, 2008 and before Jan. 1, 2010, in tax years ending after Aug. 31, 2008	907	5042
1232(b)	163(i)(1)	Beginning in 2010, IRS will be able to apply a higher rate to determine whether an obligation is an applicable high-yield discount obligation	Obligations issued after Dec. 31, 2009, in tax years ending after Dec. 31, 2009	908	5042
1241(a)	1202(a)(3)	Noncorporate taxpayers can exclude 75% (rather than 50% or 60%) of gain on the sale or exchange of QSBS held for more than 5 years and acquired after Feb. 17, 2009 and before Jan. 1, 2011	Stock acquired after Feb. 17, 2009 and before Jan. 1, 2011	902	5044
1251(a)	1374(d)(7)	S Corp built-in gain holding period shortened for 2009 and 2010	Tax years beginning after Dec. 31, 2008	903	5046
1261(a)	None	Revocation of IRS guidance exempting banks from loss limitation rules following an ownership change	For ownership changes after Jan. 16, 2009	602	5048
1261(b)	382(h)	Revocation of IRS guidance exempting banks from loss limitation rules following an ownership change	For ownership changes after Jan. 16, 2009	602	5048

Act §	Code §	Topic	Generally effective date	Analysis ¶	Com Rep ¶
1262(a)	382(n)	Code Sec. 382 loss limitation rule doesn't apply where EESA bail-out agreement requires ownership restructuring	Ownership changes made after Feb. 17, 2009	603	5049
1301(a)	144(a)(12)(C)	IDBs issued before 2011 may finance facilities used to create intangible property	Bonds issued after Feb. 17, 2009 and before Jan. 1, 2011	1310	5051
1302(a)	46(5)	30% credit is allowed for investment in qualified property used in a qualified advanced energy manufacturing project	Periods after Feb. 17, 2009	1202	5052
1302(b)	48C	30% credit is allowed for investment in qualified property used in a qualified advanced energy manufacturing project	Periods after Feb. 17, 2009	1202	5052
1302(c)(1)	49(a)(1)(C)(v)	30% credit is allowed for investment in qualified property used in a qualified advanced energy manufacturing project	Periods after Feb. 17, 2009	1202	5052
1401(a)	1400U-1	Overview of national limits on two new categories of recovery zone bonds issued in 2009 and 2010 which are allocated among states based on 2008 employment declines subject to a minimum allocation	Obligations issued after Feb. 17, 2009 and before 2011	1304	5054
1401(a)	1400U-1	National limits for recovery zone economic development bonds and recovery zone facility bonds issued in 2009 and 2010 are allocated among states based on their 2008 employment declines subject to a minimum allocation	Obligations issued after Feb. 17, 2009 and before 2011	1305	5054

Act §	Code §	Topic	Generally effective date	Analysis ¶	Com Rep ¶
1401(a)	1400U-2	Overview of national limits on two new categories of recovery zone bonds issued in 2009 and 2010 which are allocated among states based on 2008 employment declines subject to a minimum allocation	Obligations issued after Feb. 17, 2009 and before 2011	1304	5054
1401(a)	1400U-2	U.S. Treasury will pay the issuer 45% of the interest the issuer pays to the holder of a taxable recovery zone economic development bond issued before 2011	Obligations issued after Feb. 17, 2009 and before 2011	1306	5054
1401(a)	1400U-3	Overview of national limits on two new categories of recovery zone bonds issued in 2009 and 2010 which are allocated among states based on 2008 employment declines subject to a minimum allocation	Obligations issued after Feb. 17, 2009 and before 2011	1304	5054
1401(a)	1400U-3	Recovery zone facility bonds are authorized for issuance in 2009 and 2010	Obligations issued after Feb. 17, 2009 and before 2011	1307	5054
1402(a)	7871(f)	Indian tribal governments can issue $2 billion of tribal economic development bonds	Bonds issued after Feb. 17, 2009	1313	5056
1403(a)(3)	45D(f)(1)	New markets tax credit national limit is raised for 2008 and 2009 with a preferential allocation rule for the 2008 increase	Feb. 17, 2009	905	5057
1403(b)	45D(f)(2)	New markets tax credit national limit is raised for 2008 and 2009 with a preferential allocation rule for the 2008 increase	Feb. 17, 2009	905	5057
1404	42(i)(9)	States can elect grants, instead of tax credits, to finance low-income housing for 2009, but tax credit allocations are reduced	Feb. 17, 2009	906	5058

Act §	Code §	Topic	Generally effective date	Analysis ¶	Com Rep ¶
1501(a)	265(b)(7)	Tax-exempt interest expense safe harbors for banks and small issuers are expanded for obligations issued in 2009 and 2010	Obligations issued after Dec. 31, 2008	1309	5060
1501(b)	291(e)(1)(B)(iv)	Tax-exempt interest expense safe harbors for banks and small issuers are expanded for obligations issued in 2009 and 2010	Obligations issued after Dec. 31, 2008	1309	5060
1502(a)	265(b)(3)(G)	Tax-exempt interest expense safe harbors for banks and small issuers are expanded for obligations issued in 2009 and 2010	Obligations issued after Dec. 31, 2008	1309	5060
1503(a)	57(a)(5)(C)(vi)	Interest on tax-exempt bonds issued in 2009 or 2010 isn't subject to AMT	Bonds issued after Dec. 31, 2008 and before Jan. 1, 2011	202	5062
1503(b)	56(g)(4)(B)(iv)	Corporate ACE adjustment isn't required for tax-exempt bonds issued in 2009 or 2010	Bonds issued after Dec. 31, 2008 and before Jan. 1, 2011	203	5062
1504(a)	142(i)(1)	Vehicles must be capable of attaining a maximum speed in excess of 150 m.p.h. under amended definition of high-speed intercity rail facilities	Bonds issued after Feb. 17, 2009	1312	5063
1511	3402(t)	Withholding tax on government contractors is delayed for one year until 2012	Feb. 17, 2009	703	5065
1521(a)	54F	Qualified school construction bond is a new type of tax credit bond	Bonds issued after Feb. 17, 2009	1302	5067
1521(b)(1)	54A(d)(1)(E)	Qualified school construction bond is a new type of tax credit bond	Bonds issued after Feb. 17, 2009	1302	5067
1521(b)(2)	54A(d)(2)(C)(v)	Qualified school construction bond is a new type of tax credit bond	Bonds issued after Feb. 17, 2009	1302	5067

Act §	Code §	Topic	Generally effective date	Analysis ¶	Com Rep ¶
1522(a)	54E(c)(1)	Credit for QZABs is extended through 2010; national bond volume limitation is increased to $1.4 billion for 2009 and 2010	Bonds issued after Dec. 31, 2008	1303	5068
1531(a)	54AA	New tax credit bond option is added for "Build America Bonds" issued in 2009 and 2010; issuer may claim alternative, refundable credit for "qualified bonds"	Obligations issued after Feb. 17, 2009 and before Jan. 1, 2011	1301	5070
1531(b)	6431	New tax credit bond option is added for "Build America Bonds" issued in 2009 and 2010; issuer may claim alternative, refundable credit for "qualified bonds"	Obligations issued after Feb. 17, 2009 and before Jan. 1, 2011	1301	5070
1531(c)(1)	6431	New tax credit bond option is added for "Build America Bonds" issued in 2009 and 2010; issuer may claim alternative, refundable credit for "qualified bonds"	Obligations issued after Feb. 17, 2009 and before Jan. 1, 2011	1301	5070
1531(c)(2)	54A(c)(1)(B)	New tax credit bond option is added for "Build America Bonds" issued in 2009 and 2010; issuer may claim alternative, refundable credit for "qualified bonds"	Obligations issued after Feb. 17, 2009 and before Jan. 1, 2011	1301	5070
1531(c)(3)	54(c)(2)	New tax credit bond option is added for "Build America Bonds" issued in 2009 and 2010; issuer may claim alternative, refundable credit for "qualified bonds"	Obligations issued after Feb. 17, 2009 and before Jan. 1, 2011	1301	5070
1531(c)(3)	1397E(c)(2)	New tax credit bond option is added for "Build America Bonds" issued in 2009 and 2010; issuer may claim alternative, refundable credit for "qualified bonds"	Obligations issued after Feb. 17, 2009 and before Jan. 1, 2011	1301	5070

Act §	Code §	Topic	Generally effective date	Analysis ¶	Com Rep ¶
1531(c)(3)	1400N(1)(3)(B)	New tax credit bond option is added for "Build America Bonds" issued in 2009 and 2010; issuer may claim alternative, refundable credit for "qualified bonds"	Obligations issued after Feb. 17, 2009 and before Jan. 1, 2011	1301	5070
1531(c)(4)	6211(b)(4)(A)	New tax credit bond option is added for "Build America Bonds" issued in 2009 and 2010; issuer may claim alternative, refundable credit for "qualified bonds"	Obligations issued after Feb. 17, 2009 and before Jan. 1, 2011	1301	5070
1531(c)(5)	6401(b)(1)	New tax credit bond option is added for "Build America Bonds" issued in 2009 and 2010; issuer may claim alternative, refundable credit for "qualified bonds"	Obligations issued after Feb. 17, 2009 and before Jan. 1, 2011	1301	5070
1531(d)	54AA	New tax credit bond option is added for "Build America Bonds" issued in 2009 and 2010; issuer may claim alternative, refundable credit for "qualified bonds"	Obligations issued after Feb. 17, 2009 and before Jan. 1, 2011	1301	5070
1541(a)	853A	Pass-through of tax credit bond credits by RICs and REITs is modified and expanded	Tax years ending after Feb. 17, 2009	1308	5072
1541(b)	54A(h)	Pass-through of tax credit bond credits by RICs and REITs is modified and expanded	Tax years ending after Feb. 17, 2009	1308	5072
1601(1)	54C	Prevailing wage requirements are applied to projects financed with specified bonds	Bonds issued after Feb. 17, 2009	1311	5074
1601(2)	54D	Prevailing wage requirements are applied to projects financed with specified bonds	Bonds issued after Feb. 17, 2009	1311	5074
1601(3)	54E	Prevailing wage requirements are applied to projects financed with specified bonds	Bonds issued after Feb. 17, 2009	1311	5074

Act §	Code §	Topic	Generally effective date	Analysis ¶	Com Rep ¶
1601(4)	54F	Prevailing wage requirements are applied to projects financed with specified bonds	Bonds issued after Feb. 17, 2009	1311	5074
1601(5)	1400U-2	Prevailing wage requirements are applied to projects financed with specified bonds	Bonds issued after Feb. 17, 2009	1311	5074
1602	None	States can elect grants, instead of tax credits, to finance low-income housing for 2009, but tax credit allocations are reduced	Feb. 17, 2009	906	5058
1603	45	Grants in lieu of Code Sec. 45 electricity production credit and Code Sec. 48 energy credit for specified energy property placed in service or under construction in 2009 or 2010	Feb. 17, 2009	1204	5016
1603	48	Grants in lieu of Code Sec. 45 electricity production credit and Code Sec. 48 energy credit for specified energy property placed in service or under construction in 2009 or 2010	Feb. 17, 2009	1204	5016
1603	50	Grants in lieu of Code Sec. 45 electricity production credit and Code Sec. 48 energy credit for specified energy property placed in service or under construction in 2009 or 2010	Feb. 17, 2009	1204	5016
1899A(a)(1)	35(a)	Refundable HCTC for eligible individuals' health insurance costs is increased from 65% to 80% through 2010	Coverage months beginning on or after May 1, 2009 and before Jan. 1, 2011	502	5078
1899A(a)(2)	7527(b)	Refundable HCTC for eligible individuals' health insurance costs is increased from 65% to 80% through 2010	Coverage months beginning on or after May 1, 2009 and before Jan. 1, 2011	502	5078

Act §	Code §	Topic	Generally effective date	Analysis ¶	Com Rep ¶
1899B(a)	7527(e)	IRS is required to pay premiums due before start of HCTC advance payments in 2009 and 2010	For coverage months beginning after Dec. 31, 2008 and before Jan. 1, 2011	503	5078
1899C(a)	35(c)(2)(B)	Eligible TAA recipients not enrolled in training programs are eligible for the HCTC	Coverage months beginning after Feb. 17, 2009 and before Jan. 1, 2011	504	5078
1899D(a)	9801(c)(2)(D)	Pre-certification period after TAA-related loss of health coverage is temporarily ignored for certain HIPAA and HCTC purposes	Plan years beginning after Feb. 17, 2009 and before Jan. 1, 2011	505	5078
1899E(a)	35(g)(9)	Family members will continue to qualify for the HCTC after certain events for coverage months beginning in 2010	Coverage months beginning after Dec. 31, 2009 and before Jan. 1, 2011	506	5078
1899F(b)	4980B(f)(2)(B)(i)	Eligibility for COBRA continuation coverage extended up to Dec. 31, 2010 for PBGC recipients and TAA-eligible individuals who lose employment or work hours	Coverage periods that would otherwise end on or after Feb. 17, 2009; through Dec. 31, 2010	507	5078
1899G(a)	35(e)(1)(K)	HCTC allowed for VEBA coverage before 2011	Coverage months beginning after Feb. 17, 2009 and before Jan. 1, 2011	508	5078
1899H(a)	7527(d)	Additional information is required on qualified health insurance cost eligibility certificates issued before 2011	For certificates issued on or after Aug. 18, 2009 and before Jan. 1, 2011	509	5078

Act §	Code §	Topic	Generally effective date	Analysis ¶	Com Rep ¶
2201	None	One-time $250 payment to be made to recipients of social security, SSI, railroad retirement, and veterans disability or pension benefits	Feb. 17, 2009	102	5079
2202	36A(c)	Refundable $250 credit is allowed to certain government retirees ($500 for joint return where both spouses are eligible)	Feb. 17, 2009	103	5080
2202	None	Refundable $250 credit is allowed to certain government retirees ($500 for joint return where both spouses are eligible)	Feb. 17, 2009	103	5080
2202(b)(2)	6213(g)(2)	Refundable $250 credit is allowed to certain government retirees ($500 for joint return where both spouses are eligible)	Feb. 17, 2009	103	5080
2202(c)(2)	6211(b)(4)(A)	Refundable $250 credit is allowed to certain government retirees ($500 for joint return where both spouses are eligible)	Feb. 17, 2009	103	5080
3001	None	COBRA premium subsidy provided for 9 months to workers involuntarily terminated between Sept. 10, 2008 through Dec. 31, 2009	For periods of COBRA coverage provided beginning on or after Feb. 17, 2009	301	5082
3001(a)(1)(B)	None	COBRA-subsidized individuals may elect to change COBRA continuation coverage to a different plan where employer so permits	For periods of COBRA continuation coverage beginning after Feb. 17, 2009	303	5082
3001(a)(2)(C)	None	Penalty imposed on COBRA-subsidized individuals who fail to notify group health plan when they become eligible for other health coverage	Feb. 17, 2009	309	5082

Act §	Code §	Topic	Generally effective date	Analysis ¶	Com Rep ¶
3001(a)(4)	None	Certain unemployed workers have an extended 60-day period to elect subsidized COBRA continuation coverage	For periods of COBRA continuation coverage beginning after Feb. 17, 2009	302	5082
3001(a)(7)	4980B(f)(6)(D)	Terminated workers must be notified of right to COBRA continuation benefits subsidy	Feb. 17, 2009	307	5082
3001(a)(12)(A)	6432	Reimbursement mechanism provided to plans for COBRA premiums that are not paid by COBRA subsidized individuals	For COBRA premiums provided for periods of coverage beginning on or after Feb. 17, 2009.	308	5082
3001(a)(13)(A)	6720C	Penalty imposed on COBRA-subsidized individuals who fail to notify group health plan when they become eligible for other health coverage	Feb. 17, 2009	309	5082
3001(a)(14)(A)	35(g)(9)	Eligible individuals receiving COBRA premium assistance cannot claim the health coverage tax credit	Tax years ending after Feb. 17, 2009	306	5082
3001(a)(15)(A)	139C	COBRA subsidy excluded from income	Tax years ending after Feb. 17, 2009	305	5082
3001(b)	None	Recapture of COBRA premium assistance provided to high income taxpayers	Tax years ending after Feb. 17, 2009	304	5082
7001	162(m)(5)	Scope of $500,000 compensation deduction limit on TARP recipients is broadened; other non-tax executive compensation restrictions are imposed	Feb. 17, 2009	401	5084
7002	None	Scope of $500,000 compensation deduction limit on TARP recipients is broadened; other non-tax executive compensation restrictions are imposed	Feb. 17, 2009	401	5084

¶ 6001. Code Section Cross Reference Table

Act § cites are to the 2009 American Recovery and Reinvestment Act unless otherwise indicated. * denotes 2009 Children's Health Insurance Program Reauthorization Act.

Code §	Act §	Topic	Generally effective date	Analysis ¶	Com Rep ¶
23(b)(4)	1011(a)(1)	Nonrefundable personal credits can offset AMT through 2009 (instead of 2008)	Tax years beginning in 2009	204	5010
24(b)(3)	1011(a)(1)	Nonrefundable personal credits can offset AMT through 2009 (instead of 2008)	Tax years beginning in 2009	204	5010
24(b)(3)(B)	1004(b)(1)	Hope credit is increased and expanded (and re-named the "American Opportunity Tax Credit") for 2009 and 2010	Tax years beginning in 2009 and 2010	107	5004
24(b)(3)(B)	1142(b)(1)(A)	Qualified plug-in electric vehicle credit is provided for certain low-speed vehicles and 2- or 3-wheeled vehicles acquired before Jan. 1, 2012	Vehicles acquired before Jan. 1, 2012 and after Feb. 17, 2009	1003	5027
24(b)(3)(B)	1144(b)(1)(A)	Alternative motor vehicle credit (AMVC) is treated as a personal credit allowed against AMT for tax years beginning after 2008	Tax years beginning after Dec. 31, 2008	205	5027
24(d)(4)	1003(a)	Refundable portion of child tax credit is increased for 2009 and 2010	Tax years beginning in 2009 and 2010	109	5003
25(e)(1)(C)	1011(a)(1)	Nonrefundable personal credits can offset AMT through 2009 (instead of 2008)	Tax years beginning in 2009	204	5010
25(e)(1)(C)(ii)	1004(b)(2)	Hope credit is increased and expanded (and re-named the "American Opportunity Tax Credit") for 2009 and 2010	Tax years beginning in 2009 and 2010	107	5004

Code §	Act §	Topic	Generally effective date	Analysis ¶	Com Rep ¶
25(e)(1)(C)(ii)	1142(b)(1)(B)	Qualified plug-in electric vehicle credit is provided for certain low-speed vehicles and 2- or 3-wheeled vehicles acquired before Jan. 1, 2012	Vehicles acquired before Jan. 1, 2012 and after Feb. 17, 2009	1003	5027
25(e)(1)(C)(ii)	1144(b)(1)(B)	Alternative motor vehicle credit (AMVC) is treated as a personal credit allowed against AMT for tax years beginning after 2008	Tax years beginning after Dec. 31, 2008	205	5027
25A	1004(b)(8)	Hope credit is increased and expanded (and re-named the "American Opportunity Tax Credit") for 2009 and 2010	Tax years beginning in 2009 and 2010	107	5004
25A	1004(c)	Hope credit is increased and expanded (and re-named the "American Opportunity Tax Credit") for 2009 and 2010	Tax years beginning in 2009 and 2010	107	5004
25A(i)	1004(a)	Hope credit is increased and expanded (and re-named the "American Opportunity Tax Credit") for 2009 and 2010	Tax years beginning in 2009 and 2010	107	5004
25A(i)(5)	1011(a)(1)	Nonrefundable personal credits can offset AMT through 2009 (instead of 2008)	Tax years beginning in 2009	204	5010
25B(g)	1011(a)(1)	Nonrefundable personal credits can offset AMT through 2009 (instead of 2008)	Tax years beginning in 2009	204	5010
25B(g)(2)	1004(b)(4)	Hope credit is increased and expanded (and re-named the "American Opportunity Tax Credit") for 2009 and 2010	Tax years beginning in 2009 and 2010	107	5004
25B(g)(2)	1142(b)(1)(C)	Qualified plug-in electric vehicle credit is provided for certain low-speed vehicles and 2- or 3-wheeled vehicles acquired before Jan. 1, 2012	Vehicles acquired before Jan. 1, 2012 and after Feb. 17, 2009	1003	5027

Code §	Act §	Topic	Generally effective date	Analysis ¶	Com Rep ¶
25B(g)(2)	1144(b)(1)(C)	Alternative motor vehicle credit (AMVC) is treated as a personal credit allowed against AMT for tax years beginning after 2008	Tax years beginning after Dec. 31, 2008	205	5027
25C(a)	1121(a)	Nonbusiness energy property credit is increased from 10% to 30% and extended for one year	Tax years beginning after Dec. 31, 2008	1101	5021
25C(b)	1121(a)	Nonbusiness energy property credit is increased from 10% to 30% and extended for one year	Tax years beginning after Dec. 31, 2008	1101	5021
25C(c)(2)(A)	1121(d)(2)	Standards are modified for property qualifying for the nonbusiness energy property credit	Property placed in service after Feb. 17, 2009	1102	5021
25C(c)(4)	1121(d)(1)	Standards are modified for property qualifying for the nonbusiness energy property credit	Property placed in service after Feb. 17, 2009	1102	5021
25C(d)(2)(A)(ii)	1121(c)(2)	Standards are modified for property qualifying for the nonbusiness energy property credit	Property placed in service after Feb. 17, 2009	1102	5021
25C(d)(3)(B)	1121(b)(1)	Standards are modified for property qualifying for the nonbusiness energy property credit	Property placed in service after Feb. 17, 2009	1102	5021
25C(d)(3)(C)	1121(b)(2)	Standards are modified for property qualifying for the nonbusiness energy property credit	Property placed in service after Feb. 17, 2009	1102	5021
25C(d)(3)(D)	1121(b)(3)	Standards are modified for property qualifying for the nonbusiness energy property credit	Property placed in service after Feb. 17, 2009	1102	5021
25C(d)(3)(E)	1121(b)(4)	Standards are modified for property qualifying for the nonbusiness energy property credit	Tax years beginning after Dec. 31, 2008	1102	5021
25C(d)(4)	1121(c)(1)	Standards are modified for property qualifying for the nonbusiness energy property credit	Property placed in service after Feb. 17, 2009	1102	5021

Code §	Act §	Topic	Generally effective date	Analysis ¶	Com Rep ¶
25C(e)(1)	1103(b)(2)(A)	Expenditures from subsidized energy financing can qualify for REEP credit and nonbusiness energy property credit	Tax years beginning after Dec. 31, 2008	1103	5021, 5022
25C(g)(2)	1121(e)	Nonbusiness energy property credit is increased from 10% to 30% and extended for one year	Tax years beginning after Dec. 31, 2008	1101	5021
25D(b)(1)	1122(a)(1)	Dollar caps on REEP credit are eliminated for solar hot water, geothermal, and wind property expenditures	Tax years beginning after Dec. 31, 2008	1104	5022
25D(c)	1011(a)(1)	Nonrefundable personal credits can offset AMT through 2009 (instead of 2008)	Tax years beginning in 2009	204	5010
25D(e)(4)	1122(a)(2)	Dollar caps on REEP credit are eliminated for solar hot water, geothermal, and wind property expenditures	Tax years beginning after Dec. 31, 2008	1104	5022
25D(e)(9)	1103(b)(2)(B)	Expenditures from subsidized energy financing can qualify for REEP credit and nonbusiness energy property credit	Tax years beginning after Dec. 31, 2008	1103	5021, 5022
26(a)(1)	1004(b)(3)	Hope credit is increased and expanded (and re-named the "American Opportunity Tax Credit") for 2009 and 2010	Tax years beginning in 2009 and 2010	107	5004
26(a)(1)	1142(b)(1)(D)	Qualified plug-in electric vehicle credit is provided for certain low-speed vehicles and 2- or 3-wheeled vehicles acquired before Jan. 1, 2012	Vehicles acquired before Jan. 1, 2012 and after Feb. 17, 2009	1003	5027
26(a)(1)	1144(b)(1)(D)	Alternative motor vehicle credit (AMVC) is treated as a personal credit allowed against AMT for tax years beginning after 2008	Tax years beginning after Dec. 31, 2008	205	5027

Code §	Act §	Topic	Generally effective date	Analysis ¶	Com Rep ¶
26(a)(2)	1011(a)(1)	Nonrefundable personal credits can offset AMT through 2009 (instead of 2008)	Tax years beginning in 2009	204	5010
30	1142(a)	Qualified plug-in electric vehicle credit is provided for certain low-speed vehicles and 2- or 3-wheeled vehicles acquired before Jan. 1, 2012	Vehicles acquired before Jan. 1, 2012 and after Feb. 17, 2009	1003	5027
30B(a)(5)	1143(b)	Alternative motor vehicle credit (AMVC) is expanded to include a plug-in conversion credit for property placed in service after Feb. 17, 2009 and before Jan. 1, 2012	Property placed in service after Feb. 17, 2009 and conversions made before Jan. 1, 2012	1004	5027
30B(d)(3)(D)	1141(b)(1)	"New qualified plug-in electric drive motor vehicle credit" will be modified for vehicles acquired after Dec. 31, 2009	Vehicles acquired after Dec. 31, 2009	1002	5027
30B(g)(2)	1144(a)	Alternative motor vehicle credit (AMVC) is treated as a personal credit allowed against AMT for tax years beginning after 2008	Tax years beginning after Dec. 31, 2008	205	5027
30B(h)(1)	1142(b)(2)	Qualified plug-in electric vehicle credit is provided for certain low-speed vehicles and 2- or 3-wheeled vehicles acquired before Jan. 1, 2012	Vehicles acquired before Jan. 1, 2012 and after Feb. 17, 2009	1003	5027
30B(h)(8)	1143(c)	Alternative motor vehicle credit (AMVC) is expanded to include a plug-in conversion credit for property placed in service after Feb. 17, 2009 and before Jan. 1, 2012	Property placed in service after Feb. 17, 2009 and conversions made before Jan. 1, 2012	1004	5027

Code §	Act §	Topic	Generally effective date	Analysis ¶	Com Rep ¶
30B(i)	1143(a)	Alternative motor vehicle credit (AMVC) is expanded to include a plug-in conversion credit for property placed in service after Feb. 17, 2009 and before Jan. 1, 2012	Property placed in service after Feb. 17, 2009 and conversions made before Jan. 1, 2012	1004	5027
30C(d)(2)(A)	1142(b)(3)	Qualified plug-in electric vehicle credit is provided for certain low-speed vehicles and 2- or 3-wheeled vehicles acquired before Jan. 1, 2012	Vehicles acquired before Jan. 1, 2012 and after Feb. 17, 2009	1003	5027
30C(d)(2)(A)	1144(b)(2)	Alternative motor vehicle credit (AMVC) is treated as a personal credit allowed against AMT for tax years beginning after 2008	Tax years beginning after Dec. 31, 2008	205	5027
30C(e)(6)	1123(a)	Credit for QAFV refueling property is increased for property placed in service in tax years beginning in 2009 or 2010	Tax years beginning after Dec. 31, 2008	1001	5023
30D	1141(a)	"New qualified plug-in electric drive motor vehicle credit" will be modified for vehicles acquired after Dec. 31, 2009	Vehicles acquired after Dec. 31, 2009	1002	5027
30D(d)(2)(B)	1011(a)(1)	Nonrefundable personal credits can offset AMT through 2009 (instead of 2008)	Tax years beginning in 2009	204	5010
32(b)(3)(A)	1002(a)	EIC credit percentage is increased for families with three or more qualifying children for 2009 and 2010	Tax years beginning in 2009 and 2010	110	5002
32(b)(3)(B)	1002(a)	Beginning point of EIC phaseout range is increased for joint filers for 2009 and 2010	Tax years beginning in 2009 or 2010	111	5002
35		Overview of the health coverage tax credit (HCTC)	Feb. 17, 2009	501	5078

Code §	Act §	Topic	Generally effective date	Analysis ¶	Com Rep ¶
35(a)	1899A(a)(1)	Refundable HCTC for eligible individuals' health insurance costs is increased from 65% to 80% through 2010	Coverage months beginning on or after May 1, 2009 and before Jan. 1, 2011	502	5078
35(c)(2)(B)	1899C(a)	Eligible TAA recipients not enrolled in training programs are eligible for the HCTC	Coverage months beginning after Feb. 17, 2009 and before Jan. 1, 2011	504	5078
35(e)(1)(K)	1899G(a)	HCTC allowed for VEBA coverage before 2011	Coverage months beginning after Feb. 17, 2009 and before Jan. 1, 2011	508	5078
35(g)(9)	1899E(a)	Family members will continue to qualify for the HCTC after certain events for coverage months beginning in 2010	Coverage months beginning after Dec. 31, 2009 and before Jan. 1, 2011	506	5078
35(g)(9)	3001(a)(14)(A)	Eligible individuals receiving COBRA premium assistance cannot claim the health coverage tax credit	Tax years ending after Feb. 17, 2009	306	5082
36(b)	1006(b)(1)	First-time homebuyer credit is extended to purchases before Dec. 1, 2009 and increased to $8,000 ($4,000 for marrieds filing separately); recapture is waived unless residence is sold or ceases to be a principal residence within 36 months of purchase	Residences purchased after Dec. 31, 2008 and before Dec. 1, 2009	104	5006

Code §	Act §	Topic	Generally effective date	Analysis ¶	Com Rep ¶
36(b)(1)(B)	1006(b)(2)	First-time homebuyer credit is extended to purchases before Dec. 1, 2009 and increased to $8,000 ($4,000 for marrieds filing separately); recapture is waived unless residence is sold or ceases to be a principal residence within 36 months of purchase	Residences purchased after Dec. 31, 2008 and before Dec. 1, 2009	104	5006
36(d)	1006(e)	First-time homebuyer credit is extended to purchases before Dec. 1, 2009 and increased to $8,000 ($4,000 for marrieds filing separately); recapture is waived unless residence is sold or ceases to be a principal residence within 36 months of purchase	Residences purchased after Dec. 31, 2008 and before Dec. 1, 2009	104	5006
36(f)(4)(D)	1006(c)(1)	First-time homebuyer credit is extended to purchases before Dec. 1, 2009 and increased to $8,000 ($4,000 for marrieds filing separately); recapture is waived unless residence is sold or ceases to be a principal residence within 36 months of purchase	Residences purchased after Dec. 31, 2008 and before Dec. 1, 2009	104	5006
36(g)	1006(a)(2)	First-time homebuyer credit is extended to purchases before Dec. 1, 2009 and increased to $8,000 ($4,000 for marrieds filing separately); recapture is waived unless residence is sold or ceases to be a principal residence within 36 months of purchase	Residences purchased after Dec. 31, 2008 and before Dec. 1, 2009	104	5006

Code §	Act §	Topic	Generally effective date	Analysis ¶	Com Rep ¶
36(g)	1006(c)(2)	First-time homebuyer credit is extended to purchases before Dec. 1, 2009 and increased to $8,000 ($4,000 for marrieds filing separately); recapture is waived unless residence is sold or ceases to be a principal residence within 36 months of purchase	Residences purchased after Dec. 31, 2008 and before Dec. 1, 2009	104	5006
36(h)	1006(a)(1)	First-time homebuyer credit is extended to purchases before Dec. 1, 2009 and increased to $8,000 ($4,000 for marrieds filing separately); recapture is waived unless residence is sold or ceases to be a principal residence within 36 months of purchase	Residences purchased after Dec. 31, 2008 and before Dec. 1, 2009	104	5006
36A	1001(a)	Refundable "making work pay credit" of up to $400 ($800 on joint return) is allowed for 2009 and 2010	Tax years beginning after Dec. 31, 2008, and before Jan. 1, 2011	101	5001
36A	1001(b)	Refundable "making work pay credit" of up to $400 ($800 on joint return) is allowed for 2009 and 2010	Tax years beginning after Dec. 31, 2008, and before Jan. 1, 2011	101	5001
36A	1001(c)	Refundable "making work pay credit" of up to $400 ($800 on joint return) is allowed for 2009 and 2010	Tax years beginning after Dec. 31, 2008, and before Jan. 1, 2011	101	5001
36A(c)	2202	Refundable $250 credit is allowed to certain government retirees ($500 for joint return where both spouses are eligible)	Feb. 17, 2009	103	5080
38(b)(35)	1141(b)(2)	"New qualified plug-in electric drive motor vehicle credit" will be modified for vehicles acquired after Dec. 31, 2009	Vehicles acquired after Dec. 31, 2009	1002	5027

Code §	Act §	Topic	Generally effective date	Analysis ¶	Com Rep ¶
42(i)(9)	1404	States can elect grants, instead of tax credits, to finance low-income housing for 2009, but tax credit allocations are reduced	Feb. 17, 2009	906	5058
45	1603	Grants in lieu of Code Sec. 45 electricity production credit and Code Sec. 48 energy credit for specified energy property placed in service or under construction in 2009 or 2010	Feb. 17, 2009	1204	5016
45(d)(1)	1101(a)(1)	Placed-in-service end date is extended for three years through Dec. 31, 2012 for qualified wind facilities for purposes of the electricity production credit	Property placed in service after Feb. 17, 2009	1208	5013
45(d)(2)	1101(a)(2)	Placed-in-service end date is extended for three years through Dec. 31, 2013 for certain qualified facilities for purposes of the electricity production credit	Property placed in service after Feb. 17, 2009	1207	5013
45(d)(3)	1101(a)(2)	Placed-in-service end date is extended for three years through Dec. 31, 2013 for certain qualified facilities for purposes of the electricity production credit	Property placed in service after Feb. 17, 2009	1207	5013
45(d)(4)	1101(a)(2)	Placed-in-service end date is extended for three years through Dec. 31, 2013 for certain qualified facilities for purposes of the electricity production credit	Property placed in service after Feb. 17, 2009	1207	5013
45(d)(6)	1101(a)(2)	Placed-in-service end date is extended for three years through Dec. 31, 2013 for certain qualified facilities for purposes of the electricity production credit	Property placed in service after Feb. 17, 2009	1207	5013

Code §	Act §	Topic	Generally effective date	Analysis ¶	Com Rep ¶
45(d)(7)	1101(a)(2)	Placed-in-service end date is extended for three years through Dec. 31, 2013 for certain qualified facilities for purposes of the electricity production credit	Property placed in service after Feb. 17, 2009	1207	5013
45(d)(9)	1101(a)(2)	Placed-in-service end date is extended for three years through Dec. 31, 2013 for certain qualified facilities for purposes of the electricity production credit	Property placed in service after Feb. 17, 2009	1207	5013
45(d)(11)(B)	1101(a)(3)	Placed-in-service end date is extended for two years through Dec. 31, 2013 for qualified marine and hydrokinetic renewable energy facilities for purposes of the electricity production credit	Property placed in service after Feb. 17, 2009	1209	5013
45D(f)(1)	1403(a)(3)	New markets tax credit national limit is raised for 2008 and 2009 with a preferential allocation rule for the 2008 increase	Feb. 17, 2009	905	5057
45D(f)(2)	1403(b)	New markets tax credit national limit is raised for 2008 and 2009 with a preferential allocation rule for the 2008 increase	Feb. 17, 2009	905	5057
45Q(a)(1)(B)	1131(b)(2)	Secure geological storage disposal requirement to apply to the $10 per metric ton component of the carbon dioxide sequestration credit	Carbon dioxide captured after Feb. 17, 2009	1212	5025
45Q(a)(2)(C)	1131(a)	Secure geological storage disposal requirement to apply to the $10 per metric ton component of the carbon dioxide sequestration credit	Carbon dioxide captured after Feb. 17, 2009	1212	5025
45Q(d)(2)	1131(b)(1)(A)	Secure geological storage disposal requirement to apply to the $10 per metric ton component of the carbon dioxide sequestration credit	Carbon dioxide captured after Feb. 17, 2009	1212	5025

Code §	Act §	Topic	Generally effective date	Analysis ¶	Com Rep ¶
45Q(d)(2)	1131(b)(1)(B)	Secure geological storage disposal requirement to apply to the $10 per metric ton component of the carbon dioxide sequestration credit	Carbon dioxide captured after Feb. 17, 2009	1212	5025
45Q(d)(2)	1131(b)(1)(C)	Secure geological storage disposal requirement to apply to the $10 per metric ton component of the carbon dioxide sequestration credit	Carbon dioxide captured after Feb. 17, 2009	1212	5025
45Q(e)	1131(b)(3)	Secure geological storage disposal requirement to apply to the $10 per metric ton component of the carbon dioxide sequestration credit	Carbon dioxide captured after Feb. 17, 2009	1212	5025
46(5)	1302(a)	30% credit is allowed for investment in qualified property used in a qualified advanced energy manufacturing project	Periods after Feb. 17, 2009	1202	5052
48	1603	Grants in lieu of Code Sec. 45 electricity production credit and Code Sec. 48 energy credit for specified energy property placed in service or under construction in 2009 or 2010	Feb. 17, 2009	1204	5016
48(a)(4)(D)	1103(b)(1)	Business energy tax credit basis reduction rule for property financed by tax-exempt government subsidies or private activity bonds is retroactively terminated for periods after Dec. 31, 2008	Periods after Dec. 31, 2008	1206	5015
48(a)(5)	1102(a)	Taxpayers can irrevocably elect 30% business energy credit instead of electricity production credit for qualified property that is part of qualified investment credit facilities placed in service after 2008 and before 2014 (2013 for wind facilities)	Facilities placed in service after Dec. 31, 2008 and before Jan. 1, 2014 (2013 for wind facilities)	1203	5014

Code §	Act §	Topic	Generally effective date	Analysis ¶	Com Rep ¶
48(c)(4)(B)	1103(a)	$4,000 annual limitation on business energy tax credit for qualified small wind energy property is repealed for periods after Dec. 31, 2008	Periods after Dec. 31, 2008	1201	5015
48(d)	1104	Coordination of Code Sec. 48 energy credit and Code Sec. 45 electricity production credit with re-newable energy grants	Feb. 17, 2009	1205	5016
48A(b)(2)	1103(b)(2)(C)	Business energy tax cred-it basis reduction rule for property financed by tax-exempt government subsidies or private activ-ity bonds is retroactively terminated for periods af-ter Dec. 31, 2008	Periods after Dec. 31, 2008	1206	5015
48B(b)(2)	1103(b)(2)(D)	Business energy tax cred-it basis reduction rule for property financed by tax-exempt government subsidies or private activ-ity bonds is retroactively terminated for periods af-ter Dec. 31, 2008	Periods after Dec. 31, 2008	1206	5015
48C	1302(b)	30% credit is allowed for investment in qualified property used in a quali-fied advanced energy manufacturing project	Periods after Feb. 17, 2009	1202	5052
49(a)(1)(C)(v)	1302(c)(1)	30% credit is allowed for investment in qualified property used in a quali-fied advanced energy manufacturing project	Periods after Feb. 17, 2009	1202	5052
50	1603	Grants in lieu of Code Sec. 45 electricity pro-duction credit and Code Sec. 48 energy credit for specified energy property placed in service or under construction in 2009 or 2010	Feb. 17, 2009	1204	5016

Code §	Act §	Topic	Generally effective date	Analysis ¶	Com Rep ¶
51(d)(14)	1221(a)	Work opportunity credit is expanded to apply to new target group of un-employed veterans and disconnected youth who begin work in 2009 or 2010	Individuals who begin work for the employer af-ter Dec. 31, 2008 and before Jan. 1, 2011	904	5039
53(d)(1)(B)(iii)	1142(b)(4)(A)	Qualified plug-in electric vehicle credit is provided for certain low-speed ve-hicles and 2- or 3-wheeled vehicles ac-quired before Jan. 1, 2012	Vehicles ac-quired before Jan. 1, 2012 and after Feb. 17, 2009	1003	5027
54(c)(2)	1531(c)(3)	New tax credit bond op-tion is added for "Build America Bonds" issued in 2009 and 2010; issuer may claim alternative, re-fundable credit for "qual-ified bonds"	Obligations issued after Feb. 17, 2009 and before Jan. 1, 2011	1301	5070
54A(c)(1)(B)	1531(c)(2)	New tax credit bond op-tion is added for "Build America Bonds" issued in 2009 and 2010; issuer may claim alternative, re-fundable credit for "qual-ified bonds"	Obligations issued after Feb. 17, 2009 and before Jan. 1, 2011	1301	5070
54A(d)(1)(E)	1521(b)(1)	Qualified school con-struction bond is a new type of tax credit bond	Bonds issued after Feb. 17, 2009	1302	5067
54A(d)(2)(C)(v)	1521(b)(2)	Qualified school con-struction bond is a new type of tax credit bond	Bonds issued after Feb. 17, 2009	1302	5067
54A(h)	1541(b)	Pass-through of tax credit bond credits by RICs and REITs is modified and expanded	Tax years ending after Feb. 17, 2009	1308	5072
54C	1601(1)	Prevailing wage require-ments are applied to projects financed with specified bonds	Bonds issued after Feb. 17, 2009	1311	5074
54C(c)(4)	1111	National bond volume limitation for new CREBs is increased by up to $1.6 billion	Bonds issued after Feb. 17, 2009	1210	5018

Code §	Act §	Topic	Generally effective date	Analysis ¶	Com Rep ¶
54D	1601(2)	Prevailing wage requirements are applied to projects financed with specified bonds	Bonds issued after Feb. 17, 2009	1311	5074
54D(d)	1112(a)	National bond volume limitation for qualified energy conservation bonds is increased by $2.4 billion; bonds for green community programs can fund loans or grants to individuals	Bonds issued after Feb. 17, 2009	1211	5019
54D(e)(4)	1112(b)(2)	National bond volume limitation for qualified energy conservation bonds is increased by $2.4 billion; bonds for green community programs can fund loans or grants to individuals	Bonds issued after Feb. 17, 2009	1211	5019
54D(f)(1)(A)(ii)	1112(b)(1)	National bond volume limitation for qualified energy conservation bonds is increased by $2.4 billion; bonds for green community programs can fund loans or grants to individuals	Bonds issued after Feb. 17, 2009	1211	5019
54E	1601(3)	Prevailing wage requirements are applied to projects financed with specified bonds	Bonds issued after Feb. 17, 2009	1311	5074
54E(c)(1)	1522(a)	Credit for QZABs is extended through 2010; national bond volume limitation is increased to $1.4 billion for 2009 and 2010	Bonds issued after Dec. 31, 2008	1303	5068
54F	1521(a)	Qualified school construction bond is a new type of tax credit bond	Bonds issued after Feb. 17, 2009	1302	5067
54F	1601(4)	Prevailing wage requirements are applied to projects financed with specified bonds	Bonds issued after Feb. 17, 2009	1311	5074

Code §	Act §	Topic	Generally effective date	Analysis ¶	Com Rep ¶
54AA	1531(a)	New tax credit bond option is added for "Build America Bonds" issued in 2009 and 2010; issuer may claim alternative, refundable credit for "qualified bonds"	Obligations issued after Feb. 17, 2009 and before Jan. 1, 2011	1301	5070
54AA	1531(d)	New tax credit bond option is added for "Build America Bonds" issued in 2009 and 2010; issuer may claim alternative, refundable credit for "qualified bonds"	Obligations issued after Feb. 17, 2009 and before Jan. 1, 2011	1301	5070
55(c)(3)	1144(b)(3)	Alternative motor vehicle credit (AMVC) is treated as a personal credit allowed against AMT for tax years beginning after 2008	Tax years beginning after Dec. 31, 2008	205	5027
55(d)(1)(A)	1012(a)(1)	AMT exemption amounts for 2009 are increased to $46,700 for unmarrieds, to $70,950 for joint filers, and to $35,475 for marrieds filing separately	Tax years beginning in 2009	201	5010
55(d)(1)(B)	1012(a)(2)	AMT exemption amounts for 2009 are increased to $46,700 for unmarrieds, to $70,950 for joint filers, and to $35,475 for marrieds filing separately	Tax years beginning in 2009	201	5010
56(b)(1)(E)	1008(d)	Standard or itemized deduction is allowed for sales and excise taxes imposed on most new vehicles purchased on or after Feb. 17, 2009 and before 2010	Purchases on or after Feb. 17, 2009 and before 2010	105	5008
56(g)(4)(B)(iv)	1503(b)	Corporate ACE adjustment isn't required for tax-exempt bonds issued in 2009 or 2010	Bonds issued after Dec. 31, 2008 and before Jan. 1, 2011	203	5062
57(a)(5)(C)(vi)	1503(a)	Interest on tax-exempt bonds issued in 2009 or 2010 isn't subject to AMT	Bonds issued after Dec. 31, 2008 and before Jan. 1, 2011	202	5062

Code §	Act §	Topic	Generally effective date	Analysis ¶	Com Rep ¶
63(c)(1)(E)	1008(c)(1)	Standard or itemized deduction is allowed for sales and excise taxes imposed on most new vehicles purchased on or after Feb. 17, 2009 and before 2010	Purchases on or after Feb. 17, 2009 and before 2010	105	5008
63(c)(9)	1008(c)(2)	Standard or itemized deduction is allowed for sales and excise taxes imposed on most new vehicles purchased on or after Feb. 17, 2009 and before 2010	Purchases on or after Feb. 17, 2009 and before 2010	105	5008
85(c)	1007(a)	Up to $2,400 of unemployment compensation is excludible from recipient's gross income for 2009	Tax years beginning in 2009	106	5007
108(i)	1231(a)	Income from reacquisitions of business debt at a discount in 2009 and 2010 is deferred for up to five years, then included ratably over five years	Discharges in tax years ending after Dec. 31, 2008, for reacquisitions after Dec. 31, 2008, and before Jan. 1, 2011	901	5041
132(f)(2)	1151(a)	Monthly exclusion for employer-provided transit passes and vanpooling benefits increased to same level as employer-provided parking, for the rest of 2009 and 2010	Months beginning on or after Feb. 17, 2009	402	5032
139C	3001(a)(15)(A)	COBRA subsidy excluded from income	Tax years ending after Feb. 17, 2009	305	5082
142(i)(1)	1504(a)	Vehicles must be capable of attaining a maximum speed in excess of 150 m.p.h. under amended definition of high-speed intercity rail facilities	Bonds issued after Feb. 17, 2009	1312	5063
144(a)(12)(C)	1301(a)	IDBs issued before 2011 may finance facilities used to create intangible property	Bonds issued after Feb. 17, 2009 and before Jan. 1, 2011	1310	5051

Code §	Act §	Topic	Generally effective date	Analysis ¶	Com Rep ¶
162(m)(5)	7001	Scope of $500,000 compensation deduction limit on TARP recipients is broadened; other non-tax executive compensation restrictions are imposed	Feb. 17, 2009	401	5084
163(e)(5)(F)	1232(a)	Rules for high-yield OID obligations are suspended for obligations issued from Sept. 1, 2008 to Dec. 31, 2009	Obligations issued after Aug. 31, 2008 and before Jan. 1, 2010, in tax years ending after Aug. 31, 2008	907	5042
163(i)(1)	1232(b)	Beginning in 2010, IRS will be able to apply a higher rate to determine whether an obligation is an applicable high-yield discount obligation	Obligations issued after Dec. 31, 2009, in tax years ending after Dec. 31, 2009	908	5042
164(a)(6)	1008(a)	Standard or itemized deduction is allowed for sales and excise taxes imposed on most new vehicles purchased on or after Feb. 17, 2009 and before 2010	Purchases on or after Feb. 17, 2009 and before 2010	105	5008
164(b)(6)	1008(b)	Standard or itemized deduction is allowed for sales and excise taxes imposed on most new vehicles purchased on or after Feb. 17, 2009 and before 2010	Purchases on or after Feb. 17, 2009 and before 2010	105	5008
168(k)(2)(A)(iii)	1201(a)(1)(B)	50% bonus depreciation and AMT depreciation relief are extended one year through Dec. 31, 2009 (Dec. 31, 2010 for certain property)	Property placed in service before Jan. 1, 2010 and after Dec. 31, 2008	801	5034
168(k)(2)(A)(iv)	1201(a)	$8,000 increase in first-year depreciation limit for passenger automobiles that are "qualified property" is extended through Dec. 31, 2009	Property placed in service before Jan. 1, 2010 and after Dec. 31, 2008	803	5034

Code §	Act §	Topic	Generally effective date	Analysis ¶	Com Rep ¶
168(k)(2)(A)(iv)	1201(a)(1)	50% bonus depreciation and AMT depreciation relief are extended one year through Dec. 31, 2009 (Dec. 31, 2010 for certain property)	Property placed in service before Jan. 1, 2010 and after Dec. 31, 2008	801	5034
168(k)(2)(A)(iv)	1201(a)(1)	Election to trade bonus and accelerated depreciation for otherwise-deferred credits is optionally extended through Dec. 31, 2009 (Dec. 31, 2010 for certain property)	Property placed in service before Jan. 1, 2010 and after Dec. 31, 2008	804	5034
168(k)(2)(B)(ii)	1201(a)(1)(B)	50% bonus depreciation and AMT depreciation relief are extended one year through Dec. 31, 2009 (Dec. 31, 2010 for certain property)	Property placed in service before Jan. 1, 2010 and after Dec. 31, 2008	801	5034
168(k)(2)(E)(i)	1201(a)(1)(B)	50% bonus depreciation and AMT depreciation relief are extended one year through Dec. 31, 2009 (Dec. 31, 2010 for certain property)	Property placed in service before Jan. 1, 2010 and after Dec. 31, 2008	801	5034
168(k)(4)(D)(ii)	1201	Election to trade bonus and accelerated depreciation for otherwise-deferred credits is optionally extended through Dec. 31, 2009 (Dec. 31, 2010 for certain property)	Property placed in service before Jan. 1, 2010 and after Dec. 31, 2008	804	5034
168(k)(4)(D)(ii)	1201(a)(3)(A)(iii)	Binding contract rule and tax deficiency rule for the election to trade bonus and accelerated depreciation for certain otherwise-deferred credits are corrected	Tax years ending after Mar. 31, 2008	806	5034
168(k)(4)(H)	1201(b)(1)(B)	Election to trade bonus and accelerated depreciation for otherwise-deferred credits is optionally extended through Dec. 31, 2009 (Dec. 31, 2010 for certain property)	Property placed in service before Jan. 1, 2010 and after Dec. 31, 2008	804	5034

Code §	Act §	Topic	Generally effective date	Analysis ¶	Com Rep ¶
168(k)(4)(H)(ii)	1201(b)(1)(B)	Post-Dec. 31, 2008 election to trade bonus and accelerated depreciation for otherwise-deferred credits is allowed if an earlier election wasn't made	Property placed in service before Jan. 1, 2010 and after Dec. 31, 2008	805	5034
172	1211(c)	Carryback period for 2008 NOLs is increased to three, four, or five years (from two years) for electing small businesses	NOLs arising in tax years ending after Dec. 31, 2007	601	5037
172	1211(d)(2)	Carryback period for 2008 NOLs is increased to three, four, or five years (from two years) for electing small businesses	NOLs arising in tax years ending after Dec. 31, 2007	601	5037
172(b)(1)(H)	1211(a)	Carryback period for 2008 NOLs is increased to three, four, or five years (from two years) for electing small businesses	NOLs arising in tax years ending after Dec. 31, 2007	601	5037
179(b)(7)	1202(a)	Regular Code Sec. 179 deduction limit of $250,000 and beginning of phaseout amount of $800,000 for 2008 are each extended to apply to tax years beginning in 2009	Tax years beginning in 2009	802	5035
265(b)(3)(G)	1502(a)	Tax-exempt interest expense safe harbors for banks and small issuers are expanded for obligations issued in 2009 and 2010	Obligations issued after Dec. 31, 2008	1309	5060
265(b)(7)	1501(a)	Tax-exempt interest expense safe harbors for banks and small issuers are expanded for obligations issued in 2009 and 2010	Obligations issued after Dec. 31, 2008	1309	5060

Code §	Act §	Topic	Generally effective date	Analysis ¶	Com Rep ¶
291(e)(1)(B)(iv)	1501(b)	Tax-exempt interest expense safe harbors for banks and small issuers are expanded for obligations issued in 2009 and 2010	Obligations issued after Dec. 31, 2008	1309	5060
382(h)	1261(b)	Revocation of IRS guidance exempting banks from loss limitation rules following an ownership change	For ownership changes after Jan. 16, 2009	602	5048
382(n)	1262(a)	Code Sec. 382 loss limitation rule doesn't apply where EESA bail-out agreement requires ownership restructuring	Ownership changes made after Feb. 17, 2009	603	5049
529(e)(3)(A)	1005(a)	Computer technology and equipment, and Internet access and related services, qualify as higher education expenses under 529 plans for 2009 and 2010	Expenses paid or incurred after Dec. 31, 2008	108	5005
853A	1541(a)	Pass-through of tax credit bond credits by RICs and REITs is modified and expanded	Tax years ending after Feb. 17, 2009	1308	5072
904(i)	1004(b)(5)	Hope credit is increased and expanded (and re-named the "American Opportunity Tax Credit") for 2009 and 2010	Tax years beginning in 2009 and 2010	107	5004
904(i)	1011(a)(1)	Nonrefundable personal credits can offset AMT through 2009 (instead of 2008)	Tax years beginning in 2009	204	5010
904(i)	1142(b)(1)(E)	"New qualified plug-in electric drive motor vehicle credit" will be modified for vehicles acquired after Dec. 31, 2009	Vehicles acquired after Dec. 31, 2009	1002	5027
904(i)	1142(b)(1)(E)	Qualified plug-in electric vehicle credit is provided for certain low-speed vehicles and 2- or 3-wheeled vehicles acquired before Jan. 1, 2012	Vehicles acquired before Jan. 1, 2012 and after Feb. 17, 2009	1003	5027

Code §	Act §	Topic	Generally effective date	Analysis ¶	Com Rep ¶
904(i)	1144(b)(1)(E)	Alternative motor vehicle credit (AMVC) is treated as a personal credit allowed against AMT for tax years beginning after 2008	Tax years beginning after Dec. 31, 2008	205	5027
1016(a)(25)	1141(b)(3)	"New qualified plug-in electric drive motor vehicle credit" will be modified for vehicles acquired after Dec. 31, 2009	Vehicles acquired after Dec. 31, 2009	1002	5027
1016(a)(25)	1142(b)(6)	Qualified plug-in electric vehicle credit is provided for certain low-speed vehicles and 2- or 3-wheeled vehicles acquired before Jan. 1, 2012	Vehicles acquired before Jan. 1, 2012 and after Feb. 17, 2009	1003	5027
1202(a)(3)	1241(a)	Noncorporate taxpayers can exclude 75% (rather than 50% or 60%) of gain on the sale or exchange of QSBS held for more than 5 years and acquired after Feb. 17, 2009 and before Jan. 1, 2011	Stock acquired after Feb. 17, 2009 and before Jan. 1, 2011	902	5044
1374(d)(7)	1251(a)	S Corp built-in gain holding period shortened for 2009 and 2010	Tax years beginning after Dec. 31, 2008	903	5046
1397E(c)(2)	1531(c)(3)	New tax credit bond option is added for "Build America Bonds" issued in 2009 and 2010; issuer may claim alternative, refundable credit for "qualified bonds"	Obligations issued after Feb. 17, 2009 and before Jan. 1, 2011	1301	5070
1400C(d)	1011(a)(1)	Nonrefundable personal credits can offset AMT through 2009 (instead of 2008)	Tax years beginning in 2009	204	5010
1400C(d)(2)	1004(b)(6)	Hope credit is increased and expanded (and re-named the "American Opportunity Tax Credit") for 2009 and 2010	Tax years beginning in 2009 and 2010	107	5004

Code §	Act §	Topic	Generally effective date	Analysis ¶	Com Rep ¶
1400C(d)(2)	1142(b)(1)(F)	Qualified plug-in electric vehicle credit is provided for certain low-speed vehicles and 2- or 3-wheeled vehicles acquired before Jan. 1, 2012	Vehicles acquired before Jan. 1, 2012 and after Feb. 17, 2009	1003	5027
1400C(d)(2)	1144(b)(1)(F)	Alternative motor vehicle credit (AMVC) is treated as a personal credit allowed against AMT for tax years beginning after 2008	Tax years beginning after Dec. 31, 2008	205	5027
1400C(e)(4)	1006(d)(1)	First-time homebuyer credit is extended to purchases before Dec. 1, 2009 and increased to $8,000 ($4,000 for marrieds filing separately); recapture is waived unless residence is sold or ceases to be a principal residence within 36 months of purchase	Residences purchased after Dec. 31, 2008 and before Dec. 1, 2009	104	5006
1400N(l)(3)(B)	1531(c)(3)	New tax credit bond option is added for "Build America Bonds" issued in 2009 and 2010; issuer may claim alternative, refundable credit for "qualified bonds"	Obligations issued after Feb. 17, 2009 and before Jan. 1, 2011	1301	5070
1400U-1	1401(a)	Overview of national limits on two new categories of recovery zone bonds issued in 2009 and 2010 which are allocated among states based on 2008 employment declines subject to a minimum allocation	Obligations issued after Feb. 17, 2009 and before 2011	1304	5054
1400U-1	1401(a)	National limits for recovery zone economic development bonds and recovery zone facility bonds issued in 2009 and 2010 are allocated among states based on their 2008 employment declines subject to a minimum allocation	Obligations issued after Feb. 17, 2009 and before 2011	1305	5054

Code §	Act §	Topic	Generally effective date	Analysis ¶	Com Rep ¶
1400U-2	1401(a)	Overview of national limits on two new categories of recovery zone bonds issued in 2009 and 2010 which are allocated among states based on 2008 employment declines subject to a minimum allocation	Obligations issued after Feb. 17, 2009 and before 2011	1304	5054
1400U-2	1401(a)	U.S. Treasury will pay the issuer 45% of the interest the issuer pays to the holder of a taxable recovery zone economic development bond issued before 2011	Obligations issued after Feb. 17, 2009 and before 2011	1306	5054
1400U-2	1601(5)	Prevailing wage requirements are applied to projects financed with specified bonds	Bonds issued after Feb. 17, 2009	1311	5074
1400U-3	1401(a)	Overview of national limits on two new categories of recovery zone bonds issued in 2009 and 2010 which are allocated among states based on 2008 employment declines subject to a minimum allocation	Obligations issued after Feb. 17, 2009 and before 2011	1304	5054
1400U-3	1401(a)	Recovery zone facility bonds are authorized for issuance in 2009 and 2010	Obligations issued after Feb. 17, 2009 and before 2011	1307	5054
3402(t)	1511	Withholding tax on government contractors is delayed for one year until 2012	Feb. 17, 2009	703	5065
4980B		Overview of the health coverage tax credit (HCTC)	Feb. 17, 2009	501	5078
4980B(f)(2)(B)(i)	1899F(b)	Eligibility for COBRA continuation coverage extended up to Dec. 31, 2010 for PBGC recipients and TAA-eligible individuals who lose employment or work hours	Coverage periods that would otherwise end on or after Feb. 17, 2009; through Dec. 31, 2010	507	5078

Code §	Act §	Topic	Generally effective date	Analysis ¶	Com Rep ¶
4980B(f)(6)(D)	3001(a)(7)	Terminated workers must be notified of right to COBRA continuation benefits subsidy	Feb. 17, 2009	307	5082
6211(b)(4)(A)	1001(e)(1)	Refundable "making work pay credit" of up to $400 ($800 on joint return) is allowed for 2009 and 2010	Tax years beginning after Dec. 31, 2008, and before Jan. 1, 2011	101	5001
6211(b)(4)(A)	1004(b)(7)	Hope credit is increased and expanded (and re-named the "American Opportunity Tax Credit") for 2009 and 2010	Tax years beginning in 2009 and 2010	107	5004
6211(b)(4)(A)	1201(a)(3)(B)	Binding contract rule and tax deficiency rule for the election to trade bonus and accelerated depreciation for certain otherwise-deferred credits are corrected	Tax years ending after Mar. 31, 2008	806	5034
6211(b)(4)(A)	1201(b)(2)	Binding contract rule and tax deficiency rule for the election to trade bonus and accelerated depreciation for certain otherwise-deferred credits are corrected	Tax years ending after Mar. 31, 2008	806	5034
6211(b)(4)(A)	1531(c)(4)	New tax credit bond option is added for "Build America Bonds" issued in 2009 and 2010; issuer may claim alternative, refundable credit for "qualified bonds"	Obligations issued after Feb. 17, 2009 and before Jan. 1, 2011	1301	5070
6211(b)(4)(A)	2202(c)(2)	Refundable $250 credit is allowed to certain government retirees ($500 for joint return where both spouses are eligible)	Feb. 17, 2009	103	5080
6213(g)(2)	2202(b)(2)	Refundable $250 credit is allowed to certain government retirees ($500 for joint return where both spouses are eligible)	Feb. 17, 2009	103	5080

Code §	Act §	Topic	Generally effective date	Analysis ¶	Com Rep ¶
6213(g)(2)(N)	1001(d)	Refundable "making work pay credit" of up to $400 ($800 on joint return) is allowed for 2009 and 2010	Tax years beginning after Dec. 31, 2008, and before Jan. 1, 2011	101	5001
6401(b)(1)	1531(c)(5)	New tax credit bond option is added for "Build America Bonds" issued in 2009 and 2010; issuer may claim alternative, refundable credit for "qualified bonds"	Obligations issued after Feb. 17, 2009 and before Jan. 1, 2011	1301	5070
6431	1531(b)	New tax credit bond option is added for "Build America Bonds" issued in 2009 and 2010; issuer may claim alternative, refundable credit for "qualified bonds"	Obligations issued after Feb. 17, 2009 and before Jan. 1, 2011	1301	5070
6431	1531(c)(1)	New tax credit bond option is added for "Build America Bonds" issued in 2009 and 2010; issuer may claim alternative, refundable credit for "qualified bonds"	Obligations issued after Feb. 17, 2009 and before Jan. 1, 2011	1301	5070
6432	3001(a)(12)(A)	Reimbursement mechanism provided to plans for COBRA premiums that are not paid by COBRA subsidized individuals	For COBRA premiums provided for periods of coverage beginning on or after Feb. 17, 2009.	308	5082
6501(m)	1141(b)(4)	"New qualified plug-in electric drive motor vehicle credit" will be modified for vehicles acquired after Dec. 31, 2009	Vehicles acquired after Dec. 31, 2009	1002	5027
6501(m)	1142(b)(7)	Qualified plug-in electric vehicle credit is provided for certain low-speed vehicles and 2- or 3-wheeled vehicles acquired before Jan. 1, 2012	Vehicles acquired before Jan. 1, 2012 and after Feb. 17, 2009	1003	5027

Code §	Act §	Topic	Generally effective date	Analysis ¶	Com Rep ¶
6654(d)(1)(D)	1212	Decreased required estimated tax payments in 2009 for certain small businesses	Tax years beginning in 2009	701	5038
6655	704*	Estimated tax payments due from corporations with assets of $1 billion or more are increased for installments due in July, Aug., Sept. 2013	Feb. 4, 2009	702	5101
6720C	3001(a)(13)(A)	Penalty imposed on COBRA-subsidized individuals who fail to notify group health plan when they become eligible for other health coverage	Feb. 17, 2009	309	5082
7527		Overview of the health coverage tax credit (HCTC)	Feb. 17, 2009	501	5078
7527(b)	1899A(a)(2)	Refundable HCTC for eligible individuals' health insurance costs is increased from 65% to 80% through 2010	Coverage months beginning on or after May 1, 2009 and before Jan. 1, 2011	502	5078
7527(d)	1899H(a)	Additional information is required on qualified health insurance cost eligibility certificates issued before 2011	For certificates issued on or after Aug. 18, 2009 and before Jan. 1, 2011	509	5078
7527(e)	1899B(a)	IRS is required to pay premiums due before start of HCTC advance payments in 2009 and 2010	For coverage months beginning after Dec. 31, 2008 and before Jan. 1, 2011	503	5078
7871(f)	1402(a)	Indian tribal governments can issue $2 billion of tribal economic development bonds	Bonds issued after Feb. 17, 2009	1313	5056
9801		Overview of the health coverage tax credit (HCTC)	Feb. 17, 2009	501	5078

Code §	Act §	Topic	Generally effective date	Analysis ¶	Com Rep ¶
9801(c)(2)(D)	1899D(a)	Pre-certification period after TAA-related loss of health coverage is temporarily ignored for certain HIPAA and HCTC purposes	Plan years beginning after Feb. 17, 2009 and before Jan. 1, 2011	505	5078
9801(f)(3)	311(a) *	Special enrollment and notification requirements for group health plans for Medicaid- or CHIP-eligible employees or dependents	April 1, 2009	403	5102
None	3001	COBRA premium subsidy provided for 9 months to workers involuntarily terminated between Sept. 10, 2008 through Dec. 31, 2009	For periods of COBRA coverage provided beginning on or after Feb. 17, 2009	301	5082
None	1261(a)	Revocation of IRS guidance exempting banks from loss limitation rules following an ownership change	For ownership changes after Jan. 16, 2009	602	5048
None	1602	States can elect grants, instead of tax credits, to finance low-income housing for 2009, but tax credit allocations are reduced	Feb. 17, 2009	906	5058
None	2201	One-time $250 payment to be made to recipients of social security, SSI, railroad retirement, and veterans disability or pension benefits	Feb. 17, 2009	102	5079
None	2202	Refundable $250 credit is allowed to certain government retirees ($500 for joint return where both spouses are eligible)	Feb. 17, 2009	103	5080
None	3001(a)(2)(C)	Penalty imposed on COBRA-subsidized individuals who fail to notify group health plan when they become eligible for other health coverage	Feb. 17, 2009	309	5082

Code §	Act §	Topic	Generally effective date	Analysis ¶	Com Rep ¶
None	3001(a)(4)	Certain unemployed workers have an extended 60-day period to elect subsidized COBRA continuation coverage	For periods of COBRA continuation coverage beginning after Feb. 17, 2009	302	5082
None	3001(b)	Recapture of COBRA premium assistance provided to high income taxpayers	Tax years ending after Feb. 17, 2009	304	5082
None	3001(a)(1)(B)	COBRA-subsidized individuals may elect to change COBRA continuation coverage to a different plan where employer so permits	For periods of COBRA continuation coverage beginning after Feb. 17, 2009	303	5082
None	7002	Scope of $500,000 compensation deduction limit on TARP recipients is broadened; other non-tax executive compensation restrictions are imposed	Feb. 17, 2009	401	5084

¶ 6002. Act Section ERISA Cross Reference Table

Act § cites are to the 2009 American Recovery and Reinvestment Act unless otherwise indicated. * denotes 2009 Children's Health Insurance Program Reauthorization Act.

Act §	ERISA §	Topic	Generally effective date	Analysis ¶	Com Rep ¶
311(b)(1)(A)*	701(f)(3)	Special enrollment and notification requirements for group health plans for Medicaid- or CHIP-eligible employees or dependents	April 1, 2009	403	5102
311(b)(1)(B)*	102(b)	Special enrollment and notification requirements for group health plans for Medicaid- or CHIP-eligible employees or dependents	April 1, 2009	403	5102
311(b)(1)(E)*	502	Special enrollment and notification requirements for group health plans for Medicaid- or CHIP-eligible employees or dependents	April 1, 2009	403	5102
1899D(b)	701(c)(2)(C)	Pre-certification period after TAA-related loss of health coverage is temporarily ignored for certain HIPAA and HCTC purposes	Plan years beginning after Feb. 17, 2009 and before Jan. 1, 2011	505	5078

Act §	ERISA §	Topic	Generally effective date	Analysis ¶	Com Rep ¶
1899F(a)	602(2)(A)	Eligibility for COBRA continuation coverage extended up to Dec. 31, 2010 for PBGC recipients and TAA-eligible individuals who lose employment or work hours	Coverage periods that would otherwise end on or after Feb. 17, 2009; through Dec. 31, 2010	507	5078
3001(a)(7)	606(4)	Terminated workers must be notified of right to COBRA continuation benefits subsidy	Feb. 17, 2009	307	5082

¶ 6003. ERISA Section Cross Reference Table

Act § cites are to the 2009 American Recovery and Reinvestment Act unless otherwise indicated. * denotes 2009 Children's Health Insurance Program Reauthorization Act.

ERISA §	Act §	Topic	Generally effective date	Analysis ¶	Com Rep ¶
102(b)	311(b)(1)(B) *	Special enrollment and notification requirements for group health plans for Medicaid- or CHIP-eligible employees or dependents	April 1, 2009	403	5102
502	311(b)(1)(E) *	Special enrollment and notification requirements for group health plans for Medicaid- or CHIP-eligible employees or dependents	April 1, 2009	403	5102
602(2)(A)	1899F(a)	Eligibility for COBRA continuation coverage extended up to Dec. 31, 2010 for PBGC recipients and TAA-eligible individuals who lose employment or work hours	Coverage periods that would otherwise end on or after Feb. 17, 2009; through Dec. 31, 2010	507	5078
606(4)	3001(a)(7)	Terminated workers must be notified of right to COBRA continuation benefits subsidy	Feb. 17, 2009	307	5082

ERISA §	Act §	Topic	Generally effective date	Analysis ¶	Com Rep ¶
701(c)(2)(C)	1899D(b)	Pre-certification period after TAA-related loss of health coverage is temporarily ignored for certain HIPAA and HCTC purposes	Plan years beginning after Feb. 17, 2009 and before Jan. 1, 2011	505	5078
701(f)(3)	311(b)(1)(A)*	Special enrollment and notification requirements for group health plans for Medicaid- or CHIP-eligible employees or dependents	April 1, 2009	403	5102

¶ 6004. Code Sections Amended by Act

Act § cites are to the 2009 American Recovery and Reinvestment Act unless otherwise indicated. * denotes 2009 Children's Health Insurance Program Reauthorization Act.

Code Sec.	Act Sec.	Code Sec.	Act Sec.
24(b)(3)(B)	1004(b)(1)	30D	1141(a)
24(b)(3)(B)	1142(b)(1)(A)	32(b)(3)	1002(a)
24(b)(3)(B)	1144(b)(1)(A)	35(a)	1899A(a)(1)
24(d)(4)	1003(a)	35(c)(2)(B)	1899C(a)
25(e)(1)(C)(ii)	1004(b)(2)	35(e)(1)(K)	1899G(a)
25(e)(1)(C)(ii)	1142(b)(1)(B)	35(g)(9)	1899E(a)
25(e)(1)(C)(ii)	1144(b)(1)(B)	35(g)(9)	3001(a)(14)(A)
25A(i)	1004(a)	35(g)(10)	1899E(a)
25A(j)	1004(a)	35(g)(10)	3001(a)(14)(A)
25B(g)(2)	1004(b)(4)	36(b)	1006(b)(1)
25B(g)(2)	1142(b)(1)(C)	36(b)(1)(B)	1006(b)(2)
25B(g)(2)	1144(b)(1)(C)	36(d)(1)	1006(d)(2)
25C(a)	1121(a)	36(d)(2)	1006(e)
25C(b)	1121(a)	36(d)(3)	1006(e)
25C(c)(2)(A)	1121(d)(2)	36(d)(4)	1006(e)
25C(c)(4)	1121(d)(1)	36(f)(4)(D)	1006(c)(1)
25C(d)(2)(A)(ii)	1121(c)(2)	36(g)	1006(a)(2)
25C(d)(3)(B)	1121(b)(1)	36(g)	1006(c)(2)
25C(d)(3)(C)	1121(b)(2)	36(h)	1006(a)(1)
25C(d)(3)(D)	1121(b)(3)	36A	1001(a)
25C(d)(3)(E)	1121(b)(4)	38(b)(35)	1141(b)(2)
25C(d)(4)	1121(c)(1)	42(i)(9)	1404
25C(e)(1)	1103(b)(2)(A)	45(d)(1)	1101(a)(1)
25C(g)(2)	1121(e)	45(d)(2)	1101(a)(2)
25D(b)(1)	1122(a)(1)	45(d)(3)	1101(a)(2)
25D(e)(4)	1122(a)(2)(A)	45(d)(4)	1101(a)(2)
25D(e)(4)(C)	1122(a)(2)(B)	45(d)(5)	1101(b)
25D(e)(9)	1103(b)(2)(B)	45(d)(6)	1101(a)(2)
26(a)(1)	1004(b)(3)	45(d)(7)	1101(a)(2)
26(a)(1)	1142(b)(1)(D)	45(d)(9)	1101(a)(2)
26(a)(1)	1144(b)(1)(D)	45(d)(11)(B)	1101(a)(3)
26(a)(2)	1011(a)(1)	45D(f)(1)(C)	1403(a)(1)
26(a)(2)	1011(a)(2)	45D(f)(1)(D)	1403(a)(2)
30	1142(a)	45D(f)(1)(E)	1403(a)(3)
30B(a)(3)	1143(b)	45D(f)(1)(F)	1403(a)(3)
30B(a)(4)	1143(b)	45Q(a)(1)(B)	1131(b)(2)
30B(a)(5)	1143(b)	45Q(a)(2)(A)	1131(a)
30B(b)(3)(D)	1141(b)(1)	45Q(a)(2)(B)	1131(a)
30B(g)(2)	1144(a)	45Q(a)(2)(C)	1131(a)
30B(h)(1)	1142(b)(2)	45Q(d)(2)	1131(b)(1)(A)
30B(h)(8)	1143(c)	45Q(d)(2)	1131(b)(1)(B)
30B(i)	1143(a)	45Q(d)(2)	1131(b)(1)(C)
30B(j)	1143(a)	45Q(e)	1131(b)(3)
30B(k)	1143(a)	46(3)	1302(a)
30C(d)(2)(A)	1142(b)(3)	46(4)	1302(a)
30C(d)(2)(A)	1144(b)(2)	46(5)	1302(a)
30C(e)(6)	1123(a)	48(a)(4)(D)	1103(b)(1)

1,063

Code Sec.	Act Sec.	Code Sec.	Act Sec.
48(a)(5)	1102(a)	144(a)(12)(C)(iii)	1301(a)(2)
48(c)(4)(B)	1103(a)	163(e)(5)(F)	1232(a)
48(c)(4)(C)	1103(a)	163(i)(1)	1232(b)(1)
48(c)(4)(D)	1103(a)	163(i)(1)	1232(b)(2)
48(d)	1104	164(a)(6)	1008(a)
48A(b)(2)	1103(b)(2)(C)	164(b)(6)	1008(b)
48B(b)(2)	1103(b)(2)(D)	168(k)	1201(a)(2)(A)
48C	1302(b)	168(k)(2)	1201(a)(1)(A)
49(a)(1)(C)(iii)	1302(c)(1)	168(k)(2)	1201(a)(1)(B)
49(a)(1)(C)(iv)	1302(c)(1)	168(k)(2)(B)(ii)	1201(a)(2)(B)
49(a)(1)(C)(v)	1302(c)(1)	168(k)(4)(D)(i)	1201(a)(3)(A)(i)
51(d)(14)	1221(a)	168(k)(4)(D)(ii)	1201(a)(3)(A)(iii)
53(d)(1)(B)(iii)	1142(b)(4)(A)	168(k)(4)(D)(iii)	1201(a)(3)(A)(ii)
53(d)(1)(B)(iii)(II)	1142(b)(4)(B)	168(k)(4)(D)(iii)	1201(b)(1)(A)
53(d)(1)(B)(iv)	1142(b)(4)(A)	168(k)(4)(H)	1201(b)(1)(B)
54(c)(2)	1531(c)(3)	168(l)(5)(B)	1201(a)(2)(C)
54(l)(4)	1541(b)(1)	168(n)(2)(C)	1201(a)(2)(D)
54(l)(5)	1541(b)(1)	172(b)(1)(H)	1211(a)
54(l)(6)	1541(b)(1)	172(k)	1211(b)
54A(c)(1)(B)	1531(c)(2)	172(l)	1211(b)
54A(d)(1)(C)	1521(b)(1)	179(b)(7)	1202(a)(1)
54A(d)(1)(D)	1521(b)(1)	179(b)(7)	1202(a)(2)
54A(d)(1)(E)	1521(b)(1)	265(b)(3)(G)	1502(a)
54A(d)(2)(C)(iii)	1521(b)(2)	265(b)(7)	1501(a)
54A(d)(2)(C)(iv)	1521(b)(2)	291(e)(1)(B)(iv)	1501(b)
54A(d)(2)(C)(v)	1521(b)(2)	382(n)	1262(a)
54A(h)	1541(b)(2)	529(e)(3)(A)	1005(a)
54C(c)(4)	1111	529(e)(3)(A)(i)	1005(a)
54D(d)	1112(a)	529(e)(3)(A)(ii)	1005(a)
54D(e)(4)	1112(b)(2)	529(e)(3)(A)(iii)	1005(a)
54D(f)(1)(A)(ii)	1112(b)(1)	853A	1541(a)
54E(c)(1)	1522(a)	904(i)	1004(b)(5)
54F	1521(a)	904(i)	1142(b)(1)(E)
54AA	1531(a)	904(i)	1144(b)(1)(E)
55(c)(3)	1142(b)(5)	1016(a)(25)	1141(b)(3)
55(c)(3)	1144(b)(3)	1016(a)(25)	1142(b)(6)
55(d)(1)(A)	1012(a)(1)	1202(a)(3)	1241(a)
55(d)(1)(B)	1012(a)(2)	1374(d)(7)	1251(a)
56(b)(1)(E)	1008(d)	1397E(c)(2)	1531(c)(3)
56(g)(4)(B)(iv)	1503(b)	1400C(d)(2)	1004(b)(6)
57(a)(5)(C)(vi)	1503(a)	1400C(d)(2)	1142(b)(1)(F)
63(c)(1)(C)	1008(c)(1)	1400C(d)(2)	1144(b)(1)(F)
63(c)(1)(D)	1008(c)(1)	1400C(e)(4)	1006(d)(1)
63(c)(1)(E)	1008(c)(1)	1400N(d)(3)(B)	1201(a)(2)(E)
63(c)(9)	1008(c)(2)	1400N(l)(3)(B)	1531(c)(3)
85(c)	1007(a)	1400U-1	1401(a)
108(i)	1231(a)	1400U-2	1401(a)
132(f)(2)	1151(a)	1400U-3	1401(a)
139C	3001(a)(15)(A)	4980B(f)(2)(B)	1899F(b)(1)
142(i)(1)	1504(a)	4980B(f)(2)(B)(V)	1899F(b)(2)
144(a)(12)(C)	1301(a)(1)	4980B(f)(2)(B)(VI)	1899F(b)(2)
144(a)(12)(C)	1301(a)(2)	4980B(f)(2)(B)(VII)	1899F(b)(2)
144(a)(12)(C)(ii)	1301(a)(2)	4980B(f)(2)(B)(VIII)	1899F(b)(2)

Code Sec.	Act Sec.	Code Sec.	Act Sec.
5701(a)(1)	701(a)(1) *	6103(o)(1)	702(f)(1) *
5701(a)(2)	701(a)(2) *	6103(o)(1)(B)	702(f)(1) *
5701(a)(2)	701(a)(3) *	6103(p)(4)	702(f)(2) *
5701(b)(1)	701(b)(1) *	6211(b)(4)(A)	1001(e)(1)
5701(b)(2)	701(b)(2) *	6211(b)(4)(A)	1004(b)(7)
5701(c)	701(c) *	6211(b)(4)(A)	1201(a)(3)(B)
5701(d)	701(d) *	6211(b)(4)(A)	1201(b)(2)
5701(e)(1)	701(e)(1) *	6211(b)(4)(A)	1531(c)(4)
5701(e)(2)	701(e)(2) *	6213(g)(2)(L)(ii)	1001(d)
5701(f)	701(f) *	6213(g)(2)(M)	1001(d)
5701(g)	701(g) *	6213(g)(2)(N)	1001(d)
5702(h)	702(a)(5)(A) *	6401(b)(1)	1531(c)(5)
5702(j)	702(a)(5)(B) *	6431	1531(b)
5702(o)	702(d)(1) *	6432	3001(a)(12)(A)
5702(p)	702(a)(4) *	6501(m)	1141(b)(4)
5703(b)(2)(F)	702(e)(1) *	6501(m)	1142(b)(7)
5704(k)	702(a)(5)(B) *	6654(d)(1)(D)	1212
5712	702(a)(1)(A) *	6720C	3001(a)(13)(A)
5712(3)	702(b)(1) *	7527(b)	1899A(a)(2)
5713(a)	702(a)(1)(B) *	7527(d)	1899H(a)
5713(b)	702(b)(2) *	7527(e)	1899B(a)
5721	702(a)(2)(A) *	7871(f)	1402(a)
5722	702(a)(2)(B) *	9801(c)(2)(D)	1899D(a)
5723	702(a)(2)(C) *	9801(f)(3)	311(a) *
5741	702(a)(3) *		

¶ 6005. Act Sections Amending Code

Act § cites are to the 2009 American Recovery and Reinvestment Act unless otherwise indicated. * denotes 2009 Children's Health Insurance Program Reauthorization Act.

Act Sec.	Code Sec.	Act Sec.	Code Sec.
1001(a)	36A	1101(a)(2)	45(d)(6)
1001(d)	6213(g)(2)(L)(ii)	1101(a)(2)	45(d)(7)
1001(d)	6213(g)(2)(M)	1101(a)(2)	45(d)(9)
1001(d)	6213(g)(2)(N)	1101(a)(3)	45(d)(11)(B)
1001(e)(1)	6211(b)(4)(A)	1101(b)	45(d)(5)
1002(a)	32(b)(3)	1102(a)	48(a)(5)
1003(a)	24(d)(4)	1103(a)	48(c)(4)(B)
1004(a)	25A(i)	1103(a)	48(c)(4)(C)
1004(a)	25A(j)	1103(a)	48(c)(4)(D)
1004(b)(1)	24(b)(3)(B)	1103(b)(1)	48(a)(4)(D)
1004(b)(2)	25(e)(1)(C)(ii)	1103(b)(2)(A)	25C(e)(1)
1004(b)(3)	26(a)(1)	1103(b)(2)(B)	25D(e)(9)
1004(b)(4)	25B(g)(2)	1103(b)(2)(C)	48A(b)(2)
1004(b)(5)	904(i)	1103(b)(2)(D)	48B(b)(2)
1004(b)(6)	1400C(d)(2)	1104	48(d)
1004(b)(7)	6211(b)(4)(A)	1111	54C(c)(4)
1005(a)	529(e)(3)(A)	1112(a)	54D(d)
1005(a)	529(e)(3)(A)(i)	1112(b)(1)	54D(f)(1)(A)(ii)
1005(a)	529(e)(3)(A)(ii)	1112(b)(2)	54D(e)(4)
1005(a)	529(e)(3)(A)(iii)	1121(a)	25C(a)
1006(a)(1)	36(h)	1121(a)	25C(b)
1006(a)(2)	36(g)	1121(b)(1)	25C(d)(3)(B)
1006(b)(1)	36(b)	1121(b)(2)	25C(d)(3)(C)
1006(b)(2)	36(b)(1)(B)	1121(b)(3)	25C(d)(3)(D)
1006(c)(1)	36(f)(4)(D)	1121(b)(4)	25C(d)(3)(E)
1006(c)(2)	36(g)	1121(c)(1)	25C(d)(4)
1006(d)(1)	1400C(e)(4)	1121(c)(2)	25C(d)(2)(A)(ii)
1006(d)(2)	36(d)(1)	1121(d)(1)	25C(c)(4)
1006(e)	36(d)(2)	1121(d)(2)	25C(c)(2)(A)
1006(e)	36(d)(3)	1121(e)	25C(g)(2)
1006(e)	36(d)(4)	1122(a)(1)	25D(b)(1)
1007(a)	85(c)	1122(a)(2)(A)	25D(e)(4)
1008(a)	164(a)(6)	1122(a)(2)(B)	25D(e)(4)(C)
1008(b)	164(b)(6)	1123(a)	30C(e)(6)
1008(c)(1)	63(c)(1)(C)	1131(a)	45Q(a)(2)(A)
1008(c)(1)	63(c)(1)(D)	1131(a)	45Q(a)(2)(B)
1008(c)(1)	63(c)(1)(E)	1131(a)	45Q(a)(2)(C)
1008(c)(2)	63(c)(9)	1131(b)(1)(A)	45Q(d)(2)
1008(d)	56(b)(1)(E)	1131(b)(1)(B)	45Q(d)(2)
1011(a)(1)	26(a)(2)	1131(b)(1)(C)	45Q(d)(2)
1011(a)(2)	26(a)(2)	1131(b)(2)	45Q(a)(1)(B)
1012(a)(1)	55(d)(1)(A)	1131(b)(3)	45Q(e)
1012(a)(2)	55(d)(1)(B)	1141(a)	30D
1101(a)(1)	45(d)(1)	1141(b)(1)	30B(b)(3)(D)
1101(a)(2)	45(d)(2)	1141(b)(2)	38(b)(35)
1101(a)(2)	45(d)(3)	1141(b)(3)	1016(a)(25)
1101(a)(2)	45(d)(4)	1141(b)(4)	6501(m)

Act Sec.	Code Sec.	Act Sec.	Code Sec.
1142(a)	30	1231(a)	108(i)
1142(b)(1)(A)	24(b)(3)(B)	1232(a)	163(e)(5)(F)
1142(b)(1)(B)	25(e)(1)(C)(ii)	1232(b)(1)	163(i)(1)
1142(b)(1)(C)	25B(g)(2)	1232(b)(2)	163(i)(1)
1142(b)(1)(D)	26(a)(1)	1241(a)	1202(a)(3)
1142(b)(1)(E)	904(i)	1251(a)	1374(d)(7)
1142(b)(1)(F)	1400C(d)(2)	1262(a)	382(n)
1142(b)(2)	30B(h)(1)	1301(a)(1)	144(a)(12)(C)
1142(b)(3)	30C(d)(2)(A)	1301(a)(2)	144(a)(12)(C)
1142(b)(4)(A)	53(d)(1)(B)(iii)	1301(a)(2)	144(a)(12)(C)(ii)
1142(b)(4)(A)	53(d)(1)(B)(iv)	1301(a)(2)	144(a)(12)(C)(iii)
1142(b)(4)(B)	53(d)(1)(B)(iii)(II)	1302(a)	46(3)
1142(b)(5)	55(c)(3)	1302(a)	46(4)
1142(b)(6)	1016(a)(25)	1302(a)	46(5)
1142(b)(7)	6501(m)	1302(b)	48C
1143(a)	30B(i)	1302(c)(1)	49(a)(1)(C)(iii)
1143(a)	30B(j)	1302(c)(1)	49(a)(1)(C)(iv)
1143(a)	30B(k)	1302(c)(1)	49(a)(1)(C)(v)
1143(b)	30B(a)(3)	1401(a)	1400U-1
1143(b)	30B(a)(4)	1401(a)	1400U-2
1143(b)	30B(a)(5)	1401(a)	1400U-3
1143(c)	30B(h)(8)	1402(a)	7871(f)
1144(a)	30B(g)(2)	1403(a)(1)	45D(f)(1)(C)
1144(b)(1)(A)	24(b)(3)(B)	1403(a)(2)	45D(f)(1)(D)
1144(b)(1)(B)	25(e)(1)(C)(ii)	1403(a)(3)	45D(f)(1)(E)
1144(b)(1)(C)	25B(g)(2)	1403(a)(3)	45D(f)(1)(F)
1144(b)(1)(D)	26(a)(1)	1404	42(i)(9)
1144(b)(1)(E)	904(i)	1501(a)	265(b)(7)
1144(b)(1)(F)	1400C(d)(2)	1501(b)	291(e)(1)(B)(iv)
1144(b)(2)	30C(d)(2)(A)	1502(a)	265(b)(3)(G)
1144(b)(3)	55(c)(3)	1503(a)	57(a)(5)(C)(vi)
1151(a)	132(f)(2)	1503(b)	56(g)(4)(B)(iv)
1201(a)(1)(A)	168(k)(2)	1504(a)	142(i)(1)
1201(a)(1)(B)	168(k)(2)	1521(a)	54F
1201(a)(2)(A)	168(k)	1521(b)(1)	54A(d)(1)(C)
1201(a)(2)(B)	168(k)(2)(B)(ii)	1521(b)(1)	54A(d)(1)(D)
1201(a)(2)(C)	168(l)(5)(B)	1521(b)(1)	54A(d)(1)(E)
1201(a)(2)(D)	168(n)(2)(C)	1521(b)(2)	54A(d)(2)(C)(iii)
1201(a)(2)(E)	1400N(d)(3)(B)	1521(b)(2)	54A(d)(2)(C)(iv)
1201(a)(3)(A)(i)	168(k)(4)(D)(i)	1521(b)(2)	54A(d)(2)(C)(v)
1201(a)(3)(A)(ii)	168(k)(4)(D)(iii)	1522(a)	54E(c)(1)
1201(a)(3)(A)(iii)	168(k)(4)(D)(ii)	1531(a)	54AA
1201(a)(3)(B)	6211(b)(4)(A)	1531(b)	6431
1201(b)(1)(A)	168(k)(4)(D)(iii)	1531(c)(2)	54A(c)(1)(B)
1201(b)(1)(B)	168(k)(4)(H)	1531(c)(3)	54(c)(2)
1201(b)(2)	6211(b)(4)(A)	1531(c)(3)	1397E(c)(2)
1202(a)(1)	179(b)(7)	1531(c)(3)	1400N(l)(3)(B)
1202(a)(2)	179(b)(7)	1531(c)(4)	6211(b)(4)(A)
1211(a)	172(b)(1)(H)	1531(c)(5)	6401(b)(1)
1211(b)	172(k)	1541(a)	853A
1211(b)	172(l)	1541(b)(1)	54(l)(4)
1212	6654(d)(1)(D)	1541(b)(1)	54(l)(5)
1221(a)	51(d)(14)	1541(b)(1)	54(l)(6)

Act Sec.	Code Sec.	Act Sec.	Code Sec.
1541(b)(2)	54A(h)	701(b)(1) *	5701(b)(1)
1899A(a)(1)	35(a)	701(b)(2) *	5701(b)(2)
1899A(a)(2)	7527(b)	701(c) *	5701(c)
1899B(a)	7527(e)	701(d) *	5701(d)
1899C(a)	35(c)(2)(B)	701(e)(1) *	5701(e)(1)
1899D(a)	9801(c)(2)(D)	701(e)(2) *	5701(e)(2)
1899E(a)	35(g)(9)	701(f) *	5701(f)
1899E(a)	35(g)(10)	701(g) *	5701(g)
1899F(b)(1)	4980B(f)(2)(B)	702(a)(1)(A) *	5712
1899F(b)(2)	4980B(f)(2)(B)(V)	702(a)(1)(B) *	5713(a)
1899F(b)(2)	4980B(f)(2)(B)(VI)	702(a)(2)(A) *	5721
1899F(b)(2)	4980B(f)(2)(B)(VII)	702(a)(2)(B) *	5722
1899F(b)(2)	4980B(f)(2)(B)(VIII)	702(a)(2)(C) *	5723
1899G(a)	35(e)(1)(K)	702(a)(3) *	5741
1899H(a)	7527(d)	702(a)(4) *	5702(p)
3001(a)(12)(A)	6432	702(a)(5)(A) *	5702(h)
3001(a)(13)(A)	6720C	702(a)(5)(B) *	5702(j)
3001(a)(14)(A)	35(g)(9)	702(a)(5)(B) *	5704(k)
3001(a)(14)(A)	35(g)(10)	702(b)(2) *	5713(b)
3001(a)(15)(A)	139C	702(d)(1) *	5702(o)
311(a) *	9801(f)(3)	702(e)(1) *	5703(b)(2)(F)
701(a)(1) *	5701(a)(1)	702(f)(1) *	6103(o)(1)
701(a)(2) *	5701(a)(2)	702(f)(1) *	6103(o)(1)(B)
701(a)(3) *	5701(a)(2)	702(f)(2) *	6103(p)(4)

¶ 6006. ERISA Sections Amended by Act

Act § cites are to the 2009 American Recovery and Reinvestment Act unless otherwise indicated. * denotes 2009 Children's Health Insurance Program Reauthorization Act.

ERISA Sec.	Act Sec.	ERISA Sec.	Act Sec.
102(b)	311(b)(1)(B)(i) *	602(2)(A)(v)	1899F(a)(1)
102(b)	311(b)(1)(B)(ii) *	602(2)(A)(vi)	1899F(a)(3)
502(a)(6)	311(b)(1)(E)(i) *	602(2)(A)(vii)	1899F(a)(3)
502(c)(9)	311(b)(1)(E)(ii) *	602(2)(A)(viii)	1899F(a)(2)
502(c)(10)	311(b)(1)(E)(ii) *	701(c)(2)(C)	1899D(b)
602(2)(A)	1899F(a)(2)		

¶ 6007. Act Sections Amending ERISA

Act § cites are to the 2009 American Recovery and Reinvestment Act unless otherwise indicated. * denotes 2009 Children's Health Insurance Program Reauthorization Act.

Act Sec.	ERISA Sec.	Act Sec.	ERISA Sec.
1899D(b)	701(c)(2)(C)	311(b)(1)(B)(i) *	102(b)
1899F(a)(1)	602(2)(A)(v)	311(b)(1)(B)(ii) *	102(b)
1899F(a)(2)	602(2)(A)	311(b)(1)(E)(i) *	502(a)(6)
1899F(a)(2)	602(2)(A)(viii)	311(b)(1)(E)(i) *	502(a)(6)
1899F(a)(3)	602(2)(A)(vi)	311(b)(1)(E)(ii) *	502(c)(9)
1899F(a)(3)	602(2)(A)(vii)	311(b)(1)(E)(ii) *	502(c)(10)

¶ 6008. FTC 2nd ¶s Affected by Act

FTC 2d ¶	Analysis ¶	FTC 2d ¶	Analysis ¶	FTC 2d ¶	Analysis ¶
A-2800	105	A-4781.1	204	H-3823	401
A-2801	105	A-4782	1103	H-4237	505
A-4000	1003	A-4785	1104	H-4870	306, 501,
A-4010	204, 205,	A-4872	509		505
	1003	A-4900	204	H-4871	306, 502,
A-4050	109, 204,	A-4901	107, 204		503, 505
	1003	A-4902	107	H-4872	509
A-4054	204, 205,	A-4903	204	I-9100	902
	1003	A-8160	201	I-9100.1	902
A-4055	109	A-8162	201	I-9100.1A	902
A-4200	110, 111	A-8163	201	J-3000	1301
A-4201	110	A-8201	202	J-3001	1301
A-4202	111	A-8300	105, 204	J-3101	1304
A-4230	306, 501,	A-8305	105	J-3150	1304, 1310,
	504, 505	A-8320	204		1312, 1313
A-4231	306, 501,	A-8406	203	J-3153	1304
	502, 505	A-8800	1003	J-3177	1312
A-4232	504	A-8802	1003	J-3233.3	1310
A-4236	508	D-1640	903	J-3241	1313
A-4250	1003	D-1643	903	J-3242	1313
A-4255	204, 205,	D-1655	903	J-3252	1304
	1003	E-3100	1309	J-3253	1304, 1307
A-4270	104	E-3111	1309	J-3274	1304
A-4271	104	E-3112	1309	J-3277	1310
A-4272	104	E-3124	1309	J-7016	901
A-4279	104	E-3127	1309	J-7204.1	901
A-4280	104	E-3128	1309	J-7400	901
A-4281	104	E-3131	1309	J-7404	901
A-4400	204	E-3133	1309	J-7205	901
A-4405	204	E-6150	1308	J-8700	703
A-4450	204, 1003	E-6151	1308	K-4000	105
A-4455	204, 205,	E-6600	1308	K-4001	105
	1003	E-6616	1308	K-4500	105
A-4500	107	F-7360	602	K-4510	105
A-4501	107	F-7383	602, 603	K-5520	1309
A-4517	107	H-1250	301, 302,	K-5522.1	1309
A-4523	107		303, 307,	K-5700	908
A-4524	107		308, 309,	K-5754	907
A-4530	107		507	K-5755.1	907
A-4537	107	H-1293	302	K-5763	907, 908
A-4700	108	H-1296	507	K-5764	907
A-4711	108	H-1325	403, 505	K-5765	907
A-4750	1101, 1102,	H-1325.5	505	K-5766	907
	1103	H-2217	402	K-5768	907
A-4751	1101	H-3000	106	L-9310	801, 803,
A-4753	1102	H-3007	106		804
A-4756	1101, 1103	H-3775	401	L-9312	801, 803,
A-4780	204, 1103,	H-3821	401		804
	1104	H-3821.1	401	L-9315	801
A-4781	1104	H-3821.3	401		

FTC 2d ¶	Analysis ¶	FTC 2d ¶	Analysis ¶	FTC 2d ¶	Analysis ¶
L-9316	801, 803, 804	L-15580	1303	L-18031.1	1002
		L-15586	1303	L-18031.2	1002
L-9316.1	801, 804	L-16000	906	L-18032	1002
L-9365	802	L-16006	906	L-18032.1	1002
L-9366	802	L-16400	1201, 1203, 1204, 1205, 1206	L-18033.1	1002
L-9900	802			L-18034.1	204
L-9907	802			L-18034.7	1002
L-9907.1	802	L-16401	1203	L-18040	1001, 1003
L-9909	802	L-16415	1206	L-18041	1001
L-9950	802	L-16436.4	1201	L-18042	205, 1003
L-9951	802	L-16480	1308	L-18102	1002, 1003
L-9952	802	L-16482	1308	L-18400	1212
L-9985	802	L-16483	1308	L-18401	1212
L-9986	802	L-16500	1202	L-18405	1212
L-9988.1	802	L-16501	1202	M-4300	601
L-9995	802	L-17750	1204, 1205, 1207, 1208, 1209	M-4301	601
L-9996	802			M-4308	601
L-9996.1	802			O-4400	1002, 1003
L-10000	803	L-17771	1207	O-4401	204, 1002, 1003
L-10004.1A	803	L-17771.1	1207		
L-15200	804, 805, 806	L-17771.2	1207	O-4411	205
		L-17771.4	1207	P-1600	1202
L-15201	1002, 1003	L-17771.5	1208	P-1611	1202
L-15213	804	L-17771.6	1207	S-5200	701
L-15213.1	805	L-17771.9	1209	S-5203	701
L-15213.2	804, 806	L-17775	904	S-5204	701
L-15530	1302, 1308, 1311	L-17776	904	S-5204.1	701
		L-17920	905	S-5233	701
L-15532	1308	L-17927	905	S-5301	701
L-15533	1308	L-18010	1003	S-5353	702
L-15560	1210	L-18020	205, 1003, 1004	T-1500	806
L-15564	1210			T-1505	806
L-15570	1211	L-18021	205, 1003	T-5500	1301
L-15571	1211	L-18022	205	T-5511	1301
L-15572	1211	L-18030	204, 1002, 1003		
L-15573	1211				

¶ 6009. USTR ¶ s Affected by Act

USTR ¶	Analysis ¶	USTR ¶	Analysis ¶	USTR ¶	Analysis ¶
234	204	454.14	1208	1684.027	801, 803, 804
244	109	454.15	1207		
244.01	204, 205, 1003	454.18	1209	1684.085	802
		45D4	905	1684.0281	803
244.02	109	45Q4	1212	1684.0293	804, 805, 806
254	205	464	1202		
254.01	204, 1003	484	1201, 1203, 1204, 1205, 1206	1724.30	601
25A4	107			1794.01	802
25A4.02	107			2654	1309
25A4.03	107	494	1202	280F4	803
25A4.04	107	514	904	3541	502
25A4.07	107	534	1003	3824.25	602, 603
25B4	204, 205, 1003	544	1308	5294	108
		54A4	1302, 1311	8524.02	1308
25C4	1101, 1102, 1103	54A4.01	1308	8574.02	1308
		54C4.02	1210	9044.01	204, 205, 1002, 1003
25D4	204, 1103, 1104	54D4	1211		
		54D4.01	1211	12,024	902
264	107, 204, 1002, 1003	54E4	1303	13,744.01	903
		54E4.01	1303	13,97A4	802
30B4	205, 1003, 1004	554.01	201	14,00C4	204, 205, 1003
		564.03	203		
30C4	1001	574	202	14,00J4	802
30C4.01	205, 1003	594	201	14,00N4.025	802
30D4	1002, 1003	634	105	268,413	802
30D4.01	1002	854	106	34,024.29	703
30D4.02	1002	1034	1301	49,80B4.04	301, 303, 307
30D4.03	1002	1084.01	901		
30D4.04	1002	1084.02	901	4980B4.04	308
30D4.07	204	1084.04	901	49,80B4.04	309
304	1003	1324.08	402	49,80B4.07	507
324.01	110, 111	1424.01	1304	49,80B4.09	302
354	306, 502, 504, 505	1424.04	1312	62,114	806
		1444.01	1310	64,014	1301
354	501, 508	1464.01	1304, 1307	66,544.03	701
364	104	1624.009	401	66,554	702
364.01	104	1634.051	907, 908	75,274	306, 502, 503, 505, 509
384.01	1002, 1003	1644	105		
424.70	906	1644.01	105		
454	1204, 1205	1644.03	105		
454.09	1207	1684.025	801		
454.10	1207	1684.026	801, 803, 804	78,714.02	1313
454.11	1207			98,014	403, 505
454.13	1207				

¶ 6010. Tax Desk ¶s Affected by Act

TaxDesk ¶	Analysis ¶	TaxDesk ¶	Analysis ¶	TaxDesk ¶	Analysis ¶
132,506	106	381,402	1202	569,104	204, 205
134,591	402	381,601	1203, 1204,	569,105	109
158,001	1301		1205	569,205	204, 205,
158,010	1304	381,603	1206		1003
173,000.1	1308	383,001	906	569,400	306, 501,
173,006	1308	383,012	906		505
186,002	901	384,054	1204, 1205	569,401	306, 501,
186,004	901	384,711	905		502, 504,
186,022	901	393,001	204, 205,		505
188,010	901		1002, 1003	569,405	508
188,016	901	397,000	1003	569,408	501, 503
246,601	902	397,101	205, 1003,	569,505	204
246,602	902		1004	569,550	1101, 1102,
267,602.2	803	397,106	205		1103
268,400	802	397,130	1002, 1003	569,551	1101
268,411	802	397,132	1002	569,553	1102
268,413	802	397,133	1002	569,556	1101, 1103
268,414	802	397,134	1002	569,560	1103, 1104
268,600	802	397,135	1002	569,561	1104
268,704	802	397,139	1002	569,561.1	204
269,341	801	397,143	204	569,562	1103
269,342	801, 803,	397,149	1002	569,565	1104
	804	397,201	1001	569,601	107, 204
269,345	801	397,202	205, 1003	569,602	107, 1002,
269,346	801, 803,	528,924	107		1003
	804	528,930	107	569,603	204
269,346.1	801, 804	554,101	703	569,604	204
276,001.2	401	562,001	105	571,303	701
276,001.3	401	568,509	205, 1003	571,304	701
276,001.5	401	568,521	1211, 1311	571,305	701
276,001.8	401	568,805	204, 205,	571,328	701
316,009	1309		1003	580,511	804
319,730	907	568,851	104	580,512	805
319,731	907	568,852	104	580,513	804, 806
319,734	907, 908	568,859	104	609,201	702
319,735	907	568,860	104	615,002	903
319,736	907	568,861	104	615,014	903
319,737	907	568,901	107	658,501	701
319,738	907	568,917	107	666,005	701
326,006	105	568,923	107	666,006	701
326,019.1	105	568,924	107	672,310	108
356,000	601	568,930	107	691,302	201
356,001	601	568,937	107	691,303	201
380,501	1002, 1003	569,001	110	696,501	202
380,502	204	569,002	111	698,006	203
380,513	804	569,100	109	801,008	1301
380,700	904	569,101	1003	822,501	806
381,401	1202				

¶ 6011. Pension Explanations ¶ s Affected by Act

PE ¶	Analysis ¶
49,80B4.04	307
132-4.08	402
4980B4.04	309
4980B-4.04	301, 303, 308
4980B-4.09	302
9801-4	403

¶ 6012
Current and Prospective Effective Dates

Arranged in Code section order, this table shows the topic related to a change to each specified Code section made by a Tax Act passed by the 108th, 109th, 110th or the 111th Congress, the current and/or prospective effective date of that change, and the Complete Analysis in which the topic is or has been analyzed.

Code	Topic	Effective Date	Complete Analysis
1(h)(1)(B)	5% and 15% tax rates on adjusted net capital gain are extended for two years	Tax years beginning after Dec. 31, 2008 and before Jan. 1, 2011	¶ 101 Tax Increase Prevention and Reconciliation Act of 2005
1(h)(1)(B)	Post-2007 0% tax rate on adjusted net capital gains is extended for two years	Tax years beginning after Dec. 31, 2008 and before Jan. 1, 2011	¶ 102 Tax Increase Prevention and Reconciliation Act of 2005
1(h)(1)(B)	5% tax rate on adjusted net capital gains is reduced to 0% for tax years beginning in 2008	Tax years beginning after 2007, and beginning before Jan. 1, 2009	¶ 102 Jobs and Growth Tax Relief Reconciliation Act of 2003
1(h)(1)(C)	5% and 15% tax rates on adjusted net capital gain are extended for two years	Tax years beginning after Dec. 31, 2008 and before Jan. 1, 2011	¶ 101 Tax Increase Prevention and Reconciliation Act of 2005
1(h)(1)(D)(i)	5% and 15% adjusted capital gains rates on noncorporate taxpayers' qualified dividend income are extended for two years	Tax years beginning after Dec. 31, 2008 and before Jan. 1, 2011	¶ 107 Tax Increase Prevention and Reconciliation Act of 2005
1(h)(3)(B)	5% and 15% adjusted capital gains rates on noncorporate taxpayers' qualified dividend income are extended for two years	Tax years beginning after Dec. 31, 2008 and before Jan. 1, 2011	¶ 107 Tax Increase Prevention and Reconciliation Act of 2005
1(h)(11)	5% and 15% adjusted capital gains rates on noncorporate taxpayers' qualified dividend income are extended for two years	Tax years beginning after Dec. 31, 2008 and before Jan. 1, 2011	¶ 107 Tax Increase Prevention and Reconciliation Act of 2005

Code	Topic	Effective Date	Complete Analysis
1(h)(11)(D)(ii)	Long-term capital loss treatment for losses of individuals, trusts, and estates on stock to the extent extraordinary dividends were taxed as capital gains is extended for two years	Tax years beginning after Dec. 31, 2008 and before Jan. 1, 2011	¶ 108 Tax Increase Prevention and Reconciliation Act of 2005
1(i)(1)	IRS will issue cash rebates in 2008 to eligible individuals to stimulate the economy	Tax years beginning after Dec. 31, 2007	¶ 101 Economic Stimulus Act of 2008
23(b)(4)	Nonrefundable personal credits can offset AMT through 2009 (instead of 2008)	Tax years beginning in 2009	¶ 204 American Recovery and Reinvestment Act of 2009
23(b)(4)	Nonrefundable personal credits can offset AMT through 2008 (instead of 2007)	Tax years beginning in 2008	¶ 102 Tax Provisions of H.R. 1424 (Including the Emergency Economic Stabilization, Energy Improvement and Extension, and Tax Extenders and AMT Relief Acts of 2008)
23(b)(4)(B)	Residential energy efficient property credit may be claimed against AMT	Tax years beginning after Dec. 31, 2007	¶ 513 Tax Provisions of H.R. 1424 (Including the Emergency Economic Stabilization, Energy Improvement and Extension, and Tax Extenders and AMT Relief Acts of 2008)
24(a)	"Qualifying child" must be younger than claimant and be unmarried; qualifying child benefits restricted to child's parents	Tax years beginning after Dec. 31, 2008	¶ 516 Tax Provisions of H.R. 1424 (Including the Emergency Economic Stabilization, Energy Improvement and Extension, and Tax Extenders and AMT Relief Acts of 2008)
24(b)(3)	Nonrefundable personal credits can offset AMT through 2009 (instead of 2008)	Tax years beginning in 2009	¶ 204 American Recovery and Reinvestment Act of 2009

Code	Topic	Effective Date	Complete Analysis
24(b)(3)	Nonrefundable personal credits can offset AMT through 2008 (instead of 2007)	Tax years beginning in 2008	¶ 102 Tax Provisions of H.R. 1424 (Including the Emergency Economic Stabilization, Energy Improvement and Extension, and Tax Extenders and AMT Relief Acts of 2008)
24(b)(3)(B)	Hope credit is increased and expanded (and re-named the "American Opportunity Tax Credit") for 2009 and 2010	Tax years beginning in 2009 and 2010	¶ 107 American Recovery and Reinvestment Act of 2009
24(b)(3)(B)	Alternative motor vehicle credit (AMVC) is treated as a personal credit allowed against AMT for tax years beginning after 2008	Tax years beginning after Dec. 31, 2008	¶ 205 American Recovery and Reinvestment Act of 2009
24(b)(3)(B)	Residential energy efficient property credit may be claimed against AMT	Tax years beginning after Dec. 31, 2007	¶ 513 Tax Provisions of H.R. 1424 (Including the Emergency Economic Stabilization, Energy Improvement and Extension, and Tax Extenders and AMT Relief Acts of 2008)
24(b)(3)(B)	"New qualified plug-in electric drive motor vehicle credit" is allowed for tax years beginning after Dec. 31, 2008 for property purchased before Jan. 1, 2015	Tax years beginning after Dec. 31, 2008 for property purchased before Jan. 1, 2015	¶ 926 Tax Provisions of H.R. 1424 (Including the Emergency Economic Stabilization, Energy Improvement and Extension, and Tax Extenders and AMT Relief Acts of 2008)
24(d)(4)	Refundable portion of child tax credit is increased for 2009 and 2010	Tax years beginning in 2009 and 2010	¶ 109 American Recovery and Reinvestment Act of 2009

Code	Topic	Effective Date	Complete Analysis
24(d)(4)	Refundable amount of child tax credit is increased for 2008	Tax years beginning in 2008, but only for tax years beginning in 2008	¶ 502 Tax Provisions of H.R. 1424 (Including the Emergency Economic Stabilization, Energy Improvement and Extension, and Tax Extenders and AMT Relief Acts of 2008)
25(e)(1)(C)	Nonrefundable personal credits can offset AMT through 2009 (instead of 2008)	Tax years beginning in 2009	¶ 204 American Recovery and Reinvestment Act of 2009
25(e)(1)(C)	Nonrefundable personal credits can offset AMT through 2008 (instead of 2007)	Tax years beginning in 2008	¶ 102 Tax Provisions of H.R. 1424 (Including the Emergency Economic Stabilization, Energy Improvement and Extension, and Tax Extenders and AMT Relief Acts of 2008)
25(e)(1)(C)(ii)	Hope credit is increased and expanded (and re-named the "American Opportunity Tax Credit") for 2009 and 2010	Tax years beginning in 2009 and 2010	¶ 107 American Recovery and Reinvestment Act of 2009
25(e)(1)(C)(ii)	Alternative motor vehicle credit (AMVC) is treated as a personal credit allowed against AMT for tax years beginning after 2008	Tax years beginning after Dec. 31, 2008	¶ 205 American Recovery and Reinvestment Act of 2009
25(e)(1)(C)(ii)	"New qualified plug-in electric drive motor vehicle credit" is allowed for tax years beginning after Dec. 31, 2008 for property purchased before Jan. 1, 2015	Tax years beginning after Dec. 31, 2008 for property purchased before Jan. 1, 2015	¶ 926 Tax Provisions of H.R. 1424 (Including the Emergency Economic Stabilization, Energy Improvement and Extension, and Tax Extenders and AMT Relief Acts of 2008)

Code	Topic	Effective Date	Complete Analysis
25A	Hope credit is increased and expanded (and re-named the "American Opportunity Tax Credit") for 2009 and 2010	Tax years beginning in 2009 and 2010	¶ 107 American Recovery and Reinvestment Act of 2009
25A(i)	Hope credit is increased and expanded (and re-named the "American Opportunity Tax Credit") for 2009 and 2010	Tax years beginning in 2009 and 2010	¶ 107 American Recovery and Reinvestment Act of 2009
25A(i)(5)	Nonrefundable personal credits can offset AMT through 2009 (instead of 2008)	Tax years beginning in 2009	¶ 204 American Recovery and Reinvestment Act of 2009
25B(g)	Nonrefundable personal credits can offset AMT through 2009 (instead of 2008)	Tax years beginning in 2009	¶ 204 American Recovery and Reinvestment Act of 2009
25B(g)	Nonrefundable personal credits can offset AMT through 2008 (instead of 2007)	Tax years beginning in 2008	¶ 102 Tax Provisions of H.R. 1424 (Including the Emergency Economic Stabilization, Energy Improvement and Extension, and Tax Extenders and AMT Relief Acts of 2008)
25B(g)(2)	Hope credit is increased and expanded (and re-named the "American Opportunity Tax Credit") for 2009 and 2010	Tax years beginning in 2009 and 2010	¶ 107 American Recovery and Reinvestment Act of 2009
25B(g)(2)	Alternative motor vehicle credit (AMVC) is treated as a personal credit allowed against AMT for tax years beginning after 2008	Tax years beginning after Dec. 31, 2008	¶ 205 American Recovery and Reinvestment Act of 2009

Code	Topic	Effective Date	Complete Analysis
25B(g)(2)	Residential energy efficient property credit may be claimed against AMT	Tax years beginning after Dec. 31, 2007	¶ 513 Tax Provisions of H.R. 1424 (Including the Emergency Economic Stabilization, Energy Improvement and Extension, and Tax Extenders and AMT Relief Acts of 2008)
25B(g)(2)	"New qualified plug-in electric drive motor vehicle credit" is allowed for tax years beginning after Dec. 31, 2008 for property purchased before Jan. 1, 2015	Tax years beginning after Dec. 31, 2008 for property purchased before Jan. 1, 2015	¶ 926 Tax Provisions of H.R. 1424 (Including the Emergency Economic Stabilization, Energy Improvement and Extension, and Tax Extenders and AMT Relief Acts of 2008)
25C(a)	Nonbusiness energy property credit is increased from 10% to 30% and extended for one year	Tax years beginning after Dec. 31, 2008	¶ 1101 American Recovery and Reinvestment Act of 2009
25C(b)	Nonbusiness energy property credit is increased from 10% to 30% and extended for one year	Tax years beginning after Dec. 31, 2008	¶ 1101 American Recovery and Reinvestment Act of 2009
25C(c)	Credit for nonbusiness energy property includes biomass fuel stoves and excludes geothermal heat pumps; changes to water heater and roofing requirements	Expenditures made after Dec. 31, 2008 for property placed in service after Dec. 31, 2008 and before Jan. 1, 2010	¶ 511 Tax Provisions of H.R. 1424 (Including the Emergency Economic Stabilization, Energy Improvement and Extension, and Tax Extenders and AMT Relief Acts of 2008)
25C(c)(2)(A)	Standards are modified for property qualifying for the nonbusiness energy property credit	Property placed in service after Feb. 17, 2009	¶ 1102 American Recovery and Reinvestment Act of 2009
25C(c)(4)	Standards are modified for property qualifying for the nonbusiness energy property credit	Property placed in service after Feb. 17, 2009	¶ 1102 American Recovery and Reinvestment Act of 2009

Code	Topic	Effective Date	Complete Analysis
25C(d)(2)(A)(ii)	Standards are modified for property qualifying for the nonbusiness energy property credit	Property placed in service after Feb. 17, 2009	¶ 1102 American Recovery and Reinvestment Act of 2009
25C(d)(2)(C)	Credit for nonbusiness energy property includes biomass fuel stoves and excludes geothermal heat pumps; changes to water heater and roofing requirements	Expenditures made after Dec. 31, 2008 for property placed in service after Dec. 31, 2008 and before Jan. 1, 2010	¶ 511 Tax Provisions of H.R. 1424 (Including the Emergency Economic Stabilization, Energy Improvement and Extension, and Tax Extenders and AMT Relief Acts of 2008)
25C(d)(3)(B)	Standards are modified for property qualifying for the nonbusiness energy property credit	Property placed in service after Feb. 17, 2009	¶ 1102 American Recovery and Reinvestment Act of 2009
25C(d)(3)(C)	Standards are modified for property qualifying for the nonbusiness energy property credit	Property placed in service after Feb. 17, 2009	¶ 1102 American Recovery and Reinvestment Act of 2009
25C(d)(3)(C)	Credit for nonbusiness energy property includes biomass fuel stoves and excludes geothermal heat pumps; changes to water heater and roofing requirements	Expenditures made after Dec. 31, 2008 for property placed in service after Dec. 31, 2008 and before Jan. 1, 2010	¶ 511 Tax Provisions of H.R. 1424 (Including the Emergency Economic Stabilization, Energy Improvement and Extension, and Tax Extenders and AMT Relief Acts of 2008)
25C(d)(3)(D)	Standards are modified for property qualifying for the nonbusiness energy property credit	Property placed in service after Feb. 17, 2009	¶ 1102 American Recovery and Reinvestment Act of 2009
25C(d)(3)(D)	Credit for nonbusiness energy property includes biomass fuel stoves and excludes geothermal heat pumps; changes to water heater and roofing requirements	Expenditures made after Dec. 31, 2008 for property placed in service after Dec. 31, 2008 and before Jan. 1, 2010	¶ 511 Tax Provisions of H.R. 1424 (Including the Emergency Economic Stabilization, Energy Improvement and Extension, and Tax Extenders and AMT Relief Acts of 2008)

Code	Topic	Effective Date	Complete Analysis
25C(d)(3)(E)	Standards are modified for property qualifying for the nonbusiness energy property credit	Property placed in service after Feb. 17, 2009	¶ 1102 American Recovery and Reinvestment Act of 2009
25C(d)(3)(E)	Credit for nonbusiness energy property includes biomass fuel stoves and excludes geothermal heat pumps; changes to water heater and roofing requirements	Expenditures made after Dec. 31, 2008 for property placed in service after Dec. 31, 2008 and before Jan. 1, 2010	¶ 511 Tax Provisions of H.R. 1424 (Including the Emergency Economic Stabilization, Energy Improvement and Extension, and Tax Extenders and AMT Relief Acts of 2008)
25C(d)(3)(F)	Credit for nonbusiness energy property includes biomass fuel stoves and excludes geothermal heat pumps; changes to water heater and roofing requirements	Expenditures made after Dec. 31, 2008 for property placed in service after Dec. 31, 2008 and before Jan. 1, 2010	¶ 511 Tax Provisions of H.R. 1424 (Including the Emergency Economic Stabilization, Energy Improvement and Extension, and Tax Extenders and AMT Relief Acts of 2008)
25C(d)(4)	Standards are modified for property qualifying for the nonbusiness energy property credit	Property placed in service after Feb. 17, 2009	¶ 1102 American Recovery and Reinvestment Act of 2009
25C(d)(6)	Credit for nonbusiness energy property includes biomass fuel stoves and excludes geothermal heat pumps; changes to water heater and roofing requirements	Expenditures made after Dec. 31, 2008 for property placed in service after Dec. 31, 2008 and before Jan. 1, 2010	¶ 511 Tax Provisions of H.R. 1424 (Including the Emergency Economic Stabilization, Energy Improvement and Extension, and Tax Extenders and AMT Relief Acts of 2008)
25C(e)(1)	Expenditures from subsidized energy financing can qualify for REEP credit and nonbusiness energy property credit	Tax years beginning after Dec. 31, 2008	¶ 1103 American Recovery and Reinvestment Act of 2009

Code	Topic	Effective Date	Complete Analysis
25C(g)	Nonbusiness energy property credit, which expired Dec. 31, 2007, will be reinstated after Dec. 31, 2008 through Dec. 31, 2009	Expenditures made after Dec. 31, 2008 through Dec. 31, 2009	¶ 510 Tax Provisions of H.R. 1424 (Including the Emergency Economic Stabilization, Energy Improvement and Extension, and Tax Extenders and AMT Relief Acts of 2008)
25C(g)(2)	Nonbusiness energy property credit is increased from 10% to 30% and extended for one year	Tax years beginning after Dec. 31, 2008	¶ 1101 American Recovery and Reinvestment Act of 2009
25D(a)(4)	Residential energy efficient property credit is allowed for residential wind property and geothermal heat pumps	Tax years beginning after Dec. 31, 2007	¶ 515 Tax Provisions of H.R. 1424 (Including the Emergency Economic Stabilization, Energy Improvement and Extension, and Tax Extenders and AMT Relief Acts of 2008)
25D(a)(5)	Residential energy efficient property credit is allowed for residential wind property and geothermal heat pumps	Tax years beginning after Dec. 31, 2007	¶ 515 Tax Provisions of H.R. 1424 (Including the Emergency Economic Stabilization, Energy Improvement and Extension, and Tax Extenders and AMT Relief Acts of 2008)
25D(b)(1)	Dollar caps on REEP credit are eliminated for solar hot water, geothermal, and wind property expenditures	Tax years beginning after Dec. 31, 2008	¶ 1104 American Recovery and Reinvestment Act of 2009
25D(b)(1)	Credit for solar electric property expenditures is allowed without limit	Tax years beginning after Dec. 31, 2008	¶ 514 Tax Provisions of H.R. 1424 (Including the Emergency Economic Stabilization, Energy Improvement and Extension, and Tax Extenders and AMT Relief Acts of 2008)

Code	Topic	Effective Date	Complete Analysis
25D(b)(1)(D)	Residential energy efficient property credit is allowed for residential wind property and geothermal heat pumps	Tax years beginning after Dec. 31, 2007	¶ 515 Tax Provisions of H.R. 1424 (Including the Emergency Economic Stabilization, Energy Improvement and Extension, and Tax Extenders and AMT Relief Acts of 2008)
25D(b)(1)(E)	Residential energy efficient property credit is allowed for residential wind property and geothermal heat pumps	Tax years beginning after Dec. 31, 2007	¶ 515 Tax Provisions of H.R. 1424 (Including the Emergency Economic Stabilization, Energy Improvement and Extension, and Tax Extenders and AMT Relief Acts of 2008)
25D(c)	Nonrefundable personal credits can offset AMT through 2009 (instead of 2008)	Tax years beginning in 2009	¶ 204 American Recovery and Reinvestment Act of 2009
25D(c)	Residential energy efficient property credit may be claimed against AMT	Tax years beginning after Dec. 31, 2007	¶ 513 Tax Provisions of H.R. 1424 (Including the Emergency Economic Stabilization, Energy Improvement and Extension, and Tax Extenders and AMT Relief Acts of 2008)
25D(c)(2)	Nonrefundable personal credits can offset AMT through 2008 (instead of 2007)	Tax years beginning in 2008	¶ 102 Tax Provisions of H.R. 1424 (Including the Emergency Economic Stabilization, Energy Improvement and Extension, and Tax Extenders and AMT Relief Acts of 2008)
25D(d)(4)	Residential energy efficient property credit is allowed for residential wind property and geothermal heat pumps	Tax years beginning after Dec. 31, 2007	¶ 515 Tax Provisions of H.R. 1424 (Including the Emergency Economic Stabilization, Energy Improvement and Extension, and Tax Extenders and AMT Relief Acts of 2008)

Code	Topic	Effective Date	Complete Analysis
25D(d)(5)	Residential energy efficient property credit is allowed for residential wind property and geothermal heat pumps	Tax years beginning after Dec. 31, 2007	¶ 515 Tax Provisions of H.R. 1424 (Including the Emergency Economic Stabilization, Energy Improvement and Extension, and Tax Extenders and AMT Relief Acts of 2008)
25D(e)(4)	Dollar caps on REEP credit are eliminated for solar hot water, geothermal, and wind property expenditures	Tax years beginning after Dec. 31, 2008	¶ 1104 American Recovery and Reinvestment Act of 2009
25D(e)(4)(A)	Credit for solar electric property expenditures is allowed without limit	Tax years beginning after Dec. 31, 2008	¶ 514 Tax Provisions of H.R. 1424 (Including the Emergency Economic Stabilization, Energy Improvement and Extension, and Tax Extenders and AMT Relief Acts of 2008)
25D(e)(4)(A)(iv)	Residential energy efficient property credit is allowed for residential wind property and geothermal heat pumps	Tax years beginning after Dec. 31, 2007	¶ 515 Tax Provisions of H.R. 1424 (Including the Emergency Economic Stabilization, Energy Improvement and Extension, and Tax Extenders and AMT Relief Acts of 2008)
25D(e)(4)(A)(v)	Residential energy efficient property credit is allowed for residential wind property and geothermal heat pumps	Tax years beginning after Dec. 31, 2007	¶ 515 Tax Provisions of H.R. 1424 (Including the Emergency Economic Stabilization, Energy Improvement and Extension, and Tax Extenders and AMT Relief Acts of 2008)
25D(e)(9)	Expenditures from subsidized energy financing can qualify for REEP credit and nonbusiness energy property credit	Tax years beginning after Dec. 31, 2008	¶ 1103 American Recovery and Reinvestment Act of 2009

Code	Topic	Effective Date	Complete Analysis
25D(g)	Residential energy efficient property credit is extended for eight years, through 2016	Tax years beginning after Dec. 31, 2007	¶ 512 Tax Provisions of H.R. 1424 (Including the Emergency Economic Stabilization, Energy Improvement and Extension, and Tax Extenders and AMT Relief Acts of 2008)
26(a)(1)	Hope credit is increased and expanded (and re-named the "American Opportunity Tax Credit") for 2009 and 2010	Tax years beginning in 2009 and 2010	¶ 107 American Recovery and Reinvestment Act of 2009
26(a)(1)	Alternative motor vehicle credit (AMVC) is treated as a personal credit allowed against AMT for tax years beginning after 2008	Tax years beginning after Dec. 31, 2008	¶ 205 American Recovery and Reinvestment Act of 2009
26(a)(1)	Residential energy efficient property credit may be claimed against AMT	Tax years beginning after Dec. 31, 2007	¶ 513 Tax Provisions of H.R. 1424 (Including the Emergency Economic Stabilization, Energy Improvement and Extension, and Tax Extenders and AMT Relief Acts of 2008)
26(a)(1)	"New qualified plug-in electric drive motor vehicle credit" is allowed for tax years beginning after Dec. 31, 2008 for property purchased before Jan. 1, 2015	Tax years beginning after Dec. 31, 2008 for property purchased before Jan. 1, 2015	¶ 926 Tax Provisions of H.R. 1424 (Including the Emergency Economic Stabilization, Energy Improvement and Extension, and Tax Extenders and AMT Relief Acts of 2008)
26(a)(2)	Nonrefundable personal credits can offset AMT through 2009 (instead of 2008)	Tax years beginning in 2009	¶ 204 American Recovery and Reinvestment Act of 2009

Code	Topic	Effective Date	Complete Analysis
26(a)(2)	Nonrefundable personal credits can offset AMT through 2008 (instead of 2007)	Tax years beginning in 2008	¶ 102 Tax Provisions of H.R. 1424 (Including the Emergency Economic Stabilization, Energy Improvement and Extension, and Tax Extenders and AMT Relief Acts of 2008)
26(b)(2)(W)	First-time homebuyers get refundable credit for 10% of purchase price up to $7,500 ($3,750 on separate return); credit must be recaptured over 15 years	Residences purchased after April 8, 2008, and before July 1, 2009	¶ 102 Housing Assistance Tax Act of 2008
26(b)(2)(X)	Nonqualified deferred compensation (NQDC) from certain tax-indifferent corporations and partnerships is includible in gross income when not subject to substantial forfeiture risk	Deferred amounts attributable to services performed after Dec. 31, 2008	¶ 401 Tax Provisions of H.R. 1424 (Including the Emergency Economic Stabilization, Energy Improvement and Extension, and Tax Extenders and AMT Relief Acts of 2008)
30	Qualified plug-in electric vehicle credit is provided for certain low-speed vehicles and 2- or 3-wheeled vehicles acquired before Jan. 1, 2012	Vehicles acquired before Jan. 1, 2012 and after Feb. 17, 2009	¶ 1003 American Recovery and Reinvestment Act of 2009
30A	Possessions tax credit for American Samoa extended through 2009 for existing claimants	Tax years beginning after Dec. 31, 2007 and before Jan. 1, 2010	¶ 308 Tax Provisions of H.R. 1424 (Including the Emergency Economic Stabilization, Energy Improvement and Extension, and Tax Extenders and AMT Relief Acts of 2008)

Code	Topic	Effective Date	Complete Analysis
30B(a)(5)	Alternative motor vehicle credit (AMVC) is expanded to include a plug-in conversion credit for property placed in service after Feb. 17, 2009 and before Jan. 1, 2012	Property placed in service after Feb. 17, 2009 and conversions made before Jan. 1, 2012	¶ 1004 American Recovery and Reinvestment Act of 2009
30B(d)(3)(D)	"New qualified plug-in electric drive motor vehicle credit" will be modified for vehicles acquired after Dec. 31, 2009	Vehicles acquired after Dec. 31, 2009	¶ 1002 American Recovery and Reinvestment Act of 2009
30B(d)(3)(D)	"New qualified plug-in electric drive motor vehicle credit" is allowed for tax years beginning after Dec. 31, 2008 for property purchased before Jan. 1, 2015	Tax years beginning after Dec. 31, 2008 for property purchased before Jan. 1, 2015	¶ 926 Tax Provisions of H.R. 1424 (Including the Emergency Economic Stabilization, Energy Improvement and Extension, and Tax Extenders and AMT Relief Acts of 2008)
30B(g)(2)	Alternative motor vehicle credit (AMVC) is treated as a personal credit allowed against AMT for tax years beginning after 2008	Tax years beginning after Dec. 31, 2008	¶ 205 American Recovery and Reinvestment Act of 2009
30B(h)(8)	Alternative motor vehicle credit (AMVC) is expanded to include a plug-in conversion credit for property placed in service after Feb. 17, 2009 and before Jan. 1, 2012	Property placed in service after Feb. 17, 2009 and conversions made before Jan. 1, 2012	¶ 1004 American Recovery and Reinvestment Act of 2009
30B(i)	Alternative motor vehicle credit (AMVC) is expanded to include a plug-in conversion credit for property placed in service after Feb. 17, 2009 and before Jan. 1, 2012	Property placed in service after Feb. 17, 2009 and conversions made before Jan. 1, 2012	¶ 1004 American Recovery and Reinvestment Act of 2009

Code	Topic	Effective Date	Complete Analysis
30C(c)(2)(C)	Electricity is treated as a clean burning fuel for purposes of the QAFV refueling property credit	Property placed in service after Oct. 3, 2008	¶ 928 Tax Provisions of H.R. 1424 (Including the Emergency Economic Stabilization, Energy Improvement and Extension, and Tax Extenders and AMT Relief Acts of 2008)
30C(d)(2)(A)	Alternative motor vehicle credit (AMVC) is treated as a personal credit allowed against AMT for tax years beginning after 2008	Tax years beginning after Dec. 31, 2008	¶ 205 American Recovery and Reinvestment Act of 2009
30C(e)(6)	Credit for QAFV refueling property is increased for property placed in service in tax years beginning in 2009 or 2010	Tax years beginning after Dec. 31, 2008	¶ 1001 American Recovery and Reinvestment Act of 2009
30C(g)(2)	Termination date of the credit for non-hydrogen QAFV refueling property is extended for one year to apply to property placed in service before Jan. 1, 2011	Property placed in service after Oct. 3, 2008	¶ 929 Tax Provisions of H.R. 1424 (Including the Emergency Economic Stabilization, Energy Improvement and Extension, and Tax Extenders and AMT Relief Acts of 2008)
30D	"New qualified plug-in electric drive motor vehicle credit" will be modified for vehicles acquired after Dec. 31, 2009	Vehicles acquired after Dec. 31, 2009	¶ 1002 American Recovery and Reinvestment Act of 2009
30D	"New qualified plug-in electric drive motor vehicle credit" is allowed for tax years beginning after Dec. 31, 2008 for property purchased before Jan. 1, 2015	Tax years beginning after Dec. 31, 2008 for property purchased before Jan. 1, 2015	¶ 926 Tax Provisions of H.R. 1424 (Including the Emergency Economic Stabilization, Energy Improvement and Extension, and Tax Extenders and AMT Relief Acts of 2008)

Code	Topic	Effective Date	Complete Analysis
30D(d)(2)(B)	Nonrefundable personal credits can offset AMT through 2009 (instead of 2008)	Tax years beginning in 2009	¶ 204 American Recovery and Reinvestment Act of 2009
32(b)(3)(A)	EIC credit percentage is increased for families with three or more qualifying children for 2009 and 2010	Tax years beginning in 2009 and 2010	¶ 110 American Recovery and Reinvestment Act of 2009
32(b)(3)(B)	Beginning point of EIC phaseout range is increased for joint filers for 2009 and 2010	Tax years beginning in 2009 or 2010	¶ 111 American Recovery and Reinvestment Act of 2009
32(c)(2)(B)(vi)	Election to include combat pay as earned income for EITC purposes is made permanent	Tax years beginning after Dec. 31, 2007	¶ 101 Heroes Earnings Assistance and Relief Tax Act of 2008
35	Overview of the health coverage tax credit (HCTC)	Feb. 17, 2009	¶ 501 American Recovery and Reinvestment Act of 2009
35(a)	Refundable health coverage tax credit for eligible individuals' health insurance costs is increased from 65% to 80% through 2010	Coverage months beginning on or after May 1, 2009 and ending Dec. 31, 2010	¶ 502 American Recovery and Reinvestment Act of 2009
35(c)(2)	Eligible TAA recipients not enrolled in training programs are eligible for the health coverage tax credit	Coverage months beginning after Feb. 17, 2009	¶ 504 American Recovery and Reinvestment Act of 2009
35(e)(1)(K)	Health coverage tax credit allowed for VEBA coverage before 2011	Coverage months beginning after Feb. 17, 2009 and before 2011	¶ 508 American Recovery and Reinvestment Act of 2009
35(g)(9)	Family members will continue to qualify for the health coverage tax credit after certain events for coverage months beginning in 2010	Coverage months beginning in 2010	¶ 506 American Recovery and Reinvestment Act of 2009

Code	Topic	Effective Date	Complete Analysis
35(g)(9)	Eligible individuals receiving COBRA premium assistance cannot claim the health coverage tax credit	Tax years ending after Feb. 17, 2009	¶ 306 American Recovery and Reinvestment Act of 2009
36	First-time homebuyers get refundable credit for 10% of purchase price up to $7,500 ($3,750 on separate return); credit must be recaptured over 15 years	Residences purchased after April 8, 2008, and before July 1, 2009	¶ 102 Housing Assistance Tax Act of 2008
36(b)	First-time homebuyer credit extended to residences purchased before Dec. 1, 2009 and increased to $8,000 ($4,000 for married filing separately); credit recapture waived, unless the residence is sold or ceases to be a principal residence within 36 months of purchase	Residences purchased after Dec. 31, 2008 and before Dec. 1, 2009	¶ 104 American Recovery and Reinvestment Act of 2009
36(b)(1)(B)	First-time homebuyer credit extended to residences purchased before Dec. 1, 2009 and increased to $8,000 ($4,000 for married filing separately); credit recapture waived, unless the residence is sold or ceases to be a principal residence within 36 months of purchase	Residences purchased after Dec. 31, 2008 and before Dec. 1, 2009	¶ 104 American Recovery and Reinvestment Act of 2009

Code	Topic	Effective Date	Complete Analysis
36(d)	First-time homebuyer credit extended to residences purchased before Dec. 1, 2009 and increased to $8,000 ($4,000 for married filing separately); credit recapture waived, unless the residence is sold or ceases to be a principal residence within 36 months of purchase	Residences purchased after Dec. 31, 2008 and before Dec. 1, 2009	¶ 104 American Recovery and Reinvestment Act of 2009
36(d)(1)	First-time homebuyer credit extended to residences purchased before Dec. 1, 2009 and increased to $8,000 ($4,000 for married filing separately); credit recapture waived, unless the residence is sold or ceases to be a principal residence within 36 months of purchase	Residences purchased after Dec. 31, 2008 and before Dec. 1, 2009	¶ 104 American Recovery and Reinvestment Act of 2009
36(f)(4)(D)	First-time homebuyer credit extended to residences purchased before Dec. 1, 2009 and increased to $8,000 ($4,000 for married filing separately); credit recapture waived, unless the residence is sold or ceases to be a principal residence within 36 months of purchase	Residences purchased after Dec. 31, 2008 and before Dec. 1, 2009	¶ 104 American Recovery and Reinvestment Act of 2009

Code	Topic	Effective Date	Complete Analysis
36(g)	First-time homebuyer credit extended to residences purchased before Dec. 1, 2009 and increased to $8,000 ($4,000 for married filing separately); credit recapture waived, unless the residence is sold or ceases to be a principal residence within 36 months of purchase	Residences purchased after Dec. 31, 2008 and before Dec. 1, 2009	¶ 104 American Recovery and Reinvestment Act of 2009
36(h)	First-time homebuyer credit extended to residences purchased before Dec. 1, 2009 and increased to $8,000 ($4,000 for married filing separately); credit recapture waived, unless the residence is sold or ceases to be a principal residence within 36 months of purchase	Residences purchased after Dec. 31, 2008 and before Dec. 1, 2009	¶ 104 American Recovery and Reinvestment Act of 2009
36A	Refundable "making work pay credit" of up to $400 ($800 on joint return) is allowed for 2009 and 2010	Tax years beginning after Dec. 31, 2008	¶ 101 American Recovery and Reinvestment Act of 2009
36A(c)	Refundable $250 credit is allowed to certain government retirees ($500 for joint return where both spouses are eligible)	Feb. 17, 2009	¶ 103 American Recovery and Reinvestment Act of 2009
38(b)(32)	Agricultural chemicals security credit is available for qualified expenditures paid or incurred after May 22, 2008 and before Jan. 1, 2013	Amounts paid or incurred after May 22, 2008 and before Jan. 1, 2013	¶ 301 Heartland, Habitat, Harvest, and Horticulture Act of 2008

Code	Topic	Effective Date	Complete Analysis
38(b)(33)	Employers are allowed a differential wage payment credit for certain amounts paid before Jan. 1, 2010 to military personnel on active duty	Amounts paid after June 17, 2008 and before Jan. 1, 2010	¶ 103 Heroes Earnings Assistance and Relief Tax Act of 2008
38(b)(34)	Income tax credit is provided for qualified carbon dioxide captured after Oct. 3, 2008	Carbon dioxide captured after Oct. 3, 2008	¶ 918 Tax Provisions of H.R. 1424 (Including the Emergency Economic Stabilization, Energy Improvement and Extension, and Tax Extenders and AMT Relief Acts of 2008)
38(b)(35)	"New qualified plug-in electric drive motor vehicle credit" will be modified for vehicles acquired after Dec. 31, 2009	Vehicles acquired after Dec. 31, 2009	¶ 1002 American Recovery and Reinvestment Act of 2009
38(b)(35)	"New qualified plug-in electric drive motor vehicle credit" is allowed for tax years beginning after Dec. 31, 2008 for property purchased before Jan. 1, 2015	Tax years beginning after Dec. 31, 2008 for property purchased before Jan. 1, 2015	¶ 926 Tax Provisions of H.R. 1424 (Including the Emergency Economic Stabilization, Energy Improvement and Extension, and Tax Extenders and AMT Relief Acts of 2008)
38(c)(4)(B)(ii)	Low-income housing credit can offset AMT liability for buildings placed in service after 2007	Low-income housing credit can offset AMT liability for buildings placed in service after 2007	¶ 202 Housing Assistance Tax Act of 2008
38(c)(4)(B)(ii)	Overview of AMT changes for low-income housing, changes to the low-income housing tax credit, and related tax-exempt bond financing provisions	Various effective dates	¶ 201 Housing Assistance Tax Act of 2008
38(c)(4)(B)(v)	Rehabilitation credit can offset AMT liability for expenditures taken into account for periods after 2007	Qualified rehabilitation expenditures properly taken into account for periods after Dec. 31, 2007	¶ 502 Housing Assistance Tax Act of 2008

Code	Topic	Effective Date	Complete Analysis
38(c)(4)(B)(v)	The energy credit can offset 100% of the alternative minimum	Credits determined in tax years beginning after Oct. 3, 2008	¶ 901 Tax Provisions of H.R. 1424 (Including the Emergency Economic Stabilization, Energy Improvement and Extension, and Tax Extenders and AMT Relief Acts of 2008)
38(c)(4)(B)(v)	Railroad track maintenance credit can offset AMT liability for qualified railroad track expenditures paid or incurred during tax years beginning after Dec. 31, 2007 and before Jan. 1, 2010	Qualified railroad track maintenance credits determined in tax years beginning after Dec. 31, 2007 (and before 2010), including carrybacks	¶ 306 Tax Provisions of H.R. 1424 (Including the Emergency Economic Stabilization, Energy Improvement and Extension, and Tax Extenders and AMT Relief Acts of 2008)
38(c)(4)(B)(vi)	The energy credit can offset 100% of the alternative minimum tax	Credits determined in tax years beginning after Oct. 3, 2008	¶ 901 Tax Provisions of H.R. 1424 (Including the Emergency Economic Stabilization, Energy Improvement and Extension, and Tax Extenders and AMT Relief Acts of 2008)
40(a)(4)	Credit of $1.01 per gallon is allowed for qualified cellulosic biofuel produced after Dec. 31, 2008 and before Jan. 1, 2013	Qualified cellulosic biofuel produced after Dec. 31, 2008 and before Jan. 1, 2013	¶ 302 Heartland, Habitat, Harvest, and Horticulture Act of 2008
40(b)(4)(C)	Credit of $1.01 per gallon is allowed for qualified cellulosic biofuel produced after Dec. 31, 2008 and before Jan. 1, 2013	Qualified cellulosic biofuel produced after Dec. 31, 2008 and before Jan. 1, 2013	¶ 302 Heartland, Habitat, Harvest, and Horticulture Act of 2008
40(b)(6)	Credit of $1.01 per gallon is allowed for qualified cellulosic biofuel produced after Dec. 31, 2008 and before Jan. 1, 2013	Qualified cellulosic biofuel produced after Dec. 31, 2008 and before Jan. 1, 2013	¶ 302 Heartland, Habitat, Harvest, and Horticulture Act of 2008

Code	Topic	Effective Date	Complete Analysis
40(d)(3)(D)	Credit of $1.01 per gallon is allowed for qualified cellulosic biofuel produced after Dec. 31, 2008 and before Jan. 1, 2013	Qualified cellulosic biofuel produced after Dec. 31, 2008 and before Jan. 1, 2013	¶ 302 Heartland, Habitat, Harvest, and Horticulture Act of 2008
40(d)(3)(E)	Credit of $1.01 per gallon is allowed for qualified cellulosic biofuel produced after Dec. 31, 2008 and before Jan. 1, 2013	Qualified cellulosic biofuel produced after Dec. 31, 2008 and before Jan. 1, 2013	¶ 302 Heartland, Habitat, Harvest, and Horticulture Act of 2008
40(d)(4)	Percentage of allowable denaturants will be lowered from 5% to 2% of volume of alcohol for the alcohol fuels credit for fuel sold or used after Dec. 31, 2008	Fuel sold or used after Dec. 31, 2008	¶ 304 Heartland, Habitat, Harvest, and Horticulture Act of 2008
40(d)(6)	Credit of $1.01 per gallon is allowed for qualified cellulosic biofuel produced after Dec. 31, 2008 and before Jan. 1, 2013	Qualified cellulosic biofuel produced after Dec. 31, 2008 and before Jan. 1, 2013	¶ 302 Heartland, Habitat, Harvest, and Horticulture Act of 2008
40(d)(7)	Alcohol, biodiesel, renewable diesel, and alternative fuel income and excise tax incentives are made inapplicable to fuel produced outside the U.S. for use outside the U.S.	Claims for credit or payment made after May 14, 2008	¶ 924 Tax Provisions of H.R. 1424 (Including the Emergency Economic Stabilization, Energy Improvement and Extension, and Tax Extenders and AMT Relief Acts of 2008)
40(e)(2)	Credit of $1.01 per gallon is allowed for qualified cellulosic biofuel produced after Dec. 31, 2008 and before Jan. 1, 2013	Qualified cellulosic biofuel produced after Dec. 31, 2008 and before Jan. 1, 2013	¶ 302 Heartland, Habitat, Harvest, and Horticulture Act of 2008
40(e)(3)	Credit of $1.01 per gallon is allowed for qualified cellulosic biofuel produced after Dec. 31, 2008 and before Jan. 1, 2013	Qualified cellulosic biofuel produced after Dec. 31, 2008 and before Jan. 1, 2013	¶ 302 Heartland, Habitat, Harvest, and Horticulture Act of 2008

Code	Topic	Effective Date	Complete Analysis
40(h)(2)	Alcohol mixture credit rates and alcohol credit rates will be lowered for 2009 and 2010 if 7.5 billion-gallon-per-year ethanol production/ importation quota is met	May 22, 2008	¶ 303 Heartland, Habitat, Harvest, and Horticulture Act of 2008
40(h)(3)	Alcohol mixture credit rates and alcohol credit rates will be lowered for 2009 and 2010 if 7.5 billion-gallon-per-year ethanol production/ importation quota is met	May 22, 2008	¶ 303 Heartland, Habitat, Harvest, and Horticulture Act of 2008
40A(b)	Income and excise tax credits for biodiesel are increased by 50 cents per gallon to one dollar per gallon	Fuel produced, and sold or used, after Dec. 31, 2008 and before Jan. 1, 2010	¶ 920 Tax Provisions of H.R. 1424 (Including the Emergency Economic Stabilization, Energy Improvement and Extension, and Tax Extenders and AMT Relief Acts of 2008)
40A(d)(1)	Credit of $1.01 per gallon is allowed for qualified cellulosic biofuel produced after Dec. 31, 2008 and before Jan. 1, 2013	Qualified cellulosic biofuel produced after Dec. 31, 2008 and before Jan. 1, 2013	¶ 302 Heartland, Habitat, Harvest, and Horticulture Act of 2008
40A(d)(2)	Income and excise tax credits for biodiesel and renewable diesel are extended to apply through Dec. 31, 2009	Fuel produced, and sold or used, after Dec. 31, 2008 and before Jan. 1, 2010	¶ 919 Tax Provisions of H.R. 1424 (Including the Emergency Economic Stabilization, Energy Improvement and Extension, and Tax Extenders and AMT Relief Acts of 2008)

1,105

Code	Topic	Effective Date	Complete Analysis
40A(d)(5)	Alcohol, biodiesel, renewable diesel, and alternative fuel income and excise tax incentives are made inapplicable to fuel produced outside the U.S. for use outside the U.S.	Claims for credit or payment made after May 14, 2008	¶ 924 Tax Provisions of H.R. 1424 (Including the Emergency Economic Stabilization, Energy Improvement and Extension, and Tax Extenders and AMT Relief Acts of 2008)
40A(f)(2)	Income and excise tax credits for biodiesel are increased by 50 cents per gallon to one dollar per gallon	Fuel produced, and sold or used, after Dec. 31, 2008 and before Jan. 1, 2010	¶ 920 Tax Provisions of H.R. 1424 (Including the Emergency Economic Stabilization, Energy Improvement and Extension, and Tax Extenders and AMT Relief Acts of 2008)
40A(f)(3)	Credit of $1.01 per gallon is allowed for qualified cellulosic biofuel produced after Dec. 31, 2008 and before Jan. 1, 2013	Qualified cellulosic biofuel produced after Dec. 31, 2008 and before Jan. 1, 2013	¶ 302 Heartland, Habitat, Harvest, and Horticulture Act of 2008
40A(f)(3)	Requirement that renewable diesel fuel be made using a thermal depolymerization process is eliminated for purposes of income and excise tax incentives	Fuel produced, and sold or used, after Dec. 31, 2008 and before Jan. 1, 2010	¶ 921 Tax Provisions of H.R. 1424 (Including the Emergency Economic Stabilization, Energy Improvement and Extension, and Tax Extenders and AMT Relief Acts of 2008)
40A(f)(3)	Credit for renewable diesel fuel is modified to exclude fuel derived from coprocessing biomass with a feedstock that isn't biomass	Fuel produced, and sold or used, after Oct. 3, 2008 and before Jan. 1, 2010	¶ 923 Tax Provisions of H.R. 1424 (Including the Emergency Economic Stabilization, Energy Improvement and Extension, and Tax Extenders and AMT Relief Acts of 2008)

Code	Topic	Effective Date	Complete Analysis
40A(f)(4)	Credit for renewable diesel fuel is extended to apply to certain aviation fuel	Fuel produced, and sold or used, after Dec. 31, 2008 and before Jan. 1, 2010	¶ 922 Tax Provisions of H.R. 1424 (Including the Emergency Economic Stabilization, Energy Improvement and Extension, and Tax Extenders and AMT Relief Acts of 2008)
40A(g)	Income and excise tax credits for biodiesel and renewable diesel are extended to apply through Dec. 31, 2009	Fuel produced, and sold or used, after Dec. 31, 2008 and before Jan. 1, 2010	¶ 919 Tax Provisions of H.R. 1424 (Including the Emergency Economic Stabilization, Energy Improvement and Extension, and Tax Extenders and AMT Relief Acts of 2008)
41	One auto manufacturer can elect to receive a deemed payment of tax in lieu of claiming research credits, bonus depreciation and accelerated depreciation	Tax years ending after Mar. 31, 2008	¶ 902 Housing Assistance Tax Act of 2008
41(c)(5)(A)	Alternative simplified research credit is increased to 14% for tax years ending after Dec. 31, 2008	Tax years ending after Dec. 31, 2008	¶ 303 Tax Provisions of H.R. 1424 (Including the Emergency Economic Stabilization, Energy Improvement and Extension, and Tax Extenders and AMT Relief Acts of 2008)
41(h)(1)(B)	Research credit is retroactively extended to apply to amounts paid or incurred after Dec. 31, 2007 and before Jan. 1, 2010	Amounts paid or incurred after Dec. 31, 2007 and before Jan. 1, 2010	¶ 301 Tax Provisions of H.R. 1424 (Including the Emergency Economic Stabilization, Energy Improvement and Extension, and Tax Extenders and AMT Relief Acts of 2008)

Code	Topic	Effective Date	Complete Analysis
41(h)(2)	Elective alternative incremental research credit terminates for tax years beginning after Dec. 31, 2008	Tax years beginning after Dec. 31, 2008	¶ 302 Tax Provisions of H.R. 1424 (Including the Emergency Economic Stabilization, Energy Improvement and Extension, and Tax Extenders and AMT Relief Acts of 2008)
41(h)(2)	Computation of the research credit's base amount for a tax year in which the credit isn't in effect for the entire tax year is modified	Tax years beginning after Dec. 31, 2007	¶ 304 Tax Provisions of H.R. 1424 (Including the Emergency Economic Stabilization, Energy Improvement and Extension, and Tax Extenders and AMT Relief Acts of 2008)
42	Overview of AMT changes for low-income housing, changes to the low-income housing tax credit, and related tax-exempt bond financing provisions	Various effective dates	¶ 201 Housing Assistance Tax Act of 2008
42	Congress orders study on effect of 2008 Housing Act changes to the low-income housing tax credit	July 30, 2008	¶ 220 Housing Assistance Tax Act of 2008
42(b)(1)	Minimum low income housing credit rate of 9% applies to new non-federally subsidized buildings placed in service before Dec. 31, 2013	Buildings placed in service after July 30, 2008	¶ 205 Housing Assistance Tax Act of 2008
42(b)(2)	Minimum low income housing credit rate of 9% applies to new non-federally subsidized buildings placed in service before Dec. 31, 2013	Buildings placed in service after July 30, 2008	¶ 205 Housing Assistance Tax Act of 2008

Code	Topic	Effective Date	Complete Analysis
42(c)(2)	Prohibition against providing low-income housing credit to buildings receiving certain moderate rehabilitation assistance is eliminated	Buildings placed in service after July 30, 2008	¶ 211 Housing Assistance Tax Act of 2008
42(d)(2)(B)(ii)	"Related party" for purposes of eligible basis under low-income housing credit rules requires 50% attributed ownership rather than 10%	Buildings placed in service after July 30, 2008	¶ 215 Housing Assistance Tax Act of 2008
42(d)(2)(D)(iii)	"Related party" for purposes of eligible basis under low-income housing credit rules requires 50% attributed ownership rather than 10%	Buildings placed in service after July 30, 2008	¶ 215 Housing Assistance Tax Act of 2008
42(d)(4)(C)(ii)	Allowable community service facility space for low-income housing projects is increased	Buildings placed in service after July 30, 2008	¶ 214 Housing Assistance Tax Act of 2008
42(d)(5)(A)	Federal grants are not taken into account in determining the eligible basis of a building for purposes of the low-income housing credit	Buildings placed in service after July 30, 2008	¶ 208 Housing Assistance Tax Act of 2008
42(d)(5)(B)	A third type of high-cost area is made eligible for the enhanced low-income housing credit for buildings in high-cost areas	Buildings placed in service after July 30, 2008	¶ 213 Housing Assistance Tax Act of 2008
42(d)(5)(C)	A third type of high-cost area is made eligible for the enhanced low-income housing credit for buildings in high-cost areas	Buildings placed in service after July 30, 2008	¶ 213 Housing Assistance Tax Act of 2008

Code	Topic	Effective Date	Complete Analysis
42(d)(6)	Exception to ten-year nonacquisition period for existing buildings for purposes of the low-income housing credit applies to federally or state-assisted buildings	Buildings placed in service after July 30, 2008	¶ 216 Housing Assistance Tax Act of 2008
42(e)(3)(A)(ii)(I)	Substantial rehabilitation requirement for low-income housing credit is modified	Buildings with respect to which housing credit dollar amounts are allocated after July 30, 2008	¶ 212 Housing Assistance Tax Act of 2008
42(e)(3)(A)(ii)(II)	Substantial rehabilitation requirement for low-income housing credit is modified	Buildings with respect to which housing credit dollar amounts are allocated after July 30, 2008	¶ 212 Housing Assistance Tax Act of 2008
42(e)(3)(D)	Substantial rehabilitation requirement for low-income housing credit is modified	Buildings with respect to which housing credit dollar amounts are allocated after July 30, 2008	¶ 212 Housing Assistance Tax Act of 2008
42(f)(5)(B)(ii)(II)	Substantial rehabilitation requirement for low-income housing credit is modified	Buildings with respect to which housing credit dollar amounts are allocated after July 30, 2008	¶ 212 Housing Assistance Tax Act of 2008
42(g)(4)	Service member's "basic allowance for housing" isn't counted in determining if certain military housing qualifies for tax-exempt bond financing or the low-income housing credit	Income determinations made after July 30, 2008	¶ 221 Housing Assistance Tax Act of 2008

Code	Topic	Effective Date	Complete Analysis
42(g)(4)	Residential project's eligibility for tax-exempt bond financing or low income housing credit will be "held harmless" from reductions in area median gross income	Calendar years after 2008	¶ 222 Housing Assistance Tax Act of 2008
42(g)(4)	Annual current income determination requirement for tax-exempt bonds and low-income housing credit doesn't apply for new low-income tenants	Years ending after July 30, 2008	¶ 225 Housing Assistance Tax Act of 2008
42(g)(9)	A low-income housing project won't fail the general public use requirement because of occupancy restrictions or preferences that favor certain types of tenants	Buildings placed in service before, on, or after July 30, 2008	¶ 210 Housing Assistance Tax Act of 2008
42(h)(1)(E)(ii)	Low-income housing tax credit carryover allocation rule's time limit for incurring more than 10% of a project's cost is eased	Buildings placed in service after July 30, 2008	¶ 217 Housing Assistance Tax Act of 2008
42(h)(3)(I)	Amount of a state's allocation authority for low income housing tax credits is increased for 2008 and 2009	Low income housing credit allocations made for 2008 and 2009	¶ 204 Housing Assistance Tax Act of 2008
42(h)(4)(A)(ii)	Certain residential rental project bonds are treated as refunding bonds irrespective of obligor	Repayments of loans received after July 30, 2008	¶ 223 Housing Assistance Tax Act of 2008

Code	Topic	Effective Date	Complete Analysis
42(i)(2)(A)	Federally subsidized buildings don't include buildings financed with below market federal loans for the low income housing tax credit	Buildings placed in service after July 30, 2008	¶ 207 Housing Assistance Tax Act of 2008
42(i)(2)(B)	Federally subsidized buildings don't include buildings financed with below market federal loans for the low income housing tax credit	Buildings placed in service after July 30, 2008	¶ 207 Housing Assistance Tax Act of 2008
42(i)(2)(C)	Federally subsidized buildings don't include buildings financed with below market federal loans for the low income housing tax credit	Buildings placed in service after July 30, 2008	¶ 207 Housing Assistance Tax Act of 2008
42(i)(2)(D)	Federally subsidized buildings don't include buildings financed with below market federal loans for the low income housing tax credit	Buildings placed in service after July 30, 2008	¶ 207 Housing Assistance Tax Act of 2008
42(i)(2)(E)	Federally subsidized buildings don't include buildings financed with below market federal loans for the low income housing tax credit	Buildings placed in service after July 30, 2008	¶ 207 Housing Assistance Tax Act of 2008
42(i)(3)(D)(i)	Housing unit occupied by student who previously received certain foster care assistance can qualify for the low-income housing tax credit	Determinations made after July 30, 2008	¶ 219 Housing Assistance Tax Act of 2008

Code	Topic	Effective Date	Complete Analysis
42(i)(8)	Low-income housing tax credit income-targeting rules will be applied to projects in certain rural areas by using the greater of "area median gross income" or "national non-metropolitan median income"	Determinations made after July 30, 2008	¶ 209 Housing Assistance Tax Act of 2008
42(i)(9)	States can elect grants, instead of tax credits, to finance low-income housing for 2009, but tax credit allocations are reduced	Feb. 17, 2009	¶ 906 American Recovery and Reinvestment Act of 2009
42(j)(6)	Low-income housing credit bond-posting requirement is replaced by an extended statute of limitations of three years after the taxpayer notifies IRS of noncompliance with low-income housing credit rules	Interests in buildings disposed of after July 30, 2008	¶ 218 Housing Assistance Tax Act of 2008
42(m)(1)(C)	State housing credit agency low-income housing tax credit allocation plan criteria are expanded for post-Dec. 31, 2008 allocations to include the energy efficiency and historic nature of the project	Allocations made after Dec. 31, 2008	¶ 206 Housing Assistance Tax Act of 2008
45	Grants in lieu of Code Sec. 45 electricity production credit and Code Sec. 48 energy credit for specified energy property placed in service or under construction in 2009 or 2010	Feb. 17, 2009	¶ 1204 American Recovery and Reinvestment Act of 2009

Code	Topic	Effective Date	Complete Analysis
45(b)(2)	Credit amount for steel industry fuel qualifying for the electricity production credit is $2 per barrel-of-oil equivalent amount, indexed for inflation	Fuel produced and sold after Sept. 30, 2008	¶ 1009 Tax Provisions of H.R. 1424 (Including the Emergency Economic Stabilization, Energy Improvement and Extension, and Tax Extenders and AMT Relief Acts of 2008)
45(b)(4)(A)	Electricity production credit is expanded to include electricity produced from marine renewables	Electricity produced and sold after Oct. 3, 2008	¶ 1002 Tax Provisions of H.R. 1424 (Including the Emergency Economic Stabilization, Energy Improvement and Extension, and Tax Extenders and AMT Relief Acts of 2008)
45(c)(1)(I)	Electricity production credit is expanded to include electricity produced from marine renewables	Electricity produced and sold after Oct. 3, 2008	¶ 1002 Tax Provisions of H.R. 1424 (Including the Emergency Economic Stabilization, Energy Improvement and Extension, and Tax Extenders and AMT Relief Acts of 2008)
45(c)(7)	Steel industry fuel is added to the definition of refined coal as a qualified resource for purposes of the electricity production credit	Fuel produced and sold after Sept. 30, 2008	¶ 1008 Tax Provisions of H.R. 1424 (Including the Emergency Economic Stabilization, Energy Improvement and Extension, and Tax Extenders and AMT Relief Acts of 2008)
45(c)(7)(A)	Definition of refined coal for electricity production credit eliminates increased market value test and increases required sulfur dioxide and mercury emission reduction	Coal produced and sold after Dec. 31, 2008	¶ 1004 Tax Provisions of H.R. 1424 (Including the Emergency Economic Stabilization, Energy Improvement and Extension, and Tax Extenders and AMT Relief Acts of 2008)

Code	Topic	Effective Date	Complete Analysis
45(c)(7)(B)	Definition of refined coal for electricity production credit eliminates increased market value test and increases required sulfur dioxide and mercury emission reduction	Coal produced and sold after Dec. 31, 2008	¶ 1004 Tax Provisions of H.R. 1424 (Including the Emergency Economic Stabilization, Energy Improvement and Extension, and Tax Extenders and AMT Relief Acts of 2008)
45(c)(8)(C)	Nonhydroelectric dams providing hydropower for purposes of the electricity production credit must be operated for flood control, navigation or water supply purposes	Property originally placed in service after Dec. 31, 2008	¶ 1011 Tax Provisions of H.R. 1424 (Including the Emergency Economic Stabilization, Energy Improvement and Extension, and Tax Extenders and AMT Relief Acts of 2008)
45(c)(10)	Electricity production credit is expanded to include electricity produced from marine renewables	Electricity produced and sold after Oct. 3, 2008	¶ 1002 Tax Provisions of H.R. 1424 (Including the Emergency Economic Stabilization, Energy Improvement and Extension, and Tax Extenders and AMT Relief Acts of 2008)
45(d)(1)	Placed-in-service end date is extended for three years through Dec. 31, 2012 for qualified wind facilities for purposes of the electricity production credit	Property placed in service after Feb. 17, 2009	¶ 1208 American Recovery and Reinvestment Act of 2009
45(d)(1)	Placed-in-service date is extended through Dec. 31, 2010 for certain qualified facilities for purposes of the electricity production credit; placed-in-service dates for qualified wind and refined coal facilities are extended through Dec. 31, 2009	Property originally placed in service after Dec. 31, 2008	¶ 1001 Tax Provisions of H.R. 1424 (Including the Emergency Economic Stabilization, Energy Improvement and Extension, and Tax Extenders and AMT Relief Acts of 2008)

Code	Topic	Effective Date	Complete Analysis
45(d)(1)	Residential energy efficient property credit is allowed for residential wind property and geothermal heat pumps	Tax years beginning after Dec. 31, 2007	¶ 515 Tax Provisions of H.R. 1424 (Including the Emergency Economic Stabilization, Energy Improvement and Extension, and Tax Extenders and AMT Relief Acts of 2008)
45(d)(1)	Placed-in-service date is extended for one year through Dec. 31, 2008 for certain qualified facilities for purposes of the credit for electricity produced from renewable resources	Facilities placed in service after Dec. 31, 2007	¶ 903 Tax Provisions of the Tax Relief and Health Care Act of 2006
45(d)(2)	Placed-in-service end date is extended for three years through Dec. 31, 2013 for certain qualified facilities for purposes of the electricity production credit	Property placed in service after Feb. 17, 2009	¶ 1207 American Recovery and Reinvestment Act of 2009
45(d)(2)(A)	Placed-in-service date is extended through Dec. 31, 2010 for certain qualified facilities for purposes of the electricity production credit; placed-in-service dates for qualified wind and refined coal facilities are extended through Dec. 31, 2009	Property originally placed in service after Dec. 31, 2008	¶ 1001 Tax Provisions of H.R. 1424 (Including the Emergency Economic Stabilization, Energy Improvement and Extension, and Tax Extenders and AMT Relief Acts of 2008)
45(d)(2)(A)	Placed-in-service date is extended for one year through Dec. 31, 2008 for certain qualified facilities for purposes of the credit for electricity produced from renewable resources	Facilities placed in service after Dec. 31, 2007	¶ 903 Tax Provisions of the Tax Relief and Health Care Act of 2006

Code	Topic	Effective Date	Complete Analysis
45(d)(2)(B)	Definition of closed-loop biomass facilities is expanded for purposes of the electricity production credit	Property placed in service after Oct. 3, 2008	¶ 1007 Tax Provisions of H.R. 1424 (Including the Emergency Economic Stabilization, Energy Improvement and Extension, and Tax Extenders and AMT Relief Acts of 2008)
45(d)(3)	Placed-in-service end date is extended for three years through Dec. 31, 2013 for certain qualified facilities for purposes of the electricity production credit	Property placed in service after Feb. 17, 2009	¶ 1207 American Recovery and Reinvestment Act of 2009
45(d)(3)(A)	Placed-in-service date is extended through Dec. 31, 2010 for certain qualified facilities for purposes of the electricity production credit; placed-in-service dates for qualified wind and refined coal facilities are extended through Dec. 31, 2009	Property originally placed in service after Dec. 31, 2008	¶ 1001 Tax Provisions of H.R. 1424 (Including the Emergency Economic Stabilization, Energy Improvement and Extension, and Tax Extenders and AMT Relief Acts of 2008)
45(d)(3)(A)	Placed-in-service date is extended for one year through Dec. 31, 2008 for certain qualified facilities for purposes of the credit for electricity produced from renewable resources	Facilities placed in service after Dec. 31, 2007	¶ 903 Tax Provisions of the Tax Relief and Health Care Act of 2006
45(d)(3)(B)	Definition of open-loop biomass facilities is expanded for purposes of the electricity production credit	Property placed in service after Oct. 3, 2008	¶ 1006 Tax Provisions of H.R. 1424 (Including the Emergency Economic Stabilization, Energy Improvement and Extension, and Tax Extenders and AMT Relief Acts of 2008)

Code	Topic	Effective Date	Complete Analysis
45(d)(4)	Placed-in-service end date is extended for three years through Dec. 31, 2013 for certain qualified facilities for purposes of the electricity production credit	Property placed in service after Feb. 17, 2009	¶ 1207 American Recovery and Reinvestment Act of 2009
45(d)(4)	Placed-in-service date is extended through Dec. 31, 2010 for certain qualified facilities for purposes of the electricity production credit; placed-in-service dates for qualified wind and refined coal facilities are extended through Dec. 31, 2009	Property originally placed in service after Dec. 31, 2008	¶ 1001 Tax Provisions of H.R. 1424 (Including the Emergency Economic Stabilization, Energy Improvement and Extension, and Tax Extenders and AMT Relief Acts of 2008)
45(d)(4)	Placed-in-service date is extended for one year through Dec. 31, 2008 for certain qualified facilities for purposes of the credit for electricity produced from renewable resources	Facilities placed in service after Dec. 31, 2007	¶ 903 Tax Provisions of the Tax Relief and Health Care Act of 2006
45(d)(5)	Placed-in-service date is extended through Dec. 31, 2010 for certain qualified facilities for purposes of the electricity production credit; placed-in-service dates for qualified wind and refined coal facilities are extended through Dec. 31, 2009	Property originally placed in service after Dec. 31, 2008	¶ 1001 Tax Provisions of H.R. 1424 (Including the Emergency Economic Stabilization, Energy Improvement and Extension, and Tax Extenders and AMT Relief Acts of 2008)

Code	Topic	Effective Date	Complete Analysis
45(d)(5)	Electricity production credit is expanded to include electricity produced from marine renewables	Electricity produced and sold after Oct. 3, 2008	¶ 1002 Tax Provisions of H.R. 1424 (Including the Emergency Economic Stabilization, Energy Improvement and Extension, and Tax Extenders and AMT Relief Acts of 2008)
45(d)(5)	Placed-in-service date is extended for one year through Dec. 31, 2008 for certain qualified facilities for purposes of the credit for electricity produced from renewable resources	Facilities placed in service after Dec. 31, 2007	¶ 903 Tax Provisions of the Tax Relief and Health Care Act of 2006
45(d)(6)	Placed-in-service end date is extended for three years through Dec. 31, 2013 for certain qualified facilities for purposes of the electricity production credit	Property placed in service after Feb. 17, 2009	¶ 1207 American Recovery and Reinvestment Act of 2009
45(d)(6)	Placed-in-service date is extended through Dec. 31, 2010 for certain qualified facilities for purposes of the electricity production credit; placed-in-service dates for qualified wind and refined coal facilities are extended through Dec. 31, 2009	Property originally placed in service after Dec. 31, 2008	¶ 1001 Tax Provisions of H.R. 1424 (Including the Emergency Economic Stabilization, Energy Improvement and Extension, and Tax Extenders and AMT Relief Acts of 2008)
45(d)(6)	Placed-in-service date is extended for one year through Dec. 31, 2008 for certain qualified facilities for purposes of the credit for electricity produced from renewable resources	Facilities placed in service after Dec. 31, 2007	¶ 903 Tax Provisions of the Tax Relief and Health Care Act of 2006

Code	Topic	Effective Date	Complete Analysis
45(d)(7)	Placed-in-service end date is extended for three years through Dec. 31, 2013 for certain qualified facilities for purposes of the electricity production credit	Property placed in service after Feb. 17, 2009	¶ 1207 American Recovery and Reinvestment Act of 2009
45(d)(7)	Placed-in-service date is extended through Dec. 31, 2010 for certain qualified facilities for purposes of the electricity production credit; placed-in-service dates for qualified wind and refined coal facilities are extended through Dec. 31, 2009	Property originally placed in service after Dec. 31, 2008	¶ 1001 Tax Provisions of H.R. 1424 (Including the Emergency Economic Stabilization, Energy Improvement and Extension, and Tax Extenders and AMT Relief Acts of 2008)
45(d)(7)	Trash facility can be a qualified facility for the electricity production credit without the need for burning waste to produce electricity	Electricity produced and sold after Oct. 3, 2008	¶ 1005 Tax Provisions of H.R. 1424 (Including the Emergency Economic Stabilization, Energy Improvement and Extension, and Tax Extenders and AMT Relief Acts of 2008)
45(d)(7)	Placed-in-service date is extended for one year through Dec. 31, 2008 for certain qualified facilities for purposes of the credit for electricity produced from renewable resources	Facilities placed in service after Dec. 31, 2007	¶ 903 Tax Provisions of the Tax Relief and Health Care Act of 2006

Code	Topic	Effective Date	Complete Analysis
45(d)(8)	Placed-in-service date is extended through Dec. 31, 2010 for certain qualified facilities for purposes of the electricity production credit; placed-in-service dates for qualified wind and refined coal facilities are extended through Dec. 31, 2009	Property originally placed in service after Dec. 31, 2008	¶ 1001 Tax Provisions of H.R. 1424 (Including the Emergency Economic Stabilization, Energy Improvement and Extension, and Tax Extenders and AMT Relief Acts of 2008)
45(d)(8)	Placed-in-service date is extended through Dec. 31, 2009 for refined coal production facilities for purposes of the electricity production credit	Fuel produced and sold after Sept. 30, 2008	¶ 1003 Tax Provisions of H.R. 1424 (Including the Emergency Economic Stabilization, Energy Improvement and Extension, and Tax Extenders and AMT Relief Acts of 2008)
45(d)(9)	Placed-in-service end date is extended for three years through Dec. 31, 2013 for certain qualified facilities for purposes of the electricity production credit	Property placed in service after Feb. 17, 2009	¶ 1207 American Recovery and Reinvestment Act of 2009
45(d)(9)	Placed-in-service date is extended through Dec. 31, 2010 for certain qualified facilities for purposes of the electricity production credit; placed-in-service dates for qualified wind and refined coal facilities are extended through Dec. 31, 2009	Property originally placed in service after Dec. 31, 2008	¶ 1001 Tax Provisions of H.R. 1424 (Including the Emergency Economic Stabilization, Energy Improvement and Extension, and Tax Extenders and AMT Relief Acts of 2008)

Code	Topic	Effective Date	Complete Analysis
45(d)(9)	Placed-in-service date is extended for one year through Dec. 31, 2008 for certain qualified facilities for purposes of the credit for electricity produced from renewable resources	Facilities placed in service after Dec. 31, 2007	¶ 903 Tax Provisions of the Tax Relief and Health Care Act of 2006
45(d)(11)	Electricity production credit is expanded to include electricity produced from marine renewables	Electricity produced and sold after Oct. 3, 2008	¶ 1002 Tax Provisions of H.R. 1424 (Including the Emergency Economic Stabilization, Energy Improvement and Extension, and Tax Extenders and AMT Relief Acts of 2008)
45(d)(11)(B)	Placed-in-service end date is extended for two years through Dec. 31, 2013 for qualified marine and hydrokinetic renewable energy facilities for purposes of the electricity production credit	Property placed in service after Feb. 17, 2009	¶ 1209 American Recovery and Reinvestment Act of 2009
45(e)(8)	Credit amount for steel industry fuel qualifying for the electricity production credit is $2 per barrel-of-oil equivalent amount, indexed for inflation	Fuel produced and sold after Sept. 30, 2008	¶ 1009 Tax Provisions of H.R. 1424 (Including the Emergency Economic Stabilization, Energy Improvement and Extension, and Tax Extenders and AMT Relief Acts of 2008)
45(e)(9)(B)(ii)	Coordination of the electricity production credit for steel industry fuel produced from refined coal with the nonconventional fuel credit	Fuel produced and sold after Sept. 30, 2008	¶ 1010 Tax Provisions of H.R. 1424 (Including the Emergency Economic Stabilization, Energy Improvement and Extension, and Tax Extenders and AMT Relief Acts of 2008)

Code	Topic	Effective Date	Complete Analysis
45A(f)	Indian employment credit for wages paid to qualified Native Americans is extended for two years through Dec. 31, 2009	Tax years beginning after Dec. 31, 2007 and before Jan. 1, 2010	¶ 318 Tax Provisions of H.R. 1424 (Including the Emergency Economic Stabilization, Energy Improvement and Extension, and Tax Extenders and AMT Relief Acts of 2008)
45C(b)(1)(D)	Research credit is retroactively extended to apply to amounts paid or incurred after Dec. 31, 2007 and before Jan. 1, 2010	Amounts paid or incurred after Dec. 31, 2007 and before Jan. 1, 2010	¶ 301 Tax Provisions of H.R. 1424 (Including the Emergency Economic Stabilization, Energy Improvement and Extension, and Tax Extenders and AMT Relief Acts of 2008)
45D(f)(1)	New markets tax credit national limit is raised for 2008 and 2009 with a preferential allocation rule for the 2008 increase	Feb. 17, 2009	¶ 905 American Recovery and Reinvestment Act of 2009
45D(f)(1)(D)	New markets tax credit is extended through calendar year 2009	Oct. 3, 2008	¶ 321 Tax Provisions of H.R. 1424 (Including the Emergency Economic Stabilization, Energy Improvement and Extension, and Tax Extenders and AMT Relief Acts of 2008)
45D(f)(2)	New markets tax credit national limit is raised for 2008 and 2009 with a preferential allocation rule for the 2008 increase	Feb. 17, 2009	¶ 905 American Recovery and Reinvestment Act of 2009
45G(f)	Railroad track maintenance credit for qualified expenditures is extended two years to include qualified expenditures paid or incurred during tax years beginning before Jan. 1, 2010	Qualified railroad track expenditures paid or incurred during tax years beginning after Dec. 31, 2007 and before Jan. 1, 2010	¶ 305 Tax Provisions of H.R. 1424 (Including the Emergency Economic Stabilization, Energy Improvement and Extension, and Tax Extenders and AMT Relief Acts of 2008)

Code	Topic	Effective Date	Complete Analysis
45K(g)(2)(E)	Coordination of the electricity production credit for steel industry fuel produced from refined coal with the nonconventional fuel credit	Fuel produced and sold after Sept. 30, 2008	¶ 1010 Tax Provisions of H.R. 1424 (Including the Emergency Economic Stabilization, Energy Improvement and Extension, and Tax Extenders and AMT Relief Acts of 2008)
45L(g)	Energy efficient home credit for eligible contractors is extended one year through Dec. 31, 2009	Qualified new energy efficient homes acquired before Jan. 1, 2010	¶ 908 Tax Provisions of H.R. 1424 (Including the Emergency Economic Stabilization, Energy Improvement and Extension, and Tax Extenders and AMT Relief Acts of 2008)
45L(g)	Energy efficient home credit for eligible contractors is extended through 2008	Qualified new energy efficient homes acquired after Dec. 31, 2007 and before Jan. 1, 2009	¶ 901 Tax Provisions of the Tax Relief and Health Care Act of 2006
45M(b)	Energy efficient appliance credit is extended beyond Dec. 31, 2007 to cover appliances manufactured as late, in some cases, as Dec. 31, 2010	Appliances produced after Dec. 31, 2007	¶ 910 Tax Provisions of H.R. 1424 (Including the Emergency Economic Stabilization, Energy Improvement and Extension, and Tax Extenders and AMT Relief Acts of 2008)
45M(b)	Qualifying standards and credit amounts for dishwashers, clothes washers and refrigerators under the energy efficient appliance credit are changed for production after Dec. 31, 2007	Appliances produced after Dec. 31, 2007	¶ 909 Tax Provisions of H.R. 1424 (Including the Emergency Economic Stabilization, Energy Improvement and Extension, and Tax Extenders and AMT Relief Acts of 2008)
45M(c)(1)(B)	Eligible production limits on the energy efficient appliance credit are modified for appliances produced after Dec. 31, 2007	Appliances produced after Dec. 31, 2007	¶ 911 Tax Provisions of H.R. 1424 (Including the Emergency Economic Stabilization, Energy Improvement and Extension, and Tax Extenders and AMT Relief Acts of 2008)

Code	Topic	Effective Date	Complete Analysis
45M(c)(2)	Eligible production limits on the energy efficient appliance credit are modified for appliances produced after Dec. 31, 2007	Appliances produced after Dec. 31, 2007	¶ 911 Tax Provisions of H.R. 1424 (Including the Emergency Economic Stabilization, Energy Improvement and Extension, and Tax Extenders and AMT Relief Acts of 2008)
45M(d)	Eligible production limits on the energy efficient appliance credit are modified for appliances produced after Dec. 31, 2007	Appliances produced after Dec. 31, 2007	¶ 911 Tax Provisions of H.R. 1424 (Including the Emergency Economic Stabilization, Energy Improvement and Extension, and Tax Extenders and AMT Relief Acts of 2008)
45M(e)(1)	Aggregate limit on the energy efficient appliance credit is modified, and taxpayers get a "fresh start," for appliances manufactured after Dec. 31, 2007	Appliances produced after Dec. 31, 2007	¶ 912 Tax Provisions of H.R. 1424 (Including the Emergency Economic Stabilization, Energy Improvement and Extension, and Tax Extenders and AMT Relief Acts of 2008)
45M(e)(2)	Aggregate limit on the energy efficient appliance credit is modified, and taxpayers get a "fresh start," for appliances manufactured after Dec. 31, 2007	Appliances produced after Dec. 31, 2007	¶ 912 Tax Provisions of H.R. 1424 (Including the Emergency Economic Stabilization, Energy Improvement and Extension, and Tax Extenders and AMT Relief Acts of 2008)
45M(e)(2)	Qualifying standards and credit amounts for dishwashers, clothes washers and refrigerators under the energy efficient appliance credit are changed for production after Dec. 31, 2007	Appliances produced after Dec. 31, 2007	¶ 909 Tax Provisions of H.R. 1424 (Including the Emergency Economic Stabilization, Energy Improvement and Extension, and Tax Extenders and AMT Relief Acts of 2008)

Code	Topic	Effective Date	Complete Analysis
45M(f)(1)	Qualifying standards and credit amounts for dishwashers, clothes washers and refrigerators under the energy efficient appliance credit are changed for production after Dec. 31, 2007	Appliances produced after Dec. 31, 2007	¶ 909 Tax Provisions of H.R. 1424 (Including the Emergency Economic Stabilization, Energy Improvement and Extension, and Tax Extenders and AMT Relief Acts of 2008)
45M(f)(3)	Qualifying standards and credit amounts for dishwashers, clothes washers and refrigerators under the energy efficient appliance credit are changed for production after Dec. 31, 2007	Appliances produced after Dec. 31, 2007	¶ 909 Tax Provisions of H.R. 1424 (Including the Emergency Economic Stabilization, Energy Improvement and Extension, and Tax Extenders and AMT Relief Acts of 2008)
45M(f)(4)	Qualifying standards and credit amounts for dishwashers, clothes washers and refrigerators under the energy efficient appliance credit are changed for production after Dec. 31, 2007	Appliances produced after Dec. 31, 2007	¶ 909 Tax Provisions of H.R. 1424 (Including the Emergency Economic Stabilization, Energy Improvement and Extension, and Tax Extenders and AMT Relief Acts of 2008)
45M(f)(5)	Qualifying standards and credit amounts for dishwashers, clothes washers and refrigerators under the energy efficient appliance credit are changed for production after Dec. 31, 2007	Appliances produced after Dec. 31, 2007	¶ 909 Tax Provisions of H.R. 1424 (Including the Emergency Economic Stabilization, Energy Improvement and Extension, and Tax Extenders and AMT Relief Acts of 2008)
45M(f)(9)	Qualifying standards and credit amounts for dishwashers, clothes washers and refrigerators under the energy efficient appliance credit are changed for production after Dec. 31, 2007	Appliances produced after Dec. 31, 2007	¶ 909 Tax Provisions of H.R. 1424 (Including the Emergency Economic Stabilization, Energy Improvement and Extension, and Tax Extenders and AMT Relief Acts of 2008)

Code	Topic	Effective Date	Complete Analysis
45M(f)(10)	Qualifying standards and credit amounts for dishwashers, clothes washers and refrigerators under the energy efficient appliance credit are changed for production after Dec. 31, 2007	Appliances produced after Dec. 31, 2007	¶ 909 Tax Provisions of H.R. 1424 (Including the Emergency Economic Stabilization, Energy Improvement and Extension, and Tax Extenders and AMT Relief Acts of 2008)
45N(e)	Mine rescue team training credit is extended for one year to tax years beginning before Jan. 1, 2010	Oct. 3, 2008	¶ 307 Tax Provisions of H.R. 1424 (Including the Emergency Economic Stabilization, Energy Improvement and Extension, and Tax Extenders and AMT Relief Acts of 2008)
45O	Agricultural chemicals security credit is available for qualified expenditures paid or incurred after May 22, 2008 and before Jan. 1, 2013	Amounts paid or incurred after May 22, 2008 and before Jan. 1, 2013	¶ 301 Heartland, Habitat, Harvest, and Horticulture Act of 2008
45P	Employers are allowed a differential wage payment credit for certain amounts paid before Jan. 1, 2010 to military personnel on active duty	Amounts paid after June 17, 2008 and before Jan. 1, 2010	¶ 103 Heroes Earnings Assistance and Relief Tax Act of 2008
45Q	Income tax credit is provided for qualified carbon dioxide captured after Oct. 3, 2008	Carbon dioxide captured after Oct. 3, 2008	¶ 918 Tax Provisions of H.R. 1424 (Including the Emergency Economic Stabilization, Energy Improvement and Extension, and Tax Extenders and AMT Relief Acts of 2008)
45Q(a)(1)(B)	Secure geological storage disposal requirement to apply to the $10 per metric ton component of the carbon dioxide sequestration credit	Carbon dioxide captured after Feb. 17, 2009	¶ 1212 American Recovery and Reinvestment Act of 2009

Code	Topic	Effective Date	Complete Analysis
45Q(a)(2)(C)	Secure geological storage disposal requirement to apply to the $10 per metric ton component of the carbon dioxide sequestration credit	Carbon dioxide captured after Feb. 17, 2009	¶ 1212 American Recovery and Reinvestment Act of 2009
45Q(d)(2)	Secure geological storage disposal requirement to apply to the $10 per metric ton component of the carbon dioxide sequestration credit	Carbon dioxide captured after Feb. 17, 2009	¶ 1212 American Recovery and Reinvestment Act of 2009
45Q(e)	Secure geological storage disposal requirement to apply to the $10 per metric ton component of the carbon dioxide sequestration credit	Carbon dioxide captured after Feb. 17, 2009	¶ 1212 American Recovery and Reinvestment Act of 2009
46(5)	30% credit is allowed for investment in qualified property used in a qualified advanced energy manufacturing project	Periods after Feb. 17, 2009	¶ 1202 American Recovery and Reinvestment Act of 2009
47(c)(2)(B)(v)(I)	Rehabilitation credit tax-exempt use safe harbor for nonresidential real property is retroactively raised from 35% to 50% for expenditures properly taken into account after Dec. 31, 2007	Expenditures properly taken into account for periods after Dec. 31, 2007	¶ 901 Housing Assistance Tax Act of 2008
48	Grants in lieu of Code Sec. 45 electricity production credit and Code Sec. 48 energy credit for specified energy property placed in service or under construction in 2009 or 2010	Feb. 17, 2009	¶ 1204 American Recovery and Reinvestment Act of 2009

Code	Topic	Effective Date	Complete Analysis
48(a)(1)	10% business energy tax credit is expanded to apply to "combined heat and power system property"	Periods after Oct. 3, 2008	¶ 904 Tax Provisions of H.R. 1424 (Including the Emergency Economic Stabilization, Energy Improvement and Extension, and Tax Extenders and AMT Relief Acts of 2008)
48(a)(1)	30% energy credit is allowed for qualified small wind energy property	Oct. 3, 2008	¶ 906 Tax Provisions of H.R. 1424 (Including the Emergency Economic Stabilization, Energy Improvement and Extension, and Tax Extenders and AMT Relief Acts of 2008)
48(a)(2)(A)	Energy credit for solar energy property will increase from 10% to 30% for property placed in service after Dec. 31, 2005 and before Jan. 1, 2008	Periods after Dec. 31, 2005, in tax years ending after Dec. 31, 2005	¶ 322 Tax Provisions of the Energy and Transportation Acts of 2005
48(a)(2)(A)(i)(II)	Business energy tax credit for solar energy property, qualified fuel cell property, and microturbine property, is extended from Dec. 31, 2008 to Dec. 31, 2016	Oct. 3, 2008	¶ 902 Tax Provisions of H.R. 1424 (Including the Emergency Economic Stabilization, Energy Improvement and Extension, and Tax Extenders and AMT Relief Acts of 2008)
48(a)(2)(A)(i)(II)	Increase in business energy tax credit for solar energy property from 10% to 30% is extended through Dec. 31, 2008, as are the 30% credit for qualified fuel cell property and the 10% credit for qualified microturbine property	Periods after Dec. 31, 2007 and before Jan. 1, 2009	¶ 902 Tax Provisions of the Tax Relief and Health Care Act of 2006

Code	Topic	Effective Date	Complete Analysis
48(a)(2)(A)(i)(IV)	30% energy credit is allowed for qualified small wind energy property	Oct. 3, 2008	¶ 906 Tax Provisions of H.R. 1424 (Including the Emergency Economic Stabilization, Energy Improvement and Extension, and Tax Extenders and AMT Relief Acts of 2008)
48(a)(3)	The energy credit is permitted for public utility property	Periods after Feb. 13, 2008, in tax years ending after Feb. 13, 2008	¶ 905 Tax Provisions of H.R. 1424 (Including the Emergency Economic Stabilization, Energy Improvement and Extension, and Tax Extenders and AMT Relief Acts of 2008)
48(a)(3)(A)(ii)	Business energy tax credit for solar energy property, qualified fuel cell property, and microturbine property, is extended from Dec. 31, 2008 to Dec. 31, 2016	Oct. 3, 2008	¶ 902 Tax Provisions of H.R. 1424 (Including the Emergency Economic Stabilization, Energy Improvement and Extension, and Tax Extenders and AMT Relief Acts of 2008)
48(a)(3)(A)(ii)	Increase in business energy tax credit for solar energy property from 10% to 30% is extended through Dec. 31, 2008, as are the 30% credit for qualified fuel cell property and the 10% credit for qualified microturbine property	Periods after Dec. 31, 2007 and before Jan. 1, 2009	¶ 902 Tax Provisions of the Tax Relief and Health Care Act of 2006
48(a)(3)(A)(v)	10% business energy tax credit is expanded to apply to "combined heat and power system property"	Periods after Oct. 3, 2008	¶ 904 Tax Provisions of H.R. 1424 (Including the Emergency Economic Stabilization, Energy Improvement and Extension, and Tax Extenders and AMT Relief Acts of 2008)

Code	Topic	Effective Date	Complete Analysis
48(a)(3)(A)(vi)	30% energy credit is allowed for qualified small wind energy property	Oct. 3, 2008	¶ 906 Tax Provisions of H.R. 1424 (Including the Emergency Economic Stabilization, Energy Improvement and Extension, and Tax Extenders and AMT Relief Acts of 2008)
48(a)(3)(A)(vii)	10% energy credit is allowed for geothermal heat pump systems	Oct. 3, 2008	¶ 907 Tax Provisions of H.R. 1424 (Including the Emergency Economic Stabilization, Energy Improvement and Extension, and Tax Extenders and AMT Relief Acts of 2008)
48(a)(4)(D)	Business energy tax credit basis reduction rule for property financed by tax-exempt government subsidies or private activity bonds is retroactively terminated for periods after Dec. 31, 2008	Periods after Dec. 31, 2008	¶ 1206 American Recovery and Reinvestment Act of 2009
48(a)(5)	Taxpayers can irrevocably elect 30% business energy credit instead of electricity production credit for qualified property that is part of qualified investment credit facilities placed in service after 2008 and before 2014 (2013 for wind facilities)	Facilities placed in service after Dec. 31, 2008 and before Jan. 1, 2014 (2013 for wind facilities)	¶ 1203 American Recovery and Reinvestment Act of 2009
48(c)(1)(B)	Credit limitation for qualified fuel cell property is increased from $500 to $1,500 for each 0.5 kilowatt of capacity	Periods after Oct. 3, 2008	¶ 903 Tax Provisions of H.R. 1424 (Including the Emergency Economic Stabilization, Energy Improvement and Extension, and Tax Extenders and AMT Relief Acts of 2008)

Code	Topic	Effective Date	Complete Analysis
48(c)(1)(D)	The energy credit is permitted for public utility property	Periods after Feb. 13, 2008, in tax years ending after Feb. 13, 2008	¶ 905 Tax Provisions of H.R. 1424 (Including the Emergency Economic Stabilization, Energy Improvement and Extension, and Tax Extenders and AMT Relief Acts of 2008)
48(c)(1)(E)	10% business energy tax credit is expanded to apply to "combined heat and power system property"	Periods after Oct. 3, 2008	¶ 904 Tax Provisions of H.R. 1424 (Including the Emergency Economic Stabilization, Energy Improvement and Extension, and Tax Extenders and AMT Relief Acts of 2008)
48(c)(1)(E)	Business energy tax credit for solar energy property, qualified fuel cell property, and microturbine property, is extended from Dec. 31, 2008 to Dec. 31, 2016	Oct. 3, 2008	¶ 902 Tax Provisions of H.R. 1424 (Including the Emergency Economic Stabilization, Energy Improvement and Extension, and Tax Extenders and AMT Relief Acts of 2008)
48(c)(1)(E)	Increase in business energy tax credit for solar energy property from 10% to 30% is extended through Dec. 31, 2008, as are the 30% credit for qualified fuel cell property and the 10% credit for qualified microturbine property	Periods after Dec. 31, 2007 and before Jan. 1, 2009	¶ 902 Tax Provisions of the Tax Relief and Health Care Act of 2006
48(c)(2)(D)	The energy credit is permitted for public utility property	Periods after Feb. 13, 2008, in tax years ending after Feb. 13, 2008	¶ 905 Tax Provisions of H.R. 1424 (Including the Emergency Economic Stabilization, Energy Improvement and Extension, and Tax Extenders and AMT Relief Acts of 2008)

Code	Topic	Effective Date	Complete Analysis
48(c)(2)(E)	Business energy tax credit for solar energy property, qualified fuel cell property, and microturbine property, is extended from Dec. 31, 2008 to Dec. 31, 2016	Oct. 3, 2008	¶ 902 Tax Provisions of H.R. 1424 (Including the Emergency Economic Stabilization, Energy Improvement and Extension, and Tax Extenders and AMT Relief Acts of 2008)
48(c)(2)(E)	10% business energy tax credit is expanded to apply to "combined heat and power system property"	Periods after Oct. 3, 2008	¶ 904 Tax Provisions of H.R. 1424 (Including the Emergency Economic Stabilization, Energy Improvement and Extension, and Tax Extenders and AMT Relief Acts of 2008)
48(c)(2)(E)	Increase in business energy tax credit for solar energy property from 10% to 30% is extended through Dec. 31, 2008, as are the 30% credit for qualified fuel cell property and the 10% credit for qualified microturbine property	Periods after Dec. 31, 2007 and before Jan. 1, 2009	¶ 902 Tax Provisions of the Tax Relief and Health Care Act of 2006
48(c)(3)	10% business energy tax credit is expanded to apply to "combined heat and power system property"	Periods after Oct. 3, 2008	¶ 904 Tax Provisions of H.R. 1424 (Including the Emergency Economic Stabilization, Energy Improvement and Extension, and Tax Extenders and AMT Relief Acts of 2008)
48(c)(4)	30% energy credit is allowed for qualified small wind energy property	Oct. 3, 2008	¶ 906 Tax Provisions of H.R. 1424 (Including the Emergency Economic Stabilization, Energy Improvement and Extension, and Tax Extenders and AMT Relief Acts of 2008)

1,133

Code	Topic	Effective Date	Complete Analysis
48(c)(4)(B)	$4,000 annual limitation on business energy tax credit for qualified small wind energy property is repealed for periods after Dec. 31, 2008	Periods after Dec. 31, 2008	¶ 1201 American Recovery and Reinvestment Act of 2009
48(d)	Coordination of Code Sec. 48 energy credit and Code Sec. 45 electricity production credit with renewable energy grants	Feb. 17, 2009	¶ 1205 American Recovery and Reinvestment Act of 2009
48A(a)	Investment credit for qualified investment in a qualifying advanced coal project expanded to include 30% credit for additional advanced coal-based generation technology projects	The 3-year period beginning after Feb. 20, 2009 or a date prescribed by IRS	¶ 916 Tax Provisions of H.R. 1424 (Including the Emergency Economic Stabilization, Energy Improvement and Extension, and Tax Extenders and AMT Relief Acts of 2008)
48A(b)(2)	Business energy tax credit basis reduction rule for property financed by tax-exempt government subsidies or private activity bonds is retroactively terminated for periods after Dec. 31, 2008	Periods after Dec. 31, 2008	¶ 1206 American Recovery and Reinvestment Act of 2009
48A(d)(2)(A)	Investment credit for qualified investment in a qualifying advanced coal project expanded to include 30% credit for additional advanced coal-based generation technology projects	The 3-year period beginning after Feb. 20, 2009 or a date prescribed by IRS	¶ 916 Tax Provisions of H.R. 1424 (Including the Emergency Economic Stabilization, Energy Improvement and Extension, and Tax Extenders and AMT Relief Acts of 2008)

Code	Topic	Effective Date	Complete Analysis
48A(d)(3)(A)	Investment credit for qualified investment in a qualifying advanced coal project expanded to include 30% credit for additional advanced coal-based generation technology projects	The 3-year period beginning after Feb. 20, 2009 or a date prescribed by IRS	¶ 916 Tax Provisions of H.R. 1424 (Including the Emergency Economic Stabilization, Energy Improvement and Extension, and Tax Extenders and AMT Relief Acts of 2008)
48A(d)(3)(B)	Investment credit for qualified investment in a qualifying advanced coal project expanded to include 30% credit for additional advanced coal-based generation technology projects	The 3-year period beginning after Feb. 20, 2009 or a date prescribed by IRS	¶ 916 Tax Provisions of H.R. 1424 (Including the Emergency Economic Stabilization, Energy Improvement and Extension, and Tax Extenders and AMT Relief Acts of 2008)
48A(d)(5)	Investment credit for qualified investment in a qualifying advanced coal project expanded to include 30% credit for additional advanced coal-based generation technology projects	The 3-year period beginning after Feb. 20, 2009 or a date prescribed by IRS	¶ 916 Tax Provisions of H.R. 1424 (Including the Emergency Economic Stabilization, Energy Improvement and Extension, and Tax Extenders and AMT Relief Acts of 2008)
48A(e)(1)(G)	Investment credit for qualified investment in a qualifying advanced coal project expanded to include 30% credit for additional advanced coal-based generation technology projects	The 3-year period beginning after Feb. 20, 2009 or a date prescribed by IRS	¶ 916 Tax Provisions of H.R. 1424 (Including the Emergency Economic Stabilization, Energy Improvement and Extension, and Tax Extenders and AMT Relief Acts of 2008)
48A(e)(3)(B)(iii)	Investment credit for qualified investment in a qualifying advanced coal project expanded to include 30% credit for additional advanced coal-based generation technology projects	The 3-year period beginning after Feb. 20, 2009 or a date prescribed by IRS	¶ 916 Tax Provisions of H.R. 1424 (Including the Emergency Economic Stabilization, Energy Improvement and Extension, and Tax Extenders and AMT Relief Acts of 2008)

Code	Topic	Effective Date	Complete Analysis
48A(e)(3)(C)	Investment credit for qualified investment in a qualifying advanced coal project expanded to include 30% credit for additional advanced coal-based generation technology projects	The 3-year period beginning after Feb. 20, 2009 or a date prescribed by IRS	¶ 916 Tax Provisions of H.R. 1424 (Including the Emergency Economic Stabilization, Energy Improvement and Extension, and Tax Extenders and AMT Relief Acts of 2008)
48A(h)	IRS must modify the certification terms for projects that have qualified for advanced coal project and gasification project credits if certain requirements are met	May 22, 2008 and applies to all competitive certification awards entered into under Code Sec. 48A or Code Sec. 48B	¶ 308 Heartland, Habitat, Harvest, and Horticulture Act of 2008
48A(i)	Investment credit for qualified investment in a qualifying advanced coal project expanded to include 30% credit for additional advanced coal-based generation technology projects	The 3-year period beginning after Feb. 20, 2009 or a date prescribed by IRS	¶ 916 Tax Provisions of H.R. 1424 (Including the Emergency Economic Stabilization, Energy Improvement and Extension, and Tax Extenders and AMT Relief Acts of 2008)
48B	IRS must modify the certification terms for projects that have qualified for advanced coal project and gasification project credits if certain requirements are met	May 22, 2008 and applies to all competitive certification awards entered into under Code Sec. 48A or Code Sec. 48B	¶ 308 Heartland, Habitat, Harvest, and Horticulture Act of 2008
48B(a)	Coal gasification investment credit is expanded and modified	Credits described in Code Sec. 48B(d)(1)(B) which are allocated or reallocated after Oct. 3, 2008	¶ 917 Tax Provisions of H.R. 1424 (Including the Emergency Economic Stabilization, Energy Improvement and Extension, and Tax Extenders and AMT Relief Acts of 2008)

Code	Topic	Effective Date	Complete Analysis
48B(b)(2)	Business energy tax credit basis reduction rule for property financed by tax-exempt government subsidies or private activity bonds is retroactively terminated for periods after Dec. 31, 2008	Periods after Dec. 31, 2008	¶ 1206 American Recovery and Reinvestment Act of 2009
48B(c)(7)(H)	Coal gasification investment credit is expanded and modified	Credits described in Code Sec. 48B(d)(1)(B) which are allocated or reallocated after Oct. 3, 2008	¶ 917 Tax Provisions of H.R. 1424 (Including the Emergency Economic Stabilization, Energy Improvement and Extension, and Tax Extenders and AMT Relief Acts of 2008)
48B(d)(1)	Coal gasification investment credit is expanded and modified	Credits described in Code Sec. 48B(d)(1)(B) which are allocated or reallocated after Oct. 3, 2008	¶ 917 Tax Provisions of H.R. 1424 (Including the Emergency Economic Stabilization, Energy Improvement and Extension, and Tax Extenders and AMT Relief Acts of 2008)
48B(d)(4)	Coal gasification investment credit is expanded and modified	Credits described in Code Sec. 48B(d)(1)(B) which are allocated or reallocated after Oct. 3, 2008	¶ 917 Tax Provisions of H.R. 1424 (Including the Emergency Economic Stabilization, Energy Improvement and Extension, and Tax Extenders and AMT Relief Acts of 2008)
48B(f)	Coal gasification investment credit is expanded and modified	Credits described in Code Sec. 48B(d)(1)(B) which are allocated or reallocated after Oct. 3, 2008	¶ 917 Tax Provisions of H.R. 1424 (Including the Emergency Economic Stabilization, Energy Improvement and Extension, and Tax Extenders and AMT Relief Acts of 2008)

Code	Topic	Effective Date	Complete Analysis
48C	30% credit is allowed for investment in qualified property used in a qualified advanced energy manufacturing project	Periods after Feb. 17, 2009	¶ 1202 American Recovery and Reinvestment Act of 2009
49(a)(1)(C)(v)	30% credit is allowed for investment in qualified property used in a qualified advanced energy manufacturing project	Periods after Feb. 17, 2009	¶ 1202 American Recovery and Reinvestment Act of 2009
50	Grants in lieu of Code Sec. 45 electricity production credit and Code Sec. 48 energy credit for specified energy property placed in service or under construction in 2009 or 2010	Feb. 17, 2009	¶ 1204 American Recovery and Reinvestment Act of 2009
51	Work opportunity credit hiring period is extended for two years for some individuals working in the Hurricane Katrina core disaster area	Individuals hired after Aug. 27, 2007 and before Aug. 28, 2009	¶ 1208 Tax Provisions of H.R. 1424 (Including the Emergency Economic Stabilization, Energy Improvement and Extension, and Tax Extenders and AMT Relief Acts of 2008)
51(d)(14)	Work opportunity credit is expanded to apply to new target group of unemployed veterans and disconnected youth who begin work in 2009 or 2010	Individuals who begin work for the employer after Dec. 31, 2008 and before Jan. 1, 2011	¶ 904 American Recovery and Reinvestment Act of 2009
53(e)	Portion of minimum tax credit attributable to years before the third immediately preceding tax year is made refundable	Tax years beginning after Dec. 20, 2006 and before Jan. 1, 2013	¶ 1201 Tax Provisions of the Tax Relief and Health Care Act of 2006

Code	Topic	Effective Date	Complete Analysis
53(e)(2)	AMT refundable credit for individuals reduces tax over maximum of two years (instead of five years)	Tax years beginning after Dec. 31, 2007 and before Jan. 1, 2013	¶ 103 Tax Provisions of H.R. 1424 (Including the Emergency Economic Stabilization, Energy Improvement and Extension, and Tax Extenders and AMT Relief Acts of 2008)
53(f)	Underpayments (and interest and penalties) attributable to pre-2008 AMT adjustments for ISOs are abated; already-paid interest and penalties increase minimum tax credits for 2008 and 2009	Oct. 3, 2008	¶ 104 Tax Provisions of H.R. 1424 (Including the Emergency Economic Stabilization, Energy Improvement and Extension, and Tax Extenders and AMT Relief Acts of 2008)
54(c)(2)	New tax credit bond option is added for "Build America Bonds" issued in 2009 and 2010; issuer may claim alternative, refundable credit for "qualified bonds"	Obligations issued after Feb. 17, 2009 and before Jan. 1, 2011	¶ 1301 American Recovery and Reinvestment Act of 2009
54(c)(2)	Nonrefundable tax credit will be allowed to holders of qualified forestry conservation bonds	Obligations issued after May 22, 2008	¶ 307 Heartland, Habitat, Harvest, and Horticulture Act of 2008
54(m)	Authority to issue clean renewable energy bonds is extended for one year through Dec. 31, 2009	Obligations issued after Oct. 3, 2008 through Dec. 31, 2009	¶ 1104 Tax Provisions of H.R. 1424 (Including the Emergency Economic Stabilization, Energy Improvement and Extension, and Tax Extenders and AMT Relief Acts of 2008)

Code	Topic	Effective Date	Complete Analysis
54(m)	Overview of modifications to rules for energy-related tax credit bonds	Obligations issued after Dec. 31, 2008	¶ 1101 Tax Provisions of H.R. 1424 (Including the Emergency Economic Stabilization, Energy Improvement and Extension, and Tax Extenders and AMT Relief Acts of 2008)
54A	Nonrefundable tax credit will be allowed to holders of qualified forestry conservation bonds	Obligations issued after May 22, 2008	¶ 307 Heartland, Habitat, Harvest, and Horticulture Act of 2008
54A(c)(1)(B)	New tax credit bond option is added for "Build America Bonds" issued in 2009 and 2010; issuer may claim alternative, refundable credit for "qualified bonds"	Obligations issued after Feb. 17, 2009 and before Jan. 1, 2011	¶ 1301 American Recovery and Reinvestment Act of 2009
54A(d)	New clean renewable energy bond is a new type of tax credit bond	Obligations issued after Oct. 3, 2008	¶ 1103 Tax Provisions of H.R. 1424 (Including the Emergency Economic Stabilization, Energy Improvement and Extension, and Tax Extenders and AMT Relief Acts of 2008)
54A(d)(1)(C)	Qualified energy conservation bond is a new type of tax credit bond	Obligations issued after Oct. 3, 2008	¶ 1102 Tax Provisions of H.R. 1424 (Including the Emergency Economic Stabilization, Energy Improvement and Extension, and Tax Extenders and AMT Relief Acts of 2008)
54A(d)(1)(D)	Credit for qualified zone academy bonds is extended for two years through 2009, is no longer restricted to financial institution holders, and is subject to the Code Sec. 54A qualified tax credit bond rules	Obligations issued after Oct. 3, 2008 and before Jan. 1, 2010	¶ 1109 Tax Provisions of H.R. 1424 (Including the Emergency Economic Stabilization, Energy Improvement and Extension, and Tax Extenders and AMT Relief Acts of 2008)

Code	Topic	Effective Date	Complete Analysis
54A(d)(1)(D)	Requirements applicable to qualified zone academy bonds by reason of their becoming qualified tax credit bonds	Obligations issued after Oct. 3, 2008	¶ 1110 Tax Provisions of H.R. 1424 (Including the Emergency Economic Stabilization, Energy Improvement and Extension, and Tax Extenders and AMT Relief Acts of 2008)
54A(d)(1)(E)	Qualified school construction bond is a new type of tax credit bond	Bonds issued after Feb. 17, 2009	¶ 1302 American Recovery and Reinvestment Act of 2009
54A(d)(2)(C)(iii)	Qualified energy conservation bond is a new type of tax credit bond	Obligations issued after Oct. 3, 2008	¶ 1102 Tax Provisions of H.R. 1424 (Including the Emergency Economic Stabilization, Energy Improvement and Extension, and Tax Extenders and AMT Relief Acts of 2008)
54A(d)(2)(C)(iv)	Credit for qualified zone academy bonds is extended for two years through 2009, is no longer restricted to financial institution holders, and is subject to the Code Sec. 54A qualified tax credit bond rules	Obligations issued after Oct. 3, 2008 and before Jan. 1, 2010	¶ 1109 Tax Provisions of H.R. 1424 (Including the Emergency Economic Stabilization, Energy Improvement and Extension, and Tax Extenders and AMT Relief Acts of 2008)
54A(d)(2)(C)(iv)	Requirements applicable to qualified zone academy bonds by reason of their becoming qualified tax credit bonds	Obligations issued after Oct. 3, 2008	¶ 1110 Tax Provisions of H.R. 1424 (Including the Emergency Economic Stabilization, Energy Improvement and Extension, and Tax Extenders and AMT Relief Acts of 2008)
54A(d)(2)(C)(v)	Qualified school construction bond is a new type of tax credit bond	Bonds issued after Feb. 17, 2009	¶ 1302 American Recovery and Reinvestment Act of 2009
54A(h)	Pass through of tax credit bond credits by RICs and REITs	Tax years ending after Feb. 17, 2009	¶ 1308 American Recovery and Reinvestment Act of 2009

Code	Topic	Effective Date	Complete Analysis
54B	Nonrefundable tax credit will be allowed to holders of qualified forestry conservation bonds	Obligations issued after May 22, 2008	¶ 307 Heartland, Habitat, Harvest, and Horticulture Act of 2008
54C	Prevailing wage requirements are applied to projects financed with specified bonds	Bonds issued after Feb. 17, 2009	¶ 1311 American Recovery and Reinvestment Act of 2009
54C	New clean renewable energy bond is a new type of tax credit bond	Obligations issued after Oct. 3, 2008	¶ 1103 Tax Provisions of H.R. 1424 (Including the Emergency Economic Stabilization, Energy Improvement and Extension, and Tax Extenders and AMT Relief Acts of 2008)
54C	Overview of modifications to rules for energy-related tax credit bonds	Obligations issued after Dec. 31, 2008	¶ 1101 Tax Provisions of H.R. 1424 (Including the Emergency Economic Stabilization, Energy Improvement and Extension, and Tax Extenders and AMT Relief Acts of 2008)
54C(c)(4)	National bond volume limitation for new CREBs is increased by up to $1.6 billion	Bonds issued after Feb. 17, 2009	¶ 1210 American Recovery and Reinvestment Act of 2009
54D	Prevailing wage requirements are applied to projects financed with specified bonds	Bonds issued after Feb. 17, 2009	¶ 1311 American Recovery and Reinvestment Act of 2009
54D	Overview of modifications to rules for energy-related tax credit bonds	Obligations issued after Dec. 31, 2008	¶ 1101 Tax Provisions of H.R. 1424 (Including the Emergency Economic Stabilization, Energy Improvement and Extension, and Tax Extenders and AMT Relief Acts of 2008)

Code	Topic	Effective Date	Complete Analysis
54D	Qualified energy conservation bond is a new type of tax credit bond	Obligations issued after Oct. 3, 2008	¶ 1102 Tax Provisions of H.R. 1424 (Including the Emergency Economic Stabilization, Energy Improvement and Extension, and Tax Extenders and AMT Relief Acts of 2008)
54D(d)	National bond volume limitation for qualified energy conservation bonds is increased by $2.4 billion; the bonds can fund loans or grants to individuals	Bonds issued after Feb. 17, 2009	¶ 1211 American Recovery and Reinvestment Act of 2009
54D(e)(4)	National bond volume limitation for qualified energy conservation bonds is increased by $2.4 billion; the bonds can fund loans or grants to individuals	Bonds issued after Feb. 17, 2009	¶ 1211 American Recovery and Reinvestment Act of 2009
54D(f)(1)(A)(ii)	National bond volume limitation for qualified energy conservation bonds is increased by $2.4 billion; the bonds can fund loans or grants to individuals	Bonds issued after Feb. 17, 2009	¶ 1211 American Recovery and Reinvestment Act of 2009
54E	Prevailing wage requirements are applied to projects financed with specified bonds	Bonds issued after Feb. 17, 2009	¶ 1311 American Recovery and Reinvestment Act of 2009
54E	Credit for qualified zone academy bonds is extended for two years through 2009, is no longer restricted to financial institution holders, and is subject to the Code Sec. 54A qualified tax credit bond rules	Obligations issued after Oct. 3, 2008 and before Jan. 1, 2010	¶ 1109 Tax Provisions of H.R. 1424 (Including the Emergency Economic Stabilization, Energy Improvement and Extension, and Tax Extenders and AMT Relief Acts of 2008)

Code	Topic	Effective Date	Complete Analysis
54E(c)(1)	Credit for QZABs is extended through 2010; national bond volume limitation is increased to $1.4 billion for 2009 and 2010	Bonds issued after Dec. 31, 2008	¶ 1303 American Recovery and Reinvestment Act of 2009
54F	Qualified school construction bond is a new type of tax credit bond	Bonds issued after Feb. 17, 2009	¶ 1302 American Recovery and Reinvestment Act of 2009
54F	Prevailing wage requirements are applied to projects financed with specified bonds	Bonds issued after Feb. 17, 2009	¶ 1311 American Recovery and Reinvestment Act of 2009
54AA	New tax credit bond option is added for "Build America Bonds" issued in 2009 and 2010; issuer may claim alternative, refundable credit for "qualified bonds"	Obligations issued after Feb. 17, 2009 and before Jan. 1, 2011	¶ 1301 American Recovery and Reinvestment Act of 2009
55(b)(3)(B)	5% (0% in 2008) and 15% maximum AMT rates on adjusted net capital gain are extended for two years	Tax years beginning after Dec. 31, 2008 and before Jan. 1, 2011	¶ 103 Tax Increase Prevention and Reconciliation Act of 2005
55(b)(3)(C)	5% (0% in 2008) and 15% maximum AMT rates on adjusted net capital gain are extended for two years	Tax years beginning after Dec. 31, 2008 and before Jan. 1, 2011	¶ 103 Tax Increase Prevention and Reconciliation Act of 2005
55(b)(4)	A temporary 15% tax rate is applied to a corporation's qualified timber gain for both regular tax and AMT purposes	Tax years ending after May 22, 2008 and beginning before May 23, 2009	¶ 401 Heartland, Habitat, Harvest, and Horticulture Act of 2008
55(c)(3)	Alternative motor vehicle credit (AMVC) is treated as a personal credit allowed against AMT for tax years beginning after 2008	Tax years beginning after Dec. 31, 2008	¶ 205 American Recovery and Reinvestment Act of 2009

Code	Topic	Effective Date	Complete Analysis
55(d)(1)(A)	AMT exemption amounts for 2009 are increased to $46,700 for unmarrieds, to $70,950 for joint filers, and to $35,475 for marrieds filing separately	Tax years beginning in 2009	¶ 201 American Recovery and Reinvestment Act of 2009
55(d)(1)(A)	AMT exemption amounts for 2008 are increased to $46,200 for unmarrieds, to $69,950 for joint filers, and to $34,975 for marrieds filing separately	Tax years beginning in 2008	¶ 101 Tax Provisions of H.R. 1424 (Including the Emergency Economic Stabilization, Energy Improvement and Extension, and Tax Extenders and AMT Relief Acts of 2008)
55(d)(1)(B)	AMT exemption amounts for 2009 are increased to $46,700 for unmarrieds, to $70,950 for joint filers, and to $35,475 for marrieds filing separately	Tax years beginning in 2009	¶ 201 American Recovery and Reinvestment Act of 2009
55(d)(1)(B)	AMT exemption amounts for 2008 are increased to $46,200 for unmarrieds, to $69,950 for joint filers, and to $34,975 for marrieds filing separately	Tax years beginning in 2008	¶ 101 Tax Provisions of H.R. 1424 (Including the Emergency Economic Stabilization, Energy Improvement and Extension, and Tax Extenders and AMT Relief Acts of 2008)
56(b)(1)(E)	Standard or itemized deduction allowed for sales and excise taxes imposed on most new vehicles purchased on or after Feb. 17, 2009 and before 2010	Purchases on or after Feb. 17, 2009 and before 2010	¶ 105 American Recovery and Reinvestment Act of 2009

1,145

Code	Topic	Effective Date	Complete Analysis
56(b)(1)(E)	Non-itemizers can take additional standard deduction for net losses from federally declared disasters for both regular tax and AMT purposes	Disasters declared in tax years beginning after Dec. 31, 2007, and occurring before Jan. 1, 2010	¶ 1202 Tax Provisions of H.R. 1424 (Including the Emergency Economic Stabilization, Energy Improvement and Extension, and Tax Extenders and AMT Relief Acts of 2008)
56(d)(3)	"Qualified disaster losses" from pre-2010 disasters can be carried back five years and are deductible against 100% of AMT income	Losses arising in tax years beginning after Dec. 31, 2007, in connection with disasters declared after that date	¶ 1204 Tax Provisions of H.R. 1424 (Including the Emergency Economic Stabilization, Energy Improvement and Extension, and Tax Extenders and AMT Relief Acts of 2008)
56(g)(4)(B)(iii)	Interest on tax-exempt housing bonds isn't subject to AMT	Bonds issued after July 30, 2008	¶ 203 Housing Assistance Tax Act of 2008
56(g)(4)(B)(iii)	Overview of AMT changes for low-income housing, changes to the low-income housing tax credit, and related tax-exempt bond financing provisions	Various effective dates	¶ 201 Housing Assistance Tax Act of 2008
56(g)(4)(B)(iv)	Corporate ACE adjustment isn't required for tax-exempt bonds issued in 2009 or 2010	Bonds issued after Dec. 31, 2008 and before Jan. 1, 2011	¶ 203 American Recovery and Reinvestment Act of 2009
57(a)(5)(C)(iii)	Interest on tax-exempt housing bonds isn't subject to AMT	Bonds issued after July 30, 2008	¶ 203 Housing Assistance Tax Act of 2008
57(a)(5)(C)(iii)	Overview of AMT changes for low-income housing, changes to the low-income housing tax credit, and related tax-exempt bond financing provisions	Various effective dates	¶ 201 Housing Assistance Tax Act of 2008

Code	Topic	Effective Date	Complete Analysis
57(a)(5)(C)(vi)	Interest on tax-exempt bonds issued in 2009 or 2010 isn't subject to AMT	Bonds issued after Dec. 31, 2008 and before Jan. 1, 2011	¶ 202 American Recovery and Reinvestment Act of 2009
57(a)(7)	7% AMT preference percentage for excluded gain on sale of qualified small business stock is extended for two years	Tax years beginning after Dec. 31, 2008 and before Jan. 1, 2011	¶ 104 Tax Increase Prevention and Reconciliation Act of 2005
62(a)(2)(D)	Up-to-$250 above-the-line deduction for teachers' out-of-pocket classroom-related expenses, scheduled to expire after 2007, is extended through 2009	Tax years beginning after Dec. 31, 2007 and before Jan. 1, 2010	¶ 508 Tax Provisions of H.R. 1424 (Including the Emergency Economic Stabilization, Energy Improvement and Extension, and Tax Extenders and AMT Relief Acts of 2008)
63	Non-itemizers can take additional standard deduction for net losses from federally declared disasters for both regular tax and AMT purposes	Disasters declared in tax years beginning after Dec. 31, 2007, and occurring before Jan. 1, 2010	¶ 1202 Tax Provisions of H.R. 1424 (Including the Emergency Economic Stabilization, Energy Improvement and Extension, and Tax Extenders and AMT Relief Acts of 2008)
63(c)	Standard or itemized deduction allowed for sales and excise taxes imposed on most new vehicles purchased on or after Feb. 17, 2009 and before 2010	Purchases on or after Feb. 17, 2009 and before 2010	¶ 105 American Recovery and Reinvestment Act of 2009
63(c)(1)(C)	Non-itemizers can take additional standard deduction for real property taxes of up to $500 ($1,000 for joint filers) for 2008	Tax years beginning in 2008 only	¶ 101 Housing Assistance Tax Act of 2008

Code	Topic	Effective Date	Complete Analysis
63(c)(1)(C)	Additional standard deduction available to non-itemizers for real property taxes in 2008 is extended through 2009	Tax years beginning after Dec. 31, 2008 and before Jan. 1, 2010	¶ 506 Tax Provisions of H.R. 1424 (Including the Emergency Economic Stabilization, Energy Improvement and Extension, and Tax Extenders and AMT Relief Acts of 2008)
63(c)(1)(D)	Non-itemizers can take additional standard deduction for net losses from federally declared disasters for both regular tax and AMT purposes	Disasters declared in tax years beginning after Dec. 31, 2007, and occurring before Jan. 1, 2010	¶ 1202 Tax Provisions of H.R. 1424 (Including the Emergency Economic Stabilization, Energy Improvement and Extension, and Tax Extenders and AMT Relief Acts of 2008)
63(c)(7)	Non-itemizers can take additional standard deduction for real property taxes of up to $500 ($1,000 for joint filers) for 2008	Tax years beginning in 2008 only	¶ 101 Housing Assistance Tax Act of 2008
63(c)(8)	Non-itemizers can take additional standard deduction for net losses from federally declared disasters for both regular tax and AMT purposes	Disasters declared in tax years beginning after Dec. 31, 2007, and occurring before Jan. 1, 2010	¶ 1202 Tax Provisions of H.R. 1424 (Including the Emergency Economic Stabilization, Energy Improvement and Extension, and Tax Extenders and AMT Relief Acts of 2008)
72(e)(11)	Qualified long-term care insurance can be provided as a rider to an annuity contract after 2009	After Dec. 31, 2009	¶ 2402 Pension Protection Act of 2006
72(t)(2)(G)(iv)	Temporary exception to 10% tax on early withdrawals made by reservists ordered or called to active duty made permanent	For individuals ordered or called to active duty on or after Dec. 31, 2007	¶ 202 Heroes Earnings Assistance and Relief Tax Act of 2008

Code	Topic	Effective Date	Complete Analysis
85(c)	Up to $2,400 of unemployment compensation is excludible from recipient's gross income for 2009	Tax years beginning in 2009	¶ 106 American Recovery and Reinvestment Act of 2009
105(j)	Payments from state HRA to deceased participant's nonspouse, nondependent designated beneficiary will not disqualify the HRA, where pre-Jan. 2, 2008 plan language so permits these payments	Payments made before, on, or after Dec. 23, 2008	¶ 802 Worker, Retiree, and Employer Recovery Act of 2008
108	Discharges of nonbusiness debt of individuals in Midwestern disaster area by financial institutions and government agencies are excluded from income for debt cancellations on or after the applicable disaster date and before Jan. 1, 2010	Debt cancellations on or after the applicable disaster date and before Jan. 1, 2010	¶ 1239 Tax Provisions of H.R. 1424 (Including the Emergency Economic Stabilization, Energy Improvement and Extension, and Tax Extenders and AMT Relief Acts of 2008)
108(a)(1)(E)	Exclusion of debt discharge income from home mortgages is extended for three years until the end of 2012	Discharges of indebtedness after Dec. 31, 2009 and before Jan. 1, 2013	¶ 501 Tax Provisions of H.R. 1424 (Including the Emergency Economic Stabilization, Energy Improvement and Extension, and Tax Extenders and AMT Relief Acts of 2008)
108(i)	Income from reacquisitions of business debt at a discount in 2009 and 2010 is deferred and included ratably over five years	Discharges in tax years ending after Dec. 31, 2008, for reacquisitions after Dec. 31, 2008, and before Jan. 1, 2011	¶ 901 American Recovery and Reinvestment Act of 2009

Code	Topic	Effective Date	Complete Analysis
121(b)(4)	Gain allocated to periods of nonqualified use will not be excluded from income for sales or exchanges of a principal residence after Dec. 31, 2008	Sales and exchanges after Dec. 31, 2008	¶ 104 Housing Assistance Tax Act of 2008
121(b)(4)	$500,000 exclusion applies to gain from certain sales or exchanges of a principal residence by a surviving spouse within two years of the death of the spouse	Sales or exchanges after Dec. 31, 2007	¶ 301 AMT Patch, Mortgage Relief, Energy, Technical Corrections, and Other Late 2007 Tax Acts
121(d)(9)	Extension of the $250,000 exclusion of gain from the sale of a decedent's principal residence to sales by estates, heirs of decedents, and qualified revocable trusts-estates of decedents dying after Dec. 31, 2009	Estates of decedents dying after Dec. 31, 2009	¶ 331 Economic Growth and Tax Relief Reconciliation Act of 2001
121(d)(9)(C)(vi)	Intelligence community employee's duty station can be inside the U.S. for the up-to-ten year testing period suspension for the Code Sec. 121 exclusion for sales or exchanges after June 17, 2008	Sales or exchanges after June 17, 2008	¶ 402 Heroes Earnings Assistance and Relief Tax Act of 2008
121(d)(9)(E)	Election for intelligence community employees to suspend, for up to ten years, the five-year testing period for the Code Sec. 121 exclusion is made permanent	Sales or exchanges after June 17, 2008	¶ 401 Heroes Earnings Assistance and Relief Tax Act of 2008

Code	Topic	Effective Date	Complete Analysis
121(d)(12)	Election to suspend five-year period for determining whether principal residence gain exclusion applies to sales or exchanges by certain Peace Corps employees or volunteers after Dec. 31, 2007	Tax years beginning after Dec. 31, 2007	¶ 403 Heroes Earnings Assistance and Relief Tax Act of 2008
125(h)	Unused health FSA balances may be distributed to reservists called to active duty	Distributions made after June 17, 2008	¶ 502 Heroes Earnings Assistance and Relief Tax Act of 2008
132(f)(1)(D)	Qualified transportation fringe benefits geared to bicycle commuters to start in 2009	Tax years beginning after Dec. 31, 2008	¶ 707 Tax Provisions of H.R. 1424 (Including the Emergency Economic Stabilization, Energy Improvement and Extension, and Tax Extenders and AMT Relief Acts of 2008)
132(f)(2)	Monthly exclusion for employer-provided transit passes and vanpooling benefits increased to same level as employer-provided parking, for the rest of 2009 and 2010	Months beginning on or after Feb. 17, 2009	¶ 402 American Recovery and Reinvestment Act of 2009
132(f)(2)(C)	Qualified transportation fringe benefits geared to bicycle commuters to start in 2009	Tax years beginning after Dec. 31, 2008	¶ 707 Tax Provisions of H.R. 1424 (Including the Emergency Economic Stabilization, Energy Improvement and Extension, and Tax Extenders and AMT Relief Acts of 2008)

Code	Topic	Effective Date	Complete Analysis
132(f)(4)	Qualified transportation fringe benefits geared to bicycle commuters to start in 2009	Tax years beginning after Dec. 31, 2008	¶ 707 Tax Provisions of H.R. 1424 (Including the Emergency Economic Stabilization, Energy Improvement and Extension, and Tax Extenders and AMT Relief Acts of 2008)
132(f)(5)(F)	Qualified transportation fringe benefits geared to bicycle commuters to start in 2009	Tax years beginning after Dec. 31, 2008	¶ 707 Tax Provisions of H.R. 1424 (Including the Emergency Economic Stabilization, Energy Improvement and Extension, and Tax Extenders and AMT Relief Acts of 2008)
134(b)(6)	State bonus payments to service members are "qualified military benefits"	Payments made before, on, or after June 17, 2008	¶ 206 Heroes Earnings Assistance and Relief Tax Act of 2008
139(c)(2)	Changes are made to the involuntary conversion rules and other Code provisions to reflect new definition of "federally declared disaster"	Disasters declared in tax years beginning after Dec. 31, 2007, and occurring before Jan. 1, 2010	¶ 1203 Tax Provisions of H.R. 1424 (Including the Emergency Economic Stabilization, Energy Improvement and Extension, and Tax Extenders and AMT Relief Acts of 2008)
139B	Tax relief and expense reimbursements provided by state and local governments to volunteer firefighters and emergency medical responders for services performed are tax-free for 2008 - 2010 tax years	Tax years beginning after Dec. 31, 2007 and before Jan. 1, 2011	¶ 302 AMT Patch, Mortgage Relief, Energy, Technical Corrections, and Other Late 2007 Tax Acts
139C	COBRA subsidy excluded from income	Tax years ending after Feb. 17, 2009	¶ 305 American Recovery and Reinvestment Act of 2009

Code	Topic	Effective Date	Complete Analysis
142	Overview of AMT changes for low-income housing, changes to the low-income housing tax credit, and related tax-exempt bond financing provisions	Various effective dates	¶ 201 Housing Assistance Tax Act of 2008
142(d)(2)(B)(ii)	Service member's "basic allowance for housing" isn't counted in determining if certain military housing qualifies for tax-exempt bond financing or the low-income housing credit	Income determinations made after July 30, 2008	¶ 221 Housing Assistance Tax Act of 2008
142(d)(2)(C)	"Next available unit" rule and rules relating to students and single-room occupancy units under tax-exempt bond provisions are conformed with low-income housing credit rules	Determinations of status of qualified residential rental projects for periods beginning after July 30, 2008	¶ 224 Housing Assistance Tax Act of 2008
142(d)(2)(D)	"Next available unit" rule and rules relating to students and single-room occupancy units under tax-exempt bond provisions are conformed with low-income housing credit rules	Determinations of status of qualified residential rental projects for periods beginning after July 30, 2008	¶ 224 Housing Assistance Tax Act of 2008
142(d)(2)(E)	Residential project's eligibility for tax-exempt bond financing or low income housing credit will be "held harmless" from reductions in area median gross income	Calendar years after 2008	¶ 222 Housing Assistance Tax Act of 2008

Code	Topic	Effective Date	Complete Analysis
142(d)(3)(A)	Annual current income determination requirement for tax-exempt bonds and low-income housing credit doesn't apply for new low-income tenants	Years ending after July 30, 2008	¶ 225 Housing Assistance Tax Act of 2008
142(d)(3)(C)	"Next available unit" rule and rules relating to students and single-room occupancy units under tax-exempt bond provisions are conformed with low-income housing credit rules	Determinations of status of qualified residential rental projects for periods beginning after July 30, 2008	¶ 224 Housing Assistance Tax Act of 2008
142(i)(1)	Vehicles must be capable of attaining a maximum speed in excess of 150 m.p.h. under amended definition of high-speed intercity rail facilities	Bonds issued after Feb. 17, 2009	¶ 1312 American Recovery and Reinvestment Act of 2009
142(l)	Tax-exempt status is extended for qualified green building and sustainable design project bonds issued before Oct. 1, 2012	Oct. 3, 2008	¶ 1108 Tax Provisions of H.R. 1424 (Including the Emergency Economic Stabilization, Energy Improvement and Extension, and Tax Extenders and AMT Relief Acts of 2008)
142(l)(8)	Tax-exempt status is extended for qualified green building and sustainable design project bonds issued before Oct. 1, 2012	Oct. 3, 2008	¶ 1108 Tax Provisions of H.R. 1424 (Including the Emergency Economic Stabilization, Energy Improvement and Extension, and Tax Extenders and AMT Relief Acts of 2008)

Code	Topic	Effective Date	Complete Analysis
142(l)(9)	Tax-exempt status is extended for qualified green building and sustainable design project bonds issued before Oct. 1, 2012	Oct. 3, 2008	¶ 1108 Tax Provisions of H.R. 1424 (Including the Emergency Economic Stabilization, Energy Improvement and Extension, and Tax Extenders and AMT Relief Acts of 2008)
143	Taxpayers whose homes are damaged or destroyed in federally declared disasters after Dec. 31, 2007 and before Jan. 1, 2010 don't have to meet first-time homebuyer or purchase-price requirements for mortgage bond assistance	Disasters occurring after Dec. 31, 2007 and before Jan. 1, 2010	¶ 1107 Tax Provisions of H.R. 1424 (Including the Emergency Economic Stabilization, Energy Improvement and Extension, and Tax Extenders and AMT Relief Acts of 2008)
143(d)(2)(D)	Veterans' exception from qualified mortgage bond first-time homebuyer requirement is made permanent	For bonds issued after Dec. 31, 2007	¶ 801 Heroes Earnings Assistance and Relief Tax Act of 2008
143(k)(11)	Mortgage bond rules for residences located in disaster areas are extended to apply to bonds issued after May 1, 2008 and before 2010	For bonds issued after May 1, 2008 and before 2010	¶ 701 Housing Assistance Tax Act of 2008
143(k)(12)	Additional $11 billion of tax-exempt housing bonds is authorized for 2008; bonds may be used to refinance subprime mortgages	Bonds issued after July 30, 2008	¶ 702 Housing Assistance Tax Act of 2008

Code	Topic	Effective Date	Complete Analysis
143(k)(12) [sic (13)]	Taxpayers whose homes are damaged or destroyed in federally declared disasters after Dec. 31, 2007 and before Jan. 1, 2010 don't have to meet first-time homebuyer or purchase-price requirements for mortgage bond assistance	Disasters occurring after Dec. 31, 2007 and before Jan. 1, 2010	¶ 1107 Tax Provisions of H.R. 1424 (Including the Emergency Economic Stabilization, Energy Improvement and Extension, and Tax Extenders and AMT Relief Acts of 2008)
143(l)(3)(B)(ii)	Volume limits on qualified veterans' mortgage bonds issued by Alaska, Oregon, and Wisconsin are increased to $100 million	For bonds issued after Dec. 31, 2007	¶ 803 Heroes Earnings Assistance and Relief Tax Act of 2008
143(l)(4)	Recent veterans are made eligible for qualified veterans' mortgage bond financing in California and Texas	For bonds issued after Dec. 31, 2007	¶ 802 Heroes Earnings Assistance and Relief Tax Act of 2008
144(a)(4)(F)	Allowance of additional $10 million capital expenditures for small issue bonds issued after Sept. 30, 2009 won't be limited to facilities financed with urban development action grants	Bonds issued after Sept. 30, 2009	¶ 1307 American Jobs Creation Act of 2004
144(a)(4)(G)	Allowance of additional $10 million capital expenditures for small issue bonds issued after Sept. 30, 2009 won't be limited to facilities financed with urban development action grants	Bonds issued after Sept. 30, 2009	¶ 1307 American Jobs Creation Act of 2004
144(a)(12)(C)	IDBs issued before 2011 may finance facilities used to create intangible property	Bonds issued after Feb. 17, 2009 and before Jan. 1, 2011	¶ 1310 American Recovery and Reinvestment Act of 2009

Code	Topic	Effective Date	Complete Analysis
146(d)(5)	Additional $11 billion of tax-exempt housing bonds is authorized for 2008; bonds may be used to refinance subprime mortgages	Bonds issued after July 30, 2008	¶ 702 Housing Assistance Tax Act of 2008
146(f)(6)	Additional $11 billion of tax-exempt housing bonds is authorized for 2008; bonds may be used to refinance subprime mortgages	Bonds issued after July 30, 2008	¶ 702 Housing Assistance Tax Act of 2008
146(i)(6)	Certain residential rental project bonds are treated as refunding bonds irrespective of obligor	Repayments of loans received after July 30, 2008	¶ 223 Housing Assistance Tax Act of 2008
146(i)(6)	Overview of AMT changes for low-income housing, changes to the low-income housing tax credit, and related tax-exempt bond financing provisions	Various effective dates	¶ 201 Housing Assistance Tax Act of 2008
147(c)(2)(A)	Maximum amount of Aggie bonds available to first-time farmers is increased to $450,000 (up from $250,000) and indexed for inflation; fair market value test is removed from the definition of substantial farmland	Bonds issued after May 22, 2008	¶ 107 Heartland, Habitat, Harvest, and Horticulture Act of 2008
147(c)(2)(C)(i)(II)	Maximum amount of Aggie bonds available to first-time farmers is increased to $450,000 (up from $250,000) and indexed for inflation; fair market value test is removed from the definition of substantial farmland	Bonds issued after May 22, 2008	¶ 107 Heartland, Habitat, Harvest, and Horticulture Act of 2008

Code	Topic	Effective Date	Complete Analysis
147(c)(2)(E)	Maximum amount of Aggie bonds available to first-time farmers is increased to $450,000 (up from $250,000) and indexed for inflation; fair market value test is removed from the definition of substantial farmland	Bonds issued after May 22, 2008	¶ 107 Heartland, Habitat, Harvest, and Horticulture Act of 2008
147(c)(2)(H)	Maximum amount of Aggie bonds available to first-time farmers is increased to $450,000 (up from $250,000) and indexed for inflation; fair market value test is removed from the definition of substantial farmland	Bonds issued after May 22, 2008	¶ 107 Heartland, Habitat, Harvest, and Horticulture Act of 2008
149(b)(3)(A)(iv)	Bonds guaranteed by federal home loan banks are eligible for treatment as tax-exempt bonds	For guarantees made after July 30, 2008	¶ 703 Housing Assistance Tax Act of 2008
149(b)(3)(E)	Bonds guaranteed by federal home loan banks are eligible for treatment as tax-exempt bonds	For guarantees made after July 30, 2008	¶ 703 Housing Assistance Tax Act of 2008
152(c)(1)(E)	"Qualifying child" must be younger than claimant and be unmarried; qualifying child benefits restricted to child's parents	Tax years beginning after Dec. 31, 2008	¶ 516 Tax Provisions of H.R. 1424 (Including the Emergency Economic Stabilization, Energy Improvement and Extension, and Tax Extenders and AMT Relief Acts of 2008)

Code	Topic	Effective Date	Complete Analysis
152(c)(3)(A)	"Qualifying child" must be younger than claimant and be unmarried; qualifying child benefits restricted to child's parents	Tax years beginning after Dec. 31, 2008	¶ 516 Tax Provisions of H.R. 1424 (Including the Emergency Economic Stabilization, Energy Improvement and Extension, and Tax Extenders and AMT Relief Acts of 2008)
152(c)(4)(A)	"Qualifying child" must be younger than claimant and be unmarried; qualifying child benefits restricted to child's parents	Tax years beginning after Dec. 31, 2008	¶ 516 Tax Provisions of H.R. 1424 (Including the Emergency Economic Stabilization, Energy Improvement and Extension, and Tax Extenders and AMT Relief Acts of 2008)
152(c)(4)(C)	"Qualifying child" must be younger than claimant and be unmarried; qualifying child benefits restricted to child's parents	Tax years beginning after Dec. 31, 2008	¶ 516 Tax Provisions of H.R. 1424 (Including the Emergency Economic Stabilization, Energy Improvement and Extension, and Tax Extenders and AMT Relief Acts of 2008)
162(m)	Executive compensation deduction is capped at $500,000 for employers selling more than $300 million of troubled assets in bailout program	Tax years ending on or after Oct. 3, 2008	¶ 402 Tax Provisions of H.R. 1424 (Including the Emergency Economic Stabilization, Energy Improvement and Extension, and Tax Extenders and AMT Relief Acts of 2008)
162(m)(5)	Scope of $500,000 compensation deduction limit on TARP recipients is broadened; other executive compensation restrictions are imposed	Feb. 17, 2009	¶ 401 American Recovery and Reinvestment Act of 2009

Code	Topic	Effective Date	Complete Analysis
162(m)(5)	Executive compensation deduction is capped at $500,000 for employers selling more than $300 million of troubled assets in bailout program	Tax years ending on or after Oct. 3, 2008	¶ 402 Tax Provisions of H.R. 1424 (Including the Emergency Economic Stabilization, Energy Improvement and Extension, and Tax Extenders and AMT Relief Acts of 2008)
163(d)(4)(B)	Exclusion of qualified dividend income from investment income for investment interest deduction limit purposes (unless taxpayer elects to include it) is extended for two years	Tax years beginning after Dec. 31, 2008 and before Jan. 1, 2011	¶ 109 Tax Increase Prevention and Reconciliation Act of 2005
163(e)(5)(F)	Rules for high yield OID obligations are suspended for obligations issued from Sept. 1, 2008 to Dec. 31, 2009 and beyond at IRS's discretion	Obligations issued after Aug. 31, 2008 and before Jan. 1, 2010, in tax years ending after Aug. 31, 2008	¶ 907 American Recovery and Reinvestment Act of 2009
163(e)(5)(G)	Rules for high yield OID obligations are suspended for obligations issued from Sept. 1, 2008 to Dec. 31, 2009 and beyond at IRS's discretion	Obligations issued after Aug. 31, 2008 and before Jan. 1, 2010, in tax years ending after Aug. 31, 2008	¶ 907 American Recovery and Reinvestment Act of 2009
163(h)(3)(E)(iv)(I)	Interest deduction for mortgage insurance premiums is extended to amounts paid or incurred after 2007 and before 2011	Amounts paid or accrued after Dec. 31, 2007	¶ 202 AMT Patch, Mortgage Relief, Energy, Technical Corrections, and Other Late 2007 Tax Acts
163(i)(1)	Beginning in 2010, IRS will be able to apply a higher rate to determine whether an obligation is an applicable high yield discount obligation	Obligations issued after Dec. 31, 2009, in tax years ending after Dec. 31, 2009	¶ 908 American Recovery and Reinvestment Act of 2009

Code	Topic	Effective Date	Complete Analysis
164(a)(6)	Standard or itemized deduction allowed for sales and excise taxes imposed on most new vehicles purchased on or after Feb. 17, 2009 and before 2010	Purchases on or after Feb. 17, 2009 and before 2010	¶ 105 American Recovery and Reinvestment Act of 2009
164(b)(5)(I)	Election to claim itemized deduction for state and local general sales taxes is extended for two years, to apply through 2009	Tax years beginning after Dec. 31, 2007 and before Jan. 1, 2010	¶ 505 Tax Provisions of H.R. 1424 (Including the Emergency Economic Stabilization, Energy Improvement and Extension, and Tax Extenders and AMT Relief Acts of 2008)
164(b)(6)	Standard or itemized deduction allowed for sales and excise taxes imposed on most new vehicles purchased on or after Feb. 17, 2009 and before 2010	Purchases on or after Feb. 17, 2009 and before 2010	¶ 105 American Recovery and Reinvestment Act of 2009
165	10%-of-AGI limit on personal casualty losses is waived for "federally declared disasters" in 2008 and 2009	Disasters declared in tax years beginning after Dec. 31, 2007, and occurring before Jan. 1, 2010	¶ 1201 Tax Provisions of H.R. 1424 (Including the Emergency Economic Stabilization, Energy Improvement and Extension, and Tax Extenders and AMT Relief Acts of 2008)
165	Individuals' per-casualty floor for personal-use property increased from $100 to $500 for 2009	Tax years beginning after Dec. 31, 2008, and before Jan. 1, 2010	¶ 503 Tax Provisions of H.R. 1424 (Including the Emergency Economic Stabilization, Energy Improvement and Extension, and Tax Extenders and AMT Relief Acts of 2008)

Code	Topic	Effective Date	Complete Analysis
165(h)(1)	Individuals' per-casualty floor for personal-use property increased from $100 to $500 for 2009	Tax years beginning after Dec. 31, 2008, and before Jan. 1, 2010	¶ 503 Tax Provisions of H.R. 1424 (Including the Emergency Economic Stabilization, Energy Improvement and Extension, and Tax Extenders and AMT Relief Acts of 2008)
165(h)(3)	10%-of-AGI limit on personal casualty losses is waived for "federally declared disasters" in 2008 and 2009	Disasters declared in tax years beginning after Dec. 31, 2007, and occurring before Jan. 1, 2010	¶ 1201 Tax Provisions of H.R. 1424 (Including the Emergency Economic Stabilization, Energy Improvement and Extension, and Tax Extenders and AMT Relief Acts of 2008)
165(h)(4)(B)	10%-of-AGI limit on personal casualty losses is waived for "federally declared disasters" in 2008 and 2009	Disasters declared in tax years beginning after Dec. 31, 2007, and occurring before Jan. 1, 2010	¶ 1201 Tax Provisions of H.R. 1424 (Including the Emergency Economic Stabilization, Energy Improvement and Extension, and Tax Extenders and AMT Relief Acts of 2008)
165(i)(1)	10%-of-AGI limit on personal casualty losses is waived for "federally declared disasters" in 2008 and 2009	Disasters declared in tax years beginning after Dec. 31, 2007, and occurring before Jan. 1, 2010	¶ 1201 Tax Provisions of H.R. 1424 (Including the Emergency Economic Stabilization, Energy Improvement and Extension, and Tax Extenders and AMT Relief Acts of 2008)
165(i)(4)	10%-of-AGI limit on personal casualty losses is waived for "federally declared disasters" in 2008 and 2009	Disasters declared in tax years beginning after Dec. 31, 2007, and occurring before Jan. 1, 2010	¶ 1201 Tax Provisions of H.R. 1424 (Including the Emergency Economic Stabilization, Energy Improvement and Extension, and Tax Extenders and AMT Relief Acts of 2008)

Code	Topic	Effective Date	Complete Analysis
168(b)(2)(C)	"Smart" electric meters and distribution grid systems are designated as MACRS ten-year property	Property placed in service after Oct. 3, 2008	¶ 914 Tax Provisions of H.R. 1424 (Including the Emergency Economic Stabilization, Energy Improvement and Extension, and Tax Extenders and AMT Relief Acts of 2008)
168(b)(3)(I)	Fifteen-year straight-line cost recovery can be used for certain improvements to retail space	Property placed in service after Dec. 31, 2008 and before Jan. 1, 2010	¶ 313 Tax Provisions of H.R. 1424 (Including the Emergency Economic Stabilization, Energy Improvement and Extension, and Tax Extenders and AMT Relief Acts of 2008)
168(e)(3)(A)(i)	Three-year MACRS depreciation will apply to all race horses placed in service after Dec. 31, 2008 and before Jan. 1, 2014	Property placed in service after Dec. 31, 2008 and before Jan. 1, 2014	¶ 104 Heartland, Habitat, Harvest, and Horticulture Act of 2008
168(e)(3)(B)(vii)	Most new farming machinery and equipment placed in service during calendar year 2009 is designated as MACRS 5-year property	Property placed in service after Dec. 31, 2008 and before Jan. 1, 2010	¶ 1402 Tax Provisions of H.R. 1424 (Including the Emergency Economic Stabilization, Energy Improvement and Extension, and Tax Extenders and AMT Relief Acts of 2008)
168(e)(3)(D)(iii)	"Smart" electric meters and distribution grid systems are designated as MACRS ten-year property	Property placed in service after Oct. 3, 2008	¶ 914 Tax Provisions of H.R. 1424 (Including the Emergency Economic Stabilization, Energy Improvement and Extension, and Tax Extenders and AMT Relief Acts of 2008)

Code	Topic	Effective Date	Complete Analysis
168(e)(3)(D)(iv)	"Smart" electric meters and distribution grid systems are designated as MACRS ten-year property	Property placed in service after Oct. 3, 2008	¶ 914 Tax Provisions of H.R. 1424 (Including the Emergency Economic Stabilization, Energy Improvement and Extension, and Tax Extenders and AMT Relief Acts of 2008)
168(e)(3)(E)(iv)	Fifteen-year straight-line cost recovery for qualified leasehold improvements and qualified restaurant improvements is extended for two years to property placed in service before Jan. 1, 2010	Property placed in service after Dec. 31, 2007 and before Jan. 1, 2010	¶ 314 Tax Provisions of H.R. 1424 (Including the Emergency Economic Stabilization, Energy Improvement and Extension, and Tax Extenders and AMT Relief Acts of 2008)
168(e)(3)(E)(v)	Fifteen-year straight-line cost recovery for qualified leasehold improvements and qualified restaurant improvements is extended for two years to property placed in service before Jan. 1, 2010	Property placed in service after Dec. 31, 2007 and before Jan. 1, 2010	¶ 314 Tax Provisions of H.R. 1424 (Including the Emergency Economic Stabilization, Energy Improvement and Extension, and Tax Extenders and AMT Relief Acts of 2008)
168(e)(3)(E)(ix)	Fifteen-year straight-line cost recovery can be used for certain improvements to retail space	Property placed in service after Dec. 31, 2008 and before Jan. 1, 2010	¶ 313 Tax Provisions of H.R. 1424 (Including the Emergency Economic Stabilization, Energy Improvement and Extension, and Tax Extenders and AMT Relief Acts of 2008)
168(e)(7)	Qualified restaurant property subject to 15-year straight-line cost recovery includes buildings as well as improvements to buildings placed in service after Dec. 31, 2008 and before Jan. 1, 2010	Property placed in service after Dec. 31, 2008 and before Jan. 1, 2010	¶ 315 Tax Provisions of H.R. 1424 (Including the Emergency Economic Stabilization, Energy Improvement and Extension, and Tax Extenders and AMT Relief Acts of 2008)

Code	Topic	Effective Date	Complete Analysis
168(e)(8)	Fifteen-year straight-line cost recovery can be used for certain improvements to retail space	Property placed in service after Dec. 31, 2008 and before Jan. 1, 2010	¶ 313 Tax Provisions of H.R. 1424 (Including the Emergency Economic Stabilization, Energy Improvement and Extension, and Tax Extenders and AMT Relief Acts of 2008)
168(g)(3)(B)	Fifteen-year straight-line cost recovery can be used for certain improvements to retail space	Property placed in service after Dec. 31, 2008 and before Jan. 1, 2010	¶ 313 Tax Provisions of H.R. 1424 (Including the Emergency Economic Stabilization, Energy Improvement and Extension, and Tax Extenders and AMT Relief Acts of 2008)
168(g)(3)(B)	Most new farming machinery and equipment placed in service during calendar year 2009 is designated as MACRS 5-year property	Property placed in service after Dec. 31, 2008 and before Jan. 1, 2010	¶ 1402 Tax Provisions of H.R. 1424 (Including the Emergency Economic Stabilization, Energy Improvement and Extension, and Tax Extenders and AMT Relief Acts of 2008)
168(i)(15)(D)	Placed-in-service deadline for the treatment of "motorsports entertainment complexes" as 7-year MACRS property is extended two years to Dec. 31, 2009	Property placed in service after Dec. 31, 2007 and before Jan. 1, 2010	¶ 316 Tax Provisions of H.R. 1424 (Including the Emergency Economic Stabilization, Energy Improvement and Extension, and Tax Extenders and AMT Relief Acts of 2008)
168(i)(18)	"Smart" electric meters and distribution grid systems are designated as MACRS ten-year property	Property placed in service after Oct. 3, 2008	¶ 914 Tax Provisions of H.R. 1424 (Including the Emergency Economic Stabilization, Energy Improvement and Extension, and Tax Extenders and AMT Relief Acts of 2008)

Code	Topic	Effective Date	Complete Analysis
168(i)(19)	"Smart" electric meters and distribution grid systems are designated as MACRS ten-year property	Property placed in service after Oct. 3, 2008	¶ 914 Tax Provisions of H.R. 1424 (Including the Emergency Economic Stabilization, Energy Improvement and Extension, and Tax Extenders and AMT Relief Acts of 2008)
168(j)(8)	Depreciation tax breaks for Indian reservation property are extended for two years to property placed in service through Dec. 31, 2009	Property placed in service after Dec. 31, 2007 and before Jan. 1, 2010	¶ 317 Tax Provisions of H.R. 1424 (Including the Emergency Economic Stabilization, Energy Improvement and Extension, and Tax Extenders and AMT Relief Acts of 2008)
168(k)	50% bonus depreciation and AMT depreciation relief are revived for most new tangible personal property and software and certain leasehold improvements acquired during 2008	Property acquired and placed in service during calendar year 2008	¶ 202 Economic Stimulus Act of 2008
168(k)	One auto manufacturer can elect to receive a deemed payment of tax in lieu of claiming research credits, bonus depreciation and accelerated depreciation	Tax years ending after Mar. 31, 2008	¶ 902 Housing Assistance Tax Act of 2008
168(k)(1)(A)	50% bonus depreciation and AMT depreciation relief are revived for most new tangible personal property and software and certain leasehold improvements acquired during 2008	Property acquired and placed in service during calendar year 2008	¶ 202 Economic Stimulus Act of 2008

Code	Topic	Effective Date	Complete Analysis
168(k)(2)(A)(iii)	50% bonus depreciation and AMT depreciation relief are extended one year through Dec. 31, 2009 (Dec. 31, 2010 for certain property)	Property placed in service before Jan. 1, 2010 and after Dec. 31, 2008	¶ 801 American Recovery and Reinvestment Act of 2009
168(k)(2)(A)(iv)	$8,000 increase in first-year depreciation limit for passenger automobiles that are "qualified property" is extended through Dec. 31, 2009	Property placed in service before Jan. 1, 2010 and after Dec. 31, 2008	¶ 803 American Recovery and Reinvestment Act of 2009
168(k)(2)(A)(iv)	50% bonus depreciation and AMT depreciation relief are extended one year through Dec. 31, 2009 (Dec. 31, 2010 for certain property)	Property placed in service before Jan. 1, 2010 and after Dec. 31, 2008	¶ 801 American Recovery and Reinvestment Act of 2009
168(k)(2)(A)(iv)	Election to trade bonus and accelerated depreciation for otherwise-deferred credits is optionally extended through Dec. 31, 2009 (Dec. 31, 2010 for certain property)	Property placed in service before Jan. 1, 2010 and after Dec. 31, 2008	¶ 804 American Recovery and Reinvestment Act of 2009
168(k)(2)(B)(i)(I)	50% bonus depreciation and AMT depreciation relief are revived for most new tangible personal property and software and certain leasehold improvements acquired during 2008	Property acquired and placed in service during calendar year 2008	¶ 202 Economic Stimulus Act of 2008

Code	Topic	Effective Date	Complete Analysis
168(k)(2)(B)(i)(IV)	50% bonus depreciation and AMT depreciation relief are revived for most new tangible personal property and software and certain leasehold improvements acquired during 2008	Property acquired and placed in service during calendar year 2008	¶ 202 Economic Stimulus Act of 2008
168(k)(2)(B)(ii)	50% bonus depreciation and AMT depreciation relief are extended one year through Dec. 31, 2009 (Dec. 31, 2010 for certain property)	Property placed in service before Jan. 1, 2010 and after Dec. 31, 2008	¶ 801 American Recovery and Reinvestment Act of 2009
168(k)(2)(C)(i)	50% bonus depreciation and AMT depreciation relief are revived for most new tangible personal property and software and certain leasehold improvements acquired during 2008	Property acquired and placed in service during calendar year 2008	¶ 202 Economic Stimulus Act of 2008
168(k)(2)(D)(iii)	50% bonus depreciation and AMT depreciation relief are revived for most new tangible personal property and software and certain leasehold improvements acquired during 2008	Property acquired and placed in service during calendar year 2008	¶ 202 Economic Stimulus Act of 2008
168(k)(2)(E)(i)	50% bonus depreciation and AMT depreciation relief are extended one year through Dec. 31, 2009 (Dec. 31, 2010 for certain property)	Property placed in service before Jan. 1, 2010 and after Dec. 31, 2008	¶ 801 American Recovery and Reinvestment Act of 2009

Code	Topic	Effective Date	Complete Analysis
168(k)(2)(F)(i)	First-year depreciation limit for passenger automobiles is increased by $8,000 if the passenger automobile is "qualified property"	Property acquired and placed in service during calendar year 2008	¶ 203 Economic Stimulus Act of 2008
168(k)(4)	50% bonus depreciation and AMT depreciation relief are revived for most new tangible personal property and software and certain leasehold improvements acquired during 2008	Property acquired and placed in service during calendar year 2008	¶ 202 Economic Stimulus Act of 2008
168(k)(4)	Corporations can elect to treat certain unused research and AMT credits as allowable and refundable in lieu of claiming bonus and accelerated depreciation for "eligible qualified property"	Tax years ending after Mar. 31, 2008	¶ 501 Housing Assistance Tax Act of 2008
168(k)(4)(D)(ii)	Election to trade bonus and accelerated depreciation for otherwise-deferred credits is optionally extended through Dec. 31, 2009 (Dec. 31, 2010 for certain property)	Property placed in service before Jan. 1, 2010 and after Dec. 31, 2008	¶ 804 American Recovery and Reinvestment Act of 2009
168(k)(4)(D)(ii)	Binding contract rule and tax deficiency rule for the election to trade bonus and accelerated depreciation for certain otherwise-deferred credits are corrected	Tax years ending after Mar. 31, 2008	¶ 806 American Recovery and Reinvestment Act of 2009

Code	Topic	Effective Date	Complete Analysis
168(k)(4)(H)	Election to trade bonus and accelerated depreciation for otherwise-deferred credits is optionally extended through Dec. 31, 2009 (Dec. 31, 2010 for certain property)	Property placed in service before Jan. 1, 2010 and after Dec. 31, 2008	¶ 804 American Recovery and Reinvestment Act of 2009
168(k)(4)(H)(ii)	Post-Dec. 31, 2008 election to trade bonus and accelerated depreciation for otherwise-deferred credits is allowed if an earlier election wasn't made	Property placed in service before Jan. 1, 2010 and after Dec. 31, 2008	¶ 805 American Recovery and Reinvestment Act of 2009
168(l)	50% bonus depreciation and AMT depreciation relief for property used to produce "cellulosic biomass ethanol" are expanded to cover property used to produce any "cellulosic biofuel"	Property placed in service after Oct. 3, 2008 and before Jan. 1, 2013	¶ 927 Tax Provisions of H.R. 1424 (Including the Emergency Economic Stabilization, Energy Improvement and Extension, and Tax Extenders and AMT Relief Acts of 2008)
168(l)(3)	50% bonus depreciation and AMT depreciation relief for property used to produce "cellulosic biomass ethanol" are expanded to cover property used to produce any "cellulosic biofuel"	Property placed in service after Oct. 3, 2008 and before Jan. 1, 2013	¶ 927 Tax Provisions of H.R. 1424 (Including the Emergency Economic Stabilization, Energy Improvement and Extension, and Tax Extenders and AMT Relief Acts of 2008)
168(l)(4)(A)	50% bonus depreciation and AMT depreciation relief are revived for most new tangible personal property and software and certain leasehold improvements acquired during 2008	Property acquired and placed in service during calendar year 2008	¶ 202 Economic Stimulus Act of 2008

Code	Topic	Effective Date	Complete Analysis
168(m)	50% bonus depreciation and AMT depreciation relief are allowed for "qualified reuse and recycling property"	Property placed in service and purchased after Aug. 31, 2008	¶ 915 Tax Provisions of H.R. 1424 (Including the Emergency Economic Stabilization, Energy Improvement and Extension, and Tax Extenders and AMT Relief Acts of 2008)
168(n)	50% bonus depreciation and AMT depreciation relief are allowed in connection with disasters federally declared after 2007 and occurring before 2010	Property placed in service after Dec. 31, 2007 for disasters declared after Dec. 31, 2007 and occurring before Jan. 1, 2010	¶ 1207 Tax Provisions of H.R. 1424 (Including the Emergency Economic Stabilization, Energy Improvement and Extension, and Tax Extenders and AMT Relief Acts of 2008)
170	Volunteers donating services for Midwestern-related relief can exclude from income mileage reimbursements during the period beginning on the applicable disaster date and ending on Dec. 31, 2008	For use of a vehicle during the period beginning on the applicable disaster date and ending on Dec. 31, 2008	¶ 1238 Tax Provisions of H.R. 1424 (Including the Emergency Economic Stabilization, Energy Improvement and Extension, and Tax Extenders and AMT Relief Acts of 2008)
170(b)(1)(E)(vi)	Rules permitting individuals to deduct qualified conservation contributions up to 50% of contribution base (100% for farmers) with 15-year carryover are retroactively extended for two years through 2009	Contributions made in tax years beginning after Dec. 31, 2007 and before Jan. 1, 2010	¶ 102 Heartland, Habitat, Harvest, and Horticulture Act of 2008
170(b)(2)(B)(iii)	Rule permitting corporate farmers and ranchers to deduct qualified conservation contributions up to 100% of taxable income is retroactively extended for two years through 2009	For contributions made in tax years beginning after Dec. 31, 2007 and before Jan. 1, 2010	¶ 103 Heartland, Habitat, Harvest, and Horticulture Act of 2008

Code	Topic	Effective Date	Complete Analysis
170(b)(3)	Special higher charitable deduction limitations on qualified conservation contributions by qualified farmers or ranchers expanded to apply to contributions of apparently wholesome food inventory through end of 2008	Tax years ending after Oct. 3, 2008 for contributions made during the period beginning on Oct. 3, 2008 and before Jan. 1, 2009	¶ 326 Tax Provisions of H.R. 1424 (Including the Emergency Economic Stabilization, Energy Improvement and Extension, and Tax Extenders and AMT Relief Acts of 2008)
170(e)(1)	Capital asset treatment for charitable contributions of creative property is determined after 2009 without regard to the modified-carryover-basis-at-death rules	Estates of decedents dying after Dec. 31, 2009	¶ 330 Economic Growth and Tax Relief Reconciliation Act of 2001
170(e)(3)(C)(iii)	Above-basis deduction for charitable contributions of apparently wholesome food inventory is extended through end of 2009	Contributions made after Dec. 31, 2007 and before Jan. 1, 2010	¶ 325 Tax Provisions of H.R. 1424 (Including the Emergency Economic Stabilization, Energy Improvement and Extension, and Tax Extenders and AMT Relief Acts of 2008)
170(e)(3)(D)(iv)	Corporate above-basis charitable deduction for book inventory contributions to schools is extended two years through 2009	Contributions made after Dec. 31, 2007 and before Jan. 1, 2010	¶ 324 Tax Provisions of H.R. 1424 (Including the Emergency Economic Stabilization, Energy Improvement and Extension, and Tax Extenders and AMT Relief Acts of 2008)
170(e)(6)(G)	Enhanced deduction for qualified computer contributions by corporations is extended for two years through 2009	Contributions made in tax years beginning after Dec. 31, 2007, and before Jan. 1, 2010	¶ 323 Tax Provisions of H.R. 1424 (Including the Emergency Economic Stabilization, Energy Improvement and Extension, and Tax Extenders and AMT Relief Acts of 2008)

Code	Topic	Effective Date	Complete Analysis
170(i)	Charitable standard mileage rate for Midwestern-related relief is increased to 70% of business mileage rate during the period beginning on the applicable disaster date and ending on Dec. 31, 2008	For use of a vehicle during the period beginning on the applicable disaster date and ending on Dec. 31, 2008	¶ 1237 Tax Provisions of H.R. 1424 (Including the Emergency Economic Stabilization, Energy Improvement and Extension, and Tax Extenders and AMT Relief Acts of 2008)
172	Carryback period for 2008 NOLs is increased to three, four, or five years (from two years) for electing small businesses	NOLs arising in tax years ending after Dec. 31, 2007	¶ 601 American Recovery and Reinvestment Act of 2009
172	"Qualified disaster losses" from pre-2010 disasters can be carried back five years and are deductible against 100% of AMT income	Losses arising in tax years beginning after Dec. 31, 2007, in connection with disasters declared after that date	¶ 1204 Tax Provisions of H.R. 1424 (Including the Emergency Economic Stabilization, Energy Improvement and Extension, and Tax Extenders and AMT Relief Acts of 2008)
172(b)(1)(F)(ii)	"Qualified disaster losses" from pre-2010 disasters can be carried back five years and are deductible against 100% of AMT income	Losses arising in tax years beginning after Dec. 31, 2007, in connection with disasters declared after that date	¶ 1204 Tax Provisions of H.R. 1424 (Including the Emergency Economic Stabilization, Energy Improvement and Extension, and Tax Extenders and AMT Relief Acts of 2008)
172(b)(1)(F)(ii)(II)	Changes are made to the involuntary conversion rules and other Code provisions to reflect new definition of "federally declared disaster"	Disasters declared in tax years beginning after Dec. 31, 2007, and occurring before Jan. 1, 2010	¶ 1203 Tax Provisions of H.R. 1424 (Including the Emergency Economic Stabilization, Energy Improvement and Extension, and Tax Extenders and AMT Relief Acts of 2008)

Code	Topic	Effective Date	Complete Analysis
172(b)(1)(F)(ii)(III)	Changes are made to the involuntary conversion rules and other Code provisions to reflect new definition of "federally declared disaster"	Disasters declared in tax years beginning after Dec. 31, 2007, and occurring before Jan. 1, 2010	¶ 1203 Tax Provisions of H.R. 1424 (Including the Emergency Economic Stabilization, Energy Improvement and Extension, and Tax Extenders and AMT Relief Acts of 2008)
172(b)(1)(H)	Carryback period for 2008 NOLs is increased to three, four, or five years (from two years) for electing small businesses	NOLs arising in tax years ending after Dec. 31, 2007	¶ 601 American Recovery and Reinvestment Act of 2009
172(b)(1)(J)	"Qualified disaster losses" from pre-2010 disasters can be carried back five years and are deductible against 100% of AMT income	Losses arising in tax years beginning after Dec. 31, 2007, in connection with disasters declared after that date	¶ 1204 Tax Provisions of H.R. 1424 (Including the Emergency Economic Stabilization, Energy Improvement and Extension, and Tax Extenders and AMT Relief Acts of 2008)
172(i)(1)	"Qualified disaster losses" from pre-2010 disasters can be carried back five years and are deductible against 100% of AMT income	Losses arising in tax years beginning after Dec. 31, 2007, in connection with disasters declared after that date	¶ 1204 Tax Provisions of H.R. 1424 (Including the Emergency Economic Stabilization, Energy Improvement and Extension, and Tax Extenders and AMT Relief Acts of 2008)
172(j)	"Qualified disaster losses" from pre-2010 disasters can be carried back five years and are deductible against 100% of AMT income	Losses arising in tax years beginning after Dec. 31, 2007, in connection with disasters declared after that date	¶ 1204 Tax Provisions of H.R. 1424 (Including the Emergency Economic Stabilization, Energy Improvement and Extension, and Tax Extenders and AMT Relief Acts of 2008)
175(a)	Deduction will be allowed to farmers for endangered species recovery expenditures paid or incurred after Dec. 31, 2008	Expenditures paid or incurred after Dec. 31, 2008	¶ 105 Heartland, Habitat, Harvest, and Horticulture Act of 2008

Code	Topic	Effective Date	Complete Analysis
175(c)(1)	Deduction will be allowed to farmers for endangered species recovery expenditures paid or incurred after Dec. 31, 2008	Expenditures paid or incurred after Dec. 31, 2008	¶ 105 Heartland, Habitat, Harvest, and Horticulture Act of 2008
175(c)(3)(A)(i)	Deduction will be allowed to farmers for endangered species recovery expenditures paid or incurred after Dec. 31, 2008	Expenditures paid or incurred after Dec. 31, 2008	¶ 105 Heartland, Habitat, Harvest, and Horticulture Act of 2008
179(b)(1)	The $100,000 Code Sec. 179 expense election limit, $400,000 phaseout threshold, and inflation adjustments are extended for two years to tax years beginning before Jan. 1, 2010	Tax years beginning after 2007 and before 2010	¶ 401 Tax Increase Prevention and Reconciliation Act of 2005
179(b)(2)	The $100,000 Code Sec. 179 expense election limit, $400,000 phaseout threshold, and inflation adjustments are extended for two years to tax years beginning before Jan. 1, 2010	Tax years beginning after 2007 and before 2010	¶ 401 Tax Increase Prevention and Reconciliation Act of 2005
179(b)(5)(A)	The $100,000 Code Sec. 179 expense election limit, $400,000 phaseout threshold, and inflation adjustments are extended for two years to tax years beginning before Jan. 1, 2010	Tax years beginning after 2007 and before 2010	¶ 401 Tax Increase Prevention and Reconciliation Act of 2005
179(b)(7)	Regular Code Sec. 179 deduction limit of $250,000 and beginning of phaseout amount of $800,000 for 2008 are each extended to apply to tax years beginning in 2009	Tax years beginning in 2009	¶ 802 American Recovery and Reinvestment Act of 2009

Code	Topic	Effective Date	Complete Analysis
179(b)(7)	Regular Code Sec. 179 expense deduction limit is increased to $250,000 and beginning of deduction phaseout is raised to $800,000 for tax years beginning in 2008	Tax years beginning in 2008	¶ 201 Economic Stimulus Act of 2008
179(c)(2)	Right to revoke or change the Code Sec. 179 expense election without IRS consent is extended for two years to tax years beginning before Jan. 1, 2010	Tax years beginning after 2007 and before 2010	¶ 402 Tax Increase Prevention and Reconciliation Act of 2005
179(d)(1)(A)(ii)	Inclusion of off-the-shelf computer software as "section 179 property" eligible for the expensing election is extended for two years to tax years beginning before Jan. 1, 2010	Tax years beginning after 2007 and before 2010	¶ 403 Tax Increase Prevention and Reconciliation Act of 2005
179(e)	Code Sec. 179 expensing is increased for qualified disaster assistance property	Property placed in service after Dec. 31, 2007, for disasters declared after Dec. 31, 2007	¶ 1206 Tax Provisions of H.R. 1424 (Including the Emergency Economic Stabilization, Energy Improvement and Extension, and Tax Extenders and AMT Relief Acts of 2008)
179C(c)(1)(B)	Election to expense certain refineries is extended for 2 years and modified to include fuel derived from shale and tar sands	Property placed in service after Oct. 3, 2008	¶ 804 Tax Provisions of H.R. 1424 (Including the Emergency Economic Stabilization, Energy Improvement and Extension, and Tax Extenders and AMT Relief Acts of 2008)

Code	Topic	Effective Date	Complete Analysis
179C(c)(1)(F)	Election to expense certain refineries is extended for 2 years and modified to include fuel derived from shale and tar sands	Property placed in service after Oct. 3, 2008	¶ 804 Tax Provisions of H.R. 1424 (Including the Emergency Economic Stabilization, Energy Improvement and Extension, and Tax Extenders and AMT Relief Acts of 2008)
179C(d)	Election to expense certain refineries is extended for 2 years and modified to include fuel derived from shale and tar sands	Property placed in service after Oct. 3, 2008	¶ 804 Tax Provisions of H.R. 1424 (Including the Emergency Economic Stabilization, Energy Improvement and Extension, and Tax Extenders and AMT Relief Acts of 2008)
179C(e)(2)	Election to expense certain refineries is extended for 2 years and modified to include fuel derived from shale and tar sands	Property placed in service after Oct. 3, 2008	¶ 804 Tax Provisions of H.R. 1424 (Including the Emergency Economic Stabilization, Energy Improvement and Extension, and Tax Extenders and AMT Relief Acts of 2008)
179D(h)	Deduction for energy efficient commercial building property is extended for five years to property placed in service after Dec. 31, 2008 and before Jan. 1, 2014	Property placed in service after Dec. 31, 2008 and before Jan. 1, 2014	¶ 913 Tax Provisions of H.R. 1424 (Including the Emergency Economic Stabilization, Energy Improvement and Extension, and Tax Extenders and AMT Relief Acts of 2008)
179E(g)	Election to expense the cost of qualified advanced mine safety equipment property is extended by one year to property placed in service before Jan. 1, 2010	Oct. 3, 2008	¶ 311 Tax Provisions of H.R. 1424 (Including the Emergency Economic Stabilization, Energy Improvement and Extension, and Tax Extenders and AMT Relief Acts of 2008)

1,177

Code	Topic	Effective Date	Complete Analysis
181(a)(2)(A)	Qualified film and TV production expense election is extended for one year and permitted for up to $15 million in cost even where cost exceeds $15 million	Qualified film and television productions commencing after Dec. 31, 2007 and before Jan. 1, 2010	¶ 312 Tax Provisions of H.R. 1424 (Including the Emergency Economic Stabilization, Energy Improvement and Extension, and Tax Extenders and AMT Relief Acts of 2008)
181(d)(3)(A)	Qualified film and TV production expense election is extended for one year and permitted for up to $15 million in cost even where cost exceeds $15 million	Qualified film and television productions commencing after Dec. 31, 2007 and before Jan. 1, 2010	¶ 312 Tax Provisions of H.R. 1424 (Including the Emergency Economic Stabilization, Energy Improvement and Extension, and Tax Extenders and AMT Relief Acts of 2008)
181(f)	Qualified film and TV production expense election is extended for one year and permitted for up to $15 million in cost even where cost exceeds $15 million	Qualified film and television productions commencing after Dec. 31, 2007 and before Jan. 1, 2010	¶ 312 Tax Provisions of H.R. 1424 (Including the Emergency Economic Stabilization, Energy Improvement and Extension, and Tax Extenders and AMT Relief Acts of 2008)
198(h)	Election to expense qualified environmental remediation expenditures is extended for two years to include expenditures paid or incurred before Jan. 1, 2010	Expenditures paid or incurred after Dec. 31, 2007 and before Jan. 1, 2010	¶ 310 Tax Provisions of H.R. 1424 (Including the Emergency Economic Stabilization, Energy Improvement and Extension, and Tax Extenders and AMT Relief Acts of 2008)
198A	Taxpayers may expense qualified disaster expenses	Amounts paid or incurred after Dec. 31, 2007	¶ 1205 Tax Provisions of H.R. 1424 (Including the Emergency Economic Stabilization, Energy Improvement and Extension, and Tax Extenders and AMT Relief Acts of 2008)

Code	Topic	Effective Date	Complete Analysis
199(b)(2)(D)	Definition of "W-2 wages" for a qualified film added, definition of "qualified film" expanded, and attribution rules added for partnerships and S corporations, for purposes of the domestic production activities deduction	Tax years beginning after Dec. 31, 2007	¶ 1404 Tax Provisions of H.R. 1424 (Including the Emergency Economic Stabilization, Energy Improvement and Extension, and Tax Extenders and AMT Relief Acts of 2008)
199(c)(6)	Definition of "W-2 wages" for a qualified film added, definition of "qualified film" expanded, and attribution rules added for partnerships and S corporations, for purposes of the domestic production activities deduction	Tax years beginning after Dec. 31, 2007	¶ 1404 Tax Provisions of H.R. 1424 (Including the Emergency Economic Stabilization, Energy Improvement and Extension, and Tax Extenders and AMT Relief Acts of 2008)
199(d)(1)(A)(iv)	Definition of "W-2 wages" for a qualified film added, definition of "qualified film" expanded, and attribution rules added for partnerships and S corporations, for purposes of the domestic production activities deduction	Tax years beginning after Dec. 31, 2007	¶ 1404 Tax Provisions of H.R. 1424 (Including the Emergency Economic Stabilization, Energy Improvement and Extension, and Tax Extenders and AMT Relief Acts of 2008)
199(d)(2)	Domestic production activities deduction is reduced for production of oil, gas, or their primary products	Tax years beginning after Dec. 31, 2008	¶ 801 Tax Provisions of H.R. 1424 (Including the Emergency Economic Stabilization, Energy Improvement and Extension, and Tax Extenders and AMT Relief Acts of 2008)

Code	Topic	Effective Date	Complete Analysis
199(d)(8)(A)	Allowance of Code Sec. 199 domestic production activities deduction for Puerto Rico activities is extended two years to taxpayer's first four tax years beginning after 2005	Tax years beginning after Dec. 31, 2007 and before Jan. 1, 2010	¶ 309 Tax Provisions of H.R. 1424 (Including the Emergency Economic Stabilization, Energy Improvement and Extension, and Tax Extenders and AMT Relief Acts of 2008)
199(d)(8)(B)	Allowance of Code Sec. 199 domestic production activities deduction for Puerto Rico activities is extended two years to taxpayer's first four tax years beginning after 2005	Tax years beginning after Dec. 31, 2007 and before Jan. 1, 2010	¶ 309 Tax Provisions of H.R. 1424 (Including the Emergency Economic Stabilization, Energy Improvement and Extension, and Tax Extenders and AMT Relief Acts of 2008)
199(d)(8)(C)	Allowance of Code Sec. 199 domestic production activities deduction for Puerto Rico activities is extended two years to taxpayer's first four tax years beginning after 2005	Tax years beginning after Dec. 31, 2007 and before Jan. 1, 2010	¶ 309 Tax Provisions of H.R. 1424 (Including the Emergency Economic Stabilization, Energy Improvement and Extension, and Tax Extenders and AMT Relief Acts of 2008)
199(d)(9)	Domestic production activities deduction is reduced for production of oil, gas, or their primary products	Tax years beginning after Dec. 31, 2008	¶ 801 Tax Provisions of H.R. 1424 (Including the Emergency Economic Stabilization, Energy Improvement and Extension, and Tax Extenders and AMT Relief Acts of 2008)
219(f)(1)	Active military service members receiving differential pay will be treated as employees with compensation for retirement plan purposes after 2008	Years beginning after Dec. 31, 2008	¶ 201 Heroes Earnings Assistance and Relief Tax Act of 2008

Code	Topic	Effective Date	Complete Analysis
222(e)	Above-the-line deduction for higher-education expenses is extended for two years through 2009	Tax years beginning after Dec. 31, 2007 and before Jan. 1, 2010	¶ 507 Tax Provisions of H.R. 1424 (Including the Emergency Economic Stabilization, Energy Improvement and Extension, and Tax Extenders and AMT Relief Acts of 2008)
223(g)(1)	Cost-of-living adjustment for HSA and HDHP dollar amounts is modified-tax years beginning after 2007	For adjustments made for tax years beginning after 2007	¶ 305 Tax Provisions of the Tax Relief and Health Care Act of 2006
265(b)(3)(G)	Tax-exempt interest expense safe harbors for banks and small issuers are expanded for obligations issued in 2009 and 2010	Obligations issued after Dec. 31, 2008	¶ 1309 American Recovery and Reinvestment Act of 2009
265(b)(7)	Tax-exempt interest expense safe harbors for banks and small issuers are expanded for obligations issued in 2009 and 2010	Obligations issued after Dec. 31, 2008	¶ 1309 American Recovery and Reinvestment Act of 2009
280C(a)	Employers are allowed a differential wage payment credit for certain amounts paid before Jan. 1, 2010 to military personnel on active duty	Amounts paid after June 17, 2008 and before Jan. 1, 2010	¶ 103 Heroes Earnings Assistance and Relief Tax Act of 2008
280C(f)	Agricultural chemicals security credit is available for qualified expenditures paid or incurred after May 22, 2008 and before Jan. 1, 2013	Amounts paid or incurred after May 22, 2008 and before Jan. 1, 2013	¶ 301 Heartland, Habitat, Harvest, and Horticulture Act of 2008

Code	Topic	Effective Date	Complete Analysis
280G(e)	Golden parachute rules apply to severance payments to top executives of employers that sell more than $300 million of troubled assets in bailout program	Payments with respect to severances occurring during the period during which the authorities under Economic Stabilization Act §101(a) are in effect	¶ 403 Tax Provisions of H.R. 1424 (Including the Emergency Economic Stabilization, Energy Improvement and Extension, and Tax Extenders and AMT Relief Acts of 2008)
291(e)(1)(B)(iv)	Tax-exempt interest expense safe harbors for banks and small issuers are expanded for obligations issued in 2009 and 2010	Obligations issued after Dec. 31, 2008	¶ 1309 American Recovery and Reinvestment Act of 2009
306(a)(1)(D)	Qualified dividend income treatment for ordinary income on disposition of Code Sec. 306 stock extended for two years	Tax years beginning after Dec. 31, 2008 and before Jan. 1, 2011	¶ 113 Tax Increase Prevention and Reconciliation Act of 2005
341	Repeal of collapsible corporation provisions is extended two years	Tax years beginning after Dec. 31, 2008 and before Jan. 1, 2011	¶ 505 Tax Increase Prevention and Reconciliation Act of 2005
382(h)	Revocation of IRS guidance exempting banks from loss limitation rules following an ownership change	For ownership changes after Jan. 16, 2009	¶ 602 American Recovery and Reinvestment Act of 2009
382(n)	Code Sec. 382 loss limitation rule doesn't apply where EESA bail-out agreement requires ownership restructuring	Ownership changes made after Feb. 17, 2009	¶ 603 American Recovery and Reinvestment Act of 2009
401(a)(9)(H)	Required minimum distributions are waived for 2009	Calendar years beginning after Dec. 31, 2008	¶ 401 Worker, Retiree, and Employer Recovery Act of 2008
401(k)(13)	Automatic contribution arrangements for 401(k) plans	Plan years beginning after Dec. 31, 2007	¶ 401 Pension Protection Act of 2006
401(m)(12)	Automatic contribution arrangements for 401(k) plans	Plan years beginning after Dec. 31, 2007	¶ 401 Pension Protection Act of 2006

Code	Topic	Effective Date	Complete Analysis
402(c)(4)	Required minimum distributions are waived for 2009	Calendar years beginning after Dec. 31, 2008	¶ 401 Worker, Retiree, and Employer Recovery Act of 2008
402(c)(11)	Plans will be required to offer nonspouse beneficiary rollovers starting in 2010	Plan years beginning after Dec. 31, 2009	¶ 403 Worker, Retiree, and Employer Recovery Act of 2008
402(c)(11)(A)(i)	Plans will be required to offer nonspouse beneficiary rollovers starting in 2010	Plan years beginning after Dec. 31, 2009	¶ 403 Worker, Retiree, and Employer Recovery Act of 2008
402(f)(2)(A)	Plans will be required to offer nonspouse beneficiary rollovers starting in 2010	Plan years beginning after Dec. 31, 2009	¶ 403 Worker, Retiree, and Employer Recovery Act of 2008
402(g)(2)(A)(ii)	Excess deferral "gap-period income" need not be distributed with corrective distribution	Plan years beginning after Dec. 31, 2007	¶ 404 Worker, Retiree, and Employer Recovery Act of 2008
404(a)(1)(A)	Defined benefit plan deduction limits increased with separate limits set for single-employer and multiemployer plans	For years beginning after Dec. 31, 2007	¶ 510 Pension Protection Act of 2006
404(a)(1)(D)	Defined benefit plan deduction limits increased with separate limits set for single-employer and multiemployer plans	For years beginning after Dec. 31, 2007	¶ 510 Pension Protection Act of 2006
404(a)(7)(A)	Deduction limit modified for contributions to combinations of plans	For years beginning after Dec. 31, 2007	¶ 701 Worker, Retiree, and Employer Recovery Act of 2008
404(a)(7)(C)(iv)	Defined benefit plan deduction limits increased with separate limits set for single-employer and multiemployer plans	For years beginning after Dec. 31, 2007	¶ 510 Pension Protection Act of 2006

Code	Topic	Effective Date	Complete Analysis
404(a)(7)(C)(v)	Defined benefit plan deduction limits increased with separate limits set for single-employer and multiemployer plans	Contributions for tax years beginning after Dec. 31, 2007	¶ 510 Pension Protection Act of 2006
404(o)	Defined benefit plan deduction limits increased with separate limits set for single-employer and multiemployer plans	For years beginning after Dec. 31, 2007	¶ 510 Pension Protection Act of 2006
408(d)(8)(F)	Rule allowing tax-free treatment of IRA distributions donated to charity is extended to 2008 and 2009	For IRA distributions made during 2008 and 2009	¶ 504 Tax Provisions of H.R. 1424 (Including the Emergency Economic Stabilization, Energy Improvement and Extension, and Tax Extenders and AMT Relief Acts of 2008)
408A(c)(3)(B)	Distributions from "designated Roth accounts" may be rolled over to a Roth IRA tax-free without meeting pre-2010 conditions for "eligible retirement plans"	For distributions made after Dec. 31, 2007	¶ 402 Worker, Retiree, and Employer Recovery Act of 2008
408A(c)(3)(B)	Rollovers to Roth IRAs from qualified plans, 403(b) annuities, and governmental section 457 plans will be permitted after 2007 if AGI-based limit is met, but tax must be paid on otherwise tax-deferred distributions	For distributions made after Dec. 31, 2007	¶ 103 Pension Protection Act of 2006
408A(c)(3)(B)	AGI limit on conversion of non-Roth IRAs to Roth IRAs is eliminated; income from conversion can be deferred and spread over two years-after 2009	For tax years beginning after Dec. 31, 2009	¶ 203 Tax Increase Prevention and Reconciliation Act of 2005

Code	Topic	Effective Date	Complete Analysis
408A(d)(3)	Rollovers to Roth IRAs from qualified plans, 403(b) annuities, and governmental section 457 plans will be permitted after 2007 if AGI-based limit is met, but tax must be paid on otherwise tax-deferred distributions	For distributions made after Dec. 31, 2007	¶ 103 Pension Protection Act of 2006
408A(d)(3)(A)(iii)	AGI limit on conversion of non-Roth IRAs to Roth IRAs is eliminated; income from conversion can be deferred and spread over two years-after 2009	For tax years beginning after Dec. 31, 2009	¶ 203 Tax Increase Prevention and Reconciliation Act of 2005
408A(d)(3)(B)	Distributions from "designated Roth accounts" may be rolled over to a Roth IRA tax-free without meeting pre-2010 conditions for "eligible retirement plans"	For distributions made after Dec. 31, 2007	¶ 402 Worker, Retiree, and Employer Recovery Act of 2008
408A(d)(3)(E)(i)	AGI limit on conversion of non-Roth IRAs to Roth IRAs is eliminated; income from conversion can be deferred and spread over two years-after 2009	For tax years beginning after Dec. 31, 2009	¶ 203 Tax Increase Prevention and Reconciliation Act of 2005
408A(e)	Rollovers to Roth IRAs from qualified plans, 403(b) annuities, and governmental section 457 plans will be permitted after 2007 if AGI-based limit is met, but tax must be paid on otherwise tax-deferred distributions	For distributions made after Dec. 31, 2007	¶ 103 Pension Protection Act of 2006

Code	Topic	Effective Date	Complete Analysis
411(b)(5)(B)(i)(II)	Violation of preservation of capital rule by cash balance plans is treated as a violation of age discrimination rules	Years beginning after Dec. 31, 2007	¶ 602 Worker, Retiree, and Employer Recovery Act of 2008
412(a)	Minimum funding rules revised for defined benefit plans	Plan years beginning after Dec. 31, 2007	¶ 501 Pension Protection Act of 2006
412(b)	Minimum funding rules revised for defined benefit plans	Plan years beginning after Dec. 31, 2007	¶ 501 Pension Protection Act of 2006
412(b)(3)	Details of special funding rules for multiemployer plans in critical status	For plan years beginning after 2007	¶ 607 Pension Protection Act of 2006
412(c)	Rules revised for obtaining a minimum funding waiver	Plan years beginning after Dec. 31, 2007	¶ 509 Pension Protection Act of 2006
412(c)(7)(A)	One-year prohibition on plan amendments that increase plan liabilities isn't triggered by a prior retroactive amendment that didn't reduce any participant's accrued benefits	Plan years beginning after Dec. 31, 2007	¶ 108 Worker, Retiree, and Employer Recovery Act of 2008
412(d)	Minimum funding rules revised for defined benefit plans	Plan years beginning after Dec. 31, 2007	¶ 501 Pension Protection Act of 2006
412(d)(1)	A change in a plan's valuation date is treated as a change in the plan's funding method for minimum funding standard purposes	Plan years beginning after Dec. 31, 2007	¶ 109 Worker, Retiree, and Employer Recovery Act of 2008
412(d)(3)	Rules revised for obtaining a minimum funding waiver	Plan years beginning after Dec. 31, 2007	¶ 509 Pension Protection Act of 2006
412(e)	Minimum funding rules revised for defined benefit plans	Plan years beginning after Dec. 31, 2007	¶ 501 Pension Protection Act of 2006

Code	Topic	Effective Date	Complete Analysis
414(u)(12)	Active military service members receiving differential pay will be treated as employees with compensation for retirement plan purposes after 2008	Years beginning after Dec. 31, 2008	¶ 201 Heroes Earnings Assistance and Relief Tax Act of 2008
414(w)	Automatic contribution arrangements for 401(k) plans	Plan years beginning after Dec. 31, 2007	¶ 401 Pension Protection Act of 2006
414(w)(3)	Definition of "eligible automatic contribution arrangements," from which permissive withdrawals can be made, is broadened	Plan years beginning after Dec. 31, 2007	¶ 406 Worker, Retiree, and Employer Recovery Act of 2008
414(w)(5)	Definition of "eligible automatic contribution arrangements," from which permissive withdrawals can be made, is broadened	Plan years beginning after Dec. 31, 2007	¶ 406 Worker, Retiree, and Employer Recovery Act of 2008
414(w)(6)	Automatic contribution permissible withdrawals disregarded for purposes of the elective deferral limit	Plan years beginning after Dec. 31, 2007	¶ 407 Worker, Retiree, and Employer Recovery Act of 2008
414(x)	Special rules established for treatment of defined benefit plans combined with 401(k) plans-after 2009	Plan years beginning after Dec. 31, 2009	¶ 402 Pension Protection Act of 2006
414(x)(1)	Defined benefit and 401(k) plan components in an "eligible combined plan" must be terminated separately	Plan years beginning after Dec. 31, 2009	¶ 703 Worker, Retiree, and Employer Recovery Act of 2008

Code	Topic	Effective Date	Complete Analysis
415(b)(2)(E)(v)	Mortality table used for adjusting defined benefit plan limits is conformed to the mortality table used for plan funding purposes	Applies to plan years beginning after Dec. 31, 2008, but may be applied during a plan year beginning in 2008	¶ 501 Worker, Retiree, and Employer Recovery Act of 2008
415(b)(2)(E)(vi)	Interest rate rules for determining lump-sum and other benefits not payable as a straight life annuity are modified for certain small (100 or fewer participant) defined benefit plans	Years beginning after Dec. 31, 2008	¶ 502 Worker, Retiree, and Employer Recovery Act of 2008
417(a)(1)(A)(ii)	Plans subject to survivor annuity requirement will have to provide "qualified optional survivor annuity" form of benefit after 2007	For plan years beginning after Dec. 31, 2007	¶ 1105 Pension Protection Act of 2006
417(a)(3)(A)(i)	Plans subject to survivor annuity requirement will have to provide "qualified optional survivor annuity" form of benefit after 2007	For plan years beginning after Dec. 31, 2007	¶ 1105 Pension Protection Act of 2006
417(e)(3)	Interest rate and mortality table to be used for calculating the lump-sum present value of a participant's accrued benefit under the cash-out rules	For plan years beginning after Dec. 31, 2007	¶ 1104 Pension Protection Act of 2006
417(g)	Plans subject to survivor annuity requirement will have to provide "qualified optional survivor annuity" form of benefit after 2007	For plan years beginning after Dec. 31, 2007	¶ 1105 Pension Protection Act of 2006

Code	Topic	Effective Date	Complete Analysis
418E(d)(1)	Multiemployer plan sponsors must make advance determinations of impending insolvencies over a five-year period, instead of a three-year period	For determinations made in plan years beginning after 2007	¶ 705 Pension Protection Act of 2006
420(e)(2)	Rules on transfer of excess pension assets to retiree health accounts are integrated with new funding rules	Plan years beginning after 2007	¶ 2004 Pension Protection Act of 2006
420(e)(4)	Rules on transfer of excess pension assets to retiree health accounts are integrated with new funding rules	Plan years beginning after 2007	¶ 2004 Pension Protection Act of 2006
430(a)	New funding standards for single-employer defined benefit plans gear minimum required contribution to "target normal cost" and "funding shortfall," upgrade valuation and actuarial standards, and add strict rules for "at-risk" plans	Plan years beginning after Dec. 31, 2007	¶ 502 Pension Protection Act of 2006
430(b)	Definition of "target normal cost" modified to account for expected plan-related expenses and mandatory employee contributions; other funding rules on interest rates, at-risk plans, and quarterly payments clarified	Plan years beginning after Dec. 31, 2008 (for target normal cost and at-risk target normal cost rules), plan years beginning after Dec. 31, 2007 (for all other provisions)	¶ 104 Worker, Retiree, and Employer Recovery Act of 2008

Code	Topic	Effective Date	Complete Analysis
430(b)	New funding standards for single-employer defined benefit plans gear minimum required contribution to "target normal cost" and "funding shortfall," upgrade valuation and actuarial standards, and add strict rules for "at-risk" plans	Plan years beginning after Dec. 31, 2007	¶ 502 Pension Protection Act of 2006
430(c)	New funding standards for single-employer defined benefit plans gear minimum required contribution to "target normal cost" and "funding shortfall," upgrade valuation and actuarial standards, and add strict rules for "at-risk" plans	Plan years beginning after Dec. 31, 2007	¶ 502 Pension Protection Act of 2006
430(c)(5)(B)	Transition rule for determining a pension plan's funding shortfall is clarified to ease impact of financial crisis	Plan years beginning after Dec. 31, 2007	¶ 101 Worker, Retiree, and Employer Recovery Act of 2008
430(d)	New funding standards for single-employer defined benefit plans gear minimum required contribution to "target normal cost" and "funding shortfall," upgrade valuation and actuarial standards, and add strict rules for "at-risk" plans	Plan years beginning after Dec. 31, 2007	¶ 502 Pension Protection Act of 2006

Code	Topic	Effective Date	Complete Analysis
430(e)	New funding standards for single-employer defined benefit plans gear minimum required contribution to "target normal cost" and "funding shortfall," upgrade valuation and actuarial standards, and add strict rules for "at-risk" plans	Plan years beginning after Dec. 31, 2007	¶ 502 Pension Protection Act of 2006
430(f)	New funding standards for single-employer defined benefit plans gear minimum required contribution to "target normal cost" and "funding shortfall," upgrade valuation and actuarial standards, and add strict rules for "at-risk" plans	Plan years beginning after Dec. 31, 2007	¶ 502 Pension Protection Act of 2006
430(g)	New funding standards for single-employer defined benefit plans gear minimum required contribution to "target normal cost" and "funding shortfall," upgrade valuation and actuarial standards, and add strict rules for "at-risk" plans	Plan years beginning after Dec. 31, 2007	¶ 502 Pension Protection Act of 2006
430(g)(3)(B)	"Smoothing" provision to allow for adjustment for expected earnings required when averaging fair market values to determine value of plan assets for purposes of the single-employer defined benefit plan funding rules	Plan years beginning after Dec. 31, 2007	¶ 102 Worker, Retiree, and Employer Recovery Act of 2008

Code	Topic	Effective Date	Complete Analysis
430(h)	New funding standards for single-employer defined benefit plans gear minimum required contribution to "target normal cost" and "funding shortfall," upgrade valuation and actuarial standards, and add strict rules for "at-risk" plans	Plan years beginning after Dec. 31, 2007	¶ 502 Pension Protection Act of 2006
430(h)(2)	Definition of "target normal cost" modified to account for expected plan-related expenses and mandatory employee contributions; other funding rules on interest rates, at-risk plans, and quarterly payments clarified	Plan years beginning after Dec. 31, 2008 (for target normal cost and at-risk target normal cost rules), plan years beginning after Dec. 31, 2007 (for all other provisions)	¶ 104 Worker, Retiree, and Employer Recovery Act of 2008
430(i)	New funding standards for single-employer defined benefit plans gear minimum required contribution to "target normal cost" and "funding shortfall," upgrade valuation and actuarial standards, and add strict rules for "at-risk" plans	Plan years beginning after Dec. 31, 2007	¶ 502 Pension Protection Act of 2006
430(i)(2)	Definition of "target normal cost" modified to account for expected plan-related expenses and mandatory employee contributions; other funding rules on interest rates, at-risk plans, and quarterly payments clarified	Plan years beginning after Dec. 31, 2008 (for target normal cost and at-risk target normal cost rules), plan years beginning after Dec. 31, 2007 (for all other provisions)	¶ 104 Worker, Retiree, and Employer Recovery Act of 2008

Code	Topic	Effective Date	Complete Analysis
430(j)	Quarterly installments of minimum contributions to underfunded single-employer DB plans are required under new funding standards; liens imposed where unpaid contributions exceed $1 million.	Plan years beginning after Dec. 31, 2007	¶ 506 Pension Protection Act of 2006
430(j)(3)	Definition of "target normal cost" modified to account for expected plan-related expenses and mandatory employee contributions; other funding rules on interest rates, at-risk plans, and quarterly payments clarified	Plan years beginning after Dec. 31, 2008 (for target normal cost and at-risk target normal cost rules), plan years beginning after Dec. 31, 2007 (for all other provisions)	¶ 104 Worker, Retiree, and Employer Recovery Act of 2008
430(k)	Quarterly installments of minimum contributions to underfunded single-employer DB plans are required under new funding standards; liens imposed where unpaid contributions exceed $1 million	Plan years beginning after Dec. 31, 2007	¶ 506 Pension Protection Act of 2006
430(k)(6)(B)	Definition of "target normal cost" modified to account for expected plan-related expenses and mandatory employee contributions; other funding rules on interest rates, at-risk plans, and quarterly payments clarified	Plan years beginning after Dec. 31, 2008 (for target normal cost and at-risk target normal cost rules), plan years beginning after Dec. 31, 2007 (for all other provisions)	¶ 104 Worker, Retiree, and Employer Recovery Act of 2008

Code	Topic	Effective Date	Complete Analysis
430(l)	Quarterly installments of minimum contributions to underfunded single-employer DB plans are required under new funding standards; liens imposed where unpaid contributions exceed $1 million	Plan years beginning after Dec. 31, 2007	¶ 506 Pension Protection Act of 2006
431(a)	Rules on minimum funding standards for multiemployer plans relocated and modified	Plan years beginning after 2007	¶ 601 Pension Protection Act of 2006
431(b)	Rules on minimum funding standards for multiemployer plans relocated and modified	Plan years beginning after 2007	¶ 601 Pension Protection Act of 2006
431(c)	Special rules for charges and credits to multiemployer plans' funding standard accounts	Plan years beginning after 2007	¶ 603 Pension Protection Act of 2006
431(c)(5)	New full funding limitation rules to apply to multiemployer plan funding standard accounts	Plan years beginning after 2007	¶ 602 Pension Protection Act of 2006
431(c)(6)	New full funding limitation rules to apply to multiemployer plan funding standard accounts	Plan years beginning after 2007	¶ 602 Pension Protection Act of 2006
431(d)	Extension of amortization periods for multiemployer plans	Plan years beginning after 2007	¶ 604 Pension Protection Act of 2006
432	Multiemployer plan sponsors may elect to retain prior plan year's status as endangered or critical-for the plan year beginning during the period beginning Oct. 1, 2008 through Sept. 30, 2009	First plan year beginning during the period Oct. 1, 2008 through Sept. 30, 2009	¶ 201 Worker, Retiree, and Employer Recovery Act of 2008

Code	Topic	Effective Date	Complete Analysis
432	Funding improvement and rehabilitation periods for multiemployer plans in endangered or critical status for plan years beginning in 2008 or 2009 may be extended three years	Plan years beginning after Dec. 31, 2007	¶ 202 Worker, Retiree, and Employer Recovery Act of 2008
432(a)	Overview of special funding rules for multiemployer plans in endangered or critical status; annual certification by plan actuary; notice requirements	For plan years beginning after 2007	¶ 605 Pension Protection Act of 2006
432(b)(1)	Special funding rules for multiemployer plans in endangered status	For plan years beginning after 2007	¶ 606 Pension Protection Act of 2006
432(b)(2)	Details of special funding rules for multiemployer plans in critical status	For plan years beginning after 2007	¶ 607 Pension Protection Act of 2006
432(b)(3)(A)	Overview of special funding rules for multiemployer plans in endangered or critical status; annual certification by plan actuary; notice requirements	For plan years beginning after 2007	¶ 605 Pension Protection Act of 2006
432(b)(3)(B)	Overview of special funding rules for multiemployer plans in endangered or critical status; annual certification by plan actuary; notice requirements	For plan years beginning after 2007	¶ 605 Pension Protection Act of 2006
432(b)(3)(C)	Overview of special funding rules for multiemployer plans in endangered or critical status; annual certification by plan actuary; notice requirements	For plan years beginning after 2007	¶ 605 Pension Protection Act of 2006

Code	Topic	Effective Date	Complete Analysis
432(b)(3)(D)(iii)	Responsibility for issuing model notices explaining multiemployer plans' critical funding status shifted from DOL to IRS	Plan years beginning after Dec. 31, 2007	¶ 208 Worker, Retiree, and Employer Recovery Act of 2008
432(c)	Special funding rules for multiemployer plans in endangered status	For plan years beginning after 2007	¶ 606 Pension Protection Act of 2006
432(c)(7)	Schedule for implementing and enforcing default funding improvement and rehabilitation plans for underfunded multiemployer plans clarified; ERISA enforcement provision added	Plan years beginning after Dec. 31, 2007	¶ 206 Worker, Retiree, and Employer Recovery Act of 2008
432(d)	Special funding rules for multiemployer plans in endangered status	For plan years beginning after 2007	¶ 606 Pension Protection Act of 2006
432(e)	Details of special funding rules for multiemployer plans in critical status	For plan years beginning after 2007	¶ 607 Pension Protection Act of 2006
432(e)(3)(C)	Schedule for implementing and enforcing default funding improvement and rehabilitation plans for underfunded multiemployer plans clarified; ERISA enforcement provision added	Plan years beginning after Dec. 31, 2007	¶ 206 Worker, Retiree, and Employer Recovery Act of 2008
432(e)(8)(C)(iii)	Responsibility for issuing model notices explaining multiemployer plans' critical funding status shifted from DOL to IRS	Plan years beginning after Dec. 31, 2007	¶ 208 Worker, Retiree, and Employer Recovery Act of 2008
432(f)	Details of special funding rules for multiemployer plans in critical status	For plan years beginning after 2007	¶ 607 Pension Protection Act of 2006

Code	Topic	Effective Date	Complete Analysis
432(f)(2)(A)(i)	Participants whose annuity starting date comes before critical status notice is sent by underfunded multiemployer plan, are not subject to restriction on accelerated benefit payments	Plan years beginning after Dec. 31, 2007	¶ 207 Worker, Retiree, and Employer Recovery Act of 2008
432(g)	Details of special funding rules for multiemployer plans in critical status	For plan years beginning after 2007	¶ 607 Pension Protection Act of 2006
432(g)	Special funding rules for multiemployer plans in endangered status	For plan years beginning after 2007	¶ 606 Pension Protection Act of 2006
432(h)	Details of special funding rules for multiemployer plans in critical status	For plan years beginning after 2007	¶ 607 Pension Protection Act of 2006
432(h)	Special funding rules for multiemployer plans in endangered status	For plan years beginning after 2007	¶ 606 Pension Protection Act of 2006
432(i)(1)	Details of special funding rules for multiemployer plans in critical status	For plan years beginning after 2007	¶ 607 Pension Protection Act of 2006
432(i)(2)	Special funding rules for multiemployer plans in endangered status	For plan years beginning after 2007	¶ 606 Pension Protection Act of 2006
432(i)(3)	Special funding rules for multiemployer plans in endangered status	For plan years beginning after 2007	¶ 606 Pension Protection Act of 2006
432(i)(4)	Special funding rules for multiemployer plans in endangered status	For plan years beginning after 2007	¶ 606 Pension Protection Act of 2006
432(i)(5)	Details of special funding rules for multiemployer plans in critical status	For plan years beginning after 2007	¶ 607 Pension Protection Act of 2006
432(i)(7)	Details of special funding rules for multiemployer plans in critical status	For plan years beginning after 2007	¶ 607 Pension Protection Act of 2006

Code	Topic	Effective Date	Complete Analysis
432(i)(8)	Overview of special funding rules for multiemployer plans in endangered or critical status; annual certification by plan actuary; notice requirements	For plan years beginning after 2007	¶ 605 Pension Protection Act of 2006
432(i)(9)	Rules changed on how to calculate excise tax imposed for failing to timely adopt a rehabilitation plan	Years beginning after Dec. 31, 2007	¶ 205 Worker, Retiree, and Employer Recovery Act of 2008
432(i)(10)	Details of special funding rules for multiemployer plans in critical status	For plan years beginning after 2007	¶ 607 Pension Protection Act of 2006
436	Funding-based limits imposed on benefits and benefit accruals under single-employer plans	Plan years beginning after Dec. 31, 2007	¶ 1102 Pension Protection Act of 2006
436(d)(5)	Lump-sum payments of $5,000 or less are not subject to funding-based limit on accelerated forms of distribution	Plan years beginning after Dec. 31, 2007	¶ 405 Worker, Retiree, and Employer Recovery Act of 2008
436(e)(1)	Temporary rule allows avoidance of future benefit accrual limitation if plan's AFTAP for the preceding plan year is 60% or more	First plan year beginning during period beginning on Oct. 1, 2008 and ending on Sept. 30, 2009	¶ 106 Worker, Retiree, and Employer Recovery Act of 2008
436(k)	IRS may prescribe rules for application of the funding-based benefit and accrual limits to small plans with alternate valuation dates	Plan years beginning after Dec. 31, 2007	¶ 503 Worker, Retiree, and Employer Recovery Act of 2008
436(l)	"Single-employer plan" defined for funding-based benefit limit purposes	Plan years beginning after Dec. 31, 2007	¶ 504 Worker, Retiree, and Employer Recovery Act of 2008

Code	Topic	Effective Date	Complete Analysis
451(i)(3)	Gain deferral election for "qualifying electric transmission transactions" is extended retroactively through Dec. 31, 2009 for dispositions by a "qualified electric utility"	Transactions after Dec. 31, 2007	¶ 1012 Tax Provisions of H.R. 1424 (Including the Emergency Economic Stabilization, Energy Improvement and Extension, and Tax Extenders and AMT Relief Acts of 2008)
451(i)(5)(C)	"Exempt utility property" for the gain deferral election for "qualifying electric transmission transactions" is modified to exclude property located outside the U.S.	Transactions after Oct. 3, 2008	¶ 1014 Tax Provisions of H.R. 1424 (Including the Emergency Economic Stabilization, Energy Improvement and Extension, and Tax Extenders and AMT Relief Acts of 2008)
451(i)(6)	Gain deferral election for "qualifying electric transmission transactions" is extended retroactively through Dec. 31, 2009 for dispositions by a "qualified electric utility"	Transactions after Dec. 31, 2007	¶ 1012 Tax Provisions of H.R. 1424 (Including the Emergency Economic Stabilization, Energy Improvement and Extension, and Tax Extenders and AMT Relief Acts of 2008)
457A	Nonqualified deferred compensation (NQDC) from certain tax-indifferent corporations and partnerships is includible in gross income when not subject to substantial forfeiture risk	Deferred amounts attributable to services performed after Dec. 31, 2008	¶ 401 Tax Provisions of H.R. 1424 (Including the Emergency Economic Stabilization, Energy Improvement and Extension, and Tax Extenders and AMT Relief Acts of 2008)
461(j)	Excess farm losses of certain taxpayers receiving applicable farm subsidies will be disallowed in tax years beginning after Dec. 31, 2009	Tax years beginning after Dec. 31, 2009	¶ 101 Heartland, Habitat, Harvest, and Horticulture Act of 2008

Code	Topic	Effective Date	Complete Analysis
512(b)(13)(E)(iv)	Rule including in UBTI to a limited extent, "specified payments" received by a tax-exempt parent from its controlled entity, is extended through 2009	Payments received or accrued after Dec. 31, 2007 and before Jan. 1, 2010	¶ 1301 Tax Provisions of H.R. 1424 (Including the Emergency Economic Stabilization, Energy Improvement and Extension, and Tax Extenders and AMT Relief Acts of 2008)
529(e)(3)(A)	Computer technology and equipment, and Internet access and related services, qualify as higher education expenses under 529 plans for 2009 and 2010	Expenses paid or incurred after Dec. 31, 2008	¶ 108 American Recovery and Reinvestment Act of 2009
531	15% accumulated earnings tax rate and 15% personal holding company tax rate are extended two years	Tax years beginning after Dec. 31, 2008 and before Jan. 1, 2011	¶ 504 Tax Increase Prevention and Reconciliation Act of 2005
541	15% accumulated earnings tax rate and 15% personal holding company tax rate are extended two years	Tax years beginning after Dec. 31, 2008 and before Jan. 1, 2011	¶ 504 Tax Increase Prevention and Reconciliation Act of 2005
584(c)	Passthrough of qualified dividend income by common trust funds is extended for two years	Tax years beginning after Dec. 31, 2008 and before Jan. 1, 2011	¶ 111 Tax Increase Prevention and Reconciliation Act of 2005
613A(c)(6)(H)	Suspension of taxable income limit on percentage depletion from marginal wells is extended for tax years beginning after Dec. 31, 2008 and before Jan. 1, 2010	Tax years beginning after Dec. 31, 2008 and before Jan. 1, 2010	¶ 803 Tax Provisions of H.R. 1424 (Including the Emergency Economic Stabilization, Energy Improvement and Extension, and Tax Extenders and AMT Relief Acts of 2008)

Code	Topic	Effective Date	Complete Analysis
684(a)	Gain recognition rule for transfers of appreciated property to non-grantor foreign trusts and foreign estates will be extended to transfers at death to nonresident aliens after 2009	For transfers after Dec. 31, 2009	¶ 313 Economic Growth and Tax Relief Reconciliation Act of 2001
691(c)(4)	5% and 15% adjusted capital gains rates on noncorporate taxpayers' qualified dividend income are extended for two years	Tax years beginning after Dec. 31, 2008 and before Jan. 1, 2011	¶ 107 Tax Increase Prevention and Reconciliation Act of 2005
702(a)(5)	Passthrough of qualified dividend income by partnerships is extended for two years	Tax years beginning after Dec. 31, 2008 and before Jan. 1, 2011	¶ 112 Tax Increase Prevention and Reconciliation Act of 2005
848(e)(6)	Qualified long-term care insurance can be provided as a rider to an annuity contract after 2009	Tax years beginning after 2009	¶ 2402 Pension Protection Act of 2006
853A	Pass through of tax credit bond credits by RICs and REITs	Tax years ending after Feb. 17, 2009	¶ 1308 American Recovery and Reinvestment Act of 2009
854(a)	Passthrough of qualified dividend income by RICs and REITs is extended for two years	Tax years beginning after Dec. 31, 2008 and before Jan. 1, 2011	¶ 110 Tax Increase Prevention and Reconciliation Act of 2005
854(b)(1)(B)	Passthrough of qualified dividend income by RICs and REITs is extended for two years	Tax years beginning after Dec. 31, 2008 and before Jan. 1, 2011	¶ 110 Tax Increase Prevention and Reconciliation Act of 2005
854(b)(1)(C)	Passthrough of qualified dividend income by RICs and REITs is extended for two years	Tax years beginning after Dec. 31, 2008 and before Jan. 1, 2011	¶ 110 Tax Increase Prevention and Reconciliation Act of 2005
854(b)(2)	Passthrough of qualified dividend income by RICs and REITs is extended for two years	Tax years beginning after Dec. 31, 2008 and before Jan. 1, 2011	¶ 110 Tax Increase Prevention and Reconciliation Act of 2005

Code	Topic	Effective Date	Complete Analysis
854(b)(5)	Passthrough of qualified dividend income by RICs and REITs is extended for two years	Tax years beginning after Dec. 31, 2008 and before Jan. 1, 2011	¶ 110 Tax Increase Prevention and Reconciliation Act of 2005
856(c)(2)(H)	Temporary liberalization of REIT provisions for timber REITs	Tax years beginning after May 22, 2008	¶ 402 Heartland, Habitat, Harvest, and Horticulture Act of 2008
856(c)(4)(B)(ii)	Temporary liberalization of REIT provisions for timber REITs	Tax years beginning after May 22, 2008	¶ 402 Heartland, Habitat, Harvest, and Horticulture Act of 2008
856(c)(4)(B)(ii)	Amendments to REIT assets tests	Gains recognized after July 30, 2008	¶ 402 Housing Assistance Tax Act of 2008
856(c)(4)(B)(iii)(III)	Amendments to REIT assets tests	Gains recognized after July 30, 2008	¶ 402 Housing Assistance Tax Act of 2008
856(c)(5)(G)	Treatment of foreign currency gains for REIT income test purposes	Gains recognized after July 30, 2008	¶ 401 Housing Assistance Tax Act of 2008
856(c)(5)(H)	Temporary liberalization of REIT provisions for timber REITs	Tax years beginning after May 22, 2008	¶ 402 Heartland, Habitat, Harvest, and Horticulture Act of 2008
856(c)(5)(I)	Temporary liberalization of REIT provisions for timber REITs	Tax years beginning after May 22, 2008	¶ 402 Heartland, Habitat, Harvest, and Horticulture Act of 2008
856(c)(5)(J)	Treatment of foreign currency gains for REIT income test purposes	Gains recognized after July 30, 2008	¶ 401 Housing Assistance Tax Act of 2008
856(c)(5)(K)	Amendments to REIT assets tests	Gains recognized after July 30, 2008	¶ 402 Housing Assistance Tax Act of 2008
856(c)(8)	Temporary liberalization of REIT provisions for timber REITs	Tax years beginning after May 22, 2008	¶ 402 Heartland, Habitat, Harvest, and Horticulture Act of 2008
856(d)(8)(B)	Taxable REIT subsidiaries may hold health care facilities	Gains recognized after July 30, 2008	¶ 404 Housing Assistance Tax Act of 2008
856(d)(9)	Taxable REIT subsidiaries may hold health care facilities	Gains recognized after July 30, 2008	¶ 404 Housing Assistance Tax Act of 2008

Code	Topic	Effective Date	Complete Analysis
856(d)(9)(D)(ii)	Hotels and motels are lodging facilities for qualified REIT subsidiaries purposes regardless of whether rentals are transient	For tax years beginning after Dec. 31, 2007	¶ 1303 AMT Patch, Mortgage Relief, Energy, Technical Corrections, and Other Late 2007 Tax Acts
856(l)(3)	Taxable REIT subsidiaries may hold health care facilities	Gains recognized after July 30, 2008	¶ 404 Housing Assistance Tax Act of 2008
856(n)	Treatment of foreign currency gains for REIT income test purposes	Gains recognized after July 30, 2008	¶ 401 Housing Assistance Tax Act of 2008
857(b)(3)(A)(ii)	A temporary 15% tax rate is applied to a corporation's qualified timber gain for both regular tax and AMT purposes	Tax years ending after May 22, 2008 and beginning before May 23, 2009	¶ 401 Heartland, Habitat, Harvest, and Horticulture Act of 2008
857(b)(4)(B)(i)	Amendments to REIT prohibited transactions income rules	Gains recognized after July 30, 2008	¶ 403 Housing Assistance Tax Act of 2008
857(b)(6)(B)(i)	Amendments to REIT prohibited transactions income rules	Gains recognized after July 30, 2008	¶ 403 Housing Assistance Tax Act of 2008
857(b)(6)(C)	Amendments to REIT prohibited transactions income rules	Gains recognized after July 30, 2008	¶ 403 Housing Assistance Tax Act of 2008
857(b)(6)(D)	Amendments to REIT prohibited transactions income rules	Gains recognized after July 30, 2008	¶ 403 Housing Assistance Tax Act of 2008
857(b)(6)(D)(v)	Temporary liberalization of REIT prohibited transactions safe harbor for REIT timber properties	Dispositions in tax years beginning after May 22, 2008	¶ 403 Heartland, Habitat, Harvest, and Horticulture Act of 2008
857(b)(6)(G)	Temporary liberalization of REIT prohibited transactions safe harbor for REIT timber properties	Dispositions in tax years beginning after May 22, 2008	¶ 403 Heartland, Habitat, Harvest, and Horticulture Act of 2008
857(b)(6)(G)	Amendments to REIT prohibited transactions income rules	Gains recognized after July 30, 2008	¶ 403 Housing Assistance Tax Act of 2008

Code	Topic	Effective Date	Complete Analysis
857(b)(6)(H)	Temporary liberalization of REIT prohibited transactions safe harbor for REIT timber properties	Dispositions in tax years beginning after May 22, 2008	¶ 403 Heartland, Habitat, Harvest, and Horticulture Act of 2008
857(b)(6)(I)	Temporary liberalization of REIT prohibited transactions safe harbor for REIT timber properties	Dispositions in tax years beginning after May 22, 2008	¶ 403 Heartland, Habitat, Harvest, and Horticulture Act of 2008
857(c)(2)	Passthrough of qualified dividend income by RICs and REITs is extended for two years	Tax years beginning after Dec. 31, 2008 and before Jan. 1, 2011	¶ 110 Tax Increase Prevention and Reconciliation Act of 2005
864(f)	Election to allocate interest and certain other expenses on worldwide basis will be available after 2008	Tax years beginning after Dec. 31, 2008	¶ 731 American Jobs Creation Act of 2004
864(f)	Election will be available after 2008 to treat bank and financial holding companies as includible corporations if worldwide interest allocation election is made	Tax years beginning after Dec. 31, 2008	¶ 732 American Jobs Creation Act of 2004
864(f)(5)(D)	Election to allocate interest expense on a worldwide basis delayed until after 2010	Tax years beginning after Dec. 31, 2008	¶ 801 Housing Assistance Tax Act of 2008
864(f)(6)	Election to allocate interest expense on a worldwide basis delayed until after 2010	Tax years beginning after Dec. 31, 2008	¶ 801 Housing Assistance Tax Act of 2008
864(f)(7)	Election to allocate interest expense on a worldwide basis delayed until after 2010	Tax years beginning after Dec. 31, 2008	¶ 801 Housing Assistance Tax Act of 2008

Code	Topic	Effective Date	Complete Analysis
871(k)(1)(C)	Withholding tax exemption for RIC interest-related dividends and short-term capital gains dividends paid to foreign persons extended for tax years beginning in 2008 and 2009	Dividends for tax years of regulated investment companies beginning after Dec. 31, 2007 and before Jan. 1, 2010	¶ 327 Tax Provisions of H.R. 1424 (Including the Emergency Economic Stabilization, Energy Improvement and Extension, and Tax Extenders and AMT Relief Acts of 2008)
871(k)(2)(C)	Withholding tax exemption for RIC interest-related dividends and short-term capital gains dividends paid to foreign persons extended for tax years beginning in 2008 and 2009	Dividends for tax years of regulated investment companies beginning after Dec. 31, 2007 and before Jan. 1, 2010	¶ 327 Tax Provisions of H.R. 1424 (Including the Emergency Economic Stabilization, Energy Improvement and Extension, and Tax Extenders and AMT Relief Acts of 2008)
877(e)(1)	Expatriates recognize mark-to-market gain upon expatriation	Expatriations on or after June 17, 2008	¶ 301 Heroes Earnings Assistance and Relief Tax Act of 2008
877(h)	Expatriates recognize mark-to-market gain upon expatriation	Expatriations on or after June 17, 2008	¶ 301 Heroes Earnings Assistance and Relief Tax Act of 2008
877A	Election to defer the tax upon expatriation	Expatriations on or after June 17, 2008	¶ 302 Heroes Earnings Assistance and Relief Tax Act of 2008
877A	Exceptions for deferred compensation items, specified tax deferred accounts, and nongrantor trusts	Expatriations on or after June 17, 2008	¶ 303 Heroes Earnings Assistance and Relief Tax Act of 2008
877A	Expatriates recognize mark-to-market gain upon expatriation	Expatriations on or after June 17, 2008	¶ 301 Heroes Earnings Assistance and Relief Tax Act of 2008
897(h)(4)(A)(ii)	Inclusion of regulated investment company in definition of qualified investment entity extended through Dec. 31, 2009	Jan. 1, 2008 and before Jan. 1, 2010	¶ 329 Tax Provisions of H.R. 1424 (Including the Emergency Economic Stabilization, Energy Improvement and Extension, and Tax Extenders and AMT Relief Acts of 2008)

Code	Topic	Effective Date	Complete Analysis
904(i)	Hope credit is increased and expanded (and re-named the "American Opportunity Tax Credit") for 2009 and 2010	Tax years beginning in 2009 and 2010	¶ 107 American Recovery and Reinvestment Act of 2009
904(i)	Nonrefundable personal credits can offset AMT through 2009 (instead of 2008)	Tax years beginning in 2009	¶ 204 American Recovery and Reinvestment Act of 2009
904(i)	Alternative motor vehicle credit (AMVC) is treated as a personal credit allowed against AMT for tax years beginning after 2008	Tax years beginning after Dec. 31, 2008	¶ 205 American Recovery and Reinvestment Act of 2009
904(i)	Nonrefundable personal credits can offset AMT through 2008 (instead of 2007)	Tax years beginning in 2008	¶ 102 Tax Provisions of H.R. 1424 (Including the Emergency Economic Stabilization, Energy Improvement and Extension, and Tax Extenders and AMT Relief Acts of 2008)
907(a)	Different treatment of foreign oil and gas extraction income (FOGEI) and foreign oil-related income (FORI) is eliminated	Tax years beginning after Dec. 31. 2008	¶ 802 Tax Provisions of H.R. 1424 (Including the Emergency Economic Stabilization, Energy Improvement and Extension, and Tax Extenders and AMT Relief Acts of 2008)
907(b)	Different treatment of foreign oil and gas extraction income (FOGEI) and foreign oil-related income (FORI) is eliminated	Tax years beginning after Dec. 31. 2008	¶ 802 Tax Provisions of H.R. 1424 (Including the Emergency Economic Stabilization, Energy Improvement and Extension, and Tax Extenders and AMT Relief Acts of 2008)

Code	Topic	Effective Date	Complete Analysis
907(c)(4)	Different treatment of foreign oil and gas extraction income (FOGEI) and foreign oil-related income (FORI) is eliminated	Tax years beginning after Dec. 31. 2008	¶ 802 Tax Provisions of H.R. 1424 (Including the Emergency Economic Stabilization, Energy Improvement and Extension, and Tax Extenders and AMT Relief Acts of 2008)
907(f)	Different treatment of foreign oil and gas extraction income (FOGEI) and foreign oil-related income (FORI) is eliminated	Tax years beginning after Dec. 31. 2	¶ 802 Tax Provisions of H.R. 1424 (Including the Emergency Economic Stabilization, Energy Improvement and Extension, and Tax Extenders and AMT Relief Acts of 2008)
953(e)(10)	Exceptions under Subpart F for active banking, financing and insurance income expiring after 2008 extended through tax years beginning before 2010	For tax years beginning after Dec. 31, 2008 and before Jan. 1, 2010	¶ 330 Tax Provisions of H.R. 1424 (Including the Emergency Economic Stabilization, Energy Improvement and Extension, and Tax Extenders and AMT Relief Acts of 2008)
954(c)(6)	Look-through treatment for payments between related CFCs under foreign personal holding company income rules extended through 2009	Tax years of foreign corporations beginning after Dec. 31, 2007 and before Jan. 1, 2010, and tax years of U.S. shareholders with or within which such tax years of foreign corporations end	¶ 331 Tax Provisions of H.R. 1424 (Including the Emergency Economic Stabilization, Energy Improvement and Extension, and Tax Extenders and AMT Relief Acts of 2008)
954(h)(9)	Exceptions under Subpart F for active banking, financing and insurance income expiring after 2008 extended through tax years beginning before 2010	For tax years beginning after Dec. 31, 2008 and before Jan. 1, 2010	¶ 330 Tax Provisions of H.R. 1424 (Including the Emergency Economic Stabilization, Energy Improvement and Extension, and Tax Extenders and AMT Relief Acts of 2008)

Code	Topic	Effective Date	Complete Analysis
1012(c)	Basis of securities sold, disposed of, or exchanged starting Jan. 1, 2011 will be determined on an account-by-account basis, but a fund or dividend reinvestment plan can elect to treat acquired shares as one account	Jan. 1, 2011	¶ 202 Tax Provisions of H.R. 1424 (Including the Emergency Economic Stabilization, Energy Improvement and Extension, and Tax Extenders and AMT Relief Acts of 2008)
1012(d)	Basis of securities sold, disposed of, or exchanged starting Jan. 1, 2011 will be determined on an account-by-account basis, but a fund or dividend reinvestment plan can elect to treat acquired shares as one account	Jan. 1, 2011	¶ 202 Tax Provisions of H.R. 1424 (Including the Emergency Economic Stabilization, Energy Improvement and Extension, and Tax Extenders and AMT Relief Acts of 2008)
1014(f)	Step-up basis and step-down basis will end and modified carryover basis rules will apply for property acquired from a deceased individual after Dec. 31, 2009	Estates of decedents dying after Dec. 31, 2009 for property acquired from a decedent dying after Dec. 31, 2009	¶ 326 Economic Growth and Tax Relief Reconciliation Act of 2001
1016(a)(25)	"New qualified plug-in electric drive motor vehicle credit" will be modified for vehicles acquired after Dec. 31, 2009	Vehicles acquired after Dec. 31, 2009	¶ 1002 American Recovery and Reinvestment Act of 2009
1016(a)(37)	"New qualified plug-in electric drive motor vehicle credit" is allowed for tax years beginning after Dec. 31, 2008 for property purchased before Jan. 1, 2015	Tax years beginning after Dec. 31, 2008 for property purchased before Jan. 1, 2015	¶ 926 Tax Provisions of H.R. 1424 (Including the Emergency Economic Stabilization, Energy Improvement and Extension, and Tax Extenders and AMT Relief Acts of 2008)

Code	Topic	Effective Date	Complete Analysis
1022	Step-up basis and step-down basis will end and modified carryover basis rules will apply for property acquired from a deceased individual after Dec. 31, 2009	Estates of decedents dying after Dec. 31, 2009 for property acquired from a decedent dying after Dec. 31, 2009	¶ 326 Economic Growth and Tax Relief Reconciliation Act of 2001
1022(g)	Liabilities in excess of the basis of property acquired from a decedent or an estate will be excluded from gain and basis after Dec. 31, 2009	Estates of decedents dying after Dec. 31, 2009	¶ 327 Economic Growth and Tax Relief Reconciliation Act of 2001
1031(i)	Like-kind exchanges of stock in mutual ditch, reservoir, or irrigation companies can qualify for nonrecognition of gain or loss	Exchanges completed after May 22, 2008	¶ 501 Heartland, Habitat, Harvest, and Horticulture Act of 2008
1033(a)(2)(B)(i)	Replacement period is extended to five years (from two years) for involuntarily converted property located in the Kansas disaster area	May 22, 2008	¶ 606 Heartland, Habitat, Harvest, and Horticulture Act of 2008
1033(a)(2)(B)(i)	Replacement period is extended to five years (from two years) for involuntarily converted property located in the Midwestern disaster area on or after the applicable disaster date	Property that was compulsorily or involuntarily converted on or after the applicable disaster date	¶ 1240 Tax Provisions of H.R. 1424 (Including the Emergency Economic Stabilization, Energy Improvement and Extension, and Tax Extenders and AMT Relief Acts of 2008)
1033(h)(1)	Changes are made to the involuntary conversion rules and other Code provisions to reflect new definition of "federally declared disaster"	Disasters declared in tax years beginning after Dec. 31, 2007, and occurring before Jan. 1, 2010	¶ 1203 Tax Provisions of H.R. 1424 (Including the Emergency Economic Stabilization, Energy Improvement and Extension, and Tax Extenders and AMT Relief Acts of 2008)

Code	Topic	Effective Date	Complete Analysis
1033(h)(2)	Changes are made to the involuntary conversion rules and other Code provisions to reflect new definition of "federally declared disaster"	Disasters declared in tax years beginning after Dec. 31, 2007, and occurring before Jan. 1, 2010	¶ 1203 Tax Provisions of H.R. 1424 (Including the Emergency Economic Stabilization, Energy Improvement and Extension, and Tax Extenders and AMT Relief Acts of 2008)
1033(h)(3)	Changes are made to the involuntary conversion rules and other Code provisions to reflect new definition of "federally declared disaster"	Disasters declared in tax years beginning after Dec. 31, 2007, and occurring before Jan. 1, 2010	¶ 1203 Tax Provisions of H.R. 1424 (Including the Emergency Economic Stabilization, Energy Improvement and Extension, and Tax Extenders and AMT Relief Acts of 2008)
1035(a)	Qualified long-term care insurance can be provided as a rider to an annuity contract after 2009	Tax years beginning after 2009	¶ 2402 Pension Protection Act of 2006
1035(a)(4)	Qualified long-term care insurance can be provided as a rider to an annuity contract after 2009	Tax years beginning after 2009	¶ 2402 Pension Protection Act of 2006
1035(b)(2)	Qualified long-term care insurance can be provided as a rider to an annuity contract after 2009	Tax years beginning after 2009	¶ 2402 Pension Protection Act of 2006
1035(b)(3)	Qualified long-term care insurance can be provided as a rider to an annuity contract after 2009	Tax years beginning after 2009	¶ 2402 Pension Protection Act of 2006
1040	Beginning in 2010, an estate or trust will recognize gain if it distributes appreciated property to satisfy a pecuniary bequest, but only to the extent the property has appreciated between the dates of death and of distribution	Estates of decedents dying after Dec. 31, 2009	¶ 328 Economic Growth and Tax Relief Reconciliation Act of 2001

Code	Topic	Effective Date	Complete Analysis
1201(b)	A temporary 15% tax rate is applied to a corporation's qualified timber gain for both regular tax and AMT purposes	Tax years ending after May 22, 2008 and beginning before May 23, 2009	¶ 401 Heartland, Habitat, Harvest, and Horticulture Act of 2008
1202(a)(3)	Noncorporate taxpayers can exclude 75% (rather than 50% or 60%) of gain on the sale or exchange of QSBS held for more than 5 years and acquired after Feb. 17, 2009 and before Jan. 1, 2011	Stock acquired after Feb. 17, 2009 and before Jan. 1, 2011	¶ 902 American Recovery and Reinvestment Act of 2009
1221	Gain or loss from the sale or exchange of certain preferred stock is treated as ordinary income or loss after Dec. 31, 2007	Sales or exchanges after Dec. 31, 2007, in tax years ending after Dec. 31, 2007	¶ 205 Tax Provisions of H.R. 1424 (Including the Emergency Economic Stabilization, Energy Improvement and Extension, and Tax Extenders and AMT Relief Acts of 2008)
1221(a)(3)(C)	Capital gain treatment for inherited artwork or similar property will not be disallowed after 2009 solely because heir to property takes decedent's carryover basis	Estates of decedents dying after Dec. 31, 2009	¶ 329 Economic Growth and Tax Relief Reconciliation Act of 2001
1246(e)	Basis reduction for foreign investment company stock acquired from decedent repealed after 2009	Estates of decedents dying after 2009	¶ 312 Economic Growth and Tax Relief Reconciliation Act of 2001
1250(b)(3)	No recapture of additional depreciation for energy efficient commercial building property deduction	Property placed in service after Dec. 31, 2005	¶ 703 Gulf Opportunity Zone and Katrina Emergency Tax Relief Acts of 2005

Code	Topic	Effective Date	Complete Analysis
1367(a)(2)	Rule that S corporation's charitable contribution of property reduces shareholder's basis only by contributed property's basis extended for tax years beginning in 2008 and 2009	Contributions made in tax years beginning after Dec. 31, 2007 and before Jan. 1, 2010	¶ 322 Tax Provisions of H.R. 1424 (Including the Emergency Economic Stabilization, Energy Improvement and Extension, and Tax Extenders and AMT Relief Acts of 2008)
1374(d)(7)	S Corp built-in gain holding period shortened for 2009 and 2010	Tax years beginning after Dec. 31, 2008	¶ 903 American Recovery and Reinvestment Act of 2009
1397E(c)(2)	New tax credit bond option is added for "Build America Bonds" issued in 2009 and 2010; issuer may claim alternative, refundable credit for "qualified bonds"	Obligations issued after Feb. 17, 2009 and before Jan. 1, 2011	¶ 1301 American Recovery and Reinvestment Act of 2009
1397E(c)(2)	Nonrefundable tax credit will be allowed to holders of qualified forestry conservation bonds	Obligations issued after May 22, 2008	¶ 307 Heartland, Habitat, Harvest, and Horticulture Act of 2008
1400(f)(1)	DC Enterprise Zone and enterprise community designations are extended for one year through Dec. 31, 2009	Periods beginning after Dec. 31, 2007 and ending before Jan. 1, 2010	¶ 319 Tax Provisions of H.R. 1424 (Including the Emergency Economic Stabilization, Energy Improvement and Extension, and Tax Extenders and AMT Relief Acts of 2008)
1400(f)(2)	DC Enterprise Zone and enterprise community designations are extended for one year through Dec. 31, 2009	Periods beginning after Dec. 31, 2007 and ending before Jan. 1, 2010	¶ 319 Tax Provisions of H.R. 1424 (Including the Emergency Economic Stabilization, Energy Improvement and Extension, and Tax Extenders and AMT Relief Acts of 2008)

Code	Topic	Effective Date	Complete Analysis
1400A(b)	Higher tax-exempt enterprise zone facility bond limit for DC Zone bonds is extended to apply to bonds issued before Jan. 1, 2010	Bonds issued after Dec. 31, 2007 and before Jan. 1, 2010	¶ 1105 Tax Provisions of H.R. 1424 (Including the Emergency Economic Stabilization, Energy Improvement and Extension, and Tax Extenders and AMT Relief Acts of 2008)
1400B(b)(2)(A)(i)	Zero percent capital gains rate for DC Zone assets is extended for two years to apply to assets acquired before Jan. 1, 2010, and thus includes gain attributable to the period before Jan. 1, 2015	Acquisitions after Dec. 31, 2007 and before Jan. 1, 2010	¶ 320 Tax Provisions of H.R. 1424 (Including the Emergency Economic Stabilization, Energy Improvement and Extension, and Tax Extenders and AMT Relief Acts of 2008)
1400B(b)(3)(A)	Zero percent capital gains rate for DC Zone assets is extended for two years to apply to assets acquired before Jan. 1, 2010, and thus includes gain attributable to the period before Jan. 1, 2015	Acquisitions after Dec. 31, 2007 and before Jan. 1, 2010	¶ 320 Tax Provisions of H.R. 1424 (Including the Emergency Economic Stabilization, Energy Improvement and Extension, and Tax Extenders and AMT Relief Acts of 2008)
1400B(b)(4)(A)(i)	Zero percent capital gains rate for DC Zone assets is extended for two years to apply to assets acquired before Jan. 1, 2010, and thus includes gain attributable to the period before Jan. 1, 2015	Acquisitions after Dec. 31, 2007 and before Jan. 1, 2010	¶ 320 Tax Provisions of H.R. 1424 (Including the Emergency Economic Stabilization, Energy Improvement and Extension, and Tax Extenders and AMT Relief Acts of 2008)
1400B(b)(4)(B)(i)(I)	Zero percent capital gains rate for DC Zone assets is extended for two years to apply to assets acquired before Jan. 1, 2010, and thus includes gain attributable to the period before Jan. 1, 2015	Acquisitions after Dec. 31, 2007 and before Jan. 1, 2010	¶ 320 Tax Provisions of H.R. 1424 (Including the Emergency Economic Stabilization, Energy Improvement and Extension, and Tax Extenders and AMT Relief Acts of 2008)

Code	Topic	Effective Date	Complete Analysis
1400B(e)(2)	Zero percent capital gains rate for DC Zone assets is extended for two years to apply to assets acquired before Jan. 1, 2010, and thus includes gain attributable to the period before Jan. 1, 2015	Acquisitions after Dec. 31, 2007 and before Jan. 1, 2010	¶ 320 Tax Provisions of H.R. 1424 (Including the Emergency Economic Stabilization, Energy Improvement and Extension, and Tax Extenders and AMT Relief Acts of 2008)
1400B(g)(2)	Zero percent capital gains rate for DC Zone assets is extended for two years to apply to assets acquired before Jan. 1, 2010, and thus includes gain attributable to the period before Jan. 1, 2015	Acquisitions after Dec. 31, 2007 and before Jan. 1, 2010	¶ 320 Tax Provisions of H.R. 1424 (Including the Emergency Economic Stabilization, Energy Improvement and Extension, and Tax Extenders and AMT Relief Acts of 2008)
1400C(d)	Nonrefundable personal credits can offset AMT through 2009 (instead of 2008)	Tax years beginning in 2009	¶ 204 American Recovery and Reinvestment Act of 2009
1400C(d)	Nonrefundable personal credits can offset AMT through 2008 (instead of 2007)	Tax years beginning in 2008	¶ 102 Tax Provisions of H.R. 1424 (Including the Emergency Economic Stabilization, Energy Improvement and Extension, and Tax Extenders and AMT Relief Acts of 2008)
1400C(d)(2)	Hope credit is increased and expanded (and re-named the "American Opportunity Tax Credit") for 2009 and 2010	Tax years beginning in 2009 and 2010	¶ 107 American Recovery and Reinvestment Act of 2009
1400C(d)(2)	Alternative motor vehicle credit (AMVC) is treated as a personal credit allowed against AMT for tax years beginning after 2008	Tax years beginning after Dec. 31, 2008	¶ 205 American Recovery and Reinvestment Act of 2009

Code	Topic	Effective Date	Complete Analysis
1400C(d)(2)	"New qualified plug-in electric drive motor vehicle credit" is allowed for tax years beginning after Dec. 31, 2008 for property purchased before Jan. 1, 2015	Tax years beginning after Dec. 31, 2008 for property purchased before Jan. 1, 2015	¶ 926 Tax Provisions of H.R. 1424 (Including the Emergency Economic Stabilization, Energy Improvement and Extension, and Tax Extenders and AMT Relief Acts of 2008)
1400C(e)(4)	First-time homebuyer credit extended to residences purchased before Dec. 1, 2009 and increased to $8,000 ($4,000 for married filing separately); credit recapture waived, unless the residence is sold or ceases to be a principal residence within 36 months of purchase	Residences purchased after Dec. 31, 2008 and before Dec. 1, 2009	¶ 104 American Recovery and Reinvestment Act of 2009
1400C(i)	Credit for first time DC homebuyer is extended for two years to property bought before Jan. 1, 2010	Property bought after Dec. 31, 2007 and before Jan. 1, 2010	¶ 509 Tax Provisions of H.R. 1424 (Including the Emergency Economic Stabilization, Energy Improvement and Extension, and Tax Extenders and AMT Relief Acts of 2008)
1400N(a)	Tax-exempt bond financing for Midwestern disaster area for bonds issued after Oct. 3, 2008 and before 2013	For bonds issued after Oct. 3, 2008	¶ 1213 Tax Provisions of H.R. 1424 (Including the Emergency Economic Stabilization, Energy Improvement and Extension, and Tax Extenders and AMT Relief Acts of 2008)
1400N(a)	Issuance of tax-exempt bonds is permitted through Dec. 31, 2012 to finance construction and rehabilitation of property damaged by Hurricane Ike	Oct. 3, 2008, for bonds issued before Jan. 1, 2013	¶ 1106 Tax Provisions of H.R. 1424 (Including the Emergency Economic Stabilization, Energy Improvement and Extension, and Tax Extenders and AMT Relief Acts of 2008)

Code	Topic	Effective Date	Complete Analysis
1400N(c)	Additional low-income housing limitations for Midwestern disaster area for 2008 through 2010	For the 2008, 2009 and 2010 calendar years	¶ 1215 Tax Provisions of H.R. 1424 (Including the Emergency Economic Stabilization, Energy Improvement and Extension, and Tax Extenders and AMT Relief Acts of 2008)
1400N(c)	Additional allocations of low income housing credit are available for the "Hurricane Ike disaster area" for calendar years 2008, 2009 and 2010	Calendar years 2008, 2009 and 2010	¶ 1210 Tax Provisions of H.R. 1424 (Including the Emergency Economic Stabilization, Energy Improvement and Extension, and Tax Extenders and AMT Relief Acts of 2008)
1400N(d)(3)(B)	Dec. 31, 2007 deadline to start manufacture, construction or production of certain "qualified GO Zone property" is retroactively eliminated	Property placed in service after Dec. 31, 2007	¶ 601 Housing Assistance Tax Act of 2008
1400N(d)(6)(E)	50% bonus depreciation and AMT depreciation relief are revived for most new tangible personal property and software and certain leasehold improvements acquired during 2008	Property acquired and placed in service during calendar year 2008	¶ 202 Economic Stimulus Act of 2008
1400N(f)	Taxpayers may elect to expense 50% of demolition and debris-removal costs paid or incurred in the Midwestern disaster area on or after the applicable disaster date and before Jan. 1, 2011	Amounts paid or incurred on or after the applicable disaster date and before Jan. 1, 2011	¶ 1216 Tax Provisions of H.R. 1424 (Including the Emergency Economic Stabilization, Energy Improvement and Extension, and Tax Extenders and AMT Relief Acts of 2008)

Code	Topic	Effective Date	Complete Analysis
1400N(g)	Expensing of qualified environmental remediation expenditures is extended through Dec. 31, 2010 and modified as applied to the Midwestern disaster area	Amounts paid or incurred during the period beginning on the applicable disaster date and ending on Dec. 31, 2010	¶ 1217 Tax Provisions of H.R. 1424 (Including the Emergency Economic Stabilization, Energy Improvement and Extension, and Tax Extenders and AMT Relief Acts of 2008)
1400N(h)	Increased rehabilitation credit for qualified structures in the Gulf Opportunity (GO) Zone is extended for one year to Dec. 31, 2009	Expenditures paid or incurred after Oct. 3, 2008 and before Jan. 1, 2010	¶ 1209 Tax Provisions of H.R. 1424 (Including the Emergency Economic Stabilization, Energy Improvement and Extension, and Tax Extenders and AMT Relief Acts of 2008)
1400N(h)	Rehabilitation credit for expenditures for qualified rehabilitated structures and certified historic structures in the Midwestern disaster area increased for period beginning on the applicable disaster date and ending on Dec. 31, 2011	Amounts paid or incurred during the period beginning on the applicable disaster date and ending on Dec. 31, 2011	¶ 1218 Tax Provisions of H.R. 1424 (Including the Emergency Economic Stabilization, Energy Improvement and Extension, and Tax Extenders and AMT Relief Acts of 2008)
1400N(k)	NOL carryback period is extended from two to five years for Midwestern disaster area losses incurred on or after the applicable disaster date and before 2011	Amounts paid or incurred on or after the applicable disaster date and before Jan. 1, 2011	¶ 1219 Tax Provisions of H.R. 1424 (Including the Emergency Economic Stabilization, Energy Improvement and Extension, and Tax Extenders and AMT Relief Acts of 2008)
1400N(k)(1)(B)	100% (instead of 90%) ATNOLD is allowed for Midwestern disaster area loss amounts paid or incurred on or after the applicable disaster date and before 2011	Amounts paid or incurred on or after the applicable disaster date and before 2011	¶ 1220 Tax Provisions of H.R. 1424 (Including the Emergency Economic Stabilization, Energy Improvement and Extension, and Tax Extenders and AMT Relief Acts of 2008)

Code	Topic	Effective Date	Complete Analysis
1400N(l)	Tax credit bond financing for Midwestern disaster area for bonds issued after Dec. 31, 2008 and before 2010	For bonds issued after Dec. 31, 2008 and before Jan. 1, 2010	¶ 1221 Tax Provisions of H.R. 1424 (Including the Emergency Economic Stabilization, Energy Improvement and Extension, and Tax Extenders and AMT Relief Acts of 2008)
1400N(l)(3)(B)	New tax credit bond option is added for "Build America Bonds" issued in 2009 and 2010; issuer may claim alternative, refundable credit for "qualified bonds"	Obligations issued after Feb. 17, 2009 and before Jan. 1, 2011	¶ 1301 American Recovery and Reinvestment Act of 2009
1400N(l)(3)(B)	Nonrefundable tax credit will be allowed to holders of qualified forestry conservation bonds	Obligations issued after May 22, 2008	¶ 307 Heartland, Habitat, Harvest, and Horticulture Act of 2008
1400N(n)	Reliance on representations of tenants displaced in the Kansas Disaster Area is allowed in determining compliance with income limits, etc. for qualified residential rental project bonds	May 22, 2008	¶ 616 Heartland, Habitat, Harvest, and Horticulture Act of 2008
1400N(n)	Reliance on representations of tenants displaced in the Midwestern disaster area is allowed in determining compliance with income limits, etc. for qualified residential rental project bonds	Oct. 3, 2008	¶ 1214 Tax Provisions of H.R. 1424 (Including the Emergency Economic Stabilization, Energy Improvement and Extension, and Tax Extenders and AMT Relief Acts of 2008)

Code	Topic	Effective Date	Complete Analysis
1400N(o)	Taxpayers may elect to deduct public utility property losses attributable to May 4, 2007 Kansas storms and tornadoes in fifth tax year before year of loss	May 22, 2008	¶ 610 Heartland, Habitat, Harvest, and Horticulture Act of 2008
1400O	Hope credit and Lifetime Learning credit maximums are doubled for higher education expenses of students attending eligible education institutions located in the Midwestern disaster area in 2008 and 2009	Tax years beginning in 2008 and 2009	¶ 1222 Tax Provisions of H.R. 1424 (Including the Emergency Economic Stabilization, Energy Improvement and Extension, and Tax Extenders and AMT Relief Acts of 2008)
1400P	Employer housing credit for lodging provided to employees and their families by employers in the Midwestern disaster area for six-month period	Lodging furnished during the period (1) beginning on Nov. 1, 2008 and (2) ending on May 1, 2009	¶ 1224 Tax Provisions of H.R. 1424 (Including the Emergency Economic Stabilization, Energy Improvement and Extension, and Tax Extenders and AMT Relief Acts of 2008)
1400P	Value of lodging provided to employees and their families is excluded from employees' income for employees in the Midwestern disaster area for six-month period	Lodging furnished beginning on Nov. 1, 2008 and ending on May 1, 2009	¶ 1223 Tax Provisions of H.R. 1424 (Including the Emergency Economic Stabilization, Energy Improvement and Extension, and Tax Extenders and AMT Relief Acts of 2008)
1400Q	Tax relief for "qualified Disaster Recovery Assistance distributions" made under an eligible retirement plan for individuals living in the "Midwestern disaster area" during 2008 Midwestern storms	Oct. 3, 2008	¶ 1225 Tax Provisions of H.R. 1424 (Including the Emergency Economic Stabilization, Energy Improvement and Extension, and Tax Extenders and AMT Relief Acts of 2008)

Code	Topic	Effective Date	Complete Analysis
1400Q	Recontributions of retirement plan withdrawals taken for home purchases that were cancelled because of 2008 Midwestern storms, tornados, and flooding, which entitle the withdrawals to tax-free treatment	Oct. 3, 2008	¶ 1226 Tax Provisions of H.R. 1424 (Including the Emergency Economic Stabilization, Energy Improvement and Extension, and Tax Extenders and AMT Relief Acts of 2008)
1400Q	Plan loan limits increased and repayment deadlines postponed for individuals who sustained loss due to 2008 Midwestern storms, tornados and flooding	Oct. 3, 2008	¶ 1227 Tax Provisions of H.R. 1424 (Including the Emergency Economic Stabilization, Energy Improvement and Extension, and Tax Extenders and AMT Relief Acts of 2008)
1400Q	Relief for qualified retirement plans due to 2008 Midwestern storms, tornados, and flooding can take effect before plan amendments are adopted-for retroactive amendments made before 2011 plan year	Oct. 3, 2008	¶ 1228 Tax Provisions of H.R. 1424 (Including the Emergency Economic Stabilization, Energy Improvement and Extension, and Tax Extenders and AMT Relief Acts of 2008)
1400R(a)	Employee retention credit is allowed for the Midwestern disaster area for 40% of up to $6,000 of qualified wages for each eligible employee for qualified wages paid or incurred after the applicable disaster date and before Jan. 1, 2009	For qualified wages paid or incurred after the applicable disaster date and before Jan. 1, 2009	¶ 1229 Tax Provisions of H.R. 1424 (Including the Emergency Economic Stabilization, Energy Improvement and Extension, and Tax Extenders and AMT Relief Acts of 2008)

Code	Topic	Effective Date	Complete Analysis
1400S(a)	Temporary suspension of limitations on charitable deductions is extended to the Midwestern disaster area for 2008	For contributions beginning on the earliest applicable disaster date for all States and ending on Dec. 31, 2008	¶ 1230 Tax Provisions of H.R. 1424 (Including the Emergency Economic Stabilization, Energy Improvement and Extension, and Tax Extenders and AMT Relief Acts of 2008)
1400S(b)	Suspension of certain limitations on personal casualty losses is extended to the Midwestern disaster area	For casualty losses arising on or after the applicable disaster date	¶ 1231 Tax Provisions of H.R. 1424 (Including the Emergency Economic Stabilization, Energy Improvement and Extension, and Tax Extenders and AMT Relief Acts of 2008)
1400S(c)	Disaster relief for filing and payment of taxes is extended to the Midwestern disaster area	Oct. 3, 2008	¶ 1232 Tax Provisions of H.R. 1424 (Including the Emergency Economic Stabilization, Energy Improvement and Extension, and Tax Extenders and AMT Relief Acts of 2008)
1400S(d)	Look-back election for earned income credit and refundable child credit extended to Midwestern disaster area	Tax years that include the applicable date	¶ 1233 Tax Provisions of H.R. 1424 (Including the Emergency Economic Stabilization, Energy Improvement and Extension, and Tax Extenders and AMT Relief Acts of 2008)
1400S(e)	IRS authority to adjust rules to prevent loss of deductions, credits, and favorable filing status due to temporary relocations is extended to the Midwestern disaster area for tax years 2008 and 2009	Tax years beginning after Dec. 31, 2007 and before Jan. 1, 2010	¶ 1234 Tax Provisions of H.R. 1424 (Including the Emergency Economic Stabilization, Energy Improvement and Extension, and Tax Extenders and AMT Relief Acts of 2008)

Code	Topic	Effective Date	Complete Analysis
1400T	Qualified mortgage bond rules liberalized for Midwestern disaster area	Financing provided on or after Oct. 3, 2008 and before Jan. 1, 2011	¶ 1235 Tax Provisions of H.R. 1424 (Including the Emergency Economic Stabilization, Energy Improvement and Extension, and Tax Extenders and AMT Relief Acts of 2008)
1400U-1	Overview of national limits on two new categories of recovery zone bonds issued in 2009 and 2010 which are allocated among States based on 2008 employment declines subject to a minimum allocation	Obligations issued after Feb. 17, 2009 and before 2011	¶ 1304 American Recovery and Reinvestment Act of 2009
1400U-1	National limits for recovery zone economic development bonds and recovery zone facility bonds issued in 2009 and 2010 are allocated among States based on their 2008 employment declines subject to a minimum allocation	Obligations issued after Feb. 17, 2009 and before 2011	¶ 1305 American Recovery and Reinvestment Act of 2009
1400U-2	Overview of national limits on two new categories of recovery zone bonds issued in 2009 and 2010 which are allocated among States based on 2008 employment declines subject to a minimum allocation	Obligations issued after Feb. 17, 2009 and before 2011	¶ 1304 American Recovery and Reinvestment Act of 2009
1400U-2	U.S. Treasury will pay the issuer 45% of the interest the issuer pays to the holder of a taxable recovery zone economic development bond issued before 2011	Obligations issued after Feb. 17, 2009 and before 2011	¶ 1306 American Recovery and Reinvestment Act of 2009

Code	Topic	Effective Date	Complete Analysis
1400U-2	Prevailing wage requirements are applied to projects financed with specified bonds	Bonds issued after Feb. 17, 2009	¶ 1311 American Recovery and Reinvestment Act of 2009
1400U-3	Overview of national limits on two new categories of recovery zone bonds issued in 2009 and 2010 which are allocated among States based on 2008 employment declines subject to a minimum allocation	Obligations issued after Feb. 17, 2009 and before 2011	¶ 1304 American Recovery and Reinvestment Act of 2009
1400U-3	Recovery zone facility bonds are authorized for issuance in 2009 and 2010	Obligations issued after Feb. 17, 2009 and before 2011	¶ 1307 American Recovery and Reinvestment Act of 2009
1402(a)	Dollar thresholds for optional methods of computing net earnings from self-employment are increased to $4,200 and $6,300 (from $1,600 and $2,400) for 2008 and then indexed for inflation	Tax years beginning after Dec. 31, 2007	¶ 201 Heartland, Habitat, Harvest, and Horticulture Act of 2008
1402(a)(1)	Conservation Reserve Program payments made to retired or disabled farmers aren't subject to self-employment tax	Payments made after Dec. 31, 2007	¶ 202 Heartland, Habitat, Harvest, and Horticulture Act of 2008
1402(l)	Dollar thresholds for optional methods of computing net earnings from self-employment are increased to $4,200 and $6,300 (from $1,600 and $2,400) for 2008 and then indexed for inflation	Tax years beginning after Dec. 31, 2007	¶ 201 Heartland, Habitat, Harvest, and Horticulture Act of 2008
1445(b)(7)	Changes in nonforeign affidavit requirements on transfers of USRPIs	Dispositions of USRPI after July 30, 2008	¶ 802 Housing Assistance Tax Act of 2008

Code	Topic	Effective Date	Complete Analysis
1445(b)(9)	Changes in nonforeign affidavit requirements on transfers of USRPIs	Dispositions of USRPI after July 30, 2008	¶ 802 Housing Assistance Tax Act of 2008
1445(d)(1)	Changes in nonforeign affidavit requirements on transfers of USRPIs	Dispositions of USRPI after July 30, 2008	¶ 802 Housing Assistance Tax Act of 2008
1445(d)(2)	Changes in nonforeign affidavit requirements on transfers of USRPIs	Dispositions of USRPI after July 30, 2008	¶ 802 Housing Assistance Tax Act of 2008
1445(e)(1)	15% withholding rate that IRS may impose on USRPI gains passed through to foreign persons by U.S. partnerships, trusts or estates is extended for two years	Tax years beginning after Dec. 31, 2008 and before Jan. 1, 2011	¶ 105 Tax Increase Prevention and Reconciliation Act of 2005
1445(f)(6)	Changes in nonforeign affidavit requirements on transfers of USRPIs	Dispositions of USRPI after July 30, 2008	¶ 802 Housing Assistance Tax Act of 2008
2105(d)(3)	Estate tax look-through rule for RIC stock owned by nonresident aliens is extended through 2009	Applies to decedents dying after Dec. 31, 2007 and before Jan. 1, 2010	¶ 328 Tax Provisions of H.R. 1424 (Including the Emergency Economic Stabilization, Energy Improvement and Extension, and Tax Extenders and AMT Relief Acts of 2008)
2210	Estate tax will be repealed after 2009	For estates of decedents dying after Dec. 31, 2009	¶ 306 Economic Growth and Tax Relief Reconciliation Act of 2001
2502(a)	Top gift tax rate will be reduced to the top individual income tax rate of 35% on the repeal of the estate tax after 2009	For gifts made after Dec. 31, 2009	¶ 308 Economic Growth and Tax Relief Reconciliation Act of 2001
2511	Transfers to non-grantor trusts will be treated as gifts after 2009	For gifts made after Dec. 31, 2009	¶ 310 Economic Growth and Tax Relief Reconciliation Act of 2001

Code	Topic	Effective Date	Complete Analysis
2511(c)	Provision governing transfers to non-grantor trusts after 2009 clarified; these transfers will be treated as transfers of property by gift	For gifts made after Dec. 31, 2009	¶ 702 Job Creation and Worker Assistance Act of 2002
2664	Generation-skipping transfer (GST) tax will be repealed after 2009	For GSTs made after Dec. 31, 2009	¶ 307 Economic Growth and Tax Relief Reconciliation Act of 2001
2801	New transfer tax is imposed on U.S. citizens and residents who receive gifts and bequests from expat	Applies to covered gifts and bequests received on or after June 17, 2008	¶ 304 Heroes Earnings Assistance and Relief Tax Act of 2008
3121(a)(23)	Tax relief and expense payments provided by state or local governments to volunteer emergency responders aren't subject to withholding or employment taxes	Tax years beginning after Dec. 31, 2007 and before Jan. 1, 2011	¶ 603 Heroes Earnings Assistance and Relief Tax Act of 2008
3121(z)	FICA taxes are imposed on wages for services performed abroad under U.S. government contracts by U.S. citizens and residents employed by U.S.-controlled foreign persons	Services performed in calendar months beginning more than 30 days after June 17, 2008	¶ 601 Heroes Earnings Assistance and Relief Tax Act of 2008
3301	Additional 0.2% FUTA surtax is extended to apply through 2009	For wages paid after Dec. 31, 2008, and before 2010	¶ 1401 Tax Provisions of H.R. 1424 (Including the Emergency Economic Stabilization, Energy Improvement and Extension, and Tax Extenders and AMT Relief Acts of 2008)
3301	Additional 0.2% FUTA surtax is extended to apply through 2008	Wages paid in 2008	¶ 1201 AMT Patch, Mortgage Relief, Energy, Technical Corrections, and Other Late 2007 Tax Acts

Code	Topic	Effective Date	Complete Analysis
3306(b)(20)	Tax relief and expense payments provided by state or local governments to volunteer emergency responders aren't subject to withholding or employment taxes	Tax years beginning after Dec. 31, 2007 and before Jan. 1, 2011	¶ 603 Heroes Earnings Assistance and Relief Tax Act of 2008
3401(a)(23)	Tax relief and expense payments provided by state or local governments to volunteer emergency responders aren't subject to withholding or employment taxes	Tax years beginning after Dec. 31, 2007 and before Jan. 1, 2011	¶ 603 Heroes Earnings Assistance and Relief Tax Act of 2008
3401(h)	Differential military pay will be treated as wages for income tax withholding purposes after 2008	Remuneration paid after Dec. 31, 2008	¶ 602 Heroes Earnings Assistance and Relief Tax Act of 2008
3402(t)	Withholding tax on government contractors delayed for one year until 2012	Feb. 17, 2009	¶ 703 American Recovery and Reinvestment Act of 2009
3402(t)	Government entities will have to report and withhold income tax on certain payments made after 2010	For payments made after Dec. 31, 2010	¶ 802 Tax Increase Prevention and Reconciliation Act of 2005
3406(b)(3)(F)	Reportable payment transactions will be subject to backup withholding beginning in 2012	For amounts paid after Dec. 31, 2011	¶ 303 Housing Assistance Tax Act of 2008
4053(9)	Idling reduction units and advanced insulation are exempted from the retail truck excise tax	Sales or installations after Oct. 3, 2008	¶ 1503 Tax Provisions of H.R. 1424 (Including the Emergency Economic Stabilization, Energy Improvement and Extension, and Tax Extenders and AMT Relief Acts of 2008)

Code	Topic	Effective Date	Complete Analysis
4053(10)	Idling reduction units and advanced insulation are exempted from the retail truck excise tax	Sales or installations after Oct. 3, 2008	¶ 1503 Tax Provisions of H.R. 1424 (Including the Emergency Economic Stabilization, Energy Improvement and Extension, and Tax Extenders and AMT Relief Acts of 2008)
4101(a)(1)	Credit of $1.01 per gallon is allowed for qualified cellulosic biofuel produced after Dec. 31, 2008 and before Jan. 1, 2013	Qualified cellulosic biofuel produced after Dec. 31, 2008 and before Jan. 1, 2013	¶ 302 Heartland, Habitat, Harvest, and Horticulture Act of 2008
4121(e)(2)(A)	Reduction in coal excise tax rates from $1.10/55¢ per ton to 50¢/25¢ per ton is postponed until Jan. 1, 2019 (from Jan. 1, 2014)	Oct. 3, 2008	¶ 1501 Tax Provisions of H.R. 1424 (Including the Emergency Economic Stabilization, Energy Improvement and Extension, and Tax Extenders and AMT Relief Acts of 2008)
4121(e)(2)(B)	Reduction in coal excise tax rates from $1.10/55¢ per ton to 50¢/25¢ per ton is postponed until Jan. 1, 2019 (from Jan. 1, 2014)	Oct. 3, 2008	¶ 1501 Tax Provisions of H.R. 1424 (Including the Emergency Economic Stabilization, Energy Improvement and Extension, and Tax Extenders and AMT Relief Acts of 2008)
4161(b)(2)(B)	Wooden arrows designed for use by children are exempted from manufacturer's excise tax on arrows	Shafts first sold after Oct. 3, 2008	¶ 1505 Tax Provisions of H.R. 1424 (Including the Emergency Economic Stabilization, Energy Improvement and Extension, and Tax Extenders and AMT Relief Acts of 2008)

Code	Topic	Effective Date	Complete Analysis
4611(c)(2)(B)	Oil spill liability excise tax is extended to apply through Dec. 31, 2017, and is increased (from 5¢ per barrel) to 8¢ from Jan. 1, 2009 through 2016, and to 9¢ for 2017	For rate increase Jan. 1, 2009; for extension of tax, Oct. 3, 2008	¶ 1504 Tax Provisions of H.R. 1424 (Including the Emergency Economic Stabilization, Energy Improvement and Extension, and Tax Extenders and AMT Relief Acts of 2008)
4611(f)(2)	Oil spill liability excise tax is extended to apply through Dec. 31, 2017, and is increased (from 5¢ per barrel) to 8¢ from Jan. 1, 2009 through 2016, and to 9¢ for 2017	For rate increase Jan. 1, 2009; for extension of tax, Oct. 3, 2008	¶ 1504 Tax Provisions of H.R. 1424 (Including the Emergency Economic Stabilization, Energy Improvement and Extension, and Tax Extenders and AMT Relief Acts of 2008)
4971(a)	Excise tax on failure to meet minimum funding standards integrated with new funding rules	Plan years beginning after 2007	¶ 505 Pension Protection Act of 2006
4971(b)	Excise tax on failure to meet minimum funding standards integrated with new funding rules	Plan years beginning after 2007	¶ 505 Pension Protection Act of 2006
4971(c)(4)	Excise tax on failure to meet minimum funding standards integrated with new funding rules	Plan years beginning after 2007	¶ 505 Pension Protection Act of 2006
4971(g)	New excise tax scheme applies to multiemployer plans in critical or endangered status	For plan years beginning 2007	¶ 608 Pension Protection Act of 2006
4971(g)(4)(B)	Rules changed on how to calculate excise tax imposed for failing to timely adopt a rehabilitation plan	Years beginning after Dec. 31, 2007	¶ 205 Worker, Retiree, and Employer Recovery Act of 2008
4979(f)	Automatic contribution arrangements for 401(k) plans	Plan years beginning after Dec. 31, 2007	¶ 401 Pension Protection Act of 2006
4980B	Overview of the health coverage tax credit (HCTC)	Feb. 17, 2009	¶ 501 American Recovery and Reinvestment Act of 2009

Code	Topic	Effective Date	Complete Analysis
4980B(f)(2)(B)(i)	Eligibility for COBRA continuation coverage extended up to Dec. 31, 2010 for PBGC recipients and TAA-eligible individuals who lose employment or work hours	Coverage periods that would otherwise end on or after Feb. 17, 2009, through Dec. 31, 2010	¶ 507 American Recovery and Reinvestment Act of 2009
4980B(f)(6)(D)	Terminated workers must be notified of right to COBRA continuation benefits subsidy	Feb. 17, 2009	¶ 307 American Recovery and Reinvestment Act of 2009
4980F(e)(1)	Pension plans will have to provide additional information in annual reports but not send summary annual reports; multiemployer plans will have to provide new summary reports to employers and unions, and give plan information to participants or employers upon request	For plan years beginning after Dec. 31, 2007	¶ 901 Pension Protection Act of 2006
4999	Golden parachute rules apply to severance payments to top executives of employers that sell more than $300 million of troubled assets in bailout program	Payments with respect to severances occurring during the period during which the authorities under Economic Stabilization Act §101(a) are in effect	¶ 403 Tax Provisions of H.R. 1424 (Including the Emergency Economic Stabilization, Energy Improvement and Extension, and Tax Extenders and AMT Relief Acts of 2008)
6018	"Large transfers" (generally over $1.3 million) at death will have to be reported to IRS when estate tax repealed after 2009	For estates of decedents dying after Dec. 31, 2009	¶ 332 Economic Growth and Tax Relief Reconciliation Act of 2001
6019(b)	Donors will be required to provide donees with information about property reported on gift tax returns after 2009	For transfers after 2009	¶ 333 Economic Growth and Tax Relief Reconciliation Act of 2001

Code	Topic	Effective Date	Complete Analysis
6033(b)(14)	Exempt organizations that file annual information returns must include information on their disaster relief activities as IRS may require, effective for returns due after Dec. 31, 2008	Returns due (without regard to extensions) after Dec. 31, 2008	¶ 1302 Tax Provisions of H.R. 1424 (Including the Emergency Economic Stabilization, Energy Improvement and Extension, and Tax Extenders and AMT Relief Acts of 2008)
6039G	Expatriates recognize mark-to-market gain upon expatriation	Expatriations on or after June 17, 2008	¶ 301 Heroes Earnings Assistance and Relief Tax Act of 2008
6045(b)	Brokers must report customer's adjusted basis and character of gain or loss for sales of certain securities acquired after Dec. 31, 2010	Jan. 1, 2011	¶ 201 Tax Provisions of H.R. 1424 (Including the Emergency Economic Stabilization, Energy Improvement and Extension, and Tax Extenders and AMT Relief Acts of 2008)
6045(d)	Brokers must report customer's adjusted basis and character of gain or loss for sales of certain securities acquired after Dec. 31, 2010	Jan. 1, 2011	¶ 201 Tax Provisions of H.R. 1424 (Including the Emergency Economic Stabilization, Energy Improvement and Extension, and Tax Extenders and AMT Relief Acts of 2008)
6045(g)	Brokers must report customer's adjusted basis and character of gain or loss for sales of certain securities acquired after Dec. 31, 2010	Jan. 1, 2011	¶ 201 Tax Provisions of H.R. 1424 (Including the Emergency Economic Stabilization, Energy Improvement and Extension, and Tax Extenders and AMT Relief Acts of 2008)

Code	Topic	Effective Date	Complete Analysis
6045(h)	Brokers must report customer's adjusted basis and character of gain or loss for sales of certain securities acquired after Dec. 31, 2010	Jan. 1, 2011	¶ 201 Tax Provisions of H.R. 1424 (Including the Emergency Economic Stabilization, Energy Improvement and Extension, and Tax Extenders and AMT Relief Acts of 2008)
6045A	Brokers that transfer covered securities to other brokers will have to provide statements starting Jan. 1, 2011 to facilitate basis and holding period reporting	Jan. 1, 2011	¶ 203 Tax Provisions of H.R. 1424 (Including the Emergency Economic Stabilization, Energy Improvement and Extension, and Tax Extenders and AMT Relief Acts of 2008)
6045B	Issuers of specified securities will have to provide information starting Jan. 1, 2011 about organizational actions that affect basis	Jan. 1, 2011	¶ 204 Tax Provisions of H.R. 1424 (Including the Emergency Economic Stabilization, Energy Improvement and Extension, and Tax Extenders and AMT Relief Acts of 2008)
6049(d)(9)	Nonrefundable tax credit will be allowed to holders of qualified forestry conservation bonds	Obligations issued after May 22, 2008	¶ 307 Heartland, Habitat, Harvest, and Horticulture Act of 2008
6050W	Banks and online payment networks will have to report credit card sales to IRS and participating merchants on returns for calendar years beginning after Dec. 31, 2010	Returns for calendar years beginning after Dec. 31, 2010	¶ 301 Housing Assistance Tax Act of 2008
6075(a)	"Large transfers" (generally over $1.3 million) at death will have to be reported to IRS when estate tax repealed after 2009	For estates of decedents dying after Dec. 31, 2009	¶ 332 Economic Growth and Tax Relief Reconciliation Act of 2001

Code	Topic	Effective Date	Complete Analysis
6103(i)(3)(C)(iv)	IRS's authority to disclose tax information without request, in terrorism investigations, is extended permanently, effective for disclosures after Oct. 3, 2008	Disclosures after Oct. 3, 2008	¶ 1601 Tax Provisions of H.R. 1424 (Including the Emergency Economic Stabilization, Energy Improvement and Extension, and Tax Extenders and AMT Relief Acts of 2008)
6103(i)(7)(E)	IRS's authority to disclose tax information on request, in terrorism investigations, is extended permanently, effective for disclosures after Oct. 3, 2008	Disclosures after Oct. 3, 2008	¶ 1602 Tax Provisions of H.R. 1424 (Including the Emergency Economic Stabilization, Energy Improvement and Extension, and Tax Extenders and AMT Relief Acts of 2008)
6103(l)(7)	IRS's authority to disclose tax return information to the Department of Veterans Affairs for purposes of certain veterans' programs is made permanent	June 17, 2008	¶ 703 Heroes Earnings Assistance and Relief Tax Act of 2008
6103(l)(7)(D)(viii)(III)	IRS's authority to disclose tax return information to the Department of Veterans Affairs for purposes of certain veterans' programs is made permanent	June 17, 2008	¶ 703 Heroes Earnings Assistance and Relief Tax Act of 2008
6211(b)(4)(A)	Refundable "making work pay credit" of up to $400 ($800 on joint return) is allowed for 2009 and 2010	Tax years beginning after Dec. 31, 2008	¶ 101 American Recovery and Reinvestment Act of 2009
6211(b)(4)(A)	Hope credit is increased and expanded (and re-named the "American Opportunity Tax Credit") for 2009 and 2010	Tax years beginning in 2009 and 2010	¶ 107 American Recovery and Reinvestment Act of 2009

Code	Topic	Effective Date	Complete Analysis
6211(b)(4)(A)	Binding contract rule and tax deficiency rule for the election to trade bonus and accelerated depreciation for certain otherwise-deferred credits are corrected	Tax years ending after Mar. 31, 2008	¶ 806 American Recovery and Reinvestment Act of 2009
6211(b)(4)(A)	New tax credit bond option is added for "Build America Bonds" issued in 2009 and 2010; issuer may claim alternative, refundable credit for "qualified bonds"	Obligations issued after Feb. 17, 2009 and before Jan. 1, 2011	¶ 1301 American Recovery and Reinvestment Act of 2009
6211(b)(4)(A)	Refundable $250 credit is allowed to certain government retirees ($500 for joint return where both spouses are eligible)	Feb. 17, 2009	¶ 103 American Recovery and Reinvestment Act of 2009
6211(b)(4)(A)	IRS will issue cash rebates in 2008 to eligible individuals to stimulate the economy	Tax years beginning after Dec. 31, 2007	¶ 101 Economic Stimulus Act of 2008
6211(b)(4)(A)	First-time homebuyers get refundable credit for 10% of purchase price up to $7,500 ($3,750 on separate return); credit must be recaptured over 15 years	Residences purchased after April 8, 2008, and before July 1, 2009	¶ 102 Housing Assistance Tax Act of 2008
6213(g)(2)	Refundable $250 credit is allowed to certain government retirees ($500 for joint return where both spouses are eligible)	Feb. 17, 2009	¶ 103 American Recovery and Reinvestment Act of 2009
6213(g)(2)(L)	IRS will issue cash rebates in 2008 to eligible individuals to stimulate the economy	Tax years beginning after Dec. 31, 2007	¶ 101 Economic Stimulus Act of 2008

Code	Topic	Effective Date	Complete Analysis
6213(g)(2)(N)	Refundable "making work pay credit" of up to $400 ($800 on joint return) is allowed for 2009 and 2010	Tax years beginning after Dec. 31, 2008	¶ 101 American Recovery and Reinvestment Act of 2009
6401(b)	One auto manufacturer can elect to receive a deemed payment of tax in lieu of claiming research credits, bonus depreciation and accelerated depreciation	Tax years ending after Mar. 31, 2008	¶ 902 Housing Assistance Tax Act of 2008
6401(b)(1)	New tax credit bond option is added for "Build America Bonds" issued in 2009 and 2010; issuer may claim alternative, refundable credit for "qualified bonds"	Obligations issued after Feb. 17, 2009 and before Jan. 1, 2011	¶ 1301 American Recovery and Reinvestment Act of 2009
6401(b)(1)	Nonrefundable tax credit will be allowed to holders of qualified forestry conservation bonds	Obligations issued after May 22, 2008	¶ 307 Heartland, Habitat, Harvest, and Horticulture Act of 2008
6426(b)(2)(A)	Excise tax credit or refund for ethanol used in qualifying alcohol-fuel mixture will be reduced (from 51¢ to 45¢ per gal.) after 2008, unless IRS determines U.S. ethanol production/importation quota isn't met	May 22, 2008	¶ 305 Heartland, Habitat, Harvest, and Horticulture Act of 2008
6426(b)(2)(C)	Excise tax credit or refund for ethanol used in qualifying alcohol-fuel mixture will be reduced (from 51¢ to 45¢ per gal.) after 2008, unless IRS determines U.S. ethanol production/importation quota isn't met	May 22, 2008	¶ 305 Heartland, Habitat, Harvest, and Horticulture Act of 2008

Code	Topic	Effective Date	Complete Analysis
6426(b)(5)	Percentage of allowable denaturants in volume of alcohol will be lowered (from 5% to 2%) for purposes of alcohol fuel mixture excise tax credit or refund	Fuel sold or used after Dec. 31, 2008	¶ 306 Heartland, Habitat, Harvest, and Horticulture Act of 2008
6426(c)(2)	Income and excise tax credits for biodiesel are increased by 50 cents per gallon to one dollar per gallon	Fuel produced, and sold or used, after Dec. 31, 2008 and before Jan. 1, 2010	¶ 920 Tax Provisions of H.R. 1424 (Including the Emergency Economic Stabilization, Energy Improvement and Extension, and Tax Extenders and AMT Relief Acts of 2008)
6426(c)(6)	Income and excise tax credits for biodiesel and renewable diesel are extended to apply through Dec. 31, 2009	Fuel produced, and sold or used, after Dec. 31, 2008 and before Jan. 1, 2010	¶ 919 Tax Provisions of H.R. 1424 (Including the Emergency Economic Stabilization, Energy Improvement and Extension, and Tax Extenders and AMT Relief Acts of 2008)
6426(d)(1)	Alternative fuel excise tax credits/ refunds are extended through Dec. 31, 2009, qualifying fuels are expanded, and carbon capture is required for certain fuels	Fuel sold or used after Oct. 3, 2008	¶ 925 Tax Provisions of H.R. 1424 (Including the Emergency Economic Stabilization, Energy Improvement and Extension, and Tax Extenders and AMT Relief Acts of 2008)
6426(d)(2)(E)	Alternative fuel excise tax credits/ refunds are extended through Dec. 31, 2009, qualifying fuels are expanded, and carbon capture is required for certain fuels	Fuel sold or used after Oct. 3, 2008	¶ 925 Tax Provisions of H.R. 1424 (Including the Emergency Economic Stabilization, Energy Improvement and Extension, and Tax Extenders and AMT Relief Acts of 2008)

Code	Topic	Effective Date	Complete Analysis
6426(d)(2)(F)	Alternative fuel excise tax credits/ refunds are extended through Dec. 31, 2009, qualifying fuels are expanded, and carbon capture is required for certain fuels	Fuel sold or used after Oct. 3, 2008	¶ 925 Tax Provisions of H.R. 1424 (Including the Emergency Economic Stabilization, Energy Improvement and Extension, and Tax Extenders and AMT Relief Acts of 2008)
6426(d)(4)	Alternative fuel excise tax credits/ refunds are extended through Dec. 31, 2009, qualifying fuels are expanded, and carbon capture is required for certain fuels	Fuel sold or used after Oct. 3, 2008	¶ 925 Tax Provisions of H.R. 1424 (Including the Emergency Economic Stabilization, Energy Improvement and Extension, and Tax Extenders and AMT Relief Acts of 2008)
6426(e)(3)	Alternative fuel excise tax credits/ refunds are extended through Dec. 31, 2009, qualifying fuels are expanded, and carbon capture is required for certain fuels	Fuel sold or used after Oct. 3, 2008	¶ 925 Tax Provisions of H.R. 1424 (Including the Emergency Economic Stabilization, Energy Improvement and Extension, and Tax Extenders and AMT Relief Acts of 2008)
6426(i)	Alcohol, biodiesel, renewable diesel, and alternative fuel income and excise tax incentives are made inapplicable to fuel produced outside the U.S. for use outside the U.S.	Claims for credit or payment made after May 14, 2008	¶ 924 Tax Provisions of H.R. 1424 (Including the Emergency Economic Stabilization, Energy Improvement and Extension, and Tax Extenders and AMT Relief Acts of 2008)
6427(e)(5)	Alcohol, biodiesel, renewable diesel, and alternative fuel income and excise tax incentives are made inapplicable to fuel produced outside the U.S. for use outside the U.S.	Claims for credit or payment made after May 14, 2008	¶ 924 Tax Provisions of H.R. 1424 (Including the Emergency Economic Stabilization, Energy Improvement and Extension, and Tax Extenders and AMT Relief Acts of 2008)

Code	Topic	Effective Date	Complete Analysis
6427(e)(5)(B)	Income and excise tax credits for biodiesel and renewable diesel are extended to apply through Dec. 31, 2009	Fuel produced, and sold or used, after Dec. 31, 2008 and before Jan. 1, 2010	¶ 919 Tax Provisions of H.R. 1424 (Including the Emergency Economic Stabilization, Energy Improvement and Extension, and Tax Extenders and AMT Relief Acts of 2008)
6427(e)(5)(C)	Alternative fuel excise tax credits/refunds are extended through Dec. 31, 2009, qualifying fuels are expanded, and carbon capture is required for certain fuels	Fuel sold or used after Oct. 3, 2008	¶ 925 Tax Provisions of H.R. 1424 (Including the Emergency Economic Stabilization, Energy Improvement and Extension, and Tax Extenders and AMT Relief Acts of 2008)
6427(e)(6)	Alternative fuel excise tax credits/refunds are extended through Dec. 31, 2009, qualifying fuels are expanded, and carbon capture is required for certain fuels	Fuel sold or used after Oct. 3, 2008	¶ 925 Tax Provisions of H.R. 1424 (Including the Emergency Economic Stabilization, Energy Improvement and Extension, and Tax Extenders and AMT Relief Acts of 2008)
6428	IRS will issue cash rebates in 2008 to eligible individuals to stimulate the economy	Tax years beginning after Dec. 31, 2007	¶ 101 Economic Stimulus Act of 2008
6428(h)(3)	Military families can get recovery rebate credit on joint return without a spouse's social security number	Tax years beginning after Dec. 31, 2007	¶ 102 Heroes Earnings Assistance and Relief Tax Act of 2008
6431	New tax credit bond option is added for "Build America Bonds" issued in 2009 and 2010; issuer may claim alternative, refundable credit for "qualified bonds"	Obligations issued after Feb. 17, 2009 and before Jan. 1, 2011	¶ 1301 American Recovery and Reinvestment Act of 2009

Code	Topic	Effective Date	Complete Analysis
6432	Reimbursement mechanism provided to plans for COBRA premiums that are not paid by COBRA subsidized individuals	For COBRA premiums provided for periods of coverage beginning on or after Feb. 17, 2009	¶ 308 American Recovery and Reinvestment Act of 2009
6501(m)	"New qualified plug-in electric drive motor vehicle credit" will be modified for vehicles acquired after Dec. 31, 2009	Vehicles acquired after Dec. 31, 2009	¶ 1002 American Recovery and Reinvestment Act of 2009
6501(m)	"New qualified plug-in electric drive motor vehicle credit" is allowed for tax years beginning after Dec. 31, 2008 for property purchased before Jan. 1, 2015	Tax years beginning after Dec. 31, 2008 for property purchased before Jan. 1, 2015	¶ 926 Tax Provisions of H.R. 1424 (Including the Emergency Economic Stabilization, Energy Improvement and Extension, and Tax Extenders and AMT Relief Acts of 2008)
6511(d)(8)	Limitations period for filing credit or refund claims is extended for claims relating to Department of Veterans Affairs' disability determinations	Credit or refund claims filed after June 17, 2008	¶ 702 Heroes Earnings Assistance and Relief Tax Act of 2008
6651(a)	Minimum penalty for failure to file a tax return is increased from $100 to $135	Tax returns required to be filed after Dec. 31, 2008	¶ 701 Heroes Earnings Assistance and Relief Tax Act of 2008
6654(d)(1)(D)	Decreased required estimated tax payments in 2009 for certain small businesses	Tax years beginning in 2009	¶ 701 American Recovery and Reinvestment Act of 2009
6655	Estimated tax payments due from corporations with assets of $1 billion or more are increased for installments due in July, Aug., Sept. 2013	Feb. 4, 2009	¶ 702 American Recovery and Reinvestment Act of 2009

Code	Topic	Effective Date	Complete Analysis
6655	Estimated tax payment amounts due from corporations with assets of $1 billion or more are increased for installments due in July, Aug., or Sept. of 2012	May 22, 2008	¶ 502 Heartland, Habitat, Harvest, and Horticulture Act of 2008
6655	Estimated tax payment amounts due from corporations with assets of $1 billion or more are decreased for installments due in July, Aug., or Sept. of 2012 and increased for installments due in July, Aug., or Sept. of 2013	July 30, 2008	¶ 903 Housing Assistance Tax Act of 2008
6698(b)(1)	Penalty for failure to file partnership return is increased by $4 a month per partner to $89 a month per partner	Returns required to be filed after Dec. 31, 2008	¶ 904 Worker, Retiree, and Employer Recovery Act of 2008
6699(b)(1)	Penalty for failure to file S corporation return is increased from $85 to $89 a month per shareholder	Returns required to be filed after Dec. 31, 2008	¶ 905 Worker, Retiree, and Employer Recovery Act of 2008
6716	"Large transfers" (generally over $1.3 million) at death will have to be reported to IRS when estate tax repealed after 2009	For estates of decedents dying after Dec. 31, 2009	¶ 332 Economic Growth and Tax Relief Reconciliation Act of 2001
6716	Donors will be required to provide donees with information about property reported on gift tax returns after 2009	For transfers after 2009	¶ 333 Economic Growth and Tax Relief Reconciliation Act of 2001

Code	Topic	Effective Date	Complete Analysis
6720C	Penalty imposed on COBRA-subsidized individuals who fail to notify group health plan when they become eligible for other health coverage	Feb. 17, 2009	¶ 309 American Recovery and Reinvestment Act of 2009
6724(d)	Qualified long-term care insurance can be provided as a rider to an annuity contract after 2009	After Dec. 31, 2009	¶ 2402 Pension Protection Act of 2006
6724(d)(1)(B)(iv)	Issuers of specified securities will have to provide information starting Jan. 1, 2011 about organizational actions that affect basis	Jan. 1, 2011	¶ 204 Tax Provisions of H.R. 1424 (Including the Emergency Economic Stabilization, Energy Improvement and Extension, and Tax Extenders and AMT Relief Acts of 2008)
6724(d)(1)(B)(xxii)	Penalties will apply to failure to file returns for calendar years beginning after Dec. 31, 2010 and to provide related statements with respect to payment card transactions and third party network transactions	Returns for calendar years beginning after Dec. 31, 2010	¶ 302 Housing Assistance Tax Act of 2008
6724(d)(2)(DD)	Penalties will apply to failure to file returns for calendar years beginning after Dec. 31, 2010 and to provide related statements with respect to payment card transactions and third party network transactions	Returns for calendar years beginning after Dec. 31, 2010	¶ 302 Housing Assistance Tax Act of 2008

Code	Topic	Effective Date	Complete Analysis
6724(d)(2)(I)	Brokers that transfer covered securities to other brokers will have to provide statements starting Jan. 1, 2011 to facilitate basis and holding period reporting	Jan. 1, 2011	¶ 203 Tax Provisions of H.R. 1424 (Including the Emergency Economic Stabilization, Energy Improvement and Extension, and Tax Extenders and AMT Relief Acts of 2008)
6724(d)(2)(J)	Issuers of specified securities will have to provide information starting Jan. 1, 2011 about organizational actions that affect basis	Jan. 1, 2011	¶ 204 Tax Provisions of H.R. 1424 (Including the Emergency Economic Stabilization, Energy Improvement and Extension, and Tax Extenders and AMT Relief Acts of 2008)
7508A(a)	Changes are made to the involuntary conversion rules and other Code provisions to reflect new definition of "federally declared disaster"	Disasters declared in tax years beginning after Dec. 31, 2007, and occurring before Jan. 1, 2010	¶ 1203 Tax Provisions of H.R. 1424 (Including the Emergency Economic Stabilization, Energy Improvement and Extension, and Tax Extenders and AMT Relief Acts of 2008)
7518(g)(6)(A)	15% maximum tax rate on individuals' nonqualifying withdrawals from Merchant Marine capital gain accounts of capital construction funds (CCFs) is extended for two years	Tax years beginning after Dec. 31, 2008 and before Jan. 1, 2011	¶ 106 Tax Increase Prevention and Reconciliation Act of 2005
7527	Overview of the health coverage tax credit (HCTC)	Feb. 17, 2009	¶ 501 American Recovery and Reinvestment Act of 2009
7527(b)	Refundable health coverage tax credit for eligible individuals' health insurance costs is increased from 65% to 80% through 2010	Coverage months beginning on or after May 1, 2009 and ending Dec. 31, 2010	¶ 502 American Recovery and Reinvestment Act of 2009

Code	Topic	Effective Date	Complete Analysis
7527(d)	Information required before 2011 for qualified health insurance cost eligibility certificates	For certificates issued after Aug. 18, 2009 and before 2011	¶ 509 American Recovery and Reinvestment Act of 2009
7527(e)	IRS is required to pay premiums due before start of HCTC advance payments in 2009 and 2010	For coverage months beginning in 2009 and 2010	¶ 503 American Recovery and Reinvestment Act of 2009
7608(c)	IRS's authority to churn income earned from undercover operations is reinstated and made permanent	Operations conducted after Oct. 3, 2008	¶ 1603 Tax Provisions of H.R. 1424 (Including the Emergency Economic Stabilization, Energy Improvement and Extension, and Tax Extenders and AMT Relief Acts of 2008)
7701(a)(47)	Definition of "executor" that applies for estate tax purposes will apply for tax purposes generally, after 2009.	Estates of decedents dying after Dec. 31, 2009	¶ 606 Economic Growth and Tax Relief Reconciliation Act of 2001
7701(a)(50)(A)	Expatriates recognize mark-to-market gain upon expatriation	Expatriations on or after June 17, 2008	¶ 301 Heroes Earnings Assistance and Relief Tax Act of 2008
7701(b)(6)	Expatriates recognize mark-to-market gain upon expatriation	Expatriations on or after June 17, 2008	¶ 301 Heroes Earnings Assistance and Relief Tax Act of 2008
7701(n)	Expatriates recognize mark-to-market gain upon expatriation	Expatriations on or after June 17, 2008	¶ 301 Heroes Earnings Assistance and Relief Tax Act of 2008
7704(d)(1)(E)	Certain income related to industrial source carbon dioxide, and alcohol, biodiesel, and alternative fuels treated as qualifying income for publicly traded partnerships	Oct. 3, 2008 in tax years ending after Oct. 3, 2008	¶ 1403 Tax Provisions of H.R. 1424 (Including the Emergency Economic Stabilization, Energy Improvement and Extension, and Tax Extenders and AMT Relief Acts of 2008)

Code	Topic	Effective Date	Complete Analysis
7871(f)	Indian tribal governments can issue $2 billion of tribal economic development bonds	Bonds issued after Feb. 17, 2009	¶ 1313 American Recovery and Reinvestment Act of 2009
9801	Overview of the health coverage tax credit (HCTC)	Feb. 17, 2009	¶ 501 American Recovery and Reinvestment Act of 2009
9801(c)(2)(D)	Pre-certification period after TAA-related loss of health coverage is temporarily ignored for certain HIPAA and HCTC purposes	Plan years beginning after Feb. 17, 2009 and before Jan. 1, 2011	¶ 505 American Recovery and Reinvestment Act of 2009
9801(f)(3)	Special enrollment and notification requirements for group health plans for Medicaid- or CHIP-eligible employees or dependents	April 1, 2009	¶ 403 American Recovery and Reinvestment Act of 2009
9812(a)	Mental health parity rules amended to require parity in financial and treatment limits, and to require parity for addiction services; new disclosure and out-of-network provisions added	Plan years beginning after Oct. 3, 2009	¶ 702 Tax Provisions of H.R. 1424 (Including the Emergency Economic Stabilization, Energy Improvement and Extension, and Tax Extenders and AMT Relief Acts of 2008)
9812(c)(1)	"Small employer" exemption from the mental health and substance abuse parity requirements is moved and modified	Plan years beginning after Oct. 3, 2009	¶ 703 Tax Provisions of H.R. 1424 (Including the Emergency Economic Stabilization, Energy Improvement and Extension, and Tax Extenders and AMT Relief Acts of 2008)
9812(c)(2)	Increased cost exemption from the mental health and substance abuse benefits parity requirements modified	Plan years beginning after Oct. 3, 2009	¶ 704 Tax Provisions of H.R. 1424 (Including the Emergency Economic Stabilization, Energy Improvement and Extension, and Tax Extenders and AMT Relief Acts of 2008)

Code	Topic	Effective Date	Complete Analysis
9812(e)(4)	Mental health parity rules amended to require parity in financial and treatment limits, and to require parity for addiction services; new disclosure and out-of-network provisions added	Plan years beginning after Oct. 3, 2009	¶ 702 Tax Provisions of H.R. 1424 (Including the Emergency Economic Stabilization, Energy Improvement and Extension, and Tax Extenders and AMT Relief Acts of 2008)
9812(e)(5)	Mental health parity rules amended to require parity in financial and treatment limits, and to require parity for addiction services; new disclosure and out-of-network provisions added	Plan years beginning after Oct. 3, 2009	¶ 702 Tax Provisions of H.R. 1424 (Including the Emergency Economic Stabilization, Energy Improvement and Extension, and Tax Extenders and AMT Relief Acts of 2008)
9812(f)	Mental health parity requirements made permanent	Jan. 1, 2009	¶ 701 Tax Provisions of H.R. 1424 (Including the Emergency Economic Stabilization, Energy Improvement and Extension, and Tax Extenders and AMT Relief Acts of 2008)
9812(f)(3)	Mental health parity requirements extended for services furnished after June 17, 2008 and through 2008	June 17, 2008, for benefits for services furnished after June 17, 2008 and through 2008	¶ 501 Heroes Earnings Assistance and Relief Tax Act of 2008
9812(f)(4)	Mental health parity requirements extended for services furnished after June 17, 2008 and through 2008	June 17, 2008, for benefits for services furnished after June 17, 2008 and through 2008	¶ 501 Heroes Earnings Assistance and Relief Tax Act of 2008
9813	Group health plans must continue to cover dependent college students during medically necessary leaves of absence	Plan years beginning on or after Oct. 9, 2009, for medically necessary leaves of absence beginning during those plan years	¶ 706 Tax Provisions of H.R. 1424 (Including the Emergency Economic Stabilization, Energy Improvement and Extension, and Tax Extenders and AMT Relief Acts of 2008)

Code	Topic	Effective Date	Complete Analysis
None	COBRA premium subsidy provided for 9 months to workers involuntarily terminated between Sept. 10, 2008 through Dec. 31, 2009	For periods of COBRA coverage provided beginning on or after Feb. 17, 2009	¶ 301 American Recovery and Reinvestment Act of 2009
None	Revocation of IRS guidance exempting banks from loss limitation rules following an ownership change	For ownership changes after Jan. 16, 2009	¶ 602 American Recovery and Reinvestment Act of 2009
None	States can elect grants, instead of tax credits, to finance low-income housing for 2009, but tax credit allocations are reduced	Feb. 17, 2009	¶ 906 American Recovery and Reinvestment Act of 2009
None	One-time $250 payment to be made to recipients of social security, SSI, railroad retirement, and veterans disability or pension benefits	Feb. 17, 2009	¶ 102 American Recovery and Reinvestment Act of 2009
None	Refundable $250 credit is allowed to certain government retirees ($500 for joint return where both spouses are eligible)	Feb. 17, 2009	¶ 103 American Recovery and Reinvestment Act of 2009
None	Penalty imposed on COBRA-subsidized individuals who fail to notify group health plan when they become eligible for other health coverage	Feb. 17, 2009	¶ 309 American Recovery and Reinvestment Act of 2009
None	Certain unemployed workers have an extended 60-day period to elect subsidized COBRA continuation coverage	For periods of COBRA continuation coverage beginning after Feb. 17, 2009	¶ 302 American Recovery and Reinvestment Act of 2009

Code	Topic	Effective Date	Complete Analysis
None	Recapture of COBRA premium assistance provided to high income taxpayers	Tax years ending after Feb. 17, 2009	¶ 304 American Recovery and Reinvestment Act of 2009
None	COBRA-subsidized individuals may elect to change COBRA continuation coverage to a different plan where employer so permits	For periods of COBRA continuation coverage beginning after Feb. 17, 2009	¶ 303 American Recovery and Reinvestment Act of 2009
None	Overview: tax relief for qualified distributions, plan loans, and withdrawals for home purchases-response to May 4, 2007 Kansas storms and tornados	May 22, 2008	¶ 611 Heartland, Habitat, Harvest, and Horticulture Act of 2008
None	Plan loan limits increased and repayment deadlines postponed for individuals who sustained loss due to May 4, 2007 Kansas storms and tornados	May 22, 2008, (a) for loans made during the period beginning on May 22, 2008, and ending before 2009; and (b) for loan repayments with due dates beginning after May 3, 2007, and before 2009	¶ 614 Heartland, Habitat, Harvest, and Horticulture Act of 2008
None	Recontributions of retirement plan withdrawals taken for home purchases that were cancelled because of May 4, 2007 storms and tornados in Kansas make the withdrawals tax-free	May 22, 2008, for recontributions made during the period beginning on May 4, 2007, and ending on Oct. 22, 2008	¶ 613 Heartland, Habitat, Harvest, and Horticulture Act of 2008

Code	Topic	Effective Date	Complete Analysis
None	Relief for qualified retirement plans due to May 4, 2007 Kansas storms and tornados can take effect before plan amendments are adopted-for retroactive amendments made before 2010 plan year	May 22, 2008 through the "2009" plan year	¶ 615 Heartland, Habitat, Harvest, and Horticulture Act of 2008
None	Overview of the temporary tax relief provisions for the "Kansas disaster area"	May 22, 2008	¶ 601 Heartland, Habitat, Harvest, and Horticulture Act of 2008
None	Homeowners can amend a return claiming a casualty loss deduction for certain hurricane damage to take into account a grant received in a later tax year	July 30, 2008	¶ 103 Housing Assistance Tax Act of 2008
None	Income averaging provided for, and tax-free retirement plan contributions may be made from, amounts received from the Exxon Valdez litigation	Oct. 3, 2008	¶ 1405 Tax Provisions of H.R. 1424 (Including the Emergency Economic Stabilization, Energy Improvement and Extension, and Tax Extenders and AMT Relief Acts of 2008)
None	GAO to report on the effect of 2008 Extenders Act changes to the mental health parity rules, and DOL to report on compliance with these rules	Oct. 3, 2008	¶ 705 Tax Provisions of H.R. 1424 (Including the Emergency Economic Stabilization, Energy Improvement and Extension, and Tax Extenders and AMT Relief Acts of 2008)

Code	Topic	Effective Date	Complete Analysis
None	Overview of the temporary tax relief provisions for the Midwestern disaster area	Oct. 3, 2008	¶ 1211 Tax Provisions of H.R. 1424 (Including the Emergency Economic Stabilization, Energy Improvement and Extension, and Tax Extenders and AMT Relief Acts of 2008)
None	Additional $500 exemption is available for taxpayers who house people displaced in Midwestern disaster area for tax years beginning in 2008 or 2009	Tax years beginning in 2008 or 2009	¶ 1236 Tax Provisions of H.R. 1424 (Including the Emergency Economic Stabilization, Energy Improvement and Extension, and Tax Extenders and AMT Relief Acts of 2008)
None	Definition of Midwestern disaster area for temporary tax relief provisions	Oct. 3, 2008	¶ 1212 Tax Provisions of H.R. 1424 (Including the Emergency Economic Stabilization, Energy Improvement and Extension, and Tax Extenders and AMT Relief Acts of 2008)
None	Volunteers donating services for Midwestern related relief can exclude from income mileage reimbursements during the period beginning on the applicable disaster date and ending on Dec. 31, 2008	For use of a vehicle during the period beginning on the applicable disaster date and ending on Dec. 31, 2008	¶ 1238 Tax Provisions of H.R. 1424 (Including the Emergency Economic Stabilization, Energy Improvement and Extension, and Tax Extenders and AMT Relief Acts of 2008)
None	PPA changes to excise tax on failure to meet minimum funding standards are effective for tax years after 2007	Tax years beginning after Dec. 31, 2007	¶ 105 Worker, Retiree, and Employer Recovery Act of 2008
None	Restrictions on the use of the shortfall funding method by multiemployer plans clarified	Plan years beginning after Dec. 31, 2007	¶ 203 Worker, Retiree, and Employer Recovery Act of 2008

Code	Topic	Effective Date	Complete Analysis
None	Rules changed on how to calculate excise tax imposed for failing to timely adopt a rehabilitation plan	Years beginning after Dec. 31, 2007	¶ 205 Worker, Retiree, and Employer Recovery Act of 2008
None	Payments received by employees of bankrupt airlines can be rolled over to Roth IRAs regardless of contribution limits	Transfers made after Dec. 23, 2008, for payments made before, on, or after Dec. 23, 2008	¶ 408 Worker, Retiree, and Employer Recovery Act of 2008
None	Airlines can use "smoothing" to determine asset values	Plan years beginning after Dec. 31, 2007	¶ 103 Worker, Retiree, and Employer Recovery Act of 2008
None	Extension of amortization periods for multiemployer plans	Plan years beginning after 2007	¶ 604 Pension Protection Act of 2006
None	Details of special funding rules for multiemployer plans in critical status	For plan years beginning after 2007	¶ 607 Pension Protection Act of 2006
None	New excise tax scheme applies to multiemployer plans in critical or endangered status	For plan years beginning after 2007	¶ 608 Pension Protection Act of 2006
None	Overview of special funding rules for multiemployer plans in endangered or critical status; annual certification by plan actuary; notice requirements	For plan years beginning after 2007	¶ 605 Pension Protection Act of 2006
None	Special funding rules for multiemployer plans in endangered status	For plan years beginning after 2007	¶ 606 Pension Protection Act of 2006
None	Repeal of collapsible corporation provisions is extended two years	Tax years beginning after Dec. 31, 2008 and before Jan. 1, 2011	¶ 505 Tax Increase Prevention and Reconciliation Act of 2005
None	15% accumulated earnings tax rate and 15% personal holding company tax rate are extended two years	Tax years beginning after Dec. 31, 2008 and before Jan. 1, 2011	¶ 504 Tax Increase Prevention and Reconciliation Act of 2005

Code	Topic	Effective Date	Complete Analysis
None	15% maximum tax rate on individuals' nonqualifying withdrawals from Merchant Marine capital gain accounts of capital construction funds (CCFs) is extended for two years	Tax years beginning after Dec. 31, 2008 and before Jan. 1, 2011	¶ 106 Tax Increase Prevention and Reconciliation Act of 2005
None	15% withholding rate that IRS may impose on USRPI gains passed through to foreign persons by U.S. partnerships, trusts or estates is extended for two years	Tax years beginning after Dec. 31, 2008 and before Jan. 1, 2011	¶ 105 Tax Increase Prevention and Reconciliation Act of 2005
None	5% (0% in 2008) and 15% maximum AMT rates on adjusted net capital gain are extended for two years	Tax years beginning after Dec. 31, 2008 and before Jan. 1, 2011	¶ 103 Tax Increase Prevention and Reconciliation Act of 2005
None	5% and 15% adjusted capital gains rates on noncorporate taxpayers' qualified dividend income are extended for two years	Tax years beginning after Dec. 31, 2008 and before Jan. 1, 2011	¶ 107 Tax Increase Prevention and Reconciliation Act of 2005
None	5% and 15% tax rates on adjusted net capital gain are extended for two years	Tax years beginning after Dec. 31, 2008 and before Jan. 1, 2011	¶ 101 Tax Increase Prevention and Reconciliation Act of 2005
None	7% AMT preference percentage for excluded gain on sale of qualified small business stock is extended for two years	Tax years beginning after Dec. 31, 2008 and before Jan. 1, 2011	¶ 104 Tax Increase Prevention and Reconciliation Act of 2005

Code	Topic	Effective Date	Complete Analysis
None	Exclusion of qualified dividend income from investment income for investment interest deduction limit purposes (unless taxpayer elects to include it) is extended for two years	Tax years beginning after Dec. 31, 2008 and before Jan. 1, 2011	¶ 109 Tax Increase Prevention and Reconciliation Act of 2005
None	Long-term capital loss treatment for losses of individuals, trusts, and estates on stock to the extent extraordinary dividends were taxed as capital gains is extended for two years	Tax years beginning after Dec. 31, 2008 and before Jan. 1, 2011	¶ 108 Tax Increase Prevention and Reconciliation Act of 2005
None	Passthrough of qualified dividend income by RICs and REITs is extended for two years	Tax years beginning after Dec. 31, 2008 and before Jan. 1, 2011	¶ 110 Tax Increase Prevention and Reconciliation Act of 2005
None	Passthrough of qualified dividend income by common trust funds is extended for two years	Tax years beginning after Dec. 31, 2008 and before Jan. 1, 2011	¶ 111 Tax Increase Prevention and Reconciliation Act of 2005
None	Passthrough of qualified dividend income by partnerships is extended for two years	Tax years beginning after Dec. 31, 2008 and before Jan. 1, 2011	¶ 112 Tax Increase Prevention and Reconciliation Act of 2005
None	Post-2007 0% tax rate on adjusted net capital gains is extended for two years	Tax years beginning after Dec. 31, 2008 and before Jan. 1, 2011	¶ 102 Tax Increase Prevention and Reconciliation Act of 2005
None	Qualified dividend income treatment for ordinary income on disposition of Code Sec. 306 stock extended for two years	Tax years beginning after Dec. 31, 2008 and before Jan. 1, 2011	¶ 113 Tax Increase Prevention and Reconciliation Act of 2005

Code	Topic	Effective Date	Complete Analysis
None	EGTRRA sunset applicability-10% bracket income levels increase to $7,000 (from $6,000) for singles and marrieds-filing-separate, and to $14,000 (from $12,000) for joint filers, for 2005-2007; 10% income levels adjusted for inflation, annually, for 2004-2010	Tax years beginning after Dec. 31, 2010	¶ 106 Working Families Tax Relief Act of 2004
None	EGTRRA sunset applicability-15% bracket for joint filers increased to twice the single bracket for 2005-2007 to eliminate marriage penalty	Tax years beginning after Dec. 31, 2010	¶ 104 Working Families Tax Relief Act of 2004
None	EGTRRA sunset applicability-Basic standard deduction for joint filers, for 2005 through 2008, increased to 200% of amount for unmarrieds, eliminating marriage penalty	Tax years beginning after Dec. 31, 2010	¶ 105 Working Families Tax Relief Act of 2004
None	EGTRRA sunset applicability-Child tax credit increased to $1,000 per child for 2005 and thereafter	Tax years beginning after Dec. 31, 2010	¶ 201 Working Families Tax Relief Act of 2004
None	EGTRRA sunset applicability-Combat pay counts as earned income in determining refundable child tax credit	Tax years beginning after Dec. 31, 2010	¶ 203 Working Families Tax Relief Act of 2004

Code	Topic	Effective Date	Complete Analysis
None	EGTRRA sunset applicability-Increase in the refundable child tax credit to 15% (from 10%) of earned income in excess of threshold amount accelerated to 2004 (from 2005)	Tax years beginning after Dec. 31, 2010	¶ 202 Working Families Tax Relief Act of 2004
None	EGTRRA sunset applicability-AMT exemption amount of $40,250 for unmarrieds, $58,000 for joint filers, continued for 2005	Tax years beginning after Dec. 31, 2010	¶ 101 Working Families Tax Relief Act of 2004
None	EGTRRA sunset applicability-Taxpayers may elect to treat combat pay as earned income for purposes of earned income credit before 2006	Tax years beginning after Dec. 31, 2010	¶ 213 Working Families Tax Relief Act of 2004
None	2001 EGTRRA sunset of reduction of tax rates for top four brackets	Tax years beginning after Dec. 31, 2010	¶ 202 Jobs and Growth Tax Relief Reconciliation Act of 2003
None	Sunset of reduction of 10%/8% and 20%/18% maximum AMT rates on adjusted net capital gains to 5% (0% in 2008) and 15%	Tax years beginning after Dec. 31, 2008	¶ 103 Jobs and Growth Tax Relief Reconciliation Act of 2003
None	Sunset of reduction of 10%/8% and 20%/18% tax rates on adjusted net capital gain to 5% and 15% for most net capital gain taken into account after May 5, 2003	Tax years beginning after Dec. 31, 2008	¶ 101 Jobs and Growth Tax Relief Reconciliation Act of 2003
None	Sunset of reduction of 5% tax rate on adjusted net capital gains to 0% for tax years beginning in 2008	Tax years beginning after Dec. 31, 2008	¶ 102 Jobs and Growth Tax Relief Reconciliation Act of 2003

Code	Topic	Effective Date	Complete Analysis
None	Sunset of reduction of AMT preference for excluded gain on sale of qualified small business stock from 28% (or 42%) to 7% for stock disposed of after May 5, 2003	Tax years beginning after Dec. 31, 2008	¶ 104 Jobs and Growth Tax Relief Reconciliation Act of 2003
None	Sunset of reduction of accumulated earnings tax and personal holding company tax rates to 15%	Tax years beginning after Dec. 31, 2008	¶ 401 Jobs and Growth Tax Relief Reconciliation Act of 2003
None	Sunset of repeal of collapsible corporation rules	Tax years beginning after Dec. 31, 2008	¶ 403 Jobs and Growth Tax Relief Reconciliation Act of 2003
None	Sunset of individual's treatment of loss on stock as long-term capital loss to the extent extraordinary dividends were taxed as capital gains	Tax years beginning after Dec. 31, 2008	¶ 108 Jobs and Growth Tax Relief Reconciliation Act of 2003
None	Sunset of reduction in maximum tax rate on individuals' nonqualifying withdrawals from Merchant Marine capital gain accounts of capital construction funds (CCFs)	Tax years beginning after Dec. 31, 2008	¶ 106 Jobs and Growth Tax Relief Reconciliation Act of 2003
None	Sunset of taxation of noncorporate taxpayers' qualified dividend income at favorable adjusted net capital gains rates, rather than ordinary income rates	Tax years beginning after Dec. 31, 2008	¶ 107 Jobs and Growth Tax Relief Reconciliation Act of 2003
None	Sunset of treatment of ordinary income on disposition of Code Sec. 306 stock as qualified dividend income	Tax years beginning after Dec. 31, 2008	¶ 113 Jobs and Growth Tax Relief Reconciliation Act of 2003

Code	Topic	Effective Date	Complete Analysis
None	Sunset of pass through of qualified dividend income by RICs and REITs	Tax years beginning after Dec. 31, 2008	¶ 110 Jobs and Growth Tax Relief Reconciliation Act of 2003
None	Sunset of pass through of qualified dividend income by common trust funds	Tax years beginning after Dec. 31, 2008	¶ 111 Jobs and Growth Tax Relief Reconciliation Act of 2003
None	Sunset of pass through of qualified dividend income by partnerships	Tax years beginning after Dec. 31, 2008	¶ 112 Jobs and Growth Tax Relief Reconciliation Act of 2003
None	Sunset of exclusion of qualified dividend income from investment income for purposes of investment interest deduction limit	Tax years beginning after Dec. 31, 2008	¶ 109 Jobs and Growth Tax Relief Reconciliation Act of 2003
None	Sunset of reduction in withholding rate that IRS may impose on USRPI gains passed through to foreign persons by U.S. partnerships, trusts or estates	Tax years beginning after Dec. 31, 2008	¶ 105 Jobs and Growth Tax Relief Reconciliation Act of 2003
None	2001 Act provisions sunset and won't apply to tax, plan, or limitation years beginning after Dec. 31, 2010; Estate, gift and transfer tax provisions sunset and won't apply to estates of decedents dying, gifts made, or generation skipping transfers, after Dec. 31, 2010	Tax, plan, or limitation years beginning after Dec. 31, 2010, or, in the case of Title V of the 2001 Act relating to estate, gift, and generation skipping transfer taxes, estates of decedents dying, gifts made, or generation skipping transfers, after Dec. 31, 2010	¶ 701 Economic Growth and Tax Relief Reconciliation Act of 2001

INDEX

References are to paragraph numbers

G

H

I